Dictionary of Anonymous and Pseudonymous
English Literature

Dictionary

OF

Anonymous and Pseudonymous English Literature

(SAMUEL HALKETT AND JOHN LAING)

NEW AND ENLARGED EDITION

BY

Dr JAMES KENNEDY

LIBRARIAN, NEW COLLEGE, EDINBURGH

W. A. SMITH AND A. F. JOHNSON

PRINTED BOOKS DEPARTMENT, BRITISH MUSEUM

VOLUME TWO

OLIVER AND BOYD

EDINBURGH: TWEEDDALE COURT

LONDON: 33 PATERNOSTER ROW, E.C.

1926

PRINTED IN GREAT BRITAIN BY
OLIVER AND BOYD, EDINBURGH

A Dictionary of the
Anonymous and Pseudonymous
Literature of Great Britain

D

D. Bancrofts rashnes in rayling. . . .
See Dr Bancrofts rashnes in rayling
. . . (p. 100).

D. E. defeated. . . . *See* D[octor]
E[dward Bagshaw] defeated . . .
(p. 101).

D. F.'s vindication. . . . *See* D[octor]
F[rancis Atterbury]'s vindication . . .
(p. 101).

D—— (the) of A——e's letter. . . . *See*
D[uke] (the) of A[rgyl]e's letter . . .
(p. 123).

D. (the) of M——: his vindication. . . .
See D[ean] (the) of M—— . . . (p. 15).

D——N (the) of W——r. . . . *See*
D[ea]n (the) of W[orceste]r.

DACOITEE in excelsis; or, the
spoliation of Oude by the East India
Company faithfully recounted, with
notes and documentary illustrations.
[By Major Robert Wilberforce Reid.]
8vo. Pp. 214. London, [1857]
Wrongly ascribed to Samuel Lucas, also
to J. R. Taylor.

DACRE. [A novel.] [By Mrs Maria
Theresa Lister, later Lady G. Cornewall Lewis.] Edited by the Countess
of Morley. Pt 8vo. [Courtney's
Secrets, p. 57.] London, 1834

DADDY Jake the runaway, and other
short stories told after dark. By
Uncle Remus [Joel Chandler Harris].
Pt 8vo. Pp. 198. [Haynes' *Pseud.*]
New York, 1896

DADDY'S darling. By Ray Cunningham [Frances Browne Arthur]. 8vo.
Stirling, [1897]

DÆNEIDS, or the noble labours of the
great dean of Notre-Dame in Paris,
for erecting in his quire a throne for
his glory, and the eclipsing the pride
of an imperious, usurping chanter. An
heroique poem in four canto's; containing a true history, and shews the
folly, foppery, luxury, laziness, pride,
ambition, and contention of the
Romish clergy. [Translated and
curtailed from the Lutrin of Nicholas
Boileau Despréaux, with alterations
by John Crowne.] 4to. [Arber's *Term
Cat.*, ii., p. 613.] London, 1692

DAGONET the Jester [a tale]. [By
Malcolm Macmillan, publisher.] 8vo.
Pp. 179. London, 1886
The author's name appears in the edition
issued in 1894.

DAGONS downfall; or, the great idol
digged up root and branch. [By
Roger Club.] 4to. Pp. 29. [Thoma-
son *Coll. of Tracts*, vol. ii., p. 193.]
[London], 1657

DAILY bread; a story of the snow
blockade. By Col. Frederic Ingham
[Edward Everett Hale]. Fcap 8vo.
[Cushing's *Init. and Pseud.*, i., p. 137.]
Boston, 1888

DAILY bread; or, taxation without
representation resisted; being a plan
for the abolition of the Bread Tax.
By one of the millions [J— Shotsky].
8vo. London, 1841

DAILY (the) course of the Christian life.
[Compiled by Rev. John Bate.] Cr
8vo. London, 1894

DAILY (the) cross. By F. C. [Faith
Chiltern]. 12mo. [*Brit. Mus.*]
London, 1877

DAILY devotions ; consisting of thanks-givings, confessions, and prayers, in two parts : for the benefit of the more devout and the assistance of weaker Christians. The third edition ; with the addition of proper devotions before, at, and after, receiving of the blessed Sacrament. By an humble penitent [Susannah Hopton]. Fcap. 8vo. [Hickes' edition of (John Austin's) *Devotions*, p. xxxvi. of Preface.]
London, 1682

The authorship has wrongly been attri-buted to Bishop Duppa. The title of the first edition (1673) begins " Dayly devo-tions . . ."

DAILY (a) directory, enlarged. [By Sir William Waller, Parliamentary General.] 8vo. Belfast, 1727
This is a reprint of what first appeared during the seventeenth century.

DAILY hymns. By A. G. R. [Alida G— Radcliffe]. Pt 8vo. [Cushing's *Init. and Pseud.*, vol. i., p. 245.]
New York, 1867

DAILY observations or meditations, divine, morall. Written by a person of honour and piety [Arthur Capel, Lord Capel]. 4to. Pp. 118. [*N. and Q.*, 16th Sept. 1865, p. 230.]
Anno Dom. 1654

DAILY (a) office for the sick ; compil'd out of the Holy Scripture, and the Liturgy of our Church : with occasional prayers, meditations, and directions. [By John Isham.] Pt 8vo. Pp. 259, [*Bodl.*] London, 1694
The third edition, revised, was pub-lished in 1702.

DAILY (the) practice of devotion ; or, the hours of prayer fitted to the main uses of a Christian life : also lamenta-tions and prayers for the peaceful re-settlement of this Church and State. By H. H. [Henry Hammond, D.D.]. 12mo. [Arber's *Term Cat.*, vol. iii., p. 189.] London, 1700

DAILY readings, consisting of devo-tional reflections on some passage of Scripture in the Lessons or Psalms appointed for every day in the year. [By Edward Feilde.] 8vo. [*Brit. Mus.*] London, [1847]
Subscribed " E. F."

DAILY readings : passages of Scripture, selected for social reading, with appli-cations. By the author of *The Listener*, etc. [Caroline Fry, later Mrs Wilson]. Fcap 8vo. Pp. viii., 303. [*Brit. Mus.*] London, 1835

DAILY (the) service of the Anglo-Catholic Church, adapted to family or private worship. By a priest [Rev. Charles Seager, M.A.]. Intended for the use of those who either have not the privilege or are prevented from attending daily service in the house of God, and who, for various reasons, would think the whole of what the Church has provided too long for their use. A service for Sundays, etc. is added. Fcap 8vo. [*Bodl.*]
Banbury, 1838

DAILY steps towards heaven ; or, practical thoughts on the Gospel history, and especially on the life and teaching of our Lord Jesus Christ : for every day in the year, accord-ing to the Christian seasons. Chiefly taken from larger works. [By Arthur H. Dyke Acland, M.A.] 8vo. Pp. xvi., 418. [*Bodl.*] London, 1849

DAILY (a) text-book ; for the use of those who have to work hard, and of children in parish schools. By the author of *Daily prayers for the use of those who have to work hard* [Rev. Sir Henry W. Baker]. 12mo. Pp. viii., 59. [*Bodl.*] Oxford, 1854

DAILYS (the) of Sodden Fen. [By Mrs Susanna C. Venn.] 3 vols. Cr 8vo. [*Lond. Lib. Cat.*] London, 1884

ΔAIMONION (τὸ); or, the spiritual medium; its nature illustrated. . . . By Traverse Oldfield [George Whitefield Samson]. Fcap 8vo. [Cushing's *Init. and Pseud.*, vol. i., p. 214.] Boston, [Mass.], 1852

DAIMONOMAGEIA : a small treatise of sickness and disease from witch-craft and supernaturall causes. . . . [By William Drage, M.D.] Fcap 4to.
London, 1665

DAIRYMAN'S (the) daughter ; an authentic narrative. Communicated by a clergyman of the Church of England [Rev. Legh Richmond]. 8vo. Pp. 48. [*Brit. Mus.*] Ottley, 1816
Many later editions have been issued.

DAISIE'S dream. [A novel.] By the author of *Recommended to mercy* [Mrs M. C. Houstoun]. 3 vols. 8vo. [*Brit. Mus.*] London, 1869

DAISY Beresford. [A novel.] By Catherine Childar [Annie Charlotte Catharine Aldrich]. 3 vols. Cr. 8vo. [*Camb. Univ. Lib.*] London, 1882

DAISY Brentwell. By Ireland Ward [Irene Widdemer]. 8vo. [Cushing's *Init. and Pseud.*, vol. i., p. 303.]
New York, 1876

DAISY (the) chain ; or, aspirations : a family chronicle. By the author of *The Heir of Redclyffe*, etc. [Charlotte Mary Yonge]. 8vo. London, 1856

DAISY in the field. By the author of *The Wide, wide world* [Susan Warner]. 8vo. Pp. 352. [*Brit. Mus.*] London, [1901]

DAISY (the) ; or, cautionary stories in verse. [By Elizabeth Turner.] Fcap 8vo. Pp. 66. [*Brit. Mus.*] London, 1810

DAISY Plains. By the author of *The Wide, wide world*, etc. [Susan Warner]. 8vo. London, 1885

DAISY (the) seekers. By W. M. L. J. Jay [Julia Louisa Matilda Woodruff]. 8vo. [Cushing's *Init. and Pseud.*, vol. i., p. 141.] New York, 1885
Initials reversed form the pseudonym.

DAISY'S companions ; or, scenes from child life. [By Mrs Eleanor Grace O'Reilly.] Fcap 8vo. [*Brit. Mus.*] London, [1859]

DAISY'S king. By Esmé Stuart [Amélie Claire Leroy]. 8vo. [*Lond. Lib. Cat.*] London, 1888

DALE End ; or six weeks at the vicarage. By the author of *The unseen hand* [Stopford James Ram]. Fcap 8vo. [*Camb. Univ. Lib.*] Dublin, 1854

DALRYMPLES (the) ; or, long credit and long cloth. [By Sibella Jones.] Fcap 8vo. [*Brit. Mus.*] London, 1860

DAMARIS Verity. [A novel.] By Lucas Malet [Mrs St Leger Harrison, *née* Mary Kingsley]. Cr 8vo. [*Brit. Mus.*] London, 1913

DAME Curtsey's book of novel entertainments for every day in the year. [By Ellye Howell Glover.] Fcap 8vo. Chicago, 1907

DAME Durden ; a novel. By " Rita " [Mrs W. Desmond Humphreys, *née* Eliza M. J. Gollan]. 3 vols. Cr 8vo. [*Lit. Year Book.*] London, 1883.

DAME Europa's letters to her monitors. [By Sampson Sandys.] 8vo. Pp. 32. London, 1877
The foregoing and the following brochures are two of the multitude evoked by the publication of *The Fight at Dame Europa's School. See below.*

DAME Europa's remonstrance, and her ultimatum. [By James Russell Endean.] 8vo. [*F. Madan.*] London, 1877

DAME Nature and her three daughters. By X. B. de Saintine [Joseph Xavier Boniface]. 8vo. [Cushing's *Init. and Pseud.*, vol. i., p. 260.] Boston, 1869

DAME Perkins and her grey mare ; or, the mount for the market. [Verse]. By Lindon Meadows [Rev. Charles Butler Greatrex]. 4to. [*Brit. Mus.*] London, 1866

DAME Rebecca Berry ; or, court scenes in the reign of Charles the Second. [By Elizabeth Isabella Spence.] 3 vols. Fcap 8vo. [*Camb. Univ. Lib.*] London, 1827

DAME Wiggins of Lea. [By Mrs —— Sharpe.] 8vo. London, 1823

DAMEN'S ghost. [By Edwin Lasseter Bynner. Fcap 8vo. [Kirk's *Supp.*] Boston, 1881

DAMFOOL Smith Sahib, Dalrymple Smith, Esq. By the Subaltern [Andrew Alexander Irvine]. 8vo. Lahore, 1899

DAMNABLE heresie discovered, and the head of God's Church uncovered, and the spirit of man from the true light distinguished, according to the scriptures of truth, and testimony of saints. [By Robert West, of Devizes.] 4to. [Smith's *Cat. of Friends' Books*, i., 39 ; ii., 875.] N.P., 1672

DAMOISELLE (the) ; or, the new ordinary. [By Richard Brome. A comedy in five acts.] 8vo. [*Biog. Dram.*] London, 1653

DAMON and Phillida ; a new ballad opera, as it was acted by the comedians at both the theatres royal : with a table of songs. [By Colley Cibber.] 8vo. Pp. 26. [*Biog. Dram.*] London, 1732

DAN Drummond of the Drummonds. By Gulielma Zollinger [William Zachery Gladwin]. Pt. 8vo. [*Amer. Cat.*] Philadelphia, 1897

DAN of Millbrook : a story of American life. By Carleton [Charles Carleton Coffin]. 8vo. [Haynes' *Pseud.*] New York, 1893

DAN Riach, Socialist. By the author of *Miss Molly* [Beatrice May Butt]. Cr 8vo. Pp. 376. [*Lond. Lib. Cat.*] London, 1908

DAN Russel the fox ; an episode in the life of Miss Rowan. By E. Œ. Somerville and Martin Ross [Violet Martin, of Ross, in Galway]. 8vo. Pp. 346. [*Brit. Mus.*] London, 1911

DANCE (la) Machabre, or deaths duell. By W. C. [Walter Coleman, O.S.F.]. 12mo. [*D. N. B.*, vol. ii., p. 396.] London, N.D., [1632 ?]

DANCE (the) of Baldarroch. [By Andrew Edward, bookseller, Stonehaven.] Fcap 8vo. Pp. 16. [*And. Jervise.*] N.P., N.D.
In the above copy, there is a MS. note by the author, signed " A. E."

DANCE (the) of death. By William Herman [William Herman Rulofsen]. 8vo. [Cushing's *Init. and Pseud.*, vol. ii., p. 73.] San Francisco, 1877

DANCE (the) of life; a poem. By the author of *Doctor Syntax* [William Combe] ; illustrated with coloured engravings, by Thomas Rowlandson. 8vo. Pp. ii., 285. [*Brit. Mus.*]
London, 1817

DANCE (the) of the hours ; a novel. By the author of *Vera* [Charlotte Louisa Hawkins Dempster]. Pt 8vo. [*Lond. Lib. Cat.*] London, 1893

DANCIAD (the) ; a poem. By a young gentleman [Thomas Grady, High Sheriff of Limerick]. 8vo. [O'Donoghue's *Poets of Ireland.*]
Limerick, 1783

DANCING (the) devils; or, the roaring dragon : a dumb farce. [By Edward Ward.] 8vo. [*Brit. Mus.*]
London, 1724

DANCING-MASTER (the) ; or plain and easie rules for the dancing of country dances, with the tune to each dance. . . . Second edition, enlarged. . . . [By John Playford.] Obl. 8vo.
London, 1652
Preface signed " J. P." Many later editions were required.

DANCING-SCHOOL (the) : with the adventures of the Easter holy-days. [By Edward Ward.] Folio. [*Bodl.*]
London, 1700

DANDIES (the) of the present, and the macaronies of the past : a rough sketch. By D in the corner [Thomas Hayes Bayly]. 8vo. [Green's *Bibl. Somers.*, vol. i., p. 56.] Bath, [1819]

DANES (the) : a prize poem. By B. F. H. [B. F. Hartshorne]. 8vo. [*Bodl.*]
Private print, 1864

DANES Abbey ; a novel. By Morice Gerard [Rev. John Jessop Teague]. Cr 8vo. Pp. 296. London, 1918

DANES (the) in England ; and other poems. [By John Benjamin Kerridge.] Fcap 8vo. Pp. 64. [Mayo's *Bibl. Dorset.*, p. 250.] Weymouth, 1863

DANGER (the) and folly of evil courses ; being a practical discourse, shewing the base and vile nature of sin. [By Francis Hewerdine.] 12mo. [Darling's *Cyclop. Bibl.*] London, 1707

DANGER (the) line. [A novel.] By Lawrence L. Lynch [Emma M. Murdoch, later Mrs Van Deventer]. 8vo. Pp. 444. [*Lit. Year Book.*]
London, [1903]

DANGER (the) of enthusiasm discovered, in an epistle to the Quakers : in which 'tis endeavoured to convince them of being guilty of changing God's method of bringing men to salvation. By one who is no more an enemy to their opinions, than their opinions are enemies to them themselves [William Allen]. 8vo. [Smith's *Cat. of Friends' Books*, i., p. 3.] London, 1674

DANGER (the) of improving physick : with a brief account of the present epidemick fever. [By William Cockburn, M.D.] 8vo. [*Brit. Mus.*]
London, 1730

DANGER (the) of mercenary Parliaments ; with a preface, shewing the infinite mischiefs of long and pack'd Parliaments. By the editor of the Earl of Shaftesbury's letters to Lord Molesworth. [John Toland.] 8vo. [*Brit. Mus.*] London, 1722

DANGER (the) of not being prepared : a sermon preached in the English Church at the Hague, by the chaplain [Rev. Edward Brine]. 8vo. [*Brit. Mus.*] The Hague, 1859

DANGER (the) of Popery discovered, with a diswasive from it ; for the use of the vulgar, who have not money to buy, or time to read larger books. [By Rev. George Meldrum.] 8vo. Pp. 54. [*Adv. Lib.*]
Edinburgh, 1705

DANGER (the) of priestcraft to religion and government ; with some politick reasons for toleration : occasion'd by a discourse of Mr Sacheverel's intitul'd, The political union, etc., lately printed at Oxford. In a letter to a new-elected Member of Parliament. [By John Dennis.] 4to. Pp. 12. [F. Madan's list in the *Bibliographer*, vol. 3, p. 138.]
London, 1702

DANGER (the) of the Church and Kingdom from foreigners considered ; in several articles of the highest importance. [By Charles Owen, D.D.] Pt. 8vo. Pp. 38. [*D. N. B.*, vol. 42, p. 401.] London, 1721

DANGER (the) of the Church-establishment of England from the insolence of Protestant Dissenters. In a letter to Sir John Smith. By the author of *The Scourge* [Thomas Lewis]. 8vo. [*Cat. Lond. Inst.*, ii., 499.]
London, 1718

DANGER (the) of the passions ; or, Syrian and Egyptian anecdotes : translated from the French of the author of *The School of Friendship* [Henri Lambert d'Erbigny, Marquis de Thibouville]. 2 vols. 12mo. [Barbier's *Dictionnaire*.] London, 1770

DANGER (the) of the Protestant religion considered from the present prospect of a religious war in Europe. [By Daniel Defoe.] 4to. [Wilson's *Life of Defoe*, 15.] London, 1700

DANGER (the) of treaties with Popish spirits ; or, a seasonable caveat and premonition to . . . Parliament, touching the frail trust in the vowes and protestations of popishly affected Princes, for peace and reconcilement with their Protestant subjects. [By John Vicars.] 4to. [*Brit. Mus.*]
N.P., N.D., [London, 1644]
Signed " J. V."

DANGER (the) of unwatchfulness and advantages of piety. [By Charlotte Rees.] 8vo. [Smith's *Cat. of Friends' Books*, ii., 477.] Bristol, 1808

DANGER signals. . . . By John Lea [John Lea Bricknell]. Illustrated by H. J. Rhodes and other artists. 4to. Pp. vii., 162. [*Brit. Mus.*] London, 1910

DANGER (the) to England observed upon its deserting the high court of Parliament, humbly desired by all loyall and dutifull subjects to be presented to his most excellent majestie. [By Henry Parker.] 4to. [*Brit. Mus.*] London, 1642

DANGER (the) wherein the kingdome now standeth, & the remedie. [By Sir Robert Bruce Cotton.] 4to. [*Brit. Mus.*] Printed 1628

DANGEROUS (the) condition of the country. . . . By a Marylander [Reverdy Johnson]. 8vo. [Cushing's *Init. and Pseud.*, vol. i., p. 184.] Baltimore, 1867

DANGEROUS Dorothy ; a novel. By Curtis Yorke [Mrs W. S. Richmond Lee, *née* —— Jex Long]. Cr 8vo. [*Brit. Mus.*] London, 1912

DANGEROUS ground ; or, the rival detectives. By Lawrence L. Lynch [Emma M. Murdoch, later Mrs Van Deventer]. Fcap 8vo. [*Lond. Lib. Cat.*] Chicago, 1892

DANGEROUS (a) guest. By the author of *Gilbert Rugge*, etc. [Henry Jackson] 2 vols. 8vo. [*Brit. Mus.*] London, 1870

DANGEROUS (a) plot discovered : by a discourse, wherein is proved, that, Mr Richard Mountague, in his two bookes ; the one, called A new gagg ; the other, A iust appeale, laboureth to bring in the faith of Rome, and Arminius, under the name and pretence of the doctrine and faith of the Church of England : a worke very necessary for all them which have received the truth of God in love, and desire to escape errour. [By Anthony Wotton, B.D.] 4to. [*Adv. Lib.*] London, 1626

DANGEROUS positions and proceedings. . . . *See* Daungerous positions and proceedings. . . .

DANGEROUS (the) vice. . . . A fragment : addressed to all whom it may concern. By a gentleman formerly of Boston [Edward Church, junior ; *or* Silvanus Bourne]. 8vo. [Cushing's *Init. and Pseud.*, vol. i., p. 112.] Columbia, [Boston], 1789

DANGEROUS (a) woman. By Margaret Blount [Mrs Mary O'Francis]. 8vo. [Cushing's *Init. and Pseud.*, vol. i., p. 37.] New York, 1864

DANGERS and duties ; a tale. By Charlotte Elizabeth [Charlotte Elizabeth Tonna]. Fcap 8vo. Pp. 163. [*D. N. B.*, vol. lvii., p. 34.] London, 1841

DANGERS (the) of British India from French invasion and missionary establishments ; with a few hints respecting the defence of the British frontiers in Hindostan. By a late resident at Bhagulpore [David Hopkins, surgeon]. 8vo. Pp. 154. [*Brit. Mus.*] London, 1808

DANGERS (the) of coquetry. [By Amelia Alderson, later Mrs Opie.] 2 vols. 12mo. [Jeaffreson's *Novelists*, ii., 20.] London, 1790

DANGERS (the) of half-preparedness ; a plea for a declaration of American policy : an address. By Norman Angell [Ralph Norman Angell Lane]. Fcap 8vo. Pp. 133. [*Lond. Lib. Cat.*] New York, 1916

DANGERS (the) of Spiritualism ; being records of personal experiences, with notes and comments, and five illustrations. By a Member of the Society of Psychical Research [Rev. Johannes G. F. Raupert]. Cr 8vo. London, 1901
The author's name is given in the second edition (1906).

DANGERS (the) of the country. By the author of *War in disguise* [James Stephen]. 8vo. [*Sig. Lib.*]
London, 1807

DANGERS (the) with which Great Britain and Ireland are now menaced by the demands of Irish Roman Catholics. [By Arthur Henry Kenney, D.D., Dean of Achonry.] 8vo.
London, 1817

DANIEL and his three friends; seven short lectures by the author of *Plain preaching to poor people* [Rev. Edmund Fowle]. Pt 8vo.   London, 1872

DANIEL (the) catcher; the life of Daniel, in a poem . . . with several other poems. By R. S. [Richard Steere]. 8vo.   Pp. 90.   [*Evans'*
Amer. Bibl., vol. 1, p. 229.]
[New York], 1713

DANIEL Deronda.   By George Eliot [Marian Evans, later Mrs Cross]. [In 8 books and 4 volumes.] Cr 8vo. [*Brit. Mus.*]   Edinburgh, 1876

DANIEL, his Chaldie visions and his Ebrew: both translated after the original, and expounded. . . . [By Hugh Broughton.] 4to. [*Brit. Mus.*]
London, 1596

DANIEL in the den; or, the Lord President's imprisonment, and miraculous deliverance: represented in a discourse from Heb. xi., v. 33. By S. J. [Stephen Jay], rector of Chinner in the county of Oxon. 4to. [*Bodl.*]
London, 1682

DANIEL, statesman and prophet. [By Henry T. Robjohns.] 8vo.
London, [1872]

DANIEL'S great period of two thousand and three hundred days discovered and determined, in a dissertation. . . . By a clergyman of the Church of England [Richard Hastings Graves, D.D., Dean of Ardagh]. 8vo. [*D. N. B.*, vol. 22, p. 435.]
London, 1854

DANIEL'S prophecy of the seventy weeks; interpreted by a layman [James Whatman Bosanquet]. Fcap 8vo. [*See his Chronology*.]
London, 1836

DANISH (a) parsonage; being an account of life and travel in Denmark. By an angler [John Fulford Vicary]. Pt 8vo. Pp. viii., 316. London, 1884

DANNY'S Captain; a novel. By E. Livingston Prescott [Edith Katherine Spicer-Jay]. Cr 8vo. Pp. 156. [*Brit. Mus.*]   London, 1903

DAN'S political note-book.   Session 1871. By D. P. (" Frank Foster ") [Daniel Puseley]. 8vo.   Pp. 79. [*D. N. B.*, vol. 47, p. 53.]
London, [1871]

DAN'S treasure; or, labour and love. By Leigh Tempest [Jane Mill]. 8vo. [*Brit. Mus.*]   London, [1868]

DANTE and Beatrice; a drama. By Norley Chester [Emily Underdown]. 8vo. [*Lond. Lib. Cat.*]
London, 1902

DANTE and Beatrice, from 1282 to 1290: a romance. By Roxburghe Lothian [Elizabeth Kerr Coulson]. 2 vols. 8vo. [*Brit. Mus.*]
London, 1876

DANTE the wayfarer. By Christopher Hare [Mrs Marion Andrews]. 8vo. Pp. 374. [*Lond. Lib. Cat.*]
London, 1905

DANTE vignettes [sonnets]. By Norley Chester [Emily Underdown]. 12mo. [*Lond. Lib. Cat.*]   London, 1895

DANTZICK, or the story of a picture; with other tales. [By A— H. Bencke.] Fcap 8vo. Pp. viii., 228. London, 1880

DANUBIAN (the) principalities, the frontier lands of the Christian and the Turk. By a British resident of twenty years in the East [James Henry Skene, English Consul at Aleppo]. Third edition. 8vo. 2 vols. [*Brit. Mus.*]
London, 1854
Incorrectly attributed to P. O'Brien.

DANVERIAN (the) history of the affairs of Europe for the memorable year 1731; with the present state of Gibraltar . . . also of Dunkirk. By Caleb D'Anvers [Nicholas Amhurst]. 8vo. [*Brit. Mus.*]   London, 1732

DANVERS (the) jewels. [A novel. By Mary Cholmondeley.] Cr 8vo. Pp. 127. [*Bodl.*]   London, [1887]

DANVERS (the) papers; an invention. By the author of *The heir of Redclyffe* [Charlotte M. Yonge]. Pt 8vo. Pp. 149.   London, 1867

DAPHNE.   By Elizabeth Hastings [Mrs Margaret E. W. Sherwood]. Pt. 8vo. [*Amer. Cat.*] Boston, 1903

DAPHNE, a poem. [By Thomas Powell, of Monmouth.] 4to. [*Brit. Mus.*]
London, 1796
Signed " T."

DAPHNE and Amintor; a comic opera: as it is performed at the Theatre Royal in Drury-Lane. [By Isaac Bickerstaffe.]   New edition.   8vo.   [*Biog.*
Dram.]   London, 1766

DAPHNE in Paris. By the author of *Daphne in the Fatherland* [Anne Topham]. Cr 8vo. Pp. 302.
London, 1913

DAPHNE in the Fatherland. [A novel illustrating German society. By Anne Topham.] Cr 8vo. Pp. 320.
London, 1912

DAPHNIS ; a pastoral elegy ; written October 1755. [By John Balfour.] [Campbell's *Introduction to the history of poetry in Scotland*, p. 287.]
Edinburgh, 1772

DAPHNIS and Amaryllis ; a pastoral [in one act. By James Harris]. 8vo. [*Biog. Dram.*] Exeter, 1760
This is the author's *Spring*, with a new title.

DAPHNIS and Chloe ; a pastoral novel ; now first selectly translated into English from the original Greek of Longus. [By Rev. Charles Valentine Le Grice, M.A.] Fcap 8vo. [*W.*]
London, 1804

ΔΑΦΝΙΣ ΠΟΛΥΣΤΕΦΑΝΟΣ. An eclog treating of Crownes, and of Garlandes, and to whom of right they appertaine. Addressed, and consecrated to the Kings Maiestie. By G. B. knight [Sir George Buck]. 4to. No pagination. [*Bodl.*] At London, 1605
The author's name [as " Georg Buc "] is in the handwriting of Wood.

DARBY and Joan. By " Rita " [Mrs W— Desmond Humphreys, *née* Eliza M. J. Gollan]. 3 vols. Cr 8vo. [*Lond. Lib. Cat.*] London, 1886

DARBY Doyle's visit to Quebec. [By Thomas Ettingsall. 8vo.
London, [about 1840]

DARE to be singular ; or the story of Ned Batlow, the miner. By S. M. H. [Sophia Matilda Holworthy]. 12mo. Pp. 72. [*Brit. Mus.*] London, [1877]

DARK ; a tale of the Down country. [By Mrs Stephen Batson.] 2 vols. Pt. 8vo. [*Bodl.*] London, 1892

DARK and fair. [A novel.] By Sir Charles Rockingham [Philippe F. A. de Rohan-Chabot, Count de Jarnac]. 3 vols. 8vo. [*Brit. Mus.*]
London, 1857

DARK and light stories. By Mark Hope [Eustace Clare Grenville Murray]. Pt 8vo. [*Cushing's Init. and Pseud.*, ii., p. 76.] London, 1879

DARK (a) chapter from New Zealand history. By a Poverty Bay survivor [James Hawthorne]. Cr 8vo. Pp 41. [*Collier's New Zeal. Lit.*, p. 101.]
Napier, [New Zealand], 1869

DARK (the) colleen ; a love story. By the author of *The Queen of Connaught* [Harriet Jay]. 3 vols. 8vo. [*Brit. Mus.*] London, 1876

DARK (the) corner ; or, behaviour in Church. [By Rev. Francis Bourdillon.] 8vo. [*Brit. Mus.*]
London, [1866]
Signed " F. B."

DARK days. [A novel.] By Hugh Conway [Frederick John Fargus]. Fcap 8vo. [*Lond. Lib. Cat.*]
Bristol, 1884

DARK deeds. . . . [By Rev. Erskine Neale, M.A.] 8vo. [*Adv. Lib.*]
London, N.D.

DARK deeds. By Dick Donovan [Joyce E. Preston Muddock]. Cr 8vo. [*Brit. Mus.*] London, 1900

DARK House. By Wynoth Dale [M. —— G. B. Ryves]. 8vo. [*Bodl.*]
London, 1909

DARK (the) lady of Doona. [A novel. By Captain (later Rev.) William Hamilton Maxwell.] Cr 8vo. [*S. J. Brown's Ireland in Fiction.*]
London, 1834

DARK (the) land, and other poems. By Alick Mashlum [A— Cunningham Fairlie]. 8vo. Pp. iii., 120. [*Brit. Mus.*] Mission Press, Lovedale, 1892

DARK (a) lantern. By C. E. Raimond [Elizabeth Robins, later Mrs Parkes]. 8vo. [*Lond. Lib. Cat.*]
New York, 1905

DARK (a) marriage-morn. By Bertha M. Clay [Charlotte M. Law, later Mrs Braeme]. Fcap 8vo. New York, 1887

DARK (the) monk of Feola ; the adventures of a Ribbon pedlar. By an Ulster Scot [Rev. Henry Henderson, Presbyterian minister in Holywood, Co. Down]. 8vo. [*S. J. Brown's Ireland in Fiction.*] Belfast, [1860]

DARK (a) plot. By Walter B Dunlap [Sylvanus Cobb, junr.]. Pt 8vo. [*Cushing's Init. and Pseud.*, ii., p. 46.]
New York, 1891

DARK Rosaleen ; a romance. By M. E. Francis [Mrs Francis Blundell, *née* Mary E. Sweetman]. Cr 8vo. Pp. 392. [*Brit. Mus.*]
London, 1915

DARK (the) side of Christianity. By C. C. C. [C— C— Cattell]. [*Gladstone Lib. Cat.* (Lib. Club).]

DARK (the) strain. By Shubael [Jennie B. Purdy]. Fcap 8vo. [*Amer. Cat.*]
New York, 1903

DARK (the) year of Dundee : a tale of the Scottish Reformation. [By Deborah Alcock.] 8vo. [*Brit. Mus.*]
London, 1871

DARKNESS and dawn, or the peaceful advent of a new age. [By Clement Wise.] 8vo. Bristol, 1898

DARKNESS and sunshine. By " Oleander " [David M'Culloch]. Dedicated by special permission to the Right Hon. the Earl of Glasgow. 8vo. Pp. 438. Glasgow, 1876

DARKNESS at noon; or the great solar eclipse, of the 16th of June, 1806, described and represented in every particular. By an inhabitant of Boston [Andrew Newell]. Cr 8vo. [Cushing's *Init. and Pseud.*, vol. i., p. 137.] Boston, 1806

DARKNESS made light; or the story of Old Sam [Hyams], the Christian Jew. By the Secretary of the Society for promoting Christianity among the Jews [Rev. Alfred Long Stackhouse, M.A.]. Fcap 8vo. Pp. 30. [*Brit. Mus.*] Launceston, Tasmania, 1859

DARKNESS (the) of atheisme expelled by the light of nature; or, the existence of a Deity, and his creation and government of the world, demonstrated from reason and the light of nature only: with an appendix touching the most proper method of preaching the gospel among the heathens. Englished by H. C. [Henry Care]. 8vo. Pp. 117. [*Bodl.*] London, 1683

DARKNESS (the) past; a sequel to " Light in darkness; a short account of a blind deaf-mute" [viz. Eliza Cooter]. By S. R. [Sarah Robinson]. 8vo. [*Brit. Mus.*] London, 1861

DARKNESS vanquished; or faith in its primitive purity: being an answer to a late book of Mr Henry Danvers, intituled, A Treatise of laying on of hands. Wherein his mistakes and cloudy apprehensions about it are rectified, his grand objections answered. . . . By B. K. [Benjamin Keach]. 8vo. [Whitley's *Bapt. Bibl.*, i., 105.] London, 1675

An enlarged edition, with the author's name and a different title, appeared in 1698.

DARKNESS visible: a brief treatise on degrees [in Free-Masonry], etc. By a brother of the Craft [Robert Steven]. Fcap 8vo. Glasgow, 1889

DARNLEY; or, the Field of the cloth of gold. By the author of *Richelieu*, etc. [George Payne Rainsford James]. 3 vols. Pt 8vo. [*Brit. Mus.*] London, 1830

DARRELL Chevasney. [A novel.] By Curtis Yorke [Mrs W. —— S. Richmond Lee, *née* —— Jex-Long]. 8vo. Pp. 253. [*Lit. Year Book.*] London, 1893

DARTMOOR (the) house that Jack built. By John Trevena [Ernest George Henham]. Cr 8vo. Pp. 426. [*Lond. Lib. Cat.*] London, 1909

DARTMOOR (the) window again. By Beatrice Chase [Olive Katharine Parr]. 8vo. Pp. viii., 211. [*Brit. Mus.*] London, 1918

DARTNELL; a bizarre incident. By Benjamin Swift [William Romaine Paterson]. 8vo. Pp. 186. [*Brit. Mus.*] London, 1899

DARWIN among the machines. By Cellarius [Samuel Butler]. [*Brit. Mus.*] S. sh. fol. London, 1863

DARWIN on trial at the Old Bailey. By Democritus [F. —— Raymond Coulson]. Royal 8vo. Pp. 210. London, 1899

DARWINIAN (the) theory of the transmutation of species examined. By a graduate of the University of Cambridge [Robert Mackenzie Beverley, LL.D.]. 8vo. London, 1867

DARWIN'S probabilities: a review of his " Descent of Man." [By William James Linton.] 8vo. [*Brit. Mus.*] London, 1896

DASHING Charlie, the Texan whirlwind. By Ned Buntline [Edward Z. C. Judson]. Fcap 8vo. [Haynes' *Pseud.*] New York, 1890

DASHING (the) little Duke; a musical play in three acts. By Seymour Hicks. Lyrics by Adrian Ross [Arthur Reed Ropes]. 8vo. [*Brit. Mus.*] London, 1909

DATE (the) of Malachi; St Paul in a new light. By " Lumen " [Major John Samuels]. 8vo. [*Lit. Year Book.*] Glasgow, 1911

DATES and data relating to religious anthropology and Biblical archæology (Primæval period). [By J— B— Mitchell.] 8vo. London, 1876

DAUGHTER (the) of a star. By Christian Reid [Mrs Frances T. Tiernan]. 8vo. Pp. vi., 349. [*Brit. Mus.*] New York, [1913]

DAUGHTER (the) of adoption; a tale of modern times. By John Beaufort, LL.D. [John Thelwall]. 4 vols. Fcap 8vo. [Wrangham's *Cat.*, p. 612.] London, 1801

DAUGHTER (the) of an Empress. From the German of Louise Mühlbach [Mrs Clara Müller Mundt]. Pt 8vo. [Haynes' *Pseud.*] New York, 1887

DAUGHTER (a) of Bohemia. By Christian Reid [Frances C. Fisher, later Mrs James N. Tiernan]. 8vo. [Cushing's *Init. and Pseud.*, vol. i., 249.] New York, 1873

DAUGHTER (a) of earth; a novel. [By Mrs E. M. Davy.] 8vo. London, 1896

DAUGHTER (a) of Eve; a novel. By Henry Hayes [Mrs Ellen Olney Kirk]. 8vo. [Kirk's *Supp.*] Boston, 1890

DAUGHTER (the) of heaven. By Pierre Loti [Captain M— J. Viaud, of the French Navy], and Judith Gautier. Translated by Ruth H. Davis. Dy 8vo. Pp. 204. [*Lond. Lib. Cat.*] London, 1913

DAUGHTER (the) of Louis XVI., Marie Thérèse Charlotte de, Duchess of Angoulême: translated from the French of G. Lenôtre [Louis L. T. Gosselin]. 8vo. [*Amer. Cat.*] New York, 1908

DAUGHTER (a) of music. By George Colmore [Mrs Gertrude Baillie-Weaver]. Cr 8vo. [*Brit. Mus.*] London, 1894

DAUGHTER (the) of Sion avvakened, and putting on strength: she is arising and shaking her self out of the dust, and putting on her beautiful garments. M. F. [Margaret Fell]. 4to. [*Smith's Cat. of Friends' Books,* i., 601.] N.P., 1677

DAUGHTER (a) of St Dominic. By Grace Ramsay [Kathleen O'Meara]. Fcap 8vo. [*Haynes' Pseud.*] Boston, 1888

DAUGHTER (a) of the Druids; a novel. By A. K. H. [Alice Kimball Hopkins]. 8vo. Pp. 297. [*Brit. Mus.*] Boston, [Mass.], 1892

DAUGHTER (a) of the gods; or, how she came into her kingdom: a romance. By Charles M. Clay [Charlotte Moon Clark]. 8vo. Pp. 337. [Cushing's *Init. and Pseud.*, i., p. 61.] New York, 1883

DAUGHTER (a) of the King; a novel. By Alien [Mrs L— A. Baker]. 8vo. [*Lond. Lib. Cat.*] London, 1894

DAUGHTER (a) of the Klephts; or a girl of modern Greece. By Edward Garrett [Isabella Fyvie, later Mrs John R. Mayo]. 8vo. [*Brit. Mus.*] Edinburgh, [1897]

DAUGHTER (a) of the manse. By Sarah Tytler [Henrietta Keddie]. Pp. 319. [*Haynes' Pseud.*] London, 1905

DAUGHTER (a) of the Philistines. [By Hjalmar Hjorth Boyesen.] 8vo. Pp. vi., 325. [*Brit. Mus.*] London, 1883

DAUGHTER (a) of the regiment. By Clara Vance [Mrs Mary Andrews Denison]. Fcap 8vo. [Cushing's *Init. and Pseud.*, i., 292.] New York, 1888

DAUGHTER (a) of the regiment: from my grandmother's journal. By Ascott R. Hope [Ascott Robert Hope Moncrieff]. Cr 8vo. Pp. 160. [*Lond. Lib. Cat.*] London, 1903

DAUGHTER (a) of the Sierra. By Christian Reid [Mrs Frances C. F. Tiernan]. 8vo. [Kirk's *Supp.*] St Louis, Mo., 1903

DAUGHTER (a) of the soil; a novel. By M. E. Francis [Margaret E. Sweetman, later Mrs Francis Blundell]. Pt 8vo. Pp. 301. [*Lit. Year Book.*] London, 1895

DAUGHTER (a) of the West; or Ruth Gurgunell, schoolmistress. By Morice Gerard [Rev. John Jessop Teague]. 8vo. [*Brit. Mus.*] London, 1911

DAUGHTERS (the); a novel. By the author of *The Gambler's wife* [Mrs Elizabeth C. Grey]. 3 vols. Fcap 8vo. London, 1847
A later edition (1884) bears the writer's name.

DAUGHTERS of heaven [nine short stories]. By Victoria Cross [Vivian Cory]. Cr 8vo. Pp. 285. [*Amer. Cat.*] London, 1920

DAUGHTERS (the) of Job. By Darley Dale [Francesca M. Steele], author of *The village blacksmith,* etc. Cr 8vo. [*Lond. Lib. Cat.*] London, 1905

DAUGHTERS (the) of Minerva; a novel of social life. By George Barlow [James Hinton]. Cr 8vo. Pp. 216. [*Lond. Lib. Cat.*] London, [1898]

DAUGHTERS (the) of Nijo. By Onoto Watanna [Mrs. B— W. Babcock]. 8vo. London, 1904

DAUGHTERS of the Revolution and their times, 1769-1776: an historical romance. By "Carleton" [Charles Carleton Coffin]. Pt 8vo. Pp. 387. [*Haynes' Pseud.*] Boston, 1895

DAUGHTERS of Thespis; a story of the green-rooms. By John Bickerdyke [Charles Henry Cook]. 8vo. Pp. vi., 312. [*Brit. Mus.*] London, 1897

DAVID: a poem. By E. S. G. S. [Emily S. G. Saunders]. Oblong 8vo. Pp. 45. [*Brit. Mus.*] London, 1880

DAVID and Bathshua. By C. Whitworth Wynne [Charles W. Cayzer, M.A. (Oxon)]. Cr 8vo. [*Bodl.*] London, 1903

DAVID and Samuel; with other poems, original and translated. By John Robertson [Sir John Robert Seeley]. 8vo. [*D. N. B.,* vol. 51, p. 192.] London, 1859

DAVID Easterbrook: an Oxford story. By Tregelles Polkinghorne [William John Hocking]. 8vo. Pp. x., 386. [*Brit. Mus.*] London, 1883

DAVID Fleming's forgiveness. [A story.] By the author of *The Bairns,* etc. [Margaret M. Robertson]. 8vo. Pp. 345. [*Brit. Mus.*] London, 1891

DAVID Kent's ambition. By Joy
Allison [Mrs Mary A. Cragin]. Fcap
8vo. [Cushing's *Init. and Pseud.*, vol.
i., p. 10.]   Philadelphia, 1877

DAVID Lloyd's last will. By Hesba
Stretton, author of *Jessica's first prayer*,
etc. [Sarah Smith]. New edition.
Fcap. 8vo. Pp. ix. 275.
London, 1877
See the note to " Alone in London."

DAVID'S choice of three evils, " the
judgments of God and the vengeance
of man"; a sermon [on 2 Sam. xxiv.
13, 14] on the distress in the cotton
districts. By a layman [Harold
Richard Bush]. 8vo. [*Brit. Mus.*]
[London], 1862

DAVID'S distress and deliverance : a
sermon on 1 Samuel xxx. 6, preached
at Edinburgh, March 22nd, 1696. [By
J. W., minister of the Gospel [John
Wilson, Episcopalian minister of Haddington.] 4to. [*Adv. Lib.*]
Edinburgh, 1696

DAUIDS harpe ful of moost delectable
armony newely strynged and set in
tune by Theodore Basille [Thomas
Becon]. 8vo. [Lowndes' *Bibl. Man.*]
London, 1543

DAVID'S learning, or the way to true
happinesse : in a commentarie upon
the 32. Psalme, preached and now
published by T. T. [Thomas Taylor,
D.D., late Fellow of Christ's College
in Cambridge.] Pt 4to. Pp. 446.
[*Camb. Univ. Cat.*]   London, 1617

DAVID'S loom ; a story of Rochdale
life in the early years of the nineteenth
century. By " The Owd Weighver "
[John Trafford Clegg]. Pt 8vo.
London, 1894

DAVID'S musick ; or psalmes of that
royall prophet, once the sweete singer
of that Israel ; unfolded logically,
expounded paraphrastically, and then
followeth a more particular explanation
of the words, with manifold doctrines
and uses briefly observed out of the
same. By R. B. [Richard Bernard]
and R. A. [Richard Alleine]. . . .
4to. [Green's *Bibl. Somers.*, vol. ii.,
p. 167.]   London, 1616

DAVID'S prophecy relating to [Cam]-
b[rid]ge, found among the papers of a
certain rabbi, famous for a collection
of all the prophesies from the beginning
of the world to this day ; with an
account of its accomplishment in that
U[niversit]y. By Isaac Van Sampson,
a learned Dutch commentator. [A
satire principally on Dr Edmund

Keene, master of Peter-House, and
vice-chancellor of the University.]
[By William Waller, B.A., who was
expelled for publishing this pamphlet.]
8vo. Pp. 54. [Bowes' *Camb. Books*,
p. 128.]   Cambridge, 1751
Attributed also to Thomas Chapman.

DAVID'S Queen. By the author of
Lady Moreton's governess (Mignon)
[Mrs —— Baseley]. 8vo. Pp. 232.
London, [1905]

DAUIDS sling against great Goliah ;
conteining diuers notable treatises.
. . . By E. H. [Edward Hake ?].
Fcap 8vo. Pp. 329. [*Brit. Mus.*]
London, 1593

DAVID'S vision ; with a preliminary
dissertation, showing David's prophecy
of Christ. By a pilgrim in the Holy
Land [Edward Falkener]. 8vo.
London, 1872

DAVIE Armstrong : a story of the
Fells. By Austin Clare [Miss W ——
M. James]. Fcap 8vo. [*Lond. Lib.
Cat.*]   London, 1871

DAVNGEROVS positions and proceedings, published and practised within
this iland of Brytaine vnder pretence
of reformation, and for the presbi-
teriall discipline. [By Richard Bancroft, D.D.] 8vo. Pp. 193. [*Bodl.*]
London, 1591
Later issues (in 1640 and 1712) bear the
author's name, and a different spelling of
the first word of the title (" Dangerous ").
The work was directed against Robert
Baillie.

DAWK (the) bungalow ; or, is his
appointment Pucka ? [A comedy.]
By H. Broughton, B.C.S. [Sir George
Otto Trevelyan]. 8vo. Pp. 48.
[*Brit. Mus.*]   Calcutta, 1863

DAWN and sunrise. By C. B. [Char-
lotte Bickersteth, later Mrs Ward].
8vo. [*Brit. Mus.*]   London, 1860

DAWN and twilight ; a tale. By the
author of *Amy Grant*, etc. [C— B—
Doggett]. 2 vols. 8vo. [*Brit. Mus.*]
Oxford, 1858

DAWN (the) by Galilee ; a story of the
Christ. By Ralph Connor [Charles
William Gordon, D.D.]. 8vo. [*Brit.
Mus.*]   London, [1909]

DAWN (the) of a new empire. By a
British American [—— Wetherby].
8vo. [Cushing's *Init. and Pseud.*,
vol. i., p. 40.]   Halifax, N.S., 1854

DAWN (the) of a new reign ; a study
of modern Russia. By Stepniak
[Sergie Michaelovitch Kravchinsky].
Third edition. Cr 8vo. [*Brit. Mus.*]
London, 1905

DAWN (the) of freedom : a political satire. By a graduate of the University of Oxford [William Charles Townsend]. Dedicated to the sovereign people. 8vo. [*Brit Mus.*]
London, 1832

DAWN (the) of hope ; a tale of the days of St Paul. By Morice Gerard [Rev. John Jessop Teague]. Cr 8vo. Pp. 219. [*Lit. Year Book.*] London, 1917

DAWN (the) of liberty ; or, cadunt regum coronae, vicit libertas : an original drama, serio-comical, in three acts [and in verse]. By Prometheus [William Bush]. 8vo. [Cushing's *Init. and Pseud.*, i., p. 125.]
Chicago, 1869

DAY (the) after the election. [In verse.] [By Thomas Binns.] 4to. [Smith's *Cat. of Friends' Books*, i., 81 ; ii., 272.] Liverpool, 1806

DAY (the) after the holidays. By Ascott R. Hope [Ascott Robert Hope Moncrieff]. Cr 8vo. London, 1906

DAY (the) after the wedding ; or a wife's first lesson ; an interlude in one act. [By Mrs Charles Kemble, *née* Marie Thérèse De Camp.] 8vo. [*Biog. Dram.*] London, 1808

DAY (the) after to-morrow ; or Fata Morgana. By William de Tyne [William Sidney Gibson, of Newcastle-on-Tyne]. 8vo. Pp. viii., 415.
London, 1858

DAY (a) ; an epistle to John Wilkes of Aylesbury, Esq. [By John Armstrong, M.D.] 4to. London, 1761

DAY (a) and a night ; a tale. By Hesba Stretton [Sarah Smith]. Fcap 8vo. London, 1876
See the note to " Alone in London."

DAY (a) at Rome ; a musical entertainment, in two acts : as it was damned at the Theatre Royal in Covent Garden, October 11th, 1798. [By Charles Smith.] 8vo. [*Biog. Dram.*]
1798

DAY (the) Book of Melisande, from December to December. [By Mrs Nora Gribble.] Cr 8vo.
London, 1905

DAY by day we worship thee ; readings and prayers. [By Misses —— Davidson.] 8vo. London, 1910

DAY (a) in Stowe gardens. [By Mrs Mary Sabilla Novello.] 8vo. [*Brit. Mus.*] London, 1825

DAY (a) in the wilderness. [By John Dunn.] 8vo. London, 1847

DAY (a) in vacation at College [in Cambridge] ; a burlesque poem. [By W. Dodd.] 4to. [Bartholomew's *Cat. of Camb. Books.*] London, 1751

DAY (the) of doom :—or a description of the great and last judgment : with a short discourse about eternity. [By Rev. Michael Wigglesworth.] 12mo. Pp. 96. [Corser's *Collectanea Anglo-Poetica*, Part v., p. 127, *et seq.*]
London, 1673

DAY (the) of Judgment ; a poem, in two Books. [By John Ogilvie, D.D., minister in Midmar.] 8vo. [Robertson's *Aberd. Bibl.*] Aberdeen, 1753

DAY (the) of Judgment ; a poetical essay. [By Dr Robert Glynn.] Fourth edition. 4to. Pp. 16. [Watt's *Bibl. Brit.*] Cambridge, 1760

DAY (the) of my life. By " Vanoc " [Arnold White]. Fcap 8vo.
London, 1912

DAY (a) of my life at Eton ; or everyday experiences at Eton. By an Eton boy [George Nugent Banks]. Pt 8vo. Pp. viii., 183. [*Lond. Lib. Cat.*]
London, 1877

DAY (a) of pleasure ; a simple story for young children. By Mrs Harriet Myrtle, author of *Pleasures of the country*, etc. [Mrs Lydia Falconer Miller]. 4to. Pp. 108. [Cushing's *Init. and Pseud.*, vol. i., p. 199.]
London, 1853

DAY (the) of rest ; and other poems. By a clergyman [Rev. Hugh Stowell, M.A.]. 8vo. London, 1835

DAY (the) of small things. By the author of *Mary Powell* [Anne Manning, later Mrs Rathbone.] Fcap 8vo. [*Brit. Mus.*] London, [1859]

DAY (the) of the dog. By R. Greaves [George B. M'Cutcheon]. Pt 8vo. [*Amer. Cat.*] New York, 1904

DAY (the) will come. . . . By the author of *Lady Audley's secret* [Mary Elizabeth Braddon, later Mrs John Maxwell]. 8vo. [*Brit. Mus.*]
London, [1889]

DAY (a) with Charles Dickens. By Maurice Clare [May Clarissa Gillington, later Mrs Byron]. 8vo. Pp. 44. [*Brit. Mus.*] London, [1910]

DAY (a) with Charles Kingsley. By Maurice Clare [May Clarissa Gillington, later Mrs Byron]. 8vo. Pp. 47. [*Brit. Mus.*] London, [1911]

DAY (a) with Ralph Waldo Emerson. By Maurice Clare [May Clarissa Gillington, later Mrs Byron]. 8vo. Pp. 47. [*Brit. Mus.*]
London, [1911]

DAY (a) with the hounds, and what came of it. By Naunton Covertside [Naunton Davies]. Cr 8vo.
London, 1896

DAY (a) with William Shakespeare. By Maurice Clare [May Clarissa Gillington, later Mrs Byron]. 8vo. [*Brit. Mus.*] London, 1913

DAYBREAK in Britain. By A. L. O. E. [*i.e.* A Lady Of England, Charlotte M. Tucker]. 8vo. Pp. 125. [*Lit. Year Book.*] London, [1880]

DAYBREAK ; or right struggling and triumphant. By Cycla [Helen Clacy]. 8vo. [Haynes' *Pseud.*] London, 1860
  The pseudonym is an anagram of the family name.

DAY-BREAKING (the) if not the sun-rising of the Gospell with the Indians in New-England. [By Thomas Shepard.] Fcap 4to. [*New Coll. Cat.*] London, 1647

DAY-DREAMS. By a butterfly [Rev. J— A. Allan]. 8vo. Pp. 156.
  Kingston, Canada, 1854

DAY-FATALITY ; or some observations on days lucky and unlucky : penn'd and publish'd whilst King James II. was Duke of York. The second impression, with additions ; to which is added, Prince-protecting providences, and the Swans welcome ; all by an officer at arms, author of a book, *Introductio ad Latinam Blasoniam* [J. Gibbon]. Two parts. Folio. [*W.* ; *Brit. Mus.*] London, 1686

DAY-HOURS (the) of the Church of England. [By John F— Mackarness, M.A.] Cr 8vo. London, 1891

DAYLEY (the) exercises of the devout Rosarists, containing several most pithy practices of devotion. By A. C. and T. V. [Arthur Anselm Crowther, O.S.B., and Thomas Vincent Faustus Sadler, O.S.B.]. Fcap 8vo. Pp. 671. [Gillow's *Bibl. Dict.*]
  Amsterdam, 1657

DAYLY devotions. . . . *See* " Daily devotions . . ."

DAYS and hours in a garden. By E. V. B. [the Hon. Mrs Eleanor Vere Boyle, *née* Gordon]. Fcap 8vo. [Haynes' *Pseud.*] London, 1894

DAYS before the Flood ; a tale. By E. C. S. [Lady Elizabeth Susan Colchester, *née* Law]. Pt 8vo. Pp. 134. [Cushing's *Init. and Pseud.*, vol. ii., p. 23.] London, 1884

DAYS errant. By Robert Aitken [G— A. Morton]. 8vo. New York, 1907

DAYS in clover. By the amateur angler [Edward Marston, publisher]. Pt 8vo. [Cushing's *Init. and Pseud.*, vol. i., p. 6.] London, 1892

DAYS in Thule, with rod, gun, and camera. By John Bickerdyke [Charles Henry Cook]. 8vo. [*Lit. Year Book.*] London, 1884

DAY'S (a) journal of a sponge. By Peter Pasquin [William Henry Pyne]. 8vo. London, 1824

DAY'S (the) message. By Susan Coolidge [Sarah Chauncey Woolsey]. Fcap 8vo. Pp. 370. [Kirk's *Supp.*] London, 1911

DAYS (the) of Auld Langsyne. By Ian Maclaren [John Watson, D.D., Liverpool]. Fcap 8vo. Pp. viii., 358. [*Lit. Year Book.*] London, 1895

DAYS (the) of battle ; or, Quatre Bras and Waterloo. By an Englishwoman resident at Brussels in June 1815 ; author of *Rome in the nineteenth century* [Charlotte Ann Waldie, afterwards Mrs Eaton]. 8vo. [*Brit. Mus.*]
  London, 1853

DAYS (the) of England not numbered ; a reply to Sir Archibald Alison. . . . By Caritas [Mrs David Urquhart]. 8vo. [*Bodl.*] London, 1867

DAYS (the) of Knox : a tale of the sixteenth century. By the author of *The dark year of Dundee* [Deborah Alcock]. 8vo. [*Brit. Mus.*]
  London, 1869

DAYS (the) of my life ; an autobiography. By the author of *Margaret Maitland*, etc. [Mrs M. O. Oliphant]. 3 vols. 8vo. London, 1857

DAYS of my life in waters fresh and salt. By John Bickerdyke [Charles Henry Cook]. 8vo. [*Lit. Year Book.*]
  London, 1895

DAYS (the) of Prince Maurice : the story of the Netherland War, from the death of William the Silent to its close. By Mary Barrett [Mary Olivia Nutting]. Cr 8vo. [Cushing's *Init. and Pseud.*, vol. i., p. 30]. New York, 1894

DAYS (the) of Queen Mary [the First, of England. By George Stokes.] Fcap 8vo. R.T.S. London, [1826]
  Afterwards combined with *The Lollards*, by the same author, to form *A brief history of the British Reformation.*

DAYS of the [Irish] Land League ; and other poems. By R. J. M. [Robert Jasper Martin]. 8vo. [O'Donoghue's *Poets of Ireland.*] Dublin, 1884

DAYS of yore. By Sarah Tytler, author of *Citoyenne Jacqueline* [Henrietta Keddie]. 2 vols. 8vo. Pp. 380.
  London, 1889

DAYS (the) we live in. By C. E. A. [Clementina Edith Aiken]. 8vo. [*Kirk's Supp.*] Boston, 1876

DAYS we remember. By Marian Douglas [Annie Douglas Robinson, *née* Greene]. 8vo. [Cushing's *Init. and Pseud.*, vol. i., p. 83.]
  Boston, 1903

DAYS (the) when we had tails on us. With fourteen coloured illustrations. Dedicated to the officers of the British infantry. [By Lieutenant Colonel Richard Hort.] Second edition. 8vo. [*Adv. Lib.*] London, 1849

DAYS with the Lothians hounds in Spring, 1872. By an old sportsman [Charles M. Barstow]. Fcap 8vo. Edinburgh, 1872

DAZZLING (a) acquaintance ; or fair words butter no parsnips. By the author of *The young engineer* [Mrs M—Douglas]. 8vo. London, [1882]

DAZZLING (the) Miss Davison. A novel. By Florence Warden [Florence Alice Price, later Mrs George E. James]. Cr 8vo. Pp. 312. [*Brit. Mus.*] London, 1908

DE causa Dei : a vindication of the common doctrine of Protestant divines, concerning predestination (*i.e.* the interest of God as the first cause, in all actions, as such of all rational creatures) from the inviduous consequences, with which it is burden'd by Mr Joh. Howe, in a late Letter and Postscript of God's prescience. By T. D. [Thomas Danson, M.A.]. 8vo. [Wood's *Athen. Oxon.*, iv., 594.] London, 1678

DE Clifford ; a romance of the Red Rose ; a poem in twelve books. [By —— Kennedy.] 8vo. [*Brit. Mus.*] London, 1826

DE Clifford ; or, the constant man. By the author of *Tremaine*, etc. [Robert Plumer Ward]. 4 vols. Fcap 8vo. *Brit. Mus.*] London, 1841

DE Cressy, a tale. By the author of *Dorothy* [Margaret Agnes Colville, afterwards Mrs Paul]. 8vo. [*Brit. Mus.*] London, 1856

DE finibus virtutis Christianæ ; or, the ends of Christian religion ; which are,—

To $\begin{Bmatrix} \text{avoid} \\ \text{obtain} \end{Bmatrix}$ eternal $\begin{Bmatrix} \text{wrath} \\ \text{happinesse} \end{Bmatrix}$ from God

By R. S. [Robert Sharrock, LL.D.]. 4to. [*Watt's Bibl. Brit.*] Oxford, 1673

DE flagello myrteo ; thoughts and fancies on love. [By Richard Garnett, LL.D.] Square 12mo. London, 1905

DE jure maritimo et navali ; or a treatise of affairs maritime, and of commerce : in three books. [By Charles Molloy.] 8vo. [Arber's *Term Cat.*, vol. i., p. 522.] London, 1676
Several editions followed, enlarged.

DE justificatione Baxteriana Coronis : being a letter to the author of a late small book intituled, A Caveat against High Church. . . . By J. H. [John Humphrey, M.A.]. 4to. [Green's *Bibl. Somers.*, vol. ii., p. 508.] London, 1707

DE justificatione : being a letter to a friend upon a passage in one of the printed sermons of his Grace the present Archbishop of York. . . . By J. H., aged eighty-five [John Humphrey, M.A.]. 4to. [Green's *Bibl. Somers.*, vol. ii., p. 508.] London, 1706

DE Lisle ; or, the distrustful man. [By Mrs E. C. Grey ?.] 3 vols. Pt 8vo. London, 1828

DE L'Orme. By the author of *Richelieu* and *Darnley* [George Payne Rainsford James]. 3 vols. Fcap 8vo. [*Brit. Mus.*] London, 1830

DE morbis capitis ; or, of the chief internall diseases of the head. By R. P. [Robert Pennell]. 4to. Pp. 141. London, 1650

DE neutralibus et mediis ; grosly Englished, Jacke of both sides : a godly . . . admonition touching those that be neuters, holding no certaine religion, nor doctrines. . . . [Translated from the Latin of J. W. [Joannes Wigand]. 4to. [*Brit. Mus.*] London, 1626

DE omnibus rebus ; an old man's discursive ramblings on the road of everyday life. By the author of *Flemish Interiors* [Mrs Julia Clara Byrne]. 8vo. Pp. xxiii., 343. [*Brit. Mus.*] London, 1889

DE Quincey ; his life and writings, with unpublished correspondence. [By Alexander Hay Japp, LL.D.] 2 vols. 8vo. [*D. N. B.*, II. Suppl., vol. 2, p. 363.] London, 1877

DE stemmate Piscatoris ; a tale of sea toilers. By the author of *The Camacs of Co. Down*, etc. [Frank Owen Fisher]. Large 8vo. [*Bodl.*] London, [1909]

DE successionibus apud Anglos ; or a treatise of hereditary descents, shewing the rise, progress and successive alterations thereof. . . . [By Sir Matthew Hale.] 8vo. [*Brit. Mus.*] London, 1699

DE Vavasour ; a tale of the fourteenth century. [By Charles John Gardiner, first Earl of Blessington.] 3 vols. 8vo. [*Brit. Mus.*] London, 1826

DE Vere ; or, the man of independence. By the author of *Tremaine* [Robert Plumer Ward]. 3 vols. Third edition. Pt 8vo. [*Brit. Mus.*] London, 1827

DEACON Brodie ; or, behind the mask. By Dick Donovan [Joyce E. Preston Muddock]. Cr 8vo. [*Lit. Year Book.*] London, 1901

DEACONESS House, Carlsruhe ; hints on village nursing. By E. A. E. [E— A. Eminson]. 8vo. [Cushing's *Init. and Pseud.*, vol. ii., p. 47.]
London, 1885

DEAD (the) bridal ; a Venetian tale of the fourteenth century. By Jonathan Freke Slingsby [John Francis Waller, barrister, LL.D.]. 8vo. [*Brit. Mus.*]
London, 1856

DEAD certainties ; a novel. By Nathaniel Gubbins [Edward Spencer Mott]. 8vo. Pp. 218. [*Brit. Mus.*]
London, 1904

DEAD (the) doll, and other verses. By Margaret Vandergrift [Margaret Thomson Janvier]. 8vo. [*Kirk's Supp.*]
Philadelphia, 1878

DEAD (the) hand in the Free Churches, with pictures of their inner life, sketched by eminent Nonconformists. Edited by the author of *The Englishman's Brief on behalf of his national Church* [Rev. Thomas Moore]. Pt 8vo. Pp. xvi., 314. [*Crockford's Cler. Directory.*]
London, 1882

DEAD (a) heart. By Bertha M. Clay [Mrs Charlotte M. Braeme, *née* Law]. Fcap 8vo.
New York, 1885

DEAD (a) letter. By Seeley Register [Metta Victoria Fuller, later Mrs Victor]. 8vo. [*Cushing's Init. and Pseud.*, ii., 249.]
New York, 1865

DEAD (the) line ; a Kansas story of society, religion and politics. By Gideon Laine [G— C— Clemens]. 8vo.
Topeka, Kansas, 1894

DEAD man's rock ; a romance. By Q. [Sir Arthur Thomas Quiller-Couch]. Cr 8vo. Pp. 372. [*Brit. Mus.*]
London, 1900

DEAD (the) man's step. By Lawrence L. Lynch [Mrs Van Deventer, *née* Emma Murdoch]. Pt 8vo. [*Brit. Mus.*]
Chicago, 1893

DEAD men's dollars. By the author of *Queenie* [May Crommelin]. 8vo. [*Brit. Mus.*]
Bristol, 1887

DEAD men's shoes ; a novel. By the author of *Lady Audley's secret*, etc. [Mary Elizabeth Braddon, later Mrs John Maxwell]. 3 vols. Cr 8vo. [*Brit. Mus.*]
London, 1876

DEAD (the) saint speaking : or a sermon preached upon occasion of the death of Matt. Newcomen. By J. F. [John Fairfax], minister of the Gospel. With a preface by J. C. [Dr John Collings]. 4to. [*Brit. Mus.*]
London, 1679

DEADHAM Hard ; a novel. By Lucas Malet [Mrs St Leger Harrison, *née* Mary Kingsley]. Cr 8vo. [*Brit. Mus.*]
London, 1918

DEAD-HEADS, financial and moral. By a stalwart Republican [Rev. Henry Clay Badger]. 8vo. [*Kirk's Supp.*]
Boston, 1884

DEAD-SEA fruit ; a novel. By the author of *Lady Audley's secret*, etc. [Mary Elizabeth Braddon, later Mrs John Maxwell]. 3 vols. Cr 8vo.
London, 1868

DEAF and dumb ; or, the orphan protected : a historical drama, acted at Drury Lane. [By Thomas Holcroft.] 8vo. [*Biog. Dram.*]
N.P., 1801

DEAFNESS ; its prevention and cure. By " Lennox " [Alfred Mellet Peirson]. 8vo.
London, 1893

DEALINGS with the dead ; contributed to the " Boston Transcript." By a sexton of the old school [Lucius Manlius Sargent]. 2 vols. Pt 8vo. [*Cushing's Init. and Pseud.*, i., p. 265.]
Boston, [Mass.], 1856

DEALINGS with the dead. . . . By Rosicrucian [Paschal Beverley Randolph]. 8vo. [*Cushing's Init. and Pseud.*, vol. i., p. 253.]
Utica, New York, 1861-62

DEAN (the) and the squire ; a political eclogue : humbly dedicated to Soame Jenyns, Esq. By the author of the Heroic epistle to Sir William Chambers, Esq. [Rev. William Mason, M.A.]. 4to. Pp. iv., 19. [*D. N. B.*, vol. 36, p. 440.]
London, 1782
Dedication signed " Malcolm Macgregor."

DEAN Jonathan's parody on the 4th chap. of Genesis. [By Jonathan Swift, D.D.] Folio. Pp. 7. [*Camb. Hist. of Eng. Lit.*, vol. ix., p. 464.]
London, 1729

DEAN Norman [M'Leod] down in the mouth, and dealing in confessions ; a Broad-Church lament, in pibroch measure. [By Rev. John Allan.] Fcap 8vo. [*And. Jervise.*]
Aberdeen, N.D.

DEAN (the) of Canterbury [Robert Payne Smith] on Science and Revelation : a letter by M. P. [John Delaware Lewis]. 8vo. [*Brit. Mus.*]
Ramsgate, [1871]

DEAN (the) of Coleraine ; a moral history, composed from the memoirs of an illustrious Irish family. By the author of the *Memoirs of a man of quality*. Now done into English by Mr Erskine. [A translation of " Le doyen de Kellerine," by Antoine François Prevost D'Exiles.] A new edition, carefully corrected and improved. 3 vols. Fcap 8vo. [*Camb. Univ. Lib.*]
London, 1780
The earlier edition was published at Dublin in 1742 (2 vols.).

D[EAN] (the) of M——, his vindication ; in answer to a pamphlet lately publish'd, call'd Bouchain [or a dialogue between the Medley and the Examiner]. [Revised by Jonathan Swift, D.D.] 8vo. [*Camb. Hist. of Eng. Lit.*, vol. ix., p. 464.] London, 1711

D——N (the) of W——r [Francis Hare, Dean of Worcester] still the same ; or, his New defence of the Lord Bishop of Bangor [Benjamin Hoadly]'s sermon, etc., consider'd as the performance of a great critick, a man of sense, and a man of probity. By an impartial hand [Sir Richard Steele]. 8vo. [*Athen. Cat.*, p. 512.] London, 1720
Ascribed also to Benjamin Hoadly, D.D. [*Adv. Lib.*]

DEAN (the) ; or the popular preacher. By Berkeley Aikin [Fanny Aikin Kortwright]. 3 vols. Pt 8vo. [*Brit. Mus.*] London, 1859

DEAN'S (the) little daughter. By the author of *A Fellow of Trinity* [Frances Marshall]. 8vo. Pp. 158. [*Lit. Year Book.*] London, [1891]

DEAR (the) bargain ; or, a true representation of the state of the English nation under the Dutch. In a letter to a friend. [By Nathaniel Johnston.] 4to. [*Adv. Lib.*] [London, 1688]

DEAR Elsie : from the German of Johannes v. Dewall [August Kuhne]. Fcap 8vo. New York, 1892

DEAR (a) fool ; an unpretentious story. By the author of *The Book of Artemas* [Arthur Telford Mason]. 8vo. Pp. 304. [*Brit. Mus.*] London, [1920]

DEAR Granny. [A tale.] By C. E. M. [Constance E. Miller]. Fcap 8vo. Pp. 128. [*Brit. Mus.*] London, [1894]

DEAR (the) neighbours. By Max O'Rell [Paul Blouet]. Pt 8vo. [*Lond. Lib. Cat.*] London, 1885

DEAR reader, step up with the utmost velocity ; and buy, if you please, an autumnal atrocity ; where each painter attacked with the greatest of valour is by a constant frequenter of Walker's art galleries. [By Edward Rimbault Vere Dibdin.] 8vo. Pp. 24.
Liverpool, N.D.

DEARER than honour : a fool's tragedy. By E. Livingston Prescott [Edith Katharine Spicer Jay]. 8vo. Pp. 367. [*Lond. Lib. Cat.*] London, 1898

DEAREST. [A novel.] By Mrs Forrester [Mrs —— Bridges]. 3 vols. Cr 8vo. Pp. 376. [*Amer. Cat.*]
London, 1893

DEARFORGIL, the Princess of Brefney; a historical romance of 1152-1172. By the author of *The last Earl of Desmond* [Rev. Charles B. Gibson, M.R.I.A.]. 8vo. [*Adv. Lib.*] London, 1857

DEARLY (a) ransomed soul at the grave of Cardinal Newman. [By Charles Kegan Paul.] Pt 8vo. Pp. 32. London, 1891

DEATH ; a poetical essay. [By Bishop Beilby Porteus.] Sixth edition. 12mo. [*Brit. Mus.*]
London, private print, 1801

DEATH and Co., wholesale and retail dealers in ales, wines, spirits, and other intoxicating drugs. [By Arthur Trevelyan. 8vo. [*Brit. Mus.*]
Edinburgh, [1862]

DEATH and life ; a record of the cholera wards in the London hospital. By the author of *Memorials of Captain Hedley Vicars*, etc. [Catherine Marsh]. 8vo. Pp. 80. London, 1867

DEATH and the Magdalen ; the Memory of Sale ; the Idle scholar's lament ; and other poems. By the author of *Crœsus, king of Lydia ; a tragedy* [Alfred Bate Richards, B.A., barrister]. 8vo. [*Brit. Mus.*]
London, 1846

DEATH and the resurrection of the two witnesses. By the Vicar of Great Carnfield [John Phillips Gurney]. 8vo. [*Camb. Univ. Lib.*] London, 1849

DEATH bed scenes and pastoral conversations. By the late John Warton, D.D. Edited by his sons. [By William Wood, B.D.] 8vo. [*Bodl.*]
London, 1826
A second volume was published in 1827, and a third in 1828. A second series in one volume appeared in 1832.

DEATH bed scenes ; or, the Christian's companion on entering the dark valley. By the author of *The Evangelical Rambler* [Timothy East]. Fcap 8vo. London, 1825

DEATH consider'd as a door to a life of glory : penn'd for the comfort of serious mourners, and occasion'd by the funerals of several friends ; particularly of one who dy'd at Easter ; and of the author's own funeral in antecessum. [By Thomas Pierce, D.D.] 4to. Pp. 130. [*Bodl.*]
Private print, London, N.D., [1690 ?]

DEATH dis-sected ; or, a fort against misfortune in a cordiall, compounded of many pious and profitable meditations on mans mortality. In severall poems written by Tho. Jordan. 8vo. No pagination.
[London], 1649
" This volume originally appeared with the engraved title-page,—A bvckler agaynst the feare of death or pyous and proffittable observations, medytations and consola-

tions on mans mortallity by E. B. minister in G. B. London Printed for Mr Sharke Junior 1640,—opposite which are fourteen verses headed " The mind of the frontispiece." After the engraved title is a plain title-page. Then a leaf containing a dedication " To the Right Worshipfull M^ris Helena Phelips and M^ris Agneta Gorges grand children to the Right Honourable Lady Helena, late Lady Marchionesse of Northampton, now with God, E. B. wisheth the happiness of grace here and of glory hereafter," etc., etc. The book, it appears, fell subsequently into the hands of Jordan, who destroyed the original titles, etc., and then put it forth as his own production ! E. B. are the initials of Edward Benlowes."—MS. note in the hand-writing of Dyce on the copy in the Dyce collection.

DEATH in the palace. [By Mary Grylls.] 8vo. London, 1861

DEATH (the) man. By Benjamin Swift [William Romaine Paterson, M.A.]. Cr 8vo. Pp. 318. [*Lit. Year Book.*] London, 1908

DEATH (the) of Abdallah. [A poem.] By Osander [Rev. Benjamin Allen, Episcopal minister]. 12mo. Pp. vi., 192. [Cushing's *Init. and Pseud.*, i., p. 220.] New York, 1814

DEATH (the) of Abel: by Salomon Gessner. Attempted from the German [by Mary Collyer]. (New idylls by S. Gessner [translated by W— Hooper] . . .) 8vo. Pp. xi., 275. [*Brit. Mus.*] London, 1797 *See below*, " The Death of Cain."

DEATH (the) of Basseville ; a poem in terza rima. By Vincenzo Monti. Translated in the same verse [by Adam Lodge]. 8vo. [*Brit. Mus.*] London, 1845

DEATH (the) of Bonaparte ; or, One pound one : a poem, in four cantos. By Cervantes [Samuel William Henry Ireland]. 8vo. [*Brit. Mus.*] York, 1812

DEATH (the) of Bucephalus ; a burlesque tragedy, in two acts : as acted at the theatre in Edinburgh. [By Ralph Schomberg, M.D.] 8vo. [*Biog. Dram.*] London, 1765

DEATH (the) of Cain, in five books : after the manner of the Death of Abel [by Salomon Gessner]. By a lady [Mary Collyer]. 8vo. Pp. xii. 147. London, 1789

DEATH (the) of Cain [a poem. By William Henry Hall.] Intended as a companion to " The Death of Abel " [by Salomon Gessner]. Fcap 8vo. [*Brit. Mus.*] London, [1810 ?]

DEATH (the) of death ; or a study of God's holiness in connection with the existence of evil. . . . By an orthodox layman [John M— Patton]. Cr 8vo. London, 1881 Another edition, revised, gives the author's name.

DEATH (the) of King Edward I. . . . [By William Dickson, solicitor.] 8vo. [*Brit. Mus.*] Alnwick, 1868

DEATH (the) of King Gerennius. By W. E. H. [Rev. William Edward Heygate]. 12mo. [Boase and Courtney's *Bibl. Corn.*, i., p. 237.] Truro, 1848

DEATH (the) of Lady Wallace. By Mac Bremen [James Bremner, native of Keiss]. 8vo. [Mowat's *Bibl. of Caithness*, p. 60.] London, 1904

DEATH (the) of Oswald, and other poems, songs, and ballads. By Old Saltbush [Walter Smith]. 8vo. Sydney, N.S.W., 1887

DEATH (the) of our Minotaur. By Theseus [Edward Hamilton]. 8vo. [Cushing's *Init. and Pseud.*, i., p. 282.] Boston, [Mass.], 1868

DEATH (the) of Pecci (Pope Leo XIII.). [By George Aislabie Procter.] 8vo. London, 1903 Signed " G. A. P."

DEATH (the) of Robert, Earle of Hvntington, otherwjse called Robin Hood of merrie Sherwodde ; with the lamentable tragedie of Chaste Matilda, his faire maid Marian, poysoned at Dunmowe by King Iohn. Acted by the Right Honourable, the Earle of Notingham, Lord High Admirall of England, his servants. [By Anthony Munday and Henry Chettle.] 4to. B. L. No pagination. London, 1601 Reprinted in Tudor Facsimile Tracts, 1913. " This second part of Robert, Earl of Huntington, containing his death, etc., has been long erroneously attributed to Thomas Heywood ; but it was written by Henry Chettle and Anthony Munday. *See* my Shakespeare."—MS. note by Malone on the Bodleian copy.

DEATH ; or Medorus's dream. By the author of *Ahasuerus* [Robert Tyler]. Fcap. 8vo. [*Brit. Mus.*] New York, 1843

DEATH'S jest-book ; or the fool's tragedy. [A poem. By Thomas Lovell Beddoes, M.A., M.D.] Fcap 8vo. [*Camb. Univ. Lib.*] London, 1850

DEATH'S vision represented in a philosophical, sacred poem ; writ at the request of the famous Mr John Lock. [By John Reynolds.] Second edition. 4to. Pp. 141. [*Bodl.*] London, 1713

DEATH'S waiting-room ; or, the Girondist's last supper : a dramatic sketch [in verse]. By Alpha [George Walker, M.D., of Sydney, New South Wales]. 8vo. [*Brit. Mus.*] London, 1851

DEBATE (the) in the House of Commons on Church reform and the Bishops' seats in Parliament, 16th Feb. 1837. . . . With an introduction by a Manchester Reformer [Rev. Alexander Thomson, M.A.]. 8vo. Pp. 62. [*Manch. Free Lib. Cat.*]
London, 1867

DEBATE (a) on the justice and piety of the present constitution under King William, in two parts. The first relating to the State ; the second to the Church : between Eucheres, a Conformist, and Dyscheres, a Nonconformist. [By Samuel Hill, Archdeacon of Wells.] 4to. [*D. N. B.*, vol. 26, p. 421.] London, 1696

DEBATES [in the Irish House of Commons] relative to the affairs of Ireland, in the years 1763 and 1764 ; taken by a military officer [Sir James Caldwell]. To which is added, an enquiry how far the restrictions laid upon the trade of Ireland, by British Acts of Parliament, are a benefit or disadvantage to the British dominions in general, and to England in particular. 2 vols. 8vo. [Watt's *Bib. Brit.*] London, 1766
    Dedication to Mr. Pitt signed " J. C."
The pagination is continuous.

DEBAUCHED (the) cavalleer; or the English Midianite : wherein are compared, by way of parallel, the carriage, or rather miscarriage of the cavalleeres in the present reigne of our King Charles, with the Midianites of old ; setting forth their diabolicall, and hyperdiabolicall blasphemies, execrations, rebellions, cruelties, rapes, and robberies. Penned by G. L. and C. L. [George Lawrence and Christopher Love] for publique good. 4to. Pp. 8. [Wood's *Athen. Oxon.*, iv., 784.]
London, 1647

DEBAUCHEE (the) ; or, the credulous cuckold ; a comedy, acted at His Highness the Duke of York's Theatre. [An alteration of Richard Brome's Mad couple well match'd, by Mrs Aphra Behn. The prologue and epilogue were written by Lord Rochester.] 4to. [*Biog. Dram.*] London, 1677

DEBAUCHRIE (the) and vices of the present age represented and taxed in a discourse. . . . By one of the ministers in Glasgow [James Clark]. Fcap 8vo. [Scott's *Fasti*.]
Edinburgh, 1707

DEBIT and credit. By Gustav Freytag. Translated . . . by L. C. C. [Lucy Caroline Cumming, later Mrs Smith]. 2 vols. 8vo. Edinburgh, 1857

DEBORAH ; an oratorio or sacred drama [in three parts, and in verse. By S— Humphreys]. The musick by Mr Handel. 4to. [*Brit. Mus.*]
London, 1764

DEBORAH Gray. By Frances C. Ingraham [Clara Ingraham Bell]. 8vo. [*Amer. Cat.*] Washington, 1903

DEBORAH'S book, and the lonely rock. . . . [By Jean Ingelow.] 12mo. [*Brit. Mus.*] London, 1867

DEBORAH'S diary ; a fragment. By the author of *Mary Powell* [Anne Manning, later Mrs Rathbone]. 8vo. Pp. 144. London, 1860

DEBTS discharge, or some considerations on Rom. xiii: 8, the former part. [By Rev. Charles Morton.] 8vo. Pp. 64. London, 1684

DECACORDON (a) of ten quodlibeticall questions concerning religion and state : wherein the authour, framing himselfe a quilibet to every quodlibet, decides an hundred cross interrogatorie doubts about the generall contentions betwixt the seminarie priests and Jesuits, at this present. [By William Watson, a secular priest.] 4to. [Dodd's *Church History*, ii., 379 ; *D. N. B.*, vol. 60, p. 44.] N.P., 1602

DECADE (a) of grievances, presented and approved to the . . . High Court of Parliament against the hierarchy or government of the Lord Bishops, and their dependant offices. [By Alexander Leighton.] 4to. 4 leaves.
        N.P., [London], 1641
    An extract from Leighton's anonymous " Appeal to the Parliament . . ."

DECADENCE (the) of Imperial Britain ; " shadows before." By the author of *Arca*, etc. [Francis Meredyth]. 8vo. Pp. ii., 56. Dublin, [1893]

DECADENT (the) ; being the Gospel of inaction ; wherein are set forth in romance form, certain reflections touching the curious characteristics of these ultimate years. . . . [By R— A. Crane.] 4to. Pp. 41. [*Brit. Mus.*]
Cambridge, Mass., [private print], 1893

DECADENTS : the story of Blackwell's Island and Newport. By Shelton Chauncey [Charles W. De Lyon Nichols]. Pt 8vo. New York, 1899

DECALOGUE (the) ; an impeachment of the ten commandments as a code of morality. By Kosmos [Edward A. Hardwicke]. 8vo. [*Brit. Mus.*]
London, [1893]

DECALOGUE (the) explain'd, in thirty-two discourses on the Ten Commandments. By J— H— C. A—D. S. [J. Howardine]. 8vo. Pp. 432. [*Bodl.*]
London, 1750

DECAMERON (the) of the West; a series of tales. [By Arthur Sinclair.] Pt 8vo.   London, 1839

DECAMERON (the), or ten days entertainment of Boccace: translated from the Italian. [By Charles Balguy, M.D.] 8vo. [*Brit. Mus.*]
London, 1741

DECAMERON (the); or ten days entertainment of Boccaccio: translated from the Italian, in two volumes. Second edition, corrected and improved. To which are prefixed, remarks on the life and writings of Boccaccio, and an advertisement, by the author of *Old Nick*, etc. [Edward Dubois]. 8vo. [*Brit. Crit.*, xxiv., 406.]   London, 1804

DECAYED (the) but reviving churchyard yew; Offwell, Devon. [By Rev. John Gay Copleston.] A poem, with notes. 8vo. Pp. 19. [Davidson's *Bibl. Devon.*, p. 131.]   N.P., 1832

DECEIT (the) and enmity of the priests manifested; likewise XX. queries propounded to George Long, high priest of Bathe, and priest Sangers of London. By T. M. [Thomas Morford]. 4to. [*Brit. Mus.*]
London, 1659

DECEIVER (the); a novel. By Leslie Keith [Grace Leslie Keith Johnston]. 8vo. Pp. 192.   London, 1907

DECEMBER tales. [By William Harrison Ainsworth.] 8vo. [*St Andrew's Univ. Cat.*, p. 536.]
London, 1823

DECENCY (the) and order of Church and State, as now established, asserted in a late visitation sermon [on 1 Corinth. chap. 14. vers. 40. By Charles Wooley, or Wolley, M.A.]. 4to. [*Bodl.*]
London, 1684

DECIMAL coinage; the necessity for its adoption. . . . [By Cornelius Walford?] 8vo.   London, 1855

DECIMAL coinage; what it ought, and what it ought not to be. By one of the million [John Edward Grey]. 8vo. [*Brit. Mus.*]   London, 1854

DECIMARUM et oblationum tabula: a tything table, or a table of tythes and oblations. . . . By W. C. [William Clark or William Crashaw?], B.C.L. 4to.   London, 1591

DECISION; a tale. By the author of *Correction*, etc. [Mrs Anne Raikes Harding]. 3 vols. 12mo. [*D. N. B.*, vol. 24, p. 335.]   London, 1819
   All Mrs Harding's publications are anonymous.

DECISION and indecision; or, the two cousins. By the wife of a Wesleyan minister [Mrs —— Parker]. Fcap 8vo. [*Brit. Mus.*]   London, 1833

DECISION (the); or religion must be all, or is nothing. [By Grace Kennedy.] Fcap 8vo.   Edinburgh, 1821

DECIUS [William Pinkney] to the Republican citizens of Maryland. 8vo. [Cushing's *Init. and Pseud.*, vol. ii., p. 43.]   Baltimore, 1812

DECK (the) of the " Crescent City ": a picture of American life. By W. G. D. [William Giles Dix]. 8vo. [Cushing's *Init. and Pseud.*, vol. i., p. 78.]
New York, 1853

DECLAMATIONS (the) of Quintilian; being an exercitation or praxis upon his twelve books, containing the Institution of an orator. [Translated by —— Warr.] 8vo. [Lowndes' *Bibl. Man.*, p. 2029.]   London, 1686

DECLARATION (a) against all professions and professors that have not the life of what they profess. . . . [By George Fox.] 4to. [Smith's *Cat. of Friends' Books*.]   London, 1654
   Signed " G. F."

DECLARATION (a) against wigs and periwigs. [By Richard Richardson.] 4to. [Smith's *Cat. of Friends' Books*, i., 42; ii., 487.]   N.P., N.D.
   Some copies have the author's name.

DECLARATION (the) and proclamation of the Army of God owned by the Lord of Hosts in many victories: whereunto is annexed seventeen necessary proposals for settling of good Judges in every city, taking off the Excise, and payment of the souldiers. [By Peter Chamberlen.] 4to. [L. F. Brown's *Baptists and Fifth Monarchy Men*, p. 220.]   London, 1659

DECLARATION (a) concerning fasting and prayer: of the true fast, also of the false fast. [By George Fox.] 8vo. [Smith's *Cat. of Friends' Books*.]
London, 1656
   Signed " G. F."

DECLARATION (a) concerning the people called Quakers, shewing what they and their ministers at first were. . . . A dialogue between a Quaker, a taylor,

and a Quaker a shooe maker. [By John Danks.] 4to. [Smith's *Cat. of Friends' Books*, i. 510.] N.P., 1674
Written under the fictitious name of "Christodulus Eccleston."

DECLARATION (a) conteyning the iust cavses and consyderations of this present warre with the Scottis; wherein alsoe appereth the trewe & right title that the kinges most royall maiesty hath to the souerayntie of Scotland. [By King Henry VIII.] 4to. No pagination. B.L. [Lowndes' *Bibl. Man.*]
London, 1542

DECLARATION (a) from the harmless & innocent people of God called Quakers; against all the plotters and fighters in the world; for the removing of the ground of jealousie and suspition from both magistrates and people in the kingdoms, concerning wars and fightings. . . . [By George Fox.] 4to. [Smith's *Cat. of Friends' Books*. i., 662.] London, 1660

DECLARATION (the) lately published by the Elector Palatine, in favour of his Protestant subjects; to which is prefix'd, an impartial account of the causes of those innovations and grievances about religion, which are now so happily redress'd by his Electoral Highness. [By John Toland.] 8vo. [*W.*] London, 1714
These tracts are entered at the end of the Life of John Toland in a list of his works: the titles are taken from the works themselves.

DECLARATION (a) made by King James in Scotland [A.D. 1585] concerning Church government and Presbyters. [Prepared by Patrick Adamson.] 4to. [*D. N. B.*, vol. 1, p. 113.]
[London], 1646

DECLARATION (a) of egregious Popish impostures, to withdraw the harts of his maiesties subiects from their allegeance, and from the truth of Christian religion professed in England, under the pretence of casting out of deuils; practised by Edmunds, alias Weston a Iesuit, & diuers Romish priestes his vvicked associates. . . . [By Samuel Harsnet, Archbishop of York.] Newly printed by Ia. Roberts, dwelling in Barbican. 4to. Pp. 292. [*Bodl.*] London, 1605
The Epistle " to the seduced catholiques of England " is signed " S. H."

DECLARATION (a) of faith of English people remaining at Amsterdam in Holland. [By Thomas Helwys.] 16mo. Pp. 44. [Whitley's *Bapt. Bibl.*, i., 6.] N.P., 1610

DECLARATION (the) of Independence: a poem accompanied by odes, songs, etc., adapted to the day. By a citizen of Boston [George Richards]. 8vo. [Cushing's *Init. and Pseud.*, vol. i., p. 58.] Boston, 1793

DECLARATION (a) of the brethren [Resolutioners] who are for the established Government and Judicatories of this Church [of Scotland]. . . . [By James Wood, Professor at St Andrews.] 4to. Pp. 12. [*New Coll. Cat.*] Edinburgh, 1658

DECLARATION (a) of the cavses mooving the qveene of England to giue aide to the defence of the people afflicted and oppressed in the Lowe Countries. [By William Cecil, Lord Burleigh.] 4to. [*Bodl.*]
London, 1585

DECLARATION (a) of the difference of the ministers of the word from the ministers of the world; who call the writings, the word. By G. F. [George Fox]. 4to. [Smith's *Cat. of Friends' Books*, i., 651.] London, 1656

DECLARATION (a) of the Faith and Order owned and practised in the Congregational Churches in England, agreed upon and consented unto by their Elders and Messengers in their meeting at the Savoy, Oct. 12, 1658. [By Philip Nye.] 4to. Pp. 27. [*Brit. Mus.*] London, 1659

DECLARATION (the) of the fathers of the councell of Trent, concerning the going unto churches at such time as hereticall service is said, or heresy preached. Edited, with a preface, by Eupater [Joseph Mendham]. Fcap 8vo. [Jones' Peck, i., 45.]
London, 1850

DECLARATION (a) of the fauourable dealing of her maiesties commissioners appointed for the examination of certaine traitours, and of tortures vniustly reported to be done vpon them for matters of religion. [By William Cecil, Lord Burleigh.] 4to. B.L. No pagination. [Mendham *Collection Cat.*, p. 50.] N.P., 1583.

DECLARATION (the) of the freeholders of Great Britain, in answer to that of the Pretender. [By John Anderson, minister of Dumbarton.] Dated Jan. 19, in the second year of our public happiness. Folio. S. sh. N.P., [1716]

DECLARATION (a) of the ground of error and errors, blasphemy, blasphemers, and blasphemies; and the ground of inchantings and seducing spirits, and the doctrine of devils, the sons of sorcerers, and the seed of the adulterer, and the ground of nicromancy, which doth defile witches and wizards. How this is all from the Spirit of God in the transgression of it. . . . By G. F. [George Fox]. 4to. [Smith's *Cat. of Friends' Books*, i., 654.] London, 1657

DECLARATION (the) of the Lord de la Noue, upon his taking armes for the iust defence of the Townes of Sedan and Iametz. . . . Truely translated, according to the French copie printed at Verdun, by A. M. [Anthony Munday]. 4to. London, 1589

DECLARATION (a) of the officers and armies, illegall, injurious, proceedings and practises against the XI. impeached Members; (not to be parallel'd in any age) and tending to the utter subversion of free Parliaments, rights, priviledges, freedome, and all common justice. . . . [By William Prynne.] 4to. [*Bodl.*] London, 1647

DECLARATION (a) of thee power of Godes worde, concerning the holy Supper of the Lord; confutynge all lyers and fals teachers, whych mayntayne theyr maskynge masse inuented agaynst the woorde of God, and the kynges maiesties most godly proceadynge, compiled Anno Dom. MDXLVIII. [By John Mardeley.] 8vo. [*W*; Lowndes' *Bibl. Man.*] London, 1548

DECLARATION (a) of the practises and treasons attempted and committed by Robert, late Earle of Essex and his complices against her maiestie and her kingdoms; together with the very confessions and other parts of the evidences themselves, taken out of the original. [By Francis, Lord Bacon.] 4to. [*Brit. Mus.*] London, 1601

DECLARATION (a) of the present sufferings of above 140. persons of the people of God (who are now in prison,) called Quakers: with a briefe accompt of above 1900. more, being but a part of many more that have suffered within these six years last past, whose names and particular sufferings are not here set down. Together with the number of 21. persons who were imprisoned and persecuted until death. All which was delivered to Tho. Bampfield, then

speaker of the parliament, on the sixth day of the second month, 1659. [By Edward Burrough.] 4to. [Smith's *Cat. of Friends' Books*, i.] London, 1659
A portion of the above is signed " E. B."

DECLARATION (a) of the sad and great persecution and martyrdom of the people of God, called Quakers, in New England, for the worshipping of God . . . also some considerations, presented to the King. [By Edward Burrough.] Fcap 4to. [Thomason, *Coll. of Tracts*, vol. ii., p. 364.] London, 1660
Attributed also to Edward Breck. Signed " E. B."

DECLARATION (a) of the state of the Colony and affaires in Virginia; with a relation of the barbarous massacre . . . treacherously executed by the native Infidels upon the English, the 22 of March last. [By Edward Waterhouse.] Fcap 4to. [Christie-Miller *Cat.*] London, 1622

DECLARATION (a) of the true causes of the great troubles presupposed to be intended against the realme of England; wherein the indifferent reader shall manifestly perceave by whome and by what meanes the realme is broughte into these pretended perills. Scene and allowed. 8vo. N.P., Anno 1592
" A libel against the queen and government, but more particularly against the Lord Burghley and his second son Sir Robert Cecil; probably written by [Robert] Parsons the Jesuit." [Lowndes' *Bibl. Man.*]
This work was answered by Lord Bacon in " Certain observations upon a libell published this present year, 1592."

DECLARATION (the) of the true Presbyterians within the Kingdom of Scotland, concerning Mr George Whitefield and the work at Cambuslang. [By William Wilson, schoolmaster.] 8vo. [*New Coll. Cat.*] Glasgow, 1742

DECLARATION (a) of truth to Benjamin Hoadly, one of the high priests of the land, and of the degree whom men call bishops. By a ministring friend, who writ to Tho. Bradbury, a dealer in many words. [By Daniel Defoe.] 8vo. [Wilson's *Life of Defoe*, 159.] London, 1717

DECLARATION (a) to all the world of our faith, and what we believe who are called Quakers. . . . [By Edward Burrough.] 4to. [*Brit. Mus.*] London, [1660]
Signed " E. B."

DECLARATION (a) to the free-born people of England concerning the government of the Commonwealth. [By John Lilburn.] 4to. [Thomason, *Coll. of Tracts*, ii., p. 66.]
London, 1654

DECLARATION (a) without doors. By the author, etc. [Daniel Defoe]. 4to. [Wilson's *Life of Defoe*, ii., 77.]
London, 1705

DECLARATIOUN (a) of the Kings Majesties [James VI.] intentioun and meaning toward the lait Actis of Parliament. [By Patrick Adamson.] 4to.
Edinburgh, 1585

DECLINE (the) and fall of the British Empire ; or the witch's cavern. . . . [By Henry C. M. Watson.] 8vo. Pp. 291. [*Brit. Mus.*]
London, 1890

DECLINE (the) of the pulpit and its causes. By a Scottish Churchman [Rev. David Kaye]. Pt 8vo. Pp. 208. [*New Coll. Cat.*]
London, 1893

DECOY (the) ; an opera as it is acted at the new theatre in Goodman's Fields. [By Henry Potter.] 8vo. [*Biog. Dram.*]
N.P., 1773

DEDICATED. By Michael Field [Katherine H. Bradley and Edith Emma Cooper]. 8vo. [*Brit. Mus.*]
London, 1915

DEDICATION (a) to a great man, concerning dedications ; discovering, amongst other wonderful secrets, what will be the present position of affairs a thousand years hence. [By Thomas Gordon, of Kirkcudbright.] Third edition. 8vo. [*Bodl.*]
London, 1718

DEEDS of dreadful note. [A drama.] By Alfred Dubois [James Stuart Bowes]. 8vo. [*Brit. Mus.*]
London [*c.* 1850]

DEEDS of the olden time ; a romance, in five volumes. By Ann of Swansea [Julia Ann Kemble], author of *Woman's a riddle*. 12mo. [*Bodl.*]
London, 1826

DEEDS that won the Empire ; historic battle scenes. By " Vedette " [Rev. William Henry Fitchett]. Fcap 8vo. [*Lib. of Col. Inst.*, Supp. I., p. 610.]
Melbourne, 1895

DEEP Glen ; a novel. By H. Morven [John Sutherland, of Dunbeath, Caithness]. 3 vols. 8vo. [Mowat's *Bibl. of Caithness*, p. 90.]
London, 1882

DEEPDALE vicarage. [A novel.] By the author of *Mark Warren* [Mrs —— Knox, *née* Isa Craig]. 8vo.
London, [1884]

DEEPE (a) groane, fetch'd at the funeral of that incomparable and glorious monarch, Charles the First, king of Great Britaine, France and Ireland, etc. ; on whose sacred person was acted that execrable, horrid & prodigious murther, by a trayterous crew and bloudy combination at Westminster, January the 30, 1648. Written by D. H. K. [Dr Henry King, Bishop of Chichester]. 4to. Pp. 8. [*Bodl.*]
N.P., printed in the yeare 1649

In the same year the above work appeared under the title, A groane at the fvnerall, etc. [the remainder of the title the same, with the exception of a slight difference in the spelling and punctuation]. Written by I. B. In all other respects the work is the same. The author's name is in the handwriting of Wood.

DEERSTALKER (the). By Frank Forester [Henry William Herbert]. 8vo. [Cushing's *Init. and Pseud.*, i., p. 104.]
London, 1850

DEESIDE tales : or, sketches of men and manners among the peasantry of Upper Deeside since 1745. [By John Grant Michie.] 8vo. [Robertson's *Aberd. Bibl.*]
Aberdeen, 1872

DEFECTION (the) consider'd, and the designs of those who divided the friends of the government, set in a true light. [By Matthew Tindal, D.C.L.] 8vo. Pp. 64. [*Bodl.*]
London, 1718

DEFECTION (the) of the Church of Scotland from her Reformation-principles considered : being a protest by some members of the General Assembly of that Church against her Act pass'd the 15th of May 1732, anent the method of planting vacant churches. With an introduction and appendix. [By Sir Thomas Gordon.] 8vo. Pp. 80. [*New Coll. Cat.*]
Edinburgh, 1733

DEFECTS in judicial machinery. Nos. 1 and 2. . . . By J. J. S. [John Joshua Sprigge]. 8vo.
London, [1890]

DEFECTS in the criminal administration and penal legislation of Great Britain. . . . [By William Tallack.] 8vo. [*Brit. Mus.*]
London, 1872

DEFECTS (the) of an University education, and its unsuitableness to a commercial people ; with the expediency and necessity of erecting at Glasgow an Academy for the instruction of youth. In a letter to J. M., Esq. [By Rev. William Thom of Govan.] 8vo. Pp. 53. [In *Coll. Works.*]

London, 1762

DEFENCE (a) and a plea; being some remarks on the criticism made by the Rev. Wm. Arthur, M.A., and in the Methodist Magazine, on the book [by the Rev. T. Hughes], "The condition of membership in the Christian Church." By T. H. [Thomas Hughes]. 8vo. Pp. viii., 110. [*Manch. Free Lib. Cat.*]

London, 1870

DEFENCE (a) and continuation of the Discourse concerning the Knowledge of Jesus Christ, and our union and communion with him: with a particular respect to the doctrine of the Church of England, and the charge of Socinianism and Pelagianism. By the same author [William Sherlock]. 8vo. [Arber's *Term Cat.*, i., 522.]

London, 1675

The discourse itself is not anonymous: it was criticised by Robert Ferguson, Samuel Rolle, and others.

DEFENCE (a) and continuation of the Ecclesiastical politie, by way of letter to a friend in London; together with a letter from the author [Dr Symon Patrick] of the Friendly debate. [By Samuel Parker, D.D.] 8vo. [Arber's *Term Cat.*, i., 522.] London, 1771

DEFENCE (a) by J. K. L. [James Warren Doyle, Roman Catholic Bishop of Kildare & Leighlin] of his Vindication of the religious and civil principles of the Irish Catholics. 8vo. [*D. N. B.*, vol. 15, p. 412.]

Dublin, 1824

DEFENCE (a) of a book intituled, The snake in the grass. In reply to several answers put out to it by George Whithead, Joseph Wyeth, etc. [By Charles Leslie.] 8vo. [Smith's *Anti-Quak.*, p. 269.] London, 1700

DEFENCE (a) of a Brief discourse of schism, designed for the satisfaction of peaceable & concientious Dissenters: being an answer to Aerius Prostratus, by Joshua Bowchier, M.A. [By George Trosse, of Exeter.] 4to. Pp. 59. [*Bodl.*] Exon, 1702

DEFENCE (a) of a congratulatory Letter to the Reverend Dr Trapp, etc. In reply to a late pamphlet, intituled, Quakero-Methodism, etc., by James Bate, M.A., Rector of St Paul, Deptford, etc.; wherein his calumnies, misrepresentations, and false reasonings are clearly demonstrated. By

T— S——y, Esq. [Richard Finch]. 8vo. 11 sh. London, 1740

This afterwards formed part of a volume, entitled, "Tracts,—By Richard Finch." [Smith's *Cat. of Friends' Books*, i. 609-10.]

DEFENCE (a) of a late pamphlet, entitled, "A treatise on the improvements made in the art of criticism:" being an answer to some Remarks made upon it. [By John Jackson.] 8vo. Pp. 80. [Sutton's *Memoirs of Jackson*, p. 185.] London, 1749

DEFENCE of a sermon, entitled, "The necessity of philosophy to the divine." [By John Clark (of Grenton).] 8vo. Pp. 47. [Smith's *Cat. of Friends' Books*, i., 95; Green's *Bibl. Somers.*, ii., 303.]

[Bridgwater], 1826

DEFENCE (a) of An Essay on the publick debts of this kingdom, etc.; in answer to a pamphlet [by W. Pulteney, Earl of Bath], entitled, A State of the national debt, etc. By the author of the Essay [Sir Nathanael Gould]. 8vo. [M'Culloch's *Lit. of Pol. Econ.*, p. 321.] London, 1727

DEFENCE (a) of Christian liberty; in a letter to the anonymous author of a late pamphlet, entitled, "A New Creed considered on the principles of the Belfast Society, alias the Presbytery of Antrim, lately published by the Rev. Dr James Kirkpatrick, briefly examined:" By a member of the General Synod [Dr James Kirkpatrick]. Pt 8vo. Pp. 102. [Witherow's *Presb. in Ireland*, i., 157.]

Belfast, 1744

Posthumously published.

DEFENCE (a) of Christianity. . . . By a blacksmith [John Witherspoon, D.D.]. 8vo. N.P., [1764]

Signed "A. T."

This attribution of authorship has been questioned.

DEFENCE (the) of conny-catching. By Cuthbert Conny-catcher [Robert Greene]. 4to. [*W.*; Lowndes' *Bibl. Man.*] London, 1597

DEFENCE (a) of [Edmund Law's] Considerations on the propriety of requiring subscription to Articles of Faith. [By William Paley, D.D.] 8vo. [*D. N. B.*, vol. 43, p. 106.]

Sunderland, 1774

DEFENCE (the) of contraries; paradoxes against common opinion debated in forme of declamations in place of public censure only to exercise yong wittes in difficult matters. Translated out of French by A. M. [Anthony Munday]. 4to. Pp. 99. [Lowndes' *Bibl. Man.*]

London, 1593

DEFENCE (a) of corporal punishment. By Moses [Moses Field Fowler]. 8vo. [Cushing's *Init. and Pseud.*, vol. i., p. 198.] Boston, 1873

DEFENCE (the) of death ; containing a discourse of life and death, written in French by Philip de Mornaye, and doone into English by E. A. [Edward Aggas]. 8vo. [*W.*; Lowndes' *Brit. Lib.*, p. 799.] London, 1576

DEFENCE (a) of Dr [Samuel] Clarke's Demonstration of the being and attributes of God ; wherein is particularly consider'd the nature of space, duration, and necessary existence ; being an answer to a late book entitul'd, A translation of Dr King's Origin of evil, and some other objections. . . . [By John Clarke, M.A., Corpus Christi Coll., Cambridge.] 8vo. Pp. iv., 165. [*Brit. Mus.*] London, 1732

DEFENCE (a) of Dr Jonathan Swift, Dean of St Patrick's, Dublin ; in answer to certain observations passed on his life and writings [by Francis Jeffrey] in the fifty-third number of the Edinburgh Review. [By Edward Berwick.] 8vo. Pp. 67. [*N. and Q.*, 19 Feb. 1859, p. 150.] London, 1819

DEFENCE (a) of Dr Kenrick's review of Dr [Samuel] Johnson's Shakespeare ; containing a number of curious and ludicrous anecdotes of literary biography. By a friend [William Kenrick, himself]. 8vo. [*D. N. B.*, vol. 31, p. 17; Wilson's *Shaksperiana*, 43.] London, 1766
Subscribed "R. R."

DEFENCE (a) of Dr Kidd's translations of Mr Fraser's Latin Epistles. [By George Melvin.] 8vo. [Robertson's *Aberd. Bibl.*] Aberdeen, 1831

DEFENCE (a) of Dr Samuel Clarke against Lewis Philip Thummig, in favour of Leibnitz. [By Gregory Sharpe, LL.D.] 8vo. [*D. N. B.*, vol. 51, p. 423.] London, 1744

DEFENCE (a) of Dr Sherlock's Preservative against Popery, in reply to a Jesuit's answer [Lewis Sabran]. . . . By W. G., a Protestant foot-man [William Giles]. 4to. [*Bodl.*] London, 1688

DEFENCE (a) of dramatick poetry ; being a review of Mr [Jeremy] Collier's View of the Immorality and Profaneness of the Stage. [By Edward Filmer.] 8vo. [Arber's *Term Cat.*, vol. iii., p. 596.] London, 1698
"A farther Defence" was published in the same year.
Ascribed also to Thomas Rymer, antiquarian.

DEFENCE (the) of Duffer's Drift ; a few experiences in field defence for detached posts which may prove useful in our next war. By "Backsight Forethought" [Col. Ernest Dunlop Swinton]. Reprinted from the *United Service Magazine*. 8vo. Pp. 39. [*Brit. Mus.*] London, 1904

DEFENCE of ecclesiastical establishments ; in reply to the Rev. Andrew Marshall's Letter to the Rev. Andrew Thomson, D.D., minister of St George's church, Edinburgh. By the reviewer [James Lewis, D.D.]. 8vo. Pp. 165. [*New Coll. Cat.*, p. 272.] Edinburgh, 1830

DEFENCE (a) of English Catholiques against a slanderous libel [by Lord Burleigh], intituled, The execution of justice in England. [By Cardinal William Allen.] 8vo. [*W.*; Lowndes' *Bibl. Man.*] [Ingolstadt, *c.* 1584]
The running title is "An Answere to the Libel of English Justice."

DEFENCE (a) of free-thinking in mathematics. In answer to a pamphlet of Philalethes Cantabrigiensis [James Jurin], intituled, Geometry no friend to infidelity, or a defence of Sir Isaac Newton and the British mathematicians. Also an appendix concerning Mr. Walton's Vindication of the principles of fluxions against the objections contained in the Analyst. . . . By the author of *The minute philosopher* [George Berkeley, D.D.]. 8vo. Pp. 71. [Williams' *Cat.*, ii., 7.] London, 1735
Not in Fraser's edition of Berkeley's works.

DEFENCE of God's sovereignty against the impious and horrible aspersions cast upon it by Elisha Coles. [By Walter Sellon.] 8vo. Pp. xi., 347. [Copinger's *Bibl. of the Five Points*, 165.] London, 1770
A later edition appeared in 1814.

DEFENCE (a) of his Royal Highness the Duke of Cumberland. By a Member of Parliament [Treysac de Vergy]. 8vo. [*Crit. Rev.*, xxx., 239.] London, 1770

DEFENCE (a) of ignorance. By the author of *How to make home unhealthy* [Henry Morley]. 8vo. [*Brit. Mus.*] London, 1851
Wrongly ascribed to Edward Fitzgerald.

DEFENCE (a) of infant baptism : embodying replies to many of the leading arguments of the late Dr Carson, Rev. Alex. Campbell, and the Hon. and Rev. B. W. Noel. By the author of *A catechism on the nature and*

design, subjects, and mode of Christian baptism [Archibald Gardner]. 8vo. Pp. 143. Paisley, 1851
Prefatory note signed " A. G." This treatise appeared originally in the *Scottish Presbyterian.*

DEFENCE (a) of infant baptism, in point of antiquity and authority. Two parts. [By —— Shephard, of Bath Chapel.] 12mo. [Whitley's *Bapt. Bibl.*, i., 197.] N.P., 1773

DEFENCE (a) of joint stock banks and country issues. By the author of *Money and its vicissitudes in value*, etc. [Samuel Bailey]. 8vo. [M'Culloch's *Lit. of Pol. Econ.*, p. 183.] London, 1840

DEFENCE (a) of lectures. [By T. Franklin.] 8vo. [*Brit. Mus.*] London, 1721

DEFENCE (the) of Lord Pigot. [By John Lind, barrister.] 4to. [London], 1777
Ascribed also to Alexander Dalrymple.

DEFENCE (a) of Louis XVI. Part I. [Translated from the French of Jacques A. M. De Cazales.] 8vo. [Corns and Sparke's *Unf. Books.*] London, 1793

DEFENCE (the) of Lucknow ; a diary recording the daily events during the siege of the Residency, 31st May to 25th Sept. 1857. By a Staff-Officer [Lieut.-General Thomas Fourness Wilson]. Fcap 8vo. [*Calc. Imp. Lib.*] London, 1858

DEFENCE (a) of ministerial Conformity to the Church of England ; in answer to the misrepresentations of the terms thereof by Mr Calamy in the tenth chapter of his " Abridgment of the History of Mr Baxter's Life and Times." [By John Ollyffe.] 8vo. [Arber's *Term Cat.*, iii. 319.] London, 1702

DEFENCE (a) of moderation in religious doctrine, practice, and opinion : applied to the circumstances of the present times. By a country vicar [F. Mereweather]. 8vo. [*Brit. Crit.*, xli., 198.] London, 1812

DEFENCE (a) of Mr Boswell's Journal of a tour to the Hebrides ; in a letter to R. James, the author of the Remarks signed Verax. 8vo. [*Bodl.*] London, 1785

DEFENCE (a) of Mr Hutchinson's plan : being an answer to the Modest apology, etc. ; in a letter to the country-clergyman. [By Rev. Julius Bate.] 8vo. Pp. 112. [*Bodl.*] London, 1748

DEFENCE (a) of Mr Locke's Essay of human understanding ; wherein its principles, with reference to morality, revealed religion, and the immortality of the soul are considered and justified : in answer to some remarks on that Essay. [By Mrs Catherine Cockburn.] 8vo. [*Works*, 1754]
First printed in the year 1702. Ascribed also to Thomas Burnet, LL.D.

DEFENCE of Mr Locke's opinion concerning personal identity ; in answer to the first part of a late Essay on that subject. [By Edmund Law, Bishop of Carlisle.] 8vo. [*Bodl.*] Cambridge, 1769

DEFENCE (a) of Mr Maccartney. By a friend [John Oldmixon]. 8vo. London, 1712
General George Maccartney, having acted as second to Lord Mohun in the duel in which the Duke of Hamilton was killed, was accused of foul play. The above tract was written with a view to exculpate him.

DEFENCE (a) of Mr M— H——'s [Matthew Henry's] Brief enquiry into the nature of Schism, and the Vindication of it ; with reflections upon a pamphlet called the Review. . . . [By Rev. William Tong.] 8vo. Pp. 160. London, 1693

DEFENCE (a) of Mr Rousseau, against the aspersions of Mr Hume, Mons. Voltaire, and their associates. [By Edward Burnaby Green.] 8vo. [Dyce *Cat.*, i., 351.] London, 1766

DEFENCE (a) of national churches ; and particularly of the national constitution of the Church of Scotland, and the conduct of our reforming ancestors, against the cavils of Independents : with a confutation of Independency, and several new opinions vented in some late pamphlets [by John Glass] intituled, A narrative of the rise and progress, etc. ; An explication of a proposition, etc. ; A letter from a lover of Zion, etc. By a minister of the Church of Scotland [John Willison]. 8vo. [*Adv. Lib.*] Edinburgh, 1719

DEFENCE (a) of our arguments against kneeling in the act of receiving the sacramentall elements of bread and wine impugned by Mr Michelsone. [By David Calderwood.] 8vo. Pp. 75. [*Adv. Lib.*] N.P., imprinted Anno 1620

DEFENCE (a) of our present happy establishment ; and the administration vindicated from the falshood and malice of several late treasonable libels, viz. " Cato's Letters," in the London Journal, and " The historical account of the advantages of the Hanover succession," etc. [By M. Tindal ?] 8vo. [*Brit. Mus.*] London, 1722

DEFENCE (a) of Palæoromaica against the strictures made on that work by the Bishop of St David's ; the Rev. J. J. Conybeare, A.M., prebendary of York, etc. ; the British Critic ; also by the Rev W. G. Broughton. M.A., and by Dr Falconer. [By Dr John Black of Edinburgh.] 8vo. [*W.*] London, 1824

DEFENCE (the) of Plevna, 1877 ; written by one who took part in it [William von Harlessem]. 8vo. Pp. xviii., 488. [*Brit. Mus.*] London, 1895

DEFENCE (a) of pluralities, or holding two benefices with cure of souls as now practised in the Church of England. [By Dr Henry Wharton and Dean Stanhope.] 8vo. [Arber's *Term Cat.*, iii., 376.] London, 1692
" This tract is usually ascribed to Henry Wharton alone, but it was written by him in conjunction with Dean Stanhope ; but the bookseller agreed not to discover the names of those who composed it. This anecdote occurs in a MS. memorandum of Wharton's among the Lambeth MSS. It was communicated to me by Mr Todd. P. B. 1819."—Note from Dr Bliss's copy. A second edition, with additions, was published in 1703.

DEFENCE (a) of praying before sermon, as directed by the 55th canon. [By William Fleetwood, Bishop of Ely.] 8vo. [*Brit. Mus.*] London, 1720

DEFENCE (a) of priestes marriages, stablyssed by the imperiall lawes of the realme of Englande, agaynst a ciuilian, namyng hymselfe Thomas Martin, doctour of the civile lawes, goyng about to disproue the saide marriages, lawfull by the eternall worde of God, and by the hygh court of parliament, only forbydden by forayne lawes and canons of the Pope, coloured with the visour of the church. Which lawes and canons, were extynguyshed by the sayde parliament, and so abrogated by the conuocation in their Sinode by their subscriptions. . . . [By Matthew Parker, Archbishop of Canterbury.] Imprinted at London by Richarde Jugge, printer to the Queenes Maiestie. N.D. 359 fol. Table, pp. 8. Contents, preface, and corrections, pp. 10. [*Bodl.*]
Reprinted by the Parker Society.

DEFENCE of religious establishments, in a dialogue between Micaiah Too-Good and Peter Utility ; with an extract from the theological lectures of the late Dr Hey. By Quid-pro-quo [Charles John Smyth, M.A.]. 8vo. [*Bodl.*] Norwich, N.D.

DEFENCE (a) of religious liberty, in a series of letters, with notes and illustrations ; from a lover of truth. By the author of *Letters on prejudice* [Arthur Henry Kenney]. 8vo. [*Camb. Univ. Lib.*] Dublin, 1825

DEFENCE (a) of [universal] Restoration ; or an answer to a letter which has appeared in the Liverpool Theological Repository for September 1807, under the signature of M. ——. By Philantropicos Philalethes [Rev. Niel Douglas]. 8vo. Pp. 196.
Glasgow, 1807

DEFENCE (a) of revelation in general, and the gospel in particular ; in answer to the objections advanced in a late book [by Francis Webb], entitled, The morality of the New Testament digested under various heads, etc., and subscribed, A rational Christian. [By William Bell, D.D., prebendary of Westminster.] 8vo. [Watt's *Bibl. Brit.*] London, 1765

DEFENCE (a) of Sir Robert Filmer, against the mistakes and misrepresentations of Algernon Sidney, Esq ; in a paper delivered by him to the Sheriffs upon the scaffold on Tower-Hill, on Fryday December the 7th 1683, before his execution there. [By Edmund Bohun.] Folio. [Watt's *Bibl. Brit.*] London, 1684

DEFENCE (a) of Some considerations concerning the Trinity, etc. in answer to the reflections made upon them, in a late pamphlet [by Anthony Collins], entituled, An essay concerning the use of reason, etc. in a letter to the author. [By Francis Gastrell.] 8vo. [*Aberd. Lib.*] London, 1707

DEFENCE (a) of subscription to the xxxix Articles, as it is required in the University of Oxford. [By Lewis Bagot.] [Watt's *Bibl. Brit.*] N.P., 1772

DEFENCE (a) of sundry positions and Scriptures. . . . Charged at first to be weak therein by R. H. [Richard Hollingworth, M.A.]. 4to. [Thomason's *Coll. of Tracts*, i., 405.] London, 1645

DEFENCE (a) of the absolution given to Sir William Perkins at the place of execution, April 3rd. [By Jeremy Collier.] 4to. [*D. N. B.*, vol. 11, p. 345.] London, 1696

DEFENCE (a) of the Account [of the reasons why many citizens of Exon have withdrawn from the ministry of Mr J. Hallet and Mr J. Peirce] : in answer to Mr Peirce's Defence of the case [of the ministers ejected at Exon]. [By Josiah Eveleigh.] 8vo. [*Brit. Mus.*] London, 1719
This is one of many pamphlets issued during the Trinitarian Controversy among the English Presbyterians. *See* Drysdale's *Hist. of the Presbyterians in England*, p. 500.

DEFENCE (a) of the Answer [by Rev. Joseph Boyse] to a paper entitled " The case of the [Presbyterian] Dissenting Protestants of Ireland in reference to a Bill of Indulgence." [By Tobias Pullen, D.D.] Pp. 28. [Witherow's *Presb. in Ireland.*]   [Dublin, 1697]

DEFENCE (a) of the Answer to the Remarks [by Daniel Waterland] upon Dr. Clarke's exposition of the church-catechism ; wherein the difference between moral and positive duties is fully stated : being a reply to a pamphlet [by Waterland] entitled, The nature, obligation and efficacy of the sacraments consider'd.   [By Arthur Ashley Sykes, D.D.] 8vo. Pp. 102. [Disney's *Memoir of Sykes*, p. xviii.]
London, 1730

DEFENCE (a) of the antient historians : with a particular application of it to the history of Ireland. [By Francis Hutchinson, D.D.] 8vo. Pp. xv., 270.   Dublin, 1734
    In the Advocates' Library, there is another copy of the above work, with the following addition to the title, " and Great-Britain, and other northern nations : in a dialogue between a Protestant and a Papist, an Englishman and an Irishman. By Francis, Lord Bishop of Down and Connor. To which are added, two sermons ; the first preached on occasion of the Union, and the other at a publick commencement at Cambridge." In all other respects, the works are exactly alike, except that, in the one having the author's name, the motto is considerably shorter.

DEFENCE (a) of the Appendix to The Antidote, or treatise of thirty controversies against [Protestant] Sectaries. [By Anthony Champney, D.D.] . . . [Gillows' *Bibl. Dict.*, ii., 465.]
N.P., [1622]
    Sylvester Norris, S.J., wrote his Antidote partly in reply to Richard Field (in his work " Of the Church ") ; this reply, published in 1618, was followed in 1619 by a Second Part, and in 1621 by the Appendix ; Protestant attacks on this drew forth from Champney the above work, which has sometimes been erroneously attributed to John Sweet, S.J.

DEFENCE (a) of the Arch-bishop's sermon on the death of her late Majesty of blessed memory : and of the sermons of the late Arch-bishop, Bp. of Lichfield and Coventry, Bp. of Ely, Bp. of Salisbury ; Dr Sherlock, Dr Wake, Mr Fleetwood, etc., preach'd upon that, and several other solemn occasions. Being a vindication of the late Queen, his present Majesty, and the Government, from the malicious aspersions cast upon them in two late pamphlets ; one [by T. Tenison] entituled, Remarks

on some late sermons, etc., the other [by T. Ken], A letter to the author of a sermon preach'd at the funeral of her late majesty Queen Mary. [By John Williams, D.D.] [*Bodl.*]
London, 1695

DEFENCE (a) of the Bishop of Ely's visitatorial jurisdiction over Trinity College [Cambridge] in general, and over the Master thereof in particular. [By John Colbatch, D.D.] 4to. [Bartholomew's *Cat. of Camb. Books.*]
N.P., 1732

DEFENCE (a) of the book, entituled " Cerinthus and Ebion," against the exceptions of a haughty, ignorant dialogue, between Eubulus and Sophronius ; in the pamphlet call'd by the proud name of " Censura Temporum." [By Benjamin Lindley.] 4to. Pp. 24. [Smith's *Anti-Quakeriana*, p. 271.]
London, 1709

DEFENCE of the British and Foreign Bible Society, by Amicus [David Brown, bookseller]. [*Edin. Select Subscription Lib. Cat.*, p. 349.]
Edinburgh, 1826

DEFENCE of the British and Foreign School Society against the remarks in the sixty-seventh number of the " Edinburgh Review." [By Richard Allen, of Dublin.] 8vo. Pp. 48. [Supp. to Smith's *Cat. of Friends' Books*, p. 7.]   London, 1821

DEFENCE (a) of the Catholic Church against the assaults of certain busy sectaries ; being a dialogue between an itinerant preacher and Sylvester Lynch. [By Dennis Taaffe.] 8vo. [*Brit. Mus.*]   Dublin, 1803

DEFENCE (a) of the Catholyke cavse. Written by T. F. [Thomas Fitzherbert] ; with an apology or defence of his innocency in a fayned conspiracy against her Majesties person, for the which one Edward Squyre was wrongfully condemned and executed in November 1598, etc.   4to.   [*Brit. Mus.*]   [St Omer], 1602

DEFENCE (a) of the censvre gyven vpon tvvo bookes of William Charke and Meredith Hanmer mynysters, whiche they wrote against M. Edmond Campian, preest, of the Societie of Iesus, and against his Offer of disputation. Taken in hand since the deathe of the said M. Campian, and broken of agayne before it could be ended, vpon the causes sett downe in an epistle to M. Charke in the begyninge. [By Robert Parsons.] 8vo. Pp 218. [Oliver's *Collections.*]
[Rouen], 1582

DEFENCE (a) of the character of Thomas Jefferson against [Dr F. L. Hawks] a writer in the New York Review. By a Virginian [George Tucker]. 8vo. [Cushing's *Init. and Pseud.*, i., p. 296.]   New York, 1838

DEFENCE (a) of the Christian Doctrines of the Society of Friends. . . . [By Thomas Evans.]   8vo.   Pp. 180. [Supp. to Smith's *Cat. of Friends' Books*, p. 117.]   Philadelphia, 1825

DEFENCE (a) of the Christian Sabbath, Part I. ; in answer to a treatise on Mr Thomas Bampfield, pleading for Saturday Sabbath. [By John Wallis, D.D.] Second edition. 4to. [Watt's *Bibl. Brit.*]   London, 1695

DEFENCE (a) of the Church Missionary Society against the objections of the Rev. Josiah Thomas, M.A., Arch-Deacon of Bath. [By Daniel Wilson, D.D., Bishop of Calcutta.]   8vo. [Green's *Bibl. Somers.*, i., 516.]   London, 1818

DEFENCE (a) of the Church of England from priestcraft, in vindication of the contested clause of the xxth Article ; extracted out of the Vindication of the Church of England from the aspersions of a late libel, entituled, Priestcraft in perfection, &c. By the author of the Vindication [Hilkiah Bedford]. 8vo. [*Brit. Mus.*]   London, 1711

DEFENCE (a) of the Church of England, from the charge of schism and heresie, as laid against it by [Henry Dodwell] the vindicator of the deprived bishops. [By Rev. Edward Welchman, M.A.] 4to. [Wood's *Athen. Oxon.*, iv., 481.] London, 1691

DEFENCE (a) of the clergy of the Church of Scotland who have appeared in opposition to an unlimited repeal of the penal laws against Roman Catholics. [By John Warden (afterwards Mac-Farlan), D.D.) 8vo. [Scott's *Fasti*.]   Edinburgh, 1779

DEFENCE (a) of the College of G——w [Glasgow], against an insidious attempt to depreciate the ability and taste of its professors. [By William Thom, minister of Govan.] 8vo. Pp. 16.   N.P., 1761
Reprinted among "The works of the Rev. William Thom . . ." Glasgow, 1799, 12mo.

DEFENCE (a) of the Communion-office of the Church of England ; proving there is neither reason nor authority for laying it aside ; in a letter to a friend. [By George Smith.] 8vo. [*Brit. Mus.*]   Edinburgh, 1744
Signed "G. S."

DEFENCE (a) of the conduct of Barba-does during the late Expedition to Martinique and Guadaloupe ; in a letter to General Barrington. By a native of the Island [Sir J— G— Alleyne]. 8vo.   London, 1760

DEFENCE (a) of the conduct of Mari-schal College. . . . [By George Camp-bell, D.D., Principal.] 8vo.
[Aberdeen, 1780]

DEFENCE (a) of the conduct of the Warden of Winchester College in accepting that Wardenship. [By Dr Christopher Golding himself.] 8vo. [*Brit. Mus.*]   London, 1759

DEFENCE (a) of [Symon Patrick] the confuter of Bellarmin's second Note of the Church antiquity, against the cavils of the adviser. [By George Tully, A.M.] 8vo. [*Brit. Mus.*] London, 1687

DEFENCE (a) of the Considerations [by Bishop Edmund Law] on the pro-priety of requiring a subscription to articles of faith : in reply to a late answer [by Thos. Randolph] from the Clarendon Press. By a friend of re-ligious liberty [William Paley, D.D.]. 8vo. Pp. 51. [*Brit. Mus.*]
London, 1724

DEFENCE (a) of the currency of Massachusetts. By a practical banker [James B— Congdon]. 8vo. [Cush-ing's *Init. and Pseud.*, i., 238.]
Boston, 1856

DEFENCE of the Dean of St Paul's apology for writing against the Socin-ians. [By William Sherlock, D.D.] 4to. [Bliss' *Cat.*, 290.] London, 1694

DEFENCE (a) of the Dissenters' educa-tion in their private academies ; in answer to Mr W——y's [Samuel Wesley's] disingenuous and unchristian reflections upon 'em. In a letter to a noble Lord. [By Samuel Palmer.] 4to. [*D. N. B.*, vol. 60, p. 315.]
London, 1703
See " A Letter from a country divine . . ." [S. Wesley].

DEFENCE (a) of the Dissertation on the validity of the English ordinations, against the several answers made to it ; with proper vouchers for the facts advanced in that work. By [Pierre François Le Courayer] the author of the *Dissertation*. 8vo. 2 vols. [*Brit. Mus.*]   London, 1728

DEFENCE (a) of the doctrin & holy rites of the Roman Catholic Church, from the calumnies and cavils of Dr Burnet's Mystery of iniquity unveiled. By J. W. [John Warner, S.J.]. Second edition. 8vo. Pp. 325. [Oliver's *Collections*.]   London, 1688
The first edition appeared in 1679 : see " Anti-Haman . . ."

DEFENCE (a) of the doctrine and practice of the Church of England against some modern innovations, with respect to I. The supremacy of the crown. II. The sacrament of the Lord's Supper as a sacrifice. III. Baptism administer'd by lay-men invalid. IV. The necessity and authority of sacerdotal absolution. In a letter to a friend. [By Thomas Turner, D.D.] 8vo. Pp. 64. [*Bodl.*]
London, 1712

DEFENCE (a) of the doctrine of the Trinity, and eternal Sonship of our Lord Jesus Christ. . . . [By Robert Walker, M.D.] 8vo.
Edinburgh, 1782

DEFENCE (a) of the doctrines of the Holy Trinity and Incarnation placed in their due light: in answer to a letter written to the clergy of both universities. [By Arthur Bury, D.D.] 4to. [*Bodl.*] [London, 1694]
See " The doctrine of the Holy Trinity placed in its true light . . ."

DEFENCE (a) of the doings of the Reverend Consociation and Association of New-Haven County respecting Mr Philemon Robbins of Branford. . . . By a member of the Consociation and Association [Rev. Jonathan Todd]. 8vo. Pp. 118. [Cushing's *Init. and Pseud.*, ii., 98.] [New London, 1748]

DEFENCE (a) of the Doubts concerning the authenticity of the last publication of The Confessional [by Rev. Francis Blackburne], etc.; in answer to Occasional remarks, etc. [By Thomas Townson, D.D.] 8vo. [*Gent. Mag.*, June 1792, p. 573.]
London, 1768

DEFENCE (a) of [George Villiers] the Duke of Buckingham, against the Answer to his book and the Reply to his Letter. By the author of the late *Considerations* [William Penn]. 4to. London, 1685

DEFENCE (a) of the Duke of Buckingham's book of religion & worship, from the exceptions of a nameless author. By the Pensilvanian [William Penn]. 4to. [Jones' Peck, p. 67.]
London, 1685

DEFENCE (a) of the ecclesiastical discipline ordayned of God to be vsed in his church. Against a replie of Maister Bridges, to a brief and plain declaration of it, which was printed An. 1584, which replie he termeth, A defence of the gouernement established in the Church of Englande, for ecclesiasticall matters. [By Walter Travers.] 4to. Pp. 228. [*Adv. Lib.*]
N.P., 1588

DEFENCE (a) of the " Eclipse of faith," by [Henry Rogers] its author; being a rejoinder to Professor Newman's " Reply." 8vo. [*D. N. B.*, vol. 49, p. 122.] London, 1854

DEFENCE (a) of the " Enquiry about the lawfulness of eating blood." By a prebendary of York [Thomas Sharp, D.D.]. 8vo. [*D. N. B.*, vol. 51, p. 416.] London, 1734

DEFENCE (a) of the Enquiry into the reasons of the conduct of Great-Britain &c.; occasioned by the paper published in the Country-Journal or Craftsman on Saturday, Jan. 4, 1728-9. By the author of the *Enquiry* [Benjamin Hoadly]. 8vo. [*Adv. Lib.*]
London, 1729

DEFENCE (a) of the [Irish] Established Church and laws; in answer to a Vindication of Presbyterian marriages in Ireland. [By Edward Synge, D.D., Archbishop; in answer to Rev. John Macbride.] Fcap 8vo. Pp. 336. [Witherow's *Presb. in Ireland*, vol. i., p. 117.] Dublin, 1705

DEFENCE (a) of the Exposition of the doctrine of the Church of England, against the exceptions of Monsieur de Meaux, late Bishop of Condom, and his vindicator. [By William Wake, D.D.] 4to. Pp. xxiv., 166. [*Brit. Mus.*]
London, 1686

DEFENCE (a) of the first head of the charge of the Committee of the Lower House of Convocation against the Right Reverend the Bishop of Bangor; being remarks upon some positions of his Lordship, contained in his Sermon, in his answer to Dr Snape, and to the Representation: wherein is shewn, that his Lordship hath denied, and doth still deny, all authority to the Church. [By Henry Stebbing, D.D.] 8vo. Pp. 100. [*Bodl.*]
London, 1718

DEFENCE (a) of the godlie ministers, against the slaunders of D. Bridges, contayned in his Ansvvere to the Preface before the Discourse of ecclesiasticall gouernement, with a declaration of the bishops proceeding against them; wherein chieflie, 1. The lawfull authoritie of her Maiestie is defended by the Scriptures, her lawes, and authorised interpretation of them, to be the same which we have affirmed, against his cauilles and slaunders to the contrarie. 2. The lawfull refusinge also of the ministers to subscribe, is maintayned by euident groundes of Gods worde, and her Maiesties lawes, against his euident wresting of both. 3. Lastlie, the forme of church-gouernement, which we propounde, is according to his demande sillogisticallie proued to be ordinarie, perpetuall, and the best. [By Dudley Fenner.] 4to. Pp. 150. [Christie-Miller *Cat.*]   N.P., 1587

DEFENCE (a) of the honorable sentence and execution of the Queene of Scots, exempled with analogies, and diuerse presidents of emperors, kings, and popes ; with the opinions of learned men in the point, and diuerse reasons gathered foorth out of both lawes ciuill and canon. . . . [By Maurice Kyffin.] 4to. [Lowndes' *Bibl. Man.*, p. 1501.] London, [1587]

DEFENCE (a) of the Humble remonstrance against the frivolous and false exceptions of Smectymnvvs. Wherein the right of leiturgie and episcopacie is clearly vindicated from the vaine cavils, and challenges of the Answerers. By the author of the said *Humble remonstrance* [Joseph Hall, D.D.]. Seconded in way of appendance with the judgement of the famous divine of the Palatinate, D. Abrahamus Scultetus, late professor of divinitie in the universitie of Heidelberg, concerning the divine right of episcopacie, and the no-right of lay-eldership : faithfully translated out of his Latine. 4to. [*New Coll. Cat.*] London, 1641
On "Smectymnuus," *see* "An Humble remonstrance."

DEFENCE (a) of the late Dr Samuel Clarke, against the Reply of Sieur Lewis-Philip Thummig, in favour of Mr Leibnitz ; with that Reply in French and English : to which is added an original letter from Mr Leibnitz. [By Rev. Gregory Sharpe, LL.D., Master of the Temple.] 8vo. [*D.N.B.*, vol. 51, p. 423.]   London, 1744

DEFENCE (a) of the lawfulnesse of baptizing infants ; as also of the present Baptisme . . . in answer to something written by John Spilsberie. By P. B. [Praisegod Barbon]. 4to. Pp. vi., 64. [Whitley's *Bapt. Bibl.*, i., 19.]   London, 1645

DEFENCE (a) of the Layman's letter [signed Y. Z., *i.e.*, H— Webster], in answer to [Rev. George Logan on] The Lawfulness and necessity [of ministers reading the Act of Parliament regarding Captain John Porteous]. . . . Pt 8vo. Pp. 60. [*New Coll. Cat.*]   Edinburgh, 1737

DEFENCE of the Letter from a gentleman at Halifax, to his friend in Rhode-Island. [By Martin Howard, Esq., afterwards Chief Justice of North Carolina.] 8vo. [*Bodl.*]
Newport, 1765

DEFENCE (a) of the Letter to Dr Waterland ; against the false and frivolous cavils of [Zachary Pearce] the author of the *Reply*. [By Conyers Middleton, D.D.] 8vo. Pp. 94. [*D. N. B.*, vol. 37, p. 347.]
London, 1732

DEFENCE (a) of the Lord Bishop of Sarum [Gilbert Burnet] in answer to a book [by William Binches] entituled A Prefatory Discourse to an Examination of the Bishop of Sarum's Exposition of the XXXIX. Articles. . . . [By John Hoadly, Archbishop of Armagh.] 4to. [*Brit. Mus.*]
London, 1703

DEFENCE (a) of the Majority in the House of Commons, on the question relating to general warrants ; in answer to the Defence of the Minority. [By Charles Lloyd.] 8vo. [Almon's *Biog. Anec.*, i., 79 ; ii., 109.]
London, 1764
See below, " A Defence of the Minority . . ."

DEFENCE (a) of the ministers of the Church of Scotland against the charge of political partisanship, and their duty in the present crisis. . . . By a minister of the Established Church [Patrick Macfarlan, D.D., Greenock]. 8vo. Pp. 24. [*New Coll. Cat.*]
Edinburgh, 1837

DEFENCE (a) of the ministers reasons for refvsall of svbscription to the Booke of Common Prayer and of Conformitie ; against the severall ansvvers, of T. Hutton, Bacheler of divinity, in his two bookes against the minist. of Dev. and Cornwell ; William Covel, D. in divinitie, in his booke against M. I. Burges ; Tho : Shark., D. in divinitie, in his Brotherly perswasion to Vnitie and Vniformitie : so farr as any thing is sayd by them concerning the Holy Scriptures, and apocrypha : Devided into two partes. . . . [By Samuel Hieron.] 4to. Pp. 234. [Brook's *Puritans*, ii., 271.]   Imprinted 1607
See further " A Dispute upon the question . . ."

DEFENCE (a) of the Minority in the House of Commons, on the question relating to general warrants. [By Charles Townshend.] Fifth edition. 8vo. [Almon's *Biog. Anec.*, i., 78.]
London, 1764
This was the first of several pamphlets on the same subject. *See above*, " A Defence of the Majority . . .; *see also* " A History of the Minority . . ." [by John Almon].

DEFENCE (a) of the Missionaries arts ; wherein the charge of disloyalty, rebellions, plots, and treasons, asserted page 76 of that book, are fully proved

against the members of the Church of Rome. . . . By the author of the *Missionaries arts* [—— Wake, minister of Grays Inn]. 4to. Pp. 106.
London, 1689
Wrongly ascribed to Dr George Hickes.

DEFENCE of the Mofussil Courts in India. By a Madras Civilian [John Holloway]. 8vo.   London, 1852

DEFENCE (a) of the Moral philosopher; against a pamphlet [by Joseph Hallet], entitled, The immorality of the Moral philosopher. By the author. [Thomas Morgan]. 8vo. [*Brit. Mus.*]
London, 1737

DEFENCE (a) of the national administration. . . . By Cato [Ezekiel Webster]. [Cushing's *Init. and Pseud.*, i., 52.]   Concord, New Hampshire, 1828

DEFENCE (a) of the New Sophonisba, a tragedy: in answer to a criticism on that play. By a friend of the author's. [James Thomson]. 8vo. [*Dyce Cat.*, ii., 364.]   London, 1730

DEFENCE of the Observations [by W. S. Powell] on the first chapter of a book [by Edward Waring] called "Miscellanea analytica." [By William Samuel Powell, D.D.] 8vo. [Bartholomew's *Cat. of Camb. Books.*]
London, 1760

DEFENCE of the old crown [of King's College in Aberdeen]. [By Sir William D. Geddes.] 8vo.   [Aberdeen], 1893

DEFENCE (a) of the ordinations and ministry of the Church of England: in answer to the scandals raised or revived against them, in several late pamphlets, and particularly in one intituled, The Church of England truly represented, &c. [By Edmund Whitfield, B.D., Fellow of King's College, Cambridge.] 4to. Pp. 71. [*Bodl.*]   London, 1688
Ascribed also to William Whitfield.

DEFENCE (a) of the original principles of the Society of Friends, in a series of letters. No. 1, by the author of *The truth vindicated* [Henry Martin]. 8vo. [Smith's *Cat. of Friends' Books*, i., 222.]   London, 1836

DEFENCE (a) of the papers written by the late King of blessed memory, and Duchess of York, against the answer made [by Bp. Stillingfleet] to them. [By John Dryden.] 4to. Pp. 135. [*New Coll. Cat.*]   London, 1686

DEFENCE (a) of the people, in reply to Lord Erskine's "Two Defences of the Whigs." [By John Cam Hobhouse, Baron Broughton.] 8vo. Pp. 204. [*D. N. B.*, vol. 27, p. 49.]
London, 1819
The second edition, published the same year, gives the author's name.

DEFENCE (a) of the people of England; by John Milton, in answer to Salmasius's Defence of the King. [Translated from the Latin by Joseph Washington, of the Temple.] 8vo. Pp. xxii., 246. [*Brit. Mus.*]
[London], 1692

DEFENCE (a) of the people's right, from Acts 14: 23, against the cavils of [the Rev. George Logan] the Continuator of the Enquiry: in a letter. . . . [By Rev. James Hill, of Kilpatrick.] 12mo. [*New Coll. Cat.*]
Edinburgh, 1733
Signed "J. H."

DEFENCE (a) of the Plain account of the nature and end of the Sacrament of the Lord's Supper, against the objections contained in the Remarks on that book; with some observations on the preface to the second edition of those Remarks: being two letters originally published in the Independent London Journal. [By Strickland Gough, A.M.] 8vo. Pp. ix., 58. [*Bodl.*]
London, 1735
Ascribed also to Benjamin Hoadly, D.D., the author of the "Plain account." (*See below.*)

DEFENCE (a) of the Plain account [by Bishop Hoadly] of the Sacrament of the Lord's Supper. [By Sayer Rudd.] 8vo. [Whitley's *Bapt. Bibl.* i., 168.]
London, 1748

DEFENCE (a) of the proceedings against Jane Winham for witchcraft. [By Francis Bragge.] 8vo.
London, 1712
See "A Full and impartial account . . ."

DEFENCE (a) of the proceedings of the House of Commons in the Middlesex election [of John Wilkes], in which are considered two late pamphlets. . . . By the author of the *Answer to the Question stated* [Nathaniel Forster, jun.]. 4to. Pp. 61. [*D. N. B.*, vol. 20, p. 20.]   London, 1770
Ascribed also to Sir William Meredith.

DEFENCE (a) of the proceedings of the Right Reverend the Visitor [Sir John Trelawney, Bishop of Exeter] and Fellows of Exeter College, Oxford: with an answer to "The Case of Exeter College related and vindicated." 2. The Account examined. [By James Harrington.] 4to. [Arber's *Term Cat.*, ii., p. 613.] London, 1691
The above followed "An account of the proceedings . . ." by the same author. The strife resulted from the publication by Dr Arthur Bury of "The Naked Gospel." See the note to the latter.

DEFENCE (a) of the profession which the Right Reverend Father in God, John [Lake], late Lord Bishop of

Chichester, made upon his death-bed ; concerning passive obedience, and the new oaths. . . . [By Robert Jenkin, D.D.] 4to. [*Adv. Lib.*]
London, 1690
Ascribed wrongly to John Milner, S.T.B.

DEFENCE (a) of the proposition : or, some reasons rendred why the Nonconformist minister who comes to his parish-church and common prayer, cannot yet yeeld to other things that are enjoyned, without some moderation. Being a full reply to the book [by Thomas Tomkins] which is a pretended answer thereunto. By the same author [John Humphrey]. 4to. Pp. 120. [Green's *Bibl. Somers.*, vol. ii., p. 500.]   London, 1668

DEFENCE (a) of the Protestant Bible. By Akroatees [Josiah S. Polk]. 8vo. [*Camb. Univ. Lib.*]   New York, 1844

DEFENCE (a) of the Protestant Christian religion against Popery, in answer to a discourse of a Roman Catholick : wherein the manifold apostasies, heresies, and schisms of the Church of Rome, as also, the weakness of her pretensions from the Scriptures and the Fathers, are briefly laid open. By an English Protestant [Samuel Mather, of Dublin]. 4to. Pp. 56. [Dix and Dugan's *Dubl. Books.*] Dublin, 1672
Advertisement signed "S. M."

DEFENCE (a) of the Reasons for restoring some prayers and directions of King Edward the Sixth's first liturgy ; being a reply to a book [by Nathaniel Spinckes], entituled, No reason for restoring them. [By Jeremy Collier.] 8vo. Pp. 122. [*Brit. Mus.*]
London, 1718

DEFENCE (a) of the Reasons of the Counter-poyson for maintenance of the Eldership ; against an aunswere made to them by Doctor Copequot, in a publike sermon at Pawles Crosse, vpon Psal. 84. 1584 ; wherein also, according to his demaunde, is proued syllogistically for the learned, and plainlie for all men, the perpetuitie of the Elders office in the Church. [By Dudley Fenner.]   8vo.   No   pagination. [*Bodl. ; W. ; Brit. Mus.*]   N.P., 1586
Ascribed also to H. Jacob.

DEFENCE (a) of the Rector and Fellows of Exeter College, from the accusations brought against them by the Reverend Dr Huddesford, Vice-Chancellor of Oxford ; in his speech to the Convocation, October 8, 1754, on account of the conduct of the said College, at the time of the late election for the county. [By Francis Webber, D.D.] 8vo. Pp. 67. [Bartholomew's *Cat. of Camb. Books.*]   London, 1754

DEFENCE (a) of the Resolution of this case, viz., Whether the Church of England's symbolizing so far as it doth with the Church of Rome, makes it unlawfull to hold communion with the Church of England : in answer to a book intituled A modest confutation of that resolution. [By Edward Fowler, D.D., Bishop of Gloucester.] 4to. [*Brit. Mus.*]   London, 1684

DEFENCE (a) of the Rev. Dr [James] Foster's Sermon of Catholic Communion ; in a letter to a friend, in which is attempted to be proved that the truly catholic is the only consistent Christian. By Philocatholicus [Rev. John Wicke, Baptist]. 8vo. Pp. 40. [*D. B. N.*, vol. 61, p. 176.]
London, 1752

DEFENCE (a) of the Rev. Mr Whitefield's doctrine of regeneration, in answer to the Rev. Mr Land ; designed to correct his mistakes, to wipe off his aspersions, and prevent his doing mischief among the common people : in a letter to Mr Land. . . . [By Richard Finch.] 8vo. 2 sh.
London, 1739
This pamphlet afterwards formed part of a volume, entitled, "Tracts, ——. By Richard Finch." [Smith's *Cat. of Friends' Books*, i. 609-10.]

DEFENCE (a) of the Right Honourable the Earl of Shelburne from the reproaches of his numerous enemies ; in a letter addressed to Sir George Saville, Bart., and intended for the direction of all other Members of Parliament, whose object is rather to restore the glory of the British Empire, than administer to the views of a faction. . . . [By Denis O'Bryen.] Seventh edition. 8vo. Pp. 96. [*Biog. Dram.*]   London, 1783

DEFENCE (a) of the right of Kings ; wherein the power of the Papacie ouer Princes is refuted, and the Oath of Allegeance iustified. (An examination of a position published by P. R. [Robert Parsons] in the preface of his Treatise . . . concerning the lawfullnesse of the Popes power ouer Princes.) [By Edward Forsett.] 4to. [*D. N. B.*, vol. 20, p. 11.]   London, 1624

DEFENCE (a) of the Right Reverend the Lord Bishop of Sarum, in answer to a book [by Wm. Binckes] entitled, A Prefatory discourse to an examination of the Bishop of Sarum's Exposition, etc. [By Benjamin Hoadly, D.D.] 4to.   London, 1703

DEFENCE of the Rights and priviledges of the University of Oxford ; containing, 1. An answer to the petition of the city of Oxford. 1649. [By Gerard

Langbaine.] 2. The case of the University of Oxford; presented to the Honourable House of Commons, Jan. 24. 16$\frac{88}{90}$. [By James Harrington.] 4to. Pp. 63. [*Bodl.*] Oxford, 1690

The author's name is in the handwriting of Wood.

The second has the following separate title:—The case of the University of Oxford; shewing, that the city is not concern'd to oppose the confirmation of their charters by Parliament. Presented to the Honourable House of Commons on Friday Jan. 24, 16$\frac{88}{90}$.

The pagination is continuous.

DEFENCE (a) of the Rights of the Christian Church; against a late visitation sermon, intitled, The rights of the clergy in the Christian Church asserted; preach'd at Newport Pagnell in the county of Bucks, by W. Wotton, B.D., and made publick at the command and desire of the Bishop of Lincoln, and the clergy of the deaneries of Buckingham and Newport. [By Matthew Tindal.] 8vo. Pp. 55. [*D. N. B.*, vol. 56, p. 405.] London, 1707

DEFENCE (a) of the Scots abdicating Darien; including an answer to the Defence of the Scots settlement there. Authore Britanno Ged Dunensi [James Hodges]. 8vo. Pp. 168.
N.P., 1700

One Walter Herries (or Harris), surgeon to the first Expedition, was supposed by the Scots Parliament to have been the author of this Defence, which was ordered to be burnt by the hands of the hangman; and the Lords of the Treasury were required to offer a reward of £6000 Scots for the arrest of the reputed author.

DEFENCE (a) of the Scots Settlement at Darien; with an answer to the Spanish memorial against it, and arguments to prove that it is the interest of England to join with the Scots and protect it: with a description of the country, and a particular account of the Scots Colony. [By Andrew Fletcher, of Saltoun.] 4to.
Edinburgh, 1699

The author's name is given in contemporary handwriting.

DEFENCE (a) of the Scripture as the only standard of faith: in answer to a preface [by William Dunlop] first publish'd at Edinburgh, before a collection of confessions, and since publish'd by itself at London: in which the prefacer's account of the ends and uses of creeds and confessions of faith is examin'd, and what is said of their justice, reasonableness, and necessity, as a publick standard of orthodoxy, is fully considered. By the author of the Occasional paper [Moses Lowman].

8vo. Pp. vi., 170. [Wodrow's *Analecta*, iv., p. 128.] London, 1721

Ascribed also to Simon Browne, Dissenting minister in the Old Jewry.

DEFENCE (a) of the Scripture-history so far as it concerns the resurrection of Jairus's daughter; the widow of Nain's son; and Lazarus: in answer to Mr. Woolston's fifth discourse on our Saviour's miracles. [By Henry Stebbing, chancellor of the diocese of Salisbury.] 8vo. Pp. xii., 68. [*Adv. Lib.*] London, 1730

Continued in *A discourse on our Saviour's miraculous power* . . .

DEFENCE (a) of the Slave trade, on the grounds of humanity, policy, and justice. [By Robert Bisset, LL.D.] 8vo. Pp. 90. [*D. N. B.*, vol. 5, p. 102.] London, 1804

DEFENCE (a) of the Society of Jesus. [By Thomas Owen, S.J.] 8vo. [Sommervogel's *Dictionnaire*; Oliver's *Collections.*] St Omer, 1610

DEFENCE (a) of the Society of the sons of the clergy, of our Church establishment, and of divine revelation; in consequence of the late attacks in the Tyne Mercury, and the recent pamphlet, by William Burdon, Esq. of Hartford, near Morpeth. . . . By a late steward of the sons of the clergy [Nathaniel John Hollingsworth, M.A.]. 8vo. Pp. xxi., 149. [*Bodl.*]
Newcastle, 1812

DEFENCE (the) of the soul against the strongest assaults of Satan. By R. C. [Roger Carr, B.A., of Pembroke Hall, Cambridge]. 8vo. London, 1578

DEFENCE (a) of the stage, or an inquiry into the real qualities of theatrical entertainments, their scope and tendency. . . . By John William Calcraft [John William Cole]. 8vo. [R. W. Lowe's *Theat. Lit.*, p. 39.]
Dublin, 1839

DEFENCE (a) of the students of prophecy; in answer to the attack of the Rev. Dr Hamilton, of Strathblane. [By Henry Drummond, M.P.] 8vo. Pp. 129. [Boase's *Cat. of Cath. Apost. Writers.*] London, 1827

Signed "H. D."

DEFENCE (a) of the Sunday Schools attempted, in a series of letters. . . . By J. M. [Joseph Mayer]. Fcap 8vo.
Stockport, 1798

DEFENCE (a) of the Treaty of Amity . . . between the United States and Great Britain. . . . By Camillus [Alexander Hamilton]. 8vo. [Cushing's *Init. and Pseud.*, i., 49.]
New York, 1795

DEFENCE (a) of the true Church called Quakers (come and coming out of the wildernesse, Babylon, and the dark night of apostacy of Antichrist into their own land, which is Sion the mountain of holinesse, there to worship the Lord in spirit and truth) ; against the several sects and sorts of people, called Independants, Separatists, or Brownists, Baptists, Fift Monarchy-men, Seekers, and High Notionists of all sorts. . . . Written by J. C. [John Crook]. . . . 4to. [Smith's *Cat. of Friends' Books*, i., 440, 483.]
London, 1659

DEFENCE (a) of the United Company of Merchants of England trading to the East Indies, and their servants (particularly those at Bengal) against the complaints of the Dutch East India Company. [By John Dunning, Lord Ashburton.] 4to. [*D. N. B.*, vol. 16, p. 214.] London, 1762

DEFENCE (a) of the veracity of Moses, in his records of the creation and general deluge ; illustrated by obser-vations in the caverns of the Peak of Derby. By Philobiblos [Thomas Rodd]. 8vo. Pp. ii., 127. [*Aber-deen Lib.*] London, 1820

DEFENCE (a) of the Vindication of K. Charles the Martyr ; justifying His Majesty's title to ΕΙΚΩΝ ΒΑΣΙΔΙΚΗ. In answer to a late pamphlet [by John Toland] intituled " Amyntor." By the author of the *Vindication* [Thomas Wagstaffe, A.M.]. 4to. Pp. 96. [*Bodl.*] London, 1699
On the whole controversy, *see* Almack's " Bibliog. of the King's Book " ; *D. N. B.*, vol. 21, pp. 70 ff. ; also the footnote to Εἰκὼν Βασιλική.

DEFENCE (a) of the Vindication of Presbyterian ordination, &c. ; con-taining a reply to I. A layman's re-flections relating to the Vindication, in a letter to the Rev. Mr Shaw ; and also to II. Mr Sturges's sermons, entitled, The divine right of episcopacy asserted. By the author of the *Vindi-cation* [Rev. John Hartley, of Ashby-de-la-Zouch]. 8vo. Pp. 88. [Dar-ling's *Cyclop. Bibl.*] London, 1716
The " Vindication " is also anonymous.

DEFENCE (a) of the Vindication of the Church of Scotland, in answer to the Apology of the clergy of Scotland. [By Gilbert Rule.] 4to. Pp. 49. [*New Coll. Cat.*] Edinburgh, 1694

DEFENCE (a) of the Vindication of the deprived Bishops : wherein the case of Abiathar is particularly considered,

and the invalidity of lay-deprivations is further proved, from the doctrine received under the Old Testament, continued in the first ages of Christi-anity, and from our own fundamental laws. In a reply to Dr Hody and another author. To which is annexed, The doctrine of the Church of England, concerning the independency of the clergy on the lay-power, as to those rights of theirs which are purely spiritual, reconciled with our oath of supremacy, and the lay-deprivations of the popish bishops in the beginning of the Reformation. By the author of the *Vindication of the deprived bishops* [Henry Dodwell]. 4to. Pp. 111. [Green's *Bibl. Somers.*, ii., 488.]
London, 1695
This pamphlet was afterwards sup-pressed, but the latter portion (" The Doctrine of the Church of England con-cerning the independency of the clergy on the lay-power ") was issued again in 1697. *See below.*

DEFENCE (a) of the war against France. [By William Fox, attorney.] 8vo. [*Brit. Mus.*] London, [1794]

DEFENCE (a) of the Whigs. By a member of the twenty-seventh Con-gress [John Pendleton Kennedy]. 8vo. [Cushing's *Init. and Pseud.*, i., 191.]
New York, 1844

DEFENCE (a) of tobacco. [By Roger Marbeck, or Merbeck.] 4to. [*D. N. B.*, vol. 36, p. 122.] London, 1602
The author's name is given in an acrostic forming the dedication.

DEFENCE (the) of trade ; in a letter to Sir Thomas Smith, Knight, Gover-nour of the East India Companie, etc., from one of that Societie [Sir Dudley Digges]. 4to. [Watt's *Bibl. Brit.*]
London, 1615

DEFENCE (a) of Ward's Errata of the Protestant Bible. By the Rev. J. L. [John Lingard, D.D.]. 12mo. [*D. N. B.*, vol. 33, p. 323.]
Dublin, 1810

DEFENCES (the) of England ; nine letters. By a journeyman shoemaker [A— Smith, of Nottingham]. 8vo. Pp. 22. London, 1862

DEFENDER (a) of the faith ; a histori-cal romance. By Marjorie Bowen [Gabrielle Margaret Vere Campbell, later Madame Long]. Cr 8vo. [*Lond. Lib. Cat.*] London, 1911

DEFENDER (a) of the faith ; the romance of a business man. By Tivoli [Horace William Bleackley, B.A.]. 8vo. Pp. 420. [*Brit. Mus.*]
London, 1892

VOL. II.

C

DEFENSATIVE against the poyson of supposed prophesies, not hitherto confuted by the penne of any man, which being grounded eyther uppon the warrant and authoritie of old paynted bookes, expositions of dreames, oracles . . . or any other kinde of pretended knowledge, have been causes of great disorder in the Commonwealth, and chiefly among the simple and unlearned people. . . . [By Henry Howard, Earl of Northampton.] 4to. [Watt's *Bibl. Brit.*] London, 1583
This work was mainly directed against the errors of astrologists : a revised edition was published in 1621.

DEFENSATIVE armour against four of Sathan's most fiery darts ; viz. temptations to atheistical and blasphemous impressions and thoughts, self-murther, despair, and presumption : wherein is discoursed the nature of these temptations . . . and some proper advice is offered to those who are exercised with them. By J. C. [John Collinges, D.D.]. 8vo. Pp. xiv., 336. [*Brit. Mus.*] London, 1680

DEFENSE (a) and declaration of the Catholike Churches doctrine, touching Purgatory and Prayers for the soules departed. [By William Allen, Cardinal.] Fcap 8vo. [Gillow's *Bibl. Dict.*, vol. i.] Antwerp, 1565

DEFENSE (a) of an argument made use of in a letter to Mr Dodwel, to prove the immateriality and natural immortality of the soul. [By Samuel Clarke.] 8vo. [*Bodl.*]
London, 1707

DEFENSE (a) of insanity. By Paul Fairchild [John A. Taylor]. 8vo. [Cushing's *Init. and Pseud.*, vol. i., p. 98.] New York, 1876

DEFENSE (a) of the ecclesiastical regiment in Englande, defaced by T. C. [Thomas Cartwright] in his Replie agaynst D. Whitgifte. [By Lord Henry Howard.] London, 1574
A note by a contemporary hand on the copy in Camb. Univ. Library attests the authorship.

DEFENSE (a) of the innocencie of the three ceremonies of the Church of England ; the surplace, crosse after Baptisme, and kneeling to receiving of the blessed Sacrament. [By T— Cestren ?] Fcap 4to. 2 pt.
London, 1618

DEFENSE (a) of the Plea for humane reason ; being a reply to a book entitled, A plea for divine revelation. In a letter to [Edmund Gibson] the Right Reverend the Lord Bishop of London. [By John Jackson.] 8vo. Pp. xvii., 95. [*Brit. Mus.*] London, 1731

DEFIANCE (a) against all arbitrary usurpations or encroachments, either of the House of Lords, or any other, upon the soveraignty of the supreme House of Commons, (the high court of judicature of the land) or upon the rights, properties and freedoms of the people in generall. Whereunto is annexed, a relation of the unjust and barbarous proceedings of the House of Lords, against that worthy Commoner, Mr. Overton, who standeth by them committed to the most contemptuous goal [*sic*] of Newgate, for refusing to answer to interrogatories, and appealing from that Court to the Honourable House of Commons (as by the great charter of England he was bound) for the triall of his cause. . . . [By John Lilburne.] 4to. [*Bodl.*]
N.P., [London], 1646

DEFIANCE (a) to fortune, proclaimed by Andrugio, noble Duke of Saxony . . . whereunto is adioyned the honorable warres of Galastino, Duke of Millaine. Written by H. R. [Henry Roberts]. B. L. 4to. [*Brit. Mus.*]
London, 1590

DEFIANT hearts : from the German of Wilhelm Heimburg [Bertha Behrens]. Pt 8vo. New York, 1898

DEFINITIONS ; or word-poems. By Lindon Meadows [Rev. Charles Butler Greatrex]. 12mo. [*Brit. Mus.*]
London, [1879]

DEFORMED (the) ; a tragedy. By J. H., junr. [James Hedderwick, journalist in Glasgow]. 8vo.
Glasgow, 1834

DEFORMED (the) ; and the Admiral's daughter [tales]. [By Mrs Anne Marsh - Caldwell.] 2 vols. 8vo. [*D. N. B.*, vol. 36, p. 219.]
London, 1834

DEFORMITIES of Dr Samuel Johnson ; selected from his works. [By John Callander, of Craigforth.] 8vo. Pp. iv., 63. [Chalmers' *Notes.*]
Edinburgh, 1782

DEFORMITIES (the) of Fox and Burke, faithfully selected from their speeches ; together with copies of the addresses presented to the king on the rejection of Fox's India Bill, and the dismission of the late administration from his Majesty's councils. [By George Chalmers.] 8vo. [*W.*]
London, 1784

DEGENERACY (the) of aristocracy. By Isaac Didwin [William A. Sturdy]. Pt 8vo. [*Amer. Cat.*]
Chartley, Mass., 1907

DEGREDATION of [the] Bengal zemindar ; an account of his folly, vice, and causes of his distress and decline. By a Well-wisher [Lalit Mohan Roy]. 8vo. [*Calc. Imp. Lib.*]
Calcutta, 1893

DEGREES (the) of the Zodiac symbolised. By Antonio Borelli. Translated from *La Volasfera* by " Sepharial " [Walter Gorn Old]. 8vo. Pp. xi., 136. [*Brit. Mus.*]
Boston, [Mass.], 1907

DEIRDRE ; a play in three acts. By Æ. [George William Russell]. [*Brit. Mus.*] 12mo. Tower Press, 1907

DEIRDRE ; a poem. [By Robert Dwyer Joyce, M.D.] 8vo. [O'Donoghue's *Poets of Ireland*.]
Boston, [Mass.], 1876

DEIRDRE and the sons of Usna. By Fiona Macleod [William Sharp]. Fcap 8vo. [*Brit. Mus.*]
Portland, [U.S.A.], 1903

DEISM and Christianity fairly consider'd ; in four dialogues : to which is added a fifth upon Latitudinarian Christianity. . . . [By John Constable, S.J.] Fcap 8vo. [Oliver's *Collections.*] London, 1739

DEISM not consistent with the religion of nature and reason. . . . [By the Rev. Capel Berrow.] 8vo. [Watt's *Bibl. Brit.*] London, 1780

DEISM refuted ; or the truth of Christianity demonstrated by infallible proof from four rules which are incompatible to any imposture that can possibly be. In a letter to a friend by a lover of truth [Charles Leslie]. 8vo. [*D. N. B.*, vol. 33, p. 83.]
London, 1755
The above title is one of several variations of the " Short and easy method with the Deists."

DEISM revealed : or, the attack on Christianity candidly reviewed in its real merits, as they stand in the celebrated writings of Lord Herbert, Lord Shaftesbury, Hobbes, Toland, Tindal, Collins, Mandeville, Dodwell, Woolston, Morgan, Chubb, and others. [By Rev. Philip Skelton, B.A.] Second edition, with amendments. 2 vols. Fcap 8vo. [*Bodl.*] London, 1751

DEITY ; a poem. [By Samuel Boyse.] Fcap 8vo. Pp. 56. [*Bodl.*]
London, 1739

DEITY'S (the) delay in punishing the guilty, considered on the principles of reason. [By Robert Bolton.] 8vo. Pp. vi., 74. [*D. N. B.*, vol. 5, p. 332.]
London, 1751

DELAMERES (the) of Delamere Court ; a love-story. By the author of *The Duchess* [Archibald Boyd]. 3 vols. Cr 8vo. [*Brit. Mus.*] London, 1852

DELAWARE ; or, the ruined family : a tale. [By George Payne Rainsford James.] 3 vols. 8vo. [*Camb. Univ. Lib.*] Edinburgh, 1833

DELAYS dangerous. No to-morrow for the repeal of the Test and Corporation Acts. [By Caleb Fleming.] 8vo. [*Bodl.*] London, 1739

DELDEE, the ward of Waringham ; or the iron hand. By Florence Warden [Florence Alice Price, later Mrs George E. James]. 8vo. London, 1885

DELECTABLE demaundes and pleasaunt questions, with their seuerall aunswers, in matters of loue, naturall causes, with morall and politique deuises : newly translated [by William Painter] out of Frenche [of Alain Chartier]. . . . B. L. Fcap 4to.
London, [1566]

DELECTABLE (the) Duchy ; stories, studies, and sketches. By Q. [Arthur Thomas Quiller-Couch]. 8vo. [*Lit. Year Book.*] London, 1893

DELENDA Carthago ; or the true interest of England, in relation to France and Holland. [By Anthony Ashley Cooper, first Earl of Shaftesbury.] No title page. 4to. [*Cat. Lond. Inst.*, ii., 554.] [c. 1695]

DELFT (the) jug, and other stories : by Silverpen [Eliza Meteyard]. Fcap 8vo. [Haynes' *Pseud.*] London, 1885

DELIBERATE thoughts on the system of our late Treaties with Hesse Cassel. . . . [By Samuel Martyn, politician.] 8vo. [*Brit. Mus.*] London, 1756

DELICATE distress. [A novel, in the form of letters.] By Frances [Mrs Elizabeth Griffith]. 2 vols. 8vo. [Watt's *Bibl. Brit.*] London, 1769
Vols. 3 and 4, entitled " The Gordian Knot. By Henry," were written by her husband.

DELICIA. By the author of *Miss Molly*, etc. [Beatrice May Butt]. 8vo. Pp. vi., 342. [*Brit. Mus.*]
Edinburgh, 1879

DELICIAE literariæ: a new book of table-talk. [By Joseph Robertson, LL.D., of the Register Office, Edinburgh.] Fcap 8vo. Pp. 273. [*N. and Q.*, 17 March 1855, p. 214.]
London, 1840

DELICIOUS (the) answer . . . a poem. By a Professor [John Gwilliam]. 8vo. [*Brit. Mus.*] London, 1812
The above was suppressed soon after publication.

DELICIOUS (the) life-saving kiss. By Verus Cassander [Henry Egbert]. Pt 8vo. [*Amer. Cat.*] New York, 1904

DELIGHT and pastime; or, pleasant diversion for both sexes: consisting of good history and morality, witty jests, smart repartees, and pleasant fancies; free from obscene and prophane expressions, too frequent in other works of this kind; whereby the age is corrupted in a great measure, and youth inflamed to loose and wanton thoughts. . . . By G. M. [Guy Miege]. 8vo. Pp. vii., 163. [*Bodl.*]
London, 1697

DELIGHT, the soul of Art. By Chauffeur [Arthur Jerome Eddy]. Pt 8vo. [*Amer. Cat.*] Philadelphia, 1902

DELIGHTFUL (the) adventures of honest John Cole, that merry old soul. . . . By a tipling philosopher of the Royal Society [William Oldisworth]. 8vo. [*D. N. B.*, vol. 42, p. 115.] London, 1732

DELIGHTFUL fables in prose and verse; none of them to be found in Æsop, but collected from divers ancient and modern authors. . . . By R. B. [Richard Burton, *i.e.* Nathaniel Crouch, the publisher]. 12mo. Pp. 178. [*Bodl.*] London, 1691
See the Note to " Admirable Curiosities."

DELIGHTFUL (the) history of Don Quixote, the most renowned Baron of Mancha; containing his noble achievements and surprizing adventures, his daring interprizes and valiant engagement for the peerless Dulcinia del Toboso. . . . [Translated from the Spanish of Miguel de Cervantes Saavedra.] 8vo. [Arber's *Term Cat.*, ii., p. 613.] London, 1689
Several other English translations and many different editions have been produced: such are " The history of the ever renowned knight, Don Quixote . . ." (1680 ?), " The history of the most renowned Don Quixote . . ." (1687), " The much esteemed history of the ever famous Knight . . ." (1704), " The life and notable adventures of that renowned Knight . . ." (1711).

DELIGHTFUL (the) life of pleasure on the Thames, and an angler's perfect sport. By " Red Quill " [James Englefield]. Fcap 8vo. London, 1912

DELIGHTS for ladies to adorne their persons, tables, closets, and distillatories, with beauties, bouquets, perfumes, and waters. Read, practise, and censure. [By Sir Hugh Plat.] 4to. [*N. and Q.*, 19 Nov. 1853, p. 495.] London, 1640

DELIGHTS for the ingenious, in above fifty select and choice emblems, divine and moral. . . . Collected by R. B. [Richard Burton, *i.e.* Nathaniel Crouch]. 12mo. London, 1684
See the note to " Admirable Curiosities."

DELIGHTS (the) of the bottle; or, the compleat vintner: with the humours of bubble upstarts, stingy wranglers, dinner spungers, jill tiplers, beef beggars, cook teasers, pan soppers, plate twirlers, table whitlers, drawer biters, spoon pinchers, and other tavern tormentors. A merry poem, to which is added, a South-sea song upon the late bubbles. By the author of the *Cavalcade* [Edward Ward]. 8vo. Pp. 56. [*Bodl.*] London, 1720

DELINEATION of the nature and obligation of morality. . . . [By James Balfour, advocate.] Fcap 8vo. [*New Coll. Cat.*] Edinburgh, 1763

DELINEATIONS of the County of Middlesex. [By William Smith, antiquary.] 8vo. [*Brit. Mus.*]
[London, 1835 ?]
No title-page; ends unfinished at p. 48.

DELINEATIONS of the heart; or, the history of Henry Bennet: a tragicomic-satiric essay, attempted in the manner of Fielding. [By John Raithby, barrister.] 3 vols. Fcap 8vo. [Watt's *Bibl. Brit.*] London, N.D.

DELIVERANCE, not pardon only. . . . By J. N. D. [John Nelson Darby]. Fcap 8vo. London, 1874

DELLA Robbia and Benvenuto Cellini. By Leader Scott [Mrs Lucy Baxter]. Cr 8vo. [*Lond. Lib. Cat.*]
London, 1883

DELL'S New Year. By Marianne Farningham [Mary Anne Hearne, of Farningham]. 8vo. [*Brit. Mus.*]
London, 1875

DELPHA; or, marriage as a failure and a success; a dramatic love-story. . . . By Roldah [Isabel Clifton Nye]. Pt 8vo. Pp. 270. New York, 1896

DELPHINE; a novel. By Curtis Yorke [Mrs W. S—— Richmond Lee, *née* . . . Jex Long]. Cr 8vo. Pp. 520. [*Lond. Lib. Cat.*] London, 1904

DELPHINE Carfrey ; a novel. By Mrs George Norman [Mrs George Blount]. Cr 8vo. Pp. 306. [*Catholic Who's Who*.] London, 1911

DELUGE (the) and other poems. By John Presland [Mrs Gladys Skelton]. Fcap 8vo. [*Lond. Lib. Cat.*] London, 1911

DELUGE (the) ; its cause, and universality, and history of the Creation from the beginning to the Covenant rainbow. [Verse.] By Professor Udiven [Henry Wesley Harkom]. 8vo. Pp. 132. [*Brit. Mus.*] Plymouth, [1914]

DELUGE (the) ; or the destruction of the world : an opera. [By Edward Ecclestone.] 4to. [Arber's *Term Cat.*, ii., p. 613.] London, 1690

DEMAGOGUE (the) ; a political novel. [By David Ross Leckie.] Fcap 8vo. Boston, 1891

DEMETER—a mask. By " Droch " [Robert Bridges]. 8vo. [*Amer. Cat.*] New York, 1905

DEMIGOD (a). [By Edward Payson Jackson.] 8vo. New York, 1886

DEMI-REP (the). By N. O., author of the *Meretriciad* [Edward Thompson, R.N]. 4to. Pp. 35. [Brydges' *Cens. Lit.*, vii., 317.] London, 1756

DEMI-ROYAL. By Ashton Hilliers [Henry M. Wallis]. Cr 8vo. Pp. 396. [*Lond. Lib. Cat.*] London, 1915

DEMOCRACY. [A novel. By Clarence King.] Cr 8vo. London, 1882

DEMOCRACY ; a novel. By Whyte Thorne [Richard Whiteing, journalist]. 3 vols. Cr. 8vo. [Kirk's Supp.] London, 1876

DEMOCRACY : an epic poem. By Aquiline Nimble-chops, democrat [Brockholst Livingston]. [Cushing's *Init. and Pseud.*, i., p. 484.] New York, 1790

DEMOCRACY unveiled, in a letter to Sir F. Burdett. [By T. Adams.] 8vo. [Watt's *Bibl. Brit.*] London, 1811

DEMOCRACY unveiled ; or, tyranny stripped of the garb of patriotism [in verse]. By Christopher Caustic, LL.D. [Thomas Green Fessenden]. Third edition. 2 vols. Fcap 8vo. [Cushing's *Init. and Pseud.*, i., p. 53.] New York, 1806

DEMOCRAT (the) : interspersed with anecdotes of well-known characters. [By Henry James Pye.] 2 vols. 8vo. [*Bodl.*] London, 1795

DEMOCRATIAD (the) ; a poem, in retaliation, for the Philadelphia Jockey Club. By a gentleman of Connecticut [Lemuel Hopkins, M.D.]. 8vo. [Cushing's *Init. and Pseud.*, ii., 65.] Philadelphia, 1796
Also ascribed to William Cobbett.

DEMOCRATIC principles illustrated by example. By Peter Porcupine [William Cobbett]. Part the first. Fcap 8vo. Pp. 23. London, 1798
—— Part II. Containing an instructive essay tracing all the horrors of the French Revolution to their real causes, the licentious politics, and infidel philosophy of the present age. By Peter Porcupine [William Cobbett]. Fcap 8vo. [*Adv. Lib.*] London, 1798

DEMOCRATIC (the) speaker's handbook. By Mathew Carey, junr. [Augustus R. Cazauran]. 8vo. [Cushing's *Init. and Pseud.*, i., p. 50.] Cincinnati, 1868

DEMOCRITUS in London ; with the mad pranks and comical conceits of Motley and Robin Good-fellow : to which are added notes festivous, etc. [By George Daniel.] 8vo. [*Gent. Mag.*, July 1852, p. 75.] London, 1852

DEMOCRITVS ; or Doctor Merry-man his medicines against melancholy humours. Written by S. R. [Samuel Rowlands]. 4to. Twenty-three leaves. London, 1607
The 1609 and the later editions are entitled " Doctor Merryman : or nothing but mirth." [Lowndes' *Bibl. Man.*]

DEMONOLOGIA ; or natural knowledge revealed ; being an exposé of ancient and modern superstitions. By J. S. F. [J— S— Forsyth]. Pt 8vo. Pp. 438. [*New Coll. Cat.*] London, 1827

DEMONSTRATION (a), from Christian principles, that the present regulation of the ecclesiastical revenues in the Church of England is directly contrary and fatally destructive to the design of Christianity. . . . By a clergyman of the same Church [John Kirkby]. 8vo. Pp. 48. [*Brit. Mus.*] Canterbury, 1743

DEMONSTRATION (a) how the Latine tongue may be learn't with far greater ease and speed then commonly it is. [By Arthur Brett, M.A.] 4to. [*Bodl.*] London, 1669
Signed " A. B. Z. W."

DEMONSTRATION (a) of the trueth of that discipline which Christe hath prescribed in his worde for the gouernement of his Church, in all times and

places, vntill the ende of the worlde.¶
Wherein are gathered into a plaine
forme of reasoning, the proofes thereof. . . . [By John Udall.] 8vo. Pp.
86. [Dexter's *Cong. Bibl.*]
N.P., [1589]

DEMONSTRATION of the will of
God by the light of nature; in eight
discourses. [By Thomas Cooke, of
Braintree.] 8vo. [*Camb. Univ. Lib.*]
London, 1733

DEMONSTRATION (a) that the
Church of Rome and her Councils
have erred; by shewing that the
Councils of Constance, Basil, and
Trent have, in all their decrees touch-
ing communion in one kind, contra-
dicted the received doctrine of the
Church of Christ: with an appendix.
[By Daniel Whitby.] 4to. [*Bodl.*]
London, 1688

DEMOS; a story of English Socialism.
[By George R. Gissing.] 3 vols. Pt 8vo.
[*Brit. Mus.*]   London, 1886

ΔΕΝΔΡΟΛΟΓΙΑ. Dodonas grove: or, the
vocall forrest. The second edition,
more exact and perfect than the
former. . . . By J. H. [James Howell],
Esquire. Fcap 4to. [*Watt's Bibl.
Brit.*]   N.P., 1644

DENISE [a novel]. By the author of
Mademoiselle Mori [Margaret Roberts].
Fcap 8vo. [*Brit. Mus.*]
London, 1883

DENMARK and the Duchies, with
the succession as Heir General in both
of the Russo-Gottorp lines: contemporary movements on the Sound
and the Bosphorus. [By David Urquhart.] 8vo. [*Brit. Mus.*]
London, 1852

DENMARK vindicated; being an
answer to a late treatise [by Viscount
Molesworth] called, An account of
Denmark as it was in the year 1692.
. . . [By Jodocus Crull, M.D.] 8vo.
Pp. 216.   London, 1694
  The dedication to Prince George of Den-
mark is signed "J. C." *See above*, the
"Account of Denmark . . ."

DENNIS Day, carpet-bagger. [By Mrs
Wm. Loving Spencer.] 8vo.
New York, 1887

DENNIS Foggarty. By Lord Gilhooley
[Frederick Henry Seymour]. 8vo.
[*Amer. Cat.*]   New York, 1903

DENNY; or from haven to haven. By
Annie Gray [Annie Grayjones]. Pt
8vo.   London, 1883

DENOMINATIONAL education *versus*
Irish Protestantism. . . . [By William
Alexander Willock.] 8vo. [*Brit.
Mus.*]   Dublin, 1862

DENOMINATIONAL (the) reason
why; giving the origin, history, and
tenets of the various Christian sects.
[By Robert Kemp Philp.] Pt 8vo.
[Boase and Courtney's *Bib. Corn.*, ii.,
494.]   London, 1860

DENOUNCED (the). By the authors
of *Tales by the O'Hara family* [John
and Michael Banim]. 3 vols. Fcap
8vo. [S. J. Brown's *Ireland in fiction.*]
London, 1830

DENTON Hall; a novel. [By Miss
—— Cross.] 8vo.   London, 1850

DENUNCIAD (the); a satire by Cynic
[Rev. Charles Jones Langston]. Dedi-
cated to the Bath Corporation. 8vo.
[Green's *Bibl. Somers.*, i., 591.]
Bath, 1898

DENZIL Place: a story in verse. By
Violet Fane [Mrs Mary (Montgomerie)
Singleton, later Lady Currie]. 8vo.
Pp. 252. [*Brit. Mus.*] London, 1875

DEO Ecclesiæ et conscientiæ ergo; or
a plea for abatement in matters of
conformity to several injunctions and
orders of the Church of England. To
which are added some considerations
of the hypothesis of a king de jure and
de facto, proving that King William is
King of England, etc., as well of right
as fact, and not by a bare actual
posession of the throne. By Irenæus
Junior, a conforming member of the
Church of England [Samuel Snow-
den, rector of Newton and Swanstrop,
in Norfolk]. 4to. Pp. xvi., 96. [*U.
P. Lib. Cat.*]   London, 1693

DEPARTURE (the) of the Israelites: a
poem. By Nemo, author of *The
Ocean Queen* [Henry Gardiner Adams].
Fcap 8vo. [*Brit. Mus.*]
Chatham, 1837

DEPLORABLE (the) life and death of
Edward the Second, king of England;
together with the downefall of the two
vnfortunate fauorits, Gaveston and
Spencer. Storied in an excellent
poem. [By Sir Francis Hubert.] 8vo.
Pp. 152.   London, 1628
  A spurious edition. The genuine
edition was published in 1629, and has
the following title:—"The historie of
Edward the Second, surnamed Carnarvan,
one of our English Kings; together with
the fatall downe-fall of his two vnfortunate
favorites, Gaveston and Spencer: now
published by the author himself, according
to the true originall copie, and purged from
those foule errors and corruptions, wherewith that spurious and surreptitious peace,
which lately came forth vnder the same
tytle, was too much defiled and deformed.

With the addition of some other observations, both of vse and ornaments. By F. H., Knight." The dedication is signed "Fran. Hubert." For an account of these two editions, and of the reprint of 1721, see Brydges' *Restituta*, i., 92; and *The Gentleman's Magazine*, xciv., pt. 2, p. 19. *See* also Bibliotheca Anglo-Poetica, No. 555, from which the title of the genuine edition has been taken.

DEPOPULATION (the) system in the Highlands : its extent, causes, and evil consequences, with practical remedies. By an eye-witness [Rev. Thomas M'Lauchlan, LL.D.]. 8vo.
This treatise appeared originally in the *Witness* newspaper.
Edinburgh, 1849

DEPORTMENT (the) of a married life ; in a series of letters. By the Hon. E— S— [Eugenia Stanhope]. 8vo. London, 1798

DEPORTMENTAL ditties. By Col. D. Streamer [*i.e.* Coldstreamer ; Capt. Harry J. C. Graham, of the Coldstream Guards]. Cr. 8vo. [*Amer. Cat.*] New York, 1909

DEPRESSION (the) of the clergy the danger of the Church ; a sermon preached in St Peter's [Episcopal] Church, Peterhead, Sept. 28, 1856. By the Incumbent [Rev. Gilbert Rorison, D.D.]. Fcap 8vo. Pp. 40. [*Brit. Mus.*] Peterhead, 1856

DEPRESSION of trade and agriculture ; its cause and remedy. By the author of *Liberal misrule in Ireland* [James Herman de Ricci]. 8vo. [*Brit. Mus.*] London, 1887

DEPTHS (the) of Satan discovered . . . being some observations on a pamphlet called, " The Swords abuse asserted," by John Vernon. Presented to the consideration of the Armie, Citie, Kingdom, by Philopatrius Philalethes [Daniel Cawdrey]. 8vo. Pp. vi., 26. [Whitley's *Bapt. Bibl.*, i., 36.] London, 1649

DERBY (the) ministry ; a series of Cabinet pictures. By Mark Rochester [William Charles Mark Kent]. Second edition. 8vo. [*Olphar Hamst*, p. 109.] London, 1859
A later edition was issued (1866) with a different title : " The lives of eminent Conservative statesmen."

DERBYITES (the) and the Coalition. [By Edward Michael Whitty.] Fcap 8vo. London, [1854]

DERELICT (the) and Tommy. By the author of '*Twixt the devil and the deep sea* [Clarence Forestier Walker]. 8vo. Pp. 131. [*Brit. Mus.*] London, 1900

DERELICT (a) Empire. By Mark Time [Henry C. Irwin, Indian Civil Service]. 8vo. London, 1912

DERICK. By Barbara Yechton [Lydia Farrington Krause]. Pt 8vo. Pp. 370. New York, 1897

DERRICK Vaughan, novelist. By Edna Lyall [Ada Ellen Bayly]. 8vo. [*Brit. Mus.*] London, 1850

DERRY ; a tale of the Revolution. By Charlotte Elizabeth, authoress of *Osric*, etc. [Mrs Charlotte Elizabeth Tonna, previously Mrs Phelan]. New edition. Fcap 8vo. Pp. 692. [*D. N. B.*, vol. 57, p. 34.] London, 1902

DERWENT ; an ode. [By John Carr, LL.D.] 4to. Pp. 14. [*Manch. Free Lib.*] London, N.D.

DERWENT ; or, recollections of young life in the country. By John Chester [Rev. John Mitchell]. 8vo. [Cushing's *Init. and Pseud.*, i., 55.] New York, 1872

DESCANT (a) on the penny postage. By X. A. P. [John Peace]. 8vo. [*Brit. Mus.*] London, 1841

DESCANT (a) upon railroads. By X. A. P. [John Peace]. 8vo. [*Brit. Mus.*] London, 1842

DESCANT (a) upon weather-wisdom. By X. A. P. [John Peace]. 8vo. London, 1845

DESCENDANT (the) ; a novel. [By Ellen Glasgow.] 8vo. London, 1897

DESCENDANTS of William Knox and of John Knox the Reformer. By a lineal descendant [William Crawford]. Fcap 4to. [*New Coll. Cat.*] Edinburgh, 1896

DESCENT (the) into hell ; a poem. [By John Abraham Heraud.] 8vo. Pp. 231. [*Adv. Lib.*] London, 1830

DESCRIPTIO Angliæ et descriptio Londini : being two poems in Latin verse, supposed to be written in the XVth century. [By G. Coryate.] 4to. [*Brit. Mus.*] London, 1763

DESCRIPTION (a), anatomical and physiological, of the sectional model of the human body, the Parisian Venus ; comprising a popular account of the parts displayed, their functions and uses. [By J. Allison.] 8vo. [*Manch. Free Lib.*] Manchester, 1844

DESCRIPTION (a) and explanation of 268 places in Jerusalem, and in the suburbs thereof, as it flourished in the time of Jesus Christ : answerable to each of the 268 figures that are in its large and most exact description in the map ; shewing the several places of the acts and sufferings of Jesus Christ, and his holy apostles ; as also of the kings, prophets, etc. . . . [By Christian Adrichomius.] Translated by T. T[ymme] ; reviewed and in many places rectified according to the Holy Scriptures, etc., by H. Fessey. 4to. [*W*.]   London, 1654

DESCRIPTION (the) and present state of Persia ; with a faithful account of the manners, religion, and government of that people. By Nicholas Sanson ; done [from the French] into English [by John Savage]. Fcap 8vo. [Watt's *Bibl. Brit.*]   London, 1695

DESCRIPTION (the) and use of a new astronomical instrument, for taking altitudes of the sun and stars at sea, with an horizon, etc. [By W. Ward and Caleb Smith.] 4to. [*Brit. Mus.*]
London, 1735

DESCRIPTION (the) and use of a portable instrument vlugarly (*sic*) known by the name of Gunters quadrant ; by which is perform'd, most propositions in astronomy, as the altitude, azimuth, right ascension, and declination of the sun, etc. Also his rising, and setting and amplitude, together with the hour of the day or night, and other conclusions exemplified at large. To which is added the use of Napiers bones in multiplication, division, and extraction of roots. . . . By a true lover of the mathematicks [William Leybourn]. 12mo. Pp. 72. [*Aberd. Lib.*]   London, 1685
The addition has a separate title-page and pagination (pp. 93), and is said to be published by W. L.

DESCRIPTION (the) and use of a quadrant ; by which all the most usefull and necessary propositions of both the globes are easily and exactly performed, as the right ascension, declination, altitude, amplitude, rising, setting, azimuth, and houre of the day. Also of a quadrant, by which you may take all manner of heights & distances, as of towers, steeples, etc. . . . Published by J. H. for the use of such as are mathematically affected [J. Hewlett]. 8vo. Pp. 60. [*Bodl.*] London, 1665
The author's name is given in the handwriting of Wood.

DESCRIPTION (the) and use of the double horizontall Dyall ; whereby not onely the hower of the day is shewne, but also the meridian line is found. . . . By W. O. [William Oughtred]. Fcap 8vo. [*Brit. Mus.*]
London, 1636

DESCRIPTION of a method of taking the differences of right ascension and declination, with the Reticule Rhomboide of Dr. Bradley, without placing the instrument in the plane of the equator. By H. E. [Sir Henry Charles Englefield]. 4to. [*W*.]
Bath, [1794 ?]

DESCRIPTION (a) of a new instrument [invented by J. Hadley] for taking the latitude or other altitudes at sea, with directions for its use. [By George Hadley.] 8vo. [*Brit. Mus.*]
London, 1734

DESCRIPTION (a) of a series of illustrations to G. P. Harding's manuscript history of the Princes of Wales, from the time of Edward of Caernarvon, to the present sovereign of England : containing a list of all the portraits, armorial bearings, royal badges, monuments, seals, illuminated views, and other decorations. [By Thomas Moule.] 8vo. [Martin's *Cat.*]
London, 1828

DESCRIPTION (a) of a strange (and miraculous) fish, cast upon the sands in the meads, in the Hundred of Worwell, in the county palatine of Chester, (or Chesshiere). The certainty whereof is here related concerning the said most monstrous fish. To the tune of Bragandary. [In two parts.] [By Martin Parker.] Folio. Single sheet. [*Bodl.*]   London, N.D. [1636 ?]
Signed " M. P."
There is a book to satisfie such as desire a larger description hereof. (Printed note.)

DESCRIPTION of a very ancient statue of Minerva, at Athens. [By Sir George Scharf.] 8vo.
London, 1851

DESCRIPTION (the) of a voyage made by certaine ships of Holland into the East Indies, who set forth on the second of April, 1595, and returned on the 14th of August 1597. Translated out of Dutch by W. P. [W— Philip]. Folio. [Watt's *Bibl. Brit.*]
London, 1598

DESCRIPTION (a) of barrow digging on Breach Downs. [A satirical ballad : by Mrs T. Crofton Croker, *née* Marianne Nicholson.] 8vo. [Smale's *Whitby Authors*, p. 114.]
Whitby, private print, 1844

DESCRIPTION (a) of Blackpool, in Lancashire ; frequented for sea bathing. [By William Hutton.] 8vo. Pp. 57. [*Bodl.*]   Birmingham, 1789

DESCRIPTION (a) of Blenheim, the seat of his Grace the Duke of Marlborough : containing a full and accurate account of the paintings, tapestry, and furniture ; a picturesque tour of the gardens and park ; a general delineation of the china gallery, private gardens, etc. ; to which are also added, an itinerary ; an account of the Roman villa, near Northleigh, etc. etc. : with a preliminary essay on landscape gardening. [By Rev. William Fordyce Mavor, LL.D.] Twelfth edition, improved ; embellished with an elegant plan of the park, six new engravings on steel, etc. etc. 8vo. Pp. 147. [*Bodl.*] Oxford, N.D.

The first edition appeared in 1787, with the following title : Blenheim, a poem. To which is added, a Blenheim guide. Inscribed to their Graces the Duke and Duchess of Marlborough. By the Rev. William Mavor. The 12th ed. wants the poem.

DESCRIPTION (the) of Britain, translated [by H— Hatcher] from Richard of Cirencester; with the original treatise, De situ Britanniæ ; and a commentary on the Itinerary [by T— Leman]. 8vo. [*Brit. Mus.*] London, 1809

DESCRIPTION of Brownsholme Hall, in the West Riding of the County of York ; and of the parish of Waddington, in the same county : also a collection of letters, from original manuscripts, in the reigns of Charles I and II and James II. . . . [Compiled by T. L. Parker.] 4to. Private print. [*W.*] London, 1815

Attributed also to T. D. Whitaker.

DESCRIPTION (a) of Brunswick, in letters. By a gentleman of South Carolina [Henry Putnam] to a friend in that State. 8vo. [Cushing's *Init. and Pseud.*, ii., 66.] Brunswick, 1820

DESCRIPTION of Chasseloup de Laubat's System of fortification, as executed at Alessandria. By an Officer of the Corps of Royal Engineers [John Shortall Macaulay]. 8vo. [*Brit. Mus.*] London, 1833

DESCRIPTION (the) of Epsom, with the humors and politicks of the place ; in a letter to Eudoxa. [By John Toland.] There is added a translation of four letters out of Pliny. 8vo. London, 1711

Signed " Britto-Batavus."
Also inserted in the second volume of his Posthumous Works ; but so much is corrected, enlarged, and explained, that the author entitled this tract " A new description of Epsom." [*Upcott.*]

DESCRIPTION (the) of Greece by Pausanias, translated from the Greek [by Thomas Taylor] ; with notes in which much of the mythology of the Greeks is unfolded from a theory which has been for many ages unknown. Second edition. 3 vols. 8vo. [*Sig. Lib. Cat.*] London, 1824

The first edition appeared in 1794.

DESCRIPTION (a) of Kentucky in North America ; to which are prefixed miscellaneous observations respecting the United States. [By Harry Toulmin.] 8vo. Pp. 121. [*Brit. Mus.*] London, 1792

DESCRIPTION of Killarney. [By —— Dunn.] 8vo. Dublin, 1776

DESCRIPTION (a) of Latium or la Campagna di Roma ; with etchings by the author [Ellis Cornelia Knight]. 4to. Pp. xii., 268. [*Brit. Mus.*] London, 1805

DESCRIPTION of Manchester : giving an historical account of those limits in which the town was formerly included. . . . By a native of the town [James Ogden]. Fcap 8vo. Pp. 94. [*Manch. Free Lib. Cat.*] Manchester, 1783

Attributed also to —— Low.

DESCRIPTION (a) of Millenium Hall, and the country adjacent ; together with the characters of the inhabitants, and such historical anecdotes and reflections as may excite in the reader proper sentiments of humanity, and lead the mind to the love of virtue. By a gentleman on his travels [Oliver Goldsmith]. Fcap 8vo. Pp. 262. London, 1762

This work bears strong internal evidence that Goldsmith wrote it (for the publishing firm of E. Newbery) ; but the authorship is also attributed by some to Christopher Smart, by others to Mrs. Sarah Scott and Lady Barbara Montagu.

DESCRIPTION (a) of Mr D——n's [John Dryden's] Funeral : a poem. [By Thomas Browne.] 8vo. [*Brit. Mus.*] London, 1700

DESCRIPTION (a) of new philosophical furnaces ; or a new art of distilling. By John Rudolph Glauber. Set forth in English by J. F. [John French], M.D. 8vo. London, 1651

DESCRIPTION of Orkney, Zetland, Pightland Firth, and Caithness. [By John Brand.] 8vo. [Cursiter's *Books on Orkney and Shetland.*] Edinburgh, 1701

DESCRIPTION (a) of Patagonia and the adjoining parts of South America ; containing an account of the soil, produce, animals, vales, mountains, rivers, lakes, etc., of those countries. By T. F. [Thomas Falkner, S.J.]. 4to. Pp. 144. [*Brit. Mus.*] Hereford, 1774

DESCRIPTION (a) of St Kilda, the most western isle of Scotland : giving an account of its situation, extent, soil, product, bay, and adjacent islands or rocks ; the ancient and modern government, religion, and customs of the inhabitants ; and other curiosities of art and nature : also their late reformation (*sic*). [By Rev. Alexander Buchan.] 8vo. [*Edin. Univ. Cat.*]   Edinburgh, 1727
Another edition appeared in 1752.

DESCRIPTION (a) of the antiquities and curiosities in Wilton House ; illustrated with twenty-five engravings of some of the capital statues, bustos, and relievos. In this work are introduced the anecdotes and remarks of Thomas Earl of Pembroke, who collected these antiques, now first published from his lordship's MSS. [By James Kennedy.] 4to. [*W.*]
Sarum, 1786

DESCRIPTION of the armorial bearings, portraits, and busts in the Mitchell Hall and picture-gallery, Marischal College, Aberdeen. By E. A. [Ellinor Arnott]. 8vo. [Mitchell and Cash's *Scot. Top.*, i., 26.]
Aberdeen, 1896

DESCRIPTION of the Beauchamp Chapel, adjoining the Church of St Mary, at Warwick, and the monuments of the Earls of Warwick. [By Richard Gough.] 4to. [*Brit. Mus.*]
London, 1804
A later edition (1809) has the author's name.

DESCRIPTION of the body of man by 10 artificial figures representing the members, and fit termes expressing the same. . . . [By Alexander Read, M.D.] 4to. [*Brit. Mus.*]
London, 1616
Later editions, enlarged, show variations in the title.

DESCRIPTION (a) of the Chanonry of Aberdeen. . . . [By William Orem.] 8vo. [Robertson's *Aberd. Bibl.*]
Aberdeen, 1830

DESCRIPTION (a) of the Church of Christ, with her peculiar priviledges, and also of her commons and intercommoners. . . . By J. H. [John Hetherington]. 4to. Pp. viii., 120. [*Eng. Hist. Rev.*, Jan. 1915.]
London, 1610

DESCRIPTION (a) of the city, college, and cathedral of Winchester ; exhibiting a complete and comprehensive detail of their antiquities and present state : the whole illustrated with several curious and authentic particulars, collected from a manuscript of Anthony Wood, preserved in the Ashmolean Museum at Oxford ; the college and cathedral registers, and other original authorities, never before published. [By Thomas Warton, B.D.] 12mo. Pp. 108.
London, N.D. [1750]
A later issue in 1857, by Sir T. Phillipps, contains additional notes by Warton.

DESCRIPTION of the coast between Aberdeen and Leith. [By William Duncan, Police Treasurer in Aberdeen.] 8vo. Pp. iv., 125. [*The selected writings of John Ramsay, M.A.*, Aberdeen, 1871, p. 168.]
Aberdeen, 1837

DESCRIPTION (a) of the county of Angus, translated from the original Latin of Robert Edward, minister of Murroes. [By Rev. James Traill, of St Cyrus.] 8vo. [*And. Jervise.*]
Dundee, 1793
Reprinted at Edinburgh in 1883.

DESCRIPTION (a) of the eastern coast of the County of Barnstable, Massachusetts, from Cape Cod, or Race Point, to Cape Malebarre. By a member of the Humane Society [Wendell Davis]. 8vo. Pp. 15. [Cushing's *Init. and Pseud.*, i., 189.]
Boston, 1802

DESCRIPTION (a) of the famous Kingdome of Macaria ; shewing its excellent government . . . in a dialogue between a scholar and a traveller. [By Samuel Hartlib.] 4to. [*Brit. Mus.*]   London, 1641

DESCRIPTION of the figures in the chart of ancient armour ; with a sketch of the progress of European armour from the eleventh to the seventeenth century. [By John Hewitt.] Fcap 8vo. [*Adv. Lib.*] London, 1847
Signed " J. H."

DESCRIPTION (a) of the gardens of Lord Viscount Cobham at Stow in Buckinghamshire. [By B—— Seeley.] Fcap 8vo.   Northampton, 1745

DESCRIPTION (a) of the genus Cinchona. [By Aylmer Bourke Lambert.] Large 4to. [*D. N. B.*, vol. 32, p. 7.]
London, 1797

DESCRIPTION of the golden altarpiece for the cathedral of Basle. [By Colonel von Theubet.] 4to. [*Brit. Mus.*]   Paris, 1842

DESCRIPTION (a) of the heart-shrine in Leybourne Church, with some account of Sir Roger de Leyburn, Kt. By L. B. L. [Lambert Blackwell Larking, M.A.]. 8vo. [*Brit. Mus.*] London, 1864

DESCRIPTION (a) of the Lake at Keswick (and the adjacent country) in Cumberland. By a late popular writer [Dr —— Brown]. 8vo. [Anderson's *Brit. Top.*] Kendal, 1771

DESCRIPTION (a) of the Leasowes. By the author of *Letters on the beauties of Hagley*, etc. [Joseph Heely]. Fcap 8vo. [*Brit. Mus.*] London, 1777

DESCRIPTION (the) of the Low Countreys, etc., gathered into an Epitome out of the Historie of Lodouico Guicciardini. [By Thomas Danett.] 8vo. [*W.*; Lowndes' *Bibl. Man.*, p. 954.] London, 1591

DESCRIPTION (a) of the parish of Melrose; in answer to Mr Maitland's queries, sent to each parish of the kingdom. [By Rev. Adam Milne.] 8vo. [Lowndes' *Bibl. Man.*] Edinburgh, 1743

DESCRIPTION (a) of the Province and Bay of Darian. By a well-wisher to the company who lived there nineteen years [Isaac Blackwell]. 4to. [*Bodl.*] Edinburgh, 1699
The preface is signed " I. B."

DESCRIPTION (a) of the Regalia of Scotland. [By Sir Walter Scott.] Pt 8vo. Pp. 34. Edinburgh, 1819
Later editions give the author's name.

DESCRIPTION (a) of the Round-head and Rattlehead. [By John Taylor, the water-poet.] 4to. London, 1642

DESCRIPTION (a) of the scenery of Dunkeld and of Blair in Atholl. [By —— MacCulloch.] 12mo. Pp. 284. [*St Andrews' Univ. Cat.*, p. 166.] London, 1823

DESCRIPTION of the settlement of the Genesee country . . . New York. In a series of letters from a gentleman [Hugh Williamson] to his friend. 8vo. [Cushing's *Init. and Pseud.*, ii., 64.] New York, 1799

DESCRIPTION of the shields of arms recently put up in the hall of Wotton House. [By Sir Charles George Young.] Imp 8vo. Private print, 1823

DESCRIPTION (a) of the Thermolamp invented by Lebon of Paris. Published with remarks by F. A. W. [Frederick Albert Winsor, junior] of London. 4to. Brunswick, 1802
English, French, and German in parallel columns.

DESCRIPTION (a) of three hundred animals : viz., beasts, birds, fishes, serpents, and insects ; with a particular account of the whale-fishery, extracted out of the best authors, illustrated with copper plates. [By T. Boreman.] Fcap 8vo. [*Brit. Mus.*] London, 1730

DESCRIPTION (a) of Tremont House, with architectural illustrations. . . . [By William Havard Eliot.] Large 4to. Boston, [Mass.], 1830

DESCRIPTION (a) of what God hath predestined concerning man, in his creation, transgression, and regeneration ; as also an answere to John Robinson, touching Baptisme. [By John Murton.] 8vo. Pp. 174. [*Brit. Mus.*] London, 1620

DESCRIPTIVE (a) account of the wood-carvings in the Church of St Michael, Cornhill. [By Alfred Thomas Layton.] Fcap 4to. London, 1887

DESCRIPTIVE (a) and historical view of Alnwick, the county town of Northumberland ; and of Alnwick Castle. . . . [By W —— Davison.] Second edition. 8vo. Alnwick, 1822

DESCRIPTIVE and pictorial outlines of geography. . . . [By T— W— Good.] 8vo. Pp. 127. London, [1895]

DESCRIPTIVE (a) catalogue of the ancient British and British-Roman coins. [By J— Doubleday.] Folio. London, [1848]

DESCRIPTIVE (a) catalogue of the minerals, and fossil organic remains of Scarborough and the vicinity, including the line of coast from Hornsea to Mulgrave, and extending into the interior as far as Malton. [By Francis Kendall.] 8vo. Pp. 319. [*Bodl.*] Scarborough, 1816

DESCRIPTIVE (a) catalogue of the original charters, royal grants, monastic chartulary, registers, and other documents constituting the muniments of Battle Abbey ; with papers relating to the families of Browne, Sidney, and Webster. . . . [By Thomas Thorpe.] 8vo. [W. D. Macray's *Cat.*] London, 1835

DESCRIPTIVE (a) catalogue of the pictures forming that portion of Her Majesty's collection deposited in the corridor of Windsor Castle. [By J. H. Glover.] 4to. [*W.*; Martin's *Cat.*] N.P., 1845

DESCRIPTIVE (a) catalogue of the prints of Rembrandt. By an amateur [Thomas Wilson]. 8vo. Pp. 266. London, 1836

DESCRIPTIVE (a) history of the steam-engine. . . . By Robert Stuart [Robert Meikleham]. Fcap 8vo. [*Brit. Mus.*]   London, 1824

DESCRIPTIVE journey through the interior parts of Germany and France, including Paris ; with anecdotes. By a young English peer of the highest rank [Francis Russell, 6th Duke of Bedford]. 12mo. [*Brit. Mus.*]
London, 1786

DESCRIPTIVE mentality, from the head, face, and hand. By Yarmo Vedra [Holmes Whittier Merton]. 8vo. [*Amer. Cat.*] Philadelphia, 1899

DESCRIPTIVE notes on Loch Maree. By J. H. D. [John H— Dixon]. 8vo. [P. J. Anderson's *Inverness Bibl.*]
Inverness, N.D.

DESCRIPTIVE notices of some of the ancient parochial and collegiate churches of Scotland. [By Thomas S. Muir.] With illustrations on wood, by Jewitt. 8vo. Pp. xxxii., 148. [*Brit. Mus.*]   London, 1848
The introduction is signed " T. S. M."

DESCRIPTIVE (a) tour in Scotland ; by C. H. T. [Rev. Chauncy Hare Townshend, M.A.]. 8vo. [Mitchell and Cash's *Scott. Topog.*]
Brussels, 1840

DESCRIPTIVE (a) tour to the lakes of Cumberland and Westmoreland in the autumn of 1804. [By Benjamin Travers.] 12mo. [*Upcott.*]
London, 1806

DESECRATED (the) Chancel. [By William Maskell, M.A.] 8vo. [*Brit. Mus.*]   London, [1864 ?]

DESERT (the) island ; a dramatic poem, in three acts : as it is acted at the Theatre-Royal in Drury-Lane. [By Arthur Murphy.] 8vo. [*Biog. Dram.*]   London, 1760

DESERT (the) journey. By the author of *Mothers in Council* [Harriet Bickersteth, later Mrs Cook]. 8vo. [*Brit. Mus.*]   London, [1866]

DESERT life : recollections of an expedition in the Soudan. By B. Soligmos [B— E— Falkonberg]. 8vo. Pp. xi., 382.   London, 1880

DESERT (the) world. From the French of Arthur Moingin ; edited and enlarged by the translator of " The bird, by Michelet " [William H. D. Adams]. 8vo. London, 1869
The addition to the preface is signed " A."

DESERTED (the) city ; a poem [describing Bath during summer. By Edward Mangin.] 4to. [Green's *Bibl. Somers.*, i., p. 333.]   Bath, 1805
The dedication is signed " E. M."

DESERTED (the) daughter ; a comedy, as it is acted at the Theatre Royal, Covent-Garden. [By Thomas Holcroft.] 8vo. Pp. 86. [*Biog. Dram.*]
London, 1795

DESERTED (the) village school ; a poem. [By Rev. Richard Polwhele.] 8vo.   London, 1813

DESERTER (the). By Charlotte Elizabeth [Charlotte Elizabeth Tonna, previously Mrs Phelan]. Fcap 8vo. [*Brit. Mus.*]   Dublin, 1836

DESERTION (the) [of the British throne by James II.] discuss'd ; in a letter to a country gentleman. [By Jeremy Collier.] No title page. 4to. [*Brit. Mus.*]   London, 1689
Edmund Bohun followed with " An Answer to The Desertion discuss'd," and William Snatt similarly with " Mr Collier's Desertion discuss'd."

DESIDERATUM (the) : or, electricity made plain and useful. By a lover of mankind and common sense [John Wesley]. 8vo. [Osborn's *Wesl. Bibl.*].
London 1759

DESIGN and prospectus for a National Gallery of history and art at Washington. [By Franklin W. Smith.] 4to. Pp. 104.   [Washington], 1891

DESIGN (the) of enslaving England discovered in the incroachments upon the powers and privileges of Parliament, by K. Charles II. Being a new corrected impression of that excellent piece, intituled, A just and modest vindication of the proceedings of the two last Parliaments of King Charles the Second. [By Robert Ferguson.] 4to. [*Bodl.*]   London, 1689
Ascribed also to Algernon Sydney.

DESIGN (the) of love. Written [in verse] by E. B. [George W— Parker]. Pp. xxxii., 562.   London, [1893]

DESIGN (the) of part of the Book of Ecclesiastes ; or, the unreasonableness of men's restless contentions for the present enjoyments, represented in an English poem. [By William Wollaston.] 8vo. [Todd's *Life of Milton*, p. 203.]   London, 1691
Preface signed " W. W."

DESIGNE (a) for bringing a navigable river from Rickmansworth in Hartfordshire to St Gyles in the Fields ; the benefits of it declared, and the objections against it answered. [By —— Ford.] 4to. [*Bodl.*]   London, 1641

DESIGNE (a) for plentie, by an universall planting of fruit-trees ; tendred by some well-wishers to the Publick [Samuel Hartlib]. Fcap 4to. [Watt's *Bibl. Brit.*]   London, [c. 1652]

DESIGN for Church embroidery. By [Miss] A[—] R[isdale], with letterpress by Alithia Wiel. 4to.   London, 1894

DESK (the) and the counter. Young men engaged in trade urged to self exertion for advancement in true dignity and excellence. By a fellow labourer [John Maclaren]. . . . 8vo.
Edinburgh, 1844
Information from the author.

DESOLATE (the) soul; poems for Holy Week. By Maria Monica [Mrs H— E— Hamilton King]. Fcap 8vo. [*Aberd. Free Lib. Cat.*]   London, 1897

DESOLATE (the) state of France demonstrated; or evident proofs that one half of the people of that kingdom are destroyed, two-thirds of its capital stock consumed, and the nation reduc'd to such a condition that it cannot be restored to the flourishing condition it was in thirty years ago, in less than two hundred years. . . . [By —— de Soligné: translated by George Ridpath.] 8vo.   London, 1697
A similar work, by the same author, was published in 1698, entitled, " The political mischief of Popery. . . ."

DESOLATION (the) of America; a poem. [By Thomas Day.] 4to. [Watt's *Bibl. Brit.*]   London, 1777

DESPERADOES (the) of the South-West [in the United States]; containing an account of the Cane-Hill murders. By Charles Summerfield [Theodore Foster]. 8vo. [Cushing's *Init. and Pseud.*, i., 277.]
New York, 1847

DESPERATE (a) adventure; and other stories. By Max Adeler [Charles Heber Clark]. Fcap 8vo. Pp. viii., 225. [*Brit. Mus.*]   London, [1886]

DESPERATE remedies: a novel. [By Thomas Hardy.] 3 vols. Cr 8vo. [*Camb. Univ. Lib.*]   London, 1871

DESPOT (the) of Broomsedge Cove. By Charles Egbert Craddock [Mary Noailles Murfree]. Pt 8vo.   Kirk's *Supp.*. p. 1157.]   Boston, 1889

DESPOTISM; or the fate of the Jesuits; a political romance, illustrated by historical anecdotes. [By Isaac D'Israeli.] 2 vols. 8vo. Pagination continuous. [*Bodl.*]   London, 1811

DESPOTISM; or, the last days of the American Republic. By Invisible Sam [Reuben Vose?]. 8vo. [Cushing's *Init. and Pseud.*, i., 260.]
New York, 1856

DESSERT (the); a poem; to which is added the Tea. By the author of *The banquet* [Hans Busk, senior]. 8vo. Pp. x., 109. [*Brit. Mus.*]
London, 1819

DESTINATION; or memoirs of a private family. [By Clara Reeve.] Fcap 8vo. [*D. N. B.*, vol. 47, p. 405.]
London, 1799

DESTINY (the) of Claude. By May Wynne [Mabel Wynne Knowles]. Cr 8vo. Pp. 314.   London, 1919

DESTINY of the human race; a Scriptural enquiry. By the author of *The study of the Bible* [Henry Dunn]. 2 vols. Cr 8vo.   London, 1863

DESTINY; or, the chief's daughter. By the author of *Marriage*, etc. [Susan Edmonstone Ferrier]. 3 vols. Fcap 8vo. [*D. N. B.*, vol. 8, p. 39.]
Edinburgh, 1831

DESTITUTION in the Highlands [of Scotland]. Letters on the present condition of the Highlands and Islands of Scotland. [By James Bruce.] Reprinted from *The Scotsman*. 8vo. Pp. 83. [*Brit. Mus.*]   Edinburgh,1847

DESTROYER (the); a novel. By Benjamin Swift [William Romaine Paterson]. Cr 8vo. [*Brit. Mus.*]
London, 1896

DESTRUCTION (the) of Gotham. By Joaquin Miller [Cincinnatus Heine Miller]. Pt 8vo. Pp. 214. [Cushing's *Init. and Pseud.*, i., p. 194.]
New York, 1886

DESTRUCTION (the) of Jerusalem, an absolute and irresistible proof of the divine origin of Christianity; including a narrative of the calamities which befel the Jews, as far as they tend to verify our Lord's predictions relative to that event. . . . [By George Peter Holford, M.P., barrister-at-law.] 8vo. Pp. iv., 96. [*Gent. Mag.*, Sept. 1839, p. 318.]   London, 1805

DESTRUCTION (the) of the French foretold by Ezekiel; or, a commentary on the thirty-fifth chapter of that prophet: intended as a specimen of Mr Romaine's manner of interpreting Scripture. [By John Douglas, D.D.] 8vo. [Watt's *Bibl. Brit.*]
London, [1756]

DESTRUCTION (the) of Troy; an essay upon the second book of Virgil's Æneis. Written in the year 1636. [By Sir John Denham.] 4to. [*Brit. Mus.*]   London, 1656
A translation into English verse of the second Book of the Æneid.

DESTRUCTION (the) of Troy; in three Books. 1. Shewing the founders of the City, with the manner how it was sacked and first destroyed by Hercules. 2. How it was re-edified, and how Hercules slew King Laomedon and destroyed it the second time; and of Hercules's death. 3. How Priamus, son of Laomedon, rebuilded Troy;

and for the ravishment of Dame Helen, wife to K. Menelaus, the city was utterly destroyed, and Priamus and Hector and his sons killed. The twelfth edition. . . . [By Robert Le Fevre.] 4to. [Arber's *Term Cat.*, iii., 684.] London, 1702

DESULTORY pieces in prose and verse. By E. L. [Mrs Lydia Lillybridge Simons, Missionary in Burmah]. Royal 8vo. Pp. 320. Calcutta, 1846

DESULTORY reflections on banks in general, and the system of keeping up a false capital, by accommodation paper, so much resorted to by monopolists and speculators ; divided into three parts, or essays. . . . By Danmoniensis [William Burt]. Fcap 8vo. [*Adv. Lib.*] London, 1810

DESULTORY reflections on the new political aspects of public affairs in the United States of America, since the commencement of the year 1799. [By John Ward Fenno.] 2 Parts. 8vo. [*Brit. Mus.*] New York, 1800

DESULTORY reminiscences of a tour through Germany, Switzerland, and France. By an American [Hezekiah Hartley Wright]. 8vo. Pp. xx., 364. [*Brit. Mus.*] Boston, 1838

DESULTORY thoughts on the national drama. By an old play-goer [Major-General Samuel Parlby]. 8vo. London, 1850

DETACHED musings on the organic, physical, and other causes which operate in the formation of the various opinions and characteristics of men. By an old cosmopolite [John Davidson]. Fcap 8vo. Pp. 193. London, [1857]

DETACHED thoughts. By J. S. [Joseph Sykes, M.A.]. To which are added, three short essays on matters which society should avoid. 8vo. Pp. 92. [*Brit. Mus.*] Brighton, 1865

DETAIL and conduct of the American War ; with a full and correct view of the evidence as given before the House of Commons. [By General Sir William Howe.] 8vo. [*D. N. B.*, vol. 28, p. 104.] London, [1780]

DETAILS of the arrest, imprisonment, and liberation of an Englishman, by the Bourbon government of France. [By Sir John Bowring.] 8vo. [*D.N.B.*, vol. 6, p. 76.] London, 1823

DETECTION of a conspiracy formed by the United Irishmen, with the evident intention of aiding the tyrants of France in subverting the government of the United States of America. By Peter Porcupine [William Cobbett]. 8vo. [*Bodl.*] Dublin, 1799

DETECTION (the) of infamy ; earnestly recommended to the justice and deliberation of the imperial Parliament of Great Britain. By an unfortunate nobleman. [By Thomas Christopher Banks.] 8vo. [*Gent. Mag.*, Feb. 1855, p. 207.] London, 1816

DETECTION of the deuils sophistrie, wherwith he robbeth the unlearned people of the true byleefe in the most blessed sacrament of the aulter. [By Stephen Gardiner, Bishop of Winchester.] Fcap 8vo. [*D. N. B.*, vol. 20, p. 424.] [London], 1546

DETECTION (a) of the love-letters lately attributed in Hugh Campbell's work to Mary Queen of Scots ; wherein his plagiarisms are proved, and his fictions fixed. [By George Chalmers.] 8vo. [*Camb. Univ. Lib.*] London, 1825

DETECTIOUN (ane) of the doingis of Marie Quene of Scottis, tuiching the murther of hir husband, and hir conspiracie, adulterie, and pretensit mariage with the Erle Bothwell. And ane defence of the trew Lordis, mantenaris of the Kingis Grace actioun and authoritie. Translatit out of the Latine quhilk was writtin be M. G. B. [George Buchanan]. 8vo. B. L. [Lowndes' *Bibl. Man.*] Sanctandrois, Anno Do. 1572

DETECTIVE (the) officer; and other tales. By "Waters" [William Russell]. 8vo. [*Brit. Mus.*] London, 1878

A modified edition of the author's "Recollections of a Detective Police-officer" (1875).

DETECTIVE'S (the) daughter ; or Madeline Payne. By Lawrence L. Lynch [Emma M. Murdoch, later Mrs. F. M. Van Deventer]. Cr 8vo. [*Brit. Mus.*] London, 1904

DETECTIVE'S (a) triumphs. By Dick Donovan [Joyce E. P. Muddock]. Cr 8vo. Pp. 310. [*Brit. Mus.*] London, 1891

DETECTOR (the) of quackery ; or analyser of medical, philosophical, political, dramatic, and literary imposture. By an observer [John Corry]. Fcap 8vo. London, 1802

Later editions give the author's name.

DEUCE (the) is in him : a farce of two acts, as it is performed at the Theatre Royal in Drury Lane. [By George Colman.] 8vo. Pp. 47. [*Biog. Dram.*] London, 1763

DEUS justificatus ; or the divine good-
ness vindicated and cleared, against
the assertors of absolute and incon-
ditionate reprobation : together with
some reflections on a late discourse of
Mr Parkers concerning the divine
dominion and goodness. [By Henry
Hallywell.] 8vo. Pp. xxxii., 280, iii.
[*N. and Q.*, 1851, p. 195.]
London, 1668
Also ascribed, doubtfully, to Laurence
Womock, D.D.

DEUTEROMELIA ; or, the second
part of Musicks melodie, or melo-
dius musicke of pleasant roundelaies.
. . . [By Thomas Ravenscroft.] 4to.
[*D.N.B.*, vol. 47, p. 318.]
London, 1609
Signed " T. R."

DEUTERONOMY the people's book ;
its origin and nature : a defence.
[By James Sime, M.A., of Craig-
mount, Edinburgh.] Pt 8vo. Pp.
viii., 295. [*New Coll. Cat.*]
London, 1877

DEUTSCHE Liebe : German love.
Translated by G. A. M. [Georgiana
Adelaide Mueller]. 8vo. [*Brit. Mus.*]
London, 1884

DEVELOPERS [in photography] ; their
use and abuse. By Richard Penlake
[Percy R— Salmon]. 8vo. Pp. 64.
[*Brit. Mus.*] Bradford, 1895

DEVELOPMENT (the) of English
literature : the Old English period.
By Brother Azarias [P. F. Mullany].
8vo. [Cushing's *Init. and Pseud.*, i.,
22.] New York, 1879

DEVEREUX ; a tale. By the author
of *Pelham*. [Edward George Earle
Lytton Bulwer-Lytton, Baron Lytton].
3 vols. 12mo. [*Brit. Mus.*]
London, 1829

DEVICE (the) of the pageant borne
before Woolstone Dixi, Lord Maior
of the citie of London. An. 1585.
October 29. [By G. Peele.] 4to. No
pagination. B. L. [*Bodl.*]
London, 1585

DEVIIL incarnate, or a satyr upon a
satyr ; being a display of the hairy
devill, countess of Bedlam. [By Joane
Fisher.] 4to. Pp. 8. [*Bodl.*]
N.P., N.D.
The author's name is given by Wood.

DEVIL (the). [Twelve lectures. By
John Epps, M.D.] 8vo. [*Brit. Mus.*]
London, [1842]

DEVIL (the) and the dying Church.
By F. G. W. [F— G. Willatt]. Pp. 20.
[*Brit. Mus.*] High Wycombe, 1912

DEVIL (the) and the inventor. By
Austin Fryers [William Edward Clery].
Pt 8vo. [*Lond. Lib. Cat.*]
London, 1900

DEVIL (the) doctor ; hitherto unpublished adventures in the career of
mysterious Dr Fu-Manchu. By Sax
Rohmer [Arthur Sarsfield Ward]. Cr
8vo. Pp. 614. London, 1916

DEVIL (the) in love. Translated from
the French [of Jacques Cazotte].
[Barbier's *Dictionnaire*, 3562 ; *Brit.
Mus.*] Fcap 8vo. Pp. vii., 170.
London, 1794

DEVIL (the) is dead ; and Scenes in
General Dayton's garden. By the
author of *Real people* [Marrion Wil-
cox]. 8vo. Pp. viii., 382. [*Brit.
Mus.*] London, 1889

DEVIL (the) of a duke ; or, Trapolin's
vagaries : a (farcical ballad) opera, as
it is acted at the Theatre-Royal in
Drury-Lane. To which is prefix'd the
musick to each song. . . . [By Robert
Drury.] 8vo. [*Brit. Mus.*]
London, 1732
An adaptation from Nahum Tate's
" Duke and No Duke."

DEVIL (the) of a wife ; or a comical
transformation : a drama. [By
Thomas Jevon.] 8vo.
London, 1715
The author's name is given in other
editions.

DEVIL (the) to pay at St James's ; or,
a full and true account of a most
horrid and bloody battle between
Madam Faustina and Madam Cuzzoni :
also of a hot skirmish between Signor
Boschi and Signor Palmacini : more-
over, how Senesino has taken snuff, is
going to leave the opera, and sing
psalms at Hanley's oratory : also
about the flying man, and how the
Doctor of St Martin's has very un-
kindly taken down the scaffold, and
disappointed a world of good company.
[By John Arbuthnot, M.D. ?] 4to.
London, 1727
The author's name, with a query, is in
the handwriting of Dr David Laing.

DEVIL (the) to pay ; or, the wives
metamorphos'd : an opera, as it is
perform'd at the theatres. [By C.
Coffey.] Fifth edition. 8vo. Pp. 28.
[*Biog. Dram.*] London, 1733

DEVIL (the) unmasked. By the little
deacon [N. B. Cooksey]. Fcap 8vo.
[*Amer. Cat.*] New York, 1900

DEVIL (the) upon two sticks. [By
Alain René Le Sage.] Translated
from the last edition at Paris, with
several additions. Cr 8vo. [Watt's
Bibl. Brit.] London, 1708
See also " Diable (le) boiteux."

DEVIL (the) upon two sticks in England : being a continuation of " Le Diable boiteux " of Le Sage. [By William Coombe.] 4 vols. 12mo. [*Gent. Mag.*, May 1852, p. 467.]
London, 1790

DEVILIAD (the) ; an heroic poem. [By —— Taswell.] 4to. [*Brit. Mus.*]
London, 1744

A satire on Sir Thomas Deveil.

DEVILISH (the) conspiracy, hellish treason, heathenish condemnation and damnable murder committed and executed by the Jewes against the Anointed of the Lord, Christ their King. . . . A sermon on the 4th Feb. 1648 [1649]. [By John Gauden, D.D., afterwards Bishop of Canterbury.] Fcap 4to. Pp. 45. [*D. N. B.*, vol. 21, p. 69.] London, 1648 [1649]

A veiled attack on those who took part in the execution of Charles I. It was reprinted later, with the author's name and various titles.

DEVIL'S (the) bargain. By Florence Warden [Florence Alice Price, later Mrs George E. James]. 8vo. Pp. 320. [*Brit. Mus.*] London, 1908

DEVIL'S (the) bridge : an operatic drama, in three acts. [By Samuel James Arnold.] 8vo. Pp. 24. [*Brit. Mus.*] London, [1825 ?]

DEVIL'S (the) die. By Cecil Power [Charles Grant Blairfindie Allen]. Fcap 8vo. [*D. N. B.*, *First Supp.*, vol. 1, p. 37.] London, 1891

DEVIL'S (the) due ; a letter to the editor of " The Examiner." By Thomas Maitland [Algernon Charles Swinburne]. Pt 8vo. [*D. N. B.*, *Second Supp.*, vol. 3, p. 462.]
Private print, 1875

DEVIL'S (the) due ; a novel. By Mark Allerton [William Ernest Cameron, LL.B.]. Cr 8vo. Pp. 186. [*Lit. Year Book.*] London, 1919

DEVIL'S (the) half-acre ; a novel. By " Alien " [Mrs L— A— Baker]. 8vo. Pp. 290. [*Lit. Year Book.*]
London, 1900

DEVILS (the) patriarck ; or a full and impartial account of the notorious life of this present Pope of Rome, Innocent the 11th : wherein is newly discovered his rise and reign ; the time and manner of his being chosen Pope ; his prime procession, consecration and coronation ; the splendour and grandeur of his court ; his most eminent and gainful cheats, by which he gulls the silly people ; his secret and open transactions with the papists in England, Scotland, France and Ireland, and other Protestant countreys to this very day. . . . [By Christopher Nesse.] 8vo. Pp. 148. [*Bodl.*]
London, 1683

The preface is signed T. O.—query, Titus Oates ? The book was printed for John Dunton.

DEVIL'S (the) plough ; a novel. By Margaret Allston [Mrs Anna Farquhar]. Pt 8vo. [*Amer. Cat.*]
New York, 1901

DEVIL'S (the) pool [a novel depicting rural life]. By George Sand [Madame Amandine L. A. Dudevant]. Translated from the French. 8vo. [*Brit. Mus.*] London, 1895

DEVIL'S (the) roar about religious liberty in Tuscany, echoed by Hugh Stowell and Co. at the Corn Exchange in Manchester, Oct. 13, 1853. [By W— E— Stutter.] Fcap 8vo.
Manchester, 1853

Signed " W. E. S."

DEVIL'S (the) visit : why he came, what he said, why he left, and the present he sent. [By Dr F— Hollick.] Square 12mo. New York, N.D.

DEVIL'S (the) wind. [A novel.] By Patricia Wentworth [Mrs —— Dillon, *née* D— O. Ellis]. Cr 8vo. Pp. 352.
London, 1912

DEVIL-TREE (the) of El Dorado ; a romance of British Guiana, etc. By Frank Aubrey [Frank Atkins]. 8vo. Pp. xx., 392. London, 1896

DEVONSHIRE sketches ; Dartmoor and its borders. By Tickler [George P. R. Pulman]. Fcap 8vo. Pp. 132. [*Brit. Mus.*] Exeter, 1869

DEVOTED (the). By the authoress of *The disinherited*, etc. [Lady Charlotte Maria Bury]. 3 vols. Fcap 8vo. [*Brit. Mus.*] London, 1836

DEVOTED (the) legions ; a poem, addressed to Lord George Germaine, and the commanders of the forces against America. [By Thomas Day.] Second edition. 4to. [Watt's *Bibl. Brit.*] London, 1776

DEVOTEE (the) ; a tale. [By Robert Mackenzie Beverley.] 8vo.
Cambridge, 1823

DEVOTIONAL aspiration. By Effie Johnson [Euphemie Johnson Richmond]. 8vo. Pp. 184. [*Lond. Lib. Cat.*]
London, 1906

DEVOTIONAL (a) diary. By the author of *Visiting my relations*, etc. [Mary Ann Kelty]. 8vo. [*Brit. Mus.*] London, 1854

DEVOTIONAL exercises ; consisting of reflections and prayers, for the use of young persons ; to which is added a treatise on the Lord's Supper. By a lady [Harriet Martineau]. Fcap 8vo. [*D. N. B.*, vol. 36, p. 313.]
London, 1823
The first publication of the authoress.

DEVOTIONAL exercises for schools and families. By J. T. B. [Joseph Tinker Buckingham]. 8vo. [Cushing's *Init. and Pseud.*, i., 26.]
Boston, 1844

DEVOTIONAL (the) life render'd familiar, easy, and pleasant, in several hymns. . . . Composed and collected by T. S. [Rev. Thomas Seaton, M.A.]. Fcap 8vo.   London, 1734

DEVOTIONAL lines ; or prayers and meditations in a metrical form. [By Ambrose Dawson, B.D.] Pp. 183. [*Bodl.*]   Chester, 1847

DEVOTIONAL offices for public worship, collected from various services, in use among Protestant Dissenters. To which are added Two services, chiefly collected from the Book of Common Prayer. [By Thos. Howe, Unitarian minister at Bridport.] Pp. 270.   Shrewsbury, 1795

DEVOTIONAL pieces from the Psalms and Job ; with thoughts on devotional taste, sects, etc. [By Mrs Anna Letitia Barbauld, *née* Aikin.] Fcap 8vo. [*Brit. Mus.*]   London, 1775

DEVOTIONAL services for the public worship of the one true God. . . . [By Rev. William Blake, of Crewkerne.] Fcap 8vo.   Sherborne, 1812

DEVOTIONS . . . [Verse]. By R. A. [Robert Aylett], D.L. 8vo. [*Brit. Mus.*]   London, 1655

DEVOTIONS : a daily office for the sick, compiled out of the Holy Scripture and the Liturgy of our Church. [By Rev. Zachary Isham, D.D.] 8vo. [Courtney's *Secrets*, p. 40.]
London, 1699

DEVOTIONS before and after Holy Communion. [By Miss M. French.] 8vo. Pp. 121.   Oxford, 1865
With preface by " J. K." [John Keble].

DEVOTIONS. First part ; in the antient way of Offices : with Psalms, hymns, and pray'rs ; for every day in the week, and every holiday in the year. [By John Austin.] Second edition, corrected and augmented [and posthumously edited by John Sergeant]. 12mo. Pp. 479. Roan, 1672
The place and the date of the first issue are unknown, but a third edition was published at Paris in 1675, and a fourth at " Roan " in 1685.
An edition (" Devotions in the ancient

way of offices . . ."), prepared anonymously for use in the English Church, through removal of Romish peculiarities, by Mrs Susannah Hopton, was first issued in 1701 with a preface by Dr George Hickes. Even more extensive alterations, however, were made earlier by Theophilus Dorrington in the edition which he published as " Reformed devotions, in meditations, hymns, and petitions. . . ."

DEVOTIONS commemorative of the Passion ; with the office of Tenebræ. [By Rev. Frederick Oakeley, M.A.] Fcap 8vo. [*D. N. B.*, vol. 41, p. 287.]
London, 1842

DEVOTIONS for Advent, Christmas, and the Epiphany. . . . By H. V. [Herbert Vaughan, D.D.]. Pt 8vo. [*Brit. Mus.*]   London, 1867

DEVOTIONS for daily use. By C. L. C. [Hon. Charles Leslie Courtenay]. 12mo. [*Brit. Mus.*]   London, 1875

DEVOTIONS for the Sacrament of the Lord's Supper ; with an appendix, containing a method of digesting the Book of Psalms, so as to be applicable to the common occurrences of life. By a layman [Thomas Falconer, of Chester]. 8vo. [*Brit. Mus.*]
Warrington, 1786

DEVOTIONS for the sick and for prisoners. [By John Gother.] 12mo. [W. D. Macray's *Cat.*]   N.P., 1756

DEVOTIONS for the sick room, and for times of trouble ; compiled from ancient liturgies and the writings of holy men. [By Robert Brett.] 12mo. Pp. xiv., 263.   London, 1743
The " Advertisement" is signed " R. B."

DEVOTIONS for the three hours of the Agony. [By the Rev. Thomas Isaac Ball.] Fcap 8vo. Pp. 40.
London, 1865

DEVOTIONS in the ancient way of offices. . . . *See, above*, the note appended to " Devotions : First part. . . ."

DEVOTIONS (the) of Bishop [Lancelot] Andrewes ; translated from the Greek, by Dean Stanhope. [Edited by George Horne, D.D., Bishop of Norwich.] 12mo. [*W.*]   London, 1798

DEVOTIONS (the) of Bishop [Lancelot] Andrewes, translated from the Greek and arranged anew. [By John Henry Newman.] Pt 8vo. Pp. vi., 169. [*D. N. B.*, vol. 1, p. 405.]
Oxford, 1848
The Preface is signed " J. H. N." This translation previously appeared as No. 88 of " Tracts for the Times."

DEVOTIONS of the ancient Church, in seven pious prayers. . . . [By Nicholas Bernard.] 8vo. [Watt's *Bibl. Brit.*]
London, 1660

DEVOTIONS to be used by Primitive Catholicks, at Church and at home : in two parts. [By Thomas Deacon, nonjuring Bishop ?] 8vo. Pp. xxvi., 152. [*New Coll. Cat.*]
Liverpool, 1747
Each part has a separate title, but the pagination is continuous throughout.

DEVOUT (the) Christian instructed how to pray and give thanks to God ; or devotions for families, and for particular persons in most of the concerns of humane life. By the author of the *Christian sacrifice* [Symon Patrick]. 12mo. [Arber's *Term Cat.*, i., 522.]
London, 1672
Reprinted in collected works.

DEVOUT (the) Christian's daily companion ; being a selection of pious exercises for the use of Catholics. [By Charles Aylmer, Paul Ferley, and Bartold Esmer, S.J.] Fcap 8vo. [Sommervogel's *Dictionnaire*.]
Palermo, 1812

DEVOUT (the) Christian's hourly companion ; consisting of holy prayers and divine meditations. By H. Drexelius. Done into English [by Robert Samber]. Second edition. Fcap 8vo. [*Brit. Mus.*]   London, 1716

DEVOUT (the) client of Mary instructed . . . how to honour and serve her in the best manner. Written in Italian by R. F. Paul Segneri, S.J., and translated into English by N. N. [Thomas Percy Plowden, S.J.]. 12mo. Pp. 340. [Sommervogel's *Dictionnaire*.]   N.P., 1724

DEVOUT (the) communicant, according to the Church of England. [By J. Ford.] 12mo. [*Brit. Mus.*]
Ipswich, 1815

DEVOUT (the) communicant exemplified in his behaviour before, at, and after the Sacrament of the Lord's Supper ; practically suited to all the parts of that solemn ordinance. [By Abednego Seller.] Seventh edition. 8vo. [Arber's *Term Cat.*, iii., 164.]
London, 1699

DEVOUT (the) companion ; containing prayers and meditations for every day in the week, and for several occasions, ordinary and extraordinary. [By Abednego Seller.] 12mo. [*D. N. B.*, vol. 51, p. 227].   London, 1688

DEVOUT contemplations, expressed in two and fortie sermons upon all ye Quadragesimall Gospells : written in Spanish by F. Ch. de Fonseca ; Englished by I. M. [James Mabbe] of Magdalen Colledge in Oxford. Folio. [*Brit. Mus.*]   London, 1629

DEVOUT entertainments of a Christian soule ; composed in French by . . . I. H. Quarre ; translated by J. [John Paulet], M. Q. [Marquis of Winchester] Prisoner in the Tower of London. 12mo. [*Brit. Mus.*]   Paris, 1648

DEVOUT (the) laugh ; or half an hours amusement to a citizen of London, from Dr Pickering's sermon at St Paul's, Jan. 30, 1749-50 ; and the compliments paid him by the Lord Mayor and aldermen, etc. The loyalty of the Doctor and the merit of his sermon are made conspicuous, and very entertaining. A letter from Rusticus to Civis. [By Caleb Fleming.] 8vo. [*Bodl.*]   London, 1750

DEVOUT meditations ; or, a collection of thoughts upon religious and philosophical subjects. By a person of honour [Charles Howe]. 8vo. [*Adv. Lib.*]   Edinburgh, 1751
Ascribed also to Charles Howard.

DEVOUT (a) paraphrase on the seven penitential Psalms ; or a practical guide to repentance. By * * * * [Francis Blyth]. 12mo. Pp. 103. [*Brit. Mus.*]   [London], 1741

DEVOUT prayers on the life and passion of the Lord Jesus. . . . [By Robert Brett.] 12mo. [*Brit. Mus.*]
London, 1861

DEVOUT (the) soul ; or rules of heavenly devotion ; also, the free Prisoner, or the comfort of restraint. By J. H., B. N. [Joseph Hall, Bishop of Norwich]. 12mo. [*Brit. Mus.*]
London, 1644

DEW of Hermon ; or, Zion's daily sacrifice. By a son of consolation [Richard Burdon Sanderson]. Fcap 8vo. [*Brit. Mus.*] Edinburgh, [1854]

DEW (the) of Hermon which fell upon the Hill of Sion ; or an answer to a book entituled, Sions groans for her distressed, etc. offered to the Kings Majesty, Parliament, and people : wherein is pretended to be proved by Scripture, reason, and authority of fifteen ancients, that equal protection under different perswasions, is the undoubted right of Christian liberty ; but hereby confuted, wherein the power and proceedings of the kings Majesty and the Church are vindicated. [By Henry Savage, D.D., Master of Balliol.] 4to. Pp. 93. [*D. N. B.*, vol. 50, p. 337.]
London, 1663
Epistle dedicatory signed " H. S."

DEWI Sant. St David. By Owen Rhoscomyl [Owen Vaughan]. Translated by Rev. J. E. Evans. [English and Welsh.] 8vo. Pp. 73.
Merthyr Tydfil, N.D., [1907]

D. F. A.'s [Doctor Francis Atterbury's] vindication of the Bp. of Sarum [Gilbert Burnet] from being the author of a late printed speech ; in a letter to a friend. 4to. [W.] London, 1704

D'HORSAY ; or the follies of the day. By a man of fashion [John Mills, novelist]. 8vo. [Brit. Mus.]
London, 1844

DIA poemata ; poetick feet standing upon holy ground : or verses on certain texts of Scripture. With epigrams, etc. By E. E. [Edmund Ellis or Elys]. 12mo. [Lowndes' Bibl. Man., p. 731.] London, 1655

DIABLE (le) boiteux ; or the Devil upon two sticks. [By Alain René Le Sage.] Translated from the last Paris edition. 2 vols. Fcap 8vo. [Brit. Mus.] London, 1741
See also " Devil (the) upon two sticks."

DIABO-LADY (the) ; or, a match in hell : a poem, dedicated to the worst woman in her Majesty's dominions. [By William Combe.] 4to. [Bodl.]
London, 1777
The dedication is signed " Belphegor."
See also, below, " The Diaboliad, part the second."

DIABOLIAD (the) ; a poem, dedicated to the worst man in His Majesty's dominions. [By William Combe.] A new edition, with large additions. 4to. [Brit. Mus.] London, 1777
—— Part the second. By the author of part the first. [William Combe.] Dedicated to the worst woman in his Majesty's dominions. 4to.
London, 1778

DIACONAL teaching [in the Catholic Apostolic Church] at Mansfield Place, Edinburgh. By T. G. D. [T— G— Dickson]. 8vo. Edinburgh, 1895

DIAL (the) of Ahaz spiritualized. By a layman in the country [David Tucker]. 8vo. Pp. 40. [Brit. Mus.]
Carmarthen, 1770

DIAL of meditation and prayer. . . . [By Mrs L— Edwards.] Second edition. 12mo. [Brit. Mus.] London, 1858
Signed " L. E."

DIALECT (the) of Craven, in the West Riding of the county of York ; with a copious glossary, illustrated by authorities from ancient English and Scottish writers, and exemplified by two familiar dialogues. By a native of Craven [Rev. William Carr]. Second edition, much enlarged. 2 vols. 8vo. [N. and Q., April 1869, p. 342.]
London, 1828
The title of the first edition (1824) begins : " Horae momenta Cravenae. . . ."
See below.

DIALECT (the) of Leeds and its neighbourhood, illustrated by conversations and tales, with glossary. . . . [By C— Clough Robinson.] Pt 8vo.
Leeds, 1862

DIALECT tales. By Sherwood Bonner [Mrs Kate Sherwood Macdowall, née Bonner]. 8vo. [Cushing's Init. and Pseud., i., p. 38.] New York, 1883

DIALL (a), wherein is contained a remembrance of death. [A poem. By William Granger.] 4to. [Thomason Coll. of Tracts, i., 596.] London, 1648

DIALOG (ane), or mutuale talking betwixt a Clerk and ane Courteour, concerning foure parische Kirks till ane minister. [By John Davidson, minister in Prestonpans ; in verse.] 4to. [Scott's Fasti, new edition, i., p. 388.]
Saint Andrews, 1573

DIALOGES (the) in Englishe ; betwene a Docter of Diuinity and a student in the lawes of England : newely corrected and imprinted, with new additions. [By Christopher Saint-Germain.] 8vo. Fol. 176, 4. B. L. [Bodl.] Londini in ædibus Richardi Tottelli anno 1580.
See also " Dyaloges. . . ." and " Doctor and Student. . . ."

DIALOGUE (a) arguing that archbishops, bishops, curates, neuters, are to be cut-off by the law of God ; therefore all these, with their service, are to be cast-out by the law of the land. Notwithstanding, the world pleads for their own, why some bishops should be spared, the government maintained, the name had in honour still ; but the word of God is cleare against all this, for the casting-of-all-forth. The great question is, which way of government now ? for two wayes are contended for, the Presbyteriall and Independent : something is said to both these wayes. . . . Presented to the Assembly of Divines. [By Hezekiah Woodward.] 4to. [Thomason Coll. of Tracts, i., p. 311.] London, 1644
This book was republished with a new title, " The sentence from Scripture and reason against arch-bishops and bishops with their curats," etc. 4to.
[London], 1644

DIALOGUE (a) between A. and B., two plain countrey-gentlemen, concerning the times. [By Rev. Alexander Irvine, of Inverkeithing.] 4to. Pp. 55. [Adv. Lib.] London, 1694

DIALOGUE (a) between a Baptist and a Churchman ; occasioned by the Baptists opening a new meeting-house for reviving old Calvanistical doctrines and spreading Antinomian and other errors, at Birmingham: Part I., by "a Consistent Protestant" [Rev. Samuel Bourn, of Coseley, near Birmingham]; Part II., by "a Consistent Christian" [Rev. Samuel Bourn]. 8vo. [Sparke's *Bibl. Bolt.*, p. 29.]   Birmingham, 1737-39

DIALOGUE (a) between a bilious patient and a physician. By a Fellow of the College of Physicians, Dublin [James Henry, M.D.]. 8vo. [*Brit. Mus.*]   Dublin, 1838

DIALOGUE (a) between a captain of a merchant ship and a farmer concerning the pernicious practice of wrecking. . . . By Jonas Salvage, gent. [Rev. James Walker, B.C.L., vicar of Perranzabuloe]. Fcap 8vo. [Boase and Courtney's *Bibl. Cornub.*]
                                     London, 1768

DIALOGUE (a) between a Christian and a Quaker, wherein is faithfully represented some of the chief and most concerning opinions of the Quakers. By T. H. [Thomas Hicks]. 8vo. Pp. 94. [Smith's *Anti-Quak.*, p. 225.]
                                     London, 1673

DIALOGUE (a) between a Churchman and a Methodist, on the writings and opinions of Baron Swedenborg. . . . [By the Rev. John Clowes, M.A.] Pp. 43. [*Manch. Free Lib.*]
                                     London, 1802

DIALOGUE (a) between a civilian and a divine concerning the present condition of the Church of England. [By George Gillespie.] 4to. [Scott's *Fasti* (new edition), i., p. 58.]
                                     London, 1644

DIALOGUE (a) between a clergyman and his parishioner on the doctrine of entire sanctification. [By Rev. John Pomeroy Gilbert.] 8vo. Pp. 23. [*Brit. Mus.*]   Bodmin, 1850

DIALOGUE (a) between a clergyman of the Church of England and a lay-gentleman; occasioned by the late application to Parliament for the repeal of certain penal laws against Antitrinitarians. [By John Disney, D.D.] 8vo. [*Bodl.*]   London, 1792

DIALOGUE (a) between a Conformist and a Nonconformist, concerning the lawfulness of private meetings in the time of the public ordinances, and going to them. By N. E. [Nicholas Estwicke]. [Whitley's *Bapt. Bibl.*, i., 94.]   London, 1668

DIALOGUE (a) between a country gentleman and a merchant, concerning the fall of guineas. . . . [By Simon Clement?] 4to. [*Brit. Mus.*]
                                     London, 1696

DIALOGUE (a) between a curat and a countrey-man concerning the English-service or common-prayerbook of England. [By Rev. John Anderson, of Dumbarton.] 4to. [*New Coll. Cat.*]   N.P., [1710]

DIALOGUE (a) between a farmer and a country gentleman, on the principles of government; written by a member of the Society for Constitutional Information [Sir William Jones]. [*Bibl. Parriana*, p. 441.] 8vo. London, 1778
  In other editions the title reads: "The Principles of Government, in a dialogue. . . ."

DIALOGUE (a) between a lawyer and a country gentleman upon the subject of game laws. . . . By a gentleman of Lincoln's Inn, a Freeholder of Middlesex [Samuel Purlewent]. 8vo. [*Brit. Mus.*]   London, 1771

DIALOGUE (a) between a Lord-Lieutenant and one of his deputies. [By Henry Booth, second Baron Delamere, and first Earl of Warrington.] 4to. [*D. N. B.*, vol. 5, p. 382.] London, 1690

DIALOGUE (a) between a master and an apprentice, occasioned by lectures on education delivered by Mr Lancaster, in Bath, in the month of February, 1810. [By Rev. Charles Daubeny, Archdeacon.] Fcap 8vo. [Green's *Bibl. Somers.*, i., 303.]   Bath, 1810

DIALOGUE (a) between a modern Courtier and an honest English gentleman regarding perversion of justice and oppression of the innocent. [By Robert Crosfeild]. Fcap 4to. [*Cat. of Lond. Inst.*, ii., p. 479.] N.P., 1696

DIALOGUE (a) between a pastor and his parishioner touching the Lord's Supper. [By Michael Altham, D.D.] Fcap 8vo.   London, 1684
  Later editions, enlarged, give the author's name.

DIALOGUE (a) between a protesting Catholic dissenter and a Catholic, on the nature, tendency, and import of the oath lately offered to the Catholics of England. [By Rev. Wm. Pilling, O.S.F.] 8vo. [Gillow's *Bibl. Dict.*, vol. 5, p. 313.]   London, 1790

DIALOGUE (a) between a Whig and a Jacobite, upon . . . the late Rebellion and the execution of the Rebel-Lords. [By Daniel Williams?] 8vo.
                                     London, 1716

DIALOGUE (a) between Alkali and Acid. . . . Wherein a late hypothesis asserting alkali the cause and acid the cure of all diseases is proved groundless; being a specimen of the mistakes and ignorance of J. Colbatch. By T. E. [Thomas Emes]. 8vo. [Arber's *Term Cat.*, iii., p. 214.] London, 1698

DIALOGUE between an Associator and a well informed Englishman, on the grounds of the late Associations and the commencement of a war with France. [By Joseph Towers, LL.D.] 8vo. [*Gent. Mag.*, lxix., 1., 528.]
London, 1793

DIALOGUE (a) between an awakened sinner and merciful Saviour, 1694. By Christophilus Philalethes [John Moore]. 8vo. [Whitley's *Bapt. Bibl.*, i., 150.]							London, 1723

DIALOGUE (a) between Billy Batten, the tailor, and Samson Brawney, the farmer, of Dungmixen village, Zummerzet. [By Rev. Richard Warner.] 8vo. [Green's *Bibl. Somers.*, iii., p. 362.]				Bath, 1844

DIALOGUE (a) between Bishop Hoadly and Bishop Sherlock, on the Corporation and Test Acts. [By Thomas Knowles, D.D.] 8vo.		London, 1790

DIALOGUE (a) between Claret and Darby ale; a poem, considered in an accidental conversation between two gentlemen. [By Edward Ward.] 4to. [Arber's *Term Cat.*, ii., p. 613.]
London, 1691

DIALOGUE (a) between Isaac Walton and Homologistes; in which the character of Bishop Sanderson is defended against [the Rev. Francis Blackburne] the author of the Confessional. [By Thomas Townson, D.D.] 8vo. Pp. iv., 66. [*Gent. Mag.*, June 1792, p. 573.]							London, 1768

DIALOGUE between Mr Demogogue (*sic*) and a sober citizen. [By Sir Robert Dean.] 8vo. [*Brit. Mus.*]
Dublin, 1766

DIALOGUE (a) between Mr Prejudice, a Dissenting country gentleman, and Mr Reason, a student in the University; being a short vindication of the University from Popery, and an answer to some objections concerning the D. of Y. [Duke of York]. [By Thomas Wood, D.C.L.] 4to. [*Bodl.*]
London, 1682

Dedication signed "T. W." "Th. Wood of New Coll. yᵉ authour."—MS. note by Wood.

A continuation appeared soon after as "The Dissenting Casuist. . . ."

DIALOGUE (a) between Philalethes and Philotimus, occasioned by a letter from J. S. [John England, Presbyterian minister at Sherborne, Dorsetshire] to F. B. [James Lacy, vicar of Sherborne]. 8vo. [Mayo's *Bibl. Dors.*]							London, 1704

DIALOGUE (a) between Sir R. L. [Sir Roger L'Estrange] Knight, and T. O. D. [Titus Oates, Dr]. 4to. [*Bodl.*]							London, 1689

DIALOGUE (a) between Sir Roger —— and Mr Rob. Ferg—— in Newgate, relating to the Plot. [By Robert Ferguson.] 4to. [*David Laing.*]
Edinburgh, reprinted 1696

DIALOGUE (a) between the Crosse in Cheap, and Charing Crosse; comforting each other, as fearing their fall in these uncertain times. By Ryhen Pameach [Henry Peacham, M.A.]. 4to. 4 leaves, unpaged. [*W.*]
N.P., 1641

DIALOGUE (a) between the devil and a Socinian divine, on the confines of the other world. [By John Jamieson, D.D.] 8vo. [Anderson's *Scottish Nation*, vol. 2, p. 566.] Edinburgh,1791

DIALOGUE (a) between the E[arl] of C[hesterfiel]d and Mr Garrick in the Elysian Shades. [Verse. By G— Butt.] 4to.				London, 1785
See also "A Dialogue in the Shades . . ."

DIALOGUE (a) between the pulpit and the reading-desk, wherein the most common errors in religion are refuted. . . . By a member of the Church of England [Rev. Charles Perronet]. Fcap 8vo. Pp. 93. [Osborn's *Method. Lit.*, p. 155.]
London, 1767
Also attributed to William Green, of Rotherham.

DIALOGUE (a) between Timotheus and Judas, concerning a pamphlet [by Rev. William Stephens], called, The growth of Deism in England. [By Henry Hill, D.D.] 4to. Pp. 58. [Watt's *Bibl. Brit.*]			London, 1696

DIALOGUE (a) between Timothy and Philatheus. In which the principles and projects of a late whimsical book [by Matthew Tindal], entituled, The Rights of the Christian Church, &c., are fairly stated and answer'd in their kind; and some attempts made towards the discovery of a new way of reasoning. Written by a layman [William Oldisworth]. 3 vols. [Arber's *Term Cat.*, iii., 650.]
London, 1709-11
Each volume has a separate dedication and preface. Vol. I. is of the 2d. ed.

DIALOGUE (a) between Tom Thomas and Bill Bilkey, two Cornish miners,— The Snake. By T. R. H. [T— R— Higham]. 8vo. Pp. 24. [Boase and Courtney's *Bibl. Corn.*, p. 239.]
Truro, N.D., [1866]

DIALOGUE (a) between two friends, occasioned by the late Revolution of affairs, and the Oath of Allegeance. By W. K., A. M. [White Kennett, Bishop of Peterborough]. 4to. [*Bodl.*]
London, 1689

DIALOGUE (a) between two gentlemen, concerning the late application to Parliament for relief in the matter of subscription to the thirty-nine Articles and Liturgy of the Church of England. [By Joseph Towers, LL.D.] 8vo. [*Gent. Mag.*, lxxiii., 1., 355.]   London, 1772

DIALOGVE (a) betweene a knyght and a clerke, concernynge the power spiritual and temporall. [By Gulielmus de Occham.] Imprinted at London in Flete-strete, in the house of Thomas Berthelet, nere to the cundite at the sygne of Lucrece. Cum privilegio. 8vo. Fol. 26. B. L. [*Bodl.*]   N.D.

DIALOGUE (a) bytwene the commune secretary and jalowsye, touchynge the unstablenesst of harlottes. [Edited by John Payne Collier.] 4to. [*W.*]
[London, 1842 ?]
Only twenty-five copies privately reprinted in black letter facsimile, with an Introduction (signed J. P. C.) in which is considered the probability of its being written by Edward Gosynhyll, the author of *The prayse of all women, called Mulierum Pean,*" published by the same printer as this tract—John Kynge.

DIALOGUE (a) betwixt a minister of the Church of Scotland, and two of the elders of his congregation, about the Abjuration-oath. [By James Smith, minister of Cramond.] 8vo. [*Adv. Lib.*]   Printed in the year 1712

DIALOGUE (a) betwixt a Quaker and a stable Christian. . . . [By William Mitchell, minister at Leslie, afterwards Dundee.] 8vo. [Robertson's *Aberd. Bibl.*]   Aberdeen, [1670]
The most if not the whole of the above was written by Mitchell [Watt's *Bibl. Brit.*].

DIALOGVE (a) betwixt a secvlar priest, and a lay gentleman ; concerning some points objected by the Iesuiticall faction against such secular priests as have shewed their dislike of M. Blackwell and the Iesuits proceedings. [By William Watson, a Roman Catholic priest.] 4to. Pp. 154. [Thomas Graves Law on *Jesuits and Seculars*, Bibl. Notes.]   Printed at Rhemes, 1601
Preface to the reader signed " W. W."

DIALOGUE (a) betwixt Cosmophilus and Theophilus anent the urging of new ceremonies upon the Kirke of Scotland. [By David Calderwood.] 8vo. Pp. 43. [*Adv. Lib.*]   N.P., 1620
Ascribed also to John Martin [*D. Laing*] and to John Murray.

DIALOGUE (a) betwixt Jack and Will, concerning the Lord Mayor [Sir Humphrey Edwin]'s going to meetinghouses with the sword carried before him, &c. [By George Ridpath.] 4to. [*Adv. Lib.*]   London, 1697

DIALOGUE (a) betwixt two Protestants (in answer to a Popish catechism, called, A short catechism against all sectaries), plainly shewing, that the members of the Church of England are no sectaries but true Catholicks ; and that our Church is a sound part of Christ's Holy Catholick Church. . . . In two parts. [By John Rawlet.] 8vo.   London, 1685
After several editions, one was published with the author's name.

DIALOGUE (a) by way of catechism, religious, moral, and philosophical, for grown men and women, piously disposed. By a Physician [Robert Willis, M.D.]. 2 parts. 8vo. [*Brit. Mus.*]   Ramsgate, 1872

DIALOGUE (a) concerning a pamphlet [by William Stephens], entitled "The Growth of Deism in England." [By Henry Hill, D.D.] 4to. [Watt's *Bibl. Brit.*]   London, 1698

DIALOGUE (a) concerning the converting tithes and offerings to secular uses. [By Lewis Southcomb, junr.] Fcap 8vo. [W. D. Macray's *Cat.*]
Exeter, 1726

DIALOGUE (a) concerning this question, where was your Church before Luther and Calvin ; giving good direction how to discover Fishers folly. By W. C. [William Crashaw]. 4to. [*Mendham Collection Cat.*, p. 86.]   N.P., 1628

DIALOGUE (a) concerning women, being a defence of the sex : written to Eugenia. [By William Walsh.] 8vo. Pp. 144.   London, 1691
Preface by John Dryden. Part of a vol. containing " Letters and poems, amorous and gallant."—MS. note by H. Hody on the Bodleian copy.

DIALOGUE (a) in the Devonshire dialect, (in three parts) by a lady [Mrs Palmer] : to which is added a glossary, by J. F. Palmer. 12mo. [The preface and Davidson's *Bibl. Devon.*, p. 11.]
London, 1837

DIALOGUE (a), in the manner of Plato, on the superiority of the pleasures of the understanding to the pleasures of the senses. [By George Stubbes.] 8vo. [*Brit. Mus.*]   London, 1734

DIALOGUE in the shades, between Dr Dodd and [Chace Price] a Welch Member of Parliament. [By William Combe.] 4to. [*Cat. Lond. Inst.*, ii., 505.]   London, 1777

DIALOGUE (a) in the shades between Lord Chesterfield and Dr Johnson. [By William Hayley.] 8vo.
London, [1780 ?]
See also " A Dialogue between the E—l of C—d . . . "

DIALOGUE (a) in the shades, recommended to every purchaser of Dr Kinglake's Dissertation [on gout]. . . . By Sir John Floyer's ghost [William Perry, M.D.]. 8vo. [*Brit. Mus.*]   Uxbridge, 1805

DIALOGUE (a) of dying wel. First written in the Italian tongue, by the Reuerend father Don Peeter of Luca, a chanon regular, a Doctor of Diuinitie and famous preacher : wherin is also contayned sundry profitable resolutions, upon some doubtful questions in diuinitie. Translated first into French, and now into English [by Richard Verstegan, *i.e.*, Richard Rowlands]. 8vo. [*D. N. B.*, vol. 49, p. 352.] Imprinted at Antwerp, by A. C.   1603
The dedication " To the Right Reverend Lady Joan Barkley, abbesse of the English monastery of nunnes of the holy order of S. Benedict, in Bruxels," is signed " R. V."

DIALOGUE (a) of the dead betwixt Lord Eglinton and Mungo Campbell. [By Dr Langhorne.] Fcap 8vo. [*Manch. Free Lib.*]   London, 1770

DIALOGUE of the knowledge of the supreme Lord, in which are compared the claims of Christianity and Hinduism. [By Rowland Williams, D.D.] 8vo. [*W.*]   Cambridge, 1856

DIALOGUE on beauty, after the manner of Plato. [By George Stubbes, painter.] 8vo. [*Lond. Lib. Cat.*] London, 1731

DIALOGUE (a) on Christian perfection. . . . By J. N. D. [John Nelson Darby]. 8vo.   London, 1861

DIALOGUE (a) on devotion, after the manner of Xenophon ; in which the reasonableness, pleasure, and advantages of it are considered. To which is prefix'd, a conversation of Socrates on the being and providence of God ; translated from the Greek. [By Thomas Amory.] 8vo. [*Biog. Brit.*]   N.P., [1745 ?]

DIALOGUE (a) on the actual state of Parliament. 8vo. [By —— Powis.] [*Bodl.*]   Dublin, 1753

DIALOGUE on the choral service. [By John Jebb, D.D.] 8vo. Leeds, 1842
Wrongly attributed to G. A. Poole.

DIALOGUE (a) on the Christian Sacraments, wherein the nature and import of an attendance on them are inquired into ; from the Scriptures. [By Joseph Bellamy. 8vo. Pp. 83. [Evans' *Amer. Bibl.*, vol. 3, p. 310.]
Boston, [Mass.], 1762

DIALOGUE (a) on the Corn Laws : scene, the steam-boat " Orwell." [By Stephen Perry, of Ipswich.] 8vo. Pp. 24. [Supp. to Smith's *Cat. of Friends' Books*, p. 18.]   London, 1841

DIALOGUE on " The Free Church Door " [for entrance of Original Seceders], between the Rev. Archibald Brown, A.M., Adam Square, and Nominis Umbra [Rev. William White, of Haddington]. 8vo. Pp. 31. [*New Coll. Cat.*]   Edinburgh, 1852

DIALOGUE (a) on the Navy. By the author of *Galba* [John Moncrieff]. 8vo. [*Brit. Mus.*]   London, 1748

DIALOGUE (a) on the plurality of worlds ; being a supplement to the Essay on that subject. [By William Whewell, D.D.] 8vo. Pp. 55. [*D. N. B.*, vol. 60, p. 462.] [London, 1854]

DIALOGUE (a) on the present prospects of agriculture. By E. W. [E— Welch]. [*Birm. Lib. Cat.*]   London, 1736

DIALOGUE (a) upon the gardens of the Right Honourable the Lord Viscount Cobham, at Stow in Buckinghamshire. [By William Gilpin, M.A.] 8vo. Pp. iv., 60. [*Bodl.*]   London, 1748

DIALOGUES, and a small portion of the New Testament in the English, Arabic, Haussa, and Bornu languages. [By Edwin Norris, of the Royal Asiatic Society.] Oblong 8vo. [*W.*]
London, 1853

DIALOGUES and detached sentences in the Chinese language ; with a free and verbal translation in English. [By Robert Morrison.] Collected from various sources [by J. Bannerman]. 8vo. [*Brit. Mus.*]   Macao, 1816

DIALOGUES and letters on morality, economy, and politeness. . . . By the author of *Dialogues on the first principles of religion* [Dorothy Kilner]. Fcap 8vo.   London, [1780 ?]

DIALOGUES between a minister and an honest countryman concerning election and predestination, very suitable to the present times. . . . By an enquirer after truth [John Checkley]. 8vo. Pp. 40. [Evans' *Amer. Bibl.*, vol. 2, p. 177.]   Philadelphia, 1741

DIALOGUES between Philerene and Philalethe, a lover of peace, and a lover of truth ; concerning the Pope's supremacy. [By Thomas Watts, vicar of Orpington.] Part I. 4to. [*Bodl.*]
London, 1688

DIALOGUES concerning education. [By David Fordyce, M.A.] 8vo. [Robertson's *Aberd. Bibl.*]
London, 1745
A second volume was published in 1758.

DIALOGUES concerning innate principles ; containing an examination of Mr Locke's doctrine on that subject. By the author of *Three dialogues concerning liberty* [Jackson Barwis]. 8vo. Pp. 99. [*Brit. Mus.*]   London, 1779

DIALOGUES concerning the ladies ; to which is added, an essay on the ancient Amazons. [By Joseph Towers, LL.D.] 8vo. [*Gent. Mag.*, lxxiii., 1., 355.]   N.P., 1785

DIALOGUES, etc., concerning the use of tobacco. By a surgeon [Henry Mudge, M.R.C.S.E.]. 8vo. [*Brit. Mus.*]   London, 1861

DIALOGUES ; containing a comparative view of the lives, characters, and writings of Lord Chesterfield and Dr. Johnson. [By William Hayley.] Folio. [Watt's *Bibl. Brit.*]   London, 1794

DIALOGUES in a library, between Polymetis, Sophronius, and Parminio. [By Dr Thomson.] 8vo. Pp. 278. [*Brit. Crit.*, xii., 559.] London, 1797

DIALOGUES (the) of Lucian : from the Greek. [By John Carr, LL.D.] 8vo. [*Brit. Mus.*]   London, 1774

DIALOGUES (the) of Mr William Richworth [Thomas White, Roman Catholic priest] on the judgment of common sense in the choice of religion. 8vo. [Lowndes' *Brit. Lib.*, p. 1073.]
Paris, 1640

DIALOGUES (the) of St Gregory ; translated into English. By P. W. [Philip Woodward]. Fcap 8vo.
Paris, 1608

DIALOGUES of the day. By Anthony Hope [Anthony Hope Hawkins] and others. [*Lit. Year Book.*]
London, N.D.

DIALOGUES of the dead. [By George Lyttelton, Lord Lyttelton.] 8vo. Pp. xii., 320. [*Brit. Mus.*] London, 1760
The last three dialogues are by Mrs Elizabeth Montague.

DIALOGUES of the dead ; relating to the present controversy concerning the epistles of Phalaris. By the author of the *Journey to London* [William King, LL.D.]. 8vo. Pp. 92. [Bartholomew's *Bibl. of Bentley*, p. 38 ; Arber's *Term Cat.*, iii., 159.]
London, 1699

DIALOGUES of the dead with the living. [By Rev. Philip Parsons.] 8vo. [*Gent. Mag.*, lxii., 2., 291.]
London, 1779

DIALOGUES on divine Providence. By a Fellow of a College [—— Newman]. Pt 8vo.   London, 1856

DIALOGUES on prophecy. [Compiled by Henry Drummond, M.P.] 3 vols.
London, 1828-29
These dialogues contain the sentiments of various modern writers on prophecy, as delivered in private discussion, or in their published works. The following is a key to some of the names—Philalethes, Lord Mandeville ; Anastasius, H. Drummond, Esq. ; Philemon, Rev. C. S. Hawtrey ; Evander, J. Bayford, Esq. ; Sophron, W. Cuninghame, Esq. ; Crito, J. H. Frere, Esq. ; Thales, Rev. H. Simonds ; Theophilus, Rev. J. H. Stewart ; Aristo, Rev. E. Irving ; Theodosius, Rev. W. Marsh ; Isocrates, Rev. H. M'Neile ; Josephus, Rev. J. Wolfe. Some of the above have complained that their sentiments have not been correctly represented. [Lowndes' *Brit. Lib.*, p. 962.]

DIALOGUES on sincerity, retirement, the golden age of Elizabeth, and the constitution of the English government. [By Richard Hurd, D.D.] 8vo.   London, 1759
Published, with the author's name, in 1765 in Hurd's " Dialogues, moral, and political, with letters on chivalry," 3 vols. 8vo. [Savage's *Librarian*, i., 40.]

DIALOGUES on the Essays and reviews. By one who values Christianity for its own sake, and believes in it as a revelation from God [John N. Darby]. Second edition, revised. 8vo. Pp. 457. [*Aberd. Lib.*] London, 1863

DIALOGUES on the Lord's Supper continued ; in which objections to its primitive mode of administration are fully answered. . . . By N. D. [Rev. Niel Douglas], Dundee. 8vo.
Dundee, 1796

DIALOGUES on the passions, habits, and affections peculiar to children ; wherein the infant state of the soul is fully displayed, the first dawnings of vice and vicious habits clearly pointed out, and plain, practicable hints given to check the growth of these. . . . [By Lieut.-Col. James Forrester.] Cr 8vo. Pp. xii. 60.
London, 1745

DIALOGUES on the rights of Britons, between a farmer, a sailor, and a manufacturer. [By John Bowles, barrister.] 8vo. [Watt's *Bibl. Brit.*]
London, 1793

DIALOGUES on the uses of foreign travel ; considered as a part of an English gentleman's education ; between Lord Shaftesbury and Mr Locke. By the editor of Moral and political dialogues [Richard Hurd, D.D.]. 8vo. [*Brit. Mus.*]   London, 1764

DIAMOND (the) arrow ; or the Post-master's wife and the Mayor's daughter : a petit comedy, in one act. By William G. Thomas [William Thomas Thomas]. 8vo. [*Brit. Mus.*]
London, 1816

DIAMOND (the) buckled shoe. By Ben Bolt [Sir Arthur T. Quiller-Couch]. 8vo. Pp. 252. [*Lit. Year Book.*] London, 1921

DIAMOND (the) button : whose was it ? By Barclay North [William C. Hudson]. Pt 8vo. [*Lond. Lib. Cat.*]
London, 1889

DIAMOND (the) coterie : a detective story. By Lawrence L. Lynch [Miss Emma M. Murdoch, later Mrs Van Deventer]. 8vo. Pp. 154. [*Lond. Lib. Cat.*] London, 1887

DIAMOND cut diamond : or observa-tions on a pamphlet [by N. Jefferys] entitled, A review of the conduct of His Royal Highness, the Prince of Wales. . . . By Philo-Veritas [Thomas Gilliland]. 8vo. [*Brit. Mus.*]
London, 1806

DIAMOND leaves from the Dimond family. By an old, old bachelor [Nathan Stone Reed Beal]. 8vo. [Cushing's *Init. and Pseud.*, i., 212.]
Macedon, New York, 1872

DIAMOND (the) pendant [a novel]. By Maxwell Gray [Mary Gleed Tuttiett]. Cr 8vo. Pp. 256. [*Lond. Lib. Cat.*]
London, 1918

DIAMOND (the) rose ; a life of love and duty. By Sarah Tytler, author of *Citoyenne Jacqueline*, etc. [Henri-etta Keddie]. 8vo. Pp. vi., 402. [*Lit. Year Book.*] London, 1867

DIAMONDS and diamond-dust ; or, what a dominie said to some school-girls. [By Wm. Moore.] Pt 8vo. [*Brit. Mus.*] London, 1878

DIAMONDS and dust, being grains from the sands of society : a novel. 3 vols. [By Henry Noel Humphreys.] Fcap 8vo. [*Camb. Univ. Lib.*]
London, 1856

DIAMONDS and gold : the three main routes to the South African Ophir, and how to equip for the journey. By W. B. L. [William Barry Lord]. 8vo. Pp. ii., 95. [*Brit. Mus.*]
London, 1871

DIAMONDS and spades : a tale of two lives. By the author of *The gentle life* [James Hain Friswell]. 8vo. [*Brit. Mus.*] London, 1858

DIAMONDS reset. By Nellie Grahame [Mrs Annie Dunning, *née* Ketchum]. Fcap 8vo. [Cushing's *Init. and Pseud.*, i., 119.] Philadelphia, 1864

DIANA Carew ; or, for a woman's sake. [A novel.] By Mrs Forrester [Mrs —— Bridges]. Fcap 8vo. [*Amer. Cat.*]
New York, 1887

DIANA, Dutchess of Mantua ; or the persecuted lover : a romance. Written by R. C. [Rowland Carleton], Gent. 8vo. [Arber's *Term Cat.*, i., p. 349.]
London, 1679

DIANA great at Ephesus ; or, the Protestant turned Papist : a sermon from Acts 19:34 preached Nov. 5, 1755, being the anniversary of the ever memorable Revolution, 1688. . . . By Taoaltt Bob [Rev. William Graham, M.A., Congregational minister at War-ley]. 8vo. London, 1756
"Taoaltt Bob" seems to be a name composed, as an acrostic, of the initials of the words forming the following sentence : —The Author Of A Letter To The Bishop Of Bangor.

DIANA of Rosenburgh ; a story of Cornwall. By Crona Temple [Miss —— Corfield]. Fcap 8vo. Pp. 128. [*Brit. Mus.*] London, 1887

DIANA of the Ephesians. By " Rita " [Mrs W. Desmond Humphreys, *née* Eliza M. J. Gollan]. 8vo. [*Lit. Year Book.*] London, 1919

DIANA of the Islands. By Ben Bolt [Sir Arthur T. Quiller-Couch]. 8vo. [*Lit. Year Book.*] London, 1921

DIANA ; or, the excellent conceitful sonnets of H. C. [Henry Constable]. Augmented with diuers quatorzains of honorable and learned personages. Deuided into viii. decads. 8vo. No pagination. [*Bodl.*]
London, 1592 or 1594
Reprinted (50 copies) in facsimile, edited by Samuel Weller Singer. 12mo. London, [1818]

DIANA Wynyard. [A novel.] By the author of *Alice Wentworth*, etc. [Noell Radcliffe]. 3 vols. 8vo. [*Brit. Mus.*]
London, 1856

DIANA'S crescent. By the author of *Mary Powell* [Anne Manning, later Mrs Rathbone]. 2 vols. Fcap 8vo.
London, 1868

DIANA'S discipline. By Bertha M. Clay [Mrs Charlotte M. Bracme]. Pt 8vo. Pp. 248. New York, [1889]

DIANNE de Poytiers. By Marie Hay [Madame de Hindenburg]. 8vo.
London, 1900

DIAPHANTA ; or, three attendants on Fiat Lux : wherein Catholik religion is further excused against the opposition of severall adversaries. 1 Epistola ad Odoenum, against Dr Owen. 2 Epistola ad Croesum, against Mr Whitby. 3 Epistola ad Ampibolum, against Dr Taylor. And by the way, an answer is given to Mr Moulin, Denton, and Stillingfleet. [By John Vincent Cane.] 8vo. Pp. 413. [Wood's *Athen. Oxon.*, iv., 107.]

N.P., 1665

Signed "J. V. C."

DIAPHANTUS, or the passions of love. By An. Sc. [Anthony Scoloker]. 4to. [*W.*] London, 1604

DIARIES of a Lady of Quality [Frances Williams Wynn] from 1797 to 1844 : edited, with notes, by A. Hayward, Esq., Q.C. Second edition. 8vo. Pp. xvi., 373. [*Brit. Mus.*]

London, 1864

DIARY and correspondence of John Evelyn, F.R.S., author of *Sylva* ; to which is subjoined the Private Correspondence between King Charles I. and Sir Edward Nicholas, and between Sir Edward Hyde, afterwards Earl of Clarendon and Sir Richard Browne ; edited from the original MSS. at Wotton by William Bray, Esq., F.A.S. A new edition [by John Forster]. 8vo. [*W.*] London, 1850-2

DIARY (the) and houres of the Lady Adolie. Edited [or rather written] by Lady Charlotte Maria Pepys. 8vo. [*Brit. Mus.*] London, 1853

DIARY and notes of Horace Templeton, Esq., late Secretary of Legation at ——. [By Charles James Lever ?] 2 vols. 8vo. London, 1848

DIARY illustrative of the times of George the Fourth, interspersed with original letters from the late Queen Caroline, and from various other distinguished persons. [By Lady Charlotte Bury.] 2 vols. 8vo. [*Adv. Lib.*] London, 1838

Two additional volumes, edited by John Galt, were published in 1839. By Lady Charlotte Bury and Miss Sheridan. [*W.*]

DIARY (the) of a bachelor. By Billy Bachelor [Christopher Ambrose Shea]. 8vo. [*Amer. Cat.*] New York, [1910]

DIARY (the) of a Blase. By the author of *Jacob Faithful*, etc. [Capt. Frederick Marryat]. Cr 8vo. [Mr Sadleir's *Victorian Literature*, p. 88.]

Philadelphia, 1836

DIARY (the) of a Church-goer. [By Leonard Henry Courtney, Lord Courtney.] Cr 8vo. London, 1904

The name is given in a later edition (1918).

DIARY (the) of a désennuyée. [By Mrs Catherine Grace Frances Gore.] Second edition. Revised by the author, with additions. 2 vols. Fcap 8vo. [*Brit. Mus.*] London, 1836

DIARY (the) of a Detective Police Officer. By "Waters" [William Russell]. 8vo. [*Brit. Mus.*]

New York, 1864

DIARY (the) of a dutiful son. By H. E. O. [Thomas George Fonnereau]. Pt 8vo. Private print. [*D. N. B.*, vol. 19, p. 366.] London, 1849

"H. E. O." are the *second* letters in the full name.

DIARY (the) of a flirt. By Clarice Laurence [Miss C. L. Hancock]. 8vo. London, 1916

DIARY (the) of a Lady-in-waiting [Lady Charlotte Susan Maria Bury], illustrative of the times of George the Fourth ; interspersed with original letters from the late Queen Caroline, and from other distinguished persons. . . . 4 vols. 8vo. [*Brit. Mus.*] London, 1838

DIARY (the) of a milliner. By Belle Otis [Caroline H— Woods]. 8vo. [Cushing's *Init. and Pseud.*, i., 220.]

New York, 1867

DIARY (the) of a musician. By Dolores Marbourg [Mrs Mary S. Hoke Bacon]. 8vo. New York, 1894

DIARY (the) of a rebel war-clerk, 1861-1865. [By John B— Jones.] 8vo. [Cushing's *Init. and Pseud.*, i., 248.]

Philadelphia, 1866

DIARY of a retired country parson (in verse). [By Richard Warner.] 4to. [Bliss' *Cat.*, 324.] Private print, 1848

DIARY (the) of a Samaritan. By a member of the Howard Association of New Orleans [William L. Robinson]. 8vo. [Cushing's *Init. and Pseud.*, i., 189.] New Orleans, 1858

DIARY (the) of a solitaire ; or sketch of a pedestrian excursion through part of Switzerland : with a prefatory address, and notes, personal and general. [By Edwin S. Rickman.] 8vo. [*Camb. Univ. Lib.*] London, 1835

DIARY (the) of a soul in the year 1901. [By David Farquharson.] Cr 8vo. Pp. 187. London, 1902

DIARY of a Southern refugee during the [Civil] War [in the United States]. By a lady of Virginia [Mrs John W. M'Guire, *née* Brockenborough]. 8vo. [Cushing's *Init. and Pseud.*, i., 163.]

New York, 1867

DIARY of a spring holiday in Cuba. [By Richard J. Levis, M.D.] 8vo. [Kirk's *Supp.*] Philadelphia, 1877

DIARY of a summer in Europe. By Porte [G. H. Mathews]. 8vo. [Kirk's *Supp.*] New York, 1866

DIARY of a tour through Southern India, Egypt, and Palestine, in the years 1821 and 1822. By a field officer of cavalry [Sir Digby Mackworth]. 8vo. Pp. viii., 372.
London, 1823

DIARY of a traveller [Murray Forbes] over Alps and Apennines ; or daily minutes of a circuitous excursion. 8vo. Pp. vii., 170. [Dobell's *Private Prints*, p. 229.]
N.P., 1824

DIARY of a working clergyman in Australia and Tasmania. [By Rev. John Davies Mereweather.] Fcap 8vo. [Cushing's *Init. and Pseud.*, vol. ii., p. 156.]
London, 1856

DIARY of an Austrian Secretary of Legation at the Court of Peter the Great. [By Johann Georg Korb.] Translated from the original Latin. 2 vols. 8vo. [*Brit. Mus.*]
London, 1863

DIARY (the) of an ennuyée. [By Mrs Anna B. Jameson, *née* Murphy.] New edition. Fcap 8vo. [*Brit. Mus.*]
London, 1826

The title of the original edition (1824) is " A Lady's diary."

DIARY of an expelled correspondent. [By —— Boyle.] 8vo. London, 1885

DIARY (the) of an idle woman in Italy. By Florentine [Mrs Frances Elliot, *née* Dickenson]. 2 vols. Pt 8vo. [Cushing's *Init. and Pseud.*, i., 135]. London, 1871

DIARY (the) of an idle woman in Spain. By Florentine [Mrs Frances Elliot, *née* Dickenson]. Cr 8vo.
London, 1884

DIARY (the) of an Officer with the 4th Northumberland Fusiliers in France and Flanders from April 20th to May 24th, 1915. [By W— J. Bunbury.] 8vo. Pp. 63. [*Brit. Mus.*]
Hexham, [1918]

Signed " W. J. B."

DIARY of Brother Bartholomew ; with other tales and sketches of Christian life in different lands and ages. By the author of *Chronicles of the Schönberg-Cotta family*, etc. [Mrs Elizabeth Charles, *née* Rundle]. Cr 8vo. Pp. 459.
London, 1870

DIARY (the) of Delia. By Onoto Watanna [Mrs Winnifred Eaton Babcock]. Fcap 8vo. [*Amer. Cat.*]
New York, 1907

DIARY (the) of Martha Bethune Baliol, from 1753 to 1754. [By Harriet Skene.] 8vo. London, 1853

DIARY of Mrs Kitty Trevylyan : a story of the times of Whitefield and the Wesleys. By the author of *Chronicles of the Schönberg-Cotta family*, etc. [Mrs Elizabeth Charles, *née* Rundle]. Cr 8vo. Pp. 304. London, 1865

DIARY of Samuel Pepys, Esq., while an undergraduate at Cambridge ; with notes and appendix. Dedicated by special permission to Benjamin Jolley, Esq., of Chesterton, better known to the members of this University as Charon. [By Charles W. R. Cooke, B.A., M.P.] Cr 8vo. Pp. viii., 52. [*Camb. Univ. Lib.*] Cambridge, 1864

DIARY (the) of Solomon Spittle. By Ziba Sproule [Lucius Manlius Sargent]. 8vo. [Cushing's *Init. and Pseud.*, i., 273.] Boston, 1847

DIARY of the besieged resident in Paris. Reprinted from " The Daily News," with several new letters and preface. [By Henry Labouchere.] 8vo. Pp. viii., 391. London, 1871

The third edition, published in 1872, has the author's name.

DIARY (a) of the Quorndon Hunt from 1791 to 1800, inclusive, giving a succinct detail of every day's sport. . . . By Thomas Jones, whipper-in to the late Hugo Meynell, Esq. ; with rhymes at end on the Billesden Coplow Hunt. [By the Rev. Robert Lowth, M.A., of Christ College, Oxford.] 8vo. Derby, 1816

DIARY (a) of the siege of Luxembourg by the French King's forces under the command of Mareschal de Créqui. [By Jean Donneau de Vizé.] Done out of French. 4to. London, [1684]

DIARY of three tours in the Northern Province of Ceylon, 1909. [By G— R. Price.] 8vo. Pp. 59. [*Brit. Mus.*] London, [1910]

Signed " G. R. P."

DIARY (a) of travels in three-quarters of the globe. By an Australian settler [—— Ogilvie]. 2 vols. Cr 8vo. London, 1856

DIATESSARON ; or, the history of our Lord Jesus Christ, compiled from the four Gospels, according to the Authorised Version. [By John David Macbride, D.C.L., Principal of Magdalene Hall.] 8vo. [Darling's *Cyclop. Bibl.*] Oxford, 1837

DIATHEEKEE, Covenant, not Testament, throughout the Book commonly called the New Testament ; or the Old and New Covenants the proper title for the Bible. [By John Linnell, artist.] Fcap 8vo. [*Brit. Mus.*] London, 1856

Signed " J. L."

ΔIATPIBH περὶ παιδο-βαπτισμοῦ, or a consideration of infant baptism ; wherein the grounds of it are laid down, and the validity of them discussed, and many things of Mr [John] Tombes

about it scanned. . . . By J. H. [John Horne], of Lynn, an unworthy servant of Jesus Christ. 4to. Pp. viii., 160. [Whitley's *Bapt. Bibl.*, i., 54.]
London, 1654

ΔIATPIBH. Wherein the iudgement of the Reformed Churches and Protestant divines is shewed, concerning ordination, laying on of hands in ordination of ministers, and preaching by those who are not ordained ministers. [By Sydrach Simpson.] 4to. [*D. N. B.*, vol. 52, p. 276.]
London, 1647

DICK. [A tale.] By May Wynne [Mabel Wynne Knowles]. 8vo. Pp. 185. [*Brit. Mus.*] London, [1919]

DICK and his cousin. By " Flecta " [Kate W. Hamilton]. Fcap 8vo. [*Haynes' Pseud.*] Philadelphia, 1891

DICK and his donkey. . . . By the author of *Jack the Conqueror* [Mrs C— E— Bowen]. 4to.
London, [1869]

DICK Diminy ; or, the life and adventures of a jockey. By Priam [Charles James Collins]. 8vo. [Cushing's *Init. and Pseud.*, i., 240.] London, 1855
In other editions the title is varied: " The Life and adventures of Dick Diminy."

DICK Distich : a novel. [By George Daniel.] 3 vols. 8vo. London, 1812

DICK Donovan : a novel. By Edna Lyall [Ada Ellen Bayly]. 8vo. [*Lit. Year Book.*] London, 1882

DICK Ford and his father. By F. C. A. [Frances Charlotte Armstrong]. 8vo. Pp. 128. [Cushing's *Init. and Pseud.* i., 3.] London, [1875]

DICK Langdon's career in Satan's schools and Christ's schools. By Herbert Newbury [Mrs Sarah A. F. Herbert]. Pt 8vo. [Cushing's *Init. and Pseud.*, i., 203.] Philadelphia, 1886

DICK Leslie's luck ; a story of shipwreck and adventure. . . . By Harry Collingwood [William Joseph Cosens Lancaster]. 8vo. Pp. 383. [*Lond. Lib. Cat.*] London, [1906]

DICK Massey. [An Irish story.] By Reginald Tierney [Thomas O'Neill Russell]. 8vo. Pp. 300. [S. J. Brown's *Ireland in Fiction.*]
Dublin, 1908
The title of an earlier edition is " The Struggles of Dick Massey. . . ."

DICK the faithful : a novel. By John Strange Winter [Mrs Henrietta E. V. Stannard, *née* Palmer]. 8vo. Pp. vi., 303. [*Brit. Mus.*] London, 1905

DICK Turpin's ride. [By Henry Llewllyn Williams.] 8vo.
London, [1890]

DICKENS' London. By Francis Miltoun [Milburg Francis Mansfield]. Post 8vo. Pp. 300. [*Amer. Cat.*]
Boston, 1903

DICKIE Winton. [A tale.] By S. G. [Selina Gaye]. Pt 8vo.
London, [1901 ?]

DICK'S dog, and other stories of country boys. By Ascott R. Hope [Ascott Robert Hope Moncrieff]. 8vo. [*Lit. Year Book.*] Edinburgh, 1887

DICK'S holidays, and what he did with them : a picture-book of country life for young folks. By James Weston [Edward Step]. Oblong 8vo. Pp. 152. London, 1883

DICK'S mistake. [A story.] By C. E. M. [Constance E. Miller]. Fcap 8vo. Pp. 123. [*Brit. Mus.*] London, [1891]

DICK'S water lilies, and other stories. By Crona Temple [Miss —— Corfield]. Fcap 8vo. Pp. 76. [*Brit. Mus.*]
London, 1893

DICTA H. N. Documentall sentences : eaven as those-same were spoken fourth by H. N. [Hendrik Niclas, or Nicholas] and writen up out of the woordes of his mouth, and are by him perused and more distinctlie declared. Translated out of Base-almayne [by C. Vitell]. B.L. Fcap 8vo. 47 leaves. [*Brit. Mus.*]
[Amsterdam, *c.* 1575]
See the note appended to " Evangelium regni."

DICTIONARIUM Polygraphicum ; or the whole body of arts, regularly digested. [By John Barrow.] 2 vols. 8vo. [*Camb. Univ. Lib.*]
London, 1735

DICTIONARIUM rusticum et urbanicum ; or a dictionary of all sorts of country affairs, handicraft, trading, and merchandizing. . . . [By John Worlidge.] 8vo. [Arber's *Term Cat.*, iii., p. 634.] London, 1704
Ascribed also to Nathaniel Bailey.
Revisions and enlargements of this dictionary were executed under subsequent editors (Richard Bradley, H. Wise, and others) for more than half a century.

DICTIONARIUM sacrum seu religiosum ; a dictionary of all religions, ancient and modern, whether Jewish, Pagan, Christian or Mahometan. . . . [By Daniel Defoe.] 8vo. [Wilson's *Life of Defoe*, 58.] London, 1704

DICTIONARY (a) of archaic and provincial words, obsolete phrases, proverbs, and ancient customs, from the fourteenth century. By J. O. H. [James Orchard Halliwell (later Halliwell-Phillipps)]. 2 vols. 4to. [Dobell's *Private Prints.*] Brixton Hill, 1852

DICTIONARY (a) of architecture alphabetically arranged. 3 vols. By Robert Stuart [Robert Meikleham]. 8vo. [*Brit. Mus.*] London, [1825 ?]

DICTIONARY (a) of arts and sciences. By George Gregory, D.D. [but really produced by Rev. Jeremiah Joyce]. 2 vols. 8vo. [W. E. A. Axon, in the *Bibliographer*, vol. 4, p. 123.]
London, 1806-7

DICTIONARY (a) of chemistry : containing the theory and practice of that science ; its application to natural philosophy, natural history, medicine, and animal economy : with full explanation of the qualities and modes of acting of chemical remedies, and the fundamental principles of the arts, trades and manufactures, dependent on chemistry. Translated from the French [of Pierre J. Macquer, in the University of Paris]. With plates, notes, and additions, by the translator [James Keir, F.R.S.]. 2 vols. 4to. [*W.*]
London, 1771

DICTIONARY (a) of daily blunders. By the author of *A handy book of synonyms*, etc. [Thomas Preston]. 12mo. [*Brit. Mus.*] London, [1880]

DICTIONARY (the) of daily wants. By the editor of *Enquire within upon everything* [Robert Kemp Philp]. 3 vols. Post 8vo [Boase and Courtney's *Bibl. Corn.*, ii., 493.] London, 1861
Issued during 1858-1860 in thirty-six monthly numbers, and forming three volumes with continuous pagination.

DICTIONARY (the) of dainty breakfasts. By Phillis Browne [Mrs Sarah Sharp Hamer]. With a tabular introduction by a mere man [F. W. Andrewes]. 8vo. Pp. xii., 139. [*Brit. Mus.*] London, 1898
Wrongly ascribed to A. G. Payne.

DICTIONARY (a) of English Proverbs. By the author of *A Dictionary of daily blunders*, etc. [Thomas Preston]. 12mo. [*Brit. Mus.*] London, [1880]

DICTIONARY of familiar sayings and phrases, with anecdotes illustrating their origin. [By Thomas Knox.] Fcap 8vo. [*Adv. Lib.*]
Edinburgh, 1856

DICTIONARY (the) of merchandize, and nomenclature in all languages, for the use of counting-houses ; containing the history, places of growth, culture, use, and marks of excellency of such natural productions as form articles of commerce. . . . By a mer-

chant [C— H— Kauffmann]. 8vo. [*Brit. Mus.*] London, 1803
Several later editions appeared.

DICTIONARY (a) of modern antisupernaturalists ; or, an account, arranged alphabetically, of those who . . . have during the last ten centuries contributed towards the diminution of superstition. Compiled by a searcher after truth [Julian Hibbert]. Vol. i. 8vo. Pp. 128. London, 1826
No more published.

DICTIONARY (a) of modern slang, cant, and vulgar words . . . preceded by a history of cant and vulgar language from the time of Henry VIII., showing its connection with the Gipsy tongue. By a London antiquary [John Camden Hotten]. Fcap 8vo. [Black's *Gypsy Bibliography*, p. 48.]
London, 1859
Several enlarged editions have followed.

DICTIONARY (a) of painters. By Philippe Daryl [Paschal Grousset]. 8vo. [*Brit. Mus.*] London, [1877]

DICTIONARY (a) of quotations, culled from the Latin and French. . . . By D. E. Macdonnel. Ninth edition by a country gentleman [—— Moore]. 8vo. [*New Coll. Lib.*]
London, 1831

DICTIONARY (a) of the English Church, ancient and modern. [By Thomas Moore, D.D.] Cr 8vo.
London, 1881

DICTIONARY (a) of the Hudson's Bay Indian language. [By Thomas Bowrey.] Folio. [*W.*]
[London, 1701]

DICTIONARY of the religious ceremonies of the Eastern nations, with historical and critical observations. [By Francis Gladwin.] 4to.
Calcutta, 1787

DICTIONARY (a) of the Scottish language. [By Ebenezer Picken.] 12mo. Edinburgh, 1818

DICTIONARY (a) of the turf, the ring, the chase, the pit, the bon-ton, and the varieties of life ; forming the completest and most authentic Lexicon Balatronicum hitherto offered to the notice of the sporting world. By Jon. Bee [John Badcock], Esq., editor of the *Fancy*, etc. Fcap 8vo. [Lowndes' *Bibl. Man.*, p. 145.] London, 1823

DICTIONARY (a) of universal history, chronology, and historical biography, etc. [By James Mitchell.] Fcap 8vo. [*Brit. Mus.*] London, 1823
Signed "J. M."

DICTIONARY (the) of useful knowledge ; uniform with and a companion to "The dictionary of daily wants." [By Robert Kemp Philp.] Post 8vo. [Boase and Courtney's *Bibl. Corn.*, ii., 493.]
London, [1858-62]
Issued in 48 monthly numbers. The pagination of the four volumes is continuous.

DICTIONARY (a) of writers on the prophecies. By the editor of the *Investigator on Prophecy* [Joshua William Brooks]. 8vo. [*Brit. Mus.*]
London, 1835

DID Francis Bacon write "Shakespeare" ? Thirty-two reasons for believing that he did. By the author of Bacon's *Promus of formularies and elegancies* [Mrs H— Potts]. Second edition. 8vo. [*Birm. Cent. Lib.*]
London, 1893

DIDASCALIAE : discourses on several places of the Holy Scriptures ; publikely delivered on sundrie occasions unto an English congregation of believers in Amsterdam. . . . By J. F. [John Ferret]. 4to. [*Brit. Mus.*]
[Amsterdam], 1643

DIDO ; a comic opera : as it is performed at the Theatre Royal in the Hay-market. [By Thomas Bridges.] 8vo. [*Biog. Dram.*] London, 1771

DIDO and Æneas ; a classical burlesque, written for representation at Saint John's College, Hurstpierpoint, on the Prince of Wales' birthday, 1870. [By George O. L. Thomson.] 8vo. Pp. 16. London, [1870]

DIDO, Queen of Carthage ; an opera : with the masque of Neptune's prophecy. [By Prince Hoare.] 8vo. [*Brit. Mus.*] London, 1792

DIE and be damned ; or an antidote against every species of Methodism and enthusiasm. [By T. Mortimer.] Second edition, revised and enlarged by the author. 8vo. Pp. 56. [*Bodl.*]
London, 1758
Another copy has the author's name.

DIES consecrati ; or, a new Christian year with the old poets. [By Henry Edward Manning, Cardinal.] 8vo. [*Brit. Mus.*] Chobham, 1855
The dedication is signed "H. E. M."

"DIES Irae" : the story of a spirit in prison. [By Mrs Margaret O. Oliphant, *née* Wilson.] 8vo. Pp. 84.
Edinburgh, 1897

DIES Novissima ; or, the last epiphany : a poem. By Philalethes [John Pomfret]. Fcap 8vo. [*Brit. Mus.*]
London, 1702

DIET and cookery for common ailments. By a Fellow of the Royal College of Physicians and Phillis Browne [Mrs Sarah S. Hamer]. 8vo. Pp. xii., 307. [*Brit. Mus.*] London, 1894

DIFFERENCE (the) about Church government ended ; by takeing auay the distinction of government into ecclesiasticall and civill ; and proveing the government of the civill magistrat, onelie sufficient in ane Christian kingdome. Wreitin by one that by making peace, preferrs to be called a blessed childe of God, befor preeminence in this worlde. J. M., D.D. [Jasper Maine]. Published according to order. 4to. [*Bodl.*] London, 1646

DIFFERENCE (the) between the Church and Court of Rome considered ; in some reflections on a dialogue entituled, A conference between two Protestants and a Papist. By the author of the late *Seasonable discourse* [William Lloyd, D.D., Bishop of Worcester]. 4to. [*D. N. B.*, vol. 33, p. 439.] London, 1674

DIFFERENCE (the) between the Church of England, and the Church of Rome ; in opposition to a late book, intituled, An agreement between the Church of England, and Church of Rome. [By John Williams, D.D., Bishop of Chichester.] Second edition. 4to. [*D. N. B.*, vol. 61, p. 420.]
London, 1687

DIFFERENCE (the) between the Nonjurors and the present public Assemblies. [By Joseph Smith, D.D., provost of Queen's College, Oxford.] 8vo. [*Brit. Mus.*] London, 1716

DIFFERENCE (the) between words esteemed synonymous in the English language, and the proper choice of them determined ; together with so much of the Abbé Gerard's treatise on this subject, as would agree with our mode of expression. . . . [By John Trusler, LL.D.] 2 vols. Fcap 8vo.
London, 1766
Later editions give the author's name.

DIFFERENCE (the) betwene the auncient phisicke, first taught by the godly forefathers, consisting in unitie, peace and concord ; and the latter phisicke proceeding from idolaters, ethnickes, and heathen, as Gallen and such other, consisting in dualitie, discorde and contrarietie ; and wherein the naturall philosophie of Aristotle doth differ from the trueth of Gods worde, and is injurious to Christianitie and sounde doctrine. . . . By R. B. Esquire [Robert Bostock]. 12mo. No pagination. 94 leaves. [*W.*] Imprinted at London for Robert Walley. 1585

DIFFERENCE (the) betwixt the Protestant and Socinian methods : in answer to a book written by a Romanist, and intituled, The Protestants plea for a Socinian. [By Thomas Tenison, D.D.] 4to. [Jones' Peck.]
[London], 1687

DIFFERENCE (the) of the case between the separation of Protestants from the Church of Rome, and the separation of Dissenters from the Church of England. [By William Clagett, D.D.] 4to. Pp. 66. [*D.N.B.*, vol. 10, p. 367.] London, 1686
Also attributed to John Williams.

DIFFERENCES (the) of the time ; in three dialogues. The first, anent episcopacy ; the second, anent the obligation of the Covenants against episcopacy ; the third, anent separation : intended for the quieting the minds of the people, and settling them in more peace and unity. [By David Forrester.] 8vo. [*Adv. Lib.*]
Edinburgh, 1679

DIFFERENT plans for improving the harbour of Bristol impartially examined. . . . By J. T. [John Thomas]. 8vo. Pp. 48. [*Brit. Mus.*]
Bristol, 1800

DIFFERENT (the) widows; or, intrigue à la mode : a comedy [by Mrs Mary Pix], as it is now acted at the New Theatre in Little Lincoln's Inn Fields. 4to. [Arber's *Term Cat.*, iii., 684.] London, 1703

DIFFICILES nugae ; or, observations touching the Torricellian experiment, and the various solutions of the same, especially touching the weight and elasticity of the air. [By Sir Matthew Hale.] Second edition, with some occasional additions. Pp. 363. [*Bodl.*]
London, 1675

DIFFICULTIES (the) and discouragements which attend the study of the Scripture in the way of private judgment ; in order to show that since such a study of the Scriptures is men's indispensable duty, it concerns all Christian societies to remove (as much as possible) these discouragements : in a letter to a young clergyman. By a presbyter of the Church of England [Francis Hare, D.D.]. 8vo. [*D.N.B.*, vol. 24, p. 366.] London, 1714

DIFFICULTIES of a young clergyman in times of division. [By Emma Newton.] Fcap 8vo. [*Brit. Mus.*]
London, 1844

DIGBY Ravelyn : a novel. By Heber K. Daniels [Farquhar Palliser]. 8vo. Pp. 242. London, 1899

DIGEST (a) of facts and principles on banking and commerce ; with a plan for preventing future reactions. [By John Wade, LL.D.] Fcap 8vo. [*Brit. Mus.*] London, 1826

DIGEST of rules and orders of the High Court of Judicature at Madras, relating to the practice of the High Court and the Courts subordinate thereto. By H. W. [Herbert Wigram]. 8vo. Madras, 1874

DIGEST (a) of the doctrine of S. Thomas [Aquinas] on the Incarnation. [By William Humphry, S.J.] Pt 8vo. Pp. xi., 443. [*New Coll. Cat.*]
London, 1868

DIGEST (a) of the duties of customs and excise, payable upon all foreign articles imported into and exported from Great Britain ; duties outwards, and countervailing duties between Great Britain and Ireland ; customs, and excise bounties ; bounties on fisheries ; duties coastwise ; quarantine laws ; tonnage duties . . . together with a copious appendix. Brought up to 1st Dec. 1818. [By Thomas Thornton.] 8vo. Pp. xviii., 526. [*Bodl.*] London, 1818

DIGEST (a) of the laws of Moses. . . . [By John P. Firmin.] 4to. [*Brit. Mus.*] London, 1851

DIGEST (a) of the proceedings of the court leet of the manor and liberty of the Savoy, parcel of the Duchy of Lancaster, in the county of Middlesex ; from the year 1682 to the present time. [By Joseph Ritson.] 8vo. [*Bodl.*]
N.P., 1789

DIGGLES ; a legend of the Victoria Docks. [Verse.] By Arthur de Cripp Elgate [Thomas Gray, steamship surveyor]. 8vo. [*Brit. Mus.*]
London, 1868

DIGITUS Dei. [By Thomas Scott, B.D.] 4to. Pp. 48. [Lowndes' *Bibl. Man.*] N.P., N.D.

DIGITUS Dei ; or, God's justice upon treachery and treason, exemplifyed in the life and death of the late James, Duke of Hamilton. Being an exact relation of his traiterous practises since the year, 1630. . . . [By Marchamont Nedham.] 4to. Pp. 31. [Lowndes' *Bibl. Man.*] London, 1694

DIGNITIE (the) of man, both in the perfections of his soule and his bodie ; shewing as well the faculties in the disposition of the one, as the senses and organs in the composition of the other. By N. A. [Anthony Nixon]. Fcap 4to. Pp. 136. [Madan's *Oxf. Books*, i., p. 106.] Oxford [?], 1616
Though ostensibly printed in Oxford, this work was really produced elsewhere. An earlier edition appeared at London in 1612.

DIGNITY (the) of human nature ; an essay. [By Edward Jerningham.] 8vo. Pp. 69. [*D. N. B.*, vol. 29, p. 347.] London, 1805

DIGNITY (the) of kingship asserted ; in answer to Mr [John] Milton's ready and easie way to establish a free commonwealth : proving that kingship is both in it self, and in reference to these nations, farre the most excellent government ; and the returning to our former loyalty or obedience thereto is the only way under God to restore and settle these three once flourishing, now languishing, broken, & almost ruined nations. By G. S., a lover of loyalty [Gilbert Sheldon, later Archbishop of Canterbury]. . . . 8vo. 12 leaves unpaged, and pp. 221. London, 1660
Mistakenly assigned to George Searle.

DIGNITY (the), use and abuse of glass-bottles ; set forth in a sermon preach'd to an illustrious assembly, and now publish'd for the use of the inferiour clergy. By the author of the *Tale of a tub* [Jonathan Swift, D.D.]. 8vo. London, 1715

DILEMMA (the). [A novel.] By the author of *The Battle of Dorking* [Col. Sir Charles Tomkins Chesney, R.E.]. 3 vols. 8vo. [*Camb. Univ. Lib.*] Edinburgh, 1876

DILEMMA (the) of Commander Brett. By Weatherby Chesney [Charles John Cutcliffe Hyne]. Fcap 8vo. Pp. 297. [*Lond. Lib. Cat.*] London, 1917

DILEMMAS of pride. By the author of *First love* [Mrs Margracia Loudon]. 3 vols. Fcap 8vo. [*Adv. Lib.*] London, 1833

DILIGENCE and sloth, the friend and the enemy of man, his blessing and his curse. By a layman [James Heywood Markland]. Fcap 8vo. [Green's *Bibl. Somers.*, i., 339.] London, [1858]
The Preface is signed " J. H. M."

DILLY and the Captain. By Margaret Sidney [Mrs Harriett Mulford Lothrop, *née* Stone]. Fcap 8vo. [Kirk's *Supp.*, p. 1019.] Boston, 1887

DIMPLETHORPE By the author of *St Olave's*, etc. [Eliza Tabor ; later Mrs Stephenson]. 3 vols. Cr 8vo. [*Brit. Mus.*] London, 1880

DINA Mite : a story of to-day. By Brenda [Mrs —— Castle Smith, *née* . . . Meyrick]. 8vo. Pp. 190. [*Brit. Mus.*] London, 1887

DINA ; or familiar faces. [By William Patrick Wilkie.] 3 vols. Cr 8vo. [*Camb. Univ. Lib.*] Edinburgh, 1865

DINARBAS ; a tale : being a continuation of Rasselas, Prince of Abissinia. [By Ellis Cornelia Knight.] Fcap 8vo. [*Adv. Lib.*] London, 1790

DINNA forget. [A novel.] By John Strange Winter [Mrs Arthur Stannard, *née* Henrietta E. V. Palmer]. 8vo. [*Brit. Mus.*] London, 1890

DINNER (the) bell : a gastronomic manual ; edited by Fin-Bec [William Blanchard Jerrold]. 8vo. [*D. N. B.*, vol. 29, p. 353.] London, 1878

DINNER for two ; an original comedietta. By Richard Claude Carton [Richard Claude Critchett]. 12mo. [*Brit. Mus.*] London, [1903]

DINNER (the) question ; or, how to dine well and economically. . . . By Tabitha Tickletooth [Charles Selby]. 8vo. [*Brit. Mus.*] London, 1860

DINNER (the) year-book. By Marion Harland [Mary Virginia Hawes, later Mrs Terhune]. Fcap 8vo. [Kirk's *Supp.*, p. 1426.] New York, 1878

DINNERS and dishes. By Wanderer [Elim H. D'Avigdor], author of *Across country*, etc. Pt 8vo. Pp. 207. [*Brit. Mus.*] London, 1885

DIOCESAN churches not yet discovered in the primitive times : or, a defence of the Answer to Dr Stillingfleets allegations out of antiquity for such churches ; against the exceptions offered in the preface to a late treatise [by Henry Maurice] called a Vindication of the primitive Church. . . . [By David Clarkson.] 4to. Pp. vi., 113, viii. [*D. N. B.*, vol. 10, p. 453.] London, 1682

DIOCESAN Synods : a paper read at a clerical meeting. . . . [By Rev. Fielder Hemmans, M.A.] 8vo. London, 1867

DIOGENES among the D.D.'s : a book of burlesques. [By Rev. David Macrae, M.A., junr.] Pt 8vo. Pp. 118. [*New Coll. Lib.*] Glasgow, 1888

DIOGENES at Athens, and other poems. By Rowland Thirlemere [John Walker]. 8vo. [*Lond. Lib. Cat.*] London, 1918

DION ; a tragedy : and miscellaneous poetry. [By George Ambrose Rhodes, M.D.] 8vo. [Watt's *Bibl. Brit.*]
London, 1806

DIORAMIC sketches, ancient and modern. [Verse.] [By Mrs Mary Anne M'Mullan, *née* Ward.] Fcap 8vo. Pp. 107. [*Brit. Mus.*]
London, 1853

DIOSCOPE (the). By a citizen [Dr —— Torry]. 8vo. [Robertson's *Aberd. Bibl.*]
Aberdeen, 1834

DIOSG Farm ; a sketch of its history during the tenancy of John Roberts and his widow. By a Llanbrynmair farmer [Samuel Roberts]. 12mo. [*Brit. Mus.*]
Newtown, 1854

DIOTREPHES admonished ; or some remarks on a Letter from the author of Pietas Oxoniensis [Sir Richard Hill] to the Rev. Dr Adams, of Shrewsbury ; occasioned by the publication of his sermon preached at St Chad's, entitled A test of true and false doctrines. By a parishioner of St Chad's [Job Orton]. 8vo. Pp. 83. [*D. N. B.*, vol. 42, p. 272.]
London, 1770
Signed " Salopiensis."
See also below, " Diotrephes re-admonished. . . ."

DIOTREPHES catechised ; or sixteen important questions touching the ecclesiastical jurisdiction and censures (contradistinct to civill) now eagerly pretended to and challenged by a divine right, by some over-rigid Presbyterians, and Independents : propounded to both these dissenting parties, for the further discovery of truth. By a well-wisher to verity and unity [William Prynne]. 4to. [*Brit. Mus.*]
London, 1646

DIOTREPHES re-admonished ; or some remarks on the second edition of a Letter from the author of Pietas Oxoniensis to the Rev. Dr Adams of Shrewsbury ; occasioned by his sermon, entitled, A test of true and false doctrines : wherein Dr Adams, the Church of England, and some evangelical doctrines, are vindicated from the misrepresentations of the letter-writer. By a parishioner of St Chad's, and author of *Diotrephes admonished* [Job Orton]. 8vo. Pp. 91. [*D. N. B.*, vol. 42, p. 272.]
London, 1770

DIP (a) of ink. By Alan St Aubyn [Mrs Frances Marshall]. Cr 8vo. [*Lond. Lib. Cat.*]
London, 1907

DIPLOMACY ; a compendious treatise on the rights, privileges, duties, and functions of diplomatic agents. [By

Thomas Hartwell Horne.] A new edition. 8vo.
London, 1848
Annexed to Polson's Principles of the law of nations, it appeared originally in the Encyclopædia Metropolitana. [From chronological list of T. H. Horne's Works, appended to the " Reminiscences."]

DIPLOMACY (the) of the United States ; being an account of the foreign relations of the country, from the treaty with France in 1778, to the treaty of Ghent in 1814, with Great Britain. [By Theodore Lyman, junr.] 8vo. Pp. 379. [Rich's *Bibl. Amer.*, ii., 185.]
Boston, 1826

DIPLOMAT (a) on diplomacy. [By Joseph Q. Nunes.] 8vo. [Cushing's *Init. and Pseud.*, vol. i., p. 81.]
Philadelphia, 1863

DIPLOMATIC (the) policy of Mr [James] Madison unveiled, in strictures upon the late correspondence between Mr Smith and Mr Jackson. By a Bostonian [John Lowell, LL.D.]. 8vo. [Cushing's *Init. and Pseud.*, vol. i., p. 38.]
London, 1810

DIPLOMATIC sketches. By an outsider [Baron Carl von Marlortie]. 8vo. [*Brit. Mus.*]
London, 1878-79

DIPLOMATIC (the) year. By a Northern man [Joseph Reed Ingersoll, LL.D.]. 8vo. [Cushing's *Init. and Pseud.*, vol. i., p. 205.]
Philadelphia, 1863

DIPLOMAT'S (a) diary. By Julien Gordon [Mrs Julie Grinnell Cruger, *née* Storrow]. 8vo. Pp. 233. [*Lond. Lib. Cat.*]
Philadelphia, 1890

DIPPER (the) plung'd ; or Thomas Hicks his feigned Dialogue between a Christian and a Quaker, proved an unchristian forgery, consisting of self-contradictions and abuses against the truth, and people called Quakers. By G. W. [George Whitehead]. 4to. [Smith's *Cat. of Friends' Books*, ii., 893.]
N.P., 1672

DIPPING not the only Scriptural and primitive manner of baptizing ; and supposing it were, yet a strict adherence to it not obligatory on us. [By Micaiah Towgood.] 8vo. Pp. iv., 44. [Whitley's *Bapt. Bibl.*, i., 170.]
London, 1751

DIRECT legislation by the people, *versus* representative government. Translated from the original Swiss pamphlets [of W— H. Dircks] by E— Oswald. 8vo.
London, 1869

DIRECT (a) way, whereby the plainest man may be guided to the waters of life. . . . By R. C. [Roger Cotton]. B. L. 8vo. [*Brit. Mus.*] London, 1610
An earlier edition (1592) bears a different title (" A direction to . . . .").

DIRECTION (a) to be observed by N. N. if hee meane to proceede in answering the booke intituled Mercy and truth, or charity maintained by Catholiks, &c. [By Edward Knott, *alias* Matthias Wilson, Jesuit.] 8vo. [*Bodl.*] Permissu superiorum, 1636
   The author's name is in the handwriting of Wood.

DIRECTIONAL astrology. By Sepharial [Walter Gorn Old]. 8vo. [*Brit. Mus.*] London, 1915

DIRECTIONS concerning the matter and style of sermons : written to W. S. by J. A. [James Arderne, D.D.]. 12mo. [*Brit. Mus.*] London, 1671

DIRECTIONS for bringing over seeds and plants from the East Indies and other distant countries in a state of vegetation. [By John Ellis, F.R.S.] 4to. [*W.*] London, 1771
   At p. 18 is " The method of catching and preserving insects for collections," also published with the author's name.

DIRECTIONS for collecting insects in foreign countries. [By Dru Drury?] 4to. [*Brit. Mus.*] [London, 1800?]

DIRECTIONS for entrance into a religious life ; written to a young person, on occasion of his entring into a religious society for promoting of religion and piety in himself and others. [By James Budd, rector of West-Horsley.] 8vo. [*Bodl.*] London, 1701
   The Epistle dedicatory is signed " J. B."

DIRECTIONS for health, natural and artificial, with medicines for all diseases of the eye. [By Walter Bayley, or Bayly.] 4to. [*Watt's Bibl. Brit.*] London, 1626

DIRECTIONS for making observations with the dipleidoscope, and requisite tables for the year 1844. [By J. M. Bloxam.] 8vo. [*Brit. Mus.*] London, 1844

DIRECTIONS for preparing manure from peat; instructions for forestors. [By Allan Maconochie, Lord Meadowbank.] 8vo. Pp. 98. [*Brit. Mus.*] Edinburgh, 1815

DIRECTIONS for renewing our covenant with God. [By John Wesley, M.A.] Fifth edition. 12mo. [Green's *Wesley Bibl.*, p. 204.] London, 1794

DIRECTIONS for the conversation of the clergy; collected from the visitation charges of the Right Reverend Father in God, Edward Stillingfleet, D.D., late Lord Bishop of Worcester. [By Dr William Assheton.] 8vo. [*Bodl.*] London, 1710

DIRECTIONS for the education of a young Prince till seven years of age, which will serve for the governing of children of all conditions. [By Peter Du Moulin.] 8vo. [Arber's *Term Cat.*, ii., p. 522.] London, 1672

DIRECTIONS for the faithful of the N. D. [Northern District] touching the future observance of holydays. [By William Walton.] 12mo.
                              Preston, 1778

DIRECTIONS for the Latine tongue. By the translator [into Latin] of [Sir Thomas Browne's] Religio Medici [John Merryweather]. Fcap 8vo. [*D. N. B.*, vol. 7, p. 66.] London, 1681

DIRECTIONS for young students in divinity. [By John Owen, D.D.] 8vo.
                              London, 1673
   Included in his collected works.

DIRECTIONS from the King [Henry III. of France] to the gouernors of the prouinces, concerning the death of the Duke of Guyse ; togither with the Kings Letter to the Lord of Taian. Translated out of French into English by E. A. [E. Aggas]. 4to. [*Bodl.*]
                              London, 1589

DIRECTIONS left by a gentleman to his sonns ; for the improvement of barren and healthy land in England and Wales. [By Gabriel Reeve.] 8vo. [Macdonald's *Agricultural Writers*, p. 197.] London, 1670

DIRECTIONS propounded, and humbly presented to the High Court of Parliament concerning the Booke of Common Prayer and episcopall governement ; written by a reverend and learned divine now resident in London [Ephraim Udall, M.A.]. 4to. [*D. N. B.*, vol. 58, p. 4.] Oxford, 1642
   Wrongly attributed to Archbishop Ussher.
   Published (Lon., 1642, 4to) with a different title, " The Bishop of Armaghes direction concerning the Lyturgy, and Episcopall Government."

DIRECTIONS to penitents and believers, for renewing their covenant with God. [By John Wesley.] Ninth edition. 12mo. [Green's *Wesley Bibl.*, p. 204.] London, 1806

DIRECTOR (the); a weekly literary journal : containing I. Essays, on subjects of literature, the fine arts and manners. II. Bibliographiana. Account of rare and curious books, and of the book sales in this country, from the close of the seventeenth

century. III. Royal Institution. Analyses of the lectures delivered weekly. IV. British gallery. Description of the principal pictures exhibited for sale, with the names of the purchasers. [Edited by Thomas Frognall Dibdin, D.D.] 2 vols. 8vo. London, 1807
   Written by Sir Humphry Davy, William Beloe, Thomas Hope, Thomas Forster, and others.

DIRECTORIE (a) teaching the way to the truth, in a briefe and plaine discourse against the heresies of this time. . . . By I. R. [John Radford]. Fcap 8vo. [Gillow's *Bibl. Dict.*, vol. 5, p. 386.] N.P., [Doway ?], 1605

DIRECTORIUM (the) Anglicanum; being a manual of directions for the right celebration of the . . . rites and ceremonies of the Church according to the ancient use. [By Rev. John Purchas.] Second edition, by Fred. G. Lee. 4to. London, 1865

DIRECTORIUM Scoticanum et Anglicanum. [Compiled by William Wright.] 8vo. [*Camb. Univ. Lib.*]
        London, private print, 1855

DIRECTORY (the); a form of prayer, according to the doctrine of the Church of England, compiled for the use of Christian congregations. [By Robert Mackenzie Beverley.] Third edition. Fcap 8vo. Pp. 68. [*Brit. Mus.*] London, 1831

DIRGE (the) of Erin. Translated from the Irish. By Owen Clarke [James Martin, of County Meath]. 8vo. [O'Donoghue's *Poets of Ireland*.]
        Dublin, [1840 ?]

DIRGES (the) of the Whig administration. By the author of *An enquiry into the origin, nature, and objects, of the government scheme of education* [Joseph Denison]. 8vo. [*Camb. Univ. Lib.*] London, 1841

DIRLETON—a sketch in Arcady. [By John Harrison.] Large 8vo. Pp. 20. [Edinburgh], 1888
   Presentation copy "printed for private circulation." No separate title. Signed "J. H."

DIRT wip't off; or a manifest discovery of the gross ignorance, erroneousness and most unchristian and wicked spirit of one John Bunyan, laypreacher in Bedford, which he hath shewed in a vile pamphlet publish't by him, against the design of Christianity. Written for the disabusing of those poor deluded people that are followers of him, and such like teachers. . . . [By Edward Fowler, D.D.] 4to. Pp. 86. [*Brit. Mus.*] London, 1672

DISAPPEARANCE (the) of Nigel Blair. [A novel.] By Florence Warden [Florence Alice Price, later Mrs George E. James]. Cr 8vo. Pp. 296. London, 1911

DISAPPEARED. [A novel.] By Sarah Tytler [Henrietta Keddie]. 8vo. [*Lit. Year Book.*] London, 1887

DISAPPOINTED (the) gallant; or, buckram in armour: a new ballad opera, as it was acted at the New Edinburgh Theatre. Written by a young Scots gentleman [Adam Thomson]. 8vo. [*Adv. Lib.*] Edinburgh, 1738

DISAPPOINTED villainy: an entertainment. [By Thomas Horde.] 8vo. [*Brit. Mus.*] London, 1775

DISAPPOINTMENT; and other poems. [By James Aikman.] 12mo. [*Adv. Lib.*] Edinburgh, 1825

DISARMED. [A novel.] By the author of *Kitty* [Matilda Betham Edwards]. 2 vols. Cr 8vo. [*Brit. Mus.*] London, 1883

DISCARDED (the) spinster; or, a plea for the poor, on the impolicy of spinning-jennies: a poem. [By Robert Sadler.] 4to. [*Brit. Mus.*] London, 1791

DISCIPLINE. By the authoress of *Letters to my unknown friends* [Sydney Warburton]. 12mo. [*Brit. Mus.*] London, 1851

DISCIPLINE; a novel. By the author of *Self control* [Mrs Mary Brunton]. 3 vols. 8vo. [Courtney's *Secrets*, p. 51.] Edinburgh, 1814

DISCIPLINE (the) of life. [By Lady Emily Ponsonby.] 3 vols. Fcap 8vo. [*Brit. Mus.*] London, 1848

DISCLOSING (a) of the great bull; and certain calues that he hath gotten, and especially the monster bull that roared at my lord byshops gate. [By Thomas Norton.] 8vo. B. L. No pagination. [*Bodl.*] Imprinted at London by John Daye, dwelling over Aldersgate. [1570]

DISCOLLIMINIUM; or, a most obedient reply to a late book [by Francis Rous], called, Bounds & bonds, so farre as concerns the first demurrer and no further: or rather, a reply to Bounds onely, leaving Bonds to the second demurrer and grand casuist. By B. [Rev. Nathaniel Ward]. 4to. Pp. 54. [*N. and Q.*, March 1867, p. 237.] London, 1650

DISCONTENTED (a) schoolgirl. By Raymond Jacberns [Georgina M. Selby Ash]. Cr 8vo. Pp. 404. [*Lit. Year Book.*] London, 1907

DISCORD; a satire. [By Richard Hurd, D.D., Bishop of Worcester.] 8vo. [*Camb. Univ. Lib.*]
London, 1773

DISCORDS. [A novel.] By George Egerton [Mrs Golding Bright]. Cr 8vo. [*Lit. Year Book.*]
London, 1894

DISCOURSE (a) about a scrupulous conscience; containing some plain directions for the cure of it. [By Benjamin Calamy, D.D.] 4to. [*New Coll. Cat.*] London, 1684

DISCOURSE (a) about ceremonies, church-government, and liturgy; humbly offered to the consideration of Convocation. By J. G. G. [John Gailhard, Gentleman]. 4to. Pp. 168. [*New Coll. Cat.*] London, 1696

DISCOURSE about church-unity; being a defence of D. Stillingfleet's Unreasonableness of separation: in answer to several late pamphlets, but principally to Dr Owen and Mr. Baxter. By a presbyter of the Church of England [William Sherlock, D.D.]. 8vo. [*D. N. B.*, vol. 52, p. 96.]
London, 1681

DISCOURSE (a) about civil government in a New Plantation. . . . By John Cotton, B.D. [really by John Davenport, of New Haven, Mass.]. 4to. [Allibone's *Dict.*, i., 434.]
Cambridge, 1663

DISCOURSE (a) about discerning and trying the spirits; wherein are laid down rules, shewing what are the essential and necessary doctrines and practices of Christianity: to which is prefixed, the life of St Mary Magdalen de Pazzi, a Carmelite nunn. . . . [By Thomas Smith, D.D.] 4to. Pp. 134. [Jones' Peck, p. 415.]
London, 1688

DISCOURSE (a) about edification; in answer to a question, whether it is lawful for any man to forsake the communion of the Church of England, and go to the Separate meetings, because he can better edifie there? [By Gregory Hascard, Dean of Windsor.] 4to. [*Brit. Mus.*] London, 1683

DISCOURSE (a) about the charge of novelty upon the reformed Church of England, made by the Papists asking us the question, where was our religion before Luther? [By Gregory Hascard, D.D., Dean of Windsor.] 4to. [*Brit. Mus.*] London, 1685

DISCOURSE (a) about the pretious blood and sacrifice of Jesus Christ. [By Thomas Moore, Baptist minister.] 8vo. Pp. 103. [Whitley's *Bapt. Bibl.*, i., 26.] London, 1646

DISCOURSE (a) about the uniting Scotland with England; containing the general advantage of such an union to both kingdoms . . . with divers original papers delivered by the Commissioners of both nations to one another about an union in 1667. [By Blackerby Fairfax.] 8vo. [*Brit. Mus.*] London, 1702

DISCOURSE (a) about trade; wherein the reduction of interest of money to 4l. per centum, is recommended; methods for the employment and maintenance of the poor are proposed; several weighty points relating to companies of merchants; the act of navigation, naturalization of strangers, our woollen manufactures, the ballance of trade; and the nature of plantations, and their consequences in relation to the kingdom, are seriously discussed. . . . [By Sir Josiah Child.] Never before printed. 8vo. Pp. 304. [*Bodl.*] [London], 1690

DISCOURSE (a) about tradition; shewing what is meant by it, and what tradition is to be received, and what tradition is to be rejected. [By Symon Patrick, D.D.] 4to. London, 1683
Reprinted in his collected works.

DISCOURSE (a) addressed to magistrates and men in authority; occasioned by the enormous license and irreligion of the times. [By George Berkeley, D.D.] 8vo. Dublin printed.
London, Reprinted 1738
Reprinted in Fraser's edition of collected works.

DISCOURSE (a) against false preaching. [By A. Castle.] 8vo. [*Camb. Univ. Lib.*] N.P., 1719

DISCOVRSE (a) against flatterie. [By Grey Brydges, Lord Chandos.] 12mo. Pp. 152. London, 1611
" This is the first draft and impression of one of the essays which afterwards appeared under the title of 'Horæ subsecivæ,' Lond. 1620. It was altogether unknown to Lord Orford or Mr. Park, nor have I yet seen another copy."—Note in the handwriting of Douce.

DISCOURSE (a) against painting and tincturing of women; wherein the abominable sinnes of murther and poysoning, pride and ambition, adultery and witchcraft, are set foorth & discouered. . . . [By Thomas Tuke, M.A.] 4to. Pp. 74. [*Bodl.*]
London, 1616
Signed " T. T."

DISCOURSE (a) against purgatory. [By John Hartcliffe, B.D.] 4to. [*Bodl.; Brit. Mus.;* Jones' Peck, ii., 398.]　　　　　　London, 1685

    Also ascribed to Tillotson in the Bodleian Catalogue, and to William Wake by Mr Halkett (authority not given).

DISCOURSE (a) against transubstantiation. [By John Tillotson, D.D.] Second edition. 4to. [Jones' Peck, p. 148.]　　　　　　London, 1684

DISCOURSE (a) against unequal marriages ; viz., old persons marrying with young ; against persons marrying without parents' or friends' consent ; against persons marrying without their own consent. [By S— Bufford.] Fcap 8vo. [Arber's *Term Cat.*, ii., p. 614.]　　　　　　London, 1696

DISCOURSE (a) and views of Virginia. [By Sir William Berkeley.] 8vo. [Trent's *Hist. of Amer. Lit.*, i., p. 367.]　　　　　　London, 1663

DISCOURSE (a) : being the substance of several sermons on the Lord's Supper, wherein the spiritual nature thereof is unfolded ; shewing in what sense true believers do eat and drink the body and blood of Christ. . . . By T. B. [Thomas Beverley]. 8vo. [Arber's *Term Cat.*, iii., 394.]　　　　　　London, 1704

DISCOURSE (a), by way of general preface to the quarto edition of Bishop Warburton's Works ; containing some account of the life, writings, and character of the author. [By Richard Hurd, D.D.] 4to. Pp. vii., 150. [Watt's *Bibl. Brit.*]　　　　　　London, 1794

DISCOURSE (a) concerning a guide in controversies ; in two letters. . . . [By Catherine Trotter, later Mrs Cockburn.] Second edition. 8vo. [Watt's *Bibl. Brit.*]　　　　　　London, 1728

DISCOURSE (a) concerning a guide in matters of faith ; with respect, especially, to the Romish pretence of the necessity of such a one as is infallible. [By Thomas Tenison.] 4to. [Jones' Peck, p. 224.]　　　　　　London, 1683

DISCOURSE (a) concerning a judge of controversies in matters of religion ; being an answer to some papers [by Lady Theophila Nelson] asserting the necessity of such a judge : with an address to wavering Protestants, shewing what little reason they have to think of any change of their religion. [By William Sherlock, D.D.] 4to. Pp. xv., 84. [Jones' Peck, p. 375.]　　　　　　London, 1686

DISCOURSE (a) concerning a lumber office ; being a true remedy for the scarcity of money. [By Charles Morton, M.D.] 4to. [*Brit. Mus.*]　　　　　　London, 1696

DISCOURSE (a) concerning a new world and another planet. The first Book, the discovery of a new world . . . tending to prove . . . there may be another habitable world in the moon. [By John Wilkins, D.D., Bishop of Chester.] 8vo. [*D. N. B.*, vol. 61, p. 266.]　　　　　　London, 1640

DISCOURSE (a) concerning auricular confession, as it is prescribed by the Council of Trent, and practised by the Church of Rome ; with a post-script on occasion of a book lately printed in France, called Historia confessionis auricularis. [By John Goodman, D.D.] 4to. Pp. 56. [*Brit. Mus.*]　　　　　　London, 1684

    In some copies, the date is incorrectly printed 1648.

DISCOURSE (a) concerning conscience ; wherein an account is given of the nature, and rule, and obligation, of it : and the case of those who separate from the communion of the Church of England as by law established, upon this pretence, that it is against their conscience to joyn in it, is stated and discussed. [By John Sharp, D.D.] 4to. Pp. 59. [*Brit. Mus.*]　　　　　　London, 1684

    A second part was published in 1689 : *see* " A Discourse of conscience."

DISCOURSE (a) concerning divine providence, in relation to national judgements. [By Thomas Smith, D.D.] 4to. [*Bodl.*]　　London, 1693

DISCOURSE (a) concerning evangelical love, church-peace and unity ; with the occasions and reasons of present differences and divisions about things sacred and religious. . . . [By John Owen, D.D.] 8vo. Pp. 258. [*Brit. Mus.*]　　　　London, 1672

DISCOURSE (a) concerning fews and superiorities ; shewing that the rigid observance of them is inconsistent with the nature of the British constitution. Humbly address'd to the parliament of Great Britain. [By —— Hepburn of Bairford.] 8vo. [*Jas. Maidment.*]　　　Edinburgh, 1716

DISCOURSE (a) concerning generosity. [By Lord John Somers.] Fcap 8vo.　　　　　　London, 1693

DISCOURSE (a) concerning God's act of adoption ; to which is added, A discourse upon the inheritance of the adopted sons of God. [By Mrs Anne Dutton.] 8vo.　London, 1735

DISCOURSE (a) concerning infallibility in religion : written by a person of quality [Sir Kenelm Digby] to an eminent Lord [Lord George Digby]. Fcap 8vo. Pp. 229. [*Brit. Mus.*]
                              Amsterdam, 1652

DISCOURSE (a) concerning invocation of saints. [By Samuel Freeman, D.D.] 4to. Pp. 72. [Jones' Peck, p. 420.]   London, 1684

DISCOURSE (a) concerning Ireland and the different interests thereof, in answer to the Exon and Barnstaple petitions. . . . [By Sir Francis Brewster.] 4to.   London, 1698

DISCOURSE concerning laws made against hereticks. [By Jacques de Daillon du Lude.] 8vo. Dublin, 1744

DISCOURSE (a) concerning Lent, in two parts. The first, an historical account of its observation : the second, an essay concerning its original ; this subdivided into two repartitions ; whereof the first is preparatory, and shews that most of our Christian ordinances are deriv'd from the Jews ; and the second conjectures that Lent is of the same original. [By George Hooper, D.D.] 8vo. [*D. N. B.*, vol. 27, p. 303.]   London, 1695

DISCOURSE (a) concerning liberty of conscience ; in which are contain'd proposals about what liberty in this kind is now politically expedient to be given, and severall reasons to shew how much the peace and welfare of the nation is concern'd therein. By R. T. [Sir Peter Pett]. 8vo. Pp. 85. [Wood's *Athen. Oxon.*, iv., 577.]
                              London, 1661

DISCOURSE (a) concerning liturgies, and their imposition. [By John Owen, D.D.] 4to. Pp. 67.
                         [London], 1662
Reprinted in his collected works.

DISCOURSE (a) concerning miracles wrought in the Roman Catholick Church, in vindication of their truth against Dr Stillingfleet's unjust cavils ; where the miraculous translation of the Holy House of Loreto is asserted, and proved an undeniable verity. By E. W. [Edward Worsley]. The second part. 8vo.   Antwerp, 1674
The first part will be found under the " Infallibility of the Roman Catholick Church," etc. The second part has a second pagination, but the signatures are continuous. *See* "A Discourse of miracles."

DISCOURSE (a) concerning penance ; shewing how the doctrine of it, in the Church of Rome, makes void true repentance. [By Peter Allix.] 4to. [Jones' Peck, p. 342.] London, 1688

DISCOURSE (a) concerning prayer, ex tempore, or, by pretence of the Spirit ; in justification of authorized and set-formes of lyturgie. [By Jeremy Taylor.] 4to.
                    Printed in the yeere, 1646
A second edition, with the author's name, was published in 1649, under the title of " An apology for authorized and set forms of liturgie."

DISCOURSE (a) concerning Puritans : a vindication of those who uniustly suffer by the mistake, abuse, and misapplication of that name ; a tract necessary and usefull for these times. [By John Ley, pastor of Budworth, in Cheshire.] 4to. Pp. 58. [*D. N. B.*, vol. 33, p. 208.]
                Printed for Robert Bostock, 1641
The address to the reader is signed " Philus Adelphus."
In Bishop Barlow's copy in the Bodleian, the above work is said by Barlow to be " writt by J. Ley." In the Thomason *Tracts*, it is ascribed to Henry Parker [of Lincoln's Inn]. Watt has it under both names.

DISCOURSE (a) concerning ridicule and irony in writing ; in a letter to the Rev. Dr Nathaniel Marshall. [By Anthony Collins.] 8vo. Pp. 77. [Darling's *Cyclop. Bibl.*]
                              London, 1729

DISCOURSE (a) concerning schools and school-masters, offered to publick consideration. By M. N. [Marchamont Nedham]. 4to. [Wood's *Athen. Oxon.*, iii., 1187.] London, 1663

DISCOURSE (a) concerning some prevailing evils of the present time : wherein Mr [Archibald] Campbell's reasonings concerning the nature and influence of religious enthusiasm are particularly examined. [By William Wilson, minister at Perth.] 8vo. [*Adv. Lib.*]   Edinburgh, 1731

DISCOURSE (a) concerning supreme power and common right : at first calculated for the year 1641, and now thought fit to be published. By a person of Quality [Sir John Monson, D.C.L.]. 8vo. Pp. 181. [*D. N. B.*, vol. 38, p. 196.]   London, 1680

DISCOURSE (a) concerning the adoration of the Host, as it is taught and practiced in the Church of Rome ; wherein an answer is given to T. G. [Thomas Godden] on that subject, and to Monsieur Boileau's late book De adoratione Eucharistiæ. Paris, 1685. [By William Payne, D.D.] 4to. Pp. 66. [Jones' Peck, p. 372.]
                              London, 1685

DISCOURSE (a) concerning the basis and original of government, with the absolute and indispensable necessity of it ; wherein the excellency of monarchy above any other kind is evidently demonstrated : as it was delivered by way of charge to the Grand-Jury, at a Quarter-Sessions of the peace held at Ipswich in the county of Suffolk. By F. T., Esq. . . . [Francis Theobald]. 4to. [*Brit. Mus.*] London, 1667
Attributed by others to Francis Thynn.

DISCOURSE (a) concerning the celebration of divine service in an unknown tongue. [By John Williams, D.D.] 4to. Pp. 56. [Jones' Peck, p. 330.] London, 1685

DISCOURSE (a) concerning the celibacy of the clergy. [By Abraham Woodhead.] 4to. [Jones' Peck, ii., 333.] Oxon., 1687

DISCOURSE (a) concerning the certainty of a future and immortal state. By a doctor of physick [William Coward ?]. 8vo. [Lowndes' *Brit. Lib.*] London, 1706
Ascribed also to —— Harris.

DISCOURSE (a) concerning the devotions of the Church of Rome, especially as compared with those of the Church of England ; in which it is shewn that whatever the Romanists pretend, there is not so true devotion among them . . . as in the Church established by law among us. [By William Stanley, D.D.] 4to. Pp. 67. [Arber's *Term Cat.*, ii., p. 110.] London, 1685

DISCOURSE (a) concerning the Ecclesiastical Commission, open'd in the Jerusalem-chamber, October the 10th, 1689. [By Thomas Tenison.] 4to. [Arber's *Term Cat.*, ii. p. 614.] London, 1689
See also below, "A Discourse concerning the illegality. . . ."

DISCOURSE (a) concerning the execution of the laws made against prophaneness, etc., which contains some account of the reasons and tendency of these laws ; the occasions, which, till of late, obstructed their execution ; the manner in which, now, they may be legally and easily made effectual ; the obligations in duty, honour, and interest, of all ranks, in their respective stations, to promote this necessary work. . . . [By Sir Francis Grant, Lord Cullen.] 8vo. Pp. 56. [*D. N. B.*, vol. 22, p. 386.] Edinburgh, 1700

DISCOURSE (a) concerning the great and wonderful events which shall come to pass in the last days. [By James Allen.] 4to. N.P., 1708

DISCOURSE (a) concerning the illegality of the late Ecclesiastical Commission, in answer to the Vindication and Defence of it : wherein the true notion of the legal supremacy is cleared ; and an account is given of the nature, original, and mischief of the dispensing power. [By Edward Stillingfleet, D.D.] Folio. [*Brit. Mus.*] London, 1689
See also above, "A Discourse concerning the Ecclesiastical Commission."

DISCOURSE (a) concerning the immediate and necessary dependence of all things upon the Deity, wherein objections to his present government are consider'd. [By William Dudgeon.] Cr 8vo. 52 pp. London, printed in the year 1731

DISCOURSE (a) concerning the law of inheritances in fee, and therein, concerning the several degrees of consanguinity, etc. To which is prefixed a kalendar of the persons inheritable. [By Robert Robinson.] 8vo. [Watt's *Bibl. Brit.*] In the Savoy, 1736

DISCOURSE (a) concerning the laws, ecclesiastical and civil, made against Hereticks, by Popes, Emperors, and Kings, Provincial and General Councils, approved by the Church of Rome. . . . By a cordial friend to the Protestant Religion now by law established in these realms [Thomas Barlow, D.D., Bishop of Lincoln]. 4to. [*D. N. B.*, vol. 3, p. 229.] London, 1682
Wrongly ascribed to Dr Daniel Whitby.

DISCOURSE (a) concerning the love of God. [By Damaris, Lady Masham.] 8vo. Pp. 132. [Watt's *Bibl. Brit.*] London, 1696
Wrongly attributed to Dr Daniel Whitby.

DISCOURSE (a) concerning the mechanical operation of the Spirit : in a letter to a friend. A fragment. [By Jonathan Swift, D.D.] 8vo. Pp. iii., 283-322. London, 1704
The pagination is continued from the last page of the *Battel of the books*, in the same volume in the Dyce collection.

DISCOURSE (a) concerning the merit of good works. [By Peter Allix, D.D.] 4to. Pp. 32. [Jones' Peck, p. 435.] London, 1688

DISCOURSE (a) concerning the nature and obligation of oaths ; wherein all the cases which have any relation to oaths enjoyned by government are briefly considered. [By Richard Russell, M.A.] 8vo. Pp. x., 71. [*Brit. Mus.*] London, 1716
See also "The Obligation of acting according to conscience. . . ."

DISCOURSE (a) concerning the nature of idolatry ; in which a late author [Bp. Samuel Parker]'s true and onely notion of idolatry is considered and confuted. [By William Wake, D.D.] 4to. [Jones' Peck, p. 21.] London, 1688

DISCOURSE (a) concerning the necessity of believing the doctrine of the Holy Trinity, as profess'd and maintain'd by the Establish'd Church of England, in the first of the thirty-nine Articles of religion. . . . [By Samuel Mather.] [*Adv. Lib.*] London, 1719
The author's name is in the handwriting of his father, Dr. Increase Mather.

DISCOURSE (a) concerning the necessity of reformation, with respect to the errors and corruptions of the Church of Rome. [By Nicholas Stratford, D.D., Dean of St Asaph, afterwards Bishop of Chester.] The first part. 4to. Pp. 60. [Jones' Peck.] London, 1685
Part II. will be found under " Necessity (the) of reformation."

DISCOURSE (a) concerning the new birth ; to which are added two poems. By A. D. [Mrs Anne Dutton]. Fcap 8vo. Pp. 144. London, 1740

DISCOURSE (a) concerning the object of religious worship ; or, a Scripture proof of the unlawfulness of giving any religious worship to any other Being besides the One Supreme God. Part I. [By William Sherlock, D.D.] 4to. Pp. 71. [Jones' Peck, p. 420.]
London, 1685
Part II. was never printed.

DISCOURSE (a) concerning the period of humane life, whether mutable or immutable. By the author of *The Duty of man* [Richard Allestree, D.D.]. Fcap 8vo. London, 1677
See the note to " The Art of contentment."

DISCOURSE (a) concerning the precedency of Kings. . . . [By James Howell.] Folio. [Watt's *Bibl. Brit.*]
London, 1664

DISCOURSE (a) concerning the pretended sacrament of extreme unction ; with an account of the occasions and beginnings of it in the Western Church. In three parts. [By William Clagett, D.D.] 4to. Pp. xii., 136. [Jones' Peck, p. 347.] London, 1688

DISCOURSE (a) concerning the priesthood of Jesus Christ ; in which the date and order of his priesthood, as also the place, time, and manner of his performing the functions thereof, are distinctly consider'd. . . . [By William Moor, woollen-draper in the Strand.] 8vo. Pp. xxii., 146. [*Camb. Univ. Lib.*] London, 1747

DISCOURSE (a) concerning the resurrection bodies ; tending to shew, from the writings of heathens, Jews, and Christians, that there are bodies called our own, which *will not* be raised from the dead ; that there are bodies, properly called our own, which *will* be raised from the dead. By Philalethes [Rev. John Gough, rector of Kirk-Ireton in Derbyshire]. 8vo. [*N. and Q.*, Dec. 29, 1866, p. 505.]
London, 1788

DISCOURSE (a) concerning the resurrection of the same body ; with two letters concerning the necessary immateriality of created thinking substance. [By Samuel Bolde.] 8vo. Pp. 218. [*Bodl.*] London, 1705

DISCOURSE (a) concerning the rise and antiquity of Cathedral worship ; in a letter to a friend. [By Edmund Calamy, D.D.] 4to. Pp. 36. [Wilson's *Hist. of Diss. Ch.*, iv., 89.]
London, 1699
Signed " N. N." Reprinted with " An account of the growth of Deism in England." Lond. 1709.

DISCOURSE (a) concerning the second Council of Nice, which first introduced and established image-worship in the Christian Church, Anno Dom. 787. [By Thomas Comber, D.D.] 4to. [Jones' Peck, p. 430.] London, 1688

DISCOURSE (a) concerning the signification of allegiance, as it is to be understood in the new Oath of Allegiance. [By Theophilus Downes.] 4to. Pp. 27. No title-page. [*Camb. Univ. Lib.*] [London ? 1689]

DISCOURSE (a) concerning the small pox ; occasioned by Dr Holland's Essay, etc. In a letter to a friend. [By John Chandler.] 8vo. Pp. 64.
London, 1729
The second edition has the author's name.

DISCOURSE (a) concerning the Spanish monarchy ; by Thomas Campanella. Translated into English [by Edmund Chilmead]. 8vo. Pp. 232. [*Brit. Mus.*] London, 1653
See also " A Discourse touching the Spanish monarchy. . . ."

DISCOVRSE (a) concerning the svccesse of former Parliaments. [By Thomas May.] 4to. [*Brit. Mus.*]
London, 1642
Reprinted in the Harleian Miscellany.

DISCOVRSE (a) concerning the trve notion of the Lord's Svpper. By R. C. [Ralph Cudworth, D.D.]. 4to. Pp. 73. [*Brit. Mus.*] London, 1642

DISCOURSE (a) concerning the unity of the Catholick Church, etc. *See* Discourse of, etc.

DISCOURSE (a) concerning the unreasonableness of a new separation, on account of the Oaths ; with an answer to the History of passive obedience [by And. Marvell], so far as relates to them. [By Edward Stillingfleet, D.D.] 4to. [*Brit. Mus.*] London, 1689

DISCOURSE concerning the worship of God towards the holy table or altar. [By Stephen Penton.] Fcap 8vo. [Leslie's *Cat.*, 1843.] London, 1682

DISCOURSE (a) concerning the worship of the Blessed Virgin and the saints ; with an account of the beginnings and rise of it amongst Christians ; in answer to M. de Meaux [Bossuet]'s Appeal to the fourth age, in his Exposition and Pastoral letter. [By William Clagett, D.D.] 4to. Pp. 114. [Jones' Peck.] London, 1686

DISCOURSE (a) concerning trade, and that in particular of the East Indies. [An abstract of " A Treatise, wherein it is demonstrated . . . that the East India trade is the most national of all foreign trades. . . .] By Φιλόπατρις [Sir Josiah Child]. 4to. [*Brit. Mus.*] London, 1689

DISCOURSE (a) concerning transubstantiation and idolatry ; being an answer to [Samuel Parker] the Bishop of Oxford's plea relating to these two points. [By Gilbert Burnet, D.D.] 4to. [*Life of Burnet*, by Clarke and Foxcroft, *Appendix*.] London, 1688

DISCOURSE concerning treasons, and bills of attainder ; explaining the true and ancient notion of treason, and shewing the natural justice of bills of attainder. [By Richard West, Lord Chancellor of Ireland.] Second edition. 8vo. [*Brit. Mus.* ; *D. N. B.*, vol. 60, p. 339.] London, 1717

DISCOURSE (a) concerning virtue and religion. [By Philip Glover.] 8vo. [*Brit. Mus.*] London, 1732

DISCOURSE (a) continued between Patricius and Peregrine touching the Civill wars of England and Ireland. [By James Howell.] 4to. [Thomason *Coll. of Tracts*, i., p. 275.] London, 1643

DISCOURSE (a) delivered in Providence, in the Colony of Rhode Island, on the 25th day of July, 1768. By a son of liberty [Silas Downer]. 8vo. [Evans' *Amer. Bibl.*] Providence, 1768

DISCOURSE (a) delivered in the Catholic Apostolic Church, Gordon Square, on the occasion of consecrating the altar, and opening the church for public worship, Christmas Eve, 1853. [By John Bates Cardale.] 8vo. [Boase's *Cath. Apost. Lit.*] London, 1854

DISCOURSE (a) historical and political, of the war of Hungary, and of the causes of the peace between Leopold the First Emperor of the Romans, and Mahomet the Fourth Sultan of Turkey. By Louis de May of Sall, His knight and counsellor of his Highness the Duke of Wirtemberg. Translated into English [by Sir James Turner]. 8vo. Pp. 131. [*David Laing.*] Glasgow, 1669

DISCOURSE (a) in derision of the teaching in Free-Schooles and other common schooles. [By Thomas Grantham, M.A., of Peter House, Cambridge.] 4to. [*Brit. Mus.*] London, 1644

DISCOURSE (a), Luke, 13. 2. 3., on the late fast. By Phileleutherus Norfolciensis [Samuel Parr, LL.D.]. 4to. [*D. N. B.*, vol. 43, p. 363.] London, 1781

DISCOURSE (a) of a cavalier gentleman, on the divine and humane laws ; with respect to the succession. By Don A. B. [Capt. Alexander Bruce]. 4to. [*Brit. Mus.*] N.P., 1706

DISCOURSE (a) of a true Englishman, free from selfe-interest, concerning the interest England hath in the siege of Graveling. [By Richard Kilvert.] 4to. [*Brit. Mus.*] London, 1644

DISCOURSE (a) of angels ; their nature and office, or ministry ; also, something touching devils and apparitions, and impulses. [By Richard Sanders, or Saunders, M.A.] 4to. [Calamy's *Nonconf. Mem.*, Palmer's ed., ii., p. 48.] London, 1701

A posthumous publication.

DISCOURSE (a) of artificial beauty, in point of conscience, between two ladies : with some satyrical censures on the vulgar errors of these times. [By Bishop John Gauden.] 8vo. Pp. 272. The censures have a separate pagination [pp. 112]. London, 1662

This is a later edition of the following.

DISCOURSE (a) of auxiliary beauty, or artificiall hansomeness : in point of conscience between two ladies. [By Bishop John Gauden.] 8vo. Pp. 208. [Wood's *Athen. Oxon.*] London, 1656

Watt and Lowndes both have the above under Jeremy Taylor, with the intimation that it has been attributed to Gauden. In Dr Bliss's Sale Catalogue (part i., p. 116), it is entered under Bishop Gauden, with the intimation that it is often ascribed to Jeremy Taylor, and occasionally to Obadiah Walker.

DISCOURSE (a) of conscience : the second part ; concerning a doubting conscience. [By John Sharp, D.D., Archbishop of York.] 4to. Pp. 99. [*D. N. B.*, vol. 51, p. 408.]
London, 1689

For the First part of this Discourse, *see* " A Discourse concerning conscience."

DISCOURSE (a) of divine assistance, and the method thereof ; shewing what assistance men receive from God in performing the condition of the promise of pardon of sin and eternal life. By W. A. [William Allen]. 8vo. Pp. 290. [*Bodl.*]   London, 1679

DISCOURSE (a) of duels ; shewing the sinful nature and mischievous effects of them, and answering the usual excuses made for them by challengers, accepters, and seconds. By T. C. [Thomas Comber, D.D.]. 4to. Pp. 68. [*Brit. Mus.*]   London, 1687

DISCOURSE (a) of earthquakes, as they are supernatural and premonitory signs to a nation ; with a respect to what hath occurred in this year 1692 : and some special reflections thereon, as also on that security and assurance of mind which is attainable in the light and power of religion, under the greatest surprizals and terrors of sense. . . . By the author of *The Fulfilling of the Scriptures* [Robert Fleming, sen.]. 8vo.   London, 1693

Erroneously ascribed to Robert Fleming, jun., by Watt in his *Bibliotheca Britannica*, and by Wilson in the *History of Dissenting churches in London.* But both correctly assign *The Fulfilling of the Scriptures* to the elder Fleming.

DISCOURSE (a) of ecclesiastical politie ; wherein the authority of the civil magistrate over the consciences of subjects in matters of external religion is asserted ; the mischiefs and inconveniences of toleration are represented, and all pretenses pleaded in behalf of liberty of conscience are fully answered. [By Samuel Parker, Bishop of Oxford.] 8vo. [Arber's *Term Cat.*, i., 522.]
London, 1670

DISCOURSE (a) of eternitie, collected and composed for the common good. By W. T. [William Typing, or Tipping, M.A.]. 4to. Pp. 80. [Madan's *Oxford Books*, i., 174.]   Oxford, 1634

A later edition (London, 1646) is also anonymous. The writer became known as " Eternity Tipping."

DISCOURSE (a) of fish and fish-ponds, under the following heads, viz. I. Of the situation and disposition of the principal waters. II. The manner of making and raising pond-heads, with their dimensions, and how to secure the banks. III. Of sluices, stews, moats, auxiliary waters, and the course of laying the great waters dry. IV. Of the breeding and feeding of fish, and the manner of stocking waters. V. Of disposing of fish, of the management for carriage, of nuisances to ponds and fish, of frosts, and the ways to save the fish in them. VI. Of the benefits and improvements by fish. Done by a person of honour [Hon. Roger North]. 8vo. Pp. 87. [Westwood and Satchell's *Bibl. Piscat.*, p. 157.]   London, 1713

DISCOURSE (a) of free - thinking ; occasion'd by the rise and growth of a sect call'd free-thinkers. [By Anthony Collins.] 8vo. Pp. 178. [Watt's *Bibl. Brit.*]   London, 1713

This was followed by " A Further discourse of free-thinking." *See below.*

DISCOURSE (a) of government, with relation to militias. [By Andrew Fletcher, of Salton.] 8vo. Pp. 66.
Edinburgh, 1698

Reprinted in his Political Works, with name. *See* his " Life," by G. W. T. Omond.

DISCOURSE (a) of joint prayer ; shewing, 1. What is meant by joynt prayer. 2. That the joint use of prayers conceived extempore hinders devotion, and consequently displeases God. . . . 3. That the Lay Dissenters are obliged, upon their own principles, to abhor the prayers offered in the separate Assemblies, and to joyn in communion with the established Church. [By Thomas Bennet, M.A.] 8vo. [Arber's *Term Cat.*, iii., 684.]
London, 1707

Reply was made by Benj. Robinson in " A Review of the case of liturgies. . . ."

DISCOURSE (a) of miracles upon the powers of the world to come ; or the miraculous powers of the Gospel and Kingdom of our Lord Jesus Christ. By T. B. [Thomas Beverley]. 8vo. [Arber's *Term Cat.*, iii., 136.]
London, 1699

DISCOURSE (a) of miracles wrought in the Roman Catholick Church ; or a full refutation of Dr Stillingfleets unjust exceptions against miracles. By E. W. [Edward Worsley, S.J.]. 8vo. [*Brit. Mus.*]   Antwerp, 1676

See also "A Discourse concerning miracles."

DISCOURSE (a) of monarchy ; more particularly of the imperial crowns of England, Scotland, and Ireland, according to the ancient, common, and statute laws of the same ; with a close from the whole as it relates to the succession of his Royal Highness, James, Duke of York. [By John Wilson, Recorder of Londonderry.] 8vo. [Arber's *Term Cat.*, ii., 49, 614.]
London, 1683

DISCOURSE (a) of money ; being an essay on that subject, historically and politically handled : with reflections on the present evil state of the coin of this kingdom, and proposals of a method for the remedy. In a letter to a nobleman. [By John Briscoe.] 8vo. Pp. 204. [*W.*]   London, 1696

DISCOURSE (a) of natural and moral impotency. By the author of *The great propitiation* [Joseph Truman, B.D.]. 8vo. Pp. 216. [Arber's *Term Cat.*, i., 522.]   London, 1671

DISCOURSE (a) of paying of tithes. By T. L. [Thomas Larkham], M.A., Pastour of the Church of Tavistocke. Fcap 8vo. [Calamy's *Nonconf. Mem.*, Palmer's ed., vol. 2, p. 79.]
London, 1656

DISCOURSE (a) of Peters lyfe, peregrination, and death : wherein is plainly proued by the order of time and place that Peter was neuer at Rome. [By Christopher Carlisle, or Carlile.] Small 4to. [*Brit. Mus.*]
London, 1582

DISCOURSE (a) of pluralities (with the attendant non-residence) ; evincing the great evil in taking, and necessary duty of forsaking them. [By William Hughes, preacher to St Thomas' Hospital in Southwark.] 4to. [*Bodl.*]
London, 1680

The author's name is in the handwriting of Barlow.

DISCOURSE (a) of profiting by sermons, and of going to hear where men think they can profit most. [By Symon Patrick, D.D.] 4to.
London, 1683

Reprinted in his collected works.

DISCOURSE (a) of schism ; design'd for the satisfaction of conscientious and peaceable Dissenters. [By George Trosse.] 4to. [Calamy's *Nonconf. Mem.*, Palmer's ed., vol. 2, p. 108.]
London, 1701

DISCOURSE (a) of sea-ports, principally of the port and haven of Dover ; written by Sir Walter Rawleigh and address'd to Queen Elizabeth : with useful remarks, &c., on that subject by command of his late majesty K. Charles the second, never before made publick. [Published by Sir H. Sheers.] 4to. [*W.*]   London, 1700

DISCOURSE (a) of self-murder, lately written, and now published as a disswasive from so horrid and inglorious a thing. By E. P. [Ezra Pierce], in a letter to his intimate friend R. F. 4to. [Arber's *Term Cat.*, ii., 379.]
London, 1691

DISCOURSE (a) of standing armies ; shewing the folly, uselessness, and danger of standing armies in Great Britain. By Cato [John Trenchard, assisted by Walter Moyle]. 8vo. Pp. 36. [*D. N. B.*, vol. 57, p. 199 ; Ryland's *Lib. Cat.*]   London, 1722

See also "An Argument shewing that a standing army is inconsistent with a free government" (1797), and "A Short history of stand-armies" (1798).

DISCOURSE (a) of subterraneal treasure ; occasioned by some late discoveries thereof in the county of Norfolk, and sent in a letter to Thomas Brown, M.D. [By Thomas Lawrence, M.A.] 8vo. Pp. 102. [*Bodl.*]
London, 1668

The address to the reader is signed "T. L."

DISCOURSE (a) of suppressing vice, and reforming the vicious ; delivered in several sermons in the moneths of June and July, 1701. By a minister of the Church of Scotland [William Wishart, D.D.]. 4to. [Scott's *Fasti*, vol. i.]   Edinburgh, 1702

DISCOURSE (a) of taxes and contributions ; shewing the nature and measures of Crown-lands, Assessments, Poll-moneys, Lotteries, Benevolences, Penalties, Monopolies . . . with several intersperst discourses and digressions. [By Sir William Petty.] 4to. [Arber's *Term Cat.*, ii., 614.]
London, 1689

DISCOURSE (a) of the communion in one kind; in answer to a treatise of the Bishop of Meaux's, of communion under both species, lately translated into English. [By William Payne, D.D.] 4to. [Jones' Peck, p. 350.]
London, 1687

DISCOURSE (a) of the contests and dissentions between the nobles and commons in Athens and Rome; with some consequences they had upon these states. [By Benjamin Swift.] 4to. [Arber's *Term Cat.*, iii., p. 684.]   London, 1701

DISCOURSE (a) of the danger of governing by one Minister: in which is demonstrated, that the most advantageous administration, both for the king and the people, consists in an establishment of many councils, or a polysynody. [By Charles Irenée Castel Saint-Pierre.] Done into English. 8vo. Pp. xvi., 144.
London, 1728
In two parts, with continuous pagination.

DISCOURSE (a) of the duties of people to their pastors; in an essay upon Hebr: 13: 17. By M. J. C., minister of the Gospel at Dirletoun [James Clark]. 4to. [*David Laing.*]
Edinburgh, 1701

DISCOURSE of the empire and of the election of a king of the Romans, the greatest business of Christendome now in agitation. . . . By J. H. [James Howell]. 8vo. [Bliss' *Cat.*, 154.] Pp. 109.   London, 1658

DISCOURSE (a) of the excellency of Christianity. [By Henry Hallywell.] 8vo. [*Camb. Univ. Lib.*]
London, 1671

DISCOURSE (a) of the excellency of the heavenly substance. [By John Hickes, minister at Saltash, Devonshire. Fcap 8vo. [Calamy's *Nonconf. Mem.*, Palmer's ed., i., 370.]
London, 1673

DISCOURSE (a) of the general notions of money, trade and exchanges, as they stand in relation each to other; attempted by way of aphorisms: with a letter to a minister of state, further explaining the aphorisms, and applying them to the present circumstances of this nation. . . . By a merchant [Simon Clement]. 4to. [*Bodl.*]
London, 1695

DISCOURSE (a) of the grounds and reasons of the Christian religion, in two parts: the first containing some considerations on the quotations made from the Old in the New Testament, and particularly on the prophesies cited from the former and said to be fulfill'd in the latter. The second containing an examination of the scheme advanc'd by Mr. Whiston, in his Essay towards restoring the true text of the Old Testament. . . . To which is prefix'd an Apology for free debate and liberty of writing. [By Anthony Collins.] 8vo. [Watt's *Bibl. Brit.*]
London, 1724

DISCOURSE (a) of the growth of England in populousness and trade since the reformation of the clerical revenue. . . . Of the numbers of the people of England . . . in . . . 1676. . . . Of the bills of mortality. . . . Of the necessity of future public taxes. . . . With various political remarks and calculations. . . . By way of letter to a Person of Honour. [By Sir Peter Pett.] Folio. [*D. N. B.*, vol. 45, p. 104.]   London, 1689
Signed " P. P."
The above is the second edition of " The Happy future state of England . . .," published in 1688.

DISCOURSE (a) of the Holy Eucharist, in the two great points of the real presence and the adoration of the host; in answer to the two discourses [by Abraham Woodhead] lately printed at Oxford on this subject. To which is prefixed a large historical preface relating to the same argument. [By William Wake, D.D.] 4to. [Jones' Peck, p. 356.]   London, 1687

DISCOURSE (a) of the judicial authority belonging to the Master of the Rolls in the High Court of Chancery. [By Philip Yorke, Earl of Hardwicke.] 8vo. [Watt's *Bibl. Brit.*]
London, 1727
Reprinted in 1728, "with large additions —together with a preface occasioned by a book [by Samuel Burroughs] entitled, The legal judicature in Chancery stated."

DISCOURSE (a) of the nationall excellencies of England. By R. H. [Richard Hawkins]. 8vo. Pp. 248. [*Brit. Mus.*]   London, 1658
See also "A Discourse upon. . . ."

DISCOURSE (a) of the nature and obligation of oaths: wherein, satisfaction is tendered touching the non-obligation and unlawfulness of the oath called, The Solemn League and Covenant. . . . Published as an appendix to the Peace-offering. By the same author [John Stileman, M.A.]. 4to. [Watt's *Bibl. Brit.*]
London, 1662

DISCOURSE (a) of the nature, ends, and difference of the two covenants ; evincing in special, that faith as justifying, is not opposed to works of evangelical obedience. . . . [By William Allen, D.D., vicar of Bridgewater.] To which is prefixed a preface, by Mr Rich. Baxter. 8vo. [Green's *Bibl. Somers.*, ii., 109.]   London, 1673
Wrongly ascribed to A. Clifford [Arber].

DISCOURSE (a) of the nature, offices, and measures of friendship, with rules of conducting it ; written in answer to a letter from M. K. P. . . . By J. T. [Jeremy Taylor, D.D.]. 12mo. [*Brit. Mus.*]   London, 1657

DISCOURSE (a) of the nature, series, and order of occurrences ; as they are prophetically represented in the 11 chap. of the Revelation. By W. A. [William Allen]. 8vo. Pp. 110. [Green's *Bibl. Somers.*, ii., 109.]
London, 1689

DISCOURSE (a) of the nature, use, and advantages of trade, proposing some considerations for the advancement thereof. [By Sir Josiah Child.] 4to. Pp. 31. [*Athen. Cat. (Supp.)*, p. 199.]
London, 1694

DISCOURSE (a) of the necessity of Church-guides, for directing Christians in necessary faith ; with some annotations on Dr Stillingfleet's Answer to N. O. By R. H. [Robert Holden, *i.e.* Abraham Woodhead]. 4to. Pp. 272. [Jones' Peck, i., 221.]   N.P., 1685

DISCOURSE (a) of the objects, advantages, and pleasures of science. [By Henry Brougham, Lord Brougham.] 8vo. [Olphar Hamst's *Bibliog. of Lord Brougham.*]   London, 1827

DISCOURSE (a) of the original, countrey, manners, government and religion of the Cossacks ; with another of the Precopian Tartars : and the history of the wars of the Cossacks against Poland. [From the French of Pierre Chevalier ; translated by Edward Brown.] 8vo. Pp. 209. [*Brit. Mus.*]   London, 1672
Ascribed also to Sir Henry Blount.

DISCOURSE (a) of the peerage and jurisdiction of the Lords Spiritual in Parliament ; proving that . . . they have no right in claiming any jurisdiction in capital matters. [By Thomas Barlow, Bishop of Lincoln.] Folio. Pp. 28. [Arber's *Term. Cat.*, i., 522.]   London, 1679
For replies, *see below*, " The Rights of Bishops . . ." and " Two Treatises. . . ."

DISCOURSE (a) of the Pope's supremacy. Part I. In answer to a treatise, intituled, St Peter's supremacy faithfully discuss'd, according to Holy Scripture, and Greek and Latin Fathers ; and to a sermon of St Peter, preached before her Majesty the Queen Dowager, on St Peter and St Paul's day, by Thomas Godden, D.D. [By Nicholas Stratford.] 4to. [Jones' Peck.]   London, 1688

DISCOURSE (a) of the religion of England ; asserting, that reformed Christianity, settled in its due latitude, is the stability and advancement of this kingdom. [By John Corbet.] 4to. Pp. viii., 148. [Whitley's *Bapt. Bibl.*, i., 92.]   London, 1667

DISCOURSE (a) of the rise & power of Parliaments, of laws, of courts of judicature, of liberty, property, and religion, of the interest of England in reference to the desines of France ; of taxes and of trade. In a letter from a gentleman in the country to a member in Parliament. [By Thomas Sheridan.] 8vo. [Arber's *Term Cat.*, i., 522.]   London, 1679

DISCOURSE (a) of the sacrifice of the Mass. [By William Payne, D.D.] 4to. [Jones' Peck, p. 373.]
London, 1688

DISCOURSE (a) of the state ecclesiasticall of this Kingdome, in relation to the civill, considered under three conclusions. . . . By C. D. [Rev. Colybute Downinge]. The revised edition, enlarged. 4to. Pp. 112. [Madan's *Oxf. Books*, i., 167.]
Oxford, 1634

DISCOURSE (a) of the terrestrial paradise ; aiming at a more probable discovery of the true situation of that happy place of our first parents habitation. [By Marmaduke Carver, rector of Harthill, Yorkshire.] 8vo. Pp. 197. [Watt's *Bibl. Brit.*]
London, 1666
The epistle dedicatory is signed " M. C."

DISCOURSE (a) of the true and visible markes of the Catholique Church. By T. B. [Theodore Beza]. 12mo. [*Brit. Mus.*]   London, 1622

DISCOURSE (a) of the truth and reasonableness of the religion delivered by Jesus Christ ; wherein the several arguments for Christianity are briefly handled ; the miracles done by our Saviour, apostles, and Christians in confirmation of this doctrine are proved. [By Sir Henry Yelverton.] 8vo. [Darling's *Cyclop. Bibl.*]
London, 1662

DISCOURSE (a) of the unity of the Catholic Church maintained in the Church of England. [By William Cave, D.D.] 4to. [Jones' Peck, p. 11.] London, 1684

" By Dr Thorp, as he told me himself." E. Sydall.—Chetham MS. in Peck, p. 11.

DISCOURSE (a) of the use of images ; in relation to the Church of England and the Church of Rome : in vindication of Nubes testium. [By John Gother.] 4to. [*Mendham Collection Cat.*, p. 132.] London, 1687

DISCOURSE (a) of the vanity of the creature, grounded on Eccles. I. 2. By a person of honour [John Robartes, Earl of Radnor]. 8vo. [*D. N. B.*, vol. 48, p. 340.] London, 1673

DISCOURSE (a) of the variation of the Compasse, or magnetical needle ; wherein is showed the manner of the observation, effects, and application thereof. Made by W. B. [Rev. William Barlowe]. . . . Fcap 4to. [Watt's *Bibl. Brit.*] London, 1596

Also ascribed, with less probability, to William Borrough. An earlier edition appeared in 1581.

DISCOURSE (a) of the warr in Lancashire. [By Major Edward Robinson.] Edited by William Beamont, Esq. 4to. Pp. xxxiv., 164. [Vol. lxii. of the Chetham Society's Publications.] [London], 1864

DISCOURSE (a) of things above reason, inquiring whether a philosopher should admit there are any such. . . . By a Fellow of the Royal Society [the Hon. Robert Boyle]. Fcap 8vo. [Arber's *Term Cat.*, i., p. 522.] London, 1681

DISCOURSE (a) of toleration ; in answer to a late book [by John Corbet, B.A.] intituled, A discourse of the religion of England. [By Richard Perrinchief.] 4to. Pp. 58. [Whitley's *Bapt. Bibl.*, i., 93.] London, 1668

DISCOURSE (a) of trade. By N. B. [Nicholas Barbon], M.D. Fcap 8vo. [*D. N. B.*, vol. 3, p. 150.] London, 1690

DISCOURSE (a) of trade, coyn, and paper credit, etc. [By Sir Henry Pollexfen, Chief Justice.] 8vo. [*Brit. Mus.*] London, 1697

DISCOVRSE (a) of trade, from England vnto the East-Indies ; answering to diuerse objections which are vsually made against the same. By T. M. [Thomas Mun]. 4to. Pp. 58. [M'Culloch's *Lit. of Pol. Econ.*, p. 98.] London, 1621

DISCOURSE (a) [on Col. 1/21] on an unconverted man's enmity against God. . . . By J. H. [John Howe]. Fcap 8vo. [*Brit. Mus.*] London, 1700

DISCOURSE (a) on baptism ; containing observations on Dr Priestley's Chapters on the same subject. By Philalethes [Rev. Thomas Twining]. 8vo. [Murch's *Dissenters*, p. 80.] London, 1788

DISCOURSE (a) on fact. . . . [By Francis Maceroni.] 8vo. Pp. 36. [*Brit. Mus.*] [London, 1827] Signed " F. M."

DISCOURSE (a) on holy water, and on the removal of the sacrament on the Lord's Day. [By John Bate Cardale, solicitor.] 8vo. [C. Boase's *Cath. Apost. Lit.*] London, 1868

DISCOURSE (a) on our Saviour's miraculous power of healing ; in which the six cases excepted against by Mr Woolston, are considered : being a continuation of the Defence of the Scripture history, etc. By the same author [Henry Stebbing, Archdeacon]. 8vo. Pp. 66. [*Adv. Lib.*] London, 1730

DISCOURSE (a) on prophesying. [By John Bate Cardale, solicitor.] 8vo. [C. Boase's *Cath. Apost. Lit.*] London, 1868

DISCOURSE (a) on Providence ; being an essay to prove that this doctrine, as delivered in the Gospel, is a demonstration of the divine original of the Christian dispensation. [By G— Littleton.] 8vo. Pp. viii., 46. [*Brit. Mus.*] London, 1747

DISCOURSE (a) on spiritual improvement from affliction. [By John Darwall.] 8vo. Walsall, 1789

DISCOURSE (a) on the Apostle Paul's mystery of godliness being made manifest in the flesh. By Bereanus Theosebes [William Hazlitt]. 4to. Pp. 24. [Cushing's *Init. and Pseud.*, ii., 233.] Falmouth, 1786

DISCOURSE (a) on the Bookland and Folkland of the Saxons ; wherein the nature of these kinds of estates is explained, and the notion of them advanced by Sir John Dalrymple, in his Essay on feudal property, examined and confuted. [By Reymer Heckford.] 8vo. Pp. viii., 54. [*Camb. Univ. Lib.*] Cambridge, 1775

The author's name is in the handwriting of Gough, in the Bodleian copy.

DISCOURSE (a) on the conduct of the government of Great-Britain, in respect to neutral nations, during the present war. [By Charles Jenkinson, Earl of Liverpool.] 4to. Pp. 86.
London, 1758
An edition with the author's name was published in 1794.

DISCOURSE (a) on the duty of mutual exhortation in the Churches of Christ. By one of the pastors of the Baptist Church at Edinburgh [William Braidwood]. 8vo. Pp. 38. [*New Coll. Cat.*] Glasgow, 1787

DISCOURSE (a) on the emigration of British birds ; or, this question at last solv'd : whence come the stork and the turtle, the crane and the swallow, when they know and observe the appointed time of their coming ? Containing a curious, particular, and circumstantial account of the respective retreats of all these birds of passage, which visit our island at the commencement of spring, and depart at the approach of winter. . . . Also, a copious, entertaining, and satisfactory relation of winter birds of passage. . . . By a naturalist [John Legg]. 8vo. Pp. xv., 64. [Courtney's *Secrets*, p. 206.] London, 1795
Mistakenly attributed to George Edwards.

DISCOURSE (a) on the English constitution ; extracted from a late eminent writer, and applicable to the present times. [By William Stevens.] 8vo. [*Gent. Mag.*, Feb. 1807, p. 173.] London, 1776

DISCOURSE (a) on the establishment of a national and constitutional force in England. [By Charles Jenkinson, first Earl of Liverpool.] 8vo. Pp. 82. [Watt's *Bibl. Brit.*] London, 1757

DISCOURSE [on II. Cor. 13/14] on the faith and hope of the Catholic Apostolic Church. By a clergyman [Rev. Robert Norton, D.D.] Fcap 8vo. [Boase's *Cath. Apost. Lit.*] London, 1854

DISCOURSE (a) on the family as an element of government : read before the American Philosophical Society, January 1864. [By Eli K. Price.] Fcap 8vo. Pp. 50. [Smith's *Cat. of Friends' Books, Supp.*, p. 2777.] Philadelphia, 1864

DISCOURSE on the husbandry of Brabant and Flanders. [By Sir R. Weston.] 4to. [Lowndes' *Bibl. Man.*, p. 250.] London, 1645

DISCOURSE (a) on the late fast. By Phileleutherus Norfolciensis. *See* A Discourse, Luke xiii., 2, 3, etc.

DISCOURSE (a) on the late funds of the Million-Act, Lottery-Act, and Bank of England ; shewing that they are injurious to the nobility and gentry, and ruinous to the trade of the nation. By J. B. [John Briscoe]. 4to. [Quaritch's *Cat.*] London, 1694

DISCOURSE (a) on the memory of that rare and truely virtuous person, Sir Robert Fletcher of Saltoun ; who died the 13. of January last, in the thirty-ninth year of his age. Written by a gentleman of his acquaintance [Gilbert Burnet, D.D.]. 8vo. [Clarke's *Life of Bp. Burnet.*] Edinburgh, 1665

DISCOURSE on the method of rightly conducting the reason, and seeking truth in the sciences. By [René] Descartes. Translated from the French ; with an introduction [by John Veitch]. Fcap 8vo. [*Adv. Lib.*] Edinburgh, 1850
The introduction is signed " J. V."

DISCOURSE (a) on the office of Apostle [in the Catholic Apostolic Church]. By Rev. John G. Francis, M.A. 8vo. Pp. 15. [Boase's *Cath. Apost. Lit.*] London, 1848

DISCOURSE (a) on the plurality of worlds ; by Bernard le Bovier de Fontenelle. Translated by Sir W. D. [William Domville], Knt. 12mo. Pp. 106. [Dix and Dugan's *Dubl. Books.*] Dublin, 1687
This was the earliest translation of the famous treatise. For later translations, *see* " A Discovery of new worlds. . . ."

DISCOURSE (a) on the real presence of the Lord in the Sacrament of the Eucharist. [By John Bate Cardale, solicitor.] 8vo. [Boase's *Cath. Apost. Lit.*] London, 1867

DISCOURSE (a) on the service of God, wherein the reasonableness of all his commands is illustrated. . . . [By John Edmonds.] 8vo. [*Brit. Mus.*] London, 1743

DISCOURSE (a) on the study of the laws, by the Hon. Roger North : now first printed from the original MS. in the Hargrave collection, with notes and illustrations by a member of the Inner Temple [Henry Roscoe]. 8vo. Pp. xv., 105. [*Lincoln's Inn Cat.*, p. 560.] London, 1824

DISCOURSE (a) on the tendency of High Church doctrines, by a layman [John Watts de Peyster]. 8vo. [Cushing's *Init. and Pseud.*, i., p. 167.] [Poughkeepsie, 1860]

DISCOURSE (a) on tithes. [By John Bate Cardale, solicitor.] 8vo. [Boase's *Cath. Apost. Lit.*] London, 1858

DISCOURSE, opening the nature of that Episcopacy which is exercised in England. [By Robert Brooke.] 4to. [Watt's *Bibl. Brit.*] London, 1641

DISCOURSE (a) plainely proving the evident utilitie and urgent necessitie of the desired happie Union of the two famous Kingdomes of England and Scotland ; by way of answer to certaine objections against the same. [By John Thornborough, Bishop of Bristol.] 4to. [Hart's *Index Expurg. Angl.*, p. 48.] London, 1604

DISCOURSE (a), proving by Scripture and reason, and the best authors, ancient and modern, that there are witches ; and how far their power extends. . . . [By John Brinley.] 8vo. [Arber's *Term Cat.*, ii., p. 614.] London, 1686

DISCOURSE (a) proving that a man who believeth in the Trinity, the Incarnation, &c., and yet believeth not all other inferior Articles, cannot be saved. By —— Smith [Sylvester Norris, S.J.]. 4to. [Gillows' *Bibl. Dict.*, v., 191.] St Omer, 1625

DISCOURSE (a) proving the divine institution of water-baptism ; wherein the Quaker-arguments against it are collected, with as much as is needful concerning the Lord's Supper. By the author of *The snake in the grass* [Charles Leslie]. 4to. Pp. 64. [Smith's *Anti-Quak.*, p. 268.] London, 1697

DISCOURSE (a) representing the liberty of conscience that is practised in foreign parts. By N. Y. [John Dury]. 8vo. [*Bodl.*] London, 1661
The finials of the name have been given, not the initials.

DISCOURSE (a) shewing in what state the three Kingdomes are in at this present. [By John Milton ?] 4to. Pp. 8. N.P., 1641

DISCOURSE (a) shewing that Protestants are on the safer side, notwithstanding the uncharitable judgment of their adversaries ; and that their religion is the surest way to heaven. [By Luke de Beaulieu.] 4to. [*D. N. B.*, vol. 4, p. 52.] London, 1687

DISCOURSE (a), shewing that the expositions which the ante-Nicene fathers have given of the texts alléged against the Reverend Dr Clarke by a learned layman [Robert Nelson], are more agreeable to the interpretations of Dr Clarke, than to the interpretations of that learned layman. By a clergyman in the country [John Jackson, M.A.]. 8vo. Pp. 72. [*Bodl.*] London, 1714
Ascribed also to Daniel Whitby, D.D.

DISCOURSE (a) shewing that the real first cause of the straits and difficulties of this province of the Massachusetts Bay is its extravagancy. . . . By Philopatria [Thomas Paine]. 8vo. [Cushing's *Init. and Pseud.*, i., 233.] Boston, 1721

DISCOURSE (a), shewing who they are that are now qualify'd to administer Baptism and the Lord's-Supper : wherein the cause of episcopacy is briefly treated. By the author of a *Discourse proving the divine institution of Water-Baptism* [Charles Leslie]. 4to. Pp. 63. [Smith's *Anti-Quak.*, p. 270.] London, 1698

DISCOURSE (a) tending to prove the Baptisme in, or under the defection of Antichrist to be the ordinance of Jesus Christ ; as also that the Baptisme of infants or children is warrantable, and agreeable to the word of God : where the perpetuity of the estate of Christs Church in the world, and the everlastingnesse of the Covenant of Almighty God to Abraham are set forth as maine grounds, and sundry other particular things are controverted and discussed. By P. B. [Praise-God Barebone]. 4to. Pp. viii., 32. [Thomason *Coll. of Tracts*, vol. I, p. 96.] London, 1642
Wrongly attributed to P. Bakewell.

DISCOURSE (a) to the Students of the Royal Academy, December 10, 1771. [By Sir Joshua Reynolds.] 4to. [*Brit. Mus.*] London, 1772

DISCOURSE (a) touching provision for the poor. [By Sir Matthew Hale.] 8vo. [M'Culloch's *Lit. of Pol. Econ.*, p. 275.] London, 1683

DISCOURSE (a) touching the peace and concord of the Church. [Translated from the Latin of Samuel Przipcovius by John Biddle.] 8vo. [Wallace's *Antitrinitarian Biog.*, iii., 186.] London, 1653

DISCOURSE (a) touching the pretended match between the Duke of Norfolke and the Queene of Scottes. [By —— Sampson, a preacher.] 8vo. [Lowndes' *Bibl. Man.*] N.P., [1571]

DISCOURSE (a) touching the Spanish monarchy : wherein we have a political glasse, representing each particular country, province, kingdome, and empire of the world, with wayes of government, by which they may be kept in obedience ; as also the causes of the rise and fall of each kingdom and empire. Written by Tho. Campanella ; newly translated into English, according to the third edition of this book in Latine [by Edmond Chilmead]. 4to. [Watt's *Bibl. Brit.*] London, 1654

The edition of 1659 has the translator's name.

DISCOURSE (a) upon an union of the two kingdoms of England and Scotland. [By Daniel Defoe?] 8vo.
London, 1707

DISCOURSE (a) upon grants and resumptions: showing how our ancestors have proceeded with such ministers as have procured to themselves grants of the crown-revenue; and that the forfeited estates ought to be applied towards the payment of the publick debts. By the author of *The Essay on ways and means* [Charles Davenant, LL.D.]. Second edition. 8vo. Pp. 470. [Arber's *Term Cat.*, iii., p. 684.]
London, 1700

DISCOURSE (a) upon improving the revenue of the state of Athens: written originally in Greek by Xenophon, and made English from the original, with some historical notes. By W. M. [Walter Moyle], Esq. 8vo. [*Brit. Mus.*] London, 1697

DISCOURSE (a) upon justification: shewing the matter, manner, time and effects of it. By the author of the *Discourse concerning the new birth* [Mrs Ann Dutton, London]. Fcap 8vo. Pp. 166. [Whitley's *Bapt. Bibliog.*, vol. ii.] London, 1740

DISCOURSE (a) upon Masonry. [By George Minty]. 8vo. Dublin, 1757

DISCOURSE (a) upon Nicholas Macchiavell; or, an impartiall examination of the justness of the censure commonly laid upon him. [By Francis Osborne.] 12mo. [Watt's *Bibl. Brit.*]
London, 1656

DISCOURSE (a) upon religion; in two parts. [By John Bethune, of Pittullie.] 8vo. Edinburgh, 1772

DISCOURSE (a) upon the earthquake that happened through this realme of Englande and other places of Christendom, the sixt of Aprill, 1580. [By Arthur Golding.] 8vo. [Lowndes' *Bibl. Man.*] London, 1580

DISCOURSE (a) upon the intermediate state: shewing that all righteous souls . . . are immediately, upon putting off their bodies, with Christ in joy and felicity. [By Dr —— Booth.] 8vo. Pp. 24. [Abbot's *Lit. of a Future Life*, No. 2567.]
London, 1760

DISCOURSE (a) upon the meanes of wel governing and maintaining in good peace a kingdome or other principalitie . . . against Nicholas Machiavell the Florentine. [By Innocent Gentillet.] Translated [from the Latin] into English by Simon Patericke. Folio. [*Edin. Univ. Lib.*]
London, 1602

DISCOURSE (a) upon the nationall excellencies of England. By R. H. [Richard Hawkins]. 4to. Pp. 248. [Thomason *Coll. of Tracts*, ii., p. 195.]
London, 1657

See also "A Discourse of. . . ."

DISCOURSE (a) upon the present state of France [1585-1588. By Michel Hurault]; togither with a copie of the Kings letters patents, declaring his mind after his departure out of Paris. . . . Translated out of French into English, and now newly reprinted and corrected by E. Aggas. 4to. [*Camb. Univ. Cat.*]
[London], 1588

An account, similarly anonymous ("An excellent discourse upon the now present state of France"), but describing a later period (1588-1591) was published in 1592. *See below.*

DISCOURSE (a) upon the prophecy of the seventy weeks of Daniel. [By William Magee.] 8vo. Pp. 96. [*Bodl.*] Salisbury, 1837

DISCOURSE (a) upon the reasons of the resolution taken in the Valteline against the tyranny of the Grisons and heretiques. . . . Written in Italian by the author of *The Councell of Trent* [Paolo Servita, *i.e.* Pietro Sarpi], and faithfully translated into English [by Sir Thomas Roe]. 4to. [*Brit. Mus.*]
London, 1628

Signed "Philo-Britannicos."

DISCOURSE (a) upon the theory of legitimate government. By a friend to truth and liberty [Henry Augustus Dillon-Lee, Viscount Dillon]. 12mo. [*Brit. Mus.*]
Private print, Florence, 1817

DISCOURSE (a) upon the union of Scotland and England. Containing, I. A brief account of the kind proposals made to the Scots by the English, in the reigns of Henry VIII. and Edward VI. II. A short history of the treatys on that head since the Union of the crowns, shewing that the English Court have insisted on harder terms since that time. III. An account of the grievances of Scotland as to religion, liberty and trade, since the Union of the crowns. IV. Proposals for an Union of the kingdoms, upon the plan of Edward VI. which was much the same agreed to by the Scots in the reign of James VI., reserving to both kingdoms their constitution in Church and State ; where the objections against this Union are consider'd. V. Proposals of a method for preserving the Union upon the plan of the treaty of Rippon, agreed to by K. Charles I. and both kingdoms. VI. A brief view of the original rights of the kingdom of Scotland. Humbly submitted to the Parliament of Scotland, by a lover of his country [George Ridpath]. 8vo. Pp. 186. N.P., 1702

DISCOURSE (a) upon the uniting Scotland with England ; containing the general advantage of such an Union to both Kingdoms ; the several ways of uniting nations ; the difference of religion, law, nobility, etc., adjusted by the law of nature and the practice of all nations in such cases. With divers original papers. . . . [By Blackerby Fairfax, M.A., M.D.] 8vo. [Arber's *Term Cat.*, iii., 684.]
London, 1702

DISCOURSE (a) upon walking with God, in a letter to a friend. Together with some hints upon Joseph's blessing . . . as also a brief account how the author was brought into Gospel liberty. By A. D. [Mrs. Ann Dutton]. 8vo. [Whitley's *Bapt. Bibl.*, i., 157.]
London, 1735

DISCOURSE (a) wherein is debated whether it is expedient that the Scripture should be in English for al men to reade that wyll. . . . [By John Standish.] B. L. 8vo. [*Brit. Mus.*]
London, 1554
Signed " J. S."

DISCOURSE (a) wherein is plainly proued by the order of time and place, that Peter was neuer at Rome ; furthermore, that neither Peter nor the Pope is the head of Christes Church ; also an interpretation vpon the second Epistle of S. Paul to the Thessalonians, the second chapter. Seene and alowed according to the order appointed. [By Christopher Carlile.] 4to. Pp. 61. B. L. London, 1572
In another edition (Lond., by Roger Ward, N.D., 4to), the author's name is given.

DISCOURSE (a) wherein the interest of the patient in reference to physick and physicians is soberly debated, many abuses of the apothecaries in the preparing their medicines are detected, and their unfitness for practice discovered. . . . [By Thomas Coxe, M.D.] Fcap 8vo. [Arber's *Term Cat.*, i., p. 522.] London, 1669
Attributed also to Daniel Cox, M.D.

DISCOURSES concerning the everblessed Trinity. . . . By the author of *The divine right of Episcopacy* [Rev. Thomas Brett, LL.D.]. 8vo. Pp. x., 290. [*Brit. Mus.*]
London, 1720

DISCOURSES concerning the ministry, tythes, etc. ; with a brief apology for the Quakers. [By Henry Stubbe, M.A., of Christ Church, Oxford.] 8vo. [Watt's *Bibl. Brit.*]
London, [1660 ?]

DISCOURSES, controversial and practical, on various subjects, proper for the consideration of the present times. By the author of *Deism revealed* [Rev. Philip Skelton, B.A.]. 2 vols. 8vo. [*W.*; Lowndes' *Brit. Lib.*] London, 1755

DISCOURSES delivered in Meadowside Baptist Chapel, Dundee. By W. H. [W—— Henderson]. Cr 8vo. Pp. 240. Dundee, 1892

DISCOURSES for the furtherance of Christian piety and devotion. [By Edward Wetenhall, D.D.] 12mo. [*D. N. B.*, vol. 60, p. 383.]
London, 1671

DISCOURSES (the) of Cleander and Eudoxe upon the Provincial Letters [of Blaise Pascal] ; to which is added an answer to the Apology for the Provincial Letters. Translated [from the French of Gabriel Daniel, by William Darell, S.J.]. 8vo. [Oliver's *Collections*, p. 80.] London, 1704

DISCOURSES of religion, between a minister of the Church of England and a country gentleman on points of controversy between England and Rome. [By Rev. Mother —— More, abbess of the English Augustinians at Bruges.] Fcap 8vo. N.P., 1716

DISCOURSES of warre and single combat ; translated out of the French [of Bertrand de Loque] by J. Eliot. 4to. [*Brit. Mus.*] London, 1631

DISCOURSES on Davila, a series of papers on political history. By an American citizen [John Adams, President of the United States]. 8vo. [*Brit. Mus.*] Boston, 1805

DISCOURSES on subjects relating to the spiritual life, translated from the French [of —— Marsay]. Fcap 8vo. Pp. 309. Edinburgh, 1749

DISCOURSES on the diversity of theological opinions ; with some notes on the age of the world, and a catalogue of the Scriptures of different nations. By a Theophilanthropist [William R. Peck]. 8vo. Pp. 55. [*Bodl.*] Doncaster, N.D.

DISCOURSES on the publick revenues, and on the trade of England. In two parts. . . . By the author of the *Essay on ways and means* [Charles Davenant, LL.D.]. Part I. To which is added, A discourse upon improving the revenue of the state of Athens, etc. 8vo. [Arber's *Term Cat.*, iii., p. 110.]
London, 1698

DISCOURSES on the publick revenues, and on the trade of England, which more immediately treat of the foreign traffick of this kingdom. . . . By the author of the *Essay on ways and means* [Charles Davenant, LL.D.]. Part II. To which is added, The late Essay on the East-India trade. By the same hand. 8vo. [*D. N. B.*, vol. 14, p. 100.]   London, 1698

DISCOURSES upon trade ; principally directed to the cases of the interest, coynage, clipping, increase of money. [By Sir Dudley North.] 4to. [Arber's *Term Cat.*, ii., pp. 385, 651.]
London, 1691

DISCOVERED (the) country. By Ernst von Himmel [Carlyle Petersilea]. 8vo. Pp. 234. [*Brit. Mus.*]
Boston, [Mass.], [1889]

DISCOVERER (the) : being an answer to a book entitled, Englands New Chain, the second part, discovered. The second part. [By John Canne.] 4to. Pp. 80. [*D. N. B.*, vol. 8, p. 412.]   London, 1649
See also "Discoverer (the); wherein . . ."

DISCOVERER (the) discovered ; or the lot cast, T. C. [Thomas Crisp] taken, and the Babylonish garment found hid under his stuff. . . . By E. P. [Edward Penington]. 8vo. [Smith's *Cat. of Friends' Books*.]
London, 1695
See below, "A Discovery of the accursed thing. . . ."

DISCOVERER (the) ; wherein is set forth to undeceive the nation [regarding] the real plots and stratagems of Richard Overton and that partie. [By John Canne.] 4to. [Whitley's *Bapt. Bibl.*, i., 39.]   London, 1649
See also above, " Discoverer (the); being . . ."

DISCOVERIE (the) and confutation of a tragical fiction devysed and played by Ed. Squyer, yeoman, soldier, hanged at Tyburne the 23rd of Nov. 1598 : written for the only love and zeal of truth against forgerie. By M. A. priest [Richard Walpole, S.J.]. [Oliver's *Collections*, p. 214.]
Dated from Rome, 1 March 1599

DISCOVERIE (the) of a gaping gvlf whereinto England is like to be swallovved by an other French mariage, if the Lord forbid not the banes, by letting her maiestie see the sin and punishment thereof. [By John Stubbes, or Stubbs, of Lincoln's Inn.] 8vo. 44 leaves. No pagination. [*Bodl.*]   [London], 1579
Soon after the publication of this pamphlet, which protested against the proposed marriage between Queen Elizabeth and the Duke of Anjou, its circulation was strictly prohibited. The author and the publisher (William Page) were severely punished.

DISCOVERIE (a) of certaine notorious shifts, evasions, and untruthes uttered by Mr. J. White, [Protestant] minister, in a booke . . . intituled, "A Defence of the way . . . in manner of a dialogue." By W. G. [William Wright, S.J.], Professor in Divinity. 4to. [Oliver's *Collections*, p. 230.]   St Omer, 1613

DISCOVERIE (a) of Edmund Campion and his confederates, their most horrible and traiterous practises, against her Majesties most royal person and the realm. Whereunto is added, the execution of Edmund Campion, Ralph Sherwin, and Alexander Brian, executed at Tiborne, the 1st of December. Published by A. M. [Anthony Munday]. 8vo. [*W.*, Lowndes' *Bibl. Man.*] London, 1582

DISCOVERIE (a) of F. J. Nicols, minister, misreported a Jesuite, latelye recanted in the Tower of London . . . By John Howlett [Robert Parsons, S.J.]. 8vo. Pp. 194. [Oliver's *Collections* ; Sommervogel's *Dictionnaire*.]
Douay [really London], 1580

DISCOVERIE (a) of infinite treasure, hidden since the world's beginning, in the way of husbandry. By G. P. [Gabriel Plattes]. 4to. [Watt's *Bibl. Brit.*]   London, 1639
See also below, " A discovery of subterranean treasure. . . ."

DISCOVERIE (a) of London's obstinacie and miserie. [By Sir John Spelman.] 4to. [*Bodl.* ; also, p. 33 of " The case of our affaires, etc.," by Spelman.]   N.P., 1643

DISCOVERIE (a) of the state of Ireland, with the trve cavses why that kingdom was neuer entirely subdued, nor brought vnder obedience of the crowne of England, vntill the beginning of his maiesties happie raigne. [By Sir John Davies.] 4to. Pp. 287. [*Bodl.*]   [London], 1612
The author's name is in the handwriting of Wood. Other editions show variations in the title.

DISCOVERIES of the French to the south-east of New Guinea, 1768-69; with accounts of the voyages and discoveries of the Spaniards to the same seas. . . . [By Capt. Charles P. Claret de Flerieu.] 4to. [*Brit. Mus.*]
London, 1791

DISCOVERY (the); a comedy: as it is performed at the Theatre-Royal in Drury-Lane. Written by the editor of Miss Sidney Bidulph [Mrs Frances Sheridan, *née* Chamberlaine]. 8vo. Pp. 95. [*Biog. Dram.*]
Edinburgh, 1763

DISCOUERY of a London monster called, the Blacke dog of Newgate: profitable for all readers to take heed by. [By Luke Hutton.] 4to. B. L. [*W.*] London, 1612

DISCOVERY (the) of a New World; or a description of the South Indies, hitherto unknowne. By an English Mercury [John Healy]. Fcap 8vo. [Watt's *Bibl. Brit.*] London, [1644]

DISCOVERY (the) of a swarme of Separatists; or, a leather-seller's sermon. . . . [By John Taylor, the water-poet.] 4to. London, 1641

DISCOVERY (the) of a world in the moone; or a discourse tending to prove that 'tis probable there may be another habitable world in that planet. [By John Wilkins, Bishop of Chester.] Fcap 8vo. [Watt's *Bibl. Brit.*]
London, 1638

DISCOVERY (a) of new worlds; from the French [of Bernard Le Bovier de Fontenelle, by Mrs Aphra Behn]; together with a preface, by way of essay, on translated prose, wherein the arguments against the system of Copernicus (as to the motion of the earth) are considered and exposed. . . . 8vo. [Arber's *Term Cat.*, ii., p. 614.] London, 1688

For other translations, *see* "A Plurality of worlds . . .," and "A discourse on the plurality of worlds."

DISCOVERY (a) of subterraneal treasure; viz. of all manner of mines and minerals . . . with plain directions for the finding of them. [By Gabriel Plattes.] 4to. Pp. 60. [Watt's *Bibl. Brit.*] London, 1653

See also above, "A discoverie of infinite treasure. . . ."

DISCOVERY (a) of the accursed thing found in the Foxonian Quakers' camp. By T. C. [Thomas Crisp]. 4to. [Smith's *Anti-Quakeriana*.]
London, 1695

See also above, "The Discoverer discovered. . . ."

DISCOVERY (a) of the author of the letters of Junius, founded on such evidence and illustrations as explain all the mysterious circumstances and apparent contradictions which have contributed to the concealment of this "most important secret of our times." [By John Taylor, publisher.] 8vo. Pp. 139. [*D. N. B.*, vol. 20, p. 170.]
London, 1813

These letters are attributed in this pamphlet to Sir Philip Francis.

DISCOVERY (a) of the errors of the English Anabaptists. By Edmond Jessop [really by John Hetherington]. 8vo. [*Eng. Hist. Review.*]
London, 1623

DISCOVERY (a) of the fraudulent practices of John Darrell, bacheler of artes, in his proceedings concerning the pretended possession and dispossession of William Somers at Nottingham: of Thomas Darling, the boy of Burton at Caldwell: and of Katherine Wright at Mansfield, and Whittington: and of his dealings with one Mary Couper at Nottingham, detecting in some sort the deceitful trade in these latter dayes of casting out deuils. [By Samuel Harsnet.] 4to. Pp. 334. [*Bodl.*]
London, 1599

The Epistle to the reader signed "S. H." "Sam. Harsnet yᵉ author, afterwards archb. of York."—MS. note by Wood.

DISCOVERY (a) of the groundlesness and insincerity of my Ld. of Down's Dissuasive; being the fourth appendix to Svre-footing. With a letter to Dr Casaubon, and another to his answerer. By J. S. [John Sergeant]. 8vo. Pp. 247-344. 24. [Gillow's *Bibl. Dict.*, vol. 5, p. 494.] London, 1665

DISCOVERY (the) of the man of sinne: wherein is set forth the changes of Gods Chvrch, in her afflictions by his raigne, in her consolations by his ruine. First preached in divers sermons [on 2 Thess. 2. 3.] to the Vniversitie and cittie of Oxon, by a reverend & iudicious divine I. R. D. of divinity and sometimes of Queenes College [John Raynolds or Rainolds]. . . . 4to. Pp. 56. [Madan's *Oxford Books*, i., p. 99.] Oxford, 1614

DISCOVERY (a) of the person and period of Antichrist. [By Christopher Ness or Nesse.] 12mo. [Watt's *Bibl. Brit.*]
London, 1679

DISCOVERY (a) of the rebels [a sermon on Luke 19/27]. By J. V. [John Vicars], Prisoner. 4to. Pp. 22. [*Brit. Mus.*] [London], 1643

DISCOVERY (a) of truth and falshood. [By Richard Farnworth.] 4to. [Watt's *Bibl. Brit.*] London, 1653

DISCOVERY (a) of two unclean spirits ; or, two priests [Henry Hean and William Wilton], by their fruits made manifest. . . . By A. H. [Anthony Holder]. 4to. London, 1657

DISCOVERY (the) ; or the mysterious separation of H. D., Esq., and Ann, his wife. By H. D. [Hugh Doherty], Esq. Fourth edition. Vol. i. Fcap 8vo. [*Brit. Mus.*] London, 1807
No more published.

DISCREPANCY and inspiration not incompatible. [By John Collyer Knight.] 8vo. [Darling's *Cyclop. Bibl.*] London, N.D.
Reprinted from the Journal of sacred literature, for April, 1854.

DISCURSIVE remarks on modern education. By E. L. [E. Lord]. Fcap 8vo. [*Olphar Hamst*, p. 47.] London, 1841

DISCURSORY considerations on St Luke's preface and other circumstances of his Gospel ; in three letters to a friend, from a country clergyman [Rev. Charles Dunster, M.A., rector of Petworth, Sussex]. Cr 8vo. Pp. 181. [*Gent. Mag.*, 1805, p. 343.] London, 1805

DISCURSORY considerations on the hypothesis of Dr Macknight and others, that St Luke's Gospel was the first written. By a country clergyman [Rev. Charles Dunster, M.A.]. Cr 8vo. Pp. vii., 180. [*Gent. Mag.*, lxxix., ii., 833.] London, 1808

DISCURSORY considerations on the supposed evidence of the early Fathers, that St Matthew's Gospel was the first written. By a country clergyman [Rev. Charles Dunster, M.A.]. Cr 8vo. Pp. vii., 105. [Darling's *Cyclop. Bibl.*] London, 1806

DISCUSSION between two readers of Darwin's Treatise on the Origin of Species [Daniel Treadwell and Asa Gray] upon natural theology. 8vo. [Cushing's *Anon. and Pseud.*, ii., p. 291.] New Haven, Conn., 1860

DISCUSSION (a) of Mr Frye's Tenents lately condemn'd in Parliament : and Socinianism proved to be an unchristian doctrine. [By Francis Cheynell.] 4to. [Calamy's *Nonconf. Mem.*, Palmer's ed., iii., 326.] N.P., N.D., [London, 1650]

DISCUSSION (a) of Parliamentary reform. By a Yorkshire freeholder [Samuel Bailey]. Fcap 8vo. Pp. vi., 55. London, 1831
Authorship acknowledged in list prefixed to the Bury edition (1881) of *Essays on Opinions.*

DISCUSSION (a) on the atonement of Christ, election, predestination, reprobation, etc., between Clericus [Rev. William Cartwright] and Honestus. Fourth edition. 8vo. [Copinger's *Bibl. of Predestination.*] London, 1866

DISCUSSIONS on the law of libels, as at present received ; in which its authenticity is examined, with incidental observations on the legal effect of precedents and authority. [By James Adair.] 8vo. [Watt's *Bibl. Brit.*] London, 1785

DISEASES (the) of the times ; or, the distempers of the Common-wealth. . . . [By John Taylor, the water-poet.] 8vo. London, [1641 ?]

DISENCHANTED. [A novel.] By Pierre Loti [Louis M. J. Viaud,— Captain in the French Navy]. 8vo. [*Brit. Mus.*] London, 1907

DISENCHANTMENT. By William Stephenson Gregg [Frances Mabel Robinson]. Cr 8vo. [*Brit. Mus.*] London, 1886

DISENTANGLED [a novel]. By Curtis Yorke [Mrs W— S— Richmond Lee, *née* —— Jex-Long]. Cr 8vo. Pp. 336. [*Lond. Lib. Cat.*] London, 1915

DISESTABLISHMENT and disendowment. By a liberal Churchman [John Ashton]. 8vo. [*Manch. Free Lib.*] Manchester, 1875

DISESTABLISHMENT ; from a Church [of England] point of view. [By William Gilbert.] 8vo. [*Camb. Univ. Lib.*] London, 1875

DISESTABLISHMENT : is it unconstitutional ? [By Edward Capel Whitehurst, attorney.] 8vo. [*Brit. Mus.*] London, [1870]

DISGUIS'D (the) Prince ; or, the beautiful Parisian : a true story. Translated from the French [or rather, written by Mrs Eliza Haywood, *née* Fowler]. 8vo. [*Brit. Mus.*] London, 1728

DISH (a) of first-fruits ; [verses] intended as an echo or supplementary addition to "An Alarm in Zion. . . ." By Zi. S. S. S. [T— L. Styles]. 8vo. Pp. 24. [*Brit. Mus.*] London, 1828

DISH (a) of hodge podge ; or, a collection of poems by Paul Bobbin, Esq., of Alt, near Oldham [James Butterworth]. 8vo. [*D. N. B.*, vol. 8, p. 97.] Manchester, 1800

DISHES and drinks ; or, philosophy in the kitchen. By an old Bohemian [Dr Gustav L. M. Strauss]. Revised edition. Cr 8vo. [Cushing's *Init. and Pseud.*, ii., p. 109.] London, 1887

DISHONOUR (the) of Frank Scott. By M. Hamilton [Mrs Churchill Luck]. Cr 8vo. Pp. 324. [*Lond. Lib. Cat.*] London, 1900

DISHONOURED : a novel. By Theo. Gift [Dora Henrietta Havers, later Mrs. Theo. Boulger]. Cr 8vo. [*Lit. Year Book.*] London, 1890

DISILLUSION ; a story with a preface. By Dorothy Leighton [Dorothy Forsyth, later Mrs Johnson]. 3 vols. Cr. 8vo. [*Brit. Mus.*] London, 1894

DISINHERITED (the) ; and The Ensnared. By the authoress of *Flirtation* [Lady Charlotte Maria Bury]. 3 vols. Fcap 8vo. [*Brit. Mus.*] London, 1834

" DISMAL England." By the author of *Merrie England* [Robert Blatchford]. Fcap 8vo. [*Lond. Lib. Cat.*] London, 1899

DISMEMBER'D (the) empire : a poem. [By Edward Rushton.] 4to. [*Sketches of obscure poets*, p. 56.] London, 1783

DISMISSAL (the) of a Free Church Teacher. [By Rev. Cameron Mackay.] 8vo. Edinburgh, 1887

DISOWNED (the). By the author of *Pelham* [Edward George Earle Lytton Bulwer - Lytton, Baron Lytton]. Second edition. 3 vols. Fcap 8vo. [*Brit. Mus.*] London, 1829

DISPASSIONATE (a) enquiry into the reasons alledged by Mr Madison for declaring an offensive and ruinous war against Great Britain ; together with some suggestions as to a peaceable and constitutional mode of averting that dreadful calamity. By a New England farmer [John Lowell]. 8vo. Pp. 87. [Rich's *Bibl. Amer.*, ii., 61.] London, 1808
Printed also at Boston, 1812.

DISPASSIONATE (a) narrative of the conduct of the English clergy, in receiving from the French King and his Parliament the administration of the College at St Omer, late under the direction of the English Jesuits. Collected from original memorials and letters. By a layman [Ralph Hodshon, or Hodgson, of Lintz]. 8vo. Pp. viii., 155. [Gillow's *Bibl. Dict.*, iii.] London, 1768

DISPASSIONATE thoughts on the American War, addressed to the moderate of all parties. [By Josiah Tucker, Dean of Gloucester.] 8vo. [*Brit. Mus.*] London, 1780

DISPENSARY (the) ; a poem. [By Sir Samuel Garth, M.D.] [In six cantos.] 4to. Pp. 84. [Bartholomew's *Bibl. of Bentley*, p. 38.] London, 1699

DISPLAY (a) of God's special grace ; in a familiar dialogue between a minister and a gentleman of his congregation, about the work of God in the conviction and conversion of sinners so remarkably of late begun and going on in these American parts. . . . [By Jonathan Dickinson, President of New Jersey College.] Fcap 8vo. Pp. vi., iii. [Evans' *Amer. Bibl.*, vol. 2, p. 205.] Boston, N.E., 1742

DISPLAY (a) of heraldrie ; manifesting a more easie accesse to the knowledge thereof than hath beene hitherto published by any, through the benefit of method whereunto it is now reduced by the study of and industry of John Guellim [or Guillim. The real author was the Rev. John Barkham, Vicar of Barking, in Essex, who, not wishing to have his name associated with the work, allowed the publisher, Guellim, to take the credit ; the latter, however, made a few trifling additions]. Folio. [Watt's *Bibl. Brit.*] London, 1610
Later editions appeared in 1632, 1638, 1660, 1724, etc.

DISPLAY (a) of the fraudulent and gross abuses committed upon the Secession-testimony, in a late publication, entitled The re-exhibition of the testimony : containing some strictures upon persecution and toleration. [By Rev. Adam Gib.] Pt 8vo. Pp. 54. [*New Coll. Cat.*] Edinburgh, 1780

DISPLAY of tyranny ; or remarks upon the illegal and arbitrary proceedings in the Courts of Westminster and Guildhall, from 1678 to the abdication of the late King James in the year 1688. [By Titus Oates.] Fcap 8vo. [Watt's *Bibl. Brit.*] London, 1689

DISPLAYING (the) of an horrible secte of grosse heretiques, naming themselves the Familie of Love ; with the lives of their authours [D. Joris and H. Niclas] : whereunto is annexed a confession of certain Articles, which was made by two of the Familie of Love . . . newely set foorth by J. R. [John Rogers]. . . . 8vo. B. L. [*Brit. Mus.*] London, [1578]
Another edition was issued in 1579.

DISPLAYING (the) of the Protestantes, and sondry their practises ; with a description of divers their abuses of late frequented within their malignaunte churche : perused and set forte with thassent of authoritie, according to the order in that behalf appointed. [By Miles Huggarde or Hogarde.] 8vo. B. L. [*D. N. B.*, vol. 28, p. 158.] London, 1556

DISPRAISE (a) of the life of a courtier, and a commendacion of the life of the labouryng man . . . drawen . . . out of the Frenche toungue [by Sir Francis Bryan]. Fcap 8vo. [Watt's *Bibl. Brit.*]   London, 1548

DISPROOFE (a) of D. Abbots covnter proofe against D. Bishops reproofe of the defence of M. Perkins Reformed Catholike. The first part. Wherein the now Roman Church is maintained to be the true ancient Catholike Church, and is cleered from the vniust imputatation of Donatisme. Where is also briefly handled, whether euery Christian can be saued in his owne religion. By W. B., P. and D. in divinity [William Bishop]. 8vo. Pp. 433. [*Bodl.*]   Paris, 1614

DISPUTANTS (the) ; or the arguments in favour of the newly established theological institution among the Methodists brought to the test. . . . By a disciple of the Old School [Rev. James Everett, Wesleyan minister]. 8vo. Pp. 107. [Osborn's *Wesl. Bibl.*. p. 100.]   London, 1835

DISPUTATIO de pace, &c.; or, a discourse touching the peace and concord of the Church. Wherein is elegantly and acutely argued, that not so much a bad opinion, as a bad life, excludes a Christian out of the kingdom of heaven ; and that the things necessary to be known for the attainment of salvation, are very few and easie : and finally, that those, who pass amongst us under the name of hereticks, are notwithstanding to be tolerated. [By John Hales, of Eton.] 8vo. Pp. 76. [*Bodl.*]
London, 1653

DISPUTATION (the) at Winchcombe, November 9th, 1653 [between Clement Barksdale and —— Helme]. [By Clement Barksdale.] 12mo. [*Brit. Mus.*]   Oxford, [1653]

DISPUTATION (a) between the body and the soul. [By Sir Theodore Martin.] 12mo. [*Adv. Lib.*]
Edinburgh, 1838

DISPVTATION (a), betweene a hee conny-catcher and a shee-conny catcher, whether a theefe or a whoore is most hurtfull in consonage to the common-wealth : discovering the secret villanies of alluring strumpets. With the conuersion of an English courtizen, reformed this present yeare, 1592. Reade, laugh, and learne. R. G. [By Robert Greene.] 4to. B. L. No pagination.   London, 1592

DISPUTATION (a) of the Church, wherein the old religion is maintained.

[By Edmund Stratford, D.D.] Fcap 8vo. [Gillow's *Bibl. Dict.*, vol. 4, p. 175.]   Doway, 1632
The author's real name was Lechmere. The Dedication is signed " V. M. C. F. E."

DISPUTATION (a) with Mr Gunning about Schisme. [By Thomas White.] 8vo. [Watt's *Bibl. Brit.*]
London, 1658

DISPUTE (the) adjusted, about the proper time of applying for a repeal of the Corporation and Test Acts ; by shewing that no time is proper. [By Edmund Gibson, D.D.] 8vo. [*Brit. Mus.*]   London, 1732
See a reply below (" The dispute better adjusted. . . .").

DISPUTE (a) against the English-popish ceremonies obtruded upon the Church of Scotland. Wherein not only our owne arguments against the same are strongly confirmed, but likewise the answeres and defences of our opposites, such as Hooker, Mortoune, Burges, Sprint, Paybody, Andrewes, Saravia, Tilen, Spotswood, Lindsey, Forbesse, &c., particularly confuted. [By George Gillespie.] 4to. [*New Coll. Cat.*]   N.P., 1637

DISPUTE (the) better adjusted, about the proper time of applying for a repeal of the Corporation and Test Acts ; by shewing that some time is proper. In a letter to [Edmund Gibson] the author of the Dispute adjusted. [By Samuel Chandler, D.D.] 8vo. [*Brit. Mus.*]
London, 1732
See, above, " The Dispute adjusted . . ."

DISPUTE (a) between [Thomas Inglefield] a Journeyman Tanner of Carrisbrook, in the Isle of Wight, and a Quaker that held forth at the sign of the Bull, Winchester. 8vo. Pp. 24. [Smith's *Anti-Quak.*, p. 242.]
Winchester, N.D., [1739]

DISPUTE (a) upon communicating at our confused communions. [By David Calderwood.] 8vo. Pp. 74. [*Adv. Lib.*]   N.P., 1624

DISPUTE (a) upon the question of kneeling in the acte of receiving the sacramental bread and wine, proving it to be unlawfull ; or a Thirde Parte of the Defence of the ministers reasons for refusall of the subscription and conformitie requyred ; against the severall answers of D. Spark, D. Covel, Th. Hutton, and Th. Rogers. [By Samuel Hieron, D.D.] 4to. Pp. 166. [Dexter's *Cong. Bibl.* ; *D. N. B.*, vol. 26, p. 362.]
London, secret print, 1608

DISQUISITION (a) of the stone and gravel, and other diseases of the bladder, kidneys, etc. By William Adams [Sampson Perry]. Second edition. 8vo. Pp. 72. [*Brit. Mus.*]
London, [1780]

DISQUISITION (a) on the elective franchise, in a series of ten letters. By [James Fraser] the author of *Duty to farm servants.* 8vo.
Aberdeen, 1859

DISQUISITION (a) on the observance of the Lord's Supper, with a view to the defence of the Presbyterian plan of administrating that ordinance. . . . [By Rev. Alexander Duncan, D.D., Mid-Calder.] 8vo. Pp. 201. [*New Coll. Cat.*]
Edinburgh, 1805

DISQUISITION (a) on the right of jurisdiction in peerage successions, particularly the peerage of Scotland; contained in Letters to the Right Hon. the Lord K——. [By Ephraim Lockhart.] With an appendix. . . . Second edition, embracing much additional material. 8vo. [*Brit. Mus.*]
London, 1830
The first edition, published in the same year, reads: 'Letters to the Right Hon. the Lord K——, on the rights of succession to Scottish peerages. . . .'

DISQUISITION (a) touching the Sibyls and the Sibylline writings; in which their number, antiquity, and by what spirit they were inspired, are succinctly discussed; the objections made by Opsopæus, Isaac Casaubon, David Blondel, and others, are examined; as also the authority of those writings asserted: which may serve as an appendix to the foregoing learned discourse touching the truth and certainty of Christian religion. [By John Twysden.] 8vo. Pp. 9, 161-250. [*Bodl.*]
London, 1662

DISQUISITION (a) upon Etruscan vases; displaying their probable connection with the shows at Eleusis, and the Chinese feast of lanterns, with explanations of a few of the principal allegories depicted upon them. [By James Christie.] 4to. Pp. vi., 99. [*Bodl.*]
London, 1806

DISQUISITION (a) upon our Saviour's sanction of tithes, Matth. 23, 23. and Luke 11, 42.; wherein the whole case is most impartially stated and resolved according to express Scripture, for the satisfaction of all scruples. [By Thomas Beverley.] 4to. [*Bodl.*] London, 1685
" Dr Crowther saies yt Mr Beuerley, a Huntingtonshire minister (now in prison, May 4. 1685) was author of yis impertinent pamphlett."—MS. note by Barlow.

DISQUISITION (a) upon the right of succession; and an historical inquiry into the origin of the Coronation ceremony. [By Sir Thomas C. Banks.] 8vo.
London, 1818

DISQUISITIONS concerning the antiquities of the Christian Church. [By David Dalrymple, Lord Hailes.] 8vo. [*Adv. Lib.*]
Glasgow, 1783

DISQUISITIONS on several subjects. [By Soame Jenyns.] Fcap 8vo. [*Brit. Mus.*]
London, 1782

DISRUPTION (the); a Scottish tale of recent times. [By William Cross, of Paisley.] Fcap 8vo. Pp. 447.
Edinburgh, 1846

DISRUPTION (the) of the Scottish Church Establishment. By an elder of the Free Church [James Craufurd, Lord Ardmillan]. Pt 8vo. Pp. 20. [*New Coll. Cat.*]
Edinburgh, 1843

DISSECTIO mentis humanæ; or a satiric essay on modern critics, stage and epic poets, translators, drolls, ill-repute, burials, great guns and gunpowder, physicians, sleep, politicians, patrons, necessity, philosophers, prophets, conjurors, witches, astrologers, stars, gypsies, cunning men, physiognomy, giants, human complexions, fictitious beings, elves or fairies, apparitions, men of business, wealth, pride and avarice, virtue and sense. [By Daniel Defoe.] 8vo. [Wilson's *Life of Defoe,* 209.]
London, 1730

DISSECTION of the Scottish Reform Bill, having the Bill annexed. By a member of the Hon. Society of the Middle Temple [Francis Scott]. 8vo. Pp. 70.
London, 1831
This was followed by " A further dissection," to which the author attached his name.

DISSECTORS (the) dissected; or a review of the opinions of certain leaders of the Free Church . . . on the Cardross case. By Scrutator [Rev. John Tyndal]. 8vo. Pp. 128. [*New Coll. Cat.*]
Edinburgh, 1860

DISSENT (a) from the Church of England fully justified and proved the . . . just consequence of the allegiance due to Christ; being the Dissenting Gentleman's Three Letters and a postscript [by Micaiah Towgood] in answer to Mr J. White's on that subject. Fcap 8vo. [*D. N. B.,* vol. 57, p. 95.]
London, 1753
Signed " A Dissenter." Many editions were required.

DISSENT ; its character, its causes, its reasons, and the way to effect its extinction ; likewise an appendix, containing records and papers not generally known. [By Robert Weaver.] 8vo. [*Brit. Mus.*] London, 1844

DISSENTER (the) exposed to himself and the Church. . . . By a friend of the people [Edward Curtis Kemp]. 8vo. Pp. 86. [*Brit. Mus.*]
London, 1834

DISSENTERS (the) and Church [of England] reform : a letter occasioned by [Dr Thomas Arnold's] " Principles of Church reform." By Vindex [—— Manney ?]. 8vo. [*Birm. Cent. Lib.*]
London, 1833

DISSENTERS' and other unauthoriz'd baptisms null and void, by the Articles, Canons and Rubricks of the Church of England. In answer to a pamphlet [by Bp. Fleetwood], call'd, The judgment of the Church of England, in the case of lay-baptism, and of Dissenters baptism. By the author of *Lay baptism invalid* [Rev. Roger Laurence]. 8vo. Pp. xvi., 70. [*Brit. Mus.*] London, 1712
Signed " R. L."

DISSENTERS (the) and Voluntary Church-men ; or, reflections on the principles and conduct of the Voluntaries. By a probationer of the Church of Scotland [William Rae]. 8vo. Pp. 81. [*And. Jervise.*]
Edinburgh, 1835

DISSENTER'S (the) answer to the High Church Challenge. [By Daniel Defoe.] Being an answer to " The Wolf stript of his shepherd's cloathing " [by Charles Leslie]. 4to. [*Arber's Term Cat.*, iii., 390.] London, 1704

DISSENTERS' (the) apology ; or their principles and conduct justified, from the groundless and severe censures lately set forth against them by the editor of Dr Warren's sermons. . . . [By Rev. Micaiah Towgood.] 8vo. Pp. 40. [*D. N. B.*, vol. 57, p. 94.]
London, 1739
Signed " A Dissenter." Many editions were required. *See also* " Dissent from the Church . . ." and " The Dissenting gentleman's answer. . . ."

DISSENTERS' (the) claim of right to a capacity for civil offices. [By Charles Owen, D.D.] 8vo. [*D. N. B.*, vol. 42, p. 401.] London, 1717

DISSENTERS (the) in England vindicated from some reflections in a late pamphlet [by James Webster], entituled, Lawful prejudices, etc. [By Daniel Defoe.] 4to. [*Wilson's Life of Defoe*, 97.] No title page. [1707]

DISSENTERS (the) misrepresented and represented. [By Daniel Defoe.] 4to. [*Wilson's Life of Defoe*, 55.]
London, 1704

DISSENTERS no schismaticks : a second letter to Mr Robert Burscough about his Discourse of Schism. . . . [By Rev. Samuel Stodden.] 8vo. [*Green's Bibl. Somers.*, vol. 3, p. 289.]
London, 1702
Signed " S. S."

DISSENTERS no schismaticks ; or dissenting Churches orthodox. [By Jeremiah Hunt, D.D.] 8vo. [Lardner's Funeral Sermon on J. H.]
London, 1714

DISSENTERS (the) represented and condemn'd by themselves, on the points of the vocation of their ministry, the constitution of their churches, and their separation from the Church of England. In a letter of Mr D. W. [Daniel Williams] a Dissenting teacher to one of his flock who went astray ; together with some farther account of their principles and practices upon those points. [By Theophilus Dorrington, M.A., rector of Wittnessham, Kent.] 8vo. Pp. 350. [*Bodl.*]
London, 1710

DISSENTERS (the) vindicated ; or, a short view of the present state of the Protestant religion in Britain, as it is now professed in the Episcopal Church of England, the Presbyterian Church of Scotland, and the Dissenters in both. In answer to some reflections on Mr Webster's two books, published in Scotland. [By Daniel Defoe.] 8vo. [*Wilson's Life of Defoe*, 98.]
London, 1707

DISSENTING (the) academies, against Mr Sacheverel's misrepresentation of 'em. . . . [By James Owen.] 4to. [*Adv. Lib.*] London, 1704

DISSENTING (the) casuist : or, the second part of a Dialogue between Prejudice, a Dissenting country gentleman, and Reason, a student in the University. Being I. A clear justification of the execution of the laws against Dissenters. II. A comparison of the arguments on both sides concerning monarchy in general. III. Concerning an elective kingdom, or whether a lawful successor or true heir upon any misdemeanours may be excluded. [By Thomas Wood, D.C.L.] 4to. [*Bodl.*]
London, 1682
The address to the reader is signed " T. W." *See above*, the note to " A Dialogue between Mr Prejudice. . . ."

DISSENTING (the) gentleman's answer to the Reverend Mr White's three letters; in which a separation from the Establishment is fully justified; the charge of schism is refuted and re-torted; and the Church of England and the Church of Jesus Christ are impartially compared, and found to be constitutions of a quite different nature. [By Micaiah Towgood.] Second edition. 8vo. [*D. N. B.*, vol. 57, p. 94.]
London, 1746
Signed "A Dissenter."

DISSENTING (the) gentleman's second letter to . . . Mr White, in answer to his three letters, in which his various misrepresentations of the Dissenters are corrected, his objections against them answer'd, and the grounds of their dissent are further represented. [By Micaiah Towgood.] 8vo.
London, 1747

DISSENTING (the) gentleman's third Letter to the Reverend Mr White, in answer to his two defences of his three Letters; in which his misrepresentations of the Dissenters are further dis-proved, etc. [By Micaiah Towgood.] 8vo. London, 1748
Signed "A Dissenter."

DISSENTING (the) ministers' friendly reply to a Second friendly address [by Robert S. Candlish, D.D.] from ministers of the Establishment. [By Hugh Heugh, D.D.] 8vo. [*New Coll. Lib.*] [Edinburgh, 1841]

DISSENTING (the) ministry still valid. [By Charles Owen, D.D., of Warrington.] 8vo. [*D. N. B.*, vol. 42, p. 401.]
London, 1716

DISSERTATION (a) against pro-nouncing the Greek language accord-ing to accents. [By Henry Gally, D.D.] 8vo. Pp. viii., 153. [*Bodl.*]
London, 1754
A second dissertation appeared in 1763.

DISSERTATION (a) concerning in-oculation of the small pox. [By William Douglass.] 8vo. [*Brit. Mus.*] Boston, N.E., 1736
Signed "W. D."

DISSERTATION (a) concerning the being of a God. [By William Sal-mon, M.D.] 8vo. Pp. 32. [Smith's *Cat. of Friends' Books*, i., 526.]
London, 1710

DISSERTATION (a) concerning the Lord's Supper. By the author of the *Dissertation concerning water-baptism* [William Salmon, M.D.]. 8vo. Pp. xix., 74. London, 1708
A Second part was published in 1709.

DISSERTATION (a) concerning the origin and antiquity of barley wine. [By Samuel Rolleston.] 8vo. [*Brit. Mus.*] Oxford, 1750
The Greek designation of the wine forms the introductory part of the title.

DISSERTATION (a) concerning the Song of Solomon; with the original text, divided according to the metre, and a poetical version. [By Andrew Gifford.] 8vo. [*Brit. Mus.*]
London, 1757

DISSERTATION (a) concerning the use and authority of ecclesiastical history. By the author of the *Snake in the grass* [Charles Leslie]. In a letter to the abridger. 8vo.
London, 1703
The above is prefixed to "Eusebius Pam-philus his ten books of ecclesiastical history, faithfully translated and abridg'd from the original. By Samuel Parker, Gent."

DISSERTATION (a) concerning water-baptism. The Second part. By the author of the First [William Salmon, M.D.]. 8vo. London, 1701
For the First part, see *A Dissertation upon water-baptism*.

DISSERTATION (a) in vindication of the antiquity of Stone Henge, in answer to the treatises of Mr Inigo Jones, Dr Charleton, and all that have written upon that subject. By a clergyman living in the neighbour-hood of that famous monument of antiquity [Rev. Stamford Wallis]. 8vo.
Sarum, 1730
The Bodleian copy, which belonged to Tho. Hearne, has the following note in his handwriting:—" 'Tis nothing but an Extract from Webb, abating some abusive expressions of the thief, who sufficiently exposeth himself by endeavouring to de-tract from the reputation of those great men Olaus Wormius, and Dr Walter Charleton. Tho I differ from Dr Charle-ton, yet I think the Dr hath supported his opinion very well, and deserved thanks rather than obloquy. At least it is very unbecoming, for such mean writers as the publisher of this extract, to attack such a worthy man as the Dr certainly was, in so rude a manner."

DISSERTATION (a) in which the de-fence of P. Sulla, ascribed to M. Tullius Cicero, is clearly proved to be spurious; after the manner of Mr Markland; with some introductory remarks on other writings of the antients never before suspected. [By John Ross, M.A., Fellow of St John's College, Cambridge.] 8vo. Pp. 82. [*Bodl.*] London, N.D.

DISSERTATION (a) ; in which the objections of a late pamphlet [by John Ross, A.M.] to writings of the antients, after the manner of Mr Markland, are clearly answer'd ; those passages in Tully corrected, on which some of the objections are founded : with amendments of a few pieces of criticism in Mr Markland's Epist. critica. [By William Bowyer.] 8vo. Pp. 60.

London, 1746

On the title page of the Bodleian copy, there is the following MS. note by Dr Parr :—" Mr Bowyear wrote, or assisted in, this pamphlet."

DISSERTATION (a) on anecdotes. By the author of *Curiosities of literature* [Isaac D'Israeli]. 8vo. Pp. vii., 83. [*D. N. B.*, vol. 15, p. 119.]

London, 1793

DISSERTATION (a) on antient tragedy. [By Thomas Francklin, D.D.] 4to. [*Brit. Mus.*] [London, 1760]

DISSERTATION (a) on comedy ; in which the rise and progress of that species of the drama is particularly consider'd. . . . By a Student of Oxford [John Hippisley, junior]. 8vo. [*D. N. B.*, vol. 27, p. 9.] London, 1750

DISSERTATION (a) on Jacob's prophecy, Gen. xlix. 10. [Here follows the passage in Hebrew, Greek, Latin, and English.] Humbly offered as a supplement to [Thomas Sherlock] the Bishop of London's admirable dissertation on the same text. [By Rev. John Skinner, Longside.] 8vo.

London, 1757

DISSERTATION (a) on liberty and necessity ; wherein the process of ideas, from their first entrance into the soul, until their production of action, is delineated : with some remarks upon the late Reverend Dr [Samuel] Clarke's reasoning on this point. And an epistle dedicatory to truth. By A. C., Esq. [Anthony Collins]. 8vo. [*Brit. Mus.*]

London, 1729

DISSERTATION (a) on Royal Societies ; in three letters from a nobleman on his travels to a person of distinction in Sclavonia. . . . [By Sir John Hill, M.D.] 8vo. [*D. N. B.*, vol. 26, p. 399.] London, 1750

DISSERTATION (a) on St Æthelwold's Benedictional, an illuminated MS. of the tenth century, *penes* the Duke of Devonshire ; and description of a Benedictional or Pontifical . . . in the Public Library at Rouen. [By John Gage Rokewode.] 4to.

N.P., [1832]

DISSERTATION on St Paul's voyage from Cæsarea to Puteoli, on the wind Euroclydon, and on the apostle's shipwreck on the island of Melite. By a layman [William Falconer, M.D.]. 8vo. Pp. 24. [*F. Madan.*]

Oxford, 1817

DISSERTATION (a) on sea-water, etc. As also an account of the nature, properties and uses of all the remarkable mineral [bath] waters in Great Britain. By an eminent physician [Richard Russel]. Fourth edition. 8vo. [Green's *Bibl. Somers.*, i., 449.] London, 1760

DISSERTATION (a) on II. Kings 10 : 22 ; translated from the Latin of Rabbi C——d [Rev. George Costard] ; with a dedication, preface and postscript, critical and expository, by the Translator [J. C.]. 8vo. [Watt's *Bibl. Brit.*] . . . 1752

DISSERTATION (a) on the ancient pagan mysteries ; wherein the opinions of Bp. Warburton and Dr Leland on this subject are particularly considered. [By Rev. John Towne, M.A.] 8vo. [Nichols' *Leicestershire*, ii., 371.]

London, 1766

DISSERTATION (a) on the ancient Service-books of the Church of England. [By Rev. William Maskell, M.A.] 8vo. Pp. 233. [*Brit. Mus.*]

Oxford, private print, 1882

Twenty-five copies printed.

DISSERTATION (a) on the antiquity and use of seals in England. Collected by * * * * 1736. [By Rev. John Lewis.] 4to. [*Bodl.*] London, 1740

DISSERTATION (a) on the antiquity, origin, and design of the principal pyramids of Egypt, particularly of the great pyramid of Ghizeeh, with its measures, as reported by various authors ; and the probable determination of the ancient Hebrew and Egyptian cubit : also, on the original form and measures of the ark of Noah. [By Thomas Yeates.] Illustrated with drawings and suitable descriptions. 4to. Pp. viii., 29, besides plates and descriptive letterpress unpaged. [*N. and Q.*, 2 June 1866, p. 460.] London, 1833

DISSERTATION (a) on the chief obstacles to the improvement of land in Scotland. [By Sir Archibald Grant.] 8vo. [Robertson's *Aberd. Bibl.*] Aberdeen, 1760

DISSERTATION (a) on the chronology of the Septuagint ; with an appendix, shewing that the Chaldean and Egyptian antiquities, hitherto esteem'd fabulous, are perfectly consistent with

the computations of that most ancient Version of the Holy Scriptures. By the author of the *Vindication of the history of the Septuagint*, and the *Critical examination of St Matthew and St Luke's Gospels* [Charles Hayes]. 8vo. Pp. xix., 300. [*Bodl.*]
London, 1741

DISSERTATION (a) on the conduct of the Jewish Sanhedrim, and the advice offered by Gamaliel, in the famous trial of the Apostles, Acts v., 17-41 ; considered as an argument for the truth of Christianity. [By Duncan Shaw, D.D.] 8vo. Pp. vi., 190. [*Scott's Fasti.*] Edinburgh, 1769
Incorrectly attributed to Robert Riccaltoun of Hobkirk.

DISSERTATION (a) on the contents, virtues and uses, of cold and hot mineral springs ; particularly, those of Scarborough : in a letter to Robert Robinson, Esq., recorder of that Corporation. [By Peter Shaw, M.D.] 8vo. Pp. 54. [*Bodl.*] London, 1735

DISSERTATION on the demoniacs in the Gospels. [By Bishop Thomas Newton.] 8vo. [Leslie's *Cat.*, 1843.]
London, 1775

DISSERTATION (a) on the Eleusinian and Bacchic mysteries. [By Thomas Taylor.] 8vo. [*Brit. Mus.*]
Amsterdam, [1791]

DISSERTATION (a) on the existence . . . of prophetic powers in the human mind ; with examples. [By Richard Brothers.] 8vo. [*Lond. Lib. Cat.*]
London, 1794

DISSERTATION (a) on the Folclande and Boclande of the Saxons. [By James Ibbetson, barrister at law.] 4to. [*Bodl.*] London, 1777

DISSERTATION (a) on the following question : In what manner do trade and civil liberty support and assist each other ? . . . By a member of Cambridge University [William Weston, B.D.]. 4to. [*Brit. Mus.*]
London, 1756
See also "Another dissertation. . . ."

DISSERTATION (a) on the geography of Herodotus, with a map. Researches into the history of the Scythians, Getæ, and Sarmatians. Translated from the German of B. G. Niebuhr [by D. A. Talboys]. 8vo.
Oxford, 1830

DISSERTATION (a) on the geometrical analysis of the antients ; with a collection of theorems and problems, without solutions, for the exercise of young students. [By John Lawson, B.D., rector of Swanscome, Kent.] 8vo. Pp. xxiv., 36. [*Brit. Mus.*] Canterbury, 1774

DISSERTATION (a) on the governments, manners, and spirit of Asia. [By Rev. John Logan.] [D'Israeli's *Calamities of authors*, i., 215.]
London, 1787

DISSERTATION (a) on the idea of universal poetry. [By Richard Hurd, Bishop of Worcester ?] 8vo. [*Brit. Mus.*] London, 1766

DISSERTATION (a) on the massacre of Glencoe. [By —— Panton.] 8vo. [Lowndes' *Bibl. Man.*, p. 910.] 1812

DISSERTATION (a) on the message from St John the Baptist to our Saviour ; St Luke vii., 19 : with remarks on the history of his life and ministry. [By Charles William Batt.] 8vo. Pp. 64. [Nichols' *Lit. Anec.*, ix., 62.] London, 1788
Another edition, with the author's name, was published in 1789.

DISSERTATION (a) on the method of inoculating the small pox ; with critical remarks on the several authors who have treated of this disease. By J. C. [J. Castro], M.D. 8vo. [*Brit. Mus.*]
London, 1721

DISSERTATION (a) on the natural evidence against a future state. . . . [By George A. Hammett.] Fcap 8vo. Pp. 46. [Abbot's *Bibliography of a future life.*] New York, 1838

DISSERTATION (a) on the nature of heresy. By a lover of truth and peace [William Nation, sen.]. 8vo. [*Brit. Mus.*] London, 1731

DISSERTATION (a) on the numbers of mankind in antient and modern times ; in which the superior populousness of antiquity is maintained : with an appendix, containing additional observations on the same subject. [By Robert Wallace, D.D.] 8vo. Pp. iv., 331. [*Brit. Mus.*]
Edinburgh, 1753

DISSERTATION (a) on the passage of Hannibal over the Alps. By a member of the university of Oxford [John Anthony Cramer, D.D.]. 8vo. [*Adv. Lib.*] Oxford, 1820
Ascribed also to H. L. Wickham.

DISSERTATION (a) on the plan, use and importance, of the Universal dictionary of trade and commerce ; translated from the French of the late celebrated Mons. Savary, inspector-general of the manufactures for the King, at the custom-house of Paris : with such considerable additions and improvements, as will appear at large throughout this dissertation. . . . [By Malachy Postlethwayt.] 4to. Pp. 57.
London, 1749

DISSERTATION (a) on the political union and constitution of the thirteen United States of North America, which is necessary to their preservation and happiness. . . . By a citizen of Philadelphia [Pelatiah Webster]. 8vo. Pp. 47. [Evans' *Amer. Bibl.*, vol. 6, p. 263.] Philadelphia, 1783

DISSERTATION (a) on the poor-laws. By a well wisher to mankind [Rev. Joseph Townsend]. 8vo. [M'Culloch's *Lit. of Pol. Econ.*, p. 281.] London, 1786

DISSERTATION (a) on the power of the Church ; in a middle way, betwixt those who screw it up to the highest, with the Papists and Scottish Presbyterians on the one hand ; and the Erastians and followers of Hugo Grotius, who on the other hand do wholly reject the intrinsic spiritual authority wherewith Jesus Christ hath vested the rulers of his Church. By P. M. [Patrick Middleton, presbyter of the Church of Scotland]. 8vo. [*New Coll. Cat.*] London, 1733

DISSERTATION (a) on the primary objects of idolatrous worship ; being a farther attempt to divest tradition of fable. [By Samuel R. Maitland.] 8vo. Pp. 56. [*Brit. Mus.*] London, 1817

DISSERTATION (a) on the religious knowledge of the antient Jews and patriarchs ; containing an inquiry into the evidences of their belief and expectation of a future state. [By Stephen Addington, D.D.] 4to. [Watt's *Bibl. Brit.*] London, 1757

DISSERTATION (a) on the rise, union, and power of poetry and music : to which is prefixed, The Cure of Saul, a sacred ode. [By John Brown, D.D., Vicar of Newcastle.] 4to. [*Camb. Univ. Lib.*] London, 1763
Reprinted at Dublin (12mo) in the same year, with the author's name.

DISSERTATION (a) on the Scripture expressions, the Angel of the Lord, and the Angel of Jesus Christ, proving that the word angel is put to signify on these occasions material bodies, and not spirit : interspersed with many other curious observations quite new ; and containing a full answer to a late essay on Spirit [by Robert Clayton], which is calculated to set aside the doctrine of the Trinity in Unity. [By Rev. William Jones, of Nayland.] 8vo. Pp. viii., 68. [*Bodl.*] London, 1752

DISSERTATION (a) on the xviith article of the Church of England ; wherein the sentiments of the compilers, and other contemporary reformers, on the subject of the divine decrees, are fully deduced from their own writings. . . . [By Thomas Winchester.] 8vo. [Watt's *Bibl. Brit.*] Oxford, 1783

DISSERTATION (a) on the Song of Solomon : with the original text, divided according to the metre ; and a poetical version. [By Andrew Gifford.] 8vo. Pp. iii., 111. [Orme's *Bibliotheca Biblica.*] London, 1751

DISSERTATION (a) on the stone in the bladder ; in which are consider'd the nature of the human calculus, the doctrine of menstruums, or the dissolvent for the stone, and how far they are agreeable to the laws of philosophy. In a letter to a physician in London. [By Wm. Shaw, M.D.] 4to. [Green's *Bibl. Somers.*, i., 147.] [Bath], 1738

DISSERTATION (a) on the unreasonableness, folly, and danger of infidelity ; occasion'd by a late virulent book [by Anthony Collins], intitul'd "A Discourse on the grounds and reasons of the Christian religion." By Theotimus Philalethes [Rev. Thomas Curteis]. 8vo. Pp. 216. [*Manch. Free Lib.*] London, 1725

DISSERTATION (a) on the weekly festival of the Christian Church, in which the principal questions concerning Sunday and the Sabbath are discussed. [By Rev. Richard Amner.] Fcap 8vo. Pp. 256. [Cox's *Lit. of the Sabbath question*, ii., 210.] London, 1768

DISSERTATION (a) on value. [By Samuel Bailey.] Pt 8vo. [List of his works in Bury edition of *Essay on Opinions.*] London, 1825

DISSERTATION (a) on weights and measures, and the best means of revising them ; published originally in the British Review, No. xvii., 1817. [By Dr Olinthus Gregory.] 8vo. [*W.*] London, 1817

DISSERTATION (a) shewing the invalidity of all proof by similitude of hands in criminal cases . . . translated from the works of an eminent French civilian [P— de Renusson, or rather F. R. Le Vayer de Boutigny]. 8vo. [*Brit. Mus.*] London, 1744

DISSERTATION (a) upon Oriuna, said to be the Empress, or Queen of England, the supposed wife of Carausius, monarch and empéror of Britain, who reigned in the time of Diocletian, the great persecutor of Christians, whom he was at war with for many years, until received as colleague with him in the Roman Empire. . . . [By John Kennedy, D.M.] 4to. [*Bodl.*] London, 1751

DISSERTATION (a) upon pamphlets, and the undertaking of Phoenix Britannicus, to revive the most excellent among them. In a letter to a nobleman ; from the original MS. [By William Oldys.] 4to. [Morgan's *Phœnix Britannicus*, i., 553.]

London, 1732
Signed " W. O."

DISSERTATION (a) upon parties, in several [xix] letters to Caleb D'Anvers, Esq. Dedicated to the Right Honourable Sir Robert Walpole. [By Henry St John, Viscount Bolingbroke.] Second edition. 8vo. Pp. xxxi., 246. [*Bodl.*] London, 1735

DISSERTATION (a) upon that species of writing called humour, when applied to sacred subjects ; occasion'd by the publication of a sermon [by Benjamin Buckler, D.D.] at All-Souls College on the second day of November last. [By Thomas Nowell, D.D.] 8vo. [*Bodl.*] London, 1760

DISSERTATION (a) upon the account supposed to have been given of Jesus Christ by Josephus ; being an attempt to shew that this celebrated passage, some slight corruptions only excepted, may reasonably be esteemed genuine. [By Nathaniel Forster, B.D.] 8vo. [*D. N. B.*, vol. 20, p. 20.]

Oxford, 1749

DISSERTATION (a) upon the argument a priori for proving the existence of a First cause. In a letter to Mr Law. [By Daniel Waterland, D.D.] 8vo. Pp. 98. [Cambridge, 1734]

DISSERTATION (a) upon the constitution and effects of a Petty Jury. [By the Rev. Philip Skelton.] 8vo. Pp. 45. [*D. N. B.*, vol. 52, p. 333.]

Dublin, 1737

DISSERTATION (a) upon the uncertainty of the Roman history during the first five hundred years. In two parts. Part I. A critical inquiry concerning the original records, memorials, treaties, and other monuments, from whence proper materials could be drawn for compiling the history of the first ages of Rome ; and of the historians who compiled the same. Part II. An examination of some of the principal events that are said to have happen'd during that period ; wherein the inconsistency of the historians with one another, and with the few original pieces that were sav'd, when Rome was burnt by the Gauls, is prov'd. Translated from the French [of Louis de Beaufort]. Fcap 8vo. [Barbier's *Dictionnaire*.]

London, 1740

DISSERTATION (a) upon water-baptism. [By William Salmon, M.D.] 8vo. Pp. 32. [Whitley's *Bapt. Bibl.*, i., 136.] London, 1700

DISSERTATIONS by Mr Dooley. By the author of *Mr Dooley's Philosophy*, etc. [Finlay Peter Dunne]. Cr 8vo. Pp. 320. [*Amer. Cat.*] London, 1906

DISSERTATIONS on the antient history of Ireland ; wherein an account is given of the origine, government, letters, sciences, religion, &c. of the antient inhabitants. [By Charles O'Conor.] 8vo. [*Athen. Cat.*, p. 226.]

Dublin, 1753

DISSERTATIONS on the following subjects, viz. The Mosaick account of the creation and fall of man ; on original sin ; the divinity and satisfaction of Christ ; justification by faith ; the sin against the Holy Ghost ; together with a paraphrase on St Paul's Epistles to the Romans and Hebrews. By Philalethes [Rev. —— Valois, rector of East Tisted]. 8vo. Pp. 317. London, 1750
Attestation of authorship in contemporary handwriting.

DISSERTATIONS on the grand dispute between Great Britain and America. [By Thomas Crowley.] 8vo. [*Brit. Mus.*] [London, 1774]
Signed " Amor Patriæ."

DISSERTATIONS on the opening of the sealed book ; illustrating the prophetic signs used in Daniel and the Revelation. Printed from a transcript of the papers signed Biblicus, published in the London Star. [By Alexander Tulloch, LL.D.] With additional notes. 8vo. Pp. viii., 192. [Orme's *Bibliotheca Biblica*.]

Arbroath, 1819
Another edition appeared at Perth in 1852.

DISSERTATIONS on the pecuniary testimonies of the Quakers relative to their refusing to pay tithes and Church rates, etc. [By Thomas Crowley.] 8vo. [*Brit. Mus.*]

[London], 1773
Signed " T. C."

DISSIPATION ; a tale of simple life. By the author of *Realities* [Mrs Anne Raikes Harding]. 4 vols. Fcap 8vo. [*D. N. B.*, vol. 24, p. 335.]

London, 1827
All the writings of this lady are anonymous.

DISSUASION (a) from crimes, comprised in two sermons. . . . By the chaplain of the County Gaol, Northampton [William Drake]. 8vo. [*Brit. Mus.*] Northampton, 1819

DISSUASIVE from enquiring into the doctrine of the Trinity ; or, the difficulties and discouragements which attend the study of that doctrine : in a letter to a friend. [By Daniel Whitby.] 8vo. [*Brit. Mus.*]
London, 1714

DISSUASIVE (a) from Jacobitism ; shewing in general what the nation is to expect from a Popish king, and in particular from the Pretender. [By John Shute Barrington, First Viscount Barrington.] Second edition corrected. 8vo. [*Bodl.*]
London, 1713

DISSUASIVE (a) from popular rioting directed against mechanical manufacturing improvements. [By Dorning Rasbotham.] 8vo.
Manchester, 1779

DISSWASIVE (a) from conformity to the world ; as also God's severity against impenitent sinners : with a farewel sermon lately preached to a congregation in London. By H. S., minister of the Gospel [Henry Stubbe, or Stubbes]. Fcap 8vo. Pp. 236. [Calamy's *Nonconf. Mem.*, Palmer's ed., ii., p. 244.] London, 1675

DISSWASIVE (a) from gaming. By a minister of the Church of England [Josiah Woodward, D.D.]. Fcap 8vo. [*Bodl.*] London, 1718

DISSWASIVE (a) from lying, chiefly as it relates to children and young people. . . . By the author of *The English Instructor* . . . [Henry Dixon, teacher]. Fcap 8vo. [Green's *Bibl. Somers.*, i., 148.] Bath, [1752]

DISSWASIVE (a) from the sin of drunkenness. By a minister of the Church of England [Josiah Woodward, D.D.]. Fcap 8vo. [*Bodl.*]
London, 1704

DISTANT (the) country ; and other prose poems. By Fiona Macleod [William Sharp]. Fcap 8vo. [*Amer. Cat.*] Portland, Maine, 1907

DISTILLED spirituous liquors the bane of the nation : being some considerations humbly offer'd to the Hon. the House of Commons. By which it will appear, I. That the landed interest suffers greatly by the distilling of spirituous liquors. II. From a physical account of the nature of all spirituous distilled liquors, and the malignant effects they have upon human bodies. III. From the several disorders and immoralities occasioned by this sort of excess. . . . [By Thomas Wilson, D.D.] 8vo. [*Adv. Lib.*]
London, 1736

DISTINCTION (the) between real and nominal Trinitarians examined, and the doctrine of a real Trinity vindicated from the charge of tritheism ; in answer to a late Socinian pamphlet, entituled, The judgment of a disinterested person, concerning the controversie about the blessed Trinity, depending between Dr S[ou]th, and Dr Sherlock. [By William Sherlock, D.D.] 4to. [*D. N. B.*, vol. 52, p. 97.]
London, 1696

DISTINCTION (the) between the ordinary and extraordinary gifts of the Holy Spirit proved to have no foundation in the New Testament. . . . By an impartial hand [Rev. William Ashdowne, Unitarian]. 8vo. [Whitley's *Bapt. Bibl.*, i., 186.] London, 1767

DISTINCTION (a) between the presence of God, as our maker and preserver ; and his presence, as our redeemer and sanctifier. [By Richard Claridge.] 8vo. [Smith's *Cat. of Friends' Books*, i., 50, 412.]
London, 1713

DISTINCTION (a) betwixt the two suppers of Christ ; namely, the last supper in the same night that he was betrayed, before he was crucified, and the supper after he was risen and ascended at the right hand of God, which he calls people to in Rev. 3, to hear his voice, and open the door, and he will sup with them, and they shall sup with him. By G. F. [George Fox]. 4to. [Smith's *Cat. of Friends' Books*, i., 685.] N.P., 1685

DISTINGUISHED persons in Russian society. [Translated from the German of Julius W. A. von Eckardt.] 8vo. [*Brit. Mus.*] London, 1873

DISTRACTED (the) state ; a tragedy, written in the year 1641. By J. T. [John Tatham], Gent. 4to. [*Brit. Mus.*] London, 1651

DISTRACTIONS (the) of Martha. By Marion Harland [Mrs Mary Virginia Terhune, *née* Hawes]. Cr 8vo. [Cushing's *Init. and Pseud.*, vol. i., p. 127.] New York, 1906

DISTRESS upon distress ; or, tragedy in true taste : a heroi- comi- parodi- tragedi- farci-cal burlesque, in two acts [and in verse] . . . with annotations. By Sir Henry Humm [George Alexander Stevens] and notes by Paulus Purgantius Pedasculus. 8vo. [*Brit. Mus.*] London, 1752

DISTRESSED (the) and destitute state of the inhabitants of Spain and Portugal, respecting moral and religious instruction. By an old officer [Walter Bromley]. 8vo. [*Brit. Mus.*] London, 1813

DISTRESSES (the) of the times, as connected with the question of Parliamentary Reform, considered. By an inhabitant of Ipswich [Thomas Harral]. 8vo. Pp. ii., 15. [*Brit. Mus.*]
Ipswich, 1817

DISTRICT (the) school as it was. By one who went to it [Rev. Warren Burton]. 8vo. [Cushing's *Init. and Pseud.*, vol. i., p. 219.]
New York, 1838

DISUNION, and its results to the South [United States]: a letter from a resident of Washington [William L. Hodge]. 8vo. [Cushing's *Init. and Pseud.*, vol. ii., p. 130.]
Washington, 1861

DIURNALL (a) of dangers, wherein are manifested many great discoveries. By T. J. [Thomas Jordan]. 4to. [Thomason *Coll. of Tracts.*]
London, 1642
A satire on the " Diurnalls."

DIVEL (the) coniured. [By Thomas Lodge.] 4to. Pp. 89. London, 1596
Address to the reader, and dedication, signed " T. L." Reprinted by the Hunterian Club, 1875.

DIVERS parts of the Holy Scriptures done into English, chiefly from Dr J. Mill's printed Greek copy ; with notes and maps. [By —— Mortimer.] 12mo. [Lowndes' *Brit. Lib.*]
London, 1761

DIVERS politique discourses of the Duke of Rohan ; render'd into English. By G. B. [George Bridges], Esq. 4to. [Quaritch's *Cat.*] London, 1660

DIVERS views, opinions and prophecies of Yours Trooly [David Ross Locke]. 8vo. Cincinnati, 1865

DIVERS voyages touching the discoverie of America and the ilands adjacent unto the same, made first of all by our Englishmen and afterwards by the Frenchmen and Britons ; with two mappes annexed hereunto. [By Richard Hakluyt.] Two parts. 4to. [*Brit. Mus.*] London, 1582
Signed " R. H."

DIVERS women. By Pansy [Mrs Isabella M. Alden] and Mrs C. M. Livingston. 8vo. Pp. 308.
London, 1887

DIVERSIONS (the) of an autograph-hunter. By J. H. [Rev. John Horne]. Fcap 8vo. Pp. 106. [Mowat's *Caithness Bibl.*, p. 24.] London, 1894

DIVERSIONS of Hollycot, or the mother's art of thinking. By the author of *Clan-Albin* and *Elizabeth de Bruce* [Mrs Christian Isobel Johnstone]. Fcap 8vo. [*Edin. Lit. Journ.*, i., 19.] Edinburgh, 1828

DIVERSIONS of the Echo Club. [By Bayard Taylor.] 8vo. London, N.D.

DIVERSITY ; a poem. By Della Crusca [Robert Merry]. 4to. [*Brit. Mus.*] London, 1788
See the note to " The Baviad."

DIVERTING (the) history of John Bull and Brother Jonathan. By Hector Bull-us [James Kirke Paulding]. Fcap 8vo. [Cushing's *Init. and Pseud.*, vol. i., p. 42.] London, 1813

DIVERTING (the) history of the Count de Gabalis [translated from the French of the Abbé de Montfaucon de Villars]. 8vo. Pp. 88. London, 1714
See the earlier editions, under " Count (the) de Gabalis. . . ."

DIVERTING (the), pathetic, and humorous adventures of Mr Sydenham Greenfinch, gentleman, and of his friends in London. By Tom Hawkins, Esq. [Theodore Alois William Buckley, B.A.]. Cr 8vo. [*D. N. B.*, vol. 7, p. 215.] London, 1854
Sometimes wrongly attributed to Rev. Arthur Bradley.

DIVERTING (the) works of the famous Miguel de Cervantes, author of the *History of Don Quixot* ; now first translated from the Spanish. With an introduction by the author of *The London Spy* [Edward Ward]. 8vo. Pp. xii., 236. London, 1709

DIVES and Lazarus ; or the adventures of an obscure medical man in a low neighbourhood. [By William Gilbert.] 8vo. Pp. iv., 208. [*Adv. Lib.*]
London, 1858

DIVES and Pavper. See A Compendiouse treetise dyalogue.

DIVES' wife, and other fragments. By Thistle Anderson [Mrs Herbert Fisher]. 8vo. [*Camb. Univ. Lib.*] Paisley, 1908

" DIVIDE and conquer " ; or, diplomacy and the Church of Scotland ; a letter to the Right Hon. Sir Robert Peel, Bart., etc. By a Presbyterian Scot [Alexander P. Stewart, M.D.]. Fcap 8vo. [*New Coll. Cat.*]
London, 1843

" DIVIDED." A novel. By the author of *Shakespeare's stories simply told*, etc. [Mary Seamer, later Mrs Seymour]. 2 vols. 8vo. [*Brit. Mus.*]
London, 1881

DIVINATIONS (the) of Kala Persad. By Headon Hill [Frank Edward Grainger]. Pt 8vo. Pp. 246. [*Brit. Mus.*] London, [1903]

DIVINE (the) adventure ; Iona ; By sundown shores : Studies in spiritual history. By Fiona Macleod [William Sharp]. 8vo. [*Lond. Lib. Cat.*]
London, 1900

DIVINE benevolence : or, an attempt to prove that the principal end of the divine providence and government is the happiness of his creatures ; being an answer to a pamphlet [by John Balguy], entitled, Divine rectitude ; or an inquiry concerning the moral perfections of the Deity. With a refutation of the notions therein advanced. [By Thos. Bayes.] 8vo. [Darling's *Cyclop. Bibl.*] London, 1731

DIVINE breathings ; or a pious soul thirsting after Christ. [By Thomas Sherman. Part I.] 12mo. [Arber's *Term Cat.*, i., p. 522]. London, 1672

DIVINE breathings ; or a manual of practical contemplations, in one century : tending to promote Gospel principles, and a good conversation in Christ. . . . The second part. By T. S. [Thomas Sherman]. 12mo. London, 1680

DIVINE (the) catastrophe of the kingly family of the House of Stuart : or, a short history of the rise, reigne, and ruine thereof. [By Sir Edward Peyton.] 8vo. [Watt's *Bibl. Brit.*] London, 1731

DIVINE (a) centvrie of spirituall sonnets. [By Barnaby Barnes.] 4to. [Watt's *Bibl. Brit.*] London, 1595

DIVINE considerations upon sin, death, heaven. . . . By J. H. [Joseph Halsey, M.A.]. 12mo. [Watt's *Bibl. Brit.*] London, 1676

DIVINE contemplations necessary for these times. By H. I. [Henry Isaacson]. 12mo. [*D. N. B.*, vol. 29, p. 61.] London, 1648

DIVINE (the) cosmographer ; a descant on the Eighth Psalme. By W. H. [William Hodson]. 8vo. [Bliss' *Cat.*, 133.] Cambridge, 1620

DIVINE decrees in their bearing upon social life and civil allegiance ; a common sense expostulation. [By Henry William Pullen, M.A.] 8vo. [*Bodl.*] Salisbury, 1874

DIVINE dialogues containing sundry disquisitions & instructions concerning the attributes and providence of God ; the three first dialogues, treating of the attributes of God, and his providence at large. Collected and compiled by the care and industry of F. P. [Franciscus Palæopolitanus, *i.e.* Henry More, D.D.]. 2 vols. 8vo. Pp. 38 unpaged, and 560. [*D. N. B.*, vol. 38, p. 422.] London, 1668
　Epistle signed Fr. Euistor, and dated Palæopolis, Novemb. 29, 1666.

VOL. II.

DIVINE eloquence : or, an essay upon the tropes and figures contained in the Holy Scriptures ; and reduced under the proper titles of rhetorick : also several texts of Scripture, which fall in with the figures, are briefly interpreted ; especially those that seem to favour the Papist or the Socinian. [By Cornelius Norwood.] Fcap 8vo. [Wood's *Athen. Oxon.*, iv., 558.] London, 1694

DIVINE emblems ; embellished with etchings on copper, after the fashion of Master Francis Quarles. Designed, and written by, Johann Abricht, A.M. [Jonathan Birch]. 8vo. Pp. 91, including plates, which are signed by Robert Cruikshank. London, 1838

DIVINE (the) feudal law, or Covenant with mankind, represented ; together with means for the uniting of Protestants : in which also the principles of the Lutheran Churches . . . are distinctly stated and defended by the late learned Baron Pufendorf. Done out of Latin [by Theophilus Dorrington]. 8vo. [Arber's *Term Cat.*, iii., 367.] London, 1703

DIVINE (the) footsteps in human history. [By Daniel Reid.] 8vo. Pp. ix., 445. [*Adv. Lib.*] Edinburgh, 1852

DIVINE glory brought to view, in the condemnation of the ungodly. . . . By a friend to truth [Joseph Eckley]. 8vo. Pp. 51. [Cushing's *Init. and Pseud.*, ii., p. 62.] Boston, 1782

DIVINE (the) grammar ; or, select rules leading to the more nice syntax and articulate construction of dreams, visions, and apparitions. . . . By W. F., Esq. [William Freke]. 8vo. [*D. N. B.*, vol. 20, p. 247.] London, 1703

DIVINE guidance : a memorial of A. W. Dodge. By Gail Hamilton [Mary Abigail Dodge]. 8vo. Pp. 328. [Haynes' *Pseud.*] New York, 1881

DIVINE harmony [being a collection of the words of anthems : arranged and edited by William Croft, organist, Mus. Doc.]. 8vo. [*D. N. B.*, vol. 13, p. 114.] London, 1712

DIVINE (the) headship and unity of Israel scripturally vindicated. [By Mrs —— Simon.] 8vo. Pp. 28. London, 1843

DIVINE healing under the lens. By " a Berean " [Charles Cyrus Cook]. Fcap 8vo. [*Amer. Cat.*] New York, 1907

G

DIVINE (the) history of the Genesis of the world explicated and illustrated. [By Samuel Gott.] 4to. Pp. 497. [*Brit. Mus.*] London, 1670

DIVINE (the) hymnal : a collection of hymns of direct homage for the use of the Church. [By Rev. Augustus Kerr B. Granville.] 12mo. [*Brit. Mus.*] London, 1860

DIVINE hymns and poems on several occasions. . . . By Philomela [Mrs Elizabeth Rowe, *née* Singer] and several other ingenious persons. 8vo. London, 1704

DIVINE (the) idea of human dress. By Ἐνδυμακριτικός [Rev. A— Marshall]. Pt 8vo. London, 1904

DIVINE immediate revelation and inspiration continued in the true Church ; in two treatises : the first being an answer to Jo. W. Bajer, Doctor and Professor of Divinity, so called, at Jena in Germany, published first in Latine and now in English : the second being an answer to George Hicks [Hickes] (of Oxford). By G. K. [George Keith]. 8vo. Pp. 224. [Smith's *Anti-Quak.*, p. 225.] London, 1684

DIVINE (the) instinct recommended to men. Translated from the French [of Béat Louis de Muralt, by William Cookworthy ?]. 8vo. [Smith's *Cat. of Friends' Books*, i., 448.] Oxon., 1751
A different translation, though bearing the same title, appeared at London in 1781.

DIVINE (the) institution of Bishops having Churches, consisting of many congregations, examined by Scripture. [By Rev. Alex. Lauder, M.A., of Mordington.] 12mo. [Scott's *Fasti*.] Edinburgh, 1707

DIVINE (the) institution of water baptism, with as much as is needful concerning the Lord's Supper. By the author of *The snake in the grass* [Charles Leslie]. 4to. London, 1697

DIVINE (the) interpretation of Scripture : a reply to Cardinal Manning. By Saladin [William Stewart Ross]. 8vo. [*Brit. Mus.*] London, [1884]

DIVINE (the) kingdom on earth as it is in heaven. [By Rev. George Smith Drew.] 8vo. London, 1871

DIVINE (the) light of Christ is man, and His mediation truly confessed by the people called Quakers. In a brief and gentle examination of John Norris, his two treatises concerning the divine light. . . . By G. W. [George Whitehead], a servant of Christ. Fcap 8vo. [Smith's *Cat. of Friends' Books*.] London, 1692

DIVINE (the) liturgies. [By Stephen G. Hatherley.] 8vo. London, 1876

DIVINE (the) liturgy for the use of the [Roman Catholic] laity. By C. C. [Charles Cordell], C. A. D. A. [*i.e.* Catholicae Academiae Duacenae Alumnus]. 2 vols. 8vo. Newcastle, 1763
See another edition below (" The Divine Office. . . .").

DIVINE love ; or the willingness of Jesus Christ to save sinners : discovered in three divine dialogues, between 1. Christ and a publican. 2. Christ and a Pharisee. 3. Christ and a doubting Christian. With several other brief tracts. By V. P. [Vavasor Powell]. 12mo. Pp. 285. [*Bodl.*] London, 1677
The other brief tracts have the following separate title : The threefold state of a Christian discovered, viz. By nature, by grace, and in glory ; with the character of a Christian. A miscellany of divine contemplations, observations, and directions to a holy life and conversation.

DIVINE (the) master. [By Felicia M. M. Skene.] 8vo. Pp. x., 155. [Courtney's *Secrets*, p. 65.] London, 1852

DIVINE meditations grounded upon severall texts of sacred Scripture, which may be divided either into pœnitentiall groans of a sorrowfull heart seeking after Christ ; or the fervent sighs of a languishing soule in love with Christ. By E. L., minister of the Gospell, sometimes student of Pembroke Hall, Cambridge [Edward Llewellin]. 4to. [Davies' *Mem. of the York press*, p. 87.] York, 1650

DIVINE meditations ; or a honey-comb to refresh weary travellers : being a collection of divine sayings . . . gathered by G. L. [George Liddell]. Second edition. 12mo. Pp. 24. [*Brit. Mus.*] London, 1700

DIVINE meditations upon several occasions ; with a daily directory. By a person of honour [Sir William Waller, Commander-in-chief of the Parliament's forces in the West]. 12mo. Pp. 109. London, 1682
See also " A Daily directory. . . ."

DIVINE (the) office for the use of the [Roman Catholic] laity. [By Charles Cordell.] 4 vols. 12mo. [Sheffield], 1763
See another edition above (" The Divine liturgy. . . .").

DIVINE (the) origin and perpetual and universal obligation of tithes. By a clergyman of the Church of Scotland [David Thorburn, D.D., Leith]. 8vo. Pp. xxiii., 610. [*New Coll. Cat.*] Edinburgh, 1841

DIVINE (the) origin of Christianity. By the author of *Persuasives to early piety* [Rev. John Gregory Pike]. Fcap 8vo. Pp. 256. London, N.D.

DIVINE (the) panoply; or a suit of armour for the soldier of Christ. [By J— Walker, of Manchester.] Fcap 8vo. [*Brit. Mus.*] London, 1846

DIVINE (the) physician; prescribing rules for the prevention, and cure of most diseases, as well of the body, as the soul: demonstrating by natural reason, and also divine and humane testimony, that, as vicious and irregular actions and affections prove often occasions of most bodily diseases, and shortness of life, so the contrary do conduce to the preservation of health, and prolongation of life. In two parts. By J. H. [John Harris], M.A. 8vo. Pp. 225. [*Camb. Univ. Lib.*] Norwich, 1676

This work is, strictly speaking, not anonymous, since amongst the recommendatory verses prefixed to it, there is a poem by G. R. of ten lines, the initial letters of which form the words Iohn Harris.

DIVINE poems; with a short description of Christian magnanimity. By E. E. [Edmund Elys, or Ellis]. 8vo. Pp. 66. [*Bodl.*] Oxon., 1658

DIVINE providence in answer to prayer. [By Woodbury M. Fernald; an adaptation, by T. Gardiner, from his treatise, *God in his providence*.] Fcap 8vo. [*Brit. Mus.*] London, 1860

DIVINE realities in the light of modern science. By Adelphos [William Harper]. 8vo. Lodiana, 1883

DIVINE rectitude; or, a brief inquiry concerning the moral perfections of the deity, particularly in respect of creation and providence. [By John Balguy, M.A.] 8vo. [*D. N. B.*, vol. 3, p. 60.] London, 1730

DIVINE (the) right of Episcopacy asserted: wherein is proved that Episcopacy is of divine and apostolical institution; and that it was the government of the Christian Church during the three first ages of it; and was design'd to be perpetual in it to the end of the world: with an account of the distinction of the three orders of bishop, presbyter, and deacon; to reconcile the dissenting parties to that form of Church-government. By a presbyter of the Church of England [—— Tremellier]. With a preface, by George Hickes, D.D. 8vo. Pp. lviii., 231. [*Bodl.*] London, 1708

DIVINE (the) right of Episcopacy demonstrated from Calvin and Beza; together with a letter to a Presbyterian minister for union. [By Rev. Alexander Cunningham.] 4to. [*Cat. Lond. Inst.*, ii., 564.] London, 1690

DIVINE (the) right of Episcopacy; wherein is shown that there can be no lawful ministry, but what comes by Apostolick succession. [By Rev. Robert Calder.] 8vo. Pp. 56. [*Adv. Lib.*] N.P., 1705

DIVINE (the) right of man to freedom of thought; an address read to the Hulme Friendly Essay and Discussion Society. . . . By a member of the Manchester Mechanics' Institution [Henry H. Swinglehurst]. 8vo. [*Manch. Free Lib. Cat.*] Preston, 1846

DIVINE (the) sacrament of the Holy Eucharist; a sermon at St Mary's Church, Exeter, in Holy Week, 1849. [By Rev. William Maskell, M.A.] Fcap 8vo. N.P., 1849

DIVINE (the) services and anthems usually sung in His Majesties Chappell, and in all Cathedrals and Collegiate choires in England and Ireland. The second edition, with large additions. Collected by J. C. [J— Clifford]. 12mo. London, 1664

DIVINE (a) tragedie lately acted, or a collection of sundry memorable examples of Gods judgements upon Sabbath-breakers, and other like libertines, in their unlawfull sports, happening within the realme of England, in the compass only of two yeares last past, since the booke was published, worthy to be knowne and considered of all men, especially such, who are guilty of the sinne or arch-patrons thereof. [By Henry Burton.] 4to. [Cox's *Lit. of the Sabbath question*, i., 187, 465.] Anno, 1636

The author's name appears on the title-page of an edition published in 1641.

DIVINE (the) vision; and other poems. By A. E. [George W. Russell]. Cr 8vo. [*Brit. Mus.*] London, 1904

DIVINE (the) wooer, or a poem setting forth the love and loveliness of the Lord Jesus, and his great desire of our welfare and happiness. . . . Composed by J. H. [John Horne]. 8vo. [Arber's *Term Cat.*, vol. i., p. 522.] London, 1673

DIVINITY no enemy to astrology. By T. S. [Thomas Swadling, D.D., Stamford, Lincoln]. 4to. [*Brit. Mus.*] London, 1653

DIVINITY (the) of Christ vindicated from the cavils and objections of Mr John Wright. By an Observer [John Emory, D.D.]. 8vo. [Cushing's *Init. and Pseud.*, vol. ii., p. 107.]
Georgetown, D.C., 1817

DIVINITY (the) of the Trinity cleared, by wiping off the false glosses put upon several places of Scripture by Mr John Biddle. . . . [By John Brayne.] Folio. [*Brit. Mus.*] London, 1654

DIVISIONS (the) of the Church of England, crept in at XV. several doores by divers. . . . [By John Taylor, the water-poet.] 4to. London, 1642

DIVORCE. [A novel.] By Guy Thorne [Cyril A. E. Ranger-Gull]. Cr 8vo. Pp. 256. [*Lit. Year Book*.]
London, 1911

DIVORCE (the) ; a farce, as it is performed at the Theatre-Royal, Drury-Lane. Written by the author of *All the world's a stage* [Isaac Jackman]. Second edition. 8vo. [*Biog. Dram.*]
London, 1782

DIVORCE in its ecclesiastical aspect ; by " Viator " [Rev. Johannes G. F. Raupert]: a rejoinder to *The question of divorce*, by Charles Gore, D.D. Cr 8vo. Pp. 79. London, 1912

DIVOTS [being poems on golf]. By H. M. F. [Helen M. Frere]. 8vo. Pp. 19. N.P., [1898]

DO afflictions come from God ? An appeal to Scripture. By W. M. [Rev. William Marshall]. Cr 8vo.
London, 1910

DO well and doubt not ; a story by the author of *Great Catches* [E— F— Blakiston]. 3 vols. Fcap 8vo. [*Brit. Mus.*] London, 1867

DOBACHI ; a tale of colonial life. By John Ayscough [Monsignor Francis Bickerstaffe-Drew]. Cr 8vo. [*Lond. Lib. Cat.*] London, 1922

DOBBIE and Dobbie's master ; a peep into the life of a very little man. By N. D'Anvers [Mrs Nancy Bell, *née* Meugens]. Cr 8vo. London, 1876

DOCTOR (the), &c. [By Robert Southey.] 7 vols. 8vo.
London, 1834-1847
Vol. 6 has the author's name.

DOCTOR and student ; or dialogues between a Doctor of Divinity and a student in the lawes of England, concerning the grounds of these lawes. [By Christopher Saint Germain.] London, printed by J. Rastall, 1523. Fcap 8vo. B. L.
Many other editions followed, containing additional material. *See also* " The Dyaloges in Englishe . . ." and "An exact abridgement of that excellent treatise called Doctor and student."

DOCTOR (the) and the apothecary ; a musical entertainment in two acts, as performed at the Theatre-Royal, Drury - Lane. [By James Cobb.] 8vo. Pp. 44. [*Brit. Mus.*]
London, 1788

DOCTOR Antonio ; a tale. By the author of *Lorenzo Benoni* [Giovanni Ruffini]. 8vo. [*Adv. Lib.*]
Edinburgh, 1855

DR Bancrofts rashnes in rayling against the Church of Scotland, noted in an answer to a letter of a worthy person of England ; and some reasons rendred why the Answere thereunto hath not hitherto come foorth. By I. D. [John Davidson], a brother of the sayde Church of Scotland. 12mo. [Watt's *Bibl. Brit.* ; Scott's *Fasti*, new ed., vol. 1, p. 388.]
Edinburgh, 1590

DOCTOR Ben. By Democritus, Junior [Rev. Orlando Witherspoon]. 8vo. [Cushing's *Init. and Pseud.*, vol. ii., p. 45.] Boston, 1882

DR Bennet's concessions to the Nonjurors prov'd to be destructive of the cause which he endeavours to defend ; as they make the Nonjurors to be the Catholicks, and his own communion to be schismatical. In a letter to a friend. [By Thomas Brett, LL.D.] 8vo. [*D. N. B.*, vol. 6, p. 285.]
London, 1717

DR Bennet's New theory of the Trinity, examined : or some considerations on his discourse of the ever - blessed Trinity in Unity ; and his examination of Dr Clarke's Scripture-doctrine of the Trinity. [By Thomas Emlyn.] 8vo. Pp. viii., 68. [*Bodl.*]
London, 1718

DR Bentley's Proposals for printing a new edition of the Greek Testament, and St Hierom's Latin version ; with a full answer to all the remarks of a late pamphleteer [Conyers Middleton]. By a member of Trinity College in Cambridge [Richard Bentley, D.D.]. 4to. [Bartholomew's *Bibl. of Bentley*, p. 27.] London, 1721
Signed " I. E.," the second letters in the author's names.

DOCTOR Birch and his young friends. By Mr M. A. Titmarsh [William Makepeace Thackeray]. 4to.
London, 1849

DOCTOR Bolus ; a serio-comick-bombastik-operatick interlude . . . [in one act, and in verse. By George Daniell]. 8vo. [*Brit. Mus.*] London, 1818
Reprinted in Cumberland's *British Theatre*.

DR Bull's Academy. [By Rev. William Henry Pullen, M.A.] Pt 8vo. [*Brit. Mus.*] London, 1886

DR Burnett's reflections upon a book, entituled, Parliamentum pacificum, (the first part) answered, by the author [John Northleigh]. 4to. Pp. 147. [*Brit. Mus.*] London, 1688

DR Campany's courtship, and other tales. By the author of *Doctor Jacob* [Matilda Betham - Edwards]. 8vo. [*Camb. Univ. Lib.*] London, 1868

DR Colenso and the Pentateuch. [By John N. Darby.] Pt 8vo. [*Aberd. Lib.*] London, N.D.

DR Colenso's objections to the historical truth of the Pentateuch reviewed and answered. By a clergyman of the Church of England [Rev. Charles Deane, D.C.L.]. Fcap 8vo. [*Brit. Mus.*] Northampton, 1862

DR Cubitt's cubs ; a story. By A. B. Romney [A— Beatrice Rambaut]. Fcap 8vo. Pp. 96. [*Lit. Year Book.*] London, 1899

DOCTOR Dale ; a story without a moral. By Marion Harland [Mrs Mary Virginia Terhune]. Pt 8vo. [Cushing's *Init. and Pseud.*, vol. i., p. 126.] New York, 1901

DR Darch's wife ; a study. By Florence Warden [Florence Alice Price, later Mrs George E. James]. 8vo. Pp. 181. London, 1896

DR D[ave]nant's forty wonderful prophecys. [By John Asgill.] 4to. [*Cat. Lib. Trin. Coll. Dub.*, p. 137.] London, [1713 ?]

DR [Samuel] Davidson : his heresies, contradictions, and plagiarisms. By two Graduates [Enoch Mellor, and John Guinness Rogers]. 8vo. [*Brit. Mus.*] London, 1857

DR Deane's way ; and other stories. By Faye Huntington [Mrs Isabella H. Foster]. Fcap 8vo. [Cushing's *Init. and Pseud.*, vol. i., p. 134.] Boston, 1875

DOCTOR Dispachemquic : a story of the great Southern Plague of 1878. By Oneida [James Dugan]. 8vo. [Cushing's *Init. and Pseud.*, vol. ii., p. 113.] New Orleans, 1879

DOCTOR (the) dissected ; or, Willy Cadogan in the Kitchen ; addressed to all invalids. . . . By Stella [Mrs —— Ireland, mother of Wm. H. Ireland]. 4to. [Green's *Bibl. Somers.*, vol. i., p. 88.] [Bath], 1771

DR Edith Romney ; a novel. [By Anne Elliot.] 3 vols. 8vo. [*Lond. Lib. Cat.*] London, 1894

D. E. [Dr Edward Bagshaw] defeated ; or a reply to a late scurrilous pamphlet vented against [Dr George Morley] the Lord Bishop of Worcester's Letter, whereby he vindicated himself from Mr [Richard] Baxter's misreports. By S. H. [Samuel Holden]. 4to. [*Bodl.*] London, 1662

D[OCTOR] F[rancis Atterbury]'s vindication of [Gilbert Burnet] the Bp. of Sarum from being the author of a late printed speech ; in a letter to a friend. 4to. [*W.*] London, 1704

DOCTOR Grey. By Stephen Andrew [Frank G. Layton, M.R.C.S.]. Cr 8vo. [*Lit. Year Book.*] London, 1910

DR Hampden's past and present statements compared. [By Edward Bouverie Pusey, D.D.] 8vo. [*Bodl.*] Oxford, 1836
Signed " E. B. P."

DOCTOR Hampden's theological statements, and the Thirty-nine Articles, compared. By a resident member of Convocation [Edward Bouverie Pusey, D.D.]. 8vo. [*D. N. B.*, vol. 47, p. 56.] Oxford, 1836
See also " Elucidations of Dr Hampden's theological statements."

DR Hermione ; a novel. By the author of *Zit and Zoe*, etc. [Henry Curwen]. Cr 8vo. Pp. 279. [*Brit. Mus.*] Edinburgh, 1890

DOCTOR Hill's funeral-sermon ; or a New-Yeers gift to all the clergie. [A satire. By Henry Hasselwood.] 2 parts. 4to. [*Brit. Mus.*] London, 1654
Only Part I. is anonymous.

DOCTOR Hookwell ; or the Anglo-catholic family. [By Rev. Robert Armitage.] 3 vols. 8vo. [*Brit. Mus.*] London, 1842

DR Howell's family. By H. B. G. [H— B. Goodwin, later Mrs Talcott]. 8vo. [Cushing's *Init. and Pseud.*, vol. i., p. 109.] Boston, 1863

DOCTOR Hugnet ; a novel. By Ignatius Donnelly [Edmund Boisgilbert]. Cr 8vo. Pp. 309. [*Brit. Mus.*] London, 1892

DR Ibbetson's case shewn to be no sufficient precedent for assessing parsons, vicars, etc., to poor - rates for tithes they don't occupy. . . . [By Rev. Caleb Parfect.] 8vo. [*Brit. Mus.*] London, 1754
Signed " R. C."

DOCTOR (a) in corduroy. [A novel.] By Max Baring [Charles Messent]. Cr 8vo. Pp. 320. [*Lond. Lib. Cat.*] London, 1905

DOCTOR indoctus ; strictures on Professor Nichol, with reference to his " English composition." [By Fitzedward Hill.] Pt 8vo. Pp. 63.
New York, 1882

DOCTOR Jacob. By the author of *John and I* [Matilda Betham Edwards]. 3 vols. 8vo. [*Camb. Univ. Lib.*]
London, 1864

DR [Robert] Jamieson weighed in his own scales ; a reply to his defence of his Biblical Criticism. By a chapel minister [John M'Gill, afterwards Professor in St Andrews]. 8vo. [*New Coll. Cat.*]
Glasgow, 1866

DR John Brown and his sister Isabella : outlines by E. T. M'L. [Elizabeth T. Maclaren]. 8vo. Pp. 63. [*Brit. Mus.*]
Edinburgh, 1889

DR Johns. By Ik Marvel [Donald G. Mitchell, LL.D.]. Fcap 8vo. [Cushing's *Init. and Pseud.*, vol. i., p. 184.]
New York, 1888

DOCTOR [Samuel] Johnson ; his religious life and his death. By the author of *Dr. Hookwell*, etc. [Robert Armitage]. Fcap 8vo. [*Brit. Mus.*]
London, 1850

DOCTOR Kemp ; the story of a life with a blemish. By the author of " Gilbert Rugge" [Henry Jackson]. 2 vols. 8vo.
London, [1866]

DOCTOR Last in his chariot ; a comedy, as it is performed at the Theatre Royal in the Hay-Market. [By Isaac Bickerstaffe.] Third edition. 8vo. [*Biog. Dram.*]
London, 1773

DR Lincoln's children. By " Fleeta " [Kate W. Hamilton]. Fcap 8vo. [Cushing's *Init. and Pseud.*, vol. i., p. 103.]
Philadelphia, 1892

DOCTOR Manton. [A novel.] By Morice Gerard [John Jessop Teague]. 8vo. [*Lit. Year Book.*]
London, 1906

DOCTOR Merry-man : or, nothing but mirth. Written by S. R. [Samuel Rowlands]. 4to. No pagination.
London, 1627

For the first edition, *see above*, " Democritus. . . ."

DR Mirabel's theory ; a psychological study. [A novel.] By Ross George Dering [Frederick Henry Balfour]. 3 vols. 8vo.
London, 1893

DR [Aldwell] Nicholson's accusation of [Henry Edward Manning] the Archbishop of Westminster [regarding his sermon on the Devotion of the Sacred Heart]. By Catholicus [H. E. Manning]. 8vo. [*D. N. B.*, vol. 36, p. 66.]
London, [1873]

A reprint of papers from *The Tablet*.

DR [Titus] Oate's Narrative of the Popish Plot, vindicated ; in an answer to a . . . libel, call'd A Vindication of the English Catholicks from the pretended Conspiracy against the life and government of His . . . Majesty. . . . [By John Phillips, Milton's nephew.] Folio. [*Brit. Mus.*]
[London], 1680

DOCTOR (the) of Crow's Nest. By Ralph Connor [Charles W. Gordon, D.D.]. Cr 8vo. [*Lit. Year Book.*]
London, 1906

DOCTOR (the) of the " Juliet." By Harry Collingwood [William J. C. Lancaster]. Cr 8vo. Pp. 368. [*Lit. Year Book.*]
London, 1905

DOCTOR (a) of the old school. By Ian MacLaren [John Watson, D.D., Liverpool]. 8vo.
London, 1897

DR Oldham at Greystones, and his talk there. [By Caleb Sprague Henry, D.D.] 8vo. [Kirk's *Supp.*]
New York, 1860

DOCTOR papa. By Sophie May [Rebecca Sophia Clarke]. Fcap 8vo. [Cushing's *Init. and Pseud.*, vol. i., p. 185.]
Boston, 1876

DR Phillips : a Maida Vale idyll. By Frank Danby [Mrs Julia Frankau]. Pt 8vo. [*Lond. Lib. Cat.*]
London, 1889

DR Pierce his preaching confuted by his practice. Sent in a letter by N. G. [John Dobson] to a friend in London. 4to. Pp. 4. [*Bodl.*]
N.P., N.D.
" Came out at Oxon Aug : 28. 1663 : yᵉ authour of it Joh. Dobson A : M : and fellow of Magd : Coll : . . ."—MS. note by Wood.

DR Pierce his preaching exemplified in his practice ; or, an antidote to the poison of a scurrilous and libellous pamphlet sent by N. G. to a friend in London, and printed without license. In a letter from a friend of truth and justice unto a worthy divine of Cambrige. [By John Dobson.] 4to. Pp. 13.
N.P., 1663
Letter signed " J. F."
" This tract was written by Dr Pierce, although, upon a close inquisition after the author, Dobson took it upon himself, to save Dr P. *See* Wood's Athenæ, vol. iv., p. 1, ed. Bliss."—MS. note in Bodl. Cat.

DR Pirie's views on episcopacy considered. [By Rev. J— J— Ball.] 8vo. [Robertson's *Aberd. Bibl.*]
Aberdeen, 1873

DR Pons. [A novel.] By Paul Gwynne [Ernest Slater, M.I.C.E.]. Cr 8vo. [*Lit. Year Book.*]
London, 1907

DR Price's notions of the nature of civil liberty, shewn to be contradictory to reason and Scripture. [By John Gray.] 8vo. Pp. 124. [Rich's *Bibl. Amer.*, i., 256.]   1777

DOCTOR Quodlibet ; a study in ethics. [By James Franklin Fuller.] Pt 8vo. Pp. 223. [*Brit. Mus.*]   London, 1894

DR [John] Radcliffe's life [by William Pittis] and letters ; with a true copy of his . . . will. Third edition. Fcap 8vo. [*Brit. Mus.*]   London, 1716

DR Rameau. [A novel.] By Georges Ohnet [Georges Hénot] ; translated from the French by Mrs C— Hoey. Cr 8vo. Pp. 304. [*Lond. Lib. Cat.*]
London, 1889

DR Renwick's medicines. By Nellie Grahame [Mrs Annie Dunning, *née* Ketchum]. 12mo. [Cushing's *Init. and Pseud.*, vol. i., p. 119.]
Philadelphia, 1879

DR Rumsey's patient. By E. T. Meade [Elizabeth Toulmin Meade] and Clifford Halifax [Edgar Beaumont], M.D. Cr 8vo.   London, 1896

DR Sacheverell's recantation ; or the fire of St Paul's quickly quenched, by a plea for the Non-conformists. [By Daniel Defoe.] 4to. [Wilson's *Life of Defoe*, p. 114.]   London, 1709

DR Sherlock sifted from his bran and chaff ; or, a certain way of finding out the true sense of the Scriptures, and discovering who are the true living members of Christ. In a dialogue. [By Lewis Sabran, S.J.] 4to. Pp. 28. [Jones' Peck.]   London, 1687

DR Sherlock's Case of allegiance considered ; with some remarks upon his Vindication. [By Jeremy Collier.] 4to. Pp. 170. [Watt's *Bibl. Brit.*]
London, 1691

DR Snape instructed in some matters, especially relating to Convocations and converts from Popery. By a member of Convocation [White Kennett, D.D.]. 8vo. Pp. 90.   London, 1718

DR Stillingfleet against Dr Stillingfleet ; or the palpable contradictions committed by him in charging the Roman Church with idolatry, &c. [By John Warner, S.J.] 8vo. [Sommervogel's *Dictionnaire*.]   N.P., 1671
Wrongly assigned to John Williams.

DR Stillingfleet still against Dr Stillingfleet ; or the examination of Dr Stillingfleet against Dr Stillingfleet examined. By I. W. [John Warner, S.J.]. 8vo. Pp. 297. [Oliver's *Collections* ; De Backer's *Bibl.*]   N.P., 1675
Mistakenly attributed to John Keynes, and by others to John Williams.

DR Stillingfleet's principles, giving an account of the faith of Protestants, considered by N. O. [Serenus Cressy]. 8vo. Pp. 110. [Gillow's *Bibl. Dict.*]
Printed at Paris, 1671
Wrongly ascribed to Abraham Woodhead.

DR Struthers on the Free Church. By a Free Churchman [Rev. Andrew Gray]. 8vo. [*New Coll. Cat.*, p. 331.]   Perth, 1845

DOCTOR Syntax in Paris ; or a tour in search of the grotesque. [By William Combe.] Roy 8vo.   London, 1820

DR Wandermann. [A novel.] By Owen Nox [Charles Barney Cory, ornithologist]. 8vo. [Cushing's *Init. and Pseud.*, vol. i., p. 206.]
Boston, [Mass.], 1887

DOCTOR Whitty. [A novel.] By George A. Birmingham [James Owen Hannay, D.D.]. Cr 8vo. Pp. 320. [*Lit. Year Book.*]   London, 1913

DOCTORS and doctors ; some curious chapters in medical history and quackery. By Graham Everitt [William Rodgers Richardson]. Cr 8vo.
London, 1888

DOCTOR'S (the) angel. [A story.] By M. C. Ramsay [Mary Ramsay Calder]. Cr 8vo. [*Lit. Year Book.*]
London, 1914

DOCTOR'S (the) daughter [a story]. By Ramsay Guthrie [Rev. John G. Bowran, Methodist minister]. Cr 8vo. [*Methodist Who's Who.*] London, 1912

DOCTOR'S (the) daughter. By Sophie May [Rebecca Sophia Clarke]. Fcap 8vo. [Cushing's *Init. and Pseud.*, vol. i., p. 185.]   Boston, 1873

DOCTOR'S (the) daughter. [A tale.] By "Vera" [E— Barry]. 8vo. Pp. 250.   Ottawa, 1885

DOCTOR'S (the) dilemma. By Hesba Stretton, author of *Paul's courtship*, etc. [Sarah Smith]. 3 vols. 8vo.
London, 1872
See the note to "Alone in London."

DOCTOR'S (a) "Do"=ings ; or, the entrapped heiress of Witham ! A satirical poem. By Quintin Queerfellow [Charles Clark]. A very limited number reprinted from the suppressed edition. Printed by Charles Clark (an amateur) at his private press. 8vo. Pp. 10.   Totham, 1848
At the end, there is The sly old W—m Miss="Do"—er ! A song. In imitation of "The fine old English gentleman" and "All in my puss !" A song. In imitation of "All round my hat."—An edition, without date, but with the author's name, was published with almost all the blanks filled up.

DOCTOR'S (the) experiment; the adventures and experiences of one of Dr Reade's pupils, as narrated by himself. By the author of *Under fire* [H— Frederick Charles]. 8vo.
London, [1884]

DOCTOR'S (the) idol. [A novel.] By Christian Lys [Percy James Brebner]. Fcap 8vo. Pp. viii., 206. [*Lond. Lib. Cat.*]
London, [1894]

DOCTOR'S (the) little daughter. By Silverpen [Eliza Meteyard]. Pt 8vo. [*Lond. Lib. Cat.*]
London, 1850

DOCTOR'S (the) secret; a novel. By "Rita" [Eliza M. J. Gollan, later Mrs Von Booth, afterwards Mrs W. Desmond Humphreys]. Fcap 8vo. [*Brit. Mus.*]
London, 1890

DOCTOR'S (the) wife. By the author of *Lady Audley's secret* [Mary Elizabeth Braddon, later Mrs John R. Maxwell]. 3 vols. 8vo. [*Brit. Mus.*]
London, 1864

DOCTRESSE (the): a plain and easie method of curing those diseases which are peculiar to women. By R. B. [Richard Bunworth]. 12mo. Pp. 150. [*Watt's Bibl. Brit.*]
London, 1656

DOCTRIN (the) of the Holy Trinity placed in its due light, by an answer to a late book [by Robert South, D.D.], entituled "Animadversions upon Dr Sherlock's book." Also the doctrin of the Incarnation of our Lord assisted and explained. [By Arthur Bury, D.D.] 4to. [Boase and Courtney's *Bibl. Corn.*, p. 722.]
London, 1694
See continuation in "A defence of the Doctrines. . . ."

DOCTRINA placitandi; or, the art and science of pleading: showing where, and in what cases, and by what persons, pleas, as well real as personal or mixed, may be properly pleaded. By S. E. [Sampson Ever], king's attorney in the marches of Wales, and king's serjeant. 4to. [Clarke's *Law Cat.*, p. 282.]
London, 1677

DOCTRINAL and historical sketches of the Jewish and Christian revelations: intended for youth. Two parts. [By James Buchanan, D.D.] 12mo. Pp. 156, 144.
Glasgow, 1824-25

DOCTRINAL (a) catechism of the Church of England; in which all the answers are given in the language of the Homilies, Articles, and Liturgy. . . . By T. B. B. [Thomas Bagnall Baker?]. Fcap 8vo. [*Brit. Mus.*]
Oxford, 1840

DOCTRINE (the) and discipline of divorce: restor'd to the good of both sexes, from the bondage of canon law, and other mistakes, to Christian freedom, guided by the rule of charity; wherein also many places of Scripture have recover'd their long-lost meaning. Seasonable to be now thought on in the Reformation intended. [By John Milton.] 4to. Pp. 52, and two pages of omissions. [Thomason *Coll. of Tracts*, i., 277.]
London, 1643

DOCTRINE and duty; from "The Gospeller." [By James Samuel Pollock, and Thomas Benson Pollock.] Cr 8vo. [Osborn's *Wesl. Bibl.*]
London, 1875

DOCTRINE (the) and practice of the Church of Scotland, anent the sacrament of baptism, vindicated from the charge of gross error exhibited in a print [by Alexander Sutherland] called, The practice and doctrine of the Presbyterian preachers, about the sacrament of baptism, examined. Part I. [By James Hadow.] 4to. [*New Coll. Lib.*]
N.P., 1704

—— Part II. [By James Hadow.] 4to. [*Adv. Lib.*]
Edinburgh, 1704

DOCTRINE (the) held by the Church of Scotland concerning the human nature of our Lord, as stated in her standards. [By Edward Irving, M.A., and Thomas Carlyle, advocate.] Fcap 8vo. [*New Coll. Cat.*]
Edinburgh, 1830

DOCTRINE (the) of absolute predestination stated and asserted, with a preliminary discourse on the divine attributes: translated in great measure from the Latin of Jerom Zanchius, with some account of his life prefixed. By the author of *The Church of England vindicated from the charge of Arminianism* [Augustus Montague Toplady]. To which is subjoined, from the Latin of Lipsius, an appendix concerning the fate of the ancients. 8vo. [Copinger's *Bibl. of Predestination.*]
London, 1769

DOCTRINE (the) of absolution. . . . By a member of the Revision Committee of the Church of Ireland [Humphrey Lloyd, D.D.]. 8vo. [*D. N. B.*, vol. 33, p. 426.]
Dublin, 1871

DOCTRINE (the) of abstinence from blood defended; in answer to two pamphlets, the one [by William Burscough] called, The question about eating blood stated and examined &c. the other intitled, The prohibition of blood a temporary precept. By the author of *Revelation examined with candour* [Patrick Delany]. 8vo. [*Brit. Mus.*]
London, 1734

DOCTRINE (the) of antiquity concerning the most blessed Eucharist plainly shewed in remarks upon Johnson's " Unbloody Sacrifice." By Clerophilus Alethes [John Constable, S.J.]. 8vo. [Dodds' *Church Hist.*]
London, 1736

DOCTRINE (the) of atonement. By Prof. I. Rivière. Authorised translation by Luigi Cappadelta [Charles Louis Dessoulary]. 8vo. [*Brit. Mus.*; *Int. Cath. Lib.*] London, 1909

DOCTRINE (the) of baptism, as taught in the Holy Scriptures and held by the Protestant Episcopal Church. . . . [By Alfred Lee, D.D., Bishop of Delaware.] 8vo. [*Brit. Mus.*]
New York, [1866]

DOCTRINE (the) of changes, as applicable both to the institutions of social life and to the progressive order of nature. By the author of *The morning and evening sacrifice*, etc. [Thomas Wright, minister in Borthwick]. Fcap 8vo. [Scott's *Fasti.*] Edinburgh, 1844
This is a reissue, with a new title, of the work originally published under the title of " My old house." *See later.*

DOCTRINE (the) of combinations, permutations, and compositions of quantities clearly and succintly demonstrated. [By William Emerson.] 8vo. [*Brit. Mus.*] London, 1770

DOCTRINE (the) of communicating worthily in the Lord's Supper : delivered by way of question and answer. . . . By A. H. [Arthur Hildersam]. The fifth edition. 12mo. Pp. 146. [*Brit. Mus.*] London, 1617

DOCTRINE (the) of demurrers ; setting forth variety of presidents of demurrers in all sorts of actions, and in all the several parts of pleadings. . . . By R. G. [Robert Gardiner]. 8vo. [*Brit. Mus.*] London, 1706

DOCTRINE (the) of eternal torment refuted. By Melampus [George Sexton]. 8vo. [*Brit. Mus.*]
London, 1863

DOCTRINE (the) of fluxions ; not only explaining the elements thereof, but also its application and use in the several parts of mathematics and natural philosophy. [By William Emerson.] 8vo. [*W.*] London, 1743

DOCTRINE (the) of Holy Scripture respecting the attaining of salvation. By Herman Heinfetter, author of *Rules for ascertaining the sense conveyed in ancient Greek manuscripts*, etc. [Frederick Parker]. Fcap 8vo. [Cushing's *Init. and Pseud.*, vol. i., p. 128.] London, 1859

DOCTRINE (the) of Holy Scripture respecting the effect of prayer. By Herman Heinfetter, author of *Rules for ascertaining the sense conveyed in ancient Greek manuscripts*, etc. [Frederick Parker]. Second edition, with an appendix. Fcap 8vo.
London, 1859

DOCTRINE (the) of immortality in its bearing on education. By Presbyter Anglicanus [Rev. Joseph Hemington Harris]. Pt 8vo. [*Brit. Mus.*]
Ramsgate, 1871

DOCTRINE (the) of justification by faith in Jesus Christ ; stated from the Scriptures and homilies of the Church of England. By a clergyman [Henry Stebbing, D.D.]. 8vo. [*Bodl.*]
London, 1757

DOCTRINE (the) of New Jerusalem respecting the Lord ; translated from the original Latin [of Emanuel Swedenborg]. 8vo. Pp. 156. [*Manch. Free Lib. Cat.*] London, 1812

DOCTRINE (the) of non-resistance or passive obedience no way concerned in the controversies now depending between the Williamites and Jacobites. By a lay gentleman, of the communion of the Church of England by law establish'd [Edmund Bohun]. 4to. [*Queen's Coll. Cat.*, p. 771.]
London, 1689

DOCTRINE (the) of passive obedience and jure divino disproved, and obedience to the present government proved, from Scripture, law, and reason ; written for the satisfaction of all those who are dissatisfyed at the present government. By a lay-man of the Church of England [George Hickes, D.D.]. Folio. [*Bodl.*]
London, 1689

DOCTRINE (the) of passive obedience and non-resistance stated, and its consistence with theology, reason, our laws and policy, . . . consider'd. [By Michael Maittaire.] 8vo. [Arber's *Term Cat.*, iii., 669.]
London, 1710

DOCTRINE (the) of philosophical necessity briefly invalidated [against Thomas Priestley. By John Dawson, surgeon, of Sedbergh]. 8vo. [*D. N. B.*, vol. 14, p. 227.] London, 1781
Wrongly attributed to Edward Dawson, and to Benjamin Dawson.

DOCTRINE (the) of salvation, faith, and good works ; extracted from the homilies of the Church of England. [By John Wesley, M.A.] Ninth edition. Fcap 8vo. [*Brit. Mus.*]
Bristol, 1748
First published in 1739.

DOCTRINE (the) of schism fully opened, and applied to gathered churches. Occasioned by a book [by Richard Baxter] entituled, Sacrilegious desertion of the holy ministry rebuked : and tolerated preaching of the Gospel vindicated. By the author of *Toleration not to be abused by the Presbyterians* [Francis Fullwood]. 8vo. Pp. 182, 175. [*Bodl.*]   London, 1672

DOCTRINE (the) of surds. . . . [By Sir Jonas Moore.] 4to. London, 1681

DOCTRINE (the) of the blessed and adorable Trinity, stated from the Holy Scriptures ; with a brief discovery of some unsound and dangerous opinions vented by Mr. John Simpson, professor of divinity in the College of Glasgow. [By —— Hunter.] 8vo. [*Adv. Lib.*]
Edinburgh, 1728

DOCTRINE (the) of the Church of England, as stated in ecclesiastical documents set forth by authority of church and state in the Reformation period between 1536 & 1662. [By John Henry Blunt, M.A.] 8vo. Pp. xvi., 220. [*New Coll. Lib.*]
London, 1868

DOCTRINE (the) of the Church of England as to the effects of Baptism in the case of infants. [By the Rev. William Goode, D.D.] 8vo.
London, 1850
The second edition gives the author's name.

DOCTRINE (the) of the Church of England at the time of the Reformation . . . briefly compared with the remarks of [Edward Burton] the Regius Professor of Divinity. By ΟΥΔΕΙΣ [Christopher Lovett Darby]. 8vo. [*Bodl.*]   Oxford, 1831

DOCTRINE (the) of the Church of England, concerning the independency of the clergy on the lay-power, as to those rights of theirs which are purely spiritual, reconciled with our oath of supremacy and the lay-deprivations of the Popish Bishops in the beginning of the Reformation. By the author of the *Vindication of the depriv'd Bishops* [Henry Dodwell]. 4to. Pp. lxxxvi. [*Cat. Lond. Inst.*, ii., 187.]
London, 1697
The second part of a pamphlet previously issued in 1695. *See* " A Defence of the Vindication of the deprived Bishops."

DOCTRINE (the) of the Church of England, concerning the Lord's day, or Sunday = Sabbath, as it is laid down in the liturgy, catechism, and book of homilies ; vindicated from the vulgar errours of modern writers, and settled upon the only proper and sure basis of God's precept to Adam, and patriarchal practice. . . . [By John Smith, rector of St. Marie's, Colchester.] 8vo. Pp. 233. [*Bodl.*]   London, 1683
Preface signed " S. J."

DOCTRINE (the) of the Cross exhibited in the faith and patience of a humble follower of Christ. [By Robert Brett.] 8vo. Pp. cxi. [*Camb. Univ. Cat.*]
London, 1843
See the next entry.

DOCTRINE (the) of the Cross illustrated. By R. B. [Robert Brett]. Third edition. Fcap 8vo.
London, 1849

DOCTRINE (the) of the Eucharist as revealed to St. Paul. [By John Bate Cardale, solicitor.] 8vo. [*Boase's Lit. of the Cath. Apost. Church.*]
London, 1876

DOCTRINE (the) of the Eucharist stated ; and the harmony between the Primitive Church and the Reformed Church of England manifested : by which the conduct of our new Essentialists is censur'd. By a presbyter of the Church of England [Samuel Walker, B.A.]. 8vo. Pp. 107. [*Brit. Mus.*]   [London], 1720
Signed " S. W."

DOCTRINE (the) of the Fathers and Schools consider'd ; concerning the articles of a Trinity of Divine Persons and the Unity of God : in answer to the Animadversions [by Robert South] on [William Sherlock] the Dean of St. Paul's Vindication of the doctrine of the blessed Trinity. . . . By J. B. [Joseph Bingham], A.M., Presbyter of the Church of England. Part I. 4to. Pp. xii., 174. [Corns and Sparke's *Bibl. of Unfin. Books*, p. 27.]
London, 1695
Assigned also to John Braddock.

DOCTRINE (the) of the gospel, by a plaine and familiar interpretation of the particular points or articles thereof, with the promises, comforts, and duties severally belonging to the same ; whereunto is added a declaration of the danger of not knowing, not believing, or not obeying any one of them. . . . [By Robert Allen.] Folio. [Darling's *Cyclop. Bibl.*] London, 1606

DOCTRINE (the) of the Holy Eucharist, as propounded by Archdeacon Wilberforce, shewn to be inconsistent alike with reason, with Scripture, and the Church ; and his unsound views of the Holy Trinity exposed. By Theophilus Secundus [Stephen Jenner]. 8vo. [*Brit. Mus.*]   London, 1854

DOCTRINE (the) of the Incarnation. [By John Bate Cardale, solicitor.] 8vo. [C. Boase's *Lit. of Cath. Apost. Ch.*]   London, 1873

DOCTRINE (the) of the light within the natural man, leading to eternal life, examined by Scripture light. By H. H. [Henoch Howet], of Lincoln. 4to. [Whitley's *Bapt. Bibl.*, i., p. 70.]   N.P., [1658]

DOCTRINE (the) of the real presence as set forth in the works of divines and others in the English Church since the Reformation. [A catena, in two parts, by Dr William Wright.] 8vo. Pp. vii., 180, 140.   Oxford, 1855
Ascribed also to E. B. Pusey, D.D.

DOCTRINE (the) of the sacraments in relation to the doctrines of grace. By an English presbyter [Rev. Nathaniel Dimock]. Cr 8vo. [*Brit. Mus.*]   London, 1871

DOCTRINE (the) of the sphere, grounded on the motion of the earth, and the ancient Pythagorean or Copernican system, &c. [By John Flamsteed.] Two parts. 4to. [*Brit. Mus.*]   London, 1680
Presentation copy from the author.

DOCTRINE (the) of the Synods of Dort and Arles reduced to the practise; with a consideration thereof, and representation with what sobriety it proceeds. [By William Twisse, D.D.] [In three parts.] 4to. Pp. 198. [*Bodl.*; Watt's *Bibl. Brit.*]   N.P., N.D.

DOCTRINE (the) of the Trinity and Transubstantiation compared, as to Scripture, reason, and tradition; in a new dialogue between a Protestant and a Papist. The first part; wherein an answer is given to the late proofs of the antiquity of Transubstantiation, in the books called, Consensus veterum, and Nubes testium, etc. [By Edward Stillingfleet, D.D.] 4to. [Jones' Peck, 376.]   London, 1687

—— The second part; wherein the doctrine of the Trinity is shewed to be agreeable to Scripture and reason, and Transubstantiation repugnant to both. [By Edward Stillingfleet, D.D.] 4to. [Jones' Peck, 377.]   London, 1687

DOCTRINE (the) of the Trinity, as usually explained, inconsistent with Scripture and reason; and the pernicious consequences that attend such misrepresentations of Christianity set forth. In a letter to [Thomas Randolph] the author of the late Vindication of the doctrine of the Trinity, in two parts. [By Robert Clayton, Bishop of Clogher.] 8vo. [*Brit. Mus.*]   London, 1754

DOCTRINE (the) of the Trinity defended against the attacks of J. F. C. [James Freeman Clarke, D.D. By John H. Edger]. 8vo.   Boston, 1861

DOCTRINE (the) of the Trinity: with some remarks on the Arian Controversy. [By Meredith Jones.] 8vo.   London, 1768

DOCTRINE (the) of the universal atonement examined; with a reference to certain views recently advanced on the subject, by the Rev. James Morison, Kilmarnock. [By Rev. David Thomas, of Mauchline.] Fcap 8vo. Pp. 28. [*New Coll. Cat.*]   Glasgow, 1841

DOCTRINES and duties; or, faith and practice. By a layman [Frederick Bolingbroke Ribbans]. 8vo. [*Brit. Mus.*]   London, [1843]

DOCTRINES (the) and practices of the Church of Rome truly represented: in answer to a book [by John Gother] intituled, A Papist misrepresented and represented, &c. [By Edward Stillingfleet, D.D.] 4to. Pp. 144. [*Bodl.*]   London, 1686

DOCTRINES (the) of a Trinity and the Incarnation of God examined upon the principles of reason and common sense. . . . By a member of the Church of England from birth and education, and a sincere disciple of Jesus Christ from choice and rational conviction [Rev. Edward Evanson]. 8vo. Pp. 188. [*Bodl.*]   N.P., 1772

DOCTRINES (the) of original sin and the Trinity discussed in a correspondence between a clergyman of the Episcopal Church in England [Rev. William Edward Heygate] and a layman of Boston, U.S. [Hon. Nathan Appleton]. 8vo. [Kirk's *Supp.*]   Boston, 1859

DOCTRINES (the) of orthodoxy recommended to the serious consideration of all Christians. By a Berean [Rev. John Cameron, M.A., minister at Dunluce]. 8vo. [Witherow's *Presb. in Ireland*, vol. ii., p. 122.]   Belfast, 1782
Republished (1817) with the title "The skeleton covered with flesh."

DOCTRINES (the) of Swedenborg and Spinoza identified. By * * *, U.S. Army [Ethan Allen Hitchcock]. 8vo.   Boston, 1846

DOCTRINES (the) of the Church of England neither Calvinistic nor Arminian, but scriptural. . . . By a beneficed clergyman of the Established Church [Hans Hamilton, D.D.]. 8vo. [*Brit. Mus.*]   London, 1819

DOCTRINES (the) of the Trinity and transubstantiation compared. By G. R. [George Ripley]. 8vo. [Cushing's *Init. and Pseud.*, vol. i., p. 245.]
Boston, 1833

DOCUMENTS connected with the history of Ludlow and the Lords Marchers. [By the Hon. Robert Henry Clive.] 4to. [*Brit. Mus.*]
London, 1841
The preface is signed " R. H. C."

DOCUMENTS illustrative of the oppressions and cruelties of the Irish Revenue Officers. [By Rev. Edward Chichester.] 8vo. Pp. 46. [*Brit. Mus.*]
London, 1818

DOCUMENTS relative to Bradford Church, the glebe-lands, the great and small tithes, together with the allotments of the pews in the year 1805 ; illustrated by extracts from Dr Whitaker's History. [Edited by John Outhwaite.] 8vo. [*Brit. Mus.*]
Bradford, 1827

DOCUMENTS relative to the reception at Edinburgh of the kings and queens of Scotland, A.D. MDLXI. [By Sir Patrick Walker.] 4to. Pp. 124. [Martin's *Cat.*] Edinburgh, 1822

DODS [*i.e.* Rev. Professor Marcus Dods] and his critics. By the Town-clerk of Ephesus [Rev. Donald J. Martin, M.A., of Oban]. 8vo. Pp. 23. [*New Coll. Cat.*]
Dingwall, 1880

DOE (the) done to death by the dog : done into verse by the Doctor [John Samuel Bewley Monsell, LL.D.]. 8vo. [*Brit. Mus.*] London, 1870

DOES it pay to smoke ? . . . By an old smoker [James Parton]. 8vo. [*Brit. Mus.*] London, [1872]
Part of an earlier pamphlet (1868), " Smoking and drinking."

DOES the Bishop of London obey his own judgment ? [By Rev. Charles Stephen Grueber, M.A.] 8vo. [Green's *Bibl. Somers.*, ii., 458.]
Oxford, [1876]

DOES the discovery of gold in Victoria, viewed in relation to its moral and social effects as hitherto developed, deserve to be considered a national blessing or a national curse ? By Colonus [Sir William A'Beckett]. 8vo. [*Lib. Royal Colon. Inst., Supp.*, i., p. 99.]
Melbourne, 1853

DOES the earth rotate ? By William Westfield [William Edgell]. 8vo. Pp. 40. [*Brit. Mus.*] London, 1914

DOES the Revised Version affect the doctrine of the New Testament ? By E. F. O. Thurcastle [Edward Falkener, of Thurcastle]. 8vo.
London, 1884

DOESTICKS : what he says. . . . [By Mortimer M. Thompson.] 8vo. [Haynes' *Pseud.*] New York, 1855

DOFFED (a) coronet. By the author of *The martyrdom of an Empress* [Margaret Cunliffe Owen]. Cr 8vo. [*Brit. Mus.*] London, 1902

DOG (the). By Dinks [Captain Jonathan Peel]. 8vo. London, 1857

DOG (the) fiend ; or, Snarley Yow, and the King's cutter. [By Captain Frederick Marryat.] 3 vols. Pt 8vo. [*Brit. Mus.*] London, 1840

DOG (the) from Clarkson's. [By Desmond Coke, B.A., Oxon.] Cr 8vo.
London, 1895

DOG (the) in health and disease ; comprising the various modes of breaking and using him for hunting, coursing, shooting, etc. . . . By Stonehenge, author of *The greyhound*, etc. [John Henry Walsh]. 8vo. Pp. xvi., 465. [*Brit. Mus.*] London, 1859

DOG (the) in health and in disease. [By Thomas Wesley Mills.] 8vo.
London, 1892

DOG (the) in health, habits, and disease. By Landseer [Bromley Murray]. 8vo. [Cushing's *Init. and Pseud.*, vol. ii., p. 86.] Philadelphia, 1886

DOG (a) of Flanders, and other stories. By Ouida, author of *Puck*, etc. [Louise De La Ramée]. With four illustrations by Enrico Mazzanti of Florence. 8vo. Pp. 299. [*Lit. Year Book.*]
London, 1872

DOG (a) with a bad name. [A novel.] By Florence Warden [Florence Alice Price, later Mrs George E. James]. 3 vols. 8vo. London, 1885

DOG (the) ; with simple directions for his treatment, and notices of the best dogs of the day and their breeders or exhibitors. By " Idstone " [Rev. Thos. Pearce, M.A.]. With twelve full-page engravings, drawn on wood, from life, by George Earl. 8vo. Pp. 258. [*Bodl.*] N.P., [1872]

DOGGER versus Bumper. [By —— Taylor, farmer in Fetteresso.] 8vo. [*And. Jervise.*] N.P., [1856]
There is, at the end, an additional poem, by the same author, called Lummie, of which the subject was George Bruce, farmer in Lumgair, who hanged himself at the back of his own door. It is signed " Auld Style," and dated 1857.

DOGMA no antidote for doubt. [By Vine Wright Kingsley, barrister.] Pt 8vo. [*Amer. Cat.*]
Philadelphia, 1885

DOGMA or doctrine ? and other Essays. By J. M. Lloyd Thomas, W. B. Carpenter, etc. Edited by W. C. B. [William Copeland Bowie]. 8vo.
London, 1906

DOGMATICAL (a) and practical treatise on Indulgences . . . abridged from a French work [written by Jean Baptiste Bouvier]. By a parish priest. 8vo. Dublin, 1839

DOGS (the) of the British Islands [chiefly written by Rev. Thomas Pearce, M.A., Rector of Charborough, Oxford]. 8vo. London, 1866

DOGS (the) of the British Islands ; being a series of articles and letters by various contributors, reprinted from the " Field " newspaper. Edited by " Stonehenge " [John Henry Walsh]. Second edition. 4to. Pp. vii., 286. [*Brit. Mus.*] London, 1872

DOG'S (a) tale. By Mark Twain [Samuel Langhorne Clemens]. 8vo. [*Lit. Year Book.*] New York, 1905

DOGS ; their management and treatment in disease. By Ashmont [Dr Joseph Franklin Perry, junr.]. 8vo. [Cushing's *Init. and Pseud.*, vol. ii., p. 9.] Boston, 1885
Attributed also to Captain Mahon.

DOING and dreaming : a tale for the young. By Edward Garrett [Isabella Fyvie, later Mrs John R. Mayo]. Pt 8vo. [*Brit. Mus.*] London, 1877

DOING their bit [in the Great War]. By Boyd Cable [Ernest A. Ewart]. Cr 8vo. [*Lit. Year Book.*] London, 1916

DOINGS of the Bodley family in town and country. By the author of *Stories from my attic* [Horace Elisha Scudder]. Fcap 4to. Boston, 1880

DOLEFULL (a) ditty, or sorowful sonet of the lord Darly, some time King of Scots, neuew to the noble and worthy king Henry the eyght, and is to be sung to the tune of " Black and yellowe." By H. C. [Henry Chettle]. [Lowndes' *Bibl. Man.*]
London, [1567]
A broadside, reprinted in the Harleian Miscellany.

DOLEFULL (the) even-song ; or, a true narration of that fearefull and sudden calamity which befell the preacher, Mr Drury a Jesiute, and the greater part of his auditory, by the downefall of the floore at an Assembly in the Black-Friers. . . . [By Thomas Goad.] 4to. [*Brit. Mus.*]
London, 1623
Preface signed " T. G."

DOLEFULL (the) fall of A. Sall, a Jesuit of the fourth vow, from the Roman Catholick Apostolick faith ; lamented by his constant friend [Nicholas French, R. C. Bishop of Ferns]. 8vo. [*Brit. Mus.*]
[Louvain], 1674
Signed " N. N."

DOLEFVLL (the) knell, of Thomas Bell. That is, a full and sounde ansvver to his pamphlet, intituled, The Pope's fvneral. VVhich he published against a treatise of myne, called, The fore-rvnner of Bels dovvne-fal. VVherein his manifest vntruthes, grosse corruptions, cunning slightes, vaine cavils, immodest railing, insolent challenging, and idle excursions, be noted, examined, and refuted. By B. C. student in diuinitye [Robert Parsons]. Diuided into two bookes, and seuerall chapters : according to Bels method. The particular contents whereof, are to be found in the end of this booke. 8vo. [Oliver's *Collections*.] Printed at Roane, 1607
Thomas Bell, reared as a Papist, became a Protestant, and thereby incurred the enmity of his earlier co-religionists, especially because of his writings against the Jesuits, one of whom issued the foregoing rejoinder. *See below*, " The Dounefall of Popery. . . ."

DOLL (the) and her friends ; or, memoirs of the Lady Seraphina. [By Julia C. Maitland.] Cr 8vo. London, 1858

DOLL Tear-sheet, alias the Countess " Je ne me rappelle pas," a match for " Non mi ricordo." [By William Hone.] 8vo. [*Camb. Univ. Lib.*]
London, [1820]

DOLLAR City ; a novel. By Lucas Cleeve [Mrs Howard Kingscote, *née* Adelina Georgina Isabella Wolff]. Cr 8vo. Pp. 320. [*Brit. Mus.*]
London, 1907

DOLLARS and cents. By Amy Lothrop [Anna B. Warner]. 8vo. Pp. 315. [Cushing's *Init. and Pseud.*, vol. i., p. 174.] London, [1854]

DOLL'S (the) pic-nic [in verse]. By M. U. [Mary Uniacke]. 8vo. [*Brit. Mus.*] London, [1860]

DOLLY : a quiet story for quiet people. By M. F. W. [M— F. Wilson]. 8vo.
London, 1888

DOLLY and her diary ; being the story of Dolly Hope, musical comedy star, as told by herself and edited by " Pan " [Leslie Beresford]. Cr 8vo. Pp. 250. [*Lit. Year Book.*] London, 1918

DOLLY and Syb. [A tale.] By E. M. B. [E— M. Browne]. Fcap 8vo. Pp. 95.
London, [1898]

DOLLY (the) dialogues. By Anthony Hope [Anthony Hope Hawkins]. Pt 8vo. [*Lit. Year Book.*] London, 1899

DOLLY Pentreath, and other humorous Cornish tales in verse. By the author of *Recreations in rhyme* [John Trenhaile]. Fcap 8vo. Pp. 46.
Plymouth, [1855]

DOLLY the romp. [A novel.] By Florence Warden [Florence Alice Price, later Mrs George E. James]. Cr 8vo. Pp. 316. London, 1897

DOLLY'S cape. By May Kingston [Sarah Lane]. Fcap 8vo. [Cushing's *Init. and Pseud.*, vol. ii., p. 82.]
Philadelphia, 1890

DOLORES. By Mrs Forrester [Mrs —— Bridges]. Fcap 8vo. [Cushing's *Init. and Pseud.*, vol. i., p. 60.]
Philadelphia, 1884

DOLORES : a historical novel of South America. . . . By Harro [Paul Harring]. 8vo. [Cushing's *Init. and Pseud.*, i., p. 126.] New York, 1847

D.O.M. ; the Triune : or the new religion. By Scrutator [Malcolm MacColl, D.D.]. 8vo. [Cushing's *Init. and Pseud.*, i., p. 263.] London, 1867
Attributed also to Knightley William Horlock.

DOMESTIC anecdotes of the French nation, during the last thirty years, indicative of the French Revolution. [By Isaac D'Israeli.] 8vo. Pp. 461. [*Bodl.*] London, 1794

DOMESTIC (the) commentary on the New Testament of our Lord and Saviour Jesus Christ [with the text]. By a clergyman of the Church of England [Robert Shittler, vicar of Alton Pancras, Dorset]. 8vo. Pp. 514. [*Brit. Mus.*] London, [1853]

DOMESTIC (the) commentary on the Old Testament of our Lord and Saviour Jesus Christ [with the text]. By a clergyman of the Church of England [Robert Shittler, vicar of Alton Pancras, Dorset]. 3 vols. 8vo. [*Brit. Mus.*] London, [1853]

DOMESTIC economy, gymnastics, and music ; an omitted clause in the Education Bill. By a bystander [Patrick Fraser, LL.D.]. 8vo. [*Camb. Univ. Cat.*] Edinburgh, 1855

DOMESTIC (a) experiment. [By Mrs M'Fall, *née* Frances E. Clarke.] Cr 8vo. Edinburgh, 1891

DOMESTIC (the) guide, in cases of insanity ; pointing out the causes, means of preventing, and proper treatment, of that disorder. . . . [By T. Bakewell.] Fcap 8vo. Pp. xv., 79. [*Brit. Crit.*, xxxviii., 321 ; xxx., 81.]
Hanley, 1805

DOMESTIC (the) habits of birds. [By James Rennie, M.A.] Fcap 8vo. Pp. xvi., 379. [*Brit. Mus.*] London, 1833
Library of entertaining knowledge.

DOMESTIC life, and other poems. [By Alexander Carlyle, of Paisley.] 8vo. Pp. 131. [*And. Jervise.*]
Edinburgh, 1829

DOMESTIC (a) liturgy ; selected and adapted from the Book of Common Prayer. . . . Compiled by a layman [Charles B. Curtis]. 8vo. [*Brit. Mus.*] Private print, [London], 1868

DOMESTIC management ; or, the healthful cookery-book : to which is prefixed a treatise on diet, as the surest means to preserve health, long life, &c. with many valuable observations on the nutritious and beneficial, as well as the injurious effects of various kinds of food ; also remarks on the wholesome and pernicious modes of cookery. . . . By a lady [Annabella Plumptre]. 12mo. [Watt's *Bibl. Brit.*]
London, 1810

DOMESTIC medicine and surgery ; or, matronly aids to medical attendance. By the editor of *Enquire within* [Robert Kemp Philp]. 8vo. [*Brit. Mus.*] London, [1878]

DOMESTIC piety. By a lady [Mary Webster]. 4to. St Andrews, 1878
Private information from a friend.

DOMESTIC rhymes. By O. H. B. [O— H. Ball]. Fcap 8vo. Pp. 34.
London, 1909

DOMESTIC stories ; a new edition. By the author of *John Halifax, Gentleman*, etc. [Dinah Maria Mulock, later Mrs Craik]. 8vo. Pp. 389. [*Brit. Mus.*] London, 1860
The stories composing this volume formed part of a collection of tales published in three volumes under the title of *Avillion and other tales.*

DOMESTIC union ; or, London as it should be. [By George Giffin, later Stonestreet.] 4to. London, 1800

DOMESTIC verses. By Delta [David Macbeth Moir]. 8vo. Pp. viii., 174. [*Adv. Lib.*] Edinburgh, 1843

DOMESTIC (the) world ; a practical guide in all the daily difficulties of the higher branches of domestic and social economy. By the author of *Enquire within* [Robert Kemp Philp]. 8vo. Pp. 396. [*Brit. Mus.*] London, N.D.

DOMESTICATED animals, considered with reference to civilization and the arts. [By Mary Roberts.] Fcap 8vo. [*Brit. Mus.*] London, 1835

DOMINICAN (a) artist; a sketch of the life of the Rev. Père Besson, of the Order of St. Dominic. By the author of *Tales of Kirkbeck*, etc. [Henrietta Louisa Farrer, later Mrs Sidney Lear]. Cr 8vo. Pp. xi., 289. [*Brit. Mus.*] Oxford, 1870

DOMINICAN (the) Tertiary's guide. By two Fathers of the same Order. 2 vols. [Vol. I. by Charles F. Palmer; Vol. II. by Robert R. Suffield.] 8vo. [F. Boase's *Mod. Eng. Biog.*, vol. 6, col. 348.] Derby, 1868

DOMINIE'S (the) disaster, and other poems. By a member of the Musomanik Society of Anstruther [William Tennant]. Fcap 8vo. Pp. 24. [*Brit. Mus.*] Cupar, 1816

DOMINIE'S (the) legacy. By the author of *The sectarian* [Andrew Picken]. 3 vols. 8vo. [*Brit. Mus.*] London, 1830

DOMINION (the) of dreams under the dark star. By Fiona Macleod [William Sharp]. 8vo. Pp. 336. [*Lit. Year Book.*] London, 1899

DOMINION (the) of the heavens; a vast commonwealth of intellects. . . . By "Rejected" [C— Inglis, M.D.]. 8vo. Pp. 467. London, [1899]

DOMINOES. By Professor Hoffmann [Angelo John Lewis, M.A.]. Fcap 8vo. [Cushing's *Init. and Pseud.*, vol. ii., p. 76.] London, 1899

DOMINOES, and how to play them: illustrated by numerous examples. [By Joseph T. Burgess.] 8vo. [*Brit. Mus.*] London, 1877

DON. [A novel.] By the author of *Laddie*, etc. [Evelyn Whitaker]. 8vo. Pp. 376. [*Amer. Cat.*] London, 1895

DON: a poem; with large notes giving an account of the ancient families, castles, and curiosities of Don and its branches; also a full account of the battles of Harlaw, Brechin, Alford, etc. [By A— Forbes.] 8vo. [Mitchell and Cash's *Scot. Top.*, i., 49.] London, 1742
  Often reprinted (at Aberdeen, Edinburgh, Peterhead, etc.).

DON Carlos; or an historical relation of the unfortunate life and tragic death of that Prince of Spain, son to Philip II.; written in French [by César Vischard de Saint Real], anno 1672, and newly Englished by H. I. 12mo. [Arber's *Term Cat.*, vol. i., p. 522.] London, 1673

DON Esteban; or, memoirs of a Spaniard: written by himself [Valentin Llanos]. 3 vols. Fcap 8vo. [*Adv. Lib.*] London, 1825

DON Finimonde [a collection of short stories]. By E. Cavazza [Elizabeth Jones, later Mrs Pullen]. 8vo. [*Amer. Cat.*] Boston, 1902

DON Garcia in England. [Scenes and characters from English life.] By George Windle Sandys [Oswald J. F. Crawfurd]. 8vo. Pp. viii., 373. London, 1879

DON Gesualdo; a novel. By Ouida [Louise De la Ramée]. Fcap 8vo. [*Lit. Year Book.*] London, 1889

DON Gordon's shooting-box. By Harry Castlemon [Charles A. Fosdick]. Fcap 8vo. [Cushing's *Init. and Pseud.*, vol. i., p. 52.] Philadelphia, 1883

DON Juan. [By George Gordon Noel Byron, Lord Byron.] 4to. [*Brit. Mus.*] London, 1819

DON Juan. By the author of *The coming K——* [Eustace Clare Grenville Murray]. 8vo. London, 1858

DON Juan Lamberto: or, a comical history of the late times. The first part. By Montelion, Knight of the Oracle, etc. [Ascribed by some to Thomas Flatman; by others to John Phillips, nephew of Milton.] 4to. No pagination. B.L. [Wood's *Athen. Oxon.*, iv., 245.] London, 1661

DON Juan, junior; a poem. By Byron's ghost [G— R— W. Baxter]. 8vo. [*Birm. Ref. Lib.*] London, 1839

DON Juan reclaimed. By W. C. [William Cowley]. 8vo. [Cushing's *Init. and Pseud.*, vol. i., p. 47.] Sheffield, 1840

DON Juan transformed. [By Louis Menzies.] 8vo. [Robertson's *Aberd. Bibl.*, p. 84.] Aberdeen, 1871

DON Malcolm. By Marion Thorne [Ida T. Thurston]. 8vo. [*Amer. Cat.*] Boston, 1898

DON Paez and other poems. By a Virginian [James H. Price]. 8vo. [Cushing's *Init. and Pseud.*, vol. i., p. 296.] New York, 1847

DON Q. in the Sierra. By E. and H. Heron [Mrs Kate O'Brien Hesketh and Hesketh Vernon Hesketh]. Cr. 8vo. [*Amer. Cat.*] Philadelphia, 1906.

DON Quixote, Jr.; the further adventures of Miltiades Peterkin Paul. By John Brownjohn [Charles Remington Talbot]. 8vo. [Cushing's *Init. and Pseud.*, vol. i., p. 42.] Boston, 1879

DON Sobre Izquierdo, or Alfredo and Florencia ; a parent's curse, or the lovers' resolve. A Richardsonian drama, of thrilling interest, written expressly for the Royal Dramatic College fête of 1864. By Cirujano, M.M.C., author of *Barbadazulo Vanagloroso* [George Borlase Childs]. 8vo. Pp. 8. [Boase and Courtney's *Bibl. Corn.*, i., 68.] [London, 1864]

DON Tarquinio ; a kataliptic, phantasmatic romance. By Fr. Rolfe [Fred. Baron Corvo]. 8vo. London, 1905

DON Tug ; and other poems. [By John Hand.] 8vo. Liverpool, 1879

DON Zara del Fogo : a mock romance. [By Samuel Holland.] Fcap 8vo. [*Brit. Mus.*] London, 1656
The title of a later edition (1719) begins : "The Spaniard . . ."

DONA Rufina ; the romance of a cycle tour. By Heber K. Daniels [Farquhar Palliser]. 8vo. Pp. 183.
London, 1898

DONALD Deane and his cross. By Glance Gaylord [Warren Ives Bradley]. Fcap 8vo. [Cushing's *Init. and Pseud.*, vol. i., p. 111.] Boston, [Mass.], 1867

DONALDSONIAD (the) ; J—n D—n [John Donaldson] detected. . . . [By Rev. William Thom.] Fcap 8vo.
Glasgow, 1763

DONE in the dark ; a novel. By the author of *Recommended to mercy, Zoe's brand*, etc. [Mrs M. C. Houstoun]. 3 vols. 8vo. [*Brit. Mus.*]
London, 1877

DONEGAL fairy stories. By "Mac" [Seumas M'Manus]. Pt 8vo. [O'Donoghue's *Poets of Ireland*.]
London, 1900

DONEGAL Highlands. [By Rev. Dr —— M'Devitt.] 8vo. Dublin, N.D.

DONNA Charitea, Queen of Castille ; a drama, in three acts. [By Lord Francis Egerton, afterwards Earl of Ellesmere.] 8vo. Pp. 67. [*Bodl.*]
Private print, London, 1843

DONNA Marina. By C. Whitworth Wynne [Charles William Cayzer, M.A.]. 8vo. [*Brit. Mus.*]
London, 1905

DONNA Teresa. By George Paston [Emily Morse Symonds]. 8vo. [*Lond. Lib. Cat.*] London, 1902

DONNELLIANA ; an appendix to "Caesar's Column." Excerpts from the wit, wisdom, poetry, and eloquence of Ignatius Donnelly [Edmund Boisgilbert]. 8vo. Pp. 265. [*Brit. Mus.*]
Chicago, [1892]

DONNY'S Captain. By E. Livingston Prescott [Edith Katherine Spicer-Jay]. Cr 8vo. Pp. 156. [*Lond. Lib. Cat.*]
London, 1903

DONOVAN : a modern English gentleman. By Edna Lyall [Ada Ellen Bayly]. Cr 8vo. Pp. 191. [*Brit. Mus.*] London, 1894

DONOVAN : a tale of sorrow and of joy. By Maxwell Gray [Mary Gleed Tuttiett]. 8vo. [*Lit. Year Book.*]
London, 1887

DON'T : a manual of mistakes and improprieties more or less prevalent in conduct and speech. By Censor [Oliver Bell Bunce]. Fcap 8vo. [Cushing's *Init. and Pseud.*, vol. i., p. 53.] New York, 1883

DON'T : or, directions for avoiding improprieties in conduct and common errors of speech. By Censor [Oliver Bell Bunce]. Fcap 8vo. [Cushing's *Init. and Pseud.*, vol. i., p. 53.]
New York, 1888

DON'T give up the ship ; or the good son. [A tale. By Timothy Flint.] 8vo. [*Brit. Mus.*] Cincinnati, 1833

DON'T-KNOW (the) family ; a story for everybody. By Noel Hope [Sarah L. Morewood]. 8vo. London, 1904

DONUM amicis ; verses on various occasions. By F. N. [Francis Newbery]. 8vo. [*Brit. Mus.*]
London, 1815

DOOMED (the). [A novel. By Alexander Hamilton, W.S.] 3 vols. 8vo. [*Camb. Univ. Cat.*] London, 1832

DOOMED (the) village ; a poem, dedicated to the Right Honourable John Bright. [By Rev. William Vernon Harcourt.] 8vo. Pp. 4. [*Bodl.*]
[London], N.D.

DOONAN : a tale of sorrow and of joy. By Melville Gray [Mary Ethel Granger]. 8vo. Pp. viii., 300. London, 1887

דוֹר דוֹרְשִׁים. Generation (the) of seekers ; or the right manner of the saints addresses to the throne of grace : in two treatises. . . . [By John Oldfield, minister at Carsington, Derbyshire.] Fcap 8vo. Pp. 466. [Palmer's edition of Calamy's *Nonconf. Mem.*, vol. i., p. 400.] London, 1671
The prefatory epistle is signed "O. J."

DOOR (the) of hope for Britain. [By Thomas Carlyle, advocate.] Fcap 8vo. Pp. 41. [Boase's *Cath. Apost. Lit.*] London, 1853

DOOR (the) of hope for Christendom. [By Thomas Carlyle, advocate.] Fcap 8vo. Pp. 125. [Boase's *Cath. Apost. Lit.*] London, 1853

DOOR (the) of salvation opened ; or a voice from heaven to regenerate sinners. . . . By T. P. [T— Passenger, the publisher]. Fcap 8vo.
London, 1666

DOOR (the) of trvth opened : or, a brief and true narrative of the occasion how Mr Henry Burton came to shut himself out of the church-doors of Aldermanbury : published in answer to a paper, called, Trvth shvt out of doors : for the vindication of the minister and people of Aldermanbury, who are in that paper most wrongfully and unjustly charged ; and also for the undeceiving of the underwriters, and of all those that are misinformed about this businesse. . . . [By Edmund Calamy, B.D.] 4to. [Hanbury's *Hist. Mem. relating to Independents.*]
London, 1645

DOOR (a) opened to the imprisoned seed in the world ; and the way of freedom, by the spirit of truth, sent out into the world in love to the sheep that have long been lost. Which may serve any who simply seek the life of what they profess ; and may shew the feigned and false in heart, the cause why they are shut out of truths power. By J. N. [James Nayler]. The second edition corrected. 4to. [Smith's *Cat. of Friends' Books*, ii., 229.]
London, 1667
The first edition appeared in 1659.

DOP (the) doctor. [A novel.] By Richard Dehan [Clotilde Graves]. 8vo. [*Brit. Mus.*] London, 1912

DOPE ; a story of Chinatown and the drug traffic. By Sax Rohmer [Arthur Sarsfield Ward]. 8vo. Pp. viii., 310. [*Brit. Mus.*] London, [1919]

DOPES : a criticism of American arts and English efforts. By Nathaniel Gubbins [Edward Spencer Mott]. 8vo. Pp. 126. [*Brit. Mus.*]
London, 1901

DORA and her papa. By Silverpen [Eliza Meteyard]. Pt 8vo. [Cushing's *Init. and Pseud.*, vol. i., p. 267.]
London, 1870

DORA darling : the daughter of the regiment. [By Jane Goodwin Austin.] Fcap 8vo. Boston, [Mass.], 1865

DORA Thorne. By Bertha M. Clay [Mrs Charlotte M. Braeme, *née* Law]. Fcap 8vo. New York, 1887

DORANDO ; a Spanish tale. [By James Boswell, of Auchinleck.] Cr 8vo. [*Brit. Mus.*] London, 1767
Another edition was published in London, and a third in Edinburgh, all within three weeks.

DORÉ. By a stroller in Europe [W— W— Wright]. 8vo. [Cushing's *Init. and Pseud.*, vol. i., p. 275.]
New York, 1857

DOREEN : the story of a singer. By Edna Lyall [Ada Ellen Bayly]. Cr 8vo. [*Brit. Mus.*] London, 1906

DORIAS (the) ; a historical drama, in five acts [and in verse. By Miss —— Strettle]. Fcap 8vo. [*Brit. Mus.*]
Edinburgh, 1835

DORINDA, a town eclogue. [By the Right Hon. Richard Fitzpatrick.] 4to. Pp. 8. [*Brit. Mus.*]
Strawberry-Hill, 1775

DORINDA and her daughter. [A novel.] By Iota [Mrs Mannington Caffyn]. Cr 8vo. [*Brit. Mus.*]
London, 1910

DORIS. By the author of *Phyllis*, etc. [Mrs Margaret Argles, later Mrs Hungerford]. 3 vols. Cr 8vo. [*Brit. Mus.*] London, 1884

DORIS and Theodora. By Margaret Vandergrift [Margaret Thomson Janvier]. 8vo. [Cushing's *Init. and Pseud.*, vol. i., p. 292.]
Philadelphia, 1870

DORIS Moore. [A novel.] By Guy Thorne [Cyril A. E. Ranger-Gull]. Cr 8vo. Pp. 304. [*Brit. Mus.*]
London, 1919

DORIS'S fortune. By Florence Warden [Florence Alice Price, later Mrs George E. James]. Pt 8vo.
London, 1886

DOROTHEA ; a story of the pure in heart. By Maarten Maartens [Joost M. W. van den Poorten Schwartz]. Cr 8vo. Pp. 580. [*Lond. Lib. Cat.*]
London, 1913

DOROTHY ; a country story, in elegiac verse, with a preface. [By Arthur J. Manby.] Cr 8vo. Boston, 1882

DOROTHY ; a tale. [By Margaret Agnes Colville, afterwards Mrs Paul.] 8vo. [*Brit. Mus.*] London, 1856

DOROTHY and her friends. By Henry Hayes [Ellen Warner Olney, later Mrs Kirk]. 8vo. [Kirk's *Supp.*]
Boston, 1900

DOROTHY Deane : a children's story. By Henry Hayes [Mrs Ellen (Olney) Kirk]. Pt 8vo. Boston, 1898

DOROTHY Firebrace ; or the armourer's daughter of Birmingham. By the author of *Whitefriars*, etc. [Emma Robinson]. 3 vols. 8vo. [*Brit. Mus.*]
London, 1865
An earlier edition (1850) bears a slightly different title.

DOROTHY Thorn, of Thornton. By Julian Warth [Mrs Julia Parsons, *née* Warth]. Pt 8vo. [Cushing's *Init. and Pseud.*, vol. ii., p. 154.]
Boston, 1887

DOROTHY Vernon of Haddon Hall. By Edwin Caskoden [Charles Major]. Pt 8vo. [*Brit. Mus.*] London, 1902

DOROTHY'S difficulties ; a story for children. [By M— C. Cordue.] 8vo. Pp. 208. London, [1903]

DOROTHY'S novelist. By Conrad Hawthorne Carroder [Walter John Tripp]. Cr 8vo. Pp. 134. [*Brit. Mus.*] London, 1902

DORRIS Farrand's vocation. By "Pansy" [Mrs Isabella Alden, *née* Macdonald]. Fcap 8vo. [*Amer. Cat.*]
Boston, 1904

DORSET Dear. By M. E. Francis [Mrs Francis Blundell, *née* Mary Evans Sweetman]. 8vo. [*Brit. Mus.*]
London, 1905

DOSIA ; a Russian story. By Henri Gréville [Madame Alice Marie C. Durand]. Translated from the French. Fcap 8vo. Pp. 260. [*Brit. Mus.*]
Philadelphia, 1878

DOSIA'S daughters ; from the French of H. Gréville [Madame Alice M. C. Durand]. Pt 8vo. Boston, 1885

DOT and Dime : two characters in ebony. By one who knows all about them [Lillie E. Barr]. 8vo. [Cushing's *Init. and Pseud.*, vol. ii., p. 113.]
Boston, 1877

DO-THE-BOYS Hall ; a drama. By John Daly [John Besemeres, merchant in Calcutta]. 8vo. London, 1874

DOTT Wynyard's revenge. By the author of *Recommended to mercy* [Mrs Margaret C. Houstoun]. Cr 8vo. 3 vols. [*Brit. Mus.*] London, 1886

DOTTY Dimple stories. Dotty Dimple at her grandmother's. By Sophie May [Rebecca Sophia Clarke]. Fcap 8vo. Pp. 190. [Cushing's *Init. and Pseud.*, i., 185.] Boston, [Mass.], 1871

DOUAY-ELDER (the) unmask'd ; or, remarks upon a pretended Letter from an elder in the country, to a gentleman in the city, intituled, A testimony against the present defections from our covenanted reformation, &c. By a minister of the Church of Scotland [William Wilson]. No title page. 8vo. [Edinburgh, 1731 ?]

DOUBLE (a) blindness ; a novel. By "Alien" [Mrs L— A— Baker]. Cr 8vo. Pp. 320. [*Lit. Year Book.*]
London, 1909

DOUBLE (the) cherry ; a story. By Margaret E. Winchester [Margaret E. Whatham]. Fcap 8vo. [*Amer. Cat.*]
New York, 1894

DOUBLE (the) coronet ; a novel. By the author of *My first season*, etc. [Elizabeth Sarah Sheppard]. 2 vols. 8vo. [*Brit. Mus.*] London, 1856

DOUBLE (the) descent ; a poem. [By Richard Ames.] 4to. London, 1692

DOUBLE (the) disappointment ; or the fortune hunters : a comedy in two acts [and in prose], written by a gentleman [Mosco Mendez]. 8vo. [*Brit. Mus.*] [London], 1755

DOUBLE (the) disguise ; a comic opera in two acts ; as performed at the Theatre-Royal in Drury-Lane. The songs set to music by Mr Hook. [By Mrs Hook.] 8vo. [*Biog. Dram.*]
London, 1784

DOUBLE (a) duel. By Walter B. Dunlap [Sylvanus Cobb, jun.]. Pt 8vo. [Cushing's *Init. and Pseud.*, vol. ii., p. 46.] New York, 1892

DOUBLE (the) Dutchman. [A novel.] By Catherine Childar [Annie Charlotte Catherine Aldrich]. 3 vols. Cr 8vo. [*Camb. Univ. Lib.*] London, 1884

DOUBLE harness : a novel. By Anthony Hope [Anthony Hope Hawkins]. Pp. 396. [*Lit. Year Book.*]
London, 1904

DOUBLE love. By William Dodson [Olive P. Fairchild]. Fcap 8vo. [*Amer. Cat.*] New York, 1888

DOUBLE (a) marriage. [A novel.] By Lucas Cleeve [Mrs Howard Kingscote, *née* Adelina G. I. Wolff]. 8vo. [*Brit. Mus.*] London, 1906

DOUBLE (a) mask. By Norman Silver [George Knight]. 8vo.
London, [1915 ?]

DOUBLE (a) masquerade ; a romance of the Revolution. [By Charles R. Talbot.] Pt 8vo. Boston, 1885

DOUBLE (the) mistake ; a comedy, as it is performed at the Theatre-Royal in Covent-Garden. [By Mrs Elizabeth Griffith.] 8vo. Pp. 84. [*Biog. Dram.*] London, 1766

DOUBLE (the) PP.—A Papist in armes.—Bearing ten seuerall shields.—Encovntred by the Protestant.—At ten seuerall weapons. A Iesuite marching before them. [By Thomas Dekker.] 4to. Pp. 43. [Corser's *Collectanea Anglo-Poetica*, part v., p. 144.] London, 1606

DOUBLE (a) wedding. By the author of *St Olave's*, etc. [Eliza Tabor, later Mrs Stephenson]. 3 vols. 8vo. [*Lond. Lib. Cat.*]   London, 1888

DOUBLE (the) welcome ; a poem to the Duke of Marlbro'. [By Daniel Defoe.] 4to. [Wilson's *Life of Defoe*, p. 57.]   London, 1705

DOUBLE-ARMED (the) man, by the new inuention ; briefly shewing some famous exploits atchieued by our Brittish bowmen ; with seuerall portraitures proper for the pike and bow. [By William Neade.] 4to. [*W.*]   London, 1625

DOUBLE-BARRELLED ; a detective story. By Mark Twain [Samuel Langhorne Clemens]. Cr 8vo. Pp. 180.   London, 1902

DOUBTER'S (a) doubts about science and religion. [By Sir Robert Anderson, K.C.B.] 8vo. [*Brit. Mus.*]   London, 1889

DOUBTFUL (the) marriage ; a narrative drawn from characters in real life. [By William Hutchinson.] 3 vols. Fcap 8vo. [Nichols' *Lit. Illust.*, i., 424.]   London, 1775

DOUBTLETS : a word-puzzle. By Lewis Carroll [Rev. Charles Lutwidge Dodgson]. 12mo. Pp. 37.   London, 1879
> Lewis and Carroll are respectively disguises of Lutwidge (Ludovicus, Ludwig) and of Charles (Carolus, Carl).

DOUBTS concerning the authenticity of the last publication of the Confessional, and the current editions of certain books cited in it ; addressed to [Francis Blackburne] the author of that learned work. [By Thomas Townson, D.D.] 8vo. [*Camb. Univ. Lib.*]   London, 1767

DOUBTS concerning the Roman infallibility : I. Whether the Church of Rome believe it. II. Whether Jesus Christ or his apostles ever recommended it. III. Whether the primitive Church knew or used that way of deciding controversie. [By Henry Maurice, D.D.] 4to. [*D. N. B.*, vol. 37, p. 106.   London, 1688
> Reprinted in Bp. Gibson's "Preservative against Popery."

DOUBTS of the infidels : submitted to the Bench of Bishops. By a weak Christian [William Nicholson (?)]. 8vo. [*Brit. Mus.*]   London, 1781

DOUBTS upon the reasoning of Dr Paley. By Juvenis [R— G. Arrowsmith]. 8vo. [Cushing's *Init. and Pseud.*, vol. i., p. 145.]   London, 1811

DOUCE (a) lass. By the author of *Citoyenne Jacqueline*, etc. [Henrietta Keddie]. 2 vols. 8vo. London, 1877

DOUGLAS ; a tragedy, as it is acted at the Theatre-Royal in Covent-Garden. [By John Home.] 8vo. Pp. 74. [*Adv. Lib.*]   Edinburgh, 1757
> As having been written by the minister of Athelstaneford, publication of this popular drama gave great offence to many in Scotland ; but prominent among friends who rallied to his defence were Dr Hugh Blair and Dr Alexander Carlyle, the latter in an ironical brochure, "An argument to prove that the tragedy of Douglas ought to be publickly burned by the common hangman." *See also* "The Players' scourge. . . ." "A Full and true history. . . ."

DOUGLAS D'Arcy ; some passages in the life of an adventurer. [By William Hayley.] 8vo. Pp. xii., 340. [*Bodl.*]   London, 1834

DOUGLAS Deane ; or, out of the deep. [By Kathleen Mary Smith.] Fcap 8vo.   London, 1883

DOUGLAS (the) family. By Cousin Kate [Catherine Douglas Bell]. 8vo. [*Adv. Lib.*]   Edinburgh, 1851

DOUGLAS ; or the field of Otterburn : a historical romance. [By Patrick Miller M'Clatchie.] 8vo.   [Dumfries ?], 1823

DOUNEFALL (the) of Popery ; proposed by way of a new challenge to all English Jesuites, etc., daring them all to make answer thereunto, if they can. [By Thomas Bell.] 4to. Pp. 167.   London, 1605
> *See* "The dolefull knell, of Thomas Bell . . ." and note.

DOVE (the) ; a poem. [By Matthew Prior.] Folio. [*Brit. Mus.*]   London, 1717

DOVE (the) and the eagle. [By George Lunt.] Fcap 8vo. [*Brit. Mus.*]   London, 1851

DOVE (the) and the serpent. [Signed "D. T.," *i.e.* Daniel Tuvil.] 4to. [Pollard and Redgrave.] London, 1614

DOVE (the) in the eagle's nest. By the author of the *Heir of Redclyffe* [Charlotte Mary Yonge]. 2 vols. 8vo.   London, 1866

DOVE (the) on the Cross, and other thoughts in verse. [By Jane Euphemia Browne, later Mrs Saxby.] Ninth edition. Fcap 8vo. Pp. viii., 136. [*Brit. Mus.*]   London, 1863
> The Dedication is signed "J. E. B."

DOVECOT (the). By Ann [Mrs Ann Thomas]. 8vo. [Cushing's *Init. and Pseud.*, i., 16.]   London, 1834

DOVEDALE ; beauties of Derbyshire. By "Tom Oakleigh" [Abraham Kershaw Kilmister]. 8vo. [Simm's *Bibl. Staff.*, p. 262.]   Macclesfield, 1865

DOVEDALE revisited; with other holiday and angling sketches. By "The Amateur Angler" [Edward Marston, publisher]. Fcap 8vo. Pp. xiv., 130. [*Brit. Mus.*] London, 1902

DOVE-LIKE (the) soule; a sermon [on Ps. 55 [6]] preached before the Princes Highnes at White Hall, Feb. 19, 1618. By I. R. [John Rainoldes], D.D. 4to. Pp. 26. [*Brit. Mus.*]
[London, 1618]

DOVER (the) patrol; the Straits; Zeebrugge; Ostend, including a narrative of the operations in the spring of 1918. By Jackstaff [J— J— Bennett]. Cr 8vo. [*Lond. Lib. Cat.*]
London, [1919]

DOVETON; or the man of many impulses. By the author of *Jerningham* [Sir John William Kaye]. 3 vols. Fcap 8vo. London, 1837
Dedication signed "J. W. K."

DOWAGER (the) Countess and the American girl. By Lilian Bell [A— H— Bogue]. Cr 8vo. London, 1903

DOWAGER'S (the) secret. Leaves from Frank Capel's diary. By "Mignon" [Mrs —— Baseley]. 8vo. [*Manch. Free Lib.*] London, 1897

DOWLAND'S Musical Banquet. [Edited by Samuel Weller Singer.] [Martin's *Cat.*] Chiswick Press, 1817
The "Musical Banquet" was first published in 1610.

DOWN a city alley: a true story. [By A— M. Guinness.] 8vo. Pp. 43. [*Brit. Mus.*] London, [1899]

DOWN East. [By T— J— Bass.] Fcap 8vo. [*Birm. Cent. Lib.*]
Birmingham, [1903]

DOWN in Tennessee, and back by way of Richmond. By Edmund Kirke [James Robert Gilmore]. Fcap 8vo. [*Haynes' Pseud.*] New York, 1864

DOWN in the depths of outcast London; being facts not recorded in "The Bitter cry." [By William C. Preston.] 8vo. [Gladstone *Lib. Cat.* (Lib. Club).]
London, [1886?]

DOWN in the world. By Florence Warden [Mrs George E. James, *née* Florence Alice Price]. Pt 8vo. [*Brit. Mus.*] London, 1892

DOWN our Street; a provincial comedy. By J. E. Buckrose [Mrs Falconer Jameson]. Cr 8vo. Pp. 352. [*Lond. Lib. Cat.*] London, 1911

DOWN right dealing, or the despised Protestant speaking plain English to the Kings most excellent Majesty, the Hon. Houses of Parliament . . . and all other peace-desiring Commons. . . .

Written by J. H. [James Howell], an impartiall observer of the present transactions. 4to. [*Brit. Mus.*]
[London], 1647
Printed in the year of discoveries.

DOWN South. [By Iza Duffus Hardy.] 8vo. London, 1883

DOWN South; or an Englishman's experience at the scat of [the Civil] War [in the United States], 1861. [By Samuel Phillips Day.] 8vo. [Cushing's *Init. and Pseud.*, vol. i., p. 91.]
London, 1862

DOWN South; or, yacht adventures in Florida. By Oliver Optic [William T. Adams]. Fcap 8vo. [*Haynes' Pseud.*]
Boston, 1877

DOWN the bayou; The Captain's story; and other poems. By Xariffa [Mrs Mary Ashley van Voorhees Townsend]. Pt 8vo. Pp. 250. [*Amer. Cat.*]
Philadelphia, 1896

DOWN the corridors of time. [A novel.] By "Nomad" [Miss Adèle Grafton-Smith]. Cr 8vo. [*Lond. Lib. Cat.*]
London, 1912

DOWN the lane and back, in search of wild flowers. By Uncle Matt [Mordecai Cubitt Cooke]. Pt 8vo. Pp. 114. New York, 1895

DOWN the line with John Henry. . . . [By George V. Hobart.] Fcap 8vo.
New York, 1901

DOWN the ravine. By Charles Egbert Craddock [Mary Noailles Murfree]. 8vo. [Cushing's *Init. and Pseud.*, vol. i., p. 70.] Boston, 1885

DOWN the river; or practical lessons under the Code Duello. By an amateur [Colonel George W. Hooper]. 8vo. [Cushing's *Init. and Pseud.*, vol. i., p. 11.] New York, 1874

DOWN the village street. . . . Scenes in a West Country hamlet. By Christopher Hare [Mrs Marion Andrews]. 8vo. [*Lond. Lib. Cat.*]
Edinburgh, 1895

DOWN with the mug; or, reasons for suppressing the mug-houses: humbly offer'd to the consideration of the Parliament of Great-Britain. By Sir H. M. [Sir Humphrey Mackworth]. 8vo. [*Bodl.*] London, 1717

DOWNAM'S Bulletin. [By Ernest James Oldmeadow.] 8vo. [*Brit. Mus.*] London, 1910

DOWNEFAL (the) of Shebna, together with an application to the bloudie Gowrie of Scotland; in two sermons, at Oxford, and now published for a warning to all ill-affected Ogilviests. By I. S. [Isaac Singleton]. 4to. [Watt's *Bibl. Brit.*] London, 1615

DOWNFALL (the) and death of King Œdipus; a drama in two acts. [By Edward FitzGerald.] 8vo.
　　Guildford, private print, [1880-81]

DOWNFALL (the) of Anti-Christ. By R. C. [Richard Carpenter]. 8vo. [Watt's *Bibl. Brit.*]　　London, 1647

DOWNFALL (the) of Grabbum. By an Ulster Clergyman [Rev. P— O'Sullivan]. 8vo. Pp. 148.　　Belfast, 1913

DOWNFALL (the) of Robert, Earle of Huntington, afterward called Robin Hood of merrie Sherwodde ; with his love to chaste Matilda, the Lord Fitzwaters daughter, afterwardes her faire maide Marian. Acted by the Right Honourable, the Earle of Notingham, Lord High Admirall of England, his seruants. [By Anthony Munday.] 4to. B. L. No pagination.
　　Imprinted at London, 1601
　" This play, upon the authority of Francis Kirkman, has been ascribed to Thomas Heywood, and I accordingly bound it up with his other pieces ; but since this volume was bound, I have learned that it was written by Anthony Mundy ; and the second part was written by him and Henry Chettle. *See* my Shakspeare, vol. i., P. II., p. 308. They were licensed by the Master of the Revels, March 28, 1598. On the 18th of Nov. 1598, Chettle received ten shillings for ' mending the first part.' "—MS. note by Malone on the Bodleian copy.

DOWNS (the) reserve : or, the mystery of the Wishing-well. By Margaret Blount [Mrs Mary O'Francis]. 8vo. [Cushing's *Init. and Pseud.*, i., p. 37.]
　　New York, 1864

ΔΟΞΑ ἐν ὑψίστοις τῷ Θεῷ. Notes relative to the Church of England, to Romanism, and some of the varieties of Dissent. By a priest of the Church of England [Edward W. Barlow, M.A.]. 8vo. [Green's *Bibl. Somers.*, i., 44.]
　　Birmingham, 1846

DOXIE Dent ; a clogshop chronicle. By John Ackworth [Rev. Frederick R— Smith, M.A.]. Cr 8vo. [*Method. Who's Who.*]　　London, 1899

DOZEN (a) ballads for the times, about white slavery. By the author of *Proverbial Philosophy* [Martin Farquhar Tupper]. 8vo. [*Brit. Mus.*]
　　London, 1854

DOZEN (a) good times. By Mrs George Archibald [Anna Campbell, later Mrs George Archibald Palmer]. 8vo.　　Boston, 1898

DRACONICA ; or an abstract of all the penal laws touching matters of religion ; and the several oaths and tests thereby enjoyned, now so much con-

troverted : with brief observations thereupon. Published for more general information and satisfaction. By H. C. [Henry Care]. Folio. [*Brit. Mus.*]
　　London, 1687

DRAFT (a) of order for evening prayer, in obedience to the resolution of the [Scottish Episcopal] Synod. [By Alexander Penrose Forbes, D.C.L., Bishop of Brechin.] Fcap 8vo.
　　Aberdeen, 1870
　Preface signed " A. P. F."

DRAGON (the) of Wantley, a burlesque opera. [By Henry Carey.] Set to musick by Mr John Frederick Lampe. 8vo. [*Biog. Dram.*]　　London, 1770

DRAGON (the) painter. [A novel.] By Sidney M'Call [Mrs Mary M'Neil Fenollosa]. Pt 8vo. [*Amer. Cat.*]
　　Boston, 1906

DRAGONESS (the) ; a burlesque opera. [By Henry Carey.] 4to. [*Biog. Dram.*]　　London, 1743
　Part of a collection of his dramatic works published in that year.

DRAGON-FLY ; or reactive passive locomotion : a vacuum theory of aerial navigation, based on the principle of the fan-blower. By a disciple of Bacon [Thaddeus Hyatt]. 4to. [*Brit. Mus.*]　　London, 1882

DRAGON'S teeth. [A novel.] By Richard Dehan [Clotilde Graves]. Cr 8vo. [*Lit. Year Book.*]
　　London, 1915

DRAGOON campaigns to the Rocky Mountains. By a dragoon [James Hildreth]. 8vo. [Cushing's *Init. and Pseud.*, vol. i., p. 83.] New York, 1836

DRAGOONING a dragoon. By E. Livingston Prescott [Edith Katherine Spicer-Jay]. Cr 8vo. Pp. 160. [*Lond. Lib. Cat.*]　　London, 1916

DRAINS and drain ventilation : three letters reprinted from the " Sanitary Record." By J. R. T. [John Robertson Turnbull]. 8vo. [*Brit. Mus.*]
　　Torquay, 1877

DRAMA (the) ; a paper. By Mrs Madge Kendall [Mrs —— Grimston]. Cr 8vo. [*Lond. Lib. Cat.*]
　　London, 1884

DRAMA (the) ; a poem. [By Frederick Pilon.] 4to. [O'Donoghue's *Poets of Ireland.*]　　London, 1775
　Mistakenly attributed to H. Downman.

DRAMA (the) brought to the test of Scripture, and found wanting. [By Robert Kaye Greville, LL.D.] Fcap 8vo. [*New Coll. Cat.*]
　　Edinburgh, 1830

DRAMA (a) in Dutch. [A novel.] By Z. Z. [Louis Zangwill]. 2 vols. Cr 8vo. [*Brit. Mus.*]　　London, 1896

DRAMA (the) in Pokerville ; and other stories. By Everpoint [Joseph M. Field]. 8vo. [Cushing's *Init. and Pseud.*, i., 94.]   Philadelphia, 1847

DRAMAS and dialogues, amusing and instructive. [By Maria Edgeworth.] 8vo. [*Brit. Mus.*]   London, [1830]

DRAMAS for children. By the author of *Home and its duties*, etc. [Mrs J— Werner Laurie]. Fcap 8vo. [*Brit. Mus.*]   London, [1869]

DRAMAS for children. By the author of *The Blind Child* [Mrs —— Pinchard]. Fcap 8vo. [*Brit. Mus.*]   London, 1807

DRAMAS for the use of young ladies. [By C— Short.] Fcap 8vo. [*Birm. Cent. Lib.*]   Birmingham, 1792

DRAMAS in duodecimo ; abstracts and brief chronicles of youth. By Ascott R. Hope [Ascott Robert Hope Moncrieff]. Cr 8vo. Pp. 328. [*Lit. Year Book.*]   London, 1907

DRAMATIC (the) author's companion. By a theatrical manager's reader [Cecil Ferard Armstrong]. 8vo. Pp. viii., 128. [*Brit. Mus.*]   London, [1910]

DRAMATIC (the) censor ; or, critical companion.   [By Francis Gentleman.] 2 vols. 8vo. [*D. N. B.*, vol. 29, p. 129.]   London, 1770

DRAMATIC (the) congress : a short state of the Stage. . . . By W. R. Ch——d [William Rufus Chetwood]. 8vo. [*Brit. Mus.*]   London, 1743

DRAMATIC criticisms. By "Pastel" [George Frederick Pardon]. 8vo. [Haynes' *Pseud.*]   London, 1865

DRAMATIC dialogues. [By Thomas Tyers.] 8vo. Pp. 130. [Martin's *Cat.*]   London, 1782

DRAMATIC dialogues, for the use of young persons. By the author of *The Blind Child* [Mrs —— Pinchard]. Fcap 8vo. [*Brit. Mus.*] London, 1792 *See also above,* " Dramas for children."

DRAMATIC (a) entertainment, called a Christmas tale ; in three acts, as performed at the Theatre-Royal in Drury-Lane. [By David Garrick.] 8vo. Pp. 36. [*Biog. Dram.*] London, 1776

DRAMATIC (the) history of Master Edward, Miss Ann . . . and others. [By George Alexander Stevens.] 8vo. [*Brit. Mus.*]   London, 1785

DRAMATIC (a) pastoral ; occasioned by the collection at Glocester on the Coronation Day, for portioning young women of virtuous characters. By a lady [Mrs Elizabeth Thomas, wife of Rev. —— Thomas, Rector of Notgrove]. Fcap 4to. [*Biog. Dram.*]   Glocester, 1762

DRAMATIC (the) puffers, a prelude ; as performed at the Theatre-Royal in Covent-Garden. [By Rev. Sir Henry Bate Dudley, Bart.] 8vo. Pp. 20. [*Biog. Dram.*]   London, 1782

DRAMATIC romances, containing the Poison tree and the Torrid zone. [By Stephen Clarke.] 8vo. [*Brit. Mus.*]   London, 1809

DRAMATIC scenes and other poems. By Barry Cornwall [Bryan Waller Procter]. Fcap 8vo. [*Brit. Mus.*]   London, 1820

DRAMATIC sketches of the new poor law, as administered by Guardians ; or, reality and fiction identified. By a surgeon [Ellison Spencer Douglas Groves]. Pt 8vo. Pp. vii., 76.   London, 1845

DRAMATIC sketches . . . written for private performance at Thomastown Castle. By Sir Charles Rockingham [Philippe F. de Rohan-Chabot, Count de Jarnac]. 8vo. [*Brit. Mus.*]   Worksop, private print, 1866

DRAMATIC stories. [By Thomas Arnold, D.D.] 3 vols. Fcap 8vo. [Cushing's *Anon.*]   London, 1832

DRAMATIC tales. By the author of *The Poetic Mirror* [James Hogg]. 2 vols. Fcap 8vo. [*Adv. Lib.*]   Edinburgh, 1817

DRAMATIC (the) works of Samuel Foote ; with remarks on each play, and an essay on the life, genius, and writings of the author. By Jon Bee [John Badcock]. 3 vols. Fcap 8vo. [*Brit. Mus.*]   London, 1830

DRAMATICK (a) entertainment, call'd Harlequin a sorcerer ; with the loves of Pluto and Proserpine : as performed at the Theatre Royal in Lincoln's-Inn-Fields. [By Lewis Theobald.] 8vo. Pp. 21. [Dyce *Cat.*, ii., 358.]   London, 1725

DRAMATICK (the) works of M. A. M. [Rev. Mark Antony Meilan]. 8vo. [Watt's *Bibl. Brit.*]   London, 1780

DRAMATISTS of the present day. By "Q." [Thomas Purnell]. Reprinted from the *Athenæum.* Cr 8vo. Pp. viii., 140. [*Brit. Mus.*] London, 1871

DRAPER (the) confuted ; or, a candid and impartial, but full answer to The Consequences of trade : humbly offer'd to the consideration of both Houses of Parliament. By a friend to the government [William Webster, D.D.]. 8vo. [*D. N. B.*, vol. 60, p. 128.]   London, 1740

DRAPER'S (the) reply to some Remarks on "The Consequences of trade as to wealth. . . ." Annexed is an essay on Mr [Samuel] Webber's scheme. [By William Webster, D.D., Vicar of Ware, in Hertfordshire.] Cr 8vo. [*D. N. B.*, vol. 60, p. 128.]
London, 1741
A refutation of the writer's own pamphlet (" The consequences of trade . . ."). *See above.*

DRAPIER'S (a) address to the good people of England, upon the causes of the present dearness of provisions. [By James Atcherley.] 8vo. [*Brit. Mus.*] London, 1773
Signed " A. D."

DRAT the boys ! By Max O'Rell [Paul Blouet]. 8vo. [*Brit. Mus.*]
London, 1886
A later edition, enlarged, appeared with the title *John Bull, junior.*

DRAUGHT (a) for a national church accommodation ; whereby the subjects of England and Scotland, however different in their judgments concerning Episcopacy and Presbytery, may yet be united, in regard to the Queen's headship over both, in one Church and kingdom of Great Britain. [By John Humphrey.] 4to. [*Bodl.*]
London, 1705

DRAUGHT (a) of eternitie. Written in French by John Peter Camus, bishope of Belley ; translated into English by Miles Car [or Carre, *alias* Pinkney]. Fcap 8vo. Pp. 479. [Gillow's *Bibl. Dict.*] Doway, 1632

DRAUGHT (a) of Lethe ; the romance of an artist. By Roy Tellet [Rev. Albert Eubule Evans, B.A.]. 3 vols. 8vo. London, 1891

DRAWING-ROOM amusements, and evening party entertainments. By Professor Hoffmann [John Angelo Lewis, M.A.]. 8vo. [*Lit. Year Book.*]
London, 1879

DRAWING-ROOM conjuring. By Professor Hoffmann [John Angelo Lewis]. Pt 8vo. [Cushing's *Init. and Pseud.*, ii., p. 76.] London, 1887

DRAWING-ROOM (a) cynic ; being a faithful account of thirty days of his career. By Lorin Kaye [Lorin Andrews Lathrop and Miss F— Konotum]. Cr 8vo. Pp. 338. London, 1897

DRAWING-ROOM plays and parlour pantomimes : collected by Almaviva [Clement Scott]. 8vo. [Cushing's *Init. and Pseud.*, vol. ii., p. 5.]
London, 1870

DRAWING-ROOM (the) table book. By the author of *Mary Powell* [Anne Manning, later Mrs Rathbone]. 4to. No pagination. [London, 1852]

DRAWINGS from living models taken at Bath. [By Rev. Thomas Martyn.] 4to. [*European Mag.*, iii., 368.]
N.P., N.D.

DRAWN (a) game ; a novel. By " Basil " [Richard Ashe King]. 3 vols. Pt 8vo. [*Brit. Mus.*]
London, 1884

DRAYTONS (the) and the Davenants ; a story of the Civil Wars. By the author of *Chronicles of the Schönberg-Cotta family*, etc. [Mrs Elizabeth Charles, *née* Rundle]. 8vo. Pp. 494. [*Brit. Mus.*] London, 1867

DREADFUL (the) character of a drunkard. [By John Hart, D.D.] Fcap 8vo. [*Brit. Mus.*] London, 1681

DREAM (a). [By Henry Richard Vassal Fox, Lord Holland.] 8vo. Pp. 47. [*Martin's Cat.*] London, 1818

DREAM (a) ; a ballad supposed to have been written about the year eighteen hundred and fifty-two. By " Etonensis " [J— H— Arkwright]. 12mo. Pp. 15. [*Harcourt's Eton Bibl.*] Windsor, 1852

DREAM (the) and the business. By John Oliver Hobbes [Pearl Teresa Richards, later Mrs Walpole Craigie]. 8vo. [*Brit. Mus.*] London, 1906

DREAM (a) book. By E. V. B. [Hon. Mrs Eleanor Vere Boyle]. 4to. [*Haynes' Pseud.*] London, 1870

DREAM (the) chintz. By the author of *A Trap to catch a sunbeam* [Matilda Anne Planché, later Mrs Mackarness]. Cr 8vo. Pp. 118. [*Brit. Mus.*]
London, 1851

DREAM (a) detective ; being some account of the methods of Moris Klaw. By Sax Rohmer [Arthur Sarsfield Ward]. 12mo. Pp. 256. [*Lond. Lib. Cat.*] London, 1921

DREAM drops ; or stories from Fairyland. By a dreamer [Amy Lowell]. 8vo. [*Amer. Cat.*] Boston, 1888

DREAM life ; a fable of the seasons. By Ik Marvel [Donald G. Mitchell, LL.D.]. 8vo. [*Haynes' Pseud.*]
London, 1890

DREAM life and real life : a little African story. By Ralph Iron [Olive Schreiner]. Fcap 8vo. Pp. 91. [*Brit. Mus.*] Boston, 1893

DREAM (the) of Alla-ad-Deen ; from the romance of Anastasia. By Charles Erskine White, D.D. [Laughton Osborn]. 8vo. [Cushing's *Init. and Pseud.*, i., p. 306.] New York, 1831

DREAM (the) of an Englishman, faithful to his king and his country. [By Trophime Gerard, Marquis de Lally-Tollendal.] 8vo. [Nichols' *Lit. Anec.*, ix., 136.] London, 1793

DREAM (the) of Gerontius. [A poem. By John Henry Newman, D.D.] Fcap 8vo. Pp. 55. [*D. N. B.*, vol. 40, p. 350.] London, 1865
Signed "J. H. N."

DREAM (the) of human life. By the author of *The Lollards*, etc. [Thomas Gaspey]. 2 vols. 8vo. [*Bodl.*]
London, [1852]

DREAM (a) of Rubens. By Austin Clare [Miss W— M. James]. 8vo. Pp. 158. [*Lond. Lib. Cat.*]
London, [1882]

DREAM (a) of the Atonement. [By Rev. Charles Lutwidge Dodgson.] Fcap 8vo. London, 1882

DREAM (the) of the King's cup-bearer; a poem. By Annagh [Miss —— Pringle]. 8vo. [O'Donoghue's *Poets of Ireland*.] Dublin, 1907

DREAM (a) of the King's gardens; an allegory. By a Protestant Churchman [Rev. William J. E. Bennett, M.A.]. Fcap 8vo. [*Brit. Mus.*]
London, 1873

DREAM (a) of the New Museum [at Oxford. By Charles Giles Bridle Daubeny]. 8vo. Pp. 15. [*Bodl.*]
Oxford, 1855
Signed "C. G. B. D."

DREAM (a) of the sea; and other poems. By Alexander Lind [John Henry Harrison]. 8vo. Pp. vi., 133. [*Brit. Mus.*] London, 1894

DREAM (the) of youth; a poem. [By Rev. Barton Bouchier.] Fcap 8vo. [*Brit. Mus.*] London, 1818

DREAM (the) woman; a novel. By Kythe Wylwynne [Miss M— E. F. Hyland]. 8vo. London, 1901

DREAM-ALPHABET (a), and other poems. By the author of *In the gloaming* [Meta Orred]. 8vo. Pp. 113. [*Brit. Mus.*] London, 1888

DREAMER (the). [By Dr William King.] 8vo. [Watt's *Bibl. Brit.*]
London, 1754

DREAMER (a). By Katharine Wylde [Helen Hester Colvill]. 3 vols. Cr 8vo. [*Lond. Lib. Cat.*]
Edinburgh, 1880

DREAMER (the); dealing with the Rosicrucians, or Knights of the Rosy Cross; Temple of Hercules, etc. [By Dr William King.] 8vo. [Gardner's *Rosicrucian Books*, p. 41.]
London, 1754

DREAMER (a) of dreams; a modern romance. By the author of *Thoth* [Professor Joseph Shield Nicholson]. Pt 8vo. [*Lond. Lib. Cat.*]
Edinburgh, 1889

DREAMERS (the); a novel. By Lucas Cleeve [Mrs Howard Kingscote, *née* Adelina G. I. Wolff]. 8vo. [*Brit. Mus.*] London, 1905

DREAMER'S (a) harvest; a novel. By Mount Houmas [Mrs —— Gill]. 8vo. London, 1905

DREAMLAND; with other poems. By Mark Rochester [William Charles M. Kent]. Pt 8vo. [Cushing's *Init. and Pseud.*, i., 252.] London, 1862

DREAMS. By Ralph Iron [Olive Schreiner]. 8vo. [*Brit. Mus.*]
London, 1900

DREAMS and deeds. By the author of *Loved into shape* [Louisa Emily Dobrée]. 8vo. [*Brit. Mus.*] London, 1877

DREAMS and gables. By E. Herrick [Elsie Herrick Warner]. Cr 8vo.
London, 1911

DREAMS and reveries of a quiet man; consisting of The little genius, and other essays. By one of the editors of the *New York Mirror* [Theodore Sedgwick Fay]. Fcap 8vo. [*W.*]
New York, 1832

DREAMS of my solitude, on the life and mechanism of the heavens and their hosts. By Joshua Prusol [Joseph Sproul]. 8vo. [*Brit. Mus.*]
Edinburgh, 1878

DREAMS of my youth; and other poems. By Berkeley Aikin [Fanny Aikin Kortwright]. Pt 8vo. [Cushing's *Init. and Pseud.*, i., 8.] London, 1848

DREAMS, waking thoughts, and incidents; in a series of letters from various parts of Europe. [By William Beckford, of Fonthill.] 4to. Pp. 334: summary of contents, 7 leaves.
London, 1783
"This work was suppressed at the request of Lord Grantham, as it contained some severe reflections on the Dutch, a nation which it was then the policy of the English Government to conciliate. Mr Beckford reprinted the substance in 1834, 2 vols, 8vo."—[Martin's *Cat.*]

DRESS. By L. T. [Louisa Twining]. 8vo. [Cushing's *Init. and Pseud.*, vol. i., p. 279.] London, 1875

DRESS, and care of the feet. [By J. L. Peck.] 8vo. London, 1872

DREYFUS, the prisoner of Devil's Island. [By William Harding.] Fcap 8vo.   New York, 1899

Because of his Jewish parentage, A. Dreyfus, a Captain in the French Army, was falsely accused of communicating military secrets to the German authorities, and condemned by Court-Martial to degradation and penal servitude for life in Devil's Island, French Guiana. His friends, who were wealthy and influential, knowing that he was innocent, demanded a new trial in a higher court. The document on which the charge was founded was proved to be a forgery, so that he was released after suffering intense bodily and mental anguish. His friends, in spite of obstacles persistently raised, further secured trial in the Civil Court, where his innocence was fully established. A large collection of pamphlets in the British Museum, on both sides, attests the deep interest taken in this case, even beyond the borders of France. *See later*, " A History of the Dreyfus case. . . ."

DRIFT from Longshore. By a son of the Marshes [Denham Jordan, and Jean A. Owen, later Mrs Visger]. 8vo. [*Lit. Year Book.*] London, 1898

DRIFTED and sifted; a domestic chronicle of the seventeenth century. By the author of *Until the shadows flee away* [Jessie Maclaren]. 8vo. Pp. vii., 391. [*Adv. Lib.*]
Edinburgh, 1871

DRIFTED away; a tale of adventure. [By Mrs Mary Charlotte Herbert.] 8vo. Pp. 247.   London, [1877]

DRIFTING: a novel. By " Vigilans " [M— N. Patrick]. 8vo.
London, 1892

DRIFTING about; or, what Jeemes Pipes of Pipeville saw-and-did: an autobiography. [By Stephen C. Massett.] 8vo. [*Cushing's Init. and Pseud.*, i., p. 235.] New York, 1863

DRIFTING and steering. By Lynde Palmer [Mary Louise Parmlee, later Mrs A. Peebles]. 8vo. [Haynes' *Pseud.*]   Boston, 1867

DRIFTWOOD. By Russ Ruscom [Russell Whitcomb]. Cr 8vo. [*Amer. Cat.*]
Boston, 1907

DRIFT-WOOD from Scandinavia. By " Speranza " [Lady Jane F. S. Wilde]. Cr 8vo. [Haynes' *Pseud.*]
London, 1884

DRINKING cups and their customs; a book for gastronomers and connoisseurs . . . [By George E. Roberts and Dr. H. Porter.] Pt 8vo. [*Brit. Mus.*]   London, 1869

The title of the first edition (1863) is briefer: " Cups and their customs."

DRINKING (the) customs of Scotland contrasted with those of England: their cost, cause, and cure; with a consideration of the Maine Law. . . . By an Excise official [John Somerville]. 8vo. Pp. 39.   Glasgow, 1855

DRIVE (a) to Habbie's Howe, July 1897, composed in Dog-Latin . . . and translated into Doric by a member of the party [Alexander Anderson, librarian in Edinburgh University]. Cr 8vo. Pp. 8.
Private print, [Edinburgh], 1897

DRIVEN from home, and other life-stories. By a Delver [Alfred Alsop]. 8vo. Pp. 124. [*Cushing's Init. and Pseud.*, i., 79.]   Manchester, 1882

DRIVEN from the path. By Polywarp Oldfellow, M.D. [Charles Smart, M.D.]. Fcap 8vo. [*Cushing's Init. and Pseud.*, i., p. 212.]   New York, 1873

DRIVEN into exile; a story of the Huguenots. By A. L. O. E. [Charlotte Maria Tucker]. Pt 8vo. Pp. 212. [*Lit. Year Book.*] London, 1888

DRIVEN to Rome. By an ex-Anglican clergyman [Henry Willis Probyn Nevins]. 8vo. [F. Boase's *Mod. Eng. Biog.*, Supp., vol. 6.] London, 1877

DRIVING (the) force. [A novel.] By George Acorn [S— Cottage]. Cr 8vo. Pp. 320.   London, 1915

DROIT le roy; or, a digest of the rights and prerogatives of the imperial crown of Great Britain. By a member of the Society of Lincoln's Inn [Timothy Brecknock]. 8vo. Pp. xii., 95. [*N. and Q.*, 11 Mar. 1854, p. 227.]
London, 1764

DROMINA; a novel. By John Ayscough [Monsignor Francis Bickerstaffe-Drew]. Cr 8vo. Pp. 438. [*Lit. Year Book.*]   London, 1909

DRONES' honey. By Sophie May [Rebecca Sophia Clarke]. Fcap 8vo. [*Cushing's Init. and Pseud.*, vol. i., p. 185.]   Boston, 1887

DRUDGE (the); or the jealous extravagant: a piece of gallantry. [By R— Le Pays.] 8vo. [Arber's *Term Cat.*, i., p. 522.]   London, 1672

DRUID (the): a series of miscellaneous essays. [By James Kennedy, M.D.] 8vo. [*Glasg. Univ. Cat.*]
Glasgow, 1812

DRUID (the) and the Holy King; a lyrical poem. By a visitor of Royal Leamington Spa [Sarah Hamilton]. 8vo. [*Brit. Mus.*] Leamington, 1838

DRUID'S (the) monument: a tribute to the memory of Dr Oliver Goldsmith. By the author of *The Cave of Morar* [John Tait]. 4to. [*Brit. Mus.*]
London, 1774

DRUMMER (the) boy. By Paul Creyton [John Townsend Trowbridge]. Fcap 8vo. [Cushing's *Init. and Pseud.*, vol. i., p. 70.] New York, 1905

DRUMMER (the); or, the haunted house: a comedy, as it is acted at the Theatre-Royal in Drury-Lane, by his Majesty's servants. [By Joseph Addison.] 4to. [*Biog. Dram.*]
London, 1716
Later editions give the author's name.

DRUMMOND (the) schism examined and exposed. By a layman of the [Scottish Episcopal] Church [William Edmonstoune Aytoun, LL.D.]. 8vo. [*New Coll. Cat.*] Edinburgh, 1842

DRUM'S house; a novel. By Ida Wild [Mrs Meynell Pearson]. Cr 8vo. Pp. 350. London, 1913

DRUMSTICKS; a little story of a sinner and a child. By Johanna Staats [Mrs Katharine M. C. Meredith]. Pt 8vo. New York, 1896

DRUNKARD (the). By Guy Thorne [Cyril A. E. Ranger Gull]. Cr 8vo. Pp. 482. [*Brit. Mus.*] London, 1912

DRUNKARDS (the) character; or a true drunkard with such sinnes as raigne in him, viz.: pride, ignorance, enmity, atheisme, idlenesse, adultery, murther, with many the like, lively set forth in their colours . . . By R. Junius [Richard Younge]. Pt 8vo. [*Brit. Mus.*] London, 1638

DRUNKARD'S (the) progress; being a panorama of the overland route from the station at Drouth, to the general terminus in the Dead Sea: in a series of thirteen views, drawn and engraved by John Adam; the descriptions given by John Bunyan, Junior [Rev. William Arnot]. 4to. Pp. 32. [*Life of Rev. Wm. Arnot*, p. 276.]
Edinburgh, 1853

DRUNKEN Barnaby's four journeys to the north of England. [By Richard Brathwait; with an advertisement to this edition by Archibald Murray.] Fifth edition. Fcap 8vo. [*Brit. Mus.*]
London, 1805

DRY leaves from young Egypt; being a glance at Sindh, before the arrival of Sir Charles Napier. By an ex-political [Edward Backhouse Eastwick]. 8vo. [*Brit. Mus.*] London, 1849

DRY sticks, fagoted by W. S. L. [Walter Savage Landor]. 8vo. [*D. N. B.*, vol. 32, p. 55.] Edinburgh, 1858

DRYDEN'S dramatic theory and practice. By Elizabeth Hastings [Mrs Margaret E. W. Sherwood]. Fcap 8vo. [*Amer. Cat.*] Boston, 1898

DRY-FLY fishing. By " Detached Badger " [Fred. M. Halford]. Eighth edition. Pt 8vo. London, 1899

DRY-FLY fishing for trout and grayling. By " Red Quill " [James Englefield]. Fcap 8vo. London, 1907

DUBLIN; a satire. [By Sir Samuel Ferguson, LL.D.] 8vo. [O'Donoghue's *Poets of Ireland*.] Dublin, 1849

DUBLIN destroyed; or the witches' cauldron of railway horrors; a mysterious Shakespeareance in one act. [A satire, in verse.] By William Scribble [William Smyth, Irish actor, and artist]. 8vo. [O'Donoghue's *Poets of Ireland*.] Dublin, 1863

DUBLIN (a) Doctor's doggerels. By A. D. [Alexander Duke]. 12mo. [O'Donoghue's *Poets of Ireland*.]
Dublin, 1890

DUBLIN (the) Mail; or intercepted correspondence: to which is added, a packet of poems, satires in verse. [By William Russell M'Donald, Irish author.] Fcap 8vo. [O'Donoghue's *Poets of Ireland*.] London, 1821

DUCHENIER; or, the Revolt of La Vendée. [A tale. By John Mason Neale, D.D.] Fcap 8vo. [*D. N. B.*, vol. 40, p. 145.] London, 1848

DUCHESS (the): a story. By the author of *Molly Bawn* [Mrs Argles, later Mrs Hungerford, *née* Margaret W. Hamilton]. Cr 8vo. Pp. 332. [*Brit. Mus.*] London, 1888

DUCHESS (the) de la Vallière; a play in five acts. By the author of *Eugene Aram*, etc. [Edward George Earle Lytton Bulwer-Lytton, Baron Lytton]. 8vo. Pp. xviii., 180. [*Brit. Mus.*]
London, 1836
Preface signed " E. L. B."

DUCHESS Eleanour; a tragedy in five acts. By the author of *Old love & new fortune*, etc. [Henry F Chorley]. 8vo. [*Brit. Mus.*] London, [1854
Signed " H. F. C."

DUCHESS Frances. By Sarah Tytler [Henrietta Keddie]. Cr 8vo. Pp. 380. [*Lit. Year Book*.] London, 1901

DUCHESS (the) of Devonshire's cow; a poem. [By William Combe.] 4to. Pp. 11. [*D. N. B.*, vol. 11, p. 433.]
London, 1777
Combe himself next published " An heroic epistle to the noble author of ' The Duchess of Devonshire's cow.' "

DUCHESS (the) of Malfey ; a tragedy, as it is now acted at the Duke's Theatre. [By John Webster.] 4to. [*Arber's Term Cat.*, i., p. 522.] London, 1677

DUCHESS (the) of Powysland. By Cecil Power [Charles Grant Blair-findie Allen]. Pt 8vo. [*D. N. B.*, First Supp., vol. i., p. 36.] London, 1892

DUCHESS (the) of Tragetto. By the author of *Mary Powell* [Anne Manning, later Mrs Rathbone]. 8vo. Pp. iv., 300. London, 1863

DUCHESS (the) ; or, woman's love and woman's hate : a romance. [By Archibald Boyd.] 3 vols. Fcap 8vo. [*Brit. Mus.*] London, 1850

DUCHINKA. By Lucas Cleeve [Mrs Howard Kingscote, *née* Adelina G. I. Wolff]. Cr 8vo. Pp. 318. [*Lit. Year Book.*] London, 1908

DUCK Creek ballads. By Commodore Rollingpin [John H. Carter]. Fcap 8vo. [Cushing's *Init. and Pseud.*, vol. i., p. 253.] New York, 1894

DUCKS and green peas ; or, the Newcastle rider : a farce of one act, founded on fact. [By Joshua Booth.] 12mo. [Maidment's copy. Authorship ascertained from the Cat. of the books of George Smith, Esq., sold in July 1867.] Edinburgh, 1788

In Baker's Biog. Dram., a farce of one act with the title, " Ducks and peas ; or, the Newcastle rider," 1777, 8vo, is ascribed to John Lund, barber in Pontefract.

DUCTOR Historicus, or a short system of universal history, and an introduction to the study of that science ; containing a chronology of the most celebrated persons and actions from the Creation till this time. . . . Partly translated from the French of M. [Pierre Le Lorraine] de Vallamont, but chiefly composed anew by W. J. [Thomas Hearne], M.A. 8vo. [Arber's *Term Cat.*, iii., p. 77.] London, 1698

DUDLEY : a novel. By Curtis Yorke [Mrs W. S. Richmond-Lee]. 8vo. Pp. 346. [*Lond. Lib. Cat.*] London, 1888

DUE correction for Mr Hobbes ; or schoole discipline for not saying his lessons right. [By John Wallis, D.D.] Fcap 8vo. [*Brit. Mus.*] Oxford, 1656

DUEL (the) ; a play, as performed at the Theatre-Royal in Drury-Lane. [By William O'Brien.] Second edition. 8vo. Pp. 100. [*Biog. Dram.*] London, 1773

DUEL (the) ; an original poem. [By Mrs Frances Dallor.] 8vo. [*Brit. Mus.*] London, 1832

DUELLING ; a poem. [By Samuel Hayes, M.A.] 4to. [Watt's *Bibl. Brit.*] London, 1775

DUELLIST (the) ; a poem, in three books. [By Charles Churchill.] 4to. [*Brit. Mus.*] London, 1764

DVELLO (the), or single combat ; from antiquities deriued into this kingdome of Englande, with seuerall kindes, and ceremonious formes thereof from good authority described. [By John Selden.] 4to. Pp. 62. [*Cat. Lond. Inst.*, ii., 404.] London, 1610
Dedication signed " J. S."

DUENNA (the) ; a comic opera, in three acts, as it is performed by His Majesty's servants. [By Israel Pottinger.] 8vo. Pp. ii., 43. [*Biog. Dram.*] London, 1776

DUENNA King. By the author of *The Duenna* [Israel Pottinger]. 4to. [*Brit. Mus.*] [London, 1775]

DUENNA (the) of a genius. By M. E. Francis [Mrs Mary Evans Blundell, *née* Sweetman]. 8vo. Pp. 368. [*Lond. Lib. Cat.*] New York, 1898

DUENNA (the) ; or the double elopement : a comic opera. [By Richard Brinsley Sheridan.] 12mo. [*W.*] [Dublin], 1786

DUFFERSVILLE ; its cycling chronicle, and other sketches. By " Faed " [A— J— Wilson] and " Nym " [——]. Pt 8vo. Pp. 98. London, 1889

DUGDALE (the) millions ; a novel. By Barclay North [William C. Hudson]. Cr 8vo. Pp. 319. [*Amer. Cat.*] New York, 1893

DUKE (the) and the doctors. By H. H. A. S. [Rev. Hely H. A. Smith]. Fcap 8vo. [*Bodl.*] London, N.D.

DUKE (the) decides ; a novel. By Headon Hill [Francis Edward Grainger]. Cr 8vo. [*Brit. Mus.*] London, 1903

DUKE (a) for a day ; or the tailor of Brussels [a drama]. By Ross Neil [Isabella Harwood]. 8vo. [*Brit. Mus.*] London, 1874

D[UKE] (the) of A[rgyl]e's letter to the Right Honourable Sir —— —— upon the present intended expeditions. 8vo. [*Bodl.*] London, 1740

DUKE (the) of Berwick : a nonsense rhyme. By the Belgian Hare, author of *Tails with a twist* [Lord Alfred Douglas]. Oblong 4to. London, 1899

DUKE (the) of Devonshire's bull to the Duchess of Devonshire's cow; a poetical epistle : to which is prefixed, a preface, containing observations on some late publications addressed to Her Grace. [By William Combe.] 4to. Pp. vii., 10. [*D. N. B.*, vol. 11, p. 433.] London, 1777
See above, "The Duchess of Devonshire's cow."

DUKE (the) of Mantua ; a tragedy. By —— [John Roby, banker]. 8vo. [*Brit. Mus.*] London, 1823

DUKE (the) of Monmouth. By the author of *The Munster festivals*, etc. [Gerald Griffin.] 3 vols. Fcap 8vo. [*Camb. Univ. Lib.*] London, 1836

DUKE (the) of Rothsay ; a tragedy. [By Samuel Macarthur.] 8vo. [*Biog. Dram.*] Edinburgh, 1780

DUKE (the) of Wellington's visit to Sunderland. [Edited by Sir Cuthbert Sharp.] 8vo. [Martin's *Cat.*] Sunderland, 1827

DUKE Ulrich. [A novel.] By the author of *Mademoiselle Mori* [Margaret Roberts]. Pt 8vo. London, 1882

DUKE'S (the) chase; or the diamond ring *vs.* the gold ring. By Forest Warbler [M— R— M'Cormick]. 8vo. [Cushing's *Init. and Pseud.*, vol. i., p. 103.] Cincinnati, 1871

DUKE'S (the) daughter ; a classic tragedy [in verse]. [By Richard William Morgan.] 8vo. [*Brit. Mus.*] London, 1867
Signed "R. W. M."

DUKE'S (the) marriage. [By James Brinsley Richards.] Cr 8vo. 3 vols. [*D. N. B.*, vol. 48, p. 214.] London, 1886

DUKE'S (the) secret. By Bertha M. Clay [Mrs Charlotte M. Braeme, *née* Law]. Fcap 8vo. New York, 1887

DUKESBOROUGH tales : chronicles of Mr Bill Williams. By Philemon Perch [Richard Malcolm Johnston]. Pt 8vo. [Cushing's *Init. and Pseud.*, vol. i., p. 228.] New York, 1892

DUKINFIELD Lodge ; a poem. [By William Hampson.] Small 4to. [Watt's *Bibl. Brit.*] London, 1793

DULCE domum. By a vagrant viator [Thomas Newton]. 8vo. [*Brit. Mus.*] London, 1884

DULCE "domum"! [By Thomas Longueville.] Fcap 8vo. [*Brit. Mus.*] London, 1886

DULL sermons ; a sermon [on 2 Cor. x. 10] preached in the Church of St Mary the Virgin, in Oxford, in Lent, 1858, by the Vicar [Drummond Percy Chase]. 8vo. [*Brit. Mus.*] Oxford, 1858

DULL (the) stone house. By Kenner Deene [Mrs Charlotte Smith, *née* Turner]. 2 vols. Fcap 8vo. [Cushing's *Init. and Pseud.*, vol. i., p. 79.] London, 1862

DULWICH College ; or the orphan and the poor defended from the errors of the Charity-Trusts Board. [By Saxe Bannister, Attorney-General of N.S. Wales.] 8vo. [*Brit. Mus.*] London, 1856

DUMARESQ'S temptation. By Bertha M. Clay [Mrs Charlotte M. Braeme]. Pt 8vo. Pp. 324. New York, [1882]

DUMAS' Paris. By Francis Miltoun [Milburg F— Mansfield]. Cr 8vo. [*Lond. Lib. Cat.*] London, 1904

DUMB friends. By Maggie Browne [Margaret Hamer, later Mrs Andrewes]. 4to. Pp. 80. [*Brit. Mus.*] London, [1889]

DUMB (the) philosopher, or Great Britains wonder, containing :—I. A faithful and very surprising account how Dickory Cronke, a tinner's son in the county of Cornwall, was born dumb, and continued so for 58 years ; and how some days before he died, he came to his speech. With memoirs of his life, and the manner of his death. II. A declaration of his faith and principles in religion, with a collection of select meditations, composed in his retirement. III. His prophetical observations on the affairs of Europe, more particularly of Great Britain, from 1720 to 1729. The whole extracted from his original papers and confirmed by unquestionable authority. . . . [By Daniel Defoe.] 8vo. [Wilson's *Life of Defoe*, p. 169.] London, 1719

DUMB (the) projector ; being a surprising account of a trip to Holland, made by Mr Duncan Campbell, with the manner of his reception and behaviour there : as also the various and diverting occurrences that happened on his departure. [By Daniel Defoe.] 8vo. [Wilson's *Life of Defoe*, p. 189.] London, 1725

DUMB (a) speech : or, a sermon made, but no sermon preached, at the funerall of the right vertuous Mrs Mary Oberman. By B. S. [Benjamin Spencer]. Fcap 8vo. London, 1646

DUMERESQ'S daughter. By Cecil Power [Charles Grant Blairfindie Allen]. Pt 8vo. [*D. N. B.*, First Supp., vol. i., p. 31.] London, 1891

"DUMPS," and other stories. By Ascott R. Hope [Ascott Robert Hope Moncrieff]. 8vo. Pp. 128. [*Lit. Year Book.*] Edinburgh, 1886

DUMPY. By Archie Fell [Mary J. Capron]. Fcap 8vo. [Cushing's *Init. and Pseud.*, i., p. 100.] Boston, 1885

DUNALLAN; or know what you judge; a story, in three volumes. By the author of *The decision*, etc. [Grace Kennedy]. Second edition. Fcap 8vo. [*Adv. Lib.*] Edinburgh, 1825

DUNALTON; a story of Jack and his guardians. By Kate Thorne [Louisa M. Gray]. 8vo. [Cushing's *Init. and Pseud.*, vol. i., p. 441.] London, 1886

DUNBAR'S Two married women and the widow; translated into English verse [by Robert Irving]. 8vo. [Martin's *Cat.*] Edinburgh, 1840

DUNBOY, and other poems. By Timothy O'Sullivan [Timothy Daniel Sullivan, M.P.]. 8vo. [O'Donoghue's *Poets of Ireland*, p. 239.] Dublin, 1868

DUNCE'S (the) dessert; or Horatian trifles and Homeric cream. [By W. Purton.] 4to. Pp. 63. [*F. Madan.*] Oxford, [1861]

DUNCIAD (the), in four books: printed according to the complete copy found in the year 1742; with the prolegomena of Scriblerus, and notes variorum. To which are added, several notes now first publish'd, the Hypercritics of Aristarchus, and his dissertation on the hero of the poem. [By Alexander Pope.] 4to. Pp. x., 247. London, 1743

DUNCIAD (the) variorum; with the prolegomena of Scriblerus. [By Alexander Pope.] 4to. Pp. 169. [*Brit. Mus.*] London, 1727

DUNIMARLE. [A historic guide.] By J. T. [John Todd, newspaper editor]. Pp. 20. [Beveridge's *Dunf. Bibl.*] Dunfermline, 1872

DUNKELD; its straths and glens: or central Perthshire, historical and descriptive, compiled, arranged, and original. [By Charles M'Lean, bookseller, Dunkeld.] 8vo. Pp. 147. [*Adv. Lib.*] Dunkeld, 1879

DUNKIRK or Dover; or, the Queen's honour, the nation's safety, the liberties of Europe and the peace of the world, all at stake till that fort and port be totally demolish'd by the French. [By John Toland (?).] 8vo. London, 1713

DUNMARA. [A novel.] By Ruth Murray [Rosa Mulholland, Lady Gilbert]. Cr 8vo. London, 1864

DUNNOTTAR Castle; a poem. By the Rev. James Walker. [Really written by Mrs Carnegie of Pittarrow.] 12mo. Pp. 7. [*And. Jervise.*] Aberdeen, N.D.
The first poem was printed in the Aberdeen Magazine for 1796, p. 143.
A second poem on the same subject, anonymous, but written by Andrew Edward, letter carrier, Stonehaven, is printed along with Mrs. Carnegie's, with continuous pagination.

DUNSTER Castle; a tale of the Great Rebellion. [By Joseph Thomas Hewlett, M.A.] 8vo. London, 1845

DUNTHORPES (the) of Westleigh. [A novel.] By Christian Lys [Percy James Brebner]. 8vo. Pp. x., 334. [*Lond. Lib. Cat.*] London, 1896

DUPE (the); a comedy, as it is now acting at the Theatre-Royal in Drury-Lane, by his Majesty's servants. By the author of *The Discovery* [Mrs Frances Sheridan, *née* Chamberlaine]. 8vo. [*Biog. Dram.*] London, 1764

DUPLICATE (the) Duke. [A novel.] By Headon Hill [Francis Edward Grainger]. Cr 8vo. Pp. 316. [*Lit. Year Book.*] London, 1921

DURATION (the) of evil: an essay. [By John Sheppard, of Frome.] Cr 8vo. London, 1855

DURGEN; or, a plain satyr upon a pompous satyrist, amicably inscrib'd by the author to those worthy and ingenious gentlemen misrepresented in a late invective poem, call'd, The Dunciad. [By Edward Ward.] 8vo. Pp. 66. [*N. and Q.*, 1857, pp. 341.] London, 1729

DURHAM Cathedral as it was before the dissolution of the monastery. . . . [By Christopher Hunter, M.D.] Fcap 8vo. [*Brit. Mus.*] Durham, 1733

DUROVERNUM; with other poems. By Arthur Brooke [John Chalk Claris]. Fcap 8vo. Pp. 168. [*Gent. Mag.*, 1866, p. 439.] London, 1818

DUST of the world; a historical novel of Belfast in the seventeenth century. By Athène [Miss S— M— Harris]. Cr 8vo. Pp. 302. [S. J. Brown's *Ireland in fiction.*] London, 1913

DUTCH (the) better friends than the French, to the monarchy, Church, and trade of England; in a letter from a citizen to a country gentleman. [By Rev. John Withers.] Second edition. 8vo. [*Brit. Mus.*] London, 1713

DUTCH (the) gardiner, or the compleat florist; containing the most successful method of cultivating all sorts of flowers; the planting, dressing and pruning all manner of fruit-trees. . . . Translated from the Dutch [of Hendrik van Oosten]. 8vo. [*Arber's Term Cat.*, iii., 442.] London, 1705

DUTCH (the) in the Medway. By the author of *The camp of refuge* [Charles Macfarlane]. Fcap 8vo. [*Brit. Mus.*] London, 1845

DUTCH stories. By Oude Heer Smits [Mark Philip Lindo]. 8vo. [*Brit. Mus.*] London, [1870 ?]

DUTCH (the) survay; wherein are related and truly discoursed the chiefest losses and acquirements which have past betweene the Dutch and the Spaniards in these last foure yeares warres of the Netherlands. By W. C. [William Crosse(?)]. 4to. London, 1625

DUTCH (the) way of toleration, most proper for our English Dissenters: written at the request of a friend. [By William Baron, chaplain to the Earl of Clarendon.] 4to. [*Bodl.*] London, 1608
The letter is signed "——m ——n," the finials of the writer's name.

DUTCHMAN'S (the) fireside; a tale. By the author of *Letters from the South*, etc. [James Kirke Paulding]. 2 vols. Fcap 8vo. [Kirk's *Supp.*] London, 1831

DUTHIE (the) Park [in Aberdeen]: a descriptive and historical sketch. [By James Mitchell.] 8vo. [*Aberd. Free Lib.*] Aberdeen, 1883

DUTIES (the) and happiness of domestic service; or a Sister of Mercy giving instructions to the inmates of the house of mercy placed under her care. [Drawn up by Henry Formby.] Fcap 8vo. [*Brit. Mus.*] London, 1851
Signed "H. F."

DUTIES (the) and powers of public officers and private persons with respect to violations of the public peace. [By the Right Hon. Spencer Percival ?] 8vo. [*W.*]
[London ? 1792 ?]

DUTIES (the) of a Royal Engineer Officer in time of peace. . . . [By Major-General Charles Edmund Webber.] 8vo. [*Brit. Mus.*] London, 1869

DUTIES (the) of man. By Joseph Mazzini. [Translated from the Italian by Mrs E. A. Venturi.] 8vo. Pp. xvi., 220. [*Brit. Mus.*] London, 1862

DUTIES (the) of the Closet; being an earnest exhortation to private devotion. [By Sir William Dawes, Bart., Archbishop of York.] Second edition, revised. 8vo. [*D. N. B.*, vol. 14, p. 216.] London, 1700

DUTIFUL (the) son; being a . . . true account of the life of W. Sellwood. [By Rev. Thomas Bogles Murray, M.A.] Fcap 8vo. London, [1860]
Signed "T. B. M."

DUTIFULL and respective considerations upon foure severall heads of Tryall in matters of religion, proposed by the high and mighty Prince James . . . in his late book of Premonition to all Christian Princes. . . . By a late minister and preacher in England [Robert Parsons, S.J.]. 4to. Pp. 243. [Oliver's *Collections*, p. 162.] St Omer, 1609
The above work was really composed by Parsons, though for Humphrey Leach.

DUTIFULL (a) letter from a prelate [Thomas Ken] to a prelate [Archbishop Tenison]: to which is adjoyn'd another [from Henry Dodwell to Dr Tillotson], to prove Non-jurors no schismaticks. Fcap 8vo. [*Bodl.*] London, 1703
The second letter is signed "H. D."

DUTY (the) and advantage of early rising. [By John Wesley.] 8vo. [Osborn's *Wesl. Bibl.*] Cambridge, 1785

DUTY (the) and blessedness of intercessory prayer; with tables of weekly intercessions at private prayer. [By Robert Brett.] 8vo. [*Bodl.*] London, 1862
Signed "R. B."

DUTY and interest united in prayer and praise for kings, and all that are in authority; from 1 Tim. 1, 2. Being a sermon preach'd at Westminster, upon the late day of thanksgiving, Sept. 8, 1695. By V. A. [Vincent Alsop], minister of the Gospel. 4to. [Calamy's *Nonconf. Mem.*, Palmer's ed., iii., p. 50.] London, 1695

DUTY (the) and qualifications of a sea-officer. [By Rev. James Ramsay, naval chaplain.] 8vo. London, [1785 ?]

DUTY, not decay; a poem. By Edwin Lewis [Edwin Lewis Martin]. 8vo. London, 1902

DUTY (the) of a Christian in the disposal of his income. [By John Bate Cardale, solicitor.] 8vo. [Boase's *Cath. Apost. Lit.*] London, 1863

DUTY (the) of a suffering Church ; a sermon preached to a congregation of the Episcopal Church of Scotland, on the ninth of February 1779 ; being a day of general humiliation in that Kingdom. [By John Skinner, Bishop of Aberdeen.] 8vo. Pp. 37. [Robertson's *Aberd. Bibliog.*] Aberdeen, 1779

DUTY (the) of an apprentice. By a late Chamberlain of London [E— Withers]. 8vo.   London, 1755

DUTY (the) of abstaining from the use of West India produce : a speech by W. A. [William Allen]. Fcap 8vo. [*Brit. Mus.*]   London, 1792

DUTY (the) of acknowledging Jesus Christ in all we do ; a sermon preached at the Wednesday lecture in St James's Church, Bury Saint Edmund's. By a country rector [Rev. Spencer Cobbold]. Fcap 8vo. [*W.*]   Ipswich, 1835

DVTY (the) of all trve subiects to their king, as also to their native countrey, in time of extremity and danger : with some memorable examples of the miserable ends of perfidious traytors. In two bookes. Collected and written by H. P. [Henry Peacham]. 4to. Pp. 63. [*Brit. Mus.*]   London, 1639

DUTY (the) of allegiance settled upon its true grounds, according to Scripture, reason, and the opinion of the Church : in answer to a late book of Dr William Sherlock, Master of the Temple, entituled, The case of the allegiance due to sovereign powers, stated and resolved, according to Scripture, &c. With a more particular respect to the oath lately injoyn'd. [By Rev. John Kettlewell.] 4to. Pp. 84. [Lathbury's *Hist. of Nonjurors*, p. 117.]   London, 1691

DUTY (the) of associating against the profanation of the Sabbath day. [By Rev. Thomas Dale.] 8vo.   Bath, [1841]

DUTY (the) of Christians, with respect to human interpretations and decisions, when propos'd to be believed and submitted to by them, as necessary parts of the Christian religion. By a clergyman in the country [Samuel Bolde]. 4to. [*Brit. Mus.*]   London, 1717

DUTY (the) of Columbia College to the Community. . . . By one of the Trustees [Samuel Bulkley Ruggles]. 8vo. [Cushing's *Init. and Pseud.*, ii., p. 112.]   New York, 1854

DUTY (the) of excommunicating the " Moderate " ministers of the Church of Scotland. [By Patrick Dove.] 8vo. Pp. 22. [*New Coll. Cat.*]   Edinburgh, 1843

DUTY (the) of holding fast the form of sound words, referred to the Assembly's Catechisms and Confession of Faith : to which is added, a list of the divines in that Assembly ; the vow taken by every member at his entrance, with a word of their character. [By Rev. Daniel Wilcox.] [Wilson's *Hist. of Diss. Ch.*, iii., 207.]   London, 1717

DUTY (the) of increasing the stipends of the Manchester clergy, stated and proved by a practical example. [By John Young Caw, banker.] 8vo. [*Manch. Free Lib. Cat.*]   Manchester, 1852

DUTY (the) of loving Christ early. . . . [By D— Grant.] 8vo. [Robertson's *Aberd. Bibl.*, p. 57.] Aberdeen, 1818

DUTY (the) of overseers of the poor, to be delivered to them at their appointment. . . . By a country magistrate [William Nelson]. 8vo. Pp. viii., 27. [Watt's *Bibl. Brit.*]   London, 1792

DUTY (the) of praying for civil magistrates, with some of those instances of loyalty that necessarily flow from it ; recommended in a discourse upon 1 Timothy ii. 1, 2. By a minister of the Church of Scotland [Alexander Campbell]. 8vo. Pp. 64. [Scott's *Fasti.*]   Edinburgh, 1726

DUTY (the) of praying for others, enforced by some arguments taken from the success of those prayers which the Church made for St Peter's deliverance from prison. [By William Romaine.] 8vo. [*Brit. Mus.*]   London, 1757

DUTY (the) of servants. [By Henry Gandy, Nonjuror Bishop.] S. Sh. [*Bodl.*]   London, 1704

DUTY (the) of servants ; containing, 1. How parents ought to breed up their children. . . . 2. How servants may wisely chuse a service. 3. How they are to behave themselves in it, discharging their duty towards God, their master, and themselves. . . . By [Richard Lucas, D.D.] the author of *Practical Christianity*. 8vo.   London, 1685

An earlier edition (1683) has a somewhat different title.

DUTY (the) of the Church in respect of Christian missions. [By Oswald Joseph Reichel.] [The Ellerton prize essay.] 8vo. Pp. 32. [*Bodl.*]   London, 1866

DUTY (the) of worthily communicating recommended and explained . . . in a letter from a minister [Rev. John Bold, B.A.] to his parishioners. 8vo. [Watt's *Bibl. Brit.*]   London, 1745

DUTY ; or, ability and present action contrasted : designed to overtake the May meetings. By a layman [William Macfarlane]. 8vo. [*Brit. Mus.*]
Edinburgh, 1856

DUTY to farm-servants : being an essay on the present condition of the agricultural population in their relation to the soil. By [James Fraser] an agricultural labourer. 8vo. Pp. 24.   Aberdeen, 1859

DUTY'S call : a story of a girl's work in the service of others, and her reward. . . . By H. N. B. [Rev. Harold Nelson Burden]. 8vo. Pp. 112. [*Brit. Mus.*]
London, 1896

DWARF (the) ; or mind and matter : a novel. By E. L. A. Berwick, Esq. [James Reynolds, surgeon]. 3 vols. Fcap 8vo. [*Bodl.*]   London, 1855

DWELL deep ; or, Hilda Thorne's life-story. By the author of *Probable Sons*, etc. [Amy Lefeuvre]. 8vo. Pp. 191. [*Brit. Mus.*]   London, [1896]

DWELLERS in Gotham : a romance of New York. By Annan Dale [Rev. James Wesley Johnstone, Wesleyan]. 8vo. [*Wesleyan Who's Who.*]
London, 1899

DYALOGES (the) in Englishe, &c.
See "Dialogues," etc.; also "Doctor and student. . . ."

DYET (the) of Poland ; a satyr [in verse]. By Anglipoloski [Daniel Defoe]. 4to. Pp. 66. [Wilson's *Life of Defoe*, 75.]   Dantzick, [London ?], 1705

DYING (the) Christian's gain : a sermon preached in the parish church of Wrotham, Kent, Nov. 17, 1723. . . . By T. C. [Rev. Thomas Curteis]. 8vo.
London, 1723

DYING (the) command of Christ ; or the duty of believers to celebrate weekly the sacrament of the Lord's Supper. By the author of *God is love*, etc. [James Grant]. 8vo. Pp. xii., 136. [*Brit. Mus.*]   London, 1863

DYING (the) faith. By Lara [George C. Griffith Jones]. . . . 8vo. Pp. 31.
London, [1884]

DYING infants sav'd by grace, proved, and the blessed man with his blessedness described : in a sermon preached near Namptwich in Cheshire. . . . July 25, 1695 [and published 1699]. By S. A. [Samuel Acton]. . . . 4to. Pp. 32. [Whitley's *Bapt. Bibl.*, i., 129.]   London, 1699

DYING (the) legacy of [the Rev. Samuel Mather] an aged minister of the everlasting Gospel to the United States of North America. 8vo. Pp. 29. [Evans' *Amer. Bibl.*, vol. 6, p. 227.]
Boston, [Mass.], 1783

DYING (the) man's last sermon. . . . By A. Jones [but rather by John Hart, D.D.]. Fcap 8vo. [*Brit. Mus.*]
London, 1662

DYING (the) negro ; a poetical epistle, supposed to be written by a black, (who lately shot himself on board a vessel in the river Thames) to his intended wife. . . . [By Thomas Day, assisted by John Bicknell, barrister.] 4to. Pp. 24. [Keir's *Life of Day*, p. 39.]   London, 1773

The poem was reprinted (after the death of the authors) with their names (London, 1793).

DYING scientifically : a key to "St Bernard's." By Aesculapius Scalpel [Edward Berdoe]. Pt 8vo. Pp. 120.
London, 1888

DYING to live. By the author of *Live and let live* [Thomas Martyn Pascoe]. 8vo. [Boase and Courtney's *Bibl. Corn.*]   Bodmin, [1869]

DYNAMICS (the) of a particle. [By Rev. Charles Lutwidge Dodgson, M.A.] 8vo. [*Brit. Mus.*]   London, 1874

DYNAMICS (the) of religion : an essay in English culture-history. By M. W. Wiseman [John M. Robertson, M.P.]. 8vo. [*Brit. Mus.*]   London, 1898

DYNEVOR Terrace : or, the clue of life. By the author of *The heir of Redclyffe* [Charlotte Mary Yonge]. 2 vols. 8vo.   London, 1857

DYSSHE (a) of sottleties ryght rychelie seasonid : or, a goodlie garland of Duresme evergreens plaited by the ingenious. [Edited by the Rev. James Raine and Richard Surtees.] Imprynted by Master Francis Humble and his Felowes for anenst ye Neptune in Foro Dunelmensi. 8vo. Pp. 50. [Martin's *Cat.*] Reprint. N.P., 1818

DYUERS frutful gatheringes of Scrypture concernyng fayth and workes. [Written in Latin by Patrick Hamilton ; translated into English by John Frith.] 8vo.
[London, by W. Copland], N.D.

Reprinted in Fox's Acts and monuments, p. 226, edit. 1641 ; also in Knox's History of the Reformation in Scotland, p. 6, etc.

E

EAGLE and dove; a tale of the Franco-Prussian War, founded on fact. By Naomi [M— E— Clements]. Fcap 8vo. [*Amer. Cat.*] New York, 1889

EAGLE (the) and the lion; and other tales [from the German of Friedrich H. C., Baron de la Motte Fouqué]. Fcap 8vo. [*Brit. Mus.*]
London, [1845]

EAGLE PASS. By Cora Montgomery [Mrs William Leslie]. Fcap 8vo. [Cushing's *Init. and Pseud.*, vol. ii., p. 102.] New York, 1852

EAGLE'S (the) nest; a novel. By Alan Macaulay [Charlotte Stewart]. 8vo. [*Lond. Lib. Cat.*] London, 1909

EAGLE'S (the) talon. By Georges Ohnet [Georges Hénot]. Adapted from the French by Helen Mayer. 8vo. Pp. vi., 372. [*Brit. Mus.*]
New York, 1913

EARINUS; a tale of antiquity. [Verse. By Thomas Bibby, B.A.] 8vo. [O'Donoghue's *Poets of Ireland*.]
[Dublin ?, 1856]

EARL Douglas; or, generosity betray'd: a tragedy. [By John Wilson.] 8vo. Pp. 116. [Leyden's *Scottish descriptive poems*.] Glasgow, 1764

EARL Grey's circular (a memento). "I have to instruct you hereafter officially to address the prelates of the Roman Catholic Church in your government by the title of 'Your Grace,' or 'Your Lordship,' as the case may be." Earl Grey, from Downing-Street, Nov. 20, 1847, as secretary of state to a Queen, who made her royal "Declaration against Popery," from her throne in the House of Lords, on Monday, Nov. 20, 1837. "I do declare, that no foreign prince, prelate, or potentate, hath, or ought to have, any jurisdiction, power, superiority, pre-eminence, or authority, ecclesiastical or spiritual, within this realm." Earl Grey's oath, as a Peer of Parliament and Minister of the Crown. [By Dudley M. Perceval.] 8vo. London, 1849

The third edition, with the title, "The Queen's ministers responsible," etc., published in 1851, has the author's name.

EARL (the) of Chester's Regiment of Yeomanry Cavalry; its formation and services, 1797-1897. [By Frederick Leary.] Large 8vo.
Edinburgh, private print, 1898

EARL (the) of Douglas; a dramatick essay. [By John Wilson.] Pp. 74.
London, 1760
Ascribed also, but with insufficient evidence, to Francis Douglas of Aberdeen. *See N. and Q.*, 9 Nov. 1861, pp. 222 and 383.

EARL (the) of Ross; a tragedy. [By Lieut. —— Munro.] 8vo. [*Bodl.*]
Yarmouth, 1823

EARL (the) of Warwick, a tragedy, adapted from the French; as it is perform'd at the Theatre Royal in Drury-lane. [By Thomas Francklin, D.D.] 8vo. Pp. 71. [*Biog. Dram.*]
London, 1766
See the following entry for another version.

EARL (the) of Warwick; or, the king and the subject: a tragedy [in five acts and in verse, adapted from the French of J. F. de La Harpe's " Comte de Warwick," by Paul Hiffernan, M.D.]. 8vo. [*Biog. Dram.*]
London, 1764

EARL Strongbow: or, the history of Richard de Clare and the beautiful Geralda. [By James White.] 2 vols. Fcap 8vo. London, 1789

EARLE (the) of Pembroke's speech in the House of Peeres, upon debate of the citie's petition for a personall treaty, to be had with His Majesty in London; and also upon debate of those reasons given by their Lordships unto the Commons, for not sending the three propositions before a treaty. [By Sir Charles Sedley.] 4to. [*Bodl.*]
N.P. Printed in the yeare 1648
Reprinted in the second edition of Somers' *Tracts*, vol. vii., p. 79.

EARLIER adventures of a Naval Officer. By Captain Charles Hunter, R.N. [really by Sir Spenser Buckingham St. John]. 8vo. [*D. N. B.*, Second Supp., vol. 3, p. 250.] London, 1906

EARL'S (the) atonement; a novel. By Bertha M. Clay [Mrs Charlotte M. Braeme, *née* Law]. Pt 8vo. Pp. 384. [Cushing's *Init. and Pseud.*, vol. ii., p. 32.] New York, 1897

EARL'S (the) cedars. By the author of . . . *The wreckers* [Mary Rosa Stewart Kettle]. 2 vols. 8vo. [*Adv. Lib.*] London, 1860

EARL'S (the) daughter. By the author of *Amy Herbert*, etc. [Elizabeth M. Sewell]. Third edition. 2 vols. Fcap 8vo. [*Brit. Mus.*] London, 1850

I

EARL'S (the) error ; a tale. By Bertha M. Clay [Mrs Charlotte M. Braeme, *née* Law]. Fcap 8vo.
New York, 1887

EARL'S (the) grand-daughter. By " Brenda " [Mrs —— Castle Smith]. Pt 8vo. Pp. 416. [*Brit. Mus.*]
Boston, 1896

EARL'S (the) revenge ; or Lady Jane Grey : a five-act historical play. By the author of *Tacitus and Bracciolini* [John Wilson Ross]. 8vo. Pp. 87. [*Brit. Mus.*]   London, 1882

EARLY (the) Church : its faith and constitution. A letter to the Dean of Carlisle. By a curate of the diocese [Rev. Thomas Fenton, M.A.]. 8vo. [*Brit. Mus.*]   London, 1866

EARLY days at Racine, Wisconsin. . . . By an outsider [Sidney S. Hurlbut]. 8vo. [Cushing's *Init. and Pseud.*, vol. ii., p. 114.]   Racine, 1872

EARLY days at Uppingham under Edward Thring. By an old boy [Willingham Franklin Rawnsley]. Cr 8vo. Pp. x., 163.   London, 1904
Presentation copy from the author.

EARLY (the) editions of King James' Bible, in folio. [Bibliographical notices. By James Lenox.] 4to. [*Brit. Mus.*]
Private print, [New York, 1861.]
Signed " L."

EARLY Egyptian history, for the young ; with descriptions of the tombs and monuments. By the author of *Sydney Grey* [Annie Keary] and her sister. Fcap 8vo. [*Brit. Mus.*]
London, 1861

EARLY engagements. By Sarah Marshall Hayden [Mary Frazer]. 8vo. [Cushing's *Init. and Pseud.*, vol. i., p. 126.]   Cincinnati, 1858

EARLY Friends and modern professors, in reply to " Strictures," by Joseph John Gurney. By the author of *The truth vindicated* [Henry Martin]. Fcap 8vo. [Smith's *Cat. of Friends' Books*, i., 221.]   London, 1836

EARLY (the) Friends ; their message and the secret of their power. [By Mrs Sarah Grace Harvey, or Mrs Hannah W. Smith.] 8vo. Pp. 16. [Supp. to Smith's *Cat. of Friends' Books*, pp. 20 and 311.]
Philadelphia, N.D., [1870 ?]

EARLY (the) history of Church patronage ; being a precise statement of the Acts of Assembly and of the Scottish Parliament before the Revolution of 1688, in relation to this subject ; also of the Acts of Parliament 1690, of the Act of Union, and of the Act, c. 12 ; with an interpretation of certain passages in the Second Book of Discipline. By a member of the faculty of advocates [Charles Ferguson, younger of Kilkerran]. Pp. vii., 70. [*Bodl.*]   Edinburgh, 1833

EARLY (the) history of the Southern [United] States. By Lambert Lilly, schoolmaster [Francis Lester Hawks]. 8vo. [Cushing's *Init. and Pseud.*, vol. i., p. 170.]   Philadelphia, 1832

EARLY (the) history of Western Pennsylvania, and of the West, and of western expeditions and campaigns from 1754 to 1833. By a gentleman of the bar [I— Daniel Rupp]. 8vo. [Cushing's *Init. and Pseud.*, vol. i., p. 114.]   Pittsburg, Pa., 1846

EARLY (the) house of Blackwood. By I. C. B. [—— Blackwood]. 4to. Pp. 13. [Edinburgh], private print, 1900

EARLY ideas ; a group of Hindoo stories, collected and collated by an Aryan [Foster Fitzgerald Arbuthnot]. 8vo. Pp. 158. [*Brit. Mus.*]
London, 1881

EARLY influences. By the author of *Truth without prejudice* [—— Wyndham, later Mrs Alfred Montgomery]. Fcap 8vo. [*Brit. Mus.*] London, 1842

EARLY (the) life of H. Grattan. [By George Noble Plunkett.] 8vo. [*Brit. Mus.*]   Dublin, 1878
Signed " G. N. P."

EARLY magnetism in its higher relations to humanity, as veiled in the poets and the prophets. By ΘΟΜΑΣ ΣΟΥΘ [Thomas South]. 8vo. [*Brit. Mus.*]
London, 1846

EARLY memories for the children. By the author of *Tom Brown's school days* [Thomas Hughes, Q.C.]. Fcap 8vo.   London, private print, 1899

EARLY musings. [Poems.] By " Myles " [Robert Smith, law-clerk in Londonderry]. 8vo. [O'Donoghue's *Poets of Ireland*.]
Londonderry, 1884

EARLY poems. By M. A. [Lady Dorothy Violet Wellesley]. 8vo. [*Bodl.*]   London, 1913

EARLY recollections ; a tale. By the author of *Annot and her pupil* [Selina Bunbury]. Fcap 8vo. [*Brit. Mus.*]   London, [1856]

EARLY recollections of James Whitcomb Riley. By Major Ridgeway [William Ross Hartpence]. Fcap 8vo. [*Amer. Cat.*]   Harrison, Ohio, 1902

EARLY recollections of Oxford . . . [1836-58]. By an old Freeman [Stephen Quelch]. Fcap 8vo. [W. D. Macray's *Cat.*]   Oxford, [1900]

EARLY records in equity. [By Sir Henry Wilmott Seton.] 8vo. Pp. 134. Calcutta, 1842

EARLY (the) saved. . . . Compiled by W. C. W. [Rev. William Chalmers Whitcomb]. 8vo. [Cushing's *Init. and Pseud.*, vol. i., p. 301.] Boston, 1861

EARLY sketches, in prose and verse. [By Mrs W— Marianne Furlong.] Fourth edition. Fcap 8vo. [O'Donoghue's *Poets of Ireland*, p. 81.] London, 1836

EARLY Victorian ; a village chronicle. By S. G. Tallentyre [E— Beatrice Hall]. Cr 8vo. Pp. 290. [*Lond. Lib. Cat.*] London, 1910

EARLY (the) works of Sir Edwin Landseer, R.A. A brief sketch of the life of the artist, illustrated by photographs of sixteen of his most popular works ; with a complete list of his exhibited pictures. [By Frederic G. Stephens.] 4to. Pp. viii., 80. [*Brit. Mus.*] London, 1869

EARNEST (an) address to his parishioners, by a minister of the Church of England. [By William Dodd, LL.D.] [*Gent. Mag.*, Sep. 1777, p. 421.] N.P., N.D.

EARNEST (an) address to men of all orders and degrees in the united Church of England and Ireland, respecting the Papists. [By Harry Bristow Wilson, B.D.] 8vo. [*New Coll. Cat.*] London, 1807

EARNEST (an) and affectionate address to his parishioners, from the minister of a parish [Samuel Glasse, D.D. (?)]. 8vo. Gloucester, 1785

EARNEST (an) and affectionate address to the common people of England, concerning their usual recreations on Shrove Tuesday. [By Josiah Tucker, Dean of Gloucester.] Fcap 8vo. [*Brit. Mus.*] London, 1787

EARNEST (an) and affectionate address to the people called Methodists. [By Henry Stebbing, D.D., Rector of Redenhall, Norfolk.] Fcap 8vo. Pp. 47. London, 1745

EARNEST (an) and compassionate suit for forbearance ; to the learned writers of some controversies at present. By a melancholy stander-by [Edward Wetenhall, D.D., Bishop of Cork and Ross]. 4to. [*Bodl.* ; *D. N. B.*, vol. 60, p. 383.] London, 1691

EARNEST (an) and solemn remonstrance, addressed to the Rev. D. T. K. Drummond, on his intention of perpetuating the schism which bears his name. By a presbyter [Berkeley Addison, A.M.]. 8vo. [*New Coll. Cat.*] Edinburgh, 1843

EARNEST (an) appeal to the Master and Seniors of Trinity College, Cambridge, on the revision of the Statutes. By two of the Fellows [Charles J. Vaughan and George E. L. Cotton]. 8vo. Pp. 38. [*Camb. Univ. Lib.*]. London, 1840

EARNEST (the) breathings of forreign Protestants, divines and others, . . . for a compleat body of practicall divinity . . . and an essay of a modell of the said body of divinity. By J. D. [John Dury]. 4to. [*Brit. Mus.*] London, 1658

EARNEST (an) call to the people of England, to beware of the temptations of the regicide Ludlow, to contract the guilt of the murther of King Charles the First, by a conceit that the shedding of that royal bloud was no murther, but an act of justice. [By Edmund Elys.] 8vo. [*Bodl.*] N.P., 1692
" Edm. Elys the author."—MS. note by Wood.

EARNEST (an) exhortation to a frequent reception of the holy sacrament of the Lord's Supper. By a layman [Sir James Allan Park]. 12mo. [Courtney's *Secrets*, p. 18.] London, 1808

EARNEST (an) exhortation to attend public worship . . . addressed by a minister [Rev. Samuel Clapham, M.A.]. Fcap 8vo. London, 1804

EARNEST (an) exhortation to forsake the devices and inventions of men, and to follow the pattern given in the word of God. By [Robert Campbell, of Skerrington] a convert from the Presbyterian religion, in a letter to his brother Scotchmen. 8vo. Pp. 20. Edinburgh, 1846

EARNEST (an) exhortation to housekeepers to set up the worship of God in their families : with daily prayers for morning and evening. [By Robert Nelson.] Fcap 8vo. [*D. N. B.*, vol. 40, p. 212.] London, 1702
Other editions followed.

EARNEST lives. [By Robert Cochrane.] 8vo. London, 1879

EARNEST (an) persuasive to unity, mostly extracted from the writings of pious and learned members of the Church. [By James Charles Stafford, B.D.] 8vo. [*Bodl.*] Oxford, 1840

EARNEST (an) perswasive to the serious observance of the Lord's day. By a minister of the Church of England [Josiah Woodward, D.D.]. 4to. [*Bodl.*] London, 1703
No separate title-page.

EARNEST (an) protest against the further circulation of certain principles contained in the pamphlet of the Hon. and Rev. B. W. Noel . . . entitled "The Unity of the Church." By Clericus Surriensis [Rev. John Courtney]. Fcap 8vo. [*Brit. Mus.*]
London, 1837

EARNEST struggles; or, the comic incidents and anxious moments in connection with the life of a Station-master. By one who endured it [Hubert Simmons]. 8vo. [*Brit. Mus.*]
London, [1880]

EARTH (the) breath, and other poems. By A. E. [George William Russell]. Fcap 8vo. Pp. 96.   London, [1897]

EARTH for a dollar. By Roof Roofer [Rufus Randell]. 8vo. [*Brit. Mus.*]
London, 1900

EARTH (the) lover. [Verse.] By Seumas O'Sullivan [James Starkey]. Fcap 8vo. [O'Donoghue's *Poets of Ireland*.]   Dublin, 1909

EARTH (the) not a globe. [Verse.] By "Common Sense" [William Carpenter, of Greenwich]. Second edition. 8vo. [*Brit. Mus.*]
London, 1864

EARTH to earth; a novel. By Richard Dehan [Clotilde Graves]. Cr 8vo. Pp. 336. [*Lit. Year Book.*]
London, 1916

EARTHEN vessels. By Archie Fell [Mary J. Capron]. Fcap 8vo. [Cushing's *Init. and Pseud.*, vol. i., p. 100.]   Boston, 1867

EARTHQUAKE (the); a tale. By the author of *The Ayrshire legatees* [John Galt]. 3 vols. Fcap 8vo. [*Brit. Mus.*]   Edinburgh, 1820

EARTHQUAKE (the) at St Thomas, November 1867. [By William Miles Maskell.] 8vo. [*Brit. Mus.*]
London, 1868
Signed "W. M. M."

EARTH'S (the) crust, and other poems. By a land surveyor [James Lawson]. Cr 8vo.   [London ?], 1863

EARTH'S many voices. [By Elizabeth M. A. F. Saxby.] Fcap 8vo. [*Brit. Mus.*]   London, 1885

EASIE (an) method not to be found hitherto in any author or history, whereby the longitude of any places at sea or land, west or east from any first meridian, e.g. London, may be found at any distance, great or small, by certain fixed stars fitly chosen for the season of the year, as hereafter specified. [By George Keith.] 4to.
N.P., [*c.* 1710]

EASIEST (the) introduction to the Hebrew language, designed for the use of young gentlemen and ladies. [By —— Kettilby.] Part I. 8vo. [*Bodl.*]   London, 1765

EAST and West India sugar; or, a refutation of the claims of the West India colonists to a protecting duty on East India sugar. [By Zachary Macaulay.] 8vo. [M'Culloch's *Lit. of Pol. Econ.*, p. 93.]   London, 1823

EAST (the); being personal impressions of a tour in Egypt, Palestine, and Syria. By W. M., Jun. [William Martin]. 4to. Pp. 126.
Dundee, 1875
For private circulation.

EAST Coast days and memories. By the author of *The recreations of a country parson* [Andrew K. H. Boyd, D.D.]. Cr. 8vo. Pp. vii., 343. [*Brit. Mus.*]   London, 1889

EAST (an) India collation; or a discourse of travels set forth in sundry observations. [By Christopher Farewell.] Fcap 8vo. [Christie-Miller *Cat.*]   London, 1633

EAST (the) India military calendar; containing the services of general and field officers of the Indian army. By the editor of the Royal military calendar [Sir John Philippart]. 3 vols. 4to. [Lowndes' *Bibl. Man.*, p. 709.]   London, 1823-26

EAST (the) India trade a most profitable trade to the Kingdom, and best secured and improved in a Company and a Joint Stock. . . . [By Thomas Papillon.] Fcap 4to. Pp. 28. [Quaritch's *Cat.*]   London, 1677

EAST Lynne; or the Earl's daughter. By the author of *The heirs of Ashley* [Mrs Henry Wood, *née* Ellen Price]. 8vo. [*Brit. Mus.*]
Richmond, [Virginia], 1864

EAST-BOURNE; being a descriptive account of that village in the County of Sussex and its environs. . . . [By —— Roger, or Royer, Clerk of the Treasury.] Fcap 8vo. Pp. 152. [*Camb. Univ. Cat.*]   London, 1787

EASTER. By Col. F. Ingham [Edward Everett Hale]. 4to. [Cushing's *Init. and Pseud.*, vol. i., p. 137.]
Boston, 1886

EASTER; a companion to the Book of Common Prayer. [By Prince Hoare.] [John Taylor, *Records of my life*, i., 318.]   London, 1825

EASTER day. By Margaret Sidney [Mrs Harriet M. Lothrop, *née* Stone]. Fcap 8vo. [Cushing's *Init. and Pseud.*, vol. i., p. 267.]   Boston, 1886

EASTER (the) eggs ; and, Red and white roses. By the author of *The Basket of flowers*, etc. [Christoph. von Schmid]. Translated from the German. Fcap 8vo. Edinburgh, [1871]

EASTER (the) gift, a religious offering. By L. E. L. [Letitia Elizabeth Landon, later Mrs. Maclean]. Fcap 8vo. [*Brit. Mus.*] London, 1832

EASTER (an) holiday in Gran Canaria and Madeira. By E. H. R. [Edward H. Robertson, Advocate]. 8vo. Pp. 56. Edinburgh, 1893

EASTER not mis-timed : a letter written out of the countrey to a friend in London concerning Easter-day. [By John Pell.] 4to. [*Brit. Mus.*] London, 1664

EASTER ; or a manual explanatory of the Latin words and phrases . . . in the Book of Common Prayer. . . . By a Layman [Peter Hoare]. Fcap 8vo. [*Brit. Mus.*] London, 1882

EASTER (an) vacation. By Moira O'Neill [Mrs Skrine, *née* Nesta Higginson]. 8vo. [S. J. Brown's *Ireland in fiction.*] London, 1893

EASTER-MONDAY ; an ode. By the author of *Lines on the opening of London Bridge*, etc. [J. Payne]. 4to. [*Brit. Mus.*] London, [1837]

EASTERN (the) Archipelago : the scenery, people, etc. [By William Davenport Adams.] Pt 8vo. London, 1880

EASTERN (the) boundary of New Jersey : a review of a paper. . . . [By Henry Barton Dawson.] 8vo. New York, 1866

EASTERN (the) Churches : containing sketches of the Nestorian, Armenian, Jacobite, Coptic, and Abyssinian communities. By the author of *Proposals for Christian union* [Ernest Silvanus Appleyard]. Second edition. Fcap 8vo. [*Adv. Lib.*] London, 1850
The advertisement prefixed is signed " E. S. A."

EASTERN eclogues ; written during a tour through Arabia, etc. [By Eyles Irwin.] 4to. [*Brit. Mus.*] London, 1780

EASTERN Europe and the Emperor Nicholas. By the author of *Revelations of Russia* [Charles Frederick Henningsen]. 3 vols. Fcap 8vo. [*Brit. Mus.*] London, 1846

EASTERN fruit on Western dishes. By Petroleum Volcano Nasby [David R. Locke]. 8vo. [*Brit. Mus.*] London, [1875 ?]

EASTERN hospitals and English nurses. By a lady volunteer [Frances Magdalen Taylor]. 2 vols. 8vo. [Gillow's *Bibl. Dict.*, vol. 5, p. 538.] London, 1856

EASTERN nights—and flights [in aeroplanes]. By " Contact " [Alan Bott]. 8vo. [*Lond. Lib. Cat.*] Edinburgh, 1920

EASTERN (the) Question : copy of letters . . . observations and comments on the Right Hon. W. E. Gladstone's paper . . . entitled " The paths of honour and of shame." By [C— Forjett] the author of *Our real danger in India*. 8vo. Pp. 64. [*Brit. Mus.*] London, 1878

EASTERN (the) Question tackled and summarily disposed of. By Ally Sloper [Charles Henry Ross]. 8vo. [F. Boase's *Mod. Brit. Biog.*, vol. vi., col. 497.] London, 1877

EASTERN (the) Question : Turkey, its mission and doom ; a prophetical instruction. By the author of *The Government of the Kingdom of Christ*, etc. [James Moir Porteous]. 8vo. London, 1876
Private information.

EASTERN (the) tourist ; being a guide through the States of Connecticut, Rhode Island, Massachusetts, Vermont, New Hampshire and Maine, also a dash into Canada, etc. [By John Disturnell.] Fcap 8vo. [*Brit. Mus.*] New York, 1848
Signed " J. D."

EASTFORD ; or, household sketches : a novel. By Wesley Brooke [George Lunt]. 8vo. [Cushing's *Init. and Pseud.*, vol. i., p. 41.] Boston, 1855

EASTON and its inhabitants ; or, sketches of life in a country town. By L. E. [Hon. Eleanor Eden]. 8vo. [*Brit. Mus.*] London, 1858

EASTWARD ho ! ! ! Or, Quoz's letters relative to the Wet-Dock Bill. . . . [By George Griffin Stonestreet.] 4to. London, 1796

EASY chair memories and rambling notes. By the Amateur Angler [Edward Marston, publisher]. Fcap 8vo. Pp. xi., 174. [*Brit. Mus.*] London, 1911

EASY (an) introduction to the Hebrew language on the principles of Pestalozzi. By Parens [Henry Craik]. Consisting of three parts . . . intended to enable parents and teachers who consider the original of the word of God the most suitable object of early instruction, to acquire it themselves in the act of teaching. Folio. London, 1831
Ascribed also to —— Synge.

EASY lessons in money matters. [By Richard Whately, D.D.] 12mo. Pp. 86. [*Brit. Mus.*]   London, 1842

EASY lessons on Christian evidences. [By Richard Whately, Archbishop of Dublin, and C. Dickinson, Bishop of Meath.] Fcap 8vo. [*Brit. Mus.*]
London, 1838

EASY (an) method of acquiring the Hebrew, without the points, according to the ancient practice. By an experienced teacher [—— Borrenstein]. Folio. [Lowndes' *Bibl. Man.*]
London, 1822

EASY outlines of the body and temperance. [By Rev. George Benjamin Charles, B.A.] 8vo.   London, 1906

EASY whist. By Aquarius [Lewis d'Aguilar Jackson]. Fcap 8vo. Pp. 48. [*Brit. Mus.*]   London, 1884

EAT not thy heart. By Julien Gordon [Julia Storrow Cruger, later Mrs Van Rennselaer]. Fcap 8vo. Pp. 319. [*Brit. Mus.*]   Chicago, 1897

EATON Chronicle : or, the salt box. [Edited by William Gifford.] 8vo. Pp. 165. [Martin's *Cat.*] N.P., 1789
A collection of contributions by the friends of Earl Grosvenor assembled at Eaton to celebrate the twenty-first birthday of Lord Belgrave.

EBB tide. . . . By Christian Reid [Frances C. Fisher, later Mrs James N. Tiernan]. 8vo. [Cushing's *Init. and Pseud.*, vol. i., p. 249.]
New York, 1872

EBONY (the) idol. [By Mrs G— M. Flanders.] Fcap 8vo.
New York, 1860

EBORACUM ; or the history and antiquities of York [abridged from the work of Francis Drake]. 2 vols. 8vo.   York, 1788

EBRIETATIS encomium ; or, the praise of drunkenness : wherein is authentically and most evidently proved, the necessity of frequently getting drunk. By Boniface Oinophilus. [A translation of *Eloge de l'yvresse*, by Albert Henri de Sallengre.] 8vo. Pp. 209. [*Brit. Mus.*]
London, 1812

ÉCARTÉ. By " Aquarius " [Lewis d'Aguilar Jackson]. 12mo. [*Brit. Mus.*]   London, 1883

ÉCARTÉ ; or, the salons of Paris. [By Major John Richardson.] 3 vols. Fcap 8vo. [*Adv. Lib.*]
London, 1829

ECCE Agnus Dei ; emblems and thoughts of Christ : poems. By A. E. H. [Anna Elizabeth Hamilton]. Fcap 8vo. [O'Donoghue's *Poets of Ireland*].
London, 1872

ECCE Christianus : or, Christ's idea of the Christian life. . . . [By Rev. William David Ground.] 8vo. [*Brit. Mus.*]   London, 1879

ECCE coelum ; or, parish astronomy. By a Connecticut pastor [Enoch Fitch Burr, D.D.]. 8vo. [Cushing's *Init. and Pseud.*, vol. i., p. 66.]   Boston, 1867

ECCE Deus : essays on the life and doctrine of Jesus Christ, with controversial notes on [Sir John R. Seeley's] *Ecce Homo*. [By Joseph Parker, D.D.] 8vo. Pp. ix., 339. [*D. N. B.*, Second Supp., vol. 3, p. 72.]   Edinburgh, 1867

ECCE Deus-Homo ; or the work and Kingdom of the Christ of Scripture. [By Alexander White Pitzer, D.D.] Pt 8vo. Pp. 207. [Kirk's *Supp.*]
Philadelphia, 1877

ECCE femina ; or, the woman Zoe. By Cuyler Pine [Ellen Peck]. 8vo. [Cushing's *Init. and Pseud.*, vol. i., p. 235.]   New York, 1865

ECCE Homo [written by Sir John R. Seeley] ; a critique. By Presbyter Anglicanus [Rev. Joseph Hemington Harris]. Pt 8vo. [Cushing's *Init. and Pseud.*, vol. i., p. 238.]
Ramsgate, 1866

ECCE Homo : a survey of the life and work of Jesus Christ. [By Sir John Robert Seeley.] 8vo. Pp. viii., 330. [*D. N. B.*, vol. 51, p. 192.]
London, 1865
See also " The Credentials of conscience. . . ."

ECCE Homo ; a treatise on the nature and personality of God, founded upon the Gospels of St Luke and St John. By the author of *An Angel's message* [Miss J— Fawcett]. 8vo.
London, 1859

ECCE Homo ! or, a critical enquiry into the history of Jesus Christ ; being a rational analysis of the Gospels. [By Paul Thyry, Baron d'Holbach.] Second edition. 8vo. Pp. viii., 344. [*Bodl.*]   London, 1813
The first edition appeared in 1799. This work, translated from the French, is sometimes attributed to Joseph Webb. The supposed translator is J— Houston.

ECCE puella ; and other prose imaginings. By Fiona Macleod [William Sharp]. Cr 8vo. [*Lit. Year Book.*]
London, 1896

ECCE Spiritus. [By E— F. Hayward.] Fcap 8vo.   London, 1885

ECCE Unitas ; or a plea for Christian unity. By Eureka [Thomas Neely Ralston, D.D.]. Fcap 8vo. [Cushing's *Init. and Pseud.*, vol. i., p. 94.]
Cincinnati, 1875

ECCENTRIC tales. By W. F. von Kosewitz [Charles Robert Forrester]. 8vo. [*D. N. B.*, vol. 20, p. 7.]
London, 1827

ECCENTRIC tales in verse. By Cornelius Crambo, Esq. [William Barnes Rhodes]. 8vo. Pp. xi., 140. [*Gent. Mag.*, xcvi., ii., 472.]   London, 1808

ECCENTRICITIES (the) of John Edwin, comedian ; collected from his manuscripts, and enriched with several hundred original anecdotes : arranged and digested by Anthony Pasquin, Esq. [John Williams]. New edition. 2 vols. 8vo. [Haynes' *Pseud.*]
[London, 1791 ?]

ECCENTRICS (the). [A novel.] By Percy Ross [Mrs Lilian Duff, *née* Peel]. 3 vols. 8vo.   London, [1894]

ECCHOES from the sixth trumpet reverberated by a review of neglected remembrances. . . . [By George Wither.] Fcap 8vo. [*D. N. B.*, vol. 62, p. 266.]   London, 1666
    The first part of the author's " Fragmenta poetica," a series of extracts from earlier works.

ECCLESIA Dei ; a vision of the Church : with a preface, notes, and illustrations. [By William John Blew.] Fcap 8vo. [*N. and Q.*, 27 July 1861, p. 80.]
London, 1848

ECCLESIA Dei ; the place and function of the Church in the divine order of the universe, and its relations with the world. [By Rev. George Smith Frew.] Pt 8vo.   London, 1866

ECCLESIA enucleata : the Temple opened ; or a clear demonstration of the true Gospel-Church, according to the doctrine and practice of Christ and his Apostles. By I. C. [Isaac Chauncey, M.A.]. Fcap 8vo. Pp. 160. [*D. N. B.*, vol. 10, p. 171.]
London, 1684

ECCLESIA et factio : a dialogue between the Bow-Steeple dragon, and the Exchange grasshopper. [By Edward Ward.] Folio. Pp. 16. [*D. N. B.*, vol. 59, p. 313.]
London, 1698

ECCLESIA gemens ; or, two discourses on the mournful state of the Church, with a prospect of her dawning glory. [By Samuel Lee, M.A.] 8vo. Pp. 92. [*Bodl.*]   London, 1677
    The dedication is signed " S. L."

ECCLESIA Sancti Pauli illustrata : the monuments, inscriptions, and epitaphs of Kings, Nobles, Bishops and others, buried in the cathedrall Church of St. Paul, London ; together with the foundation of the said Church ; a catalogue of all the Arch-bishops and Bishops of London from the beginning ; a catalogue also of all the deanes of the same Church ; and the monuments. By H. H. [Hugh Holland]. 4to. [*W.*]   London, 1633
    A second edition of the " Monumenta sepulchraria Sancti Pauli," published in 1614.

ECCLESIASTES, otherwise called the Preacher, compendiously abridged and also paraphrastically dilated in English poesie, according to the analogie of Scripture and consent of the most approved writer thereof. Composed by H. L. [Henry Lok, or Locke], Gentleman. 4to. [Boase and Courtney's *Bibl. Corn.*, i. 85.]
London, by Rich. Field, 1597

ECCLESIASTICAL antiquities of Devon ; being observations on many churches in Devonshire [and Cornwall] originally published in the Exeter and Plymouth Gazette. . . . [By Rev. John Pike Jones, and George Oliver, D.D.] Fcap 8vo. Pp. xiii., 175. [Boase and Courtney's *Bibl. Corn.*, i., 279 ; Davidson's *Bibl. Devon.*, p. 10.]
Exeter, 1828

ECCLESIASTICAL characteristics ; or, the arcana of Church policy : being an humble attempt to open up the mystery of moderation, wherein is shewn a plain and easy way of attaining to the character of a moderate man, as at present in repute in the Church of Scotland. [By John Witherspoon, D.D.] Fcap 8vo. Pp. 51. [*D. N. B.*, vol. 62, p. 272.]
Glasgow, 1753
    The author continued his satire in " A serious apology for the Ecclesiastical characteristics." (*See below.*)

ECCLESIASTICAL (the) Commission : its origin and progress, with some examination of the Report of the Select Committee of the House of Commons in 1862-3. By a clergyman in the diocese of Winchester [Arthur Garfit]. 8vo. Pp. 47. [*Brit. Mus.*]
London, 1864

ECCLESIASTICAL disclosures for the years 1842 and 1843. (Reprinted from the *Stirling Observer* of 22d Jan., 12th and 26th Feb. 1846.) [By Ebenezer Johnston, minister at Plean.]   8vo. [*New Coll. Cat.*]   N.P., N.D.

ECCLESIASTICAL (the) explanatory table. By the author of *A new and concise system of chronology* [T. Brooke]. Fcap 8vo.
Huddersfield, N.D.

ECCLESIASTICAL history epitomized; containing a faithful account of ye birth, life, & doctrine, crucifixion & ascension of ye Holy Iesus: with the lives of ye apostles, evangelists & primitive fathers & other famous men in ye Christian Church, both antient & modern, who have couragiously confessed & suffered glorious martyrdoms & persecutions under several tyrannical governours, both Heathenish and Romish. . . . Carefully collected by J. S., gent. [John Shurley, M.A.]. Two parts. 8vo. [*Bodl.*]
London, 1682

Title engraved, with likenesses of Christ and the Apostles. Each part has a separate title. Part II., with a title differing from that of part I., was published in 1683, and has the author's name at the end of the address to the Christian reader.

ECCLESIASTICAL (the) history of M. l'abbé Fleury, from the second oecumenical council, to the end of the fourth century: translated, with notes, and an essay on the miracles of the period. [By John Henry Newman, D.D.] 8vo. Pp. ccxx., 400. [*Brit. Mus.*]   Oxford, 1842

The essay was published in 1843 with the author's name.

ECCLESIASTICAL (an) history of Scotland; containing the state of the Church of that nation, from the time of Queen Mary to the union of the two kingdoms, being the space of 154 years. [By Daniel Defoe.] 8vo. Pp. 348.
London, 1734

"The author of this volume was Daniel Defoe.—In fact, it is the same book as the 'Memoirs of the Church of Scotland. In four parts &c. London 1717,' 8vo., the title-page and pages 1-2 of the text being reprinted. D. L."—MS. note in the handwriting of Dr David Laing.

ECCLESIASTICAL (the) history of the English nation, from the coming of Julius Cæsar into this island in the 60th year before the incarnation of Christ till the year of our Lord 731: written in Latin by Venerable Bede, and now translated into English from Dr Smith's edition; to which is added, the life of the author, also explanatory notes [by Capt. John Stevens]. 8vo. [Watt's *Bibl. Brit.*]   London, 1723

Later editions, revised, give the name of the translator.

ECCLESIASTICAL sketch of Lochwinnoch Parish, embracing a period of three hundred years. By a native [Matthew Gemmell]. Fcap 8vo.
Paisley, 1878

Holograph attestation by the author.

ECCLESIASTICAL (the) supremacy of the crown proved to be the common law of England: with preliminary observations, and an appendix. By Basilicus [Edmund Lewis Lenthal Swift, Irish barrister]. 8vo. [*Brit. Mus.*]   London, 1814

ECCLESIASTICAL topography; a collection of one hundred views of churches in the environs of London, from drawings expressly taken for this work, accompanied with descriptions from the best sources, both MS. and printed. [Edited by Samuel Woodburn.] 4to. [*W.*]   London, 1811

ECCLESIOLOGICAL notes on the Isle of Man, Ross, Sutherland, and the Orkneys; or a summer pilgrimage to S. Mangold and S. Magnus. By J. M. N. [John Mason Neale, D.D.]. Fcap 8vo. [*Brit. Mus.*]
London, 1848

ECHO. A novel. By Sydney Tremayne [Mrs Roger Cookson]. Cr 8vo. Pp. 297.   London, 1919

ECHO (an) from Patmos; or prophecy fulfilling: being a collection of remarkable facts illustrating the sixth and part of the seventh vials, of the Book of the Revelation of St. John. By T. D. R. [Thomas Dennis Rock]. 8vo. [*Brit. Mus.*]   Brighton, 1860

ECHO-BANK: a temperance tale. By Ervie [Emily C. Pearson]. 8vo. [Cushing's *Init. and Pseud.*, vol. i., p. 93.]   New York, 1868

ECHOES. [Three stories.] By E. M. H. [Emily Marion Harris]. 8vo. [Cushing's *Init. and Pseud.*, i., 123.]
London, 1871

ECHOES and after-thoughts [in verse. By Henry Johnstone, Edinburgh]. Pt 8vo. Pp. 105.
Private print, [Edinburgh], 1899

ECHOES from bygone days; or love lyrics and character sonnets. By Thomas Brevior [Thomas Shorter]. 8vo. Pp. 73. [*Brit. Mus.*]
London, [1889]

ECHOES from mist-land; or, the Niebelungen-lay revealed. By Auber Forestier [Annie Aubertina Woodward]. Fcap 8vo. [Cushing's *Init. and Pseud.*, vol. i., p. 598.]
New York, 1877

ECHOES from the Orient: a broad outline of theosophical doctrines. By "Occultus" [William Q— Judge]. Pt 8vo. [*Amer. Cat.*] New York, 1890

ECHOES of foreign song. By the author of *A month in the Camp before Sebastopol* [Henry Jeffreys Bushby]. 8vo. [*Lond. Lib. Cat.*] London, 1877

ECHOES of old county life. . . . By Rusticus [John Kersley Fowler]. 8vo. London, 1892

Another edition gives the author's name.

ECHOES of Old Florence : her palaces, and those who lived in them. By Leader Scott [Mrs Lucy Baxter, *née* Barnes]. 8vo. [*Lond. Lib. Cat.*] London, 1894

ECHOES of our childhood. [Verse.] By the author of *Everley*, etc. [Miss —— Cornish]. 8vo. [*Brit. Mus.*] London, 1865

ECHOES of time and tide. [Poems.] By Laura Bell [Julia May Williamson]. 8vo. New York, 1879

ECHOING and re-echoing. [A tale.] By Faye Huntington [Mrs Isabella H. Foster]. 8vo. Pp. 64. [*Brit. Mus.*] London, [1895]

ECHOISM ; a poem. [By Henry Lee.] Fcap 8vo. [Green's *Bibl. Somers.*, iii., 12.] Taunton, 1821

ECLIPSE (the) of faith ; or, a visit to a religious sceptic. [By Henry Rogers.] 8vo. [*D. N. B.*, vol. 49, p. 122.] London, 1852

Signed " F. B." This work was followed by " A Defence of the eclipse of faith." *See above.*

ECLOGUES and monodramas ; or, a collection of verses. By William P. Lancaster [John Byrne Leicester Warren, third Baron de Tabley]. 8vo. [*Brit. Mus.*] London, 1864

ECLOGUES (the) of Virgil ; a plaything of age. By a used-up Vicar [Rev. John Meyer King]. Fcap 8vo. [Green's *Bibl. Somers.*, ii., p. 549.] Exeter, 1880

ECONOMIC (the) functions of the League [of Nations]. By Norman Angell [Ralph Norman Angell Lane]. Fcap 8vo. [*Lit. Year Book.*] London, 1920

ECONOMICAL (the) causes of slavery in the United States, and obstacles to Abolition. By a South Carolinian [Henry Middleton]. 8vo. [Cushing's *Init. and Pseud.*, vol. i., p. 271.] London, 1857

ECONOMICS for Irishmen. By Pat [Patrick D. Kenny, journalist]. Fcap 8vo. [*Lond. Lib. Cat.*] London, 1906

ECONOMY (the) of human life. . . . *See* " Œconomy (the) of human life. . . ."

ECONOMY (the) of life ; self-help to practical and progressive knowledge. By Pamphilius [David Mitchell Aird]. 8vo. [F. Boase's *Mod. Brit. Biog.*, i., col. 34.] London, [1865]

ECONOMY (the) of vegetation. By a fellow of the Linnean Society [J. Murray]. 8vo. [*Brit. Mus.*] London, 1838

ED. Lee and sailor Dick. By Aunt Abbie [Miss Abby Skinner]. Fcap 8vo. [Cushing's *Init. and Pseud.*, vol. i., p. 501.] Boston, 1866

EDDA ; or, the tales of a grandmother. History of Denmark, first part, from the earliest ages to the death of Canute the Great. Edited by Philojuvenis. [C. J. Hambro]. 8vo. Pp. 127. [*Adv. Lib.*] London, 1847

EDELWEISS ; a romance. By Rita [Eliza M. J. Gollan, later Mrs Otto von Booth, later Mrs W— Desmond Humphreys]. [*Lond. Lib. Cat.*] Fcap 8vo. London, 1890

EDEN ; and other poems. By E. L. R. [Ellen Louisa Raymond]. Fcap 8vo. [*Brit. Mus.*] London, N.D., [1867?]

EDEN (an) in England. A tale by A. L. O. E., authoress of *The Claremont tales*, etc. [Charlotte Maria Tucker]. 8vo. Pp. 288. [*Lit. Year Book.*] Edinburgh, N.D.

EDEN ; or a compleat body of gardening. [By John Hill.] Folio. [*Camb. Univ. Lib.*] London, 1757

EDGAR Allan Poe : the man, the master, the martyr. By Geoffrey Quarles [Oliver Leigh]. Cr 8vo. [*Amer. Cat.*] Chicago, 1906

EDGAR and Elfrida, with the defeat of Hoel, Prince of Wales. By T. de Monmouth [Thomas Powell]. 8vo. [*W.*] London, 179—

EDGAR and Emmeline ; a fairy tale : in a dramatic entertainment of two acts ; as it is performed at the Theatre-Royal in Drury-Lane. [By John Hawkesworth.] 8vo. [*Biog. Dram.*] London, 1761

EDGAR'S wife. [A tale.] By Esmé Stuart [Amélie Claire Leroy]. Pt 8vo. Pp. 216. [*Lond. Lib. Cat.*] London, 1889

EDGED tools. By the author of *Win and Wear* [Mrs S— S— Robbins]. 8vo. [*Bodl.*] Edinburgh, 1867

EDGIANA : being a collection of some of the sayings of Edward Edge, gate-keeper of St. Patrick's Deanery, Dublin. [By H. H. West.] Small 4to. Alassio, 1899

EDINBURGH (an) eleven : pencil portraits from College life. By Gavin Ogilvy [Sir James M. Barrie]. Pt 8vo. [*Brit. Mus.*] London, 1889

EDINBURGH fugitive pieces. [Edited by William Creech.] 8vo. Pp. vi., 314. [*Sig. Lib.*] Edinburgh, 1791

EDINBURGH (the) geographical and historical atlas ; comprehending a sketch of the history of geography, a view of the principles of mathematical, physical and political geography, an account of the geography, statistics and history of each continent, state and kingdom delineated, and a tabular view of the principal mountain chains in the world. [By D. Lizars.] Folio. [*W.*] Edinburgh, 1831

EDINBURGH in pictures ; with letter-press by the author of *Romantic Edinburgh* [John Geddie]. 8vo.
London, 1908

EDINBURGH (the) literary album. [By Grace Webster.] Fcap 8vo. Pp. x., 328. [*Adv. Lib.*]
Edinburgh, 1835

EDINBURGH merchants and merchandise in old times. [By Robert Chambers, LL.D.] 8vo.
[Edinburgh, 1859]

EDINBURGH, or, the ancient Royalty ; a sketch of former manners; with notes. By Simon Gray [Sir Alexander Boswell, Bart.]. Fcap 8vo. [*Adv. Lib.*] Edinburgh, 1810

EDINBURGH (the) paradise regain'd ; or the city set at liberty, to propagate and improve her trade and commerce : being a curious dissertation thereon, and discovery of the disease that obstructs the growth and progress thereof ; and an effectual remedy and cure therefor, by redressing and removing her grievances. . . . By a merchant-citizen, long acquainted with the city's accompt of profit and loss, both before and since the incorporate Union [Robert Mein]. 8vo. [*Adv. Lib.*] [Edinburgh], 1764

EDINBURGH, past and present ; its associations and surroundings : drawn with pen and pencil. [By William Ballingall.] Royal 8vo. Pp. 153.
Edinburgh, 1877
Introductory note signed " W. B."

EDINBURGH (the) Rosciad ; for the summer season, 1834. [By W. H. Logan.] Imprinted at Modern Athens. 8vo. [Lowe's *Theat. Liter.*, p. 112.]
Edinburgh, 1834

EDINBURGH sketches during Assembly time. By Catter Thun [Rev. Hugh Mackenzie Campbell, M.A.]. 8vo. [Scott's *Fasti*.]
Edinburgh, [1890?]

EDINBURGH (the) smoke-doctor. By A. C. and J. B. [Alexander Carmichael and John Brownlie], masons. 8vo.
Edinburgh, 1757

EDINBURGH'S address to the country. [By A. Ramsay ?] 8vo. [*W.*] [Edinburgh ? 1720 ?]

EDITH — a tale of the Azores : and other poems. [By J— Cross-Buchanan.] Pt 8vo. London, 1838

EDITH and her ayah, and other stories. By A. L. O. E., author of *Exiles in Babylon*, etc. [Charlotte M. Tucker]. Pt 8vo. Pp. 120. London, 1872

EDITH and Mary, at Holly Farm. By the authoress of *The wide wide world*, etc. [Susan Warner]. 8vo. Pp. 112. 8vo. [*Brit. Mus.*]
London, [1871]

EDITH of Glammis. By Cuthbert Clutterbuck, of Kennaquhair, F.S.A., etc. [Alexander Hamilton, W.S.]. 3 vols. 8vo. [*Adv. Lib.*]
London, 1836

EDITH of Graystock : a poem. By Eleanor M. [Eleanor L. Montagu, later Mrs Hervey]. 8vo. [*Brit. Mus.*]
London, 1833

EDITH Withington : a book for girls. By H. N. W. B. [Mrs Harriet Newell (Woods) Baker]. 8vo. [Kirk's *Supp.*]
Boston, 1871

EDITORIAL wild oats. By Mark Twain [Samuel L. Clemens]. 8vo. [Kirk's *Supp.*] London, 1905

EDLEEN Vaughan ; or paths of peril : a novel. By Carmen Sylva [Elizabeth, Queen of Roumania]. 3 vols. Cr 8vo. [*Lond. Lib. Cat.*] London, 1892

EDMOND, orphan of the castle : a tragedy, in five acts ; founded on the Old English baron, a Gothic story [by Clara Reeve]. [By John Broster, F.S.A.] 8vo. [*N. and Q.*, Oct., 1855, p. 295.] London, 1799

EDMUND and Velina, a legendary tale ; and Albert and Ellen, a Danish ballad. [By Alexander Jaffray, writer in Edinburgh.] 4to. [*Brit. Mus.*]
Edinburgh, 1797

EDMUND Dawn ; or, ever forgive. By Ravenswood [Charles Washington Beebee]. 8vo. [Cushing's *Init. and Pseud.*, vol. i., p. 248.]
New York, 1873

EDNA Willis ; or, the promise fulfilled. By S. W. [Samuel Warren]. 8vo. [Cushing's *Init. and Pseud.*, vol. ii., p. 153.] London, 1866

EDUCATION and religion : their mutual connection and relative bearings. [By David Kay, F.G.S.] 8vo.
London, 1873

EDUCATION and school. By Benjamin Place [Edward Thring]. 8vo. [Cushing's *Init. and Pseud.*, vol. i., p. 235.] London, 1867

EDUCATION at home. [By Edward White Benson.] [*N. and Q.*, 10 Nov., 1866, p. 371.]   London, 1824

EDUCATION by doing ; occupations and busy work for primary classes. By Hope Daring [Anna Johnson]. Fcap 8vo. Pp. 109. [*Amer. Cat.*]
New York, 1910

EDUCATION in Europe and Japan. [By James Summers.] 4to.
[Tokio], 1879

EDUCATION of children and young students in all its branches, with a short catalogue of the best books in polite learning and the sciences, and an appendix concerning the usefulness of natural philosophy to divines. . . . [By —— Riley.] Second edition, corrected. 8vo. [Darling's *Cyclop. Bibl.*]   London, 1752

EDUCATION (the) of children in learning ; declared by the dignitie, vtilitie, and method thereof : meete to be knowne, and practised as well of parents as schoolemaisters. [By William Kemp.] 4to. No pagination. B. L. [*Bodl.*] London, 1588
The Dedication and the Address to the reader are signed " W. K."

EDUCATION (the) of Damaris Verity [a novel]. By Lucas Malet [Mrs St Leger Harrison, *née* Mary Kingsley]. Cr 8vo. [*Brit. Mus.*] London, 1913

EDUCATION (the) of girls. [By F— J— Faraday.] Reprint from the *Dublin University Magazine.* Fcap 8vo. [*Brit. Mus.*]   Manchester, 1872

EDUCATION (the) of the feelings. [By Charles Bray.] 8vo. [*Manch. Free Lib.*, p. 239.]   Coventry, 1838

EDUCATION (the) question : an appeal to the evangelical Dissenting laity, from one of their own order [R. W. Smiles]. Fcap 8vo. [*N. and Q.*, Feb. 1869, p. 168.]
Manchester, 1855

EDUCATION (the) question [in Ireland] : thoughts on the present crisis. [By Sir Joseph Napier.] 8vo. [*Camb. Univ. Lib.*]
Dublin, private print, 1860
The second edition was published in the same year with the author's name.

EDUCATION (the) (Scotland) Act, 1872. The complete text, with notes. [By Alexander Thomson.] 8vo.
Edinburgh, 1872
Private information.

EDUCATIONAL reminiscences. [By Elizabeth Jones.] 8vo. Pp. viii., 87. [*Bodl.*]   London, N.D.

EDUCATIONAL voluntaryism an amiable delusion. By James Fagg [Dr John Robertson, surgeon]. 8vo. [*Manch. Free Lib.*] Manchester, 1853
See also the following.

EDUCATIONAL voluntaryism tested. By Godfrey Topping [Dr John Robertson]. 8vo.   Manchester, 1854

EDWARD. Translated from the French of the author of *Ourika* [Claire L. R. Bonne, Duchesse de Duras]. 8vo. [*Camb. Univ. Lib.*]   London, 1826

EDWARD I. of England in the north of Scotland : being a narrative of his proceedings in that part of the kingdom, with historical and topographical remarks. By a member of the Literary and Scientific Association of Elgin [Dr Jos. Taylor]. 8vo.   Elgin, 1858

EDWARD Irving : a review. [By Rev. Wm. Watson Andrews.] Reprinted from the *New Englander*, 1863. Fcap 8vo. Pp. 166. [Boase's *Cath. Apost. Lit.*, p. 2.]   Edinburgh, 1864

EDWARD Irving and the Catholic Apostolic Church. By one of its members [Rev. John S. Davenport]. Small 8vo. Pp. 68. [Boase's *Cath. Apost. Lit.*, p. 17.]   London, 1856

EDWARD the Seventh ; a play. By the author of *The Coming K—* and *Siliad* [Eustace C. Grenville Murray]. 8vo.   London, 1876

EDWARD Somers ; a domestic story : and A Legend of the coast. By the author of *Poems, by Viator* [Thomas D'Oyly]. Fcap 8vo. [*Camb. Univ. Lib.*]   London, 1843

EDWARD the Confessor : a drama [in verse]. By Bassanio [John Arthur Coupland]. 8vo. Pp. 147. [*Brit. Mus.*]   London, 1886

EDWARD the orphan ; a tale. By Mary Pelham [Dorothy Kilner]. Fcap 8vo. [*Brit. Mus.*] London, [1824]

EDWARD Travers ; a Roman Catholic story. By Adeline [Mrs Jane Sergeant]. 8vo. [*D. N. B.*, Second Supp., vol. iii., p. 291.] London, 1849

EDWARD ; various views of human nature, taken from life and manners, chiefly in England. By the author of *Zeluco* [John Moore, M.D.]. 2 vols. 8vo. [*Brit. Mus.*] London, 1796

EDWARD Willoughby ; a tale. By the author of *The discipline of life*, etc. [Lady Emily Ponsonby]. 2 vols. 8vo. [*Camb. Univ. Lib.*]   London, 1854

EDWARD Wortley Montagu ; an autobiography [really the autobiography of Edward Vaughan Hyde Kenealy]. 3 vols. Cr 8vo. [*Brit. Mus.*]
London, 1869

EDWIN and Eltruda; a legendary tale. By a young lady [Helen Maria Williams; edited by A. Kippis]. 4to. [*Brit Mus.*] London, 1782

EDWIN and Emma. [A poem. By David Mallet.] 4to. [*Brit. Mus.*] Birmingham, 1760

EDWIN and Emma; a pastoral tale, in four parts. [By David Black, D.D., Dunfermline.] 8vo. [Beveridge's *Dunf. Bibl.*] Dunfermline, 1814

EDWIN the banished Prince: a tragedy. [By Rev. —— Douglas.] 8vo. [Watt's *Bibl. Brit.*] Privately printed, 1784

EDWY: a dramatic poem. [By Rev. Thomas Warwick, B.C.L.] 8vo. [*Biog. Dram.*] London, 1784

EDWY and Bertha. . . . [By John Corry.] Fcap 8vo. [Watt's *Bibl. Brit.*] London, 1802

EDWY and Edilda; a tale, in five parts. [By Thos. Sedgwick Whalley, D.D.] 8vo. [Watt's *Bibl. Brit.*] London, 1779

EEDIOTIC etiquette. By Gideon Wurdz [Charles Wayland Towne]. Fcap 8vo. [*Amer. Cat.*] New York, 1906

EERIE (an) he and she. By Alan Dale [Alfred J. Cohen]. Pt 8vo. Pp. 366. [*Amer. Cat.*] New York, 1889

" EFFECTS " and adventures of Raby Rattler, Gent. [By Thomas Hall.] 8vo. [*Brit. Mus.*] London, 1845
See also " The Fortunes and adventures . . ."

EFFECTS (the) of infidel principles illustrated, in some account of J. Stratford, who was executed at Norwich for the crime of murder. [By Joseph John Gurney.] 12mo. [*Brit. Mus.*] London, 1849
Signed " J. J. G."

EFFECTS (the) of sea-bathing, and directions for its use : from the French of A. M. Gaudet, M.D., with additions. [By John Dowson, M.D.] 8vo. Pp. 37. [Smale's *Whitby Authors*, p. 167.] London, 1853

EFFECTS (the) of the passions; or, memoirs of Floricourt. From the French [of Jean Gaspard Dubois-Fontanelle]. 3 vols. Fcap 8vo. [*Brit. Mus.*] London, 1788

EFFECTS of the stage on the manners of a people; and the propriety of encouraging a virtuous theatre. By a Bostonian [William Halliburton]. 8vo. Pp. 75. [Evans' *Amer. Bibl.*, vol. 8, p. 295.] Boston, 1792

EFFECTUAL (an) method for recovering our religious liberties, addressed to the elders of the Church of Scotland; shewing, that they may easily bring about a total change of administration in the Church, and thereby remove the principal grievances arising from the law of Patronage. . . . [By John Snodgrass, D.D.] 8vo. [Scott's *Fasti.*] Glasgow, 1770

EFFICACY (the) of prayer: first published in the " Unitarian Advocate." By J. B. [John Brazer, D.D.]. Fcap 8vo. [Cushing's *Init. and Pseud.*, vol. i., p. 25.] Boston, 1832

EFFIE and her Ayah. . . . By the author of *Little Tija*, etc. [Beatrice Stebbing, later Mrs Batty]. 8vo. [*Brit. Mus.*] London, [1873]

EFFIE'S and the Doctor's tales. By a lady [Lady Maria Charlotte Lees]. 8vo. London, 1854

EFFIE'S friends; or, chronicles of the woods and shore. [By Lady Augusta M. Noel.] Fcap 8vo. [*Brit. Mus.*] London, 1865

EFFIGIES (the) of love; being a translation from the Latine of Mr Robert Waring [by Robert Nightingale]. . . . 12mo. [*Brit. Mus.*] London, 1680

EFFIGIES poeticae : or the portraits of the British poets illustrated by notes, biographical, critical, and poetical. [By Bryan Waller Procter.] 8vo. Pp. 118. London, 1824
" The work of Barry Cornwall (Mr. Procter)."—MS. note in the handwriting of Dyce.

EFFINGHAMS (the); or, home as I found it. By the author of *The victim of Chancery* [F— Jackson]. 2 vols. Fcap 8vo. New York, 1841

EFFUSIONS (the) of friendship and fancy in several letters to and from select friends. [By John Langhorne, D.D.] 2 vols. Pt 8vo. [Green's *Bibl. Somers.*, iii., 5.] London, 1763

EFFUSIONS of love from Chatelar to Mary, Queen of Scotland; translated from a Gallic manuscript, in the Scotch College at Paris : interspersed with songs, sonnets, and notes explanatory, by the translator. To which is added, Historical fragments, poetry, and remains of the amours, of that unfortunate Princess. [By William Henry Ireland.] 8vo. Pp. x., 223. [Lowndes' *Bibl. Man.*, p. 1502.] London, 1808

EGERIA ; or elementary studies on the progress of nations in political economy, legislation, and government. [By Rev. David Williams.] Vol. I. 8vo. [*Brit. Mus.*]   London, 1803
No more published.

EGLANTINE. By the author of *St Olave's*, etc. [Eliza Tabor, later Mrs Stephenson]. 3 vols. Cr 8vo. [*Brit. Mus.*]   London, 1875

EGO (the) and his own. By Max Stirmer [Johann Caspar Schmidt]. Translated from the German by S. T. Byington. 8vo. Pp. xx., 506. [*Brit. Mus.*]   London, 1912

EGOMET. By E. G. O. [William Teignmouth Shore]. 8vo. Pp. 240.
London, 1904

EGOSOPHY. By the author of *The Prigment*, etc. [Thomas Longueville]. 8vo. Pp. ix., 139. [*Brit. Mus.*]
London, 1892

EGYPT. By Pierre Loti [Captain Louis M. Julien Viaud]. Translated from the French by W. P. Baines. 8vo. [*Brit. Mus.*]   London, 1909

EGYPT ; a descriptive poem with notes. By a traveller [Henry Salt, Consul General in Egypt]. Printed for the author by Alexander Draghi at the European press, 1824. 4to. Pp. 54, [Martin's *Cat.*, p. 315.]
Alexandria, 1824
The first English work printed in Alexandria. Only 50 copies printed—not for sale.

EGYPT Ennis ; or, prisons without walls. By Kelsic Etheridge [W. B. Smith]. 8vo. [Cushing's *Init. and Pseud.*, vol. i., p. 93.] New York, 1876

EGYPT under Ismail Pacha : being some chapters of contemporary history. [By William Blanchard Jerrold.] Pt 8vo. [*D. N. B.*, vol. 29, p. 353.]
London, 1879

EGYPTIAN (an) coquette. By Clive Holland [Charles J. Hankinson]. Cr 8vo. Pp. 222. [*Lond. Lib. Cat.*]
London, 1910

EGYPTIAN dynasties of Manetho. [By Edward Hincks.] 8vo.
Private print, 1863

EGYPTIAN history deduced from monuments still in existence. [By —— Tudor.] 4to. [*Brit. Mus.*]
London, 1840

EGYPTIAN (the) imbroglio. By the author of *Liberal misrule in Ireland* [James Herman De Ricci]. 8th edition. 8vo. [Gladstone *Lib. Cat.*]
Bedford, 1884

EGYPTIAN magic. By S. S. D. D. [Mrs Emery, *née* Florence Farr]. 8vo.
London, [1905 ?]

EIDYLLIA : or, miscellaneous poems. On losing Milton ; an ode. To Isabella ; an ode. The fair matron ; an ode. Virtue's expostulation ; an ode. To adversity ; an ode. Philocles ; a monody. The Muses triumphant over Venus ; a tale. With a hint to the British poets. By the author of *Animadversions upon the Reverend Doctor Brown's three Essays on the Characteristics* ; and of a *Criticism on the late Reverend Mr Holland's Sermons* [Robert Colvill]. 4to. [*Adv. Lib.*]   Edinburgh, 1757
Ascribed also to Robert Andrews.

EIGHT forms of prayer for public social worship, with occasional offices for the administration of Baptism and the Lord's Supper. . . . Composed and compiled by T. B. [Theophilus Browne, M.A., Unitarian]. Fcap 8vo. [Green's *Bibl. Somers.*, vol. i., p. 84.]
Bath, 1803

EIGHT lectures on prophecy. [By John Nelson Darby.] Fcap 8vo.
London, 1883

EIGHT letters between the people called Buchanites, and a teacher near Edinburgh. . . . [By James Purves.] 8vo. Pp. 63. [*D. N. B.*, vol. 47, p. 51.]
Edinburgh, 1785

EIGHT letters concerning the pavement of the metropolis and the adjoining turnpike road. By X. Y. [John Rickman]. [*Brit. Mus.*]
Private print, London, 1817

EIGHT letters on the management of our poor and the general administration of the poor-laws. By an Overseer [Sir George Nicholls, C.B.]. 8vo. [*D. N. B.*]   Nottingham, 1823

EIGHT letters on the subject of the Earl of Selkirk's pamphlet on Highland emigration ; as they lately appeared under the signature of Amicus in one of the Edinburgh newspapers. [By James Gordon, of Craig, advocate.] 8vo. Pp. 59. [*Camb. Univ. Lib.*]   Edinburgh, 1806

EIGHT letters to his Grace the Duke of [Newcastle], on the custom of vail giving in England ; shewing the absurdity, inconveniency, national disreputation, and many pernicious consequences of it to all ranks of the people ; with proposals for an increase of wages, and other advantages to domestic servants. [By Jonas Hanway.] 8vo. Pp. 64. [*Brit. Mus.*]
London, 1760

EIGHT months at Rome during the Vatican Council ; impressions of a contemporary. By Pomponio Leto [Francesco Nobili Vitelleschi, Cardinal]; translated [by Alice E— Kubbard]. 8vo. [*Brit. Mus.*]   London, 1876

EIGHT months on active service ; or a diary of a General Officer of Cavalry [James Thomas Brudenell, Earl of Cardigan] in [the Crimean War]. 1854. 8vo.   London, [1856]

EIGHT or nine wise words about letter writing. By Lewis Carroll [Rev. Charles Lutwidge Dodgson, M.A.]. Fcap 8vo. Pp. 35.   Oxford, 1890
   See note on " Doubtlets."

EIGHT [VIII] qveries upon the late declarations of, and letters from, the army : proposed to all true lovers of their country and parliaments, and conscientious souldiers in the army. [By William Prynne.] 4to. [*Bliss' Cat.*]   London, 1647

EIGHT sets of queries, submitted with an unusual degree of humility to the nobility, lairds, fine gentlemen, fine ladies, tenants, merchants, manufacturers, clergy, and people of Scotland, upon the subject of wool and of the woolen manufacture. By a Peer of the realm [Patrick Murray, 5th Lord Elibank]. 8vo. [*Adv. Lib.*]
                       Edinburgh, 1775

EIGHT (the) volumes of Letters writ by a Turkish spy ; . . . translated into Italian [really written in Italian by Giovanni Paolo Marana], from thence into English. Fcap 8vo. [*Brit. Mus.*]
                       London, 1734
   Later editions in 1753, 1770, etc.

EIGHT weeks in Germany ; comprising narratives, descriptions, and directions for economical tourists. By the Pedestrian [John Aiton, D.D.]. 8vo. [*Adv. Lib.*]   Edinburgh, 1842

EIGHTEEN (the) Christian centuries. By the Rev. James White [John Hill Burton, LL.D.]. 8vo. [*D. N. B.*, vol. 8, p. 10.]   Edinburgh, 1858
   A third edition was published in 1860.

EIGHTEEN imaginary dialogues : second series. By the author of *Experiences of a Convict* [J. F. Mortlock]. 8vo. Pp. 24. [*Camb. Univ. Lib.*]
                       Cambridge, 1868

EIGHTEEN maxims of neatness and order. By Theresa Tidy [Mrs Elizabeth Susanna Graham, *née* Davenport]. Fcap 8vo. [*Courtney's Secrets*, p. 53.]   London, 1845

EIGHTEEN months' imprisonment. By D— S. [Donald Shaw], late Capt. —— Regiment. Pt 8vo. [*Brit. Mus.*]
                       London, 1883

EIGHTEEN sixty-one rhymed to death. [By Henry Campkin.] 8vo. [*Brit. Mus.*]   London, [1862]

EIGHTEENTH century colour-prints. By Frank Danby [Mrs Julia Frankau]. 8vo. [*Lond. Lib. Cat.*] London, 1900

EIGHTH (the) Isthmian of Pindar in English. [By Thomas Tyrwhitt, M.A.] 8vo. [*D. N. B.*, vol. 57, p. 446.]
                       London, 1752

EIGHTH (the) note of the Church examined, viz. sanctity of doctrine. [By John Scot, D.D., rector of St Peter's Poor.] 4to. [Jones' Peck.]
                       London, 1687

EIGHTY years of Republican Government in the United States. By H. Dropper [Louis J. Jennings]. 8vo. [Cushing's *Init. and Pseud.*, vol. i., p. 84.]   London, 1865

EIGHTY - SEVEN ; a Chautauqua story. By " Pansy " [Mrs Isabella Alden, *née* Macdonald]. 8vo. Pp. v., 342.   London, 1887

ΕΙΚΩΝ ΑΚΛΑΣΤΟΣ. The image unbroaken : a perspective of the impudence, falshood, vanities, and prophannes, published in a libell [by John Milton] entitled Εἰκονοκλάστης against Εἰκὼν Βασιλικὴ, or the pourtraicture of his Sacred Majestie in his solitudes and sufferings. [By Joseph Jane.] 4to. [Wood's *Athen. Oxon.*, iv., 644.]
                       N.P., 1651

ΕΙΚΩΝ ΒΑΣΙΛΙΚΗ, or the character of Eglon, king of Moab, and his ministry ; wherein is demonstrated, the advantages of Christianity, in the exercise of civil government. From Judges iii. 22.—And the dirt came out. By the author of *Sermons to asses* [James Murray]. 8vo. [*Bodl.*]
                       Newcastle, 1773

ΕΙΚΩΝ ΒΑΣΙΛΙΚΗ. The Povrtraictvre of His Sacred Maiestie in His solitudes and sufferings. [By Charles I.] 12mo. Pp. 273. [Almack's *Bibl. of the King's Book*; *D. N. B.*, vol. 21, p. 70 ff.]
                       [London], 1648

   Internal evidence favours the view that the King himself composed this work, which is throughout written in the first person, and is pervaded by a spirit eminently dignified and devout, bravely maintained amidst manifold difficulties to which references are made. Those who cannot regard the book as a genuinely Caroline production consider that it is a literary personation, and attribute it to Dr John Gauden, Bishop of Exeter, who at least prepared it for the press and has left some proof of this in his characteristic fondness for a few Greek words with which to begin the titles of his treatises. Nearly fifty editions were soon demanded.

ΕΙΚΩΝ ΜΙΚΡΟ-ΒΙΒΛΙΚΗ, sive Icon libellorum ; or, a critical history of pamphlets : tracing out the rise, growth and different views of all sorts of small tracts or writings, both collectively and singly, in a general and gradual representation of the respective authors, collections and their several editions, &c. ; and in particular, of all those from the beginning of the Reformation, to the latter end of King Henry the Eighth's reign ; especially here in Great-Britain, . . . &c. By a gentleman of the Inns of Court [Myles Davies]. Part I. 8vo. Pp. 436. [*Brit. Mus.*]
                              London, 1715
   This work appeared in 1716 as "Athenae Britannicae, or a critical history of the Oxford and Cambridge writers and writings. . . ."

ΕΙΚΩΝ ΤΟΥ ΘΗΡΙΟΥ, or the image of the beast ; shewing, by a parallel scheme, what a Conformist the Church of Rome is to the pagan, and what a Nonconformist to the Christian Church, in its rites. . . . By T. D. [Thomas Danson]. 4to.   [London], 1684

ΕΙΚΟΝΟΚΛΑΣΤΗΣ, in answer to a book intitl'd Εἰκὼν Βασιλική, the portrature of his sacred majesty in his solitudes and sufferings. The author I. M. [John Milton]. 4to. Pp. 256. [Masson's *Life of Milton*].   London, 1649

EILEEN. [A novel.] By Lucas Cleeve [Mrs Howard Kingscote, *née* Adelina G. I. Wolff]. 8vo. [*Brit. Mus.*]
                              London, 1908

EILY O'Hartigan ; an Irish-American tale of the days of the Volunteers. By "Eblana," author of *The last monarch of Tara* [Teresa J— Rooney]. 8vo. Pp. iii., 309. [S. J. Brown's *Ireland in fiction*.]   Dublin, 1889

ΕΙΡΗΝΙΚΟΝ ; or a peaceable consideration of Christ's peaceful kingdom on earth to come. . . . [By William Sherwin.] 4to. [*Brit. Mus.*]   [London], 1665
   The Preface is signed "Munus"

ΕΙΣ ΘΕΟΣ ΕΙΣ ΜΕΣΙΤΗΣ ; or, an attempt to show how far the notion of the plurality of worlds is consistent with the Scriptures. [By Edward Nares, D.D.] 8vo. [*D. N. B.*, vol. 40, p. 91.]
                              London, 1801
   Later editions are not anonymous.

EKKOES from Kentucky. By Petroleum Vesuvius Nasby [David Ross Locke]. Pt 8vo. [Cushing's *Init. and Pseud.*, vol. i., p. 201.]   Boston, 1888

ΕΚΛΟΓΑΙ, or, excerpts from the ecclesiastical history ; in which some account is given of the Donatists, of the Novatians under Constantine the Great, and some following reigns ; and of the Arians from the council of Nice to the council of Ariminum, in the close of the reign of Constantius. To which some account of the deposition of St Chrysostom is annexed. [By Simon Lowth.] 4to. Pp. xxviii., 216. [*Brit. Mus.*]   London, 1704

ΕΚΣΚΥΒΑΛΑΤΡΟΝ, or the discovery of a most exquisite jewel more precious then diamonds inchased in gold, found in the kennel of Worcester-streets, the day after the fight, and six before the autumnal equinox, anno 1651 ; serving in this place to frontal a vindication of the honour of Scotland from that infamy whereunto the rigid Presbyterian party of that nation, out of their covetousness and ambition, most dissembledly hath involved it. [By Sir Thomas Urquhart.] 8vo. Pp. 284. [*D. N. B.*, vol. 58, p. 48.]
                              London, 1652

EL Tih ; and other poems. [By Frederick W. R. Stewart, Marquis of Londonderry.] 8vo.   London, 1859

ELA ; or, the delusions of the heart : a tale founded on facts. [By Mrs Burke.] Fcap 8vo. [Watt's *Bibl. Brit.*]   London, 1787

ELA the outcast ; or the Gipsy of Rosemary Dell : a romance. . . . [By Thomas Peckett Prest.] 8vo. [*N. and Q.*, 1922, p. 333.]
                              London, [1841]

ELABORATORY (the) laid open ; or, the secrets of modern chemistry and pharmacy revealed ; containing many particulars extremely necessary to be known to all practitioners in medicine. [By Robert Dossie.] 8vo. [*Brit. Mus.*]   London, 1758

ELAM Storm the wolfer ; or, the lost nugget. By Harry Castlemon [Charles A. Fosdick]. Pt 8vo. Pp. 356. [Cushing's *Init. and Pseud.*, vol. i., p. 52.]   Philadelphia, 1895

ELBERT'S return ; or, Foxy at home again. By Francis Forrester [Daniel Wise, D.D.]. Fcap 8vo. Pp. 280. [Cushing's *Init. and Pseud.*, i., 104.]
                              New York, 1893

ELBOW room : a novel without a plot. By Max Adeler [Charles Heber Clark]. Fcap 8vo. [*Lond. Lib. Cat.*]
                              London, 1875

ELDER (the) and his wife. . . . By the author of *Rob Lindsay and his school* [William MacGillivray, W.S.]. Fcap 8vo. [*Signet Lib.*] Edinburgh, 1910

ELDER (an) brother. By Eglanton Thorne [Emily Charlton]. Cr 8vo. Pp. 128. [*Brit. Mus.*] London, 1895

ELDER Logan's story about the Kirks ; a book for the young. By John Strathesk [John Tod, of Lasswade]. Fcap 8vo. Pp. 128. [*Lit. Year Book.*] Edinburgh, 1884

ELDER Logan's story of the United Presbyterian Church. By John Strathesk [John Tod, of Lasswade]. 8vo. Edinburgh, 1896

ELDER (the) Park, Govan ; an account of its gift, and of the erection and unveiling of the statue of John Elder . . . and historical sketches of Govan. [By A— Craig.] 4to. Glasgow, 1891

ELDER'S (the) warning ; a lay of the Convocation. (From the *Edinburgh Evening Post and Scottish Standard*.) [By William Edmonstoune Aytoun, LL.D.] 4to. [*New Coll. Cat.*] [Edinburgh], N.D.

ELDERSHIP (the) of the Church of Scotland, as it was, is, and may be again ; also, the office of deacons : with a model of a home missionary enterprise in connection with, and growing out of, an established and parochial Church. By the editor of the *Scottish Guardian* [Rev. George Lewis]. 8vo. [*New Coll. Cat.*] Glasgow, 1834

ELDEST (the) chick of the R[oya]l brood. By Peter Pindar [C. F. Lawler ?]. 8vo. [*Brit. Mus.*] London, [1813 ?]

ELDEST (the) of seven. By the author of *Katie, the fisherman's daughter* [Emma S. Pratt]. Cr 8vo. London, [1881]

ELDON Drayton ; or, crises intellectual and moral. By Reginald May [J— Lemacks Stokes]. Fcap 8vo. [*Amer. Cat.*] Nashville, Tenn., 1885

ELEAZAR and Naphtaly ; an Hebrew tale, translated from the French [of Jean P. Clavis de Florian] by H. H. Young. Fcap 8vo. [*Brit. Mus.*] London, 1827
   An earlier translation (1816, by J. Jones) gives the author's name.

ELECTION (the). [A novel.] By the author of *Hyacinth O'Gara* [Rev. George Brittaine, of Ardagh]. 8vo. Pp. 331. [S. J. Brown's *Ireland in fiction.*] Dublin, 1841
   Ascribed also to George Delany.

ELECTION (the) ; a musical interlude. [By Miles Peter Andrews.] 8vo. [*Brit. Mus.*] London, 1780

ELECTION (the) : a poem, in seven books. [By John Sterling.] 8vo. [Carlyle's *Life of Sterling.*] London, 1841

ELECTION and reprobation. [By Rev. Thomas Husband Gregg, M.A.] Fcap 8vo. [Copinger's *Bibl. of Predestination*, p. 213.] London, [1869]

ELECTION (an) ball in poetical letters, in the Zomerzetshire dialect, from Mr Inkle, a freeman of Bath, to his wife at Gloucester : with a poetical address to John Miller, Esq., at Bath-Easton Villa. By the author of the *New Bath guide* [Christopher Anstey]. 8vo. [*Watt's Bibl. Brit.*] Dublin, 1776

ELECTION (the) dialogue, between a gentleman and his neighbour in the country, concerning the choice of good members for the next Parliament. [By Benjamin Hoadly, D.D.] 8vo. [*Brit. Mus.*] London, 1710

ELECTION lays. By a Liberal layman [Robert Houstoun]. Fcap 8vo. [*Aberd. Free Lib. Cat.*] Aberdeen, [1886]

ELECTION (the) of aliens into the vacancies in Eton College an unwarrantable practice : to which are now added, two letters to the Rev. Dr Morell ; in which the cavils of a writer in the general Evening Post, and others, are considered and refuted. Part I. By a late Fellow of King's College, Cambridge [Thomas Ashton, D.D.]. 4to. [Nichols' *Lit. Anec.*, iii., 89.] London, 1771
   Part II. was never published.

ELECTION (the) of President of the United States considered. By a citizen [Hon. Timothy Fuller]. 8vo. [Cushing's *Init. and Pseud.*, vol. i., p. 57.] Boston, 1823

ELECTION rhymes. By Matthias Pearson of the Sheepfolds, Monkwearmouth [John William Fletcher, banker]. 8vo. Sunderland, 1871

ELECTIONS (the) to the Hebdomadal Council. A letter to the Rev. C. W. Sandford, M.A., has been addressed on this subject by Goldwin Smith, and may possibly reach a second edition. [By Charles Lutwidge Dodgson, M.A.] 8vo. Oxford, 1866
   A satirical poem.

ELECTORAL corruption and its remedies. [By William Dougal Christie.] 8vo. London, 1867

ELECTORS' (the) mirror; or, a second address to Englishmen, on the triumph of British right over infidel and Papal tyranny. By Henry Hornet, Esq. [James Abbott]. 8vo. [Smale's *Whitby Authors*.] Whitby, 1826

ELECTRA; a story of modern times. By the author of *Rockingham* [Count de Jarnac]; with illustrations by Lord Gerald Fitzgerald. 3 vols. Fcap 8vo. [*Brit. Mus.*] London, 1853

ELECTRA of Sophocles; presented to Her Highnesse the Lady Elizabeth, with an Epilogue shewing the parallell in two poems, the Retvrn and the Restavration. By C. W. [Christopher Wase]. 8vo. [Lowndes' *Bibl. Man.*, p. 2454.] Pp. 72. At the Hague, 1649

ELECTRA pectoris; a novel without a villain. By Spa [Thomas M. Horsburgh]. Fcap 8vo. Pp. 42. Edinburgh, 1897

ELECTRIC gas lighting. By H. S. Norrie [Norman H. Schneider]. Fcap 8vo. [*Amer. Cat.*] New York, 1901

ELECTRIC (the) light of the twentieth century; future probation proved; body, soul, and spirit defined. [By J— P— Pervin.] 8vo. London, 1895 Signed " J. P. P."

ELECTRICITY. [By Alexander Bain.] Chambers's Educational Course. Pt 8vo. Edinburgh, 1848

ELEGANT (an) and lively description of spirituall life and death; delivered in divers sermons in Lincolnes Inne. By J. P. [John Preston], D.D. 4to. Pp. 132. [*Brit. Mus.*] London, 1632

ELEGANT dishes and rare recipes. By E. F. G. [Miss E— F. Gostling]. 8vo. Pp. xiv., 167. [*Brit. Mus.*] London, 1894

ELEGANT epistles. [By Vicesimus Knox.] 8vo. [*Camb. Univ. Lib.*] London, 1790 An enlarged edition appeared in 1807. *See also* " Models of letters. . . ."

ELEGANT extracts in prose, in verse, and epistles. [By Vicesimus Knox, D.D.] 3 vols. 8vo. [Lowndes' *Bibl. Man.*, p. 770.] London, 1783

ELEGANT, instructive, and entertaining extracts, in prose and verse, selected from the best modern authors. [By Vicesimus Knox, D.D.] 6 vols. 8vo. London, 1791

ELEGANT (the) sharper; or the science of villainy display'd : being the genuine history of frauds of George R— ——. By Peter Pindar, junr. [C— F— Lawler]. Fcap 8vo. Pp. 160. [*Brit. Mus.*] London, 1804 Wrongly attributed to John Agg.

ELEGANT tales, histories, and epistles of a moral tendency; on love, friendship, matrimony, conjugal felicity, jealousy, constancy, magnanimity, chearfulness, and other important subjects. By the author of *Woman; or historical sketches of the fair sex* [Rev. John Adams ?]. Fcap 8vo. Pp. 480. [*Brit. Mus.*] London, 1791

ELEGIAC (an) ballad on the funeral of the Princess Charlotte. [By William Hamilton Drummond, D.D.] 8vo. [*D. N. B.*, vol. 16, p. 53.] Dublin, 1817

ELEGIAC (an) epistle from an unfortunate Elector of Germany to his friend Mr Pinchbeck. [By William Mason ?] 8vo. London, 1776

ELEGIAC (an) poem; in different measures, without rhime : to the memory of an amiable and virtuous wife, her disconsolate husband offers this grateful proof of his sincere affection. [By Joseph Strutt.] 4to. [Nichols' *Lit. Anec.*, v. 672.] London, 1782

ELEGIAC (an) poem, sacred to the memory and virtues of the Hon. Sir William Jones, one of the Judges in the Supreme Court . . . in Bengal. . . . [By Rev. Thomas Maurice.] 4to. Pp. 35. [*D. N. B.*, vol. 37, p. 108.] London, 1795

ELEGIAC poems. [By Archb. Richard Chenevix Trench, D.D.] Fcap 8vo. London, 1843 Afterwards (1865) included in a collection of " Poems " with the author's name.

ELEGIÆ. [By James Glassford, of Dugaldstone, advocate.] 4to. N.P., N.D. Private print. The author's name is in the handwriting of Dr David Laing.

ELEGIE (an) on the death of Mr William Dunlop, Principal of the University of Glasgow. [By Rev. James Paul.] Folio. S. Sh. N.P., N.D.

ELEGIE on the death of the Right Hon. Sir James Falconer of Phesdo, one of the Lords of the College of Justice, etc. who dyed the 9th of June 1705. [By William Whyte.] Folio. S. Sh. N.P., N.D.

K

ELEGIE (an) vpon the death of the high and renowned princesse, our late soueraigne Elizabeth. By I. L. [John Lane]. 4to. No pagination. [*Bodl.*]
London, 1603

ELEGIE (an) vpon the death of the renowned Sir Iohn Svthlin [Suckling. By William Norris]. 4to. [Christie-Miller *Cat.*] 4 leaves. London, 1642

ELEGIES and memorials [in verse]. By A. and L. [Arabella and Louisa Shore]. Fcap 8vo. Pp. 53. [*Brit. Mus.*] London, 1890

ELEGIES and sonnets. [By Samuel Knight, M.A., of Trinity College, Cambridge.] Large 4to. Pp. 68. [Watt's *Bibl. Brit.*] London, 1785
Other editions followed, in 1785, 1787.

ELEGIES (the) of C. Pedo Albinovanus, a Latin poet of the Augustan age, with an English version. [By Rev. John Plumptre.] Fcap 8vo. Pp. 121.
Kidderminster, [1807]

ELEGIES of Tyrtæus, translated into English verse ; with notes, and the original text. [By W. Cleaver.] 8vo. Pp. xxiv., 36. [Dyce *Cat.*, ii., 378.]
London, 1761

ELEGIES on different occasions. [By Henry James Pye.] 4to. [Watt's *Bibl. Brit.*] London, 1768

ELEGIES [one in English and three in Latin] on the much lamented death of the Right Honourable [Charles Coote], the Earl of Montrath. [By John Jones, B.A.] 4to. Pp. 8. [Dix and Dugan's *Dubl. Books.*]
Dublin, 1661

ELEGY (an) inscribed to the memory of Thomas Broughall, Esq. By " Yawnoc " [Frederick William Conway]. 8vo. [O'Donoghue's *Poets of Ireland.*] Dublin, 1803
The pen-name is the family name reversed.

ELEGY, occasioned by the sudden summons of a friend from the career of life, 1810. [By Simon Fraser.] 12mo. [*W.*] Inverness, 1811

ELEGY (an) on a family tomb, [by J. J. Brundish] translated into Italian verse. By a friend of the author [John Barlow Seale, of Christ College, Cambridge]. 4to. Pp. 15. [Bartholomew's *Camb. Books.*]
Cambridge, 1783

ELEGY (an) on a storm which happened in West Kent, on the 13th of August 1763. [By William Perfect, M.D., surgeon.] 8vo. London, 1764

ELEGY (an) on Her Grace Elizabeth Duchess of Ormond, who died July the 21st 1684. By E. A., M.A., of Trin. Coll. Dubl. [Edmund Arwaker]. Folio. Pp. 7. [*Bodl.*]
In the Savoy, 1684

ELEGY on Lucky Wood. [By Allan Ramsay.] Folio. S. Sh. N.P., N.D.

ELEGY (an) on the ancient Greek model. [By William Hayley.] 4to. [*Biog. Dram.*] N.P., 1779

ELEGY (an) on Mr Patrige, the almanack-maker, who died on the 29th of March last, 1708. [By Jonathan Swift, D.D.] Reprinted in 1708. Folio. S. Sh. Edinburgh, 1708

ELEGY (an) on the author of the True-born-Englishman ; with an essay on the late storm. By the author of the *Hymn to the pillory* [Daniel Defoe]. 4to. Pp. 60. [Wilson's *Life of Defoe.*]
London, 1704

ELEGY (an) on the death of A. M. Toplady. By T. W. [Th— Wilkins]. 8vo. London, 1778

ELEGY (an) on the death of an amiable young lady ; with an epistle from Menalcas to Lycidas : to which are prefixed, three critical recommendatory letters. [By James Boswell, of Auchinleck.] 4to. Pp. 24. [*Adv. Lib.*] Edinburgh, 1761

ELEGY (an) on the death of David Garrick, Esq. By the author of the *Ode to the warlike genius of great Britain* [Rev. William Tasker, B.A.]. 4to. 6 leaves, unpaged.
London, 1779

ELEGY (an) on the death of Martin Drayson of Eythorne, near Sandwich, who died Sep. 12, 1773, aged 21 years. [By John Stanger, minister of Bessels Green Chapel, near Sevenoaks.] 8vo. Pp. 20. [Smith's *Bibl. Cant.*, p. 196.]
Sevenoaks, 1774

ELEGY (an) on the death of Miss M——s, eldest daughter of D— M—, Esq., of the F— H—, C—, Berkshire ; who died the 8th of July, 1785. By a gentleman of the Inner Temple [George Monck Berkeley]. 4to. Pp. 22.
London, 1786
" Sent to me by Monck Berkeley. S. L."—MS. note by Samuel Lysons in the Dyce copy.

ELEGY (an) on the death of Mr James Bristow, late Fellow of All-Souls. [By Edward Palmer.] 4to. Pp. 10. [*Bodl.*] Oxford, 1667

ELEGY (an) on the death of Richard Reynolds ; with other poems. [By Hannah Young.] 8vo. [Smith's *Cat. of Friends' Books*, i., 88.]
London, 1818

ELEGY (an) on the death of the Honourable Mr Robert Boyle. [By Matthew Morgan, D.C.L.] Folio. Pp. 19.   Oxford, 1692
The author's name is in the handwriting of Wood.

ELEGY (an) on the fears of death. By the author of *The Difference between words reputed synonymous*, etc. [John Trusler, LL.D.]. 4to. [*Brit. Mus.*]
London, [1780 ?]

ELEGY on the late Right Honourable William Pitt. [By Thomas Maurice.] 8vo. [*D. N. B.*, vol. 37, p. 108.]
[London, 1806]
Signed " T. M."

ELEGY (an) on the much lamented death of William Beckford, Esq., late Lord-Mayor of, and representative in Parliament for, the city of London. [By Thomas Chatterton.] 4to. Pp. 14. [Dyce *Cat.*, i., 174.]
London, 1770

ELEGY (an) on the much-to-be-deplored death of . . . the Reverend Mr Nathaniel Collins. . . . [By Cotton Mather, D.D.] 8vo.   Boston, 1685

ELEGY (an) on the usurper O. C. [Oliver Cromwell]. By the author of *Absalom and Achitophel*, published to show the loyalty and integrity of the poet [John Dryden]. Folio. S. Sh.   London, 1681
Postscript signed " J. D."

ELEGY (an), sacred to the memory of Lady Wright, formerly of Ray House, Essex, but late of Bath, who, on the 6th of January, in the year of Jesus Christ, 1802, quitted the dark wilderness of this world for the happy regions of light, bliss, and immortality. By the author of *The celestial companion* [R. Woolsey]. 8vo. [*Gent. Mag.*, June 1803, p. 539.]   [1802 or 1803]

ELEGY (an), supposed to be written on the field of battle. [By Thomas Hancock, M.D.] 8vo. [Smith's *Cat. of Friends' Books*, i., 88.]
London, 1818

ELEGY (an) to the memory of the Rev. William Mason. [By the Rev. Thomas Gisborne.] 4to. [*Brit. Mus.*]
London, 1797

ELEGY (an) to the memory of the Right Honourable William, late earl of Bath.   [By Hugh Kelly.]   4to. [Green's *Bibl. Somers.*, i., 424.]
London, 1765

ELEGY upon the death of Dr Annesley. [By Daniel Defoe.] Folio. [Wilson's *Life of Defoe*, p. 12.] London, 1697

ELEGY (an) upon the death of the late Earl Granville. [By the Hon. Thomas Hervey, M.P.] 8vo.   London, 1767

ELEGY (an) upon the death of the most excellent poet Mr Iohn Cleaveland. [By Francis Vaux.] S. Sh. [*Bodl.*]   N.P., N.D.
The author's name is in the handwriting of Wood.

ELEGY (an) written among the ruins of an abbey. By the author of *The Nun* [Edward Jerningham]. 4to. [*Camb. Univ. Lib.*] London, 1765

ELEGY (an) written among the tombs in Westminster Abbey. [By Reginald Heber, D.D.] 4to. Pp. 12. [Watt's *Bibl. Brit.*] London, 1762

ELEGY (an), written in a Quakers burial ground ; to which is added The country Quaker. [By John Wagstaffe.] Folio. [Smith's *Cat. of Friends' Books*, i., 66.]
London, 1764

ELEGY (an), written on St Mark's eve. [By Richard Cumberland.] 4to. [*Gent. Mag.*, lxxxi., i., 594.]
London, 1754

ELEGY (an) written on the author's revisiting the place of his former residence. [By Rev. John Bidlake, D.D.] 8vo. [Watt's *Bibl. Brit.*]
London, 1788

ELEGY (an) wrote in a country church yard. [By Thomas Gray.] 4to. Pp. 11.   London, 1751
See an imitation in " The Nunnery . . ." and " Evening contemplations . . ." (a parody).

ELEGY (an) wrote under a gallows ; with a preface concerning the nature of elegy. [By Hugh Downman, M.D., of Balliol College.] 4to. Pp. 15. [*Bodl.*]   London, N.D.

ELEMENTARY (the) Education Act : its working and results. By a Wesleyan minister [Rev. J— R— Hargreaves]. 8vo. [*Birm. Cent. Lib.*]
Birmingham, 1872

ELEMENTARY (an) history of architecture of all countries. By N. D'Anvers [Mrs Nancy Bell, *née* Meugens]. 8vo. [*Lond. Lib. Cat.*]
London, 1883

ELEMENTARY history of art : an introduction to ancient and modern architecture, sculpture, painting, and music. By N. D'Anvers [Mrs Nancy Bell, *née* Meugens]. 8vo. Pp. xxiv., 672.   London, 1874

ELEMENTARY (an) history of art ; architecture — sculpture — painting. By N. D'Anvers [Mrs Nancy Bell, *née* Meugens]. 8vo. Pp. xxiv., 672. [*Lond. Lib. Cat.*]   London, 1882

ELEMENTARY (an) history of music. By N. D'Anvers [Mrs Nancy Bell, *née* Meugens]. Cr 8vo. Pp. 101. [*Lond. Lib. Cat.*]   London, 1882

ELEMENTARY (an) history of sculpture of all countries. By N. D'Anvers [Mrs Nancy Bell, *née* Meugens]. 8vo.   London, 1883

ELEMENTARY illustrations of the Celestial mechanics of Laplace. Part the first, comprehending the first book. [By Thomas Young, M.D., F.R.S.] 8vo. [*Brit. Mus.*]   London, 1821
No more published.

ELEMENTARY (an) introduction to the Latin grammar, with practical exercises, after a new and easy method, adapted to the capacities of young beginners. [By George Satis.] 8vo. Pp. vii., 373. [*Aberd. Lib.*]
London, 1795

ELEMENTARY practical mathematics, for technical and industrial classes. By the author of *Commercial arithmetic*, etc. [Thomas D. Craigie, M.A.]. Cr 8vo. Pp. 240.
Edinburgh, 1905
Private information.

ELEMENTARY propositions of the principles of currency. Third edition, to which are added Outlines of political economy. [By Henry Drummond, M.P.] 8vo. Pp. 69. [*Edin. Univ. Cat.*]   London, 1826

ELEMENTARY studies in mercantile law applicable to British India. By a Barrister-at-law and Advocate of the High Court, Calcutta [Harry Stokes]. 8vo. [*Calc. Imp. Lib.*] Calcutta, 1908

ELEMENTARY (an) treatise on electrical traction. . . . By the author of *The golden book of everyday reference in science and art* [J— Fonseca]. Fcap 8vo. [*Brit. Mus.*]   Madras, 1896

ELEMENTARY (an) treatise on Logic, designed chiefly for the use of schools. By the author of *An Antidote to infidelity* [Mrs Portia Young]. 8vo. Pp. 80. [*N. and Q.*, 1863, p. 430.]
London, 1852

ELEMENTS (the) and practice of rigging and seamanship. [By David Steel.] 2 vols. 4to. [*W.*]
London, 1794
The pagination is continuous.

ELEMENTS of algebra. [By William Trail, professor of mathematics, Marischal Coll., Aberdeen.] 8vo. Pp. 69. [*Aberd. Lib.*]   N.P., N.D.

ELEMENTS of algebra. By Leonard Euler: translated from the French [by Francis Horner]. 8vo. 2 vols. [*D. N. B.*, vol. 27, p. 371.]
London, 1797
Later editions give the translator's name.

ELEMENTS (the) of algebra, including Sturm's theorem. By Pierre L. M. Bourdon. Translated from the French [by —— Ross]. 8vo.
Philadelphia, 1844

ELEMENTS (the) of armories. [By Edmund Bolton.] 4to. Pp. 230. [*Bodl.*]   London, 1610
Dedication signed " E. B." The author's name is in the handwriting of Wood.

ELEMENTS (the) of curves : comprising, I. The geometrical principles of the conic sections. II. An introduction to the algebraic theory of curves. Designed for the use of students in the University. [By Baden Powell.] 8vo. [*Brit. Mus.*]   Oxford, 1827

ELEMENTS of English epithets, with illustrations and references to authorities. [By James Jermyn.] 4to. [*W.*]
[London, 1847]

ELEMENTS of English grammar in Sanskrit and English. [By James Robert Ballantyne.] Fcap 8vo. [*D. N. B.*, vol. 3, p. 82.]
Mirzapore, 1847
Signed " J. R. B."

ELEMENTS (the) of Euclid, containing the first six and the eleventh and twelfth books, chiefly from the text of Dr Simson, adapted to elementary instruction by the introduction of symbols. By a member of the university of Cambridge [Jackson Muspratt Williams]. 8vo. [*W.*] London, 1827

ELEMENTS (the) of Euclid explain'd, in a new, but most easie method ; together with the use of every proposition through all parts of the mathematicks. Written in French by that exccellent (*sic*) mathematician, F. Claud. Francis Milliet de Chales, of the Society of Jesus ; and now carefully done into English, and purg'd from a multitude of errors, which had escap'd in the original. [By William Halifax, D.D., of C. C. C., Oxford.] 8vo. Pp. 386. [*Bodl.*]   Oxford, 1685

ELEMENTS (the) of geometry. [By John Dobson.] 2 vols. 4to. [*Edin. Univ. Lib.*]   Cambridge, 1815

ELEMENTS (the) of Greek grammar ; with notes for the use of those who have made some progress in the language. [By Richard Valpy.] Sixth edition. 8vo. Pp. 218. [*Dyce Cat.*, ii., 385.]   London, 1818

ELEMENTS (the) of heraldry. . . . To which is annexed a dictionary of technical terms. By Marc Antoine Porny [Antoine Pyron Du Martre]. 8vo. [*Brit. Mus.*]   London, 1765

ELEMENTS of Japanese grammar. [By Sir Rutherford Alcock, M.R.C.S.] 8vo.   Shanghai, 1861

ELEMENTS of jurisprudence treated of in the preliminary part of a course of lectures on the laws of England. [By Richard Wooddeson, D.C.L.] 4to. [*Brit. Mus.*]   London, 1783

ELEMENTS (the) of morality for the use of children. [By Rev. C— G. Salzmann; translated from the German by Mary Wollstonecraft.] 2 vols. Fcap 8vo.   London, N.D.
   Contemporary attestation.

ELEMENTS of policy, civil and ecclesiastical, in a mathematical method. By M. E. [Matthias Earbery]. 8vo. Pp. 94. [*Bodl.*]   London, 1716

ELEMENTS of practical geometry, for schools and workmen. By the author of *Arithmetic for young children*, etc. [Horace Grant]. 8vo. Pp. viii., 96. [*Bodl.*]   London, 1852

ELEMENTS (the) of reading. . . . [By Thomas Paterson.] 8vo. [*Robertson's Aberd. Bibl.*]   Aberdeen, 1769

ELEMENTS of religion and morality, in the form of a catechism. By W. E. C. [William Ellery Channing] and S. C. T. [Samuel Cooper Thacher]. [*Cushing's Init. and Pseud.*, vol. i., p. 47.]   Boston, 1813

ELEMENTS (the) of short-hand. [By John Mitchell.] 8vo.   London 1787

ELEMENTS of shorthand. [By J— M. R. Le Jeune.] Part I. 8vo. [*Brit. Mus.*]   London, 1891

ELEMENTS of social science. [By Dr George R. Drysdale.] Nineteenth edition. 8vo. [Gladstone *Lib. Cat.*] London, 1880

ELEMENTS of tactics, and introduction to military evolutions for the infantry. By a celebrated Prussian General [—— Saltern]: translated from the original by I. L. [Isaac Landmann]. 8vo. [*Brit. Mus.*]   London, 1787

ELEMENTS of the calculus of finite differences, treated on the method of separation of symbols. [By James Pearson.] 8vo.   London, 1849
   The second edition (1850) gives the author's name.

ELEMENTS (the) of the conic sections, with the sections of the conoids. [By James Devereux Hastler.] Third edition. 8vo. [*Camb. Univ. Lib.*] Cambridge, 1826

ELEMENTS of the natural history of the animal kingdom; being an introduction to the Systema naturæ of Linnæus. [By Charles Stewart.] 2 vols. 8vo. [Lowndes' *Bibl. Man.*, p. 1366.]   Edinburgh, 1801-2

ELEMENTS of the science of botany as established by Linnæus, with examples to illustrate the classes and orders of his system. [By Richard Duppa.] 2 vols. Fcap 8vo. [*Brit. Mus.*]   London, 1809
   Signed " R.D."

ELEMENTS of trigonometry; containing the properties, relations, and calculations of Sines, Tangents, Secants, etc. [By William Emerson.] 8vo.   London, 1749
   Later editions give the author's name.

ELEMENTS of vocal music; being a progressive course of lessons in musical notation and of exercises in singing . . . intended more especially to promote the practice of devotional music. [By Thomas L. Hately.] Oblong fcap 8vo. Pp. 52.   Edinburgh, 1868
   Private information.

ELENA. By Evelyn B. Warde [William Harrison Woodward]. Pt 8vo. [*Lond. Lib. Cat.*]   London, 1910

ELENA : the story of a Russian woman. By Robert Appleton [Roman I. Zubof]. Pt 8vo. [*Amer. Cat.*]
                    New York, 1884

ELEONORA : a novel, in a series of letters; written by a female inhabitant of Leeds, in Yorkshire [Mrs A—— Gomersall]. 2 vols. Fcap 8vo. [*Watt's Bibl. Brit.*]   London, 1789

ELEPHANT (the) tamer. [By Henry Llewellyn Williams.] 8vo.
                    London, [1890]

ELEUSINIA ; a poem upon the nature, condition, affections and expectations of the human soul. [By Richard Trott Fisher.] Cr 8vo. Pp. 225.
                    London, 1836

ELEVATION (the) of the soul to God, by means of spiritual considerations and affections : translated from the French of Abbé B. [Barthelemy Beaudrand] by R. P. [Robert Plowden, S.J.]. Second edition. Fcap 8vo. 2 vols. [Oliver's *Collections*.]
                    Edinburgh, 1792

ELEVEN opinions about Mr H——y [Harley]; with observations. [By Daniel Defoe.] 8vo. [Wilson's *Life of Defoe*, p. 126.]   London, 1711

ELEVEN years at farm work. [By John Taylor.] 8vo. [*Robertson's Aberd. Bibl.*]   Aberdeen, 1879

ELEVENTH (the) epistle of the first book of Horace, imitated, and addressed to a young physician then on his travels. By S. P. [Rev. Samuel Pullen, A.M. (T.C.D.)]. 8vo. Pp. 15. [O'Donoghue's *Poets of Ireland*.] Dublin, 1749
Wrongly attributed to Jonathan Swift.

ELEVENTH (the) hour. By a consumptive [Robert S. Coffin]. 8vo. [Cushing's *Init. and Pseud.*, vol. i., p. 66.] Boston, 1827

ELEVENTH (the) hour; or a death-bed repentance. [By Rev. John Adey.] Fcap 8vo. [F. Boase's *Mod. Brit. Biog.*, i., col. 24.] London, 1835

ELEVENTH (the) note of the Church examined, viz. The glory of miracles. [By Nathaniel Resbury, D.D., minister of Putney.] 4to. [Jones' Peck, p. 438.] London, 1687

ELF (the) errant; a fairy tale. By Moira O'Neill [Mrs Skrine, *née* Nesta Higginson]. 8vo. [O'Donoghue's *Poets of Ireland*.] London, 1902

ELFINELLA, or, home from fairyland: Lord and Lady Russell. [Plays.] By Ross Neil [Isabella Harwood]. 8vo. [*Lond. Lib. Cat.*] London, 1876

ELFREIDE; a romance of the Rhineland. By George Taylor [Professor Adolf Hausrath]. 2 vols. Cr 8vo. [*Brit. Mus.*] London, 1888

ELFRIDA; written on the model of the antient Greek tragedy. [By Rev. William Mason, M.A.] 8vo. [*D. N. B.*, vol. 36, p. 440.] London, 1752

ELGIN and Phigaleian marbles. [By Sir Henry Ellis.] 2 vols. 12mo. [*Lib. of Ent. Knowledge*.] London, 1833

ELIA. Essays which have appeared under that signature in the London Magazine. [By Charles Lamb.] 8vo. Pp. 343. [*Brit. Mus.*] London, 1823

ELIDURE and Edward; two historical dramatic sketches. [By Mrs E. Fletcher.] 8vo. Pp. xii., 125. [Martin's *Cat.; Bodl.*] London, 1825
Dedication, "To my grandchildren," signed "E. F."

ELIEZER; or suffering for Christ: a tale of Jewish life. [By Charlotte Elizabeth Stern.] 8vo.
London, [1877]

ELIHU'S reply: occasioned by the Affectionate Address of W. Mason on Bible politics. By J. T. [John Towers]. Fcap 8vo. [*Brit. Mus.*]
London, 1775

ELIJAH. By the author of *Balaam* and *Modern fanaticism unveiled* [Mrs Thalia S. Henderson, *née* Kennion]. Fcap 8vo. London, 1833
Mistakenly ascribed to Isaac Taylor.

ELIJAH: a poem. By a lady [Miss R— Richings]. 8vo. Pp. 47.
London, 1818

ELIJAH, and other poems. By B. M. [Mrs Barbara Miller Macandrew], author of *Ezekiel*, and other poems. Square 12mo. Pp. 142. [*Brit. Mus.*]
London, 1880

ELIJAH the Tishbite's supplication when presented the likeness of hand &c. (1 Kings, xviii.) [By Lady Eleanor Douglas.] 4to. N.P., 1650
At the end, said to be "by Eleanor Tichet." The authoress, who believed herself to be a prophetess, was Lady Eleanor Audley (daughter of Lord George Audley, Lord Touchet and Earl of Castlehaven), who married first Sir John Davies and afterwards —— Douglas. [*W.*]

ELIJAH'S mantle; being verses occasioned by the death of that illustrious statesman, the Right Honourable William Pitt. . . . The sixth edition, corrected by the author [James Sayers]. 8vo. [*Camb. Univ. Lib.*]
London, 1807
Generally attributed to Canning. But John Taylor, in the Records of his own life, vol. 1, p. 41, says it was written by Mr James Sayers, celebrated for his talents as a caricaturist. The prefatory address, signed "J. B.," is not by Sayers.

ELIJER Goff, his Christmas book. [By William Dawes, architect.] 8vo. [Cushing's *Init. and Pseud.*, vol. i., p. 118.] London, 1872

ELIJER Goff; his travels, trubbles, and other amoozements. [By William Dawes.] Second edition. 8vo.
London, 1872

ELIJER Goff's great fite. [By William Dawes.] 8vo. London, 1881

ELIJER Goff's kronikle of a king. [By William Dawes]. 8vo. London, 1881

ELIM and Maria; a pastoral tragedy. [By Thomas Muir.] 8vo.
Glasgow, 1792

ELINOR Fulton. By the author of *Three experiments of living*, etc. [Mrs Hannah F. Lee]. Fcap 8vo. [*Brit. Mus.*] Boston, [Mass.], 1837

ELIOT, Hampden, and Pym; or a Reply of "The author of a book," entitled "Commentaries on the life and reign of Charles the First" to the author of a book entitled "Some memorials of John Hampden, his party and his times" [Lord Nugent]. [By Isaac D'Israeli.] 8vo. [*W.*]
London, 1832

ELISA Lynch. By Orion [Hector F—Varela]. 8vo. [Cushing's *Init. and Pseud.*, vol. ii., p. 219.]
Buenos Ayres, 1870

ELISA, or an elegie upon the unripe decease of Sr. Antonie Irby: composed at the request (and for a monument) of his surviving ladie. [By Phineas Fletcher.] 4to. [*D. N. B.*, vol. 19, p. 317]. Printed by the printers to the Vniversitie of Cambridge, 1633.
Dedication signed " P. F." *See* " The Purple Island ".

ELISHA'S visit to Gilgal, and his healing the pot of potage, symbolically explain'd: a sermon [on 2 Kings, iv. 38] preached before the Warden and College of All-Souls, in the University of Oxford, on Friday the second of November, 1759; being the anniversary of the founder's commemoration. [By Benjamin Buckler, D.D.] 8vo. [*Bodl.*]   London, [1759]

ELIZA; an elegy. [By G. Houghton.] 8vo. [*Brit. Mus.*]   London, 1800

ELIZA comes to stay; a farce, in three acts. By Henry Vernon Esmond [Henry Vernon Jack]. 8vo. Pp. 79. [*Brit. Mus.*]   London, [1913]

ELIZA Powell; or trials of sensibility; a series of original letters collected by a Welsh curate [Edward Davies]. 2 vols. 12mo. [*Gent. Mag.*, ci., 645.]
London, 1795

ELIZABETH and her German garden. [By Mary Beauchamp, later Countess Russell.] Cr 8vo. Pp. 175. [*Brit. Mus.*]   London, 1898

ELIZABETH; and other sketches. By the author of *Miss Molly* [Beatrice May Butt]. 8vo. [*Brit. Mus.*]
Edinburgh, 1889

ELIZABETH de Bruce. By the author of *Clan-Albin* [Mrs Christian Isobel Johnstone]. 3 vols. 8vo. [*Adv. Lib.*]   Edinburgh, 1827

ELIZABETH, Empress of Austria: a memoir . . . By A. De Burgh [Edward Morgan Alborough]. 8vo. Pp. 383.
London, 1899

ELIZABETH Evanshaw; a sequel of " Truth, a novel." [By William Pitt Scargill ?] 3 vols. Fcap 8vo. [*Brit. Mus.*]   London, 1827

ELIZABETH in her holy retirement; an essay to prepare a pious woman for her lying in, or maxims and methods of piety to direct and support an handmaid of the Lord who expects a time of travail. [By Cotton Mather.] Fcap 8vo. [*W.*]   Boston in N.E., 1710

ELIZABETH of England; a drama. By G. [Charles Gulland]. 8vo. Pp. 68.   Cupar-Fife, 1883

ELIZABETH; or, cloud and sunshine. By Henley I. Arden [Henrietta Knight]. 8vo. Pp. 207. [*Brit. Mus.*]
Edinburgh, 1891

ELIZABETH, or, the exiles of Siberia; a tale, founded on truth. [Translated from the French of Sophie Ristaud Cottin.] 12mo. Pp. 180. [*Bodl.*]
Dublin, 1825
Many editions were issued.

ELIZABETH, or the exiles of Siberia [from the French of Sophie R. Cottin]. An entire new translation, with geographical notes; to which is added the authentic history of Miss Moreton, and the Faithful Cottager; also Paul and Virginia [translated from the French of Jacques H. B. de Saint-Pierre]. 8vo. [*Brit. Mus.*]   London, [1821]

ELIZABETH, Princess Palatine and Abbess of Herford, a sister of Prince Rupert. By Elizabeth Godfrey [Jessie Bedford]. 8vo. Pp. 380. [*Lond. Lib. Cat.*]   London, 1909

ELIZABETHA quasi vivens. Eliza's funerall: a fewe Aprill drops, showred on the hearse of dead Eliza; or the funerall teares of a true hearted subiect. By H. P. [Henry Petowe]. Fcap 4to. [Christie-Miller *Cat.*]   London, 1603

ELIZABETHAN (an) Cardinal: William Allen. By Martin Haile [Marie Halle]. 8vo. Pp. 408. [*Adv. Lib.*] London, 1914

ELIZABETH'S children. [By Margaret Westrop, later Mrs Sydney Stacey.] 8vo. Pp. 364. London, 1903

ELKSWATAWA, or the prophet of the West, a tale of the frontier. [By —— French.] 2 vols. Fcap 8vo. [*Brit. Mus.*]   New York, 1836

ELLA; or, turning over a new leaf. By Walter Aimwell [William Simonds]. Fcap 8vo. [Cushing's *Init. and Pseud.*, vol. i., p. 8.]   New York, 1885

ELLAUNA; a legend of the thirteenth century, in four cantos, with notes, etc. By " Mary " [Mary St John]. 8vo. [O'Donoghue's *Poets of Ireland.*]
Dublin, 1815

ELLEN Braye; or, the fortune-teller. [By Miss —— Blackwell.] 2 vols. Fcap 8vo. [*Adv. Lib.*] London, 1841

ELLEN Clinton; or, the influence of a loving spirit. [By Mrs——Woodward.] Fcap 8vo. [Kirk's *Supp.*] London, 1867

ELLEN Fitzarthur; a metrical tale, in five cantos. [By Mrs Caroline Anne Southey, *née* Bowles.] 8vo. Pp. vii., 134. [*Brit. Mus.*]   London, 1820

ELLEN Gray; or, the dead maiden's curse. By the late Dr Archibald Macleod [really the Rev. William Lisle Bowles, M.A.]. 8vo. Pp. xiv., 40. [Cushing's *Init. and Pseud.*, vol. i., p. 181.]   London, 1828

ELLEN Montgomery's book-shelf. By
the author of *The wide, wide world*,
etc. [Susan Warner]. New edition.
Cr 8vo. Pp. 480. [*Brit. Mus.*]
London, 1905

ELLEN; or, the young godmother. . . .
By a young lady [Alicia Catherine
Mant]. 8vo. [Cushing's *Init. and
Pseud.*, vol. ii. p. 157.]
Southampton, 1812

ELLEN Terry [actress]. By Christopher Saint John [Miss —— Marshall].
8vo.   London, 1907

ELM-TREE (the) on the Mall; a novel.
By Anatole France [Jacques Anatole
Thibault]. Translated from the French
by M. P. Willocks. Cr 8vo. [*Brit.
Mus.*]   London, 1910

ELOCUTION and the art of acting.
Common sense rules. By Walter
Bentley [Walter Begg]. 8vo. Pp. 16.
Falkirk, [1888]

ELOGIUM famæ inserviens Jacci Etonensis, sive Gigantis; or, the praises
of Jack of Eton, commonly called
Jack the Giant: collected into Latin
and English metre, after the manner
of Thomas Sternhold, John Hopkins,
John Burton, and others: to which
is added a Dissertation on the Burtonic
style. By a Master of Arts [William
King, LL.D., St Mary's Hall, Ox-
ford]. 8vo. Pp. viii., 96. [Nichols'
Lit. Anec., ii., 223.]   Oxford, 1750

ELOISA en deshabille; being a new
version of that lady's celebrated Epistle
to Abelard, done into familiar English metre by a Lounger. To which is
prefixed a dedicatory address to that
respectable fraternity of which the
author has the honour to be an unworthy member. [By John Matthews,
M.D., of Belmont, Herefordshire.]
4to. Pp. 35. [*Brit. Mus.*]
London, 1801
Ascribed also, doubtfully, to Professor
Porson and —— Coffin. The first edition
appeared in 1780.

ELOISA; or a series of original letters.
By Jean Jacques Rousseau. Trans-
lated from the French [by William
Kenrick, LL.D.]. 4 vols. Fcap 8vo.
[*D. N. B.*, vol. 31, p. 17.]
Dublin, 1761

ELOISE; and other poems, on several
occasions. By a young lady [Mary
Panton?]. 8vo.   Leith, 1815

ELOPEMENT (the); or perfidy
punished: [A novel. By Henry
Colton?]. 3 vols. Fcap 8vo.
London, 1771

ELOPEMENT (the); or |the deadly
struggle. [A novel. By Rev. John
Humphrey St Aubyn, B.A.] 3 vols.
Fcap 8vo. [*Camb. Univ. Lib.*]
London, 1838

ELOQUENCE (the) of the British
Senate; or, select specimens from the
speeches of the most distinguished
Parliamentary speakers, from the beginning of the reign of Charles I. to
the present time. With notes biographical, critical, and explanatory.
[By William Hazlitt.] 2 vols. 8vo.
London, 1807

ELSEFAIR and Evander; a poem, by
S. P. [Stephen Poynter?], founded on
fact; being an historical narrative of
two unfortunate lovers whom the
author relieved in Carolina in the
year 1766. 4to.   London, 1774.

ELSIE. Translated from the German of
Wilhelm Heimburg [Martha Behrens].
Pt 8vo. [Cushing's *Init. and Pseud.*,
vol. i., p. 128.]   Chicago, 1891

ELSIE; a lowland sketch. By A. C. M.
[Agnes C. Maitland]. 8vo. Pp. viii.,
326. [*Brit. Mus.*]   London, 1875

ELSIE Lee; or, impatience cured;
and other tales. [By George Mogridge.] Fcap 8vo. [*Brit. Mus.*]
London, [1868]

ELSIE Macgregor; or a maid of the
mine. By Ramsay Guthrie [Rev.
John G. Bowran]. Cr 8vo. Pp. 168.
[*Meth. Who's Who.*]   London, 1904

ELSIE Venner; a romance of destiny.
By the author of *The Autocrat of
the breakfast table* [Oliver Wendell
Holmes]. 8vo. [Kirk's *Supp.*]
Boston, [Mass.], 1861

ELSIE'S auntie; or bearing one
another's burdens. [By Clara Main.]
8vo. Pp. 208.   London [1886]

ELTHAM (the) tragedy reviewed. By
C. [Mrs Camilla Dufour Crosland,
née Toulmin]. 8vo. [Cushing's *Init.
and Pseud.*, vol.ii., p.21.] London, 1871

ELUCIDATIONS of Dr Hampden's
theological statements. [By John
Henry Newman, D.D.] 8vo. [*Bodl.*]
Oxford, 1836
See also "Dr Hampden's past and pre-
sent statements . . . ."

ELUCIDATIONS of interesting passages in the sacred volume, drawn from
the works of celebrated commentators
and travellers; edited by the authors of
The odd volume [Misses Corbett]. 2
vols. Fcap 8vo.   Edinburgh, 1835

ELUSIVE (the) Pimpernel; a romance.
By Baroness Orczy [Mrs Montagu
Barstow]. Cr 8vo. Pp. 352.
London, 1908

ELVIRA ; a tragedy, acted at the Theatre-Royal in Drury-Lane. [By David Mallet.] 8vo. [*Biog. Dram.*]
London, 1763

ELVIRA; or, the worst not always true: a comedy, written by a person of quality [George Digby, Earl of Bristol]. 4to. Pp. 91. [*Biog. Dram.*]
London, 1667

ELYSIAN interlude, in prose and verse, of Rowley and Chatterton in the shades. [By Thomas James Mathias, M.A.] 8vo. [*D. N. B.*, vol. 37, p. 427.]
London, 1782

ELYSII Campi, a Paradice of Delights ; or an Elixir of Comforts offered to believers, in two short discourses. . . . By R. W. [Robert Wyne], sometime Pastor of Tamerton, in Devon. 12mo. [Calamy's *Nonconf. Mem.*, Palmer's ed., ii., 77.]
London, 1671

EMANCIPATION [of Catholics] ; a dialogue. [By Thomas Kelly.] Fcap 8vo.
London, N.D., [1820 ?]

EMANCIPATION (the) Bill examined. By a friend to emancipation [John Clutton, M.A.]. 8vo. [*Bodl.*]
Hereford, 1825

EMANCIPATION (the) of the soil and free trade in land. [By Robert Strong ?]. 8vo.
Edinburgh, 1845

EMANUEL ; or, Paradise regained : an epic poem, in nine books. [By James Ogden.] 8vo. Pp. 160. [*Brit. Mus.*]
Manchester, 1797

EMANUEL Swedenborg, and other poems. By M. A. C. [Mrs Anne Cursham]. 8vo.
London, [1832]

EMANUEL Swedenborg as a man of science, a mathematician and philosopher of nature, as a civilian, seer, and theologian . . . with a brief review of all his works. [By W— M. Fernald.] [*Brit. Mus.*]
Boston, [Mass.], 1860

EMANUEL Swedenborg ; the spiritual Columbus : a sketch. By U. S. E. [William Spear]. 8vo.
London, 1877

EMBASSIES and foreign courts : a history of diplomacy. By "The roving Englishman," author of the *Pictures from the battle fields*, etc. [Eustace C. Grenville Murray]. 8vo. [*Brit. Mus.*]
London, 1885

EMBASSY (the) case. By Headon Hill [Francis Edward Grainger]. Cr 8vo. Pp. 311. [*Lond. Lib. Cat.*]
London, 1915

EMBASSY (the) ; or, the key to a mystery : an historical romance. Being the second series of the Chronicles of the Bastile. [By Louis Alexis Chamerovzow.] 3 vols. Fcap 8vo. [*Bodl.*]
London, 1846

EMBASSY (an) to Provence. By Ivory Black [Thomas Allibone Janvier]. Pt 8vo. [Cushing's *Init. and Pseud.*, vol. i., p. 36.]
New York, 1893

EMBLEM (the) of ingratitude ; a true relation of the unjust, cruel, and barbarous proceedings against the English at Amboyna in the East Indies, by the Netherlandish Governour and Council there. [By —— Beaumont.] Fcap 8vo.
London, 1672

EMBLEMS of Jesus. [By Peter Grant, D.D.] Fcap 8vo.
Edinburgh, 1860

EMBLEMS of rarities ; or choyce observations out of worthy histories of many remarkable passages and renowned action of divers Princes and severall nations. . . . Collected by D. L. [Donald Lupton]. 12mo. [Jaggard's *Index*, ii.]
London, 1636

EMBLEMS, with elegant figures newly published. By J. H. [John Hall, Esquire]. 12mo. Pp. 122. [Lowndes' *Bibl. Man.*, p. 978.]
London, [1648]

EMBROIDERED (the) banner, and other marvels. By the author of *The Horse Guards* [Lieut.-Colonel Richard Hort]. 8vo. [*Brit. Mus.*]
London, 1850

EMERALD and ermine ; a tale of the Argoät. By the author of *The Martyrdom of an Empress* [Margaret Cunliffe Owen]. 8vo. Pp. 336. [*Brit. Mus.*]
London, 1907

EMERALD (the) wreath [being essays and poems by Patrick F. White, Mus. Doc.]. 8vo. [F. Boase's *Mod. Brit. Biog.*, vi., col. 852.]
Dublin, N.D., [c. 1850]

EMERALD (the) wreath [pieces in prose and verse]. By "Caviare" [John Francis O'Donnell, journalist]. 8vo. [O'Donoghue's *Poets of Ireland.*]
Dublin, 1865

EMERSON ; his life and writings. By January Searle [George Searle Phillips, B.A.]. Fcap 8vo. [*D. N. B.*, vol. 45, p. 201.]
London, 1855

EMERSON'S Orations to the Modern Athenians ; or, Pantheism. Being a glance at the chimera of the oracle of the woods. By Civis [Alexander Dunlop]. 8vo.
Edinburgh, 1848

EMIGRANT (an) boy's story. By Ascott R. Hope [Ascott Robert Hope Moncrieff]. 8vo. Pp. 128. [*Lit. Year Book.*]
London, [1889]

EMIGRANT (the) Churchman. By a pioneer of the wilderness [Rev. —— Rose]. 8vo. [Cushing's *Init. and Pseud.*, vol. i., p. 235.]
London, 1849

EMIGRANT (the) family; or, the story of an Australian settler. By the author of *Settlers and convicts* [Alexander Harris]. 3 vols. 8vo. [*Adv. Lib.*] London, 1849

EMIGRANT (the) to North America; from memoranda of a settler in Canada: being a compendium of useful practical hints to emigrants. . . . By an emigrant farmer [Rev. Joseph Abbott]. 8vo. [Cushing's *Init. and Pseud.*, vol. i., p. 90.] Edinburgh, 1844

EMIGRANTS' (the) handbook, being a guide to the various fields of emigration in all parts of the globe. [By John Cassell.] 8vo. [*Brit. Mus.*] London, 1852

EMIGRATION. By an English farmer in America [Joseph Pickering]. 8vo. [Cushing's *Init. and Pseud.*, vol. ii., 52.] London, 1830

EMIGRATION for the million: being the digest of a plan for more equally locating the population of Great Britain and Ireland throughout the British Empire. By Gershom [Alfred George Goodwyn]. 8vo. Pp. 35. [*Brit. Mus.*] London, 1849

EMIGRATION from Ireland, and immigration into the United States. [By Mathew Carey.] 8vo. Philadelphia, 1828

EMIGRATION, past and future; or the book of the Cape; edited by the author of *Five years in Kafirland* [Harriet Ward]. 8vo. Pp. vii., 279. [*Brit. Mus.*] London, 1849

EMIGRATION to America candidly considered: in a series of letters from a gentleman resident there [Thomas Clio Rickman] to his friend in England. 8vo. [*Brit. Mus.*] London, 1798

EMILIA D'Aubigné; a novel. By the author of *Ela, or the delusions of the heart* [Mrs Burke]. Fcap 8vo. [Watt's *Bibl. Brit.*] London, 1790

EMILIA Wyndham. By the author of *Two old men's tales*, etc. [Mrs Anne Marsh-Caldwell]. 3 vols. Fcap 8vo. [*D. N. B.*, vol. 36, p. 219.] London, 1846

EMILIUS; or a treatise of education. By Jean Jacques Rousseau; translated from the French [by William Kenrick, LL.D.]. 3 vols. Fcap 8vo. [*D. N. B.*, vol. 31, p. 17.] Edinburgh, 1763

EMILY of New Moon. [A novel.] By L. M. Montgomery [Letitia and M— Montgomery]. Cr 8vo. [*Brit. Mus.*] London, 1923

EMINENT men and popular books. [By Samuel Lucas.] From *The Times.* 8vo. [*N. and Q.*, 5 Dec. 1868, p. 547.] London, 1859
Ascribed also to Samuel Phillips, LL.D.

EMINENT women of the age: being narratives. By Grace Greenwood [Sara Jane Clarke, later Mrs Lippincott]. 4to. [Cushing's *Init. and Pseud.*, vol. i. p. 120.] Boston, 1868

EMIR Malek, prince of the Assassins; an historical novel of the thirteenth century. [By John Henry Barrow.] 3 vols. Fcap 8vo. [*Camb. Univ. Lib.*] London, 1827

EMLYN. [A novel.] By Allen Raine [Mrs Beynon Puddicombe, *née* Anne A. Evans]. 8vo. [*Lond. Lib. Cat.*] London, 1905

EMMA; a novel. By the author of *Pride and prejudice* [Jane Austen]. 3 vols. Fcap 8vo. [*D. N. B.*, vol. 2, p. 260.] London, 1816

EMMA Calvé. By A. Gallus [Arthur Wisner]. 4to. [*Amer. Cat.*] New York, 1902

EMMA Cheyne: a prose idyll of English life. By Ellis Brandt [Peter Bayne, LL.D.]. 8vo. [*D. N. B.*, First Supp., vol. i., p. 147.] London, 1875

EMMA Corbett; or, the miseries of Civil War: founded on some recent circumstances which happened in America. By the author of *Liberal opinions* [Samuel Jackson Pratt]. 8vo. Pp. iv., 304. [Green's *Bibl. Somer.*, i., 123.] Dublin, 1780

EMMA de Lissau; a narrative of striking vicissitudes and peculiar trials with notes . . . illustrative of the manners and customs of the Jews. [By Mrs Amelia Bristow.] 2 vols. Fcap 8vo. [*Brit. Mus.*] London, 1828

EMMA Mayfield; or, the rector's daughter. By an author of celebrity [Thomas Frost]. 8vo. [*Brit. Mus.*] London, [1858?]

EMMA; or recollections of a friend. By M. A. K. [Mary Anne Kelty]. 8vo. [*Brit. Mus.*] London, 1850

EMMA Stanley outdone: an original melodrama. By Sir Charles Rockingham [Philippe F. A. de Rohan-Chabot, Count de Jarnac]. 8vo. Pp. 15. [*Brit. Mus.*] Worksop, private print, 1867

EMMANUEL! A poem. By a graduate of Oxford [George Hughes, M.A.]. Fcap 8vo. Pp. 45. [*Adv. Lib.*] London, 1817

EMMANUEL ; a poem. By a lady [Miss E— Colthurst]. Fcap 8vo. [O'Donoghue's *Poets of Ireland*.]
Cork, 1833

EMMANUEL manifested ; or, the two natures of Christ clearly distinguished in their acts and effects. By A. C. [Ambrose Clappe]. Fcap 8vo. Pp. 97. [Watt's *Bibl. Brit.*]   London, 1655

EMMANUEL Swedenborg : a lecture. By a Bible Student [Rev. John Hyde.] 8vo.   London, 1872
Other editions followed.

EMMA'S cross, a tale. By the author of *Joe Baker*, etc. [Mrs Gertrude Parsons, *née* Hext]. 8vo. Pp. 160. [Boase and Courtney's *Bibl. Corn.*, ii., 426.]   London, N.D., [1859]

EMMY Lou ; her book and heart. By George M. Martin [Mrs Attwood R. Martin]. Fcap 8vo. [*Brit. Mus.*]
New York, 1902

EMMY Lou's road to grace ; being a little pilgrim's progress. By George Madden Martin [Mrs Attwood R. Martin]. 8vo. Pp. ix., 305. [*Brit. Mus.*]   New York, 1916

EMOTIONAL moments. [A novel.] By Sarah Grand [Mrs Haldane M'Fall, *née* Frances Elizabeth Clark]. 8vo. [*Lond. Lib. Cat.*]   London, 1908

EMPEDOCLES on Etna, and other poems. By A. [Matthew Arnold]. 8vo. [*D. N. B.*, First Supp., vol. I, p. 71.]   London, 1852

EMPEROR'S (the) boys. [A story.] By Ismay Thorn [Edith C. Pollock]. Pt 8vo. [*Brit. Mus.*] London, [1884]

EMPEROR'S (the) candlesticks ; a tale. By Baroness Orczy [Mrs Montagu Barstow]. Cr 8vo. Pp. 288.
London, 1905

EMPIRE. By Basil Ewes [P— J. Mackie, of Corraith]. 8vo. Pp. 392.
Stirling, 1906

EMPIRE (the) of music, and other poems. By Alfred Lee [John Clark Ferguson]. Fcap 8vo. [*Brit. Mus.*]
London, 1849
A second edition, enlarged, with the author's real name, was published in 1850, under the title of " The pleasures of music and other poems."

EMPLOYERS and employed. . . . By an arbitrator [T. H. Williams]. Fcap 8vo. [*Manch. Free Lib.*]
Manchester, 1856

EMPRESS (the) of Morocco ; a farce, acted by His Majesties servants. [By Thomas Duffet.] 4to. Pp. 36. [*Biog. Dram.*]   London, 1674

EMPRESS (the) of the Andes. By Florence Warden [Florence Alice Price, later Mrs George E. James]. 8vo. Pp. 330. [*Brit. Mus.*] London, 1909

EMPTY (the) heart. By Marion Harland [Mary Virginia Hawes, later Mrs Terhune]. Fcap 8vo. [Kirk's *Supp.*]   New York, 1871

EMPYREAN. [By James Alexander Smith.] 8vo. Pp. x., 165. [*Brit. Mus.*]   London, 1861

ENAMOURED (the) spirit ; a novel, translated from the French ["Le diable amoureux" of Jacques Cazotte]. Fcap 8vo.   London, 1798

ENCHANTED. [A novel.] By Curtis Yorke [Mrs W. S. Richmond Lee, *née* —— Jex-Long]. Cr 8vo. Pp. 320. [*Lond. Lib. Cat.*]   London, 1916

ENCHANTED (the) April. By the author of *Elizabeth and her German Garden* [Countess Russell, *née* Mary Beauchamp]. Cr 8vo. London, 1922

ENCHANTED (the) plants : fables in verse. [By Mrs Montolieu.] 8vo. [*Brit. Mus.*]
London, private print, 1800

ENCHANTED (the) ship : a story of mystery, with a lot of imagination. By R. Andom [Alfred Wilson Barrett]. Cr 8vo. Pp. 288. [*Brit. Mus.*]
London, 1908

ENCHANTED (the) wood ; a legendary drama, in three acts [prose and verse. By Samuel L. Francis]. 8vo. [*Brit. Mus.*]   London, 1792

ENCHANTED (the) woods ; and other essays on the genius of places. By Vernon Lee [Violet Paget]. 8vo. Pp. 332. [*Lond. Lib. Cat.*] London, 1904

ENCHANTER (the) ; or, love and magic : a musical drama as it is performed at the Theatre-Royal in Drury-Lane. [By David Garrick.] The music composed by Mr Smith. 8vo. [*Biog. Dram.*] London, 1760

ENCHEIRIDION (the) ; daily hours of private prayer, sacramental and other devotions. . . . Translated and arranged by a layman of the Church of England [John David Chambers]. Fcap 8vo. [*Brit. Mus.*] London, 1870
Signed " J. D. C."

ENCHEIRIDION geographicum ; or, a manual of geography : being a description of all the empires, kingdoms, and dominions of the earth ; shewing their situation, bounds, dimensions, commodities, ancient and modern governments, divisions, chief cities, religions, languages, chief rivers, archbishopricks, bishopricks, and universities. Collected from the best books on that subject. By M. S. [Matthew Symson, M.A.]. 8vo. No pagination.   Edinburgh, [1704]
The author's name is in the handwriting of Dr David Laing.

ENCHIRIDION clericum; or the preacher's guide [in verse], in two parts: I. The art of getting up sermons; II. Delivery and chanting. [By —— Holmes.] 8vo. London, 1812

ENCHIRIDION controversiarum; or a briefe manuele of controversies. By L. O. [Lewis Owen?]. 12mo. [*Camb. Univ. Lib.*] London, 1633

ENCHIRIDION of faith, in a dialogue concerning Christian religion. [By Christopher Davenport.] Printed under the name of Francis Coventrie. 8vo. [Wood's *Athen. Oxon.*, iii., 1226.] [Doway], 1655

ENCHIRIDION (an) of fortification; or a handful of knowledge in martial affairs: demonstrating, by rule and figure, how to fortify or attacque any place. . . . [By Nicholas Stone.] 8vo. [*Camb. Univ. Lib.*] London, 1645

ENCHIRIDION of wit: the best specimens of English conversational wit. By William Shepard [William Shepard Walsh]. Square 12mo. [Cushing's *Init. and Pseud.*, vol. i., p. 137.] Philadelphia, 1885

ENCHIRIDION theologicum; or a manual for the use of students in divinity. [Edited by John Randolph, Bishop of Oxford.] 5 vols. Fcap 8vo. [Lowndes' *Brit. Lib.*] Oxford, 1792

ENCHIRIDIUM epigrammatum, Latino - Anglicum. An epitome of essays englished out of Latin, without elucidat. explanatory, containing six classes or centuries. . . . [By Robert Vilvain.] Fcap 8vo. [Martin's *Cat.*] London, 1654

ENCHORIAL (the) language of Egypt. From the third number of the Dublin University Review. [By Edward Hincks.] 8vo. [*Brit. Mus.*] Dublin, 1833

ENCLYTICA; being the outlines of a course of instruction on the principles of universal grammar, as deduced in an analysis of the vernacular tongue. [By —— Mosse.] 8vo. [*Brit. Mus.*] London, 1814

ENCOMIUM argenti vivi: a treatise upon the use and properties of quick silver; or the natural, chymical, and physical history of that surprising mineral, extracted from the writings of the best naturalists, chymists and physicians. By a gentleman of Trinity College, Cambridge [Thomas Dover]. 8vo. [*Brit. Mus.*] London, [1733]

ENCOUNTER (the) against Mr [Robert] Parsons, by a review of his last Sober Reckoning, and his exceptions urged in the treatise of his mitigation. . . . [By Thomas Morton, D.D., Bishop of Durham.] Fcap 4to. [*D.N.B.*, vol. 39, p. 164.] London, 1610

ENCOURAGER (the). [By George Mogridge.] 8vo. [*Brit. Mus.*] London, [1835 ?]

ENCYCLOPEDIA (the) for the home . . . the best literature of the best authors. By Marshall Everett [Henry Neil]. 8vo. [*Amer. Cat.*] Chicago, 1906

ENCYCLOPÆDIA of poultry; edited by "Chanticleer" [J— T— Brown]. 2 vols. Large 8vo. London, [1910]

ENCYLICAL letter of the Bishops of Rama, Acanthos, and Centuria; to the faithful, clergy and laity, of their respective districts: with a continued commentary for the use of the vulgar. [By Alexander Geddes, LL.D.] 8vo. [Watt's *Bibl. Brit.*] London, 1791

END (the) of a coil. By the author of *The wide, wide world* [Susan Warner]. 8vo. Pp. viii., 514. London, 1880

END (the) of all things; or the coming and kingdom of Christ. By the author of *Our heavenly home*, etc. [James Grant, journalist]. Pt 8vo. [*Brit. Mus.*] London, 1866

END (the) of life, and the life that has no ending. By the author of *Village Missionaries*, etc. [Anne Steele Elliot]. 8vo. London, 1867

END (the) of oppression, or a quartern loaf for two-pence: being a dialogue . . . concerning the rights of man. [By F. Spence.] Fcap 8vo. [*Brit. Mus.*] London, [1795]
See also "A Fragment of an ancient prophecy. . . ."

END (the) of religious controversy, in a friendly correspondence between a religious society of Protestants and a Roman Catholic divine; addressed to the RR. Dr Burgess, Lord Bishop of St Davids, in answer to his Lordship's "Protestant Catechism." In three parts. By J. M. [John Milner], D.D., F.S.A. 3 vols. Cr 8vo. [Gillow's *Bibl. Dict.*, vol. 5, p. 45.] London, 1818
Frequently reprinted, with the author's full name.

END (the) of the Fight [at Dame Europa's school]. John's defence, and Dame Europa's apology; with her addresses and advice to the other boys. [By Edward Brown, Newcastle.] Fcap 8vo. [*Bodl.*] London, 1871

END (an) to controversie between the Romane Catholique and the Protestant religions, justified. . . . [By Thomas Bayly, or Baily.] 4to. Pp. 401. [*Brit. Mus.*] Doway, 1654
The writer was the fourth son of the Bishop who wrote "The practise of piety."

ENDEAVOR (an) for peace among Protestants ; earnestly recommended and humbly submitted to Christian consideration. By one that prayeth for the peace of Jerusalem [William Hughes]. 4to. [*Bodl.*]
London, 1680

ENDEAVOUR (an) of making the principles of Christian religion . . . plain and easie. [By Herbert Palmer, B.D.] Fcap 8vo. [Mitchell's *Cat. of the Second Reformation*, p. lxxv.]
Cambridge, 1640
Later editions bear the author's name.

ENDEAVOUR (an) to prove that reason is alone sufficient to the firm establishment of religion, which must in principles of faith be ever precarious. [By Henry Constantine Jennings.] Fcap 8vo. [*Bodl.*]
Chelmsford, 1785

ENDEAVOUR (an) to rectifie some prevailing opinions, contrary to the doctrine of the Church of England. By the author of *The great propitiation* [Joseph Truman, M.A.]. 8vo. Pp. 283. [Arber's *Term Cat.*, i., 522.]
London, 1671

ENDING (the) of my day. [A novel.] By " Rita " [Mrs Wm. Desmond Humphreys, *née* Eliza M. J. Gollan]. 8vo. [*Brit. Mus.*]   London, 1901

ENDLESS (an) chain. [A story.] By Pansy [Mrs Isabella Alden, *née* Macdonald]. 8vo. Pp. 497.
Boston, [Mass.], 1884

ENDS (the) of Christian religion, which are,—

To { avoid / obtain } eternal { wrath / happinesse } from God.

By R. S. [Robert Sharrock, LL.D.]. 4to. [Watt's *Bibl. Brit.*] Oxford, 1673

ENDYMION. By the author of *Lothair* [Benjamin Disraeli, Earl of Beaconsfield]. 3 vols. 8vo. [*Brit. Mus.*]   London, 1880

ENEMIES (the) of God. [By Wm. R. Barlow, D.D.] 8vo.   Doway, 1624

ENEMIES (the) of the constitution [of the United States] discovered. . . . By Defensor [William Thomas]. 8vo. [Cushing's *Init. and Pseud.*, vol. ii., p. 43.]   New York, 1835

ENGA [a tale]. By the author of *The harbour bar* [Mrs Grace Prestwich]. 2 vols. 8vo.   Oxford, 1880

ENGINEERING estimates, costs, and accounts. By a General Manager [Alfred J— Liversedge]. 8vo. Pp. 276.   London, 1911

ENGLAND [being a pamphlet on the result of a war with Russia]. By G. D. [Giuseppe Dani]. 8vo. [*Brit. Mus.*]
London, 1878

ENGLAND and America ; with a chapter on the art of colonisation : . . . a comparison of the social and political state of both nations. [By Edward Gibbon Wakefield.] 2 vols. 8vo. [M'Culloch's *Lit. of Pol. Econ.*, p. 94.]   London, 1833

ENGLAND and China. Two episodes illustrating British policy in China. [By J. W. Drummond.] 8vo.
London, 1877

ENGLAND and East India inconsistant in their manufactures ; being an answer to a treatise [by Charles Davenant] intituled, An essay on the East India trade. By the author of the *Essay on wayes and means* [John Pollexfen]. 8vo. Pp. 59. [*Camb. Univ. Lib.*]   London, 1697
In M'Culloch's *Lit. of Pol. Econ.* the title is " England and India inconsistent," etc.

ENGLAND and France : a comparative view of the social condition of both countries, from the restoration of Charles the Second to the present time ; to which are now added, Remarks on Lord Orford's Letters. The life of the Marquise Du Deffand.— The life of Rachael, Lord Russell.— Fashionable friends, a comedy. By the editor of Madame Du Deffand's Letters [Mary Berry]. A new edition. 2 vols. Fcap 8vo. [*Brit. Mus.*]
London, 1844

ENGLAND and France in the fifteenth century. By Henry Pyne [said to be Charles, Duke of Orleans]. 8vo. [*Camb. Univ. Lib.*]   London, 1870

ENGLAND and France ; or, a cure for the ministerial Gallomania. [By Benjamin Disraeli, Earl of Beaconsfield.] 8vo. [*Brit. Mus.*]   London, 1832

ENGLAND, France, Russia and Turkey. [By David Urquhart.] 8vo. [*D. N. B.*]
London, 1835

ENGLAND and Scotland united, disjoyned ; or a gentle corosive and healing plaister applied to two dying kingdoms. By Ethog Grimes [George Smith], Gent. 4to.   London, 1648
The pseudonym is an anagram of the true names.

ENGLAND as seen by an American banker [Claudius Buchanan Patten]. 8vo. Pp. 345. [Cushing's *Init. and Pseud.*, vol. ii., p. 6.]   Boston, 1885

ENGLAND day by day : a guide to efficiency, and prophetic Calendar for 1904. By the authors of *Wisdom while you wait* [Edward V. Lucas and Charles L. Graves]. 8vo. Pp. 108. [*Brit. Mus.*] London, 1903

ENGLAND, Greece, or Rome ? A letter to a friend. By a convert from Anglicanism [George John Lloyd Crawley]. 8vo. [*Bodl.*]
York, [1853]

ENGLAND hath need of thee. By Sydney C. Grier [Hilda C. Gregg]. Cr 8vo. Pp. 339. [*Brit. Mus.*]
Edinburgh, 1916

ENGLAND, Ireland, and America. By a Manchester manufacturer [Richard Cobden]. Second edition. 8vo. [*D. N. B.*, vol. 11, p. 149.] London, 1835

ENGLAND may be extricated from her [agricultural] difficulties, consistently with the strictest principles of policy, honour, and justice. By a country gentleman [Edwyn A. Burnaby]. 8vo. Pp. 60. London, 1816

ENGLAND preserved ; an historical play. By George Watson [George Watson Taylor]. 8vo. [Cushing's *Init. and Pseud.*, vol. i., p. 304.]
London, 1795

ENGLAND regenerated, through justice to Ireland ; or a programme of reforms proposed to a reformed Parliament. . . . [By Gideon J. R. Ouseley.] 8vo. Pp. 62. London, 1888

ENGLAND rendered impregnable by the practical military organisation and efficient equipment of her national forces ; and her present position, armament, coast defences, administration, and future power considered. By H. A. L., " The old Shekarry," author of *The hunting grounds of the old world*, etc. [Henry Astbury Leverson]. With illustrations. 8vo. Pp. xvi., 463. [*Brit. Mus.*] London, 1871

ENGLAND, Scotland, and Ireland's consolation and encouragement for all good Protestants to be valiant against the common enemy, for the truth and Gospel of Jesus Christ ; touching the good success of his Majesties arms, and his wonderfull preservation in his great and eminent danger, when a cannon bullet touch'd his shoulder, and did him no further harm. Contained in a view of God's providence and protection to those that fear and serve him. . . . Being the substance of a sermon [on Psal. 35. 1, 2] on the happy arrival of King William in the kingdom of Ireland. Preach'd immediately before the battel by Dr.

W. [George Walker, D.D.], rector of Donoghmoore. 4to. [Dwyer's reprint (1893) of Walker's *True Account*.]
N.P., N.D., [1690]

ENGLAND subsists by miracle. By Feltham Burghley [C. A. Ward]. 8vo. Pp. 108. [*Bodl.*] London, 1859

ENGLAND the civilizer : her history developed in its principles. . . . By a woman [Frances Wright, later Madame D'Arusmont]. 8vo. [Cushing's *Init. and Pseud.*, vol. i., p. 309.]
London, 1848

ENGLAND under the heel of the Jew ; a tale of two books . . . arranged by the author of *The Call of the sword* [John Henry Clarke]. 8vo. Pp. 111. [*Brit. Mus.*] London, 1918

ENGLAND under the Jews. . . . [By Joseph Banister.] 8vo. [*Bodl.*]
London, 1901

ENGLAND'S alarum ; being an account of God's most considerable dispensations of mercy and judgment towards these kingdoms for fourteen years last past ; and also, of the several sorts of sins and sinners therein, especially the murmurers against the present government, with an earnest call to speedy humiliation, supplication and reformation, as the chief means of prospering their majesties counsels and preparations. [By John Dunton.] Dedicated to the King and Queen. 4to. [*Bodl.*] London, 1693
The epistle dedicatory signed " J. D."

ENGLAND'S and North Britain's happiness prov'd to be greater in her present Majesties reign than in former ages. [By James Crawford.] Cr 4to.
London, 1709

ENGLAND'S appeale from the private caballe at Whitehall to the great council of the nation, the Lords and Commons in parliament assembled. By a true lover of his country [Sir William Coventry]. 4to. [*Brit. Mus.*]
London, 1673
Another edition, with a title differing slightly from the above, was published in the same year.

ENGLAND'S battles by sea and land. [By Colonel William Freke Williams.] 2 vols. 8vo. [*Brit. Mus.*]
London, [1888]

ENGLAND'S birth-right justified against all arbitrary usurpation, whether regall or parliamentary, or under what vizor soever ; with divers queries, observations, and grievances of the people, declaring this Parliament's present proceedings to be directly contrary to those fundamentall

principles, whereby their actions at first were justifyable against the king, &c. By a well-wisher to the just cause for which Lieut. Col. Lilburn is unjustly imprisoned in Newgate [J. Lilburne ?]. 4to. [*Brit. Mus.*]
[London], 1645

"Supposed to be Lilburne's, or some friend of his."—MS. note by Thomason.

ENGLAND'S changeling; or the time servers laid open in their colours; being a clear discovery of the new cheat of the thing called the Good Old Cause. By one that hopes to see better times [Humphrey Willis]. Fcap 4to. [*Brit. Mus.*]   N.P., 1659

ENGLANDS comfort, and Londons joy; expressed in the royall, triumphant, and magnificent entertainment of our dread soveraigne Lord, King Charles, at his blessed and safe returne from Scotland on Thursday the 25. of Nouemb. 1641. By the right honourable Sir Richard Gurney, Knight, Lord Major, and the recorder, Sir Thomas Gardner, who were at that present both knighted . . . also the severall speeches, and other verses presented to his sacred person at that time. [By John Taylor, the water-poet.] 4to.   London, 1641

The verses are said to be " Verses presented to the King's owne hand by John Taylor."

ENGLAND'S confusion during its interregnum; or an exact history of the government in England from the horrid murder of King Charles I. to the happy Restauration of King Charles II. By J. D. [John Dauncey]. Fcap 8vo.
London, 1660

ENGLAND'S confvsion, or a true and impartial relation of the traverses of state in England, with the counsels leading thereunto; together with a description of the present power ruling there by the name of a Parliament, under the mask of the good old cause. . . . [By Arthur Annesley, afterwards President of the Council of State.] The second impression, with new additions. [*Cat. Lond. Inst.*, ii., 550.]
London, 1659

ENGLAND'S conversion and reformation compared; or, the young gentleman directed in the choice of his religion: to which is premised, a brief enquiry into the general grounds of the Catholick faith; in a conversation between a young gentleman and his preceptor: divided into four dialogues. [By Robert Manning.] 8vo. [Gillow's *Bibl. Dict.*, iv., 456.]
Antwerp, 1725

ENGLANDS Covenant proved lawfull and necessary also at this time, both by Scripture and reason; together with sundry answers to the usuall objections made against it. By S. C. [Samuel Clarke], preacher at B. F. [Bennet Fink]. 4to. Pp. 16. [*Brit. Mus.*]   London, 1643

ENGLAND'S crisis, and her safeguard : hints to Britons. By a patriot [Isaac Mann, M.A.]. 8vo. Pp. 30. [Whitley's *Bapt. Bibl.* ii.]   London, 1831

ENGLAND'S danger; or, reform unmasked. [By W. J. Ching.] 8vo. Pp. 55. [*Bodl.*]   London, 1819

ENGLAND'S day; a war-saga, commended to Gortschakoff, Grant, and Bismarck. . . . [By Sydney Dobell.] 8vo. [*D. N. B.*]   London, 1871

ENGLAND'S educational crisis, a letter addressed to the Right Honourable Viscount Palmerston, Prime Minister of Great Britain. By the head master of an English grammar school [Edward Rupert Humphreys, LL.D.]. 8vo. [*Brit. Mus.*]   London, 1856

ENGLAND'S faithful physician : or precious soul-saving and soul-searching remedies for preserving this sinful sin-sick nation from ruine and destruction, &c. [By John Hart, D.D.] 8vo. [*Brit. Mus.*]   London, 1666

ENGLAND'S faithful reprover and monitour. [By Richard Samwaies.] Fcap 8vo. [Wood's *Athen. Oxon.*, iii., 838.]   London, 1653

Attributed also to John Adlington, B.D.

ENGLANDS Fortresse, exemplified in the most renowned . . . Lord Fairfax : [verses] humbly presented unto his Excellency. By E. C. [Edward Calver], a lover of peace. 8vo. [*Brit. Mus.*]   London, 1648

ENGLAND'S glory; or the great improvement of trade in general, by a Royal Bank, or Office of Credit, to be erected in London; wherein many great advantages . . . will thereby accrue. . . . By H. M. [Sir Humphry Mackworth]. Fcap 8vo. [*D. N. B.*, vol. 35, p. 189.]   London, 1694

ENGLAND'S great concern in the choice of this new Parliament; dedicated to all her free-holders and electors. [By William Penn.] Folio. [Smith's *Cat. of Friends' Books*, i., 40 ; ii., 297.]   N.P., [1679]

Signed " Phil'anglus." Printed in Penn's works, ii., 678.

ENGLAND'S great interest in the well planting of Ireland with English people discussed ; wherein is briefly stated the benefits that will arise thereby. . . . By R. L. [Colonel Richard Lawrence, a member of the Army in Ireland]. 4to. Pp. iv., 44. [Whitley's *Bapt. Bibl.*, i., 65.]   Dublin, 1656
   See "The great case of transplantation . . ."

ENGLAND'S Helicon ; a collection of pastoral and lyric poems. [Edited by John Bodenham.]   4to.   [*Brit. Mus.*]
                                  London, 1812

ENGLAND'S heroes ! By the author of *Belgravia*, etc. [Mrs Caroline Leigh Gascoigne]. Fcap 8vo. No pagination. [*Camb. Univ. Lib.*]
                              [London], 1855

ENGLANDS interest by trade asserted, shewing the necessity & excellency thereof ; wherein is discovered, that many hundred thousand pounds might be gained to the king and kingdom, by the due improvement of the product thereof, more particularly by wool, and the evil consequences of its exportation unmanufactured. . . . By W. C. [William Carter], a servant to his king and country. The second impression, corrected and enlarged. 4to. [*Brit. Mus.*]   London, 1671
   The title of the first edition (1669) is somewhat different : " England's interest asserted in the improvement of its native commodities . . ."
   Authorship acknowledged in " A summary of certain papers about wooll, as the interest of England is concerned in it," published, with the author's name at the dedication, in 1685.

ENGLAND'S interest ; or the great benefit to trade by Banks or Offices of Credit in London. . . . Being a brief account of the management, nature, use, advantages, of the said Offices. [By Robert Verney.] Fcap 4to.   London, 1682

ENGLANDS ioy, for suppressing the Papists, and banishing the priests and Iesuites. [By Thomas Scot, B.D.] 4to. [*Bodl.*]   N.P., 1624

ENGLANDS looking in and out, presented to the High Court of Parliament now assembled. By the author R. M. [Ralph Maddison, Knight]. 4to. [Watt's *Bibl. Brit.*]
                                  London, 1640

ENGLANDS miserie and remedie ; in a judicious letter from an Utter Barrister concerning Lieutenant Col. Lilburns imprisonment in Newgate. [By John Lilburne.] 4to. [Watts' *Bibl. Brit.*]   London, 1645

ENGLAND'S mission. [A poem.] By Rev. John Osmond Dakeyne, M.A. 8vo.   London, 1846

ENGLAND'S monarchs : or, a compendious relation of the most remarkable transactions, and observable passages, ecclesiastical, civil, and military, which have hapned during the reigns of the kings and queens of England, from the invasion of the Romans to this present : adorned with poems, and the pictures of every monarch, from William the conqueror, to his present majesty, our gracious sovereign, king Charles the Second : together with the names of his majesty's most honourable privy council, the nobility, bishops, deans, and principal officers, civil and military, in England, in the year 1684. By R. B., author of the *Admirable curiosities in England* etc. [Richard Burton, *alias* Nathaniel Crouch]. 12mo. Pp. 240. [*Bodl.*]
                                  London, 1685
   See the note to " Admirable curiosities."

ENGLAND'S mourning garment ; worn here by plain shepherds, in memory of their sacred mistress, Elisabeth, queen of virtue, while she lived, and theme of sorrow, being dead. To which is added the true manner of her imperial funeral : after which follows the shepherds spring-song, for entertainment of King James, our most potent sovereign. [By Henry Chettle.] 4to.
                                  London, N.D.
   Reprinted in the *Harleian Miscellany*, vol. iii., pp. 500-518.

ENGLAND'S old religion faithfully gathered out of the Church of England ; as it was written by Ven. Bede, almost a thousand years agoe (that is) in the year 698 after the passion of the Saviour. By H. B. [Henry Harcourt, *alias* Beaumont, S.J.]. Fcap 8vo. Pp. 242. [Oliver's *Collections*, p. 111.]
                                 Antwerp, 1650

ENGLANDS Parnassus : or, the choysest flowers of our moderne poets, with their poeticall comparisons ; descriptions of bewties, personages, castles, pallaces, mountaines, groues, seas, springs, riuers, &c. Whereunto are annexed other various discourses, both pleasaunt and profitable.   [By Robert Allot.] 8vo. Pp. 522. [Watt's *Bibl. Brit.*]   London, 1600
   The " Dedication " and the address " To the Reader " are signed " R. A."

ENGLAND'S path to wealth and honour ; in a dialogue between an English-man and a Dutch-man. [By James Puckle.] 8vo. [Watt's *Bibl. Brit.*]   London, 1718
   The first edition was published in 1699.

ENGLAND'S present interest consider'd with honour to the prince, and safety to the people, in answer to this one question ; what is most fit, easie and safe at this juncture of affairs to be done, for composing, at least quieting of differences ; allaying the heat of contrary interests, & making them subservient to the interest of the government, and consistent with the prosperity of the kingdom ? . . . [By William Penn.] 4to. [Smith's *Cat. of Friends' Books*, ii., 293.]

N.P., 1675

The second edition, printed in the same year, has the author's name.

ENGLANDS proper and onelay way to an establishment in honour, freedome, peace, and happinesse ; or the Norman yoke once more uneased. By the author of *Anti-Normanisme* [John Hare]. 4to. [Thomason *Coll. of Tracts*, i., 586.]　　London, 1648

ENGLANDS sad posture ; or a description of the present estate of poore distressed . . . England. [In verse. By Edward Calver.] 4to. [Watt's *Bibl. Brit.*]　　London, 1644

ENGLANDS selected characters, describing the good and bad worthies of this age. VVhere the best may see their graces, and the worst discerne their basenesse. . . . [By Nicholas Breton.] 4to.　　London, 1643

The address " To the reader " is signed " B. N."

ENGLAND'S son ; and other poems. By Maxwell Gray [Mary Gleed Tuttiett]. Pt 8vo. [*Lond. Lib. Cat.*]

London, 1910

ENGLAND'S teares for the present wars. [By James Howell.] 4to. [Lowndes' *Bibl. Man.*]

London, 1644

Reprinted in the Harleian Miscellany.

ENGLAND'S threatened war with the world. [By Thomas Mulock.] 8vo.

London, 1840

ENGLAND'S three wants. . . . [By Elizabeth Catherine Thomas Carne.] Fcap 8vo. Pp. 24.　London, [1871]

ENGLAND'S training : an historical sketch. By the author of *Essays on the Church* [Robert B. Seeley]. 8vo. Pp. viii., 263. [*D. N. B.*, vol. 51, p. 193.]　　London, 1885

ENGLANDS troubles anatomized ; wherein is related the rise, cause, beginning, unhappy progresse of this uncivill warr : illustrated in all the passages thereof, whence this malignancy first sprang, which hath so rent and torne this late so flourishing kingdome

VOL. II.

of England. Written by a captaine, servant to his majesty, who fights his battels with the Parliament [John Cockayne]. 4to. Pp. vi., 55. [*Brit. Mus.*]　　London, 1644

The dedication is signed " J. C."

ENGLAND'S true interest in the choice of a new Parliament, briefly considered ; in a serious address to all the freeholders in Great Britain. By a friend to true liberty [Edmund Rack]. 8vo. [Smith's *Cat. of Friends' Books*, ii., 468.]　　London, 1774

ENGLANDS wants ; or several proposals probably beneficial for England, humbly offered to the consideration of all good patriots in both Houses of Parliament. By a true lover of his country [Edward Chamberlayne, LL.D.]. 4to. [*Bodl.; Brit. Mus.*]

London, 1667

Ascribed also to W. Carey.

ENGLANDS warning-piece ; or, the unkenneling of the Old Foxes with their cubes : wherein is contained the summary of Romes late designs against England. [By Jeffrey Corbet.] 4to. [Thomason *Coll. of Tracts*, vol. 2, p. 82.]　　London, 1654

ENGLANDS witty and ingenious jester ; or the merry citizen and jocular countryman's delightful companion : in two parts. . . . By W. W. [William Winstanley, gent.]. Seventeenth edition. Pt 8vo. [*D. N. B.*, vol. 62, p. 210.]　　London, 1718

An amended form of " Poor Robin's Jests," or " The compleat Jester," often reprinted.

ENGLAND'S worthies : under whom all the civill and bloudy warres, since anno 1642 to anno 1647, are related, wherein are described, the severall battails, encounters and assaults, of cities, townes and castles, at several times and places. . . . As also, several victories by sea, by the noble admiral, Robert Earle of Warwick. [By John Vicars.] Pp. 72. 4to. [*Bodl.*] London, 1647

A reprint was issued in 1819.

ENGLISH adventures. By a person of honour [Roger Boyle, Earl of Orrery]. 8vo. [Bliss' *Cat.*]

In the Savoy, 1676

ENGLISH advice to the freeholders of England. [By Francis Atterbury, D.D.] 8vo. [*Bodl.*]　　N.P., 1714

ENGLISH Alick. [A tale.] By May Kingston [Sarah Lane]. Fcap 8vo.

Philadelphia, 1890

L

ENGLISH (the) alphabet considered philosophically and pantologically. By a great big fool [John Burley Waring, architect]. 8vo. [*Brit. Mus.*] London, 1870

ENGLISH (the) alphabet for the use of foreigners : wherein the pronunciation of the vowels is explained, as abridged from a larger work. [By Granville Sharp.] 8vo. [Watt's *Bibl. Brit.*] London, 1786

ENGLISH (the) and American cousins ; a romance of real life. By E. S. [Eaton Smith]. 8vo. Pp. 64. [*Manch. Free Lib.*] Preston, 1873

ENGLISH (the) and Australian cookery-book. By an Australian aristologist [Hon. Edward Abbott, of Tasmania]. Fcap 8vo. London, 1864

ENGLISH (an) and Dakota vocabulary. By a member of the Dakota mission [Mrs Mary Ann C. Riggs]. 8vo. New York, 1852

ENGLISH (the) and India ; new sketches by E. de Valbezen. Translated from the French . . . by a Diplomate [H— Lysley]. 8vo. Pp. xv., 498. [*Brit. Mus.*] London, 1883

ENGLISH and Latin poems. . . . [By John Latham, D.C.L., of Bradwall in Cheshire.] Pt 8vo. Private print, [London], 1853

ENGLISH and Malagasy vocabulary. [By Rev. William Ellis.] Cr 8vo. Pp. viii., 476. London, 1863

ENGLISH and Scotch sketches. By an American [Rev. O— Prescott Hiller]. 8vo. [Cushing's *Init. and Pseud.*, vol. i., p. 12.] London, 1857

ENGLISH (the) anthology. [By Joseph Ritson.] 3 vols. 8vo. [Watt's *Bibl. Brit.*] London, 1793-94

ENGLISH (the) army in France ; being the personal narrative of an officer. [By John Gordon Smith, M.D.] 2 vols. Fcap 8vo. [*Aberd. Lib.*] London, 1830

ENGLISH babes and Irish bullies ; lays of old Rome for Old England. By Storicus[Rev. William John Blew, M.A.]. 8vo. Pp. vi., 58. London, 1890

ENGLISH (an) ballad : in answer to Mr Despreaux's Pindarique ode on the taking of Namure. [By Matthew Prior.] Folio. Pp. 11. [*Bodl.*] London, 1695

Despreaux's Ode is given on the opposite pages.

ENGLISH (the) ballance, weighing the reasons of Englands present conjunction with France against the Dutch ; with some observes upon his Majesties declaration of liberty to tender consciences. [By Robert M'Ward.] 4to. [*Brit. Mus.*] N.P., 1672

ENGLISH bards, and Scotch reviewers : a satire. [By George Gordon Noel Byron, Lord Byron.] Fcap 8vo. London, N.D., [1809]

The second edition has the author's name.

ENGLISH (the) baronetage, containing a genealogical and historic account of all the English baronets now existing, their descents, marriages and issues. [By Thomas Wotton.] 8vo. 4 vols. [*Athen. Cat.*, 2nd Supp., p. 156.] London, 1741

Attributed also to Arthur Collins.

ENGLISH bells and bell lore. By Theophila North [Dorothea Hollins]. 4to. London, 1895

ENGLISH (the) Bible in the John Rylands Library, 1525 to 1640 : with 20 facsimiles and 39 engravings. [By Rev. Richard Lovett, M.A.] Folio. Pp. 275. Private print, 1899

ENGLISH (the) boy at the Cape ; an Anglo-African story. By the author of *Keeper's travels* [Edward Augustus Kendall]. 3 vols. Fcap 8vo. [*Brit. Mus.*] London, 1835

ENGLISH caricaturists and graphic humourists of the nineteenth century . . . down to 1864. By Graham Everitt [William Rodgers Richardson]. Second edition. 8vo. Pp. xix., 427. London, 1893

ENGLISH (the) cathedral service : its glory, its decline, and its designed extinction. [By Professor Edward Taylor.] 8vo. Pp. 90. London, 1845

ENGLISH (the) Catholic's Vade Mecum. A short manual of general devotion. [By Rev. T. L. Ball, LL.D.] 12mo. London, 1882

ENGLISH charity [an explanation of the Poor Law Amendment Act]. [By Major Sir Francis Bond Head.] Fcap 8vo. Pp. 406. London, 1835

Reprinted from the *Quarterly Review*.

ENGLISH children in the olden time. By Elizabeth Godfrey [Jessie Bedford]. Second edition. 8vo. [*Lond. Lib. Cat.*] London, 1910

ENGLISH (the) chronology ; being a brief chronological account of the most considerable publick occurrences that have happen'd in these kingdoms and other adjacent parts, since King William the Third's accession to the crown, from 1688 to 1696. [By Benjamin Smithurst.] 8vo. [*Brit. Mus.*] Oxford, 1696

ENGLISH (the) Church and the Roman schism. [By Rev. Alfred W. Momerie, or Mummery, LL.D.] Cr 8vo.
Edinburgh, 1896
The author's name is given in the second edition.

ENGLISH Church defence tracts. Edited by H. P. L. [Henry Parry Liddon] and W. B. [William Bright]. Pt 8vo.
London, 1872

ENGLISH (an) Churchman's reason for his hope. [By Rev. Richard Sankey, M.A.] 8vo.　London, 1851

ENGLISH (the) connoisseur; containing an account of whatever is curious in painting, sculpture, &c. in the palaces and seats of the nobility and principal gentry of England, both in town and country. [By Thomas Martyn, B.D.] 2 vols. 8vo. [*Brit. Mus.*]　　　　London, 1766

ENGLISH (the) constitution fully stated; with some animadversions on Mr [William] Higden's mistakes about it. [By George Harbin] in a letter to a friend. 8vo. Pp. 108. [Arber's *Term Cat.*, iii., 668.]　　London, 1710

ENGLISH (the) Cotijo; or the cruelties, depredations, and illicit trade charg'd upon the English, in a Spanish libel lately published, compared with the murders and robberies of the Spaniards. By a sufferer [R— Copithorne]. 8vo.
London, [1730]

ENGLISH country life. By Martingale, author of *Sporting scenes* [Charles White]. Fcap 8vo. [*Adv. Lib.*]
London, 1843

ENGLISH (the) Cratylus; or essays on language, grammar, and composition. [By Joseph Sutcliffe.] Fcap 8vo. [*Brit. Mus.*]　　　　London, 1825

ENGLISH (the) dance of death, from the designs of Thomas Rowlandson, with metrical relations, by the author of *Doctor Syntax* [William Combe]. 2 vols. 8vo. [*Brit. Mus.*]
London, 1815-16

ENGLISH (an) dictionarie, or an interpreter of hard English words. . . . Second edition. By H. C. [Henry Cockeram, gent.]. 8vo. [Lowndes' *Bibl. Man.*]　　　London, 1626

ENGLISH echoes of German song: translated by R. E. Wallis, J. D. Morell. . . . Edited by N. D'Anvers [Nancy Bell, *née* Meugens]. 8vo. [*Brit. Mus.*]　　　　London, 1877

ENGLISH emigrants in Canada: a peep at their new homes. By Septimus Scrivener [Edward Wilson Yates]. Oblong 8vo. Pp. 32. [*Brit. Mus.*]
London, 1887

ENGLISH (the) empire in America : or, a view of the dominions of the Crown of England in the West-Indies. Namely, Newfoundland, New-England, New-York, Pensilvania, New-Jersey, Maryland, Virginia, Carolina, Bermudas, Berbuda, Anguilla, Monserrat, Dominica, St Vincent, Antego, Mevis or Nevis, St Christophers, Barbadoes, Jamaica. With an account of the discovery, situation, product, and other excellencies and rarities of these countries. . . . By R. B. [Richard Burton, *alias* Nathaniel Crouch]. The fifth edition. 12mo. Pp. 191. [*Bodl.*]
London, 1711
See the note to "Admirable curiosities."

ENGLISH (the) exposé; or men and women "abroad" and "at home." By a modern antique, author of *Celia in search of a husband* [Medora Gordon Byron]. 4 vols. Fcap 8vo. [Cushing's *Init. and Pseud.*, vol. i., p. 198.]　　　　London, 1814

ENGLISH (an) expositor, or compleat dictionary; teaching the interpretation of the hardest words and most useful terms in our language. First set forth by J. B. [John Bullokar], Doctor of Physic; and now the ninth time revised, corrected, and very much augmented. Fcap 8vo. [Arber's *Term Cat.*, ii., pp. 107, 631.] London, 1695

ENGLISH fashionables abroad. A novel. [By Mrs C. D. Burdett.] 3 vols. Fcap 8vo. [*Camb. Univ. Lib.*]　　　　London, 1827

ENGLISH (the) fortune-tellers; containing several necessary questions resolved by the ablest antient philosophers and modern astrologers, gathered from their writings and manuscripts by J. P., student in astrology [John Phillips]. 4to. Pp. 158. [*D. N. B.*, vol. 45, p. 206.]　　London, 1703

ENGLISH (an) freeholder's address to his countrymen. [By Rev. Henry Zouch, M.A.] 8vo.　London, 1780

ENGLISH (an) girl in Paris. [By Constance Elizabeth Maude.] Cr 8vo. Pp. 338. [*Lond. Lib. Cat.*] London, 1902

ENGLISH (an) girl's account of a Moravian settlement in the Black Forest. Edited by [Anne Manning] the author of *Mary Powell* [but written by Beatrice Stebbing, later Mrs Batty]. Cr 8vo. Pp. viii., 311.
London, 1858
Dedication signed "Beatrice."

ENGLISH grammar, taught in plain, familiar conversations. By Uncle Jonathan [Jonathan Badgley]. 8vo. [Cushing's *Init. and Pseud.*, vol. i., p. 339.]　Utica, New York, 1867

ENGLISH (an) green box ; or the green box of . . . L——d Churlow. . . . Dedicated to the Right Hon. Edward Lord Thurlow. . . . [By Richard Tickell.] 8vo. Pp. 96. [Watt's *Bibl. Brit.*]
                                    Dublin, 1779

ENGLISH (the) Gusman ; or the history of that unparallel'd thief James Hind. By G. F. [George Fidge]. 8vo. [Thomason *Coll. of Tracts*, vol. i., p, 858.]   London, 1652.

ENGLISH (an) harmony of the four Evangelists, generally disposed after the manner of the Greek of William Newcome, Archbishop of Armagh ; with a map of Palestine divided according to the twelve tribes, explanatory notes, and indexes. [By Richard Phillips and Thomas Thompson.] 8vo. [Smith's *Cat. of Friends' Books*, i., 78.]   London, 1802

ENGLISH hearts and English hands ; or, the railway and the trenches. By the author of the *Memorials of Captain Hedley Vicars* [Catherine Marsh]. Twenty-second thousand. Fcap 8vo. Pp. xv., 356. [*Brit. Mus.*]
                                    London, 1858

ENGLISH (the) hermit ; or the unparalleled sufferings and surprising adventures of Philip Quarll. [By Peter Longueville.] 12mo. [*Lond. Mercury*, vol. v., p. 409.]
                                    London, 1786
    One of many editions varying in the form of the title.

ENGLISH (the) heroe : or, Sir Francis Drake revived. Being a full account of the dangerous voyages, admirable adventures, notable discoveries, and magnanimous atchievements of that valiant and renowned commander. By R. B. [Richard, or Robert Burton, *alias* Nathaniel Crouch]. 12mo. Pp. 210.   London, 1687
    See the note to "Admirable curiosities. . . ."

ENGLISH hexameter translations from Schiller, Goethe, Homer, Callinus, and Meleager. By W. W. [William Whewell, D.D.]. 8vo. [*D. N. B.*, vol. 60, p. 462.]   London, 1847

ENGLISH history for children. By one who loves the souls of the lambs of Christ's flock [Rev. Richard Marks]. Fcap 8vo. [*Brit. Mus.*]
                                London, 1832-33

ENGLISH history, in question and answer . . . from the Conquest to the present time. By a lady [Jane Budge]. A new edition, revised and enlarged. 8vo. [Boase and Courtney's *Bibl. Corn.*, i., 50.]   London, 1860

ENGLISH history, methodised for the pupils of Kingstown School. By their English Master [James Rowley]. Part II., 1272-1485. 8vo. [*Brit. Mus.*]
                                    Dublin, 1874
    No more published.

ENGLISH humanity no paradox ; or an attempt to prove that the English are not a nation of savages. [By Edward Long.] 8vo. [*Gent. Mag.*, May 1813, p. 490.]   London, 1778

ENGLISH (the) hymn-book. [Edited by Rev. Robert William Dale, LL.D., D.D.] Thick 12mo. [*Brit. Mus.*]
                                    London, 1874

ENGLISH (the) Iarre ; or disagreement among the Ministers of Great Brittaine, concerning the Kinges supremacy : written in Latin [by Martin Becanus] and translated into English by I. W. P. [William Wright, S.J., D.D.]. 4to. [Oliver's *Collections*, p. 230.]   [St Omer], 1612

ENGLISH (the) in America. By the author of *Sam Slick, the clockmaker*, etc. [Thomas Chandler Haliburton]. 2 vols. Fcap 8vo. [Kirk's *Supp.*]
                                    London, 1851

ENGLISH (the) in France. By the author of *The English in Italy* [Constantine Henry Phipps, Marquis of Normanby]. 3 vols. Fcap 8vo. [*Brit. Mus.*]   London, 1828

ENGLISH (the) in India. By the author of *Pandurang Hari* and *The Zenana* [Thomas Henry Ottley]. 3 vols. Pt 8vo. [*Brit. Mus.*]
                                    London, 1828

ENGLISH (the) in Italy. [By Constantine Henry Phipps, Marquis of Normanby.] 3 vols. Fcap 8vo. [*Brit. Mus.*]   London, 1825

ENGLISH Inquisition : or, money rais'd by the new Secret Extent Law, without Act of Parliament. [By Charles Povey.] 4to. [*Brit. Mus.*]   London, 1718

ENGLISH kings in a nutshell : an aid to the memory. By Gail Hamilton [Mary Abigail Dodge]. Fcap 8vo. Pp. 81. [Cushing's *Init. and Pseud.*, vol. i., p. 126.]   New York, 1893

ENGLISH lands, letters, and kings. By Ik Marvel [Donald G. Mitchell]. 3 vols. Pt 8vo. [Haynes' *Pseud.*]
                                New York, 1893-95

ENGLISH (the) language : its sources, growth, history and literature. [By Thomas Page.] 8vo. Pp. 130.
                                London, [1883]

ENGLISH law ; or a summary survey of the household of God on earth, and that before and under the Law, and that both of Moses and the Lord Jesus : with an essay of Christian government under the regiment of our Lord and King . . . the Prince of Peace, Emmanuel. [By Charles George Cock.] Folio. [Watt's *Bibl. Brit.*]
London, 1651

ENGLISH (the) lawyer. By John Gifford, Esq. [Alexander Whellier]. 8vo. [Cushing's *Init. and Pseud.*, vol. i., p. 117.]   London, 1827

ENGLISH legends, in humorous verse. By Edward Johns [R— J— Edwards, of Ruthin]. 8vo. Pp. 52.
Aberystwith, 1901

ENGLISH liberties : or, the free-born subject's inheritance, containing I. Magna Charta, the Petition of Right, the Habeas Corpus Act ; and divers other most useful statutes. . . . II. The proceedings in appeals of murther ; the work and power of Parliaments ; the qualifications necessary for such as should be chosen to that great trust. . . . III. All the laws against Conventicles and Protestant Dissenters, with notes, and an abstract of all the laws against Papists. [By Henry Care.] Fcap 8vo.   London, N.D.
A fourth edition with the author's name, and continued, with large additions, by W. N[elson], of the Middle Temple, was published, in the Savoy, 1719. 8vo.

ENGLISH (the) life of Jesus. By Thomas Scott [Sir George William Cox]. 8vo.   Ramsgate, 1872

ENGLISH life, social and domestic, in the middle of the nineteenth century, considered in reference to our position as a community of professing Christians. By the author of *Reverses* [Mrs —— Whately]. Pt 8vo. [*Camb. Univ. Lib.*]   London, 1847
Information given by a friend of the author.

ENGLISH lyrics. [By William Smyth.] 8vo. Pp. 60. [*Camb. Univ. Lib.*]
Liverpool, 1797
Later editions give the author's name.

ENGLISH (an) Madonna. By James Hinton [George Barlow]. 8vo. [*Camb. Univ. Lib.*]   London, 1884

ENGLISH (the) maiden ; her moral and domestic duties. [By Artemas B. Muzzey.] Fcap 8vo. [*Camb. Univ. Lib.*]   London, 1841
The advertisement is signed " H. G. C[larke]," the publisher.
See also " The English wife."

ENGLISH (the) martyrologe, conteyning a summary of the lives of the glorious and renowned saintes of the three kingdomes, England, Scotland, and Ireland. Collected and distributed into moneths, after the forme of a calendar, according to every saintes festivity. Whereunto is annexed in the end a catalogue of those who have suffered death in England for defence of the Catholicke cause since King Henry the 8. his breach with the Sea Apostolicke, unto this day. By a Catholicke priest [John Wilson]. Permissu Superiorum. 8vo.
[St Omer's], Anno 1608
The dedication " To the Catholickes of England, Scotland and Ireland," is signed " I. W. P."
In the preface to an anonymous work on the same subject, published at London in 1761, and entitled " A memorial of ancient British Piety : or, a British Martyrology," etc., the book is said to have been written by " Mr John Wilson, an English priest (who lived abroad in the Low Countries)." It has been incorrectly assigned to John Watson.

ENGLISH (the) martyrology, abridged from Foxe. By Charlotte Elizabeth [Mrs Charlotte Elizabeth Tonna, previously Mrs Phelan]. 2 vols. 8vo. [*D. N. B.*, vol. 57, p. 34.] London, 1837

ENGLISH (the) [Catholic] martyrs under Henry VIII. and Elizabeth (1535-1583). [By P. Strain ?] 8vo. Pp. iv., 139.   London, 1890

ENGLISH matrons, and their profession. . . . By L. F. M., writer of *My life, and what shall I do with it* [Lydia F. M. Phillipps]. 8vo. [*Brit. Mus.*]   London, 1873

ENGLISH medieval embroidery. [By Charles Henry Hartshorne.] 12mo. [*Brit. Mus.*]   Oxford, 1848
Attributed also to John Henry Parker.

ENGLISH minstrelsy ; being a selection of fugitive poetry from the best English authors, with some original pieces hitherto unpublished. [Edited by Sir Walter Scott.] 2 vols. 8vo. [*Brit. Mus.*]   Edinburgh, 1810

ENGLISH (the) mounsieur ; a comical novel, wherein his travels, amours, and other passages of his life, no less strange than delightful, are faithfully set down. By an impartial hand [the Hon. James Howard]. Fcap 8vo. [Watt's *Bibl. Brit.*]   London, 1679

ENGLISH (the) mother. By a lady [Mrs Thomas Mortimer, *née* Favell Lee Bevan]. 8vo. [*Brit. Mus.*]
London, 1860

ENGLISH neutrality : Is the Alabama a British pirate ? [By Grosvenor P— Lowrey.] 8vo. [*Amer. Cat.*]
Philadelphia, 1863

ENGLISH (the) nunne ; being a treatise wherein (by way of dialogue) the author endeavoureth to draw young and unmarried Catholike gentlewomen to imbrace a votary and religious life. Written by N. N. [Lawrence Anderton]. 8vo. [Sparke's *Bibl. Bolt.*, p. 5.]
[Lostock Hall], 1642

ENGLISH orthographie ; or the art of right spelling, reading, pronouncing, and writing all sorts of English words : wherein such as one can possibly mistake are digested in an alphabetical order, under their several, short, yet plain rules ; also some rules for the points, and pronunciation, and the using of the great letters. [By Owen Price, M.A.] 4to. Pp. 75. [Wood's *Athen. Oxon.*, ii., 490.]
Oxford, 1668
The dedication is signed " Ow. Pr."
A later edition (1670) shows considerable difference in title. *See* the following.

ENGLISH orthography ; learning. 1. The letters of every sort of print. 2. All syllables made of letters. 3. Short rules, by way of question and answer, for spelling, etc. 4. Examples of all words (that may be mistaken) spelled with their accents, etc. 5. The difference between all words of like sound. By [Owen Price] a Master of Arts, and schoolmaster of twenty years' experience. 8vo. [Arber's *Term Cat.*, i., 523.] London, 1670
See also " English orthographie " above.

ENGLISH paradise : discovered in the Latine prospect of Iacobs blessing. Gen. 27, 27. Ecce odor filij mei sicut odor agri à domino benedicti. Preached at S. Bvttolphs without Aldersgate at London, on the holy Sabboth commonly called Trinitie Sunday, in that ioifull season of the festiuall solemnities for the blessed creation of the most gracious Prince of Wales. [By John White, Caius College, Cambridge.] 4to. Pp. 67. [*Bodl.*]
London, 1612
The dedication is signed "Ih. Wh."

ENGLISH (the) Parliament represented in a vision : with an after-thought upon the speech deliver'd to his most Christian Majesty, by the deputies of the States of Britany, on the 29th. day of February last ; and the number of votes and sermons the Tories made at London for twenty seven years. To which is added at large, that memor-

able representation of the House of Commons to the Queen, in the year 17¼¼ ; from whence Great Britain and the allies now date their late misfortunes, and France all her present power and grandeur. . . . By the author of *An inquiry into the miscarriages of the four last years reign* [Charles Povey]. 8vo. [*Brit. Mus.*]
London, 1715

ENGLISH (an) party's excursion to Paris in Easter-Week, 1849. By J. B. [John Bill], barrister-at-law. 8vo. Pp. 563. London, 1850

ENGLISH (the) peerage ; or, a view of the ancient and present state of the English nobility ; to which is subjoined a chronological account of such titles as have become extinct, from the Conquest to the beginning of the year 1790. [By Charles Catton, R.A., heraldic painter.] 3 vols. 4to. [Lowndes' *Bibl. Man.*] London, 1790

ENGLISH Pharisees, French crocodiles, and other Anglo-French and typical characters. By Max O'Rell [Paul Blouet]. Pt 8vo. Pp. 234. [*Amer. Cat.*] New York, 1893

ENGLISH Philistines and their allies ; a political satire, with preface and notes. [By John Hand, journalist.] 8vo. London, 1887

ENGLISH photographs. By an American [Stephen Fiske]. 8vo. [Cushing's *Init. and Pseud.*, vol. i., p. 12.]
London, 1869

ENGLISH (the) preacher, or sermons on the principal subjects of religion and morality ; selected, revised and abridged from various authors. [By William Enfield, LL.D.] 9 vols. Fcap 8vo. [Lowndes' *Brit. Lib.*]
London, 1773-84

ENGLISH (the) Presbyterian Church ; its pedigree and principles. [By Rev. Charles G. Scott, minister in London.] 8vo. Pp. 64. London, 1868
The preliminary address is signed " C. G. S."

ENGLISH Presbyterian eloquence, &c. ; in a collection of remarkable flowers of rhetorick, humbly inscribed to those two celebrated historiasters, Mr Oldmixon, author of the History of the royal House of Stuart, etc., etc., etc., and Mr Samuel Chandler, author of the late History of persecution. Cum notis variorum. By an admirer of monarchy and episcopacy. With an appendix. [By Zachary Grey, LL.D.] 8vo. Pp. viii., 29. [*Bodl.*]
London, 1736

ENGLISH Presbyterian eloquence : or, Dissenters sayings, ancient and modern, collected from the books and sermons of the Presbyterians, &c., from the reign of Queen Elizabeth to the present time : wherein it appears, that the Presbyterians have constantly attempted to subvert the fundamental articles of the Christian faith ; to abolish the doctrine and discipline of the Church of England establish'd by law . . . and have been profess'd enemies to truth, common sense, and good manners, from their first settlement in this kingdom. With remarks upon every chapter. [By Thomas Lewis, M.A.] 8vo. Pp. 149. [*Adv. Lib.*]   London, 1720

The preface is signed " T. L—."

ENGLISH (the) press and its poets : a satire. By Cordrac Vedcllo [Richard Harris]. 8vo.   London, 1856

ENGLISH (the) princess ; or, the death of Richard the III., a tragedy : as it is now acted at his Highness the Duke of York's Theatre. [By John Caryll.] 8vo. [*Biog. Dram.*]   London, 1674

ENGLISH Protestant Dissenters not under persecution, as is suggested by dissenting teachers ; with notes on some of their sermons, since the passing of the late Act against Occasional Conformity. By the author of *The Regular clergy's sole right to administer* [—— Sharp, curate.] 8vo. [Kennett's *Wisdom, &c.*, p. 263.]
London, 1713

ENGLISH province S. J. Alphabetical catalogue of members of the English Province S. J. who assumed aliases or by-names, together with the said aliases. By a member of the same society [Henry Foley]. 8vo. Manresa Press.   [Roehampton], 1875

The advertisement is signed " H. F." For private circulation only.

ENGLISH Pvritanisme ; containeing the maine opinions of the rigidest sort of those that are called Puritanes in the realme of England. [By William Bradshaw.] 8vo. [*Brit. Mus.*]
N.P., printed 1605

ENGLISH readings ; a comic piece, in one act. Inscribed to George Colman, Esq. [By James Cobb.] 8vo. Pp. 28. [*Biog. Dram.*]   London, 1787

ENGLISH (the) Rechabite, or a defyance to Bacchus and all his works : a poem in LXVII. hexastichs, wherein is rendred a plenary and full account how wines are pejorated, (or reduced from better to worse ;) and by admixture of what heterogeneous bodies they

become corrupted and marr'd. . . . By R. W. [Robert Whitehall], a well wisher to the body natural as well as politick. London, printed by M. Flesher, for Henry Clements, bookseller in Oxon. Folio. [Wood's *Athen. Oxon.*, iv., 178.]   [1680 ?]

ENGLISH (the) rogue ; described in the life of Meriton Latroon, a witty extravagant : being a compleat history of the most eminent cheats of both sexes. [By Richard Head and Francis Kirkman.] 8vo. [*Brit. Mus.*]
London, 1665

Other editions followed : " The English rogue, or witty extravagant . . ." (Gosport, [1689]. 12mo) ; " The life and death of the English rogue, or his last legacy to the world . . ." (London, 1679. 4to).

ENGLISH (an) rose. By David Lyall [Mrs Burnett Smith, *née* Annie Swan]. Cr 8vo. Pp. 311.   London, 1918

Private information regarding the authorship.

ENGLISH roses. By F. Harald Williams [Rev. Frederick William Orde Ward, B.A.]. Cr 8vo. Pp. 600. [*Brit. Mus.*]   London, 1899

ENGLISH (the) rudiments of the Latine tongue, explained by question and answer ; which are so formed, that a child, omitting altogether the questions, may learn only the answers, and be fully instructed in the rudiments of the Latin tongue. By W. D. [William Dugard]. 8vo. Pp. 152.
London, 1665

" That this book is Dugard's is proved by the list of Egglesfield's publications at the end of the volume."—MS. note by Dr Bliss in Bodleian copy.

ENGLISH (the) Scriptures ; their first reception and effects, including memorials of Tyndall, Fryth, Coverdale, and Rogers. . . . With an appendix. [By Rev. Christopher Anderson.] 8vo. Pp. 109.   Edinburgh, 1835

ENGLISH (the) settler's guide through Irish difficulties ; or, a hand-book for Ireland, with reference to present and future prospects. By Decanus [Edward Newenham Hoare, M.A., Dean of Achonry]. [*Olphar Hamst*, p. 41.]   Dublin, 1850

ENGLISH sirnames obtained from matters of war and chivalry. [By Michael Aislabie Denham.] S. sh., folio. [*Brit. Mus.*]   [Durham, 1854]

Signed " M. A. D."

ENGLISH songs and other small poems. By Barry Cornwall [Bryan Waller Procter]. Fcap 8vo. [Haynes' *Pseud.*]
London, 1832

ENGLISH (the) spy ; an original work, characteristic, satirical, and humorous : comprising scenes and sketches in every rank of society, being portraits of the illustrious, eminent, eccentric, and notorious. Drawn from the life by Bernard Blackmantle [Charles Molloy Westmacott]. The illustrations designed by Robert Cruikshank. 8vo. [*N. and Q.*, 13 Aug. 1859, p. 131.] London, 1825
A second volume appeared in 1826.

ENGLISH (the) tavern at Berlin ; a comedy in three acts. [By Elizabeth Harlow.] 8vo. [*Brit. Mus.*]
London, 1789

ENGLISH (the) topographer ; or, an historical account, (as far as can be collected from printed books and manuscripts) of all the pieces that have been written relating to the antiquities, natural history, or topographical description of any part of England. By an impartial hand [Richard Rawlinson, LL.D.]. 8vo. [Watt's *Bibl. Brit.*] London, 1720

ENGLISH topography ; or, a series of historical and statistical descriptions of the several counties of England and Wales. . . . By the author of *Historical and descriptive delineations of London and Westminster* [Rev. Joseph Nightingale]. Folio. [*Brit. Mus.*] London, 1816

ENGLISH (an) translation of the Nannul [of Pavanandi]. . . . By a Tamil graduate of the Madras University [J— Lazarus]. Pp. 47. [*Brit. Mus.*] Madras, 1878

ENGLISH (the) translation of the New Testament by Cornelius Vary, C.F.P.D., examined and compared with the Latin Vulgate and the Greek. By R. W. [Robert Witham], D.D. 4to. Pp. 22. N.P., 1727

ENGLISH (an) translation of the Scottish Declaration against James Graham *alias* Marquess of Montrose, wherein many things are set right between the Kingdom of Scotland and Commonwealth of England. . . . [By Rev. Cuthbert Sidenham, M.A.] 4to. Pp. 28. [*D. N. B.*, vol. 55, p. 245.] London, 1650

ENGLISH (the) version of H. Grotius his catechisme . . . together with the testimonies collected out of Holy Scripture. By N. G. [Nicholas Grey]. 8vo. [*Brit. Mus.*] London, 1668

ENGLISH (an) version of the Old Testament [in Greek] from the text of the Vatican Manuscript. By Hermann Heinfetter [Frederick Parker]. 4to. Pp. 60. [*Brit. Mus.*]
London, 1865
Only Genesis was published.

ENGLISH (the) wife ; a manual of home duties. By the author of *The English maiden, her moral and domestic duties* [Artemas B. Muzzey]. Fcap 8vo. [*Camb. Univ. Lib.*] London, 1841
The advertisement is signed "H. G. C[larke]," the publisher. *See above*, " The English maiden."

ENGLISH (the) abroad. Part I. Greece, Latium, Persia, and China. Part II. Russia, Germany, Italy, France, Spain, and Portugal. [By Stephen Weston, B.D.] 8vo. [*D. N. B.*, vol. 60, p. 374.] London, 1824-25

ENGLISHMAN (the) armed against the infidel spirit of the times. By John Isherwood [Rev. Thomas Bancroft, M.A.]. 8vo. [Sparke's *Bibl. Bolt.*, p. 16.] Stockport, 1833

ENGLISHMAN (the) directed in the choice of his religion. [By the Right Hon. Edward Weston.] The second edition, corrected. Fcap 8vo. Pp. 120. [*Bodl.*] London, 1740
Ascribed also to John Chapman.

ENGLISHMAN (the) in Kansas. . . . [By Thomas H. Gladstone.] 8vo. [Cushing's *Init. and Pseud.*, vol. i., p. 438.] New York, 1857

ENGLISHMAN (the) in Paris ; notes and recollections. [By Albert D. Vandam.] Vol. I. Louis Philippe. Vol. II. The Empire. 8vo. [*Brit. Mus.*] London, 1892-93

ENGLISHMAN'S (an) answer to the Address from the Delegates to the people of Great Britain ; in a letter to the several Colonies which were represented in the late Continental Congress. [By John Lind.] 8vo. Pp. 26. [Evans' *Amer. Bibl.*, vol. 5, p. 148.]
New York, 1775
Signed " An Englishman."

ENGLISHMAN'S (the) brief on behalf of his national Church. [By Rev. Thomas Moore.] Pt 8vo. [Crockford's *Cler. Direct.*] London, 1880

ENGLISHMAN'S (an) call to arms. [By Charles Whibley.] 8vo. [*Camb. Univ. Lib.*] London, 1914
Reprinted from the *Daily Mail*.

ENGLISHMAN'S (the) fortnight in Paris ; or, the art of ruining himself there in a few days. By an observer. Translated from the French. [By Sir John James Rutlidge.] 8vo. Pp. xxii., 224. [*Bodl.*] London, 1777
The Paris edition in French was suppressed by the French Government.

ENGLISHMAN'S (the) Greek Concordance of the New Testament. [By George V. Wigram.] Imp. 8vo. [*Brit. Mus.*] London, 1839

ENGLISHMAN'S (an) home. [A drama.] By a patriot [Guy L. B. Du Maurier]. 8vo. Pp. 96. [*Brit. Mus.*] London, 1909

ENGLISHMAN'S (an) plea for the United Church [of England and Ireland. By Rev. Philip Henry Good]. 8vo. [Cushing's *Init. and Pseud.*, vol. ii., p. 53.] London, 1869

ENGLISH-MAN'S (the) right : a dialogue between a barrister-at-law and a jury-man ; plainly setting forth I. The antiquity II. The excellent designed use III. The office and just priviledges of juries, by the law of England. [By Sir John Hawles.] 8vo. [*D. N. B.*, vol. 25, p. 243 ; *Brit. Mus.*] London, 1763
There are several later editions. The original edition (1680, 4to) bears the title " The Grand Juryman's oath and office explained. . . ."

ENGLISHMAN'S (an) sketch-book ; or, letters from New York. [By Simeon De Witt Bloodgood.] 8vo. [Cushing's *Init. and Pseud.*, vol. ii., p. 53.] New York, 1828

ENGLISHMAN'S (an) tour in Ireland in the years 1813 and 1814. [By John Gough.] 8vo. [*N. and Q.*, April 1856, p. 279.] Dublin, 1816

ENGLISH-MEN for my money ; or, a pleasant comedy [in prose and verse] called, " A woman will have her will." [By William Haughton.] 4to. [Quaritch's *Cat.*] London, 1616

ENGLISHWOMAN (the) in America. [By Isabella Bird, later Mrs Bishop.] Pt 8vo. [*Brit. Mus.*] London, 1856

ENGLISHWOMAN'S (an) love-letters. [By Laurence Housman.] 8vo. [*Lond. Lib. Cat.*] London, 1900

ENIGMA. [By Rev. Charles Lutwidge Dodgson, M.A.] 8vo. Private print, Oxford, 1866

ENIGMAS, historical and geographical [in verse]. By a clergyman's daughter [Elizabeth Hitchener]. Fcap 8vo. London, 1820

ENIGMATICALL characters, all taken to the life, from severall persons, humours, and dispositions. By R. F. [Richard Flecknoe], Esq. 8vo. Pp. 125. [*Brit. Mus.*] [London], 1658

ENJOYING life, and other literary remains. By W. N. P. Barbellion [Bruce Cummings]. Cr. 8vo. Pp. 262. [*Brit. Mus.*] London, 1919

ENJOYMENT (the) ; a poem. [By John Wilmot, Earl of Rochester ?] Folio. [*Brit. Mus.*] London, 1679

ENOCH Roden's training. By Hesba Stretton [Sarah Smith]. Fcap 8vo. London, [1864]
See the note to " Alone in London."

ENQUIRE within upon everything. [By Robert Kemp Philp.] Two hundred and seventy-seventh thousand. 8vo. Pp. 379. [*Brit. Mus.*] London, 1865

ENQUIRER (the) ; a periodical work, published in Glasgow during part of years 1820 and 1821. [Edited by James M'Conechy and Rev. —— Steel.] 8vo. Pp. viii., 248. [*David Laing.*] Glasgow, 1821

ENQUIRIES to be propounded to the most ingenious of each county in my travels through England and Wales, in order to their history of nature and arts. [By R. Plot.] Folio. [*W.*] [London, 1676 ?]

ENQUIRY (an) about the lawfulness of eating blood : occasion'd by [Dr Patrick Delany's] " Revelation examin'd with candour. . . ." By a prebendary of York [Rev. Thomas Sharp]. 8vo. [*Brit. Mus.*] London, 1733
In the following year, the author published a " Defence of the Enquiry." *See above.*

ENQUIRY (an), adapted to the present crisis, in what sense the non-intrusion principle may be reconciled with the authority of the ministry, the Christian rights of the people, and the unity of the Church. By a friend to the peace of the Church of Scotland [George M'Lelland]. 8vo. Edinburgh, 1842

ENQUIRY (an) after happiness. By the author of the *Practical Christianity* [Richard Lucas]. 8vo. [Arber's *Term Cat.*, ii., p. 614.] London, 1685

ENQUIRY (an) after philosophy and theology ; tending to show when and whence mankind came at the knowledge of these two important points. [By Robert Spearman.] 8vo. [*Bodl.*] Edinburgh, 1755

ENQUIRY (an) after wit ; wherein the trifling arguing and impious raillery of the late Earl of Shaftsbury, in his Letter concerning enthusiasm, and other profane writers, are fully answer'd, and justly exposed. [By Mrs Mary Astell.] 8vo. [*W.*] London, 1722

ENQUIRY (an) concerning the nature and end of a national militia ; wherein, from first principles and a short review of our present condition, both at home and abroad, is deduced the probability, and immediate necessity, of such an establishment. [By Maurice Morgan.] 8vo. [*European Mag.*, xli., 334.] London, N.D. [About 1758]

ENQUIRY (an) how far Papists ought to be treated here as good subjects, and how far they are chargeable with the tenets commonly imputed to them. [By Arthur Ashley Sykes, D.D.] 8vo. Pp. 40. [Disney's *Memoir of Sykes*, p. xxi.]   London, 1746

ENQUIRY (an), how far the Provost of Trinity College, Dublin, is invested with a negative on the proceedings of the Senior Fellows, by the charter and statutes of the College. [By Matthew Young, Bishop of Clonfert.] 8vo. [*D. N. B.*, vol. 63, p. 384.] Dublin, 1790

ENQUIRY (an) into a late very extraordinary physical transaction at E[to]n, in a letter to an apothecary at W[indso]r. By Ch— B——n [Charles Bateman, surgeon in Chertsey]. 8vo. [*Brit. Mus.*] London, 1758

ENQUIRY (an) into, and detection of the barbarous murther of the late Earl of Essex; or a vindication of that noble person from the guilt and infamy of having destroy'd himself. [By Robert Ferguson.] 4to. Pp. 80. [*Bodl.*]   Anno 1684

ENQUIRY (an) into Mr [John] Simson's sentiments about the Trinity, from his papers in process. [By James Hadow.] 8vo. Pp. 60. [*New Coll. Lib.*]   Edinburgh, 1730
 See also below, " An Enquiry into Professor [John] Simson's sentiments. . . ."

ENQUIRY (an) into Occasional Conformity; shewing that the Dissenters are no way concern'd in it. By the author of the *Preface to Mr Howe* [Daniel Defoe]. 4to. Pp. 31. [Wilson's *Life of Defoe*, p. 33.] London, 1702

ENQUIRY (an) into Professor [John] Simson's sentiments on the doctrine of the Trinity, from his papers in the process against him. [By Allan Logan.] 8vo. Pp. 44. [*New Coll. Lib.*]   Edinburgh, 1729
 See also above, " An Enquiry into Mr [John] Simson's sentiments. . . ."

ENQUIRY (an) into religion, and the use of reason in reference to it. Part I. By a lay hand [Sir Richard Cox, Lord Chancellor of Ireland]. 8vo. [*D. N. B.*, vol. 12, p. 415.] London, 1713
 This work seems never to have been completed.

ENQUIRY (an) into the accordancy of war with the principles of Christianity, and an examination of the philosophical reasoning by which it is defended: with observations on some of the causes of war, and on some of its effects. [By Jonathan Dymond.] 8vo. [Smith's *Cat. of Friends' Books*, i., 549.]
      London, 1823

ENQUIRY (an) into the ancient and present state of the County Palatine of Durham, wherein are shewn the oppressions which attend the subjects of this County by the male-administration of the present ministers and officers. Part I. [By John Spearman.] 4to. Pp. 129. [*Brit. Mus.*]
     [Edinburgh], 1729

ENQUIRY (an) into the authority for Echard's statement in his History of England — that Lord Russell interfered to prevent the mitigation of the barbarous part of the punishment for high treason, upon the presentation of the petition of the Sheriffs Bethel and Cornish, to the House of Commons, 23rd December 1680. [By John Martin.] 8vo. [*Martin's Cat.*]
     [London], 1852

ENQUIRY (an) into the authority of the primitive Complutensian edition of the New Testament, as principally founded on the most ancient Vatican manuscript; together with some research after that manuscript: in order to decide the dispute about 1 John v. 7. In a letter to the Reverend Mr Archdeacon Bentley, Master of Trinity-College in Cambridge. [By Richard Smalbroke, D.D.] 8vo. Pp. 54. [Bartholomew's *Bibl. of Bentley*, p. 24.]   London, 1722

ENQUIRY (an) into the cause of the pestilence, and the diseases in fleets and armies: in three parts; with an appendix. [By Alexander Bruce.] 8vo. [Watt's *Bibl. Brit.*]
     Edinburgh, 1759

ENQUIRY (an) into the causes of popular discontents in Ireland. By an Irish country gentleman [William Parnell]. 8vo. [*Brit. Mus.*]
     London, 1805

ENQUIRY (an) into the causes of the alienation of the Delaware and Shawanese Indians from the British interest, and into the measures taken for recovering their friendship. . . . [By Charles Thompson, later Secretary of the Continental Congress.] 8vo. Pp. 184. [Evans' *Amer. Bibl.*]
     Philadelphia, 1759

ENQUIRY (an) into the causes of the decay of the Dissenting interest; in a letter to a Dissenting minister. [By Strickland Gough.] The second edition. 8vo. [*D. N. B.*, vol. 22, p. 282.]
     London, 1730
 Replies (similarly anonymous) to this Enquiry were " Free thoughts on the most probable means . . ." [by Philip Doddridge], and " A Letter to the author of the Enquiry . . ." [by Abraham Taylor].

ENQUIRY (an) into the causes of the late growth of infidelity; and some remedies proposed for giving a check to that prevailing mischief. [By Thomas Smith, S.T.P.] 4to. [Watt's *Bibl. Brit.*]   London, 1705

ENQUIRY (an) into the causes of the present disaffection, as also into the necessity of some standing forces, the power of judges and juries in relation to libels, and the justice of the additional tax of one hundred thousand pounds on the Papists and Popish recusants. With remarks on the Discourse of standing armies, and other papers of Cato [Dr John Trenchard, aided by Walter Moyle] the journalist. [By Matthew Tindal.] 8vo. [*Adv. Lib.*]   London, 1723

ENQUIRY (an) into the causes of the present high prices of provisions, in two parts. [By Nathaniel Forster, D.D.] 8vo. Pp. viii., 216. [M'Culloch's *Lit. of Pol. Econ.*, p. 193.]   London, 1767

ENQUIRY (an) into the causes of the present long-continued depression in the cotton trade. . . . By a cotton manufacturer [William Hoyle, of Tottington]. Third edition. 8vo. Pp. 17.   Manchester, 1869

ENQUIRY (an) into the causes which have led to our late naval disasters. By an officer in the Navy [Rear-Admiral John Toup Nicolas]. 8vo. [*D. N. B.*, vol. 41, p. 41.] London, 1814

ENQVIRY (an) into the condvct of a late Right Honovrable Commoner [William Pitt]. [By Humphrey Cotes.] The fifth impression, corrected. 8vo. [Lord Stanhope's *History of England*, v. 253.]   London, 1766

ENQUIRY (an) into the conduct of Edmond Malone concerning the manuscript papers of John Aubrey in the Ashmolean Museum, Oxford. [By James Caulfield, bookseller.] 8vo. [*Brit. Mus.*]   London, 1797

ENQUIRY (an) into the conduct of our domestick affairs, from the year 1721, to the present time; in which the case of our national debts, the sinking fund, and all extraordinary grants of money are particularly consider'd: being a sequel to " Politicks on both sides." [By William Pulteney, Earl of Bath.] 8vo. Pp. 68. [M'Culloch's *Lit. of Pol. Econ.*, p. 321.]   London, 1734

ENQUIRY (an) into the consequences of supposing baptism makes infants, dying in infancy, inheritors of the kingdom of heaven. . . . By B. D. [Benjamin Dobell]. 4to. Pp. 24. [Whitley's *Bapt. Bibl.*, i., 156.]
London, 1733

ENQUIRY (an) into the consistency of Dr Troy's pastoral instruction. By S. N. [Thomas Elrington, D.D.]. 8vo. [*D. N. B.*, vol. 11, p. 333.]
Dublin, 1783
The author has given the last letters of his name.

ENQUIRY (an) into the constitution, discipline, unity & worship of the primitive Church that flourished within the first three hundred years after Christ; faithfully collected out of the extant writings of those ages. By an impartial hand [Peter King, Lord King]. Fcap 8vo. [*D. N. B.*, vol. 31, p. 144.]   London, 1691
" Second (the) part of the Enquiry . . ." was published in 1692.
No reply was made to this treatise till 1717, when there appeared " An Original draught of the primitive Church . . ." [by William Sclater], several editions of which were published.

ENQUIRY (an) into the constitutional authority of the Supreme Federal Court over the several [United] States, in their political capacity; being an answer to " Observations upon the Government of the United States of America, by James Sullivan, Esq., Attorney-General of the State of Massachusetts." By a citizen of South Carolina [Timothy Ford]. 8vo. Pp. 49. [Evans' *Amer. Bibl.*, vol. 8, p. 288.]   Charleston, 1792
Signed " Hortensius." Ascribed also (wrongly) to David Ramsay.

ENQUIRY (an) into the customary estates- and tenant-rights of those who hold lands of the Church and other foundations, by the tenure of three lives and twenty-one years; with some considerations for restraining excessive fines. . . . By Everard Fleetwood, Esq. [Samuel Burroughs]. Third edition. 8vo. Pp. viii., 65. [*Camb. Univ. Lib.*] London printed; and Dublin reprinted.   1768
Anonymous replies include " The Rights of Churches and Colleges defended . . ." [by Roger Long], and " The Reasonableness of Church and College fines asserted . . . [by Henry Gally ——" *See below.*

ENQUIRY (an) into the disposal of the Equivalent. [By Daniel Defoe.] 8vo. [*Camb. Hist. of Eng. Lit.*]
Edinburgh, 1706

ENQUIRY (an) into the doctrine of the Trinity, the mission and sacrifice of Jesus Christ, the pre-existence of souls, and the resurrection of the body. [By Robert Bell.] 8vo. [Smith's *Cat. of Friends' Books*, i., 63, 234.]
London, 1746

ENQUIRY (an) into the effects of public punishments upon criminals and upon society. [By Benjamin Rush, M.D.] 8vo. Pp. vii., 18. [Evans' *Amer. Bibl.*, vol. 7, p. 159.]

Philadelphia, 1787

ENQUIRY (an) into the evidence of the Christian religion. [By Mrs Newcome.] 8vo. Pp. 143. [Bowes' *Camb. Books*, p. 118.]

Cambridge, 1728

ENQUIRY (an) into the evils of general suffrage and frequent elections in Lower Canada. By Camillus [J— Henry]. 8vo. [Cushing's *Init. and Pseud.*, i., 49.] Montreal, 1810

ENQUIRY (an) into the extent of the power of juries on trials of indictments or informations for publishing seditious or other criminal writings, or libels ; extracted from a miscellaneous collection of papers that were published in 1776, entitled, Additional papers concerning the province of Quebec. [By Baron Francis Maseres.] 8vo. [*Brit. Mus.*] London, 1792

ENQUIRY (an) into the force and operation of the annulling clauses in a late Act for the better preventing of clandestine marriages, with respect to conscience ; in which the rights of marriage both in and out of society are briefly discussed upon the principles of the law of nature. [By Henry Stebbing, D.D.] 8vo. [*Brit. Mus.*]

London, 1754

ENQUIRY (an) into the force of the objection made against the resurrection of Christ, from the circumstance of his not appearing openly to the rulers and people of the Jews after he rose from the dead. . . . [By John Horsley, M.A.] 8vo. London, 1730

ENQUIRY (an) into the history of tithe ; its influence upon . . . Ireland ; with a plan . . . for the Catholic and Presbyterian clergy. [By —— Nolan, a lawyer, and —— Hartigan, a surgeon.] 8vo. [*Camb. Univ. Lib.*]

Dublin, 1808

ENQUIRY (an) into the inward call to the holy ministry. [By J— Middleton.] Second edition. 8vo. Pp. 48. [Supp. to Smith's *Cat. of Friends' Books*, p. 247.] Bristol, 1743

Signed " J. M." Wrongly assigned to Josiah Martin and to Patrick Middleton.

ENQUIRY (an) into the late supposed manifestations of the Holy Spirit. By a Presbyter of the Church of England [Hon. and Rev. Arthur Philip Percival]. 8vo. Pp. 40. [C. Boase's *Cath. Apost. Lit.*, Appendix, p. 67.]

London, 1832

ENQUIRY (an) into the life and writings of Homer. [By Thomas Blackwell, M.A.] 8vo. [*Biog. Brit.*, ii., 336.]

London, 1735

ENQUIRY (an) into the meaning of demoniacks in the New Testament. By T. P. A. P. O. A. B. I. T. C. O. S. [The Precentor And Prebendary Of Alton-Borealis In The Church Of Sarum—Arthur Ashley Sykes, D.D.]. The second edition, corrected and amended. 8vo. Pp. 81. [Disney's *Memoir of Sykes*, p. xx.]

London, 1737

A reply was made [by Thomas Church] in " An Essay towards vindicating the literal sense of the Demoniacks . . ." : this called forth [from Sykes] " A Further Enquiry . . ." ; next, there came [from Church] " A reply to the Further Enquiry . . ." and " A short state of the controversy. . . ."

ENQUIRY (an) into the measures of submission to the supream authority ; and of the grounds upon which it may be lawful or necessary for subjects to defend their religion, lives and liberties. [By Gilbert Burnet, D.D.] 4to. [Mendham Coll. *Cat.*, p. 52.]

N.P., 1687

ENQUIRY (an) into the merit of assassination ; with a view of the character of Cæsar, and his designs on the Roman republick. [By Aaron Hill.] 8vo. [*Cat. Lond. Inst.*, ii., 117.]

London, 1738

ENQUIRY (an) into the method of settling parishes, conform to the Acts and practice of the Church of Scotland, through the different periods of her administration and government, from the Reformation to this present time. [By Sir Thomas Gordon, of Earlston, and Halbert Monro.] 8vo. [*Adv. Lib.*] Edinburgh, 1732

ENQUIRY (an) into the natural right of mankind to debate freely concerning religion, wherein the maxims advanced by several late writers upon this subject, are examined. By a gentleman of Lincolns-Inn [Henry Anderson]. 8vo. [Nichols' *Lit. Anec.*, ii., 104.]

London, 1737

ENQUIRY (an) into the nature and duties of the office of inquest jurymen of the City of London, together with the by-laws of the Common Council and the Articles of Charge. By a citizen [Joseph Newell]. 8vo.

London, 1824

An edition published in 1825 bears the author's name.

ENQUIRY (an) into the nature and
origin of literary property. [By
William Warburton, D.D.] 8vo.
[Dyce *Cat.*, ii., 406.]   London, 1762
   Discussion of the subject was continued,
at intervals, by other writers. — John
Maclaurin (Lord Dreghorn), Francis Har-
grave, William Enfield.

ENQUIRY (an) into the nature, necessity and evidence of Christian faith, in
several essays. Part I. Of faith in
general, and of the belief of a Deity.
By J. C. [John Cockburn], D.D. 8vo.
Pp. 72. [*D. N. B.*, vol. 11, p. 19.]
                        London, 1696
   Part II. appeared in 1692 ; both together (second edition) in 1699. Part III.
never appeared.

ENQUIRY (an) into the nature of
ghosts and other appearances supposed
to be supernatural. [By William Newnham, surgeon.] 8vo. London, [1840 ?]

ENQUIRY (an) into the nature of property and estates as defined by the
English law ; in which are considered
the opinions of Mr Justice Blackstone
and Lord Coke concerning real property. [By John Reeves, M.A.,
F.R.S. and F.S.A.] 8vo. [*Brit. Mus.*]
                        London, 1779
   Ascribed also to Ralph Bradley.

ENQUIRY (an) into the nature of the
human soul ; wherein the immateriality of the soul is evinced from the
principles of reason and philosophy.
[By Andrew Baxter.] 4to. [*Abbot's
Lit. of a Future Life*, No. 125.]
                        London, [1745]

ENQUIRY (an) into the nature of
Zemindary tenures in the landed
property of Bengal. . . . In two parts,
with an appendix. [By James Grant.]
4to. [*Calc. Imp. Lib.*]
                London, 1810, [for 1790]

ENQUIRY (an) into the new opinions
(chiefly) propagated by the Presbyterians of Scotland ; together also
with some animadversions on a late
book [by Gilbert Rule], entituled, A
Defence of the Vindications of the
Kirk : in a letter to a friend at Edinburgh. By A. M. [Alexander Monro],
D.D. 8vo. [Darling's *Cyclop. Bibl.*]
                        London, 1696

ENQUIRY (an) into the occasional and
standing similitudes of the Lord God,
in the Old and New Testament ; or,
the forms made use of by Jehovah
Aleim, to represent themselves to the
true believers, before and since the
law by Moses. . . . [By Julius Bate,
M.A.] 8vo. [Darling's *Cyclop. Bibl.*]
                        London, [1756].

ENQUIRY (an) into the Occasional
Conformity Bill. By the author of
the *True born Englishman* [Daniel
Defoe]. 4to. Pp. 14. London, 1704
   This is the same as " An enquiry into
Occasional Conformity." [Lee's *Defoe.*]

ENQUIRY (an) into the Occasional
Conformity of Dissenters in cases of
preferment ; with a preface to the
Lord Mayor, occasioned by his carry-
ing the sword to a Conventicle. [By
Daniel Defoe.] 4to. Pp. 36. [Wilson's
Life of Defoe, 8.]   London, 1697
   The preface is signed "One, Two, Three,
Four."

ENQUIRY (an) into the opinions of
the learned Christians, both ancient
and modern, concerning the generation
of Jesus Christ. . . . Now first published by [Henry Taylor] the editor of
*Benjamin Ben Mordecai's Seven letters
to Elisha Levi.* 4to. Pp. xi., 126.
[*Manch. Free Lib.*]   London, 1777

ENQUIRY (an) into the origin and
manner of creating Peers. [By
Richard West, Lord Chancellor of
Ireland.] 8vo. [*D. N. B.*, vol. 60,
p. 339.]   London, 1719
   A reprint with the author's name was
published in 1782. An answer was written
[by George St Amand], entitled " Animadversions on the Enquiry . . .", 1724.

ENQUIRY (an) into the origin, nature
and objects of the government scheme
of education, and the causes of its
failure. [By Joseph Denison.] 8vo.
                        London, 1841

ENQUIRY (an) into the origin of
honour, and the usefulness of Christianity in war. By the author of *The
fable of the bees* [Bernard de Mande-
ville]. 8vo. [*Brit. Mus.*] London, 1732

ENQUIRY (an) into the origin of the
human appetites and affections, shewing how each arises from association ;
with an account of the entrance of
moral evil into the world : to which
are added some remarks on the independent scheme which deduces all
obligation on God's part, and man's,
from certain abstract relations, truth,
etc. [By James Long.] 8vo. Pp.
196. [*New Coll. Cat.*] Lincoln, 1747
   Ascribed also to —— Barr.

ENQUIRY (an) into the physical and
literal sense of that Scripture, Jeremiah
viii., 7. . . . Written by an eminent
Professor for the use of his scholars
[Rev. Charles Morton, Charlestown,
Mass.]. Fcap 8vo. Pp. 36. [Evans'
Amer. Bibl., vol. 1, p. 105.]
                London, N.D., [1694 ?]
   Signed " C. M."

ENQUIRY (an) into the powers of ecclesiastics on the principles of Scripture and reason. [By Thomas Gordon.] 8vo. [Watt's *Bibl. Brit.*]
London, 1776

ENQUIRY (an) into the present duty of a Low-church-man; occasion'd by the late Act of Parliament: in a letter from a Dissenter in the country to a Low-church-man in the city. [By Rev. James Peirce.] 8vo. [*N. and Q.*, Feb. 1854, p. 97.]   London, 1712

ENQUIRY (an) into the present state of affairs: and in particular, whether we owe allegiance to the king in these circumstances? And whether we are bound to treat with him, and call him back again, or not? [By Gilbert Burnet, D.D.] Published by authority. 4to. [Clarke and Foxcroft's *Life of Burnet*, p. 539.] London, 1689

ENQUIRY (an) into the present state of polite learning in Europe. [By Oliver Goldsmith.] 8vo. Pp. viii., 200. [Nichols' *Lit. Anec.*, ix., 666.]
London, 1759

ENQUIRY (an) into the present system of medical education in the State of New York. By an Observer [James Macnaughton]. 8vo. [Cushing's *Init. and Pseud.*, vol. i., p. 207.] Albany, 1830

ENQUIRY (an) into the prices of wheat, malt, and occasionally of other provisions; of land and cattle, &c. as sold in England from the year 1000 to the year 1765; computed according to the Winchester measure, and to the present standard of English coin, divided into periods of ten years each, and also into periods of circumstances. [By Michael Combrune, brewer.] Folio. [*Brit. Mus.*; M'Culloch's *Lit. of Pol. Econ.*, p. 193.]
London, 1768

ENQUIRY (an) into the principles of taxation, chiefly applicable to articles of immediate consumption. [By Andrew Hamilton.] 4to. [Watt's *Bibl. Brit.*]   London, 1790

ENQUIRY (an) into the principles of Toleration, the degree in which they are admitted by our laws, and the reasonableness of the late application made by the Dissenters to Parliament for an enlargement of their religious liberties. [By Joseph Fownes.] 8vo. Pp. xxviii., 127. [*Bodl.*] London, 1772

ENQUIRY (an) into the question whether juries are, or are not, judges of law as well as of fact; with a particular reference to the case of libels. [By Joseph Towers, LL.D.] 8vo. [*Gent. Mag.*, lxix., 1, 528.]
London, 1764

ENQUIRY (an) into the real interest of princes in the person of their ambassadors, and how far the petty quarrels of ambassadors, or the servants and dependants of ambassadors one among another, ought to be resented by their principals; with an essay on what satisfaction it is necessary to give or take in such cases. . . . [By Daniel Defoe.] 8vo. [Lee's *Defoe*, p. 137.]
London, 1712

ENQUIRY (an) into the real merit of a certain popular performer; in a series of letters, first published in the Craftsman or Gray's-Inn Journal; with an introduction to D[avi]d G[arric]k, Esq. [By Thady Fitzpatrick.] 8vo. Pp. viii., 41.   London, 1760

" This Enquiry &c. was written by Mr Thady Fitzpatrick, who had been once a great friend of Garrick's. Churchhill, to revenge Garrick's cause, introduced him into one of the *late* editions of the Rosciad, describing him as a *thing* without a name." —MS. note by Malone on the Bodleian copy. The letters are signed T. F., X. Y. Z., Theatricus, Anti-theatricus, Candidus, Philo-Tragicus, Ingenuus, W. W., A lover of truth.

ENQUIRY (an) into the reasons for abrogating the test imposed on all Members of Parliament, offered by Sa. Oxon. [By Gilbert Burnet, D.D.] 4to. No separate title-page. [Clarke and Foxcroft's *Life of Burnet*, p. 536.]
N.P., [1688]

ENQUIRY (an) into the reasons of the conduct of Great Britain, with relation to the present state of affairs in Europe. [By Benjamin Hoadly.] 8vo. [*Adv. Lib.*]   London, 1727

ENQUIRY (an) into the remote cause of Cholera. [By Patrick Shand, advocate.] 8vo. Pp. iv., 57.
Edinburgh, 1832

Contemporary attestation of authorship.

ENQUIRY (an) into the revenue, credit, and commerce of France, in a letter to a member of the present Parliament. [By G— Turner.] 8vo. Pp. 64.
London, 1742

Sometimes printed as "An Inquiry . . ." Replies to this pamphlet appeared in " A Letter to the author of An Enquiry into the revenue . . ." and in " Remarks on a pamphlet intitled ' An Inquiry into the revenue. . . .' "

ENQUIRY into the state after death, and touching the certainty thereof. [By Sylvanus Hibbert.] 8vo. Pp. 31. [*Manch. Free Lib. Cat.*]
Manchester, 1771

ENQUIRY (an) into the state of the nation at the commencement of the present Administration. [By Henry Brougham, Lord Brougham.] Fourth edition, with additions. 8vo. Pp. 218, xviii. [Thomas's *Bibliog. List*, p. 6.]
London, 1806

ENQUIRY (an) into the state of the Union of Great Britain, and the past and present state of the trade and publick revenues thereof. By the Wednesday's Club in Friday-street. [By William Paterson.] 8vo. [*N. and Q.*, 1853, p. 576.]   London, 1717

ENQUIRY (an) into the time of the coming of the Messiah and the restoration of the Jews. [By Robert Clayton, Bishop of Clogher.] 8vo. [Darling's *Cyclop. Bibl.*]   London, 1751

ENQUIRY into the tripartite division of tithes in England. By a layman [John Allen]. 8vo. [*W.*]
London, 1833

ENQUIRY (an) into the validity of a late discourse, intituled, " The nature and duty of self-defence." [By Joseph Besse.] 8vo. [Smith's *Cat. of Friends' Books*, i., 257.]   London, 1747
Signed " Philanthropus."

ENQUIRY (an) into the validity of [American] Methodist Episcopacy. By an Episcopalian of Maryland [John Kewley]. 8vo. [Cushing's *Init. and Pseud.*, vol. i., p. 92.]
Wilmington, 1807

ENQUIRY (an) respecting the punctuation of ancient Greek. By Hermann Heinfetter [Frederick Parker], author of *Objections to Bishop Middleton's doctrine of the Greek article*. Fcap 8vo. [*Brit. Mus.*]   London, 1841

ENQUIRY respecting the relation of cause and effect, in which the theories of Professor Brown and Mr Hume, are examined ; with a statement of such observations as are calculated to shew the inconsistency of these theories. [By Lady Mary Shepherd.] 8vo. [*Brit. Mus.*]   Edinburgh, 1819
The title of a later edition (1824) differs somewhat : " An Essay upon the relation of cause and effect. . . ."   *See below.*

ENQUIRY (an) whether a general practice of virtue tends to the wealth or poverty, benefit or disadvantage of a people ? In which the pleas offered by [B. de Mandeville] the author of the " Fable of the bees, or private vices publick benefits," for the usefulness of vice and roguery, are considered. With some thoughts concerning a toleration of publick stews. [By George Blewitt.] 8vo. Pp. 228.
London, 1725
" Mr Blewit, the author of this answer to Mandeville, was of the   Temple and died   aged about I believe under 30 years, soon after the publication of this book."—MS. note by De Quincey.

ENQUIRY (an) whether Popery is a proper subject of toleration to Protestant countries. [By Thomas Reader.] 8vo. Pp. 8. [Green's *Bibl. Somers.*, iii., 206.]
London, 1780

ENQUIRY (an) whether the Christian religion is of any benefit, or only a useless commodity to a trading nation. [By Jonathan Swift, D.D.] 8vo. [*Camb. Hist. of Eng. Lit.*]   London, 1732

ENSEMBLE [a novel]. By Wat Bradwood [Walter Bradford Woodgate]. 3 vols. Cr 8vo. [*Lond. Lib. Cat.*]
London, 1870

ENTAIL (the) ; or the Lairds of Grippy. By the author of *Annals of the parish*, etc. [John Galt]. 3 vols. Fcap 8vo. [*D. N. B.*, vol. 20, p. 390.]
Edinburgh, 1823

ENTANGLEMENTS : a romance. By the author of *Mr Arle* [Emily Jolly]. 2 vols. Cr 8vo. [*Brit. Mus.*]
London, 1862

ENTANGLEMENTS. The Woman's weaving. [Tales.] By Francis Prevost [Henry Francis Prevost Battersby]. 8vo. Pp. 204. [*Brit. Mus.*] London, 1898

ENTER into thy closet ; or, a method and order for private devotion : with an appendix concerning the frequent and holy use of the Lords Supper. [By Edward Wetenhall, D.D.] Third edition. 8vo. Pp. 425. [*Brit. Mus.*]
London, 1670

ENTERING into his own. By Hope Daring [Anna Johnson]. Fcap 8vo. [*Amer. Cat.*]   New York, 1903

ENTERLUDE (the) of John Bon and Mast Person : a dialogue on the festival of Corpus Christi, and on transubstantiation. [By Luke Shepherd, M.D.] [Percy Society.] 8vo.
London, 1852

ENTERPRISING (the) impresario. By Walter Maynard [Thomas Willert Beale]. 8vo. Pp. 407. [*Olphar Hamst*, p. 87.]   London, 1867

ENTERTAINING (the) medley ; being a collection of true histories and anecdotes, calculated for the Cottager's fireside. [By Abigail Roberts.] 12mo. Pp. 120. [Smith's *Cat. of Friends' Books*, Supp., p. 289.]   Dublin, 1823

ENTERTAINING passages relating to Philip's War which began in the month of June, 1675 ; as also of expeditions more lately made against the common enemy, and Indian rebels, in the Eastern parts of New England. . . . By T. C. [Thomas Church]. 4to. Pp. iv., 120. [Cushing's *Init. and Pseud.*, vol. i., p. 47.]
Boston, [Mass.], 1716

ENTERTAINMENT for a winter's evening. By Me, the Hon. B. B., Esq. [Joseph Green]. 8vo. [Cushing's *Init. and Pseud.*, vol. i., p. 186.]
Boston, 1850

ENTERTAINMENTS for Lent : the delight of sinne is momentary, the torment eternal. Translated from the French [of Nicolas Caussin by Sir Basil Brook]. Fcap 8vo. [*Brit. Mus.*]
London, 1661

ENTHRALLED and released. By Ernst Werner [Elizabeth Bürstenlinden]. From the German. Fcap 8vo.
New York, 1892

ENTHUSIASM ; a poetical essay. In a letter to a friend in town. [By John Byrom.] [Watt's *Bibl. Brit.*]
London, 1751

ENTHUSIASM (the) of Methodists and Papists compar'd. [By George Lavington, Bishop of Exeter.] 8vo. [*D. N. B.*, vol. 32, p. 213.]
London, 1749
To this first part, replies were written by John Wesley, George Whitefield, and Vincent Perronet : the controversy was continued. Part II. was published in 1749, and Part III. in 1751.

ENTHUSIASM (the) of the Church of Rome demonstrated in some observations upon the life of Ignatius Loyola. [By Henry Wharton.] 4to. Pp. 139. [*D. N. B.*, vol. 60, p. 405.]
London, 1688
In reply, " A Vindication of S. Ignatius from Phanaticism " was issued by William Darrell, S.J.

ENTHUSIASMUS triumphatus ; or, a discourse of the nature, causes, kinds, and cure, of enthusiasme : written by Philophilus Parresiastes [Henry More, D.D.], and prefixed to Alazonomastix his observations and reply : whereunto is added a letter of his to a private friend, wherein certain passages in his reply are vindicated, and severall matters relating to enthusiasm more fully cleared. 8vo. Pp. 76. [*D. N. B.*, vol. 38, p. 422.]
London, 1656

ENTHUSIAST (the) ; or the lover of nature. [A poem. By Joseph Warton.] Folio. [Courtney's *Secrets*, p. 116.]
London, 1744

ENTHUSIASTICK impostors no divinely inspired prophets ; being an historical relation of the rise, progress, and present practices of the French and English pretended prophets ; wherein all their agitations, extasies, inspirations, prophetical warnings, and pretences to working miracles are proved false, counterfeit, and ridiculous impostures. . . . [By Richard Kingston, D.D.] 8vo. [Arber's *Term Cat.*, iii., 685.]   London, 1707
See also above, " A Copious account of the French and English prophets. . . ."

ENTIRE (an) and complete history, political and personal, of the boroughs of Great Britain ; to which is prefixed, an original sketch of constitutional rights, from the earliest period until the present time. [By Thomas Henton Burnley Oldfield.] 2 vols. 8vo. [*Bodl.*]
London, 1792
Vol. II. bears the following title—"An entire and complete history, political and personal, of the boroughs of Great Britain ; together with the Cinque Ports. To which is prefixed, an original sketch of political rights, from the earliest period until the present time : illustrated by a variety of notes and references. In three volumes." All the volumes are dated 1792.

ENTIRELY (an) new metrical version of the Psalms, written for the music of that in common use. By W. H. B. [William Henry Black]. Pt 8vo. Pp. viii., 512. [Taylor's *Coll. of Psalm Versions*, p. 112.]   London, 1848

ENTRANCE (the) of Mazzarini ; or, some memorials of the state of France between the death of Cardinal Richlieu and the beginning of the late regency. [By Thomas Tanner, rector of Brightstone.] 8vo. [Bliss' *Cat.*] Pp. 114.   Oxford, 1658

ENVY, a poem, addressed to Mrs Miller, at Batheaston Villa. [By Christopher Anstey.] 4to. Pp. 23. [*Brit. Mus.*]   London, [1778]

ENVY ; a poem. . . . By the author of *The Progress of freedom* [J— Champion]. 4to. Pp. 14. [Watt's *Bibl. Brit.*]   London, 1776

ENVY at arms ! or, caloric alarming the Church. [By —— Thom ?] 8vo. [*Brit. Mus.*]   Edinburgh, 1805
A satire in verse occasioned by the opposition of the ministers of Edinburgh to the election of John Leslie to the professorship of mathematics in the University of Edinburgh.

EOTHEN ; or traces of travel brought home from the East. [By Alexander William Kinglake.] 8vo. [*D. N. B.*, vol. 31, p. 172.]   London, 1844

EPHEMERA. [Poems.] By Gabrielle Carr [Mrs Anne Steele]. 8vo. [Cushing's *Init. and Pseud.*, vol. i., p. 51.] London, 1865

EPHEMERA [in verse: with a preface signed G. E. R., *i.e.* George Edward Rice, and J. H. W., *i.e.* John Howard Wainwright]. 8vo. Pp. 112. [*Brit. Mus.*] Boston, [Mass.], 1852

The initials "J. H. W." are also held to indicate John Henry Warland.

EPHEMERA, and nugamenta. By G. E. R. [George Edward Rice]. 8vo. [Cushing's *Init. and Pseud.*, i., 245.] Boston, [Mass.], 1852

EPHEMERIS Parliamentaria ; or a faithful register of the transactions in Parliament, in the third and fourth years of the reign of our late Sovereign Lord King Charles : containing the severall speeches, cases and arguments of law transacted between his Majesty and both Houses ; together with the grand mysteries of the kingdome then in agitation. [By Thomas Fuller, D.D.] Folio. [*Brit. Mus.*] London, 1645

Preface signed " T. F."

EPHESIAN (the) and Cimmerian matrons ; two notable examples of the power of love & wit. [By Walter Charleton, M.D.] 8vo. Pp. 91. [*Bodl.*] In the Savoy, 1668

The Cimmerian matron has a separate title as follows : The Cimmerian matron ; to which is added, the mysteries and miracles of love. By P. M. Gent. In the Savoy : 1668. 8vo. Pp. 101.

The Ephesian matron is sometimes wrongly ascribed to Jeremy Taylor.

EPHESIAN (the) matron ; a comic serenata, after the manner of the Italian : as it is performed at Ranelagh House. [By Isaac Bickerstaffe.] The music by Mr Dibdin. 8vo. [*Biog. Dram.*] London, 1769

EPHRAIM Holding [George Mogridge]'s homely hints to Sunday-school teachers. 12mo. Pp. 194. [*George Mogridge : his life, character, and writings.* By the Rev. Charles Williams, p. 355.] London, 1843

EPIC (the) of Hades. In three books. By the author of *Songs of two worlds* [Sir Lewis Morris]. Fourth edition. 8vo. Pp. x., 284. London, 1878

Book II. Hades, was issued in 1876 as a separate volume.

VOL. II.

EPIC (the) of the Middle Ages ; a simple account of the Divina Commedia. By a lover of Dante [—— Alexandrina]. Fcap 8vo. London, 1904

EPICEDE (an), or funerall song on the most disastrous death of Henry, Prince of Wales. [By George Chapman.] 8vo. [Lowndes' *Bibl. Man.*] London, 1612

EPICHARIS, an historical tragedy. By the author of *Granby* [Thomas Henry Lister]. Represented for the first time at Drury Lane Theatre, October 14, 1829. Second edition. 8vo. [*D. N. B.*, vol. 33, p. 353.] London, 1829

EPICS (the) of the ton ; or, the glories of the great world : a poem, in two books, with notes and illustrations. [By Lady Anne Hamilton.] 8vo. Pp. iv., 271. [*Brit. Mus.*] London, 1807

EPICTETUS Junior, or maximes of modern morality : in two centuries. By J. D. [John Davies, of Kidwelly]. 12mo. [*D. N. B.*, vol. 14, p. 145.] London, 1670

EPICURES. [A novel.] By Lucas Cleeve [Mrs Howard Kingscote, *née* Adelina G. I. Wolff]. Pp. 240. [*Lit. Year Book.*] London, 1896

EPICURE'S (the) Year-book. By Fin Bec [William Blanchard Jerrold]. 8vo. [*D. N. B.*, vol. 29, p. 353.] London, 1867-68

EPIGONIAD (the) ; a poem in nine books. [By William Wilkie, D.D.] 8vo. [Watt's *Bibl. Brit.*] Edinburgh, 1757

EPIGRAMES, serued out in 52 severall dishes for euery man to taste without surfeting. By I. C., Gent [John Can]. 8vo. No pagination. [Lowndes' *Bibl. Man.*, p. 746.] London, [1604]

EPIGRAMMES and elegies. By I. D. and C. M. [John Davies and Christopher Marlowe]. 4to. No pagination. [*Bodl.*] At Middleborugh, [1598]

EPIGRAMS. [By Rev. Francis Wrangham, M.A.] 8vo. S. Sh. [*D. N. B.*, vol. 63, p. 67.] N.P., N.D., [1800 ?] Signed " X."

EPIGRAMS. By H. P. [H— Parrot]. 4to. 32 leaves. [*Brit. Mus.*] London, 1608

EPIGRAMS. By J. D. *See* All Ovid's elegies.

EPIGRAMS and jeux d'esprit. By A. F. G. [John Lister, advocate]. 8vo. Edinburgh, 1875

M

EPIGRAMS upon the paintings of the most eminent masters, ancient and modern. By J. E. [John Elsum]. Esq. 8vo. [Lowndes' *Bibl. Man.*]
                                    London, 1700
Wrongly attributed to John Evelyn.

EPILOGUE spoken at the representation of the tragedy of Cato at the school at Reading. Dec. 11, 1759. [By William Vansittart, D.D.] 4to. [*Bodl.*]   N.P., N.D.

EPILOGUE to the late Peace [with the United States and with France. By Rev. J— Davies]. 8vo. Pp. 32.
                                    N.P., 1783

EPIPSYCHIDION : verses addressed to the noble and unfortunate lady Emilia V— now imprisoned in the convent of ——. [By Percy Bysshe Shelley.] 8vo. [Dyce *Cat.*, ii., 297.]
                                    London, 1821

EPISCOPACIE not abivred in his Maiesties realme of Scotland : containing many remarkable passages, newly published. [By John Maxwell, Bishop of Ross, afterwards of Killala.] 4to. Pp. 8, 125. [Watt's *Bibl. Brit.*]   N.P., 1641

EPISCOPACY and Presbytery considered, according to the severall respects which may commend a church - government, and oblige good Christians to it. [By Henry Ferne, D.D., of Cambridge.] 4to. [*Bodl.*]
                                    Oxford, 1644

EPISCOPACY examined. By Chorepiscopus [Rev. John Waugh]. 8vo. [Cushing's *Init. and Pseud.*, vol. i., p. 56.]   Utica, New York, 1849

EPISCOPAL (the) Church in Scotland : extracted from the " Churchman's Monthly Review." [By the Rev. Edward Bickersteth.] 8vo.
                                    Edinburgh, 1843

EPISCOPAL (the) Church of England, and its Book of Common Prayer, briefly and catechetically examined. By A. Scot, V.D.M. [William A. Thomson, D.D., Perth]. Square 12mo. Pp. 143. [*New Coll. Cat.*]
                                    Edinburgh, 1849

EPISCOPAL (the) Church of Scotland proved to be in full communion with the Church of England, from her articles and canons, and from the testimony of English Archbishops and Bishops. By a vicar of the Church of England [Joseph Bosworth, D.D.]. 8vo. [*Brit. Mus.*]   London, 1849

EPISCOPAL government instituted by Christ and confirmed by Scripture and reason. By R. R. [Robert Rollock]. 4to. [Thomason *Coll. of Tracts*, vol. i., p. 52.]   London, 1641

EPISCOPAL jurisdiction asserted, according to the right constitution thereof by His Majesties laws, etc. ; occasioned by the stating and vindicating of the Bishop of Waterford's Case with the Mayor and Sheriffs of Waterford. [By Arthur Stanhope, LL.D., Dean of Waterford.] 4to. Pp. 131. [Dix and Dugan's *Dubl. Books.*]
                                    Dublin, N.D., [1671]
Another edition of " The Bishop of Waterford's case with the Mayor and Sheriffs of Waterford stated and vindicated " (1670).

EPISCOPAL (the) oath of allegiance to the Pope, in the Church of Rome : containing the oath both in its original and in its latest form. By Catholicus [Rev. Joseph Mendham]. 8vo. [Mendham Coll. *Cat.*, p. 202.]
                                    Birmingham, [1822]

EPISCOPAL the only apostolical ordination ; or the case of ordination truly consider'd : to which is prefixed a letter from Dr George Hickes. [By William Hamilton.] 8vo. Pp. 155.
                                    London, 1713

EPISCOPALL inheritance ; or a reply to the Humble examination [by Cornelius Burges] of a printed abstract of the answers [by John Williams, Abp. of York] to nine reasons of the House of Commons against the votes of Bishops in parliament : also a determination of [John Davenant] the late learned and Reverend Bishop of Sarum, Englished. [By Gerard Langbaine.] 4to. [Madan's *Oxf. Books*, vol. ii., p. 157.]   Oxford, 1641

EPISCOPUS puerorum, in die innocentium ; or, a discoverie of an antient custom in the church of Sarum, making an anniversarie Bishop among the choristers. [By John Gregory, Bishop of Salisbury.] 4to. [*Bodl.*]
                                    London, 1649

EPISODE (the) of Hector and Andromache (Iliad, Book vi., 369-502), attempted in English verse. By C. C. [Charles Chorley]. 8vo. Pp. 8. [Boase and Courtney's *Bibl. Corn.*]
                                    Truro, 1867

EPISODE (the) of Olimpia, translated from Orlando Furioso, Canto x. [By E. Davenport.] 8vo. [*Brit. Mus.*]
                                    London, 1824

EPISODE (an) on a desert island. By the author of *Miss Molly* [Beatrice May Butt]. Cr 8vo. Pp. 176. [*Brit. Mus.*]   London, 1901

EPISODES from François le Champi. By George Sand [Madame Amandine L. A. Dudevant]. 12mo. Pp. 136. [*Brit. Mus.*]   London, 1893

EPISODES in an obscure life. By a Curate [Richard Rowe]. 3 vols. 8vo. [Cushing's *Init. and Pseud.*, vol. ii., p. 39.]   Philadelphia, 1871

EPISODES of insect life. By Acheta Domestica, M. E. S. [Miss L. M. Budgen]. 8vo. Pp. xviii., 320. [*Bodl.*]   London, 1849
—— Second series. 8vo. Pp. xvi., 326.   London, 1850
—— Third series. 8vo. Pp. xvii., 434.   London, 1851

EPISTEL (the) exhortatorye of an Jnglyshe Chrystian vnto his derely beloved countrey of Jngland agaynst the pompouse Popysh bisshops therof, as yet the true membres of theyre fylthye father the great Antychryst of Rome. Made by Henry Stalbrydge [John Bale, Bishop of Ossory]. 8vo. [Lowndes' *Bibl. Man.*] Basyle, [1544]

EPISTLE apologetical of S. C. [Serenus Cressy], to a person of honour [Edward Hyde, Earl of Clarendon], touching his vindication of Dr Stillingfleet. 12mo. [*Brit. Mus.*]   N.P., 1674

EPISTLE (the) congratulatorie of Lysimachus Nicanor, of the Societie of Jesu to the Covenanters in Scotland : wherein is paralleled our sweet harmony and correspondency in divers materiall points of doctrine and practice. [By John Corbet, minister in Bonhill, Dumbarton.] 4to. Pp. 78. [*D. N. B.*, vol. 12, p. 199.] N.P., 1640
   Erroneously ascribed to John Maxwell, Archbishop of Tuam, and to Henry Lesley, Bishop of Down and Connor.

EPISTLE (an) declaratorie, or manifest ; written by G. L. [George Leyburn] to his brethren residing in England. 12mo. Pp. 51. [*Brit. Mus.*]   [Douai], 1657

EPISTLE (an) directed to all Justices of the Peace in England and Wales. [By Richard Bernard, minister at Batcombe]. 4to. [Green's *Bibl. Somers.*, ii., 169.]   London, 1642

EPISTLE (an) directed to the Parliament of the Commonwealth of England. [By Samuel Chidley.] No separate title. 4to. Pp. 4. N.P., [1652]

EPISTLE (the) exhortatorye of an Englyshe Christyane vnto his derelye beloued contreye of Englande, against the pompouse popyshe Bysshoppes thereof. . . . By Henrye Stalbrydge [John Bale, Bishop of Ossory]. 12mo. [*Camb. Univ. Lib. Cat.*]   [London, 1544]

EPISTLE (an) from a country parson, to a residentiary of St Paul's. [By William Salisbury.] 4to. [*Bodl.*]   Chelmsford, N.D.

EPISTLE (an) from a lady in England, to a gentleman at Avignon. [By Thomas Tickell, M.A.] Folio. [*Watt's Bibl. Brit.*]   London, 1717

EPISTLE (an) [in verse] from a nobleman [Lord John Hervey] to a Doctor of Divinity : in answer to a Latin Letter in verse. Folio. 4 leaves.   London, 1733

EPISTLE (an) from a student at Oxford, to the Chevalier ; occasioned by his removal over the Alps, and the discovery of the Swedish conspiracy. [By Nicholas Amherst.] 8vo. [*Bodl.*]   London, 1717

EPISTLE (an) from G— E— H—rd [Gorges Edmund Howard, really by Capt. Robert Jephson] to Alderman George Faulkner. Third edition. 8vo. [O'Donoghue's *Poets of Ireland*.]   Dublin, 1772
   See also below, " An Epistle [in verse] to Gorges Edmond Howard. . . ."

EPISTLE (an) [in verse] from John More, apothecary [George Bubb Dodington, Baron Melcombe] to L— C— [Lord Carteret] upon his Treatise of Worms [the Treaty of Worms]. Folio. [*Brit. Mus.*]   London, [1743 ?]

EPISTLE from Lady Grange to Edward D—, Esq. ; written during her confinement in the island of St Kilda. [By William Erskine, W.S.] 4to. [*D. N. B.*, vol. 17, pp. 413 ff.]   London, 1798

EPISTLE (an) from Mademoiselle D'Eon to the Right Honorable L—d M—d, [Lord Mansfield] C—f J—e of the C—t of K—g's B—h, on his determination in regard to her sex. [By James Perry.] 4to.   London, 1778

EPISTLE (an) from Oberea, Queen of Otaheite, to Joseph Banks, Esq. ; translated by T. Q. Z. Esq. professor of the Otaheite language in Dublin, and of all the language of the undiscovered islands in the South Sea ; and enriched with historical and explanatory notes. [By Major John Scott.] 4to. [*Bodl.*]   London, 1774

EPISTLE (an) from Sempronia to Cethegus, with reply. [By George Sewell, M.D. ?] 8vo. [*Brit. Mus.*]   London, 1713
   A satire on the Duke and Duchess of Marlborough.

EPISTLE (an) from the Elector of Bavaria to the French King, after the battel of Ramillies. [By Matthew Prior.] Folio.   London, 1706

EPISTLE from the Honourable Charles Fox, partridge shooting, to the Honourable John Townsend, cruising. [By Richard Tickell.]   4to.   [*Adv. Lib.*]
London, 1779

EPISTLE from the Marquis de la Fayette to General Washington [a fictitious production, in verse. By Anne Bannerman.] Fcap 8vo. Pp. iv., 32.   Edinburgh, 1800

EPISTLE (an) from the Rev. William M—n [Mason] to the Right Hon. William Pitt, Chancellor of the Exchequer, petitioning for the vacant Laureatship.   [By   Richard   Polwhele.]   4to.   [Boase and Courtney's *Bibl. Corn.*, ii., 507.]   [London], 1785

EPISTLE (an) from the spirit of love and peace, unto all the upright Israelites, who are born of the seed that is blessed for evermore ; with some things opened concerning the two seeds : to be read amongst Friends, when in the fear of God they are met together in the same spirit. . . . This is only to goe amongst Friends, and not otherwise.   W. S. [William Smith].   4to. [Smith's *Cat. of Friends' Books*, ii., 607.]   N.P., 1663

EPISTLE (an) from Timoleon to all the honest freeholders and other electors of Members of Parliament ; wherein the great mischief and danger of corruption are set forth, and proved from its operations in Greece and Rome. [By William Bollan.] 4to. [Rich's *Bibl. Amer.*, p. 163.]   London, 1768

EPISTLE (an) general containing wholsome exhortations and good counsel from the Spirit of truth, unto all such as are or may be under the judgment or sentence of banishment, for the testimony of Jesus Christ (which is held in a tender conscience) throughout the nation of England ; as also, unto all them that are yet at liberty (to be faithful to the Lord, and meet often together in the fear of his name, and not to fear man, that shall be made as grass) and to all in bonds, prisons, and holes every-where throughout the world, who are bearing (and suffering for) the same testimony of truth and righteousness. . . . By a servant of the Churches of Christ Jesus, W. B. [W. Bayly]. 4to. [Smith's *Cat. of Friends' Books*, i., 218.]   N.P., 1664

EPISTLE (an) general to them who are of the royal priest-hood and chosen generation ;   given forth from the movings of the power and spirit of truth, and now made publick to be sent abroad among the saints scattered in Old and New England, Germany, Holland, Ireland, Scotland, Barbadoes, and Virginia, for them to read in the fear of the Lord. [By George Fox.] 4to.   London, 1660
Signed " G. F."

EPISTLE (an) humbly address'd to the right honourable the Earl of Oxford, &c. ; with a discourse on the usefulness, and some proposals, of a supplement to Bishop Walton's polyglott Bible ; with a reconciliation of the Hebrew and Septuagint, and several remarks on the Oriental versions of the Scripture, particularly the Ethiopic, whereby some observable and difficult passages are illustrated. . . . [By John Mawyer,   M.A.]   8vo.   Pp.   64. [Davies' *Mem. of the York Press*, p. 181.]   York, N.D.

EPISTLE (an) in verse to the Rev. Dr [Francis] Randolph, occasioned by the publication of the correspondence between the Earl and Countess of Jersey and the Doctor upon . . . some letters belonging to . . . the Princess of Wales. [By Thomas James Mathias.] 8vo. [*D. N. B.*, vol. 37, p. 428.]
London, [1796]

EPISTLE (an) of a Christian brother exhorting an other to keepe himself undefiled from the present corruptions brought in to the ministration of the Lords Supper. [By David Calderwood.] 8vo. [*D. N. B.*, vol. 8, p. 245.]
N.P., 1624

EPISTLE (an) of comfort ; to the reverend priests, and to the honorable, worshipfull, and other of the lay sort, restrayned in durance for the Catholike fayth. [By Robert Southwell, S.J.] 8vo.   [*D. N. B.*, vol. 53, p. 299.]
[Douay], printed with licence, 1605
An earlier edition (1593 ?) was issued at Paris.

EPISTLE (the) of Gildas, the most ancient British author ; who flourished in the yeere of our Lord, 546, and who by his great erudition, sanctitie, and wisedome, acquired the name of Sapiens. Faithfully translated out of the originall Latine [by Thomas Habington]. 8vo. Pp. 447. [*Bodl.*]   London, 1638

EPISTLE (an) to a friend at Rome [in verse.   By Stephen Sulivan].   4to. [*Brit. Mus.*]
London, private print, 1772

EPISTLE (an) to a friend in England ; written at sea. [By Rev. —— Dent.] 4to. [*Camb. Univ. Lib.*]   N.P., N.D.

EPISTLE to a friend, on the death of John Thornton, Esq. By the author of *An Epistle to an eminent painter* [William Hayley, of Eartham]. 4to. [*Biog. Dram.*]   London, 1780

EPISTLE (an) to a friend, with other poems. By the author of *The pleasures of memory* [Samuel Rogers]. 4to. [*Brit. Mus.*]   London, 1798

EPISTLE (an) to a gentleman of the Temple, occasioned by two treatises just published, wherein the Fall of man is differently represented, viz., Mr Law's Spirit of prayer, and the Bishop of London's Appendix : shewing that, according to the plainest sense of Scripture, the nature of the Fall is greatly mistaken in the latter. [By John Byrom.] Folio. [Watt's *Bibl. Brit.*]   London, 1749

EPISTLE (an) to a lady, concerning some important and necessary truths in religion. [By William Dodd, LL.D.] 4to.   London, 1753

EPISTLE (an) to a lady who desired the author to make verses on her, in the heroick stile : also a poem, occasion'd by reading Dr Young's satires, called, " The universal passion." [By Jonathan Swift.] Folio. [Dyce *Cat.*, ii., 339.]
            Dublin printed, and reprinted at
                            London, 1734

EPISTLE (an) to a young nobleman [Lord Beauchamp] from his preceptor [Rev. John Dalton, D.D.]. 8vo. [*D. N. B.*, vol. 13, p. 427.] London, 1736

EPISTLE to Admiral Keppel. [By William Hayley, of Eartham.] 4to. [*Biog. Dram.*]   London, 1779

EPISTLE (an) to all justices of the peace in England and Wales concerning Church government. [By Richard Bernard, of Batcome.] 4to. Pp. 16. [*Brit. Mus.*]   London, 1642

EPISTLE (an) to all people on the earth ; also shewing that it was the practice of many to wait in silence upon God, to hear his word and know his voice. By G. F. [George Fox]. 4to.   London, 1657

EPISTLE (an) to an Archdeacon [Nares], Vice President of the Royal Society of literature, from R. P. [Rev. Richard Polwhele] an honorary associate. 4to. [Boase and Courtney, *Bibl. Corn.*, ii., 513.]   London, 1824

EPISTLE (an) to be read in all the assemblies of the righteous. From G. F. [George Fox]. 4to. N.P., 1666

EPISTLE (an) to Curio [Pulteney, Earl of Bath. By Mark Akenside]. 4to. [Chalmers' *Biog. Dict.*] London, 1744

EPISTLE (an) [in verse] to D. B. [D— Braithwaite]. By T. P. [T— Pearson]. 8vo. [*Brit. Mus.*]
            Private print, [London, 1795 ?]

EPISTLE (an) to Dr Shebbeare : to which is added an ode to Sir Fletcher Norton, in imitation of Horace, Ode viii. Book iv. By Malcolm Macgreggor, of Knightsbridge, Esq., author of the *Heroic epistle to Sir William Chambers*, etc. [Rev. William Mason]. Second edition. 4to. [*D. N. B.*, vol. 36, p. 440.]   London, 1777

EPISTLE (an) to Florio [Mr Ellis of Christ Church], at Oxford. [By Thomas Tyrwhitt.] 4to.
                            London, 1749

To one of the copies in the Dyce collection, an autograph letter from the author is prefixed.

EPISTLE (an) to Friends for them to read. [By George Fox.] 4to.
                    [London], 1679

Signed " G. F."

EPISTLE (an) [in verse] to Gorges Edmond Howard, with notes explanatory, critical and historical, by George Faulkner, Esq., and Alderman [really by Captain Robert Jephson]. Fifth edition. 8vo. [O'Donoghue's *Poets of Ireland*.]
                            Dublin, 1771

A satire on Faulkner. *See also above,* " An Epistle from G— E— H—rd. . . ."

EPISTLE (an) [in verse] to His Excellency John Lord Carteret, Lord Lieutenant of Ireland. [By Patrick Delany.] Folio. [*Camb. Univ. Lib.*]
                            Dublin, [1730]

EPISTLE (an) to James Boswell, Esq. occasioned by his having transmitted the moral writings of Dr Samuel Johnson, to Pascal Paoli, General of the Corsicans : with a postscript, containing thoughts on liberty. . . . By W. K. Esq. [William Kenrick]. 8vo. [*D. N. B.*, vol. 31, p. 17.]
                            London, 1768

EPISTLE (an) to Junius. [By Benjamin Hughes.] 4to. [*Brit. Mus.*]
                            London, 1774

EPISTLE (an) to . . . George, Lord Pigot, on the anniversary of the raising of the siege of Madras . . . [in verse. By Eyles Irwin, H.E.I.C.S.]. 4to. [*D. N. B.*, vol. 29, p. 58.]
                            London, 1778

EPISTLE (an) to Mr P— [Alexander Pope] in anti-heroicks. Written in 1736. [By Thomas Catesby, Lord Paget.] 8vo.   London, 1738
"A. Pope. Ex dono Autoris nobilissimi." MS. note on the half title of the Dyce copy in the handwriting of Pope. Ascribed to Lord Paget by Warton in a MS. note by him in the same copy. "On Thomas Catesby, Lord Paget, see Nichols' Anecdotes, vol. ii., p. 115."

EPISTLE (an) to Mr [Alexander] Pope from a young gentleman at Rome [Lord George Lyttelton]. 8vo. [*D. N. B.*, vol. 34, p. 372.]   London, 1730

EPISTLE (an) to Mr Warburton, occasioned by his treatment of [Mark Akenside] the author of the Pleasures of imagination. [By Jeremiah Dyson.] 8vo. [Darling's *Cyclop. Bibl.*]
London, 1744

EPISTLE to Peter Pindar. By the author of *The Baviad* [William Gifford]. Third edition, with considerable additions to the postscript. 4to. Pp. 61. [Dyce *Cat.*, i., 325.]   London, 1800
See note to "The Baviad."

EPISTLE (an) to the authour [Dr John Owen] of the "Animadversions upon 'Fiat lux,'" in excuse of Fiat lux against the said Animadversions. [By John Vincent Cane.] 8vo. [*Brit. Mus.*]   [Douay ?], 1663
Signed "J. V. C."
See "Fiat lux" and "Animadversions upon Fiat lux."

EPISTLE [an] to the Christian Indians [of North America]. . . . Written by an English minister [Cotton Mather, D.D.]. 12mo. [Evans' *Amer. Bibl.*, vol. i, p. 184.]   Boston, 1706

EPISTLE (an) to the Earl of Oxford. [By Thomas Gent.] 8vo. [*Brit. Mus.*]
York, 1731

EPISTLE to the Edinburgh Reviewers [in verse]. By A. B. [Sir Alexander Boswell]. 4to. [*D. N. B.*, vol. 5, p. 428.]   Edinburgh, 1803

EPISTLE (an) to the flock, professing the true light which lighteth every one that cometh into the world; wherein the opposers and villifiers of the true light are (by the way) expostulated with; and they that own it are exhorted to answer the light in the consciences of others by an unblamable life, and to grow it therein, both in the general, and in their particular relations. . . . From a lover of truth and righteousness, wheresoever it is found. W. T. [William Tomlinson]. 4to. [Smith's *Cat. of Friends' Books*, ii., 750.]   N.P., 1674

EPISTLE (an) to the Greeks, especially to those in and about Corinth and Athens; with certain queries propounded unto the two Churches of Greeks and Romans. By J. P. [John Perrot]. 4to. [*Brit. Mus.*]
London, 1661

EPISTLE (the) to the Hebrews; a new translation in sections, with marginal notes and an introductory syllabus. [By Josiah Conder.] 8vo. [*Brit. Mus.*]   London, 1834

EPISTLE (the) to the Hebrews; an experiment in conservative revision. By two clerks [Rev. Frederick Brooke Westcott and Rev. Henry Charles Beeching]. Royal 8vo. Pp. 42. [*Camb. Univ. Lib.*]   Cambridge, 1912

EPISTLE (the) to the Hebrews, with notes. [By Rev. Joseph Augustus Miller.] Fcap 8vo. [Darling's *Cyclop. Bibl.*]   London, 1851

EPISTLE (an) to the . . . Lord Mayor concerning the excessive use of spirituous liquors. . . . [By Bishop Isaac Maddox, D.D.] 8vo. [*D. N. B.*, vol. 35, p. 299.]   London, 1750

EPISTLE (an) to the Right Honourable Charles, Earl of Dorset and Middlesex, Lord Chamberlain of his Majesties houshold; occasion'd by his Majesty's victory in Ireland. [By Charles Montague.] Folio. [*W.*]   London, 1690

EPISTLE (an) to the Right Honourable Sir Robert Walpole. [By George Bubb Dodington, Lord Melcombe. In verse.] Second edition. Folio. Pp. 11. [*Adv. Lib.*]   London, 1726

EPISTLE (an) to the Right Honourable Sir Robert Walpole. [By Robert Nugent, M.P.] Folio. Pp. 14.
London, 1739

EPISTLE (an) to Thomas Moore, Esq., in imitation of the thirteenth Satire of Juvenal. [By Lord John, afterwards Earl Russell.] 8vo. [Courtney's *Secrets*, p. 171.]   London, 1819

EPISTLES for the ladies. [By Eliza Haywood.] 2 vols. 12mo. [*Brit. Mus.*]
London, 1749-50

EPISTLES from Bath; or, Q's letters to his Yorkshire relations, and miscellaneous poems. By Q in the corner [Thomas Haynes Bayly]. 8vo. [Green's *Bibl. Somers.*, vol. i., p. 56.]
Bath, 1817

EPISTLES in verse. [By Richard Sharp, M.P.] 8vo. Pp. 139. [*Brit. Mus.*]   London, 1828

EPISTLES (the) of Aristaenetus; a metrical version from the Greek. [By Nathaniel Brassey Halhed and Richard Brinsley Sheridan.] 8vo. [*D. N. B.*, vol. 52, p. 78.]   London, 1771

EPISTLES of Brevet-Major Pindar Puff. [By Gulian Crommelin Verplanck, LL.D.] 8vo. [Cushing's *Init. and Pseud.*, vol. i., p. 242.]
New York, 1819

EPISTLES (the) of Clio and Strephon ; being a collection of letters that passed between an English lady and an English gentleman in France. . . . [By Martha Fowke.] 8vo. [*Brit. Mus.*]   London, 1720

EPISTLES (the) of Horace ; translated into English verse. [By Charles Lloyd.] 12mo. Pp. 88. [*Martin's Cat.*]   Birmingham, 1812
The first, second, third, fourth, seventh, and tenth Epistles were printed in the *Gentleman's Magazine.*

EPISTLES (the) of Jacob Behmen, aliter Teutonicus Philosophus ; translated out of the German language. . . . [by John Ellistone]. 4to. [*Brit. Mus.*]   London, 1649
Signed " J. E."

EPISTLES (the) of Noah ; edited [or rather written] by George Umber [William Findlay, M.D.]. 8vo. Pp. xvii., 207. [*Lond. Lib. Cat.*]
Glasgow, 1883

EPISTLES (the) of Ovid, translated into verse by J. F. B. [John Francis Byrne]. 8vo. [O'Donoghue's *Poets of Ireland.*]   Dublin, 1858

EPISTLES (the) of Phalaris, translated into English from the original Greek by J. S. [Solomon Whately, of Magdalen College, Oxford], together with an appendix. . . . 8vo. Pp. iv., 223. [Bartholomew's *Bibl. of Bentley*, p. 36.]
London, 1699

EPISTLES (the) of St Paul to the Colossians, to the Thessalonians, to Timothy, and to Titus, and the general epistle of St James : a new version from the Greek, and chiefly from the text of Griesbach by Philalethes [John Jones, LL.D.]. Fcap 8vo. [Lowndes' *Brit. Lib.*, p. 254.]
London, 1819

EPISTLES ; or, the great salvation contemplated ; in a series of letters to a Christian society. By J. R. [James Relly]. 8vo. Pp. 232. [*Bodl.*]
London, 1776

EPISTLES, philosophical and moral [in verse]. [By William Kenrick.] 8vo. [*D. N. B.*, vol. 31, p. 17.] London, 1759
A fourth edition appeared in 1773 as " Epistles to Lorenzo." *See* the following.

EPISTLES to Lorenzo [in verse]. [By William Kenrick, LL.D.] 8vo. [*D. N. B.*, vol. 31, p. 17.]
London, 1756, 1773
After alteration, these were republished in 1759 as " Epistles, philosophical and

moral " (*see* the foregoing entry) ; the fourth edition, in 1773, reappeared with the original title. Censured for the sceptical spirit of the letters, the author replied anonymously in " A Scrutiny, or the critics criticised . . ." (1759). *See later.*

EPISTLES to the few ; being a real correspondence. [Edited by W. H. Miall ?] 4 vols. Fcap 8vo. [*Brit. Mus.*]   London, 1846

EPISTLES to the great, from Aristippus in retirement. [By John Gilbert Cooper.] 4to. [Watt's *Bibl. Brit.*]
London, 1757

EPISTLES to the King and Duke. [By William Wycherley.] 4to. Pp. 66. [*Bodl.*]   London, 1682
The Epistle to the Duke has a separate pagination.

EPISTOLA Macaronica ad fratrem, de iis quae gesta sunt in nupero Dissidentium conventu, Londini habito. . . . A Macaronic epistle, with an English version, for the use of the ladies and country gentlemen. [By Alex. Geddes, LL.D.] Dy 4to. Pp. 30. [*D. N. B.*, vol. 21, p. 100.]
Londini, 1790

EPISTOLA XI. H. N. [Hendrik Niclas]. Correction and exhortation, out of heartie love . . . set fourth by H. N. Translated out of Basealmayne [by C. Vitell]. B. L. Fcap 8vo. [*Brit. Mus.*]   [Amsterdam, 1574 ?]
See the note to " Evangelium regni."

EPISTOLÆ H. N. The principall Epistles of H. N. [Hendrik Niclas] which he hath set-foorth through the Holy Spirit of Love. . . . Translated out of Base-almaine. B. L. Fcap 8vo. [*Brit. Mus.*]
[Amsterdam, 1575 ?]

EPISTOLARIUM : or fasciculi of curious letters, together with a few familiar poems, and some account of the writers, as preserved among the MSS. of the Forster family. By F. [Thomas Ignatius Maria Forster, F.R.A.S., F.L.S.] Fasciculus I. Letters of particular import. 8vo. Pp. 268 (last page, in error, 168).   Bruges, 1845

EPISTOLARIUM : or the correspondence of the Forster family. Letters and Essays. Vol. II. [By Thomas Ignatius Maria Forster, F.R.A.S., F.L.S.] 8vo. Pp. xxviii., 244 (last page, in error 145). [*Martin's Cat.*]
Bruges, 1850

EPISTOLARY (an) correspondence between S. P. [Samuel Pike] and R. S. [Robert Sandeman] relating to the Letters on Theron and Aspasio. Fcap 8vo. Pp. 128. [*D. N. B.*, vol. 45, p. 290.]   Edinburgh, 1809

EPISTOLARY (an) dissertation addressed to the clergy of Middlesex : wherein the doctrine of St Austin concerning the Christian sacrifice is set in a true light ; by way of reply to Dr Waterland's late charge to them. By a divine of the University of Cambridge [George Smith, D.D.]. 8vo. [Lathbury's *Nonjurors*, p. 379.]
London, 1739

EPISTOLARY (an) letter [in verse] from T— H— [Thomas Hearne] to Sr. H— S— [Hans Sloane], who saved his life and desired him to send over all the rarities he could find in his travels. Folio. [*Brit. Mus.*]
London, 1729
A satire on Hans Sloane.

EPITAPH (an) on Don Quicksot [Charles Conquest, M.D. of Bath] ; [and] on Don Quicksilver [William Gold or Gould, M.D.]. (By a Quaker) [Thomas Guidot]. 8vo. Pp. 2. [*Bodl.*] [Bath, 1694]
All the names are given by Wood.

EPITAPH (an) upon Thomas, late Lord Fairfax ; written by a person of honour [George Villiers, 5th Duke of Buckingham]. Folio. Pp. 2. [*Bodl.*]
N.P., N.D.
The author's name is in the handwriting of Wood.

ΕΠΙΤΑΦΙΑ, or a collection of memorials inscribed to the memory of faithful servants. . . . [By J— W— Streeten, of Kempsey, Worcestershire.] 8vo.
London, 1826

EPITAPHS ; some of which have appeared in the " Literary Gazette " of March and April, 1823. [Collected by William Beckford.] 8vo. [Martin's *Cat.*]
London, 1825
Those that appeared in the *Literary Gazette* were published under the pseudonym of " Viator."

EPITHALAMIUM in honour of the marriage of their Royal Highnesses the Prince and Princess of Wales. By the author of *Whitefriars* [Emma Robinson] as recited by Miss Avonia Jones, at the Theatre Royal, New Adelphi, Tuesday, March 10, 1863. 8vo. Pp. 12.
London, 1863

EPITHALAMIUM (an) on the most auspicious nuptials of the Right Honorable the Marquis of Carmarthen, and the Lady Elizabeth Harley. By H. C. [Henry Castleton]. 8vo.
London, 1713

EPITHRENE (an), or voice of weeping ; bewailing the want of weeping. A meditation. [By John Lesley.] 12mo. [*Camb. Univ. Lib.*]
London, 1631

EPITOME of a scheme of finance, whereby a considerable revenue may be obtained without taxation or any burthen on the country. . . . [By Patrick Colquhoun, LL.D.] 8vo. Pp. 24. [*D. N. B.*, vol. 11, p. 403.]
London, 1816

EPITOME (an) of all the lives of the Kings of France. . . . Translated out of the French coppy by R. B., Esq. [Richard Braithwait]. 8vo. [*Brit. Mus.*]
London, 1639
Mistakenly ascribed, through misreading of R. B. as " Richard Burton," to Nathaniel Crouch.

EPITOME (an) of Chinese numismatics. [By John Williams.] 8vo. Pp. 34. [*Brit. Mus.*] [London, 1853]

EPITOME (an) of logic. In four parts. By N. Dralloc [John Collard]. Fcap 8vo. [*Brit. Mus.*] London, 1795
The preface is signed " J. C." The pseudonym is the reversed spelling of the true name. The second edition, improved, appeared as " The Essentials of logic . . ." with the name correctly given, 1796.

EPITOME (an) of Mr Gunton's History of Peterborough Cathedral. By C. J. [C— Jacob]. Eleventh edition. 8vo. [Cushing's *Init. and Pseud.*, vol. i., p. 140.] Peterborough, 1807

EPITOME (an) of Paley's Evidences of Christianity. . . . By a member of the University of Cambridge [Rev. Samuel Rowe]. 12mo. [Cushing's *Init. and Pseud.*, vol. ii., p. 99.]
Cambridge, 1824

EPITOME (an) of Paley's Principles of moral and political philosophy. By a member of the University of Cambridge [Rev. Samuel Rowe]. 12mo. [*Brit. Mus.*] London, 1825

EPITOME (the) of the art of husbandry ; comprising all necessary directions for the improvement of it ; plowing, gardening, directions for the use of the angle, ordering of bees, of horses, oxen, &c. . . . By J. B. [Joseph Blagrave (?)], Gent. 2 vols. Fcap 8vo. [Arber's *Term Cat.*, i. 523.] London, 1675

EPITOME (an) of the Bampton lectures of the Rev. Dr Hampden. [By William John Irons, B.D.] 8vo. [Darling's *Cyclop. Bibl.*] London, 1848

EPITOME (an) of the history of the Church of the United Brethren, in the way of question and answer. . . . [By Rev. J— Carey, of Horton.] Fcap 8vo. Pp. iv., 96. [Malin's *Cat. of Moravian Books.*] Bradford, [Yorkshire], 1850

EPITOME (an) of the history of the world, principally as it is exhibited in the fulfilment of the prophecies of the sacred writings. [By John Hoyland.] 8vo. [*Brit. Mus.*] London, 1812

EPITOME (an) of the history, statistics, etc. of Nova Scotia. By a Nova Scotian [C— B. Owen]. 8vo. [Cushing's *Init. and Pseud.*, vol. i., p. 206.]
Halifax, 1842

EPITOME (an) of the population of the counties of England. . . . [By Thomas Hill Mortimer.] 8vo. [*Brit. Mus.*]
London, 1831

EPITOME (an) of the present world, the future anticipated : or, the flowers of divinity in miniature. . . . By a layman [William Hood]. 8vo. [*Brit. Mus*]
Bristol, [1809]

EPITOME (an) of the privileges of London, including Southwark, as granted by royal charters, &c. By David Hughson, LL.D. [Edward Pugh]. 12mo. [Lowndes' *Bibl. Man.*]
London, 1816

EPITOME (an) of the whole art of war. [By Joseph Moxon, F.R.S. ?] Fcap 8vo.
London, 1692

EPITOME (an) of universal history. [By Mrs Anne Raikes Harding.] 8vo. [*D. N. B.*, vol. 24, p. 335.]
London, 1848

All Mrs Harding's publications are anonymous.

EPOCHS (the) ; a poem. By the author of *Jock o' the Knowe*, etc. [Robert W. Thom]. Pt 8vo.   Glasgow, 1884

EPPONINA ; a dramatic essay, in five acts and in verse. [By John Carr, LL.D.] 8vo. [*D. N. B.*, vol. 9, p. 170.]
London, 1765

This work, addressed to ladies, is founded on the account, given by Tacitus and Dio Cassius, of Epponina, the wife of Julius Sabinus.

EPSOM races : a poem, comic, punning, and racy. By Thomas Hood the younger [Charles Clark, Esq.] 8vo.
London, 1836

EPULLIA, and other poems. By the author of *Poems by Melanter* [Richard Doddridge Blackmore, M.A.]. Fcap 8vo. Pp. 118. [*Brit. Mus.*]
London, 1854

EPWELL (the) hunt, in Warwickshire, and Billesdon Coplow hunt, Leicestershire . . . [in verse]. By an old sportsman [Hon. Martin B. E. Hawke]. 8vo. Pp. 24. [*Brit. Mus.*]
Cheltenham, [1835]

EQUAL (an) ballance : wherein the ministers and churches of the Anabaptists (so called) are truly weighed. . . . Written by a lover of the truth [Robert Wastfield, of Brislington]. 4to. Pp. 56. [Whitley's *Bapt. Bibl.*, i., 75.]
London, 1659

EQUAL partners . . . By Howard Fielding [Charles W. Hooke]. Fcap 8vo. [*Amer. Cat.*]   New York, 1901

EQUAL to either fortune. [A novel.] By the author of *The man of mark*, etc. [Janet Maughan]. 3 vols. 8vo. [*Brit. Mus.*]
London, 1869

EQUAL to the occasion. [A novel.] By Edward Garrett [Isabella Fyvie, later Mrs John Mayo]. Pt 8vo. [*Brit. Mus.*]
London, 1887

EQUALITY (the) of the constitution. [By Edmund L. Swifte.] 8vo. [Gladstone *Lib. Cat.*]   London, 1819

EQUALL (the) wayes of God, tending to the rectifying of the crooked wayes of man. By T. H. [Thomas Hayne]. 4to. [*Brit. Mus.*]   London, 1632

EQUANIMITY in death ; a poem. By George Watson [George Watson Taylor]. 8vo. [Cushing's *Init. and Pseud.*, vol. i., p. 304.]   London, 1813

EQUESTRIAN (an) epistle in verse to the Earl of Jersey. [By Thomas James Mathias, M.A.] 8vo. [*D. N. B.*, vol. 37, p. 428.]
London, 1796

EQUITY (the) pleader's assistant ; containing a great variety of precedents and interrogatories, methodically arranged. [By Maynard Chamberlain Walker.] 2 vols. 8vo. [Watt's *Bibl. Brit.*]   London, 1796

EQUIVALENT (the) : a second poetical petition to the Right Honourable Robert Walpole, Esq. ; for the dignity of poet-laureat, in Scotland. [By Joseph Mitchell.] 8vo. [*Bodl.*]
London, 1725

Signed " J. M."

EQUIVALENT (the) explain'd. [By George Savile, Marquis of Halifax.] 4to. [*Adv. Lib.*]   N.P., N.D.

ERASTUS senior ; scholastically demonstrating this conclusion, that (admitting their Lambeth records for true) those called Bishops here in England are no Bishops, either in order or jurisdiction, or so much as legal : wherein is answered to all that hath been said in vindication of them, by Mr Mason, in his Vindiciæ Ecclesiæ Anglicanæ ; Dr Heylin, in his Ecclesia restaurata ; or Dr Bramhall (then called Bishop of Derry, now Primate of Armagh), in his last book, intituled, " The consecration -and succession of Protestant Bishops justified." With an appendix. . . . [By John Lewgar.] Fcap 8vo. [Wood's *Athen. Oxon.*, iii., 696.]   [London], 1662

Ascribed also to Peter Talbot. [*Brit. Mus.*]

ERCHIE, my droll friend (sketches). By Hugh Foulis [Neil Munro]. 8vo. Pp. viii., 191.   Edinburgh, 1904
Wrongly attributed to D. S. Meldrum.

ERCHOMENON ; or, the Republic of materialism. By * * * [Henry Cocker Marriott Watson]. 8vo. [*Brit. Mus.*]
London, 1879

ERECTING and operating : a treatise for constructing engineers. . . . By William Rogers [Nehemiah Hawkins]. 8vo. [*Amer. Cat.*]   New York, 1907

EREIGHDA Castle ; a novel. [By Geraldine Penrose Fitzgerald.]   3 vols. 8vo.   London, 1870

EREUNA ; or, an investigation of the etymons of words and names, classical and scriptural, through the medium of Celtic : together with some remarks on Hebræo-Celtic affinities.   By a Celtophile [Rev. Francis Crawford, LL.D.]. 8vo. Pp. viii., 176. [*Camb. Univ. Lib.*]   London, 1875

EREWHON ; or over the range. [By Samuel Butler.] 8vo. Pp. viii., 246. [*Bodl.*]   London, 1872

ERIC Sinclair's luck ; a story for boys. By A. B. Romney [A— Beatrice Rambaut].   Pt 8vo.   Pp. 160.   [*Lit. Year Book.*]   London, 1897

ERICK Thorburn. [A novel.   By Mary Bramston].   3 vols.   Cr 8vo.
London, 1869

ERIC'S good news. [A tale. By Amy Le Feuvre.] 8vo. Pp. 80. [*Brit. Mus.*]   London, 1895

ERIN go bragh.   By Clara Vance [Mrs Mary Andrews Denison].   Fcap 8vo. [Cushing's *Init. and Pseud.*, vol. i., p. 292.]   Boston, 1879

ERIN ; or, the cause of the Greeks ; a drama.   By an Asiatic Liberal [George Burges, M.A.]. 8vo.   London, 1823
Another edition in the same year, giving the author's name, shows variation in the title ("The Son of Erin . . .").

ERIN Quintiana ; or, Dublin Castle and the Irish Parliament, 1767-1772.   By Eblana [Teresa J. Rooney].   8vo. [S. J. Brown's *Ireland in fiction.*]
Dublin, 1898

ERIN'S fairy spell ; or the palace of industry and pleasure : a vision.   By William Scribble [William Smyth, Irish comedian and journalist].   8vo. [O'Donoghue's *Poets of Ireland.*]
Dublin, 1865

ERLACH Court : from the German of Ossip Schubin [Lola Kirschner].   Pt 8vo. [Cushing's *Init. and Pseud.*, vol. i., p. 261.]   Philadelphia, 1889

ERNALD ; or, the martyr of the Alps : and other poems.   By Adeline, author of *Scenes in the West Indies*, etc. [Mrs Emily Frances Adeline Sergeant]. 8vo. Pp. vii., 274. [*D. N. B.*, Second Supp., vol. 3, p. 291.]   London, 1843

ERNEST Dacent ; or, the purpose fulfilled.   By the author of *Stories of my pets* [Beatrice Stebbing, later Mrs Batty]. 8vo. Pp. 238. [*Brit. Mus.*]
London, 1886

ERNEST Jones ; who is he ? What has he done ? [By James Crosley, accountant.] 8vo. Pp. 16. [*Manch. Free Lib.*]   Manchester, [1868]

ERNEST Maltravers.   By the author of *Pelham*, etc. [Edward G. E. Lytton, Bulwer Lytton, Baron Lytton].   3 vols. Fcap 8vo. [*Brit. Mus.*]   London, 1837

ERNEST ; or, political regeneration [a poem.   By Capel Lofft, jun.].   12mo. Pp. 298.   [Dobell's *Private Prints*, p. 112.]   N.P., 1839
A second edition appeared in 1868 ("Ernest ; the rule of right").   *See below.*

ERNEST Singleton.   By the author of *Dr Hookwell* [Robert Armitage].   3 vols.   Fcap 8vo. [*Brit. Mus.*]
London, 1846

ERNEST ; the rule of right. [A poem. By Capel Lofft, jun.]   Second edition. 8vo.   London, 1868
See above, "Ernest ; or, political regeneration."

ERNESTINE ; a novel . . . By Wilhelmine von Hillern. [Translated from the German by Sabine Baring Gould.] 2 vols.   8vo. [*Brit. Mus.*]
London, 1879

ERNESTINE ; or, the child of mystery. By a lady of fashion. [Miss —— Blackwell].   3 vols.   Fcap 8vo. [*Camb. Univ. Lib.*]   London, 1840

ERNESTO di Ripalta ; a tale of the Italian Revolution.   By the author of *Notes of a two years' residence in Italy* [Hamilton Geale].   3 vols.   8vo. [*Camb. Univ. Lib.*]   London, 1849
The " Notes " are not anonymous.

EROTOPHUSEOS, or the love of nature : a serio-comic poem, in four scenes.   By Timotheus Pikromel, Esq. [Thomas Clarke].   8vo. [*Camb. Univ. Lib.*]   London, 1840

ERRAND-GIRL (the) : a novel.   By Flora M'Flimsey [Evelyn Kimball Johnson].   Fcap 8vo. [Cushing's *Init. and Pseud.*, vol. ii., p. 469.]
New York, 1889

ERRATA (the) to the Protestant Bible, or, the truth of their English translations examin'd ; in a treatise shewing some of the errors that are to be found in the Protestant English translations of the sacred Scriptures, against such points of Catholick doctrine as are in debate between them and the Church of Rome. . . . By T. W. [Thomas Ward]. With allowance. 4to. Pp. 100. [Cotton's *Rhemes and Doway*, p. 28.]   London, 1688
> To this work, largely based on Dr Gregorie Martin's "Discoverie of grievous errors," a reply was published by Dr William Fulke ; it was nevertheless reprinted in 1807, 1810, and 1841.

ERRATICS. By a sailor ; containing rambles in Norfolk and elsewhere : in which are interspersed some observations on the late attempts to revive the Cromwellian observance of the Sabbath. . . . [By Joshua Larwood, rector of Swanton Morley, Suffolk.] Fcap 8vo. Pp. 180. [Watt's *Bibl. Brit.*]   London, 1809

ERRORS, discrepancies, etc. of the Gospel records, with special reference to the fourth Gospel. [By Thomas Scott, of Ramsgate, or Sir George William Cox ?]. Cr 8vo.
Ramsgate, 1869

ERRORS (the) of innocence. [By Harriet Lee.] 5 vols. Fcap 8vo. [Green's *Bibl. Somers.*, i., 311.]   London, 1786

ERRORS (the) of modern theology, more especially of the Morisonian system, shown in a letter. . . . By a Christian observer [George Galloway]. Fcap 8vo. Pp. 36.   Glasgow, 1845

ERRORS of Mydar ; a poem, in two cantos : with an appendix. [By Hugh Brown, of Newhall.] 8vo.
Edinburgh, 1832

ERRORS of nature. [By B. Walwyn.] 3 vols. Fcap 8vo. [*Mon. Rev.*, lxx., 163 ; lxxiv., 473.]   London, 1783

ERRORS (the) of the Church of Rome plainly stated. By a convert from Rome [John B. Scully]. Fcap 8vo.
Oxford, 1859

ERRORS respecting Cranmer's Great Bible, 1540. By Candidus [George Cornelius Gorham]. 8vo. [Cushing's *Init. and Pseud.*, vol. ii., p. 27.]
London, 1826

ERROUR non-plust ; or, Dr Stillingfleet shown to be the man of no principles : with an essay how discourses concerning Catholick grounds bear the highest evidence. [By John Sergeant.] 8vo. [*Adv. Lib.*]   N.P., 1673

ERSILIA. By the author of *My little lady* [Eleanor Frances Poynter]. 3 vols. 8vo. [*Camb. Univ. Lib.*] London, 1876

ERSILIA ; or the ordeal. [A novel. By Ethel G. More ?].   Bath, 1867

ERUTA fragmenta : epigrams from "Deliciæ Poetarum Gallorum," translated into English verse. [By Charles R. Jackson.] 8vo. [Robertson's *Aberd. Bibl.*]   Aberdeen, 1863

ERUVIN ; or, miscellaneous essays on subjects connected with the nature, history, and destiny of man. [By Samuel Roffey Maitland, D.D.] Fcap 8vo. [*Brit. Mus.*]   London, 1831
> The author's name is given in the second edition, published in 1850.

ESKDALE ; a poem. [By Thomas Telford.] 4to. [*D. N. B.*, vol. 56, p. 9.]   London, 1781

ESOP ; a comedy [by —— Purvey], as it is acted at the Theatre-Royal in Drury Lane. 12mo. Pp. 308.
London, 1734

ESOP'S Fables, written in Chinese by the learned Mun Mooy Seen-Shang, and compiled in their present form (with a free and a literal translation) by his pupil Sloth [Robert Thom]. Folio. [*W.*]   Canton, 1840

ESPECIALLY those : a story on the prayer for all conditions of men. By Brenda [Mrs Castle Smith]. Fcap 8vo. [Haynes' *Pseud.*]   London, 1875

ESPOUSALS (the). [By Coventry D. K. Patmore.] 8vo. Pp. viii., 182.] [F. Boase's *Mod. Brit. Biog.*, vi., col. 364.]   Chiswick, 1856
> The above was revised and combined with his "Betrothal" to form "The Angel in the house" (1858).

ESQUIRE Bickerstaff's most strange and wonderful predictions for the year 1708 ; wherein the month and day of the month are set down, when several most surprising accidents shall certainly come to pass, as particularly that the present French King shall die on the 29th of July ; the Pope to die on the 11th of September ; the Dauphin, the French King's son, to dye on the 7th of May ; that Partridge, the famous astrologer, is to dye on the 29th of March ; on the 23d of May, a famous actor of the play-house will die a ridiculous death, suitable to his vocation ; upon the 26th of August, will arrive from Flanders such a welcome express of victory, that a thousand bonfires will be made in London. . . . with several other strange things too tedious to be here related. [By Jonathan Swift, D.D.] Licensed according to order. 8vo. Pp. 8.
N.P., 1708

ESSAIES politicke, and morall. By
D. T., Gent. [Attributed to Daniel
Tuvill.]   Printed by H. L. for Mathew
Lownes, dvvelling in Paules Church-
yard. 8vo. Fol. 130. [*N. and Q.*,
1860, p. 104.]   London, 1608

ESSAY (an) against uncharitableness,
wherein the secret springs of that
vice are traced, and the effects of it
briefly survey'd. [By Isaac Watts.]
Cr 8vo. [*Brit. Mus.*]   London, 1707

ESSAY (an) at a plain exposition of
that difficult phrase, A good peace. By
the author of *The Review* [Daniel
Defoe]. Fcap 8vo. Pp. 52. [Wil-
son's *Life of Defoe*, 127.]
                       [London], 1711

ESSAY (an) at removing national pre-
judices against a union with Scotland.
[By Daniel Defoe.] To be continued
during the treaty here. Part I. 4to.
Pp. 32. [*Adv. Lib.*]   London, 1706
—— Part II. 4to. Pp. 32
                         London, 1706
  A second edition of Parts I. and II. in
one was printed at Edinburgh in the same
year.
—— Part III. By the author of the two
first. 4to. Pp. 37.
                    [Edinburgh], 1706
  There were six Essays in all. The others
will be found under A Fourth essay ; A
Fifth essay ; and Two great questions con-
sidered.

ESSAY (an) concerning a fourth age of
the Church, in four parts : 1. Of the
antichristian kingdoms of Daniel and
the Revelation ; 2. Other parts of
Daniel considered, and particularly the
seventy weeks ; 3. On a fifth and sixth
antichristian kingdom ; 4. A general
review of prophecy, beginning with
Gen. 3. 15. [By Rev. E. Rouse, B.D.]
Folio. [Darling's *Cyclop. Bibl.*]
                         London, 1742

ESSAY (an) concerning Church government, out of the excellent writings of
Calvin and Beza. By A. C. [Alex-
ander Cunningham], M.A. 4to. [*New
Coll. Lib.*]   N.P., 1689

ESSAY (an) concerning critical and
curious learning ; in which are contained some short reflections on the
controversie betwixt Sir William
Temple and Mr Wotton, and that
betwixt Dr Bentley and Mr Boyl
[Robert Boyle]. By T. R., Esq.
[Thomas Rymer]. 8vo. Pp. 77. [Bar-
tholomew's *Bibliog. of Bentley, p.* 30.]
                         London, 1698

ESSAY (an) concerning human understanding. Thirty-second edition, with
notes and illustrations of the author
[John Locke], and an analysis of his

doctrine of ideas : also questions on
Locke's Essay. By A. M. [who also
signs himself T. O'M., viz. Thaddeus
O'Mahony]. 8vo. Pp. xvi., 664.
[*Brit. Mus.*]   London, 1860

ESSAY (an) concerning obedience to the
supreme powers, and the duty of subjects in all revolutions ; with some
considerations touching the present
juncture of affairs. [By Matthew
Tindal, LL.D.] 4to. Pp. 70. [*Bodl.*]
                         London, 1694

ESSAY (an) concerning pestilential con-
tagion ; occasion'd by the distemper
now raging among the cattle : with
a method proposed to prevent its progress. By Iater [John Davis, M.D.
of Bath]. [In two parts.] 8vo. Pp.
72. [Green's *Bibl. Somers.*, i., 140.]
                         London, 1748

ESSAY (an) concerning preaching, writ-
ten for the direction of a young divine.
[By Joseph Glanvil, M.A.] Fcap 8vo.
[Green's *Bibl. Somers.*, i., 210.]
                         London, 1678

ESSAY (an) concerning rational notions ;
to which is added the proof of a God.
[By Charles Mayne.] 8vo. [*Camb.
Univ. Lib.*]   London, 1733

ESSAY (an) concerning slavery, and the
dangers Jamaica is expos'd to, from
the too great number of slaves. [By
Edward Trelawney.] 8vo. Pp. 80.
                      London, [1725 ?]

ESSAY (an) concerning the divine right
of tythes. By the author of *The snake
in the grass* [Charles Leslie]. Fcap
8vo. [Watt's *Bibl. Brit.*]
                         London, 1700

ESSAY (an) concerning the human
rational soul ; in three parts. Shewing, I. The origin, II. The nature, III.
The excellency of this soul, upon
natural as well as revealed principles.
With an introduction in defence of
reveled [*sic*] religion. [By Rev.
Zachary Langton, M.A.] 8vo. Pp.
xxix., 202. [*Bodl.*]   Dublin, 1753

ESSAY (an) concerning the nature of
the priesthood. By J. S., B. K.
[Josiah Story, Bishop of Kilmore].
8vo. [Watt's *Bibl. Brit.*]
                         Dublin, 1749

ESSAY (an) concerning the necessity of
equal taxes ; and the dangerous consequences of the encouragement given
to usury among us of late years : with
some proposals to promote the former,
and give a check to the latter. By the
author of *The History of the last Parliament* [James Drake, M.D.]. 4to.
Pp. 28. [*Bodl.*]   London, 1702
  Ascribed also to Sir Richard Blackmore.
[*Manch. Free Lib. Cat.*, p. 62.]

ESSAY (an) concerning the power of the magistrate and the rights of mankind in matters of religion ; with some reasons in particular for the Dissenters not being obliged to take the Sacramental Test but in their own churches, and for a general naturalization. [By Matthew Tindal, LL.D.] 8vo [*D. N. B.*, vol. 56, p. 405.]
London, 1697

ESSAY (an) concerning the Thule of the ancients, where it is shewen that the Thule mentioned by the Roman writers was the North East part of Britain, lying over against the Isles of Orkney. [By Sir Robert Sibbald.] 8vo. [*D. N. B.*, vol. 52, p. 181.]
Edinburgh, 1693
Published afterwards (London, 1700) with some alterations.

ESSAY (an) concerning the use of reason in propositions the evidence whereof depends upon human testimony. [By Anthony Collins.] 8vo. Pp. 56. [Arber's *Term Cat.*, vol. iii., p. 685.] London, 1707

ESSAY (an) contributing to a philosophy of literature. By B. A. M. [Brother Azarias Mullany, Patrick Francis Mullany]. 8vo. [Cushing's *Init. and Pseud.*, vol. i., p. 178.]
Philadelphia, 1877

ESSAY (an) descriptive of the abbey Church of Romsey, in Hampshire, founded by King Edward the Elder. [By Charles Spence.] 8vo. Pp. 128. [Anderson's *Brit. Top.*]
Romsey, [1841]
Other editions followed.

ESSAY (an) explaining the mode of executing a useful work, entitled, A new description of England and Wales, as a continuation and illustration of Camden. [By Peter Muilman.] 8vo. [*Bodl.*] London, 1772

ESSAY (an) for a new translation of the Bible ; wherein is shewn from reason, and the authority of the best commentators, interpreters and criticks, that there is a necessity for a new translation : in two parts. By H. R. [Hugh Ross], a minister of the Church of England. Pt 8vo. Pp. 179, 212. [Arber's *Term Cat.*, iii., p. 685.]
London, 1702
A translation, without acknowledgment, of Charles Le Cène's " Projet d'une nouvelle version françoise de la Bible."

ESSAY (an) for abridging the study of physick ; to which is added a dialogue (betwixt Hygeia, Mercury, and Pluto) relating to the practice of physick as it

is managed by a certain illustrious Society ; as also an epistle from Usbek the Persian to J. W. [Joshua Ward], Esq. [By John Armstrong, M.D.] 8vo. Pp. 52. [Watt's *Bibl. Brit.*]
London, 1735

ESSAY (an) for allaying the animosities amongst British Protestants ; in a discourse founded upon the fourteenth, and part of the fifteenth chapter of the Epistle to the Romans. [By John Platts.] 8vo. Pp. 30. [*Bodl.*]
London, 1715

ESSAY (an) for composing a harmony between the Psalms and other parts of Scripture, but especially of the New Testament ; wherein the supplicatory and prophetick parts of this sacred book, are disposed under proper heads. [By Sir Edward Harley, M.D.] Second edition. 8vo. Pp. lxxxiv., 162. [*D. N. B.*, vol. 24, p. 394.] London, 1732

ESSAY (an) for peace, by union in judgement about Church-government in Scotland. In a letter from ****** to his neighbour in the countrey. [By Sir Francis Grant, Lord Cullen.] 4to. [*D. N. B.*, vol. 22, p. 386.]
Edinburgh, 1703

ESSAY for promoting of psalmody. [By Nahum Tate.] Fcap 8vo. [*D. N. B.*, vol. 55, p. 380.] London, 1710

ESSAY (an) for regulating of the coyn ; wherein is also set forth, First, how we have lost that import of plate and bullion we formerly had. Secondly, What is become of the great quantities of money coyned in the reign of King Charles II. and the preceding reigns. Thirdly, the necessity there is at this time for to rectifie the present coyn of the kingdom. Fourthly, by what methods the charge of calling in the present money, and bringing it to a designed standard may be accomplished. Fifthly, whether the method proposed for the advancing of our money (and the bullion of which its made) be convenient or inconvenient for the trade of the nation. By A. V. [A. Vickaris, of Chertsey]. 4to. [*W.*]
London, 1696
A second edition was published in the same year " with an additional proposition for the regulating the coyn, by A. V., merchant."

ESSAY (an) for the better regulation and improvement of free thinking ; in a letter to a friend. [By John Hildrop, D.D.] 8vo. Pp. 70. [In vol. 1 of his Miscellaneous works ; *D. N. B.*, vol. 26, p. 386.] London, 1754

ESSAY (an) for the conversion of the Irish ; shewing that 'tis their duty and interest to become Protestants. [By Sir Richard Cox.] Fcap 8vo. Pp. 48. [*D. N. B.*, vol. 12, p. 415.] Dublin, 1698

ESSAY (an) for the press. [By John Asgill.] 8vo. [*Brit. Mus.*]
London, 1712

ESSAY (an) for the understanding of St Paul's Epistles, by consulting St Paul himself. [By John Locke.] 4to. [*D. N. B.*, vol. 34, p. 35.] London, 1707

ESSAY (an) in defence of the female sex ; in which are inserted the characters of a pedant, a squire, a beau, a vertuoso, a poetaster, a city-critick, &c. In a letter to a lady, written by a lady [Mrs Drake]. 8vo. Pp. 148. [Watt's *Bibl. Brit.*]   London, 1696
Also ascribed to Mrs Mary Astell.

ESSAY (an) in morality ; written by G. B. to his friend H. P. Esquire. In which the nature of virtue and vice is distinctly stated, their respective reasonableness and unreasonableness demonstrated, and several useful conclusions inferred. [By George Bright, D.D., Dean of St Asaph.] Fcap 8vo. Pp. 151. [*Bodl.*]   London, 1682

ESSAY (an) in vindication of the continental colonies of America, from a censure of Mr Adam Smith, in his Theory of moral sentiments. With some reflections on slavery in general. By an American [Arthur Lee]. 8vo. [Cushing's *Init. and Pseud.*, vol. i., p. 12.]   London, 1764

ESSAY (an) of education, and the state of Ireland. By an Irish Catholic [James Warren Doyle, Bishop of Kildare]. 8vo. [Cushing's *Init. and Pseud.*, vol. i., p. 138.]   Dublin, 1825
The title of a later edition (1880) begins " An Essay on education. . . ."

ESSAY (an) of humane nature, or the creation of mankind. [By Joseph Keble, LL.B., of Gray's Inn.] 8vo. [Watt's *Bibl. Brit.*]   London, 1707

ESSAY (an) of particular advice to the young gentry, for the overcoming the difficulties and temptations they may meet with ; and the making and happy improvement of the advantages they enjoy beyond others. By the author of *Youth's grand concern* [John Graile, M.A.]. 8vo. [*Camb. Univ. Lib.*]
London, 1711

ESSAY (an) of the great effects of even languid and unheeded motion ; whereunto is annexed an experimental discourse of causes of the insalubrity of the air and its effects. [By the Hon. Robert Boyle.] 8vo. [*Brit. Mus.*]
London, 1685

ESSAY of the meanes how to make our travailles into forraine countries the more profitable and honourable. [By Thomas Palmer.] 4to. [Bliss' *Cat.*, 228.]   London, 1606

ESSAY (an) on a congress of nations. By Hamilton [George Henry Whitman]. 8vo. [Cushing's *Init. and Pseud.*, vol. i., p. 125.]   Boston, 1840

ESSAY (an) on acting ; in which will be consider'd the mimical behaviour of a certain fashionable faulty actor. . . . [By David Garrick—a criticism of himself.] 8vo. Pp. 27. [*D. N. B.*, vol. 21, p. 24.]   London, 1744

ESSAY (an) on advertising. [By Donald Nicoll.] 8vo. [Gladstone *Lib. Cat.* (Lib. Club).]   London, 1878

ESSAY (an) on aërial navigation ; with some observations on ships. By J. M'S. [Joseph Macsweeny, M.D.]. 8vo.   Cork, 1824
The second edition (1844) bears the author's name.

ESSAY (an) on American slavery. . . . By a citizen of Boston [Joshua Pollard Blanchard]. 8vo. [Cushing's *Init. and Pseud.*, vol. ii., p. 31.]   Boston, 1855

ESSAY (an) on angling. By a member of the Worcester Anglers' Society [William George]. 8vo. [Cushing's *Init. and Pseud.*, vol. i., p. 191.]
Worcester, 1840

ESSAY (an) on archery, describing the practice of that art in all ages and nations. [By Walter Michael Moseley.] 8vo. [Watt's *Bibl. Brit.*]
Worcester, [1792]

ESSAY (an) on architecture. By T. H. L. [Thomas Henry Lowth]. 8vo. [Cushing's *Init. and Pseud.*, vol. i., p. 160.]   London, 1776

ESSAY (an) on arithmo-physiology, or the chronological classification of organized matter, deduced from an inspection of the numbers employed in the divisions or subdivisions of the different parts of vegetables and animals. [By Sir Richard Rawlinson Vyvyan, Bart., Sheriff of Cornwall.] 8vo. [*D. N. B.*, vol. 58, p. 400.]
London, privately printed, 1825

ESSAY (an) on bank-tokens, bullion, &c. By a Briton [Morris Robinson, Lord Rokeby]. 8vo. [*Brit. Mus.*]
Stockton, 1811

ESSAY (an) on bashfulness. [By Samuel Charters, D.D.] 8vo. Pp. 96. [Sinton's *Hawick Bibl.*]
Hawick, 1815

ESSAY (an) on bigotry, religious inno-
vation and infidelity, as respectively
supported by Doctors Burke, Priestley,
and Toulmin ; in a letter to John
Mitford, Esq. By Falkland [Francis
Perceval Eliot]. 8vo. Pp. 55. [*Adv.
Lib.*]   London, 1791

ESSAY (an) on capacity and genius ; to
prove that there is no original mental
superiority between the most illiterate
and the most learned. . . . [By William
Andrew Mitchell, of Newcastle-on-
Tyne ?] 8vo.   London, [1820 ?]
See also " An Essay on original genius."

ESSAY (an) on Christian burial, and the
respect due to burying-grounds. By a
ruling elder of the Church of Scotland
[Robert Forbes, M.A., Bishop of Ross].
8vo. [*D. N. B.*, vol. 19, p. 410.]
                          N.P., 1765

ESSAY (an) on Christ's fear of death :
an appeal . . . from the judgment of
the Independent Church at Nottingham. [By Joseph Rawson.] 8vo.
                          London, 1737

ESSAY (an) on Church consecration,
containing a history of its origin, progress, and effects ; in answer to a
letter. . . . [By James Crombie, D.D.,
Presbyterian minister in Belfast.] Fcap
8vo. Pp. 70. [Witherow's *Presb. in
Ireland*, vol. ii., p. 212.] Dublin, 1777

ESSAY (an) on Church government.
By a layman of the [Episcopal] Church
in Scotland [John Alexander, advo-
cate]. 8vo.   Edinburgh, 1835

ESSAY on Church patronage ; or a brief
inquiry, on the ground of Scripture and
antiquity, into the people's right of
choosing their own minister. [By
John Sinclair.] 8vo. [*Lit. Gazette*,
xix., 118.]   Edinburgh, 1835

ESSAY (an) on Church reform. [By
Alexander Alison.] 8vo. [*Brit. Mus.*]
                          London, 1851

ESSAY (an) on civil government ; treating summarily of its necessity, original,
dissolution, forms and properties. [By
William Hay, M.P.] 8vo. [*Brit.
Mus.*]   London, 1728

ESSAY (an) on collateral consanguinity,
it's limits, extent, and duration ; more
particularly as it is regarded by the
statutes of All Souls College in the
University of Oxford. [By Sir William
Blackstone.] 8vo. Pp. vi., 80. [*N.
and Q.*, 1868, p. 528.] London, 1750

ESSAY (an) on comparative anatomy.
[By Alexander Monro, M.D., F.R.S.]
8vo. [*Brit. Mus.*] London, 1744

ESSAY (an) on conciliation in matters
of religion. . . . By a Bengal civilian
[John Muir, D.C.L., LL.D.]. 8vo.
                          Calcutta, 1849

ESSAY (an) on conduct and education. [By John Fry.] 8vo. [Smith's
Cat. of Friends' Books, i., 817.]
                          London, 1738

ESSAY (an) on crimes and punishments ;
translated from the Italian [of Cæsar
Bonesana, Marquis de Beccaria] : with
a commentary, attributed to Voltaire,
translated from the French. 8vo.
[Watt's *Bibl. Brit.*] London, 1767
Six editions in the original were speedily
sold ; more than sixty editions and
translations were afterwards required.
Some of the later English translations give
the author's name.

ESSAY (an) on criticism. [By Alexander Pope.] 4to. Pp. 43.
                          London, 1711
Frequently reprinted, with the author's
name.

ESSAY (an) on criticism, as it regards
design, thought, and expression in
prose and verse. By the author of
the Critical history of England [John
Oldmixon]. 8vo. [*Brit. Mus.*]
                          London, 1728

ESSAY (an) on culinary poisons : containing cautions relative to the use
of laurel-leaves, hemlock, mushrooms,
copper-vessels, earthen jars, &c. ; with
observations on the adulteration of
bread and flour, and the nature and
properties of water. [By Joseph
Robertson, vicar of Horncastle, Lin-
colnshire.] 8vo. [Watt's *Bibl. Brit.*]
                          London, 1781

ESSAY (an) on defensive war, and a
constitutional militia ; with an account
of Queen Elizabeth's arrangements
for resisting the present invasion in the
year 1588, taken from authentic records
in the British Museum, and other collections. By an officer [Capt. Dorset].
8vo. [Watt's *Bibl. Brit.*] London, 1782

ESSAY (an) on design in gardening.
[By George Mason.] 8vo. Pp. 54.
                          London, 1768
Augmented, and published with the
author's name in 1795.

ESSAY (an) on draining, more particularly with regard to the north
divisions of the great level of the
Fenns, call'd Bedford Level. [By
Sigismund Trafford.] 8vo. Pp. 23.
                          London, 1729

ESSAY (an) on drying by artificial heat ;
more particularly, on the principles of
the drying and preservation of hops.
[By John Marten.] 8vo. [*Brit. Mus.*]
                          Canterbury, 1860-61
Signed " J. M."

ESSAY (an) on ecclesiastical establishments in religion, shewing their hurtful tendency, and that they cannot be defended, either on the principles of reason or Scripture : to which are annexed, two discourses. By a Protestant Dissenter [Rev. William Christie]. Printed at Montrose. 8vo. Pp. 57. [*Mon. Rev.*, vii., 291.]
London, 1792

ESSAY (an) on education and the state of Ireland. By an Irish Catholic [James Warren Doyle, D.D.]. 8vo.
Dublin, 1880
Previously published as " An Essay of education. . . ." *See above.*

ESSAY (an) on education ; Catholic and mixed : a poem. By a Catholic priest [Rev. James Casey, of Sligo]. Fcap 8vo. [O'Donoghue's *Poets of Ireland.*]   Dublin, 1868

ESSAY (an) on electricity. [By J— B— Becket.] Fcap 8vo. [*Birm. Cent. Lib.*]   1773

ESSAY (an) on elocution, or pronunciation ; intended chiefly for the assistance of those who instruct others in the art of reading, and of those who are often called to speak in publick. [By Rev. John Mason, M.A., minister at Dorking, in Surrey.] Fourth edition. 8vo. [*Bodl.*]   London, 1757

ESSAY (an) on equitable tenancies under legal terms of years. [By John Maude Ogden.] [*Brit. Mus.*]
London, 1849

ESSAY (an) on establishments in religion ; with remarks on the Confessional [by Francis Blackburne]. [By John Rotheram, B.A.] 8vo. Pp. 148. [*D. N. B.*, vol. 49, p. 300.]
Newcastle upon Tyne, 1767

ESSAY (an) on faith, and its connection with good works. [By Rev. William Adams.] 8vo.   London, 1766
Later editions appeared in 1772, 1801.

ESSAY (an) on free trade and finance ; humbly offered to the consideration of the public. By a citizen of Philadelphia [Pelatiah Webster]. 8vo. [Cushing's *Init. and Pseud.*, vol. ii., p. 31.]   Philadelphia, 1779

ESSAY (an) on government. By Philopatria [Rachel Fanny Antonina Lee]. 8vo. [*Camb. Univ. Lib.*]
London, 1808
The name of the authoress appears on an enlarged edition published in 1809.

ESSAY (an) on Halifax. [By W. Williams.] 4to. [Newsam's *Poets of Yorkshire*, p. 201.]   Halifax, 1761

ESSAY (an) on happiness : in four books. [By John Duncan, D.D.] 4to. [Watt's *Bibl. Brit.*]   London 1762
Ascribed also to T. Newcomb. [*Brit. Mus.*]

ESSAY (an) on honour. By Timothy Hooker [John Hildrop, D.D.]. 8vo. [In vol. I. of his miscellaneous works ; *D. N. B.*, vol. 26, p. 386.]
London, 1741

ESSAY (an) on houses of industry. [By Charles Butler, barrister-at-law ?] 8vo.
London, 1773

ESSAY (an) on human life. [By Thomas Catisby Paget, Lord Paget.] Second edition, corrected and much enlarg'd by the author. 4to. [*Brit. Mus.*]
London, 1736

ESSAY (an) on hunting. By a hunting squire [Thomas Gosden]. 4to.
London, 1733

ESSAY on husbandry. [By Peter Templeman, M.D.] 8vo.
London, 1764

ESSAY (an) on immortality. By the author of a *Review of the first principles of Bishop Berkeley, Dr Reid, and Prefessor Stewart* [John Fearn]. 8vo. [*Brit. Mus.*]   London, 1814

ESSAY (an) on imposing and subscribing articles of religion ; with a postscript relating to the French clergy : in a letter to Phileleutherus Oxoniensis. By Phileleutherus Cantabrigiensis [Thomas Herne]. 8vo. [*D. N. B.*, vol. 26, p. 250.]   London, 1719

ESSAY (an) on industry ; and biographical sketches of Theophilus Radcliffe and Emma Jones. By a member of the Bar [C— W— Hart]. 8vo. [Cushing's *Init. and Pseud.*, vol. i., p. 187.]   Steubenville, Ohio, 1835

ESSAY (an) on inspiration, in two parts. [By Benjamin Bayly.] 8vo. Pp. 373. [*New Coll. Cat.*]   London, 1707
A second edition, enlarged, and with the author's name, was published in 1708.

ESSAY (an) on instinct. [By P. M. Duncan.] 8vo. [*Manch. Free Lib. Cat.*, p. 210.]   London, [1870 ?]

ESSAY (an) on intemperance, particularly hard-drinking ; wherein that spreading pest is, with its dreadful effects, justly expos'd, specify'd and diversify'd. By Theophilus Philanthropos [David Hall] 8vo. [Smith's *Cat. of Friends' Books*, i., 61, 904.]
N.P., 1742

ESSAY (an) on intuitive morals ; being an attempt to popularise ethical science. [By Frances Power Cobbe.] Part I. Theory of morals. 8vo. Pp. xii., 179. [*Brit. Mus.*] London, 1855

—— Part II. Practice of morals. Book I.—Religious duty. 8vo. Pp. xxii., 229. London, 1857

ESSAY (an) on justice, viewed as a test of religious creeds. . . . [By William Nairne.] 8vo. Pp. iv., 33.
Perth, 1832

ESSAY (an) on landscape gardening. By the author of *An essay towards a general history of feudal property*, etc. [Sir John Dalrymple]. Fcap 8vo. [*Camb. Univ. Lib.*] Greenwich, 1823

ESSAY (an) on landscape ; or, on the means of improving or embellishing the country round our habitations : translated from the French of R. L. Gerardin, Vicomte D'Ermenonville [by Daniel Malthus]. Fcap 8vo. [*Gent. Mag.*, Feb. 1800, p. 177.]
London, 1783

ESSAY (an) on landscape painting, with remarks, general and critical, on the different schools and masters, ancient and modern. [By Rev. Joseph Holden Pott, M.A., Archdeacon of London.] 8vo. [*Nichols' Lit. Anec.*, ix., 73.] London, 1783

ESSAY (an) on liberty and necessity : in answer to Augustus Toplady's tract, on (what he calls) " Christian and philosophical necessity asserted," in which John Wesley's " Thoughts on necessity " are examined and defended ; the difficulties of these subjects rendered plain and easy to common readers ; and human liberty fully proved. By Philaretus [Thomas Letchworth]. Fcap 8vo. [*Smith's Cat. of Friends' Books*, i., 70.] London, [1775]
Also ascribed to John Whitehead, M.D.

ESSAY (an) on liberty, and other poems. By J. B. F. [J— B— Farmer]. Fcap 8vo. Pp. 74. [*Cushing's Init. and Pseud.*, vol. ii., p. 57.] London, 1824

ESSAY (an) on light and shadow, on colours, and on composition in general. [By M— Garside.] Fcap. 8vo. [*Manch. Free Lib.*] Manchester, 1801

ESSAY (an) on light reading, as it may be supposed to influence moral conduct and literary taste. [By Edward Mangin.] Fcap 8vo. [*D. N. B.*, vol. 36, p. 33.] Bath, 1808

ESSAY (an) on love and matrimony. By Zadkiel [Lieut. Richard James Morrison]. 8vo. [*Cushing's Init. and Pseud.*, vol. i., p. 314.] London, 1851

VOL. II.

ESSAY (an) on man : being the first book of ethic epistles to H. St John L. Bolingbroke. [By Alexander Pope.] With the commentary and notes of W. Warburton, A.M. 4to. Pp. 115. [*Brit. Mus.*] London, 1743

ESSAY (an) on medals ; or an introduction to the knowledge of ancient and modern coins and medals, especially those of Greece, Rome, and Britain. [By John Pinkerton.] 2 vols. 8vo. [Watt's *Bibl. Brit.*] London, 1748
Later editions (1789, 1808) were enlarged.

ESSAY (an) on medical economy. [By George Darling, M.D.] 8vo.
London, 1814

ESSAY (an) on mind, with other poems. [By Elizabeth Barrett Browning.] Fcap 8vo. [*Courtney's Secrets*, p. 60.]
London, 1826

ESSAY (an) on money & bullion : wherein are considered, value intrinsick and extrinsick, money and bullion compared, Mr Locke's Considerations concerning raising the value of coin, the present state of our coin, and a scheme for raising the value of our coin, as well gold as silver. [By —— Jocelyn.] 8vo. [MS. note on the title-page of the Signet Library copy.] London, 1718

ESSAY (an) on money as a medium of commerce ; with remarks on the advantages and disadvantages of paper admitted into general circulation. By a citizen of the United States [Pelatiah Webster]. 8vo. Pp. 64. [*Cushing's Init. and Pseud.*, vol i., p. 59.]
Philadelphia, 1786
Wrongly attributed to Dr John Witherspoon.

ESSAY (an) on money ; to which is added an essay on shyness : also two letters on education. By S. G. O. [Lord Sidney Godolphin Osborne]. 8vo. [*Cushing's Init. and Pseud.*, vol. i., p. 207.] London, 1865

ESSAY (an) on moral obligation, with a view toward settling the controversy concerning moral and positive duties : in answer to two late pamphlets ; the one [by A. A. Sykes] entitled, The true foundation of natural and revealed religion asserted ; being a reply to the Supplement to the Treatise [by Daniel Waterland] on the Christian sacraments ; the other—Some reflections upon the comparative excellency and usefulness of moral and positive duties, by Mr Chubb. [By Thomas Johnson, M.A.] 8vo. Pp. 83. [*D. N. B.*, vol. 30, p. 48.] London, 1731

N

ESSAY (an) on musical expression. By Charles Avison, organist in Newcastle. The second edition, with alterations and large additions; to which is added a Letter to the author, concerning the music of the ancients, and some passages in classic writers relating to that subject [by the Rev. John Jortin, D.D.]. Likewise Mr Avison's Reply to [William Hayes] the author of "Remarks on the Essay on musical expression." In a letter from Mr Avison, to his friend in London. 8vo. [*W.*]   London, 1753

ESSAY (an) on national covenanting. [By Alexander Pirie.]   Pt 8vo. [Struthers' *Hist. of the Relief Church* (1843), p. 236.]   Edinburgh, 1767

ESSAY (an) on nothing; a discourse delivered in a society. [By Hugo Arnot.] 8vo. [*D. N. B.*, vol. 2, p. 119.]   London, 1776

ESSAY (an) on original genius, and its various modes of exertion in philosophy and the fine arts, particularly in poetry. [By Rev. William Duff, M.A., of Foveran.] Pp. xxiv., 296. [Scott's *Fasti*.]   London, 1767
    Ascribed also to —— Geddes. [*Bibl. Parriana*, p. 433.] *See also* "An essay on capacity and genius."

ESSAY (an) on paper-money and banking; from Essays on the public debt, frugality, etc. [By Patrick Murray, fifth Baron Elibank.] 8vo. [*Bodl.*] London, 1857

ESSAY (an) on politeness; wherein the benefits arising from and the necessity of being polite are clearly proved and demonstrated. . . . By a young gentleman [John Harris]. 12mo. [*Brit. Mus.*]   London, 1775
    A revised and improved edition appeared in 1820.

ESSAY (an) on Pope's Odyssey; in which some particular beauties and blemishes of that work are considered: in two parts. [By Joseph Spence, A.M.] Fcap 8vo. Part I. Pp. 168. Part II. Pp. 226. [Watt's *Bibl. Brit.*]   London, 1727

ESSAY (an) on practical federation [between Great Britain and Ireland and the British Colonies]. By Centurion [Sir Graham John Bower, K.C.M.G.]. 8vo.   London, 1887

ESSAY (an) on prayer; the nature, method, and importance of that duty; in two parts. [By John Angell.] To which is added, a variety of specimens of prayer, as delivered by several eminent Dissenting ministers in London, taken in short-hand by the editor. Fcap 8vo. [Watt's *Bibl. Brit.*]
                    London, 1761

ESSAY (an) on preaching: lately wrote in answer to the request of a young minister. [By Robert Sandeman.] Fcap 8vo. [*D. N. B.*, vol. 50, p. 256.]   Edinburgh, 1763

ESSAY (an) on private judgment in religious matters. [By William Oldisworth.] 8vo. [*D. N. B.*, vol. 42, p. 115.]   London, 1711

ESSAY (an) on Psalmody. [By Rev. William Romaine, M.A.] Fcap 8vo. Pp. 368. [In his collected works.]
                    London, 1775
    The Preface is signed "W. R."

ESSAY (an) on public happiness, investigating the state of human nature under each of its particular appearances, through the several periods of history to the present times. [Translated from the French of the Marquis F. J. de Chastellux.] 2 vols. 8vo. [*Brit. Mus.*]   London, 1774

ESSAY (an) on punctuation. [By Joseph Robertson.] The second edition. 12mo. [*Brit. Mus.*]
                    London, 1786

ESSAY (an) on railroads. [By Matthew Carey.] 8vo. [Allibone's *Dict.*]
                    Philadelphia, 1839

ESSAY (an) on reason. [By Rev. Walter Harte.] Folio. [*Brit. Mus.*]
                    London, 1735

ESSAY (an) on redemption; being the second part of Divine rectitude. By the author of the former [John Balguy]. Pt 8vo. Pp. 104. [*D. N. B.*, vol. 3, p. 60.]   London, 1741

ESSAY (an) on ridicule. [By William Whitehead.] 8vo. [Watt's *Bibl. Brit.*]   London, 1753

ESSAY (an) on satire; occasion'd by the death of Mr [Alexander] Pope. [By John Brown, D.D., Vicar of Newcastle-on-Tyne.] 4to. [*Bodl.*]
                    London, 1745

ESSAY (an) on schism, in a letter to a friend. [By C. Dewhurst.] Fcap 8vo. [*Brit. Mus.*]   London, 1833

ESSAY (an) on Scripture. [By Philip Bury Duncan.] 8vo. [*Brit. Mus.*]
                    Oxford, [1830]

ESSAY (an) on Scripture-prophecy, wherein it is endeavoured to explain the three periods contain'd in the XII. chapter of the prophet Daniel; with some arguments to make it probable, that the first of the periods did expire in the year 1715. [By William Burnet, eldest son of the Bishop.] 4to. Pp. 169. [*Bodl.*]   N.P., 1724

ESSAY (an) on sensibility : a poem, in six parts. [By William Laurence Brown, D.D.] 8vo. Pp. xviii., 183.
London, 1789
Presentation copy from the author.

ESSAY (an) on Spirit, wherein the doctrine of the Trinity is considered in the light of nature and reason, as well as in the light in which it was held by the ancient Hebrews : compared also with the doctrine of the Old and New Testament : with an inquiry into the sentiments of the primitive Fathers of the Church. . . . [By Robert Clayton, Bishop of Clogher.] 8vo.
London, 1751
In Darling's *Cyclopædia Bibliographica* is the following note—" Universally ascribed to Bp. Clayton, and not disallowed by him, but actually written by a young clergyman in his diocese." *See also* Urme's *Bibliotheca Biblica*, and *D. N. B.*, vol. II, p. 19.

ESSAY (an) on spiritual evolution, considered in its bearing upon modern Spiritualism, science, and religion. By J. P. B. [J— P— Bryce]. 12mo.
London, 1879
Presentation copy from the author. Mistakenly attributed to J. P. Brown.

ESSAY (an) on tactics. [By James F. Macpherson.] 8vo.   London, 1872

ESSAY (an) on that divine hymn, called the Doxology : wherein it's scriptural authority is proven, it's primitive use asserted, objections against it answered, and an exhortation to it's use pressed. By J. W., [John Wilson, Episcopal] minister of the Gospel at Haddingtoun. 4to. [*Adv. Lib.*]
Edinburgh, 1712

ESSAY (an) on the abolition, not only of the African slave trade, but of slavery in the British West Indies. [By John Gray.] 8vo. [*European Mag.*, xxxii., 108.]   London, 1792

ESSAY (an) on the abolition of slavery throughout the British dominions, without injury to the master or his property. [By Thomas Bunn.] 8vo. [Green's *Bibl. Somers.*, ii., 208.]
Frome, 1833

ESSAY (an) on the advantages of a polite education joined to a learned one ; with a dissertation on dancing. [By Stephen Philpot.] 8vo. [Watt's *Bibl. Brit.*]   London, 1746

ESSAY (an) on the agreeableness of Christian faith with natural reason, by way of dialogue : written in Latin by Sebastian Castellio ; Englished by C. B. [Clement Barksdale]. 8vo. [Arber's *Term Cat.*, ii., 587.]
London, 1696

ESSAY (an) on the antient and modern state of Ireland. . . . [By Henry Brooke ?] 8vo.   Dublin, 1760

ESSAY (an) on the antiquities of Great Britain and Ireland, wherein they are placed in a clearer light than hitherto : designed as an introduction to a larger work, especially an attempt to show an affinity betwixt the languages, &c. of the ancient Britains, and the Americans of the Isthmus of Darien. [By David Malcolme, D.D., minister of Duddingston.] 8vo. [Scott's *Fasti.*]
Edinburgh, 1738

ESSAY (an) on the antiquity of the Castel of Norwich, its founders and governors, from the kings of the East Angles, down to modern times. [By Thornhagh Gurdon.] 8vo. [*Upcott*, p. 980.]   Norwich, 1728

ESSAY (an) on the antiquity of the Irish language, being a collation of the Irish with the Punic language ; with a preface proving Ireland to be the Thule of the ancients : addressed to the literati of Europe. . . . [By Charles Vallancey.] 8vo. Pp. x., 64. [*Bodl.*]   Dublin, 1772

ESSAY on the application of capital to land ; with observations shewing the impolicy of any great restriction of the importation of corn, and that the bounty of 1688 did not lower the price of it. By a fellow of University College, Oxford [Edward West, M.A., later Sir Edward West, Judge in Bombay]. 8vo. Pp. 71. [*Bodl.*]
London, 1815

ESSAY (an) on the application of [Scottish] Reformation principles to the American Government. By John Knox, junr. [Rev. H— Hawthorne]. 8vo. Pp. 19.   Philadelphia, 1833

ESSAY (an) on the art of ingeniously tormenting ; with proper rules for the exercise of that pleasant art : humbly addressed, in the first part, to the master, husband, &c. ; in the second part, to the wife, friend, &c. [By Jane Collier.] 8vo. Pp. 236. [Watt's *Bibl. Brit.*]   London, 1753

ESSAY (an) on the autumnal dysentery. By a Physician [Andrew Wilson, M.D., of Newcastle and London]. 8vo. [*Brit. Mus.*]   London, 1761

ESSAY (an) on the beautiful ; from the Greek of Plotinus. [By John Taylor, LL.D.] 8vo. [Lowndes' *Bibl. Man.*, p. 1887.]   London, 1792

ESSAY (an) on the book of Nabathæan agriculture. By Ernest Renan. [Translated from the French by Sarah Symonds.] Fcap 8vo. [*Brit. Mus.*]
London, 1862

ESSAY (an) on the causes of the decline of the foreign trade, consequently of the value of lands of Britain, and of the means to restore both : begun in the year 1739. [By William Richardson.] 4to. Pp. xix., 228.
London, 1744
Ascribed by Adam Smith and others to Sir Matthew Decker, but probably written by Richardson. [M'Culloch's *Lit. of Pol. Econ.*, p. 46, 329.] Later editions appeared at Edinburgh in 1756, and at London about 1780.

ESSAY (an) on the causes of the decline of the Society of Friends. "Quantum mutatus." [By William Bigg.] 8vo. [Smith's *Cat. of Friends' Books*, ii., 216.]   London, [1858]

ESSAY (an) on the causes of the present high price of provisions, as connected with luxury, currency, taxes, and the national debt. [By Rev. Adam Dickson, of Whittinghame.] 8vo. [M'Culloch's *Lit. of Pol. Econ.*, p. 193.]   London, 1773

ESSAY (an) on the causes which have produced Dissent in Wales. [By Arthur J. Johnes.] Second edition. 8vo. [*Lond. Lib. Cat.*] London, 1832

ESSAY (an) on the certainty and causes of the earth's motion on its axis, &c. [By Sir Henry Sheere.] 4to. [*Brit. Mus.*]   London, 1698

ESSAY (an) on the character and conduct of His Excellency Lord Viscount Townshend. [By Sir James Caldwell, Bart.] 8vo. [*Brit. Mus.*]
[London], 1771

ESSAY (an) on the character and influence of Washington in the Revolution of the United States of America. . . . Translated from the French [by G. S. Hillard]. Second edition. 8vo. [*Brit. Mus.*]   Boston, [Mass.], 1851

ESSAY (an) on the character of Hamlet, as performed by Mr Henderson, at the Theatre-Royal in the Hay-market. [By Frederick Pilon.] Second edition. 8vo. [*Brit. Mus.*]
London, N.D., [1785 ?]
Wrongly ascribed to Thomas Davies.

ESSAY (an) on the character of Jonathan. [By George Hardinge.] 8vo. [Martin's *Cat.*]   London, 1813

ESSAY (an) on the Church. [By Rev. William Jones, of Nayland, F.R.S.] 8vo. [*Bodl.*]   Glocester, 1787

ESSAY (an) on the circumstances which determine the rate of wages, and the condition of the labouring classes. [By John Ramsay MacCulloch.] Cr 8vo. [*D. N. B.*, vol. 35, p. 19.]
London, 1826
Several other editions were issued.

ESSAY (an) on the constitution of the earth. [By Robert Ward.] 8vo. [*Brit. Mus.*]   London, 1844

ESSAY (an) on the construction of sleying tables, or an attempt to illustrate geometrically the fundamental principle of the art of weaving. [By Robert Barbour.] 8vo. [Watt's *Bibl. Brit.*]   Glasgow, 1759

ESSAY (an) on the danger of too much circulating cash in a State. By a Financier [Pelatiah Webster]. 8vo. [Cushing's *Init. and Pseud.*, vol. ii., p. 59.]   Boston, Mass., 1791

ESSAY (an) on the demon or divinity of Socrates. [By Robert Nares.] Cr 8vo. [*Lond. Lib. Cat.*] London, 1782

ESSAY (an) on the different stiles of poetry. [By Thomas Parnell, D.D., Archdeacon of Clogher.] 8vo. [*D. N. B.*, vol. 43, p. 350.]   London, 1737

ESSAY (an) on the discipline of Christ's house. By Theophilus [Samuel Spring, D.D.]. 8vo. [Cushing's *Init. and Pseud.*, vol. i., p. 282.]
Newburyport, 1816

ESSAY (an) on the dramatic character of Sir John Falstaff. [By Maurice Morgan.] 8vo. [*Brit. Mus.*]
London, 1777

ESSAY (an) on the duty and qualifications of a sea-officer; written originally for the use of two young officers. [By Sir Charles Knowles, Admiral.] 8vo. Pp. viii., 88. [*Bodl.*] London, 1765
Ascribed by Mr Halkett to the Rev. James Ramsay, with the note that it was reprinted with the author's name.

ESSAY (an) on the East-India-trade. By the author of *The Essay upon ways and means* [Charles Davenant, LL.D.]. 8vo. Pp. 62. [*D. N. B.*, vol. 14, p. 100.]   London, 1696

ESSAY (an) on the education of a young British nobleman, after he leaves the schools ; to which are added some observations on the office of an ambassador. [By William Keith.] 8vo. Pp. 56. [Watt's *Bibl. Brit.*] London, 1730
Attributed also to A— Millar.

ESSAY (an) on the education of young ladies ; addressed to a person of distinction. [By Rev. Joseph Robertson.] 8vo. [*Gent. Mag.*, Feb. 1802, p. 110.]   London, 1798

ESSAY (an) on the evidence from Scripture that the soul, immediately after the death of the body, is not in a state of sleep or insensibility, but of happiness or misery ; and on the moral uses of that doctrine. By Eusebius Exoniensis [Richard Polwhele]. 8vo. Pp. 59. [Boase and Courtney's *Bibl. Corn.*, ii., 512.]   London, 1819

ESSAY (an) on the factory question, occasioned by the recent votes in the House of Commons, addressed to the ladies of England. . . . [By Mrs Sibella Elizabeth Miles, *née* Hatfield.] Fcap 8vo. Pp. 42. [*Brit. Mus.*]
London, 1844

ESSAY (an) on the fall of angels and men. By E. S. [Elias Smith]. Third edition. 8vo. Boston, 1812

ESSAY (an) on the first Book of Lucretius . . . made English verse. By J. E. [John Evelyn]. 4to. [*D. N. B.*, vol. 18, p. 82.] London, 1656

ESSAY (an) on the force of imagination in pregnant women. . . . [By Giovanni Fortunato Bianchini.] 8vo. [*Edin. Univ. Cat.*] London, 1772

ESSAY (an) on the genius and writings of Pope. [By Joseph Warton.] Second edition, corrected. 8vo. [*Brit. Mus.*]
London, 1762
A second volume appeared in 1782. *See* " Essay on the writings and genius," etc.

ESSAY (an) on the genius of George Cruikshank. [Signed "θ," *i.e.* William M. Thackeray.] 8vo. [*D. N. B.*, vol. 56, p. 103.] London, 1840
Reprint from the *Westminster Review*.

ESSAY (an) on the gift of tongues, proving that it was not the gift of languages ; in a letter to a friend. [By Joseph Priestley, LL.D.] 8vo. Pp. 164. [*Bodl.*] Bath, 1786

ESSAY (an) on the governing causes of the natural rate of interest ; wherein the sentiments of Sir William Petty and Mr Locke, on that head, are considered. [By Joseph Massie.] 8vo. Pp. 62. [M'Culloch's *Lit. of Pol. Econ.*, p. 251.] London, 1750

ESSAY (an) on the great affinity and mutual agreement of the two professions of divinity and law, and on the joint interests of Church and State ; in vindication of the clergy's concerning themselves in political matters. [By William Elstob, M.A., Fellow of University College, Oxford.] Fcap 8vo. Pp. 100. [*Bodl.*]
London, 1703

ESSAY (an) on the happiness of the life to come. [By Miss —— Hunt.] 8vo. Bath, 1800

ESSAY (an) on the harmony of language, intended principally to illustrate that of the English language. [By William Mitford.] 8vo. [*Brit. Mus.*]
London, 1774

ESSAY on the headship of the Lord Jesus Christ. By an Office-bearer of the Church of Scotland as by law established [Rev. William Gregor, minister at Bonhill]. 8vo. Pp. 20. [Scott's *Fasti.*] Edinburgh, 1842

ESSAY (an) on the history and reality of apparitions ; being an account of what they are, and what they are not, whence they came, and whence they come not ; as also how we may distinguish between the apparitions of good and evil spirits, and how we ought to behave to them. [By Daniel Defoe.] 8vo. Pp. 408. [Wilson's *Life of Defoe*, 198.]
London, 1733
See a later edition (1770) with a different and fuller title : " The secrets of the invisible world laid open. . . "

ESSAY (an) on the history of parties, and persecution in Britain ; beginning with a brief account of the Test-Act, and an historical enquiry into the reasons, the original, and the consequences of the occasional conformity of Dissenters : with some remarks on the several attempts already made, and now making for an Occasional Bill. . . . [By Daniel Defoe.] 8vo. [Wilson's *Life of Defoe*, p. 129.] London, 1711

ESSAY (an) on the Holy Catholic Church. By Clericus Dorcestrensis [Rev. J— L— Jackson, M.A.]. Third edition. Fcap 8vo. Pp. v., 148.
London, 1842
Published also with the author's name, in " Two essays : the Holy Catholic Church ; the Millennial Church."

ESSAY (an) on the Holy Sacrament of the Lord's Supper, addressed to the inhabitants of a populous parish near London [viz. Mitcham, in Surrey]. By a layman [Peter Waldo]. Fcap 8vo. [Cushing's *Init. and Pseud.*, vol. i., p. 167.] London, 1771

ESSAY (an) on the human mind. [By Edward Bushby.] 8vo. [*Camb. Univ. Lib.*] Cambridge, 1829

ESSAY (an) on the human soul. [By Jean Paul Marat.] 8vo. [*Brit. Mus.*]
London, 1772

ESSAY (an) on the husbandry of Scotland, with a proposal for the further improvement thereof. By a lover of his country [William Macintosh, of Borlum]. 8vo. [*D. N. B.*, vol. 35, p. 179.] Edinburgh, 1732

ESSAY (an) on the illustration of books. [By Richard Plowman, solicitor.] 8vo.
London, 1824
Unpublished. The author's name is in the handwriting of Dawson Turner, to whom a copy was presented by the writer.

ESSAY (an) on the immateriality and immortality of the soul, and its instinctive sense of good and evil. . . . With an appendix. . . . By the author of *Letters in proof of a particular Providence.* [By —— Caulfield.] 8vo. Pp. iv. and 466. [Abbot's *Lit. on a future life.*] London, 1778

ESSAY (an) on the impolicy of a bounty on the exportation of grain, and on the principles which ought to regulate the commerce of grain. [By James Mill, author of the *History of British India.*] 8vo. [M'Culloch's *Lit. of Pol. Econ.*, p. 75.] London, 1804

ESSAY (an) on the influence of Welsh tradition upon European literature. [By Sir John Dorney Harding.] 8vo. Pp. 75. [Dobell's *Private Prints*, p. 191.] London, [1840]

ESSAY (an) on the inspection of the urine. By a physician [Theodor von Mayers]. 8vo. [*Brit. Mus.*] London, 1776

ESSAY (an) on the law of celibacy as imposed on the clergy by the Roman Catholic Church and observed in all the Orders abroad : . . . its rise and progress to the present time. [By Rev. John Hawkins.] 8vo. Worcester, [1782]

ESSAY (an) on the law of libels ; with an appendix containing authorities : to which are subjoined Remarks on the case in Ireland of attachment, and the Letter of the Hon. J. Erskine on that subject. [By Capel Lofft, senr.] 8vo. [Watt's *Bibl. Brit.*] London, 1785

ESSAY (an) on the legality of impressing seamen. [By Charles Butler.] 8vo. Pp. 128. [*Bodl.*] London, 1777
Reprinted later with the author's name.

ESSAY (an) on the liberty of the press, chiefly as it respects personal slander. [By Thomas Hayter, D.D., Bishop of London.] Second edition. 8vo. [*D. N. B.*, vol. 25, p. 306.] London, [1755]

ESSAY (an) on the liberty of the press. By Hortensius [George Hay]. 8vo. [Cushing's *Init. and Pseud.*, vol. i., p. 133.] Philadelphia, 1799

ESSAY (an) on the life and character of Petrarch ; to which are added seven of his sonnets, translated from the Italian. [By Alexander Fraser Tytler.] 8vo. Pp. 56. [Lowndes' *Bibl. Man.*] London, 1784

ESSAY (an) on the life, character, and writings of Dr Samuel Johnson. [By Joseph Towers, LL.D.] 8vo. Pp. 128. [*Brit. Mus.*] London, 1786

ESSAY (an) on the manner of writing history. [By Rev. Peter Whalley, B.C.L.] 8vo. [Watt's *Bibl. Brit.*] London, 1746

ESSAY (an) on the manufacturing interest of the United States, etc. By a member of the Society of Artists and Manufacturers of Philadelphia [Tench Coxe]. 8vo. [Cushing's *Init. and Pseud.*, vol. i., p. 190.] Philadelphia, 1804

ESSAY (an) on the means of insurance against the casualties of sickness . . . and mortality. . . . [By Sir Edwin Chadwick.] 8vo. [*Brit. Mus.*] London, 1836

ESSAY (an) on the merchandize of slaves and souls of men (Rev. 18 : 13), with an application thereof to the Church of Rome. By a Gentleman [Hon. Paul Dudley]. 8vo. [*Brit.]Mus.*] London, 1732
Another edition, in 1733, bears a different title (" A seasonable caveat against Popery . . .").

ESSAY (an) on the method of cultivating hemp and flax, with hints on the same, in the East Indies. [By Sir George Sinclair.] 8vo. Pp. 60. Edinburgh, 1797

ESSAY (an) on the Middlesex election ; in which the power of expulsion is particularly considered. [By George Rous.] 8vo. [*Brit. Mus.*] London, 1769

ESSAY (an) on the more common West-India diseases, and the remedies which that country itself produces ; to which are added some hints on the management, &c. of negroes. By a physician in the West Indies [James Grainger, M.D.]. 8vo. Pp. 80. [*Bodl.*] London, 1764

ESSAY (an) on the Mosaic account of the creation and fall of man. [By Nathaniel Lardner, D.D.] 8vo. [In his collected Works, vol. 11.] London, 1753

ESSAY (an) on the most commodious methods of marine surveying. [By Alexander Dalrymple.] 4to. [*Brit. Mus.*] London, 1771

ESSAY (an) on the National Provincial Bank of England, with a view to its improvement ; in a letter to the shareholders. By the founder of the establishment [Thomas Joplin]. 8vo. [*Camb. Univ. Lib.*] London, 1843

ESSAY (an) on the natural history of Guiana, in South America, containing a description of many curious productions in the animal and vegetable systems of that country : together with an account of the religion, manners, and customs of the several tribes of its Indian inhabitants. . . . [By Edward Bancroft, M.D.] 8vo. Pp. 402. [Rich's *Bibl. Amer.*, i., 169.] London, 1769

ESSAY (an) on the nature and conduct of the passions and affections ; with illustrations on the moral sense. By the author of the *Inquiry into the original of our ideas of beauty and virtue* [Francis Hutcheson, LL.D.]. 8vo. Pp. xxii., 335. [Scott's *Life of Hutcheson.*]   London, 1728
Other editions followed.

ESSAY (an) on the nature and constitution of the Christian Church ; wherein are set forth the form of its government, the extent of its powers, and the limits of our obedience. By a layman [William Stevens, F.S.A.]. 8vo. [Watt's *Bibl. Brit.*]
London, 1773

ESSAY (an) on the nature and existence of a material world. [By —— Russel.] 8vo. Pp. xvi., 212.
London, 1731
" This very acute essay was written by a Mr Russel."—MS. note by Dr Parr on the Signet Library copy.

ESSAY (an) on the nature and method of ascertaining the specific shares of proprietors, upon the inclosure of common fields ; with an inquiry into the means of preserving and improving the public roads of this kingdom. [By Rev. Henry Homer.] 8vo. [M'Culloch's *Lit. of Pol. Econ.*, p. 199.]
Oxford, 1766
The author's name appears in a later edition.

ESSAY (an) on the nature and operation of fines. [By William Cruise, barrister.] 8vo. [*Brit. Mus.*]
London, 1783

ESSAY (an) on the nature and principles of public credit. [By S. Gale, of Charleston, South Carolina.] 8vo. [M'Culloch's *Lit. of Pol. Econ.*, p. 333.]   London, 1784

ESSAY (an) on the nature and use of the militia ; with remarks on the Bill offered to Parliament last session for the better ordering the militia forces in the several counties of that part of Great Britain called England. By a Member of Parliament [Robert Henry Ongley, Lord Ongley]. 8vo. [Park's *Walpole.*]   London, 1757

ESSAY (an) on the nature, design, and origin, of sacrifices. [By Arthur Ashley Sykes, D.D.] 8vo. Pp. viii., 354. [Disney's *Memoir of Sykes*, p. xxii.]   London, 1748

ESSAY (an) on the nature of a loan; being an introduction to the knowledge of the public accounts. [By Thomas Howard, 3d Earl of Effingham.] 8vo. [*N. and Q.*, 18 March 1865, p. 222.]
York, 1782

ESSAY (an) on the nature of the Church [by Thomas Rattray, Bishop of Dunkeld] ; and a review [by Robert Keith, Bishop of Fife] of a work entitled, " A View of the elections of Bishops in the primitive Church" [by James Dundass, M.A.] ; together with some annexed Dissertations [by Bishop Rattray and others]. Cr 8vo. Pp. 431. [*New Coll. Cat.*]   Edinburgh, 1728

ESSAY (an) on the nature of the English verse, with directions for reading poetry. [By the author of *The Essay on punctuation*, Joseph Robertson.] 12mo. [*Brit. Mus.*]   London, 1799

ESSAY (an) on the nature of the human body, and that singular respect and veneration shewn to it, after death, among all people and nations whatsoever ; in consequence of which, on the growing evil of profaning and defiling kirks, and kirk-yards, and other burying-grounds : occasionally interpreted with several thoughts, little regarded now-a-days, though important and interesting. . . . By a ruling elder of the Church of Scotland [Robert Forbes, Bishop of Ross]. 8vo. Pp. 56. [*D. N. B.*, vol. 19, p. 410.]
Edinburgh, 1767

ESSAY (an) on the nature of true virtue. [By Jonathan Edwards, A.M., President of the College of New Jersey.] 8vo.   London, 1778
In his collected works.

ESSAY (an) on the Navy ; or England's advantage and safety prov'd dependant on a formidable and well-disciplined Navy, and the encrease and encouragement of seamen. . . . By the author of *The Seamen's Case* [John Dennis]. 4to. [Watt's *Bibl. Brit.*]   London, 1702

ESSAY (an) on the necessity of protecting Duties [in Ireland]. [By Benjamin Mendicant.] 8vo. [*Camb. Univ. Lib.*]
Dublin, 1783

ESSAY (an) on the necessity of revealed religion. [By James Hare.] 8vo. [*Brit. Mus.*]   Oxford, 1794

ESSAY (an) on the Neodruidic heresy in Britannia. Part the first. By the author of *Britannia after the Romans* [The Hon. Algernon Herbert]. 4to. [Lowndes' *Bibl. Man.*] London, 1838
No more published.

ESSAY (an) on the new project for a land-mint, proposing a proper and practicable scheme and expedient and how to put the same under due and regular management, in this conjuncture. . . . By the author of *The character of the true publick spirit* [Andrew Brown, M.D.]. 8vo. [*Adv. Lib.*]   Edinburgh, 1705

ESSAY (an) on the number seven; wherein the duration of the Church of Rome, and of the Mahometan imposture, the time also of the conversion of the Jews, and the year of the world for the beginning of the Millennium, and for the first resurrection of the martyrs, are attempted to be shewn. By a member of the Church of Christ [Rev. Richard Clarke]. 4to. [Watt's *Bibl. Brit.*]   London, 1759

ESSAY (an) on the objects of taste. . . . [By Mrs —— Glasgow.] Fcap 8vo.
London, 1823

ESSAY (an) on the origin and distribution of gold in quartz veins. By "Pick and Pen" [Henry Rosales]. 8vo.   Melbourne, 1861

ESSAY (an) on the origin of the English stage, particularly on the historical plays of Shakespeare. [By Thomas Percy, D.D.] 8vo. [*D. N. B.*, vol. 44, p. 439.]   London, 1793

ESSAY (an) on the original genius and writings of Homer; with a comparative view of the ancient and present state of the Troade. [By Robert Wood, Under Secretary of State.] 4to. [Watt's *Bibl. Brit.*]
London, 1775

ESSAY (an) on the original of funeral sermons, orations and odes. [By John Gill, D.D.] [Wilson's *Hist. of Diss. Ch.*, iv., 218.]   London, 1729

ESSAY (an) on the Oxford tracts. By the author of *Letters to the authors of the Plain tracts for critical times* [John Sibbald Edison, barrister]. Fcap 8vo. [*Camb. Univ. Lib.*]   London, 1839

ESSAY (an) on the philosophical writings of Cicero. [By Arthur Henry Hallam.] 8vo. Pp. 56. [*D. N. B.*, vol. 24, p. 98.]   Cambridge, 1832

ESSAY (an) on the policy of appropriations being made by the government of the United States, for purchasing, liberating, and colonizing the slaves thereof. By a citizen of Maryland [Rev. John Allen]. 8vo. [Cushing's *Init. and Pseud.*, vol. i., p. 58.]
Baltimore, 1826

ESSAY (an) on the polity of England, with a view to discover the true principles of the government. . . . [By Christopher Keld.] 8vo. Pp. 538. [*Brit. Mus.*]   London, 1785

ESSAY (an) on the possibility of a child being born alive, and living in the later end of the fifth solar month. [By David Dickson, M.D.] Fcap 8vo. Pp. 120. [Watt's *Bibl. Brit.*]
Edinburgh, 1712

ESSAY (an) on the power and harmony of prosaic numbers: being a sequel to one on the Power of Numbers. . . [By Rev. John Mason, M.A.] 8vo. [Watt's *Bibl. Brit.*]   London, 1749
See also the following.

ESSAY (an) on the power of numbers, and the principles of harmony in poetical compositions. [By Rev. John Mason, M.A.] 8vo. [*D. N. B.*, vol. 36, p. 432.]   London, 1749

ESSAY (an) on the present state of manners and education among the lower class of the people of Ireland, and the means of improving them. [By the Rev. James Dunn.] 8vo. [*Camb. Univ. Lib.*]   Dublin, 1799

ESSAY (an) on the principle of population, as it affects the future improvement of society; with remarks on the speculations of Mr Godwin, M. Condorcet, and other writers. [By Rev. Thomas Robert Malthus.] 8vo. Pp. 396. [Courtney's *Secrets*, p. 26.]
London, 1798
The second edition (1803) gives the author's name.

ESSAY (an) on the principle of population; in refutation of the theory of the Rev. Thomas Robert Malthus. [By William Edward Hickson.] Pp. iv., 77. 8vo. [*Brit. Mus.*]
London, 1849

ESSAY (an) on the principles of human action, being an argument in favour of the natural disinterestedness of the human mind; to which are added some remarks on the systems of Hartley and Helvetius. [By William Hazlitt.] 8vo. [*Brit. Mus.*]
London, 1805

ESSAY on the principles of translation. [By Alexander Fraser Tytler.] The second edition, corrected, and considerably enlarged. 8vo. Pp. ix., 416. [*Adv. Lib.*]   London, 1797

ESSAY on the progressive improvement of mankind; an oration, delivered in the Chapel of Trinity College, Cambridge, on the day of commemoration. Monday, Dec. 17, 1798. [By the Hon. W. Lamb, second son of Viscount Melbourne.] 4to.   London, 1799

ESSAY (an) on the proper lessons appointed by the liturgy of the Church of England to be read on Sundays and chief festivals throughout the year . . . together with such reflections on the several passages therein, as may serve to enforce the duties and doctrines propounded to our faith and practice; and also some explanatory notes. [By William Wogan.] 4 vols. 8vo. [*Brit. Mus.*]   London, 1753

ESSAY (an) on the prophecies of Daniel, and the Revelation of St John. . . . By Philo-Britannicus [Samuel Toovey]. 8vo. Pp. 80.   London, 1813

ESSAY (an) on the publick debts of this kingdom; wherein the importance of discharging them is considered; the provisions for that purpose by the Sinking Fund, and the progress therein hitherto made, are stated and explained. . . . To which is subjoined, an enquiry into the general convenience of reducing farther the interest of our publick debts below 4 per cent per annum. . . . [By Sir Nathanael Gould.]   Third edition. 8vo. [M'Culloch's *Lit. of Pol. Econ.*, p. 320.]   London, 1726

ESSAY (an) on the repeal of the malt tax. [By W— Holloway.] 8vo.
London, 1846

ESSAY (an) on the resources of Portugal, and especially considered as to her relations with foreign countries. [By John Whitehead.] 8vo. [*Brit. Mus.*]
London, 1853

ESSAY (an) on the revenues of the Church of England. [By Rev. Morgan Cove, LL.B.] 8vo. Pp. 390.
London, 1795
The author's name appears in the second edition, 1797.

ESSAY (an) on the right of conquest. [By Allan Ramsay.] 8vo. [*Bodl.*]
N.P., 1783

ESSAY (an) on the right of property in land, with respect to its foundation in the law of nature; its present establishment by the municipal laws of Europe; and the regulations by which it might be rendered more beneficial to the lower ranks of mankind. [By William Ogilvie.] 8vo. [*Brit. Mus.*]
London, [1781]

ESSAY (an) on the rights and duties of nations, relative to fugitives from justice : considered with reference to the affair of the Chesapeake. By an American [David Everett]. 8vo. Pp. 62. [*Brit. Mus.*]
Boston, [Mass.], 1807

ESSAY (an) on the science of acting. By a veteran stager [G— Grant]. 12mo. Pp. 211. [*W.*] London, 1828

ESSAY (an) on the seat of Federal Government, and the exclusive jurisdiction of Congress over a ten miles District; with observations on the economy and delicate morals necessary to be observed in infant States. By a citizen of Philadelphia [Pelatiah Webster]. Fcap 8vo. Pp. 36. [Evans' *Amer. Bibl.*, vol. 7, p. 378.]
Philadelphia, 1789

ESSAY (an) on the several dispensations of God to mankind, in the order in which they lie in the Bible. . . . [By John Shute Barrington, Viscount Barrington.] 8vo.   London, 1725
Reprinted in his collected works.

ESSAY (an) on the simplicity of truth; being an attempt to ascertain the use and extent of discipline in the Church of Christ; to which is added, a postscript on tithes, particularly addressed to the people called Quakers. By Catholicus, a peaceable member of that society [Henry Portsmouth. With postscript written by the editor, William Matthews]. 8vo. [Smith's *Cat. of Friends' Books*, i., 71; ii., 427.]
London, 1779

ESSAY (an) on the slave trade. [By Grímur Jónsson Thorkelin, LL.D.] 8vo. [*Adv. Lib.*]   London, 1788

ESSAY (an) on the slavery and commerce of the human species, particularly the African; translated from a Latin dissertation. [By Thomas Clarkson.] Second edition. 8vo.
London, 1788

ESSAY (an) on the source of the pleasures received from literary compositions, [By William Greenfield, M.A.] 8vo. [Scott's *Fasti*, vol. 1.]
Weybridge, 1809
Wrongly attributed to Edward Mangin. *See also* " Essays on the source. . . ."

ESSAY (an) on the South-Sea trade; with an enquiry into the grounds and reasons of the present dislike and complaint against the settlement of a South-Sea Company. By the author of the *Review* [Daniel Defoe]. 8vo. [*Brit. Mus.*]   London, 1712

ESSAY (an) on the state of the country in respect to the condition and conduct of the husbandry labourers, and to the consequences likely to result therefrom. [By Francis Place.] 8vo.
Private print, [1831]

ESSAY on the state of the labouring poor, with some hints for improvement. [By John Struthers, librarian in Glasgow.] 8vo. [*Mitchell Lib.*]
Glasgow, 1816

ESSAY (an) on the study of antiquities. [By Thomas Burgess, D.D., Bishop of Salisbury.] The second edition, corrected and enlarged. 8vo. Pp. v., 144. [*Brit. Mus.*]   Oxford, 1782

ESSAY on the toleration of Papists. [By Thomas Lloyd.] 8vo. [*Brit. Mus.*]   London, 1779

ESSAY (an) on the transmutation of blood, containing the ætiology ; or, an account of the immediate cause of putrid fever or agues, as also observations upon cortex Peruvianus. [By Thomas Knight, M.D.] 8vo. [*Brit. Mus.*] London, 1725
In answer to objections, the author issued a " Vindication " in 1731, with his name.

ESSAY (an) on the treaty of commerce with France: with necessary expositions. [By Daniel Defoe.] 8vo. [Wilson's *Life of Defoe.*] London, 1713

ESSAY (an) on the true interests and resources of the Empire of the King of Great Britain and Ireland. . . . By [Edward Stratford], the Earl of A—h [Aldborough]. 8vo. [*Brit. Mus.*] Dublin, 1783

ESSAY (an) on the use and necessity of establishing a militia in Ireland, and some hints towards a plan for that purpose. By a country gentleman [Sir Charles Bingham]. 8vo. Dublin, 1767

ESSAY (an) on the usefulness of mathematical learning ; in a letter from a gentleman in the city to his friend in Oxford. [By Martin Strong.] 8vo. Pp. 59. [*Bodl.*; *Brit. Mus.*] Oxford, 1701
Ascribed also to John Arbuthnot, M.D. ; to John Keill, M.A., M.D.
" By Dr Arbuthnot & Mr Kiel."—MS. note, evidently contemporary.

ESSAY (an) on the usefulness of Oriental learning. [By Gregory Sharpe, LL.D.] 8vo. Pp. 60. London, 1739
The dedication to the Rector and Fellows of Lincoln College, Oxford, is signed " Philoglottus." Attributed also, with less probability, to Richard Parker.

ESSAY (an) on the utility of Classical learning in subserviency to theological studies. [By Abel D. Hendy.] 4to. [*Brit. Mus.*] Oxford, [1804]
Afterwards (at Oxford, 1808, 8vo) appended to " Three Sermons," with the author's name.

ESSAY (an) on the wages paid to females for their labour ; in the form of a letter from a gentleman in Boston to his friend in Philadelphia. [By Joseph Tuckerman, D.D.] 8vo. [Cushing's *Init. and Pseud.*, vol. ii., p. 65.] Boston, [Mass.], 1830

ESSAY (an) on the West-India dry-gripes, with the method of preventing and curing that cruel distemper ; to which is added, an extraordinary case in physick. [By Thomas Cadwalader ; revised by Dr A. Spencer.] 4to. [*W.*] Philadelphia, 1745

ESSAY (an) on the writings and genius of Pope. [By Joseph Warton, D.D.] 2 vols. 8vo. [*Bodl.*] London, 1756-1782

ESSAY (an) on the writings and genius of Shakespeare, compared with the Greek and French dramatic poets ; with some remarks upon the misrepresentations of Mons. de Voltaire. [By Mrs Elizabeth Montagu.] Second edition. 8vo. Pp. 288. [Courtney's *Secrets*, p. 47.] London, 1770

ESSAY (an) on trade and commerce ; containing observations on taxes, as they are supposed to affect the price of labour in our manufactories ; together with some reflections on our trade to America. . . . By the author of *Considerations on taxes* [J. Cunningham ?]. 8vo. [*Brit. Mus.*] London, 1770

ESSAY (an) on trade in general, and on that of Ireland in particular. By the author of *Seasonable Remarks* . . . [Sir John Browne of Dublin]. 8vo. [*Lond. Lib. Cat.*] Dublin, 1728

ESSAY (an) on ways and means for inclosing, fallowing, and planting lands in Scotland, and that in sixteen years at farthest. By a lover of his country [William Macintosh (or Mackintosh) of Borlum, Brigadier-General]. 8vo. Pp. lii., 339. [*D. N. B.*, vol. 35, p. 179.] Edinburgh, 1729
This treatise was written while he was a prisoner in Edinburgh Castle for participation in the Rebellion of 1715.

ESSAY (an) on ways and means for raising money for the support of the present war, without increasing the public debts. Inscribed to the right Honourable George Lord Anson, first Lord Commissioner of the Admiralty, &c. By F. F. [Francis Fauquier]. 8vo. [*Brit. Mus.*] London, 1756
The author's name is given in a later edition.

ESSAY (an) on woman, in three epistles. [By John Wilkes, with notes by Thomas Potter.] 8vo. Pp. 40. [Martin's *Cat.*] London, 1763
See also *N. and Q.*, 18 July 1857, p. 41.

ESSAY (an) on wool and woollen manufacture, for the improvement of trade, to the benefit of landlords, feeders of sheep, clothiers, and merchants. [By Sir Josiah Child] in a letter to a Member of Parliament. 4to. Pp. 18. [*D. N. B.*, vol. 10, p. 245.] London, 1693

ESSAY (an) on worship, more particularly on public worship; wherein some common objections are answer'd : with an hint on the Christian Sabbath. [By Caleb Fleming, D.D.] 8vo. [*Bodl.*]
London, 1730

ESSAY (an) presented; or a method humbly proposed, to the consideration of the Honourable the Members of both Houses of Parliament, by an English woolen manufacturer; to pay the national debts, without a new tax, to inlarge trade in general, by reviving and securing for time to come, the British woolen exportation trade. [By Daniel Webb.] 8vo. [*Brit. Mus.*]
London, 1744

ESSAY (an) proving that inclosing commons and common fields is contrary to the interest of the nation. [By John Cowper.] 8vo. *Manch. Free Lib. Cat.*, p. 166.] London, 1732

ESSAY (an), proving we shall know our friends in heaven. [By John Dunton ?] Fcap 8vo.   London, 1698

ESSAY (an), shewing that there is no probability of there being so much French interest, as it's certain there's English influence in our present Parliament of Scotland. [By William Alexander, M.D.] 4to. [*David Laing.*]   Printed in the year 1704

ESSAY (an) to a continuation of Iter Boreale; attempting something upon the happy influence which that seasonable and successefull march of the Lord Gen. Monck out of the North had upon the arts and sciences. By a lover of learning [Dr Robert Wild]. 4to. [*Brit. Mus.*]   London, 1660

ESSAY (an) to ascertain the value of leases, and annuities for years and lives, and to estimate the chances of the duration of lives. [By Weyman Lee.] 8vo. [*Camb. Univ. Lib.*]
London, 1737
Signed " W. L."

ESSAY (an) to discover who are the true fools and fanaticks in the world. [By Richard Cameron.] 4to. [*David Laing.*]   Edinburgh, 1708
On internal grounds, others attribute this work to a different writer, unknown.

ESSAY (an) to illustrate the foundation, the necessity, the nature, and the evidences of Christianity; and to connect true philosophy with the Bible. By a layman [Thomas Carlyle, advocate]. 8vo. Pp. xviii., 384. [Boase's *Cath. Apost. Lit.*]
Edinburgh, 1827

ESSAY (an) to prove the salvation of all who die in infancy. [By Thomas Williams.] 8vo.   London, 1793

ESSAY (an) to revive the antient education of gentlewomen in religion, manners, arts, and tongues; with an answer to the objections against this way of education. [By Mrs Bathshua Makin.] [*Brit. Mus.*]
London, 1673

ESSAY (an) to solve the difficulties that attend the several accounts given by the Evangelists of our Saviour's Resurrection. . . . By a Fellow of Harvard College [Nathan Price]. 4to. [*Brit. Mus.*]   Boston, [Mass.], 1734
Signed " N. P."

ESSAY (an) to state the Scripture-account of man's redemption, by the death of Christ; wherein the doctrine is shewn to be as plain and intelligible, as it is useful and important. [By Caleb Fleming, D.D.] 8vo. [*Bodl.*]
London, 1745

ESSAY (an) to vindicate some Scripture truths in five several articles, from the danger of being corrupted at this time ; in answer of a letter from a gentleman to a minister. Published by a member of the Church of Scotland. [By James Hog, minister at Carnock.] Fcap 8vo. [*New Coll. Cat.*]   N.P., 1716

ESSAY (an) touching the gravitation, or non-gravitation of fluid bodies, and the reason thereof. [By Sir Matthew Hale.] 8vo. Pp. 92. [*Bodl.*]   London, 1673

ESSAY (an) toward a natural history of the Bible, especially of some partes which relate to the occasion of revealing Moses's Principia. [By John Hutchinson.] 8vo.   London, 1725
Reprinted in his Collected Works, vol. i.

ESSAY towards a collection of books relating to proverbs, emblems, apophthegms, epitaphs, and ana; being a catalogue of those at Keir. [By Sir William Stirling-Maxwell.] 8vo.
London, private print, 1860

ESSAY (an) towards a Comprehension ; or a persuasive to unity among Protestants. By a lover of peace and unity [Rev. Benjamin Gatton]. 8vo.
London, 1701

ESSAY (an) towards a contrast between Quakerism and Methodism; wherein the mystery of silent meetings is considered and explained : in an address to those of both denominations. By Johannes Catholicus [John Rutty]. 8vo. [Smith's *Cat. of Friends' Books*, i., 68.]   Bristol, 1771

ESSAY towards a demonstration of the Scripture-Trinity. By Philanthropus Londinensis [Daniel Scott, LL.D.]. Second edition [enlarged]. 8vo. [*D. N. B.*, vol. 51, p. 16.] London, 1738
The first edition was issued in 1725.

ESSAY (an) towards a history of the principal comets that have appeared since 1742 ; with remarks and reflections upon the present comet [by C. Burney] ; to which is prefixed by way of introduction a Letter upon comets, addressed to a lady by the late M. de Maupertuis. 8vo. [*W.*]
London, 1769

ESSAY towards a literal English version of the New Testament, on the Epistle of the Apostle Paul directed to the Ephesians. [By John Callander, of Craigforth.] 4to.   Glasgow, 1779

ESSAY (an) towards a new edition of the Elegies of Tibullus, with a translation and notes. [By Sam. Henley, D.D.] 8vo. [Lowndes' *Bibl. Man.*, p. 2683.]   London, 1792

ESSAY (an) toward a new translation of some parts of the Hebrew Scriptures. [By James Purves.] 3 parts. Fcap 8vo. [*D. N. B.*, vol. 47, p. 51.]   Edinburgh, 1780
No more published.

ESSAY (an) towards a proposal for Catholick communion ; wherein above sixty of the principal controverted points, which have hitherto divided Christendom, being call'd over, 'tis examin'd how many of them may and ought to be laid aside, and how few remain to be accommodated, for the effecting a general peace. By a minister of the Church of England [Joshua Basset, Master of Sydney College, Cambridge]. 8vo. Pp. 262. [*D. N. B.*, vol. 3, p. 383.]
London, 1704
This essay was reprinted in 1705 and 1812, and again in 1879 with an introduction by H. N. Oxenham, under the title " An Eirenicon of the eighteenth century." After its first appearance, replies were published by Samuel Grascome and by Nathaniel Spinckes, also by Edward Stephens (see the following entry). The authorship has been mistakenly attributed to Thomas Deane and to William Basset.

ESSAY (an) towards a proposal for Catholick communion [by Joshua Basset] fairly and impartially consider'd, the whole mystery and artifice detected, and the secret design expos'd and defeated. . . . [By Edward Stephens, of Cherington.] 8vo. [*New Coll. Lib.*]   London, 1705
See the preceding entry.

ESSAY (an) towards an abridgment of the English History. [By Edmund Burke.] 4to. Pp. 48. [*Brit. Mus.*]
[London, 1757]
No title-page : left unfinished.

ESSAY (an) towards an English grammar, with a dissertation on the nature and peculiar use of certain hypothetical verbs in the English language. [By Rev. John Fell.] Fcap 8vo. [*Brit. Mus.*]   London, 1784

ESSAY (an) towards an history of the ancient jurisdiction of the Marshalsea of the King's House ; to which is subjoined an account of the Court of the Palace of the King at Westminster, created by letters patent of King Charles II. [By Burton Morice, Steward of the Marshalsea.] 8vo. Pp. 47. [*Bibliographer*, vol. 5.] London, 1812

ESSAY (an) towards an universal alphabet.   [By Francis Lodwick.] 4to. [Watt's *Bibl. Brit.*] N.P., [1686]

ESSAY (an) towards attaining a true idea of the character and reign of K. Charles the First, and the causes of the Civil War ; extracted from, and delivered in the very words of some of the most authentic and celebrated historians, viz. Clarendon, Whitelock, Burnet, Coke, Echard, Rapin, Tindal, Neal, &c. [By Micaiah Towgood.] Fcap 8vo. [*Brit. Mus.*] London, 1748

ESSAY (an) towards carrying on the present war against France, and other publick occasions ; as also for paying off all debts contracted in the same or otherwise ; and for new coining of all our monies, without charge, to the great increase of the honour, strength and wealth of the nation. . . . [By Sir William Keith, Bart., Governor of Pennsylvania from 1717 to 1726.] [*Lond. Inst. Cat.*, ii., 393.]   [*c.* 1730]

ESSAY towards deciding the important question, Whether it be a national advantage to Britain to insure the ships of her enemies ? [By Corbyn Morris.] 8vo. [Watt's *Bibl. Brit.*]
London, [1747]
Another edition, amended and extended, with modified title, appeared in 1758.

ESSAY (an) towards fixing the true standard of wit, humour, raillery, satire, and ridicule. [By Corbyn Morris.] 8vo. [Watt's *Bibl. Brit.*]
London, 1744

ESSAY (an) towards illustrating the ancient history of the Britannic isles ; containing an explanation of the names Belgæ, Scythæ, Celtæ, Brittanni, Albanich, Eirinnich, Caledonii, Siluri, &c. &c.   Intended as a preface to a work entitled, A vindication of the ancient history of Ireland.   By C. V. [Charles Vallancey, LL.D.]. 8vo. Pp. 46. [Watt's *Bibl. Brit.*] London, 1786

ESSAY (an) towards illustrating the science of insurance; wherein it is attempted to fix, by precise calculations, several important maxims. By the author of *A Letter from a bystander* [Corbyn Morris]. 8vo. Pp. 76. [*Brit. Mus.*]   London, 1747

ESSAY (an) towards pointing out the eloquence and action proper for the pulpit. By Philagoretes [William Scott]. 8vo.   London, 1765

ESSAY (an) towards preventing the ruin of Great Britain. [By George Berkeley, D.D.] 8vo. [*Works*, edited by Fraser, iii., 195.]   London, 1721

ESSAY (an) towards the allaying of George Fox his spirit. [By Thomas Crisp.] 4to. [*Bodl.*]   London, 1695

ESSAY (an) towards the character of Her late Majesty Caroline, Queen Consort of Great Britain, &c. [By Alured Clarke, D.D.] 8vo. [*Brit. Mus.*]   London, 1738

ESSAY (an) towards the case of elections of Members of Parliament. [By John Bellers.] 4to. [Smith's *Cat. of Friends' Books*, i., 237.]   London, 1712

ESSAY (an) towards the present and future peace of Europe, by the establishment of an European Dyet, Parliament, or Estates. [By William Penn.] Fcap 8vo. [Smith's *Cat. of Friends' Books*, ii., 308.]   N.P., 1693

ESSAY (an) towards the proof of a separate state of souls between death and the resurrection, and the commencement of the reward of virtue and vice immediately after death. [By Isaac Watts, D.D.] Cr 8vo. Pp. 84. [Abbot's *Lit. on a future life.*]   London, 1732

ESSAY (an) towards the settlement of peace and truth in the church, as a certain foundation of lasting union. [By Sir Edward Harley.] 4to. [*Brit. Mus.*]   London, 1681

ESSAY (an) towards the theory of the intelligible world, intuitively considered. By Gabriel John [Thomas Durfey]. Designed for 49 parts. Fcap 8vo. [*W.*]   [London], N.D.
    A satire on a work by John Norris, of Bemerton, with a similar title (" An essay towards the theory of the ideal or intelligible world," in two parts. 1707).

ESSAY (an) towards vindicating the literal sense of the demoniacks, in the New Testament ; in answer to a late Enquiry [by Arthur A. Sykes] into the meaning of them. [By Thomas Church, D.D.] 8vo. Pp. 123. [*D. N. B.*, vol. 10, p. 306.]   London, 1737
    See note to " An Enquiry into the meaning of demoniacks. . . ."

ESSAY (an) upon an Union of Ireland with England : most humbly offered to the consideration of the Queen's . . . Majesty, and both Houses of Parliament.   [By Henry Maxwell, M.P.] 4to. [*Brit. Mus.*]
Dublin, 1704

ESSAY (an) upon civil government : wherein is set forth the necessity, origine, rights, boundaries, and different forms of sovereignty ; with observations on the ancient government of Rome and England, according to the principles of the late Archbishop of Cambray. Translated from the French [by Andrew Michael Ramsay, LL.D.]. Fcap 8vo. Pp. 235. [*Bodl.*]   London, 1722

ESSAY (an) upon education, intended to shew that the common method is defective, and that the custom of teaching dead languages . . . is absurd : with a plan of a new method. By a gentleman of Bristol [S— Butler]. 8vo. [*Brit. Mus.*]
London, N.D., [*c*. 1750]
    Signed " S. B."

ESSAY (an) upon feudal holdings, superiorities, and hereditary jurisdictions, in Scotland ; shewing I. The nature of feudal holdings, superiorities, and jurisdictions, with the casualties and forfeitures incident thereto. II. The errors and gross misrepresentations touching the same, in a late pamphlet, entituled, Superiorities display'd, or Scotland's grievance on account of holdings and hereditary jurisdictions, &c. III. That these holdings, superiorities and jurisdictions have not been any of the causes of the rebellions 1715, or 1745. IV. That the infringing the same may be dangerous to our happy constitution. [By Andrew M'Dowall, Lord Bankton.] 8vo. [*Camb. Univ. Lib.*]
London, 1747

ESSAY (an) upon gospel and legal preaching. By a minister of the Church of Scotland [James Ballantyne, minister at Edinburgh]. 8vo. Pp. 144. [Scott's *Fasti.*]
Edinburgh, 1723
    Wrongly assigned to George Logan.

ESSAY (an) upon harmony, as it relates chiefly to situation and building. [By John Gwynn.] 8vo.   London, 1739
    Wrongly attributed to Robert Morris.

ESSAY upon industry and trade, shewing the necessity of the one, the conveniency and usefulness of the other, and the advantages of both. [By David Black.] 4to.
Edinburgh, 1706

ESSAY (an) upon literature ; or, an enquiry into the antiquities and original of letters ; proving that the two tables written by the finger of God in Mount Sinai was the first writing in the world, and that all other alphabets derive from the Hebrew : with a short view of the methods made use of by the ancients to supply the want of letters before, and improve on them after they were known. [By Daniel Defoe.] 8vo. [Wilson's *Life of Defoe*, 193.]   London, 1726

ESSAY (an) upon loans : or, an argument proving that substantial funds settled by Parliament, with the encouragement of interests, and the advances of prompt payment usually allow'd, will bring in loans of money to the exchequer, in spight of all the conspiracies of parties to the contrary ; while a just, honourable, and punctual performance on the part of the government, supports the credit of the nation. By the author of the *Essay upon credit* [Robert Harley, Earl of Oxford, or Daniel Defoe]. 8vo. Pp. 27.
                    London, 1710
See note to the " Essay upon publick credit."

ESSAY (an) upon marriage ; in a letter address'd to a friend. [By William Forbes, of Disblair.] 4to. N.P., N.D.

ESSAY (an) upon money and coins. Part I. The theory of commerce, money and exchanges. [By Joseph Harris, Assay Master of the Mint.] 8vo. Pp. viii., 128.   London, 1757
—— Part II. Wherein is shewed, that the established standard of money should not be violated or altered, under any pretence whatever. [By Joseph Harris.] 8vo. Pp. xiv., 130. [*Brit. Mus.*]   London, 1758

ESSAY (an) upon nursing, and the management of children from their birth to three years of age. By a physician [William Cadogan, M.D.]. 8vo. [*Brit. Mus.*]   London, 1748
Several other editions were required.

ESSAY (an) upon poetry. [By John Sheffield, Duke of Buckingham.]   4to. [Arber's *Term Cat.*, i., 523.]
                    London, 1682
Republished later with the author's name.

ESSAY (an) upon predestination and grace, wherein the honour of God is defended, and the free-will of man maintained, &c. [By Francis Gordon.]   [Copinger's *Bibl. of Predestination*.]
Edinburgh, printed in the year 1712

ESSAY (an) upon prints ; containing remarks upon the principles of picturesque beauty, the different kinds of prints, and the characters of the most noted masters ; illustrated by criticisms upon particular pieces. . . . [By Rev. William Gilpin, M.A.] Fcap 8vo. Pp. iv., 269. [*Brit. Mus.*]
                    London, 1768
Several other editions were required.

ESSAY (an) upon projects. [By Daniel Defoe.]   [Wilson's *Life of Defoe*.]
                    London, 1697

ESSAY (an) upon publick credit ; being an enquiry how the publick credit comes to depend upon the change of the ministry, or the dissolutions of Parliaments, and whether it does so or no : with an argument proving that the publick credit may be upheld and maintain'd in this nation, and perhaps brought to a greater height than it ever yet arriv'd at. . . . [By Robert Harley, Earl of Oxford.] Pp. 28.   London, 1710
Reprinted under Harley's name in the first collection of *Somers' Tracts* and also in the second edition. Generally ascribed to Harley, but latterly to Defoe, and printed in the collection of Defoe's works edited by W. Hazlitt. Entered in Wilson's and Lee's list of Defoe's works. In the *Lond. Inst. Cat.*, it is ascribed to Harley, possibly assisted by Defoe.

ESSAY (an) upon Satyr, or a poem on the times ; to which is added, The Satyr against Separatists. [By John Sheffield (Duke of Buckingham) and John Dryden.] 8vo. [Arber's *Term Cat.*, i. 523.]   London, 1680

ESSAY (an) upon Statius ; or the first five books of Publius Papinius Statius, his Thebais : done into English verse by T. S. [Thomas Stephens], with the Poetick History illustrated. 8vo. [*Brit. Mus.*]   London, 1648

ESSAY (an) upon taxes, calculated for the present juncture of affairs in England. [By Sir Richard Temple, Bart.] 4to. [*Camb. Univ. Cat.*]
                    London, 1693
Wrongly ascribed to Sir William Temple.

ESSAY upon taxes ; particularly tending to shew that the ministers of the Church of Scotland cannot in law, and ought not, in justice and equity, to be subjected to the tax upon houses and lights. [By Alexander Carlyle, D.D., minister of Inveresk.] 8vo. [*David Laing*.]   N.P., 1769

ESSAY (an) upon that earliest species of idolatry, the worship of the elements. By J. C. [James Christie]. 4to. [*Brit. Mus.*]   Norwich, 1814

ESSAY (an) upon that paradox, Infallibility may sometimes mistake ;
or, a reply to a discourse concerning
episcopacy. . . . By a son of Martin
Mar-Prelate [Thomas Walter]. 8vo.
Pp. 140. [Cushing's *Init. and Pseud.*,
vol. ii., p. 139.] Boston, [Mass.], 1734

ESSAY (an) upon the action of an orator,
as to his pronunciation & gesture ;
useful both for divines and lawyers,
and necessary for all young gentlemen
that study how to speak well in publick.
Done out of French [of Michel Le
Faucheur]. Fcap 8vo. Pp. 217.
[*Brit. Mus.*] London, N.D., [1680 ?]

ESSAY (an) upon the advancement of
trade in Ireland. [By Sir William
Temple.] 4to. [*Camb. Univ. Lib.*]
Dublin, 1673

ESSAY (an) upon the British fisheries.
By a Caledonian fisher [J— Rose].
8vo. [Cushing's *Init. and Pseud.*,
vol. i., p. 48.] Edinburgh, 1705

ESSAY (an) upon the design, the reference, the penalty, and the offence of
the Abjuration Oath. [By Rev. Ebenezer Erskine.] 4to. [*Fraser's Life of
Ebenezer Erskine.*] N.P., 1713
See also " Abjuration Oath " in vol. i.

ESSAY (an) upon the duty of physicians
and patients, the dignity of medicine,
and the prudentials of practice. In
two dialogues. [By Samuel Parker,
of Lincoln College, Oxford.] 8vo.
Pp. 141. London, 1715
" Bibliothecæ Bodleyanæ dono dedit
auctor amicissi. Samuel Parker."

ESSAY (an) upon the vth of Matthew,
from verse 33rd to 37th ; with some
observations upon the present affirma-
tion. [By Joseph Skidmore.] 8vo.
[Smith's *Cat. of Friends' Books*, ii.,
579.] London, 1713
Signed at the end " A. B."

ESSAY (an) upon the XV. article of
the Treaty of Union between Scotland
and England. . . . [By Sir John
Clerk.] 4to. [*Adv. Lib.*]
[Edinburgh], 1706

ESSAY (an) upon the following Questions. *Quest.* What Power has the
Magistrate about sacred things ?
Quest. 2. Do the faults of rulers
render their authority void and null ?
Quest. 3. Are we to be obedient to
Magistrates of a different religion
from our selves ? And if so, *Quest.* 4.
What obedience is to be given unto
them ? By a well-wisher of the country's peace [John Pollock, minister
at Glencairn, afterwards at Roxburgh].
4to. Pp. 31. [*New Coll. Cat.*]
Dumfries, 1715

ESSAY (an) upon the harmony of language, intended principally to illustrate that of the English language.
[By William Mitford.] 8vo. Pp. iv.,
288. [*Brit. Mus.*] London, 1774

ESSAY (an) upon the important question,
whether there be a legislative, proper
authority in the church ; and whether
Christian discipline, truth, peace, and
good order may not be maintain'd
without it ? With a refutation of some
principles advanc'd in a late pamphlet
entituled, A brief review of a paper,
entituled, A letter from the Presbytery
of Antrim, &c., by some subscribing
ministers. By some non-subscribing
ministers in the North of Ireland
[mainly James Kilpatrick, D.D.]. 8vo.
Pp. 100. [Witherow's *Irish Presb.
Lit.*, i., p. 157.] Belfast, 1731

ESSAY (an) upon the inscription of
Macduff's crosse in Fyfe. By I. C.
[James Cunningham]. 1678. 4to.
[Lowndes' *Bibl. Man.*, p. 569.]
Edinburgh, 1678
Ascribed also to James Carmichael.

ESSAY (an) upon the interest of England
in respect to Protestants dissenting
from the establish'd Church. [By
John Shute Barrington, Viscount Barrington.] 4to. London, 1701
A second edition, corrected and enlarged,
was issued in 1703 with the author's
name and a modified title : " The interest
of England consider'd, with respect to
Protestants dissenting. . . ."

ESSAY (an) upon the King's friends ;
with an account of some discoveries
made in Italy, and found in a Virgil,
concerning the Tories. To Dr
S[amue]l J[ohnso]n. [By John Hall
Stevenson.] 8vo. [*D. N. B.*, vol. 54,
p. 239.] London, 1776

ESSAY (an) upon the national credit of
England, introductory to a proposal
prepar'd for establishing the public
credit in such a manner as to render
the same highly beneficial to the
government, trade and people of this
kingdom. . . . [By Charles Davenant,
LL.D.] 8vo. [*W.*] London, [1710]

ESSAY (an) upon the present interest of
England ; to which are added, the
proceedings of the House of Commons
in 1677, upon the French king's progress in Flanders. [By George
Stepney.] Second edition. 4to. Pp.
86. [*Bodl.*] London, 1701

ESSAY (an) upon the probable methods
of making a people gainers in the
ballance of trade ; treating of these
heads, viz. Of the people of England.
Of the land of England, and its product. Of our payments to the publick,

and in what manner the ballance of trade may be thereby affected. . . . By the author of *The Essay on ways and means* [Charles Davenant, LL.D.]. 8vo. Pp. 312. [*Brit. Mus.*]
London, 1699

ESSAY (an) upon the regulation of the press. [By Daniel Defoe.] 4to. [Wilson's *Life of Defoe*, 52.]
London, 1704

ESSAY (an) upon the relation of cause and effect, controverting the doctrine of Mr Hume concerning the nature of that relation ; with observations upon the opinions of Dr Brown and Mr Lawrence connected with the same subject. [By Lady Mary Shepherd.] 8vo. Pp. vii., 194. [*Brit. Mus.*]
London, 1824
Attributed also to J— Fearn.
An earlier edition (1819) has the title : "An Enquiry respecting the relation of cause and effect. . . ."

ESSAY (an) upon the trade to Africa. [By Daniel Defoe.] 8vo. Pp. 48. [*Camb. Hist. of Eng. Lit.*] London, 1711

ESSAY upon the Union ; shewing that the subjects of both nations have been, by the union of the two crowns, justly intitled to all manner of privileges, which the insuing Treaty can give them. Therefore the work of the ensuing Treaty is not so much to treat of new privileges, as to provide for the security of the old ones ; and the best security against incroachments on both sides, is to have separate Parliaments, with an express proviso that no laws about trade, or the other common concerns of the united nations, shall be of force, unless agreed to by both Parliaments. [By James Hodges.] 4to. Pp. 31. [*New Coll. Lib.*]
Edinburgh, reprinted 1706

ESSAY (an) upon toleration. By a sincere lover of the Church and State [James Webster, minister of the Tolbooth Church, Edinburgh]. 4to. [*Adv. Lib.*] [Edinburgh], 1703

ESSAY upon trade in general, more especially of the woollen manufactures ; with remarks upon it. [By Samuel Webber.] 8vo. [*Athen. Cat.*, p. 527.] London, 1741

ESSAY (an) upon tune ; being an attempt to free the scale of music, and the tune of instruments, from imperfection. [By Francis Kelly Maxwell, D.D.] 8vo. Pp. iv., 290.
Edinburgh, 1781
Ascribed also to John Maxwell, of Broomholm. [Watt's *Bibl. Brit.*]

ESSAY (an) upon ways and means of supplying the war. [By Charles Davenant, LL.D.] Third edition. 8vo. Pp. 160. [*Brit. Mus.*] London, 1701

ESSAY (an) upon wind ; with curious anecdotes of eminent peteurs : humbly dedicated to the Lord Chancellor [Thurlow]. [By Charles James Fox.] Sold by all the booksellers in town and country. [MS. note on Maidment's copy.]

ESSAY written to compete . . . for the Mackenzie Prize in political economy, on the best means for improving the relations between capital and labour. [By James Fairbairn Finlay, barrister.] 8vo. [*Edin. Univ. Lib.*] Edinburgh, 1876

ESSAYES about general and special grace ; occasioned by, and by way of animadversion upon, some lines of a late picture of a good old gentleman, drawn first in the Pulpit and then in the Press, by W. K., Rector of E. W. in N. Written by J. H. [John Horne, Preacher of the Gospel of Christ in the parish of Lynn Allhallowes]. 4to. Pp. 24. [Smith's *Anti-Quak.*, p. 235.]
London, 1659

ESSAYES and characters of a prison and prisoners. By G. M. [Geffray Minshull, or Mynshul]. Small 4to. [Watt's *Bibl. Brit.*] London, 1638
Earlier editions were issued in 1613 and 1618.

ESSAYES, morall and theologicall [By Daniel Tuvill]. Fcap 8vo. [*Brit. Mus.*] London, 1609
Signed " D. T."
The title of another edition (1629) begins thus : " Vade mecum. . . ."

ESSAYES of anatomy ; in which the construction of the organs and their mechanical operations are clearly explained according to the new hypotheses. By ****** [Dominique Beddevole], Dr in medicine. Written originally in French ; translated by J. Scougall. Fcap 8vo. Pp. 199. [*Edin. Univ. Lib.*] Edinburgh, 1691
The second edition, having the author's name, was published in 1696.

ESSAYES, or moral discourses on several subjects. [By Sir Thomas Culpeper, or Culpepper.] 8vo. [Bliss' *Cat.*] London, 1671

ESSAYES (the), or moral, politike, and militarie discourses of Michael de Montaigne. [Translated by John Florio.] Folio. [Watt's *Bibl. Brit.*]
London, 1632

ESSAYS. By Christopher Carr [Arthur Christopher Benson]. Fcap 8vo. [*Lond. Lib. Cat.*] London, 1895

ESSAYS. By Father Fitz-Eustace, a Mendicant Friar [W. Fraser ?] 8vo. Pp. viii., 240. [*Adv. Lib.*]
London, 1822

ESSAYS. By the author of *Véra*, etc. [Charlotte Louisa H. Dempster]. 8vo. Pp. 372. [*Bodl.*]   London, 1872
Reprinted from the *Edinburgh Review* and other periodicals, revised and enlarged by the author.

ESSAYS. By Timon Fieldmouse [William Brighty Rands]. 8vo. [Cushing's *Init. and Pseud.*, vol. i., p. 101.]   London, 1860 (?)

ESSAYS addressed to young married women. [By Mrs E. Griffith.] 8vo. [*Brit. Mus.*]   London, 1782

ESSAYS analytical and philosophical, on the history and progress of the human mind. [By Edward Grubb, barrister.] Cr 8vo. Pp. ix., 84. [*Brit. Mus.*]   Leicester, 1845

ESSAYS and criticisms. By the military correspondent of *The Times* [Charles A'Court Repington]. 8vo. Pp. 300. [*Brit. Mus.*]   London, 1911

ESSAYS and dissertations on various subjects, relating to human life and happiness ; partly reprinted from a periodical entitled "The Remembrancer," published at Bath in the year 1766. 2 vols. [By John Bethune.] Fcap 8vo. [*Watt's Bibl. Brit.*]
London, 1771

ESSAYS and leaves from a note-book. By George Eliot [Marian Evans, later Mrs Cross]. 8vo. [*Brit. Mus.*]
Edinburgh, 1884

ESSAYS and lectures on Indian historical subjects. By an Officer of the Bengal Staff Corps [Colonel George Bruce Malleson]. Pt 8vo. [*D. N. B.*, First Supp., vol. 3, p. 135.]
London, 1866
Signed "M."

ESSAYS and letters, on subjects religious, moral, and political. [By Robert Wilson, teller, British Linen Bank.] [*Jas. Maidment.*]
Edinburgh, 1857

ESSAYS and letters, with other miscellaneous pieces. By the author of *Newmarket ; or an essay on the Turf* [Philip Parsons, M.A.]. 8vo. [Watt's *Bibl. Brit.*]   Canterbury, 1775

ESSAYS and meditations on various subjects. By a physician [James Mackenzie, M.D.]. Fcap 8vo. Pp. vii., 175. [*Adv. Lib.*]
Edinburgh, 1762
The author subsequently published "Essays on retirement. . . ." *See later.*

VOL. II.

ESSAYS and reflections in Sydney, Australia. By a layman [James Norton]. 8vo. [*Brit. Mus.*]
London, 1852

ESSAYS and sermons on various subjects relative to the Deistical controversy. [By James Lunn.] 8vo. [*New Coll. Cat.*]   Edinburgh, 1790

ESSAYS and sketches of life and character. By a gentleman who has left his lodgings [Lord John, afterwards Earl Russell]. 8vo. Pp. vi., 248. [*Brit. Mus.*]   London, 1820
The preface is "signed" Joseph Skillett.

ESSAYS at large. By Solomon Eagle [Jack Collings Squire]. Cr 8vo. [*Bookman*, Feb. 1923.] London, 1923

ESSAYS by a barrister [James Fitz-James Stephen, Q.C.]. (Reprinted from *The Saturday Review*.) 8vo. Pp. iv., 335. [*Adv. Lib.*]
London, 1862

ESSAYS, chiefly theological. By Melampus [George Sexton]. Part I. 8vo. Pp. 47. [*Brit. Mus.*]
London, [1869]

ESSAYS, descriptive and moral, on scenes in Italy, Switzerland, and France. By an American [Rev. Mathias Bruen]. 8vo. [Cushing's *Init. and Pseud.*, vol. i., p. 12.]
Edinburgh, 1823

ESSAYS ; divine, moral, and political. [By Jonathan Swift.] 8vo. [*Cat. Lond. Inst.*, ii., 566.] London, 1714

ESSAYS from the Batchelor ; in prose and verse. By the authors of *The Epistle to Gorges Edmond Howard, Esq.* [John Courtenay, Robert Jephson, and the Rev. Francis Burroughs]. 2 vols. Fcap 8vo. [Lowndes' *Bibl. Man.*]   London, 1773
See another edition below ("Essays in prose and verse").

ESSAYS from the desk of Poor Robert the Scribe [Charles Miner]. 8vo. [Cushing's *Init. and Pseud.*, vol. i., p. 237.]   Philadelphia, 1845

ESSAYS from "The Times"; being a selection from the literary papers which have appeared in that journal. [By Samuel Phillips, LL.D.] [First series.] 8vo. Pp. vii., 310. [*Brit. Mus.*]   London, 1851
A second series was issued in 1854. Published afterwards with the author's name.

ESSAYS, historical and moral. [By George Gregory, D.D., F.S.A.] 8vo. London, 1785
The author's name appears in the second edition.

O

ESSAYS in paradox. By the author of *Exploded ideas* [John Hutton Balfour Browne, barrister]. Cr 8vo.
London, 1901

ESSAYS in poetical composition. [By Robert Gray.] 4to.   London, 1812

ESSAYS in prose and verse. By Jeffrey Wagstaffe [Francis Burroughs, Robert Jephson, and John Courtenay]. 8vo. [Cushing's *Init. and Pseud.*, vol. i., p. 302.]   Dublin, 1773
    See another edition above (" Essays from the Batchelor . . .").

ESSAYS in prose and verse, partly collected, and partly original, for the improvement of young minds. [By the Rev. Thomas Gibbons, D.D., Dissenting minister.] Fcap 8vo. Pp. viii., 112.   London, [1770 ?]

ESSAYS in psychical research. By Miss X. [Ada Goodrich-Freer]. Cr 8vo. Pp. xv., 330. [*Lond. Lib. Cat.*]
London, 1899

ESSAYS in verse. [By John Maclaurin, Lord Dreghorn.] 8vo.
[Edinburgh], 1769
    " These essays were presented to me by the ingenious author, John Maclaurin, Esqr., advocate. They were not only wrote but printed by him at a portable press ; and he told me the printing cost him much more labour and pains than the writing. D. R. [Rae]."—MS. note on a copy in the Advocate's Library."

ESSAYS, instructive and entertaining. By A. T. [A— Torkington]. Second edition. Fcap 8vo. Pp. 20.
Oldham, 1871

ESSAYS, meant as an offering in support of rational religion, especially as founded on ideas of the absolute and perfect benevolence of the Deity and his all comprehending providence. By a layman [John Hollis]. Fcap 8vo. [*Bibl. Parriana*, p. 56.] London, 1790

ESSAYS, moral and literary. [By Vicesimus Knox, D.D.] 8vo. Pp. vi., 326.   London, 1778
    A second volume, with the author's name, was published in 1779.

ESSAYS, moral and philosophical, on several subjects : viz. a view of the human faculties ; a short account of the world ; two discourses on decency ; an essay on self-love. [By Alexander Forbes, Baron Forbes of Pitsligo.] 8vo. Pp. xii., 385. [*Brit. Mus.*]
London, 1734

ESSAYS, moral and political. [By David Hume.] 8vo. Pp. v., 187 [*Adv. Lib.*]   Edinburgh, 1741

ESSAYS, moral, philosophical and political. [By John Mills, F.R.S.] 8vo. [Watt's *Bibl. Brit.*]
London, 1772

ESSAYS, moral, religious and miscellaneous ; to which is added, a prose translation of Mr Browne's Latin poem, De animi immortalitate. By J. H. [Joseph Highmore]. 2 vols. 8vo. [Watt's *Bibl. Brit.*]   London, 1766

ESSAYS of a recluse. [By William Benton Clulow.] 8vo. [Cushing's *Init. and Pseud.*, vol. ii., p. 248.]
London, 1865

ESSAYS of an optimist [Sir John William Kaye, F.R.S.]. 8vo. [Cushing's *Init. and Pseud.*, vol. i., p. 219.]
London, 1871

ESSAYS of certaine paradoxes. [By Sir William Cornwallis, junr.] 4to. [*Bodl.*]   London, 1616
    Part II. of the second edition bears the author's name.

ESSAYS of Shirley. [By Sir John Skelton, advocate.] 8vo. [*Adv. Lib.*]
Edinburgh, 1882

ESSAYS on conversation, and on quackery. [By Philip Duncan.] 12mo.   London, 1836

ESSAYS on economic subjects. By Hibernicus [—— Harper]. Dy 8vo. Pp. x., 283.   Dublin, 1885

ESSAYS on English writers. By the author of *The gentle life* [James Hain Friswell]. 8vo. Pp. viii., 360. [*Brit. Mus.*]   London, 1869

ESSAYS on fashionable diseases. . . . To which is added, A dramatic dialogue. By Benjamin Goosequill and Peter Paragraph [James Makittrick Adair, M.D.]. 8vo. [Cushing's *Init. and Pseud.*, vol. i., p. 118.]
London, [1790 ?]

ESSAYS on hunting ; being an extension of Mr Gardiner's pamphlet, entitled, The pleasures of hare-hunting. [By William Blane, F.R.S.] 8vo. [Watt's *Bibl. Brit.*]   London, 1781
    The second edition, 1788, is not anonymous.

ESSAYS on hunting : containing a philosophical enquiry into the nature and properties of the scent ; observations on hounds, with the method of hare-hunting practised by the Greeks. By a sportsman of Berkshire [Peter Beckford]. Second edition. 8vo. [*Brit. Mus.*]   Southampton, [1785 ?]

ESSAYS on husbandry. Essay I. A general introduction, shewing that agriculture is the basis and support of all flourishing communities ; the antient and present state of that useful art. . . . Essay II. An account of some experiments tending to improve the culture of lucerne by transplanta-

tion ; being the first experiments of the kind hitherto made and published in England. . . . [By Rev. Walter Harte, M.A., Canon of Windsor.] 8vo. [Watt's *Bibl. Brit.*]
London, 1764
A second edition appeared in 1770, with the author's name.

ESSAYS on moral and religious subjects. By Mary Pelham [Dorothy Kilner]. Fcap 8vo. [*Brit. Mus.*]
London, 1807

ESSAYS on New South Wales. By "Capricornus" [George Ranken]. 8vo. Sydney, 1872-93

ESSAYS on political economy, in which are illustrated the principal causes of the present national distress. [By G. Robertson.] 8vo. [*Brit. Mus.*]
London, 1830

ESSAYS on practical piety and divine grace. By S. M. J. [Samuel M. Janney]. Fcap 8vo. [Supp. to Smith's *Cat. of Friends' Books*, p. 206.] Philadelphia, [*c.* 1860]

ESSAYS on public worship, patriotism, and projects of reformation. [By Rev. David Williams.] 8vo. [*Brit. Mus.*] London, 1773

ESSAYS on retirement from business ; on old age, and on the employment of the soul after death. By a physician [James Mackenzie]. Fcap 8vo. Fourth edition. Pp. xx., 130. [*Brit. Mus.*] London, 1812
The author previously published " Essays and meditations. . . ." *See above.*

ESSAYS on Romanism. By the author of *Essays on the Church* [Robert Benton Seeley]. 8vo. [*D. N. B.*, vol. 51, p. 193.] London, 1839
See also below, " Essays on the Church."

ESSAYS on several subjects ; viz. I. On the late act to prevent clandestine marriages. II. On the guilt and danger of contracting debts. III. On a prison. IV. On the price of provisions. [By James Lind, M.D.] 8vo. Pp. x., 156. [*Bodl.*] London, 1769

ESSAYS on slavery. By Vigornius [Samuel Melancthon Worcester, D.D.]. 8vo. [Cushing's *Init. and Pseud.*, vol. i., p. 295.] Boston, 1826

ESSAYS on social subjects, from the Saturday Review. [By Anne Mozley.] 2 vols. Cr 8vo. [*D. N. B.*, vol. 39, p. 249.] London, 1868-69

ESSAYS on song-writing ; with a collection of such English songs as are most eminent for poetical merit : to which are added some original pieces. [By John Aikin, M.D.] 8vo. Pp. xvi., 280. [*Brit. Mus.*]
London, [1772]

ESSAYS on taxation and reconstruction. By Diversity [William B. Scott]. 8vo. [Cushing's *Init. and Pseud.*, vol. i., p. 82.] New York, 1866

ESSAYS on the Bible. By the author of *Essays on the Church*, etc. [Robert Benton Seeley]. Pp. xv., 336. [*D. N. B.*, vol. 51, p, 193.] London, 1869
See also the following.

ESSAYS on the Church. By a layman [Robert Benton Seeley]. Second edition, revised and considerably enlarged. 8vo. London, 1834

ESSAYS on the evidence, characteristic doctrines, and influence of Christianity. [By Thomas Haweis, LL.B., M.D.] Fcap 8vo. Pp. viii., 394. [*Brit. Mus.*] Bath, 1790

ESSAYS on the following subjects : I. On miracles. II. On the extraordinary adventure of Balaam. III. On the victory gained by Joshua over Jabin, king of Hazor, written some years since by an obscure layman in town [George Psalmanazar] and now published on occasion of some late attempts made to disprove all miracles, etc. 8vo. [*Brit. Mus.*]
London, 1753
The writer was a mysterious literary adventurer born in the South of France, who travelled in Germany and the Netherlands, but spent most of his life in London. He published other works under the name indicated above.

ESSAYS on the formation and publication of opinions, and on other subjects. [By Samuel Bailey.] 8vo. Pp. xi., 284. [*D. N. B.*, vol. 2, p. 410.]
London, 1821
The name is given in a later edition (Bury, 1881).

ESSAYS on the lives of Cowper, Newton, and Heber ; or, an examination of the evidence of the course of nature being interrupted by the divine government. [By John Philips Potter.] 8vo. Pp. iv., 330. [*Brit. Mus.*] London, 1830

ESSAYS on the negro slave trade. [By Robert Bisset, LL.D.] 8vo. [*D. N. B.*, vol. 5, p. 102.] London, 1805

ESSAYS on the political circumstances of Ireland, written during the Administration of Earl Camden ; with an appendix . . . and a postscript. By a gentleman in the North of Ireland [Alexander Knox]. 8vo. [*Camb. Univ. Lib.*] Dublin, 1798
An edition issued in 1799 bears the author's name.

ESSAYS : I. On the populousness of Africa ; II. On the trade at the Forts on the Gold Coast ; III. On the necessity of erecting a Fort at Cape Appolonia. [By John Hippisley.] 8vo. [*D. N. B.*, vol. 27, p. 9.] London, 1764

ESSAYS on the present crisis in the condition of the American Indians ; first published in the National Intelligencer under the signature of William Penn [Jeremiah Evarts]. 8vo. [Cushing's *Init. and Pseud.*, vol. i., p. 227.] Boston, [Mass.], 1829

ESSAYS on the preservation and recovery of health, in two parts : wherein the late wines are suspected and censured ; malt drink, hops, cyder, artificial wines, coffee, tea, &c., as also drinking of water, and the elaborate compositions in eating, impartially examined. . . . [By Rev. Thomas Curteis.] 8vo. [Arber's *Term Cat.*, iii., 685.] London, 1704

ESSAYS on the principles of morality and natural religion ; in two parts. [By Henry Home, Lord Kames.] Second edition, with alterations and additions. Fcap 8vo. Pp. 317. [*Adv. Lib.*] London, 1758
   The third edition, published later, is not anonymous.
   Publication of this work evoked strong disapproval of some opinions expressed ; a sharp controversy followed. *See* " An Estimate of the profit and loss of religion, . . ." also " A Delineation of the nature and obligations of morality."

ESSAYS. I. On the public debt. II. On paper-money, banking, &c. III. On frugality. [By Patrick Murray, Lord Elibank.] 8vo. [*Adv. Lib.*] London, 1755

ESSAYS on the pursuit of truth, on the progress of knowledge, and on the fundamental principle of all evidence and expectation. By the author of *Essays on the formation and publication of opinions* [Samuel Bailey]. 8vo. Pp. xii., 302. [*D. N. B.*, vol. 2, p. 410.] London, 1829
   Authorship is acknowledged in the Bury edition of *Essays on Opinions*, 1881.

ESSAYS on the source of the pleasures received from literary compositions. [By William Greenfield, Professor in Edinburgh.] Second edition. 8vo. Pp. 394. [Scott's *Fasti*, new ed., vol. i., p. 61.] London, 1813
   Wrongly assigned to Rev. Edward Mangin. *See also* " An Essay on the sources. . . ."

ESSAYS on the spirit of Jacksonism. . . . By Aristides [Thomas L. M'Kenney]. 8vo. [Cushing's *Init. and Pseud.*, vol. i., p. 19.] Philadelphia, 1835

ESSAYS on the superstitions of the Highlanders of Scotland : to which are added, translations from the Gaelic ; and letters connected with those formerly published. 2 vols. By the author of *Letters from the mountains* [Mrs Anne Grant, *née* MacVicar, of Laggan]. Fcap 8vo. [*Adv. Lib.*] London, 1811

ESSAYS on various subjects. By the author of *Reflections on the seven days of the week* [Catherine Talbot]. 2 vols. Fcap 8vo. [*Bodl.*] London, 1772

ESSAYS on various subjects of taste and criticism. [By Aulay Macaulay, M.A.] 8vo. [*Gent. Mag.*, March 1819, p. 276.] London, 1780

ESSAYS on various subjects of taste, morals, and national policy. By a citizen of Virginia [George Tucker]. 8vo. [Cushing's *Init. and Pseud.*, i., p. 59.] Georgetown, D.C., 1822

ESSAYS on various subjects, religious and moral ; the practical application of their principles to the state of man in society, particularly the lower orders. . . . By a layman [Alexander Watson, Town-clerk, Port-Glasgow]. 3 vols. 8vo. [*Bodl.*] Edinburgh, 1821

ESSAYS, pastoral and elegiac : containing, Morning, or the complaint ; Noon, or the contest ; Evening, or the exclamation ; Night, or the wanderer. . . . By a gentleman, late of the Inner-Temple [Henry Baker]. 2 vols. 8vo. [Nichols' *Lit. Anec.*, v., 278.] London, 1756

ESSAYS, philosophical, historical, and literary. [By William Belsham.] 2 vols. 8vo. Pp. iv., 466. [*Brit. Mus.*] London, 1789

ESSAYS, poems, etc. ; with an elucidation of the " Bhagvat Geeta." By January Searle [George Searle Phillips, B.A.]. 8vo. [Cushing's *Init. and Pseud.*, vol. i., p. 263.] London, 1851

ESSAYS, poetical, moral, and critical. [By Brockill Newburgh.] 8vo. [*Brit. Mus.*] Dublin, 1769

ESSAYS relating to agriculture and rural affairs ; in two parts. . . . By a farmer [James Anderson, LL.D.]. 8vo. [*Brit. Mus.*] Edinburgh, 1775
   Several editions followed.

ESSAYS, religious and moral. [By Isaac Hawkins Browne.] 8vo. Pp. vii., 274. [*Gent. Mag.*, 1818, p. 179.] London, 1815

ESSAYS tending to prove the ruinous effects of the policy of the United States on the farmers, planters, and merchants. [By Matthew Carey.] 8vo. [Kirk's *Supp.*]
Philadelphia, 1826

ESSAYS towards an union between divinity and morality, reason or natural religion and revelation ; calculated to the meridian of our present differences in Church and State. [By William Freeke, or Le Freeke.] 8vo. [Wood's *Athen. Oxon.*, iv., 741.] London, 1687
This book is said in the title to be written " Per Gulielmum Liberam Clavem," *i.e.* Free K.

ESSAYS upon peace at home and war abroad, part I. [By Charles Davenant, LL.D.] 8vo. [*Athen. Cat.*, p. 87.] London, 1704

ESSAYS upon several projects ; or effectual ways for advancing the interest of the nation ; wherein are plainly laid down the means by which subjects may be enriched, the poor relieved, trade encreased, &c. [By Daniel Defoe.] 8vo. London, 1697
This is the same as " An essay upon projects . . ." [Wilson's *Life of Defoe*, i. 268.]

ESSAYS upon several subjects concerning British antiquities ; viz. I. Introduction of the feudal law into Scotland. II. Constitution of Parliament. III. Honour ; Dignity. IV. Succession or descent. With an appendix upon hereditary and indefeasible right. Composed anno M.DCC.XLV. [By Henry Home, Lord Kames.] 8vo. Pp. 217. [*Adv. Lib.*]
Edinburgh, 1747

ESSAYS upon several subjects in law, sciz., Jus tertii, Beneficium cedendarum actionum, Vinco vincentem, Prescription. [By Henry Home, Lord Kames.] 8vo. Pp. 164. [*Adv. Lib.*]
Edinburgh, 1732

ESSAYS upon I. The ballance of power. II. The right of making war, peace, and alliances. III. Universal monarchy. To which is added, an appendix containing the records referr'd to in the second essay. [By Charles Davenant, LL.D.] 8vo. Pp. 413. [Arber's *Term Cat.*, iii., 685.]
London, 1701

ESSAYS. Viz. I. On the origin of Colleges, or Universities. II. On the origin of the custom of lecturing in Latin. III. On the impropriety of this custom, at present. [By Patrick Clason.] 8vo. Pp. 61. [*Camb. Univ. Lib.*] Glasgow, 1769
MS. note on Lord Craig's copy.

ESSAYS written in the intervals of business. [By Sir Arthur Helps.] 8vo. Pp. 128. [Courtney's *Secrets*, p. 26.] London, 1841

ESSENCE (the) of Algernon Sidney's work on Government ; to which is annexed his Essay on Love. By a Student of the Inner Temple [William Scott, later Baron Stowell]. 8vo. Pp. xix., 287. [*Brit. Mus.*]
London, 1795

ESSENCE (the) of Ecclesiastes ; in metre of Omar Khayyam. By Alastair Buchanan [—— Macmillan]. Fcap 8vo. London, 1904

ESSENCE (the) of Malone ; or, the " beauties " of that fascinating writer : extracted from his immortal work . . . entitled, " Some account of the life and writings of John Dryden ! ! " [By George Hardinge.] Second edition, enlarged. 8vo. Pp. 117. [*Bodl.*]
London, 1800
The dedication is signed " Minutius Felix." The whole is signed " Minutius Felix. — With helps from Edmond, and with his mantle spread over me."

ESSENCE (the) of the Calm Observer on the subjects of the Concert of princes, the Dismemberment of Poland, and the War with France ; first published in the Morning Chronicle. [By Vicesimus Knox, D.D.] 8vo. Pp. 75. [*Manch. Free Lib. Cat.*]
London, 1793

ESSENCE (the) of the Douglas cause : to which is subjoined some observations on a pamphlet entitled, Considerations on the Douglas cause. [By James Boswell, of Auchinleck.] 8vo. [*D. N. B.*, vol. 5, p. 433.]
London, 1767

ESSENTIAL memoranda of arithmetic. By W. B. A. [W. B. Anthony]. 8vo. [*Brit. Mus.*] Derby, 1818

ESSENTIAL memoranda of English grammar. By W. B. A. [W. B. Anthony]. 8vo. London, 1881

ESSENTIAL memoranda of English history. By W. B. A. [W. B. Anthony]. 8vo. London, 1881

ESSENTIAL (the) principles of the wealth of nations, illustrated, in opposition to some false doctrines of Dr Adam Smith, and others. [By John Gray.] 8vo. Pp. 152. London, 1797
The Bodleian copy contains an autograph letter from Mr. Gray to Lord Bulkeley, asking his Lordship's acceptance of a copy. It is dated " Lottery Office, 3d June 1797."

ESSENTIAL (the) rights and liberties of Protestants : a seasonable plea for the liberty of conscience, and the right of private judgment in matters of religion, without any controul from human authority. . . . By a lover of truth and liberty [Elisha Williams]. 8vo. Pp. 68. [Evans' *Amer. Bibl.*, vol. 2, p. 277.] Boston, [Mass.], 1744
Signed "Philalethes." Credited also to Thomas Cushing, Member of the Massachusetts House of Representatives.

ESSENTIALS (the) of elocution. By Alfred Ayres [Thomas Embley Osmun]. 8vo. Pp. 174. [*Brit. Mus.*]
New York, 1897

ESSIE'S journey, and what she found in it. By Howe Benning [Mrs Mary H. Henry]. 8vo. [Kirk's *Supp.*]
New York, 1871

ESTABLISHED (the) and the Free : in what do they differ ? An answer to the articles of Mr Taylor Innes in the "Contemporary Review." [By Andrew Macgeorge.] Tenth thousand. 8vo.   Glasgow, 1874
Republished in "Papers on the principles and real position of the Free Church," Glasgow, 1875, with the author's name at the introductory note.

ESTABLISHED (the) Church [of England] : a reply to the Letters on the Voluntary principle, by [John Foster] a "Quiet looker on." In two letters. By Philalethes [William Goode, D.D.]. 8vo. [*Brit. Mus.*]   London, 1834

ESTABLISHED (the) Church [of England] : letters on the Voluntary principle. By a quiet Looker-on [John Foster]. 8vo. [*Brit. Mus.*]
London, 1834

ESTABLISHED (the) Church in Scotland : a historical study. [By Alexander Monfries, teacher.] 8vo. [*New Coll. Lib.*]   Edinburgh, 1879

ESTABLISHED (the) Church of England, the true Catholic Church, free from innovations or diminishing the Apostolic doctrines. . . . [By Mrs Catherine Willis, *née* Eliot.] Pt 8vo. Pp. 140.   London, 1718

ESTABLISHED (the) Church of Scotland, a political injustice. [By James Bridges.] 8vo. Pp. 62. Edin., 1882

ESTABLISHED (the) Church of Scotland the truly Free Church, and friend of the people. [By Rev. Robert Burns Thomson, minister at Spott.] 8vo. Pp. 12. [Scott's *Fasti*.]
Edinburgh, 1843

ESTABLISHED (the) Church question [in England] : how to deal with it. . . . By the author of *The Englishman's brief in behalf of his national Church* [Rev. Thomas Moore]. 8vo. Pp. xxiv., 135. [Crockford's *Cler. Directory*.]   London, 1883

ESTABLISHED government vindicated from all popular and republican principles. [By John Phillips, nephew of John Milton.] 4to. [*D. N. B.*, vol. 45, p. 207.]   London, 1683

ESTABLISHMENT (the) of the Turks in Europe ; an historical discourse. [By Lord John, afterwards Earl Russell.] 8vo. Pp. vi., 128. [*Camb. Univ. Lib.*]   London, 1828

ESTABLISHMENT (the) principle, as now interpreted. [By Rev. James A. Wylie, LL.D.] 8vo. [*New Coll. Cat.*]
Edinburgh, 1870

ESTABLISHMENT (the) [of the Church of England] vindicated, against the advocates for licentiousness. [By Rev. —— Herbert, military chaplain.] 8vo. Pp. 47. [*Brit. Mus.*]
London, 1730

ESTATE (the) of English fugitives under [Philip II.] the king of Spaine and his ministers. [By Thomas Scarlett.] 4to. [*Mendham Collection Cat.*, p. 274.]
London, 1595
Attributed also to Sir Lewis Lewkenor.

ESTATE (the) of the Church, with the discourse of times from the Apostles untill this present ; also of the lives of all the Emperours, Popes of Rome, and Turkes. . . . [By Jean Crespin.] Translated out of French into English by I. Patrike. Pt. 4to. [*Brit. Mus.*]
London, 1602

ESTATE (the) orators ; a town eclogue. [By William Woty.] 8vo. [*D. N. B.*, vol. 63, p. 63.]   London, 1774
A satire on London auctioneers.

ESTATES (the), empires and principallities of the world, represented by ye description of countries, maners of inhabitants, riches of provinces. . . . With the begiñing of all militarie and religious Orders. Translated out of French [of Pierre D'Avity] by E. Grimstone. 4to. [*Edin. Univ. Lib.*]   London, 1615

ESTELLE. By the author of *Four messengers*, etc. [Emily Marion Harris]. 2 vols. 8vo. [*Camb. Univ. Lib.*]   London, 1878

ESTELLE Russell. By the author of *The private life of Galileo* [Mary Allan-Olney]. 2 vols. 8vo. [*Camb. Univ. Lib.*]   London, 1870

ESTHER. [A poem. By Emily S. G. Saunders]. 12mo. Pp. 8. [*Brit. Mus.*]   N.P., [1870]
Signed "E. S. G. S."

ESTHER. [A novel.] By A. E. Jacomb [Agnes E— Jacomb Hood]. Cr 8vo. Pp. 308. [*Lit. Year Book.*]
London, 1912

ESTHER; a drama in five acts. [By A. W. Buchan.] 8vo. Pp. 103.
Glasgow, 1873

ESTHER; a tale of modern Jewish burgher life. By the author of *Eliezer* [Charlotte Elizabeth Stern]. 8vo. Pp. 217. [*Brit. Mus.*]   London, [1880]

ESTHER; an oratorio or sacred drama. [By Samuel Humphreys.] With the last improvements by Mr Handel. 4to. [*Brit. Mus.*]   London, [1761 ?]

ESTHER Reid. By Pansy [Mrs Isabella Alden, *née* Macdonald]. 8vo. Pp. 238. [*Lit. Year Book.*]
London, [1909]

ESTHER Reid yet speaking. By Pansy [Mrs Isabella Macdonald]. 8vo. [Kirk's *Supp.*] Cincinnati, 1880

ESTIMATE (an) of the manners and principles of the times. By the author of *Essays on the characteristics*, etc. [John Brown, D.D., vicar of Newcastle]. 8vo. Pp. 221. [*Brit. Mus.*]
London, 1757
Seven editions were required.
This was followed, in 1758, by "An explanatory defence of the Estimate." (*See below.*) The *Essays on the characteristics* is not anonymous.

ESTIMATE (an) of the profit and loss of religion, personally and publicly stated : illustrated with reference to [Henry Home, Lord Kames'] Essays on morality and natural religion. [By George Anderson, chaplain to George Watson's Hospital, Edinburgh.] 8vo. Pp. 397. [*New Coll. Cat.*]
Edinburgh, 1753
See "Essays on the principles of morality and natural religion."

ESTIMATE (an) of the religion of the fashionable world. By one of the laity [Hannah More]. Fourth edition. Fcap 8vo. [Courtney's *Secrets*, p. 47.]
London, 1791

ESTIMATE (an) of the value of South-Sea stock; with some remarks relating thereto. By a member of the House of Commons [Archibald Hutcheson]. Folio. Pp. 15. [*Brit. Mus.*]
London, 1720

ESTIMATING : a method of pricing builders' quantities for competitive work. By a practical estimator [George Stephenson]. 8vo. [*Brit. Mus.*]   London, 1883

ESTRANGED; or love unquenchable. By Derek Vane [Mrs Eaton Back]. 8vo. [*Lit. Year Book.*]
London, [1894]

ESTRAY (the); a collection of poems. [Edited by Henry Wadsworth Longfellow.] Fcap. [*Brit. Mus.*]
Boston, 1847

ETCHINGS in America. . . . By J. R. W. H. [James R. W. Hitchcock]. 8vo. [Cushing's *Init. and Pseud.*, vol. ii., p. 70.]   New York, 1886

ETCHINGS of views in the vicarage of Leatherhead, Surrey. By H. D. [Harriet Dallaway]. 8vo. [Cushing's *Init. and Pseud.*, vol. i., p. 74.]
London, 1821

ETERNAL conflict : an essay. By Benjamin Swift [Wm. Romaine Paterson]. 8vo. [*Lond. Lib. Cat.*]
London, 1901

ETERNAL death in the literal sense is eternal punishment. [By Charles Frederick Hudson.] Fcap 8vo. Pp. 24. [Abbot's *Lit. on a future life.*]
[New York, 1861]

ETERNAL (the) felicitie of the saints; written in Latin by the most illustrious Cardinall Bellarmin, of the Society of Jesus : translated into English. [By Thomas Everard, or Everett, S.J.] Fcap 8vo. [Oliver's *Collections.*]
St Omer, 1638

ETERNAL (the) fires. [A novel.] By Victoria Cross [Miss Vivian Cory]. Cr 8vo. [*Amer. Cat.*]   London, 1910

ETERNAL hope and eternal punishment. [By Henry Smith Sutton.] 8vo. [Kirk's *Supp.*]
Manchester, 1870

ETERNAL life and the Holy Ghost. By A. P. C. [Lord Adelbert Percy Cecil]. Fcap 8vo. Pp. 30.
London, [1893]

ETERNAL (the) obligation of natural religion; or, the foundation of morality to God and man : being an answer to Dr Wright's remarks upon Mr Mole's sermon. By Phil-orthos [George Johnstone]. 8vo. Pp. 48. [Darling's *Cyclop. Bibl.*]   London, 1732

ETERNAL (the) peace of the Church only attainable by a zeal for Scripture in its just latitude, and by mutual charity, not by a pretense of uniformity of opinions. . . . By a lover of truth and peace [Arthur Ashley Sykes, D.D.]. 8vo. [Disney's *Memoir of Sykes.*]
London, 1716

ETERNAL (the) priestess : a novel of China manners. By B. L. Putnam Weale [Bertram Lenox Simpson]. 8vo. Pp. 404. [*Brit. Mus.*]   London, 1914

ETERNAL purpose : a study of the Scripture doctrine of immortality. [By William R. Hart.] Cr 8vo. Pp. 325. [Abbot's *Lit. on a future life.*]
Philadelphia, 1882
The second edition, also in 1882, gives the author's name.

ETERNAL (the) question : shall a man live again ? By Averna [Allen Clarke]. Cr 8vo.   London, 1902
A later edition (1919) has the author's name and a modified title.

ETERNAL (the) religion. By J. B. [Rev. J— Brierley.] Cr 8vo. [*Amer. Cat.*]   New York, 1906

ETERNAL Spring. By Neith Boyce [Mrs Hutchins Hapgood]. 8vo. [*Amer. Cat.*]   New York, 1906

ETERNITY (the) of future punishment of the wicked illustrated and proved ; in a letter to a friend. By a clergyman of Massachusetts [Enoch Pond, D.D.]. 8vo. [Cushing's *Init. and Pseud.*, vol. ii., p. 33.]
Worcester, Mass., 1819

ETERNITY (the) of hell torments. [By Charles Povey.] [Abbot's *Lit. on a future life.*]   [1723 ?]

ETHEL. By J. J. B. [John Joy Bell], author of *Wee MacGreegor*. 8vo. Pp. 180. [*Lit. Year Book.*]
Edinburgh, [1903]

ETHEL Churchill ; or, the two brides. By the author of *The improvisatrice*, etc. [Letitia Elizabeth Landon, later Mrs Maclean]. 3 vols. Fcap 8vo. [*Camb. Univ. Lib.*]   London, 1837

ETHEL Dutton. By Mattie May [Mrs C— R— Brown, of Concord, N.H.]. 8vo. [Cushing's *Init. and Pseud.*, vol. i., p. 185.]   Boston, 1880

ETHEL Mildmay's follies ; a story. By the author of *Petite's romance* [Katherine King]. 3 vols. 8vo. [*Camb. Univ. Lib.*]   London, 1872

ETHEL Somers ; or, the fate of the Union. By a Southerner [James M. Smythe]. [Cushing's *Init. and Pseud.*, vol. i., p. 272.] Augusta, Georgia, 1857

ETHEL Wilton ; a chapter from a life's history. By Adeline [Mrs Richard Sergeant, *née* Jane Hall]. Fcap 8vo. [*D. N. B.*, Second Supp., vol. 3, p. 291.]   London, [1861]

ETHEL Woodville ; or woman's ministry : a tale for the times. [By Mrs —— Hollings.] 2 vols. 8vo. [*Brit. Mus.*]   London, 1859

ETHELENA ; or self-sacrifice : a poem. By the author of *Friendship's offering*, etc. [Rev. William A. Des Brisay]. 8vo. [*Brit. Mus.*]
[New Canaan, Conn.], 1871

ETHEL'S comforter. [A tale.] By J. A. Owen [Mrs Jane Allan Visger, *née* Pinder]. Fcap 8vo. [*Lit. Year Book.*]
London, 1880

ETHICA ; or the ethics of reason. By Scotus Novanticus [Simon S. Laurie, LL.D., Professor in Edinburgh]. 8vo. [*Edin. Univ. Lib.*]   London, 1885

ETHICS and æsthetics of modern poetry. By J. B. Selkirk [John Brown, Selkirk]. Cr 8vo. Pp. 237.   London, 1878

ETHICS (the) of education. By Beatrice de Normann [. . .] and George Colmore [Mrs Gertrude Dunn]. 8vo. Pp. 73. [*Brit. Mus.*]
London, [1918]

ETHICS (the) of quotation : with a preliminary letter to the secretaries of the Congregational Union. By Silent Long [Thomas T. Lynch]. 8vo. [William White's *Memoir of T. T. Lynch* ; *D. N. B.*, vol. 34, p. 338.]
London, 1856
The author, a Congregationalist minister, had previously (in 1855) published " The Rivulet, a contribution to sacred song," the third edition of which, in 1868, contains 167 hymns by him. Strong exception was soon taken to the collection, on the ground that it was largely unsuited for Christian worship, and more pantheistic than theologically sound ; thus began " The Rivulet controversy." In reply, the author published the above, and in the same year a small doggerel production " Songs controversial," under the same pseudonym.

ETHICS (the) of war. [By Alfred C. Dewar.] Cr 8vo.   Ramsgate, [1915]

ETHICS or anarchy ; an essay concerning the relation of modern philosophy to morals and religion. [By B— F. C. Costelloe.] 8vo. Pp. vii., 100. [*Brit. Mus.*]   London, 1895
Preface signed " B. F. C. C."

ETHIOPIAN dramas. By J. C. Stewart [J— S— Crossey]. 8vo. [Cushing's *Init. and Pseud.*, vol. i., p. 274.]   New York, 1875

ETON. The founder's pageant, and play of St Nicholas. [By Montague Rhodes James.] 8vo. [*Camb. Univ. Lib.*]   Eton, [1919]

ETON and Oxford ; a few familiar scenes sketched from recollection after an interval of several years. . . . By a contemporary [Rev. George Robert Winter, M.A.]. Two series. 8vo. [Harcourt's *Eton Bibl.*]
Oxford, [1854]

ETON (an) boy's letters. By the author of *A day of my life at Eton* [George Nugent Banks]. 8vo. [*Brit. Mus.*]
London, 1901

ETON College; an explanation of the various local passages and allusions in the appeal, &c., of King's College versus Eton College. By a late scholar . . . [—— Hond]. Second edition. 8vo. Pp. 58. [*W.*] London, 1819

ETON idylls. By C. R. S. [Christopher Reynolds Stone]. 8vo. Pp. 92. [*Brit. Mus.*] London, 1902

ETON in the forties. By an old Colleger [Arthur Duke Coleridge]. Cr 8vo. [Bartholomew's *Cat. of Camb. Books.*] London, 1896
A revised edition appeared in 1898.

ETON memories. By an old Etonian [Rev. William Hill Tucker, M.A.]. 8vo. Pp. 348. London, 1909
See also below, " Eton of old."

ETON (an) miscellany; edited by Bartholomew Bouverie [William Ewart Gladstone]. 2 vols. 8vo. [Gladstone *Lib. Cat.* (Lib. Club).]
Eton, 1827

ETON of old; or eighty years since (1811-1822). By an old Colleger [Rev. William Hill Tucker]. Royal 8vo.
London, 1892
See also above, " Eton memories."

ETON of to-day. [By Arthur C. Benson.] 4to. [Bartholomew's *Cat. of Camb. Books.*] London, 1892

ETON reform. [By William Johnson, afterwards Cory, M.A.] 8vo. Pp. 34. [Bowes' *Cat. of Camb. Books.*]
Cambridge, 1861

ETON school days. By an old Etonian [Samuel Bracebridge Hemyng]. 8vo. [*Brit. Mus.*] London, 1864

ETONIAN (the). [A magazine edited by Wilfrid Blunt and Winthrop M. Praed.] 2 vols. 8vo.
Windsor, 1820-21

ETONIANA, ancient and modern; being notes of the history and conditions of Eton College, republished from Blackwood's Magazine, with additions. [By William Lucas Collins.] Pt 8vo. Pp. viii., 238. [*Edin. Univ. Lib.*] Edinburgh, 1865
The preface is signed " W. L. C." The work is wrongly ascribed to William L. Courtenay.

ETTIE Knott; or silver-lined clouds. By Winter Daisy [Miss —— Whiteway]. Fcap 8vo. [Cushing's *Init. and Pseud.*, vol. i., p. 77.] London, 1877

ETYMOLOGICON universale; or, an universal etymological dictionary. [By Rev. Walter Whiter, M.A.] 2 vols. 4to. [Watt's *Bibl. Brit.*]
Cambridge, 1811

ETYMOLOGY made easy; being familiar conversations on the derivation and meaning of some words in common use. [By Fanny Elizabeth Burnett.] 8vo. London, 1856

EUBULUS, or a dialogue, where-in a rugged Romish Ryme (inscrybed, Catholicke questions to the Protestaut) is confuted, and the questions there-of answered. By P. A. [Patricius Aberdonensis, *i.e.* Patrick Forbes, Bishop of Aberdeen]. With priviledge. 4to. Pp. 166, and one page—Escapes in printing. [J. P. Edmond's *Aberdeen Printers*, p. 25.]
Aberdene, by Edward Raban, 1627

EUCHARISTIC homilies. By Presbuteros [Rev. W— B. Moore]. Fcap 8vo. London, 1907

EUCHARISTIC (the) manual, consisting of instructions and devotions . . . from various sources. . . . [By Rev. George Rundle Prynne, M.A., Plymouth.] 12mo. Pp. viii., 104.
London, 1864

EUCHARISTICAL adoration. By Vincentius Lirinensis [William Vanderpool]. 8vo. N.P., 1874

EUCHOLOGION, or a Book of Common Order; being forms of worship issued by the Church [of Scotland] Service Society. [Chiefly prepared by George W. Sprott, D.D., and John Macleod, D.D.] Second edition, revised and enlarged. Pt 8vo. Pp. xi., 317. Edinburgh, 1869

EUCHRE; or, the game of life. By the X Y Z Club [John Godfrey Saxe, A— Livien Douglas, and George W. Pettes]. Fcap 8vo. London, N.D.

EUDOKIA; or the Angels' song: a vindication of the New Testament (English and Greek) of our blessed Lord and Saviour Jesus Christ, as affected by the work of the Bible Revision Company, 1870. . . . By Theophilus, A.M., of Glasgow University [Rev. Robert R— Rae, M.A.]. 8vo. Pp. 127. London, 1883
Information from a friend of the author.

EUGENE Aram: a tale. By the author of *Pelham*, &c. [Edward George Earle Lytton Bulwer-Lytton, Baron Lytton]. 3 vols. Fcap 8vo. [*Brit. Mus.*] London, 1832

EUGENE Vidocq, soldier, thief, spy, detective : a romance. By Dick Donovan [Joyce Emerson Preston Muddock]. Cr 8vo. [*Lit. Year Book.*]
London, 1895

EUGENIA'S teares for Great Brittaynes distractions, or some slender observations reflecting on those sad times. Written by E. R. [Edward Reynolds, Bishop of Norwich]. 8vo. [*Brit. Mus.*] London, 1642

EUGÉNIE. By the author of *Miss Molly* [Beatrice May Butt]. 8vo. Pp. 247. [*Brit. Mus.*]
Edinburgh, 1877

EUGENIO and Epenetus ; or conversations respecting the evidence in support of infant baptism : containing an attempt towards an impartial statement of the arguments for this practice and against it. [By William Innes, Baptist minister in Edinburgh.] Fcap 8vo. [*New Coll. Cat.*]
Edinburgh, 1811

EUGENIO ; or, the man of sorrow : a legendary tale. By a young gentleman of seventeen [Ambrose Pitman]. 4to. [*Brit. Mus.*] London, 1780

EUGENIO ; or, a virtuous and happy life : a poem. [By Thomas Beach.] Inscrib'd to Mr Pope. 4to. [Watt's *Bibl. Brit.*] London, 1737

EUGENIUS ; or, anecdotes of the Golden Vale. By the author of *The Spiritual Quixote* [Rev. Richard Graves, B.A.]. 2 vols. 12mo. [Watt's *Bibl. Brit.*] London, 1785

EULOGIES (the) of Howard ; a vision. [By William Hayley.] 8vo. [Nichols' *Lit. Anec.*, ix., 89.] London, 1791

EULOGIES ; or, political characters : a poem, embracing several topics ; with some sketches of Grenville, Pitt, Fox, Earl Moira, Petty, Windham, Erskine, the jeweller, &c. Addressed to the Right Hon. Lord Sidmouth. By the author of *Hezekiah*, a sacred drama [William Allen]. 8vo. Pp. 55. [Nichols' *Lit. Anec.*, ix., 205.]
London, 1806

EUNICE [A novel.] By the author of *The Bairns* [Margaret M. Robertson]. 8vo. Pp. 312. [*Brit. Mus.*]
London, 1887

EUNOMUS ; or dialogues concerning the law and constitution of England : with an essay on dialogue. [By Edward Wynne, barrister.] 4 vols. 8vo. [*Brit. Mus.*] London, 1774

EUNUCHISM display'd : describing all the different sorts of eunuchs ; the esteem they have met with in the world, and how they came to be made so : wherein principally is examin'd, whether they are capable of marriage, and if they ought to be suffer'd to enter into that state ; the whole confirm'd by the authority of Civil, Canon, and Common Law, and illustrated with many remarkable cases by way of precedent. . . . Written by a person of honour [Charles Ancillon]. Fcap 8vo.
London, 1718
The original was published in 1707 under the pseudonym of C. D'Ollincan, an anagram of the author's name.

EUPHEMIA and Salem ; a tale. By the author of *An afternoon's walk* [Pithie Booth]. Fcap 8vo. Pp. 110. [Robertson's *Aberd. Bibl.*]
Aberdeen, 1863

EUPHORION : being studies of the antique and mediæval in the Renaissance. By Vernon Lee [Violet Paget]. 2 vols. 8vo. [*Lond. Lib. Cat.*]
London, 1884

EUPHRANOR ; a dialogue on youth. [By Edward Fitzgerald, B.A.] 8vo. Pp. 81. [*Brit. Mus.*] London, 1851

EUPHRANOR : a May-day conversation at Cambridge. " 'Tis forty years since." [By Edward Fitzgerald, B.A.] 8vo. Pp. 69. Guildford, [1882]

EUPHRASIA ; songs of trust and cheer. By Frederick Vincent [Rev. William Dunlop, M.A.]. 8vo. Pp. 39. Glasgow, 1903
Information from a friend of the author.

EVPHRATES, or the waters of the East ; being a short discourse of that secret fountain whose water flows from fire, and carries in it the beams of the sun and moon. By Eugenius Philalethes [Thomas Vaughan]. 8vo. Pp. 137. [Gardner's *Rosicrucian Books*, p. 75.] London, 1655
A modern reprint was edited by Dr W. W. Westcott (1895).

EUPHROSYNE, an ode to beauty ; addressed to Mrs Crouch. By Sylvester Otway [John Oswald]. 4to. [Watt's *Bibl. Brit.*] London, 1788

EUPHROSYNE ; or, amusements on the road of life. By the author of *The Spiritual Quixote* [Rev. Richard Graves]. 2 vols. 8vo. Pp. viii., 308. [Green's *Bibl. Somers.*, ii., 445.]
London, 1776

EUPHUES shadow, the battaile of the sences : hereunto is annexed the deafe mans dialogue. By T. L. [Thomas Lodge, M.D.], Gent. 4to. [Lowndes' *Bibl. Man.*] London, 1592

EUREKA. [A novel.] By Owen Hall [Hugh H. Lusk]. Cr 8vo. Pp. 308. [*Lond. Lib. Cat.*]   London, 1899

EUREKA ; a prophecy of the future. By the author of *Mephistopheles in England* [Robert Folkestone Williams]. 3 vols. Fcap 8vo. [*Camb. Univ. Lib.*]   London, 1837

EUREKA ; a sequel to Lord John Russell's Post-bag : respectfully dedicated to the senior member of the University of Oxford. [By James T. B. Landon, M.A.] 8vo. Pp. 32. [*Falconer Madan.*]   Oxford, 1851

EUREKA, No. II. ; a sequel to a sequel to Lord John Russell's Post-bag. Respectfully dedicated to him " From whom alone of the heads of Colleges, no answer was received to any of the communications of the commission." Report, p. 9, Appendix B. [By J. T. B. Landon.] 8vo. Pp. 42.
Oxford, 1853

EURIDICE ; a tragedy. [By David Mallet.] 8vo. [*Edin. Univ. Lib.*]
London, 1731

EURIPIDES. Hecuba ; a tragedy, as it is acted at the Theatre-Royal in Drury-Lane. [Translated by Richard West.] [*Camb. Univ. Lib.*]
London, 1761

EUROPÆ speculum ; or view of the state of religion in the westerne parts of the world : wherein the Roman religion, and the pregnant policies of the Church of Rome to support the same are notably displayed. [By Sir Edwin Sandys.] 8vo. [Bliss *Cat.*]
London, 1605

EUROPE : a prophecy. By Augur [William Blake]. Pt 8vo.   [*Watt's Bibl. Brit.*]   London, 1794

EUROPE a slave, unless England break her chains ; discovering the grand designs of the French Popish party in England for several years past. [Translated from the French of Jean P— De Cerdan.] Fcap 8vo. [Arber's *Term Cat.*, vol. i., p. 523.]   London, 1681

EUROPE ; or, a general survey of the present situation of the principal powers, with conjectures on their future prospects. By a citizen of the United States [Alex. Hill Everett]. 8vo. Pp. 411. [*Brit. Mus.*] London, 1822

EUROPEAN breezes. By Margery Deane [Mrs Marie J. Pitman, *née* Davis]. 8vo. [Cushing's *Init. and Pseud.*, vol. i., p. 78.]   Boston, 1882

EUROPEAN commerce ; new channels of trade with the Continent. . . . By J. Oddy Jepson [William Playfair]. 4to.   London, 1805

EUROPEAN leaflets, for young ladies. By Evangeline [Mrs A. E. Newman]. 8vo. [Cushing's *Init. and Pseud.*, vol. i., p. 94.]   New York, 1861

EUROPEAN politics. A series of letters by the Political Key [H— I. Jenkinson]. 8vo. [Gladstone *Lib. Cat.* (Lib. Club).]   Keswick, 1879

EUROPEAN (the) traveller in America ; contained in three letters to his friend in London. [By Rev. Thomas Brockway.] 8vo. [Evans' *Amer. Bibl.*, vol. 6, p. 345.] Hartford, Conn., 1785

EUROPE'S optical illusion. By Norman Angell [Ralph Norman Angell Lane]. 8vo. Pp. 120. [*Brit. Mus.*]
London, 1909

EURYDICE ; a tragedy ; acted at the Theatre-Royal in Drury-Lane by his Majesty's servants. [By David Mallet.] 8vo. Pp. iv., 80. [*Biog. Dram.*]   London, 1731

EUSEBIUS inermatus. Just remarks on a late book, intitled, Eleutherius Enervatus, or an answer to a pamphlet intituled, The Divine Right of Presbyterian Ordination, &c., argued. By Phileleutherus Bangor, V. E. B. [Thomas Foxcroft]. Fcap 8vo. Pp. 158. [Evans' *Amer. Bibl.*, vol. 2, p. 53.]   Boston, [Mass.], 1733

EUSEBIUS Pamphilus his ten books of Ecclesiastical history, faithfully translated and abridg'd from the original. By Samuel Parker, Gent. To which is prefixed a dissertation concerning the use and authority of Ecclesiastical History. By the author of the Snake in the grass [Charles Leslie] in a letter to the abridger : with the life of Eusebius, abstracted from the best authors ; also an account of his works, and a large index. 8vo. Pp. xxx., 211. [Arber's *Term Cat.*, vol. iii., p. 357.]
London, 1703

EUSTACE Conway ; or, the brother and sister : a novel. [By John Frederick Denison Maurice.] 3 vols. Fcap 8vo. [*Maurice's Life.*] London, 1834

EUTAW ; a sequel to " The Forayers " : a tale of the Revolution. By Frank Cooper [William Gilmore Simms]. Pt 8vo. [Cushing's *Init. and Pseud.*, vol. i., p. 67.]   New York, 1885

EUTAXIA, or the Presbyterian liturgies : historical sketches. By a minister of the Presbyterian Church [Charles W. Baird, D.D.]. Fcap 8vo.
New York, 1855
Reprinted (London, 1856) with the author's name, under the title " A Chapter on Liturgies."

EVA O'Connor; a poem in three cantos. By an author yet unknown [John De Jean Frazer]. 8vo. [O'Donoghue's *Poets of Ireland*.] Dublin, 1826

EVA ; or, the bridal spectre : a tale. [By Mrs W. Johnson.] With engravings. 8vo. Pp. 311. [*Aberd. Lib.*] London, 1830

EVANGELIA nolana; the story of the Gospels. By the author of *Charles Lowder* [Maria M. Trench]. Fcap 8vo. [*Brit. Mus.*] London, 1909

EVANGELICA. By Apollo Belvedere [Katherine Russell]. Pt 8vo. Pp. 181. [*Amer. Cat.*] New York, 1897

EVANGELICAL (the) champions : a satire . . . [By Andrew Robson.] 8vo. [*Brit. Mus.*] Newcastle, 1827
The preface is signed " Laicus."

EVANGELICAL Churchmen and Evangelical Nonconformists : an address on the subject of Christian Union. By Delta [Henry Dunn]. Fcap 8vo. [Green's *Bibl. Somers.*, i., 142.] Bath, 1859

EVANGELICAL (the) Rambler. [By Timothy East.] 3 vols. 8vo. [*New Coll. Lib.*] London, 1824, 1825
Each volume consists of 36 tracts, of 12 pages, with the general title, as well as an addition indicating the subject. A new edition, in two volumes, was published in 1836. In 1857, a new and thoroughly revised edition was issued in two volumes, under the title of " The sheepfold and the common : or, within and without."

EVANGELICAL (the) Spectator. By the author of " The Evangelical Rambler " [Timothy East]. 3 vols. [*Brit. Mus.*] London, 1829-31.

EVANGELICAL summary of corroborating evidences concerning the birth, death, resurrection and ascension of Jesus Christ. By a member of the Church of England [Rev. Christopher Hodgson, LL.B., rector of Marholm, Northampton]. 8vo. Pp. xx., 68. [Watt's *Bibl. Brit.*] Peterborough, 1788

EVANGELICAL (an) view of the nature and means of regeneration. By Evangelus Pacificus [Rev. Hubbard Winslow]. 8vo. [Cushing's *Init. and Pseud.*, vol. ii. p. 55.] Boston, 1830

EVANGELIST (the) of the day. [By François M. Arouet de Voltaire.] Translated from the French. 8vo. [Watt's *Bibl. Brit.*] London, 1769

EVANGELISTS (the) : reprinted from " The Christian Witness." By J. G. B. [John George Bellett]. Fcap 8vo. London, 1859

EVANGELIUM armatum; a specimen, or short collection of several doctrines and positions destructive to our government, both civil and ecclesiastical ; preached and vented by the known leaders and abetters of the pretended Reformation, such as Mr Calamy, Mr Jenkins, Mr Case, Mr Baxter, Mr Caryll, Mr Marshall, and others, &c. [By William Assheton or Asheton.] Pp. 68. [*Bodl.*] London, 1663

EVANGELIUM regni. A joyfull message of the kingdom, published by the holie Spirit of the loue of Iesu Christ, and sent-fourth vnto all nations of people, which love the trueth in Iesu Christ. Set-fourth by H. N. [Henry Nicholas], and by him pervsed a-new and more-distinctlie declared. Translated out of Base-almayne [by C— Vitall]. 8vo. B. L. 100 leaves, including title and preface. Only the first side of the leaf is paged. [? Amsterdam, 1575]
The author, originally known as Hendrik Niklas, spent his early years in Holland, but afterwards migrated to England, where, with David Doris, he was a prominent leader in the mystic sect styled the " Family of love." Other productions of his pen are " Exhortation I.," " A Figure of the true and spiritual tabernacle," " The First Epistle : a crying voice . . .," " The First exhortation . . ." " The Prophetic of the Spirit of love," " Proverbia H. N.," " A Publishing of the peace." *See below.*

EVANS of Suffolk. By Margaret Allston [Mrs Anna Farquhar]. Pt 8vo. [*Amer. Cat.*] New York, 1904

EVE : a novel. By the author of *John Herring* [Rev. Sabine Baring Gould]. 8vo. [*Lond. Lib. Cat.*] London, 1888

EVE ; an incident of Paradise Regained. By Maarten Maartens [Joost M. W. Van der Poorten Schwartz]. Cr 8vo. Pp. 368. [*Lond. Lib. Cat.*] London, 1912

EVE in earnest. By John Barnett [John Reginald Stagg]. Cr 8vo. Pp. 307. [*Brit. Mus.*] London, 1910

EVE (the) of Pascua, and other stories. By Richard Dehan [Clotilde Graves]. Cr 8vo. [*Lit. Year Book.*] London, 1920

EVE (the) of St. Hippolyto ; a play, in five acts. [By Dr and Mrs Manson.] 8vo. Pp. 70. Nottingham, 1821

EVELEEN. By E. L. A. Berwick, author of *The Dwarf*, etc. [James Reynolds, surgeon]. 3 vols. 8vo. [*Bodl.*] London, 1856

EVELINA ; or, the history of a young lady's entrance into the world. [By Mrs Frances D'Arblay *née* Burney.] New edition. 2 vols. 8vo. [Court-ney's *Secrets*, p. 46.]   London, 1791

EVELINE. [A novel]. By the author of *Forest Keep* [Alice King]. 3 vols. Post 8vo. [*Brit. Mus.*] London, 1863

EVELYN Clare ; or the wrecked home-steads : an Irish story of love and landlordism. By Erigena [J— G. Barrett]. 8vo. Pp. viii., 274. [S. J. Brown's *Ireland in fiction*, p. 24.]
Derby, 1870

EVELYN Harcourt ; a novel. By the author of *Temptation* ; *or, a wife's perils*, etc. [Mrs M— A— Gas-coigne] 3 vols. Fcap 8vo. [*Camb. Univ. Lib.*]   London, 1847

EVELYN Hastings. [A novel.] By Victoria Cross [Miss Vivian Cory]. Cr 8vo. Pp. 157. [*Amer. Cat.*]
London, 1917

EVELYN Marston. By the author of *Emilia Wyndham*, etc. [Mrs Anne Marsh-Caldwell]. 3 vols. 8vo. [*D. N. B.*, vol. 36, p. 219.]
London, 1856

EVELYN Stuart ; or, might *versus* right. By Adrian [Anne Kent]. 3 vols. Fcap 8vo. [Cushing's *Init. and Pseud.*, vol. i., p. 6.]
London, 1846

EVELYN'S career. [A novel.] By the author of *Dr Edith Romney* [Anne Elliot]. Cr 8vo. [*Lond. Lib. Cat.*]
London, 1891

EVELYN'S folly. By Bertha M. Clay [Mrs Charlotte M. Braeme]. Fcap 8vo.
New York, 1886

EVELYN'S Quest. [A novel.] By Elsie Feild [Lilian Cecil Streatfeild]. 8vo. Pp. ix., 231.   London, 1906

EVENING communions contrary to the teaching and practice of the Church in all ages : an article [by Dr Henry Parry Liddon] reproduced from the *Christian Remembrancer*. 8vo.
London, 1872
Signed " H. P. L."

EVENING contemplations in a College ; being a parody on the Elegy in a country church-yard. By another gentleman of Cambridge [John Dun-combe]. 4to. [*Camb. Univ. Lib.*]
London, 1753
See "An Elegy wrote in a country churchyard."

EVENING (the) hymn. [Being a hymn and a prayer for thirty-one days. By Rev. James D. Burns.] Fcap 8vo. Pp. 128. [Julian's *Dict. of Hymno-logy.*]   London, 1857

EVENING incense. By the author of *Morning and night watches*, etc. [John Ross MacDuff, D.D.]. Fcap 8vo. Pp. 127.   London, 1856

EVENING meditations ; or, a series of reflections on various passages of Holy Scripture and scriptural poetry for every day in the year. By the author of *The retrospect*, etc. [Rev. Richard Marks]. Fcap 8vo. [*Brit. Mus.*]
London, 1838

EVENING (an) on Pelion : a poem, in three cantos. [By William Lean.] 8vo. Pp. 47. [*Brit. Mus.*]
Neath, 1872

EVENING recreations with pencil and paper. By Kunquer Phair [Frederick Edward Hulme]. 8vo. London, 1901

EVENING rest ; or, the shadow of the Great Shepherd. By Laura Loring [Laura Loring Pratt]. 8vo. [Cush-ing's *Init. and Pseud.*, vol. i., p. 173.]
Boston, 1872

EVENING (an) sacrifice ; or prayer for a family, necessary for these calamitous times. [By John Reading?] 8vo. B.L. [*Brit. Mus.*]   [London], 1643

EVENING thoughts. By a physician [Joseph Bullar, M.D.]. Fcap 8vo. Pp. vii., 144. [*Adv. Lib.*]
London, 1850
This was followed, in 1868, by a second series : " Thoughts of a physician." *See later.*

EVENING (an) with Dr Grant, master of the Teviotdale otter hounds. By " The Druid " [Henry Hall Dixon]. 8vo. [Sinton's *Bibl. of Hawick.*]
N.P., 1864

EVENINGS abroad. By the author of *Sketches of Corfu* [Frances Maclellan]. 8vo. Pp. x., x. 333. [*Bodl.*]
London, 1836

EVENINGS at home : in words of one syllable. By Mary Godolphin [Lucy Aikin]. Fcap 8vo. [Cushing's *Init. and Pseud.*, vol. i., p. 118.]
London, 1869

EVENINGS at home ; or, the juvenile budget opened : consisting of a variety of miscellaneous pieces, for the instruc-tion and amusement of young persons. [By Dr John Aikin and Mrs Anna Letitia Barbauld, *née* Aikin.] 4 vols. Fcap 8vo. [*Brit. Mus.*]
London, 1793-94

EVENINGS away from home. . . . By Ascott R. Hope [Ascott Robert Hope Moncrieff]. 8vo. Pp. 351. [*Lit. Year Book.*]   London, 1883

EVENINGS with a reviewer ; or, a free and particular examination of Mr Macaulay's article on Lord Bacon. [By James Spedding.] 2 vols. 8vo. [*Brit. Mus.*]   London, 1884
Preface signed "J. S."

EVENTFUL (the) history of the mutiny and piratical seizure of H.M.S. Bounty; its cause and consequences. [Edited by Sir John Barrow.] Illustrated by six etchings from original drawings by Lieut.-Colonel Batty. 8vo. Pp. xi., 356. [*Brit. Mus.*]   London, 1831

EVENTFUL (the) life of a soldier, during the late war in Portugal, Spain, and France. By a sergeant of the * * regiment of infantry [John Donaldson]. Fcap 8vo. Pp. vii., 369.
Edinburgh, 1827
The narrative appeared originally in separate volumes under the titles of " Recollections of an eventful life," and " The Peninsular war."

EVENTFUL (the) life of Napoleon Bonaparte. By Baron Karlo Excellmaus [William Henry Ireland]. 4 vols. 8vo. [*D. N. B.*, vol. 29, p. 36.]   London, 1828

EVENTIDE ; a series of tales and poems. By Effie Afton [Mrs Frances Ellen Watkins Harper]. 8vo. [Cushing's *Init. and Pseud.*, vol. i., p. 7.]
Boston, 1854

EVENTS in an Irish country house in 1880. By Étoile [Major-General Edward Mitchell.] 8vo. Pp. 48.
Manchester, 1886

EVENTS in Indian history ; beginning with an account of the origin of the American Indians and early settlements in North America. . . . [By James Wirner.] 8vo. Pp. 633. 1842

EVERETT'S encyclopaedia of useful knowledge. [Edited by Henry Neil.] 8vo. [*Amer. Cat.*]   New York, 1906

EVERLASTING (the) Gospel, commanded to be preached by Jesus Christ . . . unto all creatures . . . concerning the eternal redemption found out by Him. Written in German by Paul Siegvolck [Georg Klein-Nicolai]. 8vo. [*Brit. Mus.*]
London, 1792

EVERLASTING (the) joys of heaven ; or, the blessed life of a Christian in grace here and in glory hereafter. Set forth . . . by J. H. [John Hart, D.D.]. 8vo. [*Brit. Mus.*]   London, 1656

EVERLASTING (an) proof of the falsehood of Popery ; being a relation of the fearful estate of Francis Spira. . . . [By Nathaniel Bacon.] Fcap 8vo. Pp. 24. [*D. N. B.*, vol. 2, p. 365.]
Manchester, 1845

EVERLASTING punishment : do our clergy believe in it ? A plain question by a plain man [Rev. Henry William Pullen, M.A.]. 8vo. [*Brit. Mus.*]
London, 1872

EVERLEY : a tale. [By Miss —— Cornish.] 8vo. [*Brit. Mus.*]
London, 1855

EVERY adventurer in the present State lotteries his own dupe. . . . By the author of *Every man his own broker* [Thomas Mortimer]. 8vo. Pp. 77. [*Brit. Mus.*]   London, 1808

EVERY boy's book ; a complete encyclopædia of sports and amusements : edited by George Forrest, Esq., M.A. [Rev. John George Wood]. 8vo. Pp. x., 636. [Thomas on *Swimming*, p. 276.]   London, 1855
A later edition, by Professor Hoffmann [Angelo John Lewis], appeared in 1897. Pp. xix., 900.

EVERY cloud has a silver lining ; and other stories. By A. L. O. E., author of *Fairy Frisket*, etc. [Charlotte Maria Tucker]. 8vo. Pp. 63. [*Lit. Year Book*.]   London, 1875

EVERY inch a woman. [A novel.] By the author of *Recommended to mercy* [Mrs Margaret C. Houstoun]. 8vo. [*Brit. Mus.*]   London, 1885

EVERY man hath his proper gift ; a sermon preached on the death of Lord Tenterden, Lord Chief-Justice of England. [By Rev. Theodore Williams.] 4to.   London, 1853

EVERY man his own brewer : a practical treatise on brewing malt liquor. By Bonington Moubray, Esq. [John Lawrence]. Fcap 8vo. Pp. 69. [*Brit. Mus.*]   London, 1834

EVERY man his own broker ; or, a guide to Exchange Alley : in which the nature of the several funds, vulgarly called the Stocks, is clearly explained, and the mystery and iniquity of stock-jobbing laid before the public in a new and impartial light. Also, the method of transferring stock, of buying and selling India bonds, lottery tickets, life annuities, and other government securities, without the assistance of a broker. . . . By Philanthropos [Thomas Mortimer]. Fcap 8vo. [*Brit. Mus.*]   London, 1761

EVERY man his own butler. By the author of the *History and description of modern wines* [Cyrus Redding]. Fcap 8vo. Pp. xvi., 200. [*Bodl.*]
London, 1839

EVERY man his own gardener. By John Halsham [Forrester Scott]. 8vo.
London, 1904

EVERY man his own gardener; being a new and more complete gardener's Kalendar than any one hitherto published. By Mr Maw, gardener to the Duke of Leeds [really by John Abercrombie]. 8vo. [*D. N. B.*, vol. 1, p. 37.]   London, 1767

EVERY man his own guide to the Falls of Niagara. By a resident at the Falls [T— Hulett]. 8vo. [Cushing's *Init. and Pseud.*, vol. ii., p. 130.]
                                      Buffalo, 1842

EVERY man his own law-maker; or, the Englishman's complete guide to a Parliamentary reform. . . . [By Soame Jenyns.] Second edition. 8vo. Pp. 44. [*D. N. B.*, vol. 29, p. 333.]
                                      London, 1785

EVERY man his own lawyer. By a barrister [Henry Coleman Folkard]. 8vo. [Cushing's *Init. and Pseud.*, vol. i., p. 15.]   London, 1882

EVERY man his own lawyer; or, a summary of the laws of England. [By Giles Jacob.] 8vo. [*Brit. Mus.*]
                                      [London], 1736
Signed " G. J."

EVERY man his own poet; or, the inspired singer's recipe book. By a Newdigate prizeman [William Hurrell Mallock]. 8vo. [*Bodl.*]
                                      Oxford, 1872

EVERY man in his humour; a comedy. Written by Ben Jonson; with alterations and additions [by David Garrick] as it is perform'd at the Theatre-Royal in Drury-Lane. 8vo. [*W.*]
                                      London, 1752
The prologue spoken by Garrick was written by William Whitehead, afterwards poet laureate.

EVERY man's assistant, and the sick man's friend. [By Rev. Sir James Stonhouse, M.D.] 8vo. [*D. N. B.*, vol. 54, p. 418.]   London, 1788
Frequently reprinted.

EVERY woman her own flower gardener. By Daisy Eyebright [Mrs S. O. Johnson]. 8vo. [Cushing's *Init. and Pseud.*, vol. i., p. 95.] New York, 1871

EVERY woman her own house-keeper; or the ladies' library: containing the cheapest and most extensive system of cookery, etc. [By J— Perkins.] 2 vols. 8vo.   London, 1796

EVERYBODY'S business is nobody's business; or, private abuses, publick grievances: exemplified in the pride, insolence, and exorbitant wages of our women-servants, footmen, &c. . . .

By Andrew Moreton, Esq.; [Daniel Defoe]. Fourth edition, corrected. 8vo. [Cushing's *Init. and Pseud.*, i., 198.]   London, 1725

EVERYBODY'S business; or, a friend in need. By Ismay Thorn [Edith Caroline Pollock]. 8vo. Pp. 160. London, 1891

EVERYBODY'S Christmas annual. By Nat Forsith [Frank Stainforth]. 8vo. [Cushing's *Init. and Pseud.*, i., 104.]
                                      London, 1876

EVERYBODY'S favourite: a novel. By John Strange Winter [Mrs Arthur Stannard, *née* Henrietta E. V. Palmer]. Cr 8vo. Pp. 306.   London, 1897

EVERYBODY'S friend; or Josh Billing's proverbial philosophy of wit and humour. [By Henry Wheeler Shaw]. 8vo. [Cushing's *Init. and Pseud.*, vol. i., p. 35.]   New York, 1876

EVERYBODY'S question; or a few words on banking and currency. By one who for more than thirty years has dealt largely with money [George W. Chambers]. 8vo. [Cushing's *Init. and Pseud.*, vol. ii., p. 190.] London, 1864

EVERYDAY (the) book; Lotteries. [By William Hone.] 8vo. Pp. 125.
                                      [London, 1826]

EVERYDAY duties; or, the schoolmates. By Mrs Madeline Leslie [Harriet Newell Baker]. 8vo. [Cushing's *Init. and Pseud.*, vol. i., p. 171.]
                                      Boston, [Mass., 1864]

EVERYDAY etiquette. By Marion Harland [Mary Virginia Hawes, later Mrs Terhune]. 8vo. Pp. 363. [Cushing's *Init. and Pseud.*, vol. i., p. 126.]   Indianapolis, 1905

EVERYDAY (an) heroine: a story for girls. By Clara Vance [Mrs Mary Denison, *née* Andrews]. Pt 8vo. Pp. 329. [Cushing's *Init. and Pseud.*, ii., 292.]   Philadelphia, 1896

EVERYDAY lessons. By Christie Pearl [Ellen M. Perkins]. 8vo. [Cushing's *Init. and Pseud.*, vol. ii., p. 521.]
                                      Boston, [Mass.], 1865

EVERYDAY life in Cape Colony, in time of peace. By X. C. [R— Cadbury]. Cr 8vo. Pp. 128.
                                      London, 1902

EVERYDAY papers. By Andrew Halliday [Andrew Halliday Duff]. Cr 8vo. [Cushing's *Init. and Pseud.*, vol. i., p. 125.]   London, 1865

EVERYDAY (an) romance. By Raymond Jacberns [Georgina M. Selby Ash]. Cr 8vo. Pp. 324. [*Lit. Year Book.*]   London, 1910

EVERYDAY things ; or useful knowledge respecting the principal animal, vegetable, and mineral substances in common use. . . . By a lady [Ellen Saunders, later Mrs Hartigan]. Fcap 8vo. [*Brit. Mus.*]   London, 1850

EVERYDAY wonders. By Grace Graham [Mrs Sophie B. Titterington]. Fcap 8vo. [Cushing's *Init. and Pseud.* vol. i., p. 119.]   Philadelphia, 1891

EVERYDAY'S news. [By C— E— Francis.] 8vo. Pp. 224. [*Brit. Mus.*]   London, 1895

EVERYNIGHT book ; or, life after dark. By the author of *The Cigar* [William Clarke]. 8vo. [Thomas on *Swimming*, p. 240.]   London, 1827

EVERYTHING new ? or nothing new ? A satirical comicality in verse. By William Scribble [William Smyth]. 8vo. [O'Donoghue's *Poets of Ireland.*]   Dublin, 1864

EVERYWOMAN and war : shall this be the final war ? It can be done ! A suggestion. . . . By John Oxenham [William Arthur Dunkerley]. 8vo. Pp. 39. [*Brit. Mus.*] London, [1916]

EVE'S adventures ; a submarine fantasy. By S. Ashton [Eustace F. Bosanquet]. 4to. Pp. 142.
London, 1904

EVE'S daughters : common sense for maids, wives, etc. By Marion Harland [Mary Virginia Hawes, later Mrs Terhune]. Fcap 8vo. [Cushing's *Init. and Pseud.*, vol. i., p. 126.]
New York, 1881

EVE'S diary. By Mark Twain [Samuel Langhorne Clemens]. Cr 8vo. Pp 114. [*Lit. Year Book.*]
New York, 1906

EVE'S glossary : a book of gossip about women, for women. By the Marquise de Fontenoy [Marguerite Cunliffe-Owen]. 8vo.   New York, 1898

EVESHAMS (the) : a novel. By Edmund White [James Blythe Patton]. Cr 8vo. [*Lond. Lib. Cat.*]
London, 1902

EVIDENCE (the) for baptism ; being the substance of a sermon. By the author of *Notitiæ Ludæ* [Robert S. Bayley]. 8vo.   London, 1835

EVIDENCE (the) for our Saviour's resurrection consider'd ; with the improvement of this important doctrine. [By Henry Grove, of Taunton.] 8vo. Pp. vi., 72. [Watt's *Bibl. Brit.*]
London, 1730

EVIDENCE (the) for the authenticity and divine inspiration of the Apocalypse, stated, and vindicated from the objections of the late Professor F. D. Michaelis ; in letters addressed to the Rev. Herbert Marsh, B.D., F.R.S., Fellow of St John's College, Cambridge. [By John Chappel Woodhouse.] 8vo. Pp. iv., 92. [*Bodl.*]
London, 1802

EVIDENCE (the) for the resurrection of Jesus Christ, as given by the four Evangelists, critically examined. [By Samuel Butler.] 8vo. [*Brit. Mus.*]
London, 1865

EVIDENCE of miracles : or, an exhibition of the testimony by which we are informed that miracles were wrought in attestation of Christianity. [By George Murray, minister at North Berwick.] Fcap 8vo. [*New Coll. Cat.*]   Edinburgh, 1802

EVIDENCE (the) of the resurrection cleared from the exceptions of a late pamphlet [by Peter Annet], entitled, The resurrection of Jesus considered by a moral philosopher ; in answer to the Tryal of the witnesses, &c. [By Charles Moss, D.D., Bishop of Bath and Wells.] 8vo. Pp. 164. [*Brit. Mus.*]   London, 1744
    The dedication to the learned author of the Tryal of the witnesses of the resurrection is signed " C. M."

EVIDENCE that the relation of Josephus concerning Herod's having new built the temple at Jerusalem is either false or misinterpreted. [By Charles Hawtrey.] 8vo. Pp. 96. [*Bodl.*]   Oxford, 1786

EVIDENCES of Christianity ; or, Uncle Philip's conversations . . . about the truth of the Christian religion. [By Francis Lister Hawks.] Fcap 8vo. [Cushing's *Init. and Pseud.*, vol. i., p. 232.]   London, 1834

EVIDENT (the) approach of a war ; and something of the necessity of it, in order to establish peace, and preserve trade. [By Daniel Defoe.] To which is added, an exact plan and description of the bay and city of Gibraltar. 8vo. Pp. 63. [*Camb. Hist. of Eng. Lit.*]   London, 1727

EVIL and evolution ; an attempt to turn the light of modern science on to the ancient mystery of evil. By the author of *The social horizon* [George Francis Millin]. Cr 8vo. Pp. x., 184. [*Lond. Lib. Cat.*]
London, 1896

EVIL (the) eye : a novel. By Daniel Woodroffe [Mrs J. C. Woods]. Cr 8vo. [*Lond. Lib. Cat.*]   London, 1902

EVIL (the) speaking and ignorance of C. H. Spurgeon on the subject of Baptismal Regeneration. By the author of *The Teacher's Companion* [Robert Nelson Collins]. 8vo. [*Brit. Mus.*] London, [1864]

EVIL (the) tongue. By Nellie Graham [Mrs Annie Dunning, *née* Ketchum]. Fcap 8vo. [Cushing's *Init. and Pseud.*, vol i., p. 119.] Philadelphia, 1865

EVILS (the) inseparable from a mixed currency, and the advantages to be secured by introducing an inconvertible national paper circulation. [By William Blacker.] Third edition. 8vo. London, 1847

EVILS (the) of England, social & economical. By a London physician [James Howard]. 8vo. Second edition, with additions. [*Bodl.*] London, 1865

EVOLUTION (the) of a life. By Major Seth Eyland [Major Silas E. Reynolds]. 8vo. [*Lib. Journ.*, ix., 164.] New York, 1884
Attributed also to David E. Cronin.

EVOLUTION of animal life. By Robertson Gray [Rossiter W. Raymond]. Pt 8vo. [Cushing's *Init. and Pseud.*, vol. i., p. 120.] Boston, 1889

EVOLUTION (the) of Christianity. [By Charles Gill.] 8vo. [*Lond. Lib. Cat.*] London, 1883

EVOLUTION of property, from savagery to civilization. By Philip Lafargue [Joseph Henry Philpot, M.D.]. Cr 8vo. Pp. 182. [*Lond. Lib. Cat.*] London, 1902

EVOLUTION (the) of the steam locomotive (1803 to 1898). By G. A. Sekon [George A. Nokes]. 8vo. Pp. 327. London, 1899

EVOLUTION or revolution; a problem of forces. By Ironicus [William Henry Butlin]. 8vo. London, [1918]
Name given by a friend of the author.

EVOLUTION versus reason and theology. By a working man [—— Lindsay]. 8vo. Pp. vi., 96. Belfast, [1892]

E. W. [E— Wilkinson], his Thamescidos, devided into three bookes or cantos. 4to. [*Brit. Mus.*] London, 1600
VOL. II.

E. W. Montagu: an autobiography. Edited [or rather written] by Y. [*i.e.*, Edward Vaughan Kenealy, LL.D.]. 8vo. [*Brit. Mus.*] London, 1869

EX Oriente; sonnets on the Indian rebellion. [By James Innes Minchin.] 8vo. London, 1858

EXACT (an) abridgement of that excellent treatise [by Christopher St Germain, on the Laws of England] called Doctor and Student. Fcap 8vo. B. L. London, 1630
For the full work, in earlier editions, *see* "Doctor and student," and "The Dyaloges in Englishe."

EXACT (an) abridgment in English of the Commentaries of Edmond Plowden. By F. H. [Fabian Hicks]. 2 parts. 8vo. [*Watt's Bibl. Brit.*] London, 1650

EXACT (an) account of the charge for supporting the poor of the city of Norwich, contain'd in the following tables: viz. I. Tables of the yearly charge for maintenance of the poor in each respective parish, from the beginning of this century, to the present year. . . . II. A table of the discretional disbursements only, separated from the weekly allowances, for the years 1711, and 1718. . . . III. Tables of the yearly charge of the poor, and number of the collectioners, for a compleat 100 years, viz. from 1620 to 1720, for fourteen parishes. Lastly, A table for these fourteen parishes, containing the yearly charge, number of poor, and weeks throughout the 100 years. [By John Fransham]. 8vo. [*Bodl.*] London, 1720
The Introduction is signed "J. F."

EXACT (an) and authentic account of the greatest white-herring-fishery in Scotland, carried on yearly in the island of Zetland, by the Dutch only; the method the Dutch use in catching the herrings, and an exact account of their way of curing, and lasting, or casking them; and a method laid down whereby we may easily engross that profitable trade into our own hands. . . . By a gentleman who resided five years on the island [John Campbell, LL.D.]. 8vo. [*Adv. Lib.*] London, 1750

EXACT (an) and most impartial accompt of the indictment, arraignment, trial, and judgment (according to law) of nine and twenty regicides, the murtherers of his late Sacred Majesty of most glorious memory; began at Hicks-Hall on Tuesday, the 9th of October, 1660, and continued at the Sessions-House in the Old-Bayley

P

until Friday, the nineteenth of the same moneth. [By Heneage Finch, Earl of Nottingham.] 4to. Pp. 257. [Whitley's *Bapt. Bibl.*, vol. i., p. 78.]

London, 1660

EXACT (an) book of entries of the most select judiciall writs used in the common law; translated from the originall manuscript, which was collected by . . . Robert Moyle. By J. H. [John Hearne], Gent. 4to. Pp. 214. [Watt's *Bibl. Brit.*]

London, 1658

EXACT (an) collection of choice declarations, with pleas, replications, rejoynders, demurrers, assignement of errours; and the entries of judgments thereupon affirmed: collected by W. S. [William Sheppard], one of the clerks of the Upper Bench office. Diligently perused, and translated into English, for the benefit and helpe of young clerkes. 4to. [*Bodl.*]

London, 1653

EXACT (an) collection of the most considerable debates in the Honourable House of Commons, at the Parliament held at Westminster the one and twentieth of October, 1680. . . . [Sir William Jones is credited with the last part.] 8vo. [Watt's *Bibl. Brit.*]

London, 1681

Later editions were issued in 1689 and 1725.

EXACT (an) collection or catalogue of our English writers on the Old and New Testament, either in whole or in part. . . . [By William Crowe.] Fcap 8vo. [*New Coll. Cat.*]

London, 1663

The second edition (1668), likewise anonymous, begins: " A catalogue of our English writers."

EXACT (the) constable, with his original, and power in all cases belonging to his office; as also, the office of church wardens, overseers of the poor, surveyors of the highways, treasurers of the county stock, parish clerks, governours of fairs, and other inferiour officers, as they are at this day establisht both by the common laws and statutes of this kingdom. By E. W. [Edmund Wingate] of Grays Inne, Esq. Fourth edition. Fcap 8vo. Pp. 176. [Wood's *Athen. Oxon.*, iii., 426.]

London, 1677

EXACT (an) copy of an epistolary correspondence between the Rev. Mr M— [Martin Madan] and S— B— [Samuel Brewer], concerning the living of A. [Aldwinkle. By Martin Madan, B.A.]. 8vo. [*D. N. B.*, vol. 35, p. 289.]

London, 1768

EXACT (the) dealer refined; being a useful companion for all traders. [By John Hill.] Fcap 8vo. [Watt's *Bibl. Brit.*]

London, 1702

EXACT (an) description of the manner how his Maiestie and his nobles went to the Parliament on Munday, the thirteenth day of Aprill, 1640, to the comfortable expectation of all loyall subiects. [By Martin Parker.] Single Sheet. Folio. B. L. [*Bodl.*]

London, N.D.

Signed " M. P."

EXACT (an) diary of the late expedition of His Illustrious Highness the Prince of Orange (now King of Great Britain) from his palace at the Hague to his landing at Torbay, and from thence to his arrival at White Hall. . . . By a minister, Chaplain to the army [John Whittie]. 4to. [Watt's *Bibl. Brit.*]

London, 1689

EXACT (an) discoverie of Romish doctrine in the case of conspiracie and rebellion, by pregnant obseruations; collected (not without direction from our superiours) out of the expresse dogmaticall principles of Popish priests and doctors. [By Thomas Morton, Bishop of Durham.] 4to. Pp. 58. [Watt's *Bibl. Brit.*; *D. N. B.*, vol. 39, p. 164.]

London, 1605

Signed " T. M."

EXACT (an) diurnall of the Parliament of ladyes; ordered by the ladyes in Parliament, that they declare that Prince Rupert, Lord Digby, Lord Capell, Lord Cottington, Dr Williams, Mr Walter, L. Hopton, L. Culpepper, Dr Duppa; Sir R. Grenvill, L. Jermine, and Major Gen. Vrrey, have all their pardons granted to them by this covrt clericus. [By Henry Neville.] 4to. [*Adv. Lib.*]

N.P., 1647

EXACT (an) historie of the late Revolutions in Naples, and of their monstrous successes . . . By Alexander Giraffi: rendered to English by J. H., Esq. [James Howell]. 4to. [Dobell's *Cat.*]

London, 1647

EXACT (an) history of the several changes of government in England, from the horrid murther of King Charles I. to the happy restauration of King Charles II.; with the renowned actions of General Monck: being the second part of Florus Anglicus, by J. D., Gent. [John Dauncy]. 8vo. Pp. 400. [*Bodl.*]

London, 1660

Ascribed also to J. Davies. [Bliss' *Cat.*] The first part was written by Lambert Wood.

EXACT (an) narration of the life and death of the Reverend and learned prelate, and painfull divine, Lancelot Andrewes, late Bishop of Winchester. [By Henry Isaacson.] 4to. No pagination. [*Bodl.*]   London, 1650

EX-ALE-TATION (the) of ale. Written by a learned pen [in verse. By Peter Mews, D.D., Bishop of Bath and Wells.]. 4to. [*D. N. B.*, vol. 37, p. 315.]   London, 1671

EXAMEN confectionis pacificae ; or, a friendly examination of the Pacifick Paper [by John Humphrey] : chiefly concerning the consistency of absolute election of particular persons with the universality of redemption. . . . [By Isaac Chauncy, or Chauncey, M.A.] 4to. [*D. N. B.*, vol. 10, p. 171.]   London, 1692

     Signed " I. C."

EXAMEN de ingenios : the examination of mens wits, in which by discovering the varietie of natures, is shewed for what profession each one is apt and how far he shall profit therein. By John Huarte. Translated out of the Spanish tongue by M. Camillo Camilli. Englished out of his Italian by R. C. [Richard Carew], Esquire. 4to. Pp. 348. [*W.*] Printed by Adam Islip, for Thomas Adams.   London, 1616

     The Dedication to " Sir Francis Godolphin, Knight " is also signed " R. C."; but Wood attributes the translation to Thomas Carew.

EXAMEN legum Angliæ : or, the laws of England examined by Scripture, antiquity, and reason. Cujus author anagrammatôs est, Ἄνομος βοᾷ ὡς βαρύ. [By A. Booth.] 4to. [*Lincoln's Inn Cat.*]   London, 1656

     Ascribed also to A. Boon. [*Adv. Lib.*]

EXAMINATION (an) into the conduct of the Delegates to the Grand Convention [of North American Colonists opposed to the action of the British Government. By Samuel Seabury, D.D.]. 8vo. [Beardsley's *Life of Seabury*, p. 25.]   Boston, 1774

     Signed " A W. Farmer," *i.e.* A Westchester farmer.
     Several replies, similarly anonymous, were made to this defence of the British Government. *See* " The Farmer refuted."

EXAMINATION (an) into the Scriptural lawfulness of marriage with a deceased wife's sister, and the principles and enactments of English law respecting such marriages ; embracing a notice of the course pursued by the religious Society of Friends, with reference to such connexions. By a member of the Society of Friends [James Bowden]. 8vo. [Smith's *Cat. of Friends' Books*, i. 121, 304.]   London, [1863]

EXAMINATION (an) into the significations and senses of the Greek prepositions. By Hermann Heinfetter [Frederick Parker], author of *Rules for ascertaining the sense conveyed in ancient Greek manuscripts*, etc. Fcap 8vo. [*Adv. Lib.*]   London, 1850

EXAMINATION (an) of a book [by Wm. Dalgleish, D.D., Peebles], entitled The true Son-ship of Christ investigated. . . . [By David Brown.] 8vo. [*New Coll. Lib.*]   Edin., 1778

EXAMINATION of a book printed by the Quakers, and distributed to the members of both Houses of Parliament, entitled, " An account of the prosecutions of the people called Quakers, in the Exchequer, ecclesiastical, and other courts, &c.," in defence of the clergy of the diocese of York. [By Thomas Hayter, D.D., Bishop of London.] 8vo. [*D. N. B.*, vol. 25, p. 306.]   London, 1741

EXAMINATION (an) of a discourse on baptism with the Holy Ghost ; lately published by James Rudd. By Philalethes Candaliensis [Rev. Thomas Lancaster]. 8vo.   Kendal, 1741

EXAMINATION (an) of a discourse or sermon published by Daniel Dobel, of Cranbrook, in Kent, on the subject of water-baptism, with remarks on his preface to the same. By one of the people called Quakers [Joseph Besse]. 8vo. [Smith's *Cat. of Friends' Books*, i. 256.]   London, 1744

EXAMINATION (an) of a late edition of Shakespeare. By a country gentleman [Zachary Grey, LL.D.]. 8vo. [*D. N. B.*, vol. 23, p 219.]   London, 1752

EXAMINATION (an) of a late Vindication of a Defence of baptism with water and infant-baptism asserted : wherein the validity of a former reply to that Defence, and the insufficiency of its vindication, are demonstrated. With a postscript relating to the Protestant reformation, academical learning, and a declaration of George Fox, against Popery. [By Joseph Besse.] 8vo. [Smith's *Cat. of Friends' Books*, i., 59, 255.]   London, 1739

EXAMINATION [by George Kerr] of a pamphlet [by Alexander Gerard], entitled, " Plan of education in the Marischal College and University of Aberdeen, with the reasons of it drawn up by order of the Faculty, 1755." 8vo. Pp. 56. [Anderson's *Aberd. Univ. Bibl.*, p. 447.]
Aberdeen, 1826

EXAMINATION (an) of a pamphlet entituled, A Narration of the siege of Leicester. [By James Innes.] 4to. [Thomason *Coll. of Tracts*, i. 378.]
London, 1645

EXAMINATION of a sermon preached before the Lord Mayor, &c., May 25, 1788, by the Rev. Richard Harrison, chaplain to his lordship. [By R. E. Garnham, Fellow of Trin. Coll. Cambridge.] 8vo. Pp. 56. [Darling's *Cyclop. Bibl.*]
London, 1789

EXAMINATION (an) of an account of the erection of the Marischal College of Aberdeen by Dr Thomas Blackwell, by order and appointment of the Honourable the Magistrates of Aberdeen : shewing, from the foundation Charter and Acts of Parliament that the Marischal College is not an University, and has no pretensions to the privilege of granting the degrees of Batchelor, Licentiate, or Doctor in the Faculties of Divinity, Law, or Medicine. [By Thomas Gordon.] 4to. [Anderson's *Aberd. Univ. Bibl.*, p. 432.]
Aberdeen, 1786

EXAMINATION of an announcement made in the Prussian State Gazette, concerning " the relations of the Bishop of the United Church of England and Ireland in Jerusalem," with " the German congregation of the evangelical religion in Palestine." By a member of the Church of England [William Palmer, M.A., of Magdalen College, Oxford]. 8vo. Pp. 176. [*Bodl.* ; *D. N. B.*, vol. 43, p. 167.]
Oxford, 1842

EXAMINATION (an) of articles contributed by Professor W. Robertson Smith to the Encyclopædia Britannica, the Expositor, and the British Quarterly Review, in relation to the truth, inspiration, and authority of the Holy Scriptures. By a minister of the Free Church of Scotland [John Montgomery]. 8vo. Pp. 77. [*New Coll. Lib.*]
Edinburgh, 1877

EXAMINATION (an) of Bishop Berkeley's celebrated Theory of vision. [By Samuel Bailey.] 8vo. [*D. N. B.*, vol. 2, p. 410.]
N.P., 1841

EXAMINATION (an) of Canon Liddon's Bampton Lectures on the divinity of our Lord and Saviour Jesus Christ. By a clergyman of the Church of England [Rev. Charles Voysey, B.A.]. Cr 8vo. Pp. xiv., 337.
London, 1871

EXAMINATION of certain opinions advanced by Bp. Burgess in two recent publications, entitled Christ and not Peter the rock. [By John Lingard, D.D.] 8vo. [*D. N. B.*, vol. 33, p. 323.]
Manchester, 1813

EXAMINATION of conscience. Safe advice about this duty drawn from the writings of the Saints. [By Frederick William Faber, D.D.] 8vo. Second edition. [*Bodl.*]
London, 1846

EXAMINATION (an) of Dr Comber's Scholastical history of the primitive and general use of liturgies in the Christian Church. By S. B. [Samuel Bold, or Bolde]. 4to. Pp. 66. [*New Coll. Cat.*]
London, 1690

This was followed by " A Second examination . . ." (1691).

EXAMINATION (an) of Dr [John] MacCulloch's work on the Highlands. [By Dr James Browne.] 8vo. [*Brit. Mus.*]
Edinburgh, 1825

EXAMINATION (an) of Dr Rutherforth's argument respecting the right of Protestant Churches to require the clergy to subscribe to an established confession of faith and doctrines ; wherein is considered, the tendency and force of the argument. By a clergyman of the Church of England [Benjamin Dawson, LL.D.]. Second edition. 8vo. [*Brit. Mus.*]
London, 1766

See the note to " The Confessional. . . ."

EXAMINATION (an) of Dr Woodward's Account of the Deluge, &c. ; with a comparison between Steno's philosophy and the Doctor's, in the case of marine bodies dug out of the earth. By J. A., M.D. [John Arbuthnot]. With a letter to the author concerning an abstract of Agostino Scilla's book on the same subject, printed in the Philosophical Transactions. By W. W., F.R.S. 8vo. Pp. 90. [*Bodl.*]
London, 1697

EXAMINATION (the) of Joseph Galloway, Esq', late speaker of the House of Assembly in Pennsylvania, before the House of Commons, in a committee on the American papers. With explanatory notes. [By Joseph Galloway.] 8vo. Pp. 89.
London, 1780

EXAMINATION (an) of Lord Bolingbroke's Letters on history . . . proving that the best way to defend Christianity would be to abandon the Old
Testament. [By Alexander Campbell.]
The second edition. Fcap 8vo. [*Brit.
Mus.*]   London, 1753

EXAMINATION (an) of M. La Place's
theory of capillary attraction. [By T.
Knight, of Papcastle.] 8vo. [*Bodl.*]
                          London, 1809
Advertisement signed " T. K."

EXAMINATION (the) of men's wits ;
in which, by discovering the variety
of natures, is showed for what professions each one is apt, and how far
he shall profit therein. Written originally in Spanish by John Huarte, translated into Italian by C. Camilli :
Englished by R. C— [Richard Carew].
4to. [Jaggard's *Index* ; Watt's *Bibl.
Brit.*]   London, 1594

EXAMINATION (an) of Mr Campbell's principles as laid down in his
Enquiry into the original of moral
virtue. With an appendix, containing
short remarks on his Discourse proving
that the Apostles were no enthusiasts.
[By John Hunter.] 8vo. [*Adv. Lib.*]
                          Edinburgh, 1731

EXAMINATION (an) of Mr Chubb's
Discourse on miracles [in six sections].
Address'd to Mr Thomas Chubb. By
a layman [Caleb Fleming]. 8vo. Pp.
ii., 85. [*Bodl.*]   London, 1742
Letter signed " A. X."

EXAMINATION (an) of Mr Dugald
Stewart's pamphlet, relative to the
late election of a mathematical pro-
fessor in the University of Edinburgh.
By one of the ministers of Edinburgh
[John Inglis, D.D.]. Second edition.
With an appendix. 8vo. Pp. 152.
[*Adv. Lib.*]   Edinburgh, 1806

EXAMINATION (an) of Mr [John]
Hutchinson's Remarks, and Mr Catcott's Answer to the Observations on
his sermon, preached before the Corporation of Bristol ; in which the
pernicious consequences of their
notions to all revealed religion, together with their pride and unchari-
ableness, is fully shewn ; the integrity
of the Hebrew text is so proved, that
no one in this age ought to presume
to make any alterations. . . . By the
author of the *Observations* [Arthur
Bedford, M.A., chaplain to Haber-
dashers' Hospital]. 8vo. Pp. 110.
[Green's *Bibl. Somers.*, ii., 156.]
                          London, 1738

EXAMINATION (an) of Mr Kenrick's
Review of Mr Johnson's edition of
Shakespeare. [By —— Barclay, a
student of Oxford.] 8vo. [Chalmers'
Biog. Dict.]   London, 1766
Ascribed also to —— Barker. [Wilson's
Shaksperiana, 42.]

EXAMINATION (an) of Mr [Charles]
Leslie's last Dialogue, relating to the
satisfaction of Jesus Christ ; together
with remarks on Dr Stillingfleet's
True Reasons of Christ's sufferings.
[By Thomas Emlyn.] 4to. [*Bodl.*]
                          London, 1708

EXAMINATION (an) of Mr Pitt's
plan for diminishing the Public Debts
by means of a Sinking Fund. [By
Thomas Howard, Earl of Effingham.]
2 parts. 8vo. [*Brit. Mus.*]
                          London, 1787

EXAMINATION (an) of Mr Pope's
Essay on man . . . translated from
the French of Mr Crousaz. [By Eliza-
beth Carter, assisted by Dr Samuel
Johnson.] Fcap 8vo. [Watt's *Bibl.
Brit.*]   London, 1739

EXAMINATION of Mr Robertson's
Remarks on a reply to his letter on
the Sonship of Christ. [By Rev.
Ebenezer Ritchie, of Kirkwall.] 8vo.
Pp. 33. [*New Coll. Lib.*]
                          Edinburgh, 1827

EXAMINATION (an) of Mr Robinson
of Cambridge's Plea for the divinity
of our Lord Jesus Christ. By a late
member of the university [Theophilus
Lindsey, M.A.]. 8vo. Pp. xlviii.,
206. [*Bodl.*]   London, 1785

EXAMINATION (an) of Mr Samuel
Chandler's History of persecution, so
far as relates to (what he calls) persecution in Great Britain ; in which
his great prejudice and partiality are
detected and exposed in the manner
they deserve. By a sincere admirer
of true liberty [Zachary Grey, LL.D.].
8vo. Pp. 84. [*D. N. B.*, vol. 23,
p. 219.]   London, 1736

EXAMINATION (an) of Mr W. H.
Gillespie's Argument a priori for the
existence of a great first cause. By
T. S. B., Associate in Arts, of the Uni-
versity of Oxford [Thomas Squire
Barrett]. 8vo. [*Bodl.*] London, 1869
A later reprint (1871) gives the author's
name.

EXAMINATION (an) of Mr Warburton's second proposition, in his projected Demonstration of the divine
legation of Moses. In which the faith
of the ancient Jewish Church, touching
the doctrine of a future state, is asserted
and cleared from the author's objections. [By Henry Stebbing.] 8vo.
Pp. 169. [*Brit. Mus.*] London, 1744

EXAMINATION (an) of precedents and principles, by which it appears that the impeachment of Warren Hastings, Esq. is determined by the dissolution of Parliament. . . . [By Edward Christian, of Gray's Inn.] [*W.*]
               London, 1790
   Republished in 1791 with the author's name.

EXAMINATION (an) of Professor [George] Skene's " Chronology of the Old Testament, and its connection with profane history." [By James Laurie.] Fcap 8vo. [Orme's *Bibliotheca Biblica.*]   Edinburgh, 1838

EXAMINATION (an) of Scripture evidence respecting the Lord's Supper. By a member of the Society of Friends [George Brantingham]. 8vo. [*Aberd. Pub. Lib.*]   Aberdeen, 1872

EXAMINATION (an) of some of the astronomical and theological opinions of Dr Chalmers. . . . By a Scotch presbyter [Henry Fergus, D.D., Dunfermline]. 8vo. [*New Coll. Cat.*]
              Edinburgh, 1818

EXAMINATION (an) of such particulars in the solemne leagve and covenant, as concerne the lavv ; proving it to be destructive of the lavves of England, both ancient and modern. [By Griffith Williams, D.D., Bishop of Ossory.] 4to. [Madan's *Oxf. Books*, vol. ii., p. 388.]   Oxford, 1644
   The authorship has not been fully established.

EXAMINATION (an) of sundry scriptures alleadged by our brethren, in defence of some particulars of their Church-way ; humbly submitted to the sight and censure of any judicious divine; espccially of such of the reverend godly-learned Assembly as vouchsafe to read it. By R. H., M.A., of Magd. Col. Camb. [Richard Hollinworth]. 4to. [*Bodl.*] London, 1645

EXAMINATION (an) of the arguments contained in a late Introduction [by James Macpherson] to the history of the ancient Irish and Scots. [By Thomas Leland, D.D.] 4to. [Lowndes' *Bibl. Man.*]   London, 1772

EXAMINATION (an) of the arguments drawn from Scripture and reason, in Dr Sherlock's Case of allegiance, and his Vindication of it. [By Theophilus Downes, M.A.] 4to. Pp. 78. [*Brit. Mus.*]   London, 1691

EXAMINATION of the British doctrine which subjects to capture a neutral trade not open in time of peace [by James Madison]; with a letter to Lord Mulgrave on neutral trade [by James Monroe]. 8vo. [*Brit. Mus.*]
             London, 1806

EXAMINATION (an) of the calumnies which have been assigned as reasons for the opposition to Dr Browne's election into the office of Vice-Chancellor [of the University of Cambridge]. [By Thos. Browne, D.D.] 8vo. Pp. 55. [Bowe's *Cat. of Camb. Books*, p. 274.]   Cambridge, 1810

EXAMINATION (an) of the case on which Mr Arthur Charles, Q.C., has given an opinion as to . . . the cathedral body at Exeter. [By Rev. Francis C. Hingeston-Randolph, M.A.] 8vo. Pp. 26. [*Bodl.*] [Exeter, 1887]
   Private print. Signed " F. C. H. R."

EXAMINATION of the claim of John Lindsay Craufurd to the title and estates of Craufurd and Lindsay, with refutation of " The Craufurd peerage," etc. [By James Dobie.] 4to. [Martin's *Cat.*]   N.P., 1831

EXAMINATION (an) of the conduct of Great Britain respecting neutrals since the year 1791. By Juriscola [Tench Coxe]. 8vo. [Cushing's *Init. and Pseud.*, vol. i., p. 144.]   Boston, 1808

EXAMINATION (an) of the conduct of the Executive of the United States towards the French Republic. By a citizen of Pennsylvania [Albert Gallatin]. 8vo. [Cushing's *Init. and Pseud.*, vol. i., p. 59.]   Philadelphia, 1797

EXAMINATION of the considerations, submitted to the householders of Edinburgh, on the state of their representation in Parliament. [By John Borthwick, advocate.] 8vo. [On the authority of a letter from Mr B. accompanying a presentation copy to Sir Henry Jardine.]   Edinburgh, 1824

EXAMINATION (an) of the Edinburgh Review, Numb. I. especially of Art. VI. Concerning Mr Ebenezer Erskine's sermons. [By David Erskine.] 8vo. No separate title-page.
            [Edinburgh, 1803]

EXAMINATION (an) of the equity and expediency of ecclesiastical establishments. [By David King, LL.D.] 8vo. [*New Coll. Cat.*]
             Edinburgh, 1832

EXAMINATION (an) of the expediency and constitutionality of prohibiting slavery in the State of Missouri. By Marcus [Joseph Blunt]. 8vo. [Cushing's *Init. and Pseud.*, vol. i., p. 183.]
            New York, 1819

EXAMINATION (an) of the first part of a pamphlet, called, " An appeal to the Society of Friends." By Vindex [Joseph Gurney Bevan]. 8vo. [Smith's *Cat. of Friends' Books*, i., 79.]
            London, 1802

EXAMINATION (an) of the leading principles of the new system of morals, as that principle is stated and applied in Mr Godwin's Enquiry concerning political justice, in a letter to a friend. [By Thomas Green.] 8vo. Pp. 60. [*Bodl.*] London, [1798]

EXAMINATION (an) of the letter addressed to Principal Hill, on the case of Mr Leslie; in a letter to [Dr. Andrew Thomson] its anonymous author. With remarks on Mr Stewart's postscript, and Mr Playfair's pamphlet. By a calm observer [Sir David Brewster]. 8vo. Pp. 86. [*Adv. Lib.*] Edinburgh, 1806

EXAMINATION (an) of the new tariff proposed by the Hon. Henry Baldwin, a member of Congress. By one of the people [C. Churchhill, Cambreleng]. 8vo. Pp. 268. [*Brit. Mus.*] New York, 1821

EXAMINATION (an) of the Newtonian argument for the emptiness of space, and of the resistance of subtile fluids. [By George Martin.] 8vo. [*Adv. Lib.*] London, 1740

EXAMINATION (an) of the Observations upon His Majesties answers [by Henry Parker]; wherein the absurdities of the observators positions, and inferences are discovered. [By John Jones.] 4to. [*Bodl.*] Printed in the yeare of our Lord 1643
"Written by Mr John Jones, now prisoner in Southampton for loyalty to his sovereign, Jul. 1643."—Barlow.

EXAMINATION (an) of the passages contained in the Gospels, and other books of the New Testament, respecting the Person of Jesus. . . . By J. Smith, Gentleman [Charles Baring]. 8vo. [*Brit. Mus.*] London, 1807
A second edition, enlarged, was published in 1811.

EXAMINATION of the President's reply to the New Haven Remonstrance. By Lucius Junius Brutus [William Cranch]. 8vo. [Cushing's *Init. and Pseud.*, vol. i., p. 42.] New York, 1801
The President was T— Jefferson.

EXAMINATION (an) of the principles, and an enquiry into the conduct, of the two B*****rs [the Duke of Newcastle and Mr Pelham]; in regard to the establishment of their power, and their prosecution of the war, 'till the signing of the preliminaries. In a letter to a member of Parliament. [By John Perceval, 2d Earl of Egmont.] The third edition. This was followed by "Facts and arguments." 8vo. Pp. 79. [*Brit. Mus.*] London, 1749

EXAMINATION (an) of the principles and boasted disinterestedness of a late Right Hon. gentleman [William Pitt, Earl of Chatham]; in a letter from an old man of business to a noble lord. [By Charles Lloyd.] 8vo. [Almon's *Anecdotes*, ii., 111.] London, 1766

EXAMINATION of the principles and policy of the government of British India : embracing a particular inquiry concerning the tenure of lands, strictures on the administration of justice, and suggestions for the improvement of the character and condition of the natives in general. By a gentleman in the service of the East India Company [Major Henry D. Robertson]. 8vo. London, 1829

EXAMINATION (an) of the principles of the French Revolution. By a late dignitary of the Gallican Church [Bishop Jean Baptiste Duvoisin. Translated from the French]. 8vo. [*Edin. Univ. Lib.*] London, 1796

EXAMINATION (an) of the principles of the Scoto-Oxonian philosophy. By Timologus [M— P. W. Bolton]. Part I. 8vo. Pp. 68. London, 1861
A revised edition (1869) gives the author's name.

EXAMINATION (the) of the private spirit of Protestants. By I. S. [James (or John) Sharpe, S.J., *alias* Pollard]. 4to. [Oliver's *Collections*, p. 189; Sommervogel's *Dictionnaire*.] N.P., 1640

EXAMINATION (an) of the question now in discussion between the American and British Governments, concerning the right of search. By an American [Lewis Cass, LL.D.]. Fcap 8vo. [*Brit. Mus.*] Baltimore, 1842

EXAMINATION of the "Remarks on the Glossary to the ancient metrical romance of Havelok the Dane . . . by S. W. Singer. . . ." By the editor of Havelok [Sir Frederic Madden]. 4to. Pp. 39. [*Cat. of Eng. Dialect Lib.*, Manch., 1850, p. 18.] London, 1829

EXAMINATION (an) of the Rev. F. D. Maurice's strictures on the Bampton Lectures of 1858. By the Lecturer [Rev. Henry Longueville Mansel, LL.B.]. 8vo. Pp. 108. [*Brit. Mus.*] London, 1859

EXAMINATION of the Rev. Mr Burke's Letter of instruction to the Catholic missionaries of Nova Scotia. By Robert Stanser [Sir Alexander Croke]. 8vo. [Cushing's *Init. and Pseud.*, vol. i., p. 274.] Halifax, 1804

EXAMINATION (an) of the Rev. R. I. Wilberforce's charges against the Church of England, contained in his " Inquiry into the principles of Church authority." [By Frederick Meyrick, M.A.] Reprint from " The Christian Remembrancer " of April, 1855 ; with a reply to his " Seven letters." 8vo. Pp. 100. [*Bodl.*]   London, 1855

EXAMINATION (an) of the scheme of Church-power laid down [by Edmund Gibson] in the Codex juris ecclesiastici Anglicani. [By Sir Michael Foster.] 8vo. Pp. 168. [*Brit. Mus.*]
          London, 1735
     See also the next entry.

EXAMINATION (the) [by Sir Michael Foster] of the Scheme of Church Power laid down [by Edmund Gibson, D.D.] in the Codex Juris Ecclesiastici Anglicani set in its proper light. [By John Andrews.] 8vo. Pp. x., 52. [*Brit. Mus.*]   London, 1736

EXAMINATION (an) of the scruples of those who refuse to take the Oath of Allegiance. By a divine of the Church of England [Peter Allix, D.D.]. 4to. [*Bodl.*]   London, 1689

EXAMINATION of the statements [by Robert S. Candlish, D.D.] in the lectures on " The Fatherhood of God," regarding the human nature of Christ and the sonship of his people. [By George M'Clelland.] 8vo. [*New Coll. Cat.*]   Edinburgh, 1865

EXAMINATION of the Treaty of Amity between the United States and Great Britain. . . . By Cato [Stephen Higginson]. 8vo. [Cushing's *Init. and Pseud.*, vol. i., p. 52.]
          New York, 1795

EXAMINATION (an) of the various charges exhibited against Aaron Burr, Esq. By Aristides [William P. Van Ness]. 8vo. [Cushing's *Init. and Pseud.*, vol. i., p. 19.]
          Washington, 1804

EXAMINATION (an) of those plavsible appearances which seeme most to commend the Romish Church, and to preiudice the Reformed ; discovering them to be but meere shifts, purposely invented, to hinder an exact triall of doctrine by the Scriptures. By Mr John Cameron.   Englished out of French [by William Pinke]. 4to. Pp. 173. [Wood's *Athen. Oxon.*, ii., 476.]
          Oxford, 1626
     The Dedication is signed " W. P."

EXAMINATION (an) of three prelatical pamphlets, viz. I. A full and final answer &c. [by J— Skene].   II. Imparity among pastors, in so far as it entrencheth upon the Remarks on the case &c. [by Dr John Hay].   III. And the Short character of the Presbyterian spirit, in a letter to a friend [by Matthias Symson].   [By James Ramsay, minister in Eyemouth.]   4to.   Pp. 46. [Stewart's *History vindicated in the case of the Wigtown Martyrs*, 2d ed., p. 72.]   Edinburgh, 1703

EXAMINATION (the) of Tilenus before the triers ; in order to his intended settlement in the office of a publick preacher in the commonwealth of Utopia : whereunto are annexed the tenents of the Remonstrants touching those five Articles voted, stated, and imposed, but not disputed, at the Synod of Dort ; together with a short essay . . . upon the Fundamental theses of Mr Thomas Parker. [By Laurence Womock, D.D.] 8vo. Pp. 283. [*Brit. Mus.*]   London, 1658

EXAMINATION (the) of Vsurie, in two sermons ; taken by Characterie, and after examined. [By Henry Smith.] 8vo.   Imprinted at London by Thomas Orwin for Thomas Man, dwelling in Paternoster row, at the signe of the Talbot. [*Brit. Mus.*]   1591
     Address to the reader signed " H. S." Each sermon has a separate pagination.

EXAMINATION (an) of William Notcutt's Reply to H. B.'s " Vindication of R. Barclay's Apology " ; wherein the deceit of the said W. N. is farther manifested, his many abuses of the people call'd Quakers detected, and the genuine sense of their writers asserted against his gross and palpable perversions of them.   By H. B. [Henton Brown]. 8vo. Pp. 204. [Smith's *Anti-Quakeriana*, p. 343.]
          London, 1735

EXAMINATIONAL (the) directory ; or, student's guide to pass competitive examinations on the basis of the system of the University of London. By [the Rev. A— H— Killick] a graduate in first class honours of the University. 8vo. Pp. xv., 194.
          London, 1871

EXAMINER (the) and the tax on newspapers : from the Radical of Saturday, March 26, 1836. [By Francis Place.] Fcap 8vo.   London, [1836]
     Signed " F. P."

EXAMINER (the) examined ; being a vindication of the History of liturgies. By T. C. [Thomas Comber, D.D., Dean of Durham]. 4to. [*Brit. Mus.*]
          London, 1691

     The " Examiner " was the Rev. Samuel Bold, who followed with " A Second examination of the History of Liturgies."

EXAMINER (the) examin'd, in a letter to the "Englishman," occasioned by the "Examiner" of Friday, Dec. 18, 1713, upon the Canto of Spencer. [By Samuel Croxall, D.D.] 4to. [*D.N.B.*, vol. 13, p. 246.] London, 1713

EXAMINER (the) examined; or logic vindicated: addressed to Junior Students of Oxford University. By a Graduate [Edward Copleston, D.D., afterwards Bishop of Oxford]. 8vo. [*Memoirs*, by W. J. Copleston.]
Oxford, 1809

A criticism of "Logic made easy . . .," by Henry Kett, who afterwards suppressed the work. *See D. N. B.*, vol. 31, p. 76.

EXAMINER (the) examined; or the Examination of the Remarks [by John Hutchinson] upon, and Mr [A. S.] Catcott's Answer to the Observations [by Arthur Bedford] upon his sermon considered. . . . [By Arthur Bedford.] 8vo. Pp. 113. [Green's *Bibl. Somers.*, ii., 157.] London, 1739

Ascribed also to Julius Bate, rector of Sutton.

EXAMINER (the); or Gilbert against Tennent: containing a computation of the Rev. Mr Gilbert Tennent, and his adherents. . . . By Philalethes [John Hancock]. 8vo. Pp. 32. [Cushing's *Init. and Pseud.*, i., p. 230.]
Boston, [Mass.], 1743

EXAMPLE better than precept. By the author of *A trap to catch a sun-beam*, etc. [Mrs H. S. Mackarness, *née* Matilda Anne Planché]. Fcap 8vo. Pp. 107. [*Brit. Mus.*] London, 1867

EXAMPLES of lathes, apparatus, and work. By the author of *Lathes and turning* [W— Henry Northcott, C.E.]. 8vo. [*Brit. Mus.*] London, 1889

EXAMPLES of the ornamental heraldry of the sixteenth century. [By Sir William Stirling - Maxwell.] Folio. [*Brit. Mus.*] London, 1867-68

EXCELLENCE (the) of the Holy Scriptures an argument for their more general dispersion at home and abroad. [By Joseph Hughes.] Second edition. 8vo. [*Brit. Mus.*] London, 1803

EXCELLENCIE (the) of a free state above kingly government; or the right constitution of a Commonwealth. Published by a well-wisher to posterity [Marchamont Nedham]. 4to. Pp. 246. [*Brit. Mus.*] London, 1656

EXCELLENCY (the) of the Christian religion. [By James Bell.] 8vo. [Robertson's *Aberd. Bibl.*]
Aberdeen, 1737

EXCELLENCY (the) of the true spirit of salt, etc. [By R. Barker.] 4to. [*Brit. Mus.*] London, 1663

EXCELLENCY (the) of theology compar'd with natural philosophy, (as both are objects of men's study). Discours'd of in a letter to a friend by T. H. R. B. E. [The Hon. Robert Boyle, Esq.], Fellow of the Royal Society. To which are annex'd some occasional thoughts about the excellency and grounds of the mechanical hypothesis, by the same author. 8vo. Pp. 272. London, 1674

EXCELLENT (an) discourse upon the now present state of France [1588-1591. By Michel Hurault]; faithfully translated out of French, by E. A. [Edward Aggas]. 4to. London, 1592

See also "A Discourse upon the present state of France."

EXCELLENT (an) knave. [A novel.] By Ernest Wilding [Joseph Fitzgerald Molloy]. 3 vols. 8vo. [O'Donoghue's *Poets of Ireland*.]
London, 1893

EXCELLENT (the) woman, as described in the Book of Proverbs. [By Anne Pratt, later Mrs Pearless.] Fcap 8vo. [London, 1846]

EXCELLENT (the) woman described by true characters and their opposites. By the author of *Reformed Devotions* [Theophilus Dorrington]. Two parts. 8vo. [*N. and Q.*, Dec. 1859, p. 505.]
London, 1692-95

EXCELLENT (the) woman discoursed from Proverbs xxxi, 29-31, upon occasion of the death of the Lady Frances Hobart. By J. C. [John Collinges, D.D.]. 8vo. [*Brit. Mus.*]
London, 1669

EXCELSIOR: a truthful sketch of a lovely youth. By B. G. L. R. [Bernard Glanville Lyndon Rolls]. By his mother [Mrs M. N. Rolls]. Fcap 8vo. London, 1855

"EXCELSIOR," or the realms of poesie. By Alastor [James Orton]. 4to. Pp. xvi., 148. [Dobell's *Private Prints*, p. 136.] London, 1852

EXCEPTIONS against some passages or expressions in our introduction and first treatise, relating to infant baptism, examined. [By Hezekiah Woodward.] [*Trin. Coll. Dub. Cat.*, 9. 193.] 4to. [London ?], 1656

EXCEPTIONS, many and just, against two injurious petitions exhibited to the Parliament ; the one, Iuly 16 ; the other, Aug. 4, 1653 : both of them not only against tithes, but against all forced or constrained maintenance of ministers, examined and found many waies faulty against piety and justice, and as such now discovered. By Theophilus Philadelphus [John Ley]. 4to. Pp. 64. [*Bodl.*] Oxford, 1653

EXCERPTA historica ; or illustrations of English history. [By S. Bentley.] 8vo. [Quaritch's *Cat.*]
London, 1833

EXCERPTS from the most approved authors who have treated of the laws of England with respect to the office and duty of grand juries. [By James Ferguson, Lord Pitfour.] 8vo. [*Brit. Mus.*] [Edinburgh ? 1764 ?]

EXCESSIVE sensibility : a novel. By Mrs Thomson [Harriet Pigott]. Fcap 8vo. London, [1840 ?]

EXCHANGE no robbery ; or, the diamond ring : a comedy in three acts. . . . By the author of *Killing no murder*, etc. [Theodore Edward Hook]. 8vo. Pp. 71. [*D. N. B.*, vol. 27, p. 274.] London, 1820

EXCIDIUM Angliæ : or a view of the fatal consequences attending the smuggling of wool. By the Cheshire weaver [James Latouche]. 4to. [*Brit. Mus.*] London, 1727

EXCISE (the) rectify'd ; or a plain demonstration that the revenue now raised thereby is capable of being improved at least four or five thousand Pounds per annum. . . . [By John Farthing.] Fcap 4to. [Quaritch's *Cat.*] London, 1695-96

EXCITEMENT (the) ; or, a collection of amusing and instructive lessons. . . . By a teacher and friend to youth [Adam Keys]. 8vo. [*Brit. Mus.*]
Prescot, 1831

EXCLAMATION (an) to all those that love the Lord Jesus in sincerity, against an Apology written by an ingenious person [Thomas Sprat] for Mr Cowley's lascivious and prophane verses. By a dutiful son of the Church of England [Edmund Elys, M.A.]. 4to. [*Brit. Mus.*] London, 1670

EXCLUSIVES (the). [A novel.] [By Lady Charlotte Maria Bury.] 3 vols. Fcap 8vo. [*Camb. Univ. Lib.*]
London, 1830

EXCOMMUNICATED (the) prince ; or, the false relique : a tragedy, as it was acted by His Holiness's servants. Being the Popish plot in a play. By Capt. William Bedloe. [By Thomas Walter, M.A., of Jesus College, Oxford.] Folio. Pp. 58. London, 1769

EXCURSION (the) ; a poem, in two books. [By David Mallet.] 8vo. [*Brit. Mus.*] London, 1728

EXCURSION (an) from Jericho to the ruins of the ancient cities of Geraza and Amman, in the country east of the river Jordan. [By George Hall.] 8vo. [*Brit. Mus.*] London, 1852
Signed " G. H.," at the end of the book

EXCURSION (an) from Paris to Fontainebleau ; to which is added an adventure in the Champs Elisées near Paris ; also an interesting account of the unfortunate disaster which befel Monsieur Pilatre de Rozier at Boulogne; with a translation of the elegant eulogium upon him, by the Marquis of Maisonfort. By a gentleman, late of Bath [Sir John Harington]. 8vo. [*D. N. B.*, vol. 24, p. 383.]
London, 1786

EXCURSION (the) of a village curate ; or, the fruits and gleanings of a month's ramble in quest of health. [By George Henry Taylor.] Fcap 8vo. [*Brit. Mus.*] London, 1827

EXCURSION through the starry heavens. [By Rev. Dr [Robert] Boog, late minister of Paisley.] Fcap 8vo. [Paisley, 1835]
" The reprint. First published about twenty years ago."—MS. note by Dr David Laing.

EXCURSION (an) through the United States and Canada during the years 1822-23. By an English gentleman [William Newnham Blane]. 8vo. Pp. 511. [*N. and Q.*, Dec. 1864, p. 482.]
London, 1824

EXCURSION (an) to Cockthorp Park, near Witney, in Oxfordshire, the seat of Maximilian Western, Esq. on the 3d of September, 1769. . . . [By Thomas May, of Witney.] 8vo. [*Bodl.*]
N.P., N.D.

EXCURSION (an) to the lakes in Westmoreland and Cumberland, August 1773. [By William Hutchinson.] 8vo. [Nichols' *Lit. Illust.*, i., 421.]
London, 1773

EXCURSIONS from Helston to Lizard, Kynans, Porthleven, Wheal Vor &c. [By William Penaluna.] 12mo. [Boase and Courtney's *Bibl. Corn.*, ii., 443.] Helston, 1834

EXCURSIONS in America described in letters from a gentleman and his young companions to their friends in England. [By Priscilla Wakefield.] 8vo. London, 1806

Later editions give the writer's name.

EXCURSIONS in Normandy; edited from the journals of a recent traveller [Jacob Venedey] by F. Shoberl. 2 vols. Cr 8vo. London, 1841

EXCURSIONS in Surrey and Sussex. [By Thomas Kitson Cromwell.] 2 vols. 8vo. [*Brit. Mus.*] London, 1821-22

EXCURSIONS of an evolutionist. [By John Fiske.] Pt 8vo. [Cushing's *Init. and Pseud.*, vol. i., p. 94.]
Boston, 1883

EXCUSES (the) urged by the absenters from public worship examined: a dialogue between Mr Alamode, a young gentleman of fortune, and Mr Freeman, an aged country gentleman. [By Rev. William Peterkin, of Elgin.] 8vo. Pp. vi., 56. Aberdeen, 1729

EXECUTION (the) of iustice in England for maintenance of publique and Christian peace, against certeine stirrers of sedition, and adherents to the traytors and enemies of the Realme, without any persecvtion of them for questions of religion, as is falsely reported and published by the fautors and fosterers of their treasons. [By William Cecil, Lord Burleigh.] 4to. B. L. No pagination. [*Brit. Mus.*] London, 1583

EXECUTOR (the): a novel. By Mrs Alexander [Mrs Alexander Hector, *née* Annie French]. Fcap 8vo. [*Brit. Mus.*] London, 1886

EXELLENT (the) historie of Theseus and Ariadne. . . . [By Thomas Underdowne.] 4to. [*N. and Q.*, 1922, p. 225.] London, 1566

EXEMPLARIE novells, in six books: The two damosels; the ladie Cornelia; the libcrall lover; the force of bloud; the Spanish ladie; the jealous husband; full of various accidents both delightfull and profitable. By Miguel de Cervantes Saavedra. . . . Turned into English by Don Diego Puede-Ser [James Mabbe, " May-be "]. Folio. Pp. 323. [*W.*]
London, 1640

See also the following translation.

EXEMPLARY (the) novels of M. de Cervantes Saavedra, translated into English. [By Miss —— Moore.] 2 vols. Fcap 8vo. London, 1822

EXERCISE (an) for children, on the inimitable virtues of Christ; collected from Mr Burkit on the New Testament. By the author of *The English Instructor* [Henry Dixon]. Fcap 8vo. [Green's *Bibl. Somers.*, vol. i., p. 149.] Bath, [1754 ?]

EXERCISE (the) of a Christian life; being the first ground and foundation whence the two Treatises appartaining to Resolution were made and framed by R. P. [Robert Parsons, S.J.]. 8vo. [Sommervogel's *Dictionnaire.*]
N.P., 1594

See also " The Book of resolution . . .," " A Booke of Christian exercise . . .," " A Christian directorie . . .," and " The First Booke of the Christian exercise. . . ."

EXERCISES in arithmetic for elementary schools, after the method of Pestalozzi, under the sanction of the Committee of Council on Education. [By Thomas Tate.] 8vo. Pp. 172. [*Bodl.*] London, 1844

EXERCISES of a recumbent vacation, 1860-61; with a few of earlier date: in verse. By J. T. [James B. Tomalin]. 12mo. Pp. 44. [*Brit. Mus.*]
London, private print, 1841

EXERCITATION (an) concerning usurped powers; wherein the difference betwixt civil authority and usurpation is stated. That the obedience due to lawfull magistrates, is not owing, or payable, to usurped powers, is maintained. The obligation of oaths, and other sanctions to the former, notwithstanding the antipolitie of the latter is asserted. . . . By one studious of truth and peace both in Church and State. [By Richard Hollinworth.] 8vo. [Watt's *Bibl. Brit.*] N.P., 1650

Ascribed also to Charles Herle [*Adv. Lib.*].

EXERCITATION (an) on that historical relation, Matth. 15. 1-9, Mark 7. 1-13, concerning eating with unwashen hands; by way of appendix or supplement to the Discourse concerning indifferencies; and more particularly, to argument or reason the fourth. . . . [By Vincent Alsop.] 8vo. [*Bodl.*] London, 1680

EXERCITATIONS concerning the resolution of faith against some exceptions. [By Abraham Woodhead.] 4to. [*D. N. B.*] N.P., 1674

EXETER change for the British lions; edited by Snug the joiner [John C. Brough]. 4to. Pp. 29. London, 1869

Relates to the visit of the British Association to Exeter.

EXETER (the) register ; or, collections towards a survey, ecclesiastical and statistical, of the counties of Devon and Cornwall. . . . [By Rev. John Wallis, M.A., vicar of Bodmin.] No. 1 [all published]. 8vo. Pp. 16. [Boase and Courtney's *Bibl. Corn.*]
Bodmin, 1831

EXHIBITION of illuminated manuscripts, 1908. [By Sydney Carlyle Cockerell.] Pp. xxxix., 135. [Quaritch's *Cat.*]   London, 1908

EXHORTATION I. The first exhortation of H. N. [Hendrik Niclas] to his children, and to the Familye of Love. Translated out of Base-almayne into English. B. L. Fcap 8vo. 56 leaves. [*Brit. Mus.*]   [Amsterdam ? 1575]
See note to " Evangelium Regni."

EXHORTATION (an) in Christian love to all who frequent horse-racing, cock-fighting . . . plays, . . . or any other vain diversions. [By Abiah Darby.] 8vo. [*Brit. Mus.*]
Shrewsbury, 1769
Signed " A. D."

EXHORTATION (an) of the particular Kirks of Christ in Scotland to their Sister Kirk in Edinburgh. [By David Calderwood.] 8vo. [*Adv. Lib.*]
Printed Anno 1624

EXHORTATION (an) or warning to the inhabitants of Woodbridge, and the villages adjacent. By a well-wisher [Mary Maw]. Folio. [Smith's *Cat. of Friends' Books*, i., 71 ; ii., 168.]
N.P., [1778]

EXHORTATION (an) to all Christian people to refrain from Trinitarian worship. [By Joshua Toulmin, D.D.] The second edition. Fcap 8vo. [Watt's *Bibl. Brit.*]   London, 1789

EXHORTATION (an) to all people, to pureness, cleanness, and holiness, and faithfulness to the Lord. By G. F. [George Fox]. 4to. [Smith's *Cat. of Friends' Books*, i. 685.]
London, 1685

EXHORTATION to students in divinity, from Arrian's discourses of Epictetus ; in Greek, Latin, and English : for the use of candidates for orders in the diocese of Salisbury. [By Thomas Burgess, D.D., Bishop of Salisbury.] Fcap 8vo. [*Bodl.*]   Salisbury, 1832
Advertisement signed " T. S." The English translation is by Mrs Elizabeth Carter.

EXHORTATION (an) to the diligent studye of Scripture, made by Erasmus Roterodamus, and translated in to inglissh [by William Roy]. An ex-

position in to the seventh chaptre of the first pistle to the Corinthians. B. L. Fcap 8vo. At Malborow [really Antwerp] in the londe of Hesse, M.D.xxix. xx. daye Janÿ by my Hans Luft.
This work was denounced as heretical in a proclamation by Henry VIII. ; copies are now exceedingly rare.

EXHORTATION (an) to the inhabitants of the Province of South Carolina to bring their deeds to the light of Christ, in their own consciences. By S. H. [Sophia Hume]. 8vo. Pp. 158. [Cushing's *Init. and Pseud.*, vol. i., p. 124.]   Philadelphia, [1748]

EXHORTATION (an) to the restoring of brotherly communion betwixt the Protestant Churches, founded in this, that they do not differ in any fundamentall article of the Catholique faith. [By John Davenant, D.D., Bishop of Salisbury.] 12mo. Pp. 173. [*New Coll. Cat.*]   London, 1641

EXILE (the) from Paradise. Translated by the author of *The Life of S. Teresa* [Maria M. Trench]. Fcap 8vo. [*Brit. Mus.*]   Oxford, 1872

EXILE (the) of Erin ; or, the sorrows of a bashful Irishman. [By William Frederick Deacon.] Fcap 8vo. 2 vols. [S. J. Brown's *Ireland in fiction.*]
London, 1835
The title of a later edition (1862) is " The Adventures of a bashful Irishman."

EXILE (the) of Idria ; a German tale : in three cantos. [By John George Hamilton Bourne.] 8vo. Pp. viii., 86.   London, 1833
The preface is signed " J. G. H. B." (John Gervase Hutchinson Bourne?). Compare *Gent. Mag.*, March 1846, p. 324, with the list of Oxford Graduates.)

EXILE (the) of St Helena. By D. F. A. [David Francis Atcherley]. 8vo. [*Brit. Mus.*]   London, 1861

EXILED from Erin. [A tale.] By M. E. T. [M— Doyle]. 8vo. Pp. 266. [S. J. Brown's *Ireland in fiction.*]
Dublin, N.D.

EXILED (the) soul. [A translation of " L'âme exilée." By Mme la Comtesse E. D'Hautefeuille.] Fcap 8vo. [*Brit. Mus.*]   London, 1852

EXILES (the). [A novel.] By " Talvi " [Thérèse A. L. von Jakob, later Mrs Robinson]. 8vo. [Allibone's *Dict.*]
New York, 1854
The pseudonym is formed of the writer's initials.

EXILES in Babylon ; or, children of light. By A. L. O. E., author of *The Shepherd of Bethlehem*, etc. [Charlotte M. Tucker]. 8vo. Pp. 358.
London, 1869

EXILES of France. By Ascott R. Hope [Ascott Robert Hope Moncrieff]. Sm 8vo.   Edinburgh, 1870

EXILES (the) of Italy. By C. G. H., author of *The curate of Linwood*, etc. [Mrs Charles G. Hamilton]. 8vo. Pp. xxxii., 502. [*Adv. Lib.*]
Edinburgh, 1857

EXILES (the) of Lucerna ; or, the sufferings of the Waldenses during the persecution of 1636. [By John Ross MacDuff, D.D.] Post 8vo.
Edinburgh, 1841
Several other editions were issued.

EXILES (the) of Palestine ; a tale of the Holy Land. By the author of *Letters from the East*, etc. [John Carne]. 3 vols. Fcap 8vo. [*Camb. Univ. Lib.*]   London, 1831

EXILES (the) of the Cevenna. By Aurelius Gratianus [John Mason Neale, D.D.]. Fcap 8vo. [*D. N. B.*, vol. 4, p. 145].   Oxford, [1850 ?]

EXILE'S (the) return, and other poems. By E. H. B. [Edward Henry Blakeney]. 8vo. Pp. vii., 158. [*Camb. Univ. Lib.*]   Cambridge, 1890

EXISTENCE (the) of the Deity proved from the structure of the human mind ; a lecture. [By Thomas Bunn.] 8vo. [Green's *Bibl. Somers.*, vol. i., p. 209.]
Frome, 1845

EXISTING (the) laws of the United States, of a general and permanent character, and relating to the survey and disposition of the public domain, December 1880. [By A— T— Britton.] 8vo.   New York, 1884

EXMOOR (an) scolding between two sisters, Wilmot Moreman and Thomasin Moreman ; also, an Exmoor Courtship : to which is prefixed a translation of the same into plain English. [By Peter Lock.] Fcap 8vo. [*Camb. Univ. Lib.*]   Exeter, 1795

EXMOUTH and its neighbourhood, ancient and modern ; being notices, historical, biographical, and descriptive, of a corner of South Devon. [By Edward Edwards.] Fcap 8vo. Pp. 361. [*Manch. Free Lib.*]
Exmouth, 1868

EXODIAD (the) ; a poem. By the authors of *Calvary* and *Richard the First* [Richard Cumberland and Sir James Bland Burgess]. 4to. [*D. N. B.*, vol. 13, p. 292.]   London, 1807

EXOTICS. By J. F. and L. C. [James Freeman Clarke and Lilian (his daughter) Clarke]. 8vo. [Cushing's *Init. and Pseud.*, vol. i., p. 387.]
Boston, 1875

EXOTICS [being short poems, translated from various Continental languages. By William E. A. Axon]. Cr 8vo. Pp. 25.
Manchester, private print, 1876

EXPECTATIONS (the) formed by the Assyrians that a great deliverer would appear about the time of our Lord's Advent, demonstrated. [By Rev. Frederick Nolan, LL.D.] 8vo. [*D. N. B.*, vol. 41, p. 96.] London, 1826

EXPEDIENCY (the) of a free exportation of corn at this time ; with some observations on the bounty, and its effects. By the author of the *Farmer's Letters to the people of England* [Arthur Young]. Second edition. 8vo. Pp. 74. [*Brit. Mus.*]   London, 1770

EXPEDIENCY (the) of a secure provision for the ministers of the Gospel, a few suggestions for the improvement of the Established Church, and illustrations of voluntaryism. By a sincere friend of the people [Maurice Lothian]. 8vo. [*New Coll. Cat.*] Edinburgh, 1834

EXPEDIENCY of reform in the Court of Session in Scotland. [By Henry Erskine, advocate.] 8vo. [*D. N. B.*, vol. 17, p. 412.]   London, 1807

EXPEDIENCY (the) of relieving the Bishops from attendance in Parliament, illustrated by Episcopal speeches and votes in the Irish Church debates of 1868 and 1869. Published by George Hadfield, Esq., M.P. With an introductory review by a Manchester reformer [Rev. Alex. Thomson, M.A.]. 8vo. Pp. 75. [*New Coll. Cat.*]   London, 1870

EXPEDIENT (an) for composing differences in religion. [By Henry Hammond, D.D.] 4to. [*Watt's Bibl. Brit.*]   London, 1649

EXPEDIENT (an) propos'd ; or, the occasion of the late controversie in Convocation consider'd, and a method of adjournments pointed out consistent with the claims of both Houses, whereby all disputes in that matter may for the future be avoided : in a letter to the author of a late book [by Edmund Gibson] entitled, The Right of the Archbishop to continue and prorogue the whole Convocation asserted, &c. By a country divine [William Binckes, D.D.]. 4to. [*Arber's Term Cat.*, iii., 685.]   London, 1701
The author's name is also in the handwriting of Dr J. Walker, of Exeter.

EXPEDITION (the) against Roche-fort . . . fully stated and considered in a letter to the Right Hon. author of the "Candid reflections." By a country gentleman [Thomas Potter, M.P.]. 8vo. Pp. 70. London, 1758
The author of the "Candid reflections" was Henry Fox. *See above.*

EXPEDITION (the) of his Highness the Prince of Orange for England ; giving an account of the most remark-able passages thereof, from the day of his setting sail from Holland, to the first day of this instant December, 1688. In a letter to a person of quality. [By Gilbert Burnet, D.D.] No separate title-page. 4to. [Clarke and Foxcroft's *Life of Bp. Burnet.*]
Letter signed " N. N.," and dated 1 Dec. 1688.

EXPEDITION (the) of Humphry Clinker. By the author of *Roderick Random* [Tobias George Smollett]. 3 vols. Fcap 8vo. [*Brit. Mus.*]
London, 1671 [1771]

EXPEDITIONS on the glaciers : in-cluding an ascent of Mont Blanc, Monte Rosa, Col du Géant, and Mont Buét. By a private of the thirty-eighth artists', and member of the Alpine Club [John Barrow]. 8vo. Pp. 126. London, 1864
" Presented to the Bodleian Library by the author, John Barrow."

EXPENCE (the) of university education reduced. In a letter to A. B., Fellow of E. C. [Exeter College. By Richard Newton, D.D.]. 8vo. [*Bodl.*]
London, 1733
A fourth edition was published in 1741.

EXPERIENC'D (the) angler, or angling improv'd ; being a general discourse of angling, imparting many of the aptest wayes and choicest ex-periments for the taking of most sorts of fish in pond or river. [By Colonel Robert Venables.] First edition. 12mo. Pp. xvi., 106. [*W.*] London, 1662
The engravings are the same as those in Walton's Angler ; the recommenda-tory letter is signed " J. W.," which is supposed to be Isaac Walton. Only the first and second editions of this work are anonymous.

EXPERIENCE ; a tale for all ages. By the author of *Correction*, etc. [Mrs Anne Raikes Harding]. 4 vols. Fcap 8vo. [*Brit. Mus.*] London, 1828
All Mrs Harding's publications are anonymous.

EXPERIENCE (the) of life. By the author of *Amy Herbert*, etc. [Elizabeth Missing Sewell]. Fcap 8vo. Pp. 475. [*Brit. Mus.*] London, 1853

EXPERIENCE, the test of government : in eighteen ways . . . [By W. Duane ?] 8vo. Philadelphia, 1807

EXPERIENCED (the) butcher ; show-ing the respectability and usefulness of his calling, the religious considera-tions arising from it, the law relating to it, and various profitable sugges-tions for the rightly carrying it on. . . . [By J. Plumptree, assisted by T. Lan-taffe, butcher.] Fcap 8vo. Pp. viii., 198. [*Brit. Mus.*] London, 1816

EXPERIENCES of a backwoods preacher. [By Rev. S— H. Hilts.] 8vo. [*Camb. Univ. Cat.*]
Toronto, 1888

EXPERIENCES of a colonist forty years ago : a journey from Port Phillip to South Australia in 1839, and voyage from Port Phillip to Adelaide in 1846. By an old hand [George Hamilton]. 8vo. [*Col. Inst. Lib. Cat.*] Adelaide, 1880

EXPERIENCES of a convict, trans-ported for twenty-one years ; an auto-biographical memoir. By an ex-military officer [John F. Mortlock]. 5 parts. Cr 8vo. Pp. 233. [*Camb. Univ. Lib.*] London, 1864-65

EXPERIENCES (the) of a French detective officer ; adapted from the manuscripts of T. Duhamel. By " Waters " [William Russell]. Fcap 8vo. [*Brit. Mus.*] London, [1861]

EXPERIENCES of a gaol chaplain ; comprising recollections of ministerial intercourse with criminals of various classes. [By Rev. Erskine Neale, M.A.] 3 vols. Fcap 8vo. [*D. N. B.*, vol. 40, p. 141.] London, 1847
A work of fiction : other two editions followed.

EXPERIENCES (the) of a lady help. By John Strange Winter [Henrietta E. V. Palmer, later Mrs Arthur Stannard]. 8vo. New York, 1895

EXPERIENCES (the) of a native of the forest, written by himself [William Apes]. 8vo. [Cushing's *Init. and Pseud.*, vol. i., p. 201.]
New York, 1831

EXPERIENCES of a real detective. By Inspector F. ; edited by " Waters " [William Russell]. 8vo. [*Brit. Mus.*]
London, 1862

EXPERIENCES of an aged convert to Catholicism. By herself [Mrs Isabella Newlands]. 8vo.
Edinburgh, [1905]

EXPERIMENT (the) ; a farce in one act. By X., author of *Nothing* [Major George Ranken]. 8vo. [Cushing's *Init. and Pseud.*, i., 310.] Quebec, 1854

EXPERIMENT (an) in altruism. By Elizabeth Hastings [Margaret Pollock Sherwood]. Third edition. Pt 8vo. Pp. 215. [*Amer. Cat.*]
New York, 1895

EXPERIMENT (the) ; or, the shortest way with the Dissenters exemplified : being the case of Mr Abraham Gill, a Dissenting minister in the Isle of Ely, and a full account of his being sent for a soldier, by Mr Fern (an ecclesiastical Justice of the Peace) and other conspirators. To the eternal honour of the temper and moderation of High-Church principles. Humbly dedicated to the Queen. [By Daniel Defoe.] 4to. Pp. 58. [Wilson's *Life of Defoe*, 74.]   London, 1705

EXPERIMENTAL proofs that the surface of standing water is not convex but horizontal ; with an examination of the question, Is the earth a globe or a plane ? between J. Hampden and A. R. Wallace. By Parallax [Samuel Birley Rowbotham].   8vo. [*Brit. Mus.*]   London, 1870

EXPERIMENTAL Spiritism. The Mediums' Book . . . being the sequel to " The Spirits' Book." By Allan Kardac [Léon H. D. Rivail]. Translated [from the French] by A. Blackwell. 8vo. [*Brit. Mus.*]
London, 1876

EXPERIMENTALL (an) discoverie of Spanish practises ; or the counsell of a well-wishing souldier, for the good of his prince and state : wherein is manifested, from known experience, both the cruelty, and policy of the Spaniard to effect his own ends ; chiefly swelling with multiplicity of glorious titles, as one of the greatest monarchs of the earth, that, being admired of all, his greatnesse might amaze all, and so by degrees seeking covertly to tyrannize over all. [By Thomas Scott, B.D.] 4to. Pp. 58. [*Camb. Univ. Cat.*]   N.P., 1623

EXPERIMENTS and observations on light and colours ; to which is prefixed, the " Analogy between heat and motion." [By John Elliot, M.D.] 8vo. [*Edin. Univ. Lib.*]   London, 1786

EXPERIMENTS and observations on the Malvern waters. [By John Wall, M.D.] 8vo. [*Upcott.*]
Worcester, 1763

EXPERIMENTS made for the purpose of ascertaining the stability of bodies floating on the surface of the water. By C. B. [Charles Beaufoy]. 8vo. [*Brit. Mus.*]   London, 1806

EXPIATED. [A novel.] By the author of *Six months hence* [Herman Ludolph Prior]. 3 vols. 8vo. [*Camb. Univ. Lib.*]   Salisbury, 1872
Wrongly ascribed to Mrs Hamilton [*née* Celia V. Dakin].

EXPIATED (an) sin. [A novel.] By the author of *My Lady's folly* [Carl Andrews]. Cr 8vo.   London, 1903
Signed, at the end, " Carl Swerdna," of which the second name shows reversed spelling.

EXPIATION [an Arkansas novel]. By Octave Thanet [Alice French]. Pt 8vo. Pp. vi., 215. [*Brit. Mus.*]
New York, 1890

EXPIATION. From the French of Théodore Bentzon [Madame Thérèse Blanc]. Fcap 8vo. [Cushing's *Init. and Pseud.*, vol. i., 34.]   Boston, 1889

EXPIATION (the) of a sinner ; in a commentary vpon the Epistle to the Hebrewes. [By Thomas Lushington, M.A.] Folio. Pp. 369. [*Darling's Cyclop. Bibliog.*]   London, 1646
This work is substantially a translation, with alterations and additions, from the Latin of John Crellius and Jonas Schlichtingius. The epistle to the reader is signed " F. M."

EXPLANATION (an) and vindication of the rubricks before the new office for the eleventh day of June, more particularly as they concern the festival of St Barnabas, Whitsun Tuesday, and Trinity Sunday. [By —— Davis.] 8vo. [Watt's *Bibl. Brit.*]
Oxford, 1731

EXPLANATION, explicatory and practical, of the parable of the sower. [By Robert Brown.] Fcap 8vo.
London, [about 1865]

EXPLANATION of a passage in an article on certain works of Bishop Jewel, published in the British Critic, for July, 1841 ; a letter to the Rev. Charles Smith Bird, M.A., author of a " Plea for the Reformed Church." By the writer of the article [Frederick Oakeley, M.A.]. 8vo. Pp. 75. [*D. N. B.*, vol. 41, p. 287.]
London, 1842

EXPLANATION (an) of Dr Watts' Hymns for children. By a lady [Mrs E— Cockle]. Fcap 8vo. [*Brit. Mus.*]   London, 1836

EXPLANATION (an) of fluxions, in a short essay on the theory. [By Francis Blake.] 4to.   London, 1741

EXPLANATION (an) of Mr Kilham's Statement of the [Wesleyan] Preachers' allowance. [By Rev. Thomas Hanby.] Fcap 8vo. Pp. 24.
Nottingham, 1796

EXPLANATION (an) of Say-Brook platform. . . . By one who heartily desires the order, peace, and purity of the Churches [Thomas Fitch, M.A.]. 8vo. [Cushing's *Init. and Pseud.*, vol. ii., p. 219.]   Hartford, Conn., 1863

EXPLANATION (an) of some scriptural and ecclesiastical terms; for the use of Maghull School. [By Rev. George Holden, M.A.] Fcap 8vo. [*Brit. Mus.*]   Liverpool, 1855

EXPLANATION (an) of some truths of the carriage of things about this great work: A short view of the present condition of Scotland. [By David Buchanan.]   4to.   Pp. 58. [*Brit. Mus.*]   London, 1646

EXPLANATION (an) of the Bill proposed in the House of Commons, 1785, respecting the Judges in Scotland. [By Sir Ilay Campbell, LL.D.] 8vo. [*D. N. B.*, vol. 8, p. 361.]
[Edinburgh, 1785]

EXPLANATION (an) of the case of Edinburgh representation in Parliament. [By Henry Cockburn.] 8vo. [*Brit. Mus.*]   Edinburgh, 1826

EXPLANATION (an) of the duties of religion, for the use of Boldre School in New Forest. [By William Gilpin, M.A.] 12mo. [*Brit. Mus.*]
Lymington, 1798

EXPLANATION (an) of the holy ordinance of Confirmation. [By Thomas Henry Ashhurst, D.C.L.] Third edition. 8vo. [*Bodl.*]
Oxford, 1844

EXPLANATION (an) of the interesting prophecy respecting the two apocalyptic witnesses, as fulfilled by the institution and progress of the British and Foreign Bible Society; and illustrating the termination of the twelve hundred and sixty days, or prophetic years, referred to in that and other relative prophecies. By an observer of the times [Alexander Shand, advocate in Aberdeen]. 8vo. [*Bodl.*]
London, 1817

EXPLANATION of the plates contained in the first publication of the British Zoology. [By Thomas Pennant.] 8vo. [*Brit. Mus.*]
London, 1763

EXPLANATION (an) of the prophecy of the seven vials, or the seven last plagues, contained in the Revelation of St John, chapters xv. xvi. By a country clergyman [Robert Ingram, vicar of Wormingford and Boxted, Essex]. 8vo. [*Mon. Rev.*, lxiii., 554; lxxiii., 75.]   London, 1780

EXPLANATION (an) of the Roman Catholick's belief, concerning the principal points controverted; charitably offered to all moderate persons. [By Francis Davenport, commonly known as Francis a Sancta Clara.] Fourth edition. 8vo. [*Bodl.*]
N.P., 1670

EXPLANATIONS: a sequel to "Vestiges of the natural history of Creation." By the author of that work [Robert Chambers]. Second edition. 8vo. Pp. vii., 205. [*Brit. Mus.*] London, 1846
See "Vestiges . . .," also "An Expository outline. . . ."

EXPLANATIONS and emendations of some passages in the text of Shakespeare and of Beaumont and Fletcher. By Martinus Scriblerus [Rev. Robert Morehead]. 8vo. Pp. 60. [*And. Jervise.*]   Edinburgh, 1814

EXPLANATIONS of the new map of Nova Scotia. [By Thomas Jefferys, map-engraver.] 4to.   London, 1755

EXPLANATORY (an) analysis of St Paul's First Epistle to Timothy. By H. P. L. [Henry Parry Liddon, D.D.]. 8vo. Pp. 66. [*Brit. Mus.*]
Oxford, 1877
A later edition (London, 1897, pp. 93) bears the author's name.

EXPLANATORY and practical comments on the New Testament. . . . [By the Rev. —— Hardman, of the Catholic Apostolic Church in Dublin.] 8vo. [Boase's *Cath. Apost. Lit.*]
Edinburgh, 1834

EXPLANATORY (an) defence of the Estimate of the manners and principles of the times; being an appendix to that work, occasioned by the clamours lately raised against it. By the author of the Estimate [John Brown, D.D., vicar of Newcastle.] 8vo. Pp. 84. [*Brit. Mus.*]   London, 1758
See above, "An Estimate. . . ."

EXPLICATION (an) and vindication of the first section of the Short observations on the first principles and moving powers of the present system of philosophy. In a letter to a lady. [By Andrew Wilson, M.D.] 8vo. [Orme's *Bibliotheca Biblica.*]
Edinburgh, 1764
See below, "Short observations. . . ."

EXPLICATION (an) of passages excepted against in the Marrow of modern divinity, taken from the book it self; contained in a letter to a minister of the gospel. [By James Hog, minister at Carnock.] Fcap 8vo. [*New Coll. Cat.*]   Edinburgh, 1719
Signed "J. H."

EXPLICATION (an) of that proposition contained in Mr Glass's answers to the Synod's queries, A congregation or church of Jesus Christ, with its Presbytery, is, in its discipline subject to no jurisdiction under heaven ; together with a letter concerning communion in the Lord's Supper. . . . [By John Glas, M.A.] 8vo. Pp. 86. [*Adv. Lib.*]   Edinburgh, 1728

EXPLICATION (an) of the Creed, the Ten Commandments, and the Lord's Prayer ; with the addition of some forms of prayer. The second edition, with some prayers added. By J. R. [John Rawlet]. 8vo. [Watt's *Bibl. Brit.*]   London, 1679
Sometimes wrongly attributed to John Rawley or J— Rawlinson.

EXPLICATORY (an) catechism ; or an explanation of the [Westminster] Assemblies Shorter Catechism, wherein those principles are enlarged upon especially which obviate the great and growing errors of Popery. [By Thomas Vincent.] 8vo. [Arber's *Term Cat.*, vol. i., p. 523.]
London, 1675

EXPLICIT (an) avowal of Nothingarianism, in a sermon, March 4, 1823. By Egomet Demeres [Rev. Thomas Williams]. Printed and published nowhere, by nobody. 8vo. [Cushing's *Init. and Pseud.*, vol. ii., p. 51.]
Providence, R.I., 1823

EXPLODED ideas, and other essays. By the author of *Times and days* [John Hutton Balfour Browne]. Fcap 8vo.   London, 1900

EXPLOITS and anecdotes of the most remarkable Gypsies in the southern counties of Scotland ; together with traits of their origin, character, and manners. [By William Chambers.] 12mo.   Edinburgh, 1821
This is really an unacknowledged reproduction of material from the *Edinburgh Monthly Magazine*, 1817. [Black's *Gypsy Bibliog.*, p. 36.]

EXPLOITS (the) and triumphs in Europe of Paul Morphy, the chess champion ; including . . . various information and anecdote relating to the noble game of chess. By Paul Morphy's late secretary [Frederick Milnes Edge]. Fcap 8vo. Pp. viii., 203. [*Brit. Mus.*]   New York, 1859

EXPLOITS (the) of Captain O'Hagan. By Sax Rohmer [Arthur Sarsfield Ward]. Cr 8vo. Pp. 323. [*Lond. Lib. Cat.*]   London, 1919

EXPLOITS (the) of Miles Standish. By Muirhead Robertson [Henry Johnson]. Pt 8vo. [*Amer. Cat.*] New York, 1897

VOL. II.

EXPLOSION (the) ; or an alarming providential check to immorality : a poem occasioned by the late dreadful explosion of gunpowder on the 15th day of November 1772 in the City of Chester. . . . By a citizen of Chester [Thomas Brackenbury]. 8vo.
Chester, 1773

EXPOSÉ (the) ; or Napoleon Buonaparte unmasked : in a condensed statement of his career and atrocities. [By Peter Coxe.] [*Gent. Mag.*, Dec. 1844, p. 653.]   London, 1809

EXPOSÉ (an), touching their various mysteries, from the times of Boyd, the martyred Goldschmidt, &c. to those of Bowles, Aslett, Lord Peterborough, Cochrane, &c. ; including bulls, bears, time bargains, stock exchange telegraphs, lotteries, hoaxes, bullion, and exchanges ; illustrated by various anecdotes : with a plan for the indubitable advantage of the Minister, by the daily purchases for the Sinking Fund being made openly. . . . [By J. Lancaster.] 8vo. Pp. 112. [*Edin. Univ. Cat.*]   London, 1821

EXPOSITION (an), critical and explanatory, of Heb. vi., 4-8. [By Robert Brown.] Fcap 8vo.
London, [1870 ?]

EXPOSITION (the) given by my Lord Bishop of Sarum [Gilbert Burnet] of the second Article of our religion, examined. [By Jonathan Edwards, D.D., Principal of Jesus College, Oxford.] 8vo. Pp. 100. [Watt's *Bibl. Brit.*]   London, 1702

EXPOSITION (an) of certaine difficult and obscure wordes, and termes of the lawes of this realme, newly set foorth & augmented, both in French and English, for the helpe of such yonge studentes as are desirous to attaine the knowledge of the same. VVhereunto are also added the olde tenures. [By William Rastall.] 8vo. Folio. Pp. 216. [*Bodl.*]   London, 1579

EXPOSITION (an) of Chapters XII., XIII. and XIV. of I. Corinthians ; with observations on the present state of the Church. By the author of *Explanatory and practical comments on the New Testament* [Rev. —— Hardman, Catholic Apostolic Church in Dublin]. Second edition. Dy 8vo. Pp. 86. [Boase's *Cath. Apost. Lit.*]
Edinburgh, 1835

EXPOSITION (an) of Ecclesiastes, or the Preacher. [By George Sykes, mystic.] 4to. Pp. 478.
London, 1680

Q

EXPOSITION (an) of part of the patent laws. By a native-born citizen of the United States [Oliver Evans]. 8vo. [Cushing's *Init. and Pseud.*, vol. i., p. 201.]   Philadelphia, 1816

EXPOSITION of Psalm CXXXIX. [By John Morier.] 8vo. Pp. 24.
Tunbridge Wells, 1833

EXPOSITION (an) of some late reveries concerning the Sonship of Christ, which are fundamentally subversive of the Christian religion. [By Adam Gib.] 8vo. [*New Coll. Cat.*]   Edinburgh, 1780

EXPOSITION (an) of the Apocalypse. [By D— L— Shirres.] 8vo. [Robertson's *Aberd. Bibl.*]   Aberdeen, 1871

EXPOSITION of the Book of Revelation, chapters vi., vii., viii., ix. By H. H. [Henry Hewetson]. 8vo. [*Brit. Mus.*]   London, [1869]

EXPOSITION (an) of the causes and character of the late war between the United States and Great Britain. [By Alexander James Dallas.] 8vo. [*Brit. Mus.*]   Boston, 1815

EXPOSITION (an) of the Church Catechism, from our modern authors, and the Holy Scriptures, in words at length. By the author of the *Devout communicant* [Abednego Seller]. 8vo. [*Brit. Mus.*]   London, 1695

EXPOSITION (an) of the Church Catechism, or the practice of divine love ; revised : composed for the diocese of Bath and Wells. [By Thomas Ken, Bishop of Bath and Wells.] 8vo. [*Brit. Mus.*]   London, 1686
See also below, " An Exposition on the Church. . . ."

EXPOSITION (an) of the Church, in view of recent difficulties and controversies. [By J. T. Hecker.] 8vo.
London, 1875

EXPOSITION (an) of the doctrine of the Catholic Church in matters of controversie. By the Right Reverend James Benigne Bossuet, counsellor to the King [of France], Bishop of Meaux, formerly of Condom. . . . Done into English from the 5th edition in French. [By Henry Joseph Johnston, O.S.B.] 4to. [Jones' Peck, i., 112.]   London, 1685

EXPOSITION (an) of the doctrine of the Catholique Church in the points of controversie with those of the pretended Reformation. By James Benigne Bossuet, Bishop and Lord of Condom. . . . Translated into English by W. M. [Walter Montagu, O.S.B.]. Fcap 8vo. Pp. 230. [Gillow's *Bibl. Dict.*, vol. v., p. 78.]   Paris, 1672

EXPOSITION (an) of the doctrine of the Church of England, in the several articles proposed by Monsieur [J. B. Bossuet] de Meaux, late Bishop of Condom, in his Exposition of the doctrine of the Catholic Church. To which is prefix'd a particular account of Monsieur de Meaux's book. [By William Wake, D.D.] 4to. Pp. xxxvi., 87. [*Brit. Mus.*]   London, 1686

EXPOSITION (an) of the Epistle of Saint Paul to the Colossians. By the Rev. Jean Daillé. . . . Translated from the French by F. S. [Francis Soreton]. Large 8vo. Pp. 271.   London, 1843

EXPOSITION of the false medium and barriers excluding men of genius from the public. [By Richard Henry (or Hengist) Horne.] Fcap 8vo. Pp. ii., 330. [*D. N. B.*, vol. 27, p. 558.]
London, 1833

EXPOSITION (an) of the late controversy in the Methodist Episcopal Church. . . . By a layman [Samuel K. Jennings, M.D.]. 8vo. [Cushing's *Init. and Pseud.*, vol. i., p. 468.]
Baltimore, 1831

EXPOSITION (an) of the memorial of sundry presbyters of the Protestant Episcopal Church. By one of the memorialists [William Augustus Muhlenberg, D.D.]. 8vo. [Cushing's *Init. and Pseud.*, vol. i., p. 506.]
New York, 1854

EXPOSITION (an) of the nature, force, action, and other properties of gravitation on the planets. [By Joseph Denison.] Fcap 8vo. [*Camb. Univ. Lib.*]   London, 1842

EXPOSITION (an) of the political and commercial relations of the Government of Prince of Wales Island with the States on the East Coast of Sumatra. [By John Anderson.] 4to. [*Brit. Mus.*]   London, 1824

EXPOSITION (an) of the Song of Solomon, called Canticles ; together with profitable observations collected out of the same ; perused and published by William Govge, preacher of Gods word in Black-Friers, London. [By Sir Henry Finch.] 4to. [*Bodl.*]
London, 1615

EXPOSITION of the true Christian religion [as held in the New Jerusalem Church. By Sir Isaac Pitman]. 12mo. [Green's *Bibl. Somers.*, i., 411.]
Bath, 1841

EXPOSITION (an) of the two first verses of the sixth Chapter to the Hebrews, in form of a dialogue. By T. W. [Thomas Walkington, D.D.], minister of the Word. 4to. [*D. N. B.*, vol. 59, p. 91.]   London, 1609

EXPOSITION (an) of the whole Book of the Revelation. . . . By H. K. [Hanserd Knollys]. Large 8vo. Pp. 250. [*D. N. B.*, vol. 31, p. 281.]
London, 1689

EXPOSITION of views respecting the principal facts, causes, and peculiarities involved in spirit manifestations. [By Adin Ballou], . . . with an introduction by G. W. Stone. Fcap 8vo. [*Camb. Univ. Lib.*]   London, 1852

EXPOSITION (an) on the Church [of England] Catechism ; or the practice of divine love ; composed for the diocese of Bath and Wells. [By Thomas Ken, Bishop.] 8vo. Pp. 82. [*D. N. B.*, vol. 30, p. 403.]
London, 1685
Other editions have the title " An Exposition of the Church Catechism." *See above.*

EXPOSITION (an) on the fourth chapter of the Epistle to the Romans, occasioned from the growth of Grotian errors, and . . . them who abuse that most comforting . . . doctrine of Justification. By W. C. [Walter Cross], M.A. [minister in London]. 4to. Pp. 14. [Watt's *Bibl. Brit.*]
London, 1693

EXPOSITION (an), or true state of the matters objected in England to the people known by the name of Unitas Fratrum [or Moravians]. By [Count Nicholas Louis Zinzendorf] the Ordinary of the Brethren : with notes and additions by the editor [James Hutton]. 2 parts. 8vo. Pp. 210. [Malin's *Cat. of Moravian Books*, p. 69.]   London, 1755

EXPOSITION (an) upon some select Psalms of David, written by M. Robert Rollok, and translated out of Latine into English, by C. L. [Charles Lumisden], minister of the Gospel of Christ at Duddingstone. [Lowndes' *Bibl. Man.*] 8vo.   Edinburgh, 1600

EXPOSITIONS of Raphael's Bible. By the author of *The Expositions of the cartoons of Raphael*, etc. [Richard Henry Smith, Jun.]. Square cr 8vo. [*Brit. Mus.*]   London, 1868

EXPOSITORY essays and discourses. By Carpus [Samuel Cox, D.D.]. 8vo. [*Amer. Lib. Journ.*, ii., 307.]
London, 1877

EXPOSITORY (an) outline of the " Vestiges of the natural history of Creation " [by Robert Chambers], with a comprehensive and critical analysis of the arguments. . . . [By Samuel Laing, M.P.] Fcap 8vo. Pp. 70.
London, 1846

EXPOSITORY outlines of sermons on the Miracles of the Lord Jesus. By the author of *Looking unto Jesus* [Judith Towers Grant]. Fcap 8vo.
London, 1866

EXPOSITORY outlines of sermons on the Parables of our Lord Jesus. By the author of *Looking unto Jesus* [Judith Towers Grant]. Fcap 8vo.
London, 1864

EXPOSTULATION (an) with that party in Scotland commonly known by the name of Whigs. [By James Craufurd.] 4to. [*Camb. Univ. Lib.*]
London, 1682

EXPOSTULATION (an) with the Bishops so-called in England, concerning their jurisdiction over the people of God called Quakers. [By John Whitehead.] No title. 4to. [Smith's *Cat. of Friends' Books*.]
N.P., 1662
Signed " J. W."

EXPOSTULATION (an) with the Co-operative Societies of London. By Don Pedro Verdad [Walter M'Gee]. 8vo. Pp. 16. [*Brit. Mus.*]
London, [1881]

EXPOSTULATORY (an) address endeavouring to awaken, excite, and encourage the ignorant. . . . By a private Christian [—— Dixon]. 8vo.
Edinburgh, N.D.

EXPOSTULATORY (an) address to all who frequent places of diversion and gambling. . . . By A. D. [Abiah Darby]. 4to. [*Brit. Mus.*]
[Shrewsbury, 1765]

EXPOSTULATORY address to J. R. [John Ranby, surgeon]. By a physician [James Jurin, M.D.]. 8vo.
London, 1745

EXPOSTULATORY (an) letter to Dr Moseley, on his Review of the Report of the London College of Physicians on vaccination. By T. C. M., M.B., F.L.S. [Sir Thomas Charles Morgan]. 8vo. [*W.*]   London, 1808

EXPOSTULATORY (an) letter to Mr [Thomas] Woolston, on account of his late writings. By a clergyman in the country [—— Laurence]. 8vo. [*Brit. Mus.*]   London, 1730

EXPOSTULATORY odes to a great Duke, and a little Lord. By Peter Pindar, Esquire [John Wolcot, M.D.]. 4to. Pp. 56. [*D. N. B.*, vol. 62, p. 293.]   London, 1789

EXPOSTULATORY remarks on the use of water baptism. . . . By S. T. [Samuel Treffrey]. 8vo. [*Brit. Mus.*]
London, 1847

EXPOSURE of the arguments why murder and blasphemy ought not to be forbidden. [By Charles Bonner.] 8vo. [Robertson's *Aberd. Bibl.*]
Aberdeen, 1825

EXPOSURE of the attack [in the Law Magazine and Law Review for August 1856] on Lord Cockburn's "Memorials." [By Alexander Russel, editor of the *Scotsman*.] Reprinted from the *Scotsman*, of September 3, and November 8, 15, and 29. 8vo. Edinburgh, 1856
Signed "A. R."

EXPOSURE (an) of the corruption of the Saxon name Arms Housen into Almshouses, and of some other Norman corruptions. By B. C. [Bracy Clark], vestryman of Marybone. 4to. No title-page. [*W.*] London, N.D.

EXPOSURE (an) of the late Irish miracles; comprising observations on the nature, object and evidence of Christian miracles, as opposed to the late impostures; in a letter to Dr Murray, titular archbishop of Dublin. By a rational Christian [Alexander Leopold, Prince of Hohenlohe, Bishop of Sardica]. 8vo. Pp. 90. [*Bodl.*]
Dublin, 1823

EXPOSURE (an) of the misrepresentations . . . made by the Rev. John Tod Brown, in his discourse in the Abbey Church, Dunfermline. By "Scotus" [Thomas H. Foggo]. 8vo. [Beveridge's *Dunf. Bibl.*] Dunfermline, 1843

EXPOSURE (an) of the Orton confession of the Tichborne claimant. By W. A. F. [William Alfred Frost]. 8vo. Pp. 135. [*Brit. Mus.*] London, 1913

EXPOUNDER (the) expounded. . . . By R—ph J—ph—n [Ralph Jephson], of the Inner Temple. 8vo.
London, 1740

EXQUISITE (an) fool. [A novel. By Eleanor Frances Poynter.] 8vo.
London, 1892

EXQUISITES (the). [Letterpress by John Barrow.] 8vo. London, 1839
Wrongly ascribed to W. M. Thackeray.

EXTENT (the) and limits of the subjection due to princes; a sermon [on Romans xiii. 1] preached on Jan. 30, 1746-7, being the anniversary of the martyrdom of King Charles I. By a country clergyman [Rev. John Butler]. 8vo. [*Brit. Mus.*] London, [1747]

EXTENT (the), evils, and needlessness of Sunday trading in London, as detailed in the Parliamentary evidence of 1832, 1847, & 1850, and other documents, and the measures required for its gradual suppression considered. By a layman [William Rivington]. 8vo. Pp. 71. [*Brit. Mus.*] London, 1855

EXTENT (the) of the primitive Churches enquired into; and some reasons to prove that they were congregations. With a table of all the places in the New Testament, where the word Church is used, digested under proper heads. [By Thomas Cawdwell.] 8vo. Pp. 88. [*Bodl.*] London, 1720

EXTERMINATION of love; a fragmentary study in erotics. By E. Gerard [Emily de Laszowska]. Cr 8vo. Pp. 322. Edinburgh, 1901

EXTERMINATION of the Scottish peasantry; being a reply to a letter from the most noble the Marquess of Breadalbane, wherein his Lordship denies that extensive clearances have been made upon his highland properties. By R. Alister, author of *Barriers to the national prosperity of Scotland* [Alexander Robertson, of Dundonnochie]. 8vo. [*Brit. Mus.*]
Edinburgh, 1853

EXTERNAL (the) peace of the Church only attainable by a zeal for Scripture in its just latitude, and by mutual charity; not by a pretense of uniformity of opinions. . . . By a lover of truth and peace [Arthur Ashley Sykes, D.D.]. 8vo. Pp. 61. [Disney's *Memoir of Sykes*, p. xii.]
London, 1716

EXTRA!! Fairy tales up to now. By Omar Khayyám, Jun. [Wallace Irwin]. Pt 8vo. [*Amer. Cat.*]
San Francisco, 1904

EXTRA physics, and the mystery of creation; with a brief examination of Professor Tyndall. [By Henry Larkin.] Cr 8vo. London, 1878

EXTRACT (an) from a late ingenious author [J. Law?]. Fcap 8vo. [*Brit. Mus.*] Dublin, 1757

EXTRACT (an) from a Reply to the Observations of Lieut. Gen. Sir William Howe, on a pamphlet, entitled, Letters to a nobleman. [By John Wesley, A.M.] Fcap 8vo. Pp. 104. [Green's *Wesley Bibl.*, p. 210.] London, 1781

EXTRACT from an ignorant mind, on the following questions: 1st. In speaking of the earth, does the sacred history allude only to our earth? 2d. Admitting that in some places the sacred history speaks of another earth than this, what is that unknown earth? 3d. Does the sacred history speak of this earth in some places, and of an unknown earth in others: or does it speak everywhere but of an earth different from this? [By —— Portier.] 8vo. Pp. 504. [*Bodl.*] London, 1828

EXTRACT from Captain Stormfield's Visit to heaven. By Mark Twain [Samuel Langhorne Clemens]. 8vo. Pp. 120. [*Brit. Mus.*]
New York, 1909

EXTRACT from my Remark-book. [By Sir William Symonds.] 8vo.
Paltick, 1839

EXTRACT from the Case of the electors of Eton College, to supply all vacancies in that society with Fellows of King's College, Cambridge, so long as persons properly qualified are to be had within that description. [By Thomas Ashton, D.D.] 4to. [*Nichols' Lit. Anec.*, iii., 89.]   London, 1771

EXTRACT from the Regicide, an heroic poem, in twenty-six books; with notes and a dedication to the friend of Tallien. By the author [Rev. Charles Edward Stewart]. 8vo. [*Watt's Bibl. Brit.*]   London, 1801

EXTRACT (an) of letters,—by —— [Mrs Lefevre]. Edited by J. W. [John Wesley]. [*Olphar Hamst, p. 73.*]
Dublin, 1808

EXTRACTE (an) of examples, apothegmes and histories, collected out of Lycosthenes, Brusonius, and others, translated into Englishe, and reduced into an alphabeticall order of common places. By J. P. [John Perrinchiefe or Parrincheffe]. 8vo. [*Lowndes' Bibl. Man.*]   London, [1572]

EXTRACTION (the) of man's soul. . . . A discourse proving by divine and naturall reason that the production of mans soul is by propagation and not by creation. By H. W. [Henry Woolnor], B.D. Fcap 8vo. Pp. 335. London, 1655
Other editions (1641, 1642) differ in the title : " The true originall of the soule. . . ."

EXTRACTS and original anecdotes ; for the improvement of youth. [By Mary Leadbetter.] Fcap 8vo. [*Smith's Cat. of Friends' Books*, ii., 95.]
Dublin, 1794

EXTRACTS describing the ancient manner of placing the kingdom in military array, the various modes of defence adopted for its safety in periods of danger, and the evidence of foreigners as to the national character and personal bravery of the English : taken from original state papers of the sixteenth century. [Edited with notes by W. Gunn.] 4to. [*Brit. Mus.*]
London, 1803

EXTRACTS from a journal during a tour in Italy, in 1829 and 1830. [By Thomas J. Ireland.] 8vo. Pp. 276. [Dobell's *Private Prints*, p. 94.]
Chiswick, 1836

EXTRACTS from a journal in the months of June, July, August, and September, in the year 1819. [By Stephen Weston, B.D.] 8vo. [*Bodl.*]
London, 1820

EXTRACTS from a journal kept during a voyage from Philadelphia to Calcutta. By W. J. [W. Jordan]. 8vo.
Serampore, 1812

EXTRACTS from a journal of a pilgrimage in search of the curious and beautiful in Italy, Sicily, and Greece, during the years 1845-46. [By Richard Barrington.] 8vo.   London, 1850
Preface signed " R. B."

EXTRACTS from a manuscript pamphlet intitled " The Tittle-tattle-mongers." [By R— Dawes.] 8vo.
Newcastle-upon-Tyne, 1747

EXTRACTS from Adam's diary. By Mark Twain [Samuel L. Clemens]. 8vo.   London, 1904

EXTRACTS from, and additions to, a pamphlet entitled " Tough but True." By W. A. U. [William Aitken Urie]. 12mo.   London, 1891

EXTRACTS from Bingham's Antiquities. [By Henry Drummond, M.P.] Part I. 8vo. Pp. 99. London, 1837

EXTRACTS from English and foreign authors in prose and verse. [Collected by Henry Danby Seymour, M.P.] Fcap 8vo. Pp. 202. [*W.*]
London, 1860

EXTRACTS from Journals, 1872-1881. [By Reginald Baliol Brett, Viscount Esher.] 8vo. [*Brit. Mus.*]
London, 1908
Signed " E."

EXTRACTS from letters to the " Weekly Dispatch " [on London government]. By Nemesis [James Beal]. 8vo. [Gladstone *Lib. Cat.* (Lib. Club).]   London, 1876

EXTRACTS from my journal, 1852. [By James Redford Bulwen.] 8vo. Private print.   Norwich, 1853

EXTRACTS from my note-book, from 1831 to 1854 (and 1855 to 1866). [By Josiah Forster.] 2 parts. 8vo. Private print.   [London, 1865-67]
Prefatory note signed " J. F."

EXTRACTS from the Books of the Old Testament. [By Dr Alexander Brunton.] 8vo.   Edinburgh, 1814

EXTRACTS from the diary of a huntsman. [By Thomas Assheton Smith.] 8vo.   London, 1838

EXTRACTS from the diary of a lover of literature [Thomas Green]. 4to. Pp. vii., 241. [Lowndes' *Bibl. Man.*]
Ipswich, 1810

EXTRACTS from the Edinburgh Review [regarding Methodism. By Sydney Smith]. 8vo. [*Brit. Mus.*]
Edinburgh, [1810]

EXTRACTS from the literary and scientific correspondence of Richard Richardson, M.D., F.R.S., of Brierley, Yorkshire, illustrative of the state and progress of botany ; and interspersed with information respecting the study of antiquities and general literature in Great Britain, during the first half of the eighteenth century. [Edited by Dawson Turner.] 8vo. Pp. 463. [Martin's *Cat.*]   Yarmouth, 1835

EXTRACTS from the minutes of evidence taken before the Committee of the House of Commons on the state of the Police of the Metropolis, on the subject of fires ; with suggestions for the prevention of its future destructiveness. [By George W. Manby.] 8vo. [*Brit. Mus.*] Yarmouth, [1819]

EXTRACTS from the several treaties subsisting between Great-Britain and other kingdoms and states, of such articles and clauses as relate to the duty and conduct of the commanders of the king of Great-Britain's ships of war ; together with articles of later treaties. . . . [Collected and published by Henry Edmunds, LL.D.] 4to. Pp. xxiv., 264. [*Bodl.*] London, 1741

EXTRACTS from the Spiritual Bee ; or a miscellany of spiritual, historical, natural observations, and occasional occurrencyes, applyed in divine meditations. By an university pen [Luke Howard]. 4to. Pp. xiv., 152. [*Bodl.*]
London, 1823
The advertisement to the reader is signed " L. H." Mr. Howard ascribes the Spiritual Bee, from which these extracts are taken, to William Penn ; but Wood assigns the authorship to Nicholas Horsman.

EXTRACTS from the works of travellers, illustrative of various passages in Holy Scripture. [By Mary Fawley Maude.] Pt 8vo. [*Brit. Mus.*]
London, 1842
Preface signed " M. F. M."
In the second edition, the title reads " Manners and customs noticed in various passages of Holy Scripture . . ."; and in the fourth edition (1849), " Scripture manners and customs. . . ."

EXTRACTS from various authors ; and fragments of table-talk ;—afternoons at L * * * * * * * * * [Littlemore Lunatic asylum]. [By Edward Law Hussey.] 8vo. Pp. 156.
Oxford, 1873
The dedication is signed " E. L. H."

EXTRACTS of letters [1771 - 89] to a Christian friend. By a lady [Mrs —— Campbell ; with an introductory essay by Thomas Erskine, Esq., advocate]. 12mo. Pp. 142. [*New Coll. Cat.*]   Greenock, 1830

EXTRACTS relative to the fisheries on the north-west coast of Ireland, from the several reports of the Committee of the British House of Commons . . . and from the publications of Mr Knox, Dr Anderson, and others ; with some observations, and authentic papers, to corroborate what is there asserted, of the advantage of establishments on the north-west coast of Ireland. [By the Right Hon. Wm. Conyngham.] 8vo. Pp. 73. [*Bodl.*]   London, 1787
The author's name is in the handwriting of Gough.

EXTRANEUS vapulans ; or the Observator rescued from the violent but vain assaults of Hamon L'Estrange and the back-blows of Dr Bernard, an Irish Deane. [By Peter Heylin, D.D.] 8vo. [*D. N. B.*, vol. 26, p. 321.]   London, 1656

EXTRA-OFFICIAL State papers addressed to Lord Rawdon and the Members of both Houses of Parliament. By a late Under-Secretary of State [William Knox]. 2 vols. 8vo. [*D. N. B.*, vol. 33, p. 337.]
London, 1789

EXTRAORDINARY (the) adventures and discoveries of several famous men ; with the strange events, and signal mutations and changes in the fortunes of many illustrious places and persons in all ages. . . . By R. B. [Richard Burton, *i.e.* Nathaniel Crouch]. 12mo. Pp. 237. [*Bodl.*]
London, 1683
See note on " Admirable Curiosities."

EXTRAORDINARY ascent of the enchanted mountain (Himalaya Range) by Sir E. Stanley and others. [By Captain R. H. Peel.] 4to.
London, 1834

EXTRAORDINARY (the) Black Book ; or corruption unmasked. . . . Corrected from the latest official returns, and presenting a complete view of the expenditure, patronage, influence, and abuses of the government in Church, State, Law, and Representation. By the original editor [John Wade, LL.D.]. 8vo. Pp. xx., 576. [*Brit. Mus.*]   London, 1831
See " The Black Book, or corruption unmasked," and " Appendix to the Black Book. . . ."

EXTRAORDINARY (the) case of a Piccadilly patient ; or, Dr Reece physick'd by six female physicians. [By Elias Carpenter.] 8vo. [Davidson's *Bibl. Devon.*, p. 198.]
London, 1815

EXTRAORDINARY (the) case of the Bp. of St David's, further clear'd and made plain, from the several views that have been made of it : wherein the articles against him are consider'd, and His Lordship vindicated from them. [By Robert Ferguson.] 4to. Pp. 56. [*Adv. Lib.*] N.P., 1703

EXTRAORDINARY (an) chace ; or the parson and the Cat ; a serio-comic satirical poem, embellished with various etchings. By William Cowper [James Everett]. Second edition. Fcap 8vo. [*Brit. Mus.*]
Sheffield, [1820 ?]

EXTRAORDINARY (the) experiences of little Captain Doppelkop on the shores of Bubbleland. By Irwin Longman [Ingersoll Lockwood]. Cr 8vo. [*Amer. Cat.*] Boston, 1891

EXTRAVAGANT (the) poet ; a comical novel, wherein is described his many pleasant follies. Translated out of [the] French [of César François Oudin, Sieur de Préfontaine] by G. R., Gent. 8vo. [Barbier's *Dictionnaire*.]
London, 1681

EXTREMES, or men of the day ; a comedy, in three acts. By Edmund Falconer [Edmund O'Rourke]. 8vo. [O'Donoghue's *Poets of Ireland*.]
London, 1859

EYE (an) upon the Scottish Established Church, with reference to the law of patronage and the proposed codification of the laws of Scotland. By a Free Church minister [David C. A. Agnew]. 8vo. [*New Coll. Cat.*]
Edinburgh, 1853

EYEBRIGHT ; a story. By Susan Coolidge [Sarah Chauncey Woolsey]. 12mo. [Kirk's *Supp.*] Boston, 1879

EYES and ears ; or, how I see and hear. By Aunt Yewrownckie [Mrs Henry G. Blinn]. 8vo. [Cushing's *Init. and Pseud.*, vol. i., p. 312.]
Philadelphia, 1877

EYES in solitudes. [Poems.] By Wentworth Moore [William H. Mallock]. 4to. London, 1901

EYES right : a bachelor's talks with his boys. By Adam Stevin [James Richardson]. Square 8vo. [Cushing's *Init. and Pseud.*, vol. i., p. 274.]
Boston, 1878

EYE-WITNESS ; or life-scenes in the old North State. . . . By A. O. W. [A— O— Wheeler]. 8vo. [Cushing's *Init. and Pseud.*, vol. i., p. 297.]
Boston, 1865

EZEKIEL, and other poems. By B. M. [Mrs Barbara Macandrew, *née* Miller]. Fcap 8vo. [*Brit. Mus.*]
London, 1892

EZEKIEL'S vision of God ; or the heavenly wheel of wheels of celestial fire . . . elucidated. [By William D. Forsyth.] 8vo. Pp. v., 45.
[Littleborough, 1902]
Signed " W. D. F."

EZEKIELS wheels : a treatise concerning divine Providence. By Tho: Duresme [Thomas Morton, Bishop of Durham]. Pp. 242. [*D. N. B.*, vol. 39, p. 164.] London, 1653

EZRA ; a little narrative [in verse] of Jewish faith and trial. By A. H. [Ann Hamilton]. Fcap 8vo. [O'Donoghue's *Poets of Ireland*.]
Dublin, 1840

EZRA. [A poem. By Emily S. G. Saunders.] 8vo. [*Brit. Mus.*]
[London, 1869]
Signed " E. S. G. S."

EZRA Jordan's escape from the massacre at Fort Loyall. By James Otis [James Otis Kaler]. Fcap 8vo. Pp. 109. [Kirk's *Supp.*] Boston, 1895

F

FABIAN'S Tower; a novel. By the author of *Smugglers and foresters* [Mary Rosa Stewart Kettle]. In 3 vols. Fcap 8vo.   London, 1852
   In later works, the authoress gives her name as Rosa Mackenzie Kettle.

FABIOLA; or, the Church of the catacombs. [By Nicholas Patrick Wiseman, Cardinal.] 8vo. [Gillow's *Bibl. Dict.*, vol. 5, p. 588.]   London, 1855
   Often reprinted. The title in some editions is "Fabiola; a tale of the Catacombs."

FABLE (the) of Ovid, treting of Narcissus, translated out of Latin into Englysh Mytre, with a moral ther unto, very pleasante to rede. [By Thomas Howell.] 4to. B.L. No pagination. [*Brit. Mus.*] London, 1560
   Signed "T. H."

FABLE (the) of Phaeton, translated from Ovid [into English verse. By Mrs Elizabeth Pipe Wolferstan]. 8vo. [*Brit. Mus.*]   London, 1828

FABLE (the) of the bees: or, private vices, publick benefits. The second edition, enlarged with many additions. As also an essay on charity-schools; and a search into the nature of society. [By Bernard de Mandeville, M.D.] 8vo. Pp. 437. [*D. N. B.*, vol. 36, p. 21.]   London, 1723

FABLE (the) of the sacred phœnix; or, of Prelacy revived from the ashes of its funerals [by Simon Couper], briefly examin'd and refuted. By the author of the *Funeral of Prelacy* [Robert Whyte, of Banochy, advocate]. 4to. [*Adv. Lib.*]   N.P., 1704

FABLE (a) of the widow and her cat. [By Matthew Prior and Jonathan Swift, D.D.] Folio. [Broadside.] [*Bodl.*]   London, 1711

FABLES. By George Washington Æsop [J— E. Cornewall Lewis]. 4to. Pp. 54. [*Brit. Mus.*] London, [1885]

FABLES, antient and modern, adapted for the use of children from three to eight years of age. By Edward Baldwin, Esq. [William Godwin]. 12mo. [*Adv. Lib.*]   London, 1821

FABLES for five years old. [By John Hookham Frere.] Pt 8vo. [*D. N. B.*, vol. 20, p. 269.]   Malta, 1830

FABLES for grown gentlemen; for the year 1770. [By John Hall-Stevenson.] [Part II.] 4to. Pp. 56. [*Brit. Mus.*]   London, 1770

FABLES for grown gentlemen; or, a fable for every day in the week. [By John Hall-Stevenson.] 4to. Pp. 40. [Nichols' *Lit. Anec.*, iii., 86.]   London, 1761

FABLES for little folk. By Leal [E— Disosway]. 8vo. [Cushing's *Init. and Pseud.*, vol. i., p. 170.] New York, 1871

FABLES for the female sex. [By Edward Moore and H. Brooke, in verse.] 8vo. [*Brit. Mus.*]   London, 1744

FABLES for the Holy Alliance, Rhymes on the road, &c. By Thomas Brown, the younger, secretary of the Pococurante Society; and author of *The Fudge family*, and the *Two-penny post-bag* [Thomas Moore]. New edition. Fcap 8vo. Pp. xiv., 200. [*D.N.B.*, vol. 38, p. 382.] London, 1823

FABLES from [Jean de] La Fontaine, in English verse. [By John Matthews, M.D., of Belmont, Herefordshire.] 8vo.   London, 1820
   See also below, "Fables of La Fontaine."

FABLES in verse, and other pieces. By J. B. B. [J— B. Ballantyne]. Fcap 8vo.   Edinburgh, 1859

FABLES, moral and political; with large explications: translated from the Dutch [of John De Witt]. 2 vols. 8vo. [*W.*]   London, 1703

FABLES of Æsop and others; newly done into English, with an application to each fable. [By Samuel Croxall, D.D.] 8vo. [*D. N. B.*, vol. 13, p. 247.]   London, 1722
   Some later editions bear the translator's name.

FABLES (the) of Æsop; with the moral reflexions of Monsieur Baudoin. Translated from the French [by John Toland]. To which is prefix'd, by another hand, the true life of Æsop, by Monsieur de Meziriac. 8vo. [Watt's *Bibl. Brit.*]   London, 1704

FABLES of flowers for the female sex; with Zephyrus and Flora, a vision. By the author of *Choice emblems for youth* [John Huddlestone Wynne, printer]. 12mo. [Watt's *Bibl. Brit.*]   London, 1781

FABLES (the) of [Jean de] La Fontaine; translated into English verse. By G. W. T. [George Walter Thornbury]. 4to.   London, 1867
   See also above, "Fables from La Fontaine."

FABLES of the élite. By Dorothy
Dix [Elizabeth M. Gilmer]. Fcap
8vo. [*Amer. Cat.*] New York, 1902

FABLES of the hotel profession, and
poems of good cheer. By Charles
Martyn [J— Elliott Lane]. Fcap
8vo. [*Amer. Cat.*] New York, 1904

FABLIAUX, or tales : with a preface
and notes. By G. E. [George Ellis].
8vo. [Cushing's *Init. and Pseud.*,
vol. ii., p. 47.] London, 1796

FABRICIUS ; or, letters to the people
of Great Britain, on the absurdity and
mischief of defensive operations only,
in the American War, and on the
failure in the Southern operations.
[By Joseph Galloway.] 8vo. [Rich's
Bibl. Amer., i., 336.] London, 1782

FABRICK (the) of the eye, and the
several disorders which injure or
destroy the sight, explained. . . . [By
Sir John Hill, M.D.] 8vo. [*D. N. B.*,
vol. 26, p. 399.] London, 1758

FABRICS ; a story of to-day. By M.
Emilkroob [Martha Downe Tolman].
Fcap 8vo. [Kirk's *Supp.*]
New York, 1871

FABULOUS (the) foundation of the
Popedom ; or a familiar conference
between two friends to the truth,
Philalethes and Orthologos, shewing
that it cannot be proved that Peter
was ever at Rome. . . . [By Richard
Bernard, M.A., rector of Batcombe.]
4to. [Green's *Bibl. Somers.*, vol. ii.,
p. 167.] Oxford, 1619

FACA ; an army memoir. By Major
March [Orlando Bolivar Willcox].
8vo. [Cushing's *Init. and Pseud.*,
vol. ii., p. 95.] Boston, 1857

FACE (the) and the mask. By Luke
Sharp [Robert Barr]. Fcap 8vo.
[*Lond. Lib. Cat.*] London, 1895

FACE (a) in the flash-light ; a novel.
By Florence Warden [Florence Alice
Price, later Mrs George E. James].
Cr 8vo. [*Brit. Mus.*] London, 1906

FACE (the) of the deep ; a devotional
commentary on the Apocalypse. [By
Christina G. Rossetti.] Cr 8vo.
London, 1892
Later editions bear the name of the
authoress.

FACES about ; or recrimination charged
upon Mr John Goodwin in the point
of fighting against God and opposing
the way of Christ and justification
of the Presbyterian way. . . . [By
William Prynne.] 4to. [*Brit. Mus.*]
[London], 1644

FACES (the) in the fire ; a story for
the [Christmas] season. By Redgap
[George Frederick Pardon]. Fcap
8vo. [*D. N. B.*, vol. 43, p. 202.]
London, [1849]
Mistakenly ascribed to G. P. R. James.

FACETIÆ. " Musarum deliciæ : or
the Muses recreation, conteining
several pieces of poetique wit," by
Sr. J. M. [Sir John Mennis] and
Ja. S. [James Smith], 1656, and
" Wit restor'd in severall select poems,
not formerly publish't," 1658. Also
" Wits recreations, selected from the
finest fancies of moderne muses, with
A thousand out-landish proverbs [by
George Herbert]." Printed from edi-
tion 1640. . . . To which are now
added Memoirs of Sir John Mennis
and Dr James Smith, with a preface.
[Edited by Thomas Park and Edward
Dubois.] 2 vols. 8vo. [Lowndes'
Bibl. Man.] London, 1817

FACETIAE Cantabrigienses ; consisting of anecdotes, etc., by or relating
to celebrated Cantabs. By Socius
[Richard Gooch]. Fcap 8vo. [*Brit.
Mus.*] London, 1825

FACT and fable. . . . By Effie Johnson
[Mrs Euphemia Johnson Richmond].
8vo. Pp. 117. [*Lond. Lib. Cat.*]
London, 1901

FACT and fancy : humorous poems.
By Cupid Jones [Francis S. Saltus].
8vo. [Cushing's *Init. and Pseud.*,
vol. i., p. 143.] New York, 1895

FACTA non verba ; a comparison
between the good works performed by
the ladies in Roman Catholic convents
in England, and the unfettered efforts
of their Protestant sisters. By the
author of *Contrasts* [William Gilbert].
8vo. Pp. 347. [*D. N. B.*, First Supp.,
vol. ii., p. 280.] London, 1874

FACTION detected. [By Alexander
Carlyle, D.D.] 8vo. [*Autobiography*,
p. 448.] [London, 1763]

FACTION detected, by the evidence of
facts : containing an impartial view
of parties at home, and affairs abroad.
[By John Perceval, 2d Earl of
Egmont.] Third edition. 8vo. Pp.
175. London, 1743
Sometimes ascribed to William Pulteney,
Earl of Bath. The Faction was composed
of Sir Francis Burdett and his associates.

FACTION display'd ; a poem. [By
William Shippen, M.P.] From a
correct copy. Fcap 4to. Pp. 24.
London, 1704
Said to be " from a correct copy," to
distinguish it from a counterfeit edition

previously published, " printed in old letter, hardly legible, and full of errors." [*Adv. Lib.*]

Ascribed also to Daniel Defoe. Entered, with a query, in Lowndes' list of Defoe's works.

FACTION'S overthrow ; or more fair warning and good advice to the nobility, gentry, and commonalty of Ireland. [By John Gast.] 8vo. [*Camb. Univ. Lib.*]   Dublin, 1755
    Signed " J. G."

FACTS addressed to the landholders, stockholders . . . tradesmen, proprietors of every description, and generally to all the subjects of Great Britain and Ireland. [By John Horne Tooke and Richard Price.] 8vo. Pp. 117. [*Brit. Mus.*]   London, [1780]

FACTS and arguments against the election of General Caro. By an Anti-Abolitionist [Russell Jarvis]. 8vo. [Cushing's *Init. and Pseud.*, vol. i., p. 16.]   New York, 1848

FACTS and comments bearing on Mr Morgan's Burials Bill. By G. V. [Gilbert Venables]. 8vo. [Cushing's *Init. and Pseud.*, vol. i., p. 291.]
                                London, 1873

FACTS and documents showing the alarming state of the diocese of Oxford. By a senior clergyman of the diocese [Charles Pourtales Golightly, M.A.]. 8vo. [*D. N. B.*, vol. 22, p. 100.]
                                Oxford, 1859
    This pamphlet called special attention to practices in Cuddesdon College.

FACTS and evidences on the subject of baptism, in three letters to a deacon of a Baptist church ; with an introduction. . . . By the editor of Calmet's *Dictionary of the Bible* [Charles Taylor]. 8vo. [*Brit. Mus.*]
                                London, 1815

FACTS and experiments on the use of sugar in feeding cattle ; with hints for the cultivation of waste lands, and for improving the condition of the lower classes of peasantry in Great Britain and Ireland. [By B. Orson.] 8vo. [*W.*]   London, 1809

FACTS and fallacies relative to Scottish churches and schools : twelve tracts for the times. . . . By " Free Lance," author of *The future Church of Scotland*, etc. [Alexander Richardson, journalist]. 8vo. Pp. vi., 192. [*Adv. Lib.*]   Edinburgh, 1871

FACTS and fancies, from the Koran, the Doctors, etc. By A. N. Mount Rose [Alexander Hay Japp]. 8vo. Pp. 85. [*D. N. B.*, Second Supp., vol. 2, p. 363.]   London, 1899

FACTS and fancies, in prose and verse. By Jenny Wren [Jane Atkinson]. 8vo. [Cushing's *Init. and Pseud.*, vol. i., p. 310.]   London, 1864

FACTS and fancies of salmon fishing with original illustrations. By Clericus, author of *Rambles and recollections of a fly-fisher* [Rev. William Cartwright]. 8vo. Pp. 271. [Cushing's *Init. and Pseud.*, i., 63.]
                                London, 1874

FACTS and figures from Italy. By Don Jeremy Savonarola, Benedictine monk [Francis Sylvester Mahony], addressed during the last two winters to Charles Dickens, Esq. ; being an appendix to his " Pictures." Fcap 8vo. Pp. 309. [*Olphar Hamst*, p. 112.]
                                London, 1847

FACTS and figures in favour of the proposed Manchester Ship Canal. By Mancuniensis [James W. Harvey]. 8vo. [*Brit. Mus.*]   Manchester, 1882
    See also " The Proposed Manchester Ship Canal."

FACTS and observations relating to the Temple Church and the monuments contained in it. [By Joseph Jekyll, M.A., M.P.]   4to.   [Watt's *Bibl. Brit.*]   London, 1811

FACTS and observations relative to the coinage and circulation of counterfeit or base money, with suggestions for remedying the evil. [By George Chalmers.] 8vo. [*Brit. Mus.*]
                                London, 1795

FACTS and phases of ancient and modern sex worship, as illustrated chiefly in the religions of India. . . . [By Hargrave Jennings ?] Cr 8vo.
                                London, [1860 ?]

FACTS and reflections connected with the Indian Rebellion. [By Edward Williams, an Indian Judge.] Cr 8vo. Private print.   Liverpool, 1859

FACTS and tracts in evidence of the apathy, dereliction, and degradation of the national clergy. By the incumbent of Wormegay and Tottenhill, Norfolk [William Henry Henslowe]. 8vo. [*Brit. Mus.*]
                                London, 1844

FACTS and useful hints relating to fishing and shooting ; with a great variety of useful recipes of all kinds. Edited by I. E. B. C. [Irvine E. B. Cox]. Cr 8vo. [*Brit. Mus.*]
                                London, 1866

FACTS (the) as they are ; or a comparison of certain statements recently made in Cambridge, by the Rev. Dr Candlish, and others, in behalf of the Free Church of Scotland, with Acts of Parliament and ecclesiastical documents of the Scottish Presbyterian Church. By a member of the University of Cambridge [Rev. Edward John Nixon, chaplain to the London Hospital]. 8vo. [Darling's *Cyclop. Bibl.*]   Cambridge, 1844

FACTS designed to exhibit the real character and tendency of the American Colonization Society. By Clericus [George Smith]. 8vo. [Cushing's *Init. and Pseud.*, i., 63.]   Liverpool, 1833

FACTS, figures, and fancies. [By Rev. Charles Lutwidge Dodgson, M.A.] 8vo.   Oxford, 1874

FACTS for the laboring man. By a laboring man [Thomas Robinson Hazard]. 8vo. [Allibone's *Dict.*]
      Newport, Rhode Island, 1840

FACTS from Ulster. By an Irish tenant [Miss —— Roberts]. 8vo.
      Belfast, [1888]

FACTS illustrative of the treatment of Napoleon Buonaparte in Saint Helena. . . . [By Theodore E— Hook.] 8vo. [*Brit. Mus.*]   London, 1819

FACTS, not falsehoods ; or a plain defence of the Church of Scotland, suited to the times. By a parish minister [Lawrence Lockhart, D.D.]. 8vo. Pp. iv., 52. [Scott's *Fasti.*]
      Edinburgh, 1845

FACTS of importance relative to the present state of Great Britain. [By David Wakefield.] 8vo. [*W.*]
      London, 1800

" FACTS on a thread of fiction." In prison and out. By Hesba Stretton, author of *Jessica's first prayer*, etc. [Sarah Smith]. 8vo. Pp. vii., 208.
      London, 1880

  See note to " Alone in London."

FACTS on nuns and nunneries. [By A— H. Guinness.] 8vo.
      [London], N.D.

FACTS, reflections, and queries, submitted to the consideration of the Associated Friends of the People. [By Rev. —— Heron.] 8vo. Pp. 46.
      Edinburgh, 1792

  The author's name is in handwriting of Dr Hugh Blair.

FACTS relating to the capture of Washington. . . . By an officer serving as Quarter-Master General [Sir George De Lacy Evans]. 8vo. Pp. 20. [Cushing's *Init. and Pseud.*, vol. i., p. 209.]   London, 1829

FACTS tending to show the beneficial effects of spreading religious knowledge by means of the Holy Scriptures, &c. [By Sarah Fry.] Fcap 8vo. [Smith's *Cat. of Friends' Books*, i., 823.]   N.P., 1826

FACTS without fiction. By the author of *Thoughts upon thought*, etc. [John Grigg Hewlett, Ph.D., D.D.]. 8vo. Pp. xv., 327. [*Brit. Mus.*]
      London, 1854

FACULTIES (the) of birds. [By James Rennie, M.A.] 12mo. Pp. xvi., 338. [*Brit. Mus.*]   London, 1835
  Library of entertaining knowledge.

FACULTIES (the) of the lower animals, and their claims on man ; a lecture delivered before the Durham Athenæum. [By A. R. Fausset.] Fcap 8vo. [*Brit. Mus.*]   London, 1858

FADETTE. By George Sand [Madame Amandine L. A. Dudevant] : translated. 8vo. [Cushing's *Init. and Pseud.*, i., 260.]   New York, 1893

FADING flowers. By Meta Lander [Mrs Margarette Lawrence, *née* Woods]. 8vo. [Cushing's *Init. and Pseud.*, i., 164.]   Boston, 1860

FAG-ENDS. By Bêbi [John Joseph Stephenson]. Fcap 8vo. [*Camb. Univ. Lib.*]   Cambridge, 1875

FAGGING : is it hopelessly inseparable from the discipline of a public school ? [By Rev. Frederic Wickham.] 8vo. Pp. 28.   London, 1847

FAGGOT (a) of French sticks. By the author of *Bubbles from the Brunnens of Nassau* [Sir Francis Bond Head, Bart.]. 2 vols. Fcap 8vo. [*Brit. Mus.*]   London, 1852
  The third edition gives the author's name.

FAGOT (a) from the Coliseum. By a Bostonian [William Boott]. 8vo. [Cushing's *Init. and Pseud.*, i., 38.]
      Boston, 1869

FAIENCE (the) violin ; from the French of Champfleury [Jules François Félix Fleury]. Fcap 8vo. [Cushing's *Init. and Pseud.*, i., 54.]
      New York, 1895

FAILURE (a). By " Karl " [Charles Bloomingdale, jun.]. Fcap 8vo. [*Amer. Cat.*]   Philadelphia, 1904

FAILURE (the) of Lord Curzon ; a study in " Imperialism." An open letter to the Earl of Rosebery. By " Twenty - eight years in India " [Charles James O'Donnell]. 8vo. Pp. 120. [*Brit. Mus.*]   London, 1903

FAILURE (the) of the Churches. By a Churchman [John Abbey]. Pt 8vo. Pp. 175.   London, 1903

FAILURE of the Reformation in Ireland. By a Protestant layman [William Harris, M.D.]. 8vo.
Dublin, 1837

FAINT (a) sketch of the life, character, and manners of the late Mr [Richard] Nash [" Beau Nash." By William Oliver, M.D.]. 4to. [Green's *Bibl. Somers.*, i., 371.]   Bath, 1761

FAINT yet pursuing ; thirty-two homiletical thoughts. By the author of *How to be happy though married* [Rev. Edward John Hardy, M.A.]. 8vo. [*Brit. Mus.*]   London, 1889

FAIR and false. By Bertha M. Clay [Mrs Charlotte M. Braeme, *née* Law]. 8vo.   London, 1884

FAIR and free. [A novel.] By the author of *A modern Greek heroine* [Henry Cresswell]. 8vo. [*Brit. Mus.*]
London, 1882

FAIR (a) and impartial account of the debate in the Synod of Glasgow and Air, 6th October 1748, anent employing Mr Whitefield. [By John Erskine, D.D.] 8vo. [Memoir prefixed to Erskine's *Theol. Dissertations.*]   Edinburgh, 1748

FAIR (a) and methodical discussion of the first and great controversy between the Church of England and the Church of Rome, concerning the infallible guide ; in three discourses. . . . [By George Hooper, D.D.] 4to. Pp. 138. [Wood's *Athen. Oxon.*, iv., 642.]
London, 1689
The third discourse was never published.

FAIR (a), candid, and impartial statement of the case between Sir Isaac Newton and Mr Hutchinson. [By George Horne, D.D., Bishop of Norwich.] 8vo. [*D. N. B.*, vol. 27, p. 356.]   London, 1753

FAIR Catherine. [A novel.] By Darley Dale [Francesca M. Steele]. 3 vols. Pt 8vo. [*Lond. Lib. Cat.*]
London, 1885

FAIR (the) Circassian ; a dramatic performance ; done from the original by a Gentleman-Commoner of Oxford. [By Samuel Croxall, D.D.] 4to. Title, dedication and preface, 6 leaves, pp. 28. [*D. N. B.*, vol. 13, p. 248.]
London, 1720
Several other editions followed. " A licentious versification of the Song of Soloman, frequently reprinted in 12mo " (Lowndes). The dedication to Mrs Anna Maria Mordaunt is signed " R. D."

FAIR (the) Circassian ; a tragedy. . . . By the author of *Sympathy ; a poem* [Samuel Jackson Pratt]. 8vo. Pp. ii., 75. [*Biog. Dram.*] London, 1781

FAIR (a) country maid. [A novel.] By E. Fairfax Byrnne [Miss —— Brooke]. 3 vols. Cr 8vo. [O'Donoghue's *Poets of Ireland*, new ed., p. 52.]
London, 1885

FAIR (a) deceiver. By George Paston [Emily M. Symonds]. Pt 8vo. [*Brit. Mus.*]   London, 1898

FAIR Dianas. By " Wanderer " [Elim H. D'Avigdor], author of *Across country*. 8vo. [*Lond. Lib. Cat.*]
London, 1878

FAIR Else, Duke Ulrich, and other tales. By the author of *Mademoiselle Mori*, etc. [Margaret Roberts]. With original illustrations. 8vo. Pp. vi., 369. [*Brit. Mus.*] London, [1877]

FAIR France ; impressions of a traveller. By the author of *John Halifax, Gentleman*, etc. [Dinah Maria Mulock, later Mrs Craik]. 8vo. Pp. 317. [*Brit. Mus.*]   London, 1871

FAIR (the) haven : a work in defence of the miraculous element of our Lord's ministry upon earth. By the late John Pickard Owen. With a memoir by William Bickersteth Owen [Samuel Butler]. 8vo.   London, 1873
The second edition, published in the same year, has the author's name.

FAIR (the) Hebrew. [By Mrs Eliza Haywood.] 8vo. [*D. N. B.*, vol. 25, p. 315.]   London, 1729

FAIR (a) impostor ; a story of Exmoor. By Alan St Aubyn [Mrs Frances Marshall]. 8vo. [*Lond. Lib. Cat.*]
London, 1898

FAIR (the) Isabel of Cotehele ; a Cornish romance, in six cantos. By the author of *Local attachment*, and translator of Theocritus [Rev. Richard Polwhele]. Fcap 8vo. Pp. 376.   London, 1815
One of the copies in the Dyce collection is a presentation copy with the author's autograph.

FAIR (the) maid of the Exchange ; a comedy. [By Thomas Heywood, dramatist.] 4to. [Watt's *Bibl. Brit.*]
London, 1607

FAIR (the) Mississippian. By Charles Egbert Craddock [Mary Noailles Murfree]. Cr 8vo. [*Amer. Cat.*]
Boston, 1908

FAIR (the) moralist. . . . By a gentlewoman [Mrs Charlotte MacCarthy]. Fcap 8vo. [*Brit. Mus.*]   Dublin, 1745

FAIR (the) mystery. By Bertha M. Clay [Mrs Charlotte M. Braeme]. Fcap 8vo.   New York, 1886

FAIR (the) of Mayfair. [By Mrs Catherine Grace Gore.] 3 vols. Fcap 8vo. [*Adv. Lib.*]   London, 1832

FAIR (the) one of Tunis ; or, the generous mistres ; a new piece of gallantry. Out of French. [By Charles Cotton.] 8vo. Pp. 310. [*N. and Q.*, 6 Jan. 1866, p. 15.]   London, 1674

FAIR (a) philosopher. By Henri Daugé [Mrs E. H. Hammond]. 8vo. [Cushing's *Init. and Pseud.*, vol. i., p. 78.]   New York, 1882

FAIR (a) prisoner ; a story of the Great Year. By Morice Gerard [John Jessop Teague]. 8vo. Pp. 319. [*Brit. Mus.*]   London, [1912]

FAIR (the) Puritan ; a historical romance of the days of witchcraft. By Frank Forester [Henry William Herbert]. Pt 8vo. [*Lond. Lib. Cat.*]   Philadelphia, 1890

FAIR (the) Quaker of Deal ; or, the humours of the navy : a comedy. [By Charles Shadwell.] 4to. Pp. ii., 65. [Dyce *Cat.*, ii., 282.]   London, 1710
The epistle dedicatory is signed " C. S."

FAIR (a) refugee. [A novel.] By Morice Gerard [John Jessop Teague, M.A.]. 8vo. Pp. 251. [*Lit. Year Book.*]   London, 1917

FAIR Rosamond. [An opera, in three parts, and in verse. By Joseph Addison]. 8vo. [*D. N. B.*, vol. i, p. 131.]   London, 1707

FAIR Rosamond ; a comedy drama, in four acts [and in verse]. By John Winspere [Rev. Vincent John Leatherdale, M.A.]. 8vo. Pp. 56.   London, [1882]

FAIR Rosamond, and other poems. By M. R. [Montgomerie Ranking]. 8vo. [Cushing's *Init. and Pseud.*, vol. i., p. 245.]   London, 1868

FAIR Rosamund. [A drama.] By Michael Field [Catherine Harris Bradley, and Edith E. Cooper]. 8vo. Pp. 75. [*Lond. Lib. Cat.*]   London, 1897

FAIR Rosamund. By the author of *Dr Palmer's patient* [G. P. Smith]. 8vo.   London, 1906

FAIR (the) Syrian ; a novel. By the author of *Mount Henneth*, etc. [Robert Bage]. 2 vols. Fcap 8vo. [*Watt's Bibl. Brit.*]   London, 1787

FAIR (the) villager ; a tale : with other miscellaneous poems. [By Joseph Pott.] 4to. [*Camb. Univ. Lib.*]   London, 1776

FAIR warning ; or, twenty-five reasons against toleration and indulgence of Popery. [By Richard Baxter.] With the Archbishop of Canterbury's letter to the King [Charles II.]. 4to.   London, 1662

FAIR (a) way with the Dissenters and their patrons. Not writ by Mr L—y [Lesley], or any other furious Jacobite, whether clergyman or layman ; but by a very moderate person and dutiful subject to the Queen [Mrs Mary Astell]. 4to. [*Brit. Mus.*]   London, 1704

FAIR women. By Mrs Forrester [Mrs —— Bridges]. 3 vols. Fcap 8vo. [*Amer. Cat.*]   New York, 1886

FAIRE Damzell. [A novel.] By Esmé Stuart [Amélie Claire Leroy]. 3 vols. 8vo. [*Lond. Lib. Cat.*]   London, 1892 [?]

FAIRE Emme, the miller's daughter of Manchester ; with the Love of William the Conqueror. [Attributed to Robert Greene, by Winstanley.] 4to.   London, 1631

FAIRE (a) warning, to take heed of the Scottish discipline, as being of all others most injurious to the civill magistrate, most oppressive to the subject, most pernicious to both. [By John Bramhall, D.D.] 4to. Pp. 36. [*Works* (Anglo-Cath. Lib.).]   N.P., 1649

Another edition appeared in the same year, with the author's name.

FAIRE-VIRTVE, the mistresse of Phil'arete. Written by him-selfe. [By George Wither.] 8vo. No pagination. [*Bodl.*]   London, 1622

FAIRIES (the) ; an opera : taken from A midsummer night's dream, written by Shakespear. The songs from Shakespear, Milton, Waller, Dryden, Lansdown, Hammond, etc. [By David Garrick.] The music composed by Mr Smith. 8vo.   London, 1755

FAIRY (the) book : the best popular fairy stories selected and rendered anew. By the author of *John Halifax, Gentleman* [Dinah Maria Mulock, later Mrs Craik]. 8vo. Pp. x., 368. [*Brit. Mus.*]   London, 1870

FAIRY (the) bower, or the history of a month ; a tale for young people. [By Mrs Harriet Mozley.] 8vo. Pp. 386. [*Bodl.*]   London, 1841

FAIRY (the) cup of Kirk Malew, Isle of Man. . . . [By Michael Aislabie Denham.] 8vo. [*Brit. Mus.*]   [Durham, 1849]

Signed " M. A. D." Only 50 copies printed.

FAIRY egg, and what it held. By three friends [H. H. Weston, C— Clark, and L— Gibbons]. 8vo. [Cushing's *Init. and Pseud.*, i., 283.]
Boston, 1870

FAIRY fables. By Cuthbert Bede, B.A. [Edward Bradley]. With illustrations by Alfred Crowquill [Alfred Henry Forrester]. 8vo. Pp. vii., 238. [*D. N. B.*, vol. 20, p. 6.]
London, [1857]

FAIRY (the) family : a series of ballads & metrical tales illustrating the fairy mythology of Europe. [By Archibald Maclaren.] 8vo. Pp. xv., 279. [*Adv. Lib.*]   London, 1857

FAIRY (the) favour ; a masque. [By Thomas Hull.] 8vo. Pp. 29. [Dyce *Cat.*, i., 418.]   London, 1766

FAIRY favours ; with other tales. By E. F. D. [E. F. Dagley]. Fcap 8vo. [*N. and Q.*, Feb. 1869, p. 168.]
London, 1825

FAIRY (the) feast ; written by the author of *A Tale of a Tub*, and *The Mully of Mountown* [*not* Jonathan Swift, but William King, D.C.L.]. Folio. Pp. 12. [*D. N. B.*, vol. 31, p. 162.]   London, 1704
Surreptitiously published.

FAIRY footsteps ; or, lessons from legends : with one hundred illustrations, designed by Alfred Crowquill [Alfred Henry Forrester]. 8vo. Pp. 188. [*D. N. B.*, vol. 20, p. 6.]
London, [1861]

FAIRY Frisket ; or, peeps at insect life. By A. L. O. E., author of *Fairy Know-a-bit*, etc. [Charlotte Maria Tucker]. 8vo. Pp. 196.
London, 1874

FAIRY (the) godmothers ; and other tales. By Aunt Judy [Mrs Margaret Scott Gatty]. 8vo. [*Brit. Mus.*]
London, 1851

FAIRY gold. By Henry Hayes [Mrs Ellen Warner Kirk, *née* Olney]. Fcap 8vo. [Kirk's *Supp.*, p. 956.]
Boston, 1886

FAIRY (a) in the pigskin. By G. G. [H— G. Harper]. Cr 8vo. Pp. 234. [*Brit. Mus.*]   London, 1904

FAIRY (the) in the spider's web. By A. L. O. E. [Charlotte Maria Tucker]. 8vo. Pp. 222.   London, 1887

FAIRY Know-a-bit ; or, a nutshell of knowledge. By A. L. O. E., author of *The Shepherd of Bethlehem*, etc. [Charlotte Maria Tucker]. 8vo. Pp. 196.   London, 1868

FAIRY legends and traditions of the South of Ireland. [By Thomas Crofton Croker.] 8vo.   London, 1825
Parts 2 and 3, published in 1828, have the author's name.

FAIRY (the) mythology. [By Thomas Keightley.] 2 vols. 8vo. [*D. N. B.*, vol. 30, p. 307.]   London, 1828
Preface signed " T. K." *See also* title of the author's work, " The mythology of ancient Greece and Italy." An edition was issued in 1850, with the name of the author.

FAIRY nightcaps. By Aunt Fanny, author of the six *Nightcap books* [Mrs Fanny Barrow]. 8vo. Pp. viii., 211. [Cushing's *Init. and Pseud.*, i., 98.]   Edinburgh, 1868

FAIRY (the) of misfortune ; or, the loves of Octar and Zulima ; an Eastern tale. Translated from the French [by Edward Dubois], the author of *A piece of family biography*. Fcap 8vo.
London, 1799

FAIRY (the) of the Alps ; a novel, translated from the German of E. Werner [Elizabeth Bürstenbinder]. Pt 8vo. Pp. 285. [Cushing's *Init. and Pseud.*, i., 305.]   New York, 1889

FAIRY (the) prince ; a masque [in three parts, and in verse. By George Colman, the elder]. 8vo. [*Biog. Dram.*]   London, 1771

FAIRY (the) spectator ; or, the invisible monitor. By Mrs Teachwell and her family [Lady Eleanor Fenn]. Fcap 8vo. Pp. 83. [*Brit. Mus.*]
London, [1788]
The dedication is signed " E— F—."

FAIRY (the) stepmother ; a story. By Esca Gray [Mrs Frances A. Adamson]. Pt 8vo. Pp. 76. [*Brit. Mus.*]
London, 1897

FAIRY (a) tale, entitled " John and Henry." By Abihu Baracle [William Brown, Dunfermline]. 8vo. Pp. 47. [Beveridge's *Dunf. Bibl.*]
Dunfermline, [1900]

FAIRY (a) tale ; in two acts, taken from Shakespeare. [By David Garrick.] 8vo. [*Brit. Mus.*]
London, 1763
As to Colman's share in the above, *see Biog. Dram.*, *s.v.* Midsummer night's dream.

FAIRY tales. By Holm Lee [Harriet Parr]. 8vo. [*Lond. Lib. Cat.*]
London, 1891

FAIRY tales. By Lillian [Mrs F— G— Lawford]. 8vo.   London, 1906

FAIRY tales, comprising Patty and her pitcher, Tiny and her vanity, The giant and the dwarf, The selfish man, Peter and his goose, The giant hands. Written and illustrated by Alfred Crowquill [Alfred Henry Forrester]. 8vo. [*D. N. B.*, vol. 20, p. 6.]
London, 1857

Each tale has a separate pagination.

FAIRY tales, far and near : retold by Q. [Sir Arthur T. Quiller-Couch]. 8vo. Pp. 192. [*Brit. Mus.*] London, 1895

FAIRY tales from Bible story. By a country clergyman [Rev. Sherard Montagu Statham]. Fcap 8vo.
London, 1918

FAIRY tales from the birth-stories of Buddha. By Theo. Gift [Theodora Havers, later Mrs Boulger]. 4to. [*Lond. Lib. Cat.*] London, 1892

FAIRY tales, in verse. [By Mrs Elizabeth Pipe Wolferstan.] 8vo. [*Brit. Mus.*] London, 1830

FAIRY tales that mother told. [By Mrs Craik, *née* Dinah M. Mulock.] Pt. 8vo. London, 1915

FAITH ; a poem. [By Robert Nugent Craggs, Earl Nugent.] 4to. [*Bodl.*]
London, 1774

In *Gent. Mag.*, June 1774, p. 276, there is reviewed a work with the same title as above, published by Becket. 4to. It is said to be by Lord Viscount Clare.

FAITH (the) and belief of every sincere Christian proved by reference to various texts of Holy Scripture. [By F. Capper.] Fcap 8vo. [*Brit. Mus.*]
Ipswich, [1829]

FAITH (the) and doctrine of the Roman Catholic Church, proved by the testimony of the most learned Protestants. [By the Hon. William Talbot : with a preface by Dr John Lingard.] Fcap 8vo. [*D. N. B.*, vol. 33, p. 323.]
Dublin, 1813

FAITH (the) and practice of a Church of England-man. [By William Stanley, D.D., Dean of St. Asaph.] Fcap 8vo. Pp. 198. [Watt's *Bibl. Brit.*]
London, 1688

Reprinted in 1807, with an account of the author. Other editions have followed.

FAITH and unfaith. By the author of *Phyllis* [Mrs Argles, later Mrs Hungerford, *née* Margaret C. Hamilton]. 3 vols. Cr 8vo. [*Brit. Mus.*]
London, 1881

FAITH and works, and Canon and truth. By W. H. D—y [W— H— Darby ?]. Fcap 8vo. [*Brit. Mus.*]
London, [1859]

FAITH (the) and works of Christian Science. By the writer of *Confessio Medici* [Stephen Paget, M.D.]. Cr 8vo. Pp. 254. [*Lond. Lib. Cat.*]
London, 1909

FAITH (the) by which we are justified, in Scripture-sense : according to Scripture, opened, explained, and applied, on Rom. 5. 1. In six sermons. [By George Bright, D.D., Dean of St Asaph.] 4to. Pp. 78. [*Bodl.*]
London, 1695

Attributed also to Thomas Beverley.

FAITH Gartney's girlhood. By the author of *The Gayworthys*, etc. [Mrs Adelina D. Whitney, *née* Train]. New edition. 8vo. Pp. viii., 355. [*Adv. Lib.*] London, 1866

Preface signed " A. D. T. W."

FAITH, hope, and charity. By an old author [Daniel Puseley]. 8vo. [*D. N. B.*, vol. 47, p. 53.]
London, 1863

FAITH, hope, and charity. . . . [A story.] By Anna Lisle [Annabella Crawford]. 8vo. Pp. v., 503. [*Brit. Mus.*]
London, 1882

FAITH, hope, and charity : a novel of the graces. By John Le Breton [M— Harte-Potts and T— Murray Ford]. 8vo. Pp. 288. [*Brit. Mus.*]
London, 1897

FAITH, in five fundamentall principles. By E. F. [Edward Fisher], a seeker after the truth. Fcap 8vo. [*D. N. B.*, vol. 19, p. 56.] London, 1650

FAITH (the) of a Christian. By a disciple [Bernard Lucas]. Cr 8vo. [*Brit. Mus.*] London, 1904

FAITH (the) of an Agnostic. By George Forester [Sir George G. Greenwood]. 8vo. [*Camb. Univ. Lib.*]
London, 1900

The edition of 1919 gives the author's name.

FAITH (the) of his fathers. By A. E. Jacomb [Agnes E. Jacomb Hood]. Cr 8vo. Pp. 314. [*Lond. Lib. Cat.*]
London, 1912

FAITH (the) of the Catholick Church concerning the Eucharist ; invincibly proved by the argument used against the Protestants in the books of the Faith of the perpetuity written by M. [Antoine] Arnaud : a translation from the French [of Paul Bruzeau]. 8vo. Pp. 184. [*Aberd. Lib.*]
Printed at Holy-Rood-House, 1687

FAITH (the) of the most unworthy servant of Jesus Christ concerning the Revelation. By R. S. [Robert Some ?]. 8vo. London, 1732

FAITH (the) of the true Christian, and the primitive Quakers faith ; or, religion according to sound reason and agreeable with Holy Writ, and such as every man may come to experience in himself : conformable to the new covenant brought and taught by Jesus Christ without the help of men made priests, who by all their learning know not God nor his Christ, but exclaim against the truth, and call that error, and error truth. [By William Bromfield.] 8vo. Pp. 182. [Bodl.]
N.P., 1725
Preface signed " W. B."
" This is wrote by Wm· Bromfield a favourite of K. James 11d· and inventor of the Copper Coyn in Ireland : he was a Quaker, and in this book gives some account of himself."—MS. note in the handwriting of Richard Rawlinson.

FAITH vindicated from possibility of falshood ; or, the immovable firmness and certainty of the motives to Christian faith, asserted against that tenet, which, denying infallibility of authority, subverts its foundation, and renders it vncertain. [By John Sergeant.] 8vo. Pp. 206. [Bodl.]   Lovain, 1667
Said by Barlow, in a MS. note, to be William.

FAITHFUL (a) account of Mr Archibald Bower's motives for leaving his office of secretary to the Court of Inquisition ; including also, a relation of the horrid treatment of an innocent gentleman, who was driven mad by his sufferings, in this bloudy court ; and of a nobleman who expired under his tortures : to both which inhuman and shocking scenes the author was an eye-witness ; with the difficulties he met with in escaping from thence. [Edited by Richard Barron.] 8vo. [W.]   London, 1750

FAITHFUL (a) account of some transactions, in the three last sessions of the present Convocation ; in a letter to a friend. [By Francis Atterbury, D.D.] 4to. [Arber's Term Cat., vol. iii., p. 28.]   London, 1702

FAITHFUL (a) account of what past in Convocation, Febr. the 19th. 170½ : in a second letter to a friend. [By Francis Atterbury, D.D.] 4to.
London, 1702

FAITHFUL (a) and full account of the surprising life and adventures of the celebrated Doctor Sartorius Sinegradibus [John Taylor]. 8vo.
Edinburgh, [1740]

FAITHFUL (a) appeal to parents on the education of their children. [By John St Clair.] Second edition. 8vo. [Adv. Lib.]   Glasgow, [1874]

FAITHFUL (the) bride of Granada ; a play. . . . [By William Taverner.] 4to. Pp. 60. [Brit. Mus.]
London, 1704

FAITHFUL (a) enquiry after the ancient and original doctrine of the Trinity. [By Isaac Watts, D.D.] 8vo. Pp. viii., 47. [D. N. B., vol. 60, p. 69.]
London, 1745
This treatise was withdrawn from circulation soon after being printed, but was reissued in 1816.

FAITHFUL (the) exposition of sound doctrine and ancient truths. By R. J. [Robert Jenison], Dr D.   4to. [Brit. Mus.]   Newcastle, 1649

FAITHFUL (the) few ; an ode inscribed to all lovers of their country. [By William Hamilton of Bangour.] 12mo.
Edinburgh, 1874
In his collected poems.

FAITHFUL in little ; a tale founded on fact. By M. H. [Matilda Horsburgh, later Mrs Douglas], author of The red velvet Bible. 8vo. [Brit. Mus.]   Edinburgh, 1873

FAITHFUL (a) narrative of a remarkable visitation. By a physician [John Rutty, M.D.]. Fcap 8vo. [Smith's Cat. of Friends' Books, ii., 522.]
London, 1776

FAITHFUL (a) narrative of the base and inhuman arts that were lately practised upon the brain of Habbakuk Hilding [Henry Fielding], Justice, Dealer, and Chapman, who now lies at his house in Covent Garden, in a deplorable state of lunacy, a dreadful monument of false friendship and delusion. By Alexander Drawcansir [Tobias George Smollett], fencingmaster and philomath. Fcap 8vo. Pp. 24. [D. N. B., vol. 53, p. 176.]
London, 1752

FAITHFUL (a) narrative of the conversion and death of Count Struensee, late Prime Minister of Denmark. By D. Munter. To which is added, the history of Count Enevold Brandt [by D— Hee] : the whole translated from the German. [By the Rev. Gobhardt F. A. Wendeborn.] 8vo. Pp. xii., 308. [Brit. Mus.]   London, 1773

FAITHFUL (a) narrative of the life and death of that holy and laborious preacher Mr John Machin, late of Astbury in the county of Chester. [By Henry Newcome, M.A.]   With a præfatory epistle thereunto, written by that excellent person Sir Charles Wolseley, Baronet. Fcap 8vo. Pp. 106. [Bodl.]   London, 1671

FAITHFUL (a) promise. By Brenda [Mrs —— Castle Smith, *née* Meyrick]. Cr 8vo. Pp. 128. [*Lond. Lib. Cat.*]
London, 1919

FAITHFUL (the) Promiser. By the author of *Morning and night watches* [John Ross MacDuff, D.D.]. Fcap 8vo. Pp. 128. Glasgow, [1883]

FAITHFUL (a) rebuke to a false Report [by Stephen Lobb]; lately dispersed in a letter to a friend in the country: concerning certain differences in doctrinals between some Dissenting ministers in London. [By Vincent Alsop.] 8vo. [*New Coll. Cat.*]
London, 1697

FAITHFUL records of visits to the sick and poor. [By Elizabeth Gilpin.] Fourth edition. 8vo. [*Smith's Cat. of Friends' Books*, i., 845.]
London, 1860

FAITHFUL (a) report of a genuine debate concerning the liberty of the press, addressed to a candidate at the ensuing election; wherein a sure and safe method is proposed of restraining the abuse of that liberty, without the least encroachment upon the rights and privileges of the subject. [By Francis Squire.] Fcap 8vo. Pp. 62. [*Green's Bibl. Somers.*, iii., 278.]
London, 1740
Later editions appeared in 1761, 1764.

FAITHFUL (a) report of the trial of Hurdy-Gurdy at the Bar of the Court of King's Bench. [A burlesque. By William Sampson, Irish barrister.] Fcap 8vo. Belfast, 1794
Reprinted at Dublin in the same year, under a different title. *See* "Report of the trial of the King. . . ."

FAITHFUL (the) shepherd, a dramatic pastoral, translated into English from the Pastor fido of the Cav. Guarini: attempted in the manner of the original. [By William Grove.] 8vo. [*Lowndes' Bibl. Man.*] London, 1782

FAITHFUL (a) testimony for God and my country: or, a retro-spective glass for the legislators, and the rest of the sons of the Church of England, (so called) who are found persecuting the innocent. [By Edward Billing.] 4to. [*Smith's Cat. of Friends' Books*, i., 269.] London, 1664
Signed " E. B."

FAITHFUL unto death. [A novel.] By Zandile [Frances Ellen Colenso, daughter of Bishop Colenso]. 8vo.
London, 1872 [?]

FAITHFULL (a) and seasonable advice; or, the necessity of a correspondencie for the advancement of the Protestant cause: humbly suggested

VOL. II.

to the Great Councell of England assembled in Parliament. [By Samuel Hartlib.] 4to. [Thomason *Coll. of Tracts*, vol. i., p. 231.] London, 1643

FAITHFULL (a) messenger sent after the Anti-nomians. [By Thomas Bakewell.] 4to. [Thomason *Coll. of Tracts*, vol. i., p. 317.] London, 1644

FAITHFULNESS (the) of God considered . . . or a second part of The Fulfilling of Scripture. [By Robert Fleming, senior.] 8vo. [*D. N. B.*, vol. 19, p. 285.] London, 1674
The title of the first part is more fully given later.

FAITHS (the) of the peoples. By Ernest Wilding [Joseph Fitzgerald Molloy]. 2 vols. 8vo. [O'Donoghue's *Poets of Ireland.*]
London, 1892

FAKEER (the) a tale. [By Richard Owen Cambridge.] 4to. Pp. 11. [Watt's *Bibl. Brit.*] London, 1756

FALCON (the). [A poem. By Alfred, Lord Tennyson.] 8vo. Pp. 34. [T. J. Wise's *Bibl. of Tennyson.*]
London, 1879

FALCON (the) family; or, Young Ireland. [By Marmion W. Savage, B.A.] 8vo. Pp. 348. [*Brit. Mus.*]
London, 1845

FALKENBURG; a tale of the Rhine. By the author of *Mildred Vernon*, etc. [Hamilton Murray]. 3 vols. 8vo. [*Adv. Lib.*] London, 1851

FALKLAND. [By Edward George Earle Lytton Bulwer-Lytton, Baron Lytton.] Fcap 8vo. Pp. ix., 264. [*Brit. Mus.*] London, 1827

FALKLANDS. By the author of *The Life of Sir Kenelm Digby* [Thomas Longueville]. 8vo. Pp. xiv., 194. [*Brit. Mus.*] London, 1897

FALKNER; a novel. By the author of *Frankenstein*, etc. [Mrs Mary W. Shelley]. 3 vols. Fcap 8vo. [Courtney's *Secrets*, p. 60.] London, 1837

FALL (the) and redemption of man. . . . By E. S. A. [Ernest Silvanus Appleyard]. Fcap 8vo. [*Brit. Mus.*]
London, [1861]

FALL in silver; the question discussed, and a fit remedy proposed. By a banker [J— Craddock]. 8vo. [*Calc. Imp. Lib.*] Calcutta, 1886
Signed " J. C."

FALL (the) of Babylon; or seasonable reflections on the novelties of Rome. [By Benjamin Woodroffe, D.D.] 4to. [Jones' Peck, p. 303.] London, 1690

FALL (the) of Bob; or, the oracle of gin. By Timothy Scrub, of Rag Fair, Esq. [John Kelly]. Fcap 8vo. [*Biog. Dram.*] N.P., 1736

R

FALL (the) of Lord Paddockslea. By Lionel Langton [Llewellyn Archer Atherley-Jones, K.C., M.P.]. 8vo.
London, 1902
A political satire on the Earl of Rosebery.

FALL (the) of man ; or Milton's Paradise lost, in prose, with notes. A new translation from the French [of N. F. Dupré de Saint Maur]. Second edition. 8vo. Pp. 354. [*Brit. Mus.*]
London, [1770 ?]

FALL (the) of man ; or the loves of the Gorillas. By a learned Gorilla [Richard Grant White]. 8vo. [Cushing's *Init. and Pseud.*, i. 590.]   New York, 1871

FALL (the) of Mortimer, an historical play. [By —— Hatchett.]   8vo. [Lowndes' *Bibl. Man.*, p. 1619.]
London, 1731
This play was pronounced by the grand jury for the county of Middlesex, July 7, 1731, "a false, infamous, scandalous, seditious and treasonable libel." Prefixed to the edition of 1763 is a dedication by John Wilkes to the Earl of Bute.

FALL (the) of Needwood. [A poem. By Francis Noel Clarke Mundy.]   4to. Pp. 50. [*Manch. Free Lib.*]
Derby, 1808

FALL (the) of Oswego (14th August, 1756) ; a chapter in British history. [By William Thomas Mercer.] Cr 8vo. Pp. 31.   Private print.   N.P., 1873

FALL (the) of Portugal ; or, the royal exiles : a tragedy in five acts. [By John Wolcot, M.D.] 8vo. [*European Mag.*, vol. liii., 456-7.]   London, 1808

FALL (the) of Prince Florestan of Monaco. By himself. [By Sir Charles Wentworth Dilke, Bart.] 8vo. Pp. 83. [*Bodl.*]   London, 1874

FALL (the) of scepticism and infidelity predicted ; an epistle to Dr Beattie, occasioned by his Essay on the nature and immutability of truth : to which are subjoined, by way of notes, dissertations on several metaphysical and religious subjects. [By William Cockin.]   8vo.   [*Gent. Mag.*, June 1801, p. 576.]   London, 1785

FALL (the) of Tarquin ; a tragedy. By W. H., Gent. [William Hunt]. Fcap 8vo. Pp. 71. [*Brit. Mus.*]
York, 1713

FALL (the) of the Earl of Essex ; as it is perform'd at the theatre in Goodman's-Fields. Alter'd from " The Unhappy favourite " of Mr [John] Banks [by James Ralph]. 8vo. [*Brit. Mus.*]
London, 1731

FALL (the) of the Mogul ; a tragedy, founded on an interesting portion of Indian history, and attempted partly on the Greek model. By the author of *Indian Antiquities* [Thomas Maurice, M.A.]. 8vo. Pp. 153. [*D. N. B.*, vol. 37, p. 108.]   London, 1806

FALL (the) of the Pope, and the fate of the French President. [By John Davidson.] 8vo.   London, 1852
Advertisement signed " J D."

FALL (the) of the sugar planters of Jamaica . . . [By H— Pringle.] 8vo.   Birmingham, 1869

FALL (the) of Tsardom. By Carl Joubert [Adolphus Carl Grottey]. Second edition. 8vo. Pp. 255.
London, 1905

FALL River : an authentic narrative. By the author of *Tales, national, revolutionary* . . . [Mrs C. R. Williams]. Fcap 8vo.   Boston, [Mass.], 1833

FALLEN (a) idol. By F. Anstey [Thomas Anstey Guthrie]. 8vo. [*Lond. Lib. Cat.*]   London, 1886

FALLIBILITY (the) and falshood of the Church of Rome briefly detected and made manifest ; both in several instances thereof, and in the Scripture assertion thereabout. [By Daniel Whitby, D.D.] 4to. [Arber's *Term Cat.*, i., 523.]   London, 1675

FALLIBILITY (the) of inspired Scripture, as maintained by modern criticism ; being an examination of views propounded by Professor W R Smith, of Aberdeen, in their bearing on the doctrine of inspiration. [By James Barnhill.] 8vo. Pp. 68. [*New Coll. Cat.*]   Glasgow, 1877

FALLIBILITY (the) of the Roman Church, demonstrated from the manifest error of the 2d Nicene and Trent Councils ; which assert that the veneration and honorary worship of images is a tradition, primitive and apostolical. [By Daniel Whitby, D.D.] 4to. Pp. xi., 79. [*Bodl.*]   London, 1687

FALLING (the) flag [of the Southern United States] ; evacuation of Richmond, retreat and surrender at Appomattox. By an Officer of the Rear-Guard [Edward M. Boykin]. 8vo. [Cushing's *Init. and Pseud.*, i., 209.]
New York, 1874

FALLS (the) of Clyde, and other poems. By the author of *Law Lyrics* [Robert Bird]. Cr 8vo. [*Brit. Mus.*]
Glasgow, 1888

FALLS (the) of Clyde, or, the fairies ; a Scotish dramatic pastoral, in five acts. With three preliminary dissertations. [By John Black, LL.D.] 8vo. Pp. 241. [*Adv. Lib.*] Edinburgh, 1806

FALMOUTH (a) guide ; containing a concise account of the history, trade, port, and public establishments of Falmouth. [By Richard Thomas, C.E.] Fcap 8vo. Pp. 96. Falmouth, 1815

FALMOUTH (the) rectory scandal, and the remedy. To the parishioners of Falmouth. [By Edward C— Whitehurst, attorney.] 8vo. Pp. 4.
London, [1873]
Signed "A Cornish man."

FALSE (the) alarm. [By Samuel Johnson, LL.D.] Second edition. 8vo. Pp. 53. [Simm's *Bibl. Staff.*, p. 252.]
London, 1770
The first edition appeared in the same year.

FALSE (the) alarm : addressed to the Right Honourable Richard Rigby, Esq., Paymaster General of His Majesty's forces. [By Joseph Cawthorne, "of King Street, near Hammersmith Turnpike."] 8vo. Pp. iv., 106. [*W.*] London, 1782
Signed " Cincinnatus."

FALSE and true ; a play in three acts. [By Rev. George Moultrie.] Second edition. 8vo. Pp. 60. [*Biog. Dram.*]
London, 1798

FALSE (the) brother ; or, a new mapp of Scotland, drawn by an English pencil : being a short history of the political and civil transactions between these two nations since their first friendship. [By Rev. Cuthbert Sidenham, M.A.] 4to. Pp. 64. [*D. N. B.*, vol. 55, p. 245.] London, 1650

FALSE dawn. [A tale.] By Francis Prevost [Henry Francis Prevost Battersby]. 8vo. Pp. 352. [*Brit. Mus.*]
London, 1897

FALSE (the) favourit disgrac'd : and, the Reward of loyalty ; a tragi-comedy, never acted. [By George Gerbier d'Ouvilly.] 8vo. Pp. 118. [*Bodl.*]
London, 1657

FALSE (the) friend ; a comedy. [By Sir John Vanbrugh.] 4to. Pp. 68. [*Biog. Dram.*] London, 1702

FALSE gods. [A novel.] By Guy Thorne [Cyril A. E. Ranger-Gull]. Cr 8vo. [*Lit. Year Book.*] London, 1923

FALSE (the) notion of a Christian priesthood, and the pretences to sacerdotal oblation, intercession, benediction, and authoritative absolution, examined and confuted : being an answer to Mr Law's Second letter to the Bishop of Bangor. In a letter to a friend. By Phileleutherus Cantabrigiensis [Thomas Herne]. The second edition. 8vo. Pp. 96. [Watt's *Bibl. Brit.*]
London, 1718

FALSE (a) scent. [A novel.] By Mrs Alexander [Mrs Alexander Hector, née Annie French]. Pt 8vo. [*Brit. Mus.*] New York, 1889

FALSE (the) step ; and The Sisters [Two novels. By Miss —— Jones.] 3 vols. Fcap 8vo. [*Brit. Mus.*]
London, 1832

FALSE (a) witness examin'd ; being an answer to " A Declaration concerning the Quakers," &c. By Christodulus Ecclestone [John Danks]. 4to. [Smith's *Cat. of Friends' Books.*]
[London, 1674]

FALSEHOOD and truth. By Charlotte Elizabeth [Mrs Charlotte Elizabeth Tonna, previously Mrs Phelan]. 8vo. Pp. viii., 200. [*D. N. B.*, vol. 57, p. 34.] Liverpool, 1841

FALSHOOD in friendship ; or unions vjzard ; or wolves in lambskins. [By Anthony Munday.] 8vo. [*Christie-Miller Cat.*] London, 1605

FALSHOOD (the) of human virtue ; a moral essay [by Jacques Esprit]. Done out of French. 8vo. Pp. 308. [*Bodl.*] London, 1691

FALSHOOD unmaskt, in answer to a book [by Arthur Annesley, Earl of Anglesey], called " Truth unveil'd ; " which vainly pretends to justify the charge of Mr Standish, against some persons in the Church of England. By a dutiful son of that Church [Symon Patrick, D.D.]. 4to. [*Bodl.*]
London, 1676
Ascribed also to Henry Grove, Bishop of Chichester. [*Adv. Lib.*]

FAME (the) and confession of the fraternity of R : C : commonly, of the Rosie Cross ; with a preface annexed thereto, and a short declaration of their physicall work. By Eugenius Philalethes [Thomas Vaughan]. Pp. lxviii., 64. [Gardner's *Rosicrucian Books*, p. 76.] London, 1658

FAME (the) and glory of England vindicated. By Libertas [Peter Brown, journalist]. 8vo. [Cushing's *Init. and Pseud.*, vol. i., p. 171.]
New York, 1842

FAMILIAR (the) astrologer ; an easy guide to fate, destiny, and foreknowledge. By Raphael [R— C— Smith]. 8vo. [Cushing's *Init. and Pseud.*, vol. i., p. 247.] London, 1849

FAMILIAR chats with the queens of the stage. By Alan Dale [Alfred J. Cohen]. 8vo. [*Amer. Cat.*]
New York, 1890

FAMILIAR (a) conference upon some Antinomian tenets, sometimes miscalled the doctrines of sovereign free grace. . . . [By John Beach.] 8vo. Pp. 35. [Evans' *Amer. Bibl.*, vol. 3, p. 377.] New York, 1764

FAMILIAR conversations on Faith, the Forgiveness of Sins, Purgatory, the Word of God, and the Church. [By John Nelson Darby.] Fcap 8vo.
London, [1870 ?]

FAMILIAR (a) discourse or dialogue concerning the mine-adventure [in Wales. By William Shiers or Shires]. 8vo. Pp. 198. [*Adv. Lib.*]
London, 1700

FAMILIAR discourses upon the Apostles' Creed, the Lord's Prayer, and the Litany. By a Dignitary of the Church [Dr William Langford]. 8vo. Pp. 268. [*Brit. Mus.*] London, 1809

FAMILIAR (a) epistle from a Student of the Middle Temple, London, to his friend in Dublin. . . . [By Thomas Spring, B.A. (T.C.D.), barrister.] 8vo. [*Brit. Mus.*] London, 1771 Signed " T. S."

FAMILIAR (a) epistle to Robert J. Walker . . . from an old acquaintance [George MacHenry]. 8vo. [Cushing's *Init. and Pseud.*, vol. i., p. 210.] London, 1863

FAMILIAR (a) epistle to the most impudent man living [Bishop William Warburton]. [By Henry St John, Lord Bolingbroke.] 8vo.
London, 1749
Ascribed also to David Mallet, who denied having written this tract. Cooke, in his Life of Bolingbroke (vol. ii. p. 318), says that he has the MS. in Bolingbroke's handwriting. *See* Bolingbroke MSS. in the British Museum. Mallet was merely the passive instrument in seeing the book through the press. [Carruther's *Life of Pope*, pp. 401-2.]

FAMILIAR (the) epistles of M. T. Cicero. Englished and conferred with the French, Italian and other translations [by J. Webbe]. Fcap 8vo. [*W.*]
London, [1600 ?]

FAMILIAR epistles [in verse] to F. E. J[one]s, Esq., on the present state of the Irish stage, and the leading actors. [By John Wilson Croker.] Fcap 8vo. [*Brit. Mus.*] Dublin, 1804
The dedication is signed " T. C. D." Five editions appeared within two years ; soon after publication, reply was made in " A Few reflections. . . ." *See below.*

FAMILIAR epistles to the Rev. Dr Priestley. In which it is shewn, I. That the charges brought by him against the orthodox, are applicable to none but people of the Doctor's own persuasion. II. That, notwithstanding his endeavours to destroy the doctrines of Christ's divinity, and the vicarious punishment of sin, the Doctor has established both, even to a demonstration. III. That what the Doctor calls rational religion, has, according to his own account, been productive of the most unhappy and irrational consequences. IV. That the Doctor's religious pamphlets are a full and complete refutation of themselves. By the author of the *Shaver's Sermon on the Oxford expulsion* [John Macgowan]. 8vo. [*Queen's Coll. Cat.*, 263.] London, 1771

FAMILIAR (a) explanation of some difficulties in the subjunctive mood of the Latin verb. [By William Belcher, M.D.] 8vo. [*Brit. Mus.*]
Canterbury, 1817

FAMILIAR friends. By Olive Patch [Phillis Browne, Mrs Sarah S. Hamer]. 8vo. Pp. 168. London, [1880]

FAMILIAR (a) history of British India : new edition, brought down to 1865. By James H. Siddons [Joachim Hayward Stocqueler]. 8vo. [Cushing's *Init. and Pseud.*, vol. i., p. 267.] London, 1865

FAMILIAR (a) history of the United States. By James H. Siddons [Joachim Hayward Stocqueler]. Fcap. 8vo. [Cushing's *Init. and Pseud.*, vol. i., p. 267.] London, 1865

FAMILIAR (a) illustration of certain passages of Scripture relating to the power of man to do the will of God, original sin, election and reprobation, the divinity of Christ, and atonement for sin by the death of Christ. By a lover of the Gospel [Joseph Priestley, LL.D.]. Fcap 8vo. Pp. iv., 69.
London, 1772
Printed in vol. i. of Unitarian Tracts, London, 1791.

FAMILIAR illustrations of the language of mathematics ; or a new picture alphabet for well-behaved undergraduates. [By John Louis Roget, M.A.] Oblong folio. 9 plates.
London, 1850

FAMILIAR instructions on mental prayer, from the French of Courbon ; with a preface by the editor [William Upton Richards]. Fcap 8vo. [*Brit. Mus.*] London, 1852
Signed " W. U. R."

FAMILIAR (a) introduction to the Christian religion ; in a series of letters from a father to his sons. By a Senior [John Penrose, M.A.]. Fcap. Pp. xi., 418. [Boase and Courtney's *Bibl. Corn.*, ii., 475.]   London, 1831

FAMILIAR letters, addressed to children and young persons of the middle ranks. [By Eliza Coltman.] 12mo. [Smith's *Cat. of Friends' Books*, i., 84.]
                                London, 1811

FAMILIAR letters between the principal characters in David Simple, and some others ; being a sequel to his Adventures ; to which is added, A vision. By the author of *David Simple* [Sarah Fielding]. Second edition. 2 vols. Fcap 8vo. [*Dyce Cat.*]
                                London, 1752
The preface and the last five letters in vol. 2 were written by Henry Fielding, the brother of the authoress.

FAMILIAR letters on a variety of important and interesting subjects, from Lady Harriet Morley, and others. [By Francis Douglas, bookseller.] 8vo. Pp. viii., 476. [*Adv. Lib.*]
                                London, 1773

FAMILIAR letters written to and for particular friends on the most important occasions. [By Samuel Richardson.] 8vo. [*D. N. B.*, vol. 48, p. 244.]
                                London, 1741

FAMILIAR odes and epistles, principally designed for the amusement and instruction of the young. By the father of a family [Rev. Thomas Parsons]. 8vo. [Green's *Bibl. Somers.*, i., 396.]   Chipping-Norton, 1821

FAMILIAR (a), plain, and easy explanation of the law of wills and codicils, and of the law of executors and administrators; and also the rules by which estates, freehold and copyhold, and personal estates in general, descend, and are to be distributed, in case no will is made : with instructions to every person to make his own will. . . . By a barrister of the Inner Temple [Sir Thomas Edyne Tomlins]. 8vo. [*Brit. Mus.*]   London, 1785

FAMILIAR scenes, histories, and reflections. [By Harriet Corp.] Fcap 8vo. [W. D. Macray's *Cat.*]
                                London, 1814

FAMILIAR sketches of sculpture and sculptors. By the author of *Three experiments in living* [Mrs Hannah F. Lee]. 2 vols. 8vo. [*Brit. Mus.*]
                        Boston, [Mass.], 1854

FAMILIAR verses, from the ghost of Willy Shakspeare to Sammy Ireland : to which is added, Prince Robert, an auncient ballad. [By G. M. Woodward.] 8vo. Pp. 16. London, 1796
Author's name in the handwriting of Samuel Ireland.

FAMILIAR words ; an index verborum, or quotation handbook. By the author of *The gentle life* [James Hain Friswell]. 8vo. [*D. N. B.*, vol. 20, p. 278.]   London, 1865
Several other editions followed.

FAMILIE (the) of love : acted by the children of his maiesties reuells. [By Thomas Middleton.]   At London, printed for Iohn Helmes, and are to be sold in Saint Dunstans church yard in Fleet-street. 4to. No pagination. [Dyce *Cat.*]   1608

FAMILY adventures. By the author of *The fairy bower* [Mrs Harriet Mozley]. Fcap 8vo. [*Brit. Mus.*]
                                London, 1852

FAMILY (a) affair. By Hugh Conway [Frederick John Fargus]. 3 vols. 8vo. [Cushing's *Init. and Pseud.*, vol. i., p. 66.]   London, 1885

FAMILY anecdotes. [By Francis Henry Egerton, 8th Earl of Bridgewater.] Large 8vo.
                        [Paris, 1800 ?]

FAMILY (a) arrangement. By the author of *Dr Edith Romney* [Anne Elliot]. 3 vols. 8vo. [*Lond. Lib. Cat.*]   London, 1896

FAMILY (a) Catechism ; with a morning and evening prayer. . . . To which is prefix'd an exhortation to parents and masters of families, and a discourse on the divine right of catechising. By J. W. [John Wilson], [Episcopal] minister of the Gospel at Haddingtoun. 8vo. Pp. 134. [Haddington *Lib. Cat.*]   Edinburgh, 1712

FAMILY (a) commentary, or short and plain exposition of the New Testament. By a lady [Mrs Thomson]. 4 vols. Fcap 8vo. [Lowndes' *Brit. Lib.*, p. 224.]   York, 18—

FAMILY conversations between a father and his children, on the discoveries and evidences of Christianity. By the author of *Winter evening conversations* [Rev. Alex. Arthur, Dalkeith]. 12mo. Pp. 345.
                        Edinburgh, 1824

FAMILY (the) council ; conversations on the events of home. By Edward Garrett [Isabella Fyvie, later Mrs John R. Mayo]. Pt 8vo. Pp. 234. [*Lond. Lib. Cat.*]   London, 1886

FAMILY devotion ; or, a plain exhortation to morning and evening prayer in families. [By Edmund Gibson, Bishop of London.]   8vo.   [Watt's *Bibl. Brit.*]   London, 1705

FAMILY devotions. [By Lord Forbes.] 12mo. Privately printed.   N.P., 1853

FAMILY discourses, by a country gentleman [the Right Hon. Edward Weston]. 8vo. [Nichols' *Lit. Anec.*, ix., 494.]   London, 1768
  Republished, with the author's name, in 1776.

FAMILY (the) failing. [A novel.] By Darley Dale [Francesca M. Steele]. Pt 8vo. [*Lond. Lib. Cat.*]
                                   London, 1883

FAMILY failings ; a novel. 3 vols. [By Miss —— Fisher.] Fcap 8vo. [*Adv. Lib.*]   London, 1849

FAMILY (the) feud. By Adam Hornbook, the author of *Alderman Ralph* [Thomas Cooper, Chartist leader and journalist].   Fcap 8vo.   [Cushing's *Init. and Pseud.*, vol. i., p. 133.]
                                   London, 1856

FAMILY (the) fortunes ; a domestic story. By Edward Garrett [Isabella Fyvie, later Mrs John R. Mayo]. Pt 8vo. [Cushing's *Init. and Pseud.*, vol. i., p. 111.]   London, 1885

FAMILY (a) grievance. [A tale.] By Raymond Jacberns [Georgina M— Selby Ash]. Cr 8vo. Pp. 198. [*Lit. Year Book.*]   London, 1904

FAMILY (a) history. [A novel.] By the author of *The Queen's pardon* [Mary Eyre]. 3 vols. 8vo. [*Brit. Mus.*]
                                   London, 1861

FAMILY hymns, gathered mostly out of the best translations of David's Psalms. [By Matthew Henry.] Second edition, corrected. Fcap 8vo.
                                   London, 1702

FAMILY (the) instructor ; in three parts. With a recommendatory letter by the Reverend Mr S. Wright. [By Daniel Defoe.] 8vo. Pp. 444. [Wilson's *Life of Defoe*, 154.]
                                   London, 1715

FAMILY lectures ; or, domestic divinity : being a copious collection of sermons, selected from the polite writers and sound divines of the present century. [Edited by Vicesimus Knox, D.D.] 2 vols. [Darling's *Cyclop. Bibl.*, p. 1104.]
                                   London, 1791-95

FAMILY letters, between Middlesex, Surrey, Berks, Westminster, London, and York, as published in the London Courant. [By Peregrine Phillips ?] 8vo.   London, 1780

FAMILY (the) manual of morning and evening prayers. Prayers before Mass on Sundays, Holy Days, and common days. By M. P. [Michael Pembridge, O.S.B.]. 12mo. Pp. 61. Hereford, 1777

FAMILY (the) names of the Weald of Kent, particularly Smarden. By a Smardonian [Halford L. Mills]. 8vo. Pp. 82. [*Brit. Mus.*]
                        Ashford, [Kent], 1901

FAMILY (the) of Dalmahoy of Dalmahoy, Ratho, County of Edinburgh. [By Thos. Falconer.] 8vo. Privately printed.   [Edinburgh, 1870]

FAMILY (the) of George Briton ; or, the importance of a right education. A moral tale. [By Mary Nicholl.] Fcap 8vo.   Carmarthen, 1822

FAMILY (the) of Iona, and other poems ; with historical notes. [By Rev. William Anderson, LL.D.] 8vo. Pp. viii., 232.   Edinburgh, 1850

FAMILY (the) of Lincoln. [By R— E— G— Kirk.] 8vo.   N.P., N.D.

FAMILY pastimes ; or homes made happy. [By Robert Kemp Philp.] 8vo. Pp. 64. [Boase and Courtney's *Bibl. Corn.*, ii., 492.] London, 1851

FAMILY (the) picture ; or domestic education : a poetic epistle from a country gentleman to his college-friend, the Bishop of *******.   [By Richard Polwhele.] Fcap 8vo. Pp. iv., 67. [Boase and Courtney's *Bibl. Corn.*, ii., 511.]   London, 1808

FAMILY pictures, &c. [By Anne Manning, later Mrs Rathbone.] 8vo. [*Adv. Lib.*]   London, 1861

FAMILY pictures ; a novel : containing curious and interesting memoirs of several persons of fashion in W—re. By a lady [Susanna Minifie, afterwards Mrs Gunning]. 2 vols. Fcap 8vo. [*Gent. Mag.*, Oct. 1800, p. 1000.]
                                   Dublin, 1764

FAMILY prayers. By a layman [Sir John Gladstone, of Fasque]. . . . [*See* " A manual of prayers from the Liturgy . . . (by W. E. Gladstone). Fourth impression, Preface.]

FAMILY prayers.   By the author of *Morning and night watches*, etc. [John Ross MacDuff, D.D.]. Thirty-first edition, revised and corrected. Pt 8vo. Pp. 280.   London, 1869
  The first edition appeared in 1853.

FAMILY prayers [selected from the English Book of Common Prayer] designed especially for the use of a household observing . . . daily attendance upon the services of the Church. [By Bp. Charles Wordsworth.] Fcap 8vo. Pp. 75. [*Brit. Mus.*]   London, 1845
  Preface signed " C. W."

FAMILY prayers for morning and evening. . . . By a priest of the English Church [Rev. Clement Ogle Smith]. Fcap 8vo. [Cushing's *Init. and Pseud.*, vol. i., p. 240.]
London, 1862

FAMILY prayers for the children of the Church. [By R. Gream ?] 12mo. [*Brit. Mus.*] London, 1852

FAMILY prayers for working men. By the author of *Steps to the throne of grace* [Mrs —— Cook]. 12mo.
London, 1879

FAMILY prayers; with fourteen original hymns. [By Lady Lucy Whitmore.] Fcap 8vo.
London, 1832

FAMILY pride; a novel. By the author of *Olive Varcoe*, etc. [Frances Eliza M. Notley, later Mrs Thomas]. 3 vols. 8vo. [*Camb. Univ. Lib.*]
London, 1871
Wrongly ascribed to Francis Derrick.

FAMILY (the) save-all; a system of secondary cookery, containing nearly one thousand three hundred invaluable hints for economy in the use of every article of household consumption. By the editor of *Enquire within upon everything*, etc. [Robert Kemp Philp]. 8vo. Pp. vi., 342. [*Brit. Mus.*]
London, 1869

FAMILY (the) Scripture reader; being a series of instructive lessons extracted from a large majority of the books which constitute the sacred canon, and with suitable collects taken from the Book of Common Prayer. By one of the laity of the Church of England [Thomas Newenham]. 4to. Pp. xii., 100.
London, N.D.
The dedication is signed " T—s N—m."

FAMILY (a) secret. By Elzey Hay [Fanny Andrews]. 8vo. [Cushing's *Init. and Pseud.*, vol. i., p. 127.]
Philadelphia, 1878

FAMILY (a) tour through South Holland, up the Rhine, and across the Netherlands, to Ostend. [By Sir John Barrow.] 8vo. London, 1831

FAMILY (the) tree and other stories. By Arthur Penn [James Brander Matthews]. Pt 8vo. Pp. 236. [*Lond. Lib. Cat.*] London, 1889
Some issues bear the author's true name.

FAMINE: a masque. [By William James Linton.] 8vo. [*Brit. Mus.*]
London, 1875

FAMOUS (the) and delectable history of Don Bellianis of Greece, or the honour of chivalry; containing his valiant exploits . . . now newly written by F. Kirkman [based on the romance originally written in Spanish by Geronimo Fernandez]. 3 parts. 4to. [*Edinburgh Univ. Lib.*]
London, 1673
The title of a later edition (1715) begins " The honour of Chivalry. . . ."

FAMOUS (the) and pleasant history of Parismus. [By Emanuel Foord, or Forde.] Fcap 8vo. B. L. [*Brit. Mus.*] London, [1680]
Frequently reprinted, with varied titles. See " The History of Parismus. . . ."

FAMOVS (the) and renovvned historie of Primaleon of Greece, sonne to the great and mighty Prince Palmerin d'Oliva, Emperour of Constantinople: describing his knightly deedes of armes, as also the memorable aduentures of Prince Edvvard of England: and continuing the former history of Palmendos, brother to the fortunate Prince Primaleon, &c. Three bookes. . . . Translated out of French and Italian, into English, by A. M. [Anthony Munday]. 4to. B. L. Pp. 245. [*Bodl.*] London, 1619
" Anthony Munday, at the end of his translation of the second part of Gerileon of England, says, ' In the mean while an old promise remaineth to be performed, namely, the first booke of Primaleon of Greece, which by God's permission you shall have the next tearme, if it may be finished so soone. Let then Gerileon's welcome hasten on Primaleon.' "—MS. note in the Douce copy.

FAMOUS (the) Battel of the Catts, in the Province of Ulster, June 25, 1668. [A satire, in verse. By Sir John Denham.] 4to. [O'Donoghue's *Poets of Ireland.*]
In the Savoy, [London], 1668

FAMOUS beauties of two reigns. By Mary Craven [Mrs —— Ffoulkes]. 8vo. London, 1906

FAMOUS (the) dedication to the pamphlet, entitled, A dissertation upon parties, addressed to the Rt. Hon. Sir Robert Walpole. [By Henry St. John, Viscount Bolingbroke.] To which is annexed, the memorable Daily Courant of Thursday, November 28, 1734, upon the subject of Mr Ward's Pill-plot, said to be written by Sir A. B. C. 8vo. Pp. 40.
London, N.D.

FAMOUS fighting Regiments. By George Hood [George Douglas Brown]. 8vo. Pp. 121. London, [1900]

FAMOUS historical scenes from three centuries. By Ascott R. Hope [Ascott Robert Hope Moncrieff]. Pt 8vo. [*Lond. Lib. Cat.*] Edinburgh, 1874

FAMOUS (the) historie of Montelyon, Knyghte of the Oracle. [By Emanuel Foord.] 4to. [Lowndes' *Bibl. Man.*] London, 1633
The following is a later edition.

FAMOUS (the) History of Montelion, Knight of the Oracle, Son to the True Mirrour of Princes, the most Renowned Persicles, King of Assyria, shewing his strange birth, perillous adventures in arms, and how he came to the knowledge of his royal parents. [By J— Phillips.] Sm. 4to. Printed for W. O. for E. Tracy. N.D., [*c.* 1690]

FAMOUS (the) history of Palmendos, son to the most renowned Palmerin D'Oliva. . . . [Translated into English by Anthony Munday.] B. L. 4to. [*Brit. Mus.*] London, 1653
Signed "A. M."

FAMOUS (the) history of the destruction of Troy, in three books ; shewing the original of it, its first sacking by Hercules, and re-edifying it . . . and many famous fights. [By Raoul Le Fevre. Translated from old French.] 4to. [Arber's *Term Cat.*, ii., 615.] London, 1684

FAMOUS (the) history of the noble and valiant Prince Palmerin of England and his brother Florian du Desart . . . translated out of French by A. M. [Anthony Munday]. 2 vols. Fcap 4to. [*Brit. Mus.*] London, 1664
This work was originally written in Portuguese by Luis Hurtado or F. de Moraes. Munday previously published portions (" The first Part . . .," 1609 ; " The second Part . . .," 1616 ; " The third and last Part . . .," 1602).

FAMOUS (the) history of the seaven champions of Christendome. [By Richard Johnson.] 2 parts. 4to. [Lowndes' *Bibl. Man.*]
London, by Thomas Snodham, [1670]

FAMOUS (the) hystory of Herodotus, conteyning the discourse of dywers countreys ; the succession of theyr Kyngs, etc. Deuided into nine Bookes entitled with the names of the nine Muses. [Translated by B. R., *i.e.* Barnaby Rich.] 8vo. B. L. [*Brit. Mus.*] London, 1584
Only the first two books are translated.

FAMOUS (a) prediction of Merlin, the British wizard ; written above a thousand years ago, and relating to the year 1709 : with explanatory notes. By T. N. Philomath [Jonathan Swift, D.D.]. Folio. Single leaf. London printed : Edinburgh reprinted. 1709

FAMOUS racing men ; with anecdotes and portraits. By " Thormanby " [W— Willmott Dixon]. 8vo. [*Lond. Lib. Cat.*] London, 1887

FAMOUS readings. By Leo Ross [David Anderson Moxey, M.D.]. 8vo. Edinburgh, 1878

FAMOUS (the) romance of Tarsis and Zelie, digested into ten books : written originally in French by the acute pen of a Person of Honour [Roland Le Vayer de Boutigny] ; done into English by Charles Williams, Gent. Folio. [Arber's *Term Cat.*, ii., 615.] London, 1685

FAMOUS (the) voyage of Sir Francis Drake, with a particular account of his expedition in the West Indies against the Spaniards ; being the first commander that ever sail'd round the whole globe. To which is added the prosperous voyage of Mr Thomas Candish round the world ; with an account of the vast riches he took from the Spaniards. [By Thomas Wright.] 8vo. [Davidson's *Bibl. Devon.*, p. 157.] London, 1742

FAMOUS women. [By Edward I. Ross.] 8vo. [Aberdeen], 1890

FAN ; the story of a young girl's life. By Henry Harford [W— H— Hudson]. 3 vols. 8vo. [G. F. Wilson's *Bibliog. of W. H. Hudson.*] London, 1892

" FAN Kawe " (the) at Canton, before Treaty days, 1825-44. By an old Resident [William C. Hunter]. Fcap 8vo. Pp. 157. [*Lond. Lib. Cat.*] London, 1882

FANATICISM. By the author of *Natural history of enthusiasm* [Isaac Taylor, of Stanford Rivers]. 8vo. [*Brit. Mus.*] London, 1833

FANATICISM and its results. By a Southerner [James Dabwey MacCabe]. 8vo. Richmond, 1866

FANATICISM fanatically imputed to the Catholick Church by Doctour Stillingfleet ; and the imputation refuted and retorted. By S. C., a Catholick, O. S. B. [Hugh Paulin Serenus Cressy]. Fcap 8vo. Pp. 188. [Gillow's *Bibl. Dict.*, i., 596.]
N.P., 1672

FANATICISM in the North. A Letter to the editor of " The Witness " upon the abrupt termination of his recent attempt to defend " The Men." By Investigator [Kenneth M. Phin, D.D.]. 8vo. Pp. 47. [Mowat's *Bibl. of Caithness*, p. 25.] Edinburgh, 1852

FANATICISM reviv'd; or the enthusiasm of the Camisars. [By Jean Baptiste L'Ouvreleil.] Translated from the second edition of the French. Pt 8vo. [*Brit. Mus.*]   London, 1707

FANATICK (the) history; or an exact relation and account of the old Anabaptists and new Quakers, which may prove the death and burial of the Fanatick doctrine. [Edited by Richard Blome.] 8vo. Pp. 274. [*Brit. Mus.*]
London, 1660

FANCHETTE. By one of her admirers [John Esten Cooke]. Fcap 8vo. [*Amer. Cat.*]   Boston, 1883

FANCHON, the cricket; from the French of George Sand [Madame A. L. A. D. Dudevant].   Fcap 8vo. [Haynes' *Pseud.*]   Boston, 1891

FANCIAD (the); an heroic poem, in six cantos. To his Grace the Duke of Marlborough, on the turn of his genius to arms. [By Aaron Hill.] 8vo. Pp. viii., 72. [*Bodl.*]   London, 1743

FANCIES and facts of mission progress in India; or, an episode in the history of the Madras Christian College, 1888. [By Rev. John S— Beaumont, M.A.] 8vo. Pp. 31.   Bombay, 1888

FANCIES and feelings; original poems collected and edited [really written] by H. P. [Henry Parkinson, B.A., barrister]. 8vo. [O'Donoghue's *Poets of Ireland.*]   Dublin, 1857

FANCIES (the) of a dreamer. [By Henry H. Davis.] 8vo. [Cushing's *Init. and Pseud.*, vol. ii., p. 46.]
London, 1842

FANCIES of a rhymer. [By Rev. Alfred Gatty.] 12mo. Pp. 118. [Martin's *Cat.*]   London, 1833

FANCIES of a whimsical man. [By Frederick Townsend.] 8vo. [Cushing's *Init. and Pseud.*, vol. i., p. 306.]
New York, 1855

FANCY (the); a selection from the poetical remains of the late Peter Corcoran, of Gray's Inn, student at law; with a brief memoir of his life. [By John Hamilton Reynolds, pugilist.] Fcap 8vo. [O'Donoghue's *Poets of Ireland.*]   London, 1820

FANCY drinks and popular beverages : over five hundred recipes. By "The only William" [William Schmidt]. Fcap 8vo. [*Amer. Cat.*]
New York, 1896

FANCY'D (the) Queen; an opera : as it is acted at the Theatre-Royal in Covent-Garden. [By Robert Drury.] 8vo. Pp. 43. [*Biog. Dram.*]
London, 1733

FANCY'S following. [Poems.] By Ἄνοδος [Mary Elizabeth Coleridge]. Fcap 8vo. Pp. 58. [*Brit. Mus.*]
London, 1896

FANCY'S guerdon. By Anodos [Mary Elizabeth Coleridge]. Fcap 8vo.
Oxford, 1898
Pages 1-23 are repeated from the preceding work.

FANE (the) of the Druids; a poem. [By John Ogilvie, D.D.] 4to. [MS. note on the *Brit. Mus.* copy.]
London, 1787

—— Book the second. Comprehending an account of the origin, progress, and establishment of society in North Britain. By the author of the first book [John Ogilvie, D.D.]. 4to. [Scott's *Fasti.*]   London, 1789

FANNIE'S flowers; or fun for the nursery. [By Rev. Richard Doidge Dingle, B.A.] 8vo. Pp. 32. [*Brit. Mus.*]   London, 1856

FANNY and her mamma; or easy reading lessons, with hints for nursery discipline. By the author of *Mamma's Bible stories*, etc. [C. Leicester ?]. 8vo. [*Brit. Mus.*]   London, 1848

FANNY Fern's new stories for children. By Fanny Fern, author of *Little ferns for Fanny's little friends*, etc. [Mrs Sarah Parton, *née* Eldridge]. 8vo. Pp. iv., 197. [Cushing's *Init. and Pseud.*, vol. i., p. 101.]
London, [1865]

FANNY Hervey; or, the mother's choice. [By Mrs Stirling.] 2 vols. 8vo. [*Adv. Lib.*]   London, 1849

FANNY; with other poems. [By Fitzgreene Halleck.] Cr 8vo. [*Brit. Mus.*]   New York, 1839

FANNY'S King; and other stories. By Darley Dale [Francesca M. Steele]. Fcap 8vo. [*Lond. Lib. Cat.*]
London, 1885

FANSHAWE : a romance. [By Nathaniel Hawthorne.] 8vo. [*Brit. Mus.*]
Boston, 1832

FANTASIAS. By George Egerton [Mary Chavelita Dunn, later Mrs Egerton Clairmonte]. 8vo. Pp. 156. [*Brit. Mus.*]   London, 1897

FANTASTIC fables. By Dod Grile [Ambrose Bierce, M.A.]. Fcap 8vo. [Cushing's *Init. and Pseud.*, vol. i., p. 121.]   New York, 1899

FANTASTIC stories, from the German of Richard Leander [Richard Volkmann]; translated by P. B. Granville. 8vo. [*Brit. Mus.*]
London, 1873

FANTASTICKS : seruing for a perpetvall prognostication. Descants of 1 The world. 2 The earth. 3 Water. 4 Ayre. 5 Fire. 6 Fish. 7 Beasts. 8 Man. 9 Woman. 10 Loue. 11 Money. 12 The Spring. 13 Summer. 14 Haruest. 15 Winter. 16 The 12 moneths. 17 Christmas. 18 Lent. 19 Good Friday. 20 Easter day. 21 Morning. 22 The 12 houres. 23 Midnight. 24 The conclusion. [By Nicholas Breton.] 4to. No pagination. B. L. [*Brit. Mus.*]
London, 1626
The dedication and the address to the reader are signed " N. B."

FANTASTICS (the) : a drama. By George Fleming [Julia Constance Fletcher]. 8vo. [*Lond. Lib. Cat.*]
London, 1900

FAR above rubies ; a novel. By F. G. Trafford [Mrs Charlotte E. L. Riddell]. 3 vols. Cr 8vo. [*D. N. B.*, Second Supp., vol. 3, p. 193.] London, 1867

FAR and near ; or translations and originals. By Eta Mawr [Elizabeth Colling]. Fcap 8vo. Pp. viii., 237. [*Bodl.*] London, 1856

FAR hence unto the Gentiles. By Lumen [John Samuels, Major]. 8vo. [*Lit. Year Book.*] London, 1915

FAR (the) horizon ; a novel. By Lucas Malet [Mrs St Leger Harrison, *née* Mary Kingsley]. Cr 8vo. Pp. 428. [*Lond. Lib. Cat.*] London, 1907

FAR off ; or, Africa and America described : with anecdotes and numerous illustrations. Part II. By the author of *The peep of day*, etc. [Mrs Favell Lee Mortimer]. Fcap 8vo. [*Brit. Mus.*]
London, 1854

FAR off ; or, Asia and Australia described : with anecdotes and numerous illustrations. By the author of *The peep of day*, etc. [Mrs Favell Lee Mortimer]. Fcap 8vo.
London, 1852

FAR (the) West ; or a tour beyond the mountains. By a traveller [Edmund Flagg]. 2 vols. Fcap 8vo. [Cushing's *Init. and Pseud.*, vol. i., p. 286.]
New York, 1838
The material previously appeared in the *Louisville Journal* as " Sketches of a traveller."

FAR-AWAY (a) Princess. By Christian Reid [Frances C. Tiernan]. 8vo. Pp. 406. [*Brit. Mus.*]
New York, [1914]

FARCE (a), in two acts ; called 'Tis all a farce : as performed at the Theatre-Royal, Haymarket. [By John Till Allingham.] 8vo. Pp. 36. [*Bodl.*]
London, 1800

FARCE (the) of life ; a novel. By Lord B*** [Frederick Richard Chichester, Earl of Belfast], author of *Masters and workmen*. 3 vols. Fcap 8vo. [*Camb. Univ. Lib.*] London, 1852
Mistakenly attributed to Henry, Lord Brougham.

FARE thee well. [A poem. By Lord Byron.] 4to. [*Brit. Mus.*]
Private print, [London ?], 1816

FAREWEL odes ; for the year 1786. By Peter Pindar, Esq., a distant relation of the poet of Thebes, and Laureat to the Royal Academy [John Wolcot, M.D.]. Fourth edition. 4to. Pp. 64. [*D. N. B.*, vol. 62, p. 291.]
London, 1786

FAREWELL (the). [A dialogue in verse. By Charles Churchill.] 4to. [*Brit. Mus.*] London, [1764]

FAREWELL epistles to the Right Rev. Samuel [Horsley], Lord Bishop of St David's, in which the Unitarian Dissenters, and the Dissenters in general, are vindicated. [By David Jones, of Llandovery.] 8vo. Pp. xii., 68.
London, 1794

FAREWELL ode on a distant prospect of Cambridge. By the author of *The Brunoniad* [Thomas Foster, B.A.]. 4to. [Bartholomew's *Cat. of Camb. Books.*] Cambridge, 1794
Ascribed also to William M. Heald.

FAREWELL (a) sermon addressed to a congregation in the Diocese of Oxford. [By Rev. E. Attwood.] Fcap 8vo.
Oxford, 1848

FAREWELL to Egypt : or, the departure of the Free Church of Scotland out of the Erastian Establishment. [By James Hamilton, D.D.] Fifteenth thousand. Fcap 8vo. Pp. 12.
London, 1843
Reprinted in collected works.

FAREWELL to Harold ! [An attack on Lord Byron. By Edward Smedley.] 8vo. [Bartholomew's *Cat. of Camb. Books.*] London, 1816

FAREWELL (a) to Popery ; in a letter to Dr Nicholas, Vice-Chancellor of Oxford, and Warden of New College, from W. H. [Walter Harris], M.D., lately Fellow of the same College : shewing the true motives that withdrew him to the Romish religion, and the reasons of his return to the Church of England. 4to. Pp. 43. [*D. N. B.*, vol. 25, p. 25.] London, 1679

FAREWELL to the outward bound ; addressed to members of the Church of England. By one of her ministers [Thomas Dowell]. Fcap 8vo.
London, 1849

FAREWELL to time ; or last views of life, and prospects of immortality : including devotional exercises,—a great variety of which are in the language of Scripture,—to be used by the sick, or by those who minister to them. By the author of *The morning and evening sacrifice* [Thomas Wright]. Fcap 8vo. Pp. xxiv., 499. [Scott's *Fasti*, Second edition, vol. i., p. 303.]
Edinburgh, 1828

FARINGDON Hill ; a poem, in two books. [By Rev. Henry James Pye.] 4to. Pp. 64. [Watt's *Bibl. Brit.*]
Oxford, 1774

FARM (the) and fruit of old ; a translation, in verse, of the first and second Georgics of Virgil. By a market-gardener [Richard Doddridge Blackmore, M.A., barrister]. 8vo. [*D. N. B.*, First Supp., vol. 1, p. 208.]
London, 1862

FARM and garden produce ; a treasury of information. By Martin Doyle, [Rev. William Hickey, M.A.], author of *Small farms*, etc. 8vo. Pp. 160. [Haynes' *Pseud.*] London, 1857

FARM (the) and the fireside. By Bill Arp [Charles H. Smith]. 8vo. London, 1891

FARM (the) book for little ones. By Walter Copeland [Walter Jerrold]. 12mo. Pp. 120. London, 1901

FARM (the), garden, stable, and aviary. Vol. III. of the Field Library. By I. E. B. C. [Irvine E. B. Cox]. 8vo. [*Brit. Mus.*] London, 1866

FARM (the) in the hills. [A novel.] By Florence Warden [Florence Alice Price, later Mrs George E. James]. Cr 8vo. Pp. viii. 200. London, 1899

FARMER (the) boy [George Washington], and how he became Commander-in-chief. By Uncle Juvinell [Morrison Heedy]. 8vo. [Cushing's *Init. and Pseud.*, vol. i., p. 145.] Boston, 1864

FARMER George ; an attempt to portray the character of George III., and to present him alike in his private life and in his Court. By Lewis Melville [Lewis Samuel Benjamin]. 2 vols. Dy 8vo. [*Jewish Year Book, Lit. section.*] London, 1907

FARMER (the) [Bishop Samuel Seabury] refuted ; or a more impartial and comprehensive view of the dispute between Great Britain and the Colonies, intended as a further vindication of the Congress. [By Alexander Hamilton.] 8vo. Pp. iv., 75. [Evans' *Amer. Bibl.*, vol. 5, p. 141.] New York, 1775
Signed "A sincere friend to America."
The Bishop's controversial pamphlets were usually signed "A W. Farmer" [A Westchester Farmer]. *See below*, "Free thoughts on the proceedings. . . ."

FARMER'S (the) [John Dickinson's] and Monitor's [Arthur Lee's] Letters to the inhabitants of the British Colonies. 4to. Pp. 97. [Evans' *Amer. Bibl.*, vol. 4, p. 174.]
Williamsburg, [U.S.A.], 1769

FARMER'S (the) boy ; a rural poem. By Robert Bloomfield. Fourth edition [edited by Capel Lofft, senior]. Fcap 8vo. [*W.*] London, 1801

FARMER'S (the) case of the Roman Catholics of Ireland. [By Henry Brooke.] 8vo. [*Camb. Univ. Lib.*]
Dublin, 1760

FARMER'S (the) guide in hiring and stocking farms ; containing an examination of many subjects of great importance both to the common husbandman, in hiring a farm ; and to a gentleman on taking the whole or part of his estate into his own hands. By the author of *The Farmer's letters* [Arthur Young]. 2 vols. 8vo. [Watt's *Bibl. Brit.*] London, 1770

FARMER'S Ha' ; a Scots poem. By a student of Marischal College [Charles Keith, M.D., of Montrose]. 12mo. [Anderson's *Aberd. Univ. Bibl.*]
Aberdeen, 1796

FARMER'S (the) Kalendar ; or a monthly directory for all sorts of country businesses. By an experienced farmer [Arthur Young]. 8vo. [Watt's *Bibl. Brit.*] London, 1771

FARMER'S (the) letter to the Protestants of Ireland [on the Pretender's invasion]. No. 1. [By Henry Brooke.] 8vo. [*Brit. Mus.*] Dublin, 1745
See also "The Farmer's six letters . . ."

FARMER'S (the) letters to the people of England ; containing the sentiments of a practical husbandman on various subjects of great importance : particularly the exportation of corn. [By Arthur Young.] Third edition, corrected and enlarged. 2 vols. 8vo. [Watt's *Bibl. Brit.*] London, 1771

FARMER'S (the) manual : a treasury of information. By Martin Doyle, author of *Small farms*, etc. [Rev. William Hickey, M.A.]. 8vo. Pp. 160. [*Adv. Lib.*] London, [1857]
Most of the above work was certainly written by Martin Doyle, but additions were made by others.

FARMER'S (the) New-year's gift to his countrymen, for 1757. [By Sir Archibald Grant.] 8vo. Pp. 34. [*Brit. Mus.*]   Aberdeen, 1757

FARMER'S (the) pocket calendar, [being an abridgment of " The new farmer's calendar," both by John Lawrence.] 8vo. [Watt's *Bibl. Brit.*]
London, 1800

FARMER'S (the) queries and resolutions regarding the game. . . . [By Rev. John Clubbe.] 4to. [*D. N. B.*, vol. 11, p. 136.]   Ipswich, [1770 ?]

FARMER'S (the) return from London ; an interlude : as it is performed at the Theatre Royal in Drury-Lane. [By David Garrick.] 4to. Pp. 15. [*Biog. Dram.*]   London, 1762

FARMER'S (the) six letters to the Protestants of Ireland, of equal importance to the Protestants of England. [By Henry Brooke.] 8vo. [*Brit. Mus.*]   Dublin, 1746

FARMER'S (the) son ; a moral tale. By the Rev. P. P., M.A. [Richard Graves]. 4to. [Watt's *Bibl. Brit.*]
London, 1795

FARMER'S (the) three daughters ; a novel. [By Alexander Balfour.] 4 vols. Fcap 8vo. [*Camb. Univ. Lib.*]
London, 1822

FARMER'S (the) tour through the East of England, being the register of a journey through various counties of this kingdom, to enquire into the state of agriculture, &c. By the author of *The Farmer's letters*, and the *Tours through the North and South of England* [Arthur Young, F.R.S.]. 4 vols. 8vo. [Watt's *Bibl. Brit.*]
London, 1771

FARMER'S (the) vision. [Verse. By Thomas Erskine, Lord Erskine.] 8vo. [*W.*]   London, 1819.
Privately printed. The preface is signed " E.," " Buchan Hill, Sussex, December 25th, 1818."

FARMING for ladies ; or, a guide to the poultry-yard, the dairy and piggery. By the author of *British husbandry* [John French Burke]. 8vo. Pp. xviii., 511. [*Brit. Mus.*]   London, 1844

FARMING implements ; their various uses and recent modern improvements compared with the old machines. By F. D. P. [Frederick De Porquet]. 8vo. [*Brit. Mus.*]   London, 1847

FARMINGDALE. [A novel.] By Caroline Thomas [Mrs Julia Caroline Dorr, *née* Ripley]. 8vo. [Cushing's *Init. and Pseud.*, vol. i., p. 282.]
New York, 1854

FARNELL'S folly ; a novel. By Paul Creyton [John T. Trowbridge]. Fcap 8vo. [Cushing's *Init. and Pseud.*, vol. i., p. 70.]   Boston, 1884

FARRAGO. By Pilgrim Plowden [—— Farewell]. 8vo.   London, 1733

FARRAGO : containing essays, moral, philosophical, political and historical. [By Richard Barton.] 2 vols. 8vo. [Lowndes' *Bibl. Man.*]
Tewkesbury, 1792

FARRAGO ; or miscellanies in prose and verse. [By Richard Barton.] 8vo. [*Brit. Mus.*]   London, 1739

FARRAGO ; poems and letters. [By Richard Barton.] 8vo. London, 1753

FARRIER'S (the) and horseman's complete dictionary ; containing the art of farriery in all its branches. [By Thomas Wallace.] 8vo. [Watt's *Bibl. Brit.*]   London, 1726

FARRIERY taught on a new and easy plan. By John Hinds [J— Bell]. 8vo. [Cushing's *Init. and Pseud.*, vol. i., p. 130.]   Philadelphia, 1848

FARRINGDON Hill ; a poem in two books. [By Henry James Pye.] Fcap 4to. [Watt's *Bibl. Brit.*]
Oxford, 1774

FARTHER (a) account of the Baroccian Manuscript, lately published at Oxford ; together with the canon omitted in that edition : in a letter to his friend in London. [By Samuel Grascome.] [With an appendix of six pages ; being an answer to Mr Humphrey Hody's Letter concerning the canon at the end of the Baroccian Manuscript.] No separate title. [*Bodl.*]
[Oxford ? 1691]

FARTHER additions to a small treatise called " Salt waters sweetned." [By Capt. Robert Fitzgerald.] Fcap 8vo. [Arber's *Term Cat.*, ii., 622.]
London, 1684
See " Salt waters sweetned."

FARTHER (the) adventures of Robinson Crusoe ; being the second and last part of his life, and of the strange surprizing accounts of his travels round three parts of the globe : written by himself. To which is added a map of the world, in which is delineated the voyages of Robinson Crusoe. [By Daniel Defoe.] 8vo. London, 1719

FARTHER considerations and conjectures, relative to an original universal standard for measure and weight, but more particularly as to the English standard. [By Samuel Reynardson.] 4to. [*Bodl.*]   London, 1765

FARTHER considerations on the present state of affairs at home and abroad, as affected by the late Convention, in a letter to the minister : with a postscript ; containing some reflections upon the particular situation of our merchants. [By George Lyttelton, Lord Lyttelton.] Second edition. 8vo. Pp. 61. [*D. N. B.*, vol. 34, p. 373.] London, 1739

FARTHER (a) continuation of the History of the Crown-Inn. Part III. Containing the present state of the Inn, and other particulars. [By John Arbuthnot, M.D. ?] 8vo.
London, N.D.
See below, " The History of the Crown-Inn."

FARTHER (a) defence, &c. Being an answer to a Reply [by N. Spinckes] to the Vindication of the Reasons and Defence for restoring some prayers and directions in King Edward VI's first liturgy. By [Jeremy Collier] the author of the *Reasons*, &c. 8vo. [*D. N. B.*, vol. 11, p. 347.] London, 1720
See " Reasons for restoring. . . ."

FARTHER (a) defence of infant-baptism ; wherein the infants right, upon the parents' faith, is illustrated by those miracles which Jesus performed : their claim to baptism farther supported, from their being God's heritage. [By Caleb Fleming.] 8vo. [*Bodl.*] London, [1744]

FARTHER (a) defence of the Plain account of the nature and end of the sacrament of the Lord's Supper [by Bishop Hoadly] ; in answer to the Remarker's Second letter to the author of that book. [By Strickland Gough.] 8vo. [*Bodl.*] London, 1735

FARTHER (a) defence of the present scheme of petitioning the Parliament for relief in the matter of subscription ; occasioned by a pamphlet called " Remarks upon certain proposals for an application to Parliament. . . ." By the author of *A Letter to J. Ibbetson, D.D.* [John Firebrace]. 8vo. Pp. 40. [*Brit. Mus.*] London, [? 1771]
See " A Further defence . . ."

FARTHER (a) discourse of free-thinking, in a letter to a clergy-man ; with some considerations on Mr Pycroft's Treatise upon the same subject. [By Anthony Collins ?] 8vo. Pp. 40.
London, 1713

FARTHER (a) essay relating to the female sex ; containing six characters and six perfections, with the description of self-love. [By Mrs Mary Astell ?] 8vo. London, 1696
Attributed also to Mrs Drake.

FARTHER (a) illustration of the Analysis [of ancient mythology] ; in answer to Observations [by John Richardson] ; and an apology to John Richardson. [By Jacob Bryant.] 8vo. [*Lond. Lib. Cat.*] London, 1778

FARTHER (a) inquiry into the expediency of applying the principles of Colonial policy to the government of India, &c. [By Major Gavin Young.] 8vo. [M'Culloch's *Lit. of Polit. Econ.*, p. 109.] London, 1827

FARTHER observations on the writings of the Craftsman ; or short remarks upon a late pamphlet, entituled, An Answer to the observations on the writings of the Craftsman. [By John Hervey, Lord Hervey.] 8vo. [*Bodl.*] London, 1730
See also the previous " Observations."

FARTHER remarks on Dr Waterland's Farther vindication of Christ's divinity. By Philalethes Cantabrigiensis [John Jackson]. 8vo. Pp. 96. [Sutton's *Memoirs of Jackson.*] London, 1724

FARTHER (a) search after claret ; or, a second visitation of the vintners : a poem. [By Richard Ames.] 4to.
London, 1691
See also " The Search after claret. . . ." and " Fatal friendship."

FARTHER thoughts concerning human soul, in defence of Second thoughts ; wherein the weak efforts of the Reverend Mr Turner, and other less significant writers, are occasionally answer'd. By the author of *Second thoughts* [William Coward]. 8vo. Pp. 155. [*Sig. Lib.*] London, 1703

FARTHER (a) vindication of the case of the Hanover troops, in which the uniform influence of the Hanover-Rudder is clearly detected and expos'd, being a full answer to The interest of Great Britain steadily pursued. [By Philip Dormer Stanhope, Earl of Chesterfield.] 8vo. [*Brit. Mus.*]
London, 1743
See above, " The Case of the Hanover forces. . . ."

FARTHEST from the truth. By the authors of *Hustled history* [Edward V. Lucas and Charles L. Graves]. 8vo. [*Brit. Mus.*] London, 1910

FASCICULUS [a collection of brief poems. By Rev. John Howard Marsden, M.A.] Cr 8vo. Pp. 48. [*Brit. Mus.*] Chiswick Press, 1869

FASCICULUS chemicus ; or chymical collections : expressing the ingress, progress, and egress, of the secret hermetick science, out of the choisest and most famous authors ; collected and digested. . . . Whereunto is added, The Arcanum or grant [sic] secret of hermetic philosophy ; both made English by James Hasolle, Esquire, qui est Mercuriophilus Anglicus [Elias Ashmole]. 8vo. Pp. 316. [Bodl. ; Gardner's Roscicrucian Books, p. 7.]   London, 1650

"The Arcanum" has a separate title-page, on which it is said to be "The third edition amended and enlarged."

FASCICULUS poeticus ; or new classic guide to Latin heroic verse : in which the selections are so arranged as to lead, step by step, from the terminating dactyl and spondee to the full measure of the hexameter. [By Richard Stocker.] 12mo. Pp. iv., 88. [Bodl.]   Oxford, 1824

FASHION ; a poem. [By Ralph Schomberg, M.D.] 4to.   [Green's Bibl. Somers., i., 463.]   Bath, 1775

FASHION and folly. By Aunt Hattie [Mrs Harriet Newell Baker, née Woods]. 8vo. [Cushing's Init. and Pseud., vol. i., p. 127.]   Boston, 1869

FASHION and passion ; or, life in Mayfair. By the author of The honeymoon and Through the ages [The Duke de Medina - Pomar]. 3 vols. 8vo. [Brit. Mus.] London, 1876

FASHION of windows in civil and ecclesiastical buildings. [By John Aubrey.] 4to. [Camb. Univ. Lib. Cat.]
N.P., 1765

FASHION ; or something to wear. By the author of The Lentiad [Rev. John Allan, minister in Aberdeen]. 8vo.   Glasgow, [1880 ?]

FASHIONABLE (the) daughter ; being a narrative of true and recent facts. By an impartial hand [Daniel Turner]. Fcap 8vo. [Advertisement in his Westminster Forum.]
London, 1774

FASHIONABLE (a) day. In the first chapter of Genesis it is thus written— And the evening and the morning were the first day. And the evening and the morning were the second day, &c. to the end of the chapter. A new edition, corrected, with a post-script. [By Lady Elizabeth Berkeley, afterwards Lady Craven ; latterly Margravine of Anspach.] 8vo. Pp. ix., 123.   London, 1780

FASHIONABLE follies ; a novel : containing the history of a Parisian family. 2 vols. [By T. Vaughan.] [European Mag., i., 30, 58.]
London, 1781

FASHIONABLE (the) folly ! Oh ! say not woman's skirts are short ! A parody. Air,—" Oh ! say not woman's love is bought ! " [By Charles Clark.]
N.P., 1860

Signed " Snarly Charley." A broadside, printed by Charles Clark (an amateur) at his private press.

FASHIONABLE (the) friends ; a comedy, in five acts : as performed by their Majesties servants at the Theatre Royal, Drury Lane. [By Mary Berry.] 8vo. Pp. 85. [Bodl.]
London, 1802

FASHIONABLE (the) lover ; a comedy : as it is acted at the Theatre-Royal in Drury-Lane. [By Richard Cumberland.] 8vo. [Biog. Dram.]
London, 1772

FASHIONABLE (the) tragedian ; a criticism [of Sir Henry Irving. By William Archer and Robert W. Lowe]. Fcap 8vo. Pp. 28. [Brit. Mus.]
Edinburgh, 1877

FASHIONABLE (the) wife : a dramatic sketch for the times. By the author of Neddy Fitton, etc. [Miss R. Lahee]. 8vo. Pp. 15.   Manchester, N.D.

FASHIONABLE (the) world displayed. By Theophilus Christian, Esq. [John Owen, M.A.]. Fcap 8vo. [Watt's Bibl. Brit.]   London, 1804

The author's name is given in the corrected and enlarged second edition, also published in 1804.

FASHION'S analysis ; or, the winter in town : a satirical poem. By Sir Anthony Avalanche [—— Blauvelt]. Fcap 8vo. Pp. 84. [Cushing's Init. and Pseud., vol. i., p. 22.]
New York, 1807

FAST friends ; or David and Jonathan. By H. F. E. [Evelyn Everett-Green]. 8vo. Pp. 128.   London, [1883]

FAST life ; an autobiography . . . of a man about town, who has seen all that can be seen, and knows all that can be known in London and Paris. [By J— Lennox.] Fcap 8vo. Pp. 256.
London, [1859]

FAST (a) sermon for February the 27th, 1799 ; from Isaiah, chap. x. ver. 5. [By Stephen Weston, B.D.]   4to. Pp. 16. [Bodl.]   London, 1799

The author's name is in the handwriting of Douce, to whom the copy was presented by the author.

FAST-DAY (the) ; a Lambeth eclogue. By the author of *The Auction* [William Combe]. 4to. Pp. 32. [*D. N. B.*, vol. 11, p. 433.]   London, 1780
The dedication is signed " P. Q."

FASTI Ecclesiæ Anglicanæ ; or an essay towards a regular succession of the dignitaries in each cathedral, collegiate church, or chapel, now in being in those parts in England and Wales from the first erection thereof to the year 1715. [According to Browne Willis, John Le Neve has the name and credit of this work, yet Bishop Kennett was the real author.] Folio. [Lowndes' *Bibl. Man.*]
                              London, 1716

FASTING, versus evening Communion. By F. H. D. [Francis Henry Dickinson]. 8vo.   London, [1869]

FAT (the) knight and the petition ; or, cits in the dumps ! A poem. By Peter Pindar, Esq. [John Wolcot, M.D.]. 8vo. [*D. N. B.*, vol. 62, p. 293.]   London, N.D.

FAT (the) of the land. [A novel.] By Maria Soltera [Mary Lester]. 3 vols. Cr 8vo. [*Adv. Lib. Cat.*]
                            Edinburgh, 1888

FATA mihi totvm mea sunt agitanda per orbem. [By Sir Dudley Digges.] 8vo. Pp. 30. Imprinted at London by W. W. for Iohn Barnes.   1611
Reissued in 1612 with the following English title :—" Of the circumference of the earth ; or, a treatise of the North-east [altered in MS. to North-weast] passage." Imprint the same, with the exception of the date. On the Bodl. copy of 1611, the work is ascribed in MS. to " Sir Jhon Hollis." It is however noticed in the Cat. under Sir Dudley Digges. In a MS. note by Bliss, it is said, " I have now no doubt but that this was a presentation copy from Sir D. Digges to Sir J. Hollis."

FATAL (a) affinity ; a weird story. By Stuart C. Cumberland [Charles Garner, of Oxford]. 8vo. Pp. 160. [*Brit. Mus.*]   London, 1889

FATAL (the) chain : from the Swedish of Uncle Adam [Carl Anton Wetterbergh]. 8vo. [Cushing's *Init. and Pseud.*, ii., 4.]   London, 1864

FATAL (the) consequences of minist¹. influence ; or, the difference between royal power and ministerial power truly stated : a political essay occasioned by the petition presented last session of Parliament by six noble peers of Scotland, and addressed to the noble, the ancient, and the rich families of Great Britain. With an appendix, containing copies of those accounts of illegal practices at the last election of P—s, which some N—les and others were ready to have given, and are still ready to give upon oath, if required. [By the Hon. James Erskine, of Grange.] 8vo. Pp. iv., 61. [*Adv. Lib.*]   London, 1736

FATAL (the) discovery ; a tragedy : as it is performed at the Theatre-Royal, in Drury-Lane. [By John Home.] 8vo. Pp. 76. [*Biog. Dram.*]
                              London, 1769

FATAL (the) doom ; or, the charms of divine love. By R. H. [Robert Hooke]. Fcap 8vo. Pp. 203. [*Brit. Mus.*]
                              London, 1655

FATAL (the) effects of cow-pox protection. [By John Birch, surgeon.] Fcap 8vo. [Upcott and Shoberl's *Biog. Dict.*, p. 27.]   London, 1808

FATAL (the) extravagance ; a tragedy. By Joseph Mitchell [rather Aaron Hill]. 8vo. [Cushing's *Init. and Pseud.*, i., p. 196.]   London, 1721
Afterwards wrongly included in the works of Joseph Mitchell. [Watt's *Bibl. Brit.*]

FATAL follies ; a novel. By Mrs Thomson [Miss Harriot Pigott]. Fcap 8vo.   London, N.D.

FATAL (the) friendship ; a tragedy. [By Mrs Catherine Cockburn, *née* Trotter.] 4to. [Watt's *Bibl. Brit.*]
                              London, 1698

FATAL friendship ; or the drunkard's misery : being a satyr against hard drinking. By the author of *The Search after claret* [Richard Ames]. Fcap 4to. [Dobell's *Cat.*]
                              London, 1693

FATAL (the) gift of beauty. By C. E. Raimond [Elizabeth Robins, later Mrs G. R. Parkes]. 8vo. [*Lond. Lib. Cat.*]   Chicago, 1892

FATAL (the) inheritance. By Nellie Graham [Mrs Annie Dunning, *née* Ketchum]. 12mo. [Kirk's *Supp.*]
                            Philadelphia, 1879

FATAL (the) jealousie ; a tragedy, acted at the Duke's Theatre. [By Nevil Payne.] 4to. [*Biog. Dram.*]
                              London, 1673

FATAL jealousy ; or, friendship's balm. From the German of Stockingbach. [By T. Wright Vaughan, Esq., author of a *View of the state of Sicily*, etc.] 8vo. Pp. 16. [*James Maidment.*]
                              Paris, 1816

FATAL (the) kiss ; a poem, written in the last stage of an atrophy. By a beautiful and unfortunate young lady. [By Rev. Thos. Sedgwick Whalley, D.D.] 4to. [*Mon. Rev.*, lxiv., 311 ; lxviii., 185.]   London, 1781

FATAL (the) legacy ; a tragedy : as it is acted at the Theatre-Royal in Lincolns-Inn Fields. [By J. Robe.] 8vo. [*Biog. Dram.*]   London, 1723

FATAL lilies. By Bertha M. Clay [Mrs Charlotte M. Braeme, *née* Law.] 8vo.   London, 1881

FATAL (a) misunderstanding, and other stories. By W. Heimburg [Bertha Behrens] ; translated from the German. Pt 8vo. Pp. 313.   New York, 1893

FATAL necessity ; or, liberty regain'd : a tragedy, as it was once acted in Rome for the sake of freedom and virtue. Collected from Vertot's History of the revolutions in the Roman republick. [By Robert Morris.] Fcap 8vo. [*Biog. Dram.*]   .   Dublin, 1741

FATAL (the) passion. [A novel. By Lady Caroline Lamb.]   Cr 8vo.
                                London, 1865
   A later edition of "Glenarvon." *See below*

FATAL (the) retirement ; a tragedy : as it was intended to have been acted at the Theatre-Royal in Drury-Lane, by His Majesty's servants. [By Anthony Brown.] 8vo. Pp. 86. [*Biog. Dram.*]   London, 1739

FATAL revenge ; or the family of Montorio. By Dennis Jasper Murphy [Rev. Charles Robert Maturin]. 4 vols. Fcap 8vo. [*Edin. Select Subscription Lib. Cat.*, p. 268.]
                                London, 1824

FATAL (the) ring. [A novel.] By Dick Donovan [Joyce Emerson Preston Muddock]. Cr 8vo. [*Lond. Lib. Cat.*]
                                London, 1912

FATAL (the) smile : a fairy tale. Written and illustrated by Cynicus [J. Martin Anderson]. 4to. [*Brit. Mus.*]   London, 1892

FATAL (the) three ; a novel. By the author of *Lady Audley's Secret*, etc. [Mary Elizabeth Braddon, later Mrs John Maxwell]. 3 vols. 8vo. [*Lond. Lib. Cat.*]   London, 1888

FATAL (the) wedding. By Bertha M. Clay [Mrs Charlotte M. Braeme]. Fcap 8vo.   New York, 1892

FATAL (the) woman ; a novel. By Dick Donovan [Joyce E. Preston Muddock]. Cr 8vo. Pp. 312. [*Lit. Year Book.*]   London, 1911

FATAL zero ; a diary kept at Homburg. [By Percy Hetherington Fitzgerald, M.A.] 2 vols. 8vo.   London, 1869
   An edition of 1886 has the author's name.

FATALIST (the) ; or the fortunes of Godolphin. By an essayist on the passions [Nicholas Michell]. 3 vols. Pt 8vo. [*Cushing's Init. and Pseud.*, vol. i., p. 93.]   London, 1840

FATALL (the) dovvry ; a tragedy : as it hath beene often acted in the priuate house in Blackefryers, by his maiesties seruants. Written by P. M. and N. F. [Philip Massinger, and Nathaniel Field]. 4to. No pagination. [First edition.] [Dyce *Cat.*] Printed by Iohn Norton, for Francis Constable, and are to be sold at his shop at the Crane, in Pauls churchyard.
                                London, 1632

FATALL (the) Vesper ; or a true and punctuall relation of that lamentable and fearefull accident hapning on 26th of October last by the fall of a roome in the Black-Friers, in which were assembled many people at a sermon which was to be preached by Father Drurie a Jesuite. . . . By W. C. [William Crashaw ?]. Fcap 4to. [*Brit. Mus.*]   London, 1623

FATE. [Poems.] By Robert Blake [Robert Hely Thompson]. 8vo. Pp. 63. [*Brit. Mus.*]   London, 1916

FATE (the) of Captain Patton. By Weatherby Chesney [Charles John Cutcliffe Hyne]. Fcap 8vo. Pp. 210. [*Brit. Mus.*]   London, 1917

FATE (the) of Castle Lowengard : a story of the days of Luther. By Esmé Stuart [Amélie Claire Leroy]. 8vo. [*Lond. Lit. Cat.*]   London, 1883

FATE (the) of folly. [A novel.] By Lord B*** [Frederick R— Chichester, Earl of Belfast]. 8vo. [Cushing's *Init. and Pseud.*, vol. i., p. 28.]
                                London, 1859
   Mistakenly attributed to Henry, Lord Brougham.

FATE (the) of Julia ; an elegiac poem, in two cantos, sacred to the memory of L[a]dy J[uli]a D[ou]g[la]s. [By Rev. Robert Colvill.] 4to. Edinburgh, 1769

FATE (the) of Lewellyn ; or the Druid's sacrifice : a legendary tale. To which is added, the Genius of Carnbre, a poem. By a young gentleman of Truro school. [Richard Polwhele.] 4to. Pp. 55. [Boase and Courtney's *Bibl. Corn.*, ii., 507.]   Bath, 1777

FATE (the) of the Peers ; or a few words with our Old Nobility. [By Alexander Macdonald.] 8vo. [Gladstone *Lib. Cat.* (Lib. Club).] London, 1869

FATE (the) of villany ; a play, as it is acted by the company of comedians, at the Theatre in Goodmans-Fields. [By Thomas Walker.] 8vo. Pp. 71. [*Biog. Dram.*]   London, 1730

FATE'S fetters. . . . From the French [Un Vaincu] of Jean de la Brète [Mlle A. Cherbonnel]. 8vo. Pp. 266. [*Lond. Lib. Cat.*]   London, [1897]

FATHER and son ; a study of two temperaments. [By Edmund Gosse, giving an account of himself and his father, Philip H. Gosse.] Dy 8vo. Pp. vii., 374. [*Brit. Mus.*]
London, 1907

FATHER Austin and Lewis.—A defence of the ancient principles of the Catholic Church, addressed to the clergy and people of Ireland. [By Henry Bewley.] 12mo. [Smith's *Cat. of Friends' Books*, i., 266.]
Dublin, 1829

FATHER Brighthopes ; or an old clergyman's vacation. [A novel.] By Paul Creyton [John Townsend Trowbridge]. 8vo. [Cushing's *Init. and Pseud.*, vol. i., p. 70.]
New York, 1853

FATHER Butler and the Lough Derg pilgrimage. [By William Carleton.] 8vo. Pp. 302. [S. J. Brown's *Ireland in fiction.*]
Dublin, 1829

" FATHER Clark," or the pioneer preacher. By an old pioneer [John Mason Peck, D.D.]. 8vo. [Cushing's *Init. and Pseud.*, vol. i., 212.]
New York, 1855

FATHER Clement ; a Roman Catholic story. [By Grace Kennedy.] 8vo. [*Adv. Lib.*]
Edinburgh, 1823
Later editions give the name of the writer.

FATHER Connell. By the O'Hara family. [By John Banim only.] 3 vols. Fcap 8vo. [O'Donoghue's *Poets of Ireland.*]
London, 1842

FATHER Cotton, a Iesuite . . . his two and thirtie demands to the ministers of France . . . also threescore and foure proposed to Father Cotton by way of counter-change. By Peter Moulin. Translated by I. B. [John Barnes]. 4to. [*Camb. Univ. Lib. Cat.*]
London, 1615

FATHER Darcy ; an historical romance. By the author of *Mount Sorel* [Mrs Anne Marsh-Caldwell]. 2 vols. 8vo. [*D. N. B.*, vol. 36, p. 219.]
London, 1846

FATHER Godfrey. By the author of *Anne Dysart*, etc. [Christiana Jane Douglas]. 3 vols. 8vo. [*Brit. Mus.*]
London, 1873

FATHER Hubburd's tales ; or, the ant and the nightingale. [By Thomas Middleton, dramatist.] 4to. [*Pollard and Redgrave.*]
London, 1604
Signed " T. M."

FATHER John. By Hope Daring [Anna Johnson]. Fcap 8vo. [*Amer. Cat.*]
New York, 1907

VOL. II.

FATHER Payne. [By Arthur Christopher Benson.] Cr 8vo. [*Lond. Lib. Cat.*]
London, 1915
The second edition (1916) bears the author's name.

FATHER Rhine. [An account of a summer tour. By George Gordon Coulton.] 8vo. Pp. viii., 231. [*Brit. Mus.*]
London, 1899

FATHER (the), Son, and Holy Ghost proved to be one God, or only object of adoration : in answer to thirteen queries proposed to be considered as unanswerable objections to this important doctrine. By C. S. [Samuel Codrington, of Bridgewater]. 8vo. [Green's *Bibl. Somers.*, ii., 311.]
London, 1736

FATHER Stafford. [A novel.] By Anthony Hope [Anthony Hope Hawkins, M.A.]. Cr 8vo. Pp. 316. [*Brit. Mus.*]
London, 1910

FATHER Tom and the Pope ; or a night at the Vatican, as related by Mr Michael Heffermann, master of the National School at Tally-Mactaggart, in the County of Leitrim. . . . [By Sir Samuel Ferguson, LL.D.] 8vo. [O'Donoghue's *Poets of Ireland.*]
New York, 1868
Wrongly attributed to Dr William Maginn, and to John Fisher Murray.

FATHERLESS Fanny ; or, a young lady's first entrance into life ; being the memoirs of a little mendicant and her benefactors. By the author of *The Old English baron* [Clara Reeve]. 8vo. [*Brit. Mus.*]
London, 1819
An edition, prepared by Mrs Sarah Green, with full-page engravings, was issued in 1837.

FATHER'S (the) catechism, in a legacy to his eighth [*sic*] children ; or a help for the young and ignorant, in order to their better understanding the Assembly's Catechism. By W. L. [Robert Lang] and entered conform to Act of Parliament. 12mo. [*Adv. Lib.*]
Glasgow, 1726

FATHER'S coming home ; a tale for the young. By the author of *Copsley annals* [Emily S. Elliot]. Fcap 8vo.
London, 1871

FATHER'S (a) gift to his children ; being a short view of the evidences of the Christian religion. By a layman [Robert Ainslie]. 12mo. Pp. 119. [*Brit. Mus.*]
Edinburgh, 1818
This was followed by " A Father's second present . . ." *See below.*

S

FATHER'S (the) kingdom on earth ; a social ideal condition realised by bringing up infant children : a selection from the new revelation " Oahspe." [By John Ballou.]   8vo.   Pp. 71. [*Brit. Mus.*]   Letchworth, 1911 *See later,* " Oahspe."

FATHER'S (a) legacy ; meditations written in the years 1858-1861. By a layman of the Church of England [James Malony].   2 vols. 8vo. Greenwich, 1859-64

FATHER'S (a) letters to his son. [By George Barclay to Robert Barclay.] 8vo. [Cushing's *Init. and Pseud.*, ii., 58.]   Philadelphia, 1845

FATHERS (the) of Caithness ; a poem. By W. C. [William Crowe, of Wick]. New edition. 8vo. Pp. 32. [Mowat's *Bibl. of Caithness.*]   Glasgow, 1896 The first edition was published at Wick in 1869.

FATHERS (the) of the Church. By the author of *Tales of Kirkbeck*, etc. [Henrietta Louisa Farrer, later Mrs H. Sidney Lear].   Second edition.   3 vols. 8vo. [*Brit. Mus.*]   London, 1873 Wrongly assigned to C. A. Jones.

FATHER'S (a) reasons for repose ; or details and inferences connected with the early and latter days of a youth, most affectionately beloved and deeply lamented by the surviving members of his family. [By Rev. Thomas Fry, of Emberton.]   8vo.   Pp. xvi., 230. London, 1839

FATHER'S (a) recollection of three pious young ladies. By a clergyman [Samuel Pigott].   8vo.   London, 1831

FATHER'S (a) second present to his family ; or a short demonstration of the being and attributes of God. By a layman, author of *A Father's gift to his children* [Robert Ainslie]. Fcap 8vo. Pp. xiv., 271. [*Brit. Mus.*] Edinburgh, 1820 *See above,* " A Father's gift . . ."

FATHERS (the), the Reformers, and the public formularies of the Church of England, in harmony with Calvin and against the Bishop of Lincoln ; to which is prefixed a letter to the Archbishop of Canterbury on the subject of this controversy. By a layman [John Allen].   8vo.   Pp. xxxii., 131. London, 1812 The Bishop was George P. Tomline, who had published " A Refutation of Calvinism."

FATHER'S (the) tragedy.   William Rufus. Loyalty or love ? [being three historical plays, in blank verse].   By Michael Field [Katharine H. Bradley, and Edith E. Cooper]. 8vo. Pp. 312. [*Lond. Lib. Cat.*]   London, [1885]

FATHERS (the) vindicated ; or animadversions on a late Socinian book [by Thomas Smalbroke], entituled, " The judgment of the Fathers touching the Trinity, against Dr [George] Bull's Defence of the Nicene faith." By a Presbyter of the Church of England [J— Deacon]. 8vo. [Arber's *Term Cat.*, vol. iii., p. 686.] London, 1697

FAULTS on both sides : or, an essay upon the original cause, progress, and mischievous consequences of the factions in this nation ; shewing, that the heads and leaders on both sides have always impos'd upon the credulity of their respective parties, in order to compass their own selfish designs at the expence of the peace and tranquillity of the nation.   By way of answer to The Thoughts of an honest Tory [by Benjamin Hoadly].   [By Richard Harley.]   8vo.   Pp. 56. London, 1710 Ascribed also to Daniel Defoe and to Clements, secretary to the Earl of Peterborough. [*See* note in *Adv. Lib. Cat.; Bliss Cat.*, 307.] Printed in Scott's edition of Somers' Tracts, xii., 678. It was followed by " A Vindication of the Faults on both sides . . ." There appeared in the same year a pamphlet, entitled, " Faults on both sides ; part the second ; or, an essay upon the original cause, progress, and mischievous consequences of the factions in the Church ; shewing that the clergy, of whatsoever denomination, have always been the ring-leaders and beginners of the disturbances in every state ; imposing upon the credulity of the laity, for no other end than the accomplishing their own selfish designs, at the expence of the peace and tranquillity of the nation. . . . By way of letter to a new Member of Parliament." London, 1710. 8vo. Pp. 38. It is printed in the same volume of Somers' Tracts, p. 708. It has no author's name ; and is not a continuation of Harley's pamphlet, but an answer to it. Other anonymous pamphlets in reply are " Most faults on one side," " Faults in the fault-finders."

FAUSSETT (the) collection of Anglo-Saxon antiquities. [From the " Collectanea Antiqua," Vol. III.]   [By Charles Roach Smith.] 8vo. [*Bodl.*] London, 1854

FAUST ; a dramatic poem, by Goethe : translated into English prose, with remarks on former translations, and notes. By the translator of Savigny's *Of the vocation of our age for legislation and jurisprudence* [Abraham Hayward, Q.C.]. 8vo. Pp. 279. [Martin's *Cat.*]   London, 1833 Preface signed " A. H."

FAUST ; a tragedy, by J. W. Goethe :
Part II., as completed in 1831, trans-
lated into English verse. [By William
Bell M'Donald, of Rammerscales.]
Second edition. 8vo. Pp. viii., 351.
                              London, 1840
  The 1st edition was printed at Dumfries,
1838.

FAUST, Part I., translated by C. H. B.
[Charles Hartpole Bowen]. 8vo.
[O'Donoghue's *Poets of Ireland*, p. 22.]
                              London, 1878

FAUSTINE : a novel. By " Rita "
[Mrs W. Desmond Humphreys, *née*
Eliza M. J. Gollan]. 3 vols. Cr 8vo.
[*Lond. Lib. Cat.*]   London, 1882

FAUSTULA ; in A.D. 340. By John
Ayscough [Monsignor Francis Bicker-
staffe-Drew]. Cr 8vo. Pp. 340.
[*Cath. Who's Who.*]   London, 1912

FAUSTUS ; a romantic drama [in
three acts and in verse]. [By George
Soane.] 8vo. [*Brit. Mus.*]
                              London, 1825
  Ascribed also to Daniel Terry.

FAUSTUS ; his life, death, and descent
into Hell : translated from the German
[of F. M. von Klinger. By George
Borrow]. 8vo. [*Brit. Mus.*]
                              London, 1825

FAUSTUS ; the Bride of Corinth ; the
First Walpurgis Night. Translated
from the German by J. A. [John Martin
Anster, LL.D.]. 8vo. [O'Donoghue's *Poets of Ireland*.]
                              London, 1835

FAVOURITE (the) of fortune. By
Shirley Smith [Ella J. Curtis]. 3 vols.
Pt 8vo. [Cushing's *Init. and Pseud.*,
vol. i., p. 269.]   London, 1886

FAVOURITE (the) of nature ; a tale.
[By Mary Ann Kelty.] 3 vols. Fcap
8vo. [*Brit. Mus.*]   London, 1821

FAVOVRITES (the) chronicle. [A
satire on Charles d'Albert, Constable
of France, and his brothers. By . . .
Langlois, also known as Fancan,
Canon of St Honoré. Translated
from the French.] Printed according
to the French copie. 4to. [*Brit. Mus.*]
                              London, 1621

FAVOURITES (the) of Henry of
Navarre. By " Le petit homme rouge "
[Ernest Alfred Vizetelly]. 8vo. Pp.
334. [*Lond. Lib. Cat.*] London, 1910

FAVOURITES (the) of Louis XIV.
By " Le petit homme rouge " [Ernest
A. Vizetelly]. 8vo. Pp. 294.
                              London, 1912

FAVOURS from France. [A novel.] By
Sarah Tytler [Henrietta Keddie]. 8vo.
Pp. 310.   London, 1904

FAWCETTS (the) and Garods. [A
novel.] By Säimath [Augusta A.
Varty-Smith, of Penrith]. 8vo.
                              London, [1886]

FAWKESES (the) of York in the six-
teenth century ; including notices of
the early history of Guy Fawkes, the
Gunpowder - plot conspirator. [By
Robert Davies, F.S.A.] 8vo. Pp. 67.
[Boyne's *Yorkshire Lib.*, p. 240.]
                              Westminster, 1850

FAWN (the) of Sertorius. [By Rev.
Robert Eyres Landor, M.A.] 2 vols.
12mo. [*Adv. Lib. Cat.*]
                              London, 1846

FAWNING (the) hypocrite ; a farce.
[By William Sinclair.] Fcap 8vo. Pp.
24. [*David Laing.*]   N.P., 1772

FAYOUM (the) ; or artists in Egypt.
. . . By Paul Lenoir. [Translated
from the French by Mrs F. C. Hoey.]
8vo. [*Brit. Mus.*]   London, 1873

FAYRE (the) mayde of the exchange ;
with the pleasaunt humours of the
cripple of Fanchurch : very delectable,
and full of mirth. [By Thomas Heywood.] 4to. No pagination. [*Biog.
Dram.*]   London, 1607

FEAR ; and other essays in fiction and
fact. By the author of *Times and
days* [John H. Balfour Browne]. 8vo.
Pp. vi., 229.   London, 1912

FEARS and dangers fairly display'd ;
being a New Memorial of the Church
of England. [By Elkanah Settle.]
4to. Private print.   London, 1706
  See below, the previously published
" Memorial of the Church of England."

FEARS and jealousies ceas'd : or, an
impartial discourse tending to demon-
strate, from the folly and ill success of
the Romish politicks, that there is no
reason to apprehend any danger from
Popery. In a letter to a friend, by T.
D. [Thomas Doolittle]. 4to. [Mend-
ham Collection *Cat.*, p. 96.]
                              N.P., [1688]

FEARS (the) and sentiments of all true
Britains, with respect to national
credit, interest and religion. [By
Benjamin Hoadly.] 8vo.
                              London, 1710

FEAST (the) of feasts ; or, the celebration of the nativity of our blessed Lord
and Saviour, Jesus Christ, grounded
upon the Scriptures and confirmed by
the practice of the Christian Church in
all ages. [By Edward Fisher.] 4to.
[*Bodl.*]   Oxford, 1644

FEAST (a) of fun. By Billy Burgundy
[Oliver V. Limerick]. Fcap 8vo.
[*Amer. Cat.*]   New York, 1904

FEAST (a) of literary crumbs, or poems, letters, songs, and nonsense. By Foo Foozle [James Thomson] and friends. Edited by Simon Strap, Esq. [James Myles]. Pt 8vo. Dundee, 1848

FEAST (the) of the poets ; with notes and other pieces in verse. By the editor of the *Examiner* [James Henry Leigh Hunt]. 8vo. [*Lowndes' Bibl. Man.*] London, 1814

FEASTS (the) of the Lord—Holy Convocations. By H. C. A. [Rev. Harry C. Anstey, M.A.]. 8vo. Pp. 16. London, 1902

FEATHERS from the moulting Muse. By the residuary legatee of the late Walter Anonym [Henry Jackson Sargent]. 8vo. [*Cushing's Init. and Pseud.*, vol. i., p. 250.] Boston, 1854

FEATURES from life ; or, a summer visit. By the author of *George Bateman*, and *Maria* [Elizabeth Blower]. 2 vols. Second edition. Fcap 8vo. [*Watt's Bibl. Brit.*] London, 1788

FEDERATION (the) of the world ; with which is embodied The Secret of sound finance. By the Spirit of Truth [Charles P. W. Longdill]. 8vo. Pp. 50. [*Brit. Mus.*] Auckland, N.Z., 1919

FEEDING the mind. By Lewis Carroll [Rev. Charles L. Dodgson, M.A.]. Cr 8vo. Pp. 32. London, 1907
See the note appended to " Doubtlets."

FEELING ; or sketches from life : a desultory poem. By a lady [Mrs Elizabeth Bonhote]. Fcap 8vo. Edinburgh, 1810

FELICIAN Alphery ; or, the fortunes of the Raleigh family. By the author of *Herwald de Wake* [Hewson Clark]. 3 vols. Fcap 8vo. [*Adv. Lib.*] London, 1828

FELICITÀ ; a romance of old Siena. By Christopher Hare [Mrs Marion Andrews]. Cr 8vo. Pp. 286. [*Lond. Lib. Cat.*] London, 1904

FELIX de Lisle ; an autobiography. [By Anne Flinders.] 8vo. Pp. viii., 207. [*Bodl.*] London, 1840

FELIX Dupanloup, Bishop of Orleans. By the author of *Charles Lowder* [Maria Trench]. 8vo. [*Brit. Mus.*] London, 1890

FELIX Farley rhymes, Latin and English. By Themaninthemoon [Rev. John Eagles]. 8vo. Pp. ix., 158. [*D. N. B.*, vol. 16, p. 312.] Bristol, 1826
The work has also an engraved title-page, on which there is an engraving intended to represent " Themaninthemoon."

FELIX Holt the Radical. By George Eliot, author of *Adam Bede*, etc. [Marian Evans, later Mrs Cross]. 3 vols. 8vo. [*Brit. Mus.*] Edinburgh, 1866

FELIX Lanzberg's expiation ; from the German of Ossip Schubin [Lola Kirschner]. Fcap 8vo. [*Cushing's Init. and Pseud.*, vol. i., p. 261.] New York, 1892

FELIX on the bat ; being a scientific inquiry into the use of the Cricket bat : with the history of the Catapulta ; also the laws of Cricket. [By Nicholas Wanostrocht, jun.] Fcap 4to. [*Cushing's Init. and Pseud.*, vol. i., p. 100.] London, 1845

FELIX Summerly's day's excursions out of London to Erith, Rochester, and Cobham in Kent : with illustrations and suitable maps. [By Sir Henry Cole, K.C.B.] 8vo. Pp. 130. [*D. N. B.*, vol. 11, p. 269.] London, 1843
These papers appeared in the *Athenæum*, in the year 1842.

FELIX Summerly's handbook for the City of Canterbury ; its historical associations and works of art, with numerous illustrations and a map of the City. [By Sir Henry Cole, K.C.B.] Fcap 8vo. [*D. N. B.*, vol. 11, p. 269.] Canterbury, 1842

FELIX Summerly's handbook for the National Gallery. [By Sir Henry Cole, K.C.B.] Pt 8vo. [*Brit. Mus.*] London, 1843

FELLOW (the) commoner. [By Rev. John Hobart Caunter, B.D.] 3 vols. Fcap 8vo. [*Camb. Univ. Lib.*] London, 1836
A considerable portion appeared originally in a series of papers in the *Court Magazine*, under the title of " Remarkable escapes of a predestinated rogue."

FELLOW (a) of Trinity. [A novel.] By Alan St Aubyn [Mrs Frances Marshall]. Cr 8vo. [*Lond. Lib. Cat.*] London, 1897

FELLOW travellers. [A novel.] By Graham Travers [Margaret Todd, M.D.]. 8vo. [*Lond. Lib. Cat.*] London, 1896

FELLOWSHIP : letters addressed to my sister mourners. [By Lady Elizabeth Eastlake, *née* Rigby.] 8vo. Pp. 101. [*Courtney's Secrets*, p. 63.] London, 1868
Later editions bear the name of the authoress.

FELLOWSIANA ; a dramatic sketch : dedicated without permission to the Goldthorn Hill Lodge of Odd Fellows, and to the Aldermen, Town Councillors, and Burgesses of Wolverhampton, who are opposed to the sewerage. By a sanitary reformer [John Beddows, bookseller]. 8vo. Pp. 32. Wolverhampton, N.D.

FELLOW-TRAVELLER (the) through city and countrey. [By Henry Edmundson.] Fcap 8vo. Pp. 342.
N.P., 1658

"Other copies of this book have a different title page, viz. ' Comes facundus in via ' &c. by Democritus Secundus, 1658. In all other respects it is the same. It is somewhere stated that Barton Holyday compiled this work, and that the signature " N. Mendicus hodiernus " at the end of the first address to the reader is a conundrum for his name. But these words are rather an anagram of Henricus Edmundson."—MS. note by Douce, in the Bodleian copy.

FELONIOUS (the) treaty ; or an enquiry into the reasons which moved his late majesty, King William of glorious memory, to enter into a treaty at two several times with the King of France for the partition of the Spanish monarchy. With an essay, proving that it was always the sense both of King William, and of all the confederates, and even of the grand alliance it self, that the Spanish monarchy should never be united in the person of the Emperor. By the author of the *Review* [Daniel Defoe]. 8vo. [Wilson's *Life of Defoe*, 128.]
London, 1711

FELSTED School. By an old Felstedian [Thomas Seccombe, M.A.]. 8vo. [*Brit. Mus.*] N.P., 1898

FEMALE (the) advocate : a poem. By [William Woty]. 4to. London, 1770

The second edition, published in 1771, has the author's name.

FEMALE (the) advocate ; or, a plea for the just liberty of the tender sex, and particularly of married women. Being reflections on a late rude and disingenuous discourse delivered by Mr John Sprint. . . . By a lady of Quality [Lady Mary Chudleigh]. Pt 8vo. [Green's *Bibl. Somers.*, vol. iii., p. 276.] Bath, 1700

The preface is signed " Eugenia." *See also* " The Female preacher . . ."

FEMALE (the) advocates ; or, the frantick stock-jobber : a comedy, as it is acted at the Theatre-Royal in Drury-Lane, by her Majesty's servants. [By William Taverner.] 4to. [*Biog. Dram.*] London, 1713

FEMALE (the) captive ; a narrative of facts which happened in Barbary, in the year 1756. Written by herself [Mrs Crisp, daughter of Milborn [?] Marsh, naval officer at Port-Mahon in Minorca]. Fcap 8vo. [*Brit. Mus.*] London, 1769

"This is a true story. The lady's maiden name was Marsh. She married Mr Crisp, as related in the following narrative ; but he, having failed in business, went to India, while she remained with her father, then agent victualler at Chatham, during which she wrote and published these little volumes. On her husband's success in India, she went thither to him. The book having, as it is said, been bought up by the lady's friends, is become very scarce." —Note by Sir W. Musgrave in the British Museum copy.

FEMALE education : its importance, design, and nature considered. By a labourer's daughter [Barbara H. Farquhar]. Fcap 8vo. [*Brit. Mus.*]
London, 1851

FEMALE excellency, or the ladies' glory : worthy lives and memorable actions of nine famous women. By R. B. [Robert Burton, *alias* Nathaniel Crouch]. 12mo. London, 1688

See the Note appended to " Admirable curiosities."

FEMALE (the) fire-ships ; a satyr against whoring : in a letter to a friend just come to town. [By Richard Ames.] [Arber's *Term Cat.*, ii., 615.] London, 1691

FEMALE (the) fop ; or, the false one fitted : a comedy, as it is acted at the New Theatre over-against the Opera-House in the Hay-Market. [By —— Sandford.] 8vo. Pp. 94. [*Biog. Dram.*] London, 1724

FEMALE grievances debated, in six dialogues between two young ladies concerning love and marriage, viz. I. Proving that women, as well as men, are inclin'd to love, and equally desirous of propagating their kind. II. Shewing what love is ; its sorts and power, and the difference between love and lust. III. How to discern whether a man or woman be in love. IV. Directions for young ladies prudent managing the affairs of love. V. Of marriage ; that it is the duty of every person to marry, unless there be a lawful impediment. VI. The unreasonableness and injustice of marrying for money : and the great misfortunes that frequently attend such as do. [By Edward Ward.] The second edition. 8vo. Pp. 164. [*Bodl.*] London, 1707

FEMALE (the) Inquisition. By a lady [George Alexander Stevens]. 8vo. [Cushing's *Init. and Pseud.*, vol. i., p. 161.] London, 1753

FEMALE (the) Jesuit : or, the spy in the family. [By Mrs S— Luke.] 8vo. [*Adv. Lib.*] London, 1851
This was followed by " A Sequel to the female Jesuit " (1852).

FEMALE (the) Jockey Club ; or, a sketch of the manners of the age. . . . By the author of the former Jockey Club [Charles Pigott]. Fourth edition, with corrections and material additions. 8vo. [*Brit. Mus.*] London, 1794
See also " The Jockey Club."

FEMALE life among the Mormons. By the wife of a Mormon elder [Mrs Maria Ward]. 8vo. [Cushing's *Init. and Pseud.*, vol. i., p. 307.] New York, 1855
Attributed also to Mrs Benjamin G. Ferris.

FEMALE life in prison. By a prison matron [Frederick William Robinson]. Third edition, revised. 2 vols. 8vo. [*D. N. B.*, Supp. II., vol. 3, p. 216.] London, 1863
Wrongly assigned to Mary Carpenter.

FEMALE (the) missionary advocate ; a poem. [By Mrs —— Maddocks.] Fcap 8vo. [*Brit. Mus.*] London, 1827

FEMALE (a) Nihilist. By Stepniak [Michael Ozagomanoff]. Square 8vo. London, 1885
Attributed also to Sergius Kravtchinsky. [*Lond. Lib. Cat.*]

FEMALE poems on several occasions ; written by Ephelia [Mrs Joan Phillips]. 8vo. [*W.*] London, 1679
A second edition, enlarged, was issued in 1682.

FEMALE policy detected ; or the acts of a designing woman laid open, in maxims proper to be observed by all. Divided into six chapters. [By Edward Ward.] Fcap 8vo. [*Brit. Mus.*] London, 1695
The Epistle is signed " E. W."

FEMALE (the) preacher ; being an answer to a late rude and scandalous wedding-sermon, preach'd by Mr John Sprint, May the 11th, [1699] at Sherburn, in Dorsetshire ; wherein that Levite is expos'd as he deserves. By a Lady of Quality [Lady Mary Chudleigh]. Pt 8vo. Pp. 24. [Green's *Bibl. Somers.*, vol. iii., p. 276.] London, [1699]
See also above, " The Female advocate . . ."

FEMALE (the) prelate ; being the history of the life and death of Pope Joan : a tragedy, as it is acted at the Theatre Royal. Written by a person of quality [Elkanah Settle]. 4to. Pp. 60. [*Biog. Dram.*] London, 1689
There is an earlier edition, dated 1680.

FEMALE (the) Prince ; or Frederick of Sicily. [A novel.] Translated from the French by F. S. [Ferrand Spence]. Fcap 8vo. [*Brit. Mus.*] London, 1682

FEMALE (the) Quixote ; or, the adventures of Arabella. [By Mrs Charlotte Lennox, *née* Ramsay.] 2 vols. Fcap 8vo. [*Watt's Bibl. Brit.*] London, 1752

FEMALE (the) review. By a citizen of Massachusetts [Hermann Mann]. 8vo. [Cushing's *Init. and Pseud.*, vol. i., p. 58.] Oldham, Mass., 1797

FEMALE (the) revolutionary Plutarch, containing biographical, historical, and revolutionary sketches, characters, and anecdotes. By the author of *The Revolutionary Plutarch* and *Memoirs of Talleyrand* [—— Stewarton]. Fcap 8vo. [*Lond. Lib. Cat.*] London, 1806
Assigned also to Lewis Goldsmith.

FEMALE scripture characters, exemplifying female virtue. By the author of *The Beneficial effects of the Christian temper on domestic happiness* [Mrs King]. 2 vols. 12mo. [*Gent. Mag.*, Jan. 1800, p. 90.] London, 1813

FEMALE (the) speaker ; or, the priests in the wrong : a poem. Being an epistle from the celebrated Mrs D—mm—d [Drummond] to Dr St—b—g [Stebbing] and Mr F—t—r [Foster] ; occasioned by their dispute on the subject of heresy. Folio. Pp. 22. London, 1735
The name of the authoress is in the handwriting of Dr David Laing, who states that she was a sister of Provost Drummond of Edinburgh.

FEMALE (the) Spectator. [By Mrs Eliza Haywood, *née* Fowler.] 8vo. [*Watt's Bibl. Brit.*] London, 1744-46
Published in monthly parts, of which the first appeared in April 1744, and the twenty-fourth and last in March 1746.

FEMALE (the) suffrage movement ; its claims, objects, and consequences. By a citizen [Frederick E. Bevill]. 8vo. Sydney, N.S.W., 1896

FEMALE (the) visitor to the poor. By a clergyman's daughter [Maria Louisa Charlesworth]. 8vo. [Cushing's *Init. and Pseud.*, vol. i., p. 63.] London, 1846

FEMALE (the) volunteer, or the dawning of peace ; a drama, in three acts. By Philo-nauticus [Lawrence Hynes Halloran, D.D.]. 8vo. Pp. iv., 104. [*Biog. Dram.*] [London], 1801

FEMININE (a) conviction. By George Saint George [Mrs Saint George Hare]. Cr 8vo. London, 1896

FEMININE (the) in fiction. By L. A. M. Priestley [Mrs George Mac-Cracken]. Cr 8vo. [*Lond. Lib. Cat.*, Supp.]   London, [1918]

FENCING (the) girl; a London new soul. By Roof Roofer [Rufus Randell]. 8vo. Pp. 167. [*Brit. Mus.*]
London, 1895

FENCING-MASTER'S (the) advice to his scholars; or, a few directions for the more regular assaulting in schools: published by way of dialogue, for the benefit of all who shall be so far advanced in the art, as to be fit for assaulting. By the author of *The Scots fencing - master*, and *Swords-man's vade-mecum* [Sir William Hope, Bart.]. 8vo. Pp. 96. [*David Laing.*]
Edinburgh, 1692
The Dedication is signed " W. H."

FÉNELON, Archbishop of Cambrai; a biographical sketch. By the author of *Life of Bossuet*, etc. [Henrietta Louisa Farrer, later Mrs Sidney Lear]. Cr 8vo. Pp. xi., 473. [*Brit. Mus.*]
London, 1877

FEN-FARMING. By a landowner [Frederick Apthorp Paley]. 8vo. [*Brit. Mus.*]   London, [1880]

FENIAN (the) chief; or the martyr of '65: founded on recent events in Ireland's struggle for liberty. By the author of [the drama entitled] *Arrah na-Pogue*, etc. [Henry Ll. Williams]. 8vo. Pp. 100. [*Brit. Mus.*]   New York, [1865]

FENTON'S quest; a novel. By the author of *Lady Audley's secret*, etc. [Mary Elizabeth Braddon, later Mrs John Maxwell]. 3 vols. Cr 8vo. [*Brit. Mus.*]   London, 1871

FERDINAND and Ordella, a Russian story; with authentic anecdotes of the Russian Court after the demise of Peter the Great. . . . By Priscilla Parlante [The Hon. Mary Ann Cavendish Bradshaw]. 2 vols. Fcap 8vo. [Cushing's *Init. and Pseud.*, vol. i., p. 225.]   London, 1810

FERGUSONS (the); or, woman's love and the world's favour. [By E. Phipps.] 2 vols. Fcap 8vo. [*Adv. Lib.*]   London, 1839

FERN leaves from Fanny's portfolio. [By Mrs Sarah Payson Parton.] Illustrated by Birket Foster. 8vo. Pp. 326. [Cushing's *Init. and Pseud.*, vol. i., p. 101.]   London, 1853

FERNANDO. By John Ayscough [Monsignor Francis Bickerstaffe-Drew]. Cr 8vo. [*Cath. Who's Who.*]
London, 1918

FERNFOOT; or heart portraits. By M. D. [Mrs Margaret Duns, *née* Grant]. Pt 8vo. [*New Coll. Cat.*]
Edinburgh, 1856

FERNS (the). By Norval [James Scrymgeour]. Fcap 8vo. [*And. Jervise.*]   Dundee, 1867
Reprinted from the *Dundee Advertiser* of 25th February 1867.

FERN'S hollow. [A story.] By the author of *Jessica's first prayer*, etc. [Sarah Smith]. Fcap 8vo. Pp. 194.
London, 1864
See the note on " Alone in London."

FERNS (the) of Moffat; a collection of the ferns found in the neighbourhood of Moffat; with popular descriptions. [By Mrs J— Carruthers.] Imp 8vo.
Moffat, 1863

FERNS (the) of the British Isles described and photographed. By S. C. [S— Courtauld]. [Cushing's *Init. and Pseud.*, vol. i., p. 47.]   London, 1877

FERNYHURST Court; an every-day story. By the author of *Stone Edge* [Lady Frances Parthenope Verney]. 8vo. Pp. vii., 337. [*Adv. Lib.*]
London, 1871

FERRANDINO, a tale. Translated from the German [by H. G. Bohn]. 2 vols. Fcap 8vo. [Francis Harvey's *Cat.*]   London, 1813

FERRERS Court; a novel. By John Strange Winter [Mrs Arthur Stannard, *née* Henrietta E. V. Palmer]. Fcap 8vo. [*Brit. Mus.*] London, 1890

FERRY (the) hills [at North Queensferry]: a poem in three Cantos. [By Rev. Peter Macmorland, LL.D.] 8vo. [Scott's *Fasti.*]
Edinburgh, 1863

FERRY house (the); a sketch [of Knapdale, Eilan Mor, &c.]. Addressed to P. C. E. N., Uppingham. [By Thomas S. Muir.] No separate title-page. Cr 8vo. Pp. 56. [Mitchell and Cash's *Scot. Topogr.*, i., 15.] Private print.   [Edinburgh, 1864
Signed " Unda."

FERRY (the) maid of the Chattahoochee. By Cousin Annie [Annie Maria Barnes]. Pt 8vo. [*Amer. Cat.*]
Philadelphia, 1899

FERRY (the) man's boy, and other stories. By Crona Temple [Miss —— Corfield]. Fcap 8vo. [*Brit. Mus.*]
London, 1887

FESTIVAL (a) of song: a series of evenings with the poets. By the author of *Salad for the solitary* [Frederick Saunders]. Cr 8vo. [*Brit. Mus.*]   New York, 1866

FESTIVAL (the) of wit, or small talker; a collection of bon mots, anecdotes, etc., procured by G. K. [George King], summer resident at Windsor. Fcap 8vo.   Windsor, 1800

FESTIVALS (the) and Fasts of the Church of England. By a layman [Robert Nelson]: revised by L. Howard, D.D. Pt 8vo. [*D. N. B.*, vol. 40, p. 212.]   London, 1761
   The original edition ("A Companion to the Festivals and Fasts of the Church of England") is not anonymous, nor are later reprints.

FESTOON (the); a collection of epigrams, ancient and modern, panegyrical, satyrical, amorous, moral, humorous, monumental: with an essay on that species of composition. [By Rev. Richard Graves.] Fcap 8vo. Pp. xx., 200. [Watt's *Bibl. Brit.*]
                           London, 1766

FESTORUM metropolis; or the birthday of Jesus Christ annually to be kept holy. Written by Pastor Fido [Allan Blayney]. 4to. Pp. 77. [Thomason *Coll. of Tracts*, i., 882.] London, 1652
   The second edition, with the author's name, appeared in 1654.

FESTUM voluptatis; or, the banquet of pleasure; containing divers choice songs, love posies, sonnets, odes, madrigals, satyrs, epigrams, &c. By S. P. [Samuel Pick], Gent.   4to. [Lowndes' *Bibl. Man.*]   London, 1639

FESTUS; a poem. [By Philip James Bailey.] 8vo. Pp. 361.   [*Bodl.*]
                           London, 1839

FETTERED (the) exile; a poem, in five cantos. By the author of *The noviciate; or, The Jesuit in training*, etc. [Andrew Steinmetz]. 8vo. [*Brit. Mus.*]   London, [1850]

FETTERS of gold. By Charles Eddy [Charles E. Rose]. Cr 8vo. [*Amer. Cat.*]   London, 1904

FEUDAL castles of France (Western provinces). By the author of *Flemish interiors*, etc. [Mrs William Pitt Byrne]. Illustrated from the author's sketches.   8vo.   Pp. xviii., 360. [*Bodl.*]   London, 1869

FEUDAL days; or, the freebooter's castle: a romance.   [By Mitchell Williams.] 3 vols. Fcap 8vo. [*Bodl.*]
                           London, 1826

FEUDAL times; or, the Court of James the Third. A Scottish historical play. By the author of *The Earl of Gowrie*, etc. [James White]. First represented at the Theatre Royal Sadler's Wells. 8vo. [*Adv. Lib.*]   London, 1847

FEUDALISM in Jersey. By the editor of *The Jersey Independent* [George Julian Harney]. 8vo.   Jersey, 1857

FEW (a) additional facts and observations respecting the Government plan of assisting in the education of the poor; in which reasons are advanced why the committee of the training school in Cheltenham, and that about to be established in London, should not be connected with the Government. [By Thomas J. Graham, M.D.] Second edition. 8vo. [*Bodl.*] London, 1848

FEW (a) anecdotes and observations relating to Oliver Cromwell and his family, serving to rectify several errors concerning him, published by Nicolaus Comnenus Papadopoli, in his Historia Gymnasii Patavini. By a member of the Royal Society, and of the Society of Antiquaries, of London [Sir James Burrow]. 4to. [*Brit. Mus.*]
                           London, 1763

FEW (a) brief and modest reflexions perswading a just indulgence to be granted to the Episcopal clergy and people in Scotland. [By George Mackenzie, Earl of Cromarty.]   4to. [*Adv. Lib.*]   Printed May 27th, 1703
   Ascribed also to Sir William Seton, of Pitmedden. *See also* the "Continuation of a few brief and modest reflections."

FEW (a) brief remarks on a pamphlet published by some individuals, supposed to be connected with the late Board of Admiralty, intitled Observations on the concise statements of facts, &c., in which the calumnies of those writers are examined and exposed. By Æschines [Francis William Blagdon]. 8vo. [Watt's *Bibl. Brit.*] London, 1805

FEW (a) Church matters, from different authors. By a clergyman of the Church of England [Edward W. Barlow, M.A.]. Fcap 8vo. [Green's *Bibl. Somers.*, vol. i., p. 44.]
                           Bath, [1843]

FEW (a) cursory remarks upon the state of parties, during the administration of the Right Hon. Henry Addington. By a near observer [Thomas Richard Bentley, grandson of the critic]. 8vo. [Pellew's *Life of Sidmouth*, ii., 145-6.]   London, 1803

FEW (a) earnest thoughts on the duty of communion with the [Roman] Catholic Church. . . . By a recent Convert [Edward Healy Thompson]. 8vo.   London, 1847

FEW (a) earnest words to British Methodists, from a brother Methodist [Rev. Benjamin Gough]. 8vo. [Cushing's *Init. and Pseud.*, vol. i., p. 41.]
                           Leeds, 1860

FEW (a) English notes on a late sermon preached before the sons of the clergy, by Dr Bisse, intended to vindicate the English Reformation from the charge of sacrilege, fraud, &c. In a letter to the Reverend Dr ——, Dean of ——. [By John Lewis.]   8vo. [*Bodl.*]   London, 1717

Two letters in defence of the English Liturgy and Reformation; the second edition with additions, published at London, 1717, contains also " Remarks on four sermons," etc.

FEW (a) facts and fancies touching Ritualism.   By Oxoniensis [Rev. Francis Cruse, M.A.].   8vo.   Pp. 208.
London, 1874

A second edition, enlarged, was issued in 1875.

FEW (a) facts illustrative of the efficiency and progress of the Homœopathic system of medicine, containing a description of 20 principal remedies. [By Samuel Capper, jun.] 12mo. [Smith's *Cat. of Friends' Books*, i., 381.]   Bristol, 1855

FEW (a) facts stated in answer to the Report of the Bullion Committee.   By an annuitant [James Carey].   8vo. [*Camb. Univ. Lib.*]   London, 1811

FEW (a) flowers from the Garden of Sheikh Saadi Shirazi; being translations into English verse of portions of the Būstān.   [By Major C— W— Mackinnon.]   Fcap 8vo.
Calcutta, 1877

FEW (a) hints on colours as applied to the toilet, decorations of rooms, embroidery, fancy work, and the garden. By C. H. [Charles Henfrey].   8vo.
Brighton, 1868

FEW (a) hints on the study of ecclesiastical architecture and antiquities. Fourth edition. [By Rev. John M. Neale and John Fuller Russell.]   8vo. [*Camb. Univ. Lib.*]   Cambridge, 1843

FEW (a) hints on the treatment of lunatics.   By E. L. R. [Ellen Louisa Raymond].   12mo.   [*Brit. Mus.*]
Bristol, 1867

FEW (a) hints to Freshmen.   [By Thomas Thorp.]   8vo.   [Bartholomew's *Cat. of Camb. Books.*]   Cambridge, 1841

FEW (a) historical remarks upon the supposed antiquity of Church rates, and the three-fold division of tithes. By a lay member of the Church of England [John Mitchell Kemble, M.A.]. Cr 8vo.   [*D. N. B.*, vol. 30, p. 371.]
London, 1836

This pamphlet called forth a reply from Archdeacon W. H. Hale.

FEW (a) hundred Bible contradictions. By John P. Y. M. D. [Lieutenant —— Lecount, R.N.].   8vo.   London, 1843

FEW (a) hymns and some spiritual songs, selected (1856) for the Little Flock. [By Samuel P. Tregelles, LL.D.]   12mo.   [*D. N. B.*, vol. 57, p. 171.]   London, N.D.

FEW (a) hymns and spiritual songs. By J. N. D. [John Nelson Darby]. Fcap 8vo.   London, 1870

FEW (a) Indian stories.   By L. T. C. [Lionel James], author of *Through the eye of a needle*.   8vo.   Pp. 117.   [*Brit. Mus.*]   Allahabad, 1895

FEW (a) letters and speeches on the late Civil War.   [By August Belmont.] Royal 8vo.   New York, 1870

FEW (a) letters concerning the Church government in Scotland in 1690; from the collection of the Earl of Leven and Melville.   [By W. Leslie Melville.] 8vo.   Pp. 53.   [Martin's *Cat.*]
Edinburgh, 1840

FEW (a) letters on the Indian administration of the Earl of Mayo, Viceroy and Governor-General of India.   [By Sir Owen Tudor Burne.]   Royal 8vo. Private print.   N.P., 1877

FEW (a) minutes' advice to deaf persons. By a surgeon-aurist [William Wright]. 8vo.   [*Brit. Mus.*]   London, 1839

FEW (a) months in the East; or, a glimpse of the Red, the Dead, and the Black Seas.   By a Canadian [J. Bell Forsyth].   8vo.   [*Brit. Mus.*]
Quebec, 1861

FEW (a) more verses.   By Susan Coolidge [Sarah Chauncey Woolsey].   Fcap 8vo.   [Cushing's *Init. and Pseud.*, vol. i., p. 67.]   Boston, [Mass.], 1889

FEW (a) more words on the introduction of the Italian opera into Edinburgh. [By Rev. Richard Hibbs, M.A.]   8vo. [*Brit. Mus.*]   Edinburgh, 1855

FEW (a) notes on a Letter to the Archbishops and Bishops of the Church of England, and on a charge, recently delivered by the Archdeacon of Sarum, relative to Joseph Lancaster's plan for the education of the lower orders of the community.   By Eccletus [Luke Howard, chemist, of Plaistow].   8vo. [Smith's *Cat. of Friends' Books*, i., 80.]
London, 1806

FEW (a) notes on a recent trial, illustrative of Mofussil Judicature.   [By Joykissen Mookerjea.]   8vo.   Pp. 36, clii.   [Calcutta ?], 1858

FEW (a) notes on the proposed new entail law for Scotland. By a Freeholder of Aberdeenshire [James Gordon, advocate]. 8vo. [Robertson's *Aberd. Bibl.*] [Edinburgh, 1828]

FEW (a) notes on the Temple organ. [By Edmund Macrory.] 4to. Private print. [*Brit. Mus.*] Duncairn, 1859

FEW (a) observations upon a pamphlet, intituled, Answers to the Queries, &c. [By Joseph Brodie.] Pt 8vo. Pp. 7. [*New Coll. Lib.*] [Edinburgh, 1737] Signed " Fidelio, F. A. C."

FEW (a) plain reasons for adhering to the [English Episcopal] Church. [By James Heywood Markland.] 8vo. [*D. N. B.*, vol. 36, p. 176.] London, 1807

FEW (a) plain reasons for retaining our subscription to the Articles at matriculation, in preference to the subjoined declaration, which it is proposed to substitute. " I, A. B. declare that I do, as far as my knowledge extends, assent to the doctrines of the united Church of England and Ireland as set forth in her Thirty-nine Articles ; that I will conform to her Liturgy and discipline ; and that I am ready and willing to be instructed in her Articles of religion, as required by the statutes of this university." [By Godfrey Faussett, D.D.] 4to. [*Bodl.*] [Oxford, 1835] Signed " Quinquagenarius."

FEW (a) plain reasons why a Protestant of the Church of England should not turn Roman Catholick. By a real Catholick of the Church of England [Thomas Barlow, D.D.]. 4to. Pp. 53. [Watt's *Bibl. Brit.*] London, 1688

FEW (a) plain remarks on decimal currency, respectfully submitted to the consideration of the public. By a cypher [H. Nutting]. 8vo. [*Brit. Mus.*] Bedfordshire, [Luton, 1856]

FEW (a) plain remarks on infant baptism and confirmation ; with special reference to the objections of the Baptists. [By Rev. William John Edge.] 8vo. [*Brit. Mus.*] Woodbridge, 1841
In the same year there appeared a second edition, to which is added a brief explanation of certain passages in the Burial Service.

FEW (a) plain words concerning conformity in matters of religion and worship. [By William Smith, of Besthorp.] 4to. [*Smith's Cat. of Friends' Books.*] [London], 1664 Signed " W. S."

FEW (a) plain words on the sacrament of the Lord's Supper ; more particularly addressed to the parishioners of Handsworth, Staffordshire. [By R. L. Frere.] Fcap 8vo. [*Bodl.*] Birmingham, 1831 Signed " R. L. F."

FEW (a) poetic scraps. By J. R. [James Rock]. 8vo. London, 1891

FEW (a) practical hints to printers on the treatment of rollers . . . on wetting down paper : general remarks. By " Caxton " [J— Myers]. 8vo. Southampton, 1871

FEW (a) practical suggestions for the burial of the dead in Christ. [By Robert Brett.] 8vo. [*Bodl.*] [London, 1862]

FEW (a) questions on secular education ; what it is, and what it ought to be : with an attempt to answer them. Preceded by an appeal to Richard Cobden, Esq., M.P., and the members of the late Anti-corn-law league. By the author of *The outlines of social economy* [William Ellis]. 8vo. [*Adv. Lib.*] London, 1848

FEW (a) rambling remarks on golf ; with the rules as laid down by the Royal and Ancient Club of St Andrews. [By Robert Chambers, jun.] 8vo. Edinburgh, 1862

FEW (a) reflections occasioned by the perusal of a work [signed T. C. D., *i.e.* John Wilson Croker], entitled, " Familiar Epistles to F. J. [Frederick Edward Jones], Esq. [By Lady Sydney Morgan.] Fcap 8vo. [*Brit. Mus.*] Dublin, 1804
The dedication is subscribed " S. O.," *i.e.* Sydney Owenson, the writer's early name. *See above*, " Familiar epistles."

FEW (a) remarkable events in the life of the Rev. Josiah Thomson, a Secession minister ; shewing the evil effects of Voluntary Churches in general, and the Secession Church in the North of England in particular. By Nathan Oliver, Esq. [Robert Blakey, Ph.D.]. Fcap 8vo. Pp. 208. [*Adv. Lib.*] London, 1836
Republished in 1841, under the title of " The secret history of Dissent."

FEW (a) remarks addressed to the Society of Friends on the subject of a revival of religion among them. By a member [Maria Arthington]. 8vo. Leeds, 1836

FEW (a) remarks on a pamphlet by Mr Shilleto, entitled, " Thucydides or Grote ? " [By Rev. John Grote, M.A.] 8vo. [*Brit. Mus.*] Cambridge, 1851 Signed " J. G."

FEW (a) remarks on a sermon preached in the parish Church of St Clement, Cambridge, and since printed. By a layman [T— Nicholls]. 8vo. [*Camb. Univ. Lib.*]
Cambridge, private print, 1863

FEW (a) remarks on an Address to the Roman Catholics of the United States of America. . . . By a fair inquirer [Rev. John Hawkins]. 8vo. [Cushing's *Init. and Pseud.*, vol. i., p. 98.]
Worcester, 1796
See above, the "Address . . ." [by Bishop John Carroll].

FEW (a) remarks on currency and finance. By T. H. C. [T— H. Carter]. 8vo. N.P., 1875

FEW (a) remarks on recent doctrines contained in " Notes of Readings " held in the United States and Canada : revised by F. E. R. [F— E— Raven]. 8vo. London, 1900

FEW (a) remarks on temperance, blue-ribbonism, and pseudo-religious intoxication. By Kuklos [John Harris, LL.D.]. 8vo. [Cushing's *Init. and Pseud.*, vol. i., p. 159.] London, 1885

FEW (a) remarks on the Bengal Army and furlough regulations, with a view to their improvement. By a Bengal officer [John Jacob, Brigadier-General]. 8vo. [*Brit. Mus.*] Bombay, 1851

FEW (a) remarks on the charge of [James Henry Monk] the Lord Bishop of Glocester and Bristol on the subject of reserve in communicating religious knowledge, as taught in the Tracts for the Times, No. 80, and No. 87. By the writer of those tracts [Isaac Williams, B.D.]. 8vo. [*D. N. B.*, vol. 61, p. 410.] Oxford, 1841

FEW (a) remarks on the expectant treatment of diseases. By 'Ακέστης [William Smith, surgeon]. 8vo. [*W.*]
Bristol, 1847

FEW (a) remarks on the History [by Edward Gibbon] of the decline and fall of the Roman empire ; relative chiefly to the two last chapters. By a gentleman [Francis Eyre]. 8vo. Pp. 154. [*Brit. Mus.*] London, 1778

FEW (a) remarks on the invasion of Zulu-land. By Kuklos [John Harris, LL.D.]. 4to. [Cushing's *Init. and Pseud.*, vol. i., p. 159.] [London, 1879]
See also " A Few words on the Zulu war."

FEW (a) remarks on the most fitting material and site for the memorial statue to our late Chancellor. By a member of the Cambridge Committee [Thomas Worsley]. 8vo. [Bartholomew's *Cat. of Camb. Books.*]
Cambridge, 1862

FEW (a) remarks on the " New Library " question. By a member of neither Syndicate [Henry Coddington, M.A.]. 8vo. Pp. 31. [Bartholomew's *Cat. of Camb. Books.*] Cambridge, 1831

FEW (a) remarks on the outline of a scheme for the future constitution of Downing College. By the Master [Thomas Worsley, D.D.]. [Bartholomew's *Cat. of Camb. Books.*]
Cambridge, [1860]

FEW (a) remarks on the present system of Degrees at King's College, Cambridge. [By Edward Thring.] 8vo. [Bartholomew's *Cat. of Camb. Books.*]
Cambridge, 1846

FEW (a) remarks on the principles of the new Poor Law. [By Edward Hoblyn Padler.] 8vo. Pp. 24.
Liskeard, 1842

FEW (a) remarks upon some of the notes and resolutions of the Continental Congress held at Philadelphia in September, and the Provincial Congress held at Cambridge [Mass.] in November 1774. By a friend to peace and good order [Harrison Gray]. 8vo. Pp. 20. [*Brit. Mus.*]
[Boston, Mass.], 1775

FEW (a) reverential thoughts. [By Rev. Richard Warner.] Fcap 8vo. Pp. 80. London, 1844

FEW (a) short addresses. By an officer [Lieut.-Col. William Blakeney]. Fcap 8vo. London, 1877

FEW (a) sonnets, attempted from Petrarch in early life. [By Rev. Francis Wrangham.] Italian and English. Printed at the press of Lee Priory. 4to. Pp. 110. [*D. N. B.*, vol. 63, p. 67.] Kent, 1817
Advertisement signed " F. W."

FEW (a) strictures addressed to Mr Alderman Sadler, on his correspondence with the Bishop of Oxford. By a Protestant Churchman. [By J. Ballard.] 8vo. [*F. Madan.*]
Oxford, 1851

FEW (a) suggestions to Churchwardens on Churches and Church ornaments. Nos. I. and II. [By John Mason Neale, D.D.] 8vo. Pp. 40. [*D. N. B.*, vol. 40, p. 144.] Cambridge, 1841

FEW (a) thoughts and matters of fact concerning Methodism . . . to which is subjoined an answer to a late pamphlet of Mr [John] Wesley against Mr [John] Erskine. [By Rev. Samuel Martin, D.D., minister at Monimail.] Fcap 8vo. Pp. 24. [Scott's *Fasti.*]
Edinburgh, 1766

FEW (a) thoughts on " Chaturvarnayâ," or the four-fold social system of Castes. By W. W. [W. D. S. Wickremeseksa]. 8vo. Colombo, 1886

FEW (a) thoughts upon pointing. . . . By J. B. [Sir James Burrow], F.R.S. and F.S.A. Pt 8vo. [*Brit. Mus.*]
London, 1768

FEW (a) topographical remarks, relative to the parishes of Ringwood, Ellingham, Ibbesley, Harbridge, and Fordingbridge ; and to the New Forest. [By Peter Hall, M.A.] Fcap 8vo. [*Bodl.*]   Ringwood, 1831

FEW (a) urgent words on the present crisis, addressed to the Catholics of the English Church ; and chiefly to the members of the Church Union Societies. By the writer of *A voice from the North* [Samuel Brown Harper]. 8vo. [*Bodl.*]   London, 1850

FEW (a) valuable hints for the new Ministry, shewing that peace with France is possibly attainable, without degrading the honour of Great Britain. Dedicated to Messrs Fox & Co., the servants of the king, and professedly the servants of the people. . . . By W. P. R. [William P. Russel], a political observer; author of *Verbotomy*. 8vo. [*Bodl.*]   [London], 1806

FEW (a) verses, English and Latin. [By Rev. Edward Smedley, M.A.] 8vo. [Bartholomew's *Cat. of Camb. Books.*]   London, 1812

FEW (a) verses for a few friends. [By J— Ticknor Field.] Cr 8vo. Private print.   N.P., N.D.

FEW (a) words about drawing for beginners. . . . By J. B. [Mrs Hugh Blackburn]. 8vo.   Edinburgh, 1893

FEW (a) words about Hogarth. By W. C. M. [William Cosmo Monkhouse]. 4to. [*Brit. Mus.*]   London, 1872

FEW (a) words about music, containing hints to amateur pianists ; to which is added a slight historical sketch of the rise and progress of the art of music. By M. H. [Mrs Hullah]. Fcap 8vo. Pp. 108. [*Adv. Lib.*]   London, 1851

FEW (a) words about private tuition. By a private tutor [David James Vaughan]. 8vo.   Cambridge, 1852

FEW (a) words anent the " Red " pamphlet [of Col. George B. Malleson]. By one who has served under the Marquis of Dalhousie. [Charles Allen.] 8vo.   London, 1858
    The third edition has the author's name. *See* the note to " The Mutiny of the Bengal Army."

FEW (a) words from a humane gentleman on the threatened exterminating foray upon the bird tribe. [By Rev. Edward Warren Caulfeild, M.A.] 8vo. [Green's *Bibl. Somers.*, ii., 176.]
                        Bath, 1860

FEW (a) words from an expatriated [V. S. Zorawski]. [Poems.] 8vo. [*Brit. Mus.*]   Cowes, 1844

FEW (a) words in favour of Professor Powell, and the sciences, as connected with certain educational remarks, (chiefly in the way of extract). By Philomath : Oxoniensis [Richard Walker, B.D.]. 8vo.   Oxford, 1832

FEW (a) words in support of No. 90 of the Tracts for the Times [by John Henry Newman], partly with reference to Mr Wilson's Letter. [By William George Ward, M.A.] 8vo. [*Bodl.*]
                    Oxford, 1841
    Signed " W. G. W."

FEW (a) words of advice to the mariners of England, and enterprising youths inclined for the sea service ; showing the advantages to be derived by service in the Royal Navy. By a seaman's friend [Samuel Baker, of the Board of Trade]. Fcap 8vo. [*W.*] London, 1854

FEW (a) words of plain truth, in reply to a mis-statement of facts and mis-interpretation of Scripture, contained in a letter to the Hon. and Rev. G. Noel. By a Unitarian [Lundy Foot]. 8vo. [*Brit. Mus.*]   Bridport, 1832

FEW (a) words of plain truth, on the subject of the present negotiation for peace. By a member of the University of Cambridge [William Burdon, M.A., Fellow of Emmanuel College]. 8vo. [*Bodl.*]   Cambridge, 1797

FEW (a) words [by Michael Hodsell Miller] on No. 90 of the Tracts for the Times. 8vo.   London, 1842
    The tract was written by John Henry Newman.

FEW (a) words on our relations with Russia. By a non-alarmist [Thomas Tooke]. 8vo.   London, 1828

FEW (a) words on Popery and Protestantism. By a layman [Capt. Matthew Montagu, R.N.].   Second edition. 8vo. [*Bodl.*]   London, 1854

FEW (a) words on swimming ; with practical hints to beginners. By R. Harrington [Ralph Thomas] : to which is added, a bibliographical list of works on swimming, by Olphar Hamst [anagram of Ralph Thomas]. [Second edition.] Fcap 8vo. [*Manch. Free Lib.*]   London, 1868
    The first edition (16 pages) was published in 1861.

FEW (a) words on the Bodleian Library. [By Sir Edmund Head.] 8vo. [*Bodl.*]
                    Oxford, 1833

FEW (a) words on the defence of the country from invasion. [By Sir Francis Bond Head.] 8vo. Pp. 64.
                    London, 1846
    Published later (1850) in fuller form, with a different title (" The defenceless state of Great Britain ") and the author's name.

FEW (a) words on the 80th Psalm, with reference to the Irish Church. By Charlotte Elizabeth [Mrs Charlotte Elizabeth Tonna, previously Mrs Phelan]. 8vo. [Lowndes' *Brit. Lib.*, p. 165.]   London, 1836

FEW (a) words on the last publication of the C. C. S. [Cambridge Camden Society, written by John Mason Neale], regarding Church enlargement and Church arrangement. By a late Vice-President [John James Smith]. 8vo. Pp. 19. [Bartholomew's *Cat. of Camb. Books*.]
Cambridge, 1843

FEW (a) words on the practical bearing of the Peace question, addressed especially to the thoughtful women of England. [By Ellen J. Pearce.] 8vo. Pp. 4. [Smith's *Cat. of Friends' Books*.]   London, [1875]
Signed " A Cornishwoman."

FEW (a) words on the " promotion of home industry," and cognate matters. By Kuklos [John Harris, LL.D.]. 8vo. [*Lond. Lib. Cat.*]   London, 1885

FEW (a) words on the sin of lying. [By James Heywood Markland, D.C.L.] 8vo. [*D. N. B.*, vol. 36, p. 176.]
London, 1834

FEW (a) words on the subject of Canada. By a barrister [Charles Clark]. 8vo. Pp. 52. [*Adv. Lib.*]   London, 1837

FEW (a) words on the Temperance question. By T. B. [Thomas Bates]. 8vo. [*Camb. Univ. Cat.*]
London, 1877

FEW (a) words on the Third query, &c. Affectionately addressed to the sisters of my own religious community. [By Hannah Doyle.] 8vo. [Smith's *Cat. of Friends' Books*, i., 119.]
London, 1860
Signed " H. D." The third query to women, referred to in the above, is in these terms :—III. " Do Friends endeavour, by example and precept, to train up their children, servants, and those under their care, in a religious life and conversation, consistent with their Christian profession, and in plainness of speech, behaviour, and apparel ? "

FEW (a) words on the unreasonableness of not attending to the Christian religion. [By Rev. —— Skinner, of Richmond.] 8vo. [*Bodl.*]
London, 1801
A presentation copy to John Brand, who has given the author's name.

FEW (a) words on the Zulu war. By Kuklos [John Harris, LL.D.]. 8vo. [*Lit. Year Book.*]   London, 1879
See also " A Few remarks on the invasion of Zulu-land."

FEW (a) words on women's suffrage. By E. M. L. [Mrs E— M. Lynch]. 8vo. [*Brit. Mus.*]   Dublin, 1873

FEW (a) words, that high priced bread and high wages are no evils to the working classes. By one who wishes them well [George Monckton, M.P.]. 8vo.   London, 1839

FEW (a) words to a nurse on entering an hospital. [By Priscilla Maurice.] 8vo.
London, 1853

FEVV (a) vvords to all such (whether Papists or Protestants) as observe dayes contrary to Christ and his apostles ; and several weighty things concerning the cross of Christ, and the headship of the Church ; wherein the Pope is proved to be a false and counterfeit head, and a robber of the honour due to Christ, the true head of the true Church ; also, the Quakers challenge to the Papists, and the Quakers testimony concerning magistracy. By G. F. [George Fox]. 4to.
London, 1669
The challenge to the Papists is signed James Lancaster, John Stubbs, Thomas Briggs, and G. F.

FEW (a) words to all who professe themselves to bee of the Protestant religion, whereby they may understand by what spirit they were led, that persecuted the people of God in former ages, for the exercise of their religion, and their tenderness of conscience in matters relateing to the worship of God. . . . Written by him that would have the greatest of persecutors to repent, and cease to do evil, and learn to do well, that so they might escape the judgments of the Lord. F. E. [Francis Ellington]. 4to. [Smith's *Cat. of Friends' Books*.]
N.P., Printed in the year 1665

FEW (a) words to Church builders. [By John Mason Neale, D.D.] 8vo. Pp. 32. [*D. N. B.*, vol. 40, p. 144.]
Cambridge, 1841

FEW (a) words to Churchwardens on Churches and Church ornaments. [By Charles Thorp, Archdeacon of Durham.] 8vo.   London, 1826

FEW (a) words to Freshmen. [By Thomas Thorp.] 8vo. Nos. I. and II. [Bowes' *Camb. Books.*]
Cambridge, 1841

FEW (a) words to the country parsons touching the election for the University of Oxford. By one of themselves [John Fielder Mackarness, D.D., Exeter College]. 8vo. [*Bodl.*]
London, 1847

FEW (a) words to the Jews. By one of themselves [Charlotte Montefiore]. 8vo. Pp. 210. [*Brit. Mus.*]
London, 1853

FEW (a) words to the labourers of Great Britain. [By Wm. Clubbe.] 8vo. [*Brit. Mus.*] Woodbridge, 1793
Signed " A Yeoman."

FEW (a) words to the Parish Clerks and Sextons of country parishes. [By John Mason Neale.] 8vo. [*D. N. B.*, vol. 40, p. 144.] Cambridge, 1843

FEW (a) words to the poor and to overseers on the new poor law. [By Mrs Archer Clive, *née* Caroline Wrigley.] 8vo. [*W.*] Birmingham, [1836]

FEW (a) words to the tradesmen and to the public, on the desirableness and practicability of abridging the number of the hours of business. By A. J. K. [Alfred John Kempe]. 8vo. [*Brit. Mus.*] London, 1842

FIANDER'S widow. [A novel depicting Dorsetshire rustic life.] By M. E. Francis [Mrs Francis Blundell, *née* Mary Evans Sweetman]. 8vo. [*Lond. Lib. Cat.*] London, 1901

FIANS, fairies, and Picts. [By David MacRitchie.] 8vo. London, 1893
Private information regarding the authorship.

FIAT lux ; or, a general conduct to a right understanding in the great combustions and broils about religion here in England, between Papist and Protestant, Presbyterian and Independent. By Mr J. V. C. [John Vincent Cane] a friend to men of all religions. 8vo. Pp. 368. [*Brit. Mus.*]
[Doway ?], 1661
This print called forth [from Dr John Owen] " Animadversions on a treatise intituled ' Fiat Lux ' . . ."; and Cane replied, still covertly, in " An Epistle to the author of the Animadversions," also in " Diaphanta," to other opponents. *See above.*

FICKLE fortune. By E. Werner [Emile Buerstenbinder], author of *Under a charm.* From the German by Christina Tyrrell. 2 vols. 8vo. [*Adv. Lib.*] London, 1881

FICKLE fortune in Ceylon. By F. E. F. P. [Fanny Emily F. Penny]. 8vo. Pp. ii., 69. [*Calc. Imp. Lib.*] Madras, 1887

FICTIONS of our forefathers ; Fion Mac Cumhail and his warriors : reprinted from the Irish Quarterly Review. [By Harry Whitney, *i.e.* Patrick Kennedy.] 8vo. [*Manch. Free Lib. Cat.*] Dublin, 1859

FIDALGOS (the) of Casa Mourisca ; from the Portuguese of Julio Dinez [Joaquim G. G. Coelho]. Pt 8vo.
Boston, 1891

FIDDLE-DE-DEE : a hurdy-gurdy ode ; or, pseudo Pindaric anent Presbyterian Church organs. By a Kn— Oxonian, corresponding member of the Institute of Common Sense [Rev. John Allan, Belhelvie]. 8vo. [*And. Jervise.*] Aberdeen, [1865]

FIDDLE-FADDLE (the) fashion-book. [By John Leech.] [Jaggard's *Index*, ii.] London, 1840

FIDDLER (the) of Lugau. By the author of *The Atelier du Lys* [Margaret Roberts]. 8vo. [*Brit. Mus.*] London, 1891

FIDDLING Freddy. By Neil Forrest [Mrs Cornelia Floyd]. 8vo. [Cushing's *Init. and Pseud.*, vol. i., p. 104.] New York, 1871

FIDELIA ; or, the prevalence of fashion. [By Joseph Cradock.] Fcap 8vo. [*Brit. Mus.*] London, 1821

FIDELIA [a poetical lament] ; written by G. W. [George Wither] of Lincolnes Inne, Gentleman. Fcap 8vo. [*Brit. Mus.*] London, 1617
Another edition " newely corrected and amended," was published in 1619 ; and a modern reprint, edited by Sir E. Brydges, was issued in 1815.

FIDES divina ; the ground of true faith assisted : or, a useful and brief discourse, shewing the insufficiency of humane, and the necessity of divine evidence for divine or saving faith and Christian religion to be built upon. [By Clement Writer.] 12mo. Pp. 109. [*D. N. B.*, vol. 63, p. 158.] London, 1675

FIDES laici. [A poem.] [By William Forsyth, M.A.] 8vo. [*W.*]
London, 1850

FIELD and fern ; or Scottish flocks and herds. By " The Druid " [Henry Hall Dixon]. 8vo. [Haynes' *Pseud.*] London, 1865

FIELD (the) book : or, sports and pastimes of the United Kingdom ; compiled from the best authorities, ancient and modern. By the author of *Wild sports of the West* [William Hamilton Maxwell]. 8vo. Pp. viii., 616. [*Brit. Mus.*] London, 1833

FIELD, cover, and trap shooting. By the champion wing-shot of America [Adam H. Bogardus]. 8vo. [Cushing's *Init. and Pseud.*, vol. i., p. 54.] New York, 1875

FIELD forcing it : being a reprint of letters contributed to the *Madras Mail*, from Burmah, etc. [By Capt. E— E— Forbes.] 8vo. Pp. 69. [*Brit. Mus.*] Madras, private print, 1886

FIELD, forest, and wayside flowers. By E. M. Hardinge [Ellen Maud Going]. 8vo. New York, [1901]

FIELD, fort, and fleet : sketches of the late [Civil] War, 1861–1863. By "M. Quad" [Charles B. Lewis]. 8vo. [Cushing's *Init. and Pseud.*, i., 243.] Detroit, 1885

FIELD friends and forest foes. By Phillis Browne [Mrs Sarah S. Hamer]. 4to. [*Brit. Mus.*] London, [1877] Wrongly attributed to A. G. Payne.

FIELD (the) of honour. [Short stories.] By Harold Fielding [Harold Fielding Patrick Hall]. 8vo. Pp. 134. [*Brit. Mus.*] London, 1915

FIELD sports of the United States and Canada. By Frank Forester [Henry William Herbert]. 2 vols. Fcap 8vo. [Cushing's *Init. and Pseud.*, i., 104.] London, 1848

FIELD (the), the garden, and the woodland. . . . By a lady [Anne Pratt, later Mrs Pearless]. 12mo. Third edition. [*Brit. Mus.*] London, 1847

FIELD-PATH rambles in West Kent. . . . By Walker Miles [Edmund Taylor]. 12mo. Pp. 235. [*Brit. Mus.*] London, 1893

FIELD-SPY (the) ; or, the walking observator : a poem. By the author of *The London Spy* [Edward Ward]. 8vo. [*Brit. Mus.*] London, 1714

FIEND'S (the) delight. By Dod Grile [M— H. Bierce]. 8vo. [*Brit. Mus.*] London, [1873]

FIERY (the) cross ; a tale of the Great American War. By the author of *The Black Angel* [William Stephens Hayward]. 8vo. Pp. 411. [*Brit. Mus.*] London, 1871

FIERY (the) cross ; or, a warning voice to the sons and daughters of Caledonia. [By Rev. David Carment.] 8vo. [Edinburgh, 1843]

FIERY (the) cross ; some verse for to-day and to-morrow. By John Oxenham [William Arthur Dunkerley]. 12mo. Pp. 96. [*Lond. Lib. Cat.*] London, 1917

FIERY (a) ordeal. By Bertha M. Clay [Mrs Charlotte M. Braeme]. Fcap 8vo. Pp. 282. New York, [1889]

FIERY (a) ordeal. By Tasma [Jessie C. Huybers, later Madame Couvrier]. Cr 8vo. Pp. 356. [*Lond. Lib. Cat.*] London, 1897

FIERY (a) pillar of heavenly truth, shewing the way to a blessed life ; composed by way of catechisme. [By Alex. Grosse, B.D.] 8vo. [*D.N.B.*, vol. 23, p. 274.] London, 1641

FIESCO : a tragedy. By an American [William Elliott]. 8vo. [Cushing's *Init. and Pseud.*, vol. i., p. 12.] New York, 1850

FIESCO ; or the Genoese conspiracy : a tragedy. Translated from the German of Frederick Schiller, by G. H. N., and J. S. [G. H. Noehden, and J. Stoddart]. 8vo. London, 1796 The second edition, published in 1798. gives the translators' names in full.

FIESTAS de Aranjuez ; translated from the Spanish of Antonio de Mendoza, in celebration of the birthday of Philip IV. in 1621 [by Sir Richard Fanshawe]. 4to. [Martin's *Cat.*] N.P., 1670

FIFE and drum. [Humorous verses.] By "Touchstone" of the *Daily Mail* [Claude Barton] and "C. E. B," of the *Evening News.* 8vo. London, 1915

FIFTEEN hundred miles an hour [an imaginary visit to the planet Mars]. Edited [but rather written] by Charles Dixon. 8vo. Pp. 313. [*Brit. Mus.*] London, 1895

FIFTEEN sermons. By the author of *Persuasives to early piety* [J. G. Pike]. Fcap 8vo. Pp. iv., 213. [*Bodl.*] London, 1841

FIFTEEN stamps : the story of a great enterprise. By Skelton Kuppord [J. Adams]. 8vo. Pp. 128. London, 1896

FIFTEEN vocalises. By Annibale [Anna Ballard]. 8vo. [Cushing's *Init. and Pseud.*, vol. i., p. 16.] Boston, 1870

FIFTEEN years in India ; or, sketches of a soldier's life : being an attempt to describe persons and things in various parts of Hindostan. From the journal of an officer in his Majesty's service [Robert Grenville Wallace]. 8vo. [*Adv. Lib.*] London, 1822

FIFTEEN years of "army reform." [By James F. Macpherson.] 8vo. Edinburgh, 1884

FIFTEENTH (the) note of the Church examined, viz. Temporal felicity. [By Robert Grove, D.D., Bishop of Chichester.] 4to. [Jones' Peck.] London, 1687

FIFTH (a) essay at removing national prejudices ; with a reply to some authors who have printed their objections against an union with England. [By Daniel Defoe.] 4to. N.P., 1607 [for 1707]

FIFTH (a) essay on free trade and finance, humbly offered for the consideration of the public. By a citizen of Philadelphia [Pelatiah Webster]. 8vo. Pp. 23. [Cushing's *Init. and Pseud.*, vol. ii., p. 31.] Philadelphia, 1780

FIFTH (the) gospel ; being the Pauline interpretation of the Christ. By the author of *The faith of a Christian* [Bernard Lucas]. Cr 8vo. [*Brit. Mus.*]
London, 1906

FIFTH (a) letter to the people of England, on the subversion of the constitution, and the necessity of its being restored. [By John Shebbeare, M.D.] 8vo. Pp. 99. [*Athen. Cat.*, p. 503.]
London, 1757

FIFTH (the) Monarchy : thoughts on the Kingdom of God. [By Morton Aldis.] 8vo. Pp. xiv., 91. [*Brit. Mus.*]
London, 1909

FIFTH (the) note of the Church examined, viz., The succession of bishops. [By George Thorpe, D.D., Canon of Canterbury.] 4to. [Jones' Peck.]
London, 1687

FIFTI select Psalms, paraphrastically turned into English verse [by Sir Edwin Sandys] and by Robert Taylour set to be sung in five parts. 4to. [Lowndes' *Bibl. Man.*] London, 1615

FIFTY golden years ; incidents in the Queen's reign. By the author of *John Halifax, gentleman* [Mrs George Lillie Craik, *née* Dinah Maria Mulock]. 4to. [*Brit. Mus.*] London, [1887]

FIFTY lunches. By " Wyvern " [Arthur Colonel C. Kenney-Herbert]. Pt 8vo. Pp. 172. [Oaten's *Anglo-Ind. Lit.*]
New York, [1896]

FIFTY motives for being a Reformed Catholic, and for not being a Roman Catholic : suggested by the Duke of Brunswick's fifty reasons for being a Roman Catholic. [By George Finch.] Fcap 8vo. [Mendham Collection *Cat. (Supp.)*, p. 13.] London, 1837

FIFTY pen and ink sketches in exact facsimile. By J. E. H. [John Eliot Hodgkin] ; from a copy of Polydore Vergil's *History of England*. Fcap 4to. Private print, N.P., 1860

FIFTY queries, seriously propounded to those that question or deny infants right to Baptism. [By John Brandon.] 8vo. Pp. 26. [Whitley's *Bapt. Bibl.*, i., 105.] London, 1675

FIFTY thousand miles in an hospital ship ; a chaplain's experiences in the Great War. By a Padre [Rev. Charles Steel Wallis]. Cr 8vo. Pp. 284.
London, 1917

FIFTY years of a play-goer ; or, annals of the New York stage from A.D. 1798 to 1848. [By Joseph N. Ireland.] 8vo. [Cushing's *Init. and Pseud.*, vol. i., p. 236.] New York, 1850

FIFTY years of failure : confessions of an optimist. [By Douglas George Hamilton Gordon.] 8vo. Pp. vi., 325. [*Brit. Mus.*] London, 1905

FIFTY years of the House of Lords. [By William T. Stead.] 8vo.
London, 1894

FIFTY years' recollections of an old bookseller ; consisting of anecdotes, characteristic sketches, and original traits and eccentricities, of authors, artists, actors, books, booksellers, and of the periodical press for the last half century ; with appropriate selections. [By William West.] 8vo. Pp. 200. [*N. and Q.*, Feb. 1869, p. 169.]
Cork, 1835
The preface is signed " W. W."

FIFTY years' reminiscences of New York ; or flowers from the garden of Laurie Todd. [By Grant Thorburn, seed merchant.] 8vo. [Cushing's *Init. and Pseud.*, vol. i., p. 284.]
New York, 1845

FIFTY years' rhymes and reminiscences. By A. C. B. [A— C— Barker]. Fcap 8vo. [Robertson's *Aberd. Bibl.*]
Aberdeen, 1880

FIFTY - FIVE reasons for not being a Baptist. By Timothy [Sylvester Holmes]. 8vo. [Cushing's *Init. and Pseud.*, vol. ii., p. 145.]
New Bedford, 1830

FIFTY-ONE original fables, with morals and ethical index ; written by Job Crithannah [anagram of Jonathan Birch] . . . Also a translation of Plutarch's Banquet of the seven sages, revised for this work. Second edition. 8vo. [*Brit. Mus.*] London, [1832]

FIFTY-TWO Bible stories for children : a new and revised edition of " Streaks of light." By the author of *Peep of day*, etc. [Mrs Thomas Mortimer, *née* Favell Lee Bevan]. 12mo. Pp. 212. [*Brit. Mus.*] Oxford, 1913

FIFTY-TWO five-minute sermons. . . . By E. H. L. [Rev. Edward Henry Landon, M.A.]. Fcap 8vo. [*Brit. Mus.*] London, 1876

FIG (a) for fortune. Recte securus. A. C. [Anthony Copley]. 4to. [Lowndes' *Bibl. Man.*] London, 1596

FIG (a) for Momus ; containing pleasant varietie, included in satyres, eclogues, and epistles. By T. L. [Thomas Lodge] of Lincolnes Inne, Gent. 4to. [Lowndes' *Bibl. Man.*] London, 1595

FIGARO at Hastings St Leonards. By Cuthbert Bede [Rev. Edward Bradley, B.A.]. 8vo. [*D. N. B.*, First Supp., vol. I, p. 250.] Manchester, [1878]

FIGARO'S history of England. By O. P. Q. Philander Smiff [A— A— Dowty]. Pt 8vo. [Cushing's *Init. and Pseud.*, vol. i., p. 269.]
London, 1873

FIGHT (the) at Dame Europa's school : shewing how the German boy thrashed the French boy ; and how the English boy looked on. [By Henry William Pullen, M.A.] 12mo. [*D. N. B.*, Second Supp., vol. iii., p. 145.]
London, [1870]
So great was the demand for this pamphlet on the Franco-German War of 1870 that the circulation reached nearly 200,000 copies ; it was followed by more than 200 imitations, likewise anonymous, presenting other views of the same contest. A Bibliography was prepared by F. Madan (" The Fight at Dame Europa's School, and the literature connected with it " (1882).

FIGHT (the) for a soul. [A novel.] By Florence Warden [Florence Alice Price, later Mrs George E. James]. Cr 8vo. Pp. 288.
London, 1912

FIGHT (a) for dominion : the romance of our first war with Spain. By Gay Parker [Miss M— P— Green]. Pt 8vo. [*Amer. Cat.*] New York, 1899

FIGHT (a) for the city [municipal representation]. By Francis Walton [Alfred Hodder]. 8vo. [*Amer. Cat.*]
New York, 1903

FIGHT (the) for the Republic in China. By B. L. Putnam Weale [Bertram Lenox Simpson]. 8vo. [*Lond. Lib. Cat.*] London, 1918

FIGHT for the right. By Oliver Optic [William Taylor Adams]. Fcap 8vo. [Kirk's *Supp.*] Boston, 1893

FIGHT (the) of the fair : and why John Bull kept out of it ! [By Fr. Peasgood and Edwin Spademan.] 12mo. [*Bodl.*] Stamford, [1871]

FIGHT (a) to a finish. [A novel.] By Florence Warden [Florence Alice Price, later Mrs George E. James]. Cr 8vo. Pp. 342. London, 1901

FIGHT (a) with fate. [A novel.] By Mrs Alexander [Mrs Alexander Hector, *née* Annie French]. 8vo. Pp. 300. [*Brit. Mus.*] London, 1896

FIGHTING Admirals . . . with portraits. By John Barnett [John Reginald Stagg]. Cr 8vo. Pp. viii., 309. [*Brit. Mus.*] London, 1910

FIGHTING for the Empire ; the story of the War in South Africa. By James Otis [James Otis Kaler]. 8vo. Pp. xxi., 466. [Kirk's *Supp.*]
Boston, [Mass., 1901]

FIGHTING the good fight ; or the successful influence of well-doing : a tale by H. F. E. [Evelyn Everett-Green]. 8vo. Pp. 272. [*Brit. Mus.*]
London, 1883

FIGHTING with fate : a novel, translated from the German of E. Marlitt [Eugenie John]. 8vo. Pp. 323. [Cushing's *Init. and Pseud.*, i., 184.]
London, 1881

FIGHTS for the championship. By a Tourist [Frederick W. J. Hemming]. 2 vols. 8vo. [*Lond. Lib. Cat., Supp.*]
London, [1903]
Reprinted from the *Licensed Victuallers' Gazette.*

FIGHTS for the championship, and celebrated prize battles ; or accounts of all the prize battles for the championship from the days of Figg and Broughton to the present time. . . . Compiled from " Bell's Life in London," " Boxiana," and original sources by the Editor of Bell's Life in London [Frank L. Dowling]. Fcap 8vo. [*Olphar Hamst.*] London, 1855

FIGHTS for the flag. . . . By Vedette [William Henry Fitchett]. 8vo.
London, 1898

FIG-LEAF (the) ; a satirical and admonitory poem : dedicated without permission to the fashionable world. [By B. P. Culham.] Third edition. 4to. [Watt's *Bibl. Brit.*] London, 1805

FIGURE 8 ; or the mystery of Meredete Place. By Seeley Register [Mrs Metta Victoria Victor, *née* Fuller]. 8vo. [Cushing's *Init. and Pseud.*, vol. i., p. 249.] New York, 1869

FIGVRE (the) of fovre : wherein are sweete flowers, gathered out of that fruitfull ground, that I hope will yield pleasure and profit to all sorts of people. [By Nicholas Breton.] The second part. 8vo. No pagination. [*Bodl.*] London, 1636
To the reader, signed " N. B."

FIGURE (a) of the true and spiritual Tabernacle, according to the inward Temple or House of God in the Spirit. Whereunto is added the eight vertues or godlynesses. Set forth by H. N. [Hendrik Niclas, or Henry Nicholas]. . . . 8vo. [*Brit. Mus.*] London, 1655
See the note to " Evangelium Regni."

FIGURE (the) three : shewing the (3) great laws of God and their product. [By W— D. Forsyth.] 8vo. Pp. iii., 61. Littleborough, [1901]
Signed " W. D. F."

FIGURES in rhymes ; or, metrical computations. . . . By H. R. [Henry Robson]. 8vo. [Cushing's *Init. and Pseud.*, vol. i., p. 245.] Newcastle, 1814

FILIAL piety; a poem. [By John Carr, LL.D., Master of the Free School, Hertford.] Folio. [Nichols' *Lit. Anec.*, ii., 438.] London, 1764

FILIAL (the) tribute [in verse]. [By George Hardinge, Judge.] 12mo. Pp. 46. [Martin's *Cat.*] London, 1807

FILIOLO. [By Mrs Margaret Ethel Edwards.] 12mo. [*Camb. Univ. Lib.*] [Cambridge, 1907]

FILIPPO di Ser Brunellesco [Great Masters]. By Leader Scott [Mrs Lucy Baxter]. Cr 8vo. Pp. 174. [*Brit. Mus.*] London, 1901

FILLIGAN smilers; being Patsy Filligan's letters and adventures. By Teddy Ashton [Charles Allen Clarke, journalist]. 8vo. Pp. 95. [Sparke's *Bibl. Bolt.*, p. 44.] Blackpool, 1911

FINAL (a) answer to the edition of Benjamin Ben Mordecai's Letters. [By William Burgh.] Fcap 8vo. [*Birm. Cent. Lib.*] Birmingham, 1775

FINAL (a) answer to the Remarks on the Craftsman's vindication; and to all the libels which have come, or may come, from the same quarter against the person last mentioned in the Craftsman of the 22d of May. [By Henry St John, Viscount Bolingbroke.] 8vo. [Park's *Walpole*.] London, 1731

FINAL French struggles in India and on the Indian seas. [By Colonel George B. Malleson.] Pt 8vo. [*D.N.B.*, First Supp., vol. 3, p. 135.] London, 1878

FINAL (the) goal; a novel. By Bessie Dill [L— Beith Dalzell]. Pt 8vo. [*Amer. Cat.*] Philadelphia, 1900

FINAL restoration demonstrated from the Scriptures of truth. . . . By Philo-Bereanus [Enoch B. Kenrick]. Fcap 8vo. Pp. 69. [Cushing's *Init. and Pseud.*, vol. ii., p. 121.] Boston, 1821

FINALE (the) to Dame Europa's School; the consequences of John's policy, and a peep into futurity. [By John R. Pennefather.] 12mo. [*Bodl.*] London, 1871
    See above, "The fight at Dame Europa's school."

FINANCES (the) [of the United States], panics, and specie payments. [By J— W. Schuckers.] 8vo. [*Brit. Mus.*] Philadelphia, 1874

FINANCIAL facts of the eighteenth century; or, a cursory view, with comparative statements, of the revenue, expenditure, debts, manufactures and commerce of Great Britain. [By John M'Arthur.] 8vo. [*Gent. Mag.*, Oct. 1840, p. 437.] London, 1801

FINANCIAL (the) relations of Ireland with the Imperial Exchequer. By an Irishman [Thomas T. Shaw]. 8vo. Pp. 39. [*Brit. Mus.*] Dublin, 1911

FINANCIAL (the) side of hotel-keeping. By Charles Martyn [J— Elliott Lane]. Fcap 8vo. [*Amer. Cat.*] New York, 1904

FINANCIER'S (the) wife. [A novel.] By Florence Warden [Florence Alice Price, later Mrs George E. James]. 8vo. London, 1907

FINDING her place. By Howe Benning [Mrs Mary H. Henry]. 8vo. Pp. 368. [Cushing's *Init. and Pseud.*, vol. i., p. 34.] London, [1888]

FINDING (the) of the Cross. By L. de Combes. Authorised translation by Luigi Cappadelta [Charles Louis Dessonlavy]. 8vo. [*Brit. Mus.*; *Int. Cath. Lib.*] London, 1907

FINDING the way. By Pansy [Mrs Isabella Alden, *née* Macdonald], author of *Obeying the call*, etc. Cr 8vo. Pp. 256. Glasgow, 1878

FINE arts and recreations. By Herbert Martyne [William Tait Ross]. 8vo. [Cushing's *Init. and Pseud.*, vol. i., p. 184.] London, 1895

FINE (the) lady; a novel. By the author of *Miss Melmoth* [Sophia Briscoe]. 2 vols. Fcap 8vo. [*Gent. Mag.*, xciv., 136.] London, 1772

FINE (the) lady's airs; or, an equipage of lovers: a comedy, as it is acted at the Theatre-Royal in Drury-Lane. Written by the author of the *Yeoman of Kent* [Thomas Baker]. 4to. Pp. 67. [*Biog. Dram.*] London, [1709]

FINEST (the) baby in the world. [By Thomas Ratcliffe Barnett.] 8vo. London, 1904

FINGAL; a poem in six books, by Ossian: rendered into [English] verse [by Richard Hole, LL.B.] from Mr Macpherson's translation. Second edition. 8vo. Pp. viii., 188. London, 1787
    See below, "Fragments of antient poetry . . ." and the appended note; also "Celticism a myth."

FINGER (the) of Mr Blee. By Peter Blundell [Frank Butterworth]. Cr 8vo. London, 1913.

FINGER-POSTS for cross roads; or hints on fair thinking, dedicated to doubters. [By B— Grant.] 8vo. 4 nos. [*Brit. Mus.*] London, 1852

FINISHED or not. By M. Emilkroob [Martha Downe Tolman]. Fcap 8vo. [Kirk's *Supp.*] Boston, 1873

FINISHING (the) stroke : being a vindication of the patriarchal scheme of government, in defence of the Rehearsals, Best answer, and Best of all ; wherein Mr Hoadly's examination of this scheme in his late book of the original and institution of civil government, is fully consider'd. . . . [By Charles Leslie.] 8vo. [*Brit. Mus.*]
London, 1711

FINNAN (the) haddie ; where caught and where cured. [By Andrew Christie.] 8vo. [*Aberd. Free Lib. Cat.*]   Aberdeen, 1897

FIRE (the). [A poem. By Rev. Nicholas Brown, M.A.] 4to. [O'Donoghue's *Poets of Ireland.*]   Dublin, 1722

FIRE ; a poem.   By Timothy Plain [G. W. Blaikie, heraldic painter]. 8vo. Pp. 44. [*Lowe's Dram. Lit.*]
Edinburgh, 1828

FIRE and brimstone ; or, the destruction of Sodom. [A drama. By George Lesly, Vicar of Olney, Buckinghamshire.] 8vo. [*Brit. Mus.*]
London, [1675]

" FIRE HINTS."   By a late member of the Society for the Preservation of Life [Henry T. Baylis]. 8vo.
London, 1884

FIRE (the) seeker. [A novel.]   By " Iota " [Mrs Mannington Caffyn]. 8vo. Pp. 415. [*Brit. Mus.*]
London, 1911

FIRE (the) side ; a pastoral soliloquy [in verse], on the E— of G— [Earl of Godolphin] taking the S—ls [Seals]. [By Isaac Hawkins Browne.]   Folio. Pp. 8. [*London Mercury*, vol. v., p. 406.   London, [1735 ?]

FIRE tongue. By Sax Rohmer [Arthur Sarsfield Ward]. Cr 8vo. Pp. 314. [*Lond. Lib. Cat.*]   London, 1921

FIRE (the) within. [A novel.] By Patricia Wentworth [Mrs —— Dillon, *née* D— O. Ellis]. Cr 8vo. Pp. 276.
London, 1913

FIRE-EATER (the). [By James Wilson, advocate.] Pp. xi., 368. [*Camb. Univ. Lib.*]   Edinburgh, 1823

FIREFLASH (the) : four oars and a coxswain ; where they went, how they went, and why they went ; with the stories they told last Christmas Eve.   By one of the crew [Garnet Walch]. 8vo. [*Lib. of Col. Inst., Supp.* I., 686.]
Hobart, [Tasmania], 1867

FIRELIGHT stories.   By Maggie Broune [Margaret Hamer, later Mrs Andrewes]. 4to. Pp. 80. [*Brit. Mus.*]
London, 1892

FIRES (the) continued at Oxford : or, the decree of the Convocation for burning the Naked Gospel [written by Arthur Bury], considered.   In a letter to a person of honour. [By James Parkinson.] 4to. Pp. 15. No separate title-page.   Letter dated Aug. 30, 1690.

" This pamphlet, which was written by James Parkinson, sometime Fellow of Linc. Coll., was first expos'd to sale at Oxon, 20 Sept. 1690, having been printed at London."—Wood. *See also* the note to " The Naked Gospel."

FIRES (the) of Baal. [Poems.] By Austin Clare [Miss W— M— James]. 8vo. [*Lond. Lib. Cat.*] Dublin, 1921

FIRES of green wood. [A novel.] By Francis Prevost [Harry Francis Prevost Battersby]. Fcap 8vo. London, 1887

FIRESIDE and camp stories.   By the author of *Little Women*, etc. [Louisa M. Allcott]. 8vo. [*Brit. Mus.*]
London, [1870]

FIRESIDE (a) book, or the account of a Christmas spent at Old Court.   By the author of *May you like it* [Charles Benjamin Tayler, M.A., rector of Otley, Ipswich]. 8vo. [*Adv. Lib.*]
London, 1828

FIRESIDE education.   By Peter Parley [Samuel Griswold Goodrich]. 8vo. [*Brit. Mus.*]   London, 1838

FIRESIDE fancies.   [A poem.]   By " Riddell " [Rebecca R. Williams]. Fcap 8vo. [*Amer. Cat.*]
New York, 1906

FIRESIDE (the) magician ; or, the art of natural magic made easy.   By Paul Preston [Thomas Picton]. 8vo. [Cushing's *Init. and Pseud.*, vol. i., p. 240.]   New York, 1870

FIRESIDE melodies : a love-dream. By Sylvan [Samuel Hobbs]. 8vo. [Cushing's *Init. and Pseud.*, vol. i., p. 278.]   London, 1859

FIRESIDE tales.   By the author of *Charlie Burton*, etc. [Jane Alice Sargant]. 2 series. Fcap 8vo.
London, 1857

FIRESIDE thoughts, ballads, etc.   By Claribel [Mrs Charles Barnard, *née* Arlington]. 8vo. Pp. 154. [O'Donoghue's *Poets of Ireland*, p. 15.]
London, 1865

FIRMILIAN ; or the student of Badajoz : a spasmodic tragedy. By T. Percy Jones [William Edmonstoune Aytoun, LL.D.]. 8vo. Pp. xi., 153. [*Adv. Lib.*]   Edinburgh, 1854

FIRST and second letter to a noble Earl [Guildford], on the late negotiations, the present situation, and the measures which ought to be undertaken. [By Sir John Macpherson, Bart.] 8vo. [*Brit. Mus.*] Private print. N.P., 1797

FIRST (the) and second part of the troublesome raigne of John, King of England ; with the discouerie of King Richard Cordelions base sonne (vulgarly named, The Bastard Fawconbridge) : also, the death of King Iohn at Swinstead Abbey ; as they were (sundry times) lately acted by the Queenes Maiesties players. Written by W. Sh. [Attributed by Malone to Christopher Marlowe.] Imprinted at London by Valentine Simmes for Iohn Helme, and are to be sold at his shop in Saint Dunstons churchyard in Fleetestreet. 4to. No pagination.
[London], 1611
" The title to the original edition of this play is as follows :—The troublesome Raigne of John, King of England with the discoverie of King Richard Cordelions Basc Sonne (vulgarly named the Bastard Fawconbridge) ; also, the death of King John at Swinstead Abbey. As it was (sundry times) *publikely* acted by the Queenes Maiesties players in the *honourable citye of London.*
" Imprinted at London for Sampson Clarke and are to be solde at his shop in the backe side of the Royal Exchange 1591.
" The principal title of the Second Part, in the original edition, is as follows :—The Second Part of the troublesome Raigne of King John, conteining the death of Arthur Plantagenet, the landing of Lewes, and the poysoning of King John at Swinstead Abbey. As it was (sundry times). . . .
" The re-publisher of this play in 1611, artfully omitted the words ' publikely ' and ' in the honourable citie of London '— because those words would have detected his fraud. He wished to pass this play for Shakespeare's K. John : for which purpose he inserted the words *W. Sh.* in the title. Shakespeare's Company had *no publick* theatre in the city of London. The Globe was in Southwark. E. M."

FIRST (the) and second parts of King Edward the Fourth. Containing his merie pastime with the tanner of Tamworth ; as also his loue to faire Mistress Shore, her great promotion, fall and miserie ; and lastly the lamentable death of both her and her husband. . . . As it hath diuers times beene publikely played by the Right Honourable the Earle of Derbie his seruants. [By Thomas Heywood.] 8vo. B. L. No pagination. [*Biog. Dram.*]
London, 1613

FIRST (the) and second volume of Letters writ by a Turkish spy, who lived forty-five years undiscovered at Paris . . . [by John Paul Marana] : written originally in Arabick, first translated into Italian, afterwards into French, and now into English. The third edition. Fcap 8vo. [*Brit. Mus.*]
London, 1691
A fictitious work. Full editions are numerous. *See* " Letters writ by a Turkish spy. . . ."

FIRST (the) anniversary of the Government under His Highness the Lord Protector [Oliver Cromwell : a poem by Andrew Marvell, Jun., B.A.]. 4to. [*Camb. Hist. of Eng. Lit.*]
London, 1655

FIRST appearance : a novel. By Mrs Fairfax [Mrs Emily Ernst Bell]. 2 vols. Cr 8vo. [Cushing's *Init. and Pseud.*, vol. ii., p. 58.] Dublin, 1871

FIRST the blade ; a comedy of growth. . . . By Clemence Dane [Winifred Ashton]. 8vo. [*Bodl.*]
London, [1918]

FIRST (the) blast of the trvmpet against the monstrvovs regiment of women. [By John Knox.] 8vo. Fol. 56.
N.P., 1558
Reprinted in his collected works.
The writer had specially in view the evil influence of his sovereign, Mary, Queen of Scots. Reply was made to Knox [by John Aylmer] in " An Harborrovve for faithfull subjects and trevve . . ."

FIRST (a) book for teaching the art of reading to the blind. [By James Gall.] 8vo. [*Brit. Mus.*]
Edinburgh, [1827]

FIRST (the) book of architecture. By A. Palladio ; translated out of Italian : with an appendix touching doors and windows by P. Le Muet : translated out of French by G. R. [G— Richards]. 8vo. [*Brit. Mus.*] London, 1668

FIRST book of drawing. [By John Clark.] Fcap 8vo. [*Adv. Lib.*]
Edinburgh, 1845
Chambers's educational course.

FIRST (the) book of Fontenoy ; a poem, in nine books : with four pastoral essays. [By Thomas Stratford.] 4to. [*Brit. Mus.*] London, 1782

FIRST (the) book of history, for children and youth. By the author of *Peter Parley's tales* [Samuel Griswold Goodrich]. 12mo. [*Brit. Mus.*]
Boston, [U.S.], 1846

FIRST (the) book of Martinus Scriblerus. [By John Arbuthnot, M.D.] 8vo. [*D. N. B.*, vol. 2, p. 65.]
London, 1714

FIRST (the) book of the art of mettals, in which is declared the manner of their generation, and the concomitants of them : written in Spanish by Albaro Alonso Barba, master of art. . . . Translated into English in the year 1669 [by Edward Montague, Earl of Sandwich]. 12mo. [Watt's *Bibl. Brit.*]   London, 1670

FIRST (the) Book of the Iliad of Homer, verbally rendered into English verse ; being a specimen of a new translation of that poet, with critical annotations. [By Alexander Geddes, LL.D.] 8vo. [*D. N. B.*, vol. 21, p. 100.]
                      London, 1791

FIRST (the) Book of the Royal Chronicles, with the tales and parables of Peter Pindar [John Wolcot, M.D.] to the Royal Farmer at Cheltenham Wells. 8vo. Pp. 48. [*D. N. B.*, vol. 62, p. 293.]   London, [1788]

FIRST (the) [and the Second] Book of the works of Mr Francis Rabelais, Doctor in Physick. . . . Now faithfully translated into English by S. T. U. C. [Sir Thomas Urquhart, of Cromarty]. 2 vols. 8vo. [*D. N. B.*, vol. 58, p. 50.]   London, 1653

FIRST (the) Booke of the Christian exercise, appertayning to resolution ; wherein are layed downe the causes & reasons that should moue a man to resolue hym selfe to the seruice of God : and all the impedimentes remoued which may lett the same. Translated from the Italian [of Gasper Loartes, D.D.]. With privylege. 12mo. Pp. 443. [Courtney's *Secrets*, p. 138.]   [Rouen], 1582
      The preface is signed " R. P." [Robert Parsons].
      Edmund Bunney, a Fellow of Merton College, imperfectly acquainted with the previous history of this work, made some alterations and brought out a new edition at London in 1584 ; several other editions followed. Parsons, who resented the changes, in 1585 issued another edition entitled " A Christian Directorie, with reprofe of the falsified edition published by E. Buny." (*See above.*)

FIRST (the) Booke of the historie of the discouerie and conquest of the East Indias, enterprised by the Portugales. By Hernan Lopes de Castaneda. Translated into English by N. L. [Nicholas Lichefild]. Fcap 4to. [Watt's *Bibl. Brit.*]   London, 1582

FIRST (the) capture. By Harry Castlemon [Charles A. Fosdick]. Fcap 8vo. [Cushing's *Init. and Pseud.*, vol. i., p. 52.]   Philadelphia, 1900

FIRST (the) chapters of Genesis justified by the teachings of modern science. By S. J. L. [Samuel J— Leresche]. Cr 8vo.   London, 1896

FIRST (the) claim. [A novel.] By M. Hamilton [Mrs Churchill Luck, *née* —— Spottiswoode]. Cr 8vo. Pp. 320. [*Lond. Lib. Cat.*] London, 1906

FIRST (the) confirmation at St Matthews. By S. W. [Samuel Warren]. 8vo.
                London, 1872

FIRST (the) constitutional Catechism of the Free Church of Scotland. [Prepared by Rev. Andrew Gray, of Perth.] 12mo. Pp. 24. [*New Coll. Lib.*]
                Edinburgh, 1850

FIRST (the) day in heaven. [By Professor William Knight.] 8vo. [*D. N. B.*, vol. 31, p. 266.]   London, 1820

FIRST (the) days entertainment at Rutland-house, by declamations and musick ; after the manner of the ancients. By Sir W. D. [Sir William Davenant]. Pp. 97. [*Brit. Mus.*]
                London, 1657

FIRST (the) Duke and Duchess of Newcastle-upon-Tyne. By the author of *The Life of a Prig* [Thomas Longueville]. 8vo. [*Brit. Mus.*]
                London, 1910

FIRST (the) easy rudiments of grammar, applied to the English tongue. By one who is extremely desirous to promote good literature in America [Samuel Johnson]. Fcap 8vo. Pp. 36. [Evans' *Amer. Bibl.*, vol. iv., p. 18.]   New York, 1765

FIRST (the) Epistle. A crying voice of the Holy Spirit of Love, wherewith all people are out of meer grace called and bidden by H. N. [Hendrik Niclas] to the true repentance of their sins. Fcap 8vo. [*Brit. Mus.*] [London, 1648
      See the note to " Evangelium Regni."

FIRST (the) Epistle of Clement (the apostle Paul's fellow labourer in the Gospel) to the Corinthians ; being an effectual sausory to peace, and brotherly condescention, after an unhappy scism and separation in that Church ; from whence the understanding reader may receive satisfaction concerning the businesse of Church-government, as it stood in the time of the apostles, and after. . . . [Translated from the Greek by William Burton.] 4to. [*W.*]
                London, 1652
      This is a reprint of " Clement, the blessed Paul's fellow-labourer in the Gospel, his first Epistle to the Corinthians," published in 1647, in which the translator's name is signed to " the Epistle Dedicatory."

FIRST (the) Epistle of the second Book of Horace, imitated. [By Alexander Pope.] First edition. Folio. Pp. iv., 23. [*D. N. B.*, vol. 46, p. 120.]
London, 1737

FIRST (the) exhortation of H. N. [Hendrik Niclas] to his children and the Family of Love : likewise H. N. upon the Beatitudes and the seven deadly sins : translated out of Base-Almayne into English. 8vo. Pp. 229. [*Brit. Mus.*] London, 1656
See the note to " Evangelium Regni. . . ."

FIRST (the) families of the Sierras. By Joaquin Miller [Cincinnatus Heine Miller]. 8vo. [Cushing's *Init. and Pseud.*, vol. i., p. 194.] Chicago, 1876

FIRST favourites. By Nathaniel Gubbins [Edward Spencer]. Cr 8vo. Pp. 240. [*Lit. Year Book.*] London, 1904

FIRST (the) floor ; a farce in two acts, as it is now acting at the Theatre-Royal in Drury-Lane. [By James Cobb.] 8vo. [*Biog. Dram.*]
London, 1787

FIRST (the) four voyages of Amerigo Vespucci : translated from the rare original edition [Florence, 1505-6] ; with some preliminary notices by M. K. [Michael Kerney]. Fcap 4to.
London, 1885

FIRST (the) fourteen years of King James. [By Fulke Greville, Lord Brooke ?] Fcap 4to. Pp. 192. [*D. N. B.*, vol. 23, p. 162.]
London, 1651
More probably written by Arthur Wilson.

FIRST (the) French and English grammar. . . . New edition. By Abbé Bossut [Sir Richard Phillips]. Fcap 8vo. Pp. xi., 158. [*D. N. B.*, vol. 45, p. 210.] London, 1825
See the note to " A Biographical Classbook."

FIRST (a) friendship. [A novel. By Henry Jackson.] Reprinted from *Fraser's Magazine.* 8vo. [*Brit. Mus.*]
London, 1863

FIRST fruits of Australian poetry. [By Barron Field.] 4to. Pp. 9. Private print. [*Brit. Mus.*] Sydney, 1819
Probably the first book printed in Australia.

FIRST fruits ; poems. By E. H. R. [Elizabeth Harcourt Rolls, later Mrs Mitchell]. 8vo. [*Brit. Mus.*]
London, 1857

FIRST (the) gentleman in Europe. By Lewis Melville [Lewis Samuel Benjamin]. 2 vols. 8vo. [*Jewish Year Book.*] London, 1906

FIRST (the) George [King of England] in Hanover and England. By Lewis Melville [Lewis Samuel Benjamin]. 2 vols. 8vo. [*Jewish Year Book.*]
London, 1908

FIRST (the) glass of wine. By Nellie Grahame [Mrs Annie Dunning, *née* Ketchum]. Pt 8vo. [Cushing's *Init. and Pseud.*, vol. i., p. 119.]
Boston, 1876

FIRST harvests : episodes in the life of Mrs Levison Gower : a satire without a moral. By J. S. of Dale [Frederic Jesup Stimson]. Fcap 8vo. [*Lond. Lib. Cat.*] New York, 1888

FIRST (a) history of Greece. By the author of *Amy Herbert*, etc. [Elizabeth Missing Sewell]. 12mo. Pp. xii., 345. [*Brit. Mus.*] London, 1852

FIRST (the) homily of " The former Book of homilies ; " to which is added a Defence of the Bible Society, with some accounts of its proceedings extracted from statements and documents published by the Society [by T. Boys]. 8vo. [*Brit. Mus.*]
London, 1818

FIRST (the) hundred thousand ; being the unofficial chronicle of a visit of " K (I.)." By the Junior Sub., Ian Hay [John Hay Beith, M.A.]. Cr 8vo. Pp. viii., 342. [*Brit. Mus.*]
Edinburgh, 1915

FIRST impressions in America. By John Ayscough [Monsignor Francis Bickerstaffe-Drew]. 8vo. [*Catholic Who's Who.*] London, 1921

FIRST impressions of America. [By John Walter, jun., of the London *Times*.] 8vo. Pp. 131. Private print. [*Brit. Mus.*] London, 1867
Signed " J. W."

FIRST impressions of India. [By Gwilym Evans.] 8vo. Pp. 62.
Llanelly, 1888

FIRST impressions of the New World ; or two travellers from the Old, in 1858. [By Mrs Alexander Trotter.] 8vo. Pp. xi., 308. London, 1859
Signed " T. L. T."

FIRST impressions ; or a day in India : a letter from an Assistant-Surgeon, lately arrived in Calcutta [G— Turner]. 8vo. Private print. [*Brit. Mus.*]
Yarmouth, 1841

FIRST in the field. By the author of *Recommended to mercy*, etc. [Mrs Margaret C. Houston]. 3 vols. 8vo. [*Brit. Mus.*] London, 1872

FIRST it was ordained. By Guy Thorne [Cyril A. E. Ranger-Gull]. Cr 8vo. [*Lit. Year Book.*]
London, 1905

FIRST Italian reading-book, for the use of the students of London University College. By L. Mariotti [Antonio Gallenga], author of *A practical grammar of the Italian language.* Fcap 8vo. [*Brit. Mus.*] London, 1852

FIRST (the) last, and the last first; being the substance of Lectures in the country. . . . [By John Oldfield, minister at Carsington.] Fcap 8vo. [Calamy's *Nonconf. Mem.*, Palmer's ed., vol. i., p. 400.] London, 1666

FIRST (a) legacy to Inverness; in a letter to the Rev. Duncan Stewart. By Mirabeau [Kennedy MacNab]. 8vo. [P. J. Anderson's *Inverness Bibl.*] Inverness, 1860

FIRST lessons in grammar, on the plan of Pestalozzi. By a teacher in Boston [Nathaniel Peabody]. 8vo. [Cushing's *Init. and Pseud.*, vol. i., p. 280.] Boston, 1830

FIRST lessons in Greek. By C. D. C. [Charles Dexter Cleveland]. 8vo. [Cushing's *Init. and Pseud.*, vol. i., p. 45.] Boston, 1833

FIRST lessons in Jaloof. [By Mrs Hannah Kilham.] 8vo. London, 1820

FIRST lessons in perspective, and sketching from nature. . . . By a teacher [Benjamin H. Coe]. 8vo. [Cushing's *Init. and Pseud.*, vol. ii., p. 143.] New York, 1846

FIRST lessons in Sanskrit grammar. By J. R. B. [James Robert Ballantyne]. 8vo. [*Brit. Mus.*] Mirzapore, 1851

FIRST lessons in useful things. By a Cornish lady [Mrs Emilie Earle Hickes, *née* Steele]. 8vo. [Boase and Courtney's *Bibl. Corn.*, p. 1263.] Truro, 1868

FIRST love; a novel. [By Mrs Margracia Loudon.] 3 vols. Fcap 8vo. [*Camb. Univ. Lib.*] London, 1830

FIRST (the) man; or a short discourse of Adams state; viz. 1. of his being made a living soule; 2. of the manner of his fall. [By John Greene.] 4to. [*Brit. Mus.*] London, 1643 Signed " J. G."

FIRST mate; a domestic drama. By Richard-Henry [Richard Butler and Henry Chance Newton]. Fcap 8vo. Pp. 31. London, [1850]

FIRST (the) mate; the story of a strange cruise. By Harry Collingwood [William J. C. Lancaster]. Cr 8vo. Pp. 288. [*Lond. Lib. Cat.*] London, 1914

FIRST (the) mole in Cornwall: a morality from the Stowe of Morwenstow, in the rocky land. By H. [Rev. Robert Stephen Hawker, M.A.]. 8vo. [Boase and Courtney's *Bibl. Corn.*, p. 221.] N.P., [1850]

FIRST (the) motive of T. H. [Theophilus Higgins, or Hyggons], Maister of Arts, and lately minister, to suspect the integrity of his religion . . . 4to. [*Watt's Bibl. Brit.*] Roan, 1601

FIRST (the) news; an essay. By Joseph Conrad [Joseph Conrad Korzeniowski]. 4to. Private print. Pp. 11. [*Lit. Year Book.*] London, 1919

FIRST (the) oath. . . . By F. B. [Rev. Francis Bourdillon, M.A.]. Fcap 8vo. [*Brit. Mus.*] London, [1869]

FIRST (the) ode of the second Book of Horace paraphras'd; and address'd to Richard St—le, Esq. [By Jonathan Swift.] 4to. *Camb. Hist. of Eng. Lit.*] London, 1714

FIRST (the) of a series of letters, addressed to the agriculturists of North Northumberland, which will be continued at intervals. By J. S. Donaldson, Esq., Cheswick [James Stormouth Darling, W.S.]. 8vo. [*Signet Lib.*] Berwick, 1836

FIRST (the) of April; or, the triumphs of folly: a poem, dedicated to a celebrated Dutchess. By the author of the *Diaboliad* [William Combe]. 4to. [*Dyce Cat.*] London, 1777

FIRST (the) part of a dictionary of chemistry, &c. By J. K., F.R.S. and S.A.Sc. [James Keir]. 4to. Pp. xx., 211. [*Bodl.*] Birmingham, 1789

FIRST (the) part of an Equal check to Pharisaism and Antinomianism. . . . By the author of the *Checks to Antinomianism* [Rev. John William Fletcher, originally Jean G. De la Flechere]. Second edition. Fcap 8vo. [*Brit. Mus.*] Bristol, 1774 Preface signed " J. W."

FIRST (the) part of Ieronimo; with the warres of Portugall, and the life and death of Don Andræa. [By Thomas Kyd.] 4to. No pagination. B. L. [*Bodl.*] London, 1605

FIRST (the) part of the Catalogue of Bishops, containing the succession of the Archbishops and Bishops of Canterbury. [By Robert Hall.] Fcap 8vo. London, 1641-52

FIRST (the) part of the life and raigne of King Henry the IIII., extending to the end of the first yeare of his raigne. Written by I. H. [Sir John Haywarde, D.C.L.]. 4to. Pp. 149. [*Hart's Index Expurg. Angl.*, p. 35; *D. N. B.*, vol. 25, p. 312.] London, 1559

FIRST (the) part of the mirrour of princely Deedes and Knighthood ; wherein is shewed the worthinesse of the Knight of the Sunne and his brother Rosicleer, with the straunge love of the beautiful Princesse Briana ; translated out of Spanish by M. T. [Margaret Tyler]. Fcap 4to. [*Brit. Mus.*] London, [1580 ?]

FIRST (the) part of the no lesse rare then excellent and stately Historie of the famous and fortunate Prince Palmerin of England. . . . Translated out of French by A. M. [Anthony Munday]. Fcap 4to. [*Brit. Mus.*] London, 1609
See also " The Famous history . . ."

FIRST (the) part of the Resolution of Religion, devided into two Bookes, contayning a demonstration of the necessity of a Diuine and supernaturall Worshippe. In the first, against all Atheists and Epicures ; in the second, that Christian Catholicke Religion is the same in particuler, and more certaine in euery Article thereof, then any humane or experimented Knowledge. . . . [By Robert Parsons, S.J.] Fcap 8vo. Pp. 281. [Sommervogel's *Dictionnaire.*]   N.P., 1603
Preface signed " R. B." Attributed also to Richard Broughton.

FIRST (the) parte of Pasquils Apologie ; wherein he renders a reason to his friendes of his long silence ; and gallops the fielde with the Treatise of reformation lately written by a fugitiue, Iohn Penric.   [By Thomas Nash.] Printed where I was, and where I will bee, readie by the helpe of God and my muse, to send you the May-game of Martinisme for an intermedium, betweene the first and seconde part of the Apologie.   4to.   No pagination. [*Bodl.*]   Anno Dom. 1590

FIRST (the) Prayer-Book of Edward VI. compared with the successive revisions of the Book of Common Prayer ; also a concordance to the rubricks in the several editions.   [By James Parker.] 8vo. Pp. viii., 565. [*Bodl.*]
Oxford, 1877

FIRST (the) principles of algebra, compiled for the use of mechanics and others. By a member of the Spitalfields Mechanics' Institution [J— J— Downes]. Fcap 8vo.   London, 1825

FIRST (the) principles of English grammar, in verse, for the use of young people.   By J. W. [John Williams,   Vicar of Catherington]. 8vo. [*Bodl.*]   N.P., N.D.

FIRST (the) principles of the oracles of God, explained in a brief exposition of the Creed, the Ten Commandments, the Lord's Prayer, and the Sacrament ; with several hymns or Psalms of Prayer and Praise.   [By Thomas Downe.] 8vo. [*Brit. Mus.*]
London, 1677

FIRST question : Why are you a Catholic ?   The answer follows. Second question : But why are you a Protestant ?   An answer attempted in vain. Written by the Rev. Father S. C. [Serenus Cressy], monk of the holy order of St Benedict, and of the English Congregation. First printed in 1673. 8vo. 4to. Pp. iii., 72. [Jones' Peck, ii., 462.]   London, 1686

FIRST (the) resurrection and second death ; or, the kingdom to come. By the author of *The Word made flesh* [Thomas Carlyle, advocate]. Part I. Containing, 1. The herald of Messiah. 2. The majesty of Messiah.   3. The King of the Jews. Fcap 8vo. Pp. 93. [Boase's *Cath. Apost. Lit.*]
Edinburgh, 1830

FIRST (the) resurrection. By a spiritual Watchman [Rev. Charles S. Hawtrey, M.A.]. Fcap 8vo.   London, 1820

FIRST (the) satire of the Second Book of Horace, imitated in a dialogue between Mr Pope and the ordinary of Newgate. [By William Guthry, or Guthrie.] Fcap 8vo.   London, 1733

FIRST (the) seal ; being short homilies on the Gospel according to St Matthew. [By Samuel Richard Bosanquet.] 8vo. Pp. 603. [*Brit. Mus.*]   London, 1854

FIRST series of hymns and songs for the use of Catholic schools and families. [Edited by Henry Formby.]   3 parts. 8vo. [*Brit. Mus.*]   London, [1853]

FIRST (the) sermon [on Isaiah 52/15] preach'd at the opening of the Oratory, on Sunday, July 3, 1726.   [By John Henley.] 8vo.   [London, 1726]

FIRST (the) sermon preach'd before their Majesties in English at Windsor, on the first Sunday of October 1685. By the Reverend Father Dom. P. E. [Philip Ellis], monk of the holy order of St Benedict, and of the English Congr. 4to. Pp. 31. [*Brit. Mus.*]
London, 1686

FIRST (the) settlers of New England. By a lady [Mrs Elizabeth Sanders]. 8vo. [Cushing's *Init. and Pseud.*, i., p. 161.]   Boston, 1822

FIRST (the) settlers of New England ; or the conquest of the Pequods, Narragansetts, and Pokanokets ; as related by a mother to her children. By a lady of Massachusetts [Mrs Lydia Maria Child]. Fcap 8vo. Pp. 282. [Cushing's *Init. and Pseud.*, vol. i., p. 163.]   Boston, 1829

FIRST (the) sitting of the committee on the proposed monument to Shakspeare. Carefully taken in short-hand by Zachary Craft [Charles Kelsall], amanuensis to the chairman. 8vo.
London, 1823

FIRST (the) six books of the Iliad of Homer, literally translated into English prose, with copious explanatory notes, and a preliminary dissertation on his life and writings. By a member of the University [Henry Cary]. 8vo. Pp. 230. [*Camb. Univ. Lib.*]
Cambridge, 1828

FIRST (the) state of Muhametism ; or an account of the author and doctrine of that imposture. [By Lancelot Addison, D.D.] Fcap 8vo. [Playfair's *Bibl. of Morocco*, No. 268.]
London, 1678
The author's name is given in the second edition, with a modified title, " The Life and death of Muhamed " (1679).

FIRST (the) step to knowledge : English spelling. . . . By the Rev. J. Goldsmith [Sir Richard Phillips]. New edition. Fcap 8vo.   London, [1860]
See note to "A Biographical class-book."

FIRST (the) steps in arithmetic ; or a new method of teaching the first four rules. By a Preceptor [Josiah Carver]. Second edition. 8vo. [*Brit. Mus.*]
London, 1852

FIRST steps in occultism : being 1. Practical occultism. By H. P. B. [Helena Petrovna Blavatsky] ; 2. Occultism *v.* the occult arts. By H. P. B. ; 3. Comments on " Light on the Path." By M. C. [Mabel Collins]. Fcap 8vo. Pp. 122. [*Brit. Mus.*]
London, 1895

FIRST steps towards a Church of the future. By the author of *Organized Christianity* [Henry Dunn]. 8vo. [*Brit. Mus.*]   London, 1867

FIRST (the) temptation ; or, " Eritis sicut Deus " ; a philosophical romance, translated from the German [of Marie Schwab]. 8vo. [*Brit. Mus.*]
London, 1863

FIRST (the) ten years of a sailor's life at sea. By the author of *All about ships*, etc. [Captain Charles Chapman]. 8vo. [*Brit. Mus.*]   London, 1876
" All about ships " is not anonymous.

FIRST (the) volume of a new translation of Homer's Iliad, adapted to the capacity of honest English roast beef and pudding eaters, by Caustic Barebones, a broken apothecary [Thomas Bridges] ; to which is prefixed some small account of the abovesaid Mr Barebones himself. 12mo. [Lowndes' *Bibl. Man.*]   London, 1762

FIRST-BORN (the) ; a drama. [By Rev. William Harness.] 8vo. Pp. 121. [Martin's *Cat.*]   London, 1844

FIRSTE (the) Booke of Tully's Offices, translated grammatically. [By John Brinsley.] 8vo. [*Brit. Mus.*]
London, 1631

FIRSTE (the) examination of the worthy servant of God, Mastres Anne Askew, ye yonger daughter of Syr William Askew, Knyght of Lyncolneshyre, lately martyred i Smythefelde by the Romyshe Popes upholders. . . . [By John Bale.] 8vo. B. L. [Christie-Miller *Cat.*]   N.P., N.D.
" The latter examination," following, has a separate title-page.

FIRST-FRUITS and tenths out of ecclesiastical livings . . . no present for Caesar ; or the arithmetick of Dr Thomas Bradley . . . examined. By D. B., R. V., O. G. I., E. [Rice Vaughan, of Gray's Inn]. 8vo.
London, 1657

FISCUS papalis ; sive, catalogvs indvlgentiarum & relquarum (*sic*) septem principalium Ecclesiarum vrbis Romæ. Ex vetusto manuscripto codice vere & fideliter descriptus. A part of the Popes exchequer. That is, a catalogue of the indulgences and reliques belonging to the seuen principal churches in Rome. Laying downe the spirituall riches and infinite treasure which (as sure as the Pope is holy and true) are to be found in the Catholike Roman Church, whereof the poore heretikes in England haue not one mite. Taken out of an ancient manuscript and translated : together with certaine notes and comments, explaining the more difficult places, for the ease and helpe of good Catholikes, who had best goe to Rome, to try the vertue of the glorious indulgences. By a Catholike diuine [William Crashaw]. 4to. No pagination. [*Aber. Lib.*]   London, 1621

FISH and fishing in the United States and British Provinces of North America. By Frank Forester [Henry William Herbert]. 2 vols. 8vo. [*Brit. Mus.*]   London, 1849

FISH : how to choose and how to dress. By Piscator [William Hughes, barrister]. 8vo. [*Brit. Mus.*]
London, 1843

FISH yarns, and other salt-water tales. By Captain Hawser [Julius W. Muller]. Fcap 8vo. [*Amer. Cat.*]
New York, 1904

FISHER (the) boy. By Willie Triton [Alonzo Tripp]. 8vo. [Cushing's *Init. and Pseud.*, i. 287.]   Boston, 1857

FISHER (the) boy; a poem, comprising his several avocations during the four seasons of the year. By H. C., Esq. [William Henry Ireland]. 12mo. [Watt's *Bibl. Brit.*; *D. N. B.*, vol. 29, p. 36.] London, 1808

FISHERMAN (the); or, art of angling made easy. By Guiniad Charfy [George Smeeton]. 8vo. [Lowndes' *Bibl. Man.*, p. 412.] London, [1812] Ascribed also to James Saunders.

FISHERMAN'S (the) daughter, and dreams of the past. By Theta [Maria Theresa Hoblyn]. 8vo. [Cushing's *Init. and Pseud.*, i., 282.] London, 1869

FISHERMAN'S (the) guide : a manual for professional and amateur anglers. By Frank Forester [Henry William Herbert]. Fcap 8vo. [*Brit. Mus.*] New York, N.D.

FISHER'S drawing-room scrap-book, 1843. By the author of *The Women of England* [Mrs William Ellis, neé Sarah Stickney]. 4to. [*Brit. Mus.*] London, 1843

FISHER'S drawing-room scrap-book, with poetical illustrations by L. E. L. [Letitia Elizabeth Landon, later Mrs Maclean]. 4to. Pp. 60. [Haynes' *Pseud.*] London, 1833

FISHER'S (the) garland for 1835. By W. A. C. [William Andrew Chatto]. 8vo. [*Brit. Mus.*] London, 1836

FISHERS (the) of Derby Haven. [A tale.] By Hesba Stretton [Sarah Smith], author of *The children of Cloverley*. Fcap 8vo. London, 1866 Incorrectly attributed to Hanna Smith. *See* " Alone in London."

FISHER'S River : North Carolina scenes and characters. By " Skitt " [H— E. Taliaferro], who was rais'd thar. 8vo. [Cushing's *Init. and Pseud.*, vol. i., p. 268.] New York, 1875

FISHING and travel in Spain. By Geoffrey Mortimer [Walter M. Gallichan]. Cr 8vo. [*Lond. Lib. Cat.*] London, 1904

FISHING in Derbyshire. By Geoffrey Mortimer [Walter M. Gallichan]. 8vo. London, 1905

FISHING in Wales. By Geoffrey Mortimer [Walter M. Gallichan]. London, 1903

FISHING with hook and line. By Frank Forester [Henry William Herbert]. Fcap 8vo. [*Brit. Mus.*] New York, N.D.

FISHPORT. [A novel.] By Guy Thorne [Cyril A. E. Ranger-Gull]. Cr. 8vo. [*Lit. Year Book.*] London, 1922

FISTIANA ; Fights for the Championship, and celebrated Prize Battles, from the earliest period to 1860. By the Editor of *Bell's Life in London* [Francis L. Dowling]. Pt 8vo. [*Brit. Mus.*] London, 1860 *See also* " Fights for the championship."

FISTIANA ; or the oracle of the Ring : comprising a history of pugilism, a defence of British boxing, instruction for training. . . . By the Editor of *Bell's Life in London* [Pierce Egan]. 8vo. [*Brit. Mus.*] London, 1841

FITCH (the) Club. By " Jak " [Annie Bowles Williams]. Fcap 8vo. [Cushing's *Init. and Pseud.*, vol. ii., p. 807.] New York, 1887

FITZ-ALLAN. By a blue [Robert Huish]. 2 vols. Fcap 8vo. [*Brit. Mus.*] London, 1832

FITZALLEYNE of Berkeley ; a romance of the present time. By Bernard Blackmantle, author of *The English Spy* [Charles Molloy Westmacott]. 2 vols. 8vo. [*Brit. Mus.*] London, 1825

FITZ-EDWARD. [A novel, in a series of letters. By Elizabeth Susan Law, Lady Colchester.] Cr 8vo. Pp. 262. London, 1875

FITZGEORGE ; a novel. [By John Sterling ?] 3 vols. Fcap 8vo. [*Bookseller*, 1868, p. 460 ; but see *D. N. B.*, vol. 54, p. 193.] London, 1832

FITZHERBERT ; or, lovers and fortune-hunters. By the authoress of *The Bride of Siena* [Mrs Yorick Smythies, neé Gordon]. 3 vols. Fcap 8vo. [*Camb. Univ. Lib.*] London, 1838

FITZ-RAYMOND ; or the rambler on the Rhine : a metrico-political sketch of past and present times, written during an excursion in 1830. By Caledonnicus [Whitelaw Ainslie, M.D.]. 8vo. Pp. xi., 200. [*Adv. Lib.*] Edinburgh, 1831

FITZ-STEPHEN'S Description of the city of London, newly translated from the Latin original : with a necessary commentary ; a dissertation on the author, ascertaining the exact year of the production, is prefixed ; and to the whole is subjoined a correct edition of the original, with the various readings, and some useful annotations. By an antiquary [Samuel Pegge, LL.D.]. 4to. [*Upcott.*] London, 1772

FITZWALTERS (the), Barons of Chesterton ; or, ancient times in England. By the author of *A winter's tale*, etc. [James Norris Brewer]. 4 vols. Fcap 8vo. [*Adv. Lib.*] London, 1829

FITZWIGGINS; a novel. By the
author of *Sydenham*, etc. [W. Massie].
3 vols. Fcap 8vo. [*Adv. Lib.*]
London, 1840

FIVE books of philosophical comfort,
with marginal notes : translated from
the Latin of Boethius. [By Michael
Walpole, S.J.] 8vo. Pp. 144. [Som-
mervogel's *Dictionnaire*.]
London, 1609

FIVE captious questions, propounded
by a factor for the Papacy ; answered
by a divine of the Church of God
in England, by parallel questions
and by positive resolutions. . . . [By
Charles Gataker, rector of Hoggeston,
Bucks.] 4to. Pp. 87. [*Bodl.*]
London, 1673
Preface signed " C. G."
Another edition was published in 1674,
with the title of " The Papists bait ;
or their usual method of gaining prose-
lites answered."

FIVE cases of conscience ; occasionally
determined by a late learned hand
[Robert Sanderson, D.D.]. 8vo. Pp.
129. [*D. N. B.*, vol. 50, p. 266.]
London, 1666

FIVE discourses. . . . [By Rev. William
Corson, minister at Girvan.] 8vo.
[Scott's *Fasti*, new edition, vol. iii.,
p. 43.]   Ayr, 1847

FIVE discourses on future punishment.
By the Rector [Rev. Cameron Mann].
8vo. [*Lib. Journ.*, xiv., 59.]
New York, 1888

FIVE discourses, viz. on Water baptism,
Episcopacy, Primitive heresie of the
Quakers, Reflections on the Quakers,
a brief account of the Socinian Trinity.
By the author of *The Snake in the
Grass* [Charles Leslie]. 8vo. [Whit-
ley's *Bapt. Bibl.*, i. 135.]
London, 1700

FIVE dramas. [By Daniel Puseley.]
8vo. [*D. N. B.*, vol. 47, pp. 53.]
London, 1860

FIVE friends. [A tale.] By Pansy [Mrs
Isabella Alden, *née* Macdonald]. 8vo.
Pp. 254.   Boston, [Mass.], 1882

FIVE (the) great offerings and their
law ; or the divine programme of the
Redeemer and His redeemed. By
E. M. S. [Mrs E— M— Synge, *née*
Elliott]. 8vo.   London, [1892]

FIVE hundred majority ; or, the days
of Tammany. By Willys Niles [John
Ferguson Hume]. 8vo. [Cushing's
Init. and Pseud., vol. i., p. 204.]
New York, 1872

FIVE hundred pounds reward ; a novel.
By a barrister [William Knox Wigram].
3 vols. 8vo.   London, 1867

FIVE hundred questions and exercises
on Murray's Abridgement and Mur-
ray's English Grammar. By James
Adair [Sir Richard Phillips]. 12mo.
[*Bibliographer*, vol. 4, p. 168.]
London, 1824

FIVE hundred questions deduced from
Goldsmith's History of England. By
James Adair [Sir Richard Phillips].
Fcap 8vo.   London, 1815

FIVE hundred questions on the Old
Testament. By Rev. S. Barrow [Sir
Richard Phillips]. Second edition.
12mo. [*Bibliographer*, vol. 4, p. 168.]
London, 1819

FIVE hundred questions on the social
condition of the natives of India. . . .
[By Rev. James Long.] 8vo. [*Calc.
Imp. Lib.*]   London, 1865

FIVE letters addressed to the yeomanry
of the United States. . . . By a farmer
[George Logan]. 8vo. [Cushing's
Init. and Pseud., vol. i., p. 58.]
Philadelphia, 1792

FIVE letters concerning the inspiration
of the Holy Scriptures. Translated
[by John Locke ?] out of French [of
Jean le Clerc.] Fcap 8vo. Pp. 239.
[*D. N. B.*, vol. 34, p. 35.]   N.P., 1690
" For the better understanding of these
five letters, it seems necessary, in a few
words, to explain the occasion and subject
of them. They are not, in French, one
distinct volume, as they are here made in
English, but parts of two larger volumes
written in an epistolary form. The first,
entituled, (1.) The thoughts or reflections
of some divines in Holland, upon Father
Simon's Critical history of the Old Testament. The second, (2.) A defence of
those thoughts, in answer to the Prior
of Bolleville ; who is supposed to be
also the same Mr Simon, disguised under
a borrowed name.
" (1.) Sentiments de quelques Theo-
logiens de Hollande sur l'Histoire critique
du Vieux Testament, composée par le
P. Richard Simon. (2.) Defense des
Sentimens, &c. contre la Response du
Prieur de Bolleville."—Preface.

FIVE letters, from a free merchant in
Bengal, to Warren Hastings, Esq.,
Governor General of the Honourable
East India Company's settlements in
Asia ; conveying some free thoughts
on the probable causes of the decline
of the export trade of that kingdom ;
and a rough sketch, or outline of a
plan, for restoring it to its former
splendor. [By Captain Joseph Price.]
Reprinted, 1783. 8vo. Pp. 220.
[*Brit. Mus.*]   London, 1777

FIVE letters on several subjects, religious
and historical. [By Henry James Pye.]
8vo.   London, 1768

FIVE letters on the state of the poor in the County of Kent [by John Toke] as first printed in the year 1770; to which is added a short introduction. [By N. R. Toke, of Godington.] 8vo. Pp. 72. [*Manch. Free Lib.*]
Canterbury, 1808

FIVE letters on worship. By W. T. [William Trotter]. 8vo. [*Cushing's Init. and Pseud.*, vol. i., p. 279.]
London, 1857

FIVE letters to my neighbour Smith, touching the fifteen gallon jug. [By Samuel Griswold Goodrich.] 8vo.
Boston, 1838

FIVE letters to Sir Samuel Romilly, on the subject of his motion respecting the penal laws. By Anti-Draco [John Disney]. 8vo. [*Watt's Bibl. Brit.*]
London, 1810

FIVE letters to the Reverend Mr F—r [Fletcher] relative to his Vindication of the Minutes of the Reverend Mr John Wesley; intended chiefly for the comfort of mourning backsliders, and such as may have been distressed and perplexed by reading Mr Wesley's Minutes, or the Vindication of them. By a friend [Sir Richard Hill]. 8vo. Pp. 40. [*Brit. Mus.*] London, 1771
Signed, "Author of Pietas Oxoniensis."

FIVE little partridges; or the Pilot's house. [A novel.] By Brenda [Mrs —— Castle Smith]. Pt 8vo. [*Lond. Lib. Cat.*] London, 1885

FIVE little peppers abroad. By Margaret Sidney [Mrs Harriett Mulford Lothrop, *née* Stone]. 8vo. [*Kirk's Supp.*] Boston, 1887 [?]

FIVE little peppers, and how they grew. By Margaret Sidney [Mrs Harriet M. Lothrop]. Square 8vo. Boston, 1889

FIVE little Peppers at school. By Margaret Sidney [Mrs Harriett Mulford Stone, later Mrs Lothrop]. 8vo.
Boston, 1890

FIVE little Peppers midway. By Margaret Sidney [Mrs Harriet Mulford Lothrop]. Cr 8vo. [*Kirk's Supp.*]
London, 1909

FIVE love letters from [Marianna d'Alcoforado] a [Portuguese] nun to a Cavalier [Chevalier de Chamilly]: done out of French into English by R. L'Estrange. Fcap 8vo. [*Arber's Term Cat.*, vol. i., p. 302.]
London, 1678
For titles of other editions, *see* "Love without affectation . . ." (1709), and "Letters from a Portuguese nun . . ." (1808).

FIVE miles in a mouse-trap. By the Man in the Moon [Laura E. Richards]. Square 8vo. [*Kirk's Supp.*]
Boston, 1880

FIVE nights. [A novel.] By Victoria Cross [Miss Vivian Cory]. Cr 8vo. Pp. 350. [*Lond. Lib. Cat.*]
London, 1908

FIVE (the) nights of St Albans. [By William Mudford.] 3 vols. Fcap 8vo. [*Camb. Univ. Cat.*] Edinburgh, 1829

FIVE old friends, and a young prince. By the author of *The story of Elizabeth* [Anne Isabella Thackeray, later Mrs Ritchie]. With four illustrations by Frederick Walker. 8vo. Pp. 407. [*Camb. Univ. Lib.*] London, 1868

FIVE (the) orders of the Church: a sermon [on Eph. 4/11]. [By Rev. J— E— Bromby.] 8vo.
Melbourne, 1867

FIVE pieces of Runic poetry translated from the Islandic language. [By Thomas Percy, D.D., Bishop of Dromore.] 8vo. Pp. 100. [*Adv. Lib.*]
London, 1762

FIVE sermons on the times, against Puseyism on the one hand, and Dissent on the other. [By John Edward Sabin.] 8vo. [*Brit. Mus.*]
London, [1841]

FIVE sonnets, addressed to Wootton, the spot of the author's nativity. [By Sir Samuel Egerton Brydges.] 4to. [*W.*] Kent, Lee Priory, 1819

FIVE (the) talents of woman: a book for girls and women. By the author of *How to be happy though married* [Rev. Edward J. Hardy]. 8vo. Pp. 301. [*Lond. Lib. Cat.*] London, 1888

FIVE to two; a comedy, in three acts. By the author of *Three to one* [John Lettsom Elliot]. 8vo. Pp. 118. [*Camb. Univ. Cat.*] London, 1851

FIVE (the) unexplained Parables of Matt. xiii. [By Rev. Richard Govett.] Fcap 8vo. N.P., [1850?]

FIVE (a) weeks' tour to Paris, Versailles, Marli. [By William Lucas.] 8vo. [*Manch. Free Lib. Cat.*, p. 427.]
London, 1750

FIVE years in a lottery office. By Thomas Doyle [John J. More]. 8vo. [*Cushing's Init. and Pseud.*, vol. i., p. 83.] Boston, 1841

FIVE years in Kafirland. [By Mrs Harriet Ward.] 8vo. London, 1847
A later edition (1848), enlarged, in 2 vols., gives the writer's name.

FIVE years in the West; how an inexperienced young man finds his occupation. . . . By a Texas preacher [William Allen]. 8vo. [*Kirk's Supp.*]
Nashville, Tenn., 1884

FIVE years of colliery life ; or, the adventures of a collier boy in a Somersetshire coal-mine. By Jonathan Presto [Charles Challenger, of Bristol]. 8vo. [Green's *Bibl. Somers.*, vol. iii., p. 156.]   Manchester, 1884

FIVE years of Tory rule : a lesson and a warning.   By " Nemesis " [Alfred Farthing Robins]. 8vo. Pp. x., 152. [Gladstone *Lib. Cat.*]   London, 1879

FIVE (a) years' residence in Buenos Ayres, during the years 1820-24. By an Englishman [George Thomas Love]. 8vo.   London, 1825

FIVE years within the golden gate. By Isabelle Saxon [—— Redding, later Mrs Sutherland]. 8vo.   Pp. 315. [*Lond. Lib. Cat.*]   London, 1868

FIXED as fate. [A novel.] By the author of *Recommended to mercy* [Mrs Margaret C. Houston]. 3 vols. Cr 8vo. [*Brit. Mus.*]   London, 1881

FLAG (the) of the adventurer. By Sydney C. Grier [Hilda C. Gregg]. Cr 8vo. Pp. 362. [*Lond. Lib. Cat.*] Edinburgh, 1921

FLAG (the) of truce.   By a White Republican [Hiram Fuller]. Cr 8vo. Pp. 52. [Cushing's *Init. and Pseud.*, vol. i., p. 307.]   London, 1862

FLAG (the) of truce. By the author of *The Wide, Wide World* [Susan Warner]. 8vo.   Pp. 250. [*Brit. Mus.*] London, [1892]

FLAGELLATION and the Flagellants ; a history of the rod in all countries from the earliest period to the present time.   By the Rev. Wm. U. Cooper, B.A. [James Glass Bertram]. With numerous illustrations. A new edition, revised and corrected. Pt 8vo. Pp. xi., 544. [*Adv. Lib.*] [London], N.D.

FLAGELLATOR (the) : a philippic intended as a gentle whipping for [Edward Mangin] the author of the " Intercepted Epistle," with a rod in pickle for the writer of the promised " postman." [By E— Ashe, an actor.] 8vo. [Green's *Bibl. Somers.*, i., 334.] Bath, 1815

FLAGELLUM Flagelli ; or Doctor Bastwicks quarters beaten up in two or three pomeridian exercises, by way of animadversion upon his first booke, intituled, Independency not Gods ordinance. By J. S. [John Sadler], M.A. Published by authoritie.   Printed by Matthew Simmons, dwelling in Aldersgate-streete. 4to. [Thomason, *Coll. of Tracts*, vol. i., p. 399.] London, 1645

FLAGELLUM ; or, a dry answer to Dr Hancocke's wonderfully comic liquid book, which he merely calls Febrifugium magnum, &c.   [By Daniel Defoe.] 8vo. [Wilson's *Life of Defoe*, 181.]   London, 1723
Marked ? in Lowndes' list.

FLAGELLUM ; or the life and death, birth and burial of O. Cromwell, the late usurper : faithfully described, with an exact account of his policies and successes.   Enlarged with many additions. By S. T., Gent. [James Heath]. 8vo. Pp. 192. [*Bodl.*] London, 1672
The first edition was published in 1663.

FLAGELLUM Parliamentarium ; being sarcastic notices of nearly two hundred Members of the first Parliament after the Restoration, 1661-78. [By Andrew Marvell ?] Pt 8vo.   [*D. N. B.*, vol. 36, p. 331.]   London, 1827

FLAME-BEARERS of Welsh history : being the outline of the Story of " The Sons of Cunedda." . . . By Owen Rhoscomyl [Owen Vaughan].   8vo. Pp. xii., 258. [*Lond. Lib. Cat.*] Merthyr Tydfil, 1905

FLAMING (the) hart ; or, the life of the glorious S Teresa, foundresse of the Reformation of the Order of the all-immaculate Virgin-Mother, our B. Lady of Mount Carmel.   Written by herself in Spanish, and now translated into English by M. T. [Sir Tobie Matthew]. Second edition. Fcap 8vo. Pp. 666.   [Gillow's *Bibl. Dict.*, vol. iv., p. 541.]   Antwerpe, 1642

FLANDERS ; or, the Spanish Netherlands most accurately described : shewing the several provinces, their bounds, dimensions, rivers, riches, strength, traffick, religion, languages, archbishopricks, bishopricks, universities ; and a large and exact description of the cities, and who they are at present subject to ; with a large and useful index of all the cities, towns, ports, forts, castles, rivers, &c. [By Laurence Echard, M.A.] Fcap 8vo. Pp. 114. [Watt's *Bibl. Brit.*] London, 1691

FLATLAND ; a romance of many dimensions. By A. Square [Edwin A. Abbott, D.D.].   Small 4to.   [*Lit. Year Book.*]   London, 1885

FLAWS. By a lawyer [G. S. Cline]. 8vo. [Kirk's *Supp.*]   Boston, 1885

FLAX and hemp ; their culture and manipulation. By Eugene Sebastian Delamer [Rev. Edmund Saul Dixon, M.A.]. 8vo. [Kirk's *Supp.*] London, 1854

FLAXIE Frizzle. By Sophie May [Rebecca Sophia Clarke]. Fcap 8vo. [Kirk's *Supp.*]   Boston, 1880

FLAXIE growing up. By Sophie May [Rebecca Sophia Clarke]. Fcap 8vo.   Boston, 1885

FLEDA and the voice : with other stories. By Aunt May [Mrs Mary A. Lathbury]. 8vo. [*Lib. Journ.*, iv., 171.]   New York, 1876

FLEET (the). A brief account of the ancient prison called the " Fleet," the liberty of the rules, ancient Fleet marriages. Also remarks on the emprisonment for debt. . . . [By William Brown, Jun.] 8vo. [*Manch. Free Lib. Cat.*, p. 87.]   London, 1843

FLEMISH interiors. By the writer of *A glance behind the grilles* [Mrs William Pitt Byrne, *née* Julia Clara Busk]. 8vo. [*Adv. Lib.*]
                    [London, 1856]

FLETCHER'S guide to St Andrews ; with descriptive letter-press. [By Charles Rogers, LL.D.] Third edition. Fcap 8vo.   St Andrew's, 1859
    The earlier editions appeared in 1845 and 1853. Some copies have also an engraved title, " Tourist Guide to St Andrews."

FLEURETTES : containing an ode on solitude written in the Mountains of Auvergne by Mons. de la Mothe Fénelon ; on the pleasures of retirement ; an epistle from a young lady to her lover, etc. Translated from the French. [By Rev. Richard Graves.] 8vo. [*Green's Bibl. Somers.*, ii., 445.]   London, 1784

FLEURS ; a poem. [By Nathaniel John Hollingsworth, M.A.] 4to. Pp. 188. [*Brit. Mus.*]
                    Newcastle, 1821
    See also "The Scorpion critic unmasked . . ."

FLIES in amber. [A novel.] By George Egerton [Mrs Baillie Weaver, *née* Gertrude Dunn]. Cr 8vo. Pp. 312. [*Lond. Lib. Cat.*]   London, 1905

FLIGHT (a) from the Banff baillies ; or a winter scamper to Constantine and Tunis, Jan. and Feb. 1879. [By P— H. Chalmers.] 8vo. [*Aberd. Free Lib. Cat.*]   Aberdeen, 1879

FLIGHT of fancy, folly, and fun. . . . By an old Cormorant [Constance Burdett]. 8vo. Pp. 107. [Cushing's *Init. and Pseud.*, vol. i., p. 211.]
                    London, 1878

FLIGHT (the) of the " Meteor," 1869-71. [By Lord Thos. Brassey.] Royal 4to. [*Brit. Mus.*]   London, 1872

FLIGHT (the) of the Pretender : a poem. [By Sir Richard Blackmore (?).] 8vo.   London, [1708]

FLIGHT (the) of the timorous clergyman to I[re]l[an]d [in order to avoid reading the Act of Parliament regarding the murder of Captain John Porteous. By Rev. Patrick Cuming, of the Old Kirk, Edinburgh]. 8vo.
                    Edinburgh, 1737

FLIGHT (the) of time, discerned by the dim shadow of Job's diall : explaned. . . . [By R. M. Roger Matthew]. 4to. [*Brit. Mus.*]
                    London, 1634

FLIGHTS inside and outside Paradise. By a penitent Peri [George C. Pearson]. 8vo. [Kirk's *Supp.*]
                    New York, 1886

FLIGHTS of fancy. By Ella Rodman [Eliza Rodman MacIlvaine, later Mrs Church]. 8vo. [Cushing's *Init. and Pseud.*, vol. i., 253.]   New York, 1851

FLIGHTS of fancy ; consisting of a variety of poetical pieces, satirical, humorous, pathetic, &c. By a lady [—— Marshall, afterwards Mrs Dr Cochrane]. 8vo. Pp. 83. [*A. Jervise.*]
                    Arbroath, 1844

FLIGHTS of fancy in the chess world. By A. C. W. [Alain Campbell White]. 8vo. Pp. 158. [*Brit. Mus.*]
                    Leeds, 1919

FLIGHTS of Phaedo.   [By Joseph King, solicitor.] Fcap 8vo. [*Brit. Mus.*]   London, 1859

FLIM-FLAMS ! Or, the life and errors of my uncle, and the amours of my aunt. With illustrations and obscurities, by Messieurs Tag, Rag, and Bobtail. With an illuminating index ! [By Isaac D'Israeli.] 3 vols. Fcap 8vo. [*Brit. Mus.*]   London, 1805

FLIRTATION ; a novel. [By Lady Charlotte Maria Bury.]   Second edition. 3 vols. Fcap 8vo. [Courtney's *Secrets*, p. 56.]   London, 1828

FLIRTATION ; or a young girl's good name. By Ralph Royal [Jacob Abarbanell]. 8vo. [Kirk's *Supp.*, vol. i., p. 1.]   New York, 1884

FLIRTATION : or Cupid's shoulder-strap tactics. By Hearton Drille, U.S.A. [Jeannie H. Grey]. 8vo. [Kirk's *Supp.*]   New York, 1877

FLIRTATION with truth. [A novel.] By Curtis Yorke [Mrs S— Richmond Lee, *née* —— Jex-Long]. Cr 8vo. Pp. 290. [*Lond. Lib. Cat.*]
                    London, 1905

FLIRTS and flirts ; or a season at Ryde. [A novel. By Miss A— E. N. Bewicke.] 2 vols. 8vo. London, 1868

FLITTERS, Tatters, and the Counsellor : three waifs from the Dublin streets. By the author of *Hogan, M.P.* [May Laffan, later Mrs Hartley]. Third edition. Pp. 60. [*Brit. Mus.*]
London, [1879]

FLOATING flies, and how to dress them. By Detached Badger [Frederic M. Halford]. Pt 8vo. [Kirk's *Supp.*]
London, 1886

FLOATING (the) island : or, a new discovery, relating the strange adventure on a late voyage, from Lambethana, to Villa Franca, alias Ramallia, to the eastward of Terra del Temple : by three ships, viz. the Pay-naught, the Excuse, the Least-in-sight, under the conduct of Captain Robert Owe-much : describing the nature of the inhabitants, their religion, laws and customs. Published by Franck Careless, one of the discoverers. [By Richard Head.] 4to. Pp. 43. [Lowndes' *Bibl. Man.*]
N.P., 1673

FLOATING remembrances, and sketches of a sea life. By the Old Sailor [Matthew Henry Barker, R.N.]. 8vo. [*Brit. Mus.*]   London, 1854

FLOATING treasure. By Harry Castlemon [Charles A. Fosdick]. Fcap 8vo. [Cushing's *Init. and Pseud.*, vol. i., p. 52.]   Philadelphia, 1902

FLOCK (a) of four [a story for juveniles]. By Ismay Thorn [Edith Caroline Pollock]. Pt 8vo.   London, 1889

FLODDEN Field, and the Colour ; or, Hawick Common riding. [By James Hogg.] Fcap 8vo. [Sinton's *Hawick Bibl.*]   Hawick, 1829

FLOGGING not abolished in the British Army. By E. Livingston Prescott [Edith Katharine Spicer-Jay]. 8vo. Pp. 20. [*Lit. Year Book.*]   Clapham, 1897

FLOOD (the) of Thessaly ; The girl of Provence : and other poems. By Barry Cornwall [Bryan Waller Procter]. 8vo. Pp. 248. [*Lit. Year Book.*]   London, 1823

FLOOD (a) that led on to fortune. By Old Boomerang [John Richard Houlding]. 8vo. Pp. 366. [*Lond. Lib. Cat.*]   London, 1886

FLOORISH (a) upon fancie : as gallant a glose, upon so trifling a text, as ever was written. Compiled by N. B., Gent. [Nicholas Breton]. To which are annexed The toyes of an idle head ; containing many pretie pamphlets, for pleasaunt heads to pass away idle time withall. By the same authour. Printed by Richard Ihones, dwelling at the signe of the Rose and Crowne, neere Holborne bridge. 4to. Pp. vii., 238.   London, 1582

FLORA ; an opera, as it is now acting at the Theatre Royal in Lincoln's-Inn-Fields : being Mr Dogget's Farce of the Country-Wake, alter'd after the manner of the Beggar's Opera. . . . Written by a gentleman [John Hippisley]. Third edition. 8vo. [*Biog. Dram.*]   London, 1729
The author afterwards (1732) published " A Sequel to the Opera of Flora."

FLORA domestica, or the portable flower-garden ; with directions for the treatment of plants in pots ; and illustrations from the works of the poets. [By Elizabeth Kent.] 8vo. [*Edin. Univ. Lib.*]   London, 1823
Assigned also to R. Bryant, —— Phillips, and —— Wordsworth.

FLORA ; or, self-deception. By A. L. O. E., author of *The silver casket*, etc. [Charlotte Maria Tucker]. 8vo. Pp. 182.   London, 1871

FLORA'S dictionary. . . . By a lady [Mrs Elizabeth Washington Wirt, *née* Gamble]. 8vo. [Cushing's *Init. and Pseud.*, vol. i., p. 161.]   Baltimore, 1829

FLORA'S fortune ; the second part and finishing of the Fisher-mans tale, containing the strange accidentes which chaunced to Flora and her supposed father Thirsis ; also the happie meeting with her desired Cassander. By F. S. [Francis Sabie]. Imprinted by Richard Ihones. 4to. [*Brit. Mus.*]
London, 1595

FLORA'S vagaries ; a comedy, acted at the Theatre Royal, by His Majesties servants. [By Richard Rhodes, B.A.] 4to. Pp. 56. [*Biog. Dram.*]
London, 1677

FLORENCE Baldwin's picnic, and what came of it. By Francis Forrester [Daniel Wise, D.D.]. Fcap 8vo. Pp. 266. [Cushing's *Init. and Pseud.*, vol. i., p. 104.]   New York, 1893

FLORENCE Egerton ; or, sunshine and shadow. By the author of *Aunt Edith*, etc. [J. Macgowan]. 8vo. [*Brit. Mus.*]   Edinburgh, 1854

FLORENCE ; or the aspirants. A novel. 3 vols. [By Mrs Roberton.] 8vo. [*Adv. Lib.*]   London, 1829

FLORENCE rewarded ; or, Priscilla the beautiful. By Francis Forrester [Daniel Wise, D.D.]. Fcap 8vo. Pp. 283. [Cushing's *Init. and Pseud.*, vol. i., p. 104.]   New York, 1893

FLORENTINE (the) historie written in the Italian tongue by Niccolo Macchiavelli . . . and translated into English by T. B. [Thomas Bedingfield], Esq. Folio. Pp. 222. [Watt's *Bibl. Brit.*]   London, 1595

FLORENTINE tales, with modern illustrations [largely by Thomas Powell, but after his death by J. H. Leigh Hunt]. 8vo.   London, 1847

FLORES ecclesiae: the Saints of the Catholic Church, . . . with the flowers dedicated to them. By W. H. J. W. [William Henry James Weale]. 8vo. [Quaritch's *Cat.*]   London, 1849

FLORESTON; or, the new Lord of the manor: a tale of humanity, comprising the history of a rural revolution from vice and misery to virtue and happiness. [By Thomas Dolby.] 12mo. Pp. xi., 394. [*Adv. Lib.*] London, 1839

FLORIAN'S husband. [A novel. By Barbara Gunn.] 3 vols. 8vo. [*Adv. Lib.*]   London, 1863

FLORIO, a tale, for fine gentlemen and fine ladies; and the Bas Bleu, or conversation: two poems. [By Hannah More.] 4to. [Watt's *Bibl. Brit.*]
London, 1786

FLORIST'S (the) manual; or hints for the construction of a gay flower garden, with observations on the best methods of preventing the depredations of insects. By the authoress of *Botanical dialogues* and *Sketches of the physiology of vegetable life* [Mrs Maria E. Jackson]. Fcap 8vo. Pp. vii., 74. [*Brit. Mus.*]   London, 1816
Signed " M. E. J."

FLORUS Anglicus; or, an exact history of England, from the raign of William the Conquerour to the death of the late King [Charles I.]. By Lambert Wood [Lambert van den Bos]. 8vo. Pp. 271. [Watt's *Bibl. Brit.*]   London, 1656

FLORUS Hungaricus; or the history of Hungaria and Transylvania, deduced from the original of that nation, and their setling in Europe in the year of our Lord 461, to this dangerous and suspectful period of that kingdome by the present Turkish invasion, anno 1664. [By James Howell.] 8vo. Pp. 316.   London, 1664
The Epistle dedicatory is signed " J. H."

FLOSCULUM poeticum: poems divine and humane, panegyrical, satyrical, ironical. By P. K. [Patrick Ker]. Fcap 8vo. [*Brit. Mus.*] London, 1684

FLOTSAM: a novel. By Henry Seton Merriman [Hugh Stowell Scott]. 8vo. [*Lond. Lib. Cat.*]   London, 1895

FLOTSAM and jetsam; a cargo of Christmas rhyme. By Hookanit Bee [*i.e.* Who can it be ?], Esquire [S— R— Wigram]. Fcap 8vo. [*Camb. Univ. Lib.*]   London, 1853
Attributed also to William Knox Wigram.

FLOWER (the) garden. By Eugene Sebastian Delamer [Rev. Edmund S. Dixon, M.A.]. 8vo. [*Kirk's Supp.*]
London, 1855

FLOWER (the) garden; its cultivation, arrangement, and general management. [By Charles M'Intosh, botanist.] Cr 8vo. [*Brit. Mus.*]
London, 1839

FLOWER (the) garden, or monthly calendar of practical directions for the culture of flowers. By Martin Doyle [Rev. William Hickey, M.A.]. Fcap 8vo. [*D. N. B.*, vol. 26, p. 356.]
Dublin, 1834

FLOWER lore. [By Miss —— Carruthers, of Inverness.] 8vo.
Belfast, [1879 ?]

FLOWER (the) of grass: a story for children. By E. S. G. S. [Emily S. G. Saunders]. 8vo. [*Brit. Mus.*]
London, 1865

FLOWER (the) of mirrors; essays. By Vernon Lee [Violet Paget]. Cr 8vo. [*Lit. Year Book.*]   London, 1914

FLOWER of the dust. [A novel.] By John Oxenham [William Arthur Dunkerley]. Cr 8vo. Pp. 32. [*Lit. Year Book.*]   London, 1915

FLOWER (the) of the family; a tale of domestic life. By the author of *Stepping heavenward* [Mrs Elizabeth Prentiss]. Pt 8vo. Pp. 277. [Allibone's *Dict.*, vol. i.]   London, 1873
An earlier edition (in 1854) bears a somewhat different title.

FLOWER (the) of Yarrow; a tragedy. By the author of *Kentish legends* [Rev. Ambrose Ward].   Maidstone, 1846

FLOWER stories. By Mary Muller [Lenore E. Mulets]. Pt 8vo. [*Amer. Cat.*]   Chicago, 1903

FLOWERS; a fantasy [in verse]. By Cornelia Wallace [E— C— Ricketts]. Fcap 8vo. Pp. 44. [*Brit. Mus.*]
London, 1884

FLOWERS and gardens; notes on plant beauty. By a medical man [John Forbes Watson, M.D., LL.D.]. Pt 8vo. [*Kirk's Supp.*] London, 1872

FLOWERS and plants sketched from nature. By Emile Favart [Thomas William Hammond]. Folio. 60 plates. [*Brit. Mus.*]   Nottingham, 1879-81
No letterpress.

FLOWERS culled from the Gulistan, or Rose Garden, and from the Bostan, or Pleasure Garden, of Sadi, a Persian poet. By S. R. [Samuel Robinson]. Fcap 8vo. [*D. N. B.*, vol. 49, p. 44.]
London, 1876

FLOWERS for window gardens, in town or country : what to grow, and how. By the author of *In-door plants*, etc. [Miss E. A. Maling.] 12mo. [*Brit. Mus.*] London, 1862

FLOWERS from an Indian garden. [By Mrs —— Hope.] 2 vols. Folio. Dusseldorf, 1846

FLOWERS from the garden of the Church ; or the collects of the Church of England versified. [By George Tyler Townsend.] Fcap 8vo. [*Brit. Mus.*] Oxford, 1854

FLOWERS (the) of Lodowicke of Granado : the first part, in which is handled the conuersion of a sinner. Translated out of Latine into English. By T. L. [Thomas Lodge], Doctor of Phisicke. 12mo. [*Brit. Mus.*] London, 1601

FLOWERS of loveliness ; twelve groups of female figures, emblematic of flowers : designed by various artists ; with poetical illustrations. By L. E. L. [Letitia Elizabeth Landon, later Mrs Maclean]. 4to. No pagination. [Haynes' *Pseud.*] London, 1838

FLOWERS (the) of Shakespeare. [30 coloured plates, with quotations from Shakespeare, designed and executed by E— I. Giraud.] 4to. London, [1845] Initialed " E. I. G."

FLOWERS of the forest. [By Mary Martha Butt, later Mrs Sherwood.] Fcap 8vo. [*Brit. Mus.*] London, 1839

FLOWING (the) bowl ; a treatise on drinks of all kinds and of all periods ; interspersed with sundry anecdotes and reminiscences. By Nathaniel Gubbins [Edward Spencer Mott]. 8vo. Pp. xv., 243. [*Brit. Mus.*] London, 1899

FLOWING (the) bowl : what and when to drink. . . . By the only William [William Schmidt]. Pt 8vo. [*Amer. Cat.*] New York, 1892

FLUFF ; or what a little dog did. By M. F. W. [M— F. Wilson]. 8vo. London, 1894

FLUTE (the) of Pan ; a novel. By John Oliver Hobbes [Mrs Pearl Craigie]. 8vo. [*Lit. Year Book.*] London, 1905

FLUVIAD ; or, a metrical description of the rivers of Galloway and Dumfriesshire. [By James M'Culloch.] 8vo. Dumfries, 1842

FLY (the) in the ointment. By Frances Hammond [Frances H. Croal]. 8vo. London, 1912

FLY leaves. By C. S. C., author of *Verses and translations* [Charles Stuart Calverley]. 8vo. Pp.iv.,120. [*D.N.B.*, vol. 8, p. 264.] Cambridge, 1872

FLY-FISHER (the) and his library. [An essay.] By H. R. F. [Henry Ralph Francis]. 8vo. [*Brit. Mus.*] London, 1856

FLY-FISHER'S (the) entomology ; illustrated by coloured representations of the natural and the artificial insect. By Alfred Ronalds. Fifth edition, revised, with additions by Piscator [William Hughes]. 8vo. [Cushing's *Init. and Pseud.*, vol. i., p. 235.] London, 1856

FLY-FISHER'S (the) text-book. By Theophilus South, gent. [Edward Chitty, barrister]. 8vo. Pp. vi., 231. [Cushing's *Init. and Pseud.*, vol. i., p. 271.] London, 1841

FLY-FISHING in salt and fresh water. [By —— Hutchinson.] Large 8vo. London, 1851

FLYING (the) artillerist ; or the child of the battlefield : a tale of Mexican treachery. By Harry Hazel [Justin Jones]. 8vo. [Cushing's *Init. and Pseud.*, vol. i., p. 127.] New York, 1853

FLYING (the) burgomaster ; a legend of the Black Forest. [By the Dowager Countess of Morley.] [Martin's *Cat.*] 8vo. N.P., 1832

FLYING (the) Dutchman. [A novel.] By the author of *Gentleman Jack* [William Johnson Neale, barrister]. 8vo. [*Brit. Mus.*] London, [1867]

FLYING (the) horseman. [A North American romance.] By Gustave Aimard [Ollivier Gloux]. 8vo. [*Brit. Mus.*] London, 1876

FLYING (the) of the night. By Benjamin F. Johnson, of Boone [James Whitcomb Riley]. Pt 8vo. [Cushing's *Init. and Pseud.*, vol. i., p. 143.] Indianopolis, 1892

FLYING (the) Scud : a sporting novel. By the author of *Charlie Thornhill* [Charles Clarke]. 2 vols. Cr 8vo. [*Brit. Mus.*] London, 1867 " Charlie Thornhill " is not anonymous.

FLYING sketches of the Battle of Waterloo in June 1815. By a young traveller [Newman Smith]. Written on the spot. Fcap 8vo. Private print. N.P., 1852

FLYING U ranch. By B. M. Bower [Mrs Bertrand M. Sinclair]. Cr 8vo. Pp. 281. [*Amer. Cat.*] London, 1921

FLYING (the) U's last stand. . . . By B. M. Bower [Mrs B. M. Sinclair]. 8vo. Pp. 353. [*Brit. Mus.*] Boston, [Mass.], 1915

FLYING (the) Yankee ; or the cruise of the clippers : a tale of privateering in the war of 1812 to 1815. By Harry Hazel [Justin Jones]. 8vo. [Kirk's *Supp.*]   Philadelphia, 1875

FO : the third messenger of God. [By Edward V. H. Kenealy, barrister.] Cr 8vo. Pp. 620.   London, 1878

FOAM. [Poems. By Reginald Baliol, Viscount Esher.] 8vo. Pp. viii., 101. [Bartholomew's *Camb. Books.*]
                              London, 1893

FOCALÓIR Gaoidhilge-Sax-Bhéarla ; or an Irish-English dictionary, &c. [By Bishop John O'Brien.] 4to. [*Brit. Mus.*]   Paris, 1768

FO'C'SLE yarns, including " Betsy Lee " and other poems. [By Thomas E. Browne.] Cr 8vo.   London, 1889

FOE-FARRELL. By " Q " [Sir Arthur Thomas Quiller-Couch]. Cr 8vo. Pp. vii., 422. [*Lit. Year Book.*]
                              London, 1918

FOES of freedom. By May Wynne [Mabel Wynne Knowles]. Cr 8vo. [*Lit. Year Book.*]   London, 1916

FOES of justice. By Headon Hill [Frank E. Grainger]. Cr 8vo. Pp. 319. [*Lit. Year Book.*]
                              London, 1910

FOES (the) of our faith, and how to defeat them. By the author of *God is love*, etc. [James Grant, journalist]. 8vo. Pp. viii., 400.   London, 1863

FOG (the) Princes : a novel. By Florence Warden [Florence Alice Price, later Mrs George E. James]. 8vo. Pp. 156.   London, 1889

FOILED by love. By Bertha M. Clay [Mrs Charlotte M. Braeme]. Fcap 8vo.
                              New York, 1893

FOLD (the) track. By A. M. H. [Amelia M. Hull]. Fcap 8vo. [Kirk's *Supp.*]   London, 1855

FOLIA opima ; in verse. By J. B. N. [John Bruce Norton, B.A.], of Merton College. 8vo.   Madras, 1843

FOLIE (une). A comick opera, in two acts ; being a translation [by James Wild] from the original of Love laughs at locksmiths [by George Colman, the younger ; from the French of J. N. Bouilly]. 8vo. Pp. 56. [*Bodl.*]
                              London, 1803

FOLIOUS appearances ; a consideration on our ways of lettering books. [By John Tupling.] 8vo. [*Camb. Univ. Lib.*]   [London], 1854

FOLK-LORE ; or, manners and customs of the North of England. By M. A. D. [Michael Aislabie Denham]. 3 parts. 8vo. [*Brit. Mus.*] Durham, 1850-52

FOLLE-FARINE. By Ouida, author of *Under two flags*, etc. [Louise de La Ramée]. 3 vols. Cr 8vo. [*Lit. Year Book.*]   London, 1871

FOLLIES of a day in Convocation. [By the Rev. Joseph Hemington Harris.] 8vo. [*Lit. Year Book.*]
                              London, 1865
Signed " Presbyter Anglicanus."

FOLLIES (the) of Captain Daly. By F. Norreys Connell [Conal O'Connell O'Riordan]. Cr 8vo. [O'Donoghue's *Poets of Ireland.*]   London, 1901

FOLLIES (the) of Oxford ; or cursory sketches on a university education, from an undergraduate [Richard Polwhele] to his friend in the country. 4to. [Boase and Courtney's *Bibl. Corn.*, ii., 507.]   London, 1785

FOLLOW Jesus. By the author of *Come to Jesus*, etc. [Newman Hall, D.D.]. 30th thousand. 8vo. Pp. 64. [*Brit. Mus.*]   London, N.D.

FOLLOW me ; or, lost and found : a morality, from the German. By C. E. H. [Charlotte E. Hawker], Morwenstow. 8vo. [*Adv. Lib.*]
                              London, 1844

FOLLOWING heavenward ; or, the story of Alfred Reid. By Pansy [Mrs Isabella Alden, *née* Macdonald]. 8vo. Pp. 240.   London, 1889, [1888]

FOLLOWING (the) of Christ, diuided in foure Bookes ; written in Latin by the learned and devout man Thomas à Kempis [Thomas Hämmerlein], Canon Regular of the Order of S. Augustine : whereunto also is added the Golden Epistle of S. Bernard, and also containe Rules of a Christian life, made by John Picus the elder, Earle of Mirandula. Translated into English by B. F. [Anthony Hoskins, S.J.]. 12mo. Pp. 445. [Sommervogel's *Dictionnaire.*]   [St Omer], 1615

FOLLOWING (the) of Christ ; in four Books : translated from the original Latin [of Thomas Hämmerlein, or Hämmerchen, otherwise Thomas à Kempis] by —— Richard Challoner, D.D., V.A. To which are added practical reflections and a prayer at the end of each chapter. . . . Second edition. 12mo. Pp. 504.
                              London, 1835
See other translations under " The Christian's exercise," " The Imitation of Christ," " On the imitation . . ."

FOLLOWING the equator : a journey round the world. By Mark Twain [Samuel Langhorne Clemens]. Pt 8vo. Pp. 712. [Kirk's *Supp.*]
                    Hartford, Connecticut, 1897

FOLLY and madnesse made manifest : or, some things written to shew how contrary to the word of God and practise of the saints in the Old and New Testament, the doctrines and practises of the Quakers, lately risen up amongst us, are a rayling and reviling answer made thereunto, full of falsehood and vaine shifts and devices to maintaine their errors : this discovered and made manifest. [By William Fiennes, Viscount Say and Sele.] 4to. Pp. 142. N.P., 1659
The author's name is given by Wood.

FOLLY in print ; or a book of rymes, containing songs, ballads, catches, poems, &c. [By —— Raymund.] 8vo. London, 1667
" The lucubrations of a soldier who served in the Dutch and Spanish wars, chiefly lyrical and amatory. His name was probably Raymund, and he was intimate or connected with the noble family of Bellasise " [Lowndes' *Bibl. Man.*].

FOLLY (the) of love : a new satyr against women, together with the Bachelors Letany. By the same hand [Richard Ames]. Fifth edition. Fcap 4to. [*Dobell's Cat.*] London, 1701

FOMA Gordyeeff : By Maxim Gorky [Aleksyei Maksimovitch Pyeshkov]. Cr 8vo. [*Lond. Lib. Cat.*]
London, 1904

FOND (the) lady : a comedy [in five acts, and in verse]. Written by a person of honour [Thomas Duffet]. 4to. [*Brit. Mus.*] London, 1684

FONT (the) guarded with XX. arguments, containing a compendium of that great controversie of Infant-Baptism. [By Thomas Hall.] Fcap 8vo. Pp. 136. [Thomason *Coll. of Tracts*, vol. i., p. 865.] London, 1652

FOOD for national penitence ; or, a discourse intended for the approaching fast-day. [By John Aikin, M.D.] 8vo. [*Brit. Mus.*] London, 1793

FOOD for reflection ; Mohammedanism and Christianity. [By Rev. Sigismund Wilhelm Koelle, Ph.D., C.M.S.] 8vo. London, 1865

FOOD (the) of the soul, or miscellany of devout prayers. [By Jean-Baptiste van Derker, S.J.] 12mo. Pp. 199. [Sommervogel's *Dictionnaire*.]
Mechlin, 1837

FOOD : what to buy and how to cook it ; a practical guide to housewives, combining comfort with economy and good fare at a small cost. By the author of *Enquire within*, etc. [Robert Kemp Philp]. 8vo. Pp. viii., 128. [*Brit. Mus.*] London, [1876]

FOOD-STUDIES. By " Ione " [Grace M. Brown]. Square 12mo.
London, 1902

FOOL (the) and his heart. [A novel.] By F. Norreys Connell [Conal O'Connell O'Riordan]. Cr 8vo. [O'Donoghue's *Poets of Ireland*.] London, 1896

FOOL (the) and his saying. By the author of *The Lamplighter* [Rev. Francis Bourdillon]. 8vo. [*Brit. Mus.*]
London, [1872]

FOOL (the) : being a collection of essays and epistles, moral, political, humourous, and entertaining. . . . [By W. Horsley.] 2 vols. 12mo.
London, 1748
" In Mr. Chalmers' copy is written this note, This was written by Mr W. Horsley." —MS. note in the Hope copy in the Bodleian.

FOOL divine. [A novel.] By G. B. Lancaster [Edith Lyttleton]. Cr 8vo. Pp. 327. [*Lond. Lib. Cat.*] London, 1917

FOOL (the) hath said. A reply to the New Theology [of the Rev. R. J. Campbell]. By the author of *When it was light* [Andrew Lang, LL.D.]. Cr 8vo. London, 1907

FOOL (the) of fate. [A novel.] By Mary H. Tennyson [Mary H. Folkard]. 8vo. Pp. vi., 248. [*Brit. Mus.*] London, 1869

FOOL (the) of the family, and other tales. By John Dangerfield [Oswald John Frederick Crawfurd]. 2 vols. Cr 8vo. [*Lond. Lib. Cat.*] London, 1875

FOOL (the) turn'd critick : a comedy : as it was acted at the Theatre-Royall. By his majesties servants. By T. D., Gent. [Thomas Durfey]. 4to. Pp. 602. [*Biog. Dram.*] London, 1678

FOOLES (a) bolt is soone shott. [By Samuel Rowlands.] 4to. Pp. 39.
Imprinted at London, 1614
Reprinted by the Hunterian Club, 1873.

FOOLES (the) of fate ; or, the unravelling of the Parliament and Army. [By John Taylor, the water-poet.] 4to.
London, 1648

FOOLISH etiquette. By O. B. Hayve [O, behave ! *i.e.* Charles Wayland Towne]. Pt 8vo. [*Amer. Cat.*]
Boston, [Mass.], 1906

FOOLISH finance. By Gideon Wurdz [Charles Wayland Towne]. Small 4to. [*Amer. Cat.*] Boston, [Mass.], 1905

FOOL-KILLER (the) : a novel. By Lucas Cleeve [Mrs Howard Kingscote, *née* Adelina G. I. Wolff]. 8vo. [*Brit. Mus.*] London, 1904

FOOLS and jesters : with a reprint of Robert Armin's Nest of ninnes. [By John Payne Collier.] 8vo.
London, 1842

FOOL'S (a) errand. [A novel.] By one of the fools [Albion Winegar Tourgee]. 8vo. Pp. 361. [Kirk's *Supp.*]
New York, 1880

FOOL'S (the) Gospel. [By Barton Dell, of Bristol.] 8vo. Pp. 180. [*Supp.* to Smith's *Cat. of Friends' Books*, p. 100.]
London, 1871

FOOL'S (the) opera. By Matthew Medley [Anthony Aston]. 8vo. [Cushing's *Init. and Pseud.*, vol. i., p. 186.]   London, 1731

FOOL'S (a) paradise. [Verse.] By Dum-Dum [Captain John Kendal, R.E.]. Cr 8vo. Pp. 140. [*Brit. Mus.*]
London, 1910

FOOL'S (the) tax. [A novel.] By Lucas Cleeve [Mrs Howard Kingscote, *née* Adelina G. I. Wolff]. Cr 8vo. [*Lit. Year Book.*]   London, 1907

FOOT notes ; or walking as a fine art. By Q [Alfred Barron]. Fcap 8vo.
Wallingford, 1875

FOOTE'S Prologue detected ; with a miniature prose epilogue of his manner in speaking it. By Philo-technicus Miso-mimides [Paul Hiffernan, M.D.]. 8vo.   London, 1770

FOOTFALLS of Indian history. By Sister Nivedita [Margaret E. Noble]. Pt. 8vo.   London, 1915

FOOTPRINTS. Nature seen on its human side. By Sarah Tytler [Henrietta Keddie]. Third edition. 8vo. [*Lit. Year Book.*]   London, 1885

FOOTPRINTS (the) of Abbé [Lord Byron. A poem by Edward John Brennar ?]. Part I. 8vo. [*Brit. Mus.*]   Milan, 1874
No more published.

FOOTPRINTS of Popery ; or, places where martyrs have suffered. [By George Mogridge.] Fcap 8vo. [*Brit. Mus.*]   London, [1844 ?]

FOOTPRINTS of the holy dead ; translated from the German. By A. M. [Alice Mannington]. 8vo.
London, 1863

FOOT-PRINTS of travel in France and Italy ; with occasional divagations. By an old Fogy [Judah Lee Bliss]. 8vo. [Cushing's *Init. and Pseud.*, vol. i., p. 211.]   Boston, 1858

FOOTPRINTS on the sands of time : biographies for young people. . . . By L. E. B. [Lucy Elizabeth Bather]. 8vo. [Cushing's *Init. and Pseud.*, vol. ii., p. 12.]   Oxford, 1860

FOOTSTEPS of blood ; or, the march of the republicans : being a display of the horrid cruelties, and unexampled enormities committed by the French Republican armies in all parts of the world ; containing true accounts of their savage barbarity, in the burning and plundering of towns, villages, and farms ; the murder of men, women, and children ; and in sacrilege, rape, and every other crime. [By John Adolphus.] Fcap 8vo. Pp. 81. [*Edin. Univ. Lib.*]
London, 1803

FOOTSTEPS (the) of fortune. [A tale.] By Esmé Stuart [Amélie Claire Leroy]. Fcap 8vo. Pp. 158. [*Lond. Lib. Cat.*]
London, 1896

FOOTSTEPS (the) of St Paul. By the author of *The morning and night watches*, etc. [John Ross MacDuff, D.D.]. 8vo. Pp. xii., 416.
London, 1855

FOOTSTEPS (the) of Sir William Wallace. [By Rev. Peter Sawers, Gargunnock.] 8vo. Pp. 64. [*Bibl. Wallasiana.*]   Glasgow, 1856

FOOTSTEPS of spirits. . . . [By James Augustin Stothert.] Fcap 8vo.
Edinburgh, [1859]

FOOTSTEPS on the seas. By A. D. T. W. [Mrs Adeline D. Train Whitney]. 8vo. [Cushing's *Init. and Pseud.*, vol. ii., p. 151.]
Boston, 1857

FOR another's fault : from the German of Wilhelm Heimburg [Martha Behrens]. Pt 8vo.   Chicago, 1895

FOR another's sin : a novel. By Bertha M. Clay [Mrs Charlotte M. Braeme]. Pt 8vo. Pp. 352.   New York, [1897]

FOR Auld lang syne. By the author of *Beside the bonnie brier bush* [John Watson, D.D., Liverpool]. 8vo.
London, 1895

FOR Charles the Rover. [A novel.] By May Wynne [Mabel Wynne Knowles]. Cr 8vo. Pp. 324. [S. J. Brown's *Ireland in fiction.*]
London, 1909

FOR Church and Chieftain. By May Wynne [Mabel Wynne Knowles]. 8vo. Pp. 314. [S. J. Brown's *Ireland in fiction.*]   Dublin, 1909

FOR Crown and Covenant. . . . By Cyril Grey [A— Balfour Symington]. 8vo. Pp. 320.   London, [1902]

FOR England. By Morice Gerard [John Jessop Teague]. Cr 8vo. Pp. 310. [*Lit. Year Book.*]   London, 1902

FOR ever; and other devotional poems. By —— [Rev. Charles Smith Bird]. 8vo.   London, [1835]

FOR ever; or the final state of the redeemed, considered as to its gradations of ranks and blessedness, on Scriptural grounds. [By Caroline Pearse.] 8vo. Pp. 284. [*Brit. Mus.*] London, 1862

FOR ever true. By Effie Adelaide Rowlands [E— Maria Albanesi]. 8vo. Pp. 112. [*Brit. Mus.*]
                                    Dundee, [1920]

FOR faith and Navarre. By May Wynne [Mabel Wynne Knowles]. 8vo. [S. J. Brown's *Ireland in fiction.*]
                                    London, 1904

FOR fear of his throne. [A novel.] By R. Andom [Alfred W. Barrett]. Cr 8vo. [*Lit. Year Book.*]
                                    London, 1911

FOR France. [A novel.] By Morice Gerard [Rev. John Jessup Teague]. Cr 8vo. [*Lit. Year Book.*]
                                    London, 1922

FOR Gilbert's sake. By Ray Cunningham [Mrs Frances Brown Arthur]. 8vo.   Stirling, 1899

FOR God and the Czar: a novel. By Dick Donovan [Joyce E. P. Muddock]. Cr 8vo. [*Lit. Year Book.*]
                                    London, [1895]

FOR God or the devil; or, just chastisement no persecution: being the Christian's cry . . . for punishment of that wretch Woolston. [An ironical letter by Thomas Woolston himself.] 8vo.   London, 1728

FOR Greater Britain. By C. Whitworth Wynne [Charles William Cayzer, M.A.]. 8vo. [*Amer. Cat.*]
                                    London, 1904

FOR half-a-crown: a story. By Esmé Stuart [Amélie Claire Leroy]. Pt 8vo. [*Lond. Lib. Cat.*]   London, 1887

FOR her dear sake. By Bertha M. Clay [Mrs Charlotte M. Braeme]. Fcap 8vo.   London, 1911

FOR her sake: a tale of life in Ireland. By Gordon Roy [Ellen Wallace]. Cr 8vo. Pp. 396. [*Brit. Mus.*]
                                    London, 1906

FOR His name's sake: a plea for reverence. By the author of *The Gospel and its ministry* [R— Anderson]. 8vo. Pp. 61. [*Brit. Mus.*] London, [1895]

FOR his sake: a novel. By Mrs Alexander [Mrs Alexander Hector, *née* Annie French]. 3 vols. Cr 8vo. [*Brit. Mus.*]   London, 1892

FOR home and honor. By Victor St Clair [George W. Browne]. Fcap 8vo. [*Amer. Cat.*]   New York, 1902

FOR honour or death. By Dick Donovan [Joyce E. P. Muddock]. Cr 8vo. [*Lit. Year Book.*]   London, 1910

FOR love and honour. By Allen Raine [Mrs Beynon Puddicombe]. Cr 8vo. [*Lit. Year Book.*]   London, 1904

FOR love and life. [A novel.] By Bertha M. Clay [Charlotte M. Braeme]. 8vo. Pp. 158.   London, 1912

FOR love and ransom: a story. By Esmé Stuart [Amélie Claire Leroy]. Cr 8vo. Pp. 380. [*Lit. Year Book.*]
                                    London, 1904

FOR love of a Bedouin maid: a novel. By "Le Voleur" [Rosa N. Carey]. 8vo. [*Lond. Lib. Cat.*] London, 1897

FOR love of Prue. A novel. By Leslie Keith [Grace Leslie Keith Johnston]. Cr 8vo. [*Brit. Mus.*]
                                    London, 1898

FOR plain women only. By George Fleming [Julia Constance Fletcher]. Pt 8vo. Pp. 203. [*Lit. Year Book.*]
                                    New York, 1896

FOR puir auld Scotland's sake: a book of prose essays on Scottish literary and rural subjects. By Hugh Halyburton [James Logie Robertson]. 8vo. Pp. viii., 253. [*Lond. Lib. Cat.*]
                                    Edinburgh, 1887

FOR richer, for poorer. By Holme Lee, author of *Sylvan Holt's daughter*, etc. [Harriet Parr]. 3 vols. Second edition. 8vo. [*Brit. Mus.*]
                                    London, 1870

FOR sceptre and crown. [A novel.] By Gregor Samarow [Oscar Meding]. 8vo. [Cushing's *Init. and Pseud.*, i., p. 260.] London, 1874

FOR summer afternoons: stories. By Susan Coolidge [Sarah C. Woolsey]. Fcap 8vo. [Kirk's *Supp.*] Boston, 1886

FOR the holy women who trust in God. By G. F. [George Fox]. 4to.
                                    N.P., 1686

FOR the king and his council these. [By George Fox.] 4to. N.P., [*c.* 1660] Signed "From friends of truth and innocency, G. F., J. S. [John Stubbs], and Henry Fell."

FOR the love of a lass: a novel. By Austin Clare [Miss W. M— James]. Cr 8vo. [*Lond. Lib. Cat.*]
                                    London, 1898

FOR the old love's sake. [A novel.] By the author of *Not easily jealous* [Iza Duffus Hardy]. 8vo. [*Brit. Mus.*]
                                    London, 1875

FOR the sacred memoriall of Charles Howard, Earle of Nottingham. [By John Taylor, the water-poet.] 4to. [*D. N. B.*, vol. 55, p. 434.]
                                    London, 1625

FOR the service of truth. By Philalethes, or lover of truth, T. M. [Thomas Maule]. 8vo. [Evans' *Amer. Bibl.*, vol. i., p. 168.]   Philadelphia, 1703

FOR the soul of Rafael. By Ellis Martin [Mrs Marah Ellis Martin Ryan]. Pt 8vo. [*Amer. Cat.*]   Chicago, 1906

FOR the White Rose of Arno. [A novel.] By Owen Rhoscomyl [Owen Vaughan]. Cr 8vo. [*Lit. Year Book.*]   London, 1897

FOR treasure bound. [A sea-story.] By Harry Collingwood [William J. C. Lancaster]. Cr 8vo. Pp. 400. [*Lond. Lib. Cat.*]   London, 1897

FOR triumph or truth? A tale of thrilling adventure. By Sydney C. Grier [Hilda C. Gregg]. Cr 8vo. Pp. 310. [*Lit. Year Book.*] London, 1904

FORAYERS (the). By Frank Cooper [William Gilmore Simms]. Pt 8vo. [Cushing's *Init. and Pseud.*, vol. i., p. 67.]   New York, 1886

FORAYS among salmon and deer. By James Conway [James Conway Walter]. 8vo. Pp. xii., 248.   London, 1861
    This is an enlarged edition of " Letters from the Highlands " (1859).

FORBIDDEN banns. [A novel.] By Annabel Gray [Mrs Anne Cox]. Cr 8vo. Pp. 320. [*Lit. Year Book.*]
                    London, 1899

FORBIDDEN (the) book, with new fallacies of the faculty: being the Chrono-thermalist; or, people's medical enquirer for 1850 [and 1851]. [By Samuel Dickson, M.D.] 2 vols. 8vo. [*Bodl.*]   London, N.D.

FORBIDDEN (the) boundary: and other stories. By B. L. Putnam Weale [Bertram Lenox Simpson]. Cr 8vo. Pp. 420. [*Lond. Lib. Cat.*]
                    London, 1908

FORBIDDEN (the) frvit: or a treatise of the tree of knowledge of good and evil, of which Adam at the first, and as yet all mankind doe eate death. By Augustinus Eleutherius [Sebastianus Francken]. Translated out of English. 8vo. Pp. 172. [*Bodl.*]
            Printed in the yeare 1640

FORBIDDEN (the) sacrifice. [A novel.] By W. H. de Winton [William Henry Wilkins, M.A.]. 3 vols. 8vo. [*Brit. Mus.*]   London, 1893

FORCE (the) of contrast; or, quotations accompanied with remarks, submitted to the consideration of all who have interested themselves in . . . the Blagdon Controversy [regarding Hannah More's schools. By Rev. Thomas Drewitt, curate of Cheddar]. 8vo. [Green's *Bibl. Somers.*, iii., 96.]
                    Bath, 1801

FORCE (the) of contrast continued; or, extracts and animadversions: with occasional strictures on the contraster and others of Mr [Thomas] Bere's opponents, and observations on the effects of Mrs H[annah] More's schools. . . . By a friend of the [English Church] establishment [Rev. E— Crosse]. 8vo. [Green's *Bibl. Somers.*, iii., 98.]   Bristol, 1802

FORCE (the) of truth: an oratorio. [By Rev. John Hoadly, LL.D.] 8vo. [*D. N. B.*, vol. 27, p. 22.]
                    London, 1764

FORCED (the) mariage; a tragedy. [By John Armstrong, M.D.] 12mo. [*Brit. Mus.*]   London, 1770

FORE and aft; or letters from the life of an old sailor. By Webfoot [W— D— Phelps]. 8vo. [Cushing's *Init. and Pseud.*, vol. i., p. 304.]   Boston, 1870

FORECAST (the) shadow of the mystical body. [By Joseph T. Toye.] 4to. Pp. 176. Private print. N.P., [1879]

FOREFRONT (the) of the battle. [A novel.] By Andrew Loring [Lorin Lathrop, U.S. Consul]. 8vo. Pp. 234.
                    London, 1908

FOREIGN (the) affairs of Great Britain administered by the Right Honourable Henry John Viscount Palmerston. [By William Cargill.] Not published. 8vo. Pp. viii., 276.   London, 1841

FOREIGN conspiracy against the liberties of the United States. By Brutus [Samuel Finley Breese Morse]. 8vo. [Cushing's *Init. and Pseud.*, vol. i., p. 42.]   New York, 1835

FOREIGN courts and foreign homes. By A. M. F. [Alicia Maria Falls]. Pt 8vo. [*Lond. Lib. Cat.*]
                    London, 1898

FOREIGN exchanges; being a complete set of tables, calculated from the lowest exchange to the highest usual rates, and from one penny to one thousand pounds sterling; shewing, at one view, any sum of foreign money reduced into British sterling, and British money into foreign, with those countries with which London exchanges. . . . Concluding with a table of the real and imaginary monies of the world, the mode of reckoning the same, and their value reduced into British sterling. By the editor of Mortimer's *Commercial Dictionary* [William Dickinson]. Revised by Mr W. Tate. 8vo. Pp. xvi., 1179. [*Aberd. Lib.*]   London, 1819

FOREIGN field sports. By William Henry Scott [John Lawrence]. 8vo. [Jaggard's *Index*, ii.]   London, 1819

FOREIGN (a) marriage : a novel. [By Virginia Wales Johnson.] Fcap 8vo. [Kirk's *Supp.*] New York, 1880

FOREIGN Missions ; an illustration and an appeal. By an elder [James E. Mathieson, merchant]. 8vo.
London, 1876

FOREIGN travel ; or, cautions for the first tour. By Viator Verax [Rev. George M. Musgrave, M.A.]. 8vo. [Cushing's *Init. and Pseud.*, vol. i., p. 294.] London, 1866

FOREIGNER (the) ; a tale of Saskatchewan. By Ralph Connor [Charles W. Connor, D.D.]. Cr 8vo. [*Amer. Cat.*] New York, 1909

FOREIGNERS (the) ; a poem. Part I. [By John Tutchin.] Folio. Pp. 11. [*Bodl.*] London, 1700
No more published.

FOREIGNER'S (a) evidence on the China question. [By Robert S. Sturgis.] 8vo. [*Camb. Univ. Lib.*]
London, 1859
A second edition appeared in the same year, with a preface signed by the author.

FORENOONS in the Police-court of Aberdeen. [By George Allardyce.] 8vo. [Robertson's *Aberd. Bibl.*]
Aberdeen, 1834

FORENSIC anecdotes ; or, humour and curiosities of the law, and of the men of the law. By Jacob Larwood [L. R. Sadler]. Fcap 8vo. [*Lit. Year Book.*] London, 1882

FORENSIC (a) tour in the United States. By the Hon. John Philip Refalo, Sergeant-at-law, of Gray's Inn, London [James Dunlop]. 8vo. [Cushing's *Init. and Pseud.*, vol. i., p. 130.] London, 18—[?]

FORE-RUNNER (the) of Bels dovvnefall ; wherein, is breifley answered his braggnig (*sic*) offer of disputation, and insolent late challenge : the particularities of the confutation of his bookes, shortly by goddes grace to be published, are mentioned : with a breife answere to his crakinge and calumnious confuting of Papistes by Papistes them selues ; and lastly a taste giuen of his rare pretended sinceritye, with som few examples. [By Robert Parsons.] 8vo. Pp. 63. [Gillow's *Bibl. Dict.*, vol. 5, p. 285.]
[Doway], 1605
See note to "The dolefvll knell . . ."

FORERUNNERS (the) of Christ's peaceable Kingdom upon earth. . . . [By Rev. James Sherwin, minister at Wallington, Hertford.] 4to. [Calamy's *Nonconf. Mem.*, Palmer's edition, i., 303.] London, 1665

FOREST (the). [A book of stories.] By F. Hugin [Princess Feodora, of Schleswig-Holstein]. 8vo.
London, 1904

FOREST (the) and chase of Sutton Coldfield. [By Miss —— Bracken.] Fcap 8vo. [*Birm. Cent. Lib.*]
Birmingham, 1860

FOREST (the) and the field. By H. A. L. The "Old Shekarry," author of *The hunting grounds of the old world*, etc. [Major Henry Astbury Leverson]. With illustrations. 8vo. Pp. xviii., 551. [*Brit. Mus.*] London, 1867

FOREST (the) Arcadia of Northern New York, embracing a view of its mineral, agricultural, and timber resources. [By Nathaniel W. Coffin.] 8vo. [*Brit. Mus.*] New York, 1864

FOREST birds from the woods of Maine. [Poems.] By Florence Percy [Elizabeth Chase, later Mrs Akers]. Fcap 8vo. Pp. viii., 207. Boston, 1856

FOREST (the) chapel ; and other poems. By Maxwell Gray [Mary Gleed Tuttiett]. Fcap 8vo. Pp. 136. [*Lit. Year Book.*] London, 1899

FOREST, field, and fell. By J. A. Owen [Mrs Jane Allan Visger, *née* Pinder]. 8vo. [*Lit. Year Book.*]
London, 1893

FOREST flowers and sea-shells. By the Lynn Bard [Alonzo Lewis]. 8vo. [Cushing's *Init. and Pseud.*, vol. i., p. 176.] Boston, 1831

FOREST folk. By James Prior [James Prior Kirk]. Cr 8vo. Pp. 360. [*Lond. Lib. Cat.*] London, 1901

FOREST (a) hearth. By Edwin Caskoden [Charles Major]. Pt 8vo. [Baker's *Guide to Fiction.*] London, 1903

FOREST (a) keep. [A tale. By Alice King.] 3 vols. 8vo. [*Brit. Mus.*]
London, 1862

FOREST life. By the author of *A new home* [Mrs Mary Kirkland, *née* Clavers]. 2 vols. 8vo. [*Bodl.*]
London, 1842

FOREST (the) of fancy ; wherein is contained very pretty apothegmes and pleasant histories, both in meeter and prose. . . . By H. C. [Henry Cheeke]. 4to. London, 1580
Attributed also to Henry Chettle.
The title of another edition is given later.
See "Forrest (the) of fancy . . ."

FOREST (a) of varieties [poems, letters, etc. By Francis Dudley North, third Baron North]. 3 parts. Folio. Pp. 243. London, 1645
The following is an enlarged edition.

FOREST (a) promiscuous of several seasons productions. [By Francis Dudley North, third Baron North.] 4 parts. Folio. [*Brit. Mus.*]
London, 1659

FOREST (a) ramble ; with a description of a royal stag hunt, and characteristic sketches of all the masters of the stag-hounds during His present Majesty's reign : with notices of several well-known characters in the Forest of Windsor. [By William Law, of Bagshot, Surrey.] 4to.
London, 1818

FOREST sketches : deer-stalking and other sports in the Highlands fifty years ago. [By William Robertson.] 8vo. Pp. xxxv., 352. [*Adv. Lib.*]
Edinburgh, 1865

FOREST tithes, and other studies from nature. By a son of the marshes [Mr —— Denham Jordan] : edited by J. A. Owen [Mrs Jane Allan Visger, *née* Pinder]. Cr 8vo. Pp. 216. [*Lit. Year Book.*] London, 1893

FOREST (a) tragedy, founded on fact. By Grace Greenwood, author of *Haps and mishaps*, etc. [Sarah Jane Clarke, later Mrs L. K. Lippincott]. 8vo. Pp. 196. [*Bodl.*] London, [1856]

FORESTER (le) ; a novel. By the author of *Arthur Fitz-Albini* [Sir Samuel Egerton Brydges]. 3 vols. 12mo. [Watt's *Bibl. Brit.*]
London, 1802

FORESTERS (the). By the author of *Lights and shadows of Scottish life*, and *The trials of Margaret Lyndsay* [John Wilson, " Christopher North "]. 8vo. [*Adv. Lib.*] Edinburgh, 1825

FORESTERS (the) ; an American tale, being a sequel to the History of John Bull, the Clothier. [By Rev. Jeremy Belknap, D.D.] Fcap 8vo. Pp. 216. [*Evans' Amer. Bibl.*, vol. 8, p. 251.]
Boston, [Mass.], 1792

FORESTER'S (the) daughter : a tale of the Reformation. By the authoress of *Seymour of Sudley*, etc. [Hannah D. Wolfensberger]. 3 vols. Fcap 8vo. [*Bodl.*] London, 1844

FORGE and furnace. A novel. By Florence Warden [Florence Alice Price, later Mrs Geo. E. James]. Fcap 8vo. Pp. 215. New York, 1896

FORGET and forgive ; a comedy. By John Daly [John Besemeres, merchant in Calcutta]. 8vo. London, 1874

FORGING the fetters. [A novel.] By Mrs Alexander [Mrs Alexander Hector, *née* Annie French]. 8vo. Pp. 154. [*Lit. Year Book.*] London, 1890

FORGIVENESS and liberty. By J. N. D. [John Nelson Darby]. 8vo.
London, 1879

FORGIVING (the) husband, and adulteress wife : or, a seasonable present to the unhappy pair in Fanchurch-Street. By the author of the *London Spy* [Edward Ward]. 8vo. Pp. 12. [*Brit. Mus.*] London, [1708 ?]

FORGOTTEN lives. A novel. By the author of *Olive Varcoe*, etc. [Frances Eliza M. Notley, later Mrs Thomas]. 3 vols. 8vo. [*Brit. Mus.*]
London, 1875
Wrongly ascribed to Francis Derrick.

FORKED lightning—The Green Flag : a comedy. By Keble Howard [John Keble Bell]. 8vo. Pp. 316. [*Brit. Mus.*] London, 1916

FORLORN (the) hope. By A. L. O. E. [Charlotte Maria Tucker]. 8vo. Pp. 265. London, 1893

FORLORN hope. [A novel.] By Edmund Yates [mainly, however, by Mrs Francis Sarah Hoey]. 8vo.
London, 1867

FORM (a) for Church Government and ordination of ministers, contained in CXI. propositions [drawn up by George Gillespie], propounded to the late Generall Assembly at Edinburgh, 1647. 4to. Pp. vi., 45. London, 1647
See also under " CXI. Propositions concerning the ministerie."

FORM (a) of Common Prayer [based on Theophilus Lindsey's Revision of the Book of Common Prayer] for the use of the congregation formerly of Strand Street, now of St Stephen's Green, Dublin ; together with selections from the Psalms of David. 12mo. Pp. 206. [*Brit. Mus.*] Dublin, 1863

FORM (the) of Morning and Evening Prayer, for the use of the United Church of England and Ireland ; together with the Psalms of David, and the second lessons as they are appointed to be said every morning in the year : to which are added, the first lessons to be read on Sunday ; with notes [compiled by the Hon. Charlotte Grimston, sister of the late Earl of Verulam]. 2 vols. Fcap 8vo. [Martin's *Cat.*]
London, 1827

FORM (a) of prayer, and a new collection of psalms, for the use of a congregation of Protestant Dissenters in Liverpool. [By John Collet.] Pt 8vo.
Liverpool, 1763

FORM (the) of prayer and ceremonies used at the consecration of Churches. [By Richard Bagot, D.D., Bishop of Oxford.] 8vo. [*Brit. Mus.*]
Oxford, 1832

FORM (a) of prayer and exhortation for Baptism. [By Samuel Collet.] 8vo.
London, 1721

FORM (a) of prayer and humiliation for God's blessing upon his Majesty, and his dominions, and for the removing and averting of God's judgments from his Church and State. [By Abednego Seller.] 4to. Pp. 64. [*D. N. B.*, vol. 51, p. 227.]   London, 1690

FORM (the) of prayer, with thankgiving to Almighty God, to be used daily by all devout people throughout the realm, for the happy deliverance of Her Majesty Queen Caroline from the late most traitorous conspiracy. [By William Hone.] Fourth edition. 8vo. [*Bodl.*]   London, 1820

FORM of process before the Court of Session, the new Jury Court, and the Commission of Teinds. [By James Ivory, Lord Ivory.] 2 vols. 8vo. [*Adv. Lib.*]   Edinburgh, 1815-18
The first volume only is anonymous; the author signed the dedication of the second.

FORM (a) of reciting the most holy rosary, compiled for the nuns of the Convent of our Lord of Mercy at Hull. [By Edward Francis Collins.] 8vo.
Hull, 1859

FORM (a) of thanksgiving to be used thorowout the diocese of Lincoln and in the jurisdiction of Westminster. [By the Bishop, John Williams.] 4to. [Thomason *Coll. of Tracts*, vol. i., p. 28.]   London, 1641

FORMAN : a tale. [By Henry, Lord Brougham ?] 3 vols. Fcap 8vo.
London, 1819

FORME (the) of cury, or a roll of ancient English cookery, compiled about A.D. 1390 by the master cooks of King Richard II ; with notes and a copious index or glossary. By an antiquary [Samuel Pegge, LL.D.]. 8vo. [*Brit. Mus.*]   London, 1780

FORME (the) of government of the kingdome of England, collected out of the fundamental lawes and statutes of this kingdome ; wherein is manifested the customary uses of the kings to call their peeres and barons to be b[p]artners in treatizes : likewise the names of the kings, and the times when such parliaments were called, &c. [By Sir Robert Bruce Cotton.] 4to. [*Brit. Mus.*]   London, 1642

FORMIDABLE (the) Triumvirate ; or the Malignant Club ; in the Hudibrastic manner. [By Rev. Professor Archibald Bruce, of Whitburn.] Fcap 8vo. Pp. 15.   Edinburgh, 1770

FORMS of bidding prayer, with introduction and notes. [By Henry Octavius Coxe.] 8vo. Pp. xliv., 203. [*Bodl.*]   Oxford, 1840
Preface signed " H. O. C."

FORMS of devotion for the use of families. [By John Leland, D.D., and others.] 8vo.   Dublin, 1758

FORMS of prayer, for public [Unitarian] worship. [By Rev. John James Tayler.] Third edition. 8vo. [*Brit. Mus.*]   London, 1851
Preface signed " J. J. T."

FORMS of prayer for the use of the Dissenting Congregation at Mill-Hill Chapel, in Leeds ; chiefly compiled from other Liturgies. [By William Wood.] Fcap 8vo. Pp. 94. [*Brit. Mus.*]   Leeds, 1801

FORMS of prayer to be used in families, as set forth in the [Anglican] Prayer-Book : compiled by J. S. [Josiah Swetty, D.D.]. 8vo. [*Cushing's Init. and Pseud.*, vol. i., p. 256.]
Claremont, New Hampshire, 1861

FORMS of procedure in the bill-chamber ; with a copious appendix, containing acts of sederunt, tables of fees, and various forms of styles. [By Edward Livingston.] 8vo. Pp. vi., 128. [*Sig. Lib.*]   Edinburgh, 1827

FORMS of the Ionic dialect in Homer. Translated by G. E. L. C. [George Edward Lynch Cotton, later Bishop of Calcutta]. 8vo.   London, 1846

FORMULARE Anglicanum ; or, a collection of ancient Charters and instruments of divers kinds, taken from the originals, placed under several heads, from the Norman Conquest to the end of Henry VIII. [By Thomas Madox.] Folio. [Gross's *Sources and Lit. of Eng. Hist.*]   London, 1702

FORMULARIES of faith put forth by authority during the reign of Henry VIII, viz., Articles about Religion, 1536. The Institution of a Christian man, 1537. A necessary doctrine and erudition for any Christian man, 1543. [Edited by Charles Lloyd, Bishop of Oxford.] 8vo. [*Brit. Mus.*]
Oxford, 1825

FORREST (the) of fancy. Wherein is conteined very prety apothegmes, and pleasaunt histories, both in meeter and prose, songes, sonets, epigrams and epistles, of diuerse matter and in diuerse manner. VVith sundry other deuises no lesse pithye then pleasaunt and profytable. Reade with regard, peruse each point well, and then giue

thy iudgement as reason shall moue thee. 4to. No pagination. B. L.
London, 1579

This work is written under the signature "H. C.," and is ascribed to Henry Cheeke by Malone, to Henry Chettle by Ritson, wrongly to Henry Constable by Warton.

Another edition is also indicated above. *See* "Forest (the) of fancy . . ."

FORSAKEN (the) ; an argument, in fiction, for the morality of divorce. By Ivan Trepoff [George H. D. Gossip]. Cr 8vo. [*Amer. Cat.*]
New York, 1910

FORSAKEN (the) way ; a romance. By Philip Lafargue [Joseph Henry Philpot, M.D.]. Cr 8vo. [*Lond. Lib. Cat.*]
London, 1900

FORTH feasting ; a panegyricke to the Kings Most Excellent Majestie. [By William Drummond of Hawthornden.] Printed by Andro Hart. 4to. 8 leaves unpaged. [*Adv. Lib.*]
Edinburgh, 1617

FORTNIGHT (a) in Arran. By W. M. [William Mitchell]. 8vo.
Glasgow, [1874]

FORTNIGHT (a) in the famine country of Bengal, March, 1874. [By George Smith, LL.D., C.I.E.] 8vo. [*Calc. Imp. Lib.*]
Serampore, 1874
Preface signed " G. S."

FORTNIGHT'S (a) ramble to the lakes in Westmoreland, Lancashire and Cumberland. By a rambler [Joseph Budworth, later Palmer]. Second edition. 8vo. [Anderson's *Brit. Top.*]
London, 1795
First published in 1792.

FORTRESS (the) of Yadasara. By Christian Lys [Percy James Brebner]. 8vo. Pp. 432. [*Lit. Year Book.*]
London, 1899

FORTUNA chance. [A novel.] By James Prior [James Prior Kirk]. Cr 8vo. Pp. 446. [*Amer. Cat.*]
London, 1910

FORTUNATE (the) and unfortunate lovers ; or, the history of . . . Dorastus and Fawnia, Hero and Leander : made English from the originals. By a gentleman [Hugh Stanhope]. Fcap 8vo. Pp. 66. [*Brit. Mus.*]
London, 1735

FORTUNATE (the) complaint. [A poem. By Thomas Binning Hamilton, Earl of Haddington.] 4to.
Edinburgh, 1709
The authorship is indicated in a note written by a contemporary.

FORTUNATE (the) foundlings ; being the genuine history of Colonel M—rs, and his sister, Madam du P—y, the issue of the Hon. Ch—es M—rs, son of the late Duke of R—l—d : containing many wonderful accidents that befel them in their travels, and interspersed with the characters and adventures of several persons of condition, in the most polite courts of Europe. [By Mrs Eliza Haywood ?] Fcap 8vo. [*Watt's Bibl. Brit.*]
London, 1744

FORTUNATE (the) Island, and other stories. By Max Adeler [Charles Heber Clark]. Fcap 8vo. [*Lit. Year Book.*]
London, 1880

FORTVNATE (the) isles and their vnion : celebrated in a masqve designed for the court, on the twelfth night. [By Ben Jonson.] [First edition.] 4to. No pagination. [*Dyce Cat.*]
[London, 1624]

FORTUNATE (the) mistress ; or, a history of the life and vast variety of fortunes of Mademoiselle de Beleau, afterwards call'd the Countess of Wintselsheim, in Germany : being the person known by the name of the Lady Roxana, in the time of King Charles II. [By Daniel Defoe.] 8vo. [Wilson's *Life of Defoe.*] London, 1724

FORTUNATE (the) prisoner ; a novel. By Max Baring [Charles Messent]. Cr 8vo. [*Lit. Year Book.*]
London, 1909

FORTUNATE (the) youth ; or Chippenham Croesus : containing the commencement, action, and denouement of the Newmarket hoax. [By Abraham W. Causton.] 8vo. [*Camb. Univ. Lib.*]
London, 1818

FORTUNE ; a rhapsody. [By Francis Gentleman ?] 4to. [*Brit. Mus.*]
London, 1751

FORTUNE (the) hunter ; a novel. By Mrs Helen Berkley [Mrs Anna Cora Ritchie, *née* Ogden Mowatt]. Cr 8vo [Cushing's *Init. and Pseud.*, vol. i., p. 34.]
Philadelphia, 1854

FORTUNE in her wits ; a comedy. [By Charles Johnson.] 4to. [*Biog. Dram.*]
London, 1705

FORTUNE (the) of a spendthrift ; a novel. By R. Andom [Alfred W. Barrett] and F. Harewood [Frederick George Fisher, Lieutenant in East Surrey Regiment]. Cr 8vo.
London, 1900

FORTUNE (the) tellers ; or, the world unmask'd : a medley. Written by Abel Drugger [John Hardham]. 8vo. [*Biog. Dram.*]
N.P., [1750 ?]

FORTUNE-HUNTING; a novel. By the author of *First love* [Mrs Margracia Loudon]. 3 vols. Fcap 8vo. [*Brit. Mus.*]   London, 1832

FORTUNES (the) and adventures of Raby Rattler and his man, Floss. [By Thomas Hall.] 8vo. [*Brit. Mus.*]   London, 1864
    See also " Effects and adventures."

FORTUNES (the) and misfortunes of the famous Moll Flanders, &c. who was born in Newgate, and during a life of continu'd variety for threescore years, besides her childhood, was twelve year a whore, five times a wife (whereof once to her own brother) twelve year a thief, eight year a transported felon in Virginia, at last grew rich, liv'd honest, and died a penitent. Written from her own memorandums, [By Daniel Defoe.] 8vo. [Wilson's *Life of Defoe*, 175.]   London, 1721

FORTUNE'S boats. By Barbara Yechton [Lyda Farrington Krausé]. 8vo. [*Amer. Cat.*]   Boston, 1900

FORTUNE'S gate. [A novel.] By Alan St Aubyn [Mrs Frances Marshall]. Cr 8vo. Pp. vi., 306. [*Brit. Mus.*]   London, 1898

FORTUNES (the) of Colonel Torlogh O'Brien : a tale of the wars of King James. [By Joseph Sheridan Le Fanu.] 8vo. Pp. 342. [O'Donoghue's *Poets of Ireland*.] London, 1847
    Later editions give the author's name.

FORTUNES (the) of Conrad. By Walter B. Dunlap [Sylvanus Cobb, jun.]. Pt 8vo. [*Cushing's Init. and Pseud.*, vol. ii., p. 46.] New York, 1891

FORTUNES (the) of Ey Abbey. [A poem. By Herbert Hailstone.] 8vo. Pp. 28. [*Brit. Mus.*] London, [1870 ?]

FORTUNES (the) of Francis Croft : an autobiography. [By Bayle Saint John.] 3 vols. 8vo. [*Brit. Mus.*]   London, 1852

FORTUNES (the) of Hector O'Halloran and his man, Mark Antony O'Toole. [By Capt. Wm. Hamilton Maxwell.] 8vo. [*D. N. B.*, vol. 37, p. 138.]   London, 1842

FORTUNES (the) of Mrs Simmons, of Mayfield. By Uncle George [George Monckton, M.P.]. 8vo. London, 1849

FORTUNES (the) of Nigel. By the author of *Waverley, Kenilworth*, etc. [Sir Walter Scott, Bart.]. 3 vols. 8vo.   Edinburgh, 1822

FORTUNES (the) of Perkin Warbeck ; a romance. By the author of *Frankenstein* [Mary Wollstonecraft Godwin, afterwards Mrs Shelley]. 3 vols. Fcap 8vo. [Courtney's *Secrets*, 60.]   London, 1830

FORTUNES (the) of the Anglo-Indian race considered retrospectively and prospectively. By one of fifty years' knowledge and experience [T— G. Clarke]. 8vo. [*Calc. Imp. Lib.*]   Madras, 1878
    Signed " T. G. C."

FORTUNE'S uncertainty, or youth's unconstancy; wherein is contained a true and impartial account of what hapned in the space of few years to the author, whom you will know in this ensuing discourse by the name of Rodolphus [Charles Croke]. 8vo. Pp. 99. [*Bodl.*]   London, 1667
    " Charles Croke, a younger son of Unton Croke of Merston near Oxon (made Sergeant at law by Oliver Protector), was the author of the book following, entit. ' Fortunes uncertainty ' &c."—MS. note by Wood.

FORTUNE'S wheel. By Morice Gerard [Rev. John Jessup Teague]. Cr 8vo. Pp. 305. [*Lit. Year Book.*]   London, 1921

FORTUNE-TELLING by numbers ; being an introduction to the art of the Kabalists. By Sepharial [Walter Gorn Old]. 8vo. Pp. 61. [*Brit. Mus.*]   London, 1918

FORTY days in the desert, on the track of the Israelites ; or, a journey from Cairo, by Wady Feiran, to Mount Sinai and Petra. By the author of *Walks about Jerusalem* [William Henry Bartlett]. Third edition. 8vo. [*Brit. Mus.*]   London, [1849]

FORTY family sermons. By the editor of *The Christian Observer* [Rev. Josiah Pratt ? or Rev. C. Wilks]. 8vo.   London, 1830

XLV. (the) chapter of the prophecies of Thomas the Rhymer, in verse ; with notes and illustrations. Dedicated to Doctor Silverspoon [Witherspoon], preacher of sedition in America. [By Hugo Arnot.] 4to. [*Adv. Lib.*]   Edinburgh, 1776

FORTY meditations on the Passion, for Lent. [By Sir Thomas Clifford.] Cr 8vo.   London, 1814

FORTY minutes' advice to every country farmer. [By George Harrison.] 8vo.   Gloucester, [1780 ?]

'49. The gold-seeker of the Sierras. [A novel.] By Joaquin Miller [Cincinnatus Heine Miller]. 8vo. Pp. 148. [Kirk's *Supp.*]   London, 1886

FORTY seasons of first-class cricket ; being the autobiography and reminiscences of R. G. B. [Richard Gorton Barlow] ; together with many curious and interesting anecdotes incidental to cricket. 8vo. Pp. xi., 225.   Manchester, [1908]

FORTY years a file-closer. By Captain Minus Wonbar [George A. Thurston]. 8vo. London, 1889

FORTY years ago. [A tale.] By the author of *The Lamplighter* [Maria S. Cummins]. Fcap 8vo. [*Brit. Mus.*] London, [1862]

FORTY years in the world ; or, sketches and tales of a soldier's life. [By Captain Robert Grenville Wallace.] 3 vols. Cr 8vo. [*Brit. Mus.*] London, 1825

FORTY-SIX days in Switzerland and the North of Italy. By G. C. [George Clowes], junr. Pt 8vo. Private print. N.P., 1856

FORWARD : a series of essays on metaphysical subjects, by Aristos Philadelphus [*pseud.* ——] ; with a biographical sketch of the author. By Agathos [F— E. C. Linde]. 8vo. [*Calc. Imp. Lib.*] Calcutta, 1880

FOSTER (the) brother ; a tale of the War of Chiozza. [By Thornton Leigh Hunt.] Edited by [James Henry] Leigh Hunt. 3 vols. 8vo. [*D. N. B.*, vol. 28, p. 281.] London, [1845]

FOSTER (the) brothers ; being a history of the school and college life of two young men. [By James Payn, B.A.] Pt 8vo. Pp. 423. [Bartholomew's *Cat. of Camb. Books.*] London, 1859

FOTHERINGHAY and Mary Queen of Scots ; being an account, historical and descriptive, of Fotheringhay Castle, the last prison of Mary Queen of Scots, and the scene of her trial and execution. By Cuthbert Bede [Rev. Edward Bradley, B.A.]. 8vo. [*D. N. B.*, First Supp.,* vol. 1, p. 251.] London, 1886

FOUGHT, and won : a story of Grammar-school life. By Ruth Elliott [Lillie Peck]. 8vo. Pp. 254. [Kirk's *Supp.*] London, 1885

FOUND and fettered ; detective stories. By Dick Donovan [Joyce Emerson Preston Muddock]. Cr 8vo. [*Lit. Year Book.*] London, 1894

FOUND dead. [A novel.] By the author of *Lost Sir Massingberd*, etc. [James Payn]. 8vo. Pp. iv., 348. [*Camb. Univ. Lib.*] London, 1869

FOUND in the snow. [A story.] By Ray Cunningham [Frances Browne Arthur]. Pt 8vo. Stirling, [1896]

FOUND money : a novel. By George A. Birmingham [James Owen Hannay, D.D.]. Cr 8vo. Pp. 251. [*Lit. Year Book.*] London, 1923

FOUND out ; a story. By the author of *Comin' through the rye* [Helen B. Mathers, later Mrs Henry Reeves]. 8vo. Pp. 188. [*Brit. Mus.*] London, [1885]

FOUNDATION (the) of Christian religion : comprehended in three godlie and learned treatises. 1. Faith. 2. Hope. 3. Charitie. [Translated into English by S— Veghelman.] 8vo. [*Brit. Mus.*] London, 1612

FOUNDATION (the) of moral goodness ; or a further inquiry into the original of our idea of virtue. By a clergyman [John Balguy, M.A.]. 8vo. [*D. N. B.*, vol. 3, p. 60.] London, 1728

The previous publication was entitled " A Letter to a Deist. . . ."

FOUNDATION (the) of the faith assailed in Oxford ; a letter to His Grace the Archbishop of Canterbury, &c., Visitor of the University, with particular reference to the changes in its constitution, now under consideration. By a clerical member of Convocation [Henry William Wilberforce, Oriel College]. 8vo. [*Bodl.*] London, 1835

The author's name is in the handwriting of Dr Bliss.

FOUNDATION (the) of the Universitie of Cambridge, with a catalogue of the principal founders and speciall benefactors of all the colledges, and total number of students, magistrates and officers therein being ; and how the revenues thereof are and have been increased from time to time. [By Gerard Langbaine, D.D.] 4to. [*D. N. B.*, vol. 32, p. 92.] London, 1651

FOUNDATION (the) of the Universitie of Oxford ; with a catalogue of the principall founders and speciall benefactors of all the colledges, and total number of students, magistrates and officers therein being ; and how the revenews thereof are and have been increased from time to time. [By Gerard Langbaine, D.D.] 4to. [*D. N. B.*, vol. 32, p. 92.] London, 1651

FOUNDATIONS of freedom ; or an agreement of the people proposed as a rule for future government. Drawn up by several well-affected persons, and tendered to the consideration of the General Councell of the Army. [By Richard Overton.] 4to. Pp. 15. [Whitley's *Bapt. Bibl.*, i., 35.] London, 1648

FOUNDATIONS (the) of international polity. By Norman Angell [Ralph Norman Angell Lane]. 8vo. Pp. xlviii., 235. [*Lit. Year Book.*] London, 1914

FOUNDATIONS (the) of natural and reveal'd religion asserted ; being a reply to the supplement to the treatise entitul'd, The nature, obligation, &c. of the Christian sacraments. [By Arthur Ashley Sykes, D.D.] 8vo. Pp. 96. [Disney's *Memoir of Sykes*.]
London, 1730

FOUNDATIONS (the) of reform. By the military correspondent of *The Times* [Charles A'Court Repington]. 8vo. Pp. vi., 516. London, 1908

FOUNDATION-STONES. Fifteen lessons . . . on the founding of the Church in England. By Austin Clare [Miss W. M— James]. 8vo. Pp. 187. [*Lit. Year Book*.]
London, 1895

FOUNDERED (the) galleon ; John Topp, pirate. By Weatherby Chesney [Charles John Cutcliffe Hyne]. 8vo. [*Brit. Mus.*] London, 1905

FOUNDLING (the) Chapel brawl ; a non-heroic ballad, with notes. [By I— Sayers.] 4to. London, 1804

FOUNDLING (the) hospital for wit. [By Sir Charles Hanbury Williams.] Nos. 1-4. 8vo. London, 1743-47

FOUNDLING (the) of Glenthorn ; or, the smugglers' cave : a novel. By the author of *The Farmer's three daughters* [Alexander Balfour]. 4 vols. Fcap 8vo. [*Camb. Univ. Lib*.]
London, 1823

FOUNDLING (the) ; or, the child of Providence. Written by himself [Rev. John Church]. 8vo. Pp. 70.
London, 1823
Signed " J. C."

FOUNDRESS (the). By John Ayscough [Monsignor Francis Bickerstaffe-Drew]. Cr 8vo. [*Lond. Lib. Cat*.]
London, 1920

FOUNTAIN (the) of life. By Omicron [Hugh Barclay, Sheriff of Perth]. 8vo. Edinburgh, 1850

FOUNTAIN (the) of living waters. . . . By the author of *Little Henry and his bearer* [Mary Martha Butt, later Mrs Sherwood]. Fcap 8vo. [*Brit. Mus*.]
London, [1826 ?]

FOUNTAIN (the) of living waters ; illustrated by facts in the life of a layman [in the United States, viz. Theodore Irving]. Fcap 8vo. Pp. 151. [*Mus. Brit*.] London, 1853

FOUNTAIN (the) of monition and inter-communication divine ; shewing plainly both how the Spirit of God applies himself to men, and withal shewing most clearly how men ought to conform themselves to receive such monitions from God : design'd as a brief introduction to the holy allegorick rules of grammar. By W. F., Esq., master in the holy language, and author of *The New Jerusalem*, etc. [William Freke]. 8vo. Pp. iii., 165. [*Bodl*.] London, 1703

FOUNTAIN (the) of youth ; edited [really written] by E. Dawson [Paul Devon]. Cr 8vo. London, 1891

FOUNTAINE (the) and welspring of all variance, sedition and deadlie hate : wherein is declared at large the opinion that [the Church of] Rome is signified by the panic of Babylon, mentioned in . . . the Revelation of S. John. [By Christopher Ockland.] B. L. 4to. [*Brit. Mus*.] London, 1589
Signed " Christoph. O."

FOUR (the) ages of England ; or the iron age : with other select poems, written in the year 1648. [By Abraham Cowley.] 8vo. Pp. 94. [*Brit. Mus*.]
London, 1675

FOUR (the) ages of life ; translated from General Count Paul Philippe de Ségur. By C. C. V. G. [Mrs —— Dawson Wetherelt]. 8vo.
Dublin, 1826

FOUR cards. [A novel.] By Austin Clare [Miss W— M. James]. Cr 8vo. [*Lit. Year Book*.] London, 1904

FOUR conferences concerning, 1. Reading the Holy Scriptures in the vulgar tongue. 2. Half communion. 3. Worshipping of images. 4. Invocation of saints. [By Gilbert Coles, D.D.] 4to. [*Brit. Mus*.] Oxford, 1688

FOUR crotchets to a bar. [A novel. By Mrs Susanna C. Venn.] 3 vols. Cr 8vo. [*Camb. Univ. Lib*.]
London, 1881

FOUR dialogues, between Mr Smith, a Churchman ; Mr Stedman, a Unitarian ; and Mr Wilson, a Calvinist ; relating chiefly to mystery and the Trinity, original sin . . . and the Atonement. By William Hison [William Johns]. Fcap 8vo. [*Brit. Mus*.] London, 1831
" Hison " is an anagram of " Johns."

FOUR discourses of praises to God. [By Alex. Hume, B.A., minister at Logie.] Fcap 8vo. [*Scott's Fasti*.]
Edinburgh, 1594

FOUR discourses on the following subjects : viz. I. Of obedience to the supreme powers, and the duty of subjects in all revolutions. II. Of the laws of nations, and the rights of sovereigns. III. Of the power of the magistrate, and the rights of mankind, in matters of religion. IV. Of the liberty of the press. [By Matthew Tindal.] 8vo. Pp. iv., 329. [*Watt's Bibl. Brit*.] London, 1709

FOUR discourses to young men. [By John Bate Cardale, solicitor.] 8vo. [Boase's *Cath. Apost. Lit.*]
London, 1877

FOUR (the) dispensations. [By A— C— Barclay.] Fcap 8vo. Pp. 23. [*Brit. Mus.*] London, [1845]

FOUR dissertations, moral and religious, addressed to the rising generation. I. On covetousness. II. On hypocrisy. III. On the prosperous condition of men in this world. IV. On continuance in well-doing. [By Joseph Cradock.] 8vo. Pp. 68. [*Adv. Lib.*] London, 1815

FOUR elegies, descriptive and moral. [By John Scott, of Amwell.] 4to. Pp. 23. [*Adv. Lib.*] London, 1760

FOUR essays, as improved and enlarged in the second edition of the Reliques of ancient English poetry. [By Thomas Percy, Bishop of Dromore.] 8vo. [*Brit. Mus.*] [London], 1767

FOUR essays : viz., I. On making china-ware in England. . . . II. On a method for furnishing coals at a third part of the price they are usually sold at. [By Aaron Hill.] 8vo. [*Brit. Mus.*] London, 1718

FOUR everyday girls. By Raymond Jacberns [Georgina Selby Ash]. Cr 8vo. Pp. 220. [*Lit. Year Book.*] London, 1900

FOUR (the) farthing candles ; a satire. [By Cuthbert Shaw.] 4to. [Chalmers' *Biog. Dict.*] London, 1762

FOUR (the) gardens ; a solemn imagery [in blank verse. By Henry Dartnall, of Cheltenham]. 8vo. [*Brit. Mus.*]
Gloucester, 1870
Attributed also to —— Handyside.

FOUR girls at Chautauqua. By Pansy [Mrs Isabella Alden, *née* Macdonald]. 8vo. [*Lit. Year Book.*]
Cincinnati, 1880

FOUR (the) Gospels arranged in a series of tabular parallels, on a new principle. [By the Rev. —— Cholmondeley, M.A.] 8vo. [Horne's *Introduction to the Holy Scriptures*, v., 162.]
London, 1836

FOUR (the) Gospels in one. By a Chicago Bible-class teacher [Robert A. Campbell]. 8vo. Chicago, 1871

FOUR (the) Gospels, with a comment, both Scriptural and moral [by Pasquier Quesnel] ; revised, corrected, and the Popish errors expunged, by a Presbyter of the Church of England [Rev. Clement Cruttwell]. 2 vols. 8vo. Bath, 1790

FOUR (the) great powers : England, France, Russia, and America. By a looker-on from America [Charles Brandon Boynton, D.D.]. [Cushing's *Init. and Pseud.*, vol. ii., p. 90.]
Cincinnati, 1866

FOUR hundred sketches and skeletons of sermons. [By Jabez Burns, D.D.] 2 vols. Fcap 8vo. [*D. N. B.*, vol. 7, p. 423.] London, 1836

FOUR introductory lectures in natural philosophy. [By Hugh Hamilton, Bishop of Ossory.] Fcap 8vo. [*Camb. Univ. Lib.*] London, 1774

FOUR letters concerning the study of the Hebrew Scriptures. [By Thomas Randolph, D.D.] 8vo. Pp. iv., 52. [*Manch. Free Lib.*] London, 1755

FOUR letters, occasioned by two pamphlets recently published. . . . [By Rev. John Clayton, Congregationalist.] 8vo. [*Brit. Mus.*] London, 1805
Signed " A. Z."

FOUR letters to a friend. I. Concerning assent to a revealed proposition. II. Concerning the Scripture sense of heresy. III. Containing remarks upon some passages in Mr Chubb's supplement. IV. Remarks upon his account of the Christian justification. By a country minister [Caleb Wroe]. 8vo. [Orme's *Bibliotheca Biblica.*] London, 1725
Ascribed also to Thomas Morgan, M.D.

FOUR letters to a friend in North Britain, upon the publishing the Tryal of Dr Sacheverell. [By Robert Walpole, Earl of Orford.] 8vo. Pp. 33. [*Brit. Mus.*] London, 1710
Wrongly attributed to Roger Maynwaring.

FOUR letters to the people of England, on the situation and conduct of national affairs. [By John Shebbeare, M.D.] 8vo. [*Athen. Cat.*, p. 503.]
London, 1755-56

FOUR letters to the Right Reverend Connop Thirlwall, Bishop of St David's, on the claims of the dioceses of Wales. By " Cambrensis " [Arthur James Johnes, Welsh County Judge]. 8vo. London, 1843

FOUR letters which passed between a gentleman and a clergyman, concerning the necessity of an episcopal commission for the valid administration of Gospel ordinances. [By Thomas Brett, LL.D.] 8vo. Pp. 63. [*D. N. B.*, vol. 6, p. 286.] London, 1743

FOUR little folks, and some of their doings. By E. L. S. [Mrs E— L. Sherriff]. Pt 8vo. London, 1901

FOUR marks of Antichrist; or a supplement to the Warburtonian lecture. [By Gilbert Wakefield.] 8vo. [*Adv. Lib.*]   London, 1788

FOUR men with a van. [A novel.] By R. Andom [Alfred W. Barrett]. Cr 8vo. Pp. 158. [*Brit. Mus.*]   London, 1907

FOUR messengers. By E. M. H. [Emily Marion Harris].   12mo. [*Brit. Mus.*]   London, 1870

FOUR (the) millions. [A novel.] By O. Henry [William Sydney Porter]. Cr 8vo. Pp. 256. [*Brit. Mus.*]   Chicago, 1906

FOUR months among the gold-finders in Alta California; being the diary of an expedition from San Francisco to the Gold Country. By J. Tyrwhitt Brooks, M.D. [really Henry R. Vizetelly].   Fcap 8vo.   Pp. xviii., 207. [*Brit. Mus.*]   London, 1849

FOUR months in England. By a West Indian [John Horsford, D.D., Wesleyan minister]. Fcap 8vo. Pp. 232. [Osborn's *Wesl. Bibl.*, p. 118.]   London, 1852

FOUR (a) months' tour through France. [By —— Palmer.]   2 vols.   12mo. [*Adv. Lib.*]   London, 1776

FOUR new dialogues of the dead. [By George Lyttelton, Lord Lyttelton.] 8vo. [*Brit. Mus.*]   London, 1765

FOUR oaks. By Kamba Thorpe [Mrs Elizabeth Whitfield Bellamy].   8vo. [Cushing's *Init. and Pseud.*, vol. i., p. 283.]   New York, 1867

FOUR paradoxes: of arte, of lawe, of warre, of service. By T. S. [Thomas Scott, poet].   8vo.   24 leaves. [Lowndes' *Bibl. Man.*] London, 1602

FOUR (the) pilgrims, or life's mission; and other poems. [By Thomas Young.] 12mo. Pp. 260. [*Andrew Jervise.*]   Dundee, 1849

FOUR propositions, . . . shewing, not only that the distance of the sun, as attempted to be determined from the theory of gravity, by a late author [Dr Matthew Stewart], is, upon his own principles, erroneous; but also, that it is more than probable this capital question can never be satisfactorily answered by any calculus of the kind. [By John Dawson, of Sedbergh.] 8vo. [*D. N. B.*, vol. 19, p. 150.]   Newcastle, 1769

FOUR red night-caps. [A tale.] By Weatherby Chesney [Charles John Cutcliffe Hyne].   Cr 8vo.   Pp. 342. [*Lond. Lib. Cat.*]   London, 1901

FOUR red roses; a novel.   By Sarah Tytler [Henrietta Keddie].   Cr 8vo. Pp. 314.   London, 1904

FOUR satyrs upon the Jesuites. [By John Oldham.] 8vo. [Watt's *Bibl. Brit.*]   London, 1679

FOUR schoolfellows. By Kenner Deene [Charlotte Smith].   3 vols.   Cr 8vo. [*Lit. Year Book.*]   London, 1878

FOUR (the) seasons; a short account of the structure of plants: being four lectures written for the Working Men's Institute in Paris. [By Sarah Margaret Fitton.] 8vo. [*Brit. Mus.*]   London, 1865

FOUR sermons. By a layman [Duncan Keith, of Uddingston].   8vo.   Glasgow, [1880 ?]

FOUR sermons.   By a layman [Frederick John Monson, 5th Lord Monson]. 8vo. Pp. 74. [*W.*]   London, 1842

FOUR sermons upon most important topicks; or, catechistical lectures concerning I. The necessity of water-baptism to salvation, with the requisites to the valid administration of it. II. The conditions of our baptismal covenant on God's part. III. The conditions of the baptismal covenant on man's part. IV. The lawfulness, expediency, and necessity of infant-baptism. By a presbyter of the Church of England [Robert Hall]. 8vo. Pp. iv., 82. [Whitley's *Bapt. Bibl.*, i., 145.]   London, 1715

FOUR short discourses on funeral occasions. By a minister of the Church of Scotland [John Bethune, D.D., minister of Rosskeen].   8vo. Pp. 45. [Scott's *Fasti.*]   Edinburgh, 1758

FOUR speeches against continuing the army, as they were spoken on various occasions in the House of Commons. By W. S. [William Shippen, M.P.]. 8vo. [*Cat. Lond. Inst.*, ii., 104.]   London, 1732

FOUR topographical letters written in July 1755, upon a journey through Bedfordshire, Northamptonshire, Leicestershire, Nottinghamshire, Derby, and Warwick. [By Resta Patching, or Patchen, an inn-keeper of Gracechurch Street, London.] 8vo. [*Upcott*, i., 37.]   Newcastle, 1757

FOUR (the) white swans. By Fiona Macleod [William Sharp]. Fcap 8vo. [*Lit. Year Book.*]   London, 1904

FOUR (the) winds of Eirinn; poems, by Ethna Carbery [Mrs Anna Johnston MacManus].   Ninth edition. Fcap 8vo. [Brown's *Books on Ireland*, p. 96.]   Dublin, 1902

FOUR years at Yale. By a graduate of '69 [Lyman Hotchkiss Bagg]. 8vo. [Cushing's *Init. and Pseud.*, vol. i., p. 119.] Newhaven, Conn., 1871

FOUR years in France; or, narrative of an English family's residence there during that period : preceded by some account of the conversion of the author to the Catholic faith. [By Henry Digby Beste, M.A.] 8vo. Pp. xvi., 443. [*Adv. Lib.*] London, 1826

FOUR years in Secessia : adventures within and beyond the Union lines. By Julius Henri Browne [Albert D. Richardson]. 8vo. [Cushing's *Init. and Pseud.*, vol. i., p. 42.] New York, 1865

FOUR years in the Old World; comprising the travels . . . and evangelistic labours of Dr and Mrs Palmer in England, Ireland, Scotland, and Wales. By the author of *The way to holiness* [Mrs Phoebe Palmer]. Fcap 8vo. [*Brit. Mus.*] New York, 1866

FOUR years in the [United] States. By a journeyman printer [Henry Clark]. 8vo. [Cushing's *Init. and Pseud.*, vol. ii., p. 80.] London, 1871

FOUR years' residence in the West Indies during 1826-29; with an account of the dreadful hurricanes in Barbados, St Vincent, and St Lucia, in 1839; and an appendix. By the son of a military officer [Frederick W. M. Bayley]. 8vo. [Cushing's *Init. and Pseud.*, vol. ii., p. 139.] London, 1833

FOUR years' service in India. By a private soldier [John Ryder, 32nd Foot]. Fcap 8vo. Leicester, 1834
An edition of 1853 is not anonymous.

FOUR (the) years' voyages of Capt. George Roberts : being a series of uncommon events which befel him in a voyage to the islands of the Canaries, Cape de Verd, and Barbadoes, from whence he was bound to the coast of Guiney; the manner of his being taken by three pyrate ships commanded by Low, Russell and Spriggs, who, after having plundered him and detained him ten days, put him aboard his own sloop, without provisions, water &c., and with only two boys, one of eighteen, and the other of eight years of age; the hardships he endured for above twenty days, till he arrived at the island of St Nicholas, from whence he was blown off to sea (before he could get any sustenance) without his boat and biggest boy, whom he had sent ashore : and after four days of difficulty and distress, was shipwrecked on the unfrequented island

of St John, where, when he had remained near two years he built a vessel to bring him off. . . . [By Daniel Defoe.] 8vo. [Wilson's *Life of Defoe*, 191.] London, 1726

FOUR young explorers; or, sight-seeing in the Tropics. By Oliver Optic [William Taylor Adams]. Pt 8vo. Pp. 357. [Kirk's *Supp.*] Boston, 1896

FOUR - AND - TWENTY kickabouts. [Verses.] Written by John Lea [John Lea Bricknall]. 4to. Pp. 48. [*Brit. Mus.*] London, 1920

FOURE great lyers striving who shall win the silver - whetstone. Written by W. P. [William Painter]. 8vo. London, [1585 ?]

FOURE learned and godly treatises; viz. The carnall hypocrite; the Churches deliverances; the deceitfulnesse of sinne; the benefit of afflictions. By T. H. [Thomas Hooker]. Fcap 8vo. Pp. 297. [*Bodl.*] London, 1638

FOURE serious questions of grand importance, concerning excommunication and suspention from the Sacrament, propounded to prevent schisms and settle unity. . . . By a lover of peace and truth [William Prynne]. 4to. [*D. N. B.*, vol. 46, p. 434; Thomason *Coll. of Tracts*, i., 392 ff.] [London], 1645
Replies soon published, also anonymously, were "An Antidote against Foure dangerous quaeries," "A Full answer [by Herbert Palmer] to a printed paper," "A Brotherly and friendly censure [by George Walker]." Prynne replied in "The Antidote animadverted by P.," and, with his name, "A Vindication of Foure serious questiones."

FOURE-FOULD (a) meditation, of the foure last things, viz.

1			Houre of Death,
2	}	of the {	Day of Judgement,
3			Paines of Hell,
4			Joys of Heaven.

Shewing the estate of the elect and reprobate; composed in a diuine Poeme. By R. S., the author of *S. Peters complaint* [Robert Southwell, S.J.]. 4to. [*Brit. Mus.*] London, 1606
Reprinted in 1874.

FOURFOLD (the) ministry [in the Catholic Apostolic Church. By John Bate Cardale, solicitor]. 8vo. [Boase's *Cath. Apost. Books.*] London, 1871

FOURFOLD (the) portraiture of the Heavenly King as presented in the Gospels; a new translation of the Gospels, side by side with the Authorised and Revised Versions. By "Interpreter" [Rev. Alfred Ernest Bourne]. Dy 4to. Pp. xvii., 306. London, 1907

FOUR-HANDED folk. By Olive Thorne Miller [Mrs Harriet Mann Miller]. Fcap 8vo. Pp. 201. [*Amer. Cat.*]   Boston, 1897

FOUR-LEAVED clover; a novel. By Maxwell Gray [Mary Gleed Tuttiett]. Cr 8vo. Pp. 248. [*Lit. Year Book.*]   London, 1901

FOUR-LEGG'D (the) Quaker; to the tune of the Dog and Elder's maid, or, the Lady's fall. [By John Berkenhead.] S. sh. [*Bodl.*]   N.P., N.D.
  The author's name is in the handwriting of Wood.

FOUR-POOLS (the) mystery. [A detective story. By Jane Webster.] 8vo. [*Amer. Cat.*]   New York, 1908

FOURTEEN sonnets, elegiac and descriptive; written during a storm, on a tour. [By William Lisle Bowles.] 4to. [*Dyce Cat.*]   Bath, 1789

FOURTEENTH (the) note of the Church examined, viz. The unhappy end of the Church's enemies. [By Nicholas Stratford, D.D., Bishop of Chester.] 4to. [*Jones' Peck, p. 439.*]   London, 1657

FOURTENE sermons of Barnardine Ochyne, concernyng the predestinacion and eleccion of God; very expediente to the settynge forth of hys glorye amonge hys creatures. Translated out of Italian in to oure natyue tounge by A. C. [Anne Cooke]. 8vo. No pagination. B.L. Imprinted at London by John Day dwellynge ouer Aldersgate, & Wylliam Seres, dwellyng in Peter Colledge.   N.D.
  The translator was Anne, daughter of Sir Anthony Cooke, wife to Sir Nicholas Bacon, mother of Sir Francis Bacon. [*Bliss' Cat.*]

FOURTH (the) and last part of a Caveat against the Whiggs, &c.; in a short historical account of their behaviour in the reign of Her Majesty Queene Anne. [By Charles Hornby.] Second edition. 8vo. Pp. 134. [*Bodl.*]   London, 1712

FOURTH (the) and last part of the History of the Crown-Inn; with the character of John Bull, and other novels. [By John Arbuthnot, M.D.] Part IV. 8vo.   London, N.D.
  See note to " The History of the Crown Inn. . . ."

FOURTH (the) commandment abrogated by the Gospel; or the . . . Christian's observance of the first day of the week as an holy festival. [By Caleb Fleming, D.D.] 8vo. Pp. viii., 68. [*Whitley's Bapt. Bibl.*, i., 158.]   London, 1736

FOURTH (the) commandment of the decalogue considered; and its moral and perpetual obligation asserted and vindicated from the cavils of its adversaries, and particularly of Philip Limborch. By J. S., a presbyter of the Episcopal Church of Scotland [John Small, minister in Forfar]. 4to. [*New Coll. Cat.*]   Edinburgh, 1713

FOURTH (a) essay at removing national prejudices; with some reply to Mr H[o]dges and some other authors, who have printed their objections against an union with England. [By Daniel Defoe.] 4to. [*New Coll. Lib.*]   [Edinburgh], 1706

FOURTH (a) letter to a person of quality; being an historical account of the doctrine of the Sacrament, from the primitive times, to the Council of Trent; shewing the novelty of Transubstantiation. [By Edward Pelling, D.D.] 4to. Pp. 77. [*Brit. Mus.*]   London, 1688

FOURTH (a) letter to the people of England; on the conduct of the M—rs in alliances, fleets, and armies, since the first differences on the Ohio, to the taking of Minorca by the French. [By John Shebbeare, M.D.] Second edition. 8vo. Pp. 115. [*Brit. Mus.*]   London, 1756

FOURTH (the) note of the Church examined, viz. Amplitude, or multitude and variety of believers. [By Edward Fowler, D.D., Bishop of Gloucester.] 4to. [*Jones' Peck, p. 438.*]   London, 1687

FOURTH (the) part of Naked Truth; or, the complaint of the Church to some of her sons for breach of her Articles: in a friendly dialogue between Titus and Timothy, both ministers of the Church of England. By a legal son, and sincere conformist to the Church of England, as established by law [Edmund Hickeringill]. Folio. [*Brit. Mus.*]   London, 1682

FOWLING; a poem, descriptive of grouse, partridge, pheasant, woodcock, duck, and snipe shooting. [By Rev. John Vincent, of Constantine, Cornwall.] Fcap 8vo. [*Watt's Bibl. Brit.*]   London, 1808
  A second edition was issued in 1812.

FOXES and firebrands; or a specimen of the danger and harmony of Popery and separation: wherein is proved, from undeniable matter of fact and reason, that separation from the Church of England is, in the judgment of Papists, and by sad experience, found the most compendious way to introduce Popery, and to ruine the

Protestant religion. [By John Nalson, LL.D.] 4to. Pp. 39. [*D. N. B.*, vol. 40, p. 31.] London, 1680
The dedication is signed " Philirenes." In 1682 Robert Ware reprinted it with a second part of his own ; and in 1689 he added a third and last part in 12mo.

FOXES' tails. . . . By Leo Ross [David Anderson Moxey, M.D.]. Pt 8vo. [*New Coll. Cat.*] Edinburgh, 1878

FOX-HOUND, forest, and prairie. By " Brooksby " [Capt. Edward Pennell-Elmhirst]. Royal 8vo. [*Lond. Lib. Cat.*] London, 1892

FOX-HUNTER'S (the) guide ; containing places of all the principal hunts in England and Wales. By " Cecil " [Cornelius Tongue]. Cr 8vo. [*Lit. Year Book.*] London, [1860 ?]

FOXONIAN (the) Quakers, dunces, lyars and slanderers, proved out of George Fox's Journal, and other scriblers ; particularly B. C. his Quakers no apostates, or the hammerer defeated ; amanuensis, as is said, to G. C. (as he sometime wrote himself) Gulielmus Calamus, alias William Penn : also a reply to W. C. (a Churchman, the Quakers advocate) his Trepidantium Malleus intrepidanter malleatus, &c. By Trepidantium Malleus [Samuel Young]. Fcap 8vo. Pp. 100. [*Brit. Mus.*] London, 1697

" FOX'S (a) tale : " a sketch of the hunting-field. By the author of *The autobiography of the late Salmo Salar, Esq., comprising a narrative of the life, personal adventures, and death of a Tweed salmon* [George Rooper]. 8vo. Pp. 78. [*Brit. Mus.*] London, 1867

FOXY Fielding's friend. [A novel.] By E. A. B. [E— A— Bland]. 8vo. London, [1891]

FOXY Grandpa. By " Bunny " [Carl Emil Schultze]. Fcap 8vo. [*Amer. Cat.*] New York, 1900

FOXY Grandpa up to date. By Bunny [Carl Emil Schultze]. 8vo. New York, 1904

FOXY Grandpa's mother goose. By Bunny [Carl Emil Schultze]. 8vo. New York, 1904

FOXY Grandpa's surprises. By Bunny [Carl Emil Schultze]. 8vo. New York, 1905

F. R. [Fairman Rogers] ; a memoir. By H. H. F. [Horace H— Furness]. 8vo. Privately printed. [*Amer. Cat.*] Philadelphia, 1904

FRA Angelico, and other poems. By I. G. S. [Isaac Gregory Smith, LL.D.]. Pt 8vo. [Kirk's *Supp.*] London, 1872

FRA Bartolommeo. By Leader Scott [Mrs Lucy Baxter, *née* Barnes]. 8vo. [Kirk's *Supp.*] London, 1892

FRA Dolcino ; and other poems. By A. and L. [Arabella and Louisa Shore]. 8vo. [*Brit. Mus.*] London, 1870

FRAGMENT (a) [being a satire on prominent statesmen. By Henry Stebbing, D.D., rector of Redenhall, Norfolk]. 8vo. [*D. N. B.*, vol. 54, p. 124.] [Cambridge, 1751]

FRAGMENT (a) : addressed to the sons and daughters of humanity. By a citizen of the world [Mathew Carey]. 8vo. [Cushing's *Init. and Pseud.*, vol. i., p. 59.] Philadelphia, 1796

FRAGMENT of a journal of a sentimental philosopher, during his residence in the city of New York. [By Washington Irving.] 8vo. [Cushing's *Init. and Pseud.*, vol. i., p. 265.] New York, 1809

FRAGMENT of a parallel between the history, literature, and art of Italy in the middle ages. [By William Schomberg Robert Kerr, Marquis of Lothian.] 8vo. Pp. 478. Private print. [*Boase's Mod. Brit. Biog.*, vol. vi.] Edinburgh, 1863
Preface signed " L." [Lothian].

FRAGMENT of a tour. [By Henrietta E. M. Phillipps.] 8vo. London, [1835]

FRAGMENT of a tragedy lately acted at the British Museum ; or the tears of Cracherode on the theft of his prints. [By Rev. Stephen Weston, B.D.] 4to. Pp. 3. [*D. N. B.*, vol. 60, p. 373.] N.P., [1806]
" From the author, St. Weston. 1806. Aug."—MS. note in the handwriting of Douce.

FRAGMENT (a) of an ancient prophecy, relating, as some think, to the present Revolutions : being the fourth part of the " End of oppression." [By F— Spence.] Fcap 8vo. [*Brit. Mus.*] London, 1796

FRAGMENT (a) of Church History at the Cape of Good Hope. [By —— Jardine.] 8vo. [*Brit. Mus.*] Cape Town, 1827

FRAGMENT (a) of the history of John Bull ; with the birth, parentage, education, and humours of John Radical. . . . By Horace Hombergh [Rev. W— Ettrick, M.A.]. 8vo. Pp. vii., 184. London, 1820

FRAGMENT (a) of the true religion ; being the substance of two Letters from a Methodist Preacher in Cambridgeshire [Rev. John Berridge] to a clergyman in Bedfordshire. 8vo. Pp. vi., 25. [*Camb. Univ. Lib.*] London, 1760
Preface signed " Faith Workless, editor."

FRAGMENT (a) on government ; being an examination of what is delivered, on the subject of government in general, in the introduction to Sir William Blackstone's Commentaries : with a preface, in which is given a critique on the work at large. [By Jeremy Bentham.] 8vo. [*Brit. Mus.*]
London, 1776

FRAGMENT (a) on Mackintosh ; being strictures on some passages in the Dissertation by Sir James Mackintosh, prefixed to the Encyclopædia Britannica. [By James Mill.] 8vo. Pp. vi., 431. [*Adv. Lib.*]   London, 1835

FRAGMENT (a) on the constitutional power and duties of juries, upon trials for libels. [By Sir Samuel Romilly.] 8vo. [*D. N. B.*, vol. 49, p. 188.]
[London], 1784

FRAGMENT (a) out of the sixth book of Polybius, containing a dissertation upon government . . . translated from the Greek, with notes : to which is prefixed a preface wherein the system of Polybius is applied to the government of England. By a gentleman [Edward Spelman]. 8vo. Pp. xxviii., 126. [*Brit. Mus.*]   London, 1743

FRAGMENTA antiquitatis ; antient tenures of land, and jocular customs of some mannors, made publick for the diversion of some, and instruction of others. By T. B. [Thomas Blount], of the ˙Inner Temple, Esq.   Pt 8vo. [*D. N. B.*, vol. 5, p. 255.]
London, 1679
Later editions, enlarged, were published in 1784 and 1815.

FRAGMENTA Scoto-Dramatica, 1715-1758. [Edited by William Henry Logan.] 8vo. [*On the authority of the editor.*]   Edinburgh, 1835
A very few copies were privately printed at the expense of the editor.

FRAGMENTA Scoto-Monastica : memoir of what has been already done, and what materials exist, towards the formation of a Scotish Monasticon : to which are appended sundry new instances of goodly matter. By a delver in antiquity [William Barclay David Donald Turnbull]. 8vo.   Pp. x., 31, xcvi. [*Adv. Lib.*]
Edinburgh, 1842

FRAGMENTARY (a) chapter from the most pleasant and delectable history of Robert the Fox. [By Sir Robert Peel.] 4to. [*Athen. Cat. (Supp.*), p. 241.]   N.P., 1846

FRAGMENTS. [By Alex. Cowieson.] Fcap 8vo. [Robertson's *Aberd. Bibl.*]
Aberdeen, 1825

FRAGMENTS. [By Thomas Lake Harris, M.P.] Royal 8vo. Pp. 49.
N.P., 1896

FRAGMENTS. By a lady [Adelaide Jackson]. 8vo. [*Brit. Mus.*]
London, 1826

FRAGMENTS and anecdotes proper to be read at the present crisis by every honest Englishman. [By John Wilkes ?] 8vo. [*Brit. Mus.*]
London, 1764

FRAGMENTS and fictions. By M. De Pendemots [William Howison, poet and philosopher]. 8vo.   [*D. N. B.*, vol. 28, p. 122.]   Edinburgh, 1825

FRAGMENTS and scraps of history. [By Sir George Harrison.] 2 vols. Large 4to. [*Brit. Mus.*]   London, 1834

FRAGMENTS from the history of John Bull. [By George Moir, advocate.] 8vo. Pp. 246. [*Cat. Phil. Inst., Edin.*]
Edinburgh, 1835

FRAGMENTS from the note-book of a home-missionary. [By Cyril Pearl.] 8vo. [Cushing's *Init. and Pseud.*, vol. ii., p. 76.]   Boston, 1842

FRAGMENTS from the study of a pastor. [By Gardiner Spring, D.D.] 8vo. [Cushing's *Init. and Pseud.*, vol. ii., p. 118.]   New York, 1839

FRAGMENTS, in prose and verse.   By a young lady, lately deceased [Elizabeth Smith, of Burnhall]. With some account of her life and character, by the author of *Sermons on the doctrines and duties of Christianity* [Mrs Thomas Bowdler]. 8vo. Pp. 227. [*Brit. Mus.*]
London, 1808

FRAGMENTS, in the manner of Sterne. [By Isaac Brandon.]   Fcap 8vo. [*Brit. Mus.*]   London, 1797

FRAGMENTS of a civic feast ; being a key to Volney's Ruins, or the revolutions of empires. By a reformer [Rev. Frederick Nolan]. 8vo. [*Brit. Mus.*]
London, 1826

FRAGMENTS of a life. By Frances Macnab [Agnes Fraser]. 8vo. [*Lit. Year Book.*]   London, 1893

FRAGMENTS of a prospect from a hill in Fife. [By George Wallace, advocate.] 4to. Pp. viii., 39. [Martin's *Cat.*]   [Edinburgh, 1754]
Forty copies privately printed. Published with the author's name at Edinburgh, 1796, 8vo ; a second edition, also printed at Edinburgh, was issued in 1800.

FRAGMENTS of an intended tour—July 12, 1819. [By Rev. Thomas Frognall Dibdin, D.D.] 8vo. Pp. 16. [*W.*]   N.P., N.D.

FRAGMENTS of antient poetry, collected in the Highlands of Scotland, and translated from the Galic or Erse language. [By James Macpherson.] Second edition. Fcap 8vo. [*D. N. B.*, vol. 35, p. 262.] Edinburgh, 1760

Despite urgent requests by friends and eager expectations of the public, Macpherson never produced originals from which he professed to have derived his "translations"; it was believed, however, by some that he possessed at least a few fragments of old Celtic poems.
See also "Fingal, a poem . . . ."

FRAGMENTS of essays. [By Chandos Leigh, Baron Leigh.] Fcap 8vo. Pp. 108. [Martin's *Cat.*] London, 1816

FRAGMENTS of Scotish history. [Edited, with desultory reflections on the state of ancient Scotland, by Sir John Graham Dalyell.] 4to. [*Adv. Lib.*] Edinburgh, 1798

FRAGMENTS of the table round. [By Professor Robert Buchanan, of Glasgow.] 4to. Pp. 76. Glasgow, 1859

FRAGMENTS of truth; being the exposition of several passages of Scripture [By John M'Leod Campbell, D.D.] Third edition. Pt 8vo. Pp. viii., 336. Edinburgh, 1861

Others attribute the expositions to Thomas Erskine, of Linlathen.

FRAGMENTS on ante-historic times. 1. The Arians identified with the Scythians. 2. The Hyksos identified with the Turks. [By David Urquhart.] 8vo. Private print. London, 1858

FRAGMENTS on politeness. [By David Urquhart.] 8vo. Pp. 30. [*Brit. Mus.*] London, 1870

FRAGOLETTA; a novel. By "Rita" [Mrs W— Desmond Humphreys, *née* Eliza M. J. Gollan]. 3 vols. 8vo. [*Lit. Year Book.*] London, 1881

FRAMLEIGH Hall: a novel. [By Julia Wedgwood.] 3 vols. 8vo. [Kirk's *Supp.*] London, 1858

FRANCE. By the author of *The Atelier du Lys* [Margaret Roberts]. 8vo. [*Brit. Mus.*] London, 1881

FRANCE, Alsace, and Lorraine. By Hans Breitmann [Charles Godfrey Leland]. 8vo. [*Lond. Lib. Cat.*] London, 1870

FRANCE and her people. By C. C. B. [Mrs C. C. Benton]. Pt 8vo. [Cushing's *Init. and Pseud.*, vol. i., p. 23.] Philadelphia, 1872

FRANCE; its king, court, and government. By an American [General Lewis Cass]. 8vo. [Cushing's *Init. and Pseud.*, vol. i., p. 12.] New York, 1840

FRANCE no friend to England; or the resentment of the French upon the success of the English, as it is expressed in a . . . Remonstrance to the King of France upon surrendering the maritime forts of Flanders into the hands of the English. . . . [By Cardinal de Retz.] Translated out of French. 8vo. Pp. 25. [*Manch. Free Lib.*] London, 1659

FRANCE painted to the life. By a learned and impartial hand. [Peter Heylin.] Second edition. 8vo. Pp. 368. [Lowndes' *Bibl. Man.*] London, 1657

A spurious edition of the first part of Heylin's "Two Journeys." The first edition [1656] was printed surreptitiously, and published by William Leake, a bookseller, who (says Ant. à Wood) "fathered it in Stationers Hall on one Rich. Bignall."

FRANCE, the Empire, and civilization. [By Edward Peacock, F.S.A.] 8vo. Pp. 48. [Kirk's *Supp.*] London, 1873

FRANCESCA Carrara. By the author of *Romance and reality*, etc. [Letitia Elizabeth Landon, later Mrs Maclean]. 3 vols. Fcap 8vo. [*Brit. Mus.*] London, 1834

FRANCESCA of Rimini: a poem. By A. S. H. [Arthur Sherburne Hardy]. Fcap 8vo. Pp. 48. [Cushing's *Init. and Pseud.*, vol. i., p. 122.] Philadelphia, 1878

FRANCHISE (the). What shall we do to it? [By Charles Tennant.] 8vo. [*Adv. Lib.*] London, 1858

FRANCIS Berrian, or the Mexican patriot. [By Timothy Flint.] Fcap 8vo. [*Brit. Mus.*] Boston, [Mass.], 1826

FRANCIS Deák, Hungarian statesman; a memoir. [By Florence Arnold-Forster], with a preface by Mount-Stuart E. Grant Duff, M.P. 8vo. [*Brit. Mus.*] London, 1880

FRANCIS, Lord Bacon; or, the case of private and national corruption and bribery, impartially consider'd: address'd to all South-Sea Directors, Members of Parliament, Ministers of State, and Church-dignitaries. By an Englishman [Thomas Gordon]. Fifth edition. 8vo. Pp. xvi., 62. [*Bodl.*] London, 1721

The dedication is signed "Britannicus."

FRANCIS Spira, and other poems. By the author of *The gentle life* [James Hain Friswell]. 8vo. Pp. viii., 128. [*Brit. Mus.*] London, 1865

FRANCIS the waif; a tale of French country life. By George Sand [Madame Lucile A. Dudevant]: translated from the French. 8vo. [Haynes' *Pseud.*] London, 1895

FRANCISCAN days of vigil : a narration of personal views and developments. By Brother Angelo [Richard De Bary]. Cr 8vo. [*Amer. Cat.*]
London, 1910

FRANCO-GALLIA ; or, an account of the ancient free state of France, and most other parts of Europe, before the loss of their liberties : written originally in Latin by the famous civilian Francis Hotoman, in the year 1574, and translated into English by the author of the *Account of Denmark* [Robert Molesworth, Lord Molesworth]. 8vo. [*Brit. Mus.*]
London, 1711

FRANCO-GERMANIC (the) war ; its causes and immediate effects. [By John Tecklenborough.] 8vo. [*Brit. Mus.*]
London, 1882

FRANK Fairlegh ; or, scenes from the life of a private pupil. [By Francis Edward Smedley.] With thirty illustrations on steel, by George Cruikshank. 8vo. [*Brit. Mus.*]
London, 1850

FRANK Forester's [Henry William Herbert's] Fish and fishing of the United States and British Provinces of North America. 2 vols. Fcap 4to. [Haynes' *Pseud.*]   New York, 1850

FRANK Forester's [Henry William Herbert's] Fugitive sporting sketches ; edited by "Will Wildwood" [Frederick E. Pond]. Fcap 8vo. [Cushing's *Init. and Pseud.*, vol. i., p. 30.]
Westfield, Wisconsin, 1879

FRANK Forester's [Henry William Herbert's] Sporting scenes and characters. 8vo.   Philadelphia, 1845

FRANK Hudson's hedge fence ; and other stories. By "Pansy" [Mrs Isabella Alden, *née* Macdonald]. Pt 8vo. [*Lit. Year Book.*] London, 1894

FRANK Leslie's [Frank Collier's] Pictorial history of the American Civil War. 8vo. [Haynes' *Pseud.*]
New York, 1862

FRANK Merriwell's daring. By Burt L. Standish [Gilbert Patten]. Fcap 8vo. [*Amer. Cat.*]   New York, 1908

FRANK Merriwell's victories. By Burt L. Standish [Gilbert Patten]. Fcap 8vo. [*Amer. Cat.*]   New York, 1910

FRANK Mildmay. [A novel.] By the author of *Peter Simple* [Captain Frederick Marryat]. Fcap 8vo. [*Brit. Mus.*]   London, 1836

FRANK Milward : a novel. By W. Avon [William Kenrick]. 2 vols. Pt 8vo. [Cushing's *Init. and Pseud.*, vol. i., p. 22.]   London, 1857

FRANK Nelson in the forecastle ; or, the sportsman's club among the sailors. By Harry Castlemon [Charles A. Fosdick]. 12mo. [Cushing's *Init. and Pseud.*, vol. i., p. 52.]
Philadelphia, 1876

FRANK O'Donnell ; a tale of Irish life : edited [but really written] by Allen H. Clington [Major David Power Conyngham]. 8vo. Pp. 370. [S. J. Brown's *Ireland in fiction.*]   Dublin, 1861

FRANK, the young naturalist. By Harry Castlemon [Charles Austin Fosdick]. Fcap 8vo. [*Amer. Cat.*]
New York, 1907

FRANK Warrington. [A tale.] By the author of *Rutledge*, etc. [Mrs Sidney S Harris] Fcap 8vo. New York, 1863

FRANKENSTEIN ; or, the modern Prometheus. [By Mary Wollstonecraft Godwin, afterwards Mrs Shelley.] 3 vols. Fcap 8vo. [Courtney's *Secrets*, p. 59.]   London, 1818

FRANKLEY : from the French of Henri Gréville [Madame Alice Durand]. Pt 8vo. [Haynes' *Pseud.*] London, 1887

FRANKLIN (the) family primer. By a friend of youth [Samuel Willard, D.D.]. 8vo. [Cushing's *Init. and Pseud.*, vol. i., p. 107.]   Boston, 1811

FRANK'S ranch ; or, my holidays in the Rockies. [By Edward Marston, publisher.] Sixth edition. 8vo. [*Brit. Mus.*]   London, 1885

FRATERNA correptio ; or, the saints zeale against sinful altars : delivered in a sermon preached on a day of humiliation for the errors, heresies, and schisms of our times and nations. By Z. C. [Zachary Crofton], minister of the Word. 12mo. Pp. 176. [Palmer's edition of Calamy's *Nonconf. Mem.*, i., 104.]   London, 1655

FRATERNITYE (the) of Vacabondes. As wel of ruflyng Vacabondes, as of beggerly, of women as of men, of gyrles as of boyes, with their proper names and qualities ; with a description of the crafty company of cousoners and shifters. Whercunto also is adioyned the xxv. Orders of knaues, otherwise called a quartern of knaues. Confirmed for euer by Cocke Lorell.

The Vprightman speaketh.
Our Brotherhood of Vacabondes,
If you would know where dwell :
In graues end Barge which syldome standes,
The talke wyll shew ryght well.
Cocke Lorell aunswereth.
Some orders of my Knaues also
In that Barge shall ye fynde :
For no where shall ye walk I trow,
But ye shall see their kynde

[By Thomas Harman.] 4to. No pagination. B.L. [*Bodl.*] Imprinted at London by Iohn Awdeley, dwellyng in little Britayne Streete without Aldersgate. 1575

FRATRICIDE ; or the murderer's gibbet ; being the right tragical hystorie of Sir D. Goodere. [By Richard Smith.] Pt 8vo. Bristol, 1839

FRAUD and friendship ; or the orphan and the foundling of the King's printing house. An Edinburgh tale. [By David Pae.] 8vo. [*Adv. Lib.*]
Edinburgh, 1857

FRAUD detected ; or, the Hibernian patriot : containing all the Drapier's Letters to the people of Ireland, on Wood's coinage, &c. Interspers'd with the following particulars, viz. I. The addresses of the Lords and Commons of Ireland, against Wood's coin. II. His majesty's answer to the said addresses. III. The report of his majesty's most honourable privy council. IV. Seasonable advice to the grand jury. [By Jonathan Swift, D.D.] 8vo. Pp. 242. [*Bodl.*]
Dublin, reprinted 1725

FRAUD in accounts. . . . By the editor [of The Accountants' Library, Robert Gee]. 8vo. London, 1904

FRAUDS and abuses at St Paul's [Cathedral, London] ; in a letter to a Member of Parliament. [By Francis Hare, D.D.] 8vo. [*Manch. Free Lib. Cat.*] London, 1712
See also " A Continuation of Frauds and abuses."

FRAUDS detected . . . in drugs. . . . [By John Chandler.] 8vo. Pp. 34.
London, 1748

FRAUDS (the) of Romish monks and priests, set forth in eight letters ; lately written by a gentleman, on his journey into Italy, and publish'd for the benefit of the publick. By Gabriel d'Emillianne [Antoine Gavin]. 8vo. Pp. 430. [Quérard's *Supercher. dévoil.*, 1847, ii., 24.] London, 1691
The dedication and the address to the reader are signed " G. D. E., E. A. P."

FRÄULEIN Schmidt and Mr Anstruther : being the letters of an independent woman. By the author of *Elizabeth and her German Garden* [Mary Beauchamp, Countess of Arnim, later Countess Russell]. Cr 8vo. Pp. 384. [*Brit. Mus.*]
London, 1907

FREAKS and follies of fabledom : a little Lempriere. [By Edward Leman Blanchard.] 8vo. London, 1852

FREAKS, follies, fancies, and fashions. By H. E. R., Trin. Coll. Camb. [H. E. Reynolds]. Cr 8vo. Pp. 72. [*Bodl.*]
London, 1868

FREAKS (the) of Cupid ; a novel. By an Irish bachelor [—— Abbot]. 3 vols. Fcap 8vo. [*Camb. Univ. Lib.*]
London, 1845

FRED Brenning. By Tim Trimmer [Albion H. Redford]. 8vo. [Cushing's *Init. and Pseud.*, vol. i., p. 287.]
Nashville, Tenn., 1876

FRED Freedland. By Willis Loveyouth [I. H. Anderson]. 8vo. [Cushing's *Init. and Pseud.*, vol. ii., p. 91.]
Boston, 1859

FRED Wilson's shed. By Nellie Grahame [Mrs Annie Dunning, *née* Ketchum]. Fcap 8vo. [Cushing's *Init. and Pseud.*, vol. i., p. 119.]
Philadelphia, 1870

FREDA ; a novel. By the author of *Mrs Jerningham's journal* [Mrs Fanny Hart, *née* Wheeler]. 3 vols. 8vo. [*Adv. Lib.*] London, 1878

FREDERIC Latimer : or, the history of a young man of fashion. [By J— G— Le Maistre.] 3 vols. Fcap 8vo. [*Bodl.*] London, 1799

FREDERICA and her guardians ; or, the perils of orphanhood. By the author of *Christie Redfern's Troubles* [Margaret Murray Robertson]. 8vo. Pp. 416. [Kirk's *Supp.*]
London, 1881
In an earlier edition (1874) the title begins : " The Perils of orphanhood . . ."

FREDERICK de Montford. [A novel.] By the author of *The pursuits of fashion* [Edward Goulbourne]. 3 vols. Fcap 8vo. [Watt's *Bibl. Brit.*]
London, 1812

FREDERICK Gordon ; or, principal and interest. By " Fleeta " [Kate W. Hamilton]. Fcap 8vo. [Cushing's *Init. and Pseud.*, vol. i., p. 103.]
Philadelphia, 1866

FREDERICK Morland. By the author of *Lochiel ; or, the field of Culloden*, etc. [David Carey]. 2 vols. Fcap 8vo. [*Camb. Univ. Lib.*] London, 1824

FREDERICK Rivers, Independent parson. By Mrs Florence Williamson [Rev. William Kirkus, LL.B.]. 8vo. [Cushing's *Init. and Pseud.*, vol. i., p. 155.] London, 1864

FREDERICK the Great and his court. By Louise Mühlbach [Mrs Clara Mundt, *née* Müller]. Pt 8vo. [Cushing's *Init. and Pseud.*, vol. i., p. 199.]
New York, 1887

FREDERICK the Great and his family :
translated from the German of Louise
Mühlbach [Mrs Clara Mundt, *née*
Müller]. Pt 8vo.   New York, 1867

FREE (a) address to Protestant Dissenters
as such.   By a Dissenter [Joseph
Priestley, LL.D.].   8vo.   [*D. N. B.*,
vol. 46, p. 367.]   London, 1769

FREE (a) address to those who have
petitioned for the repeal of the late Act
of Parliament, in favour of the Roman
Catholics. By a lover of peace and
truth [Joseph Priestley, LL.D.]. Fcap
8vo. [*Bodl.*]   London, 1780

FREE (the) agency of accountable
creatures examined with candour,
and defended in several letters. . . .
[By Rev. Samuel Fancourt, Dissenting minister.] 8vo. [*Brit. Mus.*]
London, 1733

FREE and calm consideration of the
misunderstandings between the Parliament of Great Britain and the American Colonies. By Philopolites [Rev.
Benjamin Prescott]. 8vo. [*Cushing's
Init. and Pseud.*, vol. i., p. 528.]
Salem, Mass., 1774

FREE (a) and candid disquisition on
religious establishments in general, and
the Church of England in particular :
occasioned by a visitation sermon
preached at Chelmsford, May 22, 1770
[by Rev. Nathaniel Forster].   To
which is prefixed, an answer to a
Letter from a clergyman [Rev. John
Firebrace] concerning subscription to
the xxxix Articles of the Church of
England. [By Rev. Benjamin Dawson,
LL.D., rector of Burgh in Suffolk.]
8vo. [*W.*]   London, 1771

FREE and candid disquisitions relating
to the Church of England, and the
means of advancing religion therein ;
addressed to the governing powers in
Church and State, and more immediately directed to the two Houses of
Convocation. [By Rev. John Jones.]
8vo. Pp. 367. [*D. N. B.*, vol. 30,
p. 127.]   London, 1749
    See below, a reply in " Free and impar-
tial considerations."

FREE (a) and candid examination of
Lord Bolingbroke's Letters on His-
tory. . . . [By Alexander Campbell.]
Part 1. 8vo. [*Brit. Mus.*]
London, [1753]
    The second edition begins, "Examina-
tion . . ."

FREE (a) and candid examination of
the principles advanced in the Right
Rev. [T. Sherlock] the Lord Bishop of
London's very elegant sermons, lately
published, and in his very ingenious
Discourses on Prophecy ; wherein the
commonly received system concerning
the natures of the Jewish and Christian
dispensations is particularly considered.
By the author of *The critical enquiry
into the opinions and practice of the
ancient philosophers*, etc. [Rev. John
Towne, M.A.]. 8vo. Pp. xii., 375.
[*D. N. B.*, vol. 57, p. 967.]

FREE and candid thoughts on the
doctrine of predestination. By T. E.
[Thomas Edwards] author of C[*a*]*n*[*o*]*ns
of* C*r*[*i*]*t*[*i*]*c*[*i*]*sm.* 8vo. [*Brit. Mus.*]
London, 1761

FREE (a) and familiar letter to that
great refiner of Pope and Shakespear,
the Rev. Mr William Warburton,
Preacher of Lincoln's-Inn ; with remarks upon the Epistle of friend A. E.,
in which his unhandsome treatment
of this celebrated writer is expos'd in
the manner it deserves. By a country
curate [Zachary Grey, LL.D.]. 8vo.
[*D. N. B.*, vol. 23, p. 219.]
London, 1750
    The " Epistle of friend A. E." is Zachary
Grey's " Word or two of advice, &c.,"
q.v.   The letters A. E. are the vowels in
Zachary Grey.

FREE and impartial considerations
upon the Free and candid disquisitions
relating to the Church of England.
Addressed to the author [John Jones]
of the Disquisitions. By a gentleman
[John White, B.D., vicar of Nayland,
Suffolk]. 8vo. Pp. 69. [*N. and Q.*,
June 1860, p. 448.]   London, 1751
    See above, the " Free and candid dis-
quisitions."

FREE (a) and impartial enquiry into
the extraordinary and advantageous
bargain, lately under the consideration
of Parliament, for remitting money
for the pay of the forces abroad [in
Hanover] for the year 1743. [By
Edmund Waller.] 8vo. [*Camb. Univ.
Cat.*]   London, 1743

FREE (a) and impartial inquiry into
the causes of that very great esteem
and honour that the Non-conforming
preachers are generally in with their
followers ; in a letter to his honoured
friend H. M. By a lover of the
Church of England, and unfeigned
piety. [By John Eachard.] Fcap 8vo.
Pp. 204. [*Aberd. Lib.*] London, 1673

FREE and impartial thoughts on the
sovereignty of God, the doctrines of
election, reprobation, and original sin ;
humbly addressed to all who believe
and profess these doctrines. [By
Richard Finch.] Second edition, corrected and enlarged. 8vo. Pp. 89.
Smith's *Cat. of Friends' Books*, i., 610.]
London, 1745

FREE (a) and necessary enquiry, whether the Church of England in her Liturgy, and many of her learned divines in their writings, have not, by some unwary expressions relating to transubstantiation and the real presence, given so great an advantage to Papists and Deists as may prove fatal to true religion, unless some remedy be speedily applied ? With remarks on the power of priestly absolution. By the author of *The System of divinity and morality* [Ferdinand Warner, LL.D.]. 8vo. [Watt's *Bibl. Brit.*]   London, 1755

FREE (the) and open Church Advocate. [Edited by Samuel Ralph Townshend Mayer.] 6 vols. 8vo. [*Brit. Mus.*]
                                London, 1872-88
New series.   London, 1893-4

FREE (a) and serious address to the Christian laity, especially such as, embracing Unitarian sentiments, conform to Trinitarian worship ; to which is prefixed an Introduction, wherein the worship of the Holy Scriptures is contrasted with the worship of the Church of England and of Dissenters. [By Joshua Toulmin, D.D.] 8vo. [*Brit. Mus.*]   London, 1781

FREE (a) and serious remonstrance to Protestant Dissenting ministers on occasion of the decay of religion ; with some observations on the education of youth for the ministry. By a layman [Nathaniel Neal]. 8vo. [*Brit. Mus.*]   London, 1746

FREE blacks, and slaves. By a Cambridge man [Henry Arthur Bright]. 8vo. [Cushing's *Init. and Pseud.*, vol. i., p. 49.]   London, 1853

FREE (the) Briton extraordinary ; or, a short review of the British affairs : in answer to a pamphlet intitled, A short view, with Remarks on the Treaty of Seville, &c., printed for R. Francklin. By Francis Walsingham, of the Inner-Temple, Esq. [William Arnall]. 8vo. Pp. 55. [Watt's *Bibl. Brit.*]   London, 1730
  Ascribed also to R— Arnold.

FREE (the) Briton's answer to the Pretender's Declaration : supposed to be wrote by . . . the Lord A—b—sh— of Y—ke [Archbishop of York]. [By Thomas Gordon.] 8vo. Dublin, 1745
  Signed " Montanus."

FREE (a) Church and a free trade. By a member of the Free Church [James Gall]. 8vo.   Edinburgh, [1844]

FREE (the) Church and her accusers in the matter of American slavery. [By Andrew Cameron, D.D.] 8vo. [*New Coll. Cat.*]   Edinburgh, 1846

FREE (the) Church and the higher criticism : being a letter to Professor W. R. Smith, on subjects treated in his contributions to the new edition of the " Encyclopaedia Britannica." By a layman [James Barnhill]. 8vo. Pp. 94. [*New Coll. Lib.*]
                                    Glasgow, 1877

FREE (the) Church hymn-book weighed in the balances and found wanting. [By William Nixon, D.D.] 8vo. [*New Coll. Lib.*]   Edinburgh, [1883]

FREE (the) Church ; its principles and pretensions examined, with special relation to the attitude of the English Presbyterian Church towards the Church of Scotland. By a layman [Andrew Macgeorge]. 8vo.
                                    Glasgow, 1873
  Republished in " Papers on the principles and real position of the Free Church," Glasgow, 1875, with the author's name at the Introductory note.

FREE Churchism. [By Rev. Charles Buchan.] 8vo.   Edinburgh, 1846

FREE Churchmen and Voluntaries ; may they honourably and consistently seek a union ? By an " Old-Light " Voluntary [Archibald Gillies, journalist]. 8vo. [*New Coll. Cat.*]
                                    Glasgow, 1853

FREE (a) disquisition concerning the law of entails in Scotland ; occasioned by some late proposals for amending that law. [By John Swinton, Senator of the College of Justice.] 8vo. Pp. 101. [*Scottish Law Tracts*, III.]
                                    Edinburgh, 1765

FREE (the) Enquirer. [By Peter Annet.] Vol. 1. Folio. Pp. 72. [*D. N. B.*, vol. 2, p. 9.]   London, 1761
  The Free Enquirer consists of nine numbers. It was published weekly, the first number being dated Saturday, October the 17th, 1761 ; and the ninth, Saturday, December the 12th, 1761. The periodical mode of weekly publication, being found inconvenient, was discontinued.

FREE (the) enquirer into the rights, privileges, franchises, bequests, funds, etc., belonging to the Fraternity of Merchant Taylors of St John the Baptist, London. [By Robert Hugh Franks.] 8vo.   London, 1831

FREE (a) enquiry into the authenticity of the first and second chapters of St Matthew's gospel. [By John Williams, LL.D.] 8vo. Pp. vii., 151. [*D. N. B.*, vol. 61, p. 421.]   London, 1771

Replies were issued by Charles Bulkley, William Magee, Caleb Fleming, and others.

FREE (a) enquiry into the enormous increase of attornies, with some serious reflections on the abuse of our excellent laws. By an unfeigned admirer of genuine British jurisprudence . . . [Henry Constantine Jennings]. 8vo. Pp. iv., 68. [*D. N. B.*, vol. 29, p. 329.]   Chelmsford, 1785

The author's name is given by Douce.

FREE (a) enquiry into the nature and origin of evil. In six letters to —— [By Soame Jenyns.] 8vo. [*D. N. B.*, vol. 29, p. 333.]   London, 1757

FREE (a) enquiry into the origin of the Fourth Gospel. By P. C. Sense [Bernard J. Sage, M.A., barrister]. 8vo. Pp. 464.   London, 1899

FREE (a) enquiry into the vulgarly receiv'd notion of nature ; made in an essay, address'd to a friend. By R. B., Fellow of the Royal Society [The Hon. Robert Boyle]. 8vo. [*Brit. Mus.*]   London, 168⅝

FREE (a) examination of the common methods employed to prevent the growth of Popery. [By James Usher.] 8vo. 2 parts. [Mendham Coll. *Cat.*, p. 312.]   London, 1766-68

FREE (a) farmer in a Free State [viz. Holland]. By "Home Counties" [J— W. Robertson Scott]. 8vo. Pp. 380. [*Lond. Lib. Cat.*]   London, 1912

FREE grace ; the experience and triumph of every true Christian. [By William Howell.] Fcap 8vo. Pp. 62.   Leeds, 1796

FREE (the) holders grand inqvest touching our soveraigne Lord the King and his Parliament. [By Sir Robert Filmer, Knt.] 4to. Pp. 71. Printed in the three and twentieth year of the raign of our Soveraigne Lord King Charles [1647].

"Ascribed to Sir Rob. Holbourne in a MS. note by Bp. Barlow in the above copy ; and by Wood in his notice of Holbourne in his Fasti ; but included in a list of Filmer's works prefixed to the tract by the latter on the Power of Kings, published in 1680."—MS. note in *Bodl. Cat.*

FREE (the) holders plea against stock-jobbing elections of Parliament men. [By Daniel Defoe.] 4to. [*Wilson's Life of Defoe*, p. 18.]   London, 1701

FREE (the) libraries of Scotland. By an Assistant librarian [Thomas Mason]. Cr 8vo. [Mitchell *Lib. Cat.*]   Glasgow, 1880

FREE notes on Herbert Spencer's "First Principles." [By —— Edmond.] Pt 8vo.   Edinburgh, 1878

Private information regarding the authorship.

FREE (a) Parliament proposed to tender consciences, and published for the use of the Members now elected. By Alazonomastix Philalethes [Henry More, D.D.]. 4to. [*Brit. Mus.*]   [London], 1660

FREE Parliaments ; or, a vindication of the Parliamentary constitution of England : in answer to certain visionary plans of modern reformers. [By John Almon.] 8vo. [*Watt's Bibl. Brit.*]   London, 1783

FREE Parliaments ; or an argument on their constitution, proving some of their powers to be independent : to which is added an Appendix of original letters and papers which passed between the Court of Hanover and a gentleman at London, touching the right of the Duke of Cumberland to reside in England and sit in Parliament. By the author of *The Britannic Constitution* [Roger Acherley]. 8vo. [*Brit. Mus.*]   London, 1731

FREE (a) Protestant people and a Popish prince incompatible : a sermon preached Nov. 10th, 1745, at the British chapel in St Petersburgh. By J. F. [James Foster], Rector of Beer Crocombe in the county of Somerset. 4to. [Green's *Bibl. Somers.*, vol. ii., p. 407.]   N.P., 1746

FREE (the) Public Library question discussed, with special reference to Aberdeen. By Sigma [James Sinclair]. 8vo. [*Aberd. Lib. Cat.*]   Aberdeen, 1883

FREE reflections on miscellaneous papers and legal instruments under the hand and seal of William Shakespeare, in the possession of Samuel Ireland, of Norfolk Street. . . . [By Francis Godolphin Waldron.] 8vo. [*Watt's Bibl. Brit.*]   London, 1796

FREE remarks on a sermon [by Richard Shepherd] entitled, "The requisition of subscription to the thirty nine Articles and liturgy of the Church of England not inconsistent with Christian liberty" : to which are prefixed, Reasons against subscribing a petition to Parliament for the abolition of such subscription. . . . By a friend to religious liberty [Rev. John Palmer, of Macclesfield]. 8vo. Pp. 63.   London, 1772

Contemporary attestation of authorship.

FREE remarks upon the conduct of the Whigs and Radical Reformers in Yorkshire. [By the Rev. William Atkinson.] 8vo.   Bradford, 1819

FREE soil, free soul. [A novel.] By Lucas Cleeve [Mrs Howard Kingscote, *née* Adelina G. I. Wolff]. Cr 8vo. [*Lit. Year Book.*]   London, 1903

FREE (the) state of the people of England maintained, in the renewed determination of three cases : 1. Concerning the Oath. 2. The association required under King William. 3. Succession. [By John Humphrey, M.A.] 4to. [Green's *Bibl. Somers.*, vol. ii., p. 507.]   London, 1701

FREE strictures on " An Address to candid and serious men," tending to refute the arguments brought forward . . . in favour of the restoration of all lapsed intelligences. [By —— Fisher, of Wisbeach.] 8vo.   London, 1799

FREE (the) Thinker : or, essays on ignorance, superstition, bigotry, enthusiasm, craft, &c. intermixed with several pieces of wit and humour. [By Ambrose Phillips, Hugh Boulter, Archb. of Armagh, Zachariah Pearce, Bp. of Rochester, the Rt. Hon. Richard West, the Rev. George Stubbs, the Rev. Gilbert Burnet, and the Rev. Henry Steele.] Second edition, with compleat indexes. 3 vols. Fcap 8vo. [Lowndes' *Bibl. Man.*, p. 839.]   London, 1733
See also below, " Freethinkers."

FREE thinking in matters of religion stated and recommended. By a Church of England divine [Edward Synge, D.D.]. 8vo.   London, 1727
Reprinted in vol. iii. of collected works.

FREE thinking rightly stated ; wherein a discourse (falsely so called) is fully considered. [By Thomas Cockman, D.D.] 8vo.   Pp. 131. [Darling's *Cyclop. Bibl.*]   London, 1763

FREE thoughts concerning souls, in four essays : I. Of the humane soul consider'd in its own nature ; II. Of the humane soul compared with the souls of brutes. III. Of the supposed prae-existent state of souls. IV. Of the future states of souls. . . . By the author of *The Impartial Inquiry*, etc. [Samuel Colliber]. 8vo. Pp. xiii., 168. [Ezra Abbot's *Lit. on a Future life*.]   London, 1734

FREE thoughts continu'd upon several points : Of predestination ; of redemption ; of the salvability of the heathen ; of the Judaical covenant ; of justification ; of the judge of faith, and the Scripture ; of venial sin ; of liturgical and conceiv'd prayer ; of demonstrative preaching ; of the authority of the laws of men ; of the power of the magistrate about religion ; of subjection to our present Queen. Unto which are added, Of free electing grace ; of this grace, its irresistibility ; of God's will, decree, and providence, in regard to sin ; of faith and works. . . . By a graue author of middle and unparty principles [John Humphrey]. 4to. Pp. iv., 64. [*Bodl.*]   London, 1712
The second part consists of 20 pages. At the end of Part II. there is a half-page containing what is called " A close to these points of controversy." This last has the author's name.

FREE thoughts in defence of a future state, as discoverable by natural reason, and stript of all superstitious appendages ; demonstrating, against the nominal Deists, that the consideration of future advantages is a just motive to virtue,—of future loss and misery, a powerful and becoming restraint of vice. By a divine of the Church of England [the Hon. Robert Day]. 8vo. Pp. 115. [Watt's *Bibl. Brit.*]   London, 1700

FREE thoughts on a general reform, addressed to every independent man : the truth, equally distant from the flimsy machinery of Messrs Burke, Reeves, and Co. as from the gross ribaldry of Thomas Paine and his party. By —— S— S. [Rev. Charles Lucas], M.A. of the University of Oxford. 8vo. [Watt's *Bibl. Brit.*]   Bath, 1796

FREE thoughts on despotic and free governments, as connected with the happiness of the governor and the governed. [By Rev. Joseph Townsend.] 8vo. Pp. 316. [Watt's *Bibl. Brit.*]   London, 1781

FREE thoughts on liberty and the Revolution in France. By the author of *A Letter to Earl Stanhope on the Test* [Rev. Charles Hawtrey, M.A.]. 8vo. [Nichols' *Lit. Anec.*, ix., 569.]   London, 1790
Ascribed also to Charles Hawkins. [*Gent. Mag.*, June 1792, p. 550.]

FREE thoughts on many subjects : a selection from " Fraser's Magazine." By a Manchester man [Rev. Robert Lamb]. 2 vols. 8vo. [*Manch. Free Lib. Cat.*]   Manchester, 1866

FREE thoughts on public affairs ; or, advice to a patriot, in a letter addressed to the old Opposition. [By William Hazlitt.] 8vo. [*D. N. B.*, vol. 25, p. 322.] London, 1806

FREE thoughts on religion, the Church and national happiness. By B. M. [Bernard de Mandeville]. 8vo. [*Brit. Mus.*] London, 1720

FREE thoughts on the Bath Missionary Society, and on the address to that Assembly by the Rev. Josiah Thomas, A.M., Archdeacon of Bath. By a friend to consistency [Edward Trapp Pilgrim]. 8vo. [Green's *Bibl. Somers.*, vol. ii., p. 516.] Bath, 1817

FREE thoughts on the late contested election for the borough of Shrewsbury. By an independent voter [Rowland Hunt]. 8vo. [*Bodl.*] [Shrewsbury], 1806

FREE thoughts on the late religious celebration of the funeral of Her Royal Highness the Princess Charlotte of Wales, and on the discussion to which it has given rise in Edinburgh. By Scoto-Britannus [Thomas M'Crie, D.D.]. 8vo. Pp. 78. [*New Coll. Lib.*] Edinburgh, 1817

FREE thoughts on the most probable means of reviving the Dissenting interest ; occasion'd by the late Enquiry into the causes of its decay [by S. Gough]. By a minister in the country [Philip Doddridge, D.D.]. 8vo. [*Brit. Mus.* ; *D. N. B.*, vol. 15, p. 163.] London, 1730
See note to the " Enquiry."

FREE thoughts on the present state of public affairs, in a letter to a friend. [By Rev. John Wesley.] 8vo. [*Brit. Mus.*] London, 1770
In reply there was published " A Letter to the Rev. J. W—." [By J. Towers, 1721.]

FREE thoughts on the proceedings of the Continental Congress, held at Philadelphia, Sept. 5, 1774 : wherein their errors are exhibited, their reasonings confuted, and the fatal tendency of their non-importation, non-exportation, and non-consumption measures, are laid open to the plainest understandings ; . . . in a letter to the farmers, and other inhabitants of North America in general, and to those of the province of New-York in particular. By a farmer [Samuel Seabury, D.D.]. 8vo. [Beardsley's *Life of Bishop Seabury*, p. 24.] N.P., 1774
Signed " A W. Farmer " [*i.e.* A Westchester farmer]. Mistakenly attributed to Isaac Wilkins.
A reply, similarly anonymous, was written by Alexander Hamilton. *See* " The Farmer refuted. . . ."

FREE thoughts on the subject of a farther reformation of the Church of England, in six numbers ; to which are added the Remarks of the editor. By the author of *A short and safe expedient for terminating the present debates about subscription* [John Jones, Rector of Sheephall, Herts]. Published by B. Dawson, LL.D., Rector of Burgh. 8vo. [*Brit. Mus.*] London, 1771

FREE thoughts on the toleration of Popery, deduced from a review of its principles and history, with respect to liberty and the interests of princes and nations ; wherein the question concerning the repeal of the penal statutes is examined, and some late acts of the British legislature are considered. By Calvinus Minor, Scoto-Britannus [Archibald Bruce, minister at Whitburn]. 8vo. [*New Coll. Cat.*] Edinburgh, 1780

FREE thoughts upon a Free enquiry [by John Williams, LL.D.] into the authenticity of the first and second chapters of St Matthew's Gospel ; addressed to the anonymous author : with a short prefatory defence of the purity and integrity of the New Testament canon. By Theophilus [Caleb Fleming, D.D.]. 8vo. London, [1772]

FREE thoughts upon Methodists, actors, and the influence of the stage. . . . By Robert Mansel [—— Hill], of the Theatres Royal, York and Hull. 8vo. [Lowe's *Bibl. of Theat. Lit.*, p. 231.] Hull, 1814

FREE thoughts upon the brute creation ; or an examination of Father Bougeant's philosophical amusement. [By John Hildrop, D.D.] 8vo. London, 1754
In vol. i. of his miscellaneous works.

FREE thoughts upon the late regulation of the post ; by which there is an arrival to, and departure of the mail from Edinburgh on the Christian Sabbath : being the substance of a letter from a gentleman in the country [Rev. John Brown, Haddington] to his friend in Edinburgh [John Watson, cooper in Leith.] 8vo. Edinburgh, 1787

FREE trade and its so-called sophisms ; a reply [by Edward Alfred Bowring and Lord Hobart] to " The Sophisms of Free trade," by a barrister [Sir John Barnard Byles]. Fcap 8vo. [*Brit. Mus.*] London, 1850
See also " The Sophisms of free trade."

FREE trade in corn the real interest of the landlord and the true policy of the State. By a Cumberland landowner [Sir James Robert George Graham]. 8vo. Pp. iv., 83. [*Brit. Mus.*] London, 1828
Attributed also to John Rooke.

FREE trade ; its failure as an economical policy. [By John Harris.] 8vo. [*Camb. Univ. Lib.*]   London, 1876

FREE trade ; or the meanes to make trade flourish. [By Edward Myselden.] 8vo.   London, 1622
Contemporary attestation of authorship.

FREE (the) trade struggle in England. By " Wheelbarrow " [M— M— Turnbull]. 8vo. [*Amer. Cat.*]
Chicago, 1895

FREE (a) translation of the preface [by Samuel Parr] to Bellendenus ; containing animated strictures on the great political characters of the present time. [By Wm. Beloc.] 8vo. London, 1788

FREE (a) ward or a free city. By C. J. B. [C— J— Burnett]. 8vo. [Robertson's *Aberd. Bibl.*]
[Aberdeen, 1882]

FREE will to freeholders. [By Charles Lucas.] 8vo. [*Camb. Univ. Lib.*]
London, 1753
Signed " C——s L——s."

FREE, yet forging their own chains. By C. M. Cornwall [Mary Abigail Roe]. Fcap 8vo. [*Cushing's Init. and Pseud.*, vol. i., p. 67.]
New York, 1876

FREEBOOTERS (the) ; a story of the Texan War. By Gustave Aimard [Ollivier Gloux : translated from the French by Sir F. C. Lascelles Wraxall]. 8vo. [*Brit. Mus.*]   London, 1861

FREE-BORN (the) subject ; or the Englishman's birthright asserted against all tyrannical usurpations, either in Church or State. [By Sir Roger Lestrange.] 4to. [Arber's *Term Cat.*, vol. i., p. 523.]   London, 1679

FREEDOM (the) of Henry Meredyth. [A novel.] By M. Hamilton [—— Spottiswoode-Ashe, later Mrs —— Churchill-Luck]. Cr 8vo. Pp. 287.
London, 1898

FREEDOM triumphant : fourth period of the war of the Rebellion, from Sept. 1864 to its close. By Carleton [Charles Carleton Coffin]. 8vo. [*Kirk's Supp.*]
New York, 1891

FREE-GRACE truths ; or, Gospel comfort for doubting minds. By the author of *The Spiritual Treasury* [William Mason, clock-maker]. 8vo. [*Darling's Cyclop. Bibl.*]   London, 1769

FREEHOLDER (the) ; or political essays. [By Joseph Addison.] 8vo. [*Biog. Brit.*, i., 51.]   London, 1716

FREEHOLDER'S (the) political catechism. [By Henry St John, Viscount Bolingbroke.] 8vo. [*Brit. Mus.*]   London, 1733
Printed in 1775 in " A collection of political tracts. By the author of the Dissertation upon parties."

FREEMAN'S (a) answer to the Freeholder's Address [signed Hibernicus, *i.e.* John D. Latouche] to the merchants, traders, and others . . . of the City of Dublin [on election of a Member of Parliament for Dublin]. [By Charles Lucas.] 8vo. [*Brit. Mus.*]   [Dublin ?], 1748
Signed " Britannicus."

FREEMASONRY ; its pretensions exposed. By a Master Mason [Henry Dana Ward]. Fcap 8vo. [*Cushing's Init. and Pseud.*, vol. i., p. 185.]
New York, 1828

FREEMASON'S (a) pocket companion ; containing a brief sketch of the history of masonry, a chronology of interesting events, etc. By a brother of the Apollo Lodge, 711, Oxford [Walter Bishop Mant, M.A.]. 8vo. Pp. vii., 116. [*Bodl.*]
London, A.L. 5831, A.D. 1831

FREEMASON'S (the) pocket companion, containing the origin, progress, and present state of the ancient fraternity ; the institution of the Grand Lodge of Scotland, list of Grand Masters, etc. [By William Auld.] 8vo.
Edinburgh, 1761

FREENESS (the) and sovereignty of God's justifying and electing grace. [By Mary Jane Graham.] 8vo. Pp. 121. [*Camb. Univ. Lib.*]
London, 1831

FREETHINKERS : a poem in dialogue. [By Anne Finch, Lady Winchilsea ?] 8vo.   London, 1811

FREEWILL, foreknowledge, and fate : a fragment. By Edward Search, Esq. [Abraham Tucker]. 8vo. Pp. xxxi., 268. [*Bodl.*]   London, 1763
The preface of the annotator is signed " Cuthbert Comment."

FREISCHUTZ (der) travestied. . . . With etchings from drawings from an amateur, A. Crowquill [Alfred Henry Forrester]. Royal 8vo. [*D. N. B.*, vol. 20, p. 6.]
London, 1824

FRENCH (the) Academie ; wherein is discoursed the institution of maners, and whatsoever els concerneth the good and happie life of all estates, and callings, by precepts of doctrine, and examples of the lives of ancient sages and famous men. By Peter de la Primaudaye, Esquire, Lord of the said place, and of Barree, one of the ordinarie gentlemen of the king's chamber : newly translated into English by T. B. [Thomas Bowes]. 4to. Second part, 1594. 4to. [Watt's *Bibl. Brit.*]
London, 1586

The translation of the first part bears the translator's name.

FRENCH (the) alphabeth ; with the Treasure of the French tung, containing the rarest sentences, prouerbes. . . . By G. D. L. M. N. [G. Delamothe, N.]. 8vo. [Lowndes' *Bibl. Man.*, p. 622.]
London, 1595

FRENCH and English exercises. . . . New edition. By M. L'Abbé Bossut [Sir Richard Phillips]. 12mo. [*Bibliographer*, vol. 4, p. 168.]
London, 1819

See the note to "A Biographical classbook."

FRENCH (the) and English impostours detected ; or Zach. Housel and D. [William] Coward tryed by the word of God and cast : wherein also the errors of D. Coward, in his late book call'd "Second thoughts," are laid open, shewing what cause he had to think again ; and the immortality of the soul fully evinced, in the form of a tryal. [By Benjamin Keach.] Fcap 8vo. [Arber's *Term Cat.*, iii., 318 ; Whitley's *Bapt. Bibl.*, i., 138.]
London, 1702

FRENCH authors at home. Episodes in the lives and works of Balzac—Madame de Girardin—George Sand—Lamartine — Léon Gozlan — Lamennais—Victor Hugo, etc. By the author of *Heroes, philosophers, and courtiers of the times of Louis XVI.*, etc. [Mrs Annie Emma Challice]. 2 vols. 8vo. [*Adv. Lib.*]
London, 1864

FRENCH (the) conjuror ; a comedy, as it is acted at the Duke of York's Theatre. Written by T. P., Gent. [Thomas Porter]. 4to. Pp. 55. [*Brit. Mus.*]
London, 1678

FRENCH (the) flogg'd ; or, the British sailors in America : a farce of two acts, as it was performed at the Theatre Royal, Covent-Garden. [Generally ascribed to George Alexander Stevens.] 8vo. Pp. 21. [*Biog. Dram.*]
London, 1767

FRENCH (the) gardiner, instructing how to cultivate all sorts of fruit trees and herbs for the garden. . . . First written [in French] by R. D. C. D. V., B. D. N. [*i.e.* N— De Bonnefons, valet de Chambre du Roi], and now translated into English by Philocepos [John Evelyn]. 8vo. [*D. N. B.*, vol. 18, p. 82.]
London, 1658

The order of the initials is reversed. A later edition (1669) gives the translator's name.

FRENCH (the) genders taught in six tables. By the master of a Grammar-school [W— R— Goodluck]. 8vo. [Cushing's *Init. and Pseud.*, vol. ii., p. 96.]
Boston, 1826

FRENCH (a) heiress in her own château. By the author of *One only* [Eleanor C. Price]. 8vo. [Kirk's *Supp.*]
London, 1878

FRENCH history for English children. By Sara Brook [Caroline Emelia Stephen]. Pt 8vo. [Kirk's *Supp.*] London, 1881

FRENCH home life ; being essays on manners, dress, language, etc. [By Frederick Marshall.] Pp. 345. [*Brit. Mus.*]
Edinburgh, 1873

Originally published in *Blackwood's Magazine.*

FRENCH (the) in Africa. Algiers and Morocco. [By David Urquhart.] From the Portfolio, etc. 8vo. Pp. 56. [*Brit. Mus.*]
London, 1844

FRENCH (the) in England ; or, both sides of the question, on both sides of the Channel. [By William Hepworth Dixon.] 8vo. [*Brit. Mus.*]
London, 1852

FRENCH Janet. By Sarah Tytler [Henrietta Keddie], the author of *Citoyenne Jacqueline.* Fcap 8vo. [*Lit. Year Book.*]
London, 1890

FRENCH (the) King's thanks to the Tories of Great Britain. [By Benjamin Hoadly.] Folio. Pp. 2. [*Bodl.*]
[London], 1710

FRENCH philosophical dictionary, in English. [By François M. Arouet de Voltaire.] 8vo. [*Brit. Mus.*]
London, 1755

FRENCH pictures in English chalk. By the author of *The member for Paris* [Eustace Clare Grenville Murray]. 8vo. Pp. 410. [*Brit. Mus.*]
London, 1876

FRENCH (the) plot found out against the English Church; or, a manifesto upon the unequalness of the distribution of the 15000l of the money of the royal beneficence given every year to the French Protestants; the sufferings of the ecclesiastick proselytes from the French committee and its league: together with their petition humbly presented to the King and Parliament against the said committee and its league. . . . By the body of the ecclesiastick proselytes. [By Michael Malard.] 8vo. [*Bodl.*]
London, 1718

FRENCH (the) Revolution; a poem. Book the first. [By William Blake.] 8vo. [Courtney's *Secrets*, p. 124.]
London, 1791

FRENCH (the) rogue; or the life of Mon. Ragoue de Versailles; containing his parentage, monstrous birth, early rogueries, witty pranks, not only in France but in other countries. . . . Done from the original [of Charles de Fieux, Chevalier de Mouhy] by J. S. Fcap 8vo. [Arber's *Term Cat.*, ii., p. 522.]
London, 1694

FRENCH (the) schoole-master . . . first collected by Mr C. H. [C— Holy-Band], and now very much inlarged. Fcap 8vo.
London, 1649
"Holy-Band" is the English rendering of Saint Liens.

FRENCH (the) spy, or the Memoires of [Jean Baptiste de] La Fontaine, Lord of Savoy and Fontenai, late Brigadeer and Surveyor of the French King's Army, now prisoner in the Bastile: containing many secret transactions relating both to England and France. Translated from the French original [of Gatien de Courtilz de Sandras], printed at Cologne. 8vo. [Arber's *Term Cat.*, iii., 171.]
London, 1700

FRENCH thoughts on Irish evils. Translated from the "Revue des deux Mondes," with notes by a son of the soil [General Sir Justin Sheil]. Pt 8vo.
London, 1868

FRENCH windows. By John Ayscough [Rev. Monsignor Francis Bickerstaffe-Drew]. Cr 8vo. Pp. 302. [*Brit. Mus.*]
London, 1917

FRENCHIFIED (the) lady never in Paris; taken from Dryden and Colley Cibber, poets laureat. Acted at the Theatre-Royal in Covent-Garden, with universal applause. [By Henry Dell.] 8vo. Pp. ii., 40. [*Biog. Dram.*]
London, 1757

FRENCHMAN (the) and the Spaniard; or, the two great lights of the world displayed in lively character. Translated . . . by R. G. [Robert Gontilis]. Fcap 8vo. [*Brit. Mus.*] London, 1642

FRENCHMAN (a) in America. By Max O'Rell [Paul Blouet]. Pt 8vo. [*Lond. Lib. Cat.*] London, 1889

FRENCHMAN'S (a) visit to England, and the Crystal Palace; all he saw there, with his remarks upon England and the English people in general, and London in particular: translated into English by a Belgian, revised and corrected by an American, printed by a Prussian, published everywhere, and dedicated to everybody. [By Henry Curling.] 8vo. [*Adv. Lib.*]
London, 1851

FRENCHMAN'S (the) ward. By Clara Vance [Mrs Mary Andrews Denison]. Pt 8vo. [Cushing's *Init. and Pseud.*, vol. i., p. 292.] New York, 1892

FREQUENT communion; or, the advantages and necessity of it asserted and proved from Scripture, authority, and tradition. By A. C. [Alexander Mackenzie, *alias* Clinton, S.J.]. Fcap 8vo. Pp. 406. London, 1780
A later edition (Dublin [1820?]) shows variation of title: "Guide (a) to the altar; or the advantages of frequent communion. . . ."

FREQUENTED (the) village; or, the prospect of liberty: a poem. By a gentleman of the Middle Temple [Anthony King, LL.D.]. 4to. [O'Donoghue's *Poets of Ireland.*]
London, 1771
A later edition appeared at Dublin, 1797.

FRERES (the): a novel. By Mrs Alexander [Mrs Alexander Hector, *née* Annie French]. 8vo. London, 1886

FRESCOES, etc. Dramatic sketches. By "Ouida" [Louise De la Ramée]. 8vo. [*Camb. Univ. Lib.*] London, 1883

FRESH air. By Amy Lothrop [Anna B— Warner]. Fcap 8vo. [*Amer. Cat.*] New York, 1900

FRESH flowers for children. By a mother [Mrs Geo. W. Gordon]. 8vo. [Cushing's *Init. and Pseud.*]
Boston, 1851

FRESH leaves and green pastures. By the author of *Leaves from a life* [Mrs Jane Ellen Panton]. 8vo. Pp. 390. [*Lond. Lib. Cat.*] London, 1909

FRESH (a) memorial of the Kingdom of Christ; demonstrating from the solemn oath of Christ, Rev. x., by express letter of Scripture, and most historical matter of fact, it must need enter its succession, 1697. By T. B. [Thomas Beverley]. 8vo. [Arber's *Term Cat.*, vol. ii., p. 584.] London, 1696

FRESH religious thoughts and truths for the people. By the author of *Studies in Divine Things* [Rev. William Newton]. 8vo. [*Brit. Mus.*]　　　London, 1865

FRESH (a) suit against Independency; or the National Church-way vindicated, the Independent Church-way condemned. . . . By the author of the *Stop to the course of Separation* [Thomas Lamb]. Fcap 8vo. [*Arber's Term Cat.*, vol. i., p. 523.]　　　London, 1677

FRESH woods and pastures new. By the author of *An amateur angler's days in Dove Dale* [Edward Marston, publisher]. Pt 4to. Pp. x., 136. [*Brit. Mus.*]　　　London, 1887
　　The dedication is signed " E. M."

FRESHER'S (the) Don't. By a sympathiser (B. A.) [Arthur John Story]. 8vo. Sixth edition. [*Camb. Univ. Lib.*]　　　Cambridge, [1902 ?]

FRIAR (the) disciplin'd; or animadversions on Friar P. Walsh his new remonstrant religion. . . . Taken out of his History and Vindication of the loyal formulary. The author R. W. [Robert Wilson, *alias* Peter Talbot, Roman Catholic Archbishop of Dublin]. 4to. [*Brit. Mus.*]　　　Gant, 1674
　　Dedication signed " N. N."

FRIAR'S (a) scourge; nonsense verses. [By Mary S. Cotton, Viscountess Combermere.] 8vo. Pp. 170. [*Brit. Mus.*]　　　London, 1876

FRIARSWOOD Post-office. By the author of *The heir of Redclyffe* [Charlotte Mary Yonge]. Sixth edition. Fcap 8vo. Pp. 290.　　　London, 1874

FRIBBLERIAD (the). [By David Garrick.] 4to. [*Gent. Mag.*, xlix., 227; *Mon. Rev.*, xxiv., 444.] N.P., 1761

FRIEND (the); a weekly essay. [By William Fox, attorney-at-law.] 8vo. Pp. 184.　　　London, [1796]
　　The above contains 22 numbers.

FRIEND and foe. . . . By Alan-a-Dale [George Curnock]. 8vo.　　　London, 1898

FRIEND (the): from the French of Henri Greville [Madame Alice Marie Celeste Fleury Durand]. Fcap 8vo. [*Lond. Lib. Cat.*]　　　New York, 1891

" FRIEND " (the) in his family; or a familiar exposition of some of the religious principles of the Society of Friends; with brief biographical notices of a few of its early members. [By James Boorne.] 8vo. Pp. vii., 309. [Smith's *Cat. of Friends' Books*, i., 298.]　　　London, 1865

FRIEND (a) in need; a romance. [By Mrs T— E— Freeman.] 8vo. [*Brit. Mus.*]　　　London, 1858

FRIEND (a) in need, and other stories. By A. L. O. E., author of *The silver casket*, etc. [Charlotte Maria Tucker]. 8vo. Pp. 120.　　　London, 1873

FRIEND MacAuslan. By the author of *The Calton ballads* [Rev. Hugh M. Campbell, M.A.]. 8vo. [Scott's *Fasti.*]　　　London, 1910

FRIEND Macdonald. By Max O'Rell [Paul Blouet]. 8vo. [*Brit. Mus.*]　　　London, 1887

FRIEND (the) of Australia; or a plan for exploring the interior and for carrying on a survey of . . . Australia. By a retired Officer of the Hon. East India Company's Service [Allen Francis Gardiner]. 8vo. [*Edin. Univ. Lib.*]　　　London, 1830

FRIEND (the) of peace: containing a special interview between the President of the United States, and Omar, an officer dismissed for duelling. . . . By Philo Pacificus [Noah Worcester, D.D.]. 8vo. [Cushing's *Init. and Pseud.*, vol. i., p. 599.]　　　Cambridge, [Mass.], 1815

FRIEND Perditus. [A novel.] By Mary H. Tennyson [Mary Howard Folkard]. 2 vols. Cr 8vo. [*Lond. Lib. Cat.*]　　　London, 1891

FRIENDLY (a) address to all reasonable Americans, on the subject of our political confusions; in which the necessary consequences of violently opposing the king's troops, and of a general non-importation, are fairly stated. [By Myles Cooper, D.D.] 8vo. Pp. 56. [Evans' *Amer. Bibl.*, vol. 5, p. 20.]　　　London, 1774
　　This London reprint of the New York edition professes to be the work of " A W. Farmer," a pseudonym assumed by Bishop Samuel Seabury. *See above*, " Free thoughts on the proceedings. . . ."

FRIENDLY address to the Dissenters of Scotland, by ministers of the Established Church. [By Robert Smith Candlish, D.D.] 8vo. [*New Coll. Cat.*]　　　Edinburgh, 1840
　　See later, the " Friendly reply."

FRIENDLY address to the poor of the Hundred of Blything. [By R. G. White.] 8vo. [*Brit. Mus.*]　　　Ipswich, 1746

FRIENDLY (a) address to the seamen of the British navy. [By Vice-Admiral Sir Charles Vinicombe Penrose.] 8vo. [Boase and Courtney's *Bibl. Corn.*, ii., 454.]　　　Bodmin, 1820

FRIENDLY (a) address to the Volunteers of Great Britain. [By Rev. Edward Patteson, of Richmond, Surrey.] 8vo. [*Mon. Rev.*, xlii., 208.]
London, 1803

FRIENDLY (a) admonition to the drinkers of gin, brandy, and other spirituous liquors. [By Stephen Hales.] 8vo. [*Brit. Mus.*]
London, 1734

FRIENDLY advice from a minister to the servants of his parish. [By Rev. Richard Cecil.] Fcap 8vo. [*Brit. Mus.*] London, 1793
Reprints have frequently been issued.

FRIENDLY advice, in the spirit of love, unto believing parents and their tender offspring, in relation to their Christian education. The third edition. With additional caution and counsel unto young men and maidens. By J. F. [John Field]. 12mo. [*Supp.* to Smith's *Cat. of Friends' Books*, p. 122.] London, 1695

FRIENDLY advice most respectfully submitted to the Lords on the Reform Bill. [By Henry, Lord Brougham.] 8vo. Pp. 31. [Ralph Thomas' *Bibl. of Lord Brougham.*] London, 1831

FRIENDLY advice to children, and all mankind in general. . . . By a lover of truth and mankind universally [Francis Hatt]. 8vo. N.P., 1765

FRIENDLY advice to labouring people and others who have small incomes, especially to those persons who have families of children, and to the overseers of the poor, &c.; shewing the great advantages, in point of comfort, health, nutriment, & economy, which may be derived by a better mode of selecting and dressing animal and vegetable food, than is commonly in use ; and by habits of sobriety, virtue, and good management. [By Frederick Smith.] 8vo. [Smith's *Cat. of Friends' Books*, i., 85 ; ii., 584.]
Chelsea, N.D.

FRIENDLY advice to parents on the management and education of their children. By the author of *Hints for the improvement of early education and nursery discipline* [Mrs Louisa Hoare]. 12mo. Pp. 32. [*Supp.* to Smith's *Cat. of Friends' Books*, p. 192.]
London, [*c.* 1830]
Other editions have slightly modified titles.

FRIENDLY advice to the Conservatives. [By Charles Theophilus Metcalfe, Baron Metcalfe.] 8vo. [*D. N. B.*, vol. 37, p. 305.] London, 1838

FRIENDLY advice to the gentlemen-planters of the East and West Indies. In three parts. I. A brief treatise of the most principal fruits and herbs that grow in the East and West Indies ; giving an account of their respective vertues both for food and physick. . . . II. The complaints of the negro-slaves against the hard usages and barbarous cruelties inflicted upon them. III. A discourse, in way of dialogues, between an Ethiopian or negro-slave and a Christian that was his master in America. By Philotheos Physiologus [Thomas Tryon]. 8vo. Pp. 226. [*Bodl.*] [London], 1684

FRIENDLY and seasonable advice to the Roman Catholics of England. [By Thomas Comber, D.D.] Fcap 8vo. [Jones' Peck, ii., 286.] London, 1685
The fourth edition, 1686, has the author's name.

FRIENDLY (a) call, or a seasonable perswasive to unity ; directed to all Nonconformists and Dissenters in religion from the Church of England, as the only secure means to frustrate and prevent all Popish plots and designs against the peace of this kingdom, both in Church and State. By a lover of the truth and a friend to peace and unity [William Allen, D.D., Vicar of Bridgwater]. 8vo. [Green's *Bibl. Somers.*, ii., 109.] London, 1679

FRIENDLY (a) call to union, addressed to the managers of St Paul's [Episcopal] chapel, Aberdeen. [By John Hay Forbes, Lord Medwyn.] Fcap 8vo. Pp. 36. [*New Coll. Cat.*]
Edinburgh, 1823

FRIENDLY (a) caution ; or first gift of Theophilus Philanthropos, Student in Physick [Robert Poole, M.D.]. Cr 8vo. Pp. viii., 71. [*New Coll. Cat.*] London, 1740

FRIENDLY (a) conclusion occasioned by the Letters of Agnostos to Andrew Fuller. [By Dan Taylor.] 8vo. [Whitley's *Bapt. Bibl.*, ii.] 1790

FRIENDLY (a) conference between a minister and a parishioner of his, inclining to Quakerism ; wherein the absurd opinions of that sect are detected, and exposed to a just censure. By a lover of truth [Edward Fowler, D.D.]. 8vo. [Smith's *Anti-Quak.*, p. 19.] London, 1676
The authorship is doubtful.

FRIENDLY (the) conference ; or, a discourse between the country man and his nephew, who having fallen off from hearing, hath for some years been a

follower of Mr [John] M'Millan : wherein his objections against the Church and State being proposed, are answered ; the conduct of the Church in the matter of the Union, and in several other publick affairs, is fairly hinted, and vindicated.   The manifold difference between Mr M'Millan & Mr James Renwick with the worthies that went before him, is clearly though briefly illustrated. . . . [By Thomas Lin, Junr.] 4to. Pp. 56. [*Adv. Lib.*]
Edinburgh, 1711

FRIENDLY (the) dæmon, or the generous apparition ; being a true narrative of a miraculous cure newly perform'd upon that famous deaf and dumb gentleman, Dr Duncan Campbel, by a familiar spirit that appear'd to him in a white surplice, like a cathedral singing boy. [By Daniel Defoe.] 8vo. [Wilson's *Life of Defoe*.]
London, 1726

FRIENDLY (a) debate between a Conformist and a Non-conformist. [By Symon Patrick, D.D.] 8vo. [*Brit. Mus.*]   London, 1669
    Several editions were issued. There appeared also " A continuation of the Friendly debate," " A further Continuation . . . " and " An appendix to the third part of the Friendly debate. . . ."

FRIENDLY (a) debate between a Roman Catholick and a Protestant, concerning the doctrine of transubstantiation ; wherein the said doctrine is utterly confuted. . . . [By Thomas Tenison, D.D.] 4to. [Jones' Peck.]
London, 1688

FRIENDLY (a) debate ; or, a dialogue between Academicus and . . . Mundungus, two eminent physicians, about some of their late performances. By Sawney [William Douglas, M.D.]. 8vo. [Cushing's *Init. and Pseud.*, vol. i., p. 261.]   Boston, 1722

FRIENDLY (a) dialogue, between a common Unitarian Christian and an Athanasian, occasioned by the behaviour of the former during some parts of the public service ; or, an attempt to restore scripture forms of worship. [By William Hopkins, Arian.] Fcap 8vo.   London, 1784
—— To which is added, a second dialogue between Eugenius and Theophilus on the same subject. [By John Disney.] Second edition. Fcap 8vo. [*Brit. Mus.*]   London, 1787

FRIENDLY (the) disputants ; or, future punishment reconsidered. By Aura, author of *Ashburn* [Mary Catharine Irvine]. 8vo. Pp. x., 490. [*Brit. Mus.*]   London, 1859

VOL. II.

FRIENDLY (a) epistle by way of reproof from one of the people called Quakers, to Thomas Bradbury, a dealer in many words. [By Daniel Defoe.]   Fourth edition. 8vo. [Wilson's *Life of Defoe*, 155.]   London, 1715

FRIENDLY (a) epistle from a Restorationist clergyman to his parishioners. [By Rev.   Charles   Hudson.] 8vo. [Cushing's *Init. and Pseud.*, vol. ii., p. 130.]   Mendon, Mass., 1834

FRIENDLY (a) epistle to Mr George Keith, and the reformed Quakers at Turner's-Hall ; with some animadversions on a Discourse about a right administrator of Baptism, and of Episcopacy. . . . By Calvin Philanax [Samuel Young]. Fcap 8vo. [Smith's *Anti-Quak.*, p. 461.]   London, 1698

FRIENDLY (a) epistle to the Reverend clergy and Nonconforming divines who greatly approve of my late epistle to Mr George Keith, against plunging, and for sprinkling in baptism.   By Trepidantium Malleus [Samuel Young]. Fcap 8vo.   [Whitley's *Bapt. Bibl.*, i., 135.]   London, 1700

FRIENDLY epistles to Mr George Keith and the reformed Quakers, who are now convinc'd that water baptism is an ordinance of Christ, to continue to the end of the world, but are inquiring about the mode and form of administration. . . . By the reformed Quakers' old friend, Trepidantium Malleus [Samuel Young]. Fcap 8vo. [Smith's *Anti-Quak.*, p. 460.]
N.P., [1699 ?]

FRIENDLY foes.   A novel.   By Sarah Tytler [Henrietta Keddie]. 8vo. [*Lit. Year Book.*]   London, 1903

FRIENDLY hints to young gentlemen who are or intend to be bound by articles to attorneys or solicitors. [By John Folton ?]   Fourth edition. 8vo. [*Brit. Mus.*]   London, 1751

FRIENDLY (a) letter from honest Tom Boggy to the Reverend Mr G—d [Thos. Goddard], Canon of Windsor ; occasion'd by a sermon against censure, preach'd in St George's Chappel. [By William King, LL.D.] 8vo. [*D. N. B.*, vol. 31, p. 162.]   London, 1710
    This was followed by " A second letter."

FRIENDLY (a) letter to Dr [Richard] Bentley, occasioned by his new edition of Paradise Lost.   By a gentleman of Christ Church College, Oxon [rather by Edmond Miller, Fellow of Trinity College,   Cambridge]. 8vo. [Bartholomew's *Cat. of Camb. Books.*]
London, 1732
    Signed " Semicolon."
    Wrongly assigned to Dr Zachary Pearce.

Y

FRIENDLY (a) letter to John and Charles Wesley, wrote for the sake of their followers who are or may be dissatisfied with their way of worship. By [Thomas Burton] a person that found occasion to withdraw from their Society and join with the people called Quakers. 8vo. [Smith's *Anti-Quak.*, p. 447.] 8vo.   London, 1747

FRIENDLY letters on the recent strikes, from a manufacturer to his own workpeople. [By Samuel Robinson.] Fcap 8vo. [*Brit. Mus.*]
London, 1854
Signed " S. R."

FRIENDLY (the) monitor ; or, dialogues for youth. . . . By the author of the *Polite Reasoner*, etc. [Mary Weightman]. Fcap 8vo. [*Brit. Mus.*]
London, 1791

FRIENDLY (a) rebuke to one Parson Benjamin ; particularly relating to his quarrelling with his own Church, and vindicating the Dissenters. By one of the people called Quakers [Daniel Defoe]. 8vo. [Lee's *Defoe*.]
London, 1719

FRIENDLY remarks occasioned by the spirit and doctrines contained in the Rev. Mr [John William] Fletcher's Vindication, and more particularly in his Second Check to Antinomianism . . . in a letter to the author. By * * *, M.A. [Rowland Hill]. 8vo. Pp. 72. [R. Green's *Anti-Meth. Publ.*, p. 118.]   London, 1772
Wrongly attributed to Sir Richard Hill.

FRIENDLY remarks upon some particulars of his administration, in a letter to Mr Pitt. By a near observer [Maurice Montagu]. 8vo. [*Lond. Lib. Cat.*]   London, 1796

FRIENDLY reply to the " Friendly address to the Dissenters of Scotland, by ministers of the Established Church." By dissenting ministers [chiefly Hugh Heugh, D.D.] 8vo. [*New Coll. Cat.*]
Edinburgh, 1841
See above, the " Friendly address to the Dissenters."

FRIENDLY thoughts. [Verse.] By Ellis Walton [Mrs F— Percy Cotton]. Fcap 8vo.   London, 1900

FRIENDLY (a) visit to the house of mourning. [By Rev. Richard Cecil.] Fcap 8vo. [*Brit. Mus.*] London, 1792
Frequently reprinted.

FRIENDS (the) ; a sentimental history ; describing love as a virtue, as well as a passion. [By William Guthrie.] 2 vols. Fcap 8vo. [Watt's *Bibl. Brit.*]
London, 1754

FRIENDS and acquaintances. By the author of *Episodes in an obscure life* [Richard Rowe]. 3 vols. 8vo. Pp. 459. [*Camb. Univ. Lib.*]   London, 1878

FRIEND'S (a) book. By Anatole France [Jacques Anatole Thibault] : a translation by J. Lewis May. 8vo. Pp. 296. [*Lit. Year Book.*]
London, 1913

FRIEND'S (a) gift. [Poems and letters.] By a lady [Mrs Elizabeth Hamilton]. Fcap 8vo. [*Aberd. Free Lib. Cat.*] Private print.
London, 1839

FRIENDS in council ; a series of readings and discourse thereon. [By Sir Arthur Helps.] Two parts. 8vo. [*D. N. B.*, vol. 25, p. 372.]
London, 1847-59

FRIENDS in council : some thoughts for next summer. [By Sir Arthur Helps.] 8vo. Private print.
[London, 1853 ?]

FRIENDS in fur and feathers. By Gwynfryn [Olive Thorne Miller]. 8vo. [Cushing's *Init. and Pseud.*, vol. ii., p. 68.]   London, 1882

FRIENDS of fate. [A novel.] By Lucas Cleeve [Mrs Howard Kingscote, *née* Adelina G. I. Wolff]. Cr 8vo. Pp. 316. [*Lit. Year Book.*]
London, 1911

FRIENDS (the) of Jesus. By the author of *Doing and suffering*, etc. [Charlotte Bickersteth, later Mrs Wheeler]. 8vo. [*Brit. Mus.*]
London, [1865]

FRIENDS (the) of Voltaire. By S. G. Tallentyre [E. Beatrice Hall]. Cr 8vo. [*Lit. Year Book.*]   London, 1906

FRIENDS or foes : a sequel to " Is Russia wrong ? " By O. K. [Olga Kiryeeva, afterwards Madame Novikoff]. 8vo. [*Brit. Mus.*]
London, 1878

FRIENDS till death. By Hesba Stretton, author of *Jessica's first prayer*, etc. [Sarah Smith]. 8vo. Pp. 52.
London, 1876
See the note to " Alone in London."

FRIENDSHIP : a poem. By Ace of Clubs [J. C. Loftin]. 8vo. [Cushing's *Init. and Pseud.*, vol. i., p. 5.]
Montgomery, Alabama, 1871

FRIENDSHIP ; a satire. [By Edward Burnaby Greene.] 4to. [*Camb. Univ. Lib.*]   London, 1763

FRIENDSHIP ; a story. By Ouida, author of *Puck*, etc. [Louise De La Ramée]. 3 vols. Cr 8vo. [*Lit. Year Book.*]   London, 1878

FRIENDSHIP, and other poems. By Hibernicus [William Edward Hartpole Lecky, M.A.]. Fcap 8vo. [*D.N.B.*, Second Supp., vol. 2, p. 436.]
London, 1859
This was the author's first publication.

FRIENDSHIP (the) and virtue of Jonathan and David ; a political sermon, which never was, nor ever will be preached. [By Caleb Fleming, D.D.] 8vo. [*Brit. Mus.*]   London, 1765

FRIENDSHIP in death ; in twenty letters [signed " Clerimont "] from the dead to the living : to which are added, Letters moral and entertaining, in prose and verse. [By Mrs Elizabeth Rowe, *née* Singer.] Fourth edition. 8vo. Pp. 259. [Courtney's *Secrets*, p. 43.]   London, 1737

FRIENDSHIP (the) of Christ ; to which is added a description of charity, as one of the most remarkable and principal fruits of this friendship, appearing in the lives of true penitent believers. By a true son of the Church of Scotland [William Cheyne]. 8vo. Pp. 82.   Edinburgh, 1718
The Dedication is signed "W. C."

FRIENDSHIP, the good and perfect gift. By Ruth Ogden [Mrs Fannie O. Ide]. Fcap 8vo. [*Amer. Cat.*]
New York, 1903

FRIERS (the) chronicle ; or, the true legend of priests and monkes lives. [By Thomas Goad.] 4to. [*Brit. Mus.*]   London, 1623
The preface is signed " T. G."

FRIEZE and fustian. [A novel.] By M. E. Francis [Mary Evans Sweetman, later Mrs Francis Blundell]. Cr 8vo. [*Lit. Year Book.*]
London, 1896

FRIGHT (the). By the author of *The heiress*, etc. [Ellen Pickering]. 3 vols. Fcap 8vo. [*Adv. Lib.*] London, 1839

FRISKY (a) matron. By Percy Lysle [William Patrick Lynam]. 8vo. [*Brit. Mus.*]   London, 1897

FRITHIOF'S Saga. . . . By Esaias Tegnér. Translated from the original Swedish by G. S. [George Stephens, archaeologist]. 8vo. [*N. and Q.*, Feb. 1869, p. 168.]   Stockholm, 1839

FRITHIOF'S Saga ; or the legend of Saga. . . . By Esaias Tegnér. Translated from the Swedish [by H. G. and W. E. F., *i.e.* William Edward Frye]. 8vo. Pp. 246. [*Brit. Mus.*]
London, 1835

FRITILLARIES : a book of verse. By W. J. F. [William John Ferrar]. 8vo.   Oxford, 1892

FRIVOLOUS Cupid. By Anthony Hope [Anthony Hope Hawkins]. Fcap 8vo. Pp. 223. [*Lit. Year Book.*]
New York, 1895

FRIVOLOUS Glasgow. By Mark Allerton [William Ernest Cameron, LL.B.]. Fcap 8vo. [*Lit. Year Book.*]
Glasgow, 1903

FROGGY'S little brother. By Brenda [Mrs Castle Smith]. 8vo. [*Brit. Mus.*]   London, 1875

FROGS (the) [of Aristophanes ; translated by John Hookham Frere]. 4to. Pp. 79. [*D. N. B.*, vol. 20, p. 269.]
[London], 1839
No separate title-page. Intended for private circulation.

FROLICK (a) to Horn-fair. With a walk from Cuckold's-Point thro' Deptford and Greenwich. [By Edward Ward.] Folio. [*Bodl.*]
London, 1700

FROLICS (the) of Puck. [A novel. By George Soane.] 3 vols. Fcap 8vo. [*Camb. Univ. Lib.*]
London, 1834

FROM a common-room window. By Orbilius [E— M— Johnstone]. 8vo.
London, 1920
The author's name is given in a later edition.

FROM a friend's garden. By A. L. W. [Mrs Alice L. Williams]. Fcap 8vo. [*Amer. Cat.*]   Boston, 1886

FROM a quiet place. Discourses by the author of *The recreations of a country parson* [Andrew K. H. Boyd, D.D.]. 8vo. [*Brit. Mus.*]   London, 1879

FROM Calcutta to the snowy range ; being the narrative of a trip through the Upper Provinces of India to the Himalayas ; containing an account of Monghyr, Benares, Allahabad, Cawnpore, Lucknow, Agra, Delhi, and Simla. By an old Indian [F— F— Wyman]. 8vo. [*Calc. Imp. Lib.*]
London, 1866
Signed " F. F. W."
Attributed also to Francis Faithful Warden.

FROM clue to capture ; a series of thrilling detective stories. By Dick Donovan [Joyce E. P. Muddock]. Cr 8vo. [*Lit. Year Book.*]
London, 1921

FROM Connaught to Chicago ; a volume of American impressions. By George A. Birmingham [James Owen Hannay, D.D.]. Cr 8vo. [*Brit. Mus.*]
London, 1914

FROM crooked roots. [A sketch.] By John Ackworth [Rev. Frederick R. Smith]. 8vo. [*Methodist Who's Who.*] London, 1903

FROM crown to cross ; a novel. By Lucas Cleeve [Mrs Howard Kingscote, *née* Adelina Georgina Isabella Wolff]. Cr 8vo. [*Brit. Mus.*] London, 1903

FROM dark to dawn ; or, the story of Warwick Roland. By the author of *The Memoir of the Rev. Wm. Marsh, D.D.,* and of *English hearts and English hands* [Catherine Marsh]. Fcap 8vo. Pp. 63. London, [1874]

FROM dark to light ; or, voices from the slums. By a Delver [Alfred Alsop]. 8vo. Pp. 107. [Kirk's *Supp.*] Manchester, 1881

FROM darkness to light ; a tale of Spanish life. [By Elizabeth Moore.] 8vo. [*Brit. Mus.*] London, 1878

FROM dawn to daylight ; a simple story of a Western home. By a minister's wife [Mrs Henry Ward Beecher, *née* Eunice White]. 8vo. [Kirk's *Supp.*] New York, 1859

FROM dawn to noon. Poems by Violet Fane [Mary Montgomerie, later Lady Currie]. 8vo. Pp. viii., 140. [*Brit. Mus.*] London, 1872

FROM dawn to sunset. [Poems.] By James Hinton [George Barlow]. 8vo. Pp. xii., 498. [*Lond. Lib. Cat.*] London, 1890

FROM Edinburgh to the Baltic, by Paris, Brussels, Antwerp, Rotterdam, the Hague, Bremen, Hamburgh, Lubeck, and home. By C. M. [Charles Mackenzie, bookseller]. Fcap 8vo. Pp. 34. Private print. Edinburgh, 1876
Information from a friend of the author.

FROM eighteen to twenty ; a novel. [By Elizabeth Jaudon Sellers.] Fcap 8vo. [Kirk's *Supp.*] Philadelphia, 1888

FROM error to truth. By Minnie Mary Lee [Mrs Julia Amanda Wood, *née* Sargent]. Fcap 8vo. [Kirk's *Supp.*] New York, 1890

FROM faith to faith : meditations in sonnet verse on Abraham, Isaac, and Jacob. [By Rev. Thomas Andrew Walker.] Cr 8vo. Oxford, 1882

FROM far lands ; poems of North and South. By Gervais Gage [J— Laurence Rentoul]. 8vo. London, 1914

FROM gloom to sunlight. By Bertha M. Clay [Mrs Charlotte M. Braeme]. 8vo. London, 1882

FROM hand to hand : a novel. From the German of Golo Raimund [Madam Bertha Heyn Friedrich]. Fcap 8vo. [Cushing's *Init. and Pseud.*, vol. ii., p. 128.] Philadelphia, 1882

FROM hay-time to hopping. By the author of *Our farm of four acres* [Miss —— Coulton]. 8vo. Pp. 244. [*Adv. Lib.*] London, 1860

FROM information received. [A detective story.] By Dick Donovan [Joyce E. P. Muddock]. Pt 8vo. [*Lit. Year Book.*] London, 1893

FROM lands of exile. By Pierre Loti [Lieut. M. Julien Viaud] : translated from the French. Fcap 8vo. [*Brit. Mus.*] New York, 1888

FROM London to Lucknow ; with memoranda of mutinies, marches, flights, fights, and conversations. To which is added, an opium-smuggler's explanation of the Peiho massacre. By a chaplain in H.M. Indian service [James Aberigh Mackay]. 2 vols. 8vo. London, 1860

FROM Madge to Margaret. By Arnold Winchester [Mrs Caroline G. Curtis]. 8vo. [Cushing's *Init. and Pseud.*, vol. i., p. 308.] Boston, 1880

FROM Madras to Delhi and back, *via* Bombay. [By Michael Cudmore Furnell, M.D.]. 8vo. Madras, 1874

FROM matter to spirit : the result of ten years' experience in spirit manifestations. By C. D. [Mrs C— De Morgan, wife of Augustus De Morgan] : with a preface by A. B. [Augustus De Morgan]. 8vo. [*D. N. B.*, vol. 14, p. 334.] London, 1863

FROM Mayfair to Marathon. [By Eustace Clare Grenville Murray.] 8vo. London, 1853

FROM my corner : looking at life in sunshine and shadow. By Dorcas Hicks [Mary H. Perkins]. Fcap 8vo. Pp. 206. [*Amer. Cat.*] New York, [1895]

FROM my youth up. By Marion Harland [Mary Virginia Hawes, later Mrs Terhune]. Fcap 8vo. [Kirk's *Supp.*] New York, [1875 ?]

FROM Olympus to Hades. By Mrs Forrester [Mrs —— Bridges]. Fcap 8vo. [*Amer. Cat.*] New York, 1887

FROM one generation to another. By Henry Seton Merriman [Hugh Stowell Scott]. Cr 8vo. [*Lond. Lib. Cat.*] London, 1920

FROM out of the deeps. By an old Cornish boy [Dr Samuel M. Christophers]. Pt 8vo. [Cushing's *Init. and Pseud.*, vol. i., p. 211.] London, 1875

FROM out the gloom. By Bertha M. Clay [Mrs Charlotte M. Braeme]. 8vo. London, 1882

FROM Oxford to Rome ; and how it fared with some who lately made the journey. By a companion traveller. [Miss E. F. S. Harris.] Pt 8vo. [*Brit. Mus.*] London, 1847

FROM prison to throne. By K. E. H. [Katharine E. Howarth]. Pt 8vo.
London, 1901

FROM Rangoon to Amherst. By Grace Graham [Mrs Sophie B. Titterington]. Fcap 8vo. [Kirk's *Supp.*]
Philadelphia, 1892

FROM Rome to Mentana. [By Emma Maria Pearson.] 8vo. [*Brit. Mus.*]
London, 1868

FROM school to stage. By Phyllis Dare [Phyllis Dones]. 8vo. Pp. 146.
London, 1907

FROM Sedan to Saarbruck, *via* Verdun, Gravelotte, and Metz. By an officer of the Royal Artillery [Sir Henry Knollys]. Cr 8vo.   London, 1870

FROM spring to fall ; or where life stirs. By a son of the Marshes [Denham Jordan]. Cr 8vo. [*Lond. Lib. Cat.*]
London, 1894

FROM stage to peerage. [A novel.] By Florence Warden [Florence Alice Price, later Mrs George E. James]. Cr 8vo. Pp. 288. [*Lit. Year Book.*]
London, 1911

FROM switch to lever. By Victor St Clair [George W. Browne]. Fcap 8vo. [*Amer. Cat.*]   New York, 1902

FROM Taplow to Taunton. By R. W. [Robert Walker]. 8vo. [Cushing's *Init. and Pseud.*, vol. i., p. 300.]
Weymouth, 1868

FROM the Book Beautiful ; being some old lights relit. By Guy Thorne [Cyril A. E. Ranger-Gull]. Cr 8vo. Pp. 192. [*Lit. Year Book.*]
London, 1908

FROM the bosom of the deep. [A novel.] By Dick Donovan [Joyce E. P. Muddock]. Cr 8vo. Pp. viii., 363. [*Lit. Year Book.*]
London, 1886

FROM the crib to the Cross: the story of Jesus . . . in words of one syllable. [By Mrs E. A. Walker.] 8vo. Pp. 318.   London, 1905

FROM the dead ; a romance. By Denzil Vane [F— Du Tertre]. 2 vols. 8vo. [*Brit. Mus.*]   London, 1888

FROM the den of a Cambridge Don : miscellaneous verses. By L. A. [Leonard Alston]. 8vo. [*Camb. Univ. Lib. Cat.*]   Cambridge, 1914

FROM the four winds. [Tales.] By John Sinjohn [John Galsworthy]. 8vo. Pp. 246. [*Lit. Year Book.*]
London, 1897

FROM the green bag. By F. M. Allen [Edmund Downey]. 8vo. [*Lit. Year Book.*]   London, 1894

FROM the hills of dream ; threnodies, songs, and later poems. By Fiona Macleod [William Sharp]. New edition. Cr 8vo. Pp. 218. [*Lit. Year Book.*]   London, 1907

FROM the hills of " Shawfieldmont." [A poem. By William Amos Bancroft.] 8vo. [*Brit. Mus.*]   London, 1903
Signed " W. A. B."

FROM the Italian of Tasso's sonnets. By C. C. [Charles Chorley]. 8vo. Pp. 11. [Boase and Courtney's *Bibl. Corn.*]   Truro, 1867

FROM the land of the wombat. By Coo-ee [Wm. Sylvester Walker]. 8vo. [*Lit. Year Book.*]   London, 1898

FROM the loom to the lawyer's gown : being incidents in the life of Mr Mark Knowles. [By Harriet Carson.] 8vo. Pp. 95. [*Brit. Mus.*]
London, [1884]

FROM the Lune to the Neva sixty years ago. By J. B. [Mrs —— Davis Benson]. 8vo.   London, 1879

FROM the Mither Kirk. [By Alexander Walker.] 8vo. [*Aber. Pub. Lib.*]
Aberdeen, 1885

FROM the North Foreland to Penzance. By Clive Holland [Charles J. Hankinson]. Royal 8vo. Pp. 350. [*Lit. Year Book.*]   London, 1908

FROM the other side ; stories of Transatlantic travel. By Stanton Page [Henry B. Fuller]. Pt 8vo. [*Amer. Cat.*]   Boston, 1898

FROM the silence. (Words from an unseen world.) By " Astra " [Mrs Jack Dale]. 8vo. [*Brit. Mus.*]
London, [1908]

FROM vineyard to decanter ; a book about sherry. . . . By Don Pedro Verdad [Walter MacGee]. Fcap 8vo. [*Brit. Mus.*]   London, 1875

FROM whose bourne. By Luke Sharp [Robert Barr]. Fcap 8vo. Pp. 210. [*Lit. Year Book.*]   New York, [1896]

FROM Wisdom Court : essays. By Henry Seton Merriman [Hugh S. Scott] and S. G. Tallentyre [E. Beatrice Hall]. 8vo. [*Lit. Year Book.*]   London, 1896

FROM year to year ; and other verses. [By Bishop William Boyd Carpenter, D.D.] Fcap 8vo.
Private print, [London], 1878

FRONDES caducæ, J. G. [James Glassford, of Dougalston]. 8vo. Pp. 44. [*D. Laing.*]   Chiswick, 1824

FRONT lines [in the Great War]. By Boyd Cable [Ernest A. Ewart]. Cr 8vo. Pp. 320. [*Lit. Year Book.*]
London, 1919

FRONTIER (a) hero. By Marion Thorne [Ida T. Thurston]. Cr 8vo. [*Amer. Cat.*] Boston, 1898

FRONTIER (the) lands of the Christian and the Turk ; comprising travels in the regions of the Lower Danube, in 1850 and 1851. By a British resident of twenty years in the East [James Henry Skene]. 2 vols. 8vo. [*Adv. Lib.*] London, 1853

FRONTIERS (the) man. By Charles Egbert Cradock [Mary Noailles Murfree]. Pt 8vo. [Kirk's *Supp.*] Boston, 1904

FRONTISPICE [*sic*] (the) of the King's Book opened ; with a poem annexed, The in-security of princes. Considered in an occasionall meditation upon the King's late sufferings and death. [By William Somner.] 4to. [*Brit. Mus.*] N.P., [1650]

FROST and fire, natural engines, tool marks and chips ; with sketches taken at home and abroad. By a traveller [John Francis Campbell]. 2 vols. 8vo. [*Adv. Lib.*] Edinburgh, 1865

FROST (the) upon the pane : a Christmas story. [By William Brighty Rands.] 8vo. [*Brit. Mus.*] London, 1854

FROUDE. [Modern English Writers' series.] By John Oliver Hobbes [Mrs Reginald W. Craigie, *née* Pearl Teresa Richards]. 8vo. Edinburgh, 1903

FRUIT (the) gardener ; containing the method of raising stocks, for multiplying of fruit-trees, by budding, grafting, &c. : as also, directions for laying out and managing fruit-gardens; to which is added, the art of training fruit-trees to a wall, in a new, easy, expeditious, and cheap manner. [By John Gibson, M.D.] 8vo. [*Bodl.*] London, 1768

FRUIT (the) of faith revealed. How to become sons of God. By W. D. F. [William D. Forsyth]. 8vo. London, 1905

FRUIT (the) of the Spirit ; or, the Christian graces. By a lady [Mrs Eliza Ann Bacon, *née* Munroe]. 8vo. [Cushing's *Init. and Pseud.*, ii. 84.] Boston, 1842

FRUIT walls improved, in inclining them to the horizon ; or, a way to build walls for fruit trees, whereby they may receive more sunshine and heat than ordinary. By a member of the Royal Society [Nicholas F. de Duillier]. 4to. Pp. xxviii., 128. [*Brit. Mus.*] London, 1699
Dedication signed " N. F. D."

FRUITFUL (a) sermon upon Romans xii., 3-8. [By Edward Dering.] Fcap 8vo. London, 1584

FRUITS of endowments : being a list of works of upwards of two thousand authors, who have from the Reformation up to the present time enjoyed prebendal or other non-cure endowments of the Church of England. [By Rev. Fred. R. A. Glover.] 8vo. [*Brit. Mus.*] London, 1840

FRUITS of enterprize exhibited in the travels of Belzoni, in Egypt and Nubia ; interspersed with the observations of a mother to her children. By the author of *The India cabinet* [Sarah Atkins, later Mrs —— Wilson]. Fcap 8vo. [Smith's *Cat. of Friends' Books*, i., 141.] London, 1822

FRUITS (the) of the morrow ; an Irish story. By A. E. Jacomb [Agnes E. Jacomb Hood]. Cr 8vo. Pp. 324. [*Lit. Year Book.*] London, 1914

FRUITS (the) of the valley. By A. E. L. [Anne Elizabeth Lee]. 8vo. [*Brit. Mus.*] London, 1855

FRUITS of the valley. By H. M. T. [H— Mary Teulon] ; with introduction and biographical sketch by the author of *Thoughts by the Way* [W— N. Nash]. 8vo. [*Brit. Mus.*] London, 1865

FRUITS (the) of victory ; a sequel to "The Great Illusion." By Norman Angell [Ralph Norman Angell Lane]. Cr 8vo. [*Lit. Year Book.*] London, 1921

FRUITS, pastes, syrups, and preserves. By Shirley Dare [Mrs Susan C. Power, *née* Dunning]. Fcap 8vo. [Cushing's *Init. and Pseud.*, vol. ii., p. 78.] Boston, 1885

FUDGE (the) family in Paris ; edited by Thomas Brown, the younger, author of *The twopenny post-bag* [Thomas Moore]. Third edition. 8vo. Pp. viii., 168. [*Brit. Mus.*] London, 1818

FUDGE in Ireland : a collection of letters, poems, and legends. . . . [By William Russell Macdonald.] Pt 8vo. [O'Donoghue's *Poets of Ireland*.] London, 1822

FUDGES (the) in England ; being a sequel to the " Fudge family in Paris." By Thomas Brown the younger, author of *The twopenny post-bag*, etc. [Thomas Moore]. Second edition. 8vo. Pp. vii., 213. London, 1835

FUGA sæculi, or the holy hatred of the world ; conteyning the liues of 17 holy Confessours of Christ, selected out of sundry authors. Written in Italian by Giovanni Pietro Maffei, and translated into English by H. H. [Henry Hawkins, S.J.]. 4to. [*Brit. Mus.*] Paris, 1632

FUGITIVE (the) ; or, family incidents. By the author of *The Private history of the court of England* [Mrs S. Green]. 3 vols. Fcap 8vo. [Watt's *Bibl. Brit.*] London, 1815

FUGITIVE pieces. [By Henry Headley.] [Nichols' *Lit. Anec.*, viii., 157.] London, 1785

FUGITIVE pieces. [By Miss —— Field.] Cr 8vo. Reading, 18——

FUGITIVE pieces, on various subjects, by several authors. [Edited by Robert Dodsley.] 2 vols. Fcap 8vo. [*D.N.B.*, vol. 15, p. 174.] London, 1761

FUGITIVE pieces ; or, reminiscences of events in the life of the writer in India, from 1833 to 1882. [By W— H. Carey.] 8vo. [*Calc. Imp. Lib.*] Simla, [1882]

FUGITIVE pieces ; poems on various subjects. By a Scotch gentleman [Colin Maclaurin, advocate]. Cr 8vo. Pp. 92. [*Adv. Lib.*] Edinburgh, 1799

FUGITIVE pieces, written during a residence in foreign parts. [By John Bell.] 8vo. Private print, [*c.* 1814]
Presentation copy from the author.

FUGITIVE poems. By Endymion [William Nash]. 8vo. [O'Donoghue's *Poets of Ireland.*] Cork, 1832

FUGITIVE political essays. [By James Scott, D.D., rector of Simonburn, Northumberland.] 8vo. London, 1770

FUGITIVE (the) slaves in Canada. [By Mrs Lucy Sarah Wilson.] Fcap 8vo. [*Brit. Mus.*] London, 1858

FUGITIVE verses. [By Joanna Baillie.] Fcap 8vo. [*D. N. B.*, vol. 2, p. 414.] London, 1790

FUGITIVE writings. By Rudolph Hertzmann [Mrs Emma Catherine Embury, *née* Manley]. 8vo. [Cushing's *Init. and Pseud.*, ii., 74.] London, 1840-45

FUGITIVES from the escritoire of a retired editor. . . . [By Rev. Dorus Clarke, D.D.] 8vo. [Cushing's *Init. and Pseud.*, i., 260.] Boston, 1864

FVIMUS Troes Æneid 2. The trve Troianes, being a story of the Britaines valour at the Romanes first invasion : publikely represented by the gentlemen students of Magdalen Colledge in Oxford. [By Jasper Fisher, D.D.] 4to. No pagination. [Madan's *Oxf. Books.*] Oxford, 1633
" This play was written by Dr Jasper Fisher, who was blind. This is the first edition."—MS. note by Malone on the Bodleian copy.

FUL (a) and round answer to N. D., *alias* Robert Parsons, the Noddie, his foolish and rude Warne-word. [By Matthew Sutcliffe, LL.D.] 4to. [*D.N.B.*, vol. 55, p. 177.] London, 1604

FULFILLING (the) of the Scripture, held forth in a discovery of the exact accomplishment of the word of God in his works of providence, performed and to be performed. . . . [By Robert Fleming, sen.] Fcap 8vo. [*Brit. Mus.*] [Rotterdam ?], 1681
A second part was issued with a different title : " The Faithfulness of God considered. . . ." *See above.*

FULFILMENT (the) of the prophecy of Isaiah, chapter ii., verse 4, as developed in the New Testament, and in the principles and practice of the early Christians. [By William Naish, *Quaker.*] 12mo. [Green's *Bibl. Somers.*, i., 370.] London, 1853

FULL (a) account of the Buddhist controversy at Pantura in 1873. . . . [By John Capper.] 8vo. Colombo, 1873

FULL (a), accurate, and impartial report of the trial of John Bagguley, of Stockport ; John Johnston, of Salford ; and Samuel Drummond, of Manchester, charged with conspiracy, and uttering seditious speeches at a public meeting. . . . [By the Rev. Joseph Harrison.] 8vo. Pp. 64. [*Manch. Free Lib. Cat.*] Manchester, 1818

FULL (a) and authentick account of Stephen Duck, the Wiltshire poet : of his education ; his methods of improving himself ; how he first engag'd in poetry ; and his great care in writing : of each of his particular poems ; of the first encouragements he met with ; and his original sentiments on several books, things, &c. . . . By J— S— [Joseph Spence] Esq., poetry professor for the University of Oxford. 8vo. [*Bodl.*] London, 1731

FULL (a) and clear answer to a book [entitled, The antient right of the Commons of England asserted] written by William Petit, Esq. printed in the year 1680 ; by which it appears that he hath mistaken the meaning of the histories and records he hath cited, and misapplyed them ; and that he hath added to, or taken from them, or left unrecited such words and matters as he thought would either advance or destroy his assertion. . . . Together with some animadversions upon a book [by Wm. Atwood] called, Jani Anglorum facies nova. [By Robert Brady, M.D.] 8vo. [Arber's *Term Cat.*, vol. i., p. 524.] London, 1681

FULL (a) and clear exposition of the Protestant rule of faith; with an excellent dialogue laying forth the large extent of true excellent charity against the uncharitable Papists. [By Andrew Pulton.]   4to.   [Jones' Peck, ii., 321.] N.P., N.D., [1688 ?]

FULL (a) and clear vindication of the Full answer to a letter from a bystander [Corbyn Morris]; in which all the Cambridge gentleman's cavils and misrepresentations of that book, in his letter to Mr Thomas Carte, are exposed and refuted.   By the author of *The Full answer* [Thomas Carte]. 8vo.   Pp. 132.   [*Bodl.*]
London, 1743

FULL (a) and compleat answer against the writer of a late volume set forth, entituled A tale in a tub or a tub lecture: with a vindication of that ridiculous name called Rounheads; together with some excellent verses on the defacing of Cheapside Crosse. Also proving that it is far better to preach in a boat than in a tub.   By Thorny Ailo—Annagram [John Taylor, the water-poet].   4to.   [*Brit. Mus.*]
London, 1642

FULL (a) and exact account of the proceedings of the Court of Directors and Council-General of Scotland trading to Africa and the Indies. . . . [By Roderick Mackenzie, Secretary to the Company.]   4to.   N.P., 1706

FULL (a) and final answer to a triffling reply made unto a paper, entituled, Plain-dealing with the Presbyterians: wherein the reasonableness and necessity of a toleration is maintained, against all that is said in the Gentleman's letter to a Member of Parliament, and Vindication thereof.   In a letter to a friend. [By J. Skene.]   4to.   [*Brit. Mus.*]   N.P., 1703

The controversy opened with " A Letter from a gentleman [James Ramsay] to a Member of Parliament concerning Toleration. . . ."   (*See below.*)

FULL (a) and impartial account of all the late proceedings in the University of Cambridge against Dr Bentley. [By Conyers Middleton, D.D.]   4to. Pp. 114.   [Bartholomew and Clark's *Bibl. of Bentley*, p. 67.]   London, 1719

A second part, entered under its proper heading, appeared in the following year.

FULL (a) and impartial account of the discovery of sorcery and witchcraft, practis'd by Jane Wenham, of Walkerne in Hertfordshire, upon the bodies of Anne Thorn, Anne Street, &c.; the proceedings against her from her being first apprehended, till she was committed to gaol by Sir Henry Chauncy: also her tryal at the assizes at Hertford before Mr Justice Powell, where she was found guilty of felony and witchcraft, and receiv'd sentence of death for the same, March 4, 1711-12.   [By Francis Bragge, B.D.]   8vo.   [*Adv. Lib.*]   London, 1712

The same writer published, in continuation, " A Defense of the proceedings against Jane Wenham . . .," and " Witchcraft farther display'd. . . ." (*See below.*) On his side there was also issued " The Belief of Witchcraft vindicated . . ." By G. R. Against the prosecution there appeared " The Case of the Hertfordshire witchcraft considered . . .," " The Impossibility of witchcraft . . .," " A Full confutation of witchcraft. . . ."   (*See below.*)

FULL (a) and impartial account of the Oxford riots.   Containing I. The behaviour of the Constitution Club, with a complete list of the rioters cited. . . . II. An order against riots, and tumults, drawn up by Bishop Smalridge.   III. An order for the strict observation of the first of August, the day of His Majesty's happy accession to the throne.   IV. The substance of Judge Dormer's excellent charge, upon opening the assizes. . . .   V. The presentment of the grand-jury, read to the court by Sir Robert Jenkinson, Bart. foreman. . . .   VI. An account of the Anabaptist-teacher at Oxford, who baptized two young women in the morning, and was found in bed between them the same night.   In a letter from a member of the University, to his friend in London.   [By Richard Rawlinson, LL.D.]   8vo.   [*D. N. B.*, vol. 47, p. 333.]   London, 1715

FULL (a) and particular account of the trial and condemnation of Mess John Presbytery, who is to be hanged on or before — day of May, 1798. By Cousin-German [Rev. Archibald Bruce, of Whitburn].   8vo.   Pp. 17. [*New Coll. Cat.*]   Edinburgh, 1798

FULL (a) and plaine declaration of ecclesiastical discipline owt off the word off God, and off the declininge off the churche off England from the same.   [By Walter Travers, D.D.] 4to.   Pp. 201.   Imprinted, 1574

The above work was published in Latin, in the same year, at Rupella [Rochelle], in 8vo.   It was also published in English at Geneva, in 1580, 8vo.   The address, " To the godly reader," was written by Thomas Cartwright, B.D.   *See* Memoir of the life and writings of Thomas Cartwright.   By the Rev. B. Brook, London, 1845, p. 217.

FULL (a) and true account of a horrid and barbarous revenge by poison, on the body of Mr Edmund Curll, bookseller, with a faithfull copy of his will and testament. Published by an eye witness. [By Alexander Pope.] Folio. [*Brit. Mus.*] [London, 173—]

FULL (a) and true account of the dreadful and melancholly earthquake which happened between twelve and one o'clock in the morning on Thursday, the fifth instant. With an exact list of such persons as have been found in the rubbish. . . . [By Richard Bentley.] Folio.   London, 1750
A satire, signed " P. D."

FULL (a) and true history of the bloody tragedy of Douglas, as it is now to be seen acting at the theatre in the Canongate. [By Alexander Carlyle, D.D.] Folio. Single leaf. N.P., N.D., [1757 ?]
See above, " Douglas, a tragedy."

FULL (a) answer and confutation of a scandalous pamphlet [by Bishop William Lloyd], called, A seasonable discourse, shewing, the necessity of maintaining the established religion in opposition to Popery ; or a clear vindication of the Catholicks of England. [By Roger Palmer, Earl of Castlemaine.] 4to. [*Brit. Mus.*]
[Antwerp, 1673]

FULL (a) answer to a late View of the internal evidence of the Christian religion [by Soame Jenyns] ; in a dialogue between a rational Christian and a friend. By the editor of *Ben Mordecai's Letters to Elisha Levi* [Rev. Henry Taylor, M.A., of Portsmouth]. 8vo. [*Brit. Mus.*]
London, 1777

FULL (a) answer to a printed paper [by William Prynne], entituled, Foure serious questions concerning excommunication, and suspension from the sacrament &c. ; wherein the severall arguments and texts of Scripture produced are particularly and distinctly discussed, and the debarring of ignorant and scandalous persons from the sacrament vindicated. [By Herbert Palmer, D.D.] 4to. [Thomason *Coll. of Tracts*, vol. i., p. 396.]
London, 1645

FULL (a) answer to all popular objections that have yet appear'd, for not taking the Oath of Allegiance to their present majesties ; particularly offer'd to the consideration of all such of the divines of the Church of England (and others) as are yet unsatisfied. . . . By a divine of the Church of England, and author of a late treatise entituled, A resolution of certain queries, concerning submission to the present government [Thomas Long, B.D.]. 4to. Pp. 83. [*Bodl.*]
London, 1689

FULL (a) answer to an infamous and trayterous pamphlet [entituled, A declaration of the Commons of England in Parliament assembled, expressing their reasons and grounds of passing the late resolutions touching no further addresse or application to the king]. [By Edward Hyde, Earl of Clarendon.] 4to. Pp. 196. [*Bodl.*]   [London], 1648

FULL (a) answer to that question, What is the Church of England ? With a defence and continuation of the " Conforming non-conformist," &c. ; wherein the present controversies about Churchgovernment and separation are further opened and discussed. By J. C. [Rev. John Cheney]. 8vo. Pp. 276. [*Bodl.*]   London, 1680
See above, " The Conforming Nonconformist."

FULL (a) answer to the country parson's Plea against the Quakers tythe-bill : the priest taken in his own craft, and confuted by his own arguments ; his ordination consider'd, and left at the gates of Rome. By the author of *The Replication to the country parson's Papers and Plea.* . . . [Joseph Besse]. 8vo. Pp. vii., 96. [Smith's *Cat. of Friends' Books*, i., 254.]
London, 1736

FULL (a) answer to the Letter from a Bystander [Corbyn Morris], &c. ; wherein his false calculations and misrepresentations of facts in the time of King Charles II. are refuted, and an historical account is given of all the Parliamentary aids in that reign, from the journals of the House of Commons ; the ancient and modern power of the Crown, and the excessive height to which it is risen of late, are clearly represented. . . . By R— H—, Esq [Rev. Thomas Carte]. 8vo. Pp. 218. [M'Culloch's *Lit. of Pol. Econ.*, p. 328.]   London, 1742
This was followed by " A Full and clear vindication " (1743).
See also the reply [by Corbyn Morris] in " A letter to the Rev. Mr Thomas Carte. . . ."

FULL (a) answer to the Second defence [by William Wake] of the Exposition of the doctrin of the Church of England ; in a letter to the defender. [By Henry Joseph Johnston.] 4to. [*Aberd. Lib.*]   London, 1687

FULL (a) confutation of all the facts advanced in Mr Bower's three defences; in which the charge brought against him is confirmed by a seventh letter to Father Sheldon, by an authentic certificate from Italy, and many other demonstrative proofs. By the author of the *Six letters illustrated*, and of *Bower and Tillemont compared* [John Douglas, D.D., Bishop of Salisbury]. 8vo. Pp. 94. [*D. N. B.*, vol. 15, p. 327.]   London, 1757

FULL (a) confutation of the Covenant lately sworne by many in Scotland ; delivered in a speech at the visitation of Downe and Connor. . . . [By Bishop Henry Lesley, or Leslie.] 4to. Pp. 38. [*Brit. Mus.*]   London, 1639

FULL (a) confutation of witchcraft, more particularly of the depositions against Jane Wenham, lately condemned for a witch, at Hertford ; in which the modern notions of witches are overthrown, and the ill consequences of such doctrines are exposed by arguments, proving that witchcraft is priestcraft. In a letter from [Arthur S. Fairman ?] a physician in Hertfordshire, to his friend in London. 8vo.   London, 1712
     This reply to "A full and impartial account of the discovery of sorcery . . ." (*see above*) has been misattributed to the writer of the works controverted.

FULL (a) declaration of all particulers concerning the march of the Forces under Collonel Fiennes to Bristoll and their carriage upon their enemies approach ; as also a relation of the late bloody abominable conspiracy against the City of Bristoll, as appeareth by the examinations of the parties discovering their plot and intention ; together with sundry letters annexed. From a noble hand [Hercules Langrish]. 4to. [Green's *Bibl. Somers.*, ii., 264.]   London, 1643

FULL (a) declaration of the true state of the secluded Members case ; in vindication of themselves and their privileges, and of the respective counties, cities and boroughs for which they were elected to serve in Parliament, against the vote of their discharge, published in print, Jan. 5. 1659. by their fellow members : compiled and published by some of the secluded members, who could meet with safety and conveniencie without danger of a forcible surprize by the redcoats. [By William Prynne.] 4to. Pp. 60. [*Bodl.*]   London, 1660
     The author's name is in the handwriting of Wood, who gives the date as " about the latter end of Jan. 1659."

FULL (a) enquiry into the power of faith, the nature of prophecy, the translation of Enoch and Elias, and the resurrection of Christ. [By William Freke.] 4to. London, 1693

FULL (a) inquiry into the original authority of that text, 1 John v., 7, There are three that bear record in heaven, &c. ; containing an account of Dr Mill's evidences from antiquity, for and against its being genuine : with an examination of his judgment thereupon. Humbly address'd to both Houses of Convocation now assembled. [By Thomas Emlyn.] 8vo. [*Brit. Mus.*]   London, 1715

FULL (a) refutation of the reasons advanced in the Defence of the petition intended to be offered to Parliament for the abolition of subscription. By no bigot to, nor against the Church of England [Samuel Cooper, D.D.]. 8vo. Yarmouth, 1772

FULL (a) satisfaction concerning a double Romish iniquitie, hainous rebellion and more then heathenish aequivocation. [By Thomas Morton, Bishop.] 4to. [*D. N. B.*, vol. 39, p. 164.]   London, 1606

FULL (the) stature of a man : a life-story. By Julian Warth [Mrs Julia Warth Parsons]. Pt 8vo. [Kirk's *Supp.*]   Boston, 1886

FULL swing. [A novel.]   By Frank Danby [Mrs Julia Frankau]. Cr 8vo. Pp. 362. [*Lit. Year Book.*]
London, 1914

FULL (a), true, and comprehensive view of Christianity ; containing a short historical account of religion from the creation to the fourth century after our Lord Jesus Christ ; as also the complete duty of a Christian in relation to faith, practice, worship and rituals, in two catechisms. . . . [By Thomas Deacon.]   Second edition.   8vo. [Darling's *Cyclop. Bibl.*]
London, 1748

FULL (a) view of Popery, in a satyrical account of the lives of the Popes. . . . To this is added a Confutation of the Mass, and a vindication of Reform'd devotion : in two parts. Written by a learned Spanish convert [Cypriano de Valera], and addressed to his countrymen : now faithfully translated from the second and best edition of the original. 8vo. Pp. vi., 488. [*Manch. Free Lib. Cat.*]
London, 1704

FULL (a) view of the doctrines and practices of the ancient Church relating to the Eucharist ; wholly different from those of the present Roman

Church, and inconsistent with the belief of transubstantiation : being a sufficient confutation of Consensus veterum, Nubes testium, and other late collections of the Fathers, pretending the contrary. [By John Patrick, D.D.] 4to. Pp. 202. [Jones' Peck.]
London, 1688

FULL (a) vindication and answer of the xi. accused members (viz. Denzell Holles, Esq. ; Sir Philip Stapleton, Sir William Lewis, Sir John Clotworthy, Sir William Waller, Sir Iohn Maynard, Kts, Major Gen. Massey, Iohn Glynne Esq., recorder of London, Walter Long, Esquire, Col. Edward Harley, Anthony Nichols, Esq.) to a late printed pamphlet intituled, A particular charge or impeachment, in the name of Sir Thomas Fairfax and the army under his command, against the said members, by his appointment and the councel of war. [By William Prynne.] 4to. Pp. 43. [*D. N. B.*, vol. 46, p. 434.]   London, 1647

FULL (a) vindication of the Manager of the Theatre Royal [in Dublin], written by himself [Thomas Sheridan]. 8vo. [Lowe's *Theat. Bibl.*, p. 302.]
Dublin, 1747

FULL (a) vindication of the measures of the Congress, from the calumnies of their enemies ; in answer to a Letter [by Bishop Samuel Seabury, D.D.] under the signature of *A. W.* Farmer ; whereby his sophistry is exposed, his cavils confuted, his artifices detected, and his wit ridiculed. [By Alexander Hamilton.] Fcap 8vo. Pp. 35. [Evans' *Amer. Bibl.*, vol. v. p. 31.]   New York, 1774
   Signed " A Friend of America."
   Seabury's pamphlet (" The Congress canvassed . . .") was published as having been written by " A W. Farmer," a designation which signified "A Westchester farmer." *See above.*

FULL (a) vindication of the overtures transmitted to Presbyteries by the Commission, November 1719 ; from the objections publish'd in several papers against them. [By Professor William Dunlop.] Fcap 8vo. [*Adv. Lib.*]   Edinburgh, 1720

FULLER (a) answer to a treatise written by Dr Ferne, entituled, " The resolving of conscience," etc. Done by another author [Rev. Charles Herle, M.A.] ; and by him revised and enlarged. 4to. Pp. 20. [Boase and Courtney's *Bibl. Corn.*] London, 1642

FULNESS (the) of time ; a key to Bible dates. By Lumen [Major John Samuel]. 8vo. [*Lit. Year Book.*]
London, 1908

FUMIFUGIUM ; or the inconvenience of the Aer, and smoake of London dissipated ; together with remedies humbly proposed by J. E. [John Evelyn], Esq. to His Sacred Majestie, and to the Parliament now assembled. 4to. Pp. viii., 49. [*D. N. B.*, vol. 18, p. 82.]   London, 1661

FUN. Edited and illustrated by Alfred Crowquill, author of *A bundle of crowquills*, etc. [Alfred Henry Forrester]. Twelfth thousand. 8vo. Pp. 224. [*D. N. B.*, vol. 20, p. 6.]
London, 1854

FUN : a parodi-tragi-comical satire ; as it was to have been perform'd at the Castle tavern in Pater-noster-row, Feb. 13th, 1752, but was suppressed by an order of the Lord Mayor. [By William Kenrick.] 8vo. [*Biog. Dram.*]   N.P., 1752

FUN o' the forge [a collection of humorous Irish stories]. By Brian na Banban [Brian O'Higgins]. Fcap 8vo. [S. J. Brown's *Ireland in fiction*, p. 205.]   Dublin, 1915

FUN with the Spoopendykes. [By Stanley Huntley.] 8vo. [*Brit. Mus.*]
London, [1884]

FUND (a) raising for the Italian gentleman [Charles Edward Stuart] ; or, a magazine filling on the scheme of frugality. What damage may arise from an explosion is calculated from the accurate observations of the famous Dr Atterbury. [By Caleb Fleming.] 8vo. [*Bodl.*]   London, 1750

FUNDAMENTA chymica : or a sure guide into the high and rare mysteries of Alchymie. By L. C. [Ludovicus Combachius], Philomedico Chymicus. [Translated by Robert Turner.] Fcap 8vo.   London, 1658

FUNDAMENTAL (the) charter of Presbytery, as it hath been lately established in the kingdom of Scotland, examin'd and disprov'd, by the history, records, and publick transactions of our nation ; together with a preface, wherein the Vindicator of the Kirk [Gilbert Rule], is freely put in mind of his habitual infirmities. [By Bishop John Sage.] 8vo. [*D. N. B.*, vol. 50, p. 115.]   London, 1695
   Included in the author's collected works.

FUNDAMENTAL (the) constitution of the English government, proving King William and Queen Mary our lawful King and Queen. [By William Atwood.] Folio. [Moule's *Bibl. Herald.*, p. 246.]   N.P., 1690

FUNDAMENTAL constitutions of Carolina. [Drawn up by the Earl of Shaftesbury and John Locke.] Folio. No separate title-page. [Christie-Miller *Cat.*] N.P., [*c.* 1680]

FUNDAMENTAL principles of the laws of Canada, as they existed under the natives, as they were changed under the French kings, and as they were modified and altered under the domination of England . . . prefaced by an historical sketch of the origin and rise of religious and political institutions amongst the principal nations of the world, etc. [By N. B. Doucet.] 8vo. [*Brit. Mus.*]
[Montreal ? 1840 ?]

FUNDAMENTALS without foundation, or a true picture of the Anabaptists in their rise, progress and practice : written for the use of such as take them for saints, when they are not so much as Christians. [By David Russan, of Hythe.] 8vo. Pp. 176. [Whitley's *Bapt. Bibl.*, i., 139; Arber's *Term Cat.*, iii., 686.]
London, 1703

FUNERAL (the) elogy and character of the late Princess Sophia, with the explication of her consecration ; written originally in Latine, translated into English, and further illustrated by Mr Toland, who has added the character of the King, the Prince and the Princess. [By Joannes F. Cramer.] 8vo. [*Brit. Mus.*] London, 1714

FUNERAL entertainments ; or, a practical discourse clearly shewing the incomparable excellency of Balaam's wish, and the infallible means for our obtaining it. [By Edward Mores, M.A.] Fcap 8vo. Pp. 172. [Watt's *Bibl. Brit.*] London, 1702

FUNERAL (a) gift, or a preparation for death ; with comforts against the fears of approaching death, and consolations against immoderate grief for the loss of friends. By the author of *The Devout Companion* [Abednego Seller]. Fcap 8vo. [Arber's *Term Cat.*, vol. ii., p. 615.] London, 1689

FUNERAL hymns. [By Charles Wesley.] Third edition. Fcap 8vo. Pp. 24. [Green's *Wesl. Bibl.*]
London, 1753

FUNERAL hymns. [By Charles Wesley.] Fcap 8vo. Pp. 70. [Green's *Wesl. Bibl.*] London, 1759
Different from those published in 1753.

FUNERAL (the) of Prelacy ; or, the modern Prelates claim to the office of an apostle or evangelist discust : where also its demonstrated by several arguments, that Presbyterian (and not Prelatick) government, is that unalterable form of Church-government instituted by Christ : in answer to a late pamphlet [by Dr John Hay] intituled, Imparity among pastors, the government of the Church by divine institution, as maintain'd in an extemporary debate, &c. [By Robert White, advocate.] 4to. Pp. 67. [*New Coll. Cat.*] N.P., 1704

FUNERAL (the) of the Mass ; or, the mass dead and buried, without hope of resurrection. Translated out of French [of David de Rodon, by S. A.]. 8vo. [*Brit. Mus.*] London, 1673
Later editions were published (in 1716 and 1836) with the author's name. In reply, there appeared " The Mass triumphant . . ." *See later.*

FUNERAL (a) oration in honour of Miss Jeany Muir [Dr John Clark], a celebrated lady of pleasure. By Miss Betty Montgomery [William Cullen, M.D.], her dear friend and successor. 8vo. Pp. 16. Amsterdam, N.D.
The author's name is in the handwriting of Dr David Laing.

FUNERAL (a) poem, sacred to the memory of John Churchill, Duke of Marlborough. [By Nicholas Amhurst.] 8vo. [*Brit. Mus.*] London, 1722

FUNERAL (a) sermon [on Job xxx. 23] at the interrment of the very great and noble Charles, late Earl of Southeske, who died at his castle of Leuchars in the shire of Fife, upon the 9th of August, and was interr'd at his burial-place near his house of Kinnaird in the shire of Angus, upon the 4th of October 1699. By R. S. [Robert Scott], D.D. 4to. [*David Laing.*]
Edinburgh, 1699

FUNERAL (a) sermon [on Cant. 8 : 5] . . . bearing testimony to the gracious life and peaceful death of a widow. [By Charles B. Smyth.] 8vo.
Fressingfield, [1829]

FUNERAL sermon on R. Herbert of Oakly-Park, Bromfield, Salop. [By J. Slade.] 4to. [Bliss' *Cat.*, 291.] 1676

FUNERAL (a) sermon upon Mr [Richard] Noble. By a neighbouring minister [William Fleetwood, Bishop of Ely]. 8vo. [*Bodl.*] London, 1713

FUNERALL (the) sermon of [Henrietta Maria] the Queen of Great Britanie [translated from the French]. By Thomas Carre [Miles Pinkney]. 8vo. Pp. 52. [Gillow's *Bibl. Dict.*]
Paris, 1670

FUNGUSIANA ; or the opinions and table-talk of the late Barnaby Fungus, Esq. [By Arthur Benoni Evans, D.D.] 8vo. [*D. N. B.*, vol. 18, p. 55.]
London, 1809

FUNNY (the) fellow's grab-bag. By Bill Nye [Edgar Wilson Nye]. Fcap 8vo. [Kirk's *Supp.*] New York, 1903

FUNNY figures. By A. Funnyman (Cuthbert Bede) [Rev. Edward Bradley, B.A.]. 8vo. [*D. N. B.*, First Supp., vol. 1, p. 251.] London, [1858]

FUNNY stories and humorous poems. By Mark Twain [Samuel Langhorne Clemens] and Oliver Wendell Holmes. Pt 8vo. Pp. 173, 192. [*Brit. Mus.*]
London, [1876]
The stories and poems have a separate pagination.

FUR (the) country; or seventy degrees north latitude. By Jules Verne: translated [from the French] by N. D'Anvers [Nancy Meughens, later Mrs Bell]. Pt 8vo. [Kirk's *Supp.*]
New York, 1876

FURIES (the); with Vertues encomium, or the Image of honour: in two bookes of epigrammes, satyricall and encomiasticke. By R. N. [Richard Niccols]. 8vo. Pp. 78. [Lowndes' *Bibl. Man.*]
London, 1614

FURIUS; or, a modest attempt towards a history of the life and surprising exploits of the famous W[illiam] L[auder] critic and thief-catcher, who has so eminently distinguish'd himself by his laudible detection of the heretofore admired John Milton: in a letter from an honest North Briton to his friend in London. . . . [By Andrew Henderson, a bookseller.] 8vo. [Lowndes' *Bibl. Man.*, p. 1319.]
London, [1754]
Letter signed " Miltonicus."
See " Calumny displayed."

FURLOUGH reminiscences. By "Wyvern " [Colonel Arthur C. Kenney]. 8vo. [Oates' *Anglo-Ind. Lit.*]
Madras, 1880

FURMETARY (the); a very innocent and harmless poem, in three cantos. [By William King, LL.D.] 4to. [Arber's *Term Cat.*, vol. iii., p. 141.]
London, 1699

FURNACE (the); a novel. By " Pan " [Leslie Beresford]. Cr 8vo. Pp. 316. [*Lit. Year Book.*] London, [1920]

FURNACE (the) of divine love sufficient to melt the hardest hearts to devotion towards our Saviour Christ. Written in Latin by Ludovicus Blosius, abbot of Lessy. . . . Englished by R. F. [Richard Flecknoe ?]. Fcap 8vo.
[London], 1642

FURNITURE (the) people. By Hope Daring [Anna Johnson]. 8vo. [*Amer. Cat.*] Philadelphia, 1903

FURNIVALLOS Furioso! and " The newest Shakespeare Society." A dram-attic squib. [By John Jeremiah.] 8vo. [*Brit. Mus.*] London, 1876

FUROR poeticus (*i.e.*) propheticus; a poetick-Phrenzie.
Some (probably) will call it so:
Thus named, therefore, let it go.
It is the result of a private-musing, occasioned by a publike report in the country, of the Parliaments restauration by General George Moncke, in February 1659. and meditated soon after the said General's arrival in London. By G. W., Esq. [George Wither]. 8vo. Pp. 48. [Dyce *Cat.*]
London, 1660

FURTH in field: essays on the life language, and literature of old Scotland. By Hugh Haliburton [James Logie Robertson, M.A.]. Pt 8vo. [*Lit. Year Book.*] Edinburgh, 1894

FURTHER (a) account of the state of the Orphan-school, Hospital and Workhouse at Edinburgh. [By Andrew Gairdner, merchant.] 8vo. Pp. 12. [*New Coll. Cat.*] Edinburgh, 1736

FURTHER (the) adventures of Foxy Grandpa. By Bunny [Carl Emil Schultze]. 8vo. [*Amer. Cat.*]
New York, 1901

FURTHER (the) adventures of the little traveller. [By George Frederick Pardon.] 8vo. [*Brit. Mus.*]
London, [1858]
Signed " G. F. P."

FURTHER considerations upon a reduction of the Land-tax; together with a state of the annual supplies of the Sinking Fund, and of the national debt at various future periods. . . . [By Robert Nugent.] 8vo. [*Brit. Mus.*] London, 1751

FURTHER (a) continuation and defence; or, a third part of the Friendly debate. By the same author [Symon Patrick, D.D.]. 8vo. Pp. xxx., 846. [*Bodl.*]
London, 1672
Included in the author's collected works.

FURTHER (a) defence of priestcraft: being a practical improvement of the Shaver's sermon on the expulsion of six young gentlemen from the University of Oxford, for praying, reading, and expounding the Scriptures; occasioned by a Vindication of that pious act by a member of the University. . . . [By John Macgowan.] Fourth edition. 8vo. [*Bodl.*]
London, 1768

FURTHER (a) defence of the present scheme for petitioning the Parliament for relief in the matter of subscription, occasioned by a pamphlet called, Remarks upon certain proposals for an application to Parliament, & c. By the author of a Letter to James Ibbetson, D.D. [Rev. John Firebrace]. 8vo. [*Brit. Mus.*]   London, [1771]

FURTHER (a) defence of the Report ; vindicating it from Mr. Alsops cavils, and shewing the difference between Mr W's [Williams] and my self to be real, and the charge in my Appeal to be true. [By Stephen Lobb.] 8vo. [*New Coll. Cat.*]   London, 1698

FURTHER (a) discoverie of the office of pvblick addresse for accommodations. [By Samuel Hartlib.] 4to. [*Bodl.*]   London, 1648

FURTHER (a) discovery of the Mystery of Jesuitisme, in a collection of severall pieces. [By Pierre Jarrige.] Translated from the French. 6 parts. 8vo. [Watt's *Bibl. Brit.*]   London, 1658
This is a supplement to " The Mystery of Jesuitism . . ." [by Blaise Pascal]. *See later.*

FURTHER (a) enquiry into the meaning of demoniacks in the New Testament ; wherein the Enquiry is vindicated against the objections of the Revd. Mr Twells, and of [Thomas Church] the author of the Essay in answer to it. [By Arthur Ashley Sykes, D.D.] 8vo. Pp. viii., 116. [Disney's *Memoir of Sykes*, p. xx.]
     London, 1737
See above, " An Enquiry into the meaning . . ." and the appended note.

FURTHER (a) essay for the amendment of the gold and silver coins ; with the opinion of Mr Gerrard de Malynes, who was an eminent merchant in the reign of Queen Elizabeth, concerning the standard of England. [By William Lowndes.] 4to. [*Adv. Lib.*]
     London, 1695
Signed " W. L."

FURTHER (a) examination of our American measures, and of the reasons and the principles on which they are founded. By the author of *Considerations on the measures carrying on with respect to the British colonies in North America* [Matthew Robinson, Lord Rokeby]. 8vo. [Park's *Walpole.*]
     London, 1776

FURTHER experiences of an Irish R. M. By Edith Œnone Somerville and Martin Ross [Violet Martin]. 8vo. Pp. viii., 315.   London, 1908
See " Some experiences . . ."

FURTHER (a) inquiry into the expediency of applying the principles of colonial policy to the government of India, and of effecting an essential change in its landed tenures and in the character of its inhabitants. [By Major Gavin Young.] 8vo. Pp. xv., 293. [*W.*]   London, 1822

FURTHER (a) inquiry into the right of appeal from the Chancellor, or Vice-Chancellor, of the University of Cambridge, in matters of discipline ; in which the objections of [Richard Hurd] the author of a late pamphlet intitled, " The opinion of an eminent lawyer concerning the right of appeal from the Vice-Chancellor of Cambridge to the Senate ; supported by a short historical account of the jurisdiction of the University," are fully obviated. [By Thomas Chapman, D.D., Fellow of King's College, Cambridge.] 8vo. Pp. 88. [Bartholomew's *Camb. Books.*]
     London, 1752
See also the previous " Inquiry into the right of appeal. . . ."

FURTHER (a) justification of the present war against the United Netherlands. [By Henry Stubbe, M.A.] Fcap 4to. [*Brit. Mus.*]   London, 1673

FURTHER observations intended for improving the culture and curing of indigo . . . in South Carolina. [By Sir Edward Leigh.] 8vo. [Jaggard's *Index.*]   London, 1747

FURTHER observations on Carausius, emperor of Britain, and Oriuna, supposed by some to be a real person ; with answers to those trifling objections made to the former discourse. Together with some new thoughts concerning his successor, Allectus, Emperor also of Britain. [By John Kennedy.] 4to. [*Bodl.*] London, 1756

FURTHER observations on the Reform Bill ; or, what are the advantages of close boroughs ? [By Montague Gore ?] 8vo.   London, 1831

FURTHER observations on the writings of the Craftsman. [By John, Lord Hervey.] 8vo. [*Brit. Mus.*]
     London, 1730

FURTHER (a) prospect of the Case in view, in answer to some new objections. [By Henry Dodwell, senior.] 8vo. Pp. 150. [*D. N. B.*, vol. 15, p. 181.]   London, 1712
See above, " The Case in view."

FURTHER remarks on Dr Waterland's Further Vindication of Christ's divinity. By Philalethes Cantabrigiensis [Rev. John Jackson, B.A., of Rossington]. 8vo. [*Brit. Mus.*]   London, 1724

FURTHER remarks on Statutes and the present system of King's College, Cambridge. [By Edward Thring.] 8vo. [Bartholomew's *Camb. Books.*]
Cambridge, 1848

FURTHER remarks on two of the most singular characters of the age. By the author of *The Critique on the conduct of the Rev. John Crosse, vicar of Bradford, and the Rev. William Atkinson Fellow of Jesus College, Cambridge* [Rev. Edward Baldwyn]. 8vo. Pp. 91. [Watt's *Bibl. Brit.*] London, 1787

FURTHER (the) surprising adventures of Lemuel Gulliver (first a surgeon, and then a captain of several ships) in Topsy-Turvey Isle. By Vivian Grey [Elliott E. Mills]. 8vo. Pp. vi., 80. Oxford, 1906

FURTHER (a) vindication of a late pamphlet, intituled " The Case of the Hanover troops considered. . . . [By Philip Dormer Stanhope, Earl of Chesterfield, and Edmund Waller.] 8vo. [*Brit. Mus.*] London, 1743

FURTHEST from the truth : a series of dashes. By the authors of *Wisdom while you wait* [Edward V. Lucas and Charles L. Graves]. 8vo.
London, 1909

FURZE the cruel. [A novel.] By John Trevena [Ernest George Henham]. Cr 8vo. Pp. 400. [*Lond. Lib. Cat.*]
London, 1913

FUTILITY (the) of Socialism : its impossibilities, its dangers, and its antidote. By a Lancashire engineer [Eustace C. Holden]. 8vo. Pp. 28.
Bolton, [1909]

FUTTEYPOOR ; or the city of victory. By A. L. O. E. [Charlotte Maria Tucker]. 8vo. London, [1859]

FUTURE (the) Church of Scotland ; an essay in favour of a national Presbyterian Church, on the basis of toleration, economy, and utility : addressed to the lay Presbyterians of Scotland, with suggestions for increasing its efficiency in the religious instruction of the people. By " Free Lance " [Alexander Richardson, journalist]. 8vo. Pp. xi., 355. [*New Coll. Lib.*]
Edinburgh, 1870

FUTURE (the) currency of the United States. . . . By an American citizen [Charles Randolph]. 8vo. [Kirk's *Supp.*] Chicago, 1877

FUTURE (the) Marquis. [A novel.] By Catherine Childar [Annie Charlotte Catherine Aldrich]. 3 vols. Cr 8vo. [*Camb. Univ. Lib.*] London, 1881

FUTURE (the) of Austria-Hungary, and the attitude of the Great Powers. By Scotus Viator [Robert William Seton-Watson, D.Litt.]. In part reprinted from *The Spectator.* 8vo. Pp. 88. [*Lond. Lib. Cat.*] London, 1907

FUTURE (the) of democracy. [By John M. Galt.] 8vo. [Kirk's *Supp.*]
Williamsburg, Virginia, 1852

FUTURE (the) of Ireland, and the awakening of the fires. By Æ. [George William Russell]. 4to. [*Lond. Lib. Cat.*] London, N.D.

FUTURE (the) of militarism ; an examination of F. Scott Oliver's " Ordeal by battle." By " Roland " [John M. Robertson, M.P.]. Cr 8vo. Pp. 185.
London, 1916

FUTURE (the) of the novel. [By Charles Grant Blairfindie Allen ?] 8vo. London, 1897

FUTURE rewards and punishments believed by the ancients, particularly the philosophers ; wherein some objections of the Rev^d. Mr Warburton, in his Divine legation of Moses, are consider'd. [By John Tillard.] 8vo. Pp. ix., 230. London, 1742
Attributed also to Henry Coventry.

FUTURITY. By the author of *Emanuel*, etc. [Miss E— Colthurst]. 8vo. [O'Donoghue's *Poets of Ireland*, p. 41.] Cork, 1837

FUTURITY continued. [A poem.] By the author of *Emanuel*, etc. [Miss E— Colthurst]. 8vo. [O'Donoghue's *Poets of Ireland.*] Cork, 1838

FYNIE'S flower. [A tale.] By Brenda [Mrs Castle Smith]. 8vo. Pp. 106. [*Lond. Lib. Cat.*] London, 1880

G

GABERLUNZIE, a periodical publication, chiefly original. [By Archibald Campbell, auctioneer in Ayr.] 8vo. Pp. iv., 188.   Paisley, 1825

GABERLUNZIE (the); a Scottish comedy, in three acts [and in verse]. [By Laurence Black.] 8vo. Pp. 75. [*Adv. Lib.*]   Edinburgh, 1839

GABERLUNZIE'S (the) wallet. With numerous illustrations on steel and wood. [By James Ballantine.] Vol. I. 8vo. Pp. 315.   Edinburgh, 1843
   No more published.

GABLE (the) house ; or, the picnic in the valley. By the author of *Sketches and stories of life in Italy* [Anna Carolina Eugenia, Contessa di Tergolina]. 8vo. Pp. 80. [*Brit. Mus.*]
London, [1885]

GAELIC (a) dictionary . . . profusely illustrated. [By Edward Dwally.] 3 vols. 8vo. [*Brit. Mus.*]
Herne Bay, 1902 11

GAELIC readings in prose and verse. By Fionn [Henry Whyte]. 8vo. [*New Coll. Cat.*]   Glasgow, 1898

GAELIC (the) topography of the Dunoon district. By the author of *Celtic etymology of the Campsie Fells* [Neil Thomson]. 8vo. Pp. 47. [*Brit. Mus.*]
Kirkintilloch, [1892]

GAGE (the) of red and white. [A novel.] By Graham Hope [Jessie Hope]. 8vo. [*Lit. Year Book.*]   London, 1904

GAGE (the) of the two civilizations : shall Christendom waver ? Causes of the rupture of the Treaties of Tientsin, and a general review of our relations with China. [By Gideon Nye.] Fcap 4to. Private print. Macao, 1860

GAGG (a) for the Quakers, speaking by the inspiration of the Papists. [By Thomas Smith, Vicar of Caldegate, Cambridgeshire.] 4to. Pp. 44. [Smith's *Bibl. Anti-Quak.*, p. 12.] London, 1659

GAGGE (a) for long hair'd rattle heads who revile all civil round heads. [By William Prynne.] 4to. Pp. 4.
London, 1646

GAGGE (the) of the reformed Gospell ; briefly discouering the errors of our time, with the refutation by expresse textes of their owne approoued English Bible. The second edition, augmented thoroughout the whole, by the author of the first [Matthew Kellison, D.D.]. Fcap 8vo. Pp. 168. [Gillow's *Bibl. Dict.*, iii., 683.]   [Douai], 1623

GAIETIES and gravities ; a series of essays, comic tales, and fugitive vagaries ; now first collected. By one of the authors of *Rejected addresses* [Horace Smith]. 3 vols. Fcap 8vo. [*D. N. B.*, vol. 53, p. 54.]
London, 1825

GAIETY (a) girl ; new musical comedy, in two acts : words by Owen Hall [James Davis.] 8vo. Pp. 33. [*Lit. Year Book.*]   London, [1894]

GAILES of '89 as imprinted on the mind of an Officer : the sketches by Twym [Alexander Stuart Boyd]. Obl. 8vo.   Glasgow, [1890]

GAIN (the) of a loss ; a novel, in three volumes. By the author of *The last of the Cavaliers* [Rose Piddington]. Fcap 8vo. [*Bodl.*]   London, 1866

GAINSAYER (the) convinced ; or an answer to a certain scandalous paper . . . in which the calling of the ministry of the Church of England, the right of tithes, with many other points now in controversy, are briefly cleared. By T. T. [Thomas Thache], preacher of the word at Kemble in Wiltshire. 4to. Pp. 45. [Thomason *Coll. of Tracts*, i., 172.] London, 1649

GALA-DAYS. By Gail Hamilton [Mary Abigail Dodge]. Fcap 8vo. [Kirk's *Supp.*]   Boston, [Mass.], 1863

GALATEA of the Wheatfield. [A novel.] By M. E. Francis [Mary Evans Sweetman, later Mrs Francis Blundell]. 8vo. [*Lit. Year Book.*]
London, 1909

GALATEO Espagnol ; or the Spanish gallant. By Lucas Gracian Dantisco. Done into English by W. S. [William Style ?]. Fcap 8vo.   London, 1640

GALATEO ; or a treatise on politeness and delicacy of manners, addressed to a young nobleman : from the Italian of Monsignor Giovanni de la Casa, Archbishop of Benevento. [Translated by Rev. Richard Graves of Claverton.] 12mo. [Green's *Bibl. Somers.*, ii., 444.]   London, 1774
   An abridged translation had previously appeared (1663 and 1686) as " The Refin'd Courtier. . . ." *See later.*

GALBA ; a dialogue on the Navy. [By John Moncrieff.] 8vo. [*Camb. Univ. Lib.*]   London, 1748

GALE Middleton ; a story of the present day. By the author of *Brambletye House,* etc. [Horace Smith]. 3 vols. Fcap 8vo. [*D. N. B.*, vol. 53, p. 54.]
London, 1833

GALERIO and Nerissa ; including original correspondence ; the history of an English nobleman and lady : several poetical effusions ; and a few domestic anecdotes. [By John Gale Jones.] 8vo. [*Brit. Mus.*]
London, 1804

GALILEO to Urban VIII. ; or, a history of error, in letters to [Robert Clayton] the Bp. of Clogher, occasioned by the tenth letter of ——. A Vindication of the Old and New Testament. Part II. [By Dr Robert Clayton.] 4to. [*Camb. Univ. Lib. Cat.*]
Dublin, 1758

GALLANT (a) fight. By Marion Harland [Mary Virginia Hawes, later Mrs Terhune]. Fcap 8vo. [*Kirk's Supp.*]
New York, 1888

GALLANT (the) Graham. [A novel.] By May Wynne [Mabel Wynne Knowles]. 8vo. Pp. 320. [*Lond. Lib. Cat.*]
London, 1911

GALLANT lords of Bois Doré : from the French of George Sand [Madame A. L. A. D. Dudevant]. Fcap 8vo. [*Lit. Year Book.*] New York, 1890

GALLANT (a) of Spain. [A novel.] By May Wynne [Mabel Wynne Knowles]. Cr 8vo. [*Lond. Lib. Cat.*]
London, 1920

GALLATHEA ; played before the queenes maiestie at Greenwich, on New-yeeres day at night, by the children of Pavls. [By John Lilly.] 12mo. No pagination. [*Bodl.*]
London, 1632

GALLIAE notitia ; or the present state of France : containing a general description of that kingdom [by Nicolas Besogne], translated from the last edition of the French. . . . By R. W. [Richard Wolley], M.A. Fcap 8vo. [Arber's *Term Cat.*, ii., p. 615.]
London, 1690

GALLIAE speculum ; or a new survey of the French Coast and Camp. By H. C. [Henry Care]. 12mo. [*D. N. B.*, vol. 9, p. 45.] London, 1673

GALLIENUS redivivus ; or, murther will out, &c. being a true account of the De-Witting of Glencoe, Gaffney, &c. [By Charles Leslie.] 4to.
Edinburgh, 1695
See the beginning of the tract, where it is said to have been printed in the Answer to Abp. King's book, ascribed by some to Leslie.

GALLOWAY gossip sixty years ago ; . . . manners, customs, etc. By Saxon [Robert de Bruce Trotter]. Fcap 8vo. Bedlington, 1877
The name was given by the author on a presentation copy. A later edition (1901) also bears his name.

GALPINE'S Church Catechism explained, and compared with Scripture : with a glossary. [By William Hewson, M.A.] Fcap 8vo. Pp. iv., 92. [Smales' *Whitby Authors*, p. 174.]
Selby, 1838

GAL'S gossip. By Pitcher [A— M— Binstead]. Cr 8vo. London, 1903

GALVANIST (the) ; a periodical paper. By Hydra Polycephalus, Esq. [W— D— Whittington and others]. 11 nos. 8vo. [*Brit. Mus.*]
Cambridge, [1804]

GAMBLERS (the) ; a poem : with notes critical and explanatory. [By Theophilus Swift, B.A.] 4to. Pp. 69. [Watt's *Bibl. Brit.*] London, 1777

GAMBLER'S (the) wife ; or murder will out. By the author of *The ordeal by touch* [Mrs Elizabeth Caroline Greig]. Cr 8vo. [*Brit. Mus.*]
London, [1851]

GAMBLING. Culverwell *v.* Sidebottom. A letter to Her Majesty's Attorney-General, with a full report of the above extraordinary trial. By a barrister [Frederick Laurence]. Second edition, to which are added, the Trial of Sidebottom *v.* Atkins, and Lord Derby's celebrated Letter to the Jockey Club. 8vo. London, 1859
The title of the first edition (1857) begins " Culverwell *v.* Sidebottom."

GAMBLING (the) world ; being anecdotic memories and stories of personal experience in the Temple of Hazard and speculation, with some mysteries and iniquities of Stock Exchange affairs. By " Rouge et Noir " [Henry Vizetelly] ; with an appendix by " Blue Gown " on turf gambling and bookmakers' practice. 8vo. Pp. viii., 373. London, 1898

GAME (a) at chæss as it was acted nine days to gether at the Globe on the banks side. [By Thomas Middleton.] 4to. No pagination. [Hart's *Index Expurg. Angl.*, p. 64.] N.P., [1624]

GAME. By Hawkeye [Major-General Richard Hamilton]. Second edition. 8vo. Madras, 1881

GAME fish of the Northern States of America, and British Provinces. By Barnwell [Robert Barnwell Roosevelt]. 8vo. Pp. 324. [*Lib. Journ.*, iv., 208.]
New York, 1862

GAME fishes. By Coquina [G— O—
Shields]. 8vo. [Kirk's *Supp.*]
Chicago, 1900

GAME (the) hen. [An Irish tale.] By
the author of *Flitters, tatters, and
the counsellor* [May Laffan, later Mrs
Hartley]. 8vo. Pp. 56. [S. J. Brown's
Ireland in fiction.]   Dublin, 1880

GAME (the) in Wall Street, and how
to play it successfully. By Hoyle
[William E. Forrest]. Pt 8vo. [*Amer.
Cat.*]   New York, 1898

GAME (the) laws. . . . [By Charles
Neate, M.A.] 8vo. [*D. N. B.*, vol.
40, p. 151.]   London, 1830

GAME (the) of Bridge. By "Cut
Cavendish" [Edwin Anthony]. Fcap
8vo. [*Lit. Year Book.*] London, 1909

GAME (a) of chance. By Shirley
Smith [Ella J— Curtis]. 3 vols. Pt
8vo. [*Lit. Year Book.*]
London, 1889

GAME (the) of cribbage: second
edition, with additions. By G. Dee
[George Henry Davidson]. 12mo.
[*Brit. Mus.*]   London, 1832

GAME (the) of croquet: its appoint-
ment and laws. By R. Fellow [Horace
Elisha Scudder]. 8vo. [Kirk's *Supp.*]
New York, 1866

GAME (the) of diplomacy. By a
European Diplomat [Baron Eugene N.
von Shel'king]. 8vo. Pp. 255. [*Brit.
Mus.*]   London, [1918]
Special reference is made to Russia.

GAME (the) of draughts; containing
one hundred games. By J— S. [J—
Sinclair]. 8vo. Pp. 40. [*Brit. Mus.*]
Glasgow, 1832

GAME (the) of lawn tennis. By
"Cavendish" [Henry Jones]; with
the authorised laws. Fcap 8vo. [*Lit.
Year Book.*]   London, 1886

GAME (the) of life. [A novel.] By
Darley Dale [Francesca M. Steele].
3 vols. Cr 8vo. [*Lond. Lib. Cat.*]
London, 1897

GAME (the) of life. [A novel.] By
"Waters" [William Russell]. 8vo.
Pp. 272. [*Lit. Year Book.*]
London, [1857]

GAME (the) of Logic. By Lewis
Carroll [Rev. Charles L. Dodgson,
M.A.]. Cr 8vo. [*Brit. Mus.*]
London, 1887
For an account of the pseudonym, *see*
the note to "Doublets."

GAME (the) of ombre. [By Henry
Hucks Gibbs, F.S.A.] Fcap 4to.
Private print, 1878

GAME-KEEPER (the) at home;
sketches of natural history and rural
life. By R. J. [Richard Jefferies].
8vo. [*Brit. Mus.*]   London, 1880

GAME-PRESERVER'S (the) manual.
By "High Elms" [Sir Edward Levett
Darwin]. 8vo.   Buxton, 1859
Later editions, enlarged, give the
author's name.

GAMES at cards for three players. . . .
By "Aquarius" [Lowis D'Aguilar
Jackson]. 12mo. Pp. 56. [*Brit. Mus.*]
London, 1883

GAMES for all seasons: consisting of
in-door and out-door sports, athletic
exercises, fireside amusements for
winter evenings, chess, draughts, back-
gammon, . . . etc. A sequel to "Parlour pastimes." [By George Frederick
Pardon.] 8vo. Pp. 280. [Thomas, on
Swimming, p. 283.]   London, [1869]
The preface is signed "G. F. P."

GAMES for gentlemen. By Captain
Crawley [George Frederick Pardon].
12mo. [*Lit. Year Book.*]
London, N.D.

GAMES for two players [at cards] of
the type of Piquet: arranged by
"Aquarius" [Lowis D'A. Jackson].
12mo. [*Brit. Mus.*]   London, 1884

GAMES of patience. By "Tarbart"
[Sir Thomas De La Rue, Bart.]. Fcap
8vo.   London, 1919
The pseudonym is formed from a
selection of letters in the author's name
and designation. (Private information.)

GAMES, pastimes, and amusements for
boys and girls. By "Gar" [Raymond
H. Garman]. 8vo. [*Amer. Cat.*]
Wausau, Wis., 1906

GAME'S (the) up! By Menenius [Digby
Pilot Starkey, LL.D.]. 8vo. [O'Don-
oghue's *Poets of Ireland.*]
Dublin, 1848

GAMESTER (the); a comedy. [By
Susanna Freeman Centlivre.] As it
is acted at the New-Theatre in
Lincolns-Inn-Fields, by her Majesty's
servants. 4to. [*Biog. Dram.*]
London, 1705

GAMESTER (the); a tragedy. [By
Edward Moore.] 8vo. Pp. 84.
[Watt's *Bibl. Brit.*]   London, 1753
Frequently reprinted.

GAMESTERS (the); a comedy, alter'd
from Shirley: as it is perform'd by
His Majesty's servants, at the Theatre
Royal in Drury Lane. [By David
Garrick.] 8vo. [*Biog. Dram.*]
London, 1758

GAMESTERS (the); a poem: addressed to the Mayor of C— [Canter-
bury]. [By Edward Wilkinson, surgeon at Bow, Middlesex.] 12mo and
4to. [*Brit. Mus.*]   London, 1774

GAMING-HUMOR (the) considered and reproved : or, the passion-pleasure, and exposing money to hazard by play, lot, or wager, examined. By a well-wisher to mankind [Rev. Charles Morton, Charlestown, Massachusetts]. Fcap 8vo. Pp. 52. [*Brit. Mus.*]
London, 1684
Wrongly ascribed to Sir John Denham.

GAMLE Norge ; or our holiday in Scandinavia. [By Robert Taylor Pritchett.] Fcap 8vo. Pp. xi., 312. [*Brit. Mus.*] London, 1862

GAMMER Grethel ; or German Fairy Tales and Popular Stories ; from the Collection of the Brothers Grimm and other sources, with illustrative notes. [Translated by Edgar Taylor.] Fcap 8vo. [*Brit. Mus.*] London, 1839

GAMMER Gurton's garland ; or, the nursery Parnassus : a choice collection of pretty songs and verses, for the amusement of all little good children who can neither read nor run. [By Joseph Ritson.] 8vo. Pp. 48.
London, 1810

GAMMER Gurton's pleasant stories of Patient Grissel, the Princess Rosetta, and Robin Goodfellow. . . . Newly revised and amended by Amb(rose) Mer(ton, Gent., F.S.A. [William John Thoms]). Fcap 8vo.
Westminster, [1846]

GAOL (the) chaplain. [By Erskine Neale, M.A.] 8vo. [*D. N. B.*, vol. 40, p. 141.] London, 1856
A work of fiction. The first edition appeared in 1847.

GAOL (the) cradle : who rocks it ? A plea for the abolition of juvenile imprisonment. By a member of the School-Board of London [Rev. Benjamin Waugh]. Fourth edition. Pt 8vo. Pp. 202. [*Brit. Mus.*]
London, 1876

GAOL (the) of the city of Bristol compared with what a gaol ought to be. . . . By a citizen [Miss —— Morgan]. 8vo. Pp. 96. Bristol, 1815

GAP (the) of Barnesmore ; a tale of the Irish Highlands, and the Revolution of 1688. [By Isaac Butt.] 3 vols. 8vo. [S. J. Brown's *Ireland in fiction*.]
London, 1848

GARCIA ; or the noble error : a tragedy [in five acts, and in verse]. [By F— G. Tomlins.] 8vo. Pp. 86. [*Brit. Mus.*] Private print, [1835]

GARDEN (the) ; a poem. By Jacques de Lille ; translated from the French [by Mrs —— Montelieu]. 4to. [*Brit. Mus.*] London, 1798

GARDEN (the) of a Commuter's wife. By " Barbara " [Mrs Mabel Osgood Wright]. 8vo. [*Brit. Mus.*]
London, 1905

GARDEN (the) of eloquence ; conteyninge the figures of grammar and rhetorick. . . . [By Henry Peacham, senior.] 4to. [Watt's *Bibl. Brit.*]
London, 1577

GARDEN (the) of Epicurus. By Anatole France [Jacques Anatole Thibault] ; translated from the French by Alfred Allinson. 8vo. Pp. 240. [*Lond. Lib. Cat.*] London, 1908

GARDEN (the) of Florence ; and other poems. By John Hamilton [John Hamilton Reynolds]. Pt 8vo. Pp. xiii., 175. [Allibone's *Dict.*, vol. ii.]
London, 1821

GARDEN (a) of girls : a novel. By Theo Gift [Mrs Theodora Boulger]. 3 vols. 8vo. [*Lit. Year Book.*]
London, 1879

GARDEN (the) of Hyères : a description of the most southern point on the French Riviera. By Adolphe Smith [Adolphe Smith Headingley]. 8vo. Pp. 135. [*Brit. Mus.*] London, [1880]

GARDEN (the) of Isleworth ; a sketch, in verse. By one formerly possessed of the place [Willoughby Lacy]. 8vo. [O'Donoghue's *Poets of Ireland*.]
London, 1794

GARDEN (the) of Kama, and other love lyrics from India. By Laurence Hope [Mrs Malcolm H. Nicolson, *née* Adela Florence Cory]. 8vo. [*Brit. Mus.*] London, 1901
Reissued in 1908, as " Songs from the Garden of Kama."

GARDEN (the) of life ; a manual of devotion. By the author of *The bread of life* [Augustine David Crake]. 12mo. [*Brit. Mus.*] London, 1873

GARDEN (the) of our B. Lady ; or a devout manner how to serve her in the rosary. Written by S. C., of the Society of Jesus [Sabin Chambers]. [Translated from the French of François De la croix.] 8vo. [Gillow's *Bibl. Dict.*, vol. i., p. 461.] [Douai ?], 1619

GARDEN (the) of Paradise ; or holy prayers and exercises . . . pursuing the design of the treatise of True Christianity [by John Arndt]. Now done into English [by A— W. Boehm]. 8vo. [*Brit. Mus.*] London, 1716
See a translation of the two preceding parts under " Of true Christianity."

GARDEN (a) of peace ; a medley in quietude. By F. Littlemore [Frank Frankfort Moore]. 8vo. Pp. vi., 271. [*Brit. Mus.*]   London, [1919]

GARDEN (a) of pleasure. By E. V. B. [Hon. Eleanor Vere Boyle, *née* Gordon], author of *Days and hours in a garden*. 8vo. [*Lit. Year Book*.] London, 1895

GARDEN (a) of spinsters. [A novel.] By Annie E. Holdsworth [Mrs E— Lee-Hamilton]. 8vo. [*Lit. Year Book*.]
London, 1904

GARDEN (the) of the bees ; and other poems. By Seosamh MacCathmaoil [Joseph Campbell]. Sq. 12mo. [*O'Donoghue's Poets of Ireland*.]
Belfast, 1905
The name in the title is really the Gaelic of Joseph Campbell.

GARDEN (the) of the Muses. . . . [By John Bodenham.] 12mo. London, 1610
This is the second edition of Bodenham's " Belvedere."

GARDEN (the) of the soul ; or a manual of spiritual exercises and instructions for Christians, who, living in the world, aspire to devotion. [By Richard Challoner, Bishop of Debra.] Fcap 8vo. [Gillow's *Bibl. Dict.*] Manchester, 1812
Several editions were published earlier.

GARDEN (a) of women.   By Sarah Tytler, author of *Citoyenne Jacqueline*, etc. [Henrietta Keddie]. 8vo. Pp. vi., 398.   London, 1875
Reprinted from the *Cornhill Magazine* and *Fraser's Magazine*, with additions by the author.

GARDEN (the) that I love. [By Alfred Austin.] 8vo. [*Brit. Mus.*]
London, 1900

GARDEN (the), the grove, and the field. By the author of *The Life of Dean [Isaac] Milner* [his widow, Mrs Mary Milner]. 12mo. [*Cat. of Bath Books*.]
Bath, [1852]

GARDEN (the) which was not. [A novel.]   By " Zack " [Gwendoline Keats]. Cr 8vo. [*Lit. Year Book*.]
London, 1902

GARDEN (the), you, and I. By Barbara, author of *The Garden of a Commuter's wife* [Mrs Mabel Osgood Wright]. Cr 8vo. Pp. xii., 307. [*Brit. Mus.*]   New York, 1906

GARDENER (the) and farmer's reason why. [By Robert K. Philp.] 8vo.
London, 1860

GARDENERS (the) labyrinth : containing a discourse of the gardeners life in the yearly travels to be bestowed on his plot of earth for the use of a garden. . . . By Didymus Mountaine [Thomas Hill]. 4to. [*Brit. Mus.*]
London, 1577

GARDENER'S (the) pocket-book ; or country gentleman's recreation. . . . By R. S., Gent. [Sir John Hill, M.D.]. Fcap 8vo. [*D. N. B.*, vol. 26, p. 400.]
London, N.D., [1770 ?]

GARDENS (the) and menagerie of the Zoological Society delineated. [T— Yarrell was a leading contributor.] 2 vols. 8vo.   Chiswick Press, 1830

GARIBALDI ; or, the rival patriots : a dramatic operetta, in two acts. By Rosalind [Rosalind Davis]. The music composed by F. H. Cowen. 8vo.
London, 1860

GARIBALDI ; recollections of his public and private life. . . . Translated from the French [of Marie Espérance von Schwartz] by Elpis Melena [Charles Edwards]. 8vo. Pp. x., 348. [Simm's *Bibl. Staff*., p. 153.]   London, 1887

GARIBALDI'S miraculous escapes ; or the exiles of Italy. By C. G. H. [Charles G— Hamilton].   Cr 8vo. [*Lit. Year Book*.]   London, 1857

GARLAND (a) for the New Royal Exchange, composed of the pieces of divers excellent poets, made in memory of the first and second opening thereof in 1571 and 1669. [By Sir W. Tite.] 4to. [Ellis and White's *Cat*.]
London, 1845

GARLAND (a) of Bon-Accord. [By William Walker.] 8vo. [Robertson's *Aberd. Bibl*.]   [Aberdeen], 1886

GARLAND (a) of Christmas carols, ancient and modern, including some never given before in any collection. Edited with notes, by Joshua Sylvester [John Camden Hotten]. 8vo. [Cushing's *Init. and Pseud*., i., 275.]
London, 1869

GARLAND (the) of Flora. [By Dorothea Lynde Dix ?] 8vo. London, 1829

GARLAND (the) of good-will ; divided into three parts, containing many pleasant songs and poems, with a table to find the names of the songs. By T— D— [Thomas Deloney]. 8vo. B. L. No pagination.
London, [*c.* 1685]
Reprinted by the Percy Society in 1842.

GARLAND (a) of good works, such as Christian laymen may perform to the glory of God. . . . [By George Jonathan Story.] 12mo. [*Brit. Mus.*]
London, 1869
Signed " G. J. S."

GARLAND (a) of poetry for the young. By Mrs Mary Clavers [Mrs Caroline Matilda Kirkland]. 8vo. [Cushing's *Init. and Pseud*., vol. i., p. 61.]
New York, 1872

GARLAND (a) of seven lilies. By Stephen Yorke [Mary Linskill]. 8vo. [*Lit. Year Book.*]   London, 1886

GARLAND (a) of thorns; a novel. By Alan St Aubyn [Frances Marshall]. Pt 8vo. [*Lit. Year Book.*]
London, 1893

GARMISCATH. By the author of *A Lunatic at large* [J. Storer Clouston]. Cr 8vo.   London, 1904

GARNER'D sheaves; or, handfu's frae far an' near. By the author of *Prairie Chickens* [Ralph Nisbet]. 8vo.
London, [1909]

GARNET'S ghost; addressing to the Jesuits, met in private caball, just after the murther of Sir Edmund-Bury Godfrey: written by [John Oldham] the author of the satyr against virtue (not yet printed). Folio. [*Camb. Univ. Lib.*]   [London, 1679 ?]
Directed against Henry Garnet.

GARRET van Horn; or, the beggar on horseback. By John S. Sauzade [James Payn]. 8vo. [Cushing's *Init. and Pseud.*, vol. ii., p. 135.]
New York, 1863

GARRICK'S looking-glass; or the art of rising on the stage: a poem, in three cantos. [By S— J. Pratt.] 4to. [Lowe's *Theat. Lit.*]   London, 1776

GARRISON gossip. By John Strange Winter [Mrs Arthur Stannard, *née* Henrietta E. V. Palmer]. 2 vols. Cr 8vo. [*Lit. Year Book.*] London, 1887

GARSTON (the) bigamy. [A novel.] By Albert Ross [Linn Boyd Porter]. Pt 8vo. [*Lit. Year Book.*]
New York, 1892

GARTHOWEN: a story of a Welsh homestead. By Allen Raine [Mrs Beynon Puddicombe]. 8vo. [*Lit. Year Book.*]   London, 1890

GASCONADO the Great: a tragi-comi, political, whimsical opera [in one act, and in verse. By James Worsdale]. 4to. [*Brit. Mus.*]   London, 1759

GASPAR Ruiz. By Joseph Conrad [Joseph Conrad Korzeniowski]. Cr 8vo. [*Lond. Lib. Cat.*] London, 1919

GASPARA Stampa . . . with a selection from her sonnets: translated by George Fleming [Julia Constance Fletcher]. 8vo. [*Lit. Year Book.*]
London, 1881

GASTON de Foix; a romance of the sixteenth century. [By George P. R. James.] 8vo. [*Brit. Mus.*]
London, 1844

GASTON de Foix; and other plays. By Max Baring [Charles Messent]. Cr 8vo. [*Lit. Year Book.*]
London, 1903

GATE (the) of death: a diary. [By Arthur Christopher Benson.] Pt 8vo. [*Camb. Univ. Lib.*]   London, 1906
The second edition (1909) bears the author's name.

GATE (the) of England; a romance of the days of Drake. By Morice Gerard [John Jessop Teague, M.A.]. Cr 8vo. Pp. 316. [*Lit. Year Book.*]
London, 1914

GATE (the) of heaven; an allegory. By "Jacia" [John Crane]. 8vo. [Gladstone *Lib. Cat.* (Lib. Club).]
Birmingham, 1860

GATE (the) of Paradise: a dream of Easter Eve. [By Edith S— Jacob.] 4to. Pp. 19.   London, [1898]

GATE (the) of the desert; a novel. By John Oxenham [William Arthur Dunkerley]. Cr 8vo. Pp. 332. [*Lond. Lib. Cat.*]   London, 1905

GATE (the) openers. [A novel.] By K. L. Montgomery [Kathleen and Letitia Montgomery]. Cr 8vo. Pp. 320. [*Brit. Mus.*]   London, 1912

GATE (the) to the French, Italian, and Spanish unlocked. [By William Goodhugh.] Fcap 8vo.   London, 1827

GATE (the) to the Hebrew, Arabic, and Syriac, unlocked by a new and easy method of acquiring the accidence. By the author of the Gate to the French, Italian, and Spanish, unlocked [William Goodhugh.] 8vo. Pp. viii., 92. [*Bodl.*]   London, 1828

GATELESS (the) barrier. By Lucas Malet [Mrs Mary St Leger Harrison, *née* Kingsley]. 8vo. [*Lit. Year Book.*]
London, 1900

GATES (the) of prayer; a book of private devotion for morning and evening. By the author of *Morning and night watches*, etc. [John Ross MacDuff, D.D.]. 8vo. Pp. 363.
London, 1874

GATHERED fragments. [By Margaret Hay Home Tough, of Ayton.] Pt 8vo.
Edinburgh, 1864

GATHERED fragments: briefly illustrative of the life of George Dillwyn, of Burlington, West New Jersey, North America. [Edited by Ann Alexander, *née* Dillwyn.] 8vo. [Smith's *Cat. of Friends' Books*, i., 9, 532.]
London, 1858

GATHERED leaves of many seasons; being the collected poems of "H. H." [Rev. Hugh Hutton]. Fcap 8vo. [O'Donoghue's *Poets of Ireland.*]
London, 1858

GATHERED thoughts : the Book of Common Prayer a national bond of peace. By an old clergyman in Wales [Edgar Arthur William Vaughan-Williams, M.A., in Radnorshire]. 8vo.
London, [1889]

GATHERING (the) of Brother Hilarius. [A novel.] By Michael Fairless [Margaret Fairless Barber]. 8vo. Pp. 180. [*Brit. Mus.*]   London, 1901

GATHERINGS ; a collection of short pieces, written at various periods by the author of *The listener*, &c. [Caroline Fry]. Fcap 8vo. Pp. ix., 275. [*Brit. Mus.*]   London, 1839

GATHERINGS [in prose and verse]. By C. E. W. [Charlotte E— Woods]. 8vo. Pp. iv., 239. [*Brit. Mus.*]
London, [1890]

GATHERINGS from Spain. . . . By the author of *The Handbook of Spain* [Richard Ford]. Pt 8vo. [*Brit. Mus.*]
London, 1846

GATHERINGS from the pit-heaps ; or, the aliens of Shiney Row. By Coleman Collier [Rev. James Everett]. 8vo. [Kirk's *Supp.*]   London, 1861

GATHERINGS of a country rambler. [By Lady Frances Elizabeth Dickens.] 8vo. [Kirk's *Supp.*]   London, 1853

GAUL, King of Ragah ; a tragic drama, in three parts. [By W. R. Hawkes.] Fcap 8vo. [Watt's *Bibl. Brit.*]
London, 1813
Assigned also to Clio Rickman.

GAVEROCKS (the) ; a tale of the Cornish coast. By the author of *John Herring* [Sabine Baring-Gould]. 3 vols. Cr 8vo. [Kirk's *Supp.*]
London, 1887

GAVIOTA (la) ; the sea-gull : or the lost beauty. By Fernando Caballero [Cicilia B. de F. Arrom]. Fcap 8vo. [Baker's *Guide to fiction.*]
Philadelphia, 1877

GAWTHORNE (the) correspondence. The Archbishop of Canterbury and the Rev. W. Brudenell Barter's " Few words." [By Henry T. James Bagge, B.A.] 8vo. [*Brit. Mus.*]
London, 1852

GAWYIM Honor ; a tragedy in five acts [and in verse]. By the author of *Waldenberg* [Margaret E. M. Jones]. 8vo. [*Brit. Mus.*]   London, [1844 ?]

GAY. By the author of *Laddie* [Evelyn Whitaker]. Cr 8vo. Pp. 316. [*Amer. Cat.*]   Edinburgh, 1903

GAY (the) deceiver ; a farce. By Arthur Griffinhoof, of Turnham Green [George Colman, jun.]. 8vo. [Cushing's *Init. and Pseud.*, vol. i., p. 120.]
London, 1808

GAY (the) life. [A novel.] By Keble Howard [John Keble Bell]. Cr 8vo. [*Lond. Lib. Cat.*]   London, 1916

GAY life in New York ! . . . By an old traveller [Henry Llewellyn Williams]. 8vo. [Cushing's *Init. and Pseud.*, vol. i., p. 213.]   New York, [1866]

GAY (a) little woman. [A novel.] By John Strange Winter [Mrs Arthur Stannard, *née* Henrietta E. V. Palmer]. Cr 8vo. Pp. 126. [*Lit. Year Book.*]
London, 1897

GAY morning. By J. E. Buckrose [Mrs Falconer Jameson]. Cr 8vo. Pp. 320. [*Lond. Lib. Cat.*]
London, 1914

GAY young creatures. By " Majude " [Louis Cohen]. 8vo. Pp. 76.
[Dutoitspan, South Africa], 1880

GAYWORTHYS (the) ; a story of threads and thrums. By the author of *Faith Gartney's girlhood* [Adelina D. Train Whitney]. New edition. 8vo. Pp. viii., 400. [*Adv. Lib.*]
London, 1866
Signed " A. D. T. W."

GAZETTEER (a) of France ; containing every city, town, and village in that extensive country. . . . [By Clement Crutwell.] 3 vols. Fcap 8vo. [*Camb. Univ. Lib.*]   London, 1793

GAZETTEER (a) of the Old and New Testaments : to which is added the natural history of the Bible. [By John Parker Lawson.] 2 vols. 8vo. [*D. N. B.*, vol. 32, p. 296.]
Edinburgh, 1838

GEBIR ; a poem, in seven books. [By Walter Savage Landor.] 8vo. Pp. 74. [*D. N. B.*, vol. 32, p. 55.]
London, 1798

GE—GE and F—st—r [George and Forster] ; a new ballad. . . .
See below, " Ge[or]ge and F[or]st[e]r. . . ."

GEISHA (the) : a story of a tea-house ; a Japanese musical play. Words by Owen Hall [James Davis, B.A.]. 8vo. Pp. 32. [*Lit. Year Book.*]
London, [1897]

GEMINI. By Toler King [Mrs Emily Fox]. Fcap 8vo. [Haynes' *Pseud.*]
Boston, 1878

GEMINI, and lesser lights. By " Kim Bilir " [A— H— Scaife]. Fcap 4to. [*Lib. of Col. Inst.*]
Victoria (B.C.), 1901

GEMMA of the Isles, a lyrical drama ; and other poems. By A. and L. [Arabella and Louisa Shore]. 8vo. [*Brit. Mus.*]   London, 1859

GEMMARIUS fidelis ; or the faithful lapidary : experimentally describing the richest treasures of nature, in an historical narration of the several natures, virtues, and qualities of all precious stones. . . . By T. N. [Thomas Nichols, or Nicols]. 4to. [*Watt's Bibl. Brit.*]   Cambridge, 1652

GEMS of art ; containing specimens of the works of Rubens, Titian, Cuyp Hobbima . . . executed in colors : with letter-press descriptions by the author of *Beauties of English scenery*, etc. [A. Thomson ?]. 4to.
London, [1861]

GEMS of sacred poetry. [Edited by Richard Cattermole.] 2 vols. Fcap 8vo. [*Brit. Mus.*]   London, 1841
Introductory essay signed " R. C."

GEMS, selected from the antique, with illustrations. [By Richard Dagley.] 4to. [*Bodl.*]   London, 1804

GEMS, talismans, and guardians : the facts, fancies, legends and lore of nativity. By Ten Alcott [Charles Adiel Lewis Totten]. 8vo. [*Kirk's Supp.*]   New York, 1887

GENDER (a) in satins. [A novel.] By " Rita " [Eliza M. J. Gollan, later Mrs Otto von Booth, afterwards Mrs W. Desmond Humphreys]. Cr 8vo. [*Lit. Year Book.*]   London, 1895

GENEALOGICAL (a) account of the Barclays of Urie, formerly of Mather ; extracted from ancient registers, and authentic documents ; together with memoirs of the life of Colonel David Barclay of Urie : collected for the information and use of their posterity. [By Robert Barclay, son of the Apologist.] 8vo. Pp. 61. [*Martin's Cat.*]   Aberdeen, 1740

GENEALOGICAL account of the descendents of James Young, merchant burgess of Aberdeen, and Rachel Cruikshank, his wife, 1697-1893 ; with notes. . . . [By Alexander Johnston, followed by Colonel W. Johnston, C.B.] 4to. [*Aberd. Free Lib.*]
Aberdeen, 1894

GENEALOGICAL and historical table of the families of Heron : verified throughout by records, and other authentic documents. [By the Rt. Hon. Sir Richard Heron.] Folio. [*W.*]   N.P., 1797

GENEALOGICAL collections concerning the Sir-Name of Baird, and the families of Auchmedden, Newbyth, and Saughton Hall. With notes. . . . [By William N. Fraser.] 4to. [*Brit. Mus.*]   N.P., 1870

GENEALOGICAL descent of the royal house of Bruce, until the accession of Robert II., 1370-1 ; of II. Marjorie, Countess of Carrick, mother of Robert the Bruce ; and III. Scheme exhibiting the collateral descent from David I. of Bruce and Baliol, the competitors for the throne in 1291-2, and of Comyn of Badenoch (slain in 1306) ; with IV. Some of the expenses of the funeral of Robert I.—1320. [By John Parker.] 8vo. Pp. 20. [*Jas. Maidment.*] N.P., N.D.

GENEALOGICAL, heraldic, and other records . . . of the family of Woodd. [By Henry Woodd]. Folio. Private print.   London, 1886

GENEALOGICAL (a) history of the families of Ogston. [By Alexander Milne Ogston.] 8vo. Edinburgh, 1876

GENEALOGICAL history of the family of Brabazon ; from its origin, down to Sir William Brabazon, Lord Treasurer, and Lord Chief Justice of Ireland, temp. Henry VIII., who died in 1552, the common ancestor of the Earl of Meath, and of the Brabazons of Brabazon Park. . . . down to Sir William John Brabazon of Brabazon Park, in the County of Mayo, Bart., now surviving. [Edited by Hercules Sharp, of Domons, Northiam, Sussex.] 4to. Pp. 21 ; Appendix, pp. lvi. ; Fragment, par le Chevalier Courcelles, pp. 4. [*W.*]   Paris, 1825

GENEALOGICAL (a) history of the house of Yvery, in its different branches of Yvery, Luvel, Perceval, and Gournay. [By J— Anderson.] 2 vols. 8vo. [*Book prices current, 1911.*]
London, private print, 1742

GENEALOGICAL history of the Savage family in Ulster ; being a revision and enlargement of certain chapters of " The Savages of the Ards," compiled by members of the family . . . and edited by G. F. A. S. A. [G— F. A. S. Armstrong]. Large 4to. Private print.
N.P., 1906

GENEALOGICAL (a) memoir of the Duffs. [By William Baird.] 8vo. [*S.S.C. Lib. Cat.*]   Aberdeen, 1869

GENEALOGICAL memoranda relating to the Browne and Hawkins families. [By Reginald Stewart Boddington.] 4to. [*Brit. Mus.*]   [London, 1878]

GENEALOGICAL memoranda relating to the family of Schank, or Shank, of Castlerig, in the County of Fife, N.B. [By Edward G. Weavring.] 4to.
London, 1885

GENEALOGICAL memoranda relating to the family of Sotheran, and to the sept of MacManus. [By Charles Sotheran.] 4to. Private print.
N.P., 1874

GENEALOGIE (the) of the Mac-
kenzies, preceeding ye year M.DC.LXI.
Wreattin in ye year M.DC.LIX. By a
persone of qualitie (Mackenzie of
Applegarth). [Printed from a MS.
written by Sir George Mackenzie
of Rosehaugh, afterward Earl of
Cromarty, Viscount Tarbet, and Lord
Clerk Register of Scotland. The
editor was J. W. Mackenzie, Esq.,
W.S.] 4to. [Martin's *Cat.*]
                              Edinburgh, 1829

GENEALOGIE (the) of the most noble . . .
    See below, " Genealogy (the) of the most
    noble . . ."

GENEALOGIES (the) recorded in the
Sacred Scriptures, according to every
family and tribe, with the line of our
Saviour Christ observed from Adam
to the Blessed Virgin Mary. By J. S.
[John Speed]. 4to. [Lowndes' *Brit.
Lib.*, p. 340.]   London, 1611, 1615

GENEALOGY (the) of Christ ; as it is
represented in the east-window in the
college chappel at Winchester ; a
poem. By a young gentleman of
Winchester School [Robert Lowth,
D.D.]. 8vo. [*Bodl.*] London, 1729

GENEALOGY of Her Majesty Queen
Victoria, through the Anglo-Saxon,
Scottish, Norman, Welsh, and Este-
Guelphic lines ; with illustrative his-
torical notes.   By an amateur
[Archibald N. Carmichael]. Third
edition. 8vo. [*Adv. Lib.*]
                              Edinburgh, 1845
    Signed " A. N. C."

GENEALOGY (the) of Queen Victoria
traced from our first parents, according
to the tradition of the Coronation-
stone ; collated, designed and drawn
by Shirley Smith [Ella Curtis]. Single
sheet.   N.P., [1885]

GENEALOGY (the) of the families of
Douglas of Milderg, and Robertson of
Kindeace, with their descendants.
[By Rev. Gustavus Aird, D.D., of
Creich.] 4to.   Dingwall, 1895

GENEALOGY (the) of the most noble
and ancient House of Drummond. By
the Honourable William Drummond,
afterwards Viscount of Strathallan
MDCLXXXI. [Reprinted and edited by
David Laing.] 4to. Pp. 331.
                              Edinburgh, 1831
    The original title is, " The Genealogie
of the most noble and ancient House of
Drummond : containing a true accompt
of the original extractione, the offspring,
and allayes of that family ; deduced from
the first of that name, ane Hungarian
gentleman, and continowed to the present
age. By a friend to vertue and the
family. Collected in the year 1681."

GENEALOGY (the) of the Stewarts
refuted : in a letter to Andrew Stuart,
Esq., M.P. [By Sir Henry Steuart,
Bart., LL.D.] 8vo. [*Adv. Lib.*]
                              Edinburgh, 179

GENEALOGY simplified and applied
to the illustrations of British history :
with a description of the changes which
have taken place in the armorial bearings of the sovereigns of England. By
Archibald Barrington, M.D. [Frederick
Glasspool]. Fcap 8vo. Pp. viii., 141.
[*Manch. Free Lib.*]   London, 1843

GENERAL (the) ; a poem : respectfully inscribed to the Right Honourable
The Marquis of Granby. By the
author of *A Trip to the moon* [Francis
Gentleman]. 4to. [*Bodl.*]
                              London, 1764

GENERAL (a) abridgement of cases in
Equity, argued and adjuged in the
High Court of Chancery, etc., digested
under proper titles, with notes and
references to the whole. By a gentle-
man of the Middle Temple. [Attributed
respectively to R. Foley, Sir G.
Gilbert, Mathew Bacon, and ——
Pooley.] Fourth edition. 2 vols. Folio.
[*W.*]   In the Savoy, 1756

GENERAL (a) account of Miranda's
Expedition [to effect a Revolution in
South America. By John N. Sher-
man]. Pp. 120. [*Brit. Mus.*]
                              New York, 1808

GENERAL (a) account of Tunbridge
Wells and its environs, historical and
descriptive. [By Rev. Richard Oneley
B.A.] Fcap 8vo. Pp. viii., 54. [Smith's
Bibl. Cant.]   London, 1771

GENERAL (a) and descriptive history
of the ancient and present state of the
town of Liverpool, comprising a review
of its government, police, antiquities
and modern improvements. . . . The
whole carefully compiled from original
manuscripts, authentic records, and
other warranted authorities. [By
James Wallace.] 8vo. [*Upcott.*]
                              Liverpool, 1795
    Reprinted in 1797.

GENERAL and equitable commutation
of tithes ; a plan for the general commutation of lay and ecclesiastical tithes
into corn rents : being a self-adjusting
mode of payment . . . three letters.
[By Richard Howlett Jago.] 8vo.
                              Wells, 1830
    The second edition (London 1833) has
the author's name.

GENERAL (a) and particular account of
the annular eclipse of the sun, which
will happen on Sunday, April 1, 1764,
in the forenoon. [By Captain Robert
Heath.] 4to. [*W.*]   London, 1764

GENERAL and rare memorials pertayning to the perfect arte of navigation; annexed to the Paradoxal cumpas, in playne : now first published ; 24 yeres after the first invention thereof. [By John Dee, D.C.L.] Folio. Pp. 107.   London, 1577
    " I have Dr Dee's autograph of this work."—F. Douce.

GENERAL (the) Assembly of the Church of Scotland vindicated ; in answer to a Letter from several elders, lovers of peace and moderation. . . . By a friend of the constitution of the Church [Rev. James Nasmith, minister at Dalmeny]. Cr 8vo. Pp. 32. [Scott's *Fasti*.]   Edinburgh, 1753

GENERAL (the) Assembly ; or a discourse of the gathering of all the saints to Christ : wherein it appears that all saints, in all places and ages, shall at last be gathered to Christ their Head : being some few meditations on II. Thess. 11/1. By O. H. [Oliver Heywood]. 8vo. [Arber's *Term Cat.*, iii., 161.]   London, 1699

GENERAL (the) [*i.e.*, Charles Lee], attacked by a Subaltern ; or, the Strictures on the Friendly Address examined, and a refutation of its principles attempted : addressed to the people of America. [By Captain Henry Barry.] 8vo. Pp. 14. [Evans' *Amer. Bibl.*, vol. 5, p. 102.]
            [Boston, Mass.], 1775

GENERAL (a) bibliographical dictionary ; from the German of Frederick Adolphus Ebert, librarian to the king of Saxony, &c. [Translated by Arthur Browne, M.A.] 4 vols. 8vo. Pp. xvii., 2050. [*W.*]   Oxford, 1837
    The pagination is continued throughout the four volumes.

GENERAL (a) biographical dictionary. By John Gorton, author of the *General Topographical Dictionary*, etc. [About one-third of the articles were written by the Rev. Richard Harris Barham.] A new edition. 3 vols. 8vo. [*W.*]
              London, 1847

GENERAL (a) chronological history of the air, weather, seasons, meteors, &c. in sundry places and different times ; more particularly for the space of 250 years. . . . [By Thomas Short, M.D.] 2 vols. 8vo. [*D. N. B.*, vol. 52, p. 154.]   London, 1749

GENERAL Confession of the true Christian Faith and Religion [by John Knox], according to God's word, and acts of our Parliament, subscribed . . . at Edinburgh 28th of Januarie 1581. 8vo. [*W.*]
    London, Rob. Waldegrave, [1581]

GENERAL (the) contents of the British Museum, with remarks, serving as a directory to that noble cabinet. [By Robert Dodsley.] 8vo. [*Cat. of Lond. Inst.*, ii., 219.]   London, 1761

GENERAL (a) corresponding, circulating and friendly letter, with particular addresses, I. To the patrons of the Presbyterian Church of Scotland, together with the officers of the crown, through whose hands the king's presentations may come. II. To the professors of divinity and teachers of youth, in the universities and other seminaries of learning. III. To the students of divinity and expectants of the ministry. IV. To the Gospel ministers and lay-elders. V. A supplement to the foregoing. VI. An address to the Christian people in all vacant congregations of the Presbyterian Church of Scotland. VII. Select thoughts and meditations. [By John Fleming.] 8vo. Pp. 84. [*David Laing.*]   Glasgow, 1771
    The Letter is signed " J. F."

GENERAL (the) delusion of Christians, touching the way of God's revealing himself, to, and by the prophets, evinced from Scripture and primitive antiquity ; and many principles of scoffers, atheists, Sadducees, and wild enthusiasts, refuted. . . . Four parts. [By John Lacy.] 8vo. Pp. ix., 508. [*G. C. Boase.*]   London, 1713
    Assigned also to Francis Lee.
    Republished, with preface and notes [by Edward Irving, M.A.]. London, 1832.

GENERAL (a) dictionary of husbandry, planting, gardening, and the vegetable part of the materia medica. . . . [By Richard Cruttwell.] 8vo. Bath, 1779

GENERAL (a) draught and prospect of government in Europe, and civil policy; shewing the antiquity, power, decay, of Parliaments : with other historical and political observations relating thereunto. [By Thomas Rymer.] 8vo. Pp. 96. [*Bodl.*]   London, 1681
    The author's name is in the handwriting of Barlow.

GENERAL (the) election : a working man's advice. [By Thomas Adolphus Trollope.] 8vo. [*Brit. Mus.*]
           London, [1892]

GENERAL (a) epistle of brotherly admonition and counsel, to the people called Quakers, in Great Britain, Ireland, and America ; issued at the time of the yearly meeting in London anno 1803, on behalf of sundry brethren concerned for the religious improvement of that Society. By Theophilus Freeman [William Matthews]. 8vo. [Smith's *Cat. of Friends' Books*, ii., 166.] London, 1803

GENERAL (a) epistle to all who have believed in the light of the Lord Jesus, and are called to follow the Lamb through the Great Tribulation. [By Francis Howgill.] 4to. [*Brit. Mus.*]
[London, 1665]
Signed " F. H."

GENERAL (a) epistle to be read in all the Christian meetings in the world. . . . By G. F. [George Fox]. 4to. [Smith's *Cat. of Friends' Books.*]　　N.P., 1662

GENERAL (a) epistle to Friends, and all people, to read over and consider in the fear of God. . . . By G. F. [George Fox]. 4to.　　N.P., 1667

GENERAL (a) epistle to the dispersed and persecuted flock of Christ Jesus in the dominion of England and all parts and regions where this shall come, who have believed in Christ. [By Francis Howgill.] 4to. [*Brit. Mus.*]
London, 1665
Signed " F. H."

GENERAL (a) essay on military tactics : with an introductory discourse. . . . Translated (from the French of Jacques Ant. Hypol. Guibert) by an officer [Lieut. Douglas]. 2 vols. 8vo. [Lowndes' *Bibl. Man.*, p. 954.]
London, 1781

GENERAL (the) Fast ; a lyric ode : with a form of prayer proper for the occasion, and a dedication to the King. By the author of *The Duenna* [Richard Brinsley B. Sheridan]. 4to. [*Brit. Mus.*]　　London, 1775

GENERAL Frankie ; a story for little folks. By Ethel Lynn [Mrs Ethelinda Beers]. Fcap 8vo. [Kirk's *Supp.*]
New York, 1863

GENERAL George ; a story of the Chouan Campaign. By Moreton Hall [Juliette Heale]. Cr 8vo. Pp. 256.　　London, 1903

GENERAL (the) grievances and oppression of the isles of Orkney and Shetland. . . . All in two parts. With an appendix of pieces. [By James Fea.] Cr 8vo. Pp. 116, vi. [Cursiter's *Lit. on Orkney and Shetland.*]
Edinburgh, 1750
The work was never continued beyond chap. i. of Part II.
Ascribed also to James Mackenzie, S.S.C.

GENERAL heads relating to the intended enlargement of the limits of the city of Edinburgh. [By Robert Wallace, D.D.] 4to. [*Adv. Lib.*]
[Edinburgh, 1760]

GENERAL hints for improving the merchant service of the United Kingdom. By a pilot who has hitherto weathered the storm [James Brown]. 8vo. [*W.*]　　Glasgow, 1825

GENERAL (a) history of Connecticut, from its first settlement under George Fenwick, Esq., to its latest period of amity with Great Britain ; including a description of the country, and many curious and interesting anecdotes. . . . By a gentleman of the Province [Samuel Andrew Peters]. 8vo. [Cushing's *Init. and Pseud.*, vol. i., p. 115.]
London, 1781

GENERAL (the) history of earthquakes ; being an account of the most remarkable and tremendous earthquakes that have happened in divers parts of the world, from the creation to this time, as they are recorded by sacred and common authors ; and particularly those lately in Naples, Smyrna, Jamaica and Sicily : with a description of the famous burning mount, Ætna, in that island. . . . By R. B. [Richard Burton, *i.e.*, Nathaniel Crouch]. 12mo. Pp. 180.
London, 1694
See the note to " Admirable curiosities."
Wrongly ascribed by some to Richard Browne.

GENERAL (the) history of printing, from the first invention of it in the city of Mentz to its progress and propagation through the most celebrated cities in Europe. . . . By S. P. [Samuel Palmer, printer ; but the most of the work was done by George Psalmanazar.] 4to. Pp. xii., 400.
London, 1729
For Psalmanazar, see note to " Essays on the following subjects . . ."

GENERAL (a) history of quadrupeds. [By Ralph Beilby.] The figures engraved on wood are by T. Bewick. Second edition. 8vo. [*Lond. Lib. Cat.*]　　Newcastle-upon-Tyne, 1791

GENERAL (a) history of Stirling ; containing a description of the town, and origin of the Castle and burgh. [By Capt. Sutherland.] Fcap 8vo.
Stirling, 1794

GENERAL history of the Christian Church, from her birth to her final triumphant state in heaven. . . . By Signor Pastorini [Charles Walmesley, D.D.]. 8vo. [Alzog's *Church History.*]　　London, 1798

GENERAL (a) history of the County of Norfolk, intended to convey all the information of a Norfolk tour, with the more extended details of antiquarian, statistical . . . and miscellaneous information. [By John Chambers.] 2 vols. 8vo. [*Brit. Mus.*]
Norwich, 1829
The pagination is continuous.

GENERAL (the) history of the highways in all parts of the world, more particularly in Great Britain. . . . [Translated from the French of Nicolas Bergier.] Book I. 8vo. [*Brit. Mus.*]
London, 1712
No more translated.

GENERAL (a) history of trade, and especially consider'd as it respects the British commerce, as well at home, as to all parts of the world ; with a discourse of the use of harbours and roads for shipping, as it relates particularly to the filling up the harbour of Dunkirk. This for the month of July. [By Daniel Defoe.] 8vo. [*Wilson's Life of Defoe.*] London, 1713

GENERAL (the) inefficacy and insincerity of a late or deathbed repentance ; with earnest disswasives from committing our eternal condition to that infinite hazard. . . . By T. B. [Thomas Beverley]. 4to. [Arber's *Term Cat.*, i., 25 and 538.] London, 1670

GENERAL instructions by way of Catechism ; in which the history and tenets of [the Roman Catholic] religion . . . are briefly explained by the Scriptures and tradition : translated from the French, and carefully compared with the Spanish approved translation. By S. Ll. [Silvester Lewis Lloyd, O.S.F.]. Part I. 8vo. [Gillow's *Bibl. Dict.*, iv., 291.] London, 1722
No more was published. The work was condemned in the Index.

GENERAL instructions for the hydrographic surveyors of the Admiralty. [By John Washington.] 8vo.
London, 1862
Signed " J. W."

GENERAL (a) introduction to the Apostolical Epistles. By a Bishop's chaplain [Rev. Frederick Martin]. 8vo. [Bartholomew's *Camb. Books.*]
Cambridge, 1861

GENERAL John Regan. By George A. Birmingham [James Owen Hannay, D.D.], author of *Spanish Gold*, etc. Cr 8vo. Pp. 324. [S. J. Brown's *Ireland in Fiction.*] London, 1913

GENERAL (the) lover : a comedy [in five acts and in prose]. By Mr [Theophilus] Moss [—— Marriot]. 8vo. [*Bibl. Dram.*] London, 1749

GENERAL (the) manager's story : old-time reminiscences of railroading in the United States. By Fred. Benton Williams [Herbert Elliott Hamblen]. Cr 8vo. [*Amer. Cat.*]
New York, 1898

GENERAL observations upon music. [By George F— Graham.] 8vo. [*Grove's Dict. of Music.*]
Edinburgh, 1817

GENERAL (the) post-bag ; or, news, foreign and domestic. By Humphrey Hedgehog [John Agg]. 8vo.
London, 1815

GENERAL principles of grammar. [By Caroline Frances Cornwallis.] Fcap 8vo. [*Brit. Mus.*] London, 1847
Small books on great subjects, No. xii.

GENERAL remarks on the British fisheries. By a North Briton [Thomas Gordon]. 8vo. [Watt's *Bibl. Brit.*]
London, 1784

GENERAL remarks on the system of government in India ; with further considerations on the present state of the Company at home and abroad. [By Captain —— Smith.] 8vo. Pp. 130. [*Manch. Free Lib. Cat.*, p. 654.]
London, 1773

GENERAL (a) sketch of the history of Pantheism. [By Constance E. Plumptre.] 2 vols. 8vo. [*Brit. Mus.*]
London, 1878

GENERAL Skobeleff and the Slavonic cause. By O. K. [Madame Olga Kireef Novikoff]. 8vo. [*Lond. Lib. Cat.*] London, 1883

GENERAL (a) theorem for A**** [Trinity] Coll. Declamation. By —— ; with copious notes by Gronovius [Rev. Charles V. Le Grice, M.A.]. 8vo. [*Camb. Univ. Lib.*] Cambridge, 1796

GENERAL (a) treatise of commerce, in which that of all nations is particularly described and consider'd ; with an account of all the foreign banks, and species and denominations of monies, with their current and intrinsick value, and of the method of foreign and domestick exchange ; with an introductory discourse on the nature and origin of exchange. . . . [By Alexander Justice.] 4to. [Watt's *Bibl. Brit.*] London, 1707
Attributed also to Samuel Rickard.

GENERAL (a) treatise of monies and exchanges ; in which those of all trading nations are particularly describ'd and consider'd : with an account of all the foreign banks and different species and denominations of monies, with their current and intrinsick value ; and of the method and practice of foreign and domestick exchanges. . . . By a well-wisher to trade [Alexander Justice]. 4to. [*Bodl.*] London, 1707
Dedication signed " A. J."

GENERAL (a) treatise of the dominion and laws of the sea, containing what is most useful upon that subject in ancient and modern authors, and particularly the excellent body of sea-laws lately publish'd in France, besides the ancient laws of the Rhodians,

and of Oleron, and other countries ;
with a collection of the marine treaties
concluded during the last century.
. . . [By Alexander Justice.]   4to.
[Arber's *Term Cat.*, iii., 686.]
London, 1706

GENERAL (a) treatise of the reduction of
the exchanges, moneys, and real species
of most places in Europe. . . . By a
well-wisher to trade [Alexander Justice].
4to. [*Camb. Univ. Lib.*] London, 1707
    See also " A General treatise of monies.
. . ."

GENERAL (a) treatise on various cold
mineral waters in England, but more
particularly those at Harrogate, Thorp-
Arch, Dorst-Hill, Wigglesworth, etc.
[By Thomas Short, M.D.]   8vo.   Pp.
viii., 248. [*Brit. Mus.*]
London, 1765

GENERAL (the) use of machinery, at
a time when the poor are starving for
want of employment, proved to be
destructive to the morals and happiness
of the nation.   [By J. Dallinger ?]
8vo. [*W.*]   Dallinghoo, 1821
    Signed " An Englishman."

GENERAL (a) view of England . . . in
a letter to A. M. L. C. D.   By
M. V. D. M. [Mons. Vivant De
Mezague] : now translated from the
French. 8vo. [*Brit. Mus.*]
London, 1766

GENERAL (a) view of the agriculture
of Hertfordshire, drawn up for the
consideration of the Board of Agriculture and internal improvement. By
the secretary of the Board [Arthur
Young]. 8vo. Pp. xix., 236. [*Upcott.*]
London, 1804

—— the county of Essex.   2 vols. 8vo.
London, 1807

—— the county of Lincoln.   8vo.   Pp.
462.   London, 1799

—— of the county of Norfolk. 8vo.
London, 1804

—— the county of Suffolk.   8vo.
London, 1804

GENERAL (a) view of the arguments
for the unity of God ; and against the
divinity and pre-existence of Christ,
from reason, from the scriptures, and
from history.   [By Joseph Priestley,
LL.D.]   Fcap 8vo.   [Bogue and
Bennett's *Hist. of Dissenters*, ii., 510.]
Birmingham, 1783.
    Wrongly ascribed to William Frend.

GENERAL (a) view of the East India
Company, written in January, 1769;
to which are added some observations
on the present state of their affairs.
[By Alexander Dalrymple, F.R.S.]
8vo. Pp. vii., 109. [*Brit. Mus.*]
London, 1772

GENERAL (a) view of the stage. By
Mr Wilkes [Samuel Derrick].   8vo.
[Watt's *Bibl. Brit.*]   London, 1759

GENERAL (a) vindication of the
Catholic's Remarks on the intolerant
charge of Shute Barrington, Bishop
of Durham, to the clergy of his diocese ;
with appropriate animadversions on
three illiberal replies attempted to be
made. . . . By a Catholic divine [John
Lingard, D.D.]. 8vo. Pp. 97. [*D.
N. B.*, vol. 33, p. 322.]   Dublin, 1808
    Another edition was issued at Newcastle
in the same year.

GENERAL (a) volume of epitaphs,
original and selected : with a large
selection of striking and appropriate
texts of Scripture, and an historical
and moral essay, on the subject. By
a clergyman [Benjamin Richings].
8vo. Pp. lxxvii., 168. [*Bodl.*]
London, 1840

GENERALL (a) bill of mortality of the
clergie of London, which have been
defunct by reason of the contagious
breath of the sectaries. [By Matthew
Griffith, D.D.] 4to. [*D. N. B.*, vol.
23, p. 234.]   London, 1646

GENERALL (the) history of women ;
containing the lives of the most holy
and profane, the most famous and infamous in all ages, exactly described
not only from poeticall fictions, but
from the most ancient, modern, and
admired historians in our times.   By
T. H. [Thomas Heywood], Gent. 8vo.
Pp. 651. [*Brit. Mus.*] London, 1657
    A new edition of the author's " Γυναικεῖον,
or nine books of various history concerning
women . . ." (1624).

GENERALL (the) Junto ; or the covn-
cell of union, chosen equally out of
England, Scotland and Ireland, for
the better compacting of three nations
into one monarchy, &c. [By Henry
Parker.] Folio. [*D. N. B.*, vol. 43,
p. 241.]   N.P., 1642
    The dedication is signed " H. P." These
initials have led to misattribution of the
work to Hugh Peters.

GENERALL (a) table of Europe, re-
presenting the present and future state
thereof ; from the Prophecies of Kol-
terus, Christiana, and Drabricius, etc.
Collected out of the originals. [By
John Amos Comenius.] 4to. [*Brit.
Mus.*]   [London], 1670
    An appendix of the " Planting of the
Christian religion in China," etc.

GENERAL'S (the) wife. [A novel.] By
M. Hamilton [Mrs Churchill-Luck,
née Spottiswoode]. Cr 8vo. Pp. 286.
[*Lond. Lib. Cat.*]   London, 1916

GENERATION (a) of Judges. By their reporter [William D. I. Foulkes, barrister]. 8vo.   London, 1886

דר דרשים. Generation (the) of seekers ; or the right manner of the saints addresses to the throne of grace : in two treatises . . . of prayer. [By John Oldfield, minister at Carsington, Derbyshire.] Fcap 8vo.   Pp. 464.   [Calamy's Nonconf. Mem., Palmer's edition, vol. i., p. 400.]   London, 1671
    The preface is signed " O. J."

GENEROUS (the) Free-mason ; or, the constant lady : with the humours of Squire Noodle, and his man Doodle. A tragi - comi - farcical ballad opera, in three acts, with the musick pre-fix'd to each song. By the author of The Lover's opera [William Rufus Chetwood]. 8vo. [Biog. Dram.]   London, 1731
    The Lover's opera is not anonymous.

GENEROUS (a) friendship ; or, the happenings of a New England summer. [By Emma Turner.] 8vo.   Pp. 308. [Brit. Mus.]   London, [1885]

GENEROUS (the) impostor ; a comedy, as it is now performing at the Theatre-Royal, Drury-Lane.   [By Thomas Lewis O'Beirne, Bishop of Meath.] 8vo. Pp. 117. [Gent. Mag., xcii., i., 472.]   London, 1781

GENESIS and modern science. . . . (Founded upon the Sorbonne Lectures of Monsignor Meignan, Bishop of Châlons-sur-Marne). By the author of Christ in the Law [Rev. Robert H. Nisbet Browne]. 8vo.   [Brit. Mus.]   London, 1881
    Signed " R. H. N. B."

GENESIS : Biblical, historical, bio-graphical, doctrinal, moral, and social truths blended. By a layman [Henry Hart]. 8vo.   Vol. I.   Pp. xvi., 232. [Brit. Mus.]   London, [1890]

GENESIS in advance of present science : a critical examination of Chapters I. to IX. By a septuagenarian bene-ficed presbyter [Rev. Henry Smith-Warleigh]. 8vo.   London, 1883
    Signed " R. H. S."

ΓΕΝΕΣΙΣ καὶ τέλος ἐξουσίας. The original and end of civil power. . . . By Eutactus Philodemius [Anthony As-cham]. Fcap 4to. [Camb. Univ. Lib. Cat.]   London, 1649

GENESIS, miracles, and the predictions according to Spiritism. By Allan Kardec [H— L. D. Rivail]. Trans-lated from the French by Anna Blackwell. 8vo. [Lond. Lib. Cat.]   London, 1883

GENESIS (the) of the angels ; or, the Mosaic narrative of creation and geo-logy reconciled. [By Patrick Buchan.] 8vo. Pp. xvi., 233. [And. Jervise.]   Glasgow, 1870

GENESIS (the) of the earth and of man. [By Edward William Lane.] 8vo.   London, 1860

GENESIS (the) of the Goldfields Law in Australia. By Rolf Boldrewood [Thomas Alexander Browne]. 8vo. [Lib. Royal Colon. Instit., Supp. I., p. 92.]   Sydney, 1897

GENESIS ; or, the details of the Austrian Revolution [of 1848]. By an officer of state [F— Hartig, Count]. 8vo.   London, 1872

GENESIS : the three first chapters and their meanings, interpreted through the study of the connexion of Jewish symbols with the Egyptian hiero-glyphics. . . . By Richard Saumarez. 8vo. [Brit. Mus.]   Bath, 1861

GENETHLIA : a poem on the blessed Nativity. [By Rev. Thomas Curteis, of Wrotham, Kent.] Folio.   London, 1727

GENEVIEVE ; or the children of Port Royal : a story of Old Spanish France. By the author of The Spanish Brothers [Deborah Alcock]. Fcap 8vo. [Brit. Mus.]   London, 1889

GENIAL (the) rascal. [A tale.] By R. Andom [Alfred Wilson Barrett] and Reginald Hodder. 8vo. [Lit. Year Book.]   London, [1910]

GENIUS ; a poem. [By James Mullin, M.D.] 8vo. [O'Donoghue's Poets of Ireland.]   Cookstown, 1880

GENIUS and fancy ; or, dramatic sketches [in verse]. By a lady [Mary Julia Young]. 4to. [Brit. Mus.]   London, 1791

GENIUS and valour ; a Scotch pastoral. [By Rev. John Langhorne.] 4to. [Watt's Bibl. Brit.]   London, 1763
    Written to defend the Scottish character.

GENIUS loci : notes on places. By Vernon Lee [Violet Paget]. 8vo. Pp. 211. [Lit. Year Book.] London, 1899

GENIUS (the) of Britain : an iambic ode ; addressed to the Right Hon. William Pitt, Esq. [By John Gilbert Cooper.] 4to. [Watt's Bibl. Brit.]   London, 1756

GENIUS (the) of Judaism. [By Isaac D'Israeli.] 8vo. Pp. 266. [D. N. B., vol. 15, p. 119.]   London, 1833

GENIUS (the) of oblivion ; and other original poems. By a lady of New Hampshire [Mrs Sarah Josepha Hale, née Buell]. 8vo. [Allibone's Dict.]   Concord, N.H., 1823

GENIUS (the) of Shakespeare ; a summer dream [in verse. By George Skene]. 4to. London, [1793]

GENOA the superb : the city of Columbus. By Cousin Virginia [Virginia Wales Johnson]. Fcap 8vo. [Cushing's *Init. and Pseud.*, vol. i., p. 469.] Chicago, 1892

GENTILE (the) sinner ; or England's brave gentleman characterised both as he is and as he should be ; in a letter to a friend. [By Clement Ellis.] Fcap 8vo. Pp. 261. [*D. N. B.*, vol. 17, p. 295.] Oxford, 1660

GENTLE and simple. [A novel. By Margaret Agnes Colville, later Mrs Paul.] 2 vols. Cr 8vo. [*Lit. Year Book.*] London, 1878

GENTLE (the) art of angling ; a practical handbook. By " Corrigeen " [Joseph Adams]. [*Camb. Univ. Lib.*] London, [1909]

GENTLE (a) Belle : a novel. By Christian Reid [Frances C. Fisher, later Mrs J. C. Tiernan]. 8vo. [Kirk's *Supp.*] New York, 1879

GENTLE bread-winners ; the story of one of them. By Catherine Owen [Mrs Helen Nitsch]. Fcap 8vo. [Cushing's *Init. and Pseud.*, vol. ii., p. 114.] Boston, 1887

GENTLE (the) craft ; a discovrse containing many matters of delight, very pleasant to be read : shewing what famous men have been shoo-makers in time past in this land, with their worthy deeds and great hospitality. . . . T. D. [Thomas Deloney]. 4to. Pp. 72. Chiefly B. L. [*Bodl.*] London, 1652

GENTLE (the) grafter. By O. Henry [William Sydney Porter]. Cr. 8vo. Pp. 252. [*Lond. Lib. Cat.*] London, 1916

GENTLE (the) knight of Old Brandenburg. By Edwin Caskoden [Charles Major]. Cr 8vo. [*Amer. Cat.*] London, 1909

GENTLE (the) life. Essays in aid of the formation of character. [By James Hain Friswell.] 8vo. [*Brit. Mus.*] London, 1864

GENTLE (a) reflection on the Modest Account, and a vindication of the loyal abhorrers from the calumnies of a factious pen. By the author of *The Parallel* [John Andrews, D.D.]. Folio. [*Bodl.*] London, 1682

GENTLE (the) sponge ; being a safe . . . and just mode of reducing the national debt of England : in a letter to His Grace the Duke of Wellington. By an old soldier [Edward Moor]. 8vo. [*Brit. Mus.*] London, 1829

GENTLE-HEART stories. By Barbara Yechton [Lydia Farrington Krausé]. 8vo. New York, 1894

GENTLEMAN (the) : a satire, written during the years 1812, 1813, 1814, and 1815. [By George Ambrose Rhodes, M.D.] 8vo. Pp. 100. [*N. and Q.*, March 1870, p. 274.] London, 1818

GENTLEMAN (the) apothecary ; being a late and true story [by J— de Villiers], turned out of French ; with several letters. [By Sir Roger L'Estrange.] 8vo. [Arber's *Term Cat.*, i., 524.] London, 1678

GENTLEMAN Clifford, and his white mare Brilliant ; or the Ladies' Highwayman : a romance. [By Edward Viles.] 8vo. [*N. and Q.*, Apr. 1922, p. 332.] London, 1866

GENTLEMAN (the) emigrant in Canada, Australia, and the United States. By Mark Tapley, jun. [William Stamer]. 2 vols. Cr 8vo. London, 1874

GENTLEMAN (the) farmer ; being an attempt to improve agriculture by subjecting it to the test of rational principles. [By Henry Home, Lord Kames.] Fifth edition. 8vo. Pp. xxxi, 438. Edinburgh, 1802

The letterpress of this work gives no indication of its authorship ; facing the title-page, however, there is normally an engraved portrait of " Lord Kames." The first edition was published in 1776.

GENTLEMAN (the) from Portland ; a novel. By the author of *When it was dark* [Cyril A. E. Ranger-Gull]. 8vo. [*Brit. Mus.*] London, 1909

GENTLEMAN (the) in black ; and tales of other days. [By J— Dalton.] Pt 8vo. London, 1845

A portion of this work appeared originally in a periodical entitled the *Literary Magnet*. Ascribed also to J. Y. Ackerman. Another edition appeared in 1845

GENTLEMAN (a) instructed in the conduct of a virtuous and happy life ; written for the instruction of a young nobleman. [By William Darrell, S.J.] Second edition. Fcap 8vo. Pp. 192. [Oliver's *Collections*, p. 80.] London, 1704

GENTLEMAN Jack: a naval story. By the author of *Cavendish* [William Johnson Neale]. 8vo. [*Brit. Mus.*]
London, 1837

GENTLEMAN Jack; or life on the road: a romance. . . . By the author of *Paul Clifford* [Edward Viles ?]. 8vo. [*N. and Q.*, 1922, p. 374.]
London, 1852
Attributed also to John Frederick Smith.

GENTLEMAN (a) of London. [A novel.] By Morice Gerard [John Jessop Teague]. Cr 8vo. Pp. 312. [*Lit. Year Book.*]   London, 1908

GENTLEMAN (a) of Virginia. By Christian Lys [Percy John Brebner]. Fcap 8vo. [*Amer. Cat.*]
New York, 1910

GENTLEMAN Roger. [A novel.] By M. E. Francis [Mrs Francis Blundell, *née* Mary Evans Sweetman]. Cr 8vo. Pp. 282. [*Lond. Lib. Cat.*]
London, 1911

GENTLEMAN Upcott's daughter. [A novel.] By Tom Cobbleigh [Walter Raymond]. Pt 8vo. [*Lit. Year Book.*]   London, 1894

GENTLEMAN - CULLY (the); a comedy: as it was acted at the Theatre Royal by His Majesty's servants. [By Charles Johnson.] 4to. Pp. 48. [*Biog. Dram.*] London, 1702

GENTLEMANS (the) academie; or, the Booke of S. Albans: containing three most exact and excellent bookes; the first of hawking, the second of all the proper termes of hunting, and the last of armorie: all compiled by Iuliana Barnes, in the yere from the incarnation of Christ 1486. And now reduced into a better method by G. M. [Gervase Markham]. 4to. Fol. 99. London, 1595
Each of the bookes has a separate title, but the pagination is continuous. The address to the reader is signed " G. M."

GENTLEMAN'S (the) accomplish'd jockey; with the compleat horseman and approved farrier. By G. M., Gent. [Gervase Markham]. Fcap 8vo. [*Brit. Mus.*]   London, 1722

GENTLEMAN'S (the) calling; written by the author of *The Whole duty of man* [Richard Allestree, D.D., Provost of Eton College]. 8vo. London, 1696
See the note appended to " The Art of Contentment."

GENTLEMANS (the) companion; or a character of true nobility and gentility: in the way of an essay. By a person of quality [William Ramesay, M.D.]. Written at first for his own private use, and now published for the benefit of all. 8vo. Pp. 264. [*Adv. Lib.*]   London, 1676

GENTLEMANS (the) exercise; or a supplement to Mr Lathams Bookes of faulconry, being the compleatest work ever yet printed in our nation of this subject, containing the ordering and training up of all hawks in generall. There is further added, in this new supplement, all the material things in Mr [Edmund] Bert's Treatise of hawks. . . . Newly published this yeere, 1662, for the publick good of the gentry of this kingdome. [By Anthony Hammond.] 12mo. Pp. 122. London, 1662
The Epistle to the Reader is signed " A. H."

GENTLEMAN'S (the) guide in his tour through France; wrote by an Officer [John Millard] who lately travelled on a principle which he most sincerely recommends to his countrymen, viz., not to spend more money in the country of our natural enemy than is required to support with decency the character of an Englishman. . . . Fourth edition, greatly enlarged. Pt 8vo. Pp. iv., 263. [*W.*] London, 1770
Further editions followed, modified in title and contents.

GENTLEMAN'S (the) guide in his tour through Italy; with a correct map, and directions for travelling in that country. [By Thomas Martyn, B.D.] Fcap 8vo. [*D. N. B.*, vol. 36, p. 323.]
London, 1787
Reprinted in 1791, after enlargement, with the author's name, under the title of *A tour through Italy.*

GENTLEMAN'S (the) handbook of poker. By " Florence " [William Jermyn Florence]. Fcap 8vo.
London, 1892

GENTLEMAN'S (the) recreation: in four parts, viz., hunting, hawking, fowling, fishing; wherein these generous exercises are largely treated of, and the terms of art for hunting and hawking more amply enlarged than heretofore; whereto is prefixt a large sculpture, giving easie directions for blowing the horn, and other sculptures inserted proper to each recreation. With an abstract at the end of each subject of such laws as relate to the same. [By Nicholas Cox.] The third edition, with the addition of a Hunting-horse. 8vo. [Arber's *Term Cat.*, i., 524.]   London, 1686
Each part has a separate title and pagination, except the second and third, in which the pagination is continuous. The " addition " in the general title has a separate title and pagination, and was printed at Oxford in 1685. The first edition was published at London in 1674. [*Bibliotheca Piscatoria, s.v.* " Cox."]

GENTLEMAN'S (a) religion : in three parts. The 1st contains the principles of natural religion. The 2d. and 3d. the doctrins of Christianity both as to faith and practice. With an appendix, wherein it is proved, that nothing contrary to our reason can possibly be the object of our belief : but that it is no just exception against some of the doctrins of Christianity, that they are above our reason. [By Edward Synge, D.D.] Fcap 8vo. Pp. 425. [Arber's *Term Cat.*, iii., 686.]
London, 1698

GENTLEMAN'S (a) tour through Monmouthshire and Wales, in the months of June and July, 1774. [By Henry Penruddock Wyndham, M.A.] 8vo. Pp. v., 223. [Anderson's *Brit. Top.*, p. 213.] London, 1775
The name is given in a later edition (Salisbury, 1781).

GENTLEMAN'S (the) tutor for the small sword ; or, the compleat English fencing master : containing the truest and plainest rules for learning that noble art. . . . [By Henry Blackwell.] Adorn'd with several curious postures. 4to. Pp. 60. [*Camb. Univ. Lib.*]
London, 1730
Preface signed " H. B."

GENTLEMEN (the) of the color. By Ben Horst [Edward G. Fast]. 8vo. [Kirk's *Supp.*] Baltimore, 1870

GENTLEMEN—the King. [Verses on the life of Christ.] By John Oxenham [William Arthur Dunkerley]. Fcap 8vo. [*Lit. Year Book.*] London, 1920

GENT'S History of Hull (Annales Regioduni Hullini) reprinted in facsimile of the original of 1735 : to which is appended notices of the life and works of Thomas Gent. . . . [By G— Ohlson.] 8vo. [Anderson's *Brit. Top.*] Hull, 1869

GENUINE (the) account of the life and trial of Eugene Aram for the murder of Daniel Clark. [By W— Bristow.] To which are added . . . his plan for a lexicon, and some pieces of poetry of Eugene Aram. 8vo. [*Brit. Mus.*]
London, [1759]

GENUINE (a) account of the Ship S[usse]x, in the service of the Honble. East India Company, from the time she was deserted by the officers and the greatest part of the crew, till she was unfortunately wrecked on the Bassas de India : with a narrative of what happened to the sixteen brave sailors who staid on board. By J. D—n [John Dean], the only one of them now alive. Pt 8vo. [*Brit. Mus.*]
London, 1740

GENUINE (a) and true journal of the most miraculous escape of the young Chevalier, from the battle of Culloden to his landing in France ; taken from the mouths and journals of the very persons who assisted him therein, partly wrote in London, and partly in Scotland : to which is added a short account of what befel the Pr. in France. By an Englishman [John Burton, M.D., of York]. 8vo. [*Bodl.*]
London, 1749

GENUINE Christianity, or the Unitarian doctrine briefly stated. By a physician [Thomas Foster Barham, M.B.]. 8vo. [Boase and Courtney's *Bibl. Corn.*, p. 13.] Penzance, 1824
The third edition (1835) has the author's name.

GENUINE (a) epistle from M. P. [Matthew Prior] at Paris to the Rev. J—n S—t [Jonathan Swift] at Windsor. 8vo. London, 1714

GENUINE (the) Grub-Street opera, as it was intended to be acted at the New Theatre in the Hay-Market. Written by Scriblerus Secundus [Henry Fielding]. 8vo. Pp. 64. [*Bodl.*]
London, 1731

GENUINE (a) lady. By Marion Thorne [Ida T. Thurston]. 8vo. [*Amer. Cat.*] Boston, 1897

GENUINE letters and memoirs relating to the natural, civil, and commercial history of the islands of Cape Breton, and Saint John, from the first settlement there, to the taking of Louisburg by the English, in 1758. . . . By an impartial Frenchman [Thomas Pichon]. Translated from the author's original manuscript. 8vo. [*Adv. Lib.*]
London, 1760

GENUINE (the) life and trial of George Barrington [George Waldron], 1755-90. Pt 8vo. [*Lond. Lib. Cat.*]
London, 1791

GENUINE (the) life of Isaac Darking, *alias* Dumas, the noted highwayman ; who was executed at Oxford, March 23, 1761. . . . [By George Smith Green.] 8vo. [*Bodl.*] London, 1761

GENUINE Methodism acquitted and spurious Methodism condemned, in 6 letters to J. Cooke. [By Edward Hare.] 8vo. [*Brit. Mus.*]
Rochdale, 1807

GENUINE (a) narrative of the life and theatrical transactions of Mr John Henderson, commonly called the Bath Roscius. [By Thomas Davies.] 8vo. Pp. 64. [*Bodl.* ; Green's *Bibl. Somers.*, i., 256.] London, 1777

GENUINE religion the best friend of the people; or, the influence of the Gospel, when known, believed, and experienced, upon the manners and happiness of the common people. . . . [By Archibald Bonar, minister of Cramond.] Fcap 8vo. Pp. xi., 96. [*New Coll. Cat.*]　　Edinburgh, 1796

GENUINE (the) sentiments of an English country-gentleman upon the present plan of the Foundling Hospital. [By Jonas Hanway.] 8vo. [*D. N. B.*, vol. 24, p. 314.]
London, 1759

GENUINE (the) sequel to the Essay on spirit. [By Robert Clayton, Bishop of Clogher.] Fcap 8vo. [*Camb. Univ. Lib.*]　　　　　　Dublin, 1752

GENUINE (the) speech of Lord L—ne [George Granville, Lord Lansdowne], against repealing the Occasional and Schism Bills. 4to. [*Brit. Mus.*]
London, 1719

GENUINE (the) speech of the Hon. Mr —— [Bathurst] at the late trial of Miss Blandy: which contains a summary of all the proofs against her; with notes on its faults, and beauties; and observations on the effects it had on the audience. 8vo. [*Brit. Mus.*]
London, 1752
Attributed also to William Murray, Earl of Mansfield.

GENUINE (the) use and necessity of the two sacraments, namely, Baptism and the Lord's Supper; with our obligation frequently to receive the latter. [By Lancelot Addison, D.D.] 8vo. Pp. 71. [*Watt's Bibl. Brit.*]
London, 1697

GEOFF and Jim. [A novel.] By Ismay Thorn [Edith Caroline Pollock]. Cr 8vo. Pp. 188. [*Brit. Mus.*]
London, 1914

GEOFFREY Cheriton. By John Barnett [John Reginald Stagg]. 8vo. Pp. 316. [*Brit. Mus.*] London, 1909

GEOFFREY Gambado; or a simple remedy for hypochondriacism and melancholy splenetic humours. By a humourist physician [Rev. Richard Cobbold, M.A.]. Fcap 4to.
London, [1850?]

GEOFFREY Harrington's adventures. By Harry Collingwood [William Joseph Cosens Lancaster]. Cr 8vo. Pp. 510. [*Lit. Year Book.*]
London, 1907

GEOFFREY the Lollard. By Frances Eastwood [Mrs D. C. Knevels]. [*Kirk's Supp.*]　　　New York, 1870

GEOFFREY'S wife; a reminiscence. By Stanley Hope [Joseph Sydney Willes Hodges, artist]. 2 vols. 8vo. [*Kirk's Supp.*]　　London, 1874

VOL. II.

GEOGRAPHICA Classica; the geography of the ancients. . . . [By Hermann Moll.] Fifth edition. 4to. [*Watt's Bibl. Brit.*]　London, 1727

GEOGRAPHICAL and historical account of places mentioned in Holy Scripture, originally composed by Edward Wells, D.D., now revised and corrected, and augmented by a series of geographical dissertations, &c. . . . By the editor of Calmet's *Dictionary of the Bible* [Charles Taylor]. 8vo. [*Lowndes' Brit. Lib.*]　London, 1824

GEOGRAPHICAL (a) and historical description of the shire of Tweeddale; with a miscelany and curious collection of select Scotish poems. By A. P., M.D. [Alexander Pennecuik, M.D., of Newhall]. 4to. Pp. 188. [*And. Jervise.*]　　　Edinburgh, 1715
The poems have a separate pagination.

GEOGRAPHICAL (the) and topographical guide to the Isle of Man; intended for the use of travellers and tourists, and of those who, visiting this fine island as sea bathing quarters, or as a cheap, pleasant, and convenient marine residence, are desirous of a succinct description of it. [By Henry Robert Oswald.] 8vo. Pp. 76. [Harrison's *Bibl. Monensis*, p. 105.]
Douglas, 1823

GEOGRAPHICAL (the) instructor's companion. [By Nicholas Richards.] Fcap 8vo. [*Brit. Mus.*]
London, [1852]

GEOGRAPHICAL (the) Magazine: by —— Martyn [Rev. William Fordyce Mavor, LL.D.]. 2 vols. 8vo. [Upcott and Shoberl's *Biog. Dict.*, p. 229.]　　　　　London, 1781

GEOGRAPHICAL (the), natural, and civil history of Chili; by Abbé Don J. Ignatius Molina; translated by an American gentleman [Richard Alsop]. 8vo. [Cushing's *Init. and Pseud.*, vol. i., p. 14.]
Middletown, Connecticut, 1808

GEOGRAPHICAL sketch of St Domingo. By a traveller [Benjamin C. Clark]. 8vo. [*Kirk's Supp.*]
Boston, 1850

GEOGRAPHY epitomized, or a tour round the world: being a short but comprehensive description of the terraqueous globe, attempted in verse (for the sake of the memory), and principally designed for the use of schools. By an American [Robert Davidson]. 8vo. [Evans' *Amer. Bibl.*, vol. 8, p. 22.]　　　　　　London, 1787

GEOGRAPHY (the) of America and the West Indies. . . . [By George Long.] 8vo.　　London, 1847

2 A

GEOGRAPHY (a) of China and the world, for use in schools : revised edition. [By George Patterson.] With maps. 8vo. Pp. vii., 376. [*Brit. Mus.*] London, 1905
The preface is signed " G. P."

GEOGRAPHY (the) of the Holy Land ; intended to serve as an explanatory key to the map of Palestine : with a copious index. [By Joseph C. Wigram, Bishop of Rochester.] Fcap 8vo. Pp. 168. [*Aberd. Lib.*]
London, 1832

GEOLOGICAL facts and observations ; with hints for the improvement of the interior of . . . Wales. By J. J. [J— Jones, of Charlotte Street, London]. 8vo. Pp. 50. [*Brit. Mus.*]
London, 1831

GEOLOGICAL (a) primer in verse : with a poetical geognosy, or feasting and fighting, and sundry right pleasant poems ; with notes. . . . [By John Scafe.] 8vo. Pp. xii., 68. [*Adv. Lib.*] London, 1820

GEOMETRIC turning simplified. By the author of *Lathes and turning* [W— Henry Northcott]. 8vo. Pp. 62. [*Brit. Mus.*] London, 1889

GEOMETRICAL deductions, riders, and exercises, based upon Euclid, books i.-iv. [By Arthur Thomas Fisher.] 8vo. [*Bodl.*] London, 1886
Preface signed " A. T. F."

GEOMETRICAL (a) system of conic sections. [By William Marrat.] 8vo.
Cambridge, 1822

GEOMETRY improv'd : 1st, by a large table of segments of circles ; with tables for finding a true proportional part and their use ; . . . 2nd, a concise treatise of polyedra, or solid bodies of many bases. By A. S. [Abraham Sharp], Philomath. 4to. [*Camb. Univ. Lib.*] London, 1717, 1718

GEOMETRY no friend to infidelity : or, a defence of Sir Isaac Newton and the British mathematicians, in a letter to [Bishop Berkeley] the author of the Analyst. . . . By Philalethes Cantabrigiensis [James Jurin, M.D.]. 8vo. Pp. 84. [Berkeley's *Works*, edited by Fraser, iii., 301.] London, 1734

GEOMETRY, plane, solid, and spherical, in six books ; to which is added, in an appendix, the theory of projection, so far as it is auxiliary to geometry ; with an account of the plane sections of the cone and cylinder. . . . [By Pierce Morton.] 8vo. Pp. viii., 272. [*Lond. Cat.*] London, 1830

GEOMETRY without axioms ; or the first book of Euclid's Elements, with alterations and familiar notes : with an intercalary book. . . . [By Thomas Perronet Thompson.] Fourth edition. 8vo. [*Brit. Mus.*] London, 1833

GEORDY'S last ; Newcastle folk-speech. By Harry Haldane [R. O. Heslop]. 8vo. Newcastle, 1875

GEORGE ; a story in drab and scarlet. By the author of *Our own Pompeii* [S— Middleton Fox]. 3 vols. Cr 8vo. [*Brit. Mus.*] London, 1890

GE—GE and F—st—r [George and Forster] ; a new ballad by way of parody on that celebrated one, intituled, " William and Margaret." . . . [By Rev. Samuel Langley.] 8vo.
Stafford, 1777

GEORGE at the wheel ; or, life in a pilot-house. By Harry Castlemon [Charles A. Fosdick]. Fcap 8vo. [Kirk's *Supp.*] Philadelphia, 1882

GEORGE Beattie, of Montrose ; poet, humorist, and a man of genius. By A. S. Mt. Cyrus [Alexander Silver], M.A. 8vo. Montrose, 1895

GEORGE Coad, the letter-carrier ; or pure religion displayed in humble life. By O. H. [Rev. Oliver Henwood]. 8vo. Plymouth, 1849

GEORGE Douglas Brown, author of " The House with the Green shutters " : a biographical memoir by Cuthbert Lennox [John H. Napier, solicitor]. Cr 8vo. Pp. 262. London, 1903
Private information from a friend.

GEORGE Eliot in Derbyshire ; a volume of gossip about passages and people in the novels of George Eliot. By Guy Roslyn [Joshua Hatton]. Fcap 8vo. Pp. 90. [*Cat. of Engl. Dialect Lib.*, Manchester, 1880, p. 9.]
London, 1876

GEORGE Fox and his friends, as leaders in the peace cause. [By William Naish.] 8vo. [Smith's *Cat. of Friends' Books*, ii., 214.]
London, 1859

GEORGE FOX digg'd out of his burrowes ; or an offer of disputation on fourteen Proposalls made this last summer 1672 (so call'd) unto G. Fox, then present on Rode-Island, in New-England, by R. W. [Roger Williams], as also, how (G. Fox slily departing) the disputation went on being managed three dayes at Newport on Rode-Island, and one day at Providence, between John Stubs, John Burnet, and William Edmundson on the one part, and R. W. on the other. 4to. Pp. 327. [Smith's *Anti-Quak.*, p. 452.]
Boston, 1676

GEORGE Fox ; his character, doctrine, and work : an essay. By a member of the Society of Friends [Edward Ash, M.D.]. 8vo. Pp. 34. [Smith's *Supp. to Cat. of Friends' Books*, p. 27.] London, 1873

GEORGE Fox : his life, travels, sufferings, and death ; wherein is plainly discovered the real origin of the people called Quakers, and what a Quaker ought to be. . . . By George R. [Railton]. 8vo. Pp. 32. [Smith's *Supp. to Cat. of Friends' Books*, p. 136.] London, 1881

GEORGE Geith of Fen Court. A novel. By F. G. Trafford, author of *Too much alone*, etc. [Mrs Charlotte Elizabeth Lawson Riddell]. 3 vols. 8vo. [*D. N. B.*, Second Supp., vol. 3, p. 193.] London, 1864

GEORGE Harris. By E. J. Y. [Edward James Young]. 8vo. [Kirk's *Supp.*] Boston, 1875

GEORGE in camp ; or, life on the plain. By Harry Castlemon [Charles A. Fosdick]. Fcap 8vo. [Kirk's *Supp.*] Philadelphia, 1879

GEORGE Malcolm ; a novel. By Gabriel Setoun [Thomas N. Hepburn, teacher in Edinburgh]. 8vo. [*Lit. Year Book*.] London, 1897

GEORGE Mandeville's husband. [A novel.] By C. E. Raimond [Elizabeth Robins, later Mrs Parkes]. Pt 8vo. Pp. 156. [*Lit. Year Book*.] London, 1894

GEORGE Mason, the young backwoodsman; or "Don't give up the ship." A story of the Mississippi. By the author of *Francis Berrian* [Timothy Flint]. Fcap 8vo. [*Brit. Mus.*] Boston, [Mass.], 1829

GEORGE Morton ; the boy and the man. Tales by the author of *Emma's cross*, etc. [Mrs Gertrude Parsons, *née* Hext]. 8vo. Pp. 162. [Boase and Courtney's *Bibl. Corn.*, ii., 426.] London, 1859

GEORGE Ready ; or, how to live for others : a Christmas story. . . . By Robert O. Lincoln [George C. Mason]. Fcap 8vo. [Cushing's *Init. and Pseud.*, vol. i., p. 496.] New York, 1858

GEORGE Romney. By George Paston [Emily Morse Symonds]. Fcap 8vo. [*Lond. Lib. Cat.*] London, 1903

GEORGE Sandford ; or, the draper's assistant. By one who has stood behind the counter [David Pae]. Fcap 8vo. [*Adv. Lib.*] Edinburgh, 1853

GEORGE Selwyn ; his life and times. [By Abraham Hayward.] 8vo. [*Brit. Mus.*] London, 1854

GEORGE Stephenson. By J. F. Layson [John Finlayson]. 8vo. Newcastle, [1881]

GEORGE the Third. [By Rev. Edward Mangin.] 3 vols. Fcap 8vo. [Green's *Bibl. Somers.*, i., 334.] Bath, 1807

GEORGE Wallis and his friends. [A tale. By Jonathan Lett Stackhouse.] 8vo. Pp. 46. London, [1865]

GEORGE'S enemies : a sequel to "My school-boy friends." By Ascott R. Hope [Ascott Robert Hope Moncrieff]. Fcap 8vo. [*Lit. Year Book*.] Edinburgh, 1872

GEORGIA (the) bequest. By a Georgia huntsman [Major W. R. Rembert]. 8vo. [Cushing's *Init. and Pseud.*, vol. i., p. 66.] Augusta, 1854

GEORGIA scenes, characters, incidents, etc., in the first half century of the Republic. By a native Georgian [Augustus Baldwin Longstreet]. Second edition. Fcap 8vo. Pp. 214. [*Brit. Mus.*] New York, 1848
Later editions in 1855 and 1884.

GEORGIA sketches. By an old man [Richard Malcolm Johnston]. 8vo. [Kirk's *Supp.*] Augusta, Georgia, 1864

GEORGIANS : a story of Southern life. [By Mrs E. H. Hammond.] 8vo. [Kirk's *Supp.*] Boston, 1881

GEORGICAL essays. By Ignotus [Alexander Hunter, M.D., F.R.S.]. 8vo. [*Lond. Lib. Cat.*] York, 1777

GEORGICS (the) of Bacchicles, in three books ; now for the first time published in English tongue. [By Francis David Morice.] 8vo. Pp. 20. Oxford, 1873

GEORGIE and Lizzie. By Cousin Kate [Catherine Douglas Bell]. 8vo. [*Lit. Year Book*.] Edinburgh, 1849

GERALD Fitzgerald ; a tale of the seventeenth century [in verse]. By D. G. [Dorothea Grubb, of Waterford]. 8vo. [O'Donoghue's *Poets of Ireland*.] Waterford, 1845

GERALD Fitzgerald ; an Irish tale. By Ann of Swansea, author of *Uncle Peregrine's heiress*, etc. [Julia Ann Kemble, otherwise Anne Hatton]. 5 vols. 12mo. [S. J. Brown's *Ireland in fiction*.] London, 1831

GERALD Marlowe's wife. A novel. By J. C. Ayrton [Mary Frances Chapman]. 3 vols. 8vo. [Cushing's *Init. and Pseud.*, vol. ii., p. 10.] London, 1876

GERALD of Kildare ; a dramatic poem. [By Thomas Bibby, B.A.] 8vo. [O'Donoghue's *Poets of Ireland*.] Dublin, 1854

GERALDINE: a romance in verse. [By William H. Carleton.] Fcap 8vo. [Kirk's *Supp.*]   Boston, 1881

GERALDINE: a souvenir of the St Lawrence. [By Alonzo Hopkins.] 8vo. [Kirk's *Supp.*]
                    Boston, [Mass.], 1887

GERALDINE; a tale of conscience. By E. C. A. [Eleanor C. Agnew]. 3 vols. Fcap 8vo. [*Brit. Mus.*]
                    London, 1837

GERALDINE Fauconberg. By the author of *Clarentine* [Sarah Harriet Burney]. 3 vols. Fcap 8vo. [Watt's *Bibl. Brit.*]   London, 1808

GERALDINE Hamilton; or, self-guidance: a tale. [By E— H— Macleod.] 2 vols. Fcap 8vo. [*Camb. Univ. Lib.*]
                    London, 1832

GERALDINE Hawthorne: a sketch. By the author of *Miss Molly* [Beatrice May Butt]. 8vo. Pp. viii., 311. [*Lond. Lib. Cat.*]   Edinburgh, 1882

GERALDINE of Desmond; or Ireland in the reign of Elizabeth: an historical romance.   [By Miss —— Crumpe.] 3 vols. Fcap 8vo. [S. J. Brown's *Ireland in fiction*.]
                    London, 1829

GERALDINE; or, modes of faith and practice: a tale. By a lady [Mary Jane Mackenzie]. 3 vols. Fcap 8vo. [*Camb. Univ. Lib.*]   London, 1820

GERALD'S dream; a Christmas story. By the author of *Earth's many voices* [Elizabeth M. A. F. Saxby]. Fcap 8vo. [*Brit. Mus.*]   London, [1883]

GERARD; or the world, the flesh, and the Devil: a novel.   [By Mary E. Braddon, later Mrs John Maxwell.] 8vo. [*Brit. Mus.*]   London, 1891

GERARDO, the unfortunate Spaniard; or a pattern for lascivious lovers; out of Spanish [of Goncalo Cespedes] into English by L. D. [Leonard Digges]. 8vo. Pp. 421. [Watt's *Bibl. Brit., s.v.* "Cespedes."]   London, 1653

GERARD'S Scottish adventures; a story in black and blue. By Ascott R. Hope [Ascott Robert Hope Moncrieff]. Cr 8vo. [*Lit. Year Book*.]
                    London, 1921

GERMAINE'S marriage: from the French of George Sand [Madame A. L. A. D. Dudevant]. Fcap 8vo. [*Lit. Year Book*.]   New York, 1892

GERMAN ambitions as they affect Britain and the United States of America; reproduced, with additions and notes, from the *Spectator*. By "Vigilans sed Aequus" [William Thomas Arnold]. Cr 8vo. Pp. xxii., 132. [*Camb. Univ. Lib.*]
                    London, 1903

GERMAN and French games at cards. By Aquarius [Lowis d'Aguilar Jackson]. 8vo. [*Brit. Mus.*]
                    London, 1888

GERMAN days: personal experiences and impressions of life, manners, and customs in Germany. By a Polish girl [Mrs —— Boyle]. Cr 8vo. Pp. 337.   London, 1919

GERMAN experiences; addressed to the English. . . . By John Hampden, jun. [William Howitt]. 8vo. [*Lit. Year Book*.]   London, 1844

GERMAN home life. Reprinted from Fraser's Magazine. [By the Countess von Bothmer.] Pt 8vo. [*Lond. Lib. Cat.*]   London, 1876

GERMAN (the) hotel; a comedy, as performed at the Theatre Royal, Covent Garden. [Translated by A. Marshall from the German of Johann Christian Brandes, and altered by Thomas Holcroft.] 8vo. Pp. 72. [*Brit. Mus.*]   London, 1790

GERMAN hymns and sacred songs selected by Her Majesty the Queen [Victoria] from the collection of Her late Royal Highness the Duchess [of Kent]; with an English translation. [By Edgar A. Bowring.] 4to. Pp. 82.
                    Private print, 1861

GERMAN love; from the papers of an alien. [By Friedrich Max Müller.] Translated. 8vo. [*Brit. Mus.*]
                    London, 1877

GERMAN (the) lyrist; or, metrical versions from the principal German lyric poets. By W. N. [William Nind, vicar of Cherryhinton]. 8vo. Pp. xv., 160. [F. Boase's *Mod. Brit. Biog.*, vol. 6, col. 297.]
                    Cambridge, [U.S.A.], 1856

GERMAN (the) national cookery for English kitchens. [By Mrs Anne Letitia Schiller.] 8vo. London, 1873

GERMAN (a) Pompadour; being the extraordinary history of Wilhelmine von Grävenitz, Landhofmeisterin of Wirtemberg: an eighteenth century narrative. By Marie Hay [Madame de Hindenburg]. Demy 8vo. Pp. 368.
                    London, 1906

GERMAN popular stories; translated [by Edgar Taylor] from the "Kinder und Haus Märchen," collected by the Brothers Grimm from oral tradition. 2 vols. 12mo. [*Brit. Mus.*]
                    London, 1824-26

GERMAN romance: specimens of its chief authors; with biographical and critical notices. By the translator of Wilhelm Meister, and author of the *Life of Schiller* [Thomas Carlyle]. 4 vols. 8vo.   Edinburgh, 1827

GERMAN (the) sausages ; or the devil to pay at Congress ! A poem. By Peter Pindar, Esq. [John Wolcot, M.D.]. Second edition. 8vo. [*D.N.B.*, vol. 62, p. 293.] London, 1815

GERMAN (the) shoemaker. [By Mrs Margaret Fison.] 8vo. [*Bodl.*] London, 1855

GERMAN (the) spy system from within. By Ex-Intelligence Officer [Colonel Lionel James]. Pt 8vo. Pp. 160. [*Lit. Year Book.*] London, 1915

GERMAN (the) watch-song ; or a new way to count. . . . [By Miss Asenath Barrows.] 8vo. Boston, [Mass.], 1855

GERMANS. By themselves. [By Theodore Andrea Cook.] 8vo. Pp. viii., 42. London, 1914
The Preface is signed " T. A. C."

GERMANS (the) in England. By Henry Dorgeel [Dr Heinrich Geehl]. 8vo. [*Brit. Mus.*] London, 1885
A translation from the German.

GERMANY and Belgium before and during the [Great] War. [By A— Lowenstein.] 8vo. London, 1915

GERMANY versus Denmark ; being a short account of the Schleswig-Holstein question. By a Liverpool merchant [Francis Prange]. 8vo. Pp. 24. Liverpool, 1864
Signed " F. P."

GERMS of a philosophy of the human mind. [By William Squibb, of the Middle Temple.] 8vo. [*W.*] London, 1827

GERSHOM, the miner. By Crona Temple [Miss —— Corfield]. 8vo. Pp. 160. [*Brit. Mus.*] London, 1889

GERTRUDE. By the author of *Amy Herbert* [Elizabeth Missing Sewell]. Edited by the Rev. William Sewell, B.D. Fifth edition. 2 vols. Fcap 8vo. [*Brit. Mus.*] London, 1846

GERTRUDE and her family. [By Selina Bunbury.] Fcap 8vo. [*Camb. Univ. Lib.*] Dublin, 1830

GERTRUDE Dacre ; a story. By the author of *The Sunbeam* [Cecilia Anne Jones]. 8vo. [*Brit. Mus.*] London, 1862
Signed " C. A. J."

GERTRUDE Morgan's adventures among the Indians of the Far West. By Wesley Bradshaw [Charles Alexander]. 8vo. [Cushing's *Init. and Pseud.*, i., 39.] Philadelphia, 1850 [?]

GERTRUDE, the Amazon. By Walter B. Dunlap [Sylvanus Cobb, jun.]. Pt 8vo. [Cushing's *Init. and Pseud.*, vol. ii., p. 46.] New York, 1894

GERTRUDE the emigrant : a tale of Colonial life. By an Australian lady [Mrs Caroline Louisa Waring Calvert, *née* Atkinson]. Cr 8vo. [*Col. Inst. Lib. Cat.*, Supp. I., p. 686.] London, 1857

GERTRUDE Waynflete : a story for Christmas. By M. J. H. [Miss Josephine Hannan]. 8vo. London, [1864]

GERTRUDE'S diary, and the cube. [A tale.] By Pansy [Mrs Isabella Alden, *née* Macdonald]. 8vo. Pp. 110. Boston, [Mass., 1885]

GERTRUDE'S love ; a legend of Gloucester Hall. [By F— W— Bourdillon.] Pt 8vo. Oxford, 1874

GESTA Grayorum ; or, the history of the high and mighty prince, Henry Prince of Purpoole [*i.e.* Henry Helmes, a Norfolk gentleman], Arch-Duke of Stapulia and Bernardia, Duke of High and Nether Holborn, Marquis of St Giles and Tottenham, Count Palatine of Bloomsbury and Clerkenwell, Great Lord of the Cantons of Islington, Kentish-Town, Paddington and Knights-bridge, Knight of the most heroical order of the helmit, and sovereign of the same ; who reigned and died A.D. 1594. . . . [By W. Canning.] 4to. Pp. 72. [*Adv. Lib.*] London, 1688
Epistle dedicatory signed " W. C."

GETHSEMANE and Calvary. [By Archibald Young.] 8vo. [Robertson's *Aberd. Bibl.*] Aberdeen, 1877

GETTING ahead. By " Pansy " [Mrs Isabella Alden, *née* Macdonald]. Fcap 8vo. [*Lit. Year Book.*] Boston, 1877

GETTING an indorser ; and other stories. By Oliver Optic [William Taylor Adams]. Fcap 8vo. Pp. 80. [Kirk's *Supp.*] Boston, [1897]

GETTING together. By Ian Hay [John Hay Beith]. 8vo. Pp. 86. [*Brit. Mus.*] London, 1917
Referring to the United States on joining in the Great War.

GEWGAW (the), or Brighton toy ; a caricature poem. By Peter Broadgrin [George Colman, jun.]. 8vo. Brighton, [1810 ?]

GEYSERS (the), or jetting fountains, near Haukadal in Iceland, as seen in the years 1814 and 1815. By E. H. [Ebenezer Henderson, D.D.]. 8vo. Pp. 22. [*New Coll. Cat.*] Edinburgh, 1818

GHAIST (the) o' Dennilair : a legend of Fyvie. [By David Scott, of Peterhead.] 8vo. Pp. 8. [*And. Jervise.*] Peterhead, 1870
Revised by Dr Longmuir.

GHEEL, the city of the simple. By the author of *Flemish Interiors* [Mrs William Pitt Byrne, *née* Julia Clara Busk]. 8vo. Pp. xvi., 195. [*Brit. Mus.*] London, 1869

GHERGHIS Mahomed ; or reports of the new Egyptian Parliament. By Sain Gon [Bayle St John, who thus ridiculed the rule of Ismail Pasha]. 8vo. Pp. 179. Jericho, [Paris ?], 1867

GHIBERTI and Donatello, with other early sculptors. By Leader Scott [Mrs Lucy Baxter]. Pt 8vo. [*Lond. Lib. Cat.*] London, 1882

GHOST (the). By the author [Charles Churchill]. 4to. Pp. 56. [*Adv. Lib.*] London, 1762

GHOST (the) Camp ; or the avenger. [A novel.] By Rolf Boldrewood [Thomas Alexander Browne]. Cr 8vo. [*Lond. Lib. Cat.*] London, 1902

GHOST (the) of an old love. [A novel.] By John Strange Winter [Mrs Arthur Stannard, *née* Henrietta E. V. Palmer]. Cr 8vo. [*Lit. Year Book.*] London, 1903

GHOST (the) of Ernest, great grandfather of her Royal Highness the Princess Dowager of Wales. With some account of his life. [By Rev. Robert Bolton, LL.D.] 8vo. Pp. xxvii., 64. [*Adv. Lib.*] London, 1757

GHOST (the) of Passy ; a sensational novel. By Captain George Z. Fighton [U— M. C. Winteler de Weindeck]. 8vo. Pp. 131. [*Brit. Mus.*] London, 1889

GHOST (the) of Redbrook. [By James George Atkinson Coulson.] 8vo. [Kirk's *Supp.*] Philadelphia, 1879

GHOST (the) of Richard the Third, expressing himself in these three parts. 1 His character. 2 His legend. 3 His tragedie. . . . [By Christopher Brooke.] Printed for G. Eld : for L. Lisle : and are to be sold in Paules Church-yard at the sign of the Tygers head. 4to. [*Bodl.*] London, 1614
The epistle dedicatory is signed " C. B."

GHOST (the) of the hollow field. By the author of *East Lynne* [Mrs Henry Wood, *née* Ellen Price]. 8vo. [*Brit. Mus.*] London, [1867]

GHOST (the) of Walter ; a poem [on the French invasion of Ireland. By John Kearney, D.D., Provost of Trinity College, Dublin]. 8vo. [O'Donoghue's *Poets of Ireland*.] Dublin, 1798

GHOST stories. By E. and H. Heron [Kate O'Brien Prichard and Hesketh Vernon Prichard]. 8vo. Pp. 117. [*Brit. Mus.*] London, 1916

GHOST stories and tales of mystery. [By Joseph Sheridan Le Fanu.] 8vo. [S. J. Brown's *Ireland in fiction*.] London, 1851

GHOST-HUNTER (the) and his family. By the O'Hara family [Michael Banim]. 8vo. [S. J. Brown's *Ireland in fiction*.] London, 1833
Reissued in 1870 with the title "Joe Wilson's Ghost."

GHOSTS (the) of the guard-room, and other stories. By Annabel Gray [Mrs Anne Cox]. Pt 8vo. [*Lit. Year Book.*] London, [1894]

GHOULS (the) of New York. By Ned Buntline [Edward Z. C. Judson]. 8vo. [Cushing's *Init. and Pseud.*, vol. i., p. 43.] New York, 1850

GIANT circumstance. [A novel.] By John Oxenham [William Arthur Dunkerley]. Pt 8vo. Pp. 256. [*Lit. Year Book.*] London, 1921

GIANT (the) cowboys. [By Henry Llewellyn Williams.] 8vo. [*Brit. Mus.*] London, [1890]

GIANT (the) dwarf. [A tale]. By "Jak" [Annie Bowles Williams]. Fcap 8vo. [Cushing's *Init. and Pseud.*, vol. ii., p. 60.] New York, 1889

GIANT-KILLER (the) ; or, the battle which all must fight. By A. L. O. E., author of *Fairy know-a-bit*, etc. [Charlotte M. Tucker]. 8vo. Pp. 165. London, 1868

GIANT-LAND ; or the wonderful adventures of Tim Pippin. By Roland Quiz [Richard H. M. Quittenton]. 8vo. Pp. 189. [*Brit. Mus.*] London, [1874]

GIANTS (the) and the sons of God ; a criticism upon Genesis vi. 1-5, etc. [By John Collyer Knight.] 8vo. London, [1867]
Signed "J. C. K."

GIANT'S (the) robe ; a novel. By F. Anstey [Thomas Anstey Guthrie]. [*Lit. Year Book.*] London, 1895

GIDDY Gusher papers. [By Mrs M— H. Fiske.] Edited by H. G. Fiske. Fcap 8vo. New York, 1889

GIDEON : a new oratorio. [By Thomas Morell, D.D.] 4to. [*Brit. Mus.*] London, [1754 ?]

GIDEON ; or the patriot : an epic poem in twelve books. [Books I., II. By Aaron Hill.] 4to. [*Brit. Mus.*] London, 1749

GIDEON, "the mighty man of valour" : a history. By H. H. [Lady Harriet Howard]. 8vo. Pp. 257. [*Brit. Mus.*] Brighton, 1839

GIDEON'S cake of barley meal: a letter [by Michael Nash] to the Rev. W. Romaine, on his preaching for the emigrant Popish clergy. . . . 8vo. [Watt's *Bibl. Brit.*]   London, 1793
Signed "M. N."

GIDEON'S fleece; or the Sieur de Frisk: an heroick poem, written on the cursory perusal of a late book [by Gideon Harvey] call'd "The Conclave of Physicians." By a friend to the Muses [Thomas Guidott].   4to. [Arber's *Term Cat.*, ii., 616.]
London, 1684
Signed "Philo-Musus."

GIFFORD'S [Alexander Whellier's] English Lawyer . . . to which is added an appendix; also a supplement. Twelfth edition. 8vo. [*Brit. Mus.*]
London, 1826

GIFT (the) of rest. By E. A. D. [E— A— Draper]. 8vo. Pp. 77.
London, [1898]

GIFT (the) of St Anthony: a novel. By Charles Granville [Francis Granville Egerton, Earl of Ellesmere]. Cr 8vo. Pp. 272. [*Brit. Mus.*] London, 1909

GIFT (the) of the gods. By J. Calder Ayrton [Mary Frances Chapman]. 2 vols. 8vo. [Cushing's *Init. and Pseud.*, vol. ii., p. 10.]   London, 1879

GIFTS and graces. By the author of *The Rose and the Lotus* [Elizabeth Thomason, later Mrs Johnston]. 8vo. [*Brit. Mus.*]   London, 1882

"GIFTS for men." By X. H. [Mrs Brewster Macpherson]. 8vo. Pp. xvi., 350. [*Adv. Lib.*]
Edinburgh, 1870

GIFTS (the) of the Holy Spirit revived: the ministries promised to the Church restored. [By William Tarbet.] 8vo. [Boase's *Cath. Apost. Lit.*]
Liverpool, 1854

GILBERT Freethorne's heritage: a romance of clerical life. By W. C. Alvary [William Erskine, jeweller in Burntisland]. Second edition. Cr 8vo.
London, 1888

GILBERT Gurney. By the author of *Sayings and Doings* [Theodore Edward Hook]. 3 vols. Fcap 8vo. [*Brit. Mus.*]   London, 1836

GILBERT Massenger. By Holme Lee [Harriet Parr], author of *Thorney Hall*. Fcap 8vo. [*Lit. Year Book.*]
London, 1855

GILBERT Midhurst, M.P. [A novel. By Charles F. Howard.] 2 vols. 8vo. [*Brit. Mus.*]   London, 1859

GILBERT; or the young carrier: an amatory rural poem. [By James Templeman.] 8vo. Pp. viii., 143. [*Brit. Mus.*]   London, 1808

GILBERT Rugge. [A novel.] By the author of *A first friendship* [Henry Jackson]. 3 vols. Cr 8vo. [*Brit. Mus.*]   London, 1866

GILBERT Starr and his lessons. By Glance Gaylord [Warren Ives Bradley]. Fcap 8vo. [Kirk's *Supp.*]
Boston, 1866

GILDED (the) age: a novel by Mark Twain [Samuel L. Clemens] and Charles Dudley Warner. 3 vols. 8vo.
London, 1874
The preface to the American edition is signed "S. L. C."

GILDED (a) serpent. By Dick Donovan [Joyce E. P. Muddock]. Cr 8vo. Pp. 316. [*Brit. Mus.*] London, 1908

GILDED sin. By Bertha M. Clay [Mrs Charlotte M. Braeme]. Fcap 8vo.
New York, 1886

GILDED vanity. [A novel.] By Richard Dehan [Clotilde Graves]. 8vo. Pp. 314. [*Lit. Year Book.*] London, 1916

GILDEROY. [A novel.] By "Ouida" [Louise de la Ramée]. Cr 8vo. [*Lit. Year Book.*]   London, 1891

GILES Witherne; or the reward of disobedience: a village tale. By Raven Witherne [John P. Parkinson, D.C.L.]. 8vo. [F. Boase's *Mod. Brit. Biog.*, vol. 6, col. 359.]   London, 1859
The sixth edition (1863) gives the author's name.

GILL'S lap; a tale. [By John Mason Neale, D.D.] Fcap 8vo. [*D. N. B.*, vol. 40, p. 145.]   London, [1850 ?]

GILLY (the) of Christ; poems. By Seosamh Mac Cathmaoil [Joseph Campbell]. 8vo. [O'Donoghue's *Poets of Ireland*.]   London, 1908
The name in the title is really the Gaelic of Joseph Campbell.

GIMCRACKIANA; or fugitive pieces on Manchester men and manners ten years ago. [By John Stanley Gregson, bookseller in Manchester.] 8vo. Pp. 195. [Fishwick's *Lancashire Lib.*, p. 128.]   Manchester, 1833

GINETTE'S happiness. [A novel.] By Gyp [Comtesse de Martel—Gabrielle de Mirabeau]. Translated. Cr 8vo. Pp. 272. [*Brit. Mus.*] London, 1908

GINEVRA; and The Duke of Guise: two tragedies. [By Francis H. H. Terrell.] Pt 8vo.   London, 1880

GINGHAM (the) bag: the tale of an heirloom. By Margaret Sidney [Mrs Harriet Mulford Lothrop]. Cr 8vo. Pp. 369. [Kirk's *Supp.*]
Boston, [1896]

GINSEY Krieder. [A novel.] By Huldah Herrick [Sarah Endicott Ober]. 8vo.   Boston, 1880

GINX'S baby; his birth and other misfortunes. [By John Edward Jenkins.] Fcap 8vo. Pp. 330. [*Brit. Mus.*]
London, 1870

GIORDANO: a tragedy. [By James Lawson.] 8vo. New York, 1867

GIORGIO, and other poems. By Stuart Sterne [Gertrude Bloede]. Fcap 8vo. [Cushing's *Init. and Pseud.*, vol. i., p. 274.] Boston, 1881

GIPHANTIA; or, a view of what has passed, what is now passing, and during the present century, what will pass, in the world. Translated from the original French [of C. F. Tiphaigne de la Roche], with explanatory notes. Fcap 8vo. [*Barbier's Dict.*]
Dublin, 1761

GIPSIES (the); a comick opera, in two acts, as it is performed at the Theatre-Royal in the Haymarket. [By Charles Dibdin.] 8vo. [*Biog. Dram.*]
London, 1778

GIPSIES of the New Forest, and other tales. By H. E. J. G. [Henry E. J. Gibbins]. 8vo. Pp. 126. [Black's *Gypsy Bibl.*, p. 65.]
Bournemouth, [1909]

GIPSY Roy; a story of early Methodism. By Harry Lindsay [Harry Lindsay Hudson]. 8vo. Pp. 320. [*Lond. Lib. Cat.*] London, 1901

GIPSY'S (the) daughter. By Bertha M. Clay [Mrs Charlotte M. Braeme]. Fcap 8vo. New York, 1890

GIPSY'S (the) daughter; a tale. [By A. M. Grey.] Edited by the author of *The Gambler's wife*, etc. [Mrs Elizabeth Caroline Grey]. 2 vols. Fcap 8vo. [*Brit. Mus.*] London, 1852

GIRALDI; or, the curse of love. By Ross George Dering [Frederic Henry Balfour]. 2 vols. 8vo.
London, 1889

GIRDING on the armour. [By Mrs H. H. Robins.] 8vo. New York, 1868

GIRDLE (the) of the globe; or the voyage of Mister Mucklemouth: being a poem descriptive of toil and travel round the world, in ten cantos. By Ralph [Lieut.-Col. John MacGregor, M.D., Bombay Army]. Pt 8vo. Pp. xii., 359. [*Brit. Mus.*]
London, 1890

GIRL (a) among the Anarchists. By Isabel Meredith [Olivia and Elena Rossetti]. 8vo. [*Brit. Mus.*]
London, 1903

GIRL (the) and the man. By Curtis Yorke [Mrs W. S. Richmond Lee]. Cr 8vo. [*Lit. Year Book.*]
London, 1906

GIRL (a) from Corsica. [A drama.] By Mark Allerton [William Ernest Cameron, LL.B.]. 8vo. [*Lit. Year Book.*] London, 1915

GIRL (the) from Gatford. [A novel.] By Olivia Ramsay [Letitia Selwyn Oliver]. Cr 8vo. Pp. 308. [*Brit. Mus.*] London, 1909

GIRL (the) from Kay's; a new and original musical play. By Owen Hall [James Davis, B.A.]. 8vo. Pp. 28. [*Lit. Year Book.*] London, 1903

GIRL (the) from the corner shop. [A tale.] By Bertha M. Clay [Mrs Charlotte M. Braeme]. 8vo. London, 1913

GIRL (the) from the farm. By Gertrude Dix [Miss —— Nicol]. Cr 8vo. [*Lond. Lib. Cat.*] London, 1895

GIRL (the) in fancy dress. By J. E. Buckrose [Mrs Falconer Jameson]. Cr 8vo. Pp. 310. [*Lit. Year Book.*]
London, 1920

GIRL (the) in grey. By Curtis Yorke [Mrs W. S. Richmond Lee]. Cr 8vo. [*Lond. Lib. Cat.*] London, 1907

GIRL (a) in London. [A novel.] By John Strange Winter [Mrs Arthur Stannard, *née* Henrietta E. V. Palmer]. Cr 8vo. [*Brit. Mus.*] London, 1903

GIRL neighbours. By Sarah Tytler [Henrietta Keddie]. Cr 8vo. [*Lit. Year Book.*] London, 1892

GIRL (a) of Klondike. [A novel.] By Victoria Cross [Vivian Cory]. Cr 8vo. [*Amer. Cat.*] London, 1899

GIRL (a) of no importance. [A novel.] By Olivia Ramsay [Letitia Selwyn Oliver]. Cr 8vo. Pp. 320. [*Brit. Mus.*] London, 1913

GIRL (a) of the multitude. [A French story.] By the author of *Letters of her mother to Elizabeth* [W— R. H. Trowbridge]. Cr 8vo. London, 1902

GIRL (the) of the name of Brown. [A story.] By Eglanton Thorne [Emily Charlton]. Cr 8vo. Pp. 222. [*Lond. Lib. Cat.*] London, 1901

GIRL (the) of the period. [By Mrs Eliza Lynn Linton.] 8vo. [*Brit. Mus.*] London, 1869

GIRL (the) on the green. [A novel.] By Mark Allerton [William Ernest Cameron]. Cr 8vo. Pp. 352. [*Lit. Year Book.*] London, 1914

GIRL (the) ranchers. By Carl Louis Kingsbury [Mrs Caroline Louise Marshall]. 8vo. Philadelphia, 1897

GIRL (a) to love. [A tale.] By Bertha M. Clay [Charlotte M. Braeme]. Fcap 8vo. London, 1911

GIRL (the) who couldn't lie. [A novel.] By Keble Howard [John Keble Bell]. 8vo. [*Lond. Lib. Cat.*]
London, 1908

GIRL (the) who waited. [A novel.] By Florence Warden [Florence Alice Price, later Mrs George E. James]. Cr 8vo. Pp. 311. London, 1922

GIRL (the) who wouldn't mind getting married. [By Harry Parkes.] 8vo.
London, 1885

GIRL (the) who wrote. [A novel.] By Alan Dale [Alfred J. Cohen]. Cr 8vo. Pp. 376. [*Amer. Cat.*]
New York, 1902

GIRL (a) with money. By Florence Warden [Florence Alice Price, later Mrs George E. James]. Cr 8vo. Pp. 316. [*Brit. Mus.*] London, 1917

GIRL (the) with the haunting eyes. By Florence Warden [Florence Alice Price, later Mrs George E. James]. Cr 8vo. Pp. 310. London, 1920

GIRLHOOD. By Marianne Farningham [Mary Anne Hearne, of Farningham]. New and revised edition. 8vo. Pp. viii., 231. [*Brit. Mus.*]
London, 1895

GIRLHOOD and womanhood : the story of some fortunes and misfortunes. By Sarah Tytler, author of *Papers for thoughtful girls*, etc. [Henrietta Keddie]. 8vo. Pp. vii., 359. [*Lit. Year Book.*] London, 1868

GIRLHOOD days ; or Auld Lang Syne. By the author of *Chaucer's stories simply told*, etc. [Mary Seamer, later Mrs Seymour]. Pt 8vo. Pp. 192. [*Brit. Mus.*] London, 1886

GIRLHOOD (the) of our Lady. By Marion J. Brunowe [Marion J. Browne]. Pt 8vo. [*Amer. Cat.*]
New York, 1903

GIRLS and women. By Eliza Chester [Harriet Eliza Paine]. 8vo.
Boston, 1890

GIRLS (the) at Quinnemont ; or, Miss Annie's butterflies. By Hope Ledyard [Mrs F. M'Cready Harris]. Cr 8vo. [Cushing's *Init. and Pseud.*, vol. i., p. 170.] London, 1885

GIRLS (the) at the Grange ; a novel. By Florence Warden [Florence Alice Price, later Mrs George E. James]. 8vo. Pp. vi., 296. London, 1897

GIRLS (the) of Beechcroft School. By May Wynne [Mabel Wynne Knowles]. Cr 8vo. Pp. 255. [*Lit. Year Book.*]
London, 1920

GIRLS (the) of Cromer Hall. [A tale.] By Raymond Jacberns [Georgina M— Selby Ash]. Cr 8vo. Pp. 240. [*Lit. Year Book.*] London, 1904

GIRLS (the) of Inverbarns. By Sarah Tytler [Henrietta Keddie]. Cr 8vo. [*Lit. Year Book.*] London, 1906

GIRLS (the) of the cottage. A novel. By Florence Warden [Florence Alice Price, later Mrs George E. James]. 8vo. London, 1924

GIRL'S (the) own cookery book. By Phillis Browne [Mrs Sarah Sharp Hamer]. 8vo. Pp. iv., 160. [*Brit. Mus.*] London, [1882]

GIRL'S (a) romance. [By Marian James.] 8vo. [*Brit. Mus.*]
Edinburgh, 1867

GIRLS will be girls. [A novel.] By Florence Warden [Florence Alice Price, later Mrs George E. James]. 8vo. Pp. vi., 296. London, 1898

GISELA ; a tragedy, in five acts. By J. J. H. [John James Holroyd]. 8vo. Pp. 96. [*Brit. Mus.*] London, 1839

GISELLA. By the author of *Second love* [John Palgrave Simpson, M.A.]. 3 vols. Fcap 8vo. [*Brit. Mus.*]
London, 1847

GITANA (the) : a tale. [By Sophia Briggs.] 3 vols. 8vo. London, 1845

GITHA of the forest. By the author of *Lord Dacre of Gilsland*, etc. [Elizabeth M. Stewart]. 3 vols. Fcap 8vo. [*Bodl.*] London, 1845

GIUSEPPE, the Italian boy. By the author of *The German shoemaker* [Margaret Fison]. Fcap 8vo. Pp. 63. [*Bodl.*] London, 1846

GIUSEPPINO ; an occidental story. [By Edward N. Shannon.] 8vo. [Boase's *Mod. Brit. Biog.*, vol. 6, col. 544.] London, 1821

GIUSTINA ; a Spanish tale of real life : a poem, in three cantos. By E. S. L. [the Hon. Elizabeth Susan Law, afterwards Lady Colchester]. 8vo. Pp. 66. [Martin's *Cat.*] [London], 1833

GIVE me thine heart. [By Azel Stevens Roe.] 8vo. New York, 1880

GIVING alms no charity, and employing the poor a grievance to the nation : being an essay upon this great question, —whether work-houses, corporations, and houses of correction for employing the poor, as now practis'd in England, . . . are not mischievous to the nation, tending to the destruction of our trade, and to increase the number and misery of the poor. Addressed to the Parliament of England. [By Daniel Defoe.] 8vo. [Wilson's *Life of Defoe*, p. 64.]
London, 1704

GIVING and keeping. By "Fleeta" [Kate W— Hamilton]. Fcap 8vo. [Cushing's *Init. and Pseud.*, vol. i., p. 103.] Philadelphia, 1891

GIVING trust. I. Bread and oranges. II. Rapids of Niagara. Tales illustrating the Lord's Prayer. By the author of *The wide, wide world*, etc. [Susan Warner]. 8vo. Pp. 428. [*Amer. Cat.*] London, 1875

GLAD tales and sad tales. By Reginald Reverie [Grenville Mellen]. 8vo. [Haynes' *Pseud.*]
Boston, [Mass.], 1829

GLAD tidings; or walks with the wonderful. By a lover of the Word [Harvey A. Ingham]. 8vo. [Cushing's *Init. and Pseud.*, vol. i., p. 175.]
Rochester, New York, 1868

GLAD (the) worshipper. By the author of *The Lamplighter* [Rev. Francis Bourdillon]. 8vo. [*Brit. Mus.*]
London, [1867]

GLADSTONE (the) almanac, 1885. [By George Stronach, M.A.] 8vo. [*Adv. Lib.*] London, 1884

GLADSTONE and Company. [By George Stronach, M.A.] 8vo. [*Adv. Lib.*] London, 1885
See also "Gleanings from Gladstone," and "More Gleanings."

GLADSTONE and the Irish Church. [By George Davidson.] 8vo. [Robertson's *Aberd. Bibl.*] Aberdeen, 1868

GLADSTONE (the) government; being cabinet pictures. By a Templar [William Charles Mark Kent]. 8vo. Pp. 340. [*Brit. Mus.*] London, 1869

GLADYS: a frivolous novel. By Tramio [Gertrude Armitage Smith]. 3 vols. 8vo. [*Brit. Mus.*]
London, 1882

GLADYS Greye. By Bertha M Clay [Mrs. Charlotte M. Braeme]. Fcap 8vo. New York, 1891

GLADYS of Harlech: an historical romance. [By Anne Beale.] 3 vols. Fcap 8vo. [*Brit. Mus.*]
London, 1858

GLAMOUR; a novel. By "Wanderer," author of *Fair Dianas*, etc. [Elim H. D'Avigdor]. 2 vols. 8vo. [*Lond. Lib. Cat.*] London, 1885

GLANCE (a) at New York; a local drama. [By Rev. Asa Greene.] 8vo. [Allibone's *Dict.*] New York, 1837

GLANCE (a) at some points in education. By one who has undergone the process [Samuel Bailey]. 8vo.
London, N.D.
Authorship indicated in Bury edition (1881) of his "Letters of an Egyptian Kafir," p. xii.

GLANCE (a) at the Exhibition of works of living Artists under the patronage of the Glasgow Dilettante Society. By Geoffrey Crayon [John Strang, LL.D.]. 8vo. [*Mitchell Lib.*] Glasgow, 1830

GLANCE (a) at the historical traditions of Pittenweem during the two last centuries. By an old residenter [James Horsburgh, provost of Pittenweem]. 12mo. [*And. Jervise.*]
Pittenweem, [1851]
Signed "J. H."

GLANCE (a) at the old world. By Lake-Elbe [Archibald Bleloch, M.D.]. 8vo.
Edinburgh, 1878
The pseudonym is a modification of the family name.

GLANCE (a) at the pictures in the hall of the worshipful Company of Ironmongers. [By Leapidge Smith.] Fcap 4to. London, 1847

GLANCE (a) at the Temple Church. By Felix Summerly [Sir Henry Cole]. Fcap 8vo. [Anderson's *Brit. Top.*]
London, [1840]

GLANCE (a) behind the grilles of religious houses in France; with an insight into the working of the Roman Church system as compared with our own. [By Mrs William Pitt Byrne, *née* Julia Clara Busk.] 8vo. [*Adv. Lib.*] London, 1855
The title-page is printed in B. L.

GLANCES at character [in verse. By J— Clarke]. 8vo. London, 1814

GLANCES of Brighton; past and present. By the authoress of *Rambles in the realms of thought* [Amelia Balcomb]. 8vo. [*Brit. Mus.*]
London, [1836]

GLANCINDA; a fairy tale in nine glintings. By Mardale [R— H— Holme]. Large 8vo. Pp. 122.
London, 1908

GLAPHYRA, and other poems. By Francis Reynolds [Francis Reginald Statham]. 8vo. [*Brit. Mus.*]
London, 1870

GLASGOW Bibliographical Society; Foulis exhibition held in the University of Glasgow, April 12-16, 1913: description of exhibits and opening ceremony. [By Wm. J. Couper.] 8vo. Pp. 23. Glasgow, 1913
Author's presentation copy.

GLASGOW in 1901. By James Hamilton Muir [James Bone, Archibald Hamilton Charteris, and Muirhead Bone]. 8vo. Pp. 255. [*Glasg. Univ. Lib.*] Glasgow, 1901
The pen-name is formed of selections from the names of the three contributors.

GLASGOW; or, the vision: a poem, in three cantos. [By Thomas Blair, Commander of the E. I. C.'s ship *William Fairlie*.] Fcap 8vo. Pp. 72. [*And. Jervise.*] London, 1824

GLASGOW, past and present ; illustrated in Dean of Guild Court reports, and in the reminiscences and communications of Senex [Robert Reid] and Aliquis [Dr Mathie Hamilton]. [By James Pagan and David Robertson.] 3 vols. Fcap 4to. [*Mitchell Lib.*]   Glasgow, 1884

GLASS (a) for the people of New England, in which they may see themselves and spirits, and if not too late, repent and turn from their abominable ways and cursed contrivances. By S. G. [S. Groome]. 4to. [Christie-Miller *Cat.*]   N.P., 1676

GLASS (the) of fashion ; some social reflections. By a gentleman with a duster [Harold Begbie]. Cr 8vo. Pp. 171. [*Brit. Mus.*]   London, 1921

GLASSE (a) for gamesters ; and namelie for suche as delight in cards and dise : wherein thei maie see not onely the vanitie, but also the vilenesse of those plaies plainly discouered and overthrown by the word of God. Written by T. W. [Thomas Wilcocks]. Imprinted at London by Ihon Kyngston, for Thomas Man. 8vo. No pagination. B. L. [*Bodl.*]   1581

GLASS-EYE. [A tale.] By " Bruin " [J— F. C. Adams]. Pt 8vo. [Cushing's *Init. and Pseud.*, vol. ii., p. 20.]   New York, 1873

GLASTONBURY Abbey ; a poem. [By C— Cookson.] Fcap 8vo. [Green's *Bibl. Somers.*, ii., 437.]   Taunton, 1828

GLASTONBURY Abbey, Somersetshire. [A history. By Dr William Robinson.] 4to. Pp. 73.   Tottenham, private print, 1844

GLEAM (a) of comfort to this distracted empire, in despite of faction, violence, and cunning ; demonstrating the fairness and reasonableness of national confidence in the present ministry. [By Thomas Lewis O'Beirne, Bishop of Meath.] Seventh edition. 8vo. [*D. N. B.*, vol. 41, p. 304.]   Dublin, 1785
Wrongly ascribed to Denis O'Bryen.

GLEAMS from the sick chamber ; memorial thoughts of consolation and hope gathered from the Epistles of Peter. By the author of *Morning and night watches* [John Ross MacDuff, D.D.]. Fcap 8vo. Pp. xx., 172.   London, 1882

GLEAMS of light and glimpses through the rift. [By T— S— Wilmot.] 4to. Pp. xv., 724. [*Brit. Mus.*]   London, 1893

GLEAMS through the mists, literary and domestic ; or a story of two lives. [By Charlotte Bickersteth, later Mrs Wheeler.] Fcap 8vo.   London, 1876

GLEANER (the) ; a miscellaneous production. By Constantia [Judith Murray]. 3 vols. Fcap 8vo. [*Brit. Mus.*]   Boston, 1798

GLEANER (the) : containing original essays in prose and verse, with extracts from various publications, particularly the reviews, and other periodical works. [Edited by James Grahame, advocate.] 8vo. [*David Laing.*] Edinburgh, 1795
One number only was published.

GLEANINGS after " Grand tour "-ists. [By Arthur Blennerhassett Rowan, D.D.] 8vo. [*Brit. Mus.*]   London, 1856

GLEANINGS and groupings from a pastor's portfolio. [By Joshua Noble Danforth.] 8vo. [Cushing's *Init. and Pseud.*, vol. i., p. 225.]   New York, 1852

GLEANINGS ; being a sequel to " Ploughing and sowing." By a clergyman's daughter [Mary E. Simpson]. 8vo. [*Brit. Mus.*]   London, 1876
Signed " M. E. S."

GLEANINGS from a Confederate Army note-book. By Personne [Felix G. De Fontaine]. 8vo. [Kirk's *Supp.*]   Columbia, S.C., 1865

GLEANINGS from a pastor's portfolio. By the author of *Scripture localities and their associations* [Henry John Betts]. Fcap 8vo. Pp. 93. [*Bodl.*]   London, 1854

GLEANINGS from fireside fancies. By Sans Souci [Mrs Nelly Nichol MacAfee]. 8vo. [Kirk's *Supp.*]   Chicago, 1866

GLEANINGS from [W. E.] Gladstone. [By George Stronach, M.A.] Fcap 4to. [*Adv. Lib.*]   Edinburgh, 1880
This was followed by " New Gleanings."

GLEANINGS from Gospel story. [By Eliza Tabor, later Mrs Stephenson.] Fcap 8vo. [*Brit. Mus.*] London, 1861

GLEANINGS from the South, East, and West. By a daughter of the late author of *The Cambrian Plutarch* [Mrs Anna Elizabeth Nightingale, *née* Parry]. 8vo. [*Brit. Mus.*]   London, 1843

GLEANINGS in Europe. England. By an American [James Fenimore Cooper]. 2 vols. Fcap 8vo. [*Brit. Mus.*]   Philadelphia, 1837

GLEANINGS in Europe. Italy. By an American [James Fenimore Cooper]. 2 vols. Fcap 8vo. Philadelphia, 1838

GLEANINGS in London, Sheffield, Glasgow, and Dublin. By the author of *The Autobiography of a beggar boy* [James Dawson Burn]. Dy 8vo. [*Brit. Mus.*] London, 1858

GLEANINGS; or the spirit of the Press. . . . [By William Lyle Keys.] 8vo. Cincinnati, 1841

GLEANINGS, pictorial and antiquarian, on the overland route. By the author of *Forty days in the desert* [William Henry Bartlett]. Second edition. 8vo. Pp. vi., 256. [*Brit. Mus.*] London, 1851

GLEANINGS respecting Battel [Battle] and its Abbey. By a native [F— W. Ticehurst]. Fcap 8vo. [Anderson's *Brit. Top.*] Battel, 1841

GLEES and madrigals. By Paddy Green [George Henry Townsend]. 8vo. London, [1862 ?]

GLEN Luna. By Amy Lothrop [Anna Bartlett Warner]. 8vo. Pp. viii., 464. [Cushing's *Init. and Pseud.*, ii., 174.] London, 1852
See also " Glen-Luna," below.

GLEN Morris stories. By Francis Forrester [Daniel Wise, D.D.]. 5 vols. 8vo. [Kirk's *Supp.*] New York, 1874

GLEN (the) o' weeping; a novel. By Marjorie Bowen [Gabrielle Vere Campbell, later Madame Long]. Cr 8vo. [*Lond. Lib. Cat.*] London, 1907

GLEN (the) of silver birches. [A novel.] By E. Owens Blackburn [Elizabeth O. B. Casey]. 8vo. [S. J. Brown's *Ireland in fiction.*] New York, 1881

GLENAIR; or life in Scotland. By H. H. Tatem [Helen Hazlett]. 8vo. [Cushing's *Init. and Pseud.*, vol. i., p. 280.] Philadelphia, 1869

GLENARVON. [By Lady Caroline Lamb.] 3 vols. Fcap 8vo. [Courtney's *Secrets*, p. 57.] London, 1816
Republished in 1865 as "The Fatal passion."

GLENATHOLE. [A novel.] By Cyril Grey [A— Balfour Symington]. Cr 8vo. Pp. iv., 364. London, 1889

GLENCAIRN; a dramatic story in three acts. By W. C. [William Chambers, LL.D.]. Fcap 4to. Pp. 42. [Corrie's *Glencairn*, p. 199.] Private print, [Edinburgh], 1875

GLENCOE; or the fate of the Macdonalds : a tragedy, in five acts. [By Thomas Noon Talfourd.] 8vo. Pp. vi., 95. [Martin's *Cat.*] [London, 1839]

GLENCREGGAN : or, a Highland home in Cantire. By Cuthbert Bede [Edward Bradley]. Illustrated with three maps, eight chromolithographs, and sixty-one woodcuts, from the author's drawings. 2 vols. 8vo. [*Brit. Mus.*] London, 1861

GLENDOVER : a novel. By Deane Roscoe [Frederic B. Yates]. Fcap 8vo. [*Lib. Journ.*, v., 187.] New York, 1880

GLENERNE. [A Temperance tale.] By Frances Palliser [Mrs Mary Wilson]. 8vo. [Cushing's *Init. and Pseud.*, vol. i., p. 224.] Glasgow, [1863]

GLENFERGUS. [By Robert Mudie.] 3 vols. Fcap 8vo. [*Gent. Mag.*, Aug. 1842, p. 214.] Edinburgh, 1820

GLENGARRY school-days. By Ralph Connor [Charles W. Gordon, D.D.]. Pt 8vo. [*Lit. Year Book.*] Chicago, 1902

GLENGOYNE; reminiscences of the parish and its people. By the late William Gairdner [or rather William MacGillivray], Writer to Her Majesty's Signet. 2 vols. Fcap 8vo. [Edinburgh], private print, 1900

GLENLONELY; or the demon fiend. [A novel. By William Henry De Merle.] 3 vols. 8vo. London, 1837

GLEN-LUNA (the) family. [A novel.] By the author of *The wide, wide world* [Susan Warner]. Pt 8vo. [*Brit. Mus.*] London, [1879]
See also above, " Glen-Luna."

GLENMORE Abbey. [By Thomas Dutton, M.A.] London, [1800 ?]

GLENMORE; or the Irish peasant [a tale of eviction]. By a member of the Irish Bar [Peter Burrowes Kelly]. 8vo. [Cushing's *Init. and Pseud.*, vol. i., p. 189.] Dublin, 1839

GLENNANDALE. By Clara Vance [Mrs Mary Andrews Denison]. 12mo. [Kirk's *Supp.*] Boston, 1882

GLENROYSDALE; a sketch. By a Celt [Mary E. Colquhoun]. Pt 8vo. Edinburgh, 1878
Private information from a friend.

GLENTIRLIE. By John Strathesk [John Tod]. 4to. [*Lit. Year Book.*] Edinburgh, 1890

GLIMPSE (a) at the army, the hospitals, and the freedman [in the United States. By the Rev. Edward James Young]. 8vo. Boston, [Mass.], 1864

GLIMPSE (a) at the social condition of the working classes during the early part of the present century; trade strikes and their consequences to the people who may be immediately connected with them. . . . By the author of *The auto-biography of a beggar boy* [James Dawson Burn]. 8vo. Pp. iv., 156. [*Brit. Mus.*] London, [1868]

GLIMPSE (a) at whist. By a glowworm [John Loraine Baldwin]. Fcap 8vo. [Kirk's *Supp.*] London, 1866

GLIMPSE (a) of eternity ; a sermon on
II. Corinthians iii., 17.   By A. C.
[Abraham Caley, B.D.].   Fcap 8vo.
[Calamy's *Nonconf. Mem.*, Palmer's
edition, ii., 212.]   London, 1667
  Later editions give the author's name.

GLIMPSE (a) of Sion's glory; or the
Churches beautie specified . . . [By
Hanserd Knollys ?] Fcap 4to. [*Brit.
Mus.*]   London, 1641
  The epistle to the reader is signed
" W. K." [William Kiffin].

GLIMPSE (a) of the great secret Society
[of the Jesuits.   By Charles N. Newde-
gate, M.P.].   Fourth edition, with
additions and notes.   Cr 8vo.   Pp. 87
and 254.   [*New Coll. Lib.*]
                            London, 1873

GLIMPSE (a) of the world.   By the
author of *Amy Herbert*, etc. [Eliza-
beth Missing Sewell].   8vo.   Pp. 540.
[*Brit. Mus.*]   London, 1863

GLIMPSE (a) through the gloom, in a
candid discussion of the policy of the
Peace. . . . [By R— Legge Willis].
8vo.   London, 1794

GLIMPSES of ancient Hackney and
Stoke Newington ; with an appendix
dealing with the conversion of a portion
of Hackney Churchyard into an open
space.   By F. R. C. S. [Dr ——
Clarke].   Large 8vo.   London, 1893

GLIMPSES of antiquity ;   being a
collection of metrical sketches.   By
George F. Preston [George Fortescue,
and the Hon. John B. L. Warren,
Baron De Tabley].   8vo.
                            London, 1862

GLIMPSES of English history [in
burlesque].   By F. M. Allen [Edmund
Downey].   Cr 8vo.   Pp. 200.   [*Lit.
Year Book.*]   London, 1901

GLIMPSES of Evangelical Europe ; or,
notes for Christian laymen, compiled
by one of themselves [Robert Sal-
mond, manufacturer, Arbroath].   With
a prefatory note by W. G. Blaikie,
D.D.   8vo.   Pp. 159.
                          Edinburgh, [1879]
  Information from a friend of the writer.

GLIMPSES of Fairy Land.   By Edith
Bateman [Edith M. Briggs].   8vo.
                            London, 1903

GLIMPSES of famine and flood in
East Bengal.   By Nivedita [Margaret
E. Noble].   8vo.   Pp. 95.   [*Brit. Mus.*]
                          Allahabad, [1907]

GLIMPSES of Glen-na-Mona.   By
Brian na Banban [Brian O'Higgins].
8vo.   Pp. 615.   [S. J. Brown's *Ireland
in Fiction*, p. 205.]   Dublin, 1908

GLIMPSES of hidden India.   By John
Law [Miss M— E. Harkness].   Fcap
8vo.   [*Lit. Year Book.*]
                          Calcutta, [1909]

GLIMPSES of life in Victoria.   By a
resident [J— H. Kerr].   8vo.
                          Edinburgh, 1872

GLIMPSES of New York City.   By a
South-Carolinian who had nothing
else to do [William M. Bobo].   8vo.
[Cushing's *Init. and Pseud.*, vol. i.,
p. 271.]   Charleston, S.C., 1852

GLIMPSES of pleasant houses.   [By
Mary Theresa Austin Carroll.]   8vo.
                            New York, 1869

GLIMPSES of real life.   By the author
of *The Burnish family* [Mrs Clara
Lucas Balfour].   8vo.   [Kirk's *Supp.*]
                          Glasgow, [1859]

GLIMPSES of real life, as seen in the
theatrical world and in Bohemia ;
being the confessions of Peter Paterson, a strolling comedian. [By James G.
Bertram, journalist.]   Cr 8vo.   [The
author's *Some memories of books*,
etc.]   Edinburgh, 1864
  An enlarged edition, with modified title,
of " Behind the scenes. . . ."

GLIMPSES of the past.   By Charlotte
Elizabeth [Mrs Charlotte Elizabeth
Tonna, previously Mrs Phelan].   8vo.
Pp. 354.   [*Brit. Mus.*]   London, 1839

GLIMPSES of the unseen ;   poems.
By A. L. O. E., authoress of *The
Claremont tales*, etc. [Charlotte M.
Tucker].   Fcap 8vo.   Pp. 108.
                          Edinburgh, [1854]

GLIMPSES within the veil ;   their
teachings and consolations.   By the
author of *The coming struggle* [David
Pae].   8vo.   [*Brit. Mus.*]
                          Edinburgh, 1855

GLOBE (the) prepared for man ;   a
guide to geology.   By the author of
The observing eye [Anne Wright].   8vo.
Pp. vi., ii., 339.   London, 1853

GLOBULES for tobacco-olaters.   [By
Thomas Reynolds, Secretary of the
British Anti-Tobacco Society.]   8vo.
                            London, 1855

GLORIA Patri.   Prayers, chants, and
responses for public worship [prepared
by T. B. Thayer, D.D., and L. J.
Fletcher, D.D.].   Fcap 8vo.   Pp. 214.
[Eddy's *Universalism in America*, ii.,
572.]   Boston, [Mass.], 1866

GLORIA victis : from the German of
Ossip   Schubin   [Lola   Kirschner].
[Cushing's *Init. and Pseud.*, i., 475.]
12mo.   Philadelphia, 1886

GLORIES (the) of heaven, and the
terrors of hell. . . . By G. L. [George
Larkin, or Larkham, M.A., minister
at Cockermouth].   Fcap 8vo.
                            London, 1699
  The authorship is indicated in contemporary handwriting.

GLORIOUS (a) espousal ; a brief essay to illustrate and prosecute the marriage wherein our Great Saviour offers to espouse unto Himself all the children of men. [By Cotton Mather, D.D.] Fcap 8vo. [Evans' *Amer. Bibl.*, vol. 1, p. 275.] Boston, [Mass.], 1719

GLORIOUS (the) Gospel of Christ : considered in its relations to the present life. By the author of *God is love*, etc. [James Grant, journalist]. 8vo. Pp. xvi., 409. [*Brit. Mus.*] London, 1861

GLORIOUS (the) lover ; a divine poem, upon the adorable mystery of sinners redemption. By B. K. [Benjamin Keach], author of *War with the devil*. 8vo. [*Bib. Angl. Poet.*, No. 410.] London, 1679

GLORIOUS (the) return : a story of the Vaudois in 1689. By Crona Temple [Miss —— Corfield]. 8vo. Pp. 157. [*Brit. Mus.*] London, [1889]

GLORIOUS (the) truth of redemption by Jesus Christ, rescued out of the hand of unrighteousness. By W. L. [William Levitt]. 8vo. [*Thomason Coll. of Tracts*, vol. i., p. 890.] London, 1652

GLORY (the) and downfall of Edom. [By Rev. Stillman Pratt.] 8vo. Boston, 1845

GLORY (the) and the shame of Britain ; a prize essay on the condition and claims of the working classes. [By Henry Dunckley.] Fcap 8vo. [*D. N. B.*, First Supp., vol. 2, p. 169.] London, 1851

GLORY Court ; the story of its light-bringers. By Charles Aver [Charles Wesley Keyworth, B.A.]. Cr 8vo. Pp. 208. [*Methodist Who's Who.*] London, 1908

GLORY (the) of Christ, and the ruine of Antichrist, unvailed as they are set forth in Revelation, by the seales, trumpets, and vialls, dialogue-wise. . . . By T. C. [Thomas Collier, or Colyer, minister at York]. Fcap 8vo. Pp. vii., 108. [*Camb. Univ. Lib.*] N.P., 1647

GLORY (the) of Christ as God-man display'd ; in three discourses. . . . [By Isaac Watts, D.D.] 8vo. Pp. xx., 276. [*D. N. B.*, vol. 60, p. 69.] London, 1746

GLORY (the) of England, or a true description of many excellent prerogatives and remarkable blessings whereby shee triumpheth over all nations in the world. By T. G. [Thomas Gainsford]. 4to. [*Brit. Mus.*] London, Edwd. Griffin, 1619

GLORY (the) of Jesus Christ ; a brief account of our Lord's life . . . in Sanskrit verse. [By] J. M. [John Muir, D.C.L.]. Second edition, with a Hindi version and an English summary. 8vo. [*Brit. Mus.*] Calcutta, 1849

GLORY (the) of love. By " Pan " [Leslie Beresford], author of *White heat*, etc. 8vo. Pp. 248. [*Lit. Year Book.*] London, [1919]

GLORY (the) of the heavenly city and blessedness of departed saints, graciously manifested in a vision to a young lady [Miss —— Field, of Bristol] as related by herself. 8vo. Bristol, 1782

GLORY (the) of the New Covenant. [By William Smith, of Besthorp.] 4to. [*Brit. Mus.*] [London, 1664] Signed " W. S."

GLORY (the) of the sea. By Darley Dale [Francesca M. Steele]. Pt 8vo. [*Brit. Mus.*] London, 1887

GLORY (the) of their times ; or the liues of yᵉ primitiue Fathers. Cōtayning their chiefest actions, workes, sentences, and deaths. [By Daniel (or Donald) Lupton, Vicar of Sumbury.] 4to. Pp. 548. [*Bodl.*] London, 1640

GLORY (the) of women ; or a looking-glasse for ladies : written first in Latine by Henricus Cornelius Agrippa ; translated into English prose, but now turned into heroicall verse by H. C. [Henry Care], Gent. 8vo. [*Thomason Coll. of Tracts*, vol. i., p. 883.] London, 1652 Attributed also to Hugh Crompton.

GLORY (the) of Zeebrugge and the " Vindictive." By Keble Howard [John Keble Bell]. Pt 8vo. Pp. 64. [*Lond. Lib. Cat.*] London, 1918

GLORY or gravity essential, and mechanical : wherein the objects and articles of the Christian faith are exhibited, as they were originally and successively reveal'd, hieroglyphically, by representations in figures. . . . With some account of the origin and present state of the doctrine of the Adversary. By J. H. [John Hutchinson]. 8vo. Pp. 261. [*New Coll. Cat.*] London, 1732 Part of the sixth volume of the collected works, published in 1749. It does not contain the " Mechanical" part, which occupies the greater portion of the eleventh volume. The Hebrew title is כבר יהוה.

GLOSSARY (a) of provincial words used in Herefordshire and some of the adjoining counties. [By Sir George Cornewall Lewis.] 12mo. Pp. xii., 132. [*D. N. B.*, vol. 33, p. 182.] London, 1839

GLOSSARY (a) of provincial words used in Teesdale in the county of Durham. [By Frederick P. Dinsdale, LL.D.] 8vo. Pp. xiv., 151. [*Brit. Mus.*]   London, 1849

GLOSSARY (a) of terms used in British heraldry ; with a chronological table, illustrative of its rise and progress. [By Henry Gough, barrister of the Middle Temple.] 8vo. [*Adv. Lib.*]
Oxford, 1847
Another edition was issued in 1894.

GLOSSARY (a) of terms used in Grecian, Roman, Italian, and Gothic architecture. [By John Henry Parker.] Third edition, enlarged. Exemplified by seven hundred woodcuts. 8vo. [*Bodl.*]   Oxford, 1840

GLOSSARY (a) of Yorkshire words and phrases, collected in Whitby and the neighbourhood ; with examples of their colloquial use, and allusions to local customs and traditions. By an inhabitant [Francis Kildale Robinson]. Fcap 8vo. Pp. x., 204. [Boyne's *Yorkshire Library*, p. 194.]   London, 1855

GLOSSARY (a) to the Canterbury Tales. [By Thomas Tyrwhitt.] 8vo. [*Brit. Mus.*]   Oxford, 1778

GLOSSOGRAPHIA ; or a dictionary, interpreting all such hard words, whether Hebrew, Greek, Latin, Italian, Spanish, French, Teutonick, Belgick, British or Saxon, as are now used in our refined English tongue : also the terms of divinity, law, physick, mathematicks, heraldry, anatomy, war, musick, architecture, and of several other arts and sciences, explicated. . . . By T. B. of the Inner-Temple, barrester [Thomas Blount]. 8vo. No pagination. [*Bodl.*]   London, 1656
A fifth edition, with additions, was published in 1681.

GLOUCESTERSHIRE Notes and Queries. Edited by B. H. B. [Rev. Beaver Henry Blacker, M.A.]. 8vo. [*Brit. Mus.*]   London, 1879

GLOWING (the) thoughts of an M.A.—*id est* Magnus Asinus—of the Calcutta University. By Max O'Tell [Daniel O'Brien Moore]. 8vo. [*Calc. Imp. Lib.*]   Calcutta, N.D., [1890 ?]

GLYGLUMGLEAGH ; a legend of the olden time. By the author of *The famine*, etc. [Thomas Hingston Harvey]. 8vo. [Boase and Courtney's *Bibl. Corn.*]   Truro, 1849

GNOME (the) hatter ! or, the elfinish wile and the well-finished tile, a "moral" impossibility. By Messrs. J. F. Sunavill and J. W. Hogo-Hunt [James Frank Sullivan and John William Houghton]. 12mo. Pp. 47.   N.P., N.D.

GNOME (the) king ; or, the giant mountains : a dramatick legend, in two acts, first perform'd at the Theatre Royal, Covent Garden, on Wednesday, October 6th, 1819. [By George Colman, the younger.] The musick by Mr Bishop ; the arrangement of the action under the direction of Mr Farley. 8vo. Pp. 56.   London, 1819
"This piece was written by George Colman (the younger)."—MS. note by Dyce.

GO forth and find. By Thomas H. Brainerd [Mrs John R. Jarboe]. Cr 8vo.   London, 1895

GO in peace ; some brief directions for young ministers in their visitation of the sick. [By John Martin, of Oriel College.] Fcap 8vo. [*D. N. B.*, vol. 36, p. 281.]   London, 1674

" GO out quickly." (Luke xiv. 21.) By ροβ ροι [John MacGregor]. 8vo. [Mendham Coll. *Cat. (Supp.*), p. 21.]
London, 1855

GOAL (the). [A novel.] By May Wynne [Mabel Wynne Knowles]. Cr 8vo. Pp. 320. [*Lit. Year Book.*]
London, 1907

GOAL (the) of life : a poem. By "Spectator" [W— H. Wingate]. 8vo. [*Brit. Mus.*]   St Ives, [1867]

GOAT'S (the) beard ; a fable. [By William Whitehead.] Third edition. 4to. Pp. 40. [*Watt's Bibl. Brit.*]
London, 1777

GO-BANG ; a musical farcical comedy in two acts. Lyrics. By Adrian Ross [Arthur Reed Ropes]. 8vo. Pp. 32. [*Brit. Mus.*]   London, [1894]

GOBLIN gold. By the author of *Queenie* [May Crommelin]. Cr 8vo. [*Brit. Mus.*]   London, [1885]

GOBLINS (the) of Neapolis. [Verses.] By Paul Puck Peeradeal [Sir William Cusack Smith, Bart.]. 8vo. [O'Donoghue's *Poets of Ireland*.]   Dublin, 1836

GOD. Conferences delivered at Notre Dame in Paris by Père Lacordaire, of the Order of St Dominic : translated by a Tertiary of the same Order [Henry D. Langdon]. 8vo. [*Brit. Mus.*]   London, 1870
See also below, "God and man."

GOD and His Book. The Bible: when did we get it, and what is it ? By Saladin [William Stewart Ross]. 8vo. Pp. viii., 302. [*Brit. Mus.*]   London, [1906]

GOD and His Wisdom. By T. [William Henry Trenwith]. 8vo. [Cushing's *Init. and Pseud.*, vol. i., p. 278.]
New York, 1877

GOD and man. [By James Alexander Smith.] 8vo. Pp. x., 165. [*Adv. Lib.*]
London, 1861
The preface is signed "J. A. S."

GOD and man : conferences delivered at Notre Dame in Paris, by Père Lacordaire, of the Order of St Dominic; translated from the French . . . by a Tertiary of the same Order [Henry D. Langdon]. 8vo. [*Brit. Mus.*]
London, 1872

GOD and the Agnostics; or, the end of the age of faith. By an Englishman [G— N. Rogers]. Cr 8vo. London, 1903

GOD and the country robbed, or the Nonconformist movement for the abolition of Church rates, briefly exposed. [By Rev. William Nicholson Kingdon, B.D.] 8vo. Pp. 15. [*Brit. Mus.*]
Launceston, 1857

GOD and the Dragon ; rhymes. By H. D. C. P. [H— Douglas C. Pepler]. Fcap 8vo. Pp. 44. [*Brit. Mus.*]
London, 1917
This is a later edition of *Concerning Dragons* (1916).

GOD and the King. By Marjorie Bowen [Gabrielle Vere Campbell, later Madame Long]. Second edition. Cr 8vo. Pp. vii., 376. [*Lond. Lib. Cat.*]
London, 1911

GOD and the King ; or a dialogue [between Theodidactus and Philalethes] shewing that our Soveraigne Lord King James, being immediate under God within his dominions, doth rightfully claime whatsoever is required by the Oath of Allegiance. [By Richard Mocket (or Moquet), D.D.] Fcap 8vo. Pp. 92. [*D. N. B.*, vol. 38, p. 91.]
London, 1615
Later editions, slightly modified, were published in 1663 and 1727 ; at Edinburgh, in 1617 and 1725, a Latin version was also printed. A royal command required that this treatise should be taught in all Universities, Schools, and Churches. *See also* the following entries.

GOD and the King ; or, a dialogue [between Aristobulus and Philanax] wherein is treated of Allegiance due to our most gracious Lord K. James within his dominions [by Richard Mocket, D.D.]. . . . Translated out of Latin [printed 1615 and 1616] into English [by John Floyd, S.J.]. Fcap 8vo. Pp. 140. Cullen, 1620
The above is the Romish edition of the preceding.

GOD and the king ; or, the divine constitution of the supreme magistrate, especially in the kingdome of England, against all popular pretenders whomsoever ; published for the satisfaction of the weake : being a private discourse of a reverend Judge [David Jenkins], with some commanders of the Army, for their satisfaction, by their desire. 4to. [*Brit. Mus.*] [London], 1649

GOD in His world ; an interpretation. [By Henry Mills Alden.] Cr 8vo. [*Brit. Mus.*] New York, 1890

GOD in Shakespeare. By Clelia [Charles Downing]. 8vo. Pp. 424. [*Brit. Mus.*] London, 1890

GOD (the) in the car : a novel. By Anthony Hope [Anthony Hope Hawkins]. Cr 8vo. [*Lond. Lib. Cat.*]
London, 1898

GOD (the) in the garden ; an August comedy. By Keble Howard [John Keble Bell]. Cr 8vo. Pp. 346. [*Lit. Year Book.*] London, 1904

GOD is all in all ; or the Kingdom of the Son delivered up to God, even the Father, by the Son Himself : leading into an exacter and clearer discovery of the Kingdom of Christ upon that great Context, I. Cor. 15 : 27, 28, etc. By T. B. [Thomas Beverley]. 8vo. [Arber's *Term Cat.*, iii., 698.]
London, 1704

GOD is love ; or, glimpses of the Father's infinite affection for his people. By the author of *The brother born for adversity* [James Grant, journalist]. Third edition. 8vo. Pp. xv., 403. [*Brit. Mus.*] London, 1858

GOD made man ; or an account of time, stating the day, hour, and minute of our Saviour's nativity, verified by the rules of practical astrology. [By John Butler, B.D.] Fcap 8vo. [Watt's *Bibl. Brit.*] London, 1671

GOD (the) of the Jews ; or Jehovah unveiled : to which is prefixed a letter to [Richard Watson] the Bishop of Llandaff. By a tradesman [William Skinner]. 8vo. Pp. v., 99. [*Brit. Mus.*] London, 1819

GOD our Father. By a Father of the Society of Jesus [Florentin J. Boudreaux], author of *The happiness of heaven.* 8vo. [Sommervogel's *Dictionnaire.*] London, 1878

GOD save the king ; or, the loyal and joyfull acclamation of subjects to their king : as it was opened in a sermon, preached in one of the congregations of the city of Edinburgh, upon the day of solemn thanksgiving for the Kings Majesty his happy return and restauration to his dominions : kept June 19, 1660, at the appointment of the presbyterie of Edinburgh. By R. L. [Robert Lawrie], one of the ministers of the city. 4to. [*Adv. Lib.*]
Edinburgh, 1660

GOD the beautiful ; an artist's creed ; and the religion of beauty contrasted with Hinduism. By E. P. B. [Emil P. Berg]. Second edition. Fcap 8vo.
London, 1905

GOD (the) Yutzo, 763 B.C. By Lord Gilhooley [Frederick Henry Seymour]. 8vo. [*Amer. Cat.*] New York, 1897

GODDESSES three; a novel. [By Daisy Hugh Price.] Cr 8vo. London, 1899

GODFREY of Bulloigne, or the recouery of Hiervsalem; an heroicall poeme written in Italian by Seig. Torquato Tasso, and translated into English by R. C. [Richard Carew], Esquire, and now the first part, containing fiue cantos, imprinted in both languages. 4to. Pp. 235. London, N.D.
The address to the reader is dated 1594, and signed " C. H.," *i.e.* Christ. Hunt.

GODFREY'S wife; a reminiscence. By Stanley Hope [Sydney Hodges]. 2 vols. 8vo. [*Brit. Mus.*]
London, 1874

GODLIE (ane) dreame compylit in Scottish meter be M. M. [Mistress Melvil] gentelvvoman in Culros at the requeist of her freindes. [By Elizabeth Melvil, Lady Culross.] 4to. No pagination. B. L. [Lowndes' *Bibl. Man.*]
Edinbvrgh, 1603

GODLIE (a) forme of hovsholde government; for the ordering of private families according to the direction of Gods word: whereunto is adioyned in a more particular manner, the seuerall duties of the husband towards his wife; and the wiues duty towards her husband; the parents duty towards their children, and the childrens towards their parents; the masters dutie towards his seruants, and also the seruants dutie towards their masters. Gathered by R. C. [Roger Carr, B.A., of Pembroke Hall, Cambridge]. 8vo. Pp. 384. [Cooper's *Athenæ Cantab.*, iii.] London, 1598
Wrongly ascribed by some to Robert Cawdrie, by others to Robert Cleaver.
Another edition was issued in 1600; a still later edition (1612) has " First gathered by R. C. and now newly perused, amended, and augmented, by J. Dod and R. Clever."

GODLIE (a) treatisse. *See* " Godly (a) treatise."

GODLY (a) and frvitefull sermon, made vpon the 20. & 21. verses of the 14. chapter of the booke of Genesis: wherein there is taught, what prouision ought to be made for the ministrie: very necessarie to be learned of all Christians. [By Eusebius Paget.] 8vo. No pagination. B. L. N.P., N.D.
The Bodleian copy contains the following MS. note : " By Eusebius Paget. See it printed by Wolfe, 1583, which, except the title page, agrees page for page with this; yet the spelling, etc., shews it to be another impression."

GODLY (a) and necessarye admonition of the decrees and canons of the Counsel of Trent, celebrated under Pius the Fourth, Byshop of Rome, in the yeares of our Lord M.D.LXII. and M.D.LXIII. Lately translated out of Latine. [Supposed to be done by Archbishop Parker, or by his appointment.] 4to. [Lowndes' *Bibl. Man.*]
London, by John Day, 1564

GODLY fear; or the nature and necessity of fear and its usefulness : both to the driving sinners to Christ and to provoking Christians on in a godly life. . . . By R. A. [Richard Alleine], author of *Vindiciae pietatis.* Fcap 8vo. [Green's *Bibl. Somers.*, vol. 2, p. 108.]
London, 1674

GODLY (the) mans portion and sanctuary; being a second part of Vindiciae pietatis. By R. A. [Richard Alleine]. 8vo. Pp. 152. [Green's *Bibl. Somers.*, ii., 107.]
N.P., printed in the year 1663

GODLY priuate praiers, for householders to meditate vpon, and to saye in their famylies. [By Edward Dering.] Imprinted at London by Iohn Charlewood. 8vo. No pagination. B. L. [*Bodl.*] 1581

GODLY (a) sermon preached at Detford the ix of June 1572. [By E. Paget ?] 8vo. B. L. [*Brit. Mus.*] London, 1586

GODLY (a) treatise declaring the benefites, frutes, and great commodities of prayer, and also the true use thereof; written in Latyn, forty yeares past, by an Englishman [John Fisher, Bishop of Rochester], and lately translated into Englyshe. 12mo. [*Brit. Mus.*]
N.P., 1560

GODLY women of the Bible. [By Ellen Elvira Gibson.] 8vo. Boston, [1830 ?]

GODODIN (the), and the odes of the month; translated from the Welsh. [By W. Probert.] [B. Pickering's *Cat.*] Alnwick, N.D.

GODOLPHIN. A novel. [By Edward George Earle Lytton Bulwer-Lytton, Baron Lytton.] 3 vols. 12mo. [*Brit. Mus.*] London, 1833

GODOLPHIN; a tragedy, in five acts: and miscellaneous poems. [By —— Hope.] Pt 8vo. Pp. x., 108.
Hertford, 1843
Information from a friend of the author

GOD'S abyss and a woman. By Charles Granville [Francis Charles Granville Egerton, Earl of Ellesmere]. 8vo. Pp. 156. [*Brit. Mus.*] London, 1908

GODS (the) are athirst. By Anatole France [Jacques Anatole Thibault] : translated by A. Allinson. Dy 8vo. Pp. 292. [*Brit. Mus.*] London, 1913

2 B

GOD'S birds [*i.e.* the birds of the Bible]. By John Priestman [Rev. John Fitzpatrick]. 8vo. Pp. 91. [O'Donoghue's *Poets of Ireland*.] London, [1893]

GODS blessing upon the providers of corne ; and Gods curse upon the hoarders. By C. F. G. [Charles Fitz-Geoffrey]. Together with the corn imported into the London port in four months. 4to. Pp. 56. [Thomason *Coll. of Tracts*, i., p. 570.]
London, 1648
Three sermons on Proverbs xi. 26.

GOD'S bottle for believers' tears. By one who has a tear for others, as well as himself [Archibald Currie, Abercorn]. 12mo. Pp. 126. [*Adv. Lib.*]
Edinburgh, 1854

GOD'S failures. By a son of the soil [Joseph Smith Fletcher]. Pt 8vo. [*Amer. Cat.*] New York, 1897

GOD'S fool : a Koopstad story. By Maarten Maartens [Joost M. W. van der Poorten-Schwartz]. Cr 8vo. [*Lond. Lib. Cat.*] London, 1894

GODS (the) give my donkey wings. By Angus Evan Abbott [James Barr]. Cr 8vo. London, 1895

GOD'S good woman. [A novel.] By Eleanore S. Terry [Mrs J— Sterry]. Cr 8vo. London, 1909

GOD'S goodness to His Israel in all ages : being the substance of some sermons on Psalm LXXIII. 1. By J. F. [James Forbes, M.A., Nonconformist minister in Gloucester]. 8vo. [Calamy's *Nonconf. Mem.*, Palmer's edition, ii., 251.]
London, 1700

GOD'S gracious presence with his Highness Richard Lord Protector. . . . [By William Kaye.] 4to.
London, 1658

GOD'S greeting ; a story of this our day. By John Garrett Leigh [John Lee]. Cr 8vo. Pp. viii., 405.
London, 1899

GOD'S heavenly family contrasted with the earthly, shewing Christ's finished work for man's redemption. . . . [By W— D. Forsyth.] 8vo. Pp. 56, xiii.
Littleborough, [1903]
Signed " W. D. F."

GOD'S holy name magnified, and His truth exalted by the testimony of His faithful servants who have the cruel penalty of banishment from their native country by the rulers thereof ; as also an abstract of their names. . . . [By] R. C. [Richard Crane]. . . . 4to. [*Brit. Mus.*] [London], 1665

GOD'S judgments upon the Gentile apostatized Church, against the modern hypothesis of some eminent apocalyptical writers ; in four parts. Together with Dr Grabe's opinion of the Scripture prophecies concerning the Church of Rome. . . . [By John Hildrop, D.D.] Reprinted from a work published in 1713. 8vo. Pp. xxxv., 204. [Darling's *Cyclop. Bibl.*] London, 1823

GOD'S lad. By Paul Cushing [Roland Alexander Wood-Seys]. Cr 8vo. [*Lit. Year Book.*] London, 1900

GODS love to mankind, manifested by dis-prooving his absolute decree for their damnation. [By Samuel Hoard, B.D.] 4to. Pp. 110. [*D. N. B.*, vol. 27, p. 24.] N.P., 1633
Reprints were issued in 1658 and 1673. Replies were written by William Twiss and Bishop Davenant.

GODS (the) of the East Indies ; or an account of the religion of the Hindoos, with a short vindication of the attempts to propagate Christianity in India. [By Thomas Perronet Thompson.] Fcap 8vo. Pp. 23. [*Brit. Mus.*]
Hull, [1810 ?]

GOD'S playthings. By Marjorie Bowen [Gabrielle Vere Campbell, later Madame Long]. Cr 8vo. Pp. 326. [*Lond. Lib. Cat.*] London, 1912

GOD'S plea for the poor : observations concerning the poor and the new Poor Law. [By Rev. Richard Hibbs, M.A.] 8vo. [*Brit. Mus.*] London, 1851

GOD'S prisoner ; the story of a crime, a punishment, a redemption. By John Oxenham [William Arthur Dunkerley]. 8vo. Pp. viii., 331. [*Brit. Mus.*]
London, 1898

GOD'S purpose in creation and the successive steps in manifesting the same. Being the substance of lectures delivered in Scotland. . . . [By Francis Sitwell, of Barmoor Castle, Northumberland.] 8vo. Pp. xvi. 356. [C. Boase's *Cath. Apost. Lit.*]
Edinburgh, 1865

GOD'S purpose with mankind and the earth. [By William R. Caird.] 8vo.
Melbourne, 1876

GOD'S revenge against murder and adultery, remarkably displayed in a variety of tragical histories, etc. [By John Reynolds, merchant in Exeter.] 8vo. Pp. vii. 188. [*Brit. Mus.*]
London, 1770

GOD'S revenge against punning ; shewing the miserable fates of persons addicted to this crying sin, in court and town. [By Alexander Pope.] Folio. [*Camb. Hist. of Eng. Lit.*]
London, 1716
Incorrectly attributed to Jonathan Swift.

GOD'S revenge against the enemies of the Church : written by T. W. [Thomas Wall, M.A.]. 8vo. Pp. 53. [*Bodl.*]
London, 1658

GOD'S safe way of obedience . . . for a humble penitent. By Sylvester Jenks, D.D. : revised and edited by a priest [Charles J. Bowen]. 12mo.
London, 1872

GOD'S scourge ; a drama. By Moreton Hall [Juliette Heale]. Cr 8vo.
London, 1902

GODS (the), some mortals, and Lord Twickenham. [A novel.] By John Oliver Hobbes [Pearl Maria Teresa Richards, later Mrs Reginald Walpole Craigie]. Cr 8vo. [*Brit. Mus.*]
London, 1895

GOD'S sovereignty and man's duty asserted : a sermon [on Ezek. 24/16], occasioned by the death of Martha Shelton. . . . By R. K. [Richard Kingston], M.A. 4to. [*Brit. Mus.*]
London, 1688

GOD'S temple. [By William Yunnie.] 8vo. [Robertson's *Aberd. Bibl.*]
Paisley, N.D.

GOD'S temple-throne : a hymn. By H. C. B. [Henry Clark Barlow, M.D.]. 8vo. [*Brit. Mus.*] Roma, 1855

GOD'S tenth. [By Caroline Woolmer Leakey.] 8vo. London, 1850

GODS terrible voice in the city ; wherein you have I. The sound of the voice, in the narration of the two late dreadful judgments of plague and fire, inflicted by the Lord upon the city of London ; the former in the year 1665, the latter in the year 1666. II. The interpretation of the voice, in a discovery, 1. of the cause of these judgments. . . . 2. Of the design of these judgments. . . . By T. V. [Thomas Vincent]. 8vo. Pp. 221. [*Wood's Athen. Oxon.* (ed. *Bliss*), iii., 1174.]
[London], 1667

GOD'S Troubadour ; the story of St. Francis of Assisi. By Ellen Burroughs [Sophie Jewett]. 8vo. [*Amer. Cat.*] New York, 1910

GOD'S universal right proclaimed : a sermon [on Psalm 24. 1. 2.] preached at Paules crosse, the 27. of March 1603. being the next Sunday after Her Maiesties departure. By I. H. [John Hayward]. 8vo. No pagination. [Strype's *Life of Whitgift*, p. 558.]
London, 1603

GOD'S unspeakable gift ; or, views of the person and work of Jesus Christ. By the author of *God is love*, etc. [James Grant, journalist]. 8vo. Pp. viii., 400. [*Brit. Mus.*]
London, 1861

GOD'S voice in the house. By the author of *The Lamplighter* [Rev. Francis Bourdillon]. 8vo. [*Brit. Mus.*]
London, 1870

GOD'S warriors, and other verses. By L. M. A. [Lucy Margaret Alden]. Fcap 8vo. [*Bodl.*] Oxford, [1902]

GÖTHE and Schiller. By Louise Mühlbach [Mrs Clara Müller Mundt]. Fcap 8vo. [Cushing's *Init. and Pseud.*, vol. i., p. 199.] New York, 1887

GOETHE'S Torquato Tasso, translated into English verse [by J— Cartwright, M.A.]. 8vo. Pp. vii., 151. [Kirk's *Supp.*] London, 1861

GOETZ of Berlichingen with the iron hand ; an historical drama, translated from the German of Goethe [by Rose D'Aguilar, later Mrs Lawrence]. 8vo. [*Brit. Mus.*] London, [1795]
Incorrectly given as " Gortz of Berlingen." *See below.*

GOFF (the) ; an heroi-comical poem, in three cantos. [By Thomas Mathison.] 8vo. [*Adv. Lib.*]
Edinburgh, 1743

GOIN' to Cyprus. By A. [Benjamin Brierly]. 8vo. [*Manch. Free Lib.*]
Manchester, 1879

GOING home. [A poem.] By R. W. [Robert White]. 8vo. [Cushing's *Init. and Pseud.*, vol. i., p. 300.]
Newcastle-on-Tyne, 1850

GOING south ; or, yachting on the Atlantic coast. By Oliver Optic [William T. Adams]. Fcap 8vo. [Kirk's *Supp.*] Boston, 1880

GOINGS (the) on of Mrs Brown at the Tichborne trial, and in her own family. [By George Rose.] 8vo. [*Brit. Mus.*]
London, 1872

GOLD ; a legendary rhyme. Illustrated with twelve outlines, by Alfred Crowquill [Alfred Henry Forrester]. Oblong Folio. No pagination. [*D. N. B.*, vol. 20, p. 6.] London, [1851]

GOLD and competition ; or, the wailings of a commission-mania satire. By J. B. [Joseph Burton]. Fcap 8vo. [*Brit. Mus.*] Hull, 1863

GOLD and dross. [A novel.] By Edward Garrett [Isabella Fyvie, later Mrs John R. Mayo]. 8vo. [*Lit. Year Book.*] London, 1874

GOLD and gilt ; or, Maybee's puzzle. By Archie Fall [Mary J. Capron]. Fcap 8vo. [Kirk's *Supp.*]
Boston, 1877

GOLD fields of Victoria in 1862. By the " Argus " Commissioner [J— C— Patterson]. Fcap 8vo. [*Lib. of Col. Inst.*, vol. i., p. 126.] Melbourne, 1862

GOLD, frankincense and myrrh. By E. R. [E— Reed]. 8vo. [Cushing's *Init. and Pseud.*, i. 245.]
Philadelphia, 1872

GOLD (the) hunter's adventures ; or, life in Australia. By a returned Australian [William H. Thomes]. Fcap 8vo. [*Lib. of Col. Inst., Supp.* I., 686.] Boston, 1864

GOLD Island ; a novel. By Noel West [Mrs M— B— Cox]. Cr 8vo. Pp. 346. London, 1904

GOLD (the) spinner. [A novel.] By Dick Donovan [Joyce E. Preston Muddock]. Cr 8vo. [*Lit. Year Book.*] London, 1907

GOLD (a) standard in India. [By E— Kleinmann.] 8vo. Paris, 1897

GOLD stories of 1849. By a Californian [Nüima Smith]. Pt 8vo. [*Amer. Cat.*] New York, 1896

GOLD (the) that perisheth. [A novel.] By David Lyall [Annie Swan, later Mrs Burnett Smith]. Cr 8vo. Pp. 320. London, 1901

GOLDBEATER (the) ; a novel. By the author of *The Blacksmith's daughter*, etc. [— M'Gauran]. 3 vols. Fcap 8vo. [*Adv. Lib.*]
London, 1852

GOLDELSE : from the German of E. Marlitt [Henriette F. C. Eugenie John]. Pt 8vo. [Cushing's *Init. and Pseud.*, i., 184.] New York, 1887

GOLDEN (the) age ; or England in 1822-23 : a poetical epistle. [By — Davenport, M.P.] 8vo.
London, 1823

GOLDEN age ; the story of four merry children. By Ismay Thorn [Edith Caroline Pollock]. Cr 8vo. Pp. 224. [*Brit. Mus.*] London, 1906

GOLDEN (a) and blessed casket of nature's marvels. By Benedictus Figulus [Benedikt Toepfer]. Now first done into English [by A. E. Waite] from the German original. . . . 8vo. Pp. xxxi., 361. [*Brit. Mus.*]
London, 1893

GOLDEN (a) anniversary. . . . [By William Alfred Hovey.] 8vo.
Boston, [Mass.], 1880

GOLDEN (a) autumn : a novel. By Mrs Alexander [Mrs Alexander Hector *née* Annie French]. Cr 8vo. Pp. 312. [*Lit. Year Book.*] London, 1896

GOLDEN (a) bar. [By E— M— Archer.] Cr 8vo. London, 1884

GOLDEN (a) bar. [A novel.] By the author of *Christina North*, etc. [Mrs Eleanor A. Towle]. 3 vols. 8vo. [*Brit. Mus.*] London, 1882

GOLDĒ (the) boke of Christen matrimonye, moost necessary & profitable for all thē that entend to liue quietly and godlye in the Christen state of holy wedlock : newly set forthe in English by Theodore Basille [Thomas Becon]. Imprinted at London in Botulph lane at the sygne of the Whyte Beare, by John Mayler for John Gough. 8vo. Fol. lxxviii. B. L.
Anno Dñi., 1543
The " preface unto the boke " and " address to the readers," as well as the table, are unpaged.

GOLDEN (the) book of St John Chrysostom, concerning the education of children : translated out of the Greek by J. E. [John Evelyn, sen.], Esq. 12mo. Pp. 96. [*Brit. Mus.*]
London, 1659

GOLDEN (the) bottle ; or the story of Ephraim Benezet of Kansas. By Ignatius Donnelly [Edmund Boisgilbert]. Cr 8vo. Pp. 313. [*Lond. Lib. Cat.*] New York, 1892

GOLDEN (the) butterfly ; a novel. By the authors of *Ready-money Mortiboy*, etc. [Sir Walter Besant and James Rice]. 3 vols. 8vo. [*Brit. Mus.*]
London, 1876

GOLDEN (the) calf : a novel. By the author of *Lady Audley's secret* [Mary Elizabeth Braddon, later Mrs John Maxwell]. 3 vols. 8vo. [*Brit. Mus.*]
London, 1883

GOLDEN (a) censer full with the pretious incense of the praiers of the Saints. [By Maurice Ewens, *alias* Keynes, *alias* Newport, S.J.] Fcap 8vo. Pp. 142. [*Gillow's Bibl. Dict.*, vol. ii., p. 193.] Paris, 1654

GOLDEN (the) chain. By the author of *The memoir of the Rev. William Marsh, D.D.*, etc. [Catherine Marsh]. 8vo. Pp. 194. London, [1875]

GOLDEN (the) chayne of salvation. By Herman Renecker ; now translated out of Latine into English [by Peter Allibond, minister of Cheynis]. Fcap 4to. [Watt's *Bibl. Brit.*]
London, 1604

GOLDEN (the) Chersonese ; or, the Logan rock restored. By an officer of the Royal Navy [Hugh C. Goldsmith]. 8vo. [Boase and Courtney's *Bibl. Corn.*] Penzance, 1824

GOLDEN (the) child : a daily chronicle. [By Thomas Lake Harris.] Royal 8vo. Fountain Grove, 1878

GOLDEN (a) curb for the mouth, which, with a headstrong folly, rushes into the sins of profane swearing and cursing. [By Cotton Mather, D.D.] 8vo. [Evans' *Amer. Bibl.*, vol. i., p. 201.]
Boston, [Mass.], 1709

GOLDEN (the) Dagon; or, up and down the Irrawaddi. [By John Williamson Palmer, M.D.] 8vo.
New York, 1856

GOLDEN (the) dawn. By Bertha M. Clay [Mrs Charlotte M. Braeme]. Fcap 8vo.　New York, 1886

GOLDEN (the) decade of a favoured town: being biographical sketches and personal recollections of the celebrated characters who have been connected with Cheltenham, from 1843 to 1853. By Contem Ignotus [Rev. Richard Glover]. Pt 8vo.
London, 1884

GOLDEN dreams and leaden realities. By Ralph Raven [George Payson]. 8vo. [Cushing's *Init. and Pseud.*, vol. i., p. 248.]　New York, 1853

GOLDEN dreams, and waking realities; being the adventures of a gold-seeker in California and the Pacific. [By William Shaw.] 8vo. [Cushing's *Init. and Pseud.*, vol. i., p. 548.]
London, 1851

GOLDEN (the) dwarf. By Norman Silver [George Knight]. 8vo.
London, [1915?]

GOLDEN feather. By the author of *Mehalah* [Rev. Sabine Baring-Gould, M.A.]. 8vo. [*Brit. Mus.*]
London, [1886]

GOLDEN (the) fleece. By A. L. O. E., author of *My neighbour's shoes*, etc. [Charlotte Maria Tucker]. 8vo. Pp. 149.　London, 1869

GOLDEN (the) fleece. By John Graham [David G. Phillips]. Fcap 8vo. [*Amer. Cat.*]　New York, 1903

GOLDEN (the) fleece diuided into three parts; vnder which are discouered the errours of religion, the vices and decayes of the kingdome, and lastly the wayes to get wealth, and to restore trading so much complayned of. Transported from Cambrioll Colchos, out of the southermost part of the Iland commonly called the New-fovndland, by Orpheus Iunior, for the generall and perpetuall good of Great Britaine. [By Sir William Vaughan, LL.D.] 4to. Pp. 350. [*Wood's Athen. Oxon.*]　London, 1626

GOLDEN fruit from Bible trees. By Old Colony [Rev. Francis Nicoll Zabriskie]. 8vo. [Haynes' *Pseud.*]
New York, 1862

GOLDEN (the) gate series of fairy tales. By May Wentworth [Mrs Mary W. Newman]. 8vo. [Cushing's *Init. and Pseud.*, vol. i., p. 305.] New York, 1867

GOLDEN gates. By Bertha M. Clay [Mrs Charlotte M. Braeme, *née* Law]. Fcap 8vo.　New York, 1888

GOLDEN girls. [A novel.] By Alan Muir [Rev. Hayes Robinson]. New edition, revised. Cr 8vo. Pp. 334. [*Lond. Lib. Cat.*]　London, [1888]

GOLDEN (the) greyhound. By Dwight Tilton [Wilder Dwight Quint]. 8vo. [*Amer. Cat.*]　Boston, [Mass.], 1906

GOLDEN (the) grove; or, a manuall of daily prayers and letanies, fitted to the dayes of the week; containing a short summary of what is to be believed, practised, desired: also festival hymns, according to the manner of the ancient Church, composed for the use of the devout, especially of younger persons. By the author of *The Great Exemplar* [Jeremy Taylor, D.D.]. 8vo. Pp. 185. [Watt's *Bibl. Brit.*]　London, 1655

GOLDEN (a) heart. By Bertha M. Clay [Mrs Charlotte M. Braeme, *née* Law]. Fcap 8vo.　Chicago, 1887

GOLDEN Hills; a tale of the Irish famine. By the author of *Cedar Creek* [Elizabeth Hely Walshe]. 8vo. Pp. viii., 272. [*Brit. Mus.*]　London, [1865]

GOLDEN (the) horse-shoe: the story of a lucky strike. By Robert Aitken [Robert Aitken Swan]. Cr 8vo. Pp. 318. [*Lit. Year Book.*]　London, 1908

GOLDEN (the) ladder: stories illustrative of the eight beatitudes. By the authors of *The wide, wide world*, etc. [Susan and Anna B. Warner]. Eighth thousand. 8vo. Pp. vii., 479. [*Brit. Mus.*]　London, 1863

GOLDEN (the) legacy; a story of life's phases. By a lady [Mrs H— J— Moore]. 8vo. [Cushing's *Init. and Pseud.*, vol. i., p. 161.] New York, 1857

GOLDEN (the) life. [By Mrs Julia Wright, *née* MacNair.] 8vo. [Allibone's *Dict.*]　Boston, [Mass.], 1867

GOLDEN links; or thoughts for the hours. [By Maria Shoemaker.] 8vo.
Philadelphia, 1869

GOLDEN lives; biographies for the day. [By Alexander Hay Japp, LL.D.] 8vo. [*D. N. B.*, Second Supp., vol. ii., p. 363.]　London, 1873

GOLDEN (the) milestone; some passages in the life of an ex-confederate officer: a novel. By Scott Graham [Miss Hazelton Black]. Pt 8vo. Pp. 547.　London, 1885

GOLDEN (the) opportunity. [By Jean Ingelow.] 12mo. [*Brit. Mus.*]
London, 1867

GOLDEN (the) pippin; an English burletta, in three acts: as it is performed at the Theatre-Royal, Covent-garden. By the author of *Midas* [Kate O'Hara]. 8vo. Pp. 51. [*Biog. Dram.*]　London, 1773

GOLDEN (the) referee : a guide to health. . . . By Medicus and Co. [Joshua T. Woodhead]. 8vo. [Kirk's *Supp.*] Liverpool, 1874

GOLDEN (the) rod ; an idyl of Mount Desert. [By Mrs Constance Harrison *née* Cary.] 8vo. New York, 1870

GOLDEN (the) rule ; or, the royal law of equity explained. [By John Goodman, D.D.] 8vo. Pp. 90. [*Bodl.*] London, 1688

GOLDEN sayings from George A. Birmingham [James Owen Hannay, D.D.]. 12mo. Pp. 95. [*Brit. Mus.*] London, [1915]

GOLDEN (the) scorpion. By Max Rohmer [Arthur Sarsfield Ward]. Cr 8vo. Pp. 256. [*Lond. Lib. Cat.*] London, 1919

GOLDEN (the) ship ; and other tales. [By Gertrude Ward.] 8vo. London, 1900
Preface signed " G. W."

GOLDEN (the) spy ; or, a political journal of the British nights' entertainments of war and peace, and love and politics : wherein are laid open the secret miraculous power and progress of gold in the courts of Europe. . . . [By Charles Gildon.] 8vo. Pp. xi., 310. London, 1709
" Charles Gildon who wrote the Golden Ass, an imitation of Apuleius, in 2 vols., 8vo, Lond., 1708, promised a continuation of it which was never published ; instead of which he seems to have intended this, as a continuation. Accordingly, in the second edition of the Golden Ass (in 2 vol. 12mo, 1724), the Golden Spy is added at the end of it."—MS. note in Dr David Laing's copy.

GOLDEN (a) straw. [A novel.] By J. E. Buckrose [Mrs Falconer Jameson]. Cr 8vo. Pp. 316. [*Lond. Lib. Cat.*] London, 1910

GOLDEN (a) sunset ; being an account of the last days of Hannah Broomfield. By the author of *Morning and night watches*, etc. [John Ross MacDuff, D.D.]. 8vo. Pp. 148. London, 1874

GOLDEN (the) treasury of thought : a gathering of quotations from the best ancient and modern authors. By Theodore Taylor, author of *Thackeray, the humourist and man of letters*, etc. [John Camden Hotten]. 8vo. Pp. vi., 466. [*Adv. Lib.*] London, [1874]

GOLDEN (the) treasury Psalter ; being an edition, with briefer notes, of " The Psalms chronologically arranged by four friends " [Alex. W. Potts, LL.D., Francis E. Kitchener, and two others]. 12mo. Pp. xii., 271. London, 1870

GOLDEN (a) trust. [A novel.] By Theo Douglas [Mrs H— D. Everett]. 8vo. [*Brit. Mus.*] London, 1905

GOLDEN (the) vase. [By J— M. Fletcher.] 8vo. Boston, [Mass.], 1851

GOLDEN (the) violet, with its tales of romance and chivalry ; and other poems. By L. E. L., author of *The improvisatrice*, etc. [Letitia Elizabeth Landon]. 8vo. Pp. 310. [*Brit. Mus.*] London, 1827

GOLDEN (the) wedding ring. . . . By a clergyman of the Church of England [Rev. John Clowes, M.A.]. Fcap 8vo. [*N. and Q.*, Feb. 1869, p. 168.] Manchester, 1813

GOLDEN (the) West. By Margaret Sidney [Mrs Harriet Mulford Lothrop]. 8vo. [Kirk's *Supp.*] Boston, 1885

GOLD-FOIL hammered from popular proverbs. By Timothy Titcomb [Josiah Gilbert Holland, M.D.]. 8vo. [Allibone's *Dict.*] London, 1890

GOLD-HEADED (the) cane. [By William Macmichael, M.D.] 8vo. Pp. 274. [*N. and Q.*, Sept. 1855, p. 194.] London, 1827

GOLDMAKERS (the). [A tale.] By Esmé Stuart [Amélie Claire Leroy]. Cr 8vo. [*Lond. Lib. Cat.*] London, 1897

GOLD-SEEKERS (the) ; a tale of California. By Gustave Aimard [Ollivier Gloux. Translated from the French by Sir Frederick Charles Wraxall]. 8vo. [*Brit. Mus.*] London, 1861

GOLD-WORSHIPPERS (the) ; or, the days we live in : a *future* historical novel. By the author of *Whitefriars* [Emma Robinson]. 3 vols. Fcap 8vo. [*Brit. Mus.*] London, 1851

GOLF ; a royal and ancient game. [Edited by Robert Clark.] 4to. Pp. xxi., 284. Edinburgh, 1875
The Introduction is signed " R. C."

GOLF ; an heroi-comical poem, in three cantos. [By Rev. Thomas Mathieson.] 8vo. Pp. 22. Edinburgh, 1753
Previously published in 1743.

GOLF (the) craze. By Cleeke Shotte, Esq., of Bunker's Hill [John Hogben]. Cr 8vo. Pp. 136. Edinburgh, [1907]
Information from a friend of the author.

GOLF faults remedied ; containing also rules worth remembering. By Mark Allerton [William Ernest Cameron, LL.B.]. 8vo. Pp. 26. [*Lit. Year Book.*] London, [1911]

GOLF in the year 2000 ; or what we are coming to. By J. A. C. K. [J— Mac-Culloch]. Pt 8vo. London, 1892

GOLF made easy. By Mark Allerton [William Ernest Cameron] and R. Browning. Cr 8vo. Pp. 146. [*Lit. Year Book.*] London, 1910

GOLFER'S (the) manual ; being an historical and descriptive account of the national game of Scotland : with an appendix. By a keen hand [Henry Brougham Farnie]. 8vo. Pp. xii., 96. [*Adv. Lib.*] Cupar, 1857

GOLFING (a) idyll ; or the skipper's round with the Deil on the links of St Andrews. By Violet Flint [Colonel J— E— Thomson]. 4to.
Edinburgh, 1892
Presentation copy from the author, with his name.

GOLIAH beheaded with his own sword ; or, a vindication of the Roman Catholic Church against the late charge of Dr Magee. . . . By Julius Vindex [Dennis Taafe]. Fcap 8vo. [*Brit. Mus.*]
London, 1824

GOLIATH slain ; being a reply to the Reverend Dr Nowell's Answer to Pietas Oxoniensis : wherein the false glosses of that gentleman's pamphlet are removed. . . . By the author of *Pietas Oxoniensis* [Sir Richard Hill]. 8vo. [*Brit. Mus.*] London, 1768

GOLIGHTLYS (the), father and son. By Laurence North [J— D-- Symon]. Cr 8vo. Pp. 356. [*Lit. Year Book.*]
London, 1912

GOMERY of Montgomery ; a family history. [By Charles A. Washburn.] 8vo. New York, 1865

GONDIBERT and Birtha ; a tragedy. [By William Thompson, M.A., of Queen's College, Oxford.] 8vo. Pp. 323-444. [*Biog. Dram.*]
Oxford, 1751

GONDOLA (the). [A novel. By Henry Stoe Van Dyk.] Fcap 8vo. Pp. vi., 246. [*Brit. Mus.*] London, 1827

GONE wrong : a new novel. By Miss Rhody Dendron [Sir Francis Cowley Burnand]. 8vo. [Kirk's *Supp.*]
London, 1881

GONVERSATIONINGS. By Diedrich Dinkelspiel [George V. Hobart]. 8vo. [*Amer. Cat.*] New York, 1900

GONZALEZ and his waking dreams. By C. S. H. [Rev. Charles Sumner Harington, M.A.]. Fcap 8vo. [Kirk's *Supp.*] London, 1868

GONZALO de Baldivia ; or, a widow's vow : a romantic legend. By the author of *Cambrian pictures*, etc. [Ann Kemble, otherwise Ann of Swansea]. 4 vols. Fcap 8vo. London, 1817

GOOD advice before it be too late ; being a breviate for the Convention. [By Major Sir John Wildman ?] 4to. [*D. N. B.*, vol. 61, p. 235.]
[Amsterdam], 1689

GOOD advice to the Church of England, Roman Catholick, and Protestant Dissenters ; in which it is endeavoured to be made appear that it is their duty, principles and interest to abolish the penal laws and tests. [By William Penn.] 4to. Pp. 61. [Smith's *Cat. of Friends' Books*, ii., 304.]
London, 1687

GOOD advice to the ladies ; shewing that, as the world goes and is like to go, the best way for them is to keep unmarried. [In verse.] By the author of *The true-born Englishman* [Daniel Defoe]. 4to. [*Brit. Mus.*]
London, 1702

GOOD advice to the pulpits, deliver'd in a few cautions for the keeping up the reputation of those chairs, and preserving the nation in peace. [By John Gother.] Published with allowance. 4to. Pp. 70. [*Brit. Mus.*]
London, 1687

GOOD (the) and evil of tobacco. [By William E. A. Axon.] 8vo. [*Manch. Free Lib.*] Manchester, [1878 ?]

GOOD (a) and necessary proposal for the restitution of Catholick communion between the Greek Churches and the Church of England. [By Edward Stephens.] 4to. [*Bodl.*]
N.P., [1703 ?]

GOOD (a) boy's diary. By the author of *A Bad boy's diary* [Mrs Metta Victoria Victor, *née* Fuller]. 8vo. Pp. 127. [*Brit. Mus.*] London, 1884

GOOD (a) character ; or a walk with God characterized. . . . By one of the ministers of Boston [Cotton Mather, D.D.]. 8vo. Pp. 31. [*Evans' Amer. Bibl.*, vol. 1, p. 322.]
Boston, N.E., 1723

GOOD conduct. By George A. Birmingham [James O. Hannay, D.D.], author of *Spanish Gold*, etc. Cr 8vo. Pp. 250. [*Lit. Year Book.*]
London, 1920

GOOD (a) expedient for innocence and peace ; being an essay concerning the great usefulness and advantage of laying aside publick oaths. [By —— Taylour.] 4to. [*Adv. Lib.*]
Edinburgh, 1704

GOOD (the) fight. By Lynde Palmer [Mary Louise Parmlee, later Mrs A. Peebles]. 12mo. [Allibone's *Dict.*]
Boston, 1866

GOOD (the) fight of faith. . . . By C. J. G. [Mrs —— Freeland]. Cr 8vo. London, 1890

GOOD for evil ; and other stories. By A. L. O. E., author of *The silver casket*, etc. [Charlotte M. Tucker]. 8vo. Pp. 120. London, 1873

GOOD Friday and Easter Sunday. By Alethphilos [Rev. Joseph Rathbone, R.C. priest]. 8vo. Pp. 28. Isle of Wight, 1839

GOOD (the) gray poet [Walt Whitman] ; a vindication. [By William Douglas O'Connor.] 8vo. Pp. 46. [O'Donoghue's *Poets of Ireland*.] New York, 1866

GOOD (the) housewife made a Doctor ; or health's sure friend : being a plain way, of nature's own prescribing, to prevent and cure most diseases . . . [By Thomas Tryon.] 8vo. [Arber's *Term Cat.*, vol. ii., p. 616.] London, 1684

GOOD (a) husband for five shillings ; or Esquire Bickerstaff's [Sir Richard Steele's] lottery for the London Ladies. Wherein those that want bed fellows, in an honest way, will have a fair chance to be well-fitted. 8vo. Pp. 18. London, 1710

GOOD Indian. By B. M. Bower [Mrs Bertha Muzzy Sinclair]. 8vo. Pp. 255. [*Brit. Mus.*] London, 1919

GOOD investment. [A tale. By Mrs —— Somerset.] 8vo. London, [1891]

GOOD little hearts. The bird's nest. Stories. By Aunt Fanny [Frances Barrow, later Mrs Gage], author of *Nightcaps*, etc. 4 vols. Square 12mo. [Kirk's *Supp.*] Edinburgh, 1870

GOOD luck ! A novel. By E. Werner [Elizabeth Bürstenbinder] : translated from the German. 8vo. Pp. 153. [*Brit. Mus.*] London, 1890

GOOD (the) man's preparation for the receiving of the Blessed Sacrament ; with an account of Passion-Week and Easter. By A. S. [Abednego Seller]. Fcap 8vo. [*D. N. B.*, vol. 51, p. 227.] London, 1704
This is a revised and enlarged edition of " The Devout Communicant."

GOOD (the) mans priviledge : a sermon lately preached at Plimmouth in Devon by I. B. [John Barlow], and now published at the request of some that then were auditors. . . . 4to. Pp. 25. [Dredge's *Devon Bibl.*] London, 1618

GOOD morning ! Good night ! By the author of *Beneath the banner* [F— J— Cross]. 8vo. London, 1895

GOOD Mrs Hypocrite. [A novel.] By " Rita " [Mrs W— Desmond Humphreys, *née* Eliza M. J. Gollan]. Cr 8vo. [*Lit. Year Book*.] London, 1904

GOOD (the) neighbours ; a tale of the Cholera in 1849. By the author of *Charlie Burton* [Jane Alice Sargant]. 12mo. Pp. 119. London, 1852

GOOD newes and bad newes. By S. R. [Samuel Rowlands]. 4to. No pagination. London, 1622
Reprinted by the Hunterian Club, 1872.

GOOD newes from New England ; or a true relation of things very remarkable at the Plantation of Plimoth in New England, shewing the wondrous providence and goodness of God in their preservation. . . . Written by E. W. [Edward Winslow]. 4to. [Christie-Miller *Cat.*] London, 1624

GOOD newes from the North, truly relating how about a hundred of the Scottish rebels, intending to plunder the house of Mr Thomas Pudsie (at Stapleton in the bishoprick of Durham), were set upon by a troupe of our horsemen, under the conduct of that truly valorous gentleman Leiutenant Smith, Leiutenant to noble Sr. Iohn Digby ; thirty nine of them (whereof some were men of quality) are taken prisoners, the rest all slaine except foure or five which fled, whereof two are drowned. . . . [By Martin Parker.] S. Sh. Folio. Chiefly B. L. [*Bodl.*] London, 1640
Signed " M.P."

GOOD news from Scotland ; or the Abjuration and the Kirk of Scotland reconcil'd. [By ? Archibald Pitcairne, M.D.] 8vo. N.P., 1712
The authorship has yet to be ascertained.

GOOD night and good morning. [Verses, with illustrations.] By R. M. M. [Richard Monckton Milnes, later Lord Houghton] and A. H. M. [Annabella Hungerford Milnes]. 4to. Private print. [*Brit. Mus.*] N.P., 1859

GOOD (the) nurse ; or hints on the management of the sick and lying-in chamber and the nursery. [By Mrs Hanbury.] Second edition. Pp. xx., 387. [*W.*] London, 1828

GOOD (the) old cause, further discuss'd. In a letter to Benjamin Hoadly, the author of the Jacobite's hopes reviv'd. [By Charles Leslie.] 8vo. [Kennett's *Wisdom*, p. 58.] London, 1710

GOOD (the) old cause ; or, lying in truth : being a second defence of the Lord Bishop of Sarum [Dr Gilbert Burnet], from a second speech ; and also, the dissection of a sermon it is said his Lordship preached in the cathedral church of Salisbury last 29th of May. By one Miso-Dolos [Charles Leslie]. 4to. Pp. 36. [*D. N. B.*, vol. 33, p. 81.] London, 1710

GOOD (the) old days; or Christmas under Queen Elizabeth. By Esmé Stuart [Amélie Claire Leroy]. 8vo. [*Lond. Lib. Cat.*]   London, 1876

GOOD (the) old times; a tale of Auvergne. By the author of *Mary Powell* [Anne Manning, later Mrs Rathbone]. Second edition. 8vo. Pp. v., 275.   London, 1857

GOOD (the) old way; or Christianity described. . . . [By Cotton Mather, D.D.] Fcap 8vo. Pp. 96. [Evans' *Amer. Bibl.*, vol. 1, p. 184.]
                            Boston, [Mass.], 1706

GOOD out of evil; or the story of Adjai, the African slave-boy. By a lady [Miss A— F. Childe]. 12mo. [*Brit. Mus.*]   London, 1850

GOOD (the) prior: a fragment of the Middle Ages. [By Thomas Crofton Croker?] Fcap 4to. Private print.
                                    N.P., 1843

GOOD Queen Anne vindicated, and the ingratitude, insolence, &c. of her Whig ministry and the Allies detected and exposed, in the beginning and conducting of the war. The English-man's memorial; containing a short history of the land wars we have been engaged in, with unanswerable arguments, proving 'tis not the interest of England to be concerned, as a principal, in a land war, upon any pretence whatsoever;—Mind the sea. . . . By the author of the *Dissertation on parties* [Henry St John, Viscount Bolingbroke]. Second edition. 8vo. Pp. 76. [*Brit. Mus.*]   London, 1748

GOOD report from bad men, no mean disparagement: together with a cordial for Christians when they receive evil for well doing. . . . [By Richard Younge, of Roxwell, Essex.] 8vo. [*Bodl.*]   London, [1670?]

GOOD (the) Shepherd; a sermon. By W. S. O'B. [Rev. William Stuart O'Brien, M.A.]. 8vo. [Green's *Bibl. Somers.*, vol. i., p. 379.]   Bath, [1875]

GOOD (the) Shepherd carrying a lamb in his bosom, out of this world into the next. [By Henry Peckwell, D.D., rector of Bloxam-cum-Digby.] 8vo. [*Brit. Mus.*]   London, 1778

GOOD (the) ship "Dove." By Florence Warden [Florence Alice Price, later Mrs George E. James]. Cr 8vo. Pp. 313. [*Brit. Mus.*]   London, 1919

GOOD (a) souldier maintaining his militia, and posturing himself as the servants of the Lord now and in all ages have postured the Kingdomes. . . . Humbly presented to the House

of Parliament and Assembly of divines. By Hez. W. [Hezekiah Woodward]. 4to. Pp. 154. [Thomason *Coll. of Tracts*, vol. i., p. 323.]
                                    London, 1644

GOOD (a) speed to Virginia. By R. G. [Robert Gray]. Fcap 4to. Pp. 32. Printed for Felix Kyngston by William Welbie at the Greyhound in Pauls church-yard. [Christie-Miller *Cat.*]
                                    London, 1609

GOOD the final goal of ill: or, the better life beyond. Four letters to the Ven. Archdeacon Farrar, D.D. By a lay-man [Alex. Harvey]. Cr 8vo. Pp. 152. [*New Coll. Cat.*]   London, 1883

GOOD (a) time coming. By the author of *Matthew Paxton* [William Wilson, minister at Etal]. 3 vols. 8vo. [M'Guffie's *Priests of Etal*.]
                                    London, 1860

1. GOOD (the) wife; or, a rare one amongst women: whereto is annexed an exquisite discourse of epitaphs, including the choisest thereof, ancient or modern. [By Richard Brathwayt.] At London, printed for Richard Red-mer. 8vo. No pagination.   1618
   Includes—

2. REMAINS after death: including, by way of introduction, diuers memorable obseruances occasioned vpon discourse of epitaphs and epycedes; their distinction and definition seconded by approued authors. Annexed there be diuers select epitaphs and hearce-attending epods worthie our obseruation. Imprinted at London by John Beale, 1618. 8vo. No pagination.
   The Epistle to the reader is signed "Mvso-philvs." Another copy, with the same imprint, has the author's name.

3. PRODIGALS (the) glasse.

4. COMPENDIOUS (a) discourse annexed by the author, touching moderate weeping, behouefull for euerie tenderly-affected reader, who many times offends in the extremitie of this passion.
   The running title is "The mourners meane."

GOOD will to men: a narrative. By Elis [Rev. Edward Payson Hammond]. 8vo. [Kirk's *Supp.*]   London, 1861

GOOD will towards men, or a treatise of the Covenants, viz. of works and grace, old & new; wherein sundry propositions are laid down concerning them, and diverse questions occasionally discussed. By a lover of truth and peace [John Barrett]. 8vo. Pp. 502. [Cresswell's *Printing in Nottingham-shire*, p. 5.]   London, 1675
   Preface signed "J. B."

GOOD wives; a story for girls: being a sequel to "Little women." By the author of *An old-fashioned girl* [Louisa May Alcott]. 8vo. Pp. iv., 313.

London, [1871]

The sixth edition, containing "Little women and Good wives," published in 1872, has the name of the authoress.

"GOOD Words"; the theology of its editor [Norman Macleod, D.D.]. [By Thomas Alexander, minister in Chelsea.] 8vo. [*New Coll. Cat.*]

London, 1863

GOOD work for a good magistrate; or, a short cut to great quiet: by honest, homely, plain English hints given from Scripture, reason, and experience. . . . By H. P. [Hugh Peters]. Printed by William Du-Gard, printer to the Council of State. 12mo. [*New Coll. Cat.*]

London, 1651

GOOD workes, if they be well handled; or certaine projects about maintenance for parochiall ministers. [By Ephraim Udall, M.A.] 4to. [*D. N. B.*, vol. 58, p. 4.]

London, 1641

GOOD-BYE. [A novel.] By John Strange Winter [Mrs Arthur Stannard, *née* Henrietta E. V. Palmer]. 8vo. [*Brit. Mus.*]

London, 1898

GOOD-BYE, proud world. By Henry Hayes [Ellen Warner Olney, later Mrs Kirk]. 8vo. [*Lit. Year Book.*]

Boston, 1903

GOODCHILD'S Garland [a story-book for juveniles]. By Henry Nemo [Henry Newbolt]. 8vo.

London, 1910

GOODLY (a) Prymer, in Englysshe; newly corrected and printed, with certeyne godly meditations and prayers added to the same, very necessarie & profitable for all them that ryghte assuredly vnderstande not ye Latine and Greke tongues. [Translated by George Joy.] 8vo. [Lowndes' *Bibl. Man.*, p. 1970.] Printed by John Byddel.

London, 1535

GOOD-NATURED (the) bear; a story for children of all ages. [By Elizabeth B. Browning.] Fcap 8vo. [*D. N. B.*, vol. 27, p. 358.]

London, 1846

GOODWIFE (the) at home; in metre, illustrating the dialect of the north-west district of Aberdeenshire. By a lady [Mrs Elizabeth Windsor Allardyce]. With a glossary. 8vo. [*And. Jervise.*]

Aberdeen, 1867

GOORKHAH (the), and other poems. By a young Officer [Henry Barkley Henderson]. 8vo. [*Brit. Mus.*]

Calcutta, 1817

GOOSTLY Psalmes and Spiritual Songes drawen out of the Holy Scripture, for the comfort and consolacyon of such as love to rejoyse in God and his Worde. [By Miles Coverdale.] Imprinted by me, Johan Gough. 4to. [*D. N. B.*, vol. 12, p. 366.]

London, [1539]

GORDIAN (the) knot. [A novel, in the form of letters.] By "Henry" [Richard Griffith]. 2 vols. 8vo.

London, 1770

GORDON League ballads. By Jim's wife [Mrs Clement Nugent Jackson]. Pt 8vo.

London, 1903

The name is given with "More Gordon League ballads" (1911).

GORDONHAVEN; scenes and sketches of fisher life in the North. By an old fisherman [George G. Green]. 8vo. Pp. 156. [*Brit. Mus.*] Edinburgh, 1887

GORGIOUS (a) gallery of gallant inuentions, garnished and decked with diuers dayntie deuises, right delicate and delightfull, to recreate eche modest minde withall; first framed and fashioned in sundrie formes, by diuers worthy workemen of late dayes, and now ioyned together and builded up. By T. P. [Thomas Proctor]. Imprinted at London, for Richard Iones. 4to. No pagination. B. L. [*Bodl.*]

1578

Reprinted in Heliconia, vol. i.

GORLAYE, or a tale of the olden tyme, in four cantos. [By John Magor Boyle.] Pp. 180. [Boase and Courtney's *Bibl. Corn.*, i., 39.]

London, 1835

The half-title reads, "Cithara Danmonii." The work contains, in addition to Gorlaye, seven miscellaneous poems occupying from p. 157 to the end.

GORSE blossoms from Dartmoor; poems. By Beatrice Chase [Olive Katharine Parr]. A new impression. 8vo. Pp. 62. [*Brit. Mus.*]

London, 1918

GORTZ of Berlingen [incorrectly for Goetz of Berlichingen] with the iron hand; an historical drama of the fifteenth century. Translated from the German of Goethe [by Mrs Rose Lawrence, *née* D'Aguilar]. 8vo. Pp. ix., 130. [*Brit. Mus.*] Liverpool, [1799]

See above, "Goetz of Berlichingen. . . ."

GOSHEN Hill; or, a life's broken pieces. By Howe Benning [Mrs Maria H. Henry]. Fcap 8vo. Pp. 319. [Cushing's *Init. and Pseud.*, vol. i., p. 34.]

New York, [1895]

GOSPEL (the). Good news to the ungodly concerning the Son of God. [By William Tait.] Third edition. Fcap 8vo. [*New Coll. Cat.*]
Edinburgh, N.D.

GOSPEL (the) according to Matthew; translated . . . and illustrated by extracts from Emanuel Swedenborg; together with notes of the translator [Rev. John Clowes]. 8vo. Pp. xxvii., 435. [*Manch. Free Lib. Cat.*]
London, 1805

GOSPEL (the) according to Peter: a study. By the author of *Supernatural Religion* [Walter R. Cassels]. Pt 8vo. [*Lond. Lib. Cat.*]   London, 1894

GOSPEL (the) according to St Matthew, with explanatory vocabulary.   [By John R. Strachan.] 8vo.
Aberdeen, 1889

GOSPEL (the) alphabet. . . . By the editor of *Footsteps of truth* [C— Russell Hurditch]. 8vo.   London, [1884]

GOSPEL (the) and the Church according to Scripture. . . . By J. N. D. [John Nelson Darby]. Pt 8vo.
London, 1876

GOSPEL Canticles; or, spiritual songs; in five parts. Part I. The believer's espousals; or, the way how a sinner is divorced from the law as a covenant, and married unto Christ, &c. Part II. The believer's jointure. . . . Part III. The believer's riddle; or, the mystery of faith; shewing the believer's twofold condition. . . . Part IV. The believer's lodging; or, his inn while here upon earth. . . . Part V. The believer's soliloquy, especially when in affliction and desertion, complaining of his own evil heart. . . . By a minister of the Gospel in the Church of Scotland [Ralph Erskine]. 8vo. Pp. 100. [*David Laing.*]   Edinburgh, 1720
     Published with the author's name in 1726 as "Gospel sonnets."

GOSPEL cordials, or the perplexed believer relieved; from the oracles of God: in ten several cases of conscience. By M. J. C., minister of the Gospel in Glasgow [James Clark]. Fcap 8vo. [*Scott's Fasti.*]
Glasgow, 1722

GOSPEL events chronologically arranged. By S. C. [Mrs S— Croft]. Fcap 8vo.   London, [1880?]
     See also "A Gospel harmony."

GOSPEL (the) for the nineteenth century. [By Thomas Gribble.] Fourth edition. Dy 8vo. [*New Coll. Cat.*]
London, 1880

GOSPEL (a) glasse; representing the miscarriages of English professors, both in their personal and relative capacities for which God is contending with them, by the sword, plague, etc. and (since the writing of the greatest part of the following treatise for the press) by the dreadful fire of London. Or a call from heaven to sinners and saints, etc. [By Lewis Stuckley.] 8vo. [*Calamy's Nonconf. Mem.*, Palmer's edition, vol. iii., p. 32.] London, 1667

GOSPEL (the) grace of faith; its nature opened, illustrated and argued from Scripture. . . . [By Thomas Beverley.] 4to. [*Watt's Bibl. Brit.*]
London, 1695

GOSPEL (a) harmony of the events of Good Friday; or, the inspired drama of the Passion: arranged as a help to meditation. By S. C. [Mrs S— Croft]. Fcap 8vo.   London, 1878
     See also "Gospel events."

GOSPEL (the) history and doctrinal teaching critically examined.   By the author of *Mankind, their origin and destiny* [Arthur Dyot Thomson, M.A.]. 8vo. [*Lond. Lib. Cat.*]
London, 1873

GOSPEL liberty, and the royal-law of love from Christ Jesus, who has all power in heaven and earth given unto him, set above Artaxerxes and Nebuchadnezer's laws and commands, and above the Medes and Persians and Darius his decrees. Also, several Scriptures opened, which the Jesuits and others used to bring for persecution, wherein their mouthes may be stopt that plead for persecution; and how God and Christ is judge in his Church, religion, worship, and faith. By G. F. [George Fox]. 4to. Pp. 51. [*Smith's Cat. of Friends' Books*, i., 669.]   N.P., printed in the year 1668

GOSPEL liberty sent down from heaven in a suffering time; or Christian toleration given by the Lord about the worship of God, and, in matters of faith and salvation, to the people of God, and primitive Christians.   By R. F. [Richard Farnworth].   4to. [*Smith's Cat. of Friends' Books*, i., 591.]   [London, 1664]

GOSPEL (the) Liturgy; a prayerbook for churches, congregations and families, prepared by direction of the General Convention of Universalists. [By Abel C. Thomas.] Fcap 8vo. Pp. 360. [*Eddy's Universalism in America*, vol. ii., p. 564.]   Philadelphia, 1857

GOSPEL musick ; or, the singing of Davids psalms, &c. in the publick congregations, or private families asserted, and vindicated, against a printed pamphlet, entitled, Certain reasons by way of confutation of singing psalms in the letter. . . . By thy loving brother, N. H., D.D., M.M.S. [Nathaniel Holmes].   Printed for Henry Overton in Popes-Head Alley. 4to.   London, 1644

GOSPEL (the) of divine humanity ; a reconsideration of Christian doctrine in the light of a central principle. [By Rev. John W. Farquhar.]   8vo.
       London, 1884
   Author's name in later edition.

GOSPEL (the) of God's Anointed, the glory of Israel and the light of revelation for the Gentiles ; or the glad tidings of the service, sacrifice, and triumph of our Lord and Saviour Jesus Christ. . . . Being a recent Version, in two parts, of the Sacred Writings commonly called the New Testament. [By Alexander Greaves.]   Fcap 8vo. [*Brit. Mus.*]   London, 1827

GOSPEL (the) of home life.   By Mark Evans [Paul Tidman].   8vo.   [*Kirk's Supp.*]   London, 1877

GOSPEL (the) of Jesus Christ.   [Sermons. By Joseph Parker, D.D.]   8vo.
       London, 1903

GOSPEL (the) of Luke ; notes of addresses.   By J. N. D. [John Nelson Darby].   Cr 8vo.   London, N.D.

GOSPEL (the) of other days ; or, thoughts on Old and New Testament Scriptures. By the writer of *Seed time and harvest* [William King Tweedie, D.D.]. Fcap 8vo. Pp. iv., 185. [*Adv. Lib.*]   London, 1854

GOSPEL (the) of Paul the Apostle ; being an attempt to render in modern English the principal writings of St Paul, and the narrative of Luke. By the author of *Vox Clamantis* [Ralph Sadler]. 8vo. [*Brit. Mus.*]   London, 1892

GOSPEL (the) of slavery ; a primer of freedom.   By Iron Gray [Abel C. Thomas].   8vo.   [*Cushing's Init. and Pseud.*, i., 120.]   New York, 1864

GOSPEL (the) of the Kingdom ; a contribution towards a liberal theology. By the minister of a country parish [Peter Hately Waddell, B.D., Whitekirk].   Cr 8vo.   Pp. 152.   [*Scott's Fasti*, new edition.]   Edinburgh, 1892

GOSPEL (the) of the Kingdom,—a Kingdom not of this world. . . . By " Senior Harvard " [Henry Dana Ward].   8vo.   [*Kirk's Supp.*]
       Philadelphia, 1870

GOSPEL (the) of the Old Testament ; an explanation of the types and figures by which Christ was exhibited under the legal dispensation : rewritten from the original work of Samuel Mather. By the author of *The listener*, etc. [Caroline Fry].   2 vols.   Fcap 8vo. [*Brit. Mus.*]   London, 1834

GOSPEL (the) of the stars ; or, wonders of astrology.   By Gabriel [James Hingston].   Pt 8vo.   New York, 1899

GOSPEL (the) ; or God's work and God's rest.   By H. C. A. [Rev. Harry Christopher Anstey, M.A.].   8vo.   Pp. 52.   London, [1902]

GOSPEL (the) Physitian, presenting (by way of meditation) divine physick. . . . By J— A. [John Anthony], Dr of Physick.   4to.   [*Watt's Bibl. Brit.*]
       London, 1655

GOSPEL (the) recovered from its captive state, and restored to its original purity.   By a Gentile Christian [John Goldie].   6 vols.   8vo.   [*Brit. Mus.*]
       London, 1784

GOSPEL (the) story ; a plain commentary on the four Gospels.   [By Rev. William Michell, M.A.]   3 vols. Fcap 8vo.   London, 1870-71

GOSPEL tydings ; wherein is shewed what the Gospel-administration was, the apostacy from it, and the restauration into it again : being a message of true & unfeigned love unto all that are seeking peace in their own way, and wearying themselves in their own wanderings, that they may come to the light of Christ Jesus, and be established in the power of the Gospel.   [By William Smith.]   4to.   [*Smith's Cat. of Friends' Books.*]   London, 1663
   Signed " W. S."

GOSPELS (the) collated ; presenting in one view the concurrent testimony of the Evangelists.   By a barrister of Lincoln's Inn [E. Boodle].   8vo.   Pp. xix., 228.   [*Lincoln's Inn Cat.*]
       London, 1843

GOSPELS (the) consolidated ; with a copious index.   By F. T. H. [Frederic Thomas Hall, solicitor].   8vo.   [*Brit. Mus.*]   London, 1869

GOSPELS of anarchy, and other contemporary studies.   By Vernon Lee [Violet Paget].   8vo.   [*Lond. Lib. Cat.*]
       London, 1908

GOSPEL - SEPARATION   separated from its abuses ; or the saints' guide in Gospel-fellowship : whereby they may be directed not only to preserve the purity, but withal the unity of the Gospel-worship.   By R. L. [Richard Lawrence].   8vo.   Pp. 141.   [*Whitley's Bapt. Bibl.*, i., 66.]   London, 1657

GOSSAMER. [A novel.] By George A. Birmingham [James Owen Hannay, D.D.]. Cr 8vo. [S. J. Brown's *Ireland in Fiction.*] London, 1915

GOSSIP. [A novel.] By Benjamin Swift [William Romaine Paterson]. Cr 8vo. Pp. 282. [*Lit. Year Book.*] London, 1905

GOSSIP from Millhall. [By T— W— Erle.] Fcap 8vo. Private print. 1858
Presentation copy from the author.

GOSSIP of the century; personal and traditional memories, social, literary, artistic, etc. [By Mrs William Pitt Byrne.] 2 vols. Royal 8vo. [*Brit. Mus.*] London, 1892

GOSSIP on dress; or half-an-hour's amusement for our friends. [By Elias Moses.] 8vo. [*Brit. Mus.*]
London, 1863

GOSSIP (the) shop. By J. E. Buckrose [Mrs Falconer Jameson]. Cr 8vo. Pp. 309. [*Lit. Year Book.*] London, 1917

GOSSIPING (the) guide to Jersey. By J. B. P. [James Bertrand Payne]. 8vo. London, 1865

GOSSIPING (a) guide to Wales: North Wales and Aberystwith. Traveller's edition. [By Askew Roberts.] 8vo. Pp. lxxxviii., 324. [*Brit. Mus.*]
London, 1889

GOSSIP'S (a) story; and a legendary tale. By the author of *Advantages of education* [Mrs Jane West]. 2 vols. Fourth edition. Fcap 8vo. [*Watt's Bibl. Brit.*] London, 1799

GOSSIP'S (the) week. By the author of *Slight reminiscences* [Mrs Mary Boddington]. With wood-cuts from original designs. 2 vols. Fcap 8vo. [*Brit. Mus.*] London, 1836

GOTHAM. [A poem. By Charles Churchill.] 4to. [*Brit. Mus.*]
London, 1764

GOTHAM and the Gothamites; a medley. [By Samuel B. H. Judah.] 8vo. New York, 1823

GOTHAM in alarm; a farce, in three acts, as performed by His Majesty's servants, at the Theatre-Royal, Gotham Square. By an Odd Fellow. [The joint production of Peter M'Kenzie, editor of the *Glasgow Gazette*, James Wallace, Glasgow, James Brown, M.D., Robert Kay, Dumbarton, Joseph Souter, Aberdeen, Alexander M'Neill, advocate, and James Duncan, bookseller, Glasgow.] Ninth edition. Fcap 8vo. Glasgow, 1816

GOTTFRIED of the iron hand; a tale of German chivalry. [Translated by Mrs —— Richardson, of Bristol.] 8vo. [*Adv. Lib.*] Edinburgh, 1865

GOURDS for the many: how to grow and cook them. By the author of *Indoor plants* [E. A. Maling]. 12mo. [*Adv. Lib.*] London, 1862

GOVERNESS (the): a first lesson book for children. . . . By a schoolmaster of twenty years' standing; author of *Botanical rambles*, etc. [Rev. Charles Alexander Johns, F.L.S.]. Fcap 8vo. [*D. N. B.*, vol. 30, p. 3.] London, [1854]

GOVERNESS (the); or, the Baroness in disguise. By C. Melnec [Clementine Boettger]: translated [from the German] by H. A. M. H. 8vo. Pp. 306. [*Brit. Mus.*] London, 1891

GOVERNESS (the); or the little female academy: being the history of Mrs Teachum and her nine girls. By the author of *David Simple* [Sarah Fielding]. Fcap 8vo. [*Brit. Mus.*]
London, 1749

GOVERNMENT (the) and order of the Church of Scotland. [By Alexander Henderson ?] 4to. Pp. 68.
[London], 1641
The preface seems to indicate that the author was an Englishman.

GOVERNMENT (the) and the Irish Roman Catholic Members [of Parliament. By Charles Purton Cooper, LL.D.]. 8vo. [*Edin. Univ. Cat.*]
London, 1851

GOVERNMENT as it is: a plea [in verse] for Parliamentary reform. By Aliquis [James Henry James]. Fcap 8vo. [*Brit. Mus.*] London, 1858

GOVERNMENT by the people. By the author of *The Story of my dictatorship* [Lewis Henry Berens]. 8vo. [Gladstone *Lib. Cat.* (Lib. Club).]
London, 1895

GOVERNMENT (the) of India: a primer for Indian schools. Second edition. By H. B. [Henry Bell, of Mozufferpore]. Fcap 8vo. Pp. 72. [*Brit. Mus.*] Calcutta, 1889

GOVERNMENT (the) of Ireland vnder the honorable, ivst, and wise gouernour Sir Iohn Perrot, knight, one of the priuy councell to Queene Elizabeth, beginning 1584. and ending 1588: being the first booke of the continvation of the Historie of that kingdome, formerly set forth to the yeare 1584, and now continued to this present 1626. . . . [By Sir Edward Cecil.] 4to. Pp. 148. [*Bodl.*] London, 1626
The epistle dedicatory is signed "E. C. S." The author's name is in the handwriting of Wood.

GOVERNMENT (the) of the [English] National Church. [By Rev. Joseph H. Harris.] Pt 8vo. Ramsgate, 1870
Signed "Presbyter Anglicanus."

GOVERNMENT (the) of the people of England, precedent and present, the same. [By John Parker.] 4to. [*Bodl.*]
London, 1650

GOVERNMENT (the) of the thoughts : a prefatory discourse to " The Government of the tongue." By the author of *The whole duty of Man* [Richard Allestree, D.D.]. 8vo. London, 1693
On the authorship of this work and the following, *see* the note to " The Art of Contentment."

GOVERNMENT (the) of the tongue. By the author of *The whole duty of man* [Richard Allestree, D.D.]. Fcap 8vo. Oxford, 1675

GOVERNMENT (the) plan of education defended. . . . By a Dissenting minister [John R. Beard, D.D.]. [*N. and Q.*, Feb. 1869, p. 169.]
London, 1839

GOVERNMENT (the) unhing'd ; or an account of many great encroachments made upon the liberties and propertie of the people of England. [By Robert Crosfeild.] 4to. Pp. 23. [*Manch. Free Lib. Cat.*] London, 1703

GOVERNOR (the) of England [a dramatic story of Oliver Cromwell]. By Marjorie Bowen [Gabrielle Vere Campbell, later Madame Long]. 8vo. Pp. 384. [*Lond. Lib. Cat.*]
London, 1913

GOVERNOR Strong's calumniator reproved. By No Bel-Esprit [John Lowell, LL.D.]. 8vo. [Cushing's *Init. and Pseud.*, vol. i., p. 204.]
Boston, 1814

GRACE and glory ; or, the believer's bliss in both worlds. By the author of *God is love*, etc. [James Grant, journalist]. 8vo. Pp. viii., 402. [*Brit. Mus.*]
London, 1873

GRACE Darling ; her true story, from unpublished papers in possession of her family. [By Daniel Hopkin Atkinson.] Cr 8vo. London, 1880
Presentation copy from the biographer : the authorship has been wrongly ascribed to T. Darling.

GRACE Darling, the maid of the isles. Dedicated to Her Grace the Duchess of Northumberland. . . . [By —— Vernon.] 8vo. Pp. 480. [*Bodl.*]
Newcastle-upon-Tyne, 1839

GRACE leading unto glory ; or, a glimpse of the glorie, excellencie, and eternity of heaven. . . . Written by J. H. [? John Hall, B.D., London]. 8vo. [*Brit. Mus.*] London, 1651

GRACE Mansfield's experiment. By Nellie Graham [Mrs Annie Dunning, *née* Ketchum]. Fcap 8vo. [Haynes' *Pseud.*] Philadelphia, 1869

GRACE Morton ; or the inheritance : a Catholic tale. By M. L. M. [Mary L— Meaney]. Fcap 8vo. [*Brit. Mus.*] Philadelphia, 1864

GRACE . . . Notes of lectures by F. E. R. [F— E— Raven]. 8vo. Pp. 88. [*Brit. Mus.*] London, 1896

GRACE (the) of God manifested in the life and death of William Sandy. By E. M. [Mrs Eleanor Moon]. 8vo.
London, 1862

GRACE O'Halloran ; a tale of to-day. [By Agnes M. Stewart.] 8vo. [S. J. Brown's *Ireland in fiction*.]
London, 1887

GRACE, the power of unity and gathering : by J. N. D. [John Nelson Darby]. 8vo. [*Brit. Mus.*] London, 1867

GRACE Tilden ; or, seven years' service for Christ. By Alpha [Mrs L. L. Phelps]. [Cushing's *Init. and Pseud.*, vol. i., p. 11.] Boston, 1869

GRACE Tolmar : a novel. By John Dangerfield [Oswald John Frederick Craufurd]. 8vo. [Haynes' *Pseud.*]
London, 1876

GRACE triumphant ; a sacred poem in nine dialogues : wherein the utmost power of nature, reason, virtue, and the liberty of the human will, to administer comfort to the awakened sinner, are impartially weighed and considered. . . . By Philanthropos [John Fellows, Baptist minister]. 8vo. [Watt's *Bibl. Brit.*] London, 1770
Later editions give the author's name.

GRACE Wardwood. [An Irish novel.] By " Athene " [Miss S— M— Harris]. Pt 8vo. Pp. 269. [S. J. Brown's *Ireland in fiction*.] Dublin, 1900

GRACECHURCH. By John Ayscough [Monsignor Francis Bickerstaffe - Drew]. Cr 8vo. Pp. 330. [*Lond. Lib. Cat.*] London, 1913

GRADUS ad Homerum ; or the A. B. C. D. of Homer : being a heteroclite translation of the First Four Books of the Iliad into English heroics, with notes. By X. Y. Z. [William Purton, M.A.]. 8vo. Pp. 181. [*F. Madan.*]
Oxford, 1862

GRAECIAN (the) story, &c.
See Grecian (the) story, &c.

GRÄFIN Rinsky, and other tales. By Hilarion [Campbell MacKellar]. 8vo. Pp. 269. London, 1892

GRAHAM Hamilton. [By Lady Caroline Lamb.] 2 vols. Fcap 8vo. [*Brit. Mus.*] London, 1822

GRAHAM of Claverhouse. [A romance.] By Ian Maclaren [John Watson, D.D., Liverpool]. 8vo. Pp. 346. [*Lit. Year Book.*] London, 1908

GRAHAME ; or, youth and manhood : a romance. By the author of *Talbot and Vernon* [John L. MacConnel]. Fcap 8vo. [*Brit. Mus.*]
New York, 1850

GRAMMAR made easy. [By Thomas Watt.] 8vo. [Robertson's *Aberd. Bibl.*] Edinburgh, 1751
Another edition was issued in Aberdeen, 1805.

GRAMMAR (the) of astrology ; containing all things necessary for calculating a nativity. By Zadkiel [William Lilly]. Fcap 8vo. [*Brit. Mus.*] London, 1840

GRAMMAR (a) of general geography . . . with maps and engravings. By the Rev. J. Goldsmith [Sir Richard Phillips]. Revised, corrected, and . . . enlarged by E. Hughes. Fcap 8vo. London, [1862]
See the note to " A Biographical dictionary."

GRAMMAR (the) of house planning : hints on arranging and modifying plans of cottages, street-houses, farmhouses, villas, mansions, and outbuildings. By an M.S.A., and M.R. A.S. [Robert Scott Burn]. 8vo. Pp. x., 190. [*Adv. Lib.*] Edinburgh, 1864

GRAMMAR of the Bornu or Kanuri language ; with dialogues, translations, and vocabulary. [Edited by Edwin Norris, of the Royal Asiatic Society.] 8vo. Pp. 101. [*Brit. Mus.*]
London, 1853

GRAMMAR (a) of the English tongue ; with the arts of logick, rhetorick, poetry, &c. Illustrated with useful notes, giving the grounds and reasons of grammar in general. . . . [By Sir Richard Steele.] Seventh edition. Fcap 8vo. Pp. x., 306. [Watt's *Bibl. Brit.*] London, 1746
The " approbation " is signed " Isaac Bickerstaff [Sir Richard Steele], censor."

GRAMMAR (a) of the English verb, founded on the Remarks by the same author on the auxiliary signs. [By William Belcher.] Two parts. Fcap 8vo. [*Brit. Mus.*] Canterbury, 1815
See continuation below : " A Grammar of the verb. . . ."

GRAMMAR of the French language. By the author of *Mademoiselle Mori* [Margaret Roberts]. Pt 8vo. [*Brit. Mus.*] London, 1887

GRAMMAR (a) of the French language for Pupil-teachers and the more advanced classes in schools. [By Margaret Roberts.] Pt 8vo. [*Brit. Mus.*] London, 1882

GRAMMAR (a) of the [Irish] Gaelic language. By E. O'C. [Edmond O'Connell, *i.e.* William Haliday]. 8vo. [Lyster's *Bibliog. of Irish Philology.*] Dublin, 1808

GRAMMAR (a) of the verb ; part the third : being an application of the former parts of the work to an explanation of the various uses of the Latin verb, particularly in the subjunctive mood, with notes on the coincidences of the Latin and English verb. [By William Belcher.] 8vo. [*Brit. Mus.*] Canterbury, 1815
A continuation of " A Grammar of the English verb . . ."

—— : part the fourth, being a collection of mistakes by distinguished writers in the use of the English verb, with its auxiliary signs, etc. [By William Belcher.] 8vo. [*Brit. Mus.*]
Canterbury, 1816

GRAMMAR (the) School of King Edward the Sixth in Birmingham ; its history, and suggestions for its improvement. By Historicus [Charles Edward Mathews]. . . . 8vo. Pp. 39. [*Brit. Mus.*] Birmingham, [1864]

GRAMMATICAL (a) chart ; or, a key to English grammar. Two parts. [By Walter William King.] 8vo. Pp. 76. [*Brit. Mus.*] London, 1841

GRAMMATICAL drollery, consisting of poems and songs ; wherein the rules of the nouns and verbs in the accedence are pleasantly made easie. By W. H. [William Hickes]. 8vo. Pp. 119. [*Bodl.*] London, 1682
Although this work is generally attributed to Captain Hickes, who was originally a tapster, this is doubted by some, Dr Bliss among the number.

GRAMMATICAL exercises, English and French . . . to which is added, an introduction to French poetry. By Marc Antoine Porny [Antoine Pyron Du Martre]. Eighth edition. Fcap 8vo. [*Brit. Mus.*] London, 1796

GRAMMATICALL miscellanies; wherein, the truth of many rules, both in the English rudiments, and Latine grammar is examined : some whereof are null'd ; others newly made, many quæres and doubts proposed, sundry errours discovered and rectified: superfluities ejected. . . . By T. M. [Thomas Merriott]. 8vo. Pp. 101. [Bliss' *Cat.*, ii., 27.] Oxford, 1660

GRANBY. A novel. [By Thomas Henry Lister.] 3 vols. Fcap 8vo. Third edition. [*Adv. Lib.*]
London, 1826

GRAND (the) and important question about the Church and parochial communion fairly and friendly debated, in a dialogue. . . . [By Rev. John Lindsay.] 8vo. [Lathbury's *Nonjurors*, p. 398.]   London, 1756

GRAND (the) and important question about the Church and parochial communion, further debated, in a fair and friendly conference. . . . [By Rev. John Lindsay.] 8vo. [Lathbury's *Nonjurors*, p. 399.]   London, 1759

GRAND (the) arcanum detected. By me, Phil Arcanos, Gent., Student in astrology [Joseph Green].   8vo. [Cushing's *Init. and Pseud.*, vol. i., p. 186.]   Boston, 1755

GRAND (the) case of conscience concerning the Engagement stated & resolved : or, a strict survey of the Solemn League & Covenant in reference to the present Engagement. [By John Milton.] 4to. Pp. 22. [*Bodl.*]
London, 1650
" Penn'd by John Milton."—MS. note in the handwriting of Barlow.

GRAND (the) case of the present ministry : whether they may lawfully declare and subscribe, as by the late Act of Vniformity is required ; and the several cases, thence arising (more especially about the Covenant) are clearly stated and faithfully resolved. [By Francis Fullwood, D.D., Archdeacon of Totness.] 8vo. Pp. 204. [*Bodl.*]   London, 1662

GRAND (the) conspiracy of Jews against their King. A demonstration that the highest insolencies proceed from men of the lowest and most base extractions. The

Husbandmen ⎫ kill ⎧ Sonne.
Vine-dressers ⎬ the ⎨ Heire.
Peasants   ⎭   ⎩ Lords Anointed.

[By John Allington.] Fcap 8vo. Pp. 218.   London, 1655
  The work consists of four sermons, each of which has a separate title. The titles of the second and third sermons differ from those of the first and fourth, of which the last bears the date, 1654. The pagination is continuous. The copy in the Advocates' Library is of the fourth edition, has a somewhat different title from the above, is dated 1655, and has the author's name.

GRAND (the) contrast, God and man, set forth in an epitome of Holy Writ ; with reflections, and a critical examination of Mr Newman's Essay on " The development of Christian doctrine." By an aged layman [Richard Poole, M.D.]. 8vo. Pp. xv., 546. [*Brit. Mus.*]   London, 1854

GRAND (the) designe ; or, a discovery of that forme of slavery entended and in part brought upon the free people of England by a powerfull party in the Parliament. . . . Written by Sirrahniho [John Harris]. 4to. [Thomason *Coll. of Tracts*, i., 577.]
[London], 1647

GRAND (the) designs of the Papists in the reigne of our late soveraign, Charles the First, and now carried on against his present Majesty, his Government, and the Protestant religion. [By Andreas ab Habernfeld ; translated by Sir W— Boswell.] 4to. [Arber's *Term Cat.*, vol. i., p. 524.]
London, 1678

GRAND (a) Duchess ; the life of Anna Amalia, Duchess of Saxe-Weimar-Eisenach, and the classical circle of Weimar. By Frances A. Gerard [Geraldine Penrose Fitzgerald]. 2 vols. 8vo.   London, 1902

GRAND (the) Duchy of Finland. By the author of *A Visit to the Russians in Central Asia* [Isabella Mary Phibbs]. Cr 8vo. [*Lond. Lib. Cat.*]
London, 1903

GRAND (the) errour of the Quakers detected and confuted : shewing how they contradict God's method of directing men to salvation by following that light within which comes by outward teaching, by their directing them to seek it by following that light within which is wrought without external teaching by the Scriptures or by men. . . . By W. A. [William Allen]. Fcap 8vo. Pp. 104. [Smith's *Anti-Quak.*, p. 3.]   London, 1680

GRAND (the) essay : or, a vindication of reason and religion against impostures of philosophy, proving according to those ideas and conceptions of things human understanding is capable of forming to it self. 1. That the existence of any immaterial substance is a philosophic imposture, and impossible to be conceived. 2. That all matter has originally created in it a principle of internal, or self-motion. 3. That matter and motion *must* be the foundation of thought in men and brutes. To which is added, a brief answer to Mr Broughton's Psycholo, &c. By W. C. [William Coward], M.D., C.M., L.C. 8vo. Pp. 248. [*D. N. B.*, vol. 12, p. 373.]   London, 1704

GRAND Fleet days. By the author of *In the northern mists* [Montagu Thomas Hainsselin]. Cr 8vo. Pp. 244. [*Lond. Lib. Cat.*]
London, 1917

GRAND (the) Highland tour. Glasgow —the Clyde—Oban—the Caledonian canal—Inverness—Highland railway. By the author of *Round the Grange farm*, etc. [Jean L. Watson]. 8vo. Pp. 112.   Edinburgh, 1875

GRAND (the) imposter discovered: or, the Quakers doctrine weighed in the ballance, and found wanting. A poem, by way of dialogue: wherein their chief and most concerning principles are laid down, and by the authority of Gods holy Word clearly refuted. By B. K. [Benjamin Keach]. 8vo. Pp. 7, 193-288. [Whitley's *Bapt. Bibl.*, i., 105; Smith's *Anti-Quak.*, p. 258.]
London, 1675

GRAND (the) impostor examined: or, the life, tryal, and examination of James Nayler, the seduced and seducing Quaker, with the manner of his riding into Bristol. [By John Deacon.] 4to. [Smith's *Cat. of Friends' Books*, ii., 233.]   London, 1656

GRAND (the) inquest; or a full and perfect answer to several reasons by which it is pretended the Duke of York may be proved to be a Roman-Catholick. [By John Garbrand.] 4to. [*Bodl.*]   London, 1680

GRAND (the) Juryman's oath and office explain'd, and the rights of Englishmen asserted: a dialogue between a barrister-at-law and a Grand Juryman. [By Sir John Hawles.] 4to. [Allibone's *Dict.*, vol. i., p. 804.]
London, 1680

Several editions were published later (1763, 1764, etc. 8vo) as " The Englishman's right; a dialogue. . . ." *See above.*

GRAND (the) mystery laid open; namely, by dividing of the Protestants to weaken the Hanover succession, and by defeating the succession to extirpate the Protestant religion: to which is added, the sacredness of Parliamentary securities against those who wou'd indirectly this year, or more directly the next (if they live so long) attack the publick funds. [By John Toland.] 8vo. [*Bodl.*]   London, 1714

GRAND (the) old man; a political random rhyme. By a loyal Irishman [William Hawkes]. Fourth edition. 8vo. [O'Donoghue's *Poets of Ireland*.]
Liverpool, 1889

A satire directed against William Ewart Gladstone.

GRAND Pluto's progresse through Great Britaine and Ireland: being a diarie or exact Journall of all his observations during the time of his walking to and fro in the said Kingdomes; found on Dunsmore Heath, and translated out

of infernall characters into English verse. By G. W., *alias* Parthenopen Esdras [Sir George Wharton]. 4to. [*Brit. Mus.*]   London, 1647

GRAND (the) politician; or the secret art of state policy discovered in evident demonstrations of unparallel'd prudence, and confirmed with wonderful advantages both in peace and war. . . . Written in Latin by Conradus Reinking . . . and now done into English. [By Patrick Ker.] Fcap 8vo. [Arber's *Term Cat.*, vol. ii., pp. 338 and 644.]
London, 1690

GRAND (the) prerogative of humane nature; namely, the souls naturall or native immortality, and freedome from corruption, shewed by many arguments, and also defended against the rash and rude conceptions of a late presumptuous authour, who hath adventured to impugne it. By G. H. [Guy Holland], Gent. 8vo. Pp. 147. [*Bodl.*]   London, 1653

" Lib. Tho. Barlow . . . ex dono D[ni] Holland, authoris."

GRAND (the) question concerning the Bishops right to vote in Parlament in cases capital, stated and argued, from the Parlament-rolls and the history of former times. With an enquiry into their peerage, and the three estates in Parlament. [By Edward Stillingfleet.] 8vo. Pp. 188. [*Brit. Mus.*]
London, 1680

GRAND (the) question concerning the judicature of the House of Peers stated and argued; and the case of T. Skinner, complaining of the East India Company, which gave occasion to that question, related. By a true well-wisher to the peace and good government of the kingdom, and to the dignity and authority of Parliament. [By Denzil, Lord Hollis.] 8vo. Pp. 219. [Moule's *Bibl. Herald.*, p. 220.] London, 1669

GRAND (the) question debated; or an essay to prove that the soul of man is not, neither can it be, immortal: the whole founded on the arguments of Locke, Newton, Pope, Burnet, Watts, &c. By Ontologos [William Kenrick, LL.D.]. 8vo. Pp. vii., 72. [*D. N. B.*, vol. 31, p. 17.]
Dublin, 1751

In the same year, and under the same pseudonym, Kenrick himself published in answer " A Reply to the grand question debated. . . ." *See below.*

GRAND (the) question whether war, or no war, with Spain, impartially consider'd: in defence of the present measures against those that delight in war. [By Horatio, Lord Walpole.] 8vo. [*Brit. Mus.*]   London, 1730

GRAND (the) serio-comic opera of Lord Bateman and his Sophia. By J. H. S. [John Henry Scourfield], later J. H. P. [John Henry Phillips]. 4to. Pp. 37. Private print. [*Brit. Mus.*] N.P., 1863

GRAND tours in many lands ; a poem. By Nomentino [John MacCosh, M.D.]. 8vo. [*Lond. Lib. Cat.*] London, 1881

GRAND university logic stakes, of two hundred and fifty sovereigns, for horses of all ages above three years, without restriction as to weight or breeding. Ten-mile course. Gentlemen riders. Second decennial meeting to come off June 14, 1849. [By James T. B. Landon.] 8vo. [*Bodl.*] Oxford, N.D.

GRANDEUR (the) of the Law ; a collection of the Nobility and Gentry of this Kingdom whose honors and estates have by some of their ancestors been acquired or considerably augmented by the practise of the Law or offices and dignities relating thereunto. By H. P. [Henry Phillips]. Fcap 8vo. [*Arber's Term Cat.*, vol. ii., p. 616.] London, 1684

GRANDFATHER'S prayer. By Mignon [Mrs Baseley]. 8vo. [*Manch. Free Lib.*] Manchester, 1901

GRANDISON Mather ; or an account of the fortunes of Mr and Mrs Thomas Gardiner. By Sidney Luska [Henry Harland]. Fcap 8vo. Pp. 391. [*D. N. B.*, Second Supp., vol. 2, p. 213.] London, [1889]

GRANDMA'S miracles ; or, stories told at six o'clock in the evening. By Pansy [Mrs Isabella Alden, *née* Macdonald]. 8vo. Pp. 128. [*Lit. Year Book.*] London, 1887

GRANDMOTHER Gwen : a tale. By the author of *Earth's many voices* [Elizabeth M. A. F. Saxby]. 8vo. Pp. 109. [*Brit. Mus.*] London, [1896]

GRANDMOTHER Normandy. By Clara Vance [Mrs Mary Andrews Denison]. Fcap 8vo. [Kirk's *Supp.*] Boston, 1882

GRANDMOTHER'S (the) advice to Elizabeth. By the author of *The letters of her mother to Elizabeth* [W— R. H. Trowbridge]. Cr 8vo. Pp. 157. [*Lond. Lib. Cat.*] London, 1902

GRANDMOTHER'S cap-strings. . . . [By Mary Charlotte Phillpotts, later Mrs Herbert.] 8vo. [Boase and Courtney's *Bibl. Corn.*, ii., 486.] London, [1864]

GRANDMOTHER'S curiosity cabinet. By Emilie Eyler [Mary Osten]. 8vo. [Kirk's *Supp.*] Boston, 1869

GRANDMOTHER'S money. By the author of *One and twenty*, etc. [Frederick William Robinson]. 3 vols. 8vo. [*Adv. Lib.*] London, 1860

GRANDMOTHER'S (the) shoe. [A tale.] By the author of *Studies for stories* [Jean Ingelow]. 12mo. [Kirk's *Supp.*] London, 1867

GRANDPA'S desk ; or, who wins ? By Howe Benning [Mrs Mary H. Henry]. 8vo. Pp. 96. [Kirk's *Supp.*] New York, [1896]

GRANGE (the) : a study in the science of history. By Gracchus Americanus [John G. Wells]. 8vo. [Cushing's *Init. and Pseud.*, vol. i., p. 119.] New York, 1874

GRANITE. [A novel.] By John Trevena [Ernest George Henham]. Cr 8vo. Pp. 488. [*Brit. Mus.*] London, 1909

GRANNY'S spectacles, and what she saw through them. By the author of " A Trap to catch a sunbeam " [Mrs H. S. Mackarness, *née* Matilda Anne Planché.] 8vo. [*Adv. Lib.*] London, [1869]

GRANTA ; or, a page from the life of a Cantab. [By D'Arcy Godolphin Osborne, M.A., of Magdalen College.] Second edition. 8vo. [Bartholomew's *Cat. of Camb. Books.*] London, 1838

GRANTLEY (the) Grange benedicts and bachelors. By Shelsley Beauchamp [T— Waldron Bradley]. 3 vols. Pt 8vo. [Kirk's *Supp.*] London, 1874

GRAPES from Canaan ; or the believer's present taste of future glory : a poem. [By Francis Taylor.] Fcap 8vo. [Calamy's *Nonconf. Mem.*, Palmer's ed., ii., 323.] London, 1658

GRAPES in the wilderness ; or the solid grounds of sweet consolation which the people of the Lord have from the precious promises in the Word, while walking through their wilderness lott in their way towards heaven : held forth as the summe of severall sermons preached some years agoe. . . . By a faithfull minister of the Gospel of Iesus Christ now deceased [Thomas Bell], " minister of the Gospel, and professor of philology in the Colledge of Edinburgh." 8vo. 11 leaves unpaged ; pp. 108. [*Adv. Lib.*] N.P., 1680

GRAPES of Eshcol ; or, gleanings from the land of promise. By the author of *Morning and night watches*, etc. [John Ross MacDuff, D.D.]. 8vo. Pp. xii., 276. London, 1861

GRAPES of wrath. By Boyd Cable [Ernest A. Ewart]. Cr 8vo. Pp. 276. [*Brit. Mus.*] London, 1917

GRAPHIC and historical description of the Cathedrals of Great Britain. [By James Sargant Storer, and H— S— Storer.] 4 vols. 8vo. London, 1814-19

G R A P H I D Æ, or characteristics of painters. [By Henry Reeve, of the Privy Council Office.] 8vo. [*Martin's Cat.*] N.P., private print, 1838
Preface signed "H. R."

GRAPHOLOGY. By Simon Arke [Clifford Howard]. 8vo. [*Amer. Cat.*] Washington, 1903

GRAPHOMANIA (the) : an epistle. By the author of *Varnishando* [F. D. Astley]. 4to. [*N. and Q.*, Feb. 1869, p. 169.] Manchester, 1809

GRASS (the) eater ; a novel. By Phyllis Austin [Mrs Edward Rigby]. Cr 8vo. Pp. 288. [*Lit. Year Book.*] London, 1921

GRASSHOPPER (the). Being some account of the banking house at 68 Lombard Street : with an introductory sketch of the history of money-lending. By J. B. M. [John Biddulph Martin]. 8vo. London, 1873

GRATEFUL (the) Non-conformist ; or, a return of thanks to Sir John Baker, Knight, and Doctor of physick, who sent the author ten crowns. [By John Wild.] Folio. A broadside. [*Bodl.*] [London, 1665]
The date and the author's name are in the handwriting of Wood.

GRATEFUL (the) sparrow ; a true story. [By Sarah Margaret Fitton.] 8vo. [*Brit. Mus.*] London, 1862

GRATITUDE'S offering : being original productions [in verse] on a variety of subjects. By the author of *Village musings* [Cornelius Whur]. 8vo. Pp. xi., 192. [*Brit. Mus.*] Norwich, 1845

GRATULATORY (a) address to his Alma Mater. By a student of Medicine [Rev. William Robb]. 8vo. [*Cushing's Init. and Pseud.*, vol. ii., p. 141.] Edinburgh, 1826

GRAVE (a) answer to Mr [John] Wesley's "Calm address to our North American Colonies." By a gentleman of Northumberland [Rev. James Murray, of Newcastle]. 8vo. [*D. N. B.*, vol. 39, p. 373.] Newcastle, 1775

GRAVE dialogues betwixt three free-thinkers, Θ, Λ and X. [By John Glas.] Fcap 8vo. Pp. 76. Edinburgh, 1738

GRAVE (the) digger ; a novel. By the author of *The Scottish heiress* [Robert Mackenzie Daniel, or Daniels]. 3 vols. Fcap 8vo. [*Adv. Lib.*] London, 1844

GRAVE Lady Jane. [A novel.] By Florence Warden [Florence Alice Price, later Mrs George E. James]. Fcap 8vo. Pp. 183. New York, 1893

G R A V E N (the) image. By David Lyall [Annie Swan, later Mrs Burnett Smith]. 8vo. Pp. 320. London, [1919]

GRAVER (the) thoughts of a country parson. By the author of *The recreations of a country parson* [Andrew Kennedy Hutchison Boyd, D.D.]. 8vo. Pp. 301. London, 1862

—— Second series. 8vo. Pp. vi., 330. London, 1865

—— Third series. 8vo. Pp. 323. London, 1876

GRAY (the) life. [A novel.] By Keble Howard [John Keble Bell]. 8vo. [*Lond. Lib. Cat.*] London, 1916

GRAY (a) mist. By the author of *The martyrdom of an Empress* [Margaret Cunliffe Owen]. Cr 8vo. Pp. 282. [*Brit. Mus.*] London, 1907

GRAY Roses. By Sidney Luska [Henry Harland]. 8vo. [*Lit. Year Book.*] Boston, 1895

GRAY versus Malthus. The principles of population and production investigated : and the questions, Does population regulate subsistence, or subsistence population ; Has the latter, in its increase, a tendency to augment or diminish the average quantum of employment and wealth ; and Should government encourage or check early marriage ; discussed by George Purves, LL.D. [Simon Gray]. 8vo. Pp. xi., 496. [*Adv. Lib.*] London, 1818

GRAY'S Elegy, translated into Latin elegiacs, by G. H. [Gavin Hamilton] (Countryman of George Buchanan). 8vo. Edinburgh, 1877

GRAY'S (the) Inn Journal. By Charles Ranger, Esq. [Arthur Murphy]. Folio. London, [1753-54]
Containing fifty - two numbers, from No. 1, Sept. 29, 1753, to No. 52, Sept. 21, 1754. "This work was reprinted and extended to 104 numbers, in two volumes 12mo, 1756. To the dedication of this edition, the author has signed his name. No. 38 of the original publication was not reprinted, as it was a translation from a French translation of the *Rambler*, No. 190 : to this he owed his introduction to Dr Johnson."—Taken from a note by Alex. Chalmers in the Brit. Mus. copy.

GREASED (the) plank ; or projected Liberal legislation for Ireland. By Hibern Pessimistes [Captain W. C. Bonaparte Wyse]. 8vo. [*Manch. Free Lib.*] Manchester, 1883

GREAT (the) acceptance ; the life story of Frederick N. Charrington. By Guy Thorne [Cyril A. E. Ranger-Gull]. Cr 8vo. Pp. 284. [*Brit. Mus.*]
London, 1913

GREAT (the) advantage of eating pure and genuine bread. [By Thomas Pownall.] 8vo. London, 1773

GREAT (the) advantages to both kingdoms of Scotland and England by an union. By a friend to Britain [Dr Hugh Chamberlayn, or Chamberlen]. Fcap 8vo. [*Adv. Lib.*] N.P., 1702

GREAT (the) alphabet, in twenty-two sonnets ; or Psalm cxix. [By W— Day.] 8vo. [*Brit. Mus.*]
Hobart Town, 1854

GREAT (the) American scout and spy. By General Bunker [C— Lorain Ruggles]. 8vo. [Cushing's *Init. and Pseud.*, vol. i., p. 43.] New York, 1870

GREAT and good deeds of Danes, Norwegians, and Holsteinians ; collected by Eva Malling. Translated by the author of *A Tour in Zealand* [Andreas Andersen Feldborg]. Large 4to. Pp. 328. London, 1807

GREAT and good ; or, Alfred the father of his people. . . . [By Deborah Alcock.] Fcap 8vo. London, [1864]

GREAT and grave questions for American politicians By Eboracus [W— W. Broom]. 8vo. [Cushing's *Init. and Pseud.*, vol. i., p. 86.]
Boston, 1866

GREAT (the) and new art of weighing vanity : or a discovery of the ignorance and arrogance of the great and new artist, in his pseudo-philosophical writings. By M. Patrick Mathers, Arch-Bedal to the University of S. Andrews. [Really written by William Sanders.] To which are annexed some Tentamina de motu penduli & projectorum. 8vo. Pp. 120. Glasgow, 1672
"Mathers was not the author of this book ; but Mr William Sanders, at that tyme one of the Regents in St Andrews, was the author, and was thereto assisted by James Gregory, author of the Optica promota ; to whom the Tentamina geometrica de motu penduli &c doth entirely belong. I knew Mr Gregory, Sanders, Sinclair and the Arch bedal. R. Gray. London Ja^y. 26. 170$\frac{9}{10}$."—MS. note on Dr David Laing's copy.

GREAT (the) and popular objection against the repeal of the penal laws and tests briefly stated and consider'd, and which may serve for answer to several late pamphlets upon that subject. By a friend to liberty for liberties sake [William Penn]. 4to. [Jones' Peck.]
London, 1688

GREAT and weighty considerations relating to the D. [Duke of York] or successor of the crown, humbly offer'd to the kings most excellent majesty, and both Houses of Parliament. By a true patriot [Thomas Hunt]. Folio. [*Bodl.*] N.P., N.D.

GREAT (the) Antichrist. By J. V. [John Vicars], Prisoner. 4to. Pp. 22. [*Brit. Mus.*] London, 1643

GREAT (the) apostacy demonstrated, in an exposé of Anti-Christian doctrines. By a Scripture student [D— C— Retallack]. 8vo. [*Brit. Mus.*]
London, [1865]

GREAT (the) assises holden in Parnassus by Apollo and his assessovrs : at which sessions are arraigned Mercurius Britanicus, Mercurius Aulicus, Mercurius Civicus. The Scout. The writer of Diurnalls. The intelligencer. The writer of occurrences. The writer of passages. The post. The spye. The writer of weekly accounts. The Scottish dove, &c. [By George Wither.] 4to. Pp. 52. London, 1645
"Assigned to Wither by Dalrymple, but not registered as such by the poet or his biographers. Mr. Pulham says it is erroneously attributed to Wither."—Lowndes.

GREAT (the) attempt. By Frederick Arthur [Col. Frederick Arthur H Lambert]. Cr 8vo. [*Brit. Mus.*]
London, 1914

GREAT (the) auk's eggs. By Darley Dale [Francesca M. Steele]. Pt. 8vo. [*Lond. Lib. Cat.*] London, 1886

GREAT (the) awakening [after death]. By a Chancery barrister. [Edited by Bishop Henry Reginald Courtenay.] 8vo. London, 1900
Reprint of part of a work written in 1843.

GREAT (the) Bank fraud ; an urgent warning to business men. By Cynicus [Martin Anderson]. Pt 8vo. Pp. 63. [*Lit. Year Book.*] Edinburgh, 1917

GREAT battles of the British Army. [By Charles Macfarlane.] 8vo.
London, 1853

GREAT (the) Boulder, Kalgoorlie, Western Australia. By "The Vagabond" [Julian Thomas]. 8vo. [*Lib. of Col. Inst.*] Melbourne, 1896

GREAT (the) bread riots ; and what came of Fair Trade. By S. L. S. [John St Loe Strachey]. 12mo. [Gladstone *Lib. Cat.*] Bristol, 1885

GREAT Britain arraigned as of felo de se, and found guilty ; in a brief chronology of commerce from its original. [By John Blanch.] 8vo.
London, 1721

GREAT Britain : England, Wales, and Scotland, as far as Loch Maree and the Cromarty Firth. Handbook for travellers by K. Baedeker [prepared by James F. Muirhead, M.A.]. Pt 8vo.
Leipzig, 1887

GREAT Britain's crisis ! Reform, retrenchment, and economy ; the hard case of the poor farmers. . . . A letter to the Right Hon. Sir James Graham, Bart. [By Richard Warner.] 8vo. [Green's *Bibl. Somers.*, vol. iii., p. 361.]   Bath, 1831

GREAT Britain's just complaint for her late measures, present sufferings, and the future miseries she is exposed to ; with the best, safest, and most effectual way of securing and establishing her religion, government, liberty and property, upon good and lasting foundations. [By Sir James Montgomery.] 4to. Pp. 61. [*Cat. Lond. Inst.*, vol. ii., p. 211.]   N.P., 1692

GREAT Britain's memorial against the Pretender and Popery. [By Samuel Chandler, D.D.] Fcap 8vo. [Mendham Coll. *Cat.*, p. 68.] London, 1745

GREAT (the) bullion robbery of May, 1855. [By Henry G. Abell.] 8vo.
London, 1856

GREAT (the) calumny of the Quakers despising the Holy Scriptures, refuted out of their printed books, unjustly perverted, confusedly curtail'd and crowded, by William Mather, in his Dagger Sheet. [By William Robinson.] Broadside. [Smith's *Cat. of Friends' Books*, i., 46 ; ii., 505.]
London, 1700

GREAT (the) case of liberty of conscience once more briefly debated and defended, by the authority of reason, scripture, and antiquity. . . . The authour W. P. [William Penn]. 4to. Pp. 55. [Smith's *Cat. of Friends' Books*.]   N.P., 1670

GREAT (the) case of tithes truly stated, clearly open'd, and fully resolv'd, by Anthony Pearson, formerly a Justice of Peace in Westmorland ; with an appendix thereto : to which is added, A defence of some other principles held by the people call'd Quakers, in which they differ from other religious denominations. . . . By J. M. [Josiah Martin]. 8vo. Pp. viii., 292. London, 1730
The " Defence " occupies from p. 131 to the end. *See* the first edition (1657) later (" The great case of Tythes . . ."), which is anonymous.

GREAT (the) case of transplantation in Ireland discussed ; or certain considerations wherein the many great inconveniences in the transplanting of the natives of Ireland generally out of the three provinces of Leinster, Ulster, and Munster into the province of Connaught are shewn. . . . By a well-wisher to the good of the Commonwealth of England [Vincent Gookin]. 4to. [*D. N. B.*, vol. 22, p. 154.]
London, 1656
This pamphlet, now very rare, elicited a counter-statement from Col. Richard Lawrence, in reply to which Gookin published a Vindication of his statements, with his name. *See* " England's great interest . . ."

GREAT (the) case of tythes and forced maintenance once more revived. . . . By F. H. [Francis Howgil]. 4to. [Smith's *Cat. of Friends' Books*.]
London, 1665

GREAT (the) case of tythes truly stated, clearly opened, and fully resolved. By a crountrey-man [*sic*], A. P. [Anthony Pearson]. 4to. [*Brit. Mus.*]
London, 1657
See also above, a later edition (1730, " The Great case of tithes "), giving the author's name.

GREAT catches ; or, grand matches. [By Eleanor Frances Blakiston.] 2 vols. Fcap 8vo. [*Adv. Lib.*]
London, 1861

GREAT (the) charter for the interpretation of the prophecy of Scriptures, with a discourse of the powers of the world to come ; or the miraculous powers of the Gospel and Kingdom of Christ. By T. B. [Rev. Thomas Beverley]. 8vo. [Arber's *Term Cat.*, vol. ii., p. 585.]   London, 1696

GREAT (the) chin episode. By Paul Cushing [Roland A. Wood-Seys]. 8vo. [*Lit. Year Book*.]
London, 1900

GREAT (the) Christian service ; a companion for those who are present at the holy sacrifice without communicating. By C. J. H. [Charles Jerram Hunt]. 8vo. Pp. 32. [*Brit. Mus.*]
London, [1894]

GREAT cities of the ancient world. By Hazel Shepard [Helen Ainslie Smith]. 8vo. [Kirk's *Supp.*]   London, 1885

GREAT cities of the modern world. By Hazel Shepard [Helen Ainslie Smith]. 8vo. [Kirk's *Supp.*]   London, 1886

GREAT (the) city problem ; the evil and remedy of New York government. [By Dorman Bridgman Eaton.] 8vo. Pp. 79.   New York, 1871

GREAT (the) commandment. By the author of *The Listener*, etc. [Caroline Fry]. Fcap 8vo. Pp. vii., 335. [*Brit. Mus.*]   London, 1847

GREAT (the) controversy of states and people. . . . [By Rev. Joseph Henry Allen.] 8vo.   Boston, [Mass.], 1851

GREAT (the) country : impressions of America.   By   Arthur   Sketchley [George Rose].   Cr 8vo. [Haynes' *Pseud.*]   London, 1868

GREAT (the) cranberry quarrel. [A story.] By J. A. Owen [Mrs Jane Allan Visger, *née* Pinder]. Pt 8vo. Pp. 122. [*Brit. Mus.*] London, [1882]

GREAT (the) crisis ; or, the mystery of the times and seasons unfolded, with relation to the late disorder and confusion of the seasons of the year : with considerations and observations, tending to better understanding the wisdom of Providence in the order of the ages ; . . . [By Richard Roach, B.D.] 8vo. [*Brit. Mus.*] London, 1725

GREAT (the) cryptogram : Francis Bacon's cipher in the so-called Shakespeare Plays. By Ignatius Donnelly [Edmund Boisgilbert]. 2 vols. 8vo. [*Brit. Mus.*]   London, 1888

GREAT (the) day at the dore ; and He cometh with clouds that shall judge the quick and the dead, and reigne on the earth with all his saints : not for a thousand yeares in this corrupt and sinfull world, as some corruptly conceive and teach, nay, but for a thousand and a thousand, and ten thousand times ten thousand thousands of yeares, even for ever and ever, eternally in the world to come, wherein righteousness and peace, incorruption, immortality and joy, shall habit and dwell for evermore, world without end. [By John Eachard, pastor of Durham, in Suffolk ?]   4to.
           Printed at London, 1648
The dedication signed " I. E."

GREAT (the) deputation ; a farce dedicated to the ratepayers of Aston. [By W— Berry.] 8vo. [*Birm. Cent. Lib.*]   London, 1879

GREAT (the) devastation ; a prophecy of the times that are coming in Europe, astrologically interpreted. By Sepharial [Walter Gorn Old]. Cr 8vo. Pp. 19. [*Brit. Mus.*] London, 1914

GREAT (the) disclosure of wickedness in high places. . . . [By Mrs Elizabeth C. Packard.] 8vo.
                       Boston, [Mass.], 1865

GREAT duties of life with respect to the Supreme Being. By S. B. [Simon Berington]. 8vo.   London, 1738

GREAT (the) duty and benefit of self-denial. . . . By a minister of the Church of England [John Howard, M.A.]. 8vo. [Watt's *Bibl. Brit.*]
                              London, 1710

GREAT (the) duty of Christians, to go forth without the Camp to Jesus ; in several sermons on Hebrews 13 : 13. By S. T. [Samuel Tomlyns], M.A. 8vo. [Calamy's *Nonconf. Mem.*, Palmer's edition, vol. ii., p. 263.]
                              London, 1682

GREAT (the) duty of communicating explain'd and enforc'd : the objections against it answered ; and the necessary preparation for it stated. . . . By the author of *The Duties of the Closet* [Sir William Dawes, Bart., Archbishop of York]. 8vo. [Arber's *Term Cat.*, vol. iii., p. 686.]   London, 1700

GREAT (the) duty of Conformity, plainly illustrated in the example of a young man who was first drawn to the Presbyterians, afterwards to the Independents, but now, from a deep sence of his sin, returned to the Church of England. . . . [By John Jones.] 8vo. [Arber's *Term Cat.*, vol. ii., p. 616.]
                              London, 1692

GREAT (the) duty of frequenting the Christian sacrifice. [By Robert Nelson.] Fcap 8vo. [*D. N. B.*, vol. 40, p. 212.]   London, 1707
   An enlarged chapter of the author's " Companion for the Festivals."

GREAT (the) Eastern's log, containing her first Transatlantic voyage. . . . By an executive officer [William A. Wallace]. 8vo. [Cushing's *Init. and Pseud.*, vol. i., p. 301.] London, 1860
   Signed " W. A. W."

GREAT (the) eater of Grayes-Inne ; or the life of Mr Marriot the cormorrant. . . . Also, a rare physicall dispensatory ; being the manner how he makes his cordiall broaths, etc. By G. F. [George Fidge], Gent. 4to. [Jaggard's *Index.*]   London, 1652

GREAT (a) Emperor ; Charles V., 1519-1588.   By Christopher Hare [Mrs Marion Andrews]. 8vo. Pp. 351. [*Lond. Lib. Cat.*]   London, 1917

GREAT events in England's history. By the author of *Our country's story* [Jane Budge]. 8vo. Pp. 223. [Smith's *Cat. of Friends' Books.*]
                              London, 1872

GREAT (the) Exhibition " wot is to be," or probable results of the industry of all nations in the year '51. . . . By Vates Secundus [George Augustus Henry Sala]. Oblong 8vo (panoramic).   London, [1850]

GREAT explorers of Africa, from the earliest times. [Edited by Dr John Scott Keltie.] 2 vols. Large 8vo.
                              London, 1894

" GREAT (the) fact " examined and disproved ; or, Homœpathy unmasked. By Chirurgus [John Dix]. A reply to Dr Horner. 8vo. [*Bodl.*]
London, 1857
The Introductory notice is signed " J. D., Chirurgus."

GREAT fun for our little friends. By the author of *The voyage of the Constance* [Mary Gillies]. 8vo. [*Brit. Mus.*]   London, 1862

GREAT (the) game ; a plea for a British imperial policy. By a British subject [Walter Millar Thorburn, B.A.]. 8vo. Pp. 215.   London, 1875
The second edition, published in the same year, has the author's name.

GREAT (the) game, and how it is played ; a treatise on the Turf, full of tales. By Nathaniel Gubbins [Edward Spencer Mott]. 8vo. [*Lit. Year Book.*]   London, 1901

GREAT (the) god success. A novel. By John Graham [David Graham Phillips]. 8vo.   London, 1901

GREAT (the) gold mine. By C. E. M. [Constance E. Miller], author of *Adam Gorlake's Will*. Fcap 8vo. Pp. 212.
London, [1897]

GREAT (the) Gorham case ; a history, in five books, including expositions of the rival baptismal theories. By a looker on : with a preface by John Search [Thomas Binney]. 8vo. Pp. xxviii., 248. [*Brit. Mus.*] London, 1850

GREAT (the) Gospel-grace of faith ; its nature opened, illustrated and argued from Scripture principally. . . . Being the substance of several discourses on John 7 : 7, 8. By a servant of the Lord Jesus Christ [Thomas Beverley]. 8vo.   [Arber's *Term Cat.*, ii., p. 616.] London, 1695

GREAT (the) grandmother. [A novel.] By George A. Birmingham [James O. Hannay, D.D.]. Cr 8vo. [*Lond. Lib. Cat.*]   London, 1923

GREAT Grenfell Gardens. By the author of *Jennie of the Prince's* [B— H— Buxton]. Post 8vo. London, 1880

GREAT (the) gulf fixed : a novel. By Gerald Grant [Gertrude Elizabeth Grant]. 3 vols. 8vo. [Kirk's *Supp.*]
London, 1877

GREAT (the) gun ; an eccentric biography. By Boswell Butt, Esq. [Charles Henry Ross]. 8vo. [F. Boase's *Mod. Brit. Biog.*, vi., col. 497.]
London, 1865

GREAT (the) honour and advantages of the East India trade to this Kingdom. By J. C. [Sir Josiah Child]. Second edition. 8vo. [*D. N. B.*, vol. 10, p. 245.]   London, 1697

GREAT (the) illusion ; a study of the relation of military power to national advantage. By Norman Angell [Ralph Norman Angell Lane, journalist]. Cr 8vo. [*Lond. Lib. Cat.*]
London, 1912

GREAT (the) image. By " Pan " [Leslie Beresford]. Cr 8vo. [*Lit. Year Book.*]   London, 1921

GREAT (the) importance and necessity of increasing tillage by an Act of Parliament, in Ireland. . . . [By Rev. Philip Skelton.] 8vo.   Dublin, 1755

GREAT (the) importance of a religious life consider'd ; to which are added some morning and evening prayers. [By William Melmoth.] Fcap 8vo. Pp. 124. [Watt's *Bibl. Brit.*]
London, 1711

Erroneously attributed to John Percival, Earl of Egmont. The nineteenth edition, corrected, was issued in 1794.

GREAT (the) Indian chief of the West ; or, the life and adventures of Black Hawk. [By Benjamin Drake.] 8vo. [Allibone's *Dict.*]   Cincinnati, 1838

GREAT is Diana of the Ephesians ; or, the original of idolatry, together with the politick institution of the Gentiles sacrifices. [By Charles Blount.] Fcap 8vo. [*Brit. Mus.*]   London, 1695
The first edition appeared in 1680.

GREAT (the) journey : a pilgrimage through the valley of tears to Mount Zion, the city of the living God. [By John Ross MacDuff, D.D.] Third edition. Fcap 8vo. Edinburgh, 1854

GREAT joy : a word to the children on Christmas Day. By E. A. W., author of *Life of Wm. F. Clarke* [Mrs Edw. Ashley Walker]. 12mo.
London, 1892

GREAT (the) law of nature ; or self-preservation examined, asserted, and vindicated from Mr Hobbes his abuses : in a small discourse ; part moral, part political, and part religious. [By J. Shafte.] Fcap 8vo. Pp. 96. [*Bodl.*]
London, 1673

GREAT (the) law of subordination consider'd ; or, the insolence and unsufferable behaviour of servants in England duly inquir'd into : illustrated with a great variety of examples, historical cases, and remarkable stories of the behaviour of some particular servants, suited to all the several arguments made use of, as they go on. In ten familiar letters. . . . [By Daniel Defoe.] 8vo. Pp. ii., 302. [Wilson's *Life of Defoe*, p. 184.] London, 1824

GREAT (the) lesson of the [Civil] War [in the United States. By Clinton Lloyd]. 8vo. Washington, 1865

GREAT lessons of the Indian famine. By a journalist [Frederick A. Towers ?]. Post 8vo. London, 1877

GREAT Lowlands. [A novel.] By Annie E. Holdsworth [Mrs —— Lee-Hamilton]. 8vo. [*Lit. Year Book.*] London, 1901

GREAT (the) man's answer to " Are these things so ? " In a dialogue between his Honour and the Englishman in his grotto. [By James Miller.] Folio. [Quaritch's *Cat.*] London, 1740

GREAT (the) match and other matches. [By Mary Prudence Wells, later Mrs —— Smith.] 8vo. Boston, [Mass.], 1877

GREAT (the) metropolis. By the author of *Random recollections of the Lords and Commons* [James Grant, of Elgin]. 2 vols. Fcap 8vo. [*Adv. Lib.*] London, 1836

—— Second series. 2 vols. Fcap 8vo. London, 1837

GREAT (the) Miss Driver. [A novel.] By Anthony Hope [Anthony Hope Hawkins]. Cr 8vo. [*Lit. Year Book.*] London, 1908

GREAT modern preachers ; sketches and criticisms. [By Rev. William Dorling.] 8vo. London, 1875

GREAT (a) mystery solved ; being a continuation and conclusion to " The Mystery of Edwin Drood," [left unfinished by Charles Dickens]. By " Gillan Vase " [——]. Cr 8vo. Pp. 318. [*Brit. Mus.*] London, 1913

GREAT (a) natural healer. By Max Adeler [Charles Heber Clark]. 12mo. [*Amer. Cat.*] Philadelphia, 1910

GREAT (the) necessaries of publick worship in the Christian Church expressly and manifestly allowed and provided for in the use of the present Liturgy ; in answer to a late pamphlet [by Richard Laurence], intituled, The indispensible obligation, &c. With an appendix [by Thomas Wagstaffe], wherein the union opposed by that author is justified. . . . [By Thomas Brett, LL.D.] 8vo. Pp. 59. London, 1733

Signed " T. B."

GREAT Pan lives : Shakespeare's Sonnets, 20-126, with paraphrase and references. By Clelia [Charles Downing]. Cr 8vo. [*Brit. Mus.*] London, 1892

GREAT (the) Paschal cycle of five hundred thirty-two years ; with other tables used in the Church of England. [By —— Bunbury.] 8vo. Pp. 135. [*Bodl.*] London, 1718

GREAT (the) point of succession discussed. [By Robert Brady, M.D.] With a full and particular answer to a late pamphlet [by John, Lord Somers], entituled, A brief history of the succession, &c. Folio. [Arber's *Term Cat.*, i., 524.] London, 1681

A second edition, also anonymous, much enlarged, bears a modified title, " A true and exact history of the succession of the crown of England . . ." (1681).

" I am inform'd that Doc^tr. Brady a Physitian was author of this Book. & y^t he writt it w^n Master of Trinity Coll. in Cambridge."—MS. note in the Bodleian copy.

GREAT (the) prayer of Christendom ; thoughts on the Lord's Prayer. By the author of *Chronicles of the Schönberg-Cotta Family* [Mrs Elizabeth Charles, *née* Rundle]. 8vo. Pp. 164. [*Brit. Mus.*] London, 1886

GREAT (the) pressures and grievances of the Protestants in France, and their Apology to the late ordinances made against them, both out of the Edict of Nantes and several other fundamental laws of France. . . . Gathered and digested by E. E. [Edmund Everard] of Gray's Inn. . . . Folio. [Arber's *Term Cat.*, i., 420.] London, 1680

GREAT (the) problem and its solution. [By Rev. S— Jennings.] Cr 8vo. London, 1905

The first edition (1898) bears a longer title. *See below.*

GREAT (the) problem of substance and its attributes. . . . [By George Jamieson.] 8vo. London, 1895

GREAT (the) problem ; or Christianity as it is. By a student of science [Rev. Walter S. Lewis, M.A.]. Cr 8vo. Pp. viii., 445. [*New Coll. Cat.*] London, [1881]

GREAT (the) problem ; or man's future place and work in the universe. By S. J. [Rev. S— Jennings]. 8vo. London, 1895

The second edition (1905) bears a briefer title. *See above.*

GREAT (the) Proconsul. By Sydney C. Grier [Hilda C. Gregg]. Cr 8vo. Pp. 450. [*Lit. Year Book.*] Edinburgh, 1904

GREAT (the) propitiation : or, Christ's satisfaction, and man's justification by it, upon his faith ; that is, belief of, and obedience to the Gospel : endeavoured to be made easily intelligible, and to appear rational and well accountable to ordinary capacities, and so more lovely and amiable. In some sermons. [By Joseph Truman, B.D.] 8vo. Pp. 235. [*Bodl.*] London, 1669

At the end there is "A discourse concerning the Apostle Paul's meaning by justification by faith," by the same author.

GREAT (the) Pyramid of Jizeh. [By James Ralston Skinner.] 8vo.
Cincinnati, 1871

GREAT (the) question between Protestants and Catholics viewed in a new light ; with an address to both parties. . . . By a member of the Church of England [Edmund Hepple]. 8vo. [*Brit. Mus.*] Newcastle-on-Tyne, 1829

GREAT (the) question concerning things indifferent in religious worship, briefly stated, and tendred to the consideration of all sober and impartial men. [By Edward Bagshaw, Jun.] 4to. Pp. 4, 16. [Whitley's *Bapt. Bibl.*, i., 78.] London, 1660

GREAT (the) question to be considered by the King and this approaching Parliament, briefly proposed, and modestly discussed : (to wit) How far religion is concerned in policy or civil government, and policy in religion ? With an essay rightly to distinguish these great interests, upon the disquisition of which a sufficient basis is proposed for the firm settlement of these nations, to the most probable satisfaction of the several interests and parties therein. By one who desires to give unto Cæsar the things that are Cæsar's, and to God the things that are God's [William Penn]. Folio. [Smith's *Cat. of Friends' Books*, i., 41 ; ii., 297.]
N.P., N.D.

Signed "Philo-Britannicus."

GREAT (the) reasons and interests consider'd anent the Spanish monarchy. I. What interest the French King has to assist the Duke d'Anjou, in respect to the Spanish monarchy. II. What English measures ought to be taken. III. What the Scots ought to do in the present juncture. [By George Ridpath.] 8vo. [*Adv. Lib.*]
Printed in the year 1701

GREAT (the) reconciler. By the author of *Miss Molly* [Beatrice May Butt]. Cr 8vo. Pp. 470. [*Brit. Mus.*]
London, 1903

GREAT (the) refusal. By Maxwell Gray [Mary Gleed Tuttiett]. 8vo. Pp. 382. [*Lit. Year Book.*]
London, 1906

GREAT (the) refusal ; a war poem. By a citizen of the United States [Melville B. Anderson, Professor in Stanford University, California]. Fcap 8vo. Pp. 28. Florence, 1916

GREAT (the) refusal : an account of the events which led to the death of General [Charles] Gordon. By Vindex [George W. Rusden]. 8vo. Pp. 36. [*Brit. Mus.*] London, 1890

GREAT riches : Nellie Rivers' story. By Aunt Fanny [Mrs Fanny Barrow]. Fcap 8vo. [Cushing's *Init. and Pseud.*, vol. ii., p. 58.] Edinburgh, 1867

GREAT (the) sacrifice of the new law, expounded by the figures of the old. [By James Dymock.] Fcap 8vo. Pp. 214. [*Bodl.*]
Printed in the year 1676

The epistle dedicatory is signed "J. D."

GREAT (the) Scanderberg ; a novel. [By Urbain Chevreaux]. Done out of French. . . . Fcap 8vo. [Arber's *Term Cat.*, ii., 616.] London, 1690

GREAT Scot ; the Chaser ; and other sporting stories. By G. G. [Charles G. Harper]. 8vo. Pp. 318. [*Lit. Year Book.*] London, 1897

GREAT (the) seals of England, from the time of Edward the Confessor to the reign of William the Fourth : with historical and descriptive notices. [Edited by E. Edwards.] Folio. [*Brit. Mus.*] London, 1837

GREAT (the) secret, and its unfoldment in Occultism : a record of forty years' experience in the modern mystery. By a Church of England clergyman [Charles Maurice Davies, D.D.]. Pt 8vo. London, 1895

GREAT shipwrecks, 1544-1877 : a record of perils and disasters at sea. [By William Henry Davenport Adams.] Pt 8vo. London, [1877]

GREAT (the) sin of great cities. . . . A reprint of an article from the Westminster and Foreign Quarterly Review for July 1850. [By William Rathbone Greg.] 8vo. London, 1853

GREAT (the) social problem. By T. L. C. [T. L. Clark]. 8vo. London, 1906

GREAT success. By S. A. F. [Sarah A. Flint]. 12mo. [Kirk's *Supp.*]
Boston, 1871

GREAT (the) Tab Dope ; and other stories. By "Ole Luk-Oie" [General Ernest Dunlop Swinton]. 8vo. Pp. 374. [*Lit. Year Book.*]
Edinburgh, 1915

GREAT thoughts for little thinkers. By Lucia True Ames [Lucia Ames Mead]. 8vo. Providence, R. I., 1890

GREAT Tom of Oxford. By the author of *Peter Priggins*, etc. [Joseph T. Hewlett]. 3 vols. Fcap 8vo. [*Adv. Lib.*] London, 1846

GREAT (the) truths of the Christian religion. 5 parts. [By Rev. William Upton Richards, M.A.] Eighth edition. Fcap 8vo. Pp. vii., 351. [*Brit. Mus.*] London, 1881

The preface is signed " W. U. R."

GREAT (the) Turf fraud, and other notable crimes. By Dick Donovan [Joyce E. P. Muddock]. 8vo. [*Lit. Year Book.*] London, 1909

GREAT (the) unwashed. By the journeyman engineer, author of *Some habits and customs of the working classes*, etc. [Thomas Wright]. 8vo. Pp. ix., 293. [*Adv. Lib.*]
London, 1868

GREAT (the) work of our redemption by Christ, and the several branches of it : as represented at one view, and in the words of Scripture, under the sixth head of the Bishop of London's Second pastoral letter. With a preface, shewing the need there is to enforce and inculcate the doctrin at this time. [By Edmund Gibson.] 8vo. [*Bodl.*]
London, 1735

GREATER (the) glory : a novel. By Maarten Maartens [Jan M. W. van de Poorten Schwartz]. Cr 8vo. Pp. 486. [*Lit. Year Book.*] London, 1902

GREATER (the) law. [A novel.] By Victoria Cross [Miss Vincent Cory]. Cr 8vo. Pp. 320. [*Brit. Mus.*]
London, 1914

GREATER (the) power. [A novel.] By Guy Thorne [Cyril A. E. Ranger-Gull]. Cr 8vo. Pp. 184. [*Lit. Year Book.*] London, 1915

GREATER Russia ; the Continental empire of the Old World. By Wirt Gerrare [William O. Greener]. Royal 8vo. Pp. 324. [*Lit. Year Book.*]
London, 1904

GREATER (the) Waterloo. By Rob. Richardson [Margaret Mower Perkins]. Pt 8vo. [*Amer. Cat.*]
New York, 1905

GREATEST (the) light in the world, far exceeding the light of the Quakers. [By John Wallis, D.D.] 8vo.
N.P., 1674

Ascribed also to J— Wigan.

GREATEST (the) of our social evils ; prostitution, as it now exists. . . . By a physician [Robert Knox, M.D.]. Pt 8vo. [*D. N. B.*, vol. 31, p. 333.]
London, 1857

Wrongly attributed to Gustav Richelot.

GREATEST (the) of the Plantagenets, Edward I. ; an historical sketch. [By Robert Benton Seeley.] 8vo. [*D. N. B.*, vol. 51, p. 193.] London, 1860

Wrongly attributed to Edmund Clifford. The title of a later edition (1872) is " The Life and reign of Edward I."

GREATEST (the) of the prophets. By the author of *Essays on the Church* [Robert Benton Seeley]. 8vo. [*D.N.B.*, vol. 51, p. 193.] London, 1875

GREATEST (the) of these. [A novel.] By Gordon Roy [Ellen Wallace]. Cr 8vo. [*Lit. Year Book.*]
London, 1902

GREATEST (the) plague of life ; or the adventures of a lady in search of a good servant. By one who has been " almost worried to death " ; edited [but rather wholly written] by the brothers [Henry and Augustus] Mayhew. 8vo. [*Brit. Mus.*]
London, [1847]

GREATEST (the) thing in the world : an address. [By Prof. Henry Drummond, F.R.S.E.] 8vo. Pp. 64. [*Brit. Mus.*] London, 1890

GREAT-HEART Gillian. By John Oxenham [William Arthur Dunkerley]. 8vo. [*Lit. Year Book.*]
London, 1912

GREATNESS (the) of Christ. By F. E. R. [F— E— Raven]. 8vo. Pp. 48. [*Brit. Mus.*] London, [1904]

GREATNESS (the) of Josiah Porlick : a novel. [By Berman Paul Neuman.] Cr 8vo. [*Jewish Year Book.*]
London, 1904

GREATNESS of mind, promoted by Christianity. In a letter to a friend. The first part. [By Hon. Robert Boyle.] 8vo. Pp. 57. [*Bodl.*]
London, 1691

GREATNESS (the) of Shiva (Mahimnastava of Pushpadanta) ; a translation and commentary by Arthur Avalon [Sir John Woodroffe], together with Sanskrit commentary of Jagaunâtha Chakravartî. Large 8vo. [*Adv. Lib.*]
London, [1912 ?]

GRECIA victrix : a lay of modern Greece. By Arculus [E— W— Bowling]. 8vo. [Bartholomew's *Cat. of Camb. Books.*] Cambridge, 1891

GRECIAN (the) courtezan ; or the adventures of Lycoris. . . . Translated from the French of Antoine Bret. Fcap 8vo. [*Brit. Mus.*] London, 1779

In an earlier edition (1761), the beginning of the title is " Lycoris . . ."

GRECIAN (the) daughter ; a tragedy [in five acts and in verse]. [By Arthur Murphy.] 8vo. Pp. 72, vii. [*Biog. Dram.*] London, 1772

GRECIAN (the) story; being an historical poem, in five books: to which is annex'd the Grove, consisting of divers shorter poems upon several subjects. By J. H., Esq. [John Harington]. 4to. Pp. 325. [*Brit. Mus.*] London, 1684
The Grove [pp. 23] has a separate pagination.

GREECE; her hopes and troubles. [By Campbell MacKellar.] 8vo. Pp. 73. [*Brit. Mus.*] Paisley, 1897

GREED'S labour lost. A novel. By the author of *Recommended to mercy*, etc. [Mrs Margaret C. Houstoun, *née* Jones]. 3 vols. Second edition. 8vo. [*Brit. Mus.*] London, 1875

GREEK (the) and Roman history illustrated by coins and medals; representing their religions, rites, manners, customs, games, feasts, arts and sciences. Together with a succinct account of their emperors, consuls, cities, colonies and families. In two parts. . . . By O. W. [Obadiah Walker]. 8vo. Pp. 378. [Watt's *Bibl. Brit.*] London, 1692

GREEK (the) Church; a sketch. By the author of *Proposals for Christian union* [Ernest Silvanus Appleyard]. Second edition. Fcap 8vo. [*Brit. Mus.*] London, 1851
The advertisement at the beginning is signed " E.S.A."

GREEK (the) Church identified by means of the English, and the Church of Scotland acquitted of the pseudoprophetical character implied in the description of the false prophet and his exploits—Rev. xvi., 13, 14. [By Richard Burdon Sanderson.] 8vo. [*Brit. Mus.*] London, 1842
Signed " R. B. S."

GREEK Grammar; translated from the German of Philip Buttmann, Professor in the University of Berlin [by Edward Everett]. 8vo. [*W.*] London, 1824

GREEK (the) Madonna. By Shelton Chauncey [Charles W. De Lyon Nichol]. Pt 8vo. New York, 1894

GREEK (a) slave; a musical comedy: words by Owen Hall [James Davis, B.A.]. 8vo. Pp. 35. [*Lit. Year Book.*] London, 1901

GREEK-ENGLISH (a) lexicon, containing the derivations and various significations of all the words in the New Testament; with a compleat index in Greek and English: Whereunto is added a praxis, or an explanation of the Second of Romans, and the Greek dialects contained in the New Testament. [By Joseph Caryl and others.] Fcap 8vo. [*D. N. B.*, vol. 9, p. 254.] London, 1658

GREEKS' (the) opinion touching the Eucharist misrepresented by Monsieur Claude in his answer to Mr Arnauld. [By Abraham Woodhead.] 4to. [Jones' Peck, ii., 385.] London, 1686

GREEN as grass. By F. M. Allen [Edmund Downey]. 8vo. [*Lit. Year Book.*] London, 1892

GREEN (the) bag; a new farce in three acts. [By David Webster.] 8vo. [*Jas. Maidment.*] N.P., 1807

GREEN bays; verses and parodies. By Q. [Sir Arthur T. Quiller-Couch]. 8vo. [*Lond. Lib. Cat.*] London, 1893

GREEN (the) book; or freedom under the snow. [A historical novel.] By Dr Mor Jokai: translated from the Hungarian by Ellis Wright [Mrs —— Waugh]. 8vo. London, 1897

GREEN (the) box of Monsieur de Sartine, found at Mademoiselle Du Thé's lodgings; from the French of the Hague edition, revised and corrected by those of Leipsic and Amsterdam. [By Richard Tickell.] 8vo. Pp. 71. [*Brit. Mus.*] London, 1779
A satire.

GREEN (the) carnation. [A novel. By Robert Smythe Hichens.] Pt 8vo. [*Brit. Mus.*] London, 1894

GREEN (the) cat; a castle-in-the-air. By S. Ashton [Eustace F. Bosanquet]. 4to. Pp. 134. London, 1901

GREEN cliffs: a summer love-story. By Rowland Grey [Lilian Kate Rowland Brown]. 8vo. Pp. viii., 310. [*Lond. Lib. Cat.*] London, 1905

GREEN (the) country. [Sketches of modern Irish life.] By Andrew Merry [Mrs Mildred H. G. Darby, *née* Gordon-Dill]. Cr 8vo. Pp. viii., 378. [S. J. Brown's *Ireland in Fiction*, p. 199.] London, 1902

GREEN (the) curve; and other stories. By " Ole Luk-Oie " [General Ernest Dunlop Swinton]. Cr 8vo. Pp. 326. [*Lond. Lib. Cat.*] Edinburgh, 1909

GREEN (the) eyes of Bâst. By Sax Rohmer [Arthur S. Ward]. Cr 8vo. Pp. 314. [*Lond. Lib. Cat.*]
London, 1920

GREEN fields and running brooks. By Benjamin F. Johnson, of Boone [James Whitcomb Riley]. Pt 8vo.
Indianapolis, 1893

GREEN fire; a story of the Western Isles. By Fiona Macleod [William Sharp]. Cr 8vo. Pp. 292. [*Lit. Year Book.*] London, 1896

GREEN gates; an analysis of foolishness. By Johanna Staats [Mrs Katharine Mary Chewer Meredith]. Pt 8vo. Pp. 257. New York, 1896

GREEN (a) hand's first cruise, roughed out from the log-book of memory, of twenty-five years' standing, together with a residence of five months in Dartmoor. By a Younker [Josiah Cobb, of U.S. Navy]. 2 vols. Fcap 8vo. [Cushing's *Init. and Pseud.*, vol. ii., p. 158.]   Baltimore, 1841

GREEN (the) Mountain boys ; a historical tale of the early settlement of Vermont. By the author of *May Martin ; or the money-diggers* [Daniel Pierce Thompson]. 2 vols. Fcap 8vo. [*Brit. Mus.*]
                Montpelier, [Vermont], 1839

GREEN Mountain girls ; a story of Vermont. By Blythe White, junr. [Solon Robinson]. 8vo. [Cushing's *Init. and Pseud.*, vol. i., p. 306.]
                New York, 1856

GREEN peas, picked from the patch of Invisible Green, Esq. [William G. Crippen]. 8vo. [Kirk's *Supp.*]
                Cincinnati, 1856

GREEN pleasure and grey grief. [A novel.] By the author of *Phyllis*, etc. [Margaret Argles, later Mrs Hungerford]. 3 vols. 8vo. [*Brit. Mus.*]
                London, 1886

GREEN (the) republic ; a visit to South Tyrone. By A. P. O'Gara [W— R. Macdermott]. Cr 8vo. Pp. 252. [*S. J. Brown's Ireland in fiction*, p. 159.]
                London, 1902

GREEN tea ; a love-story. By V. Schallenberger [Mrs E— Simmons]. Fcap 8vo. Pp. 190. New York, [1895]

GREENE in conceipt newe raised from his graue to wryte the tragique storye of his faire Valeria of London. [By John Dickenson.] 4to. [Lowndes' *Bibl. Man.*]   London, 1598

GREENES funeralls. By R. B., Gent. [Richard Barnfield]. 4to. No pagination. Printed at London by Iohn Danter. [*Bodl.*]   1594

G R E E N E S ghost havnting conycatchers : wherein is set downe The art of humouring. The art of carrying stones. Will. St. Lipt. Ja. Fost. Law. Ned Bro. Catch. and Blacke Robins kindnesse. With the merry conceits of Doctor Pinch-backe a notable makeshift. Ten times more pleasant than any thing yet published of this matter. [By Samuel Rowlands.] 4to. No pagination. B. L. [*Bodl.*]
                London, 1626
    " Epistle dedicatory signed ' S. R.,' probably Samuel Rowlands, or Samuel Rid."—Lowndes.

GREEN-EYED (the) monster. By "Kay Spen" [Henry Courtney Selous]. Pt 8vo. [Kirk's *Supp.*] London, 1871

GREEN-EYED (the) monster : a Christmas lesson. By Whatshisname [E. C. Massey]. 8vo. [*N. and Q.*, 16 Jan. 1864, p. 64.]   London, 1854

GREEN-HOUSE (the) companion ; comprising a general course of greenhouse and conservatory practice throughout the year : a natural arrangement of all the green-house plants in cultivation ; with a descriptive catalogue of the most desirable to form a collection, their proper soils, modes of propagation, management, and references to botanical works in which they are figured. . . . [By John Claudius Loudon.] 8vo. Pp. xii., 460. [*Brit. Mus.*]
                London, 1824

GREENHOUSE favourites ; a description of choice greenhouse plants. . . . [By Shirley Hibberd.] 4to.
                London, [1866]

GREEN-ROOM gossip ; or, gravity gallinipt : a gallimawfry, consisting of theatrical anecdotes, bon mots, chitchat, drollery, entertainment, fun, gibes, humour, jokes, kickshaws, lampoons, mirth, nonsense, oratory, quizzing, repartee, stories, tattle, vocality, wit, yawning, zest. . . . Gathered and garnished by Gridiron Gabble, Gent., godson to Mother Goose [Joseph Haslewood]. Fcap 8vo. Pp. 184.
                London, [1809]

GREENSTONE (the). [A novel.] By Alan St Aubyn [Mrs Frances Marshall]. Cr 8vo. Pp. 316. [*Lit. Year Book.*]   London, 1906

GREENWICH Hospital ; a series of naval sketches descriptive of the life of a Man-o-war's man. By an old sailor [Matthew Henry Barker]. 4to. [*Brit. Mus.*]   London, 1826

GREENWOOD cemetery, and other poems. By John Cramer [Joseph Lemuel Chester, LL.D.]. 8vo. [Kirk's *Supp.*]   New York, 1843

GREENWOOD leaves : a collection of sketches and letters. By Grace Greenwood [Mrs Sara Jane Lippincott, *née* Clarke]. [Allibone's *Dict.*]
                New York, 1849

GREETING to my friends. [Verses.] By Ellis Walton [Mrs F— Percy Cotton]. Fcap 4to.   London, 1898

GREEVOVS grones for the poore. Done by a well-willer, who wisheth that the poore of England might be prouided for, as none should neede to go a begging within this realme. [By Thomas Dekker, or Decker.] 4to. Pp. 27. [*Brit. Mus. ; Bodl.*]
                London, 1621
    Attributed also to Michael Sparkes.

GREGORY Father Grey-beard with his vizard off; or news from the Cabal; in some reflections upon a late pamphlet [by Andrew Marvell], entituled, "The Rehearsal transpros'd." In a letter to our old friend R. L. [Roger L'Estrange], from E. H. [Edmund Hickeringill]. 8vo. [Arber's *Term Cat.*, vol. i., pp. 142 and 511.]
London, 1673

GREGORY Hawkshaw; his character and opinions. By the author of *Colonial adventures and experiences by a University man* [George Carrington]. 8vo. Pp. xi., 379. [*Brit. Mus.*]
London, 1873

GR—LLE [Grenville] Agonistes; a dramatic poem. [By —— Hale.] 8vo. [*Lond. Lib. Cat.*]
London, 1807
A satire on the fall of the Grenville Ministry.

GRETCHEN : a novel. By "Rita" [Mrs W— Desmond Humphreys, *née* Eliza M. J. Gollan]. 3 vols. Cr 8vo. Pp. 26. [*Lit. Year Book.*]
London, 1887

GRETNA-GREEN and its traditions. By "Claverhouse" [Miss M— C. Smith]. Cr 8vo. Pp. 78.
Paisley, 1905

GREY (the) Brethren. By Michael Fairless [Margaret Fairless Barber]. 8vo. [*Brit. Mus.*]
London, 1905

GREY (the) Countess. [A Russian novel.] By Theo Douglas [Mrs H— D— Everett]. Cr 8vo. Pp. 320. [*Lit. Year Book.*]
London, 1913

GREY (the) lady : a novel. By Henry Seton Merriman [Hugh Stowell Scott]. 8vo. [*Lond. Lib. Cat.*]
London, 1894

GREY (a) life ; a romance of Bath. By "Rita" [Mrs W— Desmond Humphreys, *née* Eliza M. J. Gollan]. Cr 8vo. Pp. 348. [*Lit. Year Book.*]
London, 1913

GREY (the) moth. [A novel.] By Florence Warden [Florence Alice Price, later Mrs George E— James]. Cr 8vo. Pp. 122. [*Brit. Mus.*]
London, 1920

GREY (the) shepherd. By J. E. Buckrose [Mrs Falconer Jameson]. Cr 8vo. Pp. 187. [*Lit. Year Book.*]
London, 1916

GREYBEARD'S Colorado ; a trip to Denver in 1881-82. [By John Franklin Graff.] [*Kirk's Supp.*]
New York, 1883

GREYBEARD'S lay sermons ; a summary of the great doctrines of Holy Scripture, interpreted and illustrated by the Scriptures themselves. [By John Franklin Graff.] Fcap 8vo. [*Kirk's Supp.*]
Philadelphia, 1876

GREYCLIFFE ; and Vashti Lethby's heritage. By "Fleeta" [Kate W. Hamilton]. Fcap 8vo. [*Kirk's Supp.*]
Philadelphia, 1870

GREYDON (the) family. [A story.] By "Mignon" [Mrs —— Baseley]. 8vo. [*Manch. Free Lib.*]
Manchester, [1904]

GREYHOUND (the) ; being a treatise on the art of breeding, rearing, and training greyhounds for public running ; their diseases and treatment. . . . By Stonehenge [John Henry Walsh]. With illustrations. 8vo. Pp. xii., 400. [*Brit. Mus.*] London, 1853
Appeared originally in *Bell's Life*. See *also* the following.

GREYHOUND (the) in 1864 : being the second edition of a treatise on the art of breeding, rearing, and training greyhounds for public running ; their diseases and treatment. Containing also the national rules for the management of coursing meetings and for the decision of courses. By Stonehenge [John Henry Walsh]. With illustrations. 8vo. Pp. xvi., 435.
London, 1864

GREYSTONE and porphyry. By Rafford Pike [Harry Thurston Peck]. 8vo. [*Amer. Cat.*] New York, 1899

GRIEVANCES from Ireland. [By Lord Ashtown.] Cr 8vo.
London, [1905 ?]

GRIEVANCES (the) of the American colonies candidly examined. Printed by authority, at Providence, Rhode Island. [By Governor Samuel Ward.] 8vo. [Whitley's *Bapt. Bibl.*, i., 187.]
London, 1765
Sometimes ascribed to Stephen Hopkins.

GRIFFIN Alley folk ; or, pearls from the slums. By Ernest Gilmore [Mrs Helen H. Farley]. Fcap 8vo. [*Cushing's Init. and Pseud.*, i., 117.]
Philadelphia, 1886

GRIFFINAGE (the) of the Hon. Newman Strange. . . . By T. B. H. [T— B— Hogarth], R.A. 8vo. [*Cushing's Init. and Pseud.*, i., 124.]
London, 1862

GRIFFINHOOF. By Crona Temple [Miss —— Corfield]. 8vo. Pp. 383. [*Brit. Mus.*] London, 1884

GRILLION'S Club, from its origin in 1812 to its fiftieth anniversary. By P. G. E. [Sir Philip De Malpas Grey Egerton]. Small 4to. Private print. [Anderson's *Brit. Top.*] London, 1880

GRIM justice ; the study of a Nonconformist conscience. By "Rita" [Mrs W. Desmond Humphreys, *née* Eliza M. J. Gollan]. Cr 8vo. Pp. 430. [*Brit. Mus.*] London, 1912

GRIMALDI (the) Shakspere. Notes and emendations on the plays of Shakspere, from a recently-discovered annotated copy by the late Joseph Grimaldi, Esq., comedian. [By Frederick William Fairholt.] N.B. —These notes and emendations are copyright, and must not be used by any editor in any future edition of Shakspere. 8vo. [*N. and Q.*, 1869, p. 168.] London, 1853

GRIMELLOS fortunes, with his entertainment in his trauaile ; a discourse full of pleasure. [By Nicholas Breton.] 4to. B. L. No pagination. [*Bodl.*]
London, 1604
The address to the reader is signed " B. N."

GRINDER (the) papers : being the adventures of Miss Charity Grinder [By Mary Kyle Dallas]. 8vo.
New York, 1877

GRINS and wrinkles ; or, food for laughter. By Democritus Machiavel Brown [James MacGregor Allan]. Pt 8vo. London, 1857

GRIP. A novel. By John Strange Winter [Mrs Henrietta E. V. Stannard]. Cr 8vo. Pp. 345.
London, 1897

GRIP (the) of the wolf. [A novel.] By Morice Gerard [John Jessop Teague]. 8vo. [*Lit. Year Book.*]
London, 1907

GRISELDA. By Bertha M. Clay [Mrs Charlotte M. Braeme]. Fcap 8vo. New York, 1886

GRISELDA ; a dramatic poem ; translated from the German of Friedrich Halm [Freyherr von Münch-Bellinghausen], by Q. E. D. Fcap 8vo. [*Brit. Mus.*] London, 1844

GRISELDA ; a society novel, in rhymed verse. [By Wilfrid S. Blunt.] Fcap 8vo. [*Brit. Mus.*]
London, 1893

GRISELDA ; or La Virtu in cimento : a musical drama in two acts. . . . Italian and English. [By Angela Anelli.] 12mo. [*Brit. Mus.*]
London, 1815

GR—LLE [Grenville] Agonistes ; a dramatic poem. [By —— Hale, a retired diplomat.] 8vo. Pp. 26. [*N. and Q.*, June 1855, p. 495.]
London, 1807

GROANS from the grave ; or complaints of the dead against the surgeons for raising their bodies out of the dust. [By Alexander Pennecuik.] 4to. [*Brit. Mus.*] [Edinburgh, 1725]

GROANS (the) of believers under their burdens, evidently set forth in a sermon, from 2 Cor. v. 4. Wherein the text is most clearly and judiciously opened up, and a most apposite and very edifying point of doctrine drawn from it. . . . By a learned, faithful, zealous, and reverend minister of the Gospel in the Church of Scotland [Ebenezer Erskine]. Fcap 8vo. [*Adv. Lib.*]
Edinburgh, 1722

GROANS (the) of the plantations ; or a true account of their grievous and extreme sufferings by the heavy impositions upon sugar, and other hardships : relating more particularly to the island of Barbados. [By Edward Littleton.] 4to. [Wood's *Athen. Oxon.*, iv., 575.]
London, 1689

GROANS of the quartern loaf ; and other poems. By Peter Pindar [John Walcot, M.D.]. 8vo. [*Brit. Mus.*]
London, [1840]

GRONDALLA : a romance in verse. By Idamore [Mary Cutts]. 8vo. [*Lib. Journ.*, v., 54.] New York, 1866

GROSS (a) imposition upon the public detected ; or, Archbishop Cranmer vindicated from the charge of Pelagianism : being a brief answer to a pamphlet, intituled, A dissertation on the 17th article of the Church of England ; in a letter to the Dissertator. By the author of *Pietas Oxoniensis*, and of *Goliath slain* [Sir Richard Hill]. 8vo. [R. Green's *Anti-Meth. Publ.*, p. 122.]
London, [1775]

GROTON, Massachusetts. [A poem.] By W. A. B. [William Amos Bancroft]. 8vo. [*Brit. Mus.*]
[Boston, Mass.], 1904

GROTTO (the) : a poem. Written by Peter Drake, fisherman of Brentford [Matthew Green]. 8vo. Pp. 14. [*Brit. Mus.*] London, 1733

GROUND arms : the story of a life ; from the German of B. Oulot [Baroness Bertha von Suttner]. Pt 8vo. [*Amer. Cat.*]
Chicago, 1892

GROUND (the) ash ; a public school story. By the author of *The fight at Dame Europa's school* [Henry William Pullen, M.A.]. 8vo. Pp. 247. [*D. N. B.*, Second Supp., vol. 3, p. 146.]
Salisbury, 1874

GROUND flowers and fern leaves [chiefly translations from the German and French]. By A. S. K. [Abraham Stansfield, of Kersall in Yorkshire]. 8vo. Pp. xii., 216. Manchester, 1876

GROUND (the) of high places and the end of high places ; and a rest for the people of God above all the high places of the earth. [By George Fox.] 4to. [Smith's *Cat. of Friends' Books*.]

London, 1657

Signed " G. F."

GROUNDS (the) and occasions of the contempt of the clergy and religion enquired into. In a letter written to R. L. [By John Eachard, D.D.] 8vo. Pp. 139. [Arber's *Term Cat.*, i., 57 and 546.] London, 1670

Signed " T. B."

GROUNDS (the) and principles of the Christian religion, explain'd in a catechetical discourse for the instruction of young people. Written in French by J. F. Ostervald, pastor of the Church of Neufchatel. . . . Rendred into English by a good hand [Humphrey Wanley]. . . . Fifth edition. 8vo. Pp. 377.

Edinburgh, 1732

GROUNDS (the) and reasons of Monarchy, considered and exemplified out of the Scottish history. By J. H. [John Hall, Durham]. In two parts. 4to. Pp. 56. [*Bodl.*]

Edinburgh, 1651

Prefixed to the works of James Harrington. London, 1700. Folio.

GROUNDS (the) of Alderman Wilkes and Boydell's profound petition for peace examined and refuted. [By John Reeves, M.A., F.R.S., F.S.A.] 8vo. [*D. N. B.*, vol. 47, p. 416.]

London, 1795

GROUNDS (the) of the Christian's belief ; or the Apostles' Creed explained in twenty-three moral discourses. By J. H. [John Joseph Hornyhold, D.D., Romish Bishop]. Fcap 8vo.

Birmingham, 1771

Some of these discourses were really written by the Rev. John Johnson. *See* Gillow's *Bibl. Dict.*, vol. iii., p. 402.

GROUNDS (the) of the lawes of England, digested methodically into cases, for the use and benefit of all practisers and students. By M. H. [Michael Hawkes]. Pp. 474. [Thomason's *Coll. of Tracts*, ii., 192.]

London, 1657

GROUNDS (the) of the old religion ; or, some general arguments in favour of the Catholick, Apostolick, Roman communion collected both from antient and modern controvertists. . . . By a convert [Richard Challoner, D.D.]. Fcap 8vo. Pp. 182. [*Brit. Mus.*] Augusta, [London ?], 1742

GROUNDWORK (the) of science. By D'Arcy Drew [St George Mivart]. 8vo. [Gladstone *Lib. Cat.*]

London, 1898

The views expressed in this and other publications diverged so much from the doctrines of the Roman Catholic Church that the writer was excommunicated.

GROUP (a) of Scottish women. By Col. D. Streamer [Coldstreamer, *i.e.* Capt. Harry Graham, of the Coldstream Guards]. Cr 8vo. [*Amer. Cat.*] New York, 1908

GROVE (the) ; a satire : by the author of *Pursuits of Literature* [Thomas J. Mathias]. 4to. [*D. N. B.*, vol. 37, p. 427.] London, N.D.

GROVE Cottage ; and, The India cabinet opened. [Two stories.] By the author of *Fruits of Enterprise* [Sarah Atkins]. Fcap 8vo. Pp. 252. [*Brit. Mus.*] London, 1838

GROVE Hill : a rural and horticultural sketch (with a catalogue of fruit trees and plants in the gardens). [By John Coakley Lettsom, M.D.] 4to. Pp. 47. [Watt's *Bibl. Brit.*]

London, 1804

GROVE Hill (Camberwell) : a descriptive poem : with an Ode to Mithra. By the author of Indian antiquities [Rev. Thomas Maurice, of the British Museum]. The engravings on wood by J. Anderson from drawings by G. Samuel. 4to. Pp. 82. [*D. N. B.*, vol. 37, p. 108.] London, 1799

GROWING ; a word to the girls and boys on New Year's day. By E. A. W. [Mrs Edward Ashley Walker]. 12mo. London, 1892

GROWTH. [A novel.] By Graham Travers [Margaret Todd, M.D.], author of *Mona Maclean*. 8vo. Pp. 428. [*Lit. Year Book*.] London, 1906

GROWTH (the) of Cardiff from 1875 to 1880 ; with some particulars of Cardiff in the last century. [By Thomas Glyde.] Fcap 8vo. Pp. 70.

Cardiff, 1880

GROWTH (the) of error : being an exercitation concerning the rise and progress of Arminianism, and more especially Socinianism, both abroad, and now of late in England. By a lover of truth, and peace [Stephen Lobb]. 8vo. Pp. v., 208. [*New Coll. Cat.*] London, 1697

The preface is signed "S. L."

GROWTH (the) of knavery and Popery under the mask of Presbytery. [By Sir Roger L'Estrange.] 4to. [Arber's *Term Cat.*, i., 524.] London, 1678

GROWTH (the) of love. A poem in twenty-four sonnets. [By Robert Seymour Bridges, M.A., M.B., M.R.C.P.] 8vo. No pagination. [Kirk's *Supp.*]   London, 1876
Later editions give the author's name.

GROWTH (the) of Russian power contingent on the decay of the British constitution. [By Stewart Erskine Rolland.] 8vo. [*Brit. Mus.*]   London, 1858

GRUB STREET verses. [By Joseph Trapp, D.D.] 8vo. [*D. N. B.*, vol. 57, p. 158.]   London, 1731

GRUMBLER (the) ; a comedy. [By Sir Charles Sedley.] Fcap 8vo. [*Brit. Mus.*]   London, 1719

GRYLL Grange. By the author of *Headlong Hall* [Thomas Love Peacock]. 8vo. Pp. viii., 316. [*Adv. Lib.*]   London, 1861

GUARDIAN (the). A comedy of two acts, as it is perform'd at the Theatre-royal in Drury-Lane. [By David Garrick.] 8vo. Pp. 58. [*Biog. Dram.*]   London, 1759

GUARDIAN (the). [A novel.] By George Colmore [Mrs Baillie Weaver, *née* Gertrude Colmore Dunn]. Cr 8vo. [*Lit. Year Book.*] London, 1923

GUARDIAN (a) angel. By the author of *A Trap to catch a sunbeam* [Matilda Anne Planché, later Mrs Mackarness]. 2 vols. 8vo. [Allibone's *Dict.*]   London, 1864

GUARDIAN'S (the) instruction ; or, the gentleman's romance : written for the diversion and service of the gentry. [By Stephen Penton.] 12mo. Pp. 106. [*Bodl.*]   London, 1688
The author's name is in the handwriting of Wood.

GUARDS (the) and the Line. By the author of *The Horse Guards* [Lieut.-Colonel Richard Hort]. 8vo. [*Brit. Mus.*]   London, 1850

GUARDS, hussars, and infantry. By an officer [Harry Austin]. 8vo. [*Brit. Mus.*]   London, 1838

GUATIMOZIN'S letters on the present state of Ireland, and the right of binding it by British Acts of Parliament, &c. [By Dr Jebb and others.] 8vo. Pp. 76. [*Bodl.*]   London, 1779
The letters are signed "Guatimozin."

GUDGEON against Daniels. [By Edward Wilkinson, surgeon.] 8vo. [*Gent. Mag.*, lxxix., 1176.]   London, 1774

GUERNDALE : an old story. By J. S. of Dale [Frederic Jesup Stimson]. 8vo. [Kirk's *Supp.*] New York, 1882

GUERNSEY (the) lily ; a tale of the Jersey Islands. By Susan Coolidge [Sarah Chauncey Woolsey]. Fcap 8vo. [Kirk's *Supp.*] Boston, [Mass.], 1892

GUESS not ; an art pantomime. [By Cassius M. Coolidge.] 8vo.
            Rochester, New York, 1875

GUESSES at truth. By two brothers [Julius Charles Hare and Augustus William Hare]. The first [and second] volume. 8vo. [*Brit. Mus.*]
            London, 1827
The preface " To the Reader " is signed " U."

GUEST (the). [A novel.] By George Colmore [Mrs Baillie Weaver]. Cr 8vo. Pp. 325. [*Lit. Year Book.*]
            London, 1917

GUEST (a) at the Ludlow ; and other stories. By Bill Nye [Edgar Wilson Nye]. Fcap 8vo. Pp. 272. [Kirk's *Supp.*]   Indianapolis, 1897

GUESTS (the) of Brazil ; or the martyrdom of Frederick : a tragedy. [By Gurdon Huntington.] 8vo.
            New York, 1854

GUIDE (a) for constables and all peace officers. . . . By an acting Justice [John Hewitt]. 8vo. [Watt's *Bibl. Brit.*]   Birmingham, 1779

GUIDE (a) for the penitent ; or a modell drawn up for the help of a devout soul wounded with sin. [By Brian Duppa, Bishop of Winchester.] 8vo. Pp. 55. [*Brit. Mus.*]
            London, 1660
Ascribed also to Jeremy Taylor. Another edition appeared in 1674.

GUIDE (the) in controversies ; or, a rational account of the doctrine of Roman-Catholicks concerning the ecclesiastical guide in controversies of religion ; reflecting on the later writings of Protestants, particularly of Archbishop Lawd and Mr Stillingfleet, on this subject. By R. H. [Obadiah Walker, or Abraham Woodhead]. 4to. Pp. 24, 139-366. [Bliss' edition of Wood's *Athen. Oxon.*, iii., 1159.]
            N.P., 1667
" This vol. contains only the third and fourth parts. . . . The two first were burnt at the fire of London, and are of very great rarity."—MS. note by Dr Bliss.
Questionably ascribed to Robert Holden, but this is generally regarded as an *alias* of Woodhead. Another edition was issued in 1673. Reply was made in " A Discourse concerning 'A Guide in controversies,' " [by Mrs Catherine Cockburn].

GUIDE (the) mistaken, and temporizing rebuked ; or a brief reply to Jonathan Clapham's book, intituled, A Guide to the true religion. By W. P. [William Penn]. 4to. [Smith's *Cat. of Friends' Books*, ii.]   London, 1668

GUIDE (the) of faith ; or, a third part of the Antidote against the pestiferovs writings of all English sectaries ; and in particuler, agaynst D. Bilson, D. Fvlke, D. Reynoldes, D. Whitaker, D. Field, D. Sparkes, D. White, and M. Mason, the chiefe vpholders, some of Protestancy, and some of Puritanisme : wherein the truth, and perpetuall visible succession of the Catholique Roman Church, is cleerly demonstrated. By S. N. [Sylvester Norris], Doctour of Diuinity. 4to. Pp. 229. [Gillow's *Bibl. Dict.*]
　　　　　　　　Permissu Superiorum, 1621

GUIDE (the) of the desert ; or life in the Pampa. By Gustave Aimard [Ollivier Gloux]. Fcap 8vo. [*Brit. Mus.*]
　　　　　　　　London, [1875]

GUIDE (a) to all the watering-places and sea-bathing places, with a description of the Lakes ; a sketch of a tour in Wales, with itineraries. [By John Feltham.] Fcap 8vo.
　　　　　　　　London, [1803]

GUIDE (a) to astrology ; a complete system of genethliacal astrology. By Raphael [R— C. Smith]. 3 vols. 8vo. [Cushing's *Init. and Pseud.*, i. 247.]
　　　　　　　　London, 1884
　　Attributed also to J. Palmer.

GUIDE to Bodmin and neighbourhood. . . . [By Joseph Polsue.] Fcap 8vo. Pp. 30. [Boase and Courtney's *Bibl. Corn.*]
　　　　　　　　Truro, 1872

GUIDE (a) to Burghley House, Northamptonshire, the seat of the Marquis of Exeter ; containing a catalogue of all the paintings, antiquities, &c., with biographical notices of the artists. [By Thomas Blore.] 8vo. [Anderson's *Brit. Top.*]
　　　　　　　　Stamford, 1815

GUIDE (a) to Caerphilly Castle and the neighbourhood. [By Thomas Glyde.] 8vo. Pp. 32.
　　　　　　　　Cardiff, 1895

GUIDE (a) to confirmation and holy communion. . . . [By Robert Brett.] 8vo.
　　　　　　　　London, 1863

GUIDE to Cullen. [By William Cramond, LL.D.] 8vo.
　　　　　　　　Cullen, 1896

GUIDE (the) to Deeside. By James Brown [Dr Joseph Robertson]. Second edition. 8vo. [*Aberd. Free Lib. Cat.*]
　　　　　　　　Aberdeen, 1835
　　The title of the first edition (1831) is "A Guide to the Highlands of Deeside." *See also* "The New Deeside Guide" (1842 and later).

GUIDE (the) to Dovedale, Ilam, Alton Towers, etc. By R. H. [Robert Hobson, the publisher]. 8vo. Pp. 36. [Simm's *Bibl. Staff.*, p. 228.]
　　　　　　　　Ashbourn, 1850

GUIDE to Dunimarle. [By John Todd, journalist.] 8vo. [Beveridge's *Dunf. Bibl.*]
　　　　　　　　Dunfermline, 1884

GUIDE (the) to East Bourne and its environs ; a descriptive account of that beautiful watering-place, and the objects of interest in its vicinity. [By T. S. Gowland.] New edition. 8vo. Pp. 61. [*Bodl.*]
　　　　　　　　East Bourne, [1856]

GUIDE to Falmouth, Penryn, St Mawes, and neighbourhood. [By Joseph Polsue.] Fcap 8vo. [Boase and Courtney's *Bibl. Corn.*]
　　　　　　　　Truro, 1869

GUIDE (a) to Gretna Green ; the romance of runaway weddings, and tales of the blacksmith. By James Forbes [Richard Macdougal, of Annan]. 8vo.
　　　　　　　　Carlisle, 1908

GUIDE (a) to Harrogate ; with a correct account of the places in the neighbourhood. [By William Langdale.] 8vo.
　　　　　　　　Harrogate, [1845]

GUIDE (a) to health, beauty, riches, and honour. [By Francis Grose.] 8vo. Pp. viii., 64. [*Bodl.*]
　　　　　　　　London, 1785
　　The book consists of a preface written by Capt. Grose, and of a collection of cviii. advertisements collected by him.

GUIDE to Inverness Museum and the surrounding district. [By Thomas Wallace.] 8vo. [P. J. Anderson's *Inverness Bibl.*]
　　　　　　　　Inverness, 1909

GUIDE (the) to Jersey. [By Edward Eadon.] 8vo.
　　　　　　　　Jersey, 1881
　　Preface signed " E. E."

GUIDE to London and its suburbs. By Captain Crawley [George Frederick Pardon]. [*Brit. Mus.*]　London [1866 ?]

GUIDE (a) to Moffat ; embracing sketches of the surrounding scenery, etc. By a Visitor [J— M'Diarmid]. Fcap 8vo. [Mitchell and Cash's *Scot. Top.*]
　　　　　　　　Dumfries, 1833

GUIDE (a) to Newquay and the neighbourhood, including Perran and Bedruthen Steps : the Cornish pilchard fishery. By J. C. O. [John Cardell Oliver]. 8vo. Pp. 42. [*Brit. Mus.*]
　　　　　　　　Truro, 1872

GUIDE to official letter-writing, orders, etc. By an army schoolmaster [George L. Dunnett]. Fourth edition. 8vo. Pp. 105. [*Brit. Mus.*] London, [1891]

GUIDE to Penzance, St Michael's Mount, and neighbourhood. [By Joseph Polsue.] Fcap 8vo. Pp. 24. [Boase and Courtney's *Bibl. Corn.*]
　　　　　　　　Truro, 1869

GUIDE (a) to Peterborough cathedral. By January Searle [George Searle Phillips, B.A.]. 8vo. [*Lit. Year Book.*]
　　　　　　　　Peterborough, 1843

GUIDE to private social worship ; the duty of stated and select private Christian fellowship briefly inculcated and directed. [By Andrew Symington, D.D.] 12mo. Pp. 72. Paisley, 1840
Information from a relative of the author.

GUIDE (a) to rain betting. . . . [By J— Wilton Gonsalves.] 8vo. [Calc. Imp. Lib.] Calcutta, 1896

GUIDE to selecting plays. . . . [By Wentworth Hogg.] 8vo.
London, [1882]
Preface signed " W. H."

GUIDE (the) to service : Seventeen parts [including the Clerk, the Governers, the Groom, all signed " G. S.," i.e. Sir George Stephen]. Fcap 8vo. [Brit. Mus.] London, 1838-44

GUIDE (a) to Sherwood Forest. [By J— Stanton.] 8vo. London, 1885

GUIDE (a) to star-gazing : a familiar explanation of the first principles of astronomy by reference to the natural sphere ; showing how the aspect of the heavens may be readily calculated for every month in the year. [By Mary Jenkins.] 8vo. Pp. 63. [Bodl.]
London, 1861
Preface signed " M. J."

GUIDE to Stirling and the Trosachs, Loch Katrine and Loch Lomond, Dunkeld and Blair Athole, the Falls of the Clyde, &c. [By Patrick Maxwell.] A new edition, greatly enlarged. 8vo. Pp. vi., 170. [And. Jervise.] Edinburgh, 1849

GUIDE to successful chicken-rearing. By the author of Management of the sitting hen during incubation [H— Pritchard]. 8vo. London, [1881]

GUIDE (a) to the Acts of the Apostles. By A. D. [Rev. Alexander Robert Charles Dallas]. 8vo. London, 1847

GUIDE (a) to the altar ; or the advantages of frequent communion . . . to which is added, A Discourse on the love of God. By Alexander Clinton [Alexander Mackenzie, S.J.]. Fcap 8vo. Pp. iv., 431. [Brit. Mus.]
Dublin, [1820 ?]
See also " Frequent communion . . ."

GUIDE (a) to the Apocalypse. [By Rev. Francis John Bodfield Hooper.] 8vo. [Brit. Mus.] London, 1853

GUIDE (a) to the architectural antiquities in the neighbourhood of Oxford. [By John Henry Parker.] 8vo. [Bodl.]
Oxford, 1846

GUIDE to the Athole Highlands. By Benjie [James Brown Gillies, journalist]. Pt 8vo. Pp. 68. [Mitchell and Cash's Scot. Top.] Edinburgh, [1882]

GUIDE (a) to the blind pointed to ; or a true testimony to the light within : wherein some men are reproved, others counselled and encouraged, but all (who are ignorant of their true Guide) directed into the path of life. . . . Also some Queries to the persecuting ministers of the Church of England. Written for the truth's sake by T. F. [Thomas Forster, London]. Fcap 8vo. Pp. 96. [Smith's Cat. of Friends' Books, Supp., p. 127.] London, 1659

GUIDE (a) to the Cathedral Church of St Peter's, York, commonly called York Minster. [By Rev. Charles Wellbeloved.] Second edition. [Anderson's Brit. Top.] York, 1809

GUIDE (a) to the choice of a site for residential purposes. [By W— Gilford.] 8vo. [Brit. Architects' Lib. Cat., Supp., p. iii.] London, 1887

GUIDE (a) to the choice of books ; or a selection of more than six hundred volumes. . . . [By W— Drausfield.] Fcap 8vo. Pp. xi., 302. [Manch. Free Lib. Cat.] London, 1833

GUIDE (a) to the [English] Church. [By Thomas Tregenna Biddulph, M.A.] 8vo. [Brit. Mus.]
London, 1824

GUIDE to the city and cathedral of Worcester. By Ambrose Florence [Edwin Lees]. 8vo. Worcester, 1828

GUIDE to the Civil Service examinations ; with directions for candidates, examination papers, abstract of Commissioners' report, standards of qualification, amount of salaries, and all necessary information for those seeking employment in the government civil service. [By Henry White, B.A.] 8vo. Pp. xxxvi., 112. [Bodl.]
[London], 1856

GUIDE (a) to the Eastern escarpment of Dartmoor. [Compiled by Dr —— Crocker.] Cr 8vo. Chudleigh, 1851

GUIDE to the Fox-hounds and Staghounds of England ; with the Otterhounds and harriers of several Counties. [By —— Greville.] 8vo. London, 1849

GUIDE (a) to the Highlands of Deeside. By James Brown [Dr Joseph Robertson]. 8vo. [Aberd. Free Lib. Cat.]
Aberdeen, 1831
The title of the second edition, 1835, is : " The Guide to Deeside." See also " The New Deeside Guide " (1842).

GUIDE to the Island of Jersey. . . . To-gether with its laws, customs, and privileges. [By A— J— Le Cras.] Fcap 8vo. [*Brit. Mus.*] Jersey, 1834

GUIDE (a) to the lakes in Cumberland, Westmorland, and Lancashire. By the author of the *Antiquities of Furness* [Thomas West, S.J.]. Tenth edition. 8vo. [*Upcott*, i., 123.]
Kendal, 1812

GUIDE to the Land's End, St Ives, and neighbourhood. [By Joseph Polsue.] Fcap 8vo. Pp. 28. [Boase and Court-ney's *Bibl. Corn.*] Truro, 1869

GUIDE (a) to the law ; for general use. By a barrister [Edward Reynolds]. Twenty-third edition. Cr 8vo. Pp. xiii., 305. [*Brit. Mus.*] London, 1880

GUIDE (a) to the Mount's Bay and the Land's End ; comprehending the topography, botany, agriculture, fish-eries, antiquities, mining, mineralogy and geology of Western Cornwall. Second edition. . . . By a physician [John Ayrton Paris, M.D.]. 8vo. [*Lit. Gazette*, xii., 611.] London, 1824
    The first edition was published at Pen-zance in 1816.

GUIDE (a) to the musical tuition of very young children. By an old lady [A— Dawson]. 8vo. London, 1868

GUIDE (a) to the paintings of Venice . . . with short lives of Venetian masters. By Karl Koly [F. Tryon Charles]. Fcap 8vo. London, 1895

GUIDE (a) to the stage. . . . By Austin Fryers [William Edward Clery]. 8vo. Pp. xv., 101. [*Brit. Mus.*]
London, [1904]

GUIDE (a) to the town and port of Cardiff. [By William Edward Winks.] 8vo. Manchester, [1883]

GUIDE (a) to the town of Tenby and its neighbourhood. [By Richard Mason.] Third edition. 8vo.
Tenby, [1854]
    Later editions give the author's name.

GUIDE (a) to the unprotected in every-day matters relating to property and income. By a banker's daughter [M. S. Welsman]. Cr 8vo. London, 1863

GUIDE (a) to the watering-places. . . . By A. Crowquill [Alfred Henry For-rester]. 8vo. London, N.D., [1837 ?]

GUIDE (a) to those who are ignorant of law ; or justice and injustice con-trasted. [By James Millar, Elgin.] Fcap 8vo. Edinburgh, 1814
    Only vol. i. was published.

GUIDE (the) to trade. [By Thomas Carter, tailor.] Fcap 8vo.
London, 1838

GUIDE (a) to Wemyss Bay, Skelmorlie, Inverkip, Largs, and surrounding districts. [By Rev. John Boyd, M.A., minister at Skelmorlie.] Square cr 8vo. Glasgow, 1879
    Information from a friend of the author·

GUIDING lights for young pilgrims. [By William Yunnie.] 8vo. [Robert-son's *Aberd. Bibl.*] Paisley, [1884]

GUIDING (a) star. By Austin Clare [Miss W— M— James]. 8vo. Pp. 127. [*Lit. Year Book.*]
London, [1880]

GUIDING (the) star. By Bertha M. Clay [Mrs Charlotte M. Braeme]. Fcap 8vo. New York, 1887

GUIDING stars. [By Sarah Sprague Jacobs.] 8vo. Boston, [Mass.], 1848

GUIDO ; and other poems. By Ianthe [Mrs Emma Catherine Embury, *née* Manley]. Fcap 8vo. [Cushing's *Init. and Pseud.*, vol. i., p. 135.]
New York, 1828

GUIDO Reni. [By Moses Foster Sweetser.] 8vo.
Boston, [Mass.], 1878

GUILDEROY. [A novel.] By "Ouida" [Louise De La Ramée]. Cr 8vo. [*Lit. Year Book.*] London, 1891

GUILDFORD (the) farce : a satirical poem. [By Joseph King, solicitor.] Fcap 8vo. London, 1860

GUILE. [A novel.] By Headon Hill [Francis Edward Grainger]. Cr 8vo. Pp. 319. [*Lond. Lib. Cat.*]
London, 1920

GUILLOTINA (the) ; or a democratic dirge : a poem. By the author of *The Democratiad* [William Cobbett]. 8vo. Pp. 14. [*Brit. Mus.*]
Philadelphia, [1796 ?]

GUILLOTINE the Great and her suc-cessors ; some fresh memorials of the French Republic, one and indivisible. By Graham Everitt [William Rodgers Richardson]. 8vo. Pp. xiii., 302.
London, 1890

GUILT (the) of democratic scheming fully proved against the Dissenters, at the particular request of Mr Parsons, Dissenting Minister of Leeds, by the Inquirer : a reply to E. Parson's " Vindication of the Dissenters against the charge of democratic scheming." By the author of *A candid inquiry into the democratic schemes of Dis-senters* [Rev. William Atkinson]. 8vo. [*Brit. Mus.*] Bradford, 1802

GUILT ; or the anniversary : a tragedy, in four acts, from the German of Adolphus Mullner. [Translated by R. P. Gillies, author of *Childe Alarique*.] 4to. Pp. 104. [Martin's *Cat.*]
Edinburgh, 1819

GUILTY gold ; a romance of financial fraud and city crime. By Headon Hill [Francis Edward Grainger]. Cr 8vo. Pp. 358. [*Lit. Year Book.*]
London, 1897

GUILTY, or not guilty ; or, a lesson for husbands : a tale. By Ann of Swansea, author of *Conviction*, etc. [Julia Ann Kemble]. 5 vols. Fcap 8vo.
London, 1822

GUINEA (the) note ; a poem. By Timothy Twig, Esq. [Alexander Campbell]. 4to. [Roger's *Modern Scot. Minstrel*, i., 162.] Edinburgh, 1797

GUINEA (the) outfit ; or the sailor's farewell : a comedy in three acts [and in prose. By Thomas Boulton]. New edition. Fcap 8vo. [*Brit. Mus.*]
London, 1800

GUISACHAN ; a legend of St Marjory. [By William Hugh Logan, banker in Berwick-on-Tweed.] 8vo. Pp. 8. Printed for the Flying Stationers.
N.P., Christmas, 1859
A burlesque, edited by James Maidment. *See Maidment Bibliography*, p. 15.

GUISEPPINO ; an occidental story in verse. [By Edward N. Shannon.] 8vo. [*Brit. Mus.*] London, 1821

GULF (the) bridged ; or the everlasting Gospel in the world to come : with a note on the creation of the universe. [By Charles Craddock Underwood.] 8vo. Pp. iv., 76. [*Brit. Mus.*]
London, 1885
Signed " C. C. U."

GULLANE : a poem. By J. F. Lysander [W. T. M. Hogge, teacher of shorthand]. 8vo. Edinburgh, 1887
Information from a friend of the author.

GULLIVER Joe. By Jonathan Quick, Dean of St Rattrick's [Cecil Eldred Hughes and Harold Begbie]. Cr 8vo. Pp. 108. [*Brit. Mus.*] London, 1903
A satirical variation of Jonathan Swift's *Gulliver's Travels*, directed against the Right Hon. Joseph Chamberlain.

GULLIVER revived ; containing singular travels, campaigns, voyages, and adventures. By Baron Munchausen [Rudolf Eric Raspe]. Fifth edition. 12mo. Pp. xxiv., 208. London, 1787
See above, " Adventures (the) of Baron Munchausen. . . ."

GULLIVERIANA ; or, a fourth volume of miscellanies : being a sequel of the three volumes published by Pope and Swift : to which is added Alexander-iana ; or, a comparison between the

ecclesiastical and poetical Pope ; and many things, in verse and prose, relating to the latter. [By Jonathan Smedley, Dean of Clogher.] 8vo. Pp. xliv., 344. [Dyce *Cat.*, ii., 340.]
London, 1727

GUN, rifle, and hound, in East and West. By " Snaffle " [Robert Dunkin]. 8vo. [*Brit. Mus.*]
London, 1894

GUN, rod, and saddle ; personal experiences. By Ubique [Parker Gillmore]. 8vo. Pp. viii., 295. [Kirk's *Supp.*] London, 1869

GUN trial and field trial records of America. By Will Wildwood [Frederick Eugene Pond]. 8vo. [Kirk's *Supp.*] Cincinnati, 1883

ΓΥΝΑΙΚΕΙΟΝ, or nine books of various history concerning women ; containing lives of the most holy and profane, the most famous and infamous in all ages, exactly described. . . . [By Thomas Heywood.] 8vo. [*Brit. Mus.*]
London, 1624
A later edition (1657) begins thus : " The generall history of women ." *See above.*

GUNNER'S (a) aid to instruction ; compiled in a handy form for the use of Volunteer Gunners. By Frederick Page [Duncan Blanckley Shaw]. Sixth thousand. 8vo. London, 1873

GUNTER'S modern confectioner [written by John Camden Hotten, from data supplied], by William Jeanes. Cr 8vo. London, [1871]

GURNEY married ; a sequel to " Gilbert Gurney." By the author of *Sayings and Doings* [Theodore Edward Hook]. 3 vols. Fcap 8vo. [*D. N. B.*, vol. 27, p. 275.]
London, 1839

GUTTA podagrica ; a treatise of the Gout : the several sorts thereof, what diet is good for such as are troubled therewith, and some approved medicines and remedies for the same. By P. H. [Philemon Holland], Dr in Physick. Fcap 4to. London, 1633

GUY de Maupassant. By Joseph Conrad [Joseph Conrad Korzeniowski]. 8vo. Private print. [*Lond. Lib. Cat.*] [London], 1919

GUY Harris, the runaway. By Harry Castlemon [Charles A. Fosdick]. Fcap 8vo. [Kirk's *Supp.*] New York, 1887

GUY Livingstone ; or, " Thorough." [By George Alfred Lawrence.] 8vo. [*Brit. Mus.*] London, 1857

GUY Mannering ; or, the astrologer. By the author of *Waverley* [Sir Walter Scott, Bart.]. 3 vols. Sixth edition. Fcap 8vo. Edinburgh, 1820

GUY Mervin. [A novel.] By Brandon Roy [Mrs Florence Barclay]. 8vo.
London, 1891

GUY Rivers, the outlaw; a tale of Georgia. By the author of *Martin Faber* [William Gilmore Simms, LL.D.]. 3 vols. Pt 8vo. [*Brit. Mus.*]
New York, 1835
The title is varied in later editions.

GUYDOS Questions, newly corrected; whereunto is added the thirde and fourth Booke of Galen, with a treatise for the helps of all the outward part of mans body, and also an excellent antidotary. . . . [By George Baker, surgeon.] Fcap 4to. [Watt's *Bibl. Brit.*] London, 1579

GWEN; a drama in monologue, in six Acts. By the author of *The Epic of Hades* [Sir Lewis Morris]. Fcap 8vo. [*Brit. Mus.*] London, 1879

GWEN; an idyll of the Canyon. By Ralph Connor [Charles W. Gordon, D.D.]. Cr 8vo. Pp. 128. [*Lit. Year Book.*] London, 1904

GWEN Dale's ordeal. By the author of *A harvest of weeds*, etc. [Clara Lemore]. 8vo. Pp. 206. [*Brit. Mus.*]
London, [1891]

GWENDOLINE'S harvest; a novel. By the author of *Lost Sir Massingberd*, etc. [James Payn]. 2 vols. 8vo. [*Brit. Mus.*] London, 1870

GYFTE (a) for the newe yeare; or, a playne, pleasaunt, and profytable pathe waie to the Black-letter paradyse. [By the Rev. C. H. Hartshorne.] Emprynted over the grete gate-waie offe Saincte Jhonnes Colledge, Cambridge, by Wyntonne Hattfelde. 12mo. Pp. 20. [Martin's *Cat.*] 1825

" GYM (the) " [*i.e.* The Gymnasium, Old Aberdeen]; or sketches from school. By an old boy [J— Buckley Allan]. 8vo. Pp. 40. [Robertson's *Aberd. Bibl.*] Aberdeen, 1889

GYMNASIAD (the), or boxing-match; a very short but very curious epic poem, with the prolegomena of Scriblerus Tertius and notes variorum. By the E—l of C—d [Paul Whitehead]. 8vo. [*Lond. Lib. Cat.*] Dublin, 1744

GYMNASTIC competition and display exercises. [By F. Graf.] 8vo.
London, 1897

GYMNASTICS, physical education, and muscular exercises, including walking, running, and leaping; with a chapter on training. By Captain Crawley, author of *Manly games for boys*, etc. [George Frederick Pardon]. 8vo. Pp. 62. [*Brit. Mus.*] London, [1866]

GYPSY Roy: a story of early Methodism. By Harry Lindsay [Harry Lindsay Hudson]. Cr 8vo. Pp. 320. [*Lit. Year Book.*] London, 1904

PRINTED BY OLIVER AND BOYD, EDINBURGH